ISBN 978-1-334-26543-3
PIBN 10760445

RELIGIOUS AND LITERARY JOURNAL.

EDITED BY ROBERT SMITH.

VOLUME XIII.

PHILADELPHIA—PRINTED BY ADAM WALDIE.
1840.

INDEX.

EDITED

PUBLI
Price one dollar p
Subscription
GEORGE
No. 29, North

PU

The Life and P

It is a most ret
part of our mental
constitution of ev
to have put those
conversations o
ties of Christ,
how to wish not
a pleasing inst
their remembran
which come and
trials, and when
of true religion
urges that, in ea
can, these sudden
quietly been nev
movements, which
which are many o
of "truth and sob
rest that there is
clearest, and the
becoming "religi
serious deductions
are liable, from it
ing in the vast stre
pilgrimage. B
bless enthusiasm h
possibly have gro
that a work of g
on. A process of
a considerable ex
sense of most ans
suddenly become
field, already wea
the influence of a
the intervention o
cause he has pa
truth," we may
we mistake the ef
piety and sin, for
neither, or the o
push what is real
to encourage or a
deception of our
ject of "renewal
of course, foun
nection with the

THE FRIEND.

A RELIGIOUS AND LITERARY JOURNAL.

VOL. XIII.   **SEVENTH DAY, TENTH MONTH, 5, 1839.**   **NO. 1.**

EDITED BY ROBERT SMITH.

PUBLISHED WEEKLY.

Price two dollars per annum, payable in advance.

Subscriptions and Payments received by

GEORGE W. TAYLOR,

NO. 50, NORTH FOURTH STREET, UP STAIRS,

PHILADELPHIA.

From the Dublin Christian Examiner.

The Life and Times of Selina, Countess of Huntingdon.

It is a most refreshing and truly gratifying part of our monthly labours, to turn from the contentions of criticism and controversy, and to have our thoughts directed to the walk and conversation of some heavenly-minded servant of Christ, who has left us an example *how* to walk and to please God. It is equally a pleasing duty to meditate occasionally on those remarkable eras of religious history, which come under the denomination of revivals, and which usher in a wider extension of true religion and piety. We are well aware that, through the snares of the evil one, these sudden transitions have not unfrequently been accompanied by some visionary movements, which we cannot commend, and which are quite inconsistent with a profession of "truth and soberness." We are not ignorant that there is such a thing as social excitement, and that there is great danger of becoming "religious in a crowd." To this serious deduction all ecclesiastical movements are liable, from the registry of a camp meeting to the records of a popish altar or a foreign pilgrimage. But amidst all the fanaticism and false enthusiasm to which sudden changes may possibly have given rise, it cannot be denied that a work of true piety may still be going on. A process of internal renovation may, to a considerable extent, be in operation; a scene of most interesting pastoral labour may suddenly assume a cheering aspect; and a field, already white to harvest, may exhibit the influence of a power quite independent of the intervention of human means. While we cannot be too jealous of what are called "revivals," we must also be on our guard lest we mistake the steadily burning light of true piety and zeal for an *ignis fatuus*. We are neither, on the one hand, to despise or impede what is really good; nor, on the other, to encourage or open a door to the insidious deceptions of our spiritual enemy. The subject of "revivals in religion" has, as a matter of course, forced itself on our notice in connection with the name of the departed saint,

a memoir of whose "life and times" is now presented to the public by a member of her distinguished family. "Among the illustrious characters of the eighteenth century, no one has shone more conspicuously in the religious world, or enjoyed a greater share of heartfelt esteem and love, than the venerable Countess of Huntingdon. Above all her celebrated contemporaries, she was honoured with a life of continued usefulness, protracted to the utmost period of mortal existence; with extraordinary talents, ample means, and a head and heart alike devoted to promote the glory of God in the highest, on earth peace, and good will towards men." At the period when this eminent and useful servant of God took a prominent part in advancing the tone of religion in England, there was a visible lifelessness, a darkness, which might be felt prevailing, to an alarming extent, amongst its inhabitants. Both the clergy and laity, as if by mutual consent, were satisfied to ascend no higher in religion than to a cold and chilling formality, or a heartless orthodoxy; and "the vital feeling and zealous activity of Christianity were known to the few only, and these rather mourned over the state of things in secret, than exerted themselves in public to effect an alteration." At this moment of torpid insensibility with regard to the things of God, the subject of this memoir shone forth as a brilliant star in our spiritual firmament, and with a decision, the happy result of a deep-seated principle, "determined to throw all the weight of her influence into the scale of the gospel." Fired with zeal for the glory of God, and anxious to employ her various talents as a means to encourage the growth and expansion of vital godliness throughout the land, she seconded the efforts of the "Oxford band," and gave the right hand of fellowship to "pious ministers of various denominations," who, with an energy and boldness commensurate with the occasion, "brought the deadness of mere ly formal Christianity into juxta-position with the living truth of the gospel." The history of her life and ardent exertions to cherish and promote the noble object which exclusively engaged her thoughts, is closely interwoven with the biographies of Whitfield, Wesley, Romaine, and other eminently pious individuals, whose works of faith and labours of love occupy a conspicuous and prominent place in the pages of ecclesiastical history during the last century. The anonymous biographer of Lady Huntingdon informs us, that a common zeal for the gospel was a sufficient passport to her affections, and constrained her to unite with men, like-minded with herself, for the furtherance of the common object which each had in view.

"Lady Huntingdon had now become the

open and avowed patroness of all the zealous clergy of the church of England who dared to be singular in the unambiguous preaching of the gospel, many of whom exposed themselves, particularly at this period, to much obloquy, abuse, and persecution. She became a shelter, and the companion of all those who were so used. A difference on some doctrinal points caused a separation between Whitfield and Wesley, and their disciples soon after became divided. 'They parted, indeed,' says Dr. Haweis, 'like Paul and Barnabas; but the extent of the sphere of their usefulness was thereby enlarged.' Her ladyship's correspondence with Howel Harris, and several of the Welsh clergy who had been awakened under Whitfield's ministry, was the means, under God, of leading her into more consistent views of divine truth, which she ever after maintained, and in the firm belief of which she ended her days. Her zealous heart embraced with cordiality all whom she esteemed real Christians, whatever their denomination or opinions might be; but from this period her connections with ministers and Christians of the Calvinistic persuasion, according to the liberal sense of the articles of the church of England, became greatly enlarged.

"Lady Huntingdon's heart expanded towards all the children of God—she loved all those whom she had reason to believe loved her Divine Master—and considering herself as a 'debtor both to the Greeks and barbarians,' she was ready, had it been possible, to have visited the uttermost parts of the earth with the glorious truths of the gospel of God our Saviour."

It appears that the famous Dr. Doddridge was frequently a visiter at her house; and the testimony of so eminent a man to the Christian character of his host, cannot, with propriety, be omitted. In a letter to his wife, he says:—

"I can conclude with telling you, that I am now come to the conclusion of one of the most pleasant days I shall ever spend without you. After an hour's charming conversation with Lady Huntingdon and Mrs. Edwin, I preached in her family, by her express desire, and met Colonel Gumley, who is really a second Colonel Gardiner. Such a monument of the power and sovereignty of Divine grace, as truly I have hardly ever met with since I was acquainted with his story.

"Lady Huntingdon is quite a mother to the poor; she visits them, and prays with them in their sicknesses; and they leave their children to her for a legacy when they die, and she takes care of them. I was really astonished at the traces of religion I discovered in her and Mrs. Edwin, and cannot but

More cheerfulness I
with devotion."
the opinion expressed
, her ladyship's bio-
at "a great cloud of
testify, that from her
ith the truths of the
and elect Countess of
brough every stage of
age to walk worthy of
rowing in grace, and
f God her Saviour in

I at an interesting mo-
of Lady Huntingdon,
'hich existed between
assumed a prominent
er ladyship was sensi-
nd fearful of the con-
ined on an endeavour
l to nip in the bud the
versy which those dif-

It appears that her
n produced the desired
dated 12th January,
ed her ladyship that
sley to assist occasion-

' (says he) but it may
ship will hear soon. O
all I see to desire to
k it my highest privi-
to all, but the head of
f power sometimes in-
wn dear children, and
a passion for zeal, and
or an authority given
my own part, I find
than govern, and that
dden under foot than
er to serve others so.
m that which, at our
e too apt to court.
f all lords for taking
rving me! I cannot
o dear a rate. This
your ladyship pants,
'd will delight to fill
our ladyship's letter
e who know and do
and do least: If it
elf would prove our
d zeal, through the
f our hearts, be our
madam, my hands and
ted up for you, that
more in every good
clothed with that hu-
ship delights to wear
humble mind which

been already noticed,
f doctrine ultimately
ween these two emi-
Wesley seems to have
ompanion with great
ear that each itinerat-
walk without a viola-
f Christian love, by
sed to be guided.
warm attachment to
her zeal to promote

the cause of her Redeemer, led her to associate with men of a kindred spirit, and equally
ardent with herself in an earnest desire to promote the glory of God. This volume abounds
with a list of Christian worthies whose meat
and drink it was to accelerate the benevolent
current of true godliness, and whose testimony
will outlive monuments of bronze and marble.
Some of these men of God have already passed in review before us; and their agency, as
instruments in the hands of God, in effecting
a change throughout the moral world, cannot
be dwelt on without giving rise to feelings of
gratitude and a sense of our own unworthiness. "Had their successors in the great
work been warmed with their zeal, and secured the aid of the Almighty with prayer,
united and continued as theirs," the church
would now present a different appearance.

POPERY ENCOURAGES VICE.

The following testimony upon the common
effects of Romanism is of value, because on
no point is there so much error propagated
as concerning the moral attributes of popery.
It is extracted from Fisk's travels in Europe;
and proves that the descriptions of "the spirit
of prophecy concerning the anti-christian
Babylon have literally been accomplished.—
Episcopal Recorder.

That "popery encourages vice" might not
strike the superficial observer, when for the
first time he was introduced into a popish
country, and saw all the array of devotional
exercises and religious associations, together
with all the terrors that are hung out as motives of alarm and fear to the ignorant popu-
lace. If, therefore, he should be informed
that the history of the church shows her to
have been very corrupt both in her laity and
clergy; and that the history of those nations
which have been the most fully under the influence of popery shows them to be among
the most notorious for moral corruption, this
would lead to an enquiry for the reason.
There are various causes which produce this,
in the very constituent principles of popery.
The law of celibacy, which is binding on so
many priests and monastic orders of both
sexes, has a direct tendency to licentiousness.

The doctrines are not suited to eradicate
sin. The doctrines of penance, and of works
of supererogation, and of clerical absolution,
and of purgatory, and of masses for the dead,
and of transubstantiation, not only leave the
passions of the heart unsubdued, but substitute
something else for personal holiness. Spread
those doctrines over the world, and give them
the ascendency in every heart, and you have
gained nothing towards the moral renovation
of man. Let a man believe that a priest can
procure absolution, and that he will do it for
money or for penance, and will he give himself the trouble to forsake his sins? Let him
believe that he can be prayed out of purgatory if he goes there, and will he be very
anxious about his course of life? Let him believe that, by partaking of the sacrament, he
eats the body of Christ, and that whosoever
eats it shall live for ever, and will he not
trust to this rather than to personal holiness?

Romanism being true, it is difficult to see
how any one dying within the pale of the
church can be finally lost. He may have to
do penance in purgatory a long time, but he
will sooner or later come out. When he sees
on a church door or over an altar, "Indulgences given here daily," or every Tuesday
and Friday, &c., as the case may be; "for
the living and the dead—*pro vivis et defunc-
tis*;" and over another altar, "Two souls are
released from purgatory every time mass is
celebrated here;" or when he learns that,
"by climbing the holy staircase on his knees,
he may reduce the period of his purgatorial
pains two hundred years;" when he becomes
acquainted, in fine, with the various ways of
escaping from the punishment of sin without
forsaking sin, he will be very likely to sin on,
trusting to his membership in "the only true
church" for ultimate and final deliverance,
and to some of those various devices for an
early escape from the flames of purgatory.
In that way a man may be very superstitious
and yet very wicked. He may fear that he
shall hazard his salvation by neglecting his
"*Ave Maria*," although he rises from it to
go and commit robbery and murder without
compunction. Our *vetturino* would swear
most blasphemously, and the next moment
would raise his hat to a *madonna* rudely
painted by the way side. I am far from
thinking that the present race of Italians are
sinners above all, yet licentiousness prevails
and dishonesty. My convictions are, that the
tendency of *Romanism* is to encourage vice
rather than to restrain it; and while I give
due credit to individual character for morality
and piety wherever found, still I believe a
careful examination will show, that protestant
communities, other circumstances being equal,
have the decided advantage in point of moral
character.—*Fisk's Travels in Europe.* Page
283, 285.

THE INTELLIGENCE OF ANIMALS.

In the forests of Tartary and South America
where the wild horse is gregarious, there are
herds of five or six hundred, which being ill
prepared for fighting, or indeed for any resistance, and knowing that their safety is in
flight, when they sleep, appoint one in rota-
tion who acts as sentinel while the rest are
asleep. If a man approaches, the sentinel
walks towards him as if to reconnoitre, or
see whether he can be deterred from coming
near; if the man continues, he neighs aloud
and in a peculiar tone, which rouses the herd,
and all gallop away, the sentinel bringing up
the rear. Nothing can be more judicious or
rational than this arrangement, simple as it
is. So a horse belonging to a smuggler in
Dover, used to be laden with rum spirits, and
sent on the road, unattended, to reach the
rendezvous. When he descried a soldier, he
would jump off the highway, and hide himself in a ditch, and when discovered would
fight for his load. The cunning of foxes is
proverbial; but I know not if it was ever
more remarkably displayed than in the Duke
of Beaufort's county, where Reynard being
hard pressed, disappeared suddenly, and was

after a strict search, found immersed in a water-pool up to the snout, by which he held a willow bough hanging over the pond. The cunning of a dog, which Sergeant Wilde tells me of, as known to him, is equal. He used to be tied up, as a precaution against hunting sheep. At night he slipped his head out of the collar, and returning before dawn, put on the collar again, in order to conceal his nocturnal excursion. Nobody has more familiarity with various animals (besides his great knowledge of his own species) than my excellent learned, and ingenious friend the Sergeant; and he possessed many curious ones himself. His anecdote of a drover's dog is striking, as he gave it me, when we happened, near his place, to meet a drove. The man had brought seventeen out of twenty oxen from a field, leaving the remaining three mixed with another herd. He then said to the dog, "Go fetch them," and he went and singled out those very three. The Sergeant's brother, however, a highly respectable man, lately sheriff of London, has a dog that distinguishes Saturday night, from the practice of tying him up for the Sunday, which he dislikes. He will escape on Saturday night, and return on Monday morning. The Sergeant himself had a gander which was at a distance from the goose, and, hearing her make an extraordinary noise, ran back and put his head into the cage, then brought back the goslings one by one, and put them into it with the mother, whose separation from their brood had occasioned her clamour. He then returned to the place whence her cries had called him. A swallow had slipped its foot into the noose of a cord attached to a spout in the College des Quatre Nations at Paris, and, by endeavouring to escape, had drawn the knot tight. Its strength being exhausted in vain attempts to fly, it uttered piteous cries, which assembled a vast flock of other swallows from a basin between the Tuileries and Pont Neuf. They seemed to crowd and consult together for a little while, and then one of them darted at the string, and struck at it with his beak as he flew past; and others, following in quick succession, did the same, striking at the same part, till, after continuing this combined operation for half an hour, they succeeded in severing the cord, and freeing their companion. They all continued flocking and hovering till night; only, instead of the tumult and agitation in which they had been at their first assembling, they were chattering as if without any anxiety at all, but conscious of having succeeded.—*Lord Brougham's Dissertations on Science.*

Languages of the United Kingdom.

It is worthy of remark, that there is no civilized country in Europe in which not only so many different dialects prevail, but so many different languages, as in Great Britain. Yorkshire has its peculiar dialect; Lancashire, Northumberland, and Cumberland, theirs. The peasant of Worcestershire, understands not him of Westmoreland; and still less can he of the latter county hold any intelligible communication with the cockney.

In the vicinity of Cambridge, if you talk good English to a labouring man or small farmer, they touch their hat, beg your pardon, and, passing on, in evident reluctance to continue the conversation, avow themselves to be "no scholars." In Scotland, the dialects, and especially the "twangs," are as various as in England. Your native of Aberdeen understands not him of Glasgow; and your Paisley "budy," learned in politics and cunning at the loom, gapes, stares, and looks unutterable astonishment, when he is addressed by a man of Tweeddale. The Irish are more uniform in their dialect when they do speak English; the thing remarkable to them being the accent. All this is anomalous; but not so much as the fact that we have, in the two islands denominated Great Britain and Ireland five distinct languages cut up into so many dialects that it would be endless to enumerate them. There is the English language, properly so called; the Scotch language; and there are the Gaelic, the Welsh, and the Irish languages.—*Late paper.*

From a useful chart, or "Ecclesiastical Directory," just published, we perceive that the number of places of public worship in the city and liberties of Philadelphia is 127; not including the public charitable institutions where worship is held. The several denominations are as follows,—

Roman Catholic,	6
Protestant Episcopal,	19
Reformed Episcopal,	1
Methodist Episcopal,	22
Methodist Protestant,	4
Presbyterian,	24
Reformed Presbyterian,	3
Associate Presbyterian,	2
Baptist,	17
German Baptist	1
German Lutheran,	2
Evangelical Lutheran,	2
German Reformed,	3
Reformed Dutch,	2
Orthodox Friends,	4
Hicks Friends,	3
Free Quakers,	1
Universalists,	2

The following denominations have each one place of worship,—Moravian, Congregational, Independent, Unitarian, Jews, Christian Society, Philadelphia Christians, Bible Christians. We believe there is one Swedenborgian omitted in the chart.

There is also a Mariners' church, besides two that are included in the number of Baptist and Methodist churches.

The number of names set down as pastors or assistants is 126.

A similar chart, published in 1830, gives the number of places worship 83, and of ministers 72. Of the names of ministers only twelve are the same in both charts.

The population supplied as above numbers more than 200,000; but in estimating the sufficiency of church-room for the inhabitants, the number of infants, and sick and infirm persons should be considered, also the number of domestics and others who cannot attend but

one service on the Lord's day. The population of the prisons, alms-houses, &c., should also be deducted from the aggregate of the census.

Of the places of worship in the above list, eleven are exclusively occupied by coloured persons, viz. 4 Methodists, 3 Baptists, 3 Presbyterians, and 1 Episcopal.—*S. S. Journal.*

The British parliamentary report on drunkenness, states, that the number of persons that went into fourteen gin-shops in one week, were—142,453 men, 180,593 women, and 8,391 children; total, 269,438.

Judge Erskine made a very impressive charge to the grand jury of the Dorchester assizes, last week, upon the necessity of a *religious* education. He said the question of general education was one of the greatest importance; it had occupied the minds of the most eminent men, and it was to be regretted that some unobjectionable plan for affording necessary instruction to all classes had not been devised. It was known, however, from experience, in this country, and more so from the state of other countries, where extended plans had been carried into operation, that mere education, unaccompanied by the instilment of sound *religious* principles, did not tend to lessen crime. His lordship continued, with much emphasis, "If you wish to lessen crime by extending education, the education you give the people must be based upon the revealed will of God."—*English paper.*

THE SEA SERPENT.

On Saturday, Sept. 7, the schr. Planet, of Sag Harbour, Capt. David Smith, when about thirty miles off Seguin, coming into the Kennebec, ran within forty feet of the sea serpent. The captain and all the hands had a distinct view of him. They could see his whole length. His colour and shape were very nearly like a black snake, without any thing like fluke or fins. Most of the time he had his head out of water four or five feet. He was as long as the schooner, about seventy feet, and his body appeared as large as a barrel, but the captain thought it was larger in the middle. When first noticed, he was close to the schooner, and swimming quickly. As he passed toward the stern, he fell into the wake, then turned and followed the vessel for fifteen or twenty minutes, all the time being in full view of the crew, and so near them as to preclude all possibility of their being deceived.

Captain Smith has been many years in the whale fishery, and spent all his whole life at sea; yet he never saw such an animal before. He had harpooned a great many whales, and had then a harpoon on board; but he was without the necessary lines and lances to capture such an ugly looking customer as this. The serpent was quick in his motions, and evidently a very powerful creature. His body appeared smooth—nothing like bunches upon his back, as some have described him.

They were probably deceived by his undulatory or wriggling motion in swimming, his back appearing above the water at regular distances.

Captain Smith is well known here as a man of strict veracity and unimpeachable character. His statement is implicitly believed by those who know him.

After this, and the numerous other accounts we have had, we see no loophole on which to hang a doubt of the existence of a sea serpent of prodigious size inhabiting the sea. There cannot be many of them, or they would be seen oftener. Probably there is more than one, but it is remarkable that no one has ever seen two of them in company.—*Kennebec Journal.*

Religion enhances every Enjoyment.

We may see how completely religion is adapted to the nature of man, by observing that even the elements of enjoyment (and they are many, though fleeting) which this world contains, are never fully tasted but by religious persons. Those abundant sources of pure delight which are to be found in the heart, the intellect, and the imagination, are never received in their fulness but by them; and why? because they are the germs of their future and more glorious being, and can only flourish in a soil akin to that ultimately destined for them. In a worldly mind, like plants removed from their original soil and climate, they exist, indeed, but with a blighted existence; and produce, but how degenerate is the production! Every thing that wants religion wants vitality. Philosophy without religion is crippled and impotent; poetry without religion has no heart-stirring powers; life without religion is a complex and unsatisfactory riddle; the very arts which address themselves to the senses never proceed so far towards perfection as when employed on religious subjects. Religion, then, can be no obstacle to enjoyment, since the only sources of it which are confessedly pure are all enhanced by its possession. Even in the ordinary commerce with the world, what a blessing awaits an exemption from the low and sordid spirit, the petty passions and paltry feelings, which abound in it!

COLONIZATION AT TRINIDAD.

It is stated in the Boston Daily Advertiser, that the governor of Nova Scotia has given public notice, that the government of the island of Trinidad will pay twenty-five dollars for the passage of each labouring person of African descent, whether male or female, from Nova Scotia or either of the neighbouring provinces to Trinidad; and the same sum for the passage of two children between seven and fourteen years of age, or for three from one to seven years of age. This sum is to be paid as a free gift, and no claim will be made at any time for its repayment.

The notice remarks, that according to the rate of wages given on the island, a labourer, whether male or female, may easily earn daily, between sunrise and sunset, wages equal to four shillings, or five shillings Nova Scotia currency. Such labourers as do not choose to work the whole day, may be at liberty to work as much time during the day as will entitle them to half the allowance. They will have, in addition, the use of a good cottage and half an acre of productive ground, free from rent or any other charge. The soil is stated to be of great fertility, and land may be procured at from four dollars to sixteen dollars an acre in the best districts. An industrious labourer, by the earnings of a short period, may become the owner of a productive farm.

It is also stated that there are at the present time large sugar estates, and also estates producing cocoa and coffee, in Trinidad, owned by coloured persons, among whom are some who have risen into offices of honour and emolument under the royal government. Many coloured persons in Trinidad went from Nova Scotia several years ago, and are contented with their condition, supporting themselves comfortably. Exertions are making to give instruction to the whole of the labouring people, seventy-six public schools, besides many private schools, having been opened. Children whose parents cannot afford to pay are taught without charge. Religious sects are equally protected and assisted by the government. Ministers of every church receive moderate annual allowances from the colonial treasury: and it is customary to encourage the building of churches and chapels, by giving as large an amount of public money as the people may at any time raise among themselves for that purpose.

ART OF WRITING OR PRINTING.

That eminent Christian philosopher, Dr. Mason Good, draws the following contrast between oral tradition and the art of writing or printing.

"Such is a brief history of the noblest art that has ever been invented by the unassisted efforts of human understanding; an art that gives stability to thought, forms a cabinet for our ideas, and presents, in imperishable colours, a speaking portraiture of the soul. Without this, hard indeed would be the separation of friends, and the traveller would become an exile from his native home, vainly languishing for the consolatory information, that his wife, his children, his kinsmen, his country, were in a state of health and prosperity, and he himself still embalmed in their affections; without this, what to us would be the wisdom of past ages, or the history of former states? The chain of nature would be broken through all its links, and every generation become an isolated and individual world, equally cut off, as by an irremediable abyss, from its ancestors and from posterity. While the language of the lips is fleeting as the breath itself, and confined to a single spot, as well as to a single moment; the language of the pen enjoys, in many instances, an adamantine existence, and will only perish amidst the ruins of the globe. Before its mighty touch, time and space become annihilated; it joins epoch to epoch, and pole to pole; it gives unity to the works of creation and Providence, and enables us to trace from the beginning of things to the end. It is the great sun of the moral world, that warms, and stimulates, and vivifies, and irradiates, and developes, and matures the best virtues of the heart, and the best faculties of the intellect. But for this, every thing would be doubt, and darkness, and death-shade; all knowledge would be traditionary, and all experience local; civilized life would relapse into barbarism, and man would have to run through his little and comparatively insignificant round of existence, the perpetual sport of ignorance and error."

THE BALKING HORSE.

Who has not seen and been pained at the cruel punishment inflicted on a horse, which, taking what is called the "studs," refuses to move an inch forward, albeit he will back a horse took the studs in one of our principal streets. He was, as the bystanders all agreed, provokingly stubborn. He was coaxed and patted, but without effect—there was no "go-along" in him. It was distressing to see how he was whipped, now over the head, now on the back, again on the knees; and every one was pleased when a stranger, with a benevolent face and intelligent eye, interfered. "This is all wrong," he said, "you must not beat this horse any more. He has already been punished too severely." "What are we to do then?" asked the drayman, "I have been here for two hours trying to get him along. Must I let the horse stand here all day?" "No," replied the gentleman, "the horse must go along, but without any more punishment." "But he won't," expostulated the drayman. "O yes, he will, he must. The horse, I say, must go. He has but a reasonable load, looks as if he is fed well, and he must go along." "That is what I think," said the drayman. "Very well, I have seen how they make jackasses move in South America, and they are reputed more stubborn even than horses. I shall, therefore, make this horse go. Now get me a rope about twice as long as the horse." The rope was brought, and every body stood gaping, expecting, of course, that some hocus-pocus was about to be performed. The gentleman directed the rope to be tied to the horse's tail, and passed between his legs out in the front. He then took hold of it, and gave it a pull. The horse looked wild for an instant as if taken by surprise, and at the same time, gave strong indications, by kicking up behind, that he disliked the new plan of driving. The rope was pulled strongly, and the horse with a very quick motion, started off! The triumph was complete; one square's driving in that way, enabled him to return to the old mode, and the drayman drove off "amidst the shouts of the multitude."

"We live and learn," may well be said. Here, by a simple expedient, a horse was cured of the "studs," which, but for the timely arrival of the strange gentleman, might have been the subject of cruel and continued punishment for hours longer. The cause of humanity gained by it, and there was also a positive gain of "time, which is money."—*Balt. Patriot.*

For "The Friend."
ROBERT BARROW.
(Concluded from page 413.)

They found Solomon Cresson in Augustine, who gave them an account of his journey. The old cacique having, whilst at the town where the Dutch crew had been eaten the year before, discovered that he was not a Spaniard, the Indians began to look angrily upon him, and would allow him no food. In the morning they started on as if towards Augustine, but from their looks and conduct, he had no doubt but that they intended to kill him. A little after noon they put to shore, and kindled up a large fire. At this moment the sound of oars was heard, and the Spanish boat glided to the land. The Indians looked confounded, whilst the joy of Solomon was extreme. The Spaniards immediately ordered the cacique to return with them, taking his spoil from him, whilst they directed two Indians to show Solomon to the nearest Spanish settlement. The natives not appearing inclined to accompany him, he left them, and succeeded in reaching the place alone.

The necessary stock of clothing and provisions having been obtained, the whole company were soon ready to leave Augustine for Charleston. The governor, was desirous that Lopez and his boat might arrive before the departure took place, in order that the Englishmen might be furnished with whatever of their property had been saved from the wreck. J. Dickinson and Joseph Kirle told the governor, that they had given up all for lost, and if any thing was saved, they presented it to him, and to Lopez, and the company who had gone to their rescue. The governor replied he could have naught to do with it, for that all he had done had been for Christ's sake. They then told the governor that believing all that could be saved would be of little value, they had thought of making Lopez and his men an additional present of one hundred pieces of eight. This pleased the governor, and he promised to deliver it for them.

Robert Barrow was grievously disordered in his bowels from a cold which had fallen on them, which reduced him very low. Many of the men had been affected in a similar manner since having a sufficiency of food, and if their chief sustenance had not been vegetable, it is probable they would have lost more from over-eating than from all the hardships they had previously endured. After signing an obligation to pay four hundred pieces of eight for the provisions and clothing they had purchased, they on the 29th of the 9th month departed, accompanied by captain Francisco de Roma and six soldiers. The governor walked down to see them embark. He told them that they would forget him when they were among their own nation, but that God would not. With mutual courtesies and kind feelings they parted some time after noon, and sailed to Santa Cruz, where they were to remain for the night. They were directed to the Indian warehouse, which appears to have been a large circular building composed of sixteen cabins. Before these

they found fires were already kindled. They were here abundantly supplied by the Indians with what provisions they needed. There was in this town a large place of worship built by the Spaniards, on the services of which the Indians were constant attenders. In passing along they were surprised at the marks of industry apparent in the natives, who had plenty of hogs and fowls, and large corn houses, which bore testimony to heavy crops. About sunset of the 2d of 10th month they reached the town of St. Mary. Here they found the Indian warehouse to consist of thirty-two cabins, each painted, and well covered with mats. The native women here showed great dexterity in manufacturing a coarse cloth out of the moss obtained from some of their trees. From this cloth they made petticoats and gowns for themselves, which looked very neat at a short distance. The Indian boys were all kept at school, the teacher of which was the priest. This was the largest town our travellers saw. They remained here several days, making what provisions they could for their journey to Carolina.

With seven large canoes in which were seven Spaniards, and more than thirty Indians to pilot and to row them, they left St. Mary on the 5th of the 10th month. They passed along very pleasantly for several days, and on the tenth sent a letter express to the governor of Carolina, by an Indian. On the eleventh and twelfth the weather was exceedingly stormy, wet and cold. Their booths, in which they were obliged to remain during those days, did not keep out the rain, and Robert Barrow could neither be made warm, nor obtain any natural rest. Yet, through all he was cheerful and contented. On the fourteenth, it being the evening of the Spaniards' Christmas,* they used various ceremonies, tinkling a piece of iron, and begging presents from the Indians, who, in turn, begged of them. So that what the Indians gave the Spaniards the Spaniards returned to the Indians. After much wet and cold travelling, they on the 22d reached the first settlement in Carolina. This belonged to Richard Bennet, who received them in a very kind manner, provided for them plentifully, and treated their Spanish conductors with great hospitality. On the morning of the 24th, they reached the country seat of Governor Blake, who showed them much kindness, and sent Robert Barrow to the house of his neighbour, Margaret Bammers, an ancient Friend, who, he said, would be careful of him, and nurse him. The rest of the company went on to Charleston, where they soon separated; the most of the mariners obtaining employment in the vessels then in port. Joseph Kirle took passage for Providence, in hopes of a speedy return to Philadelphia. Robert Barrow continued very weak, and early in the 1st month, 1697, he was brought into Charleston, where he lay at the house of Mary Cross. He was anxious to live to reach Philadelphia, and although the captain, who had engaged to

* It should be observed, that these dates are all old style, and that two months and eleven days should be added, to bring each date to the time, according to the present mode of reckoning.

take J. Dickinson and family, was unwilling to receive him on board in his weak condition, yet his earnest entreaties prevailed, and having embarked on the 18th of 1st month, he was carried to Philadelphia in fourteen days.

The vessel reached the city on fifth day, the 1st of 2d month, about eight o'clock in the evening. Many Friends came on board to see him; but they found him so reduced by the disorder, which had now been on him fourteen weeks, that they were afraid to attempt his removal that night. But although very weak in body, his mind was strong, and he remarkably cheerful—rejoicing to see his friends, and to feel himself amongst those with whom he could enjoy the blessed fellowship of the gospel. He said, "It gives me great satisfaction that the Lord hath granted my request, in bringing me to this place, that I may lay down my body here. But my heart is strong, and I hope I may see you at your meeting first. He then extolled the merciful kindness which the Lord had displayed towards him, in that His presence had attended him through every exercise. The next morning, sixth day, the 2d, many Friends came early on board, and whilst the vessel was drawing to the wharf, and preparations making for his removal, he again testified his satisfaction in being with his friends, and his grateful sense of the Lord's goodness to him. Having wrapped him in a blanket, and placed him in a hammock, divers Friends assisted in carrying him to the dwelling of Samuel Carpenter. Here being laid on a bed, and having many of his friends around him, his heart seemed to overflow, and he could but again extol the goodness of his God. He said, "My heart is yet strong, and my memory and understanding good." He added, That he had not had any pain in his head through all his long illness and many exercises, and hoped Friends would yet see him at meeting. His mind then turned to his wife and family in much love, and whilst speaking in tenderness about them, he declared, "that his dear wife was a good woman, and his children were good children, and that he did not doubt but that they were well in the truth. I married my wife for truth's sake; she was God's gift to me, and I was God's gift to her; we parted in the love of God—nothing should have moved me there. to but to keep my peace with the Lord."

He then sank into a sweet slumber, and having slept the greater part of the day, he awoke towards evening, much refreshed. He then conversed freely with those Friends who visited him. The thankful emotions of his heart still prompted his tongue to pour forth the praises of Him, who had been near him through all his late difficulties and dangers.

On 7th day, the 3d, on being removed out of bed, he fainted; when he recovered, he said, "My heart never failed me before. I had thought I might have had one more harmonious meeting amongst you, but now I think it may be otherwise. But I am content in the will of the Lord, having finished the work he has given me to do. I have had

y heart's *desire* in coming here." After-
ards many Friends came in to see him, and
eir presence caused the heart of this lover
the brethren to rejoice. He put forth his
nd, and seemed ready to embrace them.
n some of the Friends expressing their glad-
ss to see him, and their sorrow at finding
m so weak, he replied, "Although my body
weak, my mind is sound, and my memory
od. The Lord has been very good to me
l along unto this very day; and this very
orning hath sweetly refreshed me. The
ord hath answered my desire, for I desired
ntent, and that I might reach this place, to
ing to have a conscience void of offence
wards God and towards men." In the
ening other Friends having called to
sit him, he inquired of them what had
come of George Keith's people. He was
ld that they were strangely divided; many
them were turned baptists, and the honest
earted had returned to Friends. After a
me, he said, " They have split upon that
ock, they have rejected; and it may yet
ease God to try you many other ways.
our neighbouring governments may tempt
ou to settle, or establish the national ministry
ere. Friends, stand fast in faithfulness against
, and touch not therewith. I believe they
ill also endeavour to persuade you to join
ith them in establishing and maintaining a
ilitia amongst you. Neither touch with
is. If you are faithful to the Lord, he will
efend and preserve you, and you need no
her means of preservation. If your way
eases the Lord, he will make your enemies
be at peace with you. That promise is
lfilled, and a remnant now witness it, swords
all be beaten into ploughshares, and spears
to pruning hooks. I have been convinced
out forty-five years, and have borne a faith-
l testimony against the hireling priests. I
ve been seven times in prison for my testi-
ony. The Lord has always been my pre-
rver and deliverer by ways that I thought
t of. So, Friends, he will be to you, if you
e but faithful to Him. Several who have
en committed as prisoners with me, have
ed indirect means to obtain their liberty ;
t it was always my resolution not to bow a
nee to Baal; and the Lord wrought my de-
verance. In my late affliction amongst
vage Indians, I have seen more of the
onders and dealings of the Lord, and more
to the mysteries of his kingdom than I ever
d before, or ever should have done, if I had
ot gone through it. The Lord's presence
as with me, which outbalanced all. I can
y as David did, it is good that I have been
fflicted. The Lord gave me patience in my
te sufferings, and I felt his power to sup-
ort me over all. On seeking to him, his
nswer was, let patience have her perfect
ork. This is a great work. I have found
at saying fulfilled, ' all things work to-
ether for good to those who love God.' I
as sick near twenty weeks in Jamaica, and
iissed but one meeting during that time.
Vhilst I was amongst the barbarous Indians,
ho thirsted or longed after our flesh, as
uch as we ever did after meat, I desired of

the Lord that I might not die by them, and
so be buried in oblivion.
"In Jamaica and Carolina there are but
few Friends; but this place is God's plantation; the Lord hath made you as a standard.
This place has a great fame abroad wherever
I have been since I left you, for an honest,
laborious, and good people. Friends keep up
your fame ! The way is by being faithful to
God, and keeping in love one with another.
Forgive the trespasses one against another,
and love one another ; for by this ye may
know if ye be the disciples of Christ. Meet
often together—for they that feared the Lord
met often together, and spake often one unto
another, and a book of remembrance was
written. The Lord in bringing me hither
hath given me the desire of my heart, and if
I die here, I am very well satisfied, and believe my wife will be satisfied also. For as
the Lord gave her to me, and gave me to her,
even so have we given one another up. When
I came from her, it was as if I was going to
my grave. Neither gold nor silver, riches
nor honour should have parted us. I only
did it in obedience to the Lord, and to keep
my peace with God. The Lord is with me,
and all is well. I have nothing of guilt upon
me, and have nothing to do but to die ; and if
I die now, I shall die like an innocent child.
"Many Friends that were round us in
Westmoreland who were rich men, and had
public testimonies, were much cumbered with
their worldly concerns, which proved a great
hinderance to them, and to their public service. I often spoke to them about it, for, I
had found mine a hinderance to me, and had
given all up into my son's hand ; he allowing
me and my wife so much by the year. Then
I was at liberty, and had the world under my
feet."
This deeply interesting and solemn season
in which Robert Barrow was enabled to clear
his mind of the exercise he felt, in the hearing of many of the principal Friends of Philadelphia, seemed a remarkable fulfilment of
his desire to have one more religious opportunity with them. It would appear that
having thus relieved his mind, he rested,
quietly waiting for his change. There are
none of his expressions recorded until the
next evening, first day, the 4th. He then desired a Friend who was sitting near him to
write for him to his wife. To remember his
dear love to her, to make her acquainted
with his travels and exercises. To let her
know that he was in Philadelphia, the Lord
being with him, and all well. That he was
as well nursed as if he were at home. That
his outward affairs were all settled, and that
she would have wherewithal to live on. This
message was delivered about the fifth hour.
The Friend promised to attend to it, after
which Robert seemed gradually to sink. At
six, a friend who stood by his bedside, remarking, in a low voice, he believed that
" I have my senses very perfect, and thank
the Lord that he hath not left me, but preserved me in my understanding to this moment." It was now difficult to understand
his speech through the declension of his

strength; but th
gone," were dist
last brief sentenc
still." After th
weaker and weak
away, to compel
that infinite good
celebrate on eart

From th
Tracts at the l

Mr. Lacey, of
in Orissa, says,
paired to the lar
of a large pakka
raised about sev
From this veran
the number of
Oriya, Bengali,
was immense, a
tracts very great
together, to obta
labour, I may v
never exerted b
house admitted o
in three places
other. After ea
we stayed our ha
Sometimes we w
seriousness. So
scattered in the s
but their numbe
the numbers give
." The cars of
moved past us as
surrounded by a v
living mass mov
consequence of
people, they also
scene was sorro
hearers were ca
tude, and the pa
came to our aid
' Hari bol !' and
sneer of bitterne
had passed, we a
work, and our c
must have been
cars. A good m
being eaten near
to the town, whic
the last night.
" Early this m
gadhar to the
distributed tract
We addressed a
passed. Afterw
cars on the large
the front of the h
and evergreens;
about in their g
decorated with
most brilliant c
glittering tinsel ;
the plain dry.
employed in the
evening; great
ceived tracts.
" This mornin
ed to the Athar
150 tracts, the l

when the sun became hot, completely exhausted by walking over the loose hot sand. Here our labours close, for this season, at Puri. A great number of persons have heard the word of God; and 11,000 books have been taken away, which contain the word of God able to save the soul.* This allows 500 for loss by tearing up, &c. And may God bless and succeed his word by imparting his Holy Spirit, which is promised in connection with the preaching of the gospel. This Spirit was given in the first times of the gospel, and hence the glorious effects which succeeded; this Spirit is now promised; and until it shall be poured forth, we shall preach in vain and labour in vain. O for a universal effort of prayer, faithful, believing prayer, instead of coldness and disbelief!"

POPERY AND THE BIBLE.

At the last anniversary of the British and Foreign Bible Society, the following statements were made by T. S. Grimshave:

During the time I was in Rome, but a few months ago, there were two Augustine friars who had received Bibles, and the effect had been that their minds had been enlightened; the character of their preaching was immediately changed; and (on the principle that, when a man once perceives the value of divine truth himself, he feels a desire to communicate that blessing to others) these Augustine friars went through different parts of the country, as we should say, preaching the gospel, and producing a powerful effect. At length they were checked by the power of the church of Rome, and lodged in the castle of St. ——, and there I left them, imprisoned for the great crime of reading the Bible! and preaching according to its divine contents. And further, to show what the degree of prosecution is, I would beg briefly to mention that a Swiss minister, distributing the Bible in a part of Italy, the name of which, perhaps it may be more prudent not to disclose, was in consequence visited by the police, and commanded to leave the country in forty-eight hours. I may also state that though he had distributed only a small portion of his books —I think about twenty-three Bibles and Testaments—those that had received them were actually imprisoned, some for six weeks, some for seven, and one for ten weeks, in consequence of having a copy in their possession.

KIDNAPPING.

The Massachusetts Spy, of 9th month, 25th, contains the following:

On the 12th inst. two persons, calling themselves Perly or Perlin Shearer, and —— Dickinson, came to the house of John F. Francis, a coloured man, in this town, and stated that Shearer was in want of a boy to live with him, and offered to take a son of Francis and "bring him up." Shearer, as he was called, represented himself as a trader in Palmer, which was confirmed by Dickinson, who professed to be Shearer's clerk, and recommended him as a very excellent person

* Portions of Scripture, we suppose, are meant.

with whom to place a boy. The parents finally consented to let them take a little boy of theirs, about eight years old. After they were gone, the parents became uneasy, and, finally, on the morning of the fifteenth, the father went in pursuit of his son. He wrote from Springfield, a day or two after, stating, that his son had gone to some place over the mountains, about forty miles from that place, whither he was going after him. Since that time nothing has been heard from him. He left home with but about three dollars of money, which sum must have been soon exhausted.

In the mean time, on the morning of the 23d instant, a letter was received from the mayor of Fredericksburg, Virginia, dated the 19th instant, informing, that on the 15th a man, calling himself Dickinson Shearer, arrived there, with a negro boy whom he called his slave, and that on the night of the 18th he parted with him, and it was feared had sold him to a slave trader. The circumstances were so suspicious as to lead to his arrest. On examination, he admitted that the boy was free, and that he came with him from Worcester, and that, when he obtained him from his parents, he did not inform them that he was going to take him to Virginia.

The story which he told, adds the writer, was "so absurd as to create a strong impression that he is a kidnapper, and information is sent to you that proper inquiries be made, and, if possible, evidence sent here to prove the boy's freedom, and to identify him. This, of course, must be some white person, and the abolitionists, if there be any among you, have now an opportunity of displaying their humane feelings. This man says he came from Pelham, [Palmer?] Massachusetts, and has a brother, a Doctor Shearer, residing there. Inquiries of the truth of this statement may be material. All that humanity requires will be done here to recover the unfortunate boy. A messenger will be despatched to-night in pursuit, and the constituted authorities invoked to aid him. This man is in custody, but cannot be long detained without evidence."

On receipt of this letter, immediate measures were taken to procure all the necessary dispositions, &c., and yesterday morning two of our inhabitants started for Fredericksburg, one of whom knows the boy, and will be able to identify him if he is to be found.

The circumstance has produced a strong sensation here, and much indignation is felt at the commission of so daring an outrage. The humane feelings displayed by the mayor of Fredericksburg, and the promptitude of his action in the case, are worthy of especial commendation. There is reason to believe that the name of Perly or Perlin Shearer was a false one, and that the person assuming it was merely an instrument in the hands of Dickinson, or Dickinson Shearer, who is unquestionably the principal in the transaction. We are not certain what the penalty for the offence is in Virginia, to the laws of which state he will be amenable for selling the boy, but we believe the crime is punishable with death.

POLITENESS.

The following anecdote is related of President Finley, of Princeton college. At a certain time he gave out *politeness*, as a theme for discussion, to one of the classes in college. The students were highly delighted with the subject, and discovered much ability and ingenuity in treating it. They read their dissertations, and expected he would, as usual, comment on their productions, examine the various opinions and arguments at length, and give his own judgment with his reason for it. They were, however, much surprised to hear him say, he had but a single remark to make, and that would be barely a definition of the term. Politeness, said he, is *real kindness, kindly expressed.*

The Wonders of Horticulture.

Innumerable are the advantages which mankind have derived from the horticulturists. Few would suppose that the peach (from which branched the nectarine) had its origin in the almond; or that the lemon proceeded from the diminutive wild lime. That favourite edible, celery, springs from a rank and acid root denominated smallage, which grows in all sides of ditches, and in the neighbourhood of the sea. The hazle-nut was the ancestor of the filbert and cub-nut; while the luscious plum can claim no higher source than the sloe. From the sour crab issues the golden pippin; and the pear and cherry originally grew in the forest. The garden asparagus, which grows, though not very commonly, in stony and gravelly situations near the sea, when growing spontaneously is a diminutive plant; and none indeed but a practised eye, examining into the species which is reared by artificial culture, can discern the least resemblance. Wondrous to relate, the cauliflower, of which the broccoli is a sub-variety, derives, together with the cabbage, from the colewort; a plant, in its natural state, and scanty leaves, not weighing half an ounce. The Crambe Maratima, which is found wild adjacent to the sea, has been improved into sea-kale; the invaluable potato is the offspring of a bitter American root of spontaneous growth; and the all-tempting pineapple descends from a fruit which "in foreign climates grows wild by the side of rivulets, and under the shade of lofty trees."—*Gardener's Gazette.*

KNOWLEDGE IS POWER.

At a meeting which took place the other evening for the purpose of forming a North London Mechanics' Institution, Basil Montagu, as an illustration of the maxim that knowledge is power, related the following anecdote. He was walking a few months ago in Portland-place, when he observed a large crowd of people assembled, and found that it was in consequence of a large mastiff dog having a lesser one in his gripe. Several persons tried, by splitting the mastiff's ear, and by biting and pinching its tail, to make it let go its hold, but in vain. At last a delicate and dandied young gentleman came up, and

...aking his way through the crowd, into the circle, requested to be allowed to separate the dogs; assent was given amidst jeers and laughter; when the dandy slowly drew from his pocket a large snuff box, and having taken a pinch himself, inserted his fingers again into the box and withdrawing a larger pinch deliberately applied it to the mastiff's nose. The snuff operated so powerfully on the animal's olfactory nerves, that it not only immediately let go its hold, but made its escape as fast as it could. The dandy was loudly jeered, upon which he stopped for a moment and said, "Gentlemen, I have merely given you a proof that ! Knowledge is Power."—*London paper.*

From an Irish Magazine.

THE OCEAN,

Likeness of Heaven !
Agent of power!
Man is thy victim !
Shipwrecks thy dower |
Spices and jewels
From valley and sea,
Armies and banners
Are buried in thee.

What are the riches
Of Mexico's mines,
To the wealth that far down
In the deep water shines ?
The proud navies that cover
The conquering west—
Thou fling'st them to death
With one heave of thy breast.

From the high hills that view
Thy wreck-making shore,
When the bride of the mariner
Shrieks at thy roar;
When like lambs in the tempest,
Or mews in the blast,
O'er thy ridge broken billows
The canvass is cast.

How humbling to one
With a heart and a soul,
To look on thy greatness
And list to its roll;
To think how that heart
In cold ashes shall be,
While the voice of eternity
Rises from thee !

Yes! where are the cities
Of Thebes and of Tyre ?
Swept from the nations
Like sparks from the fire;
The glory of Athens,
The splendour of Rome,
Dissolved—and for ever—
Like dew in thy foam.

But thou art almighty,
Eternal—sublime—
Unweakened—unwasted—
Twin brother of Time !
Fleets, tempests, nor nations
Thy glory can bow;
As the stars first beheld thee,
Still chainless art thou !

But hold! when the surges
No longer shall roll,
And that firmament's length
Is drawn back like a scroll;
Then—*then* shall the spirit
That sighs by thee now,
Be more mighty—more lasting,
More chainless than thou.

HONESTY REWARDED.

A friend of ours in the city of New York had in his possession a few days since, among other money, *a thousand dollar bill* on a southern bank. As he was looking over his funds for the purpose of making a deposite in a bank, he missed this bill, and was utterly at a loss to know by what means it was out of his hands. Endeavouring to recollect the last time he had seen it, he called to mind the fact that during the evening previous, he had shown the bill to a friend, in his parlour up town. As this was the last recollection he could catch of his lost money, he hurried to his friend's house, and without ceremony entered the parlour and made search, supposing that he might have dropped it upon the carpet. Not finding it, he was about giving it up in despair, but ringing for the servant, a coloured woman, he asked her if she had found any thing on the floor. "Yes," said she, "I've got it, I've got it," and immediately produced the thousand dollar bill rolled carefully in a bit of paper. It had actually blown out of the window, and was found detained by the iron railing of the piazza, with the face of the bill towards the house. The gentleman, as may be imagined, was not a little pleased to receive his money, and gave the coloured woman twenty dollars for her honesty. She was delighted with her reward, and expressed her determination always to do the thing that is right.—*Newburg Journal.*

Mix Straw with Clover.—Farmers who have straw or coarse old hay, will find a great advantage in mixing them in layers, with hay that is not thoroughly made; the dry stuff will prevent the clover from injuring by moisture, and it imbibes sweetness, so that the cattle will eat it with a good relish.—*Yankee Farmer.*

THE FRIEND.

TENTH MONTH, 5, 1839.

In entering upon another year of editorial labour and responsibility, we derive encouragement from the fact, that our subscription list, both in point of stability and numerically, wears a better aspect than at any former period. But yet the amount of support is but an approximation to what it should be, seeing that "The Friend" is the only periodical of the kind, in this country, exclusively devoted to the interests of our religious Society. We therefore remind our agents every where that this is a suitable time to revive their exertions for the obtainment of new subscribers. We give them credit for the success in this way which has attended former exertions, and this success should animate them to renovated efforts, at least sufficient to fill up the blanks occasioned by death and otherwise. A revised list of agents is in preparation, and will be inserted next week. The index for Vol. XII., it is expected, will accompany next number.

At the risk of being laughed at for easy credulity, we have copied from an exchange paper a recent account of the long talked of sea serpent, which has on the face of it all the appearance of truth and soberness. In fact, we do not hesitate to avow our belief that such a monster has occasionally visited our shores, and our conviction rests upon the testimony of an intelligent and very estimable minister of our religious Society, now gone to his final rest, who, in our hearing, circumstantially, and in a way entirely to remove all previous scruples on the subject, related what he saw himself of this strange visitant.

BINDING.

Volume XII being now completed, those who wish to have the work bound, can have it neatly done by sending their numbers to this office. The sooner the better, if any numbers are to be supplied. Other binding done also to any pattern.

Respectfully,
GEO. W. TAYLOR.

The winter term of Franklin Park School will commence on second day, the 7th of 10th month next.

MAYBERRY M'VAUGH,
BENJAMIN H. DEACON.

9mo. 16th, 1839.

The winter term of Haverford School will commence on fourth day, the 9th of tenth month next, under the direction of the following Friends as its officers, viz. John Gummeré, Superintendent of the institution and Teacher of Mathematics; Daniel B. Smith, Teacher of Moral Philosophy, English Literature, &c. ; William Dennis, Teacher of the Latin and Greek Languages and Ancient Literature; Saml. J. Gummeré, Teacher of Mathematics and Natural Philosophy; Benjamin V. Marsh, Assistant Superintendent.

The terms are $250 per annum, payable as follows, viz. $75 at the commencement, and $75 at the middle of the winter term, and $100 at the opening of the summer term. Copies of the last annual report, with such further information as may be desired, will be furnished by the undersigned, to whom applications for admission are to be addressed,

By direction of the managers.

CHARLES YARNALL, Secretary,
No. 39 Market street, Philadelphia.

Philadelphia, 8 mo. 29, 1839.

WANTED, a Friend to act as Steward of the above Institution. Also, one to take charge of the Farm. Apply to

KIMBER & SHARPLESS,
No. 8 South Fourth street.

COAL.

Schuylkill, Lehigh, Hazleton, and Laurel Hill Coal for sale by George W. Taylor, at the office of "The Friend."

PRINTED BY ADAM WALDIE,
Carpenter Street, below Seventh, Philadelphia.

THE FRIEND.

A RELIGIOUS AND LITERARY JOURNAL.

VOL. XIII.   **SEVENTH DAY, TENTH MONTH, 12, 1839.**   **NO. 2.**

EDITED BY ROBERT SMITH.

PUBLISHED WEEKLY.

Price two dollars per annum, payable in advance.

Subscriptions and Payments received by

GEORGE W. TAYLOR,

NO. 50, NORTH FOURTH STREET, UP STAIRS,

PHILADELPHIA.

SCENES IN SOUTHERN AFRICA.

The subject of an article in a late number of the London Quarterly Review, is a narrative by Capt. W. C. Harris " Of an Expedition into Southern Africa during the years 1836 and 1837, from the Cape of Good Hope through the territories of the chief Moselekatse to the tropic of Capricorn, &c. &c." We have marked off some portions for insertion in " The Friend," interesting at least for their novelty.

The travellers now entered upon the nearly flat and entirely treeless Chooi desert, all suffering, the poor oxen especially, from want of water. During the night the hyænas, attracted by the smell of their mutton, devoured a spring-buck within the very limits of their camp. As they advanced, the game became hourly more abundant, though very wild.

" Groups of hartebeests [*Acronotus Caama*], quaggas, and brindled gnoos, were every where to be seen. A short chase was sufficient to seal the fate of three quaggas—all males, averaging thirteen hands high. During the run I had not seen a human being, and fancied myself all alone: but I had scarcely dismounted to secure my game, when a woolly head protruded itself from every bush, and in an instant I was surrounded by thirty Baralongs, who, having by signs expressed their approbation of my performance, proceeded to devour the carcass with the greatest avidity—greedily drinking the blood, rubbing the fat upon their bodies, and not leaving so much even as the entrails for the birds of prey."

On they went among the broken remnants of various Bechuana tribes conquered by Moselekatse, and now destitute of cattle, and depending entirely for subsistence on locusts and the produce of their pitfalls. These desolate wretches hovered round the captain's little band to divide a portion of the spoil with the vultures, hyænas, and jackals. The winged scavengers wheeling in circles above their heads " were ever ready to pounce upon game that had been shot, or upon the carcasses of oxen that perished on the road—devouring the largest bodies with a promptitude truly surprising."

The Chooi desert was now passed, and before reaching the Siklagole river they journeyed by many ruined though recently inhabited villages. Two days had now elapsed since they had seen a human being not of their own party ; and when, on the morning of the 9th of October, the wagons had started for the Meritsane river, the captain, led by the love of sport, made a deviation that had nearly terminated his career, and wanted but little of leaving his bones to bleach on the arid sands :—

> " The sun's eye had a sickly glare,
> The earth with age was wan ;
> The skeletons of nations were
> Around that lonely man."

Surely this little episode is given with admirable ease, simplicity, and energy.

" I turned off the road in pursuit of a troop of brindled gnoos, and presently came upon another, which was joined by a third still larger—then by a vast herd of zebras, and again by more gnoos, with sassaybys and hartebeests, pouring down from every quarter, until the landscape literally presented the appearance of a moving mass of game. Their incredible numbers so impeded their progress, that I had no difficulty in closing with them, dismounting as opportunity offered, firing both barrels of my rifle into the retreating phalanx, and leaving the ground strewed with the slain. Still unsatisfied, I could not resist the temptation of mixing with the fugitives, loading and firing, until my jaded horse suddenly exhibited symptoms of distress, and shortly afterwards was unable to move. At this moment I discovered that I had dropped my pocket-compass, and, being unwilling to lose so valuable an ally, I turned loose my steed to graze, and retraced my steps several miles without success, the prints of my horse's hoofs being at length lost in those of the countless herds which had crossed the plain. Completely absorbed in the chase, I had retained but an imperfect idea of my locality, but, returning to my horse, I led him in what I believed to be a north-easterly direction, knowing, from a sketch of the country which had been given me by our excellent friend Mr. Moffat, and which, together with drawing materials, I carried about me, that that course would eventually bring me to the Meritsane. After dragging my weary horse nearly the whole of the day under a burning sun, my flagging spirits were at length revived by the appearance of several villages. Under other circumstances, I should have avoided intercourse with their inhospitable inmates, but, dying with thirst, I eagerly entered each in succession, and, to my inexpressible disappointment, found them deserted. The same evidence existing of their having been recently inhabited, I shot a hartebeest, in the hope that the smell of meat would as usual attract some straggler to the spot. The keen-sighted vultures, that were my only attendants, descended in multitudes, but no woolly-headed negro appeared to dispute the prey. In many of the trees I observed large thatched houses resembling hay-stacks ; and, under the impression that these had been erected in so singular a position by the natives as a measure of security against the lions, whose recent tracks I distinguished in every direction, I ascended more than one in the hope of at least finding some vessel containing water. Alas, they proved to be the habitations of large communities of social grosbeaks, those winged republicans of whose architecture and magnificent edifices I had till now entertained a very inadequate conception. Faint and bewildered, my prospects began to brighten as the shadows of evening lengthened. Large troops of ostriches running in one direction plainly indicated that I was approaching water ; and immediately afterwards I struck into a path impressed with the foot-marks of women and children—soon arriving at a nearly dry river, which, running east and west, I at once concluded to be that of which I was in search.

" Those only who have suffered, as I did during this day, from prolonged thirst, can form a competent idea of the delight, and, I may add, energy, afforded me by the first draught of the putrid waters of the Meritsane. They equally invigorated my exhausted steed, whom I mounted immediately, and cantered up the bank of the river, in order, if possible, to reach the wagons before dark. The banks are precipitous—the channel deep, broken, and rocky—clusters of reeds and long grass indicating those spots which retain the water during the hot months. It was with no small difficulty, after crossing the river, that I forced my way through the broad belt of tangled bushes which margined the edge. The moonless night was fast closing around, and my weary horse again began to droop. The lions, commencing their nightly prowl, were roaring in all directions, and, no friendly fire or beacon presenting itself to my view, the only alternative was to bivouac where I was, and to renew my search in the morning. Kindling a fire, I formed a thick bush into a pretty secure hut, by cutting away the middle and closing the entrance with thorns ; and, having knee-haltered my horse to prevent his straying, I proceeded to dine upon a guinea-fowl that I had killed, comforting myself with another draught of *aqua pura*. The monarchs of the forest roared incessantly, and so alarmed my horse, that I was obliged repeatedly to fire my rifle to give him confidence. It was piercingly cold, and, all my fuel being expended, I suffered as much from chill as I had during the day from the scorching heat. About three o'clock, completely overcome by fatigue, I could keep my eyes open no longer, and, commending myself to the protecting care of Providence, fell into a profound sleep.

"On opening my eyes my first thought was of my horse. I started from my heathy bed in the hope of finding him where I had last seen him; but his place was empty. I roamed every where in search of him, and ascended trees which offered a good look-out, but he was no where to be seen. It was more than probable he had been eaten by lions, and I had almost given up the search in despair, when I at length found his foot-mark, and traced him to a deep hollow near the river, where he was quietly grazing. The night's rest, if so it could be called, had restored him to strength, and I pursued my journey along the bank of the river, which I now recrossed opposite to the site of some former scene of strife, marked by numerous human skeletons, bleached by exposure. A little further on I disturbed a large lion, which walked slowly off, occasionally stopping and looking over his shoulder, as he deliberately ascended the opposite bank. In the course of half an hour I reached the end of the dense jungle, and immediately discovered the wagon-road; but, as I could detect no recent traces upon it, I turned to the southward, and, after riding seven or eight miles in the direction of Siklagole, had the unspeakable satisfaction of perceiving the wagons drawn up under a large tree in the middle of the plain. The discharge of my rifle at a little distance had relieved the anxiety of my companions and followers, who during the night had entertained the most gloomy forebodings on my account, being convinced that I had either been torn piecemeal by lions, or speared by the assagais of the cannibals! A cup of coffee was immediately offered me, which, as I had scarcely tasted nourishment for thirty hours, proved highly grateful."—pp. 67–73.

Nothing daunted, however, we find our sportsman, soon after passing the river, leaving the wagons again—with a companion however. Sallying through a magnificent park of *Kameel dorn* trees—many of which were groaning under the huge nests of the social grosbeak, whilst others were decorated with green clusters of misletoe with bright scarlet berries—they soon came upon large herds of quaggas and brindled gnoos; which continued to join each other until the whole plain seemed alive. We quote another masterly piece of writing :—

"The clatter of their hoofs was perfectly astounding, and I could compare it to nothing but the din of a tremendous charge of cavalry, or the rushing of a mighty tempest. I could not estimate the accumulated numbers at less than 15,000 ; a great extent of country being actually chequered black and white with their congregated masses. As the panic caused by the report of our rifles extended, clouds of dust hovered over them ; and the long necks of troops of ostriches were also to be seen,

towering above the heads of their less gi tic neighbours, and sailing past with asto ing rapidity. Groups of purple sass [*Acronotus Lunata*], and brilliant red yellow hartebeests, likewise lent their ai complete the picture, which must have seen to be properly understood, and w beggars all attempt at description.

savages kept in our wake, dexterously patching the wounded gnoos by a touch the spine with the point of an assagai, instantly covering up the carcasses bushes, to secure them from the voraci the vultures, which hung about us like sp in the firmament, and descended with the locity of lightning, as each discharge of artillery gave token of prey. As we ceeded, two strange figures were perce standing under the shade of a tree ; these instantly knew to be elands [*Bosela; Oreas*], the savages at the same moment claiming with evident delight, *Impoofo, poofo*, and, pressing our horses to the utr speed, we found ourselves for the first t at the heels of the largest and most beau species of the antelope tribe. Notwithsta ing the unwieldy shape of these animals, t had at first greatly the speed of our je horses, but, being pushed, they soon s: rated ; their sleek coats turned first blue then white with froth ; the foam fell, f their mouths and nostrils, and the persp tion from their sides. Their pace gradu slackened, and, with their full brilliant e turned imploringly towards us, at the enc a mile, each was laid low by a single l They were young bulls, measuring upw of seventeen hands at the shoulder.

"I was engaged in making a sketch of one I had shot, when the savages came and, in spite of all my remonstrances, | ceeded with cold-blooded ferocity to stab unfortunate animal, stirring up the blood, shouting with barbarous exultation as it iss from each newly-inflicted wound, regard of the eloquent and piteous appeal, expres in the beautiful clear black eye of the n and inoffensive eland. In size and shape body of the male eland resembles that o well-conditioned Guzerat ox, not unfreque attaining the height of nineteen hands, weighing 2000 pounds. The head is stri: that of the antelope, light, graceful, and bc with a pair of magnificent straight hor about two feet in length, spirally ringed, pointed backwards. A broad and deep dew fringed with brown hair reaches to the kr The colour varies considerably with the s being dun in some—in others an ashy b with a tinge of ochre—in many sandy g approaching to white.

"The flesh is esteemed by all classes Africa above that of any other animal ; grain and colour it resembles beef, but is l ter tasted and more delicate, possessin; pure game flavour ; and the quantity of with which it is interlarded is surprisi greatly exceeding that of any other ga quadruped with which I am acquainted. female is smaller and slighter of form, w less ponderous horns. The stoutest of savage attendants could with difficulty tra

10 feet high, though Tournefort says that in some places he was obliged to stoop a little, and that at one point, about the middle of the road, they found the passage so low and so narrow, that they were obliged to crawl on their hands and knees, one by one. This passage neither ascends nor descends very much; the floor is smooth and level from side to side; the walls or sides are perfectly perpendicular, and formed of the solid rock, except here and there, where they are cased with masonry most carefully executed. At every ten or twelve paces new passages of the same sort present themselves, and they, in their turn, either break off into other passages, or return to the original passage from which they had diverged. After an apparent progression in this subterranean puzzle of nearly an hour, North Douglas's party, who thought themselves in the very heart of the mountain, came back upon their packthread at the very place whence they had started. This gentleman remarked as a striking peculiarity, that, instead of finding any close or unwholesome air in these narrow recesses, they breathed as freely when they were nearly a mile from its mouth as when they first entered the labyrinth. He also observed that all the angles in this singular excavation were as sharp as if they had just been cut. In one of the passages he, with great difficulty, discovered, through a narrow aperture, a small octagonal room, remarkable for the elegance of its form. Tournefort speaks of two small chambers, almost round (presque rondes), cut in the rock, at what he considered the most distant or innermost part of the labyrinth. On the walls of these rooms he found several names of visiters, which had been written with charcoal during the time that the Venetians were masters of Candia. He copied two or three of these; for example:—"Qui fu el strenuo Signor Zan de Como, Capno. dela Fanteria, 1526." (Here was the bold Signor Zan de Como, a captain of infantry.) "P. Francesco Maria Pesaro, Capucino (a Capuchin friar); Frater Taddeus Nicolaus (another friar), 1539." In these rooms, and in the passages leading to them, were several other dates (written or cut out by the chisel), ranging from the year 1495 to 1579, and Tournefort added 1700, the year of his visit. According to this correct old traveller, the most tortuous and difficult part of the labyrinth is that which branches off to the left at about thirty paces from the entrance, where an infinitude of passages, some crossing each other, and some having no outlet, perfectly bewilder the explorer. Sandys, who visited the island of Candia more than two centuries ago, but whose curiosity did not lead him to the labyrinth, tells us, that he "had heard an English merchant (who hath seen it) say, that it was so intricate and vast, that a guide which used to show it unto others for twenty years together, lost himself therein, and was never more heard of." There is no water dripping through the rocks, no congelation of any kind, but, through-out, the labyrinth is dry, and the air of an equal and pleasant temperature.

According to the early part of Grecian history or tradition, where fable is mingled with fact, or nearly every thing is to be taken in an allegorical sense, the key to which we have lost, the labyrinth was made, in imitation of a similar work in Egypt, by Dædalus, the Athenian, for the second Minos, king of Crete, who flourished some thirteen centuries before the Christian era. The story of the monstrous Minotaur that ranged through these recesses, and of Theseus, who was shut up in them to be devoured, and of the fair Ariadne, who extricated her lover by giving him a clue of thread, belongs to the most imaginative part of mythology, and will hardly assist us in conjecturing what the place was really intended for. It has been called a catacomb, but no remains of any kind, indicating that it was put to such a use, have ever been found in it or about it. "The labyrinth," says North Douglas, "could never have been intended for a burial place, as we find none of those recesses in the walls which were used as sepulchres in the catacombs of Italy and Malta, nor, indeed, any other place fitted for the reception of a corpse." Belon, and other old travellers, concluded it was merely a stone quarry. Sandys says, "But by most this is thought to have been but a quarry, where they had the stone that built both Cnossus and Gortyus; being forced to leave such walls for the support of the roof, and by following of the veins, to make it so intricate."

A modern traveller, Monsieur Sonnini, who, however, like Sandys, never visited the labyrinth, adopts this opinion, and unnecessarily refers the quarry to a much more modern date. North Douglas, who, Theseus-like, explored the passage with a clue of thread in 1812, objects to these conclusions. He says, "Independently of there being no city nearer to it than Gortyna, which in comparatively modern times could never have required so large a quantity of materials, is it likely that there would have been such extreme regularity of design, such handsome chambers and entrances, and above all, such artful intricacy, so evidently intended to mislead, if the object to recommend it—that precisely the same material is found in the hill directly above Gortyna, and close to Cnossus. Was it then probable that people would seek at a distance across rude mountains and deep valleys for what they had close at hand? Would they make a choice of all kinds of difficulties rather than cut stone on the spot they wanted it, and where there were no difficulties at all? After a good deal more to the same purpose, Tournefort concluded that the labyrinth was originally the work of nature—a lusus naturæ, but that man, whose handiwork is every where visible in it, had taken delight, or had found some advantage, in enlarging it where it was narrow, and in giving regularity to its sides, roof, &c. "The ancient Cretans," he continues, "a people highly civilized and much attached to the fine arts, were disposed to finish what nature had only sketched out. Without doubt some shepherds having discovered these subterranean passages, gave room to greater men to make out of them this marvellous labyrinth, which might serve as an asylum to many families; during civil wars or the reigns of tyrants, although they now only serve as a retreat to the bats." He might have added, that in ages when robbery and violence were held to be heroic virtues, and the seas of Crete swarmed in an especial manner with pirates, the people flying from the coast at times would be happy to have so excellent a hiding place for themselves and their goods.

He conjectures that the ancient Cretans did not touch that part of the passage where it is necessary to crawl on hands and knees, because they wished posterity should know, by seeing it, how all the rest was made originally by nature, and how much their art and industry had done to improve it. Beyond that narrow passage the labyrinth is as regular and beautiful as it is before reaching that point. In support of Tournefort's hypothesis it should be mentioned, that many natural grottoes and long caverns exist in this volcanic island, and that Mount Ida, close by, is in many places quite honey-combed with them.

We will offer no conjecture of our own, but leave that pleasant field open to our readers. One thing is certain, that whether it be the labyrinth so often referred to by ancient writers (and we are inclined to think it is), or whether it be wholly, or only in part, the work of man, the labyrinth visited and described by Tournefort and North Douglas, is an exceedingly curious and interesting place.
—Penny Magazine.

From the National Gazette of seventh day, the 5th inst.

EXTENSIVE FIRE AND LOSS OF LIFE.

About eleven o'clock last night a fire was discovered in the basement story of W. J. Stroup's provision store, No. 14 South Wharves, between Chestnut and Market streets, facing the Delaware river. Three custom house watchmen, William Abel, Pierson Horn, and James Lenten, broke open the door, and state that a few buckets of water would have extinguished the fire, but the draught created by opening the door instantly increased it, and extended to various combustible merchandize. In a few minutes the flames burst out and reached the adjoining store of D. W. Prescott. This house was built back to Water street, facing No. 19 on that street. In the same range the store of George Merrill took fire immediately afterwards.

Although the fire companies were promptly on the ground, the progress of the flames was so rapid, that the prospect of arresting them was, even at that early hour, very doubtful. The grocery stores of C. Cheese. borough and of George A. Wood, No. 15 south wharves, the oil store of Newlin and Allibone, and the commission store of J.

rew
the
the
ing
ped

was
uni-
ier,
i to
ion
A.
the
ier-
uc-

est-
ad-
i is
iive
l7 ;
r of
ire-
H.
No.
ire-
Co.
ise,
ter
the
de-
or
his
o.'s
by
J.
ind

as
the
the
nut
ind

ld-
ing
ere
vas
ho-
ek-
d ;
is-
it ;
he
hn
im
nt-
y's
o.
7 ;
19,
of
oy
M.
on
se
ofs
o.
st
of
ly
is

direction, beyond the expectations of the
spectators. Meanwhile the flames had extended to the Steamboat Hotel, on the south
side of Chestnut street, at the corner, of
Water. Next door a cooper's shop was
destroyed, and the office and baggage depot
of the Camden and Amboy line was materially injured. At the south-west corner of
Water and Chestnut streets the fire reached
the clothing store of Enoch Allen ; next the
barber shop of William Gorgas, next to
Martin's tavern, No. 57 Front street, and to
the German commission house of Meisgies
& Unkart, No. 59. These houses were
wholly consumed. The other stores in the
same range, of J. B. M'Ilvaine, Wm. P.
Hanna, and Charles Field & Son were slightly
injured.

The sparks set several buildings on fire in
Taylor's alley. J. Rowland's liquor store
was seriously damaged, and a large four story
building also injured.

In Chestnut street above Front the store
of Durden B. Carter was considerably burnt,
and the store of Henry Risborough partially.

We have not yet been able to ascertain the
names of the owners of the buildings which
were injured or destroyed by this calamitous
fire. All which were within the circle of the
flames were burnt literally to the ground.
Not a particle of wood work is left in them,
and the walls of many have fallen entirely.
There prevailed during the whole night a
strong north-east wind, which rapidly extended the conflagration and greatly increased
the difficulties of operating against it efficiently.

In several of the stores the oil, liquors, and
other combustibles, blazed for hours with intense violence. Explosions were frequent,
and several are said to have been kegs of
gunpowder. At six o'clock this morning the
indefatigable and daring exertions of the firemen had reduced the flames, and further destruction of property ceased to be apprehended. It is impossible to commend, in
terms too ardent or grateful, the labours of
the firemen on this occasion. When they
had no opportunity of working at the engines
or performing other duties, they got drays
and carts in the neighbourhood, loaded them
with goods and furniture, and dragged them
with infinite toil to places of secure deposit.
The mayor and the whole body of watchmen
were on the ground, protecting the property
scattered about the streets, and preserving
order among the thousands of spectators who
thronged to the disastrous scene.

The amount of property of various kinds
thus destroyed it is impossible to estimate
with precision, but it may be reasonably
stated at about 600,000 dollars. This loss is
most untimely. Never, we learn, have the
merchants of this city stood more in need of
regular and prosperous trade.

The extensive warehouse of David S.
Brown, commission merchant, we omitted to
mention among the buildings slightly injured.
Although greatly exposed, it was saved by
the use of wet blankets on the roof and in the
windows.

The most painful portion of this recital yet
remains. *Several, we know not how many,
have been killed or severely wounded.* At
eight o'clock this morning the walls of Enoch
Allen's house fell with a tremendous crash,
and buried in the ruins, as we learn positively,
a fireman named W. Moreland, a member of
the Good Will Engine. He was instantly
killed. Others it is feared were also mortally
hurt. Two of the wounded were carried to
the hospital.

William Field, a fireman, was severely
injured.

James Smiley, a member of the Diligent
Hose Company, fell into a burning cellar,
and had his head much cut and his hands
burned.

James Barber and John Douglass, members of the Good Will Engine Company, and
a member of the Hope Hose Company, whose
name we did not learn, are missing, and the
worst is feared concerning them.

Bernard Timmins, also of the latter company, is severely burnt.

Jacob Kugler, fireman, badly burnt.

We have just learned that *Thomas* not
James Barber was an engineer at the Mint,
and not a fireman. He was taken to the
hospital, and died in about three hours, leaving a wife and three children.

Robert Reynolds and Charles Herman,
members of the Weccacoe Engine, were both
seriously injured by a bale of cotton thrown
from the upper window of one of the stores.

Many poor families have been thus turned
from their homes, and have lost a great portion of their furniture and clothing. There
was generally insurance on the property as
far as we have been able to ascertain, but the
particulars on this head we cannot yet state
with accuracy. It is proper to mention,
however, that the disaster will *not cause any
failures.* There are various surmises concerning the cause of the fire, which many
suppose was the work of an incendiary. The
firemen are now—twelve o'clock, M. leaving
the scene of conflagration with their apparatus.

This, we believe, is the most destructive
fire which has ever occurred in Philadelphia.
Of fifty-two buildings which were on fire,
forty are in total ruin, many of them large
new warehouses.

American Free Produce Association.

The first annual meeting of the American
Free Produce Association will be held in
Philadelphia on 15th of 10th mo. at Clarkson Hall. Societies auxiliary to this are requested to send large delegations, and the
friends of the cause generally are invited to
attend. On behalf of the executive committee.

ABM. L. PENNOCK, Chairman.
DANL. L. MILLER, Jr. Secretary.

HAVERFORD SCHOOL.

WANTED, a Friend to act as Steward of
this Institution. Also, one to take charge of
the Farm. Apply to
KIMBER & SHARPLESS,
No. 8 South Fourth street.

For "The Friend."

THOMAS COLLEY.

Thomas Colley, of Sheffield, England, who visited this country in the year 1785, was a friend extensively known, and highly esteemed as a faithful and diligent minister of the gospel of Christ, in which he laboured during a period of more than forty years.

He was born at Smeaton, a village near Pontefract, in Yorkshire, in the year 1742, and was educated in the principles of the established church of England, and at the early age of eleven years was placed as an apprentice in Sheffield. During his minority his mind was awakened to the importance of a religious life, and he joined in communion with the Methodists, amongst whom he was zealous, active, and held in good esteem.

In the year 1764 he married. About this period the performances and observations in which he had been engaged, failing to satisfy that travail, which, in divine mercy, had been raised in his soul, he sought for something more inward and substantial, and in this disposition of mind was drawn to attend the meetings of Friends. Waiting reverently before the Lord, he became further acquainted with the operation of divine grace, and was engaged to press after a deeper knowledge of those things which accompany salvation.

He continued his attendance of the religious meetings of Friends diligently, until he observed that some, who were active in the concerns of the Society, absented themselves from those held near the middle of the week. Reflecting on his own circumstances, which were then low in the world, and influenced by their example, he for a time followed their practice, but found that by so doing he suffered loss in a spiritual sense, and was therefore engaged diligently to attend meetings for divine worship. We are admonished by this incident of the importance of a consistent life in all those who are making a high profession of religion; by the want of it such often become, in different ways, stumbling blocks in the path of honest inquirers, and not only suffer loss, but are in danger of bringing upon themselves the reproof addressed by our Lord to some of old, "Ye enter not in yourselves, and them that were entering in ye hindered." At the same time it is highly important for those who are seeking the way to Zion not to look out at the example of others, but to keep a single eye to the Shepherd and Bishop of their souls, who is the author of eternal salvation to all who obey him.

Having given proof of his sincere attachment to our religious principles, Thomas Colley was in due time received into membership with Friends, and in the year 1768 he was first engaged in public labour as a minister; and being careful to occupy the talents committed to him, his services were acceptable and edifying. Not long afterwards, he felt himself called upon to travel in the service of the gospel; and performed several journeys, with the unity of his friends.

In 1779, in company with his friend Philip Madin, also of Sheffield, he paid a visit to the then remaining members of our Society on the island of Barbadoes, and also on a few of the other British West India Islands. He was brought very low when on his passage across the Atlantic; but his mind appears, by a memorandum made at the time, to have been greatly consoled in this season of conflict of spirit, in the fresh remembrance of the sufferings of the unconquered Captain of our salvation; and he was enabled to look, in faith, unto Him, and to lay hold on his gracious promises.

Being permitted to return home in safety, he penned the following reflections: "Under a grateful remembrance of the many favours of the Almighty, graciously extended to us, through the course of this long and perilous journey, in preserving us in the midst of a raging and tumultuous war, in opening our way in the service in which we were engaged, and affording ability and strength to discharge the duty of the day, are our spirits humbly bowed in deep reverence and thankfulness to the Father and Fountain of all our living mercies."

A few years after his return from this voyage, he again left his near connections, and travelled extensively in North America, where his gospel labours were well received, and made a deep and instructive impression on the minds of many of those whom he visited, some of whom yet remain amongst us, retaining in advanced life a lively remembrance of this devoted servant of Christ.

In his native land he travelled much afterwards as a minister; and was often concerned, more particularly in the latter part of life, to labour, in word and doctrine, among those of other religious societies. In reference to one of these journies he wrote thus from London : " I have laboured many weeks in this populous place; visited all the meetings in this city, and most of them on first days; and also have attended their quarterly and monthly meetings, and have had public meetings at all the meeting-houses, and in other places ; in which service, I may with reverence acknowledge, that the Lord has been near, and his ancient promise fulfilled, 'As the day is, so shall my strength be.' The meetings have generally been large; neither unfavourable weather, nor snow on the ground, prevented the people from attending ; and that living power, which is both ancient and new, was a crown and diadem to our assemblies."

When not engaged in religious service, he was diligent in attention to his business, which was that of a cutler, and of which the superintendance, during the periods of his absence from home, devolved in great measure upon his wife, who, not only in a religious sense, but also in regard to temporal concerns, was truly a " help-meet," and the honest industry of both was attended with the blessing of Providence.

In the year 1796 he felt his mind engaged to address an affectionate epistle to the youth of Sheffield meeting, which is subjoined to this memoir, not only as exhibiting his concern for this interesting class, but as being appropriate to the circumstances of the youth amongst us, and particularly that description of them, who, coming from a distance to acquire a knowledge of business, are removed from under the care of their natural guardians, and are often exposed to many temptations. To such and to our youth in general, these Christian councils and advices are tenderly recommended.

Thomas Colley was a man whose deportment in life was such as becometh one employed in preaching the glad tidings of salvation; his manners were grave and unaffected, though on suitable occasions he was cheerful and communicative. He was desirous to keep himself unspotted from the world, and his general demeanour manifested on whom his confidence was placed. In religious meetings his reverent silent waiting was obvious to others, and had a tendency to draw them into the same frame of spirit. He was uprightly concerned for the due preservation of our Christian discipline, and careful to keep his place in the meetings established for its support. In the exercise of the ministry he was diligent in waiting for the renewed influence of divine power ; and was thereby often eminently qualified to set forth the blessing of salvation through our Lord Jesus Christ, who came as a sacrifice for sin, and as the light of the world ; fervently endeavouring, in the ability received, to gather all to the inward, immediate teachings of the Holy Spirit.

In the year 1810, he attended the yearly meeting in London, near the close of which he had a dangerous attack of illness ; but was restored to his family and friends. He afterwards held a few public meetings in his own neighbourhood, and diligently attended other meetings at home. Towards the latter end of the year there were obvious symptoms of a declining state of health, which occasioned him to remark to a friend : " I have for a considerable time apprehended I should have a lingering illness, and have never desired it might be otherwise. I do not, as some have done, wish for a sudden removal, as I think, divine providence, as well as divine grace, is as much manifested in times of sickness, as in times of health ; and it now yieldeth me great consolation, that I worked while health and ability were afforded. I now see but little to be done ; and it is cause of great satisfaction, that I was enabled to perform my last religious visit to London."

For some time he had been seldom heard in his own meeting, but he now frequently spoke, both in testimony and supplication, with clearness, and in the power and love of the gospel, manifesting, as a father in the church, his continued and increasing solicitude for the spiritual progress of those amongst whom he had long and faithfully laboured. The solemnity which prevailed on these occasions, made a deep and instructive impression on his friends.

In the eleventh month, 1811, he was seized with violent illness, which he expected to survive only a few days; but being a little revived, he said to a friend who visited him, " I am a poor weak creature, uncertain how this attack may terminate; nor am I anxious about it. For some time past, I have been concerned to use the strength afforded, in discharging manifested duties; and, on retrospect, I do not see one religious duty or service left undone."

After this he gradually declined; and in the sixth month, 1812, he became very weak. On the 10th of that month, when one of his friends, who had called on him, was about to take his leave, having to attend a meeting of ministers and elders that evening, he said, with a calm and expressive countenance, "The Lord bless thee; and may He be with you in all your movements, in the promotion of his work. How long the taper may glimmer in the socket is uncertain; I think it will not be long. My love to Friends. Farewell."

He spoke but little afterwards, appearing to be in a state of patient waiting for the full accomplishment of the divine will concerning him; and, on the 12th of the sixth month, 1812, he expired, in the seventieth year of his age, having been a minister forty-four years. "Mark the perfect man, and behold the upright, for the end of that man is peace,"

                             T. K

The following is the epistle mentioned in the preceding memoir; it is addressed to "The Youth of Sheffield Meeting."

Dear Young Friends,—Having often felt my mind drawn in tender affection towards you, with desires for your preservation in the truth; that you might know an advancement in righteousness and holiness, and a growth in sound experience; so at this time, I feel a freedom to address you in a degree of that love, which is both ancient and new, and which extends over all the Lord's heritage; desiring to guard you against the dangerous snares of the enemy, and encourage you to persevere in the way of truth and righteousness.

We are called with an high and holy calling, even that in our lives and conversation we should glorify God, the object of worship, and the author of every good and perfect gift.

The profession which many of you have derived from education, is awful; that of believing in, and living under, the government of the spirit of Christ; and great have been the advantages which you have been partakers of, in that your minds are directed, both by precept and example, to a certain evidence of divine truth in your hearts. This hath been the guide of the faithful in all generations, through the slippery paths of life, and hath clothed them with strength and salvation, in proportion to their attention and obedience thereunto: whilst those who disregard this law of the spirit of life, which alone can set free from the law of sin and death, and follow lying vanities, are left in a state of uncertainty, and are strangers to that good, which the Lord hath in store for them that love him.

Your situations and circumstances in this place are rather peculiar. Youth are brought from distant parts, of different dispositions, whose minds may have received impressions from various kinds of examples, before they come. This hath been the cause of much solicitude, in the minds of well-concerned Friends. Example is very prevalent, and if you measure yourselves by the standard of those who are not careful to live in the fear of the Lord, you may soon become wrapped up in an unsafe confidence, and gradually settle in a state of insensibility, like some of old, whose apprehension of divine things was so darkened that they said, "the Lord will not do good, why should we love him?—neither will he do evil, why should we fear him"—Whenever a mind becomes so estranged from God, as to have no true sense of his love and power in their hearts, who is the fountain of happiness and true centre of the soul, such will then be seeking to draw satisfaction from things without them, and propose to themselves, that which they will not be able to obtain; encouraging themselves, and one another, in the pursuit thereof, in a disposition like that which is described in Solomon's recantation, when, representing the language of flesh and spirit, which are in continual opposition to each other, he saith, "Rejoice, O young man, in thy youth, and let thine heart cheer thee in the days of thy youth. Walk in the ways of thine heart, and in the sight of thine eyes." But they do not consider the following sentence, viz.—"But, know thou, that for all these things God will bring thee into judgment. Therefore, remove sorrow from thy heart, and put away evil from thy flesh; for childhood and youth are vanity."

Truly the situation of some is to be lamented, who, notwithstanding all the care of pious parents, and religiously concerned friends, and against all the checks and remonstrances of the spirit of truth in their own minds, continue to slight the reproofs of instruction from within, and the admonitions of their friends, as instrumentally applied. These will become like the heath in the desert, who see not when good cometh, and like unto the salt which has lost its savour, that is henceforth good for nothing. How much better would it be, in the early stage of life, before the ramparts of the mind become weakened by wrong impressions, or evil habits, by custom, be established, to take the counsel of the wise man, "Remember now thy Creator in the days of thy youth; whilst the evil days come not, and the years draw nigh, when thou shalt say, I have no pleasure in them;" as also the doctrine of our Lord, who certainly knew what was best for us to do. He said, "Seek first the kingdom of heaven, and the righteousness thereof."

An early acquaintance with the Lord, and dedication of heart to him, prepares their tender minds, according to their capacities, for filling up their respective duties in life; first to God, to whom we are accountable for our time in this world, and from whom we must receive a recompense in the world to come; and next, our relative duties in social life. First, then, our duty to God is a surrender of our hearts and affections to him, who hath called in the language of wisdom, "My son, give me thy heart, and let thine eyes observe my ways." This will bring to

a state of
daily cros
and reduc
cence with
Though
stations in
watchfulne
pective po
principle c
contribute,
advancem
in righteo
Holy Gho
ed with h
filling up
There is g
rectitude c
Humility
people, are
esteem. I
" that bef
haughty, c
And it wa
writing to
sober-min
tended to, i
tion; for i
as well as
and of the
and advice
the paths o
acquainted
steps, and
qualified t
in, and by
them. Fo
formerly,
honour of
confirmed
the sons."
As one
succeedeth
the Almig
will attain
whom the
of truth m
fear: and
different g
pain of mi
cerned to
" Likewise
unto the
that have
selves, for
that must
As you
blishment,
dience to,
seek after
Be diligen
divine wor
the Lord,
ever a slac
in the atte
dicates a l
to the Lor
more liber
self will, a
their own
friends.
Let oth
cherish a

near to the spring of divine life. Thus, as you advance in years, you may grow in grace, and in the knowledge of the truth; that, when the elders are removed from works to rewards, their seats may not remain empty; but that you, being prepared by the Lord's forming hand, may fill up the places of the faithful, in the promotion of the work of righteousness in the earth. With the salutation of gospel love, I remain, your friend,

THOMAS COLLEY.

Testimony of Infidels to the character of Jesus Christ.

Vanina, an Italian scholar, who suffered death for his atheism, frankly acknowledged that he could find nothing in the history and actions of our Saviour that he could charge with secular interest or design, by which to blast him or his religion. Bolingbroke allows that Jesus taught, in all cases, one continued lesson of the strictest morality, of justice, benevolence and universal charity. Paine acknowledges the leading trait of the character of Jesus to be philanthropy. Gibbon records "his mild constancy in the midst of cruel and voluntary sufferings, his universal benevolence, and the sublime simplicity of his actions and characters." Lequino, a French unbeliever, speaks of him as the wisest and best man that ever lived, as a generous philanthropist; as having wholly sacrificed himself to the public good, giving his whole existence to the unhappy, never lying to his persecutors, but teaching them virtue. Voltaire and Rosseau both acknowledge him to be "infinitely superior" to Socrates. Rosseau's memorable words are often quoted: "If the life and death of Socrates are those of a philosopher, the life and death of Jesus Christ are those of a God."

Glass Works at Sandwich, Massachusetts.

The yards and buildings of this establishment cover six acres of ground. It employs two hundred and twenty-five workmen, who, with their families, occupy sixty dwelling houses.

The raw material used, per annum, are, glass, 600 tons; red lead, 700,000 pounds; pearl-ash, 450,000 pounds; saltpetre, 70,000 pounds. They consume 1,100 cords of pine wood, 700 cords of oak ditto, and 100,000 bushels of bituminous coal.

Seventy tons of hay and straw are used for packing the glass.

The amount of glass ware manufactured is $300,000 per annum, said to be superior to any other manufactured in America, and equal to any in Europe.

By the application of heated air from the steam-engine, to pans containing sea water, they manufacture about 3,000 bushels of salt per annum; and all the ashes are bleached, and the lye converted to potash. It is said that the mere saving to the company by this species of economy, which is carried through every department, is sufficient to pay a handsome dividend on the stock.

PUNISHMENT OF DEATH.

The following important statement has been recently published by the committee of the British Anti-Capital Punishment Society. In the year 1821, there were 114 executions in England and Wales. In 1828 the number was reduced to 59; in 1836, to 17; and in 1838 it was only 6. That this change has been effected without diminishing, even in the slightest degree, the security of the persons and properties of men, is a matter of the clearest evidence, the evidence of actual experience, which cannot be disputed or falsified. The government returns prove that there have been fewer highway robberies the last five years, with 5 executions, than in the preceding five years with 36 executions;—that there have been fewer acts of burglary and housebreaking in the last six years, with only 3 executions, than in the preceding six years, when 56 persons suffered death for those crimes;—that there has been less horse-stealing in the last nine years, without any execution, than in the preceding nine years, during which, for that offence alone, 46 convicts were sent to the scaffold.

BAKED TOMATOES.

Those who find the tomato too acid, when stewed, &c., may relish them when cooked as follows:

Cut the tomato in two, and removing a part of the contents, fill them with crumbs of grated bread, and season parsley, salt, pepper, a little butter, &c. Then bake them like apples, for twenty or thirty minutes, and they will be a dish to set before the sultan himself. In this and other forms, any one may raise in his garden, cheaper and more palatable medicine, than under this popular name is to be obtained from the apothecary.

STRAWBERRIES.

A writer in the New England Farmer states that one of his neighbours in Dedham (Mass.) has received from the sale of strawberries the present year, an amount that would be equal to $1120. an acre. The ground cultivated measured 10 rods, has a southern aspect, and is of ordinary quality. This patch was planted with the Methven Castle four years since, has been well taken care of, and is now well covered with vines. From June 18th to July 19th, was sold strawberries to the amount of $77. The quantity gathered during this period, weighed 258 lbs. and measured 9 bushels and 3 pecks. The amount of expense for labour, manure, and sending to market, was $6 44. These strawberries were sold at the Astor House, N. Y., and none were sent measuring less than two and a half inches in circumference. The writer very justly remarks:

"This cultivator reaped more from his little patch of ground than many of our farmers do from acres; and so it will be till they can learn to cultivate less land, and that, from their bad management, generally half starved."

A farm should be an extended garden; and then every inch of ground, for the care we have taken of it will bountifully repay our labour. Mother earth is better than her children; she is grateful for favours and returns them.

CIRCULAR.

Philadelphia, Ninth Mo. 1839.

Esteemed Friend,—It has long been a subject of deep concern to many Friends, that the people of colour who are amongst us, are deprived of so many of the advantages partaken of by other members of the community. The Managers of the "Institute for Coloured Youth," impressed with these views, have the satisfaction to state they have purchased a farm, which is considered very eligible for the purposes of the proposed Institute, being about seven miles north of the city, on the Willow Grove or Old York Turnpike Road. On this place it is intended to receive a limited number of coloured children, who will be instructed in farming, some of the useful arts, and the elementary branches of an English education; in the hope that if the young be thus prepared to enter on the duties of life, they will be qualified to take their station as useful members in the community.

In taking this preliminary step towards carrying out the wishes of the benevolent individual to whose liberal bequest, in connection with the contributions of other friends, we are indebted for the means of making a commencement in this effort, the funds have been nearly exhausted; but trusting that the sympathies of the members of our Religious Society will be increasingly awakened in behalf of the oppressed portion of the human family, for whose benefit this fund is intended, we are encouraged to hope that an appeal will not be made in vain, but that ample means will be afforded to carry on this important work. We respectfully request thy pecuniary assistance for this desirable object, as well as thy influence and exertion in procuring the aid of others.

Signed by direction and on behalf of the Board of Managers.

CASPAR WISTAR, Secretary.

Donations or subscriptions will be gratefully received by either of the undersigned managers:

Benjamin Cooper, near Camden, N. J.; George Williams, No. 71 North Seventh street; Philip Garrett, Noble above Sixth street; Blakey Sharpless, No. 8 South Fourth street; Thomas Evans, No. 129 South Third street; John G. Hoskins, No. 50 North Fourth street; Saml. Mason, jr. No. 68 North Seventh street; John Elliott, Race above Seventh street; Thomas Wistar, jr. Abington; Caspar Wistar, No. 184 Arch street; Mordecai L. Dawson, N. W. corner Tenth and Filbert streets; Marmaduke C. Cope, No. 286, Filbert street; Stephen P. Morris, N. E. corner Eighth and Spruce streets; Joseph Scattergood, No. 14 Minor street; Wm. Biddle, N. W. corner Eleventh and Arch streets.

For "The Friend."

THOUGHTS IN A GROVE.

"The retiring of the mind into itself, is the state most susceptible of divine impressions."—LORD BACON.

How beautiful ye are—green trees! green trees!
How nobly beautiful! Fain would I rest
'Neath the broad shadow of your mantling arms—
And lose the world's unquiet imagery
In the soft mist of dreams. Your curtaining veil
Shuts out the revelry and toil that chafe
The city's denizens. Man wars with men,
And brethren forage on each other's hearts,
Throwing their life-blood in that crucible
Which brings forth gold.
    Perchance we vaunt ourselves
Among our fellow-worms, and reach and strive,
And gaze at gauds, and cling to wind-swept reeds,—
Then darkly sink and die,—
    But here ye stand,
Your moss grown roots by hidden moisture fed,
And on your towering heads the dews that fall
From God's right hand. I love your sacred lore,
And to the silence you have learned of Him
Bow down my spirit. Not a whispering leaf
Uplifts itself, to mar the holy pause
Of meditation.
    Doth not wisdom dwell
With silence and with nature? From the throng
Of fierce commanding or of feverish joys,
So the sweet mother of the Lord of life
Turned to the manger and its lowly train;
And, mid their quiet ruminations, found
Refuge and room.
    Methinks an angel's wing
Floats o'er your arch of verdure, glorious trees,
Luring the soul above. Oh! ere we part—
For soon I leave your blessed company,
And seek the dusty paths of life again—
Give me some gift—some token of your love—
One holy thought, in heavenly silence born—
That I may nurse it till we meet again.   L. H. S.

Hartford, Connecticut, Sept. 30th.

THE FRIEND.

TENTH MONTH, 12, 1839.

We rejoice that the benevolent and beautiful conception which was among the last thoughts of the late Richard Humphreys of this city; and of which his legacy, amounting with the interest to fourteen or fifteen thousand dollars, will form the foundation, is now in a likely way to be realized. The proof of this will be found in the circular on another page, to which we invite the attention of all our readers. Here is presented a fair and appropriate occasion for the exercise of a liberal spirit, and of giving tangible evidence of good feeling towards a greatly injured portion of the human family.

We learn with pleasure that at the request of a number of our most respectable fellow citizens, Dr. James Espy of this city, previously to his intended departure for Europe, has concluded to deliver a course of lectures before such of the literary and scientific societies and citizens of Philadelphia, as feel an interest in the science of meteorology. Having enjoyed the privilege of attending several of the interesting lectures delivered by him on this his favourite pursuit, at Friends' Reading Room, some two or three winters ago, we were agreeably entertained, and incited to admiration at the extent and variety of curious and valuable information which in

familiar language he unfolded to the class. Since that period the doctor has devoted much time to the subject, and we are informed has accumulated a large accession to the amount of facts corroborative of the theories or discoveries which he hopes to establish; and we therefore entertain the expectation that the proposed course of lectures will be rendered peculiarly entertaining and instructive. In our next number we shall probably be able to announce the time, place, and terms of the course.

The continued solicitude evinced by the managers of Friends' Reading Room to provide liberally for the improvement and rational entertainment of our young Friends, of which the following notice is a fresh proof, we hope will be met by a corresponding readiness on their part diligently to avail themselves of the proffered benefit. The qualifications of Dr. Bryan as a lecturer are already advantageously known.

Lectures at Friends' Reading Room.

Dr. J. Bryan will commence a course of sixteen lectures on Anatomy and Physiology, in the lower room occupied by Friends' Reading Room Association on Apple-tree alley, near Fourth street, on fifth day evening next, the 17th instant, at 7½ o'clock.

LIST OF AGENTS.

MAINE.
  Peter W. Morrell, Portland.
  Daniel Taber, Vassalborough.
  William Cobb, South Windham.
  Stephen Jones, Jr., Palermo.
NEW HAMPSHIRE.
  Moses Gove, Jr., Weare.
  Jonathan Beede, Poplin.
MASSACHUSETTS.
  Abijah Chase, Salem.
  James Austin, Nantucket.
  William C. Taber, New Bedford.
  Stephen Dillingham, P. M., Falmouth, Cape Cod.
  John M. Earle, Worcester.
  Thomas Akin, P. M., S. Yarmouth.
VERMONT.
  Dr. Harris Otis, Danby, Rutland Co.
  John Knowles, Monkton, Addison Co.
RHODE ISLAND.
  R. J. Peckham, Providence.
  Job Sherman, Newport.
NEW YORK.
  Mahlon Day, City of New York.
  Joshua Kimber, Flushing, L. I.
  William Willis, Jericho, L. I.
  John F. Hull, Stanfordville.
  Asa B. Smith, Farmington.
  Jesse P. Haines, Lockport.
  Charles Field, Saw Pit.
  Joseph Bowne, Butternuts.
  Thomas Townsend, Lowville.
  Elihu Ring, Tromansburg.
  Thomas Bedell, Coxsackie.
  Moses Sutton, Jr., Pinesbridge.
  Samuel Adams, New Paltz Landing, Ulster Co.
  Ephraim Potter, Granville, Washington Co.
  Isaac Moshec, Queensbury, Warren Co.
  William Keese 3d, Keeseville, Essex Co.
  Nathaniel Adams, Canterbury.
  James Congdon, Poughkeepsie.
NEW JERSEY.
  Charles Atherton, Burlington.
  John Bishop, Columbus.
  Samuel Bunting, Crosswicks.
  David Roberts, Moorestown.
  Caspar Wistar, Salem.
  Josiah Tatum, Woodbury.
  Hugh Townsend, Plainfield.
  Jacob Parker, Rahway.
  John N. Reeve, Medford.
  Benjamin Sheppard, Greenwich.
PENNSYLVANIA.
  George Malin, Whiteland.
  Charles Lippincott, Westchester.
  George G. Ashbridge, Downingtown.
  Isaac Pusey, Londongrove.
  Solomon Lukens, Coatesville.
  Jesse Spencer, Gwynedd.
  Jesse J. Maris, Chester.
  Thomas Wistar, Jr., Abington.
  Joel Evans, Springfield.
  James Moon, Fallsington, Bucks Co.
  Thomas Mendenhall, Berwick, Columbia Co.
  Jonathan Binns, Brownsville, Fayette Co.
  Jacob Haines, Muncy, Lycoming Co.
DELAWARE.
  John W. Tatum, Wilmington.
MARYLAND.
  John P. Balderston, Baltimore.
  Dr. Thomas H. Dawson, Easton.
  Dr. Thomas Worthington, Darlington, Ha
VIRGINIA.
  Micajah Bates, Richmond.
  William Davis, Jr., Lynchburg.
  Robert White, Barber's X Roads P. O
    Wight Co.
  Aaron H. Griffith, Winchester.
NORTH CAROLINA.
  Phineas Nixon, P. M., Nixon's, Randolph
  Jesse Hinshaw, New Salem.
  Nathan Hunt, Jr., P. M., Hunt's Store.
  Lambert Moore, P. M., New Garden.
SOUTH CAROLINA.
  Benjamin B. Hussey, Charleston.
OHIO.
  Ephraim Morgan, Cincinnati.
  Lemuel Jones, Mount Pleasant.
  James Stanton, Barnesville.
  Henry Crew, P. M., Richmond.
  John Street, Salem, Columbiana Co.
  John Negus, Upper Springfield, Columbi
  Thomas Talbert, Jacksonburg.
  Micajah Bailey, Wilmington.
  Gersham Perdue, Leesburgh, Highland C
  Aaron L. Benedict, Bennington, Delawar
  David Mote, West Milton, Miami Co.
  James W. Marmon, Zainesfield, Logan C
  William S. Bates, M. D., Smithfield, Jeffe
  William Foulke, Pennsville, Morgan Co.
INDIANA.
  Elijah Coffin, Richmond.
  William Hobbs, Canton.
  William Hadley, Mooresville, Morgan Co
  Richard Gordon, Spiceland.
  Jeremiah H. Siler, Rockville, Parke Co.
  Henry Hendley, Carthage, Rush Co.
  Joel Parker, P. M., New Garden.
MICHIGAN.
  Joseph Gibbons, Jr., Adrian.
UPPER CANADA.
  Augustus Rogers, New Market.
  Gilbert Dorland, Hallowell.
  Frederick Stover, Norwich.
LIVERPOOL, ENGLAND.
  Thomas Hodgson, No. 80, Lord street.

MARRIED, at Friends' meeting, Twelfth fourth day, ninth month, 25th, ISRAEL Mo ELIZABETH LONGSTRETH, both of this city. —— at the same meeting, on fourth instant, JOHN COLLINS, to ANNA BAILY, dau late Joshua Baily, of this city, merchant.

DIED, on the 11th of ninth month, at he in Wheeling, Va., very suddenly, FATIENC in the 61st year of her age, a member of of Friends, and formerly of New Bedford.

PRINTED BY ADAM WALDI
Carpenter Street, below Seventh, Phila

THE FRIEND.

A RELIGIOUS AND LITERARY JOURNAL.

VOL. XIII.   **SEVENTH DAY, TENTH MONTH, 19, 1839.**   NO. 3.

EDITED BY ROBERT SMITH.

PUBLISHED WEEKLY.

Price two dollars per annum, payable in advance.

Subscriptions and Payments received by

GEORGE W. TAYLOR,

NO. 50, NORTH FOURTH STREET, UP STAIRS,

PHILADELPHIA.

SCENES IN SOUTHERN AFRICA.

(Continued from p. 19.)

Pursuing their course, our travellers entered a pass which conducted them between two ranges of the Kurrichane hills, and here our strenuous captain met with a serious accident:—

"The ground was broken and stony, and in parts abounded with deep holes. In the act of killing a sassayby, my horse put his feet into one of these, and came down with frightful violence, cutting my knees and elbows to the bone, breaking his own nose, and, what was a far greater misfortune, and one that I had long anticipated, fracturing the stock of my only and especially favourite rifle. I could have wept if the doing so would have availed any thing. A strip of the sassayby's hide rectified the damage for the present at least; and, having packed the flesh in the wagon, we continued winding among the hills, constantly assured by the guides that the kraal at which they had resolved we should pass the night was close at hand, but still not reaching it until we had travelled full thirty miles from Mosega, by which time it was fairly dark. At last we perceived fires in the valley beneath us, and soon drew up under the fence of a little village."

Their arrival at the Moriqua was marked by a prize of some magnitude:—

"The approach to this small but beautiful river is picturesque in the highest degree. Emerging suddenly from an extensive wood of magnificent thorn-trees, we passed a village surrounded by green corn-fields, and then descended by a winding path into a lawn covered with a thick and verdant carpet of the richest grass, bounded by a deep and shady belt of the many-stemmed acacia, which margined the river on either hand far as the view extended—and clothed with a vest of golden blossoms, diffusing a delicious and grateful odour around. Single mokaalas, and detached clumps of slender mimosas, hung with festoons of flowering creepers, heightened the effect, screening with their soft and feathery foliage considerable portions of the refreshing sward, across which troops of querulous pintadoes and herds of graceful pallahs [*Antelope Melampus*] were to be seen hurrying from our approach.

"As we threaded the mazes of the parasol-topped acacias, which completely excluded the sun's rays, a peep of the river itself was unexpectedly obtained. A deep and shaded channel, about twenty yards in breadth, with precipitous banks overgrown with reeds, was lined with an unbroken tier of willows. These extended their drooping branches so as nearly to entwine, had they not been forbidden by the force of the crystal current, which swayed them with it as it foamed and bubbled over the pebbly bottom. A plain on the opposite side, bounded by a low range of blue hills, was dotted over with mokaala-trees, beneath which troops of gnoos, sassaybies, and harte-beests were reposing.

"We drew up the wagons on a verdant spot on the river-bank, at a convenient distance from an extensive kraal constructed on the slope. Although the sun shone, the cold occasioned by a dry cutting wind was scarcely to be endured even with the assistance of a great-coat; and the inhabitants being clamorous for food, I readily placed myself under the guidance of their chief with ten of his men, and, diving into the heart of the extensive groves, soon furnished them with the carcass of a black rhinoceros, upon which to whet their appetites. This huge beast crossed the river twice after being mortally wounded at duelling distance; and I was compelled, cold as it was, to wade after him, through water reaching to my middle—following his trail by the blood, until, from single drops, the traces became splashes of frothy crimson. Struggling to force his tottering frame through the tangled cover, the wounded monster at length sank upon his knees; another bullet from the grooved bore ending his giant struggles, while he was yet tearing up the ground with his ponderous horn."

Our sportsman was now to be gratified with the sight of game as unlike the heavy mass of life which he had lately extinguished as can well be imagined. He had crossed the river in search of elands, and had passed over a great extent of country without sport: but he can speak for himself.

"Beginning to despair of success, I had shot a hartebeest for the savages, when an object which had repeatedly attracted my eye, but which I had as often persuaded myself was nothing more than the branchless stump of some withered tree, suddenly shifted its position, and the next moment I distinctly perceived that singular form, of which the apparition had oft-times visited my slumbers—but upon whose reality I now gazed for the first time. It passed rapidly among the trees, above the topmost branches of many of which its graceful head nodded like some lofty pine—it was the stately, the long-sought *giraffe*. Putting spurs to my horse, and directing the Hottentots to follow, I presently found myself half choked with excitement, rattling at the heels of the tallest of all the Mammiferes, whom thus to meet, free on his native plains, has fallen to the lot of few of the votaries of the chase. Sailing before me with incredible velocity, his long swan-like neck keeping time to the eccentric motion of his stilt-like legs—his ample black tail curled above his back, and whisking in ludicrous concert with the rocking of his disproportioned frame, he glided gallantly along 'likes some tall ship upon the ocean's bosom,' and seemed to leave whole leagues behind him at each stride. The ground was of the most treacherous description; a rotten black soil overgrown with long coarse grass, which concealed from view innumerable cracks and fissures that momentarily threatened to throw down my horse. For the five minutes I rather lost than gained ground, and despairing, over such a country, of ever diminishing the distance, or improving my acquaintance with this ogre in seven-league boots, I dismounted, and had the satisfaction of hearing two balls tell roundly upon his plank-like stern. But I might as well have fired at a wall: he neither swerved from his course nor slackened his pace, and had pushed on so far ahead during the time I was reloading, that, after remounting, I had some difficulty in even keeping sight of him amongst the trees. Closing again, however, I repeated the dose on the other quarter, and spurred along my horse, ever and anon sinking to his fetlock; the giraffe now flagging at each stride, until, as I was coming up hand over hand, and success seemed certain, down I came headlong—my horse having fallen into a pit, and lodged me close to an ostrich's nest, in which the old birds were sitting.

"There were no bones broken, but the violence of the shock had caused the lashings of my rifle to give way, and had doubled it in half—the barrels only now hanging to the stock by the trigger guard. Nothing dismayed by this heavy calamity, I remounted my jaded beast, and one more effort brought me ahead of my wearied victim, which stood still and allowed me to approach. In vain I attempted to bind my fractured rifle with a pocket handkerchief, in order to admit of my administering the *coup de grace*—it was so bent that the hammer could not by any means be brought down upon the nipple. In vain I looked around for a stone, and sought in every pocket for my knife, with which to strike the copper cap, and bring about ignition, or hamstring the colossal but harmless animal, by whose side I appeared the veriest pigmy in the creation—alas, I had lent it to the Hottentots to cut off the head of the hartebeest. Vainly did I wait for the tardy and rebellious villains to come to my assistance, making the air ring, and my throat tingle, with reiterated shouts—not a soul appeared—and, in a few minutes, the giraffe, having recovered his wind, and being only slightly wounded in the hind quarters, shuffled his long legs—twisted his tail over his back—walked a few steps—then broke into a gallop, and, diving into the mazes of the forest, disappeared from my sight. Disappointed and annoyed, I returned towards the wagons, now eight miles distant, and on my way overtook the Hottentots, who, smoking their pipes, were leisurely returning, having come to the conclusion that 'Sir could not catch the camel,' for which reason they did not think it worth while to follow as I had directed.

"My defeat did not cause me to lose sight of the flesh-pots. Any change from the monotony of an unvaried bread and meat diet being highly agreeable, I went back to the nest of the ostrich with a view of obtaining the eggs. So alarmed were the old birds by my unceremonious intrusion in the morning, that they had not returned. Twenty-three gigantic eggs were laid on the bare ground, without either bush or grass to conceal them, or any attempt at a nest beyond a shallow concavity which had been scraped out with the feet. Having broken one, to ascertain if they were worth carrying home, a Hottentot took off his trousers, in which (the legs being first tied at the lower end) the eggs were securely packed, and placed on the saddle. Although each of these enormous eggs is equivalent to twenty-four of the domestic fowl's, many of our followers could devour two at a single meal, first mixing the contents, and then broiling them in the shell. When dressed in a more orthodox manner, we found them a highly palatable omelette."

Richardson, who had kept to the right, while Harris had advanced on the left, had been engaged in close conflict with a rhinoceros, which, infuriated by being aroused from a comfortable siesta by the smart of a gun-shot wound, attacked his unceremonious flapper so closely that it became necessary to discharge the second barrel into his mouth, "an operation by which the stock was much disfigured." The captain employed the rest of the day repairing his own rifle with an iron clamp from a box, and a strip of green hide from an eland's carcass.

Shortly after they had crossed the Mariqua they had some pleasant light shooting at sassaybies and quaggas, which were charged by the captain so close that one of the latter fell at each discharge of his patched-up rifle; but the savages who had followed in hopes of dried meat looked down upon such trifles, although delighted at the performance: presently, however, the gallant captain crept within thirty yards of a white rhinoceros, (Rhinoceros simus,) and, after putting in six two-ounce bullets behind his shoulder, whilst the unwieldy victim made frequent charges, with his snout almost touching the ground,

but in so clumsy a manner that it was only necessary to step on one side to be perfectly safe, made him bite the dust. His friends, the savages, had pointed out this pretty piece of game, standing stupidly under the shade of a spreading acacia, whilst, in eulogy of the expected dainty, they smacked their thick lips, and patted their stomachs, repeatedly exclaiming "chickore! chickore!" the native name for the huge beast.

Conversion of Dr. Capadose, a Portuguese Jew.

The following account we transfer, with a few verbal variations, from the Episcopal Recorder, wherein it is stated to be "selected by a friend from letters from Europe." Having ourselves perused it with lively interest, we did not question that it would prove equally acceptable to our readers.

Two celebrated men, Capadose and Dacosta, Portuguese Jews by birth, and settled in Holland, were converted to the gospel some years ago. These conversions have produced a very lively sensation, not only among Jews, but among Christians in this part of Europe. It is, I believe, no exaggeration to say, that these two proselytes, as eminent for their learning as for the rank they occupy in the world, have greatly contributed to the religious revival which now pervades all the provinces of Holland.

Men of the world, seeing Dr. Capadose and the poet Dacosta renouncing their family connections and exposing themselves to cruel insults to confess Jesus Christ, feel that there must be in the Christian religion more than human force, and begin to examine seriously the things relating to salvation. Pastors and laymen feel a holy jealousy when they see these children of Israel according to the flesh, showing such generous courage. Genuine religion appears again upon the ancient soil of Batavia, bedewed with the blood of so many martyrs of the sixteenth century, and a breath from on high begins to animate these dry bones which had crumbled to dust under the fatal embrace of a degenerate Arminianism.

The friends of the gospel long urged Dr. Capadose to publish an account of his conversion, but his modesty, and perhaps also some family consideration, prevented till now his complying with this wish. Finally, at the repeated requests of most estimable Christians, he determined to write a narrative of his religious experience. A pamphlet has appeared at Neufchatel, (Switzerland,) entitled: "Conversion of Dr. Capadose, the Portuguese Jew;" and I hasten to communicate to you what is most striking in this interesting publication.

I will let Capadose himself speak; but as the pamphlet comprises more than fifty pages, I will suppress many details, and will abridge the rest, without essentially altering the ideas.

A Portuguese Jew by birth, I was far from being zealous for the religion of my fathers. My education was rather moral than religious; the aim was to inspire me with a dread of vice, and to make me love what they

world call virtue; but I owe it to the goodness of God that I was preserved from open impiety. Literature and the sciences employed me from my infancy. Though living among the worldly and having an enthusiastic love for public shows, balls, and other vanities, I still felt more satisfaction in my studies. I read the writings of Voltaire and Rousseau; but the superficial tone, the dishonesty, and especially the dreadful consequences of their system in the French revolution, fortified me, by divine grace, against their pernicious influence.

My parents destined me to the profession of medicine, and I therefore made it a duty to acquire the knowledge necessary for this calling; but I felt more attraction towards philosophical studies. Our conversations, at the University of Leyden, ran almost always, between my friends and myself, upon the metaphysics of Plato, the system of Descartes, in short, on the most abstruse questions. Happily, I became acquainted with a professor in the academy, the illustrious Bilderdeck, a man of extraordinary genius, a great poet, an excellent historian, a profound philosopher, and, more than all, a true disciple of Christ. Bilderdeck honoured us, my friend Dacosta and myself, with particular affection, and though he never spoke to us directly of Christianity before our conversion, his conversations contributed not a little, in the hand of God, to direct our minds to serious things. His vivacity, ardour of mind, noble sentiments, powerful logic, depth and extent of knowledge, joined to an earnest desire to be useful to youth, all these fine qualities captivated us.

But the religious element, if I may so speak, had not yet entered my mind. Already, indeed, in my childhood, about the age of nine years, I felt a certain desire to pray, and I asked my Jewish parents for a prayer-book in French or Dutch. Since then, in spite of the changes occurring in my external condition, and even during my studies, I never neglected to discharge this duty, and I may say that a few short prayers composed my whole worship, till the moment when the Lord awakened me. I keep this book, and cannot look at it without being affected, and without adoring the goodness of God, my deliverer, who deigned to give me, in mature age, what as a child of nine years I had constantly asked every night, without knowing what I asked.

During my studies, I had moments of special emotion, which left deep traces in my soul. I recollect that, on Saturday evening, a poor woman used to sing psalms in the street, to excite the pity of passengers. More than once, when the sounds of her pious songs reached my ears, I left my books, irresistibly drawn to the window, and there remained a long time motionless with undefinable feelings. The same thing happened to me when, on Sunday morning, I heard the singing of psalms resound from the arches of a church near my dwelling.

The tempter suggested to our minds, to Dacosta and myself, to change our mode of life. Both of us being enemies to half-measures, unable to conform ourselves to that modern Judaism which has invented the art of observing or laying aside, according to convenience, the various prescriptions of the Mosaic law, we firmly resolved to become true Israelites, rigid observers of the law, not allowing ourselves to be intimidated by any authority, and thus compelling Christians to have more respect for the Jewish nation. National pride, that feeling which, in my early youth, made me say to my good mother, when I observed her disconsolate: "Be cheerful, mamma, when I grow up, I will take you to Jerusalem;" this national pride took the place of every thing else.

With this disposition of mind and these resolutions, we set about the diligent reading of the Bible. But, O shame! O the wretchedness of the unconverted soul! we could not proceed further than Genesis! Constant jests, a disposition to scoff, and often (Lord, enter not into judgment with us!) blasphemies were upon our lips instead of prayer. This proceeded to such a point, that at last I told my friend we had better give up our reading than perform it thus.

Dr. Capadose returned to Amsterdam in 1818, and went to live in the house of his uncle, one of the most distinguished physicians of Holland. He felt much alarm and compunction of conscience, and a sullen despair seized all the powers of his soul, he thirsted for the truth, but knew not where to find it. He resolved at last to resume the reading of the Scriptures.

One night I read the prophet Isaiah. When I came to the 53d chapter, the reading made so deep an impression upon me, and I saw with so much clearness, and exactly, line for line, which I had read in the gospel of the sufferings of Christ, that I really believed some one had substituted another Bible for my own. I could not persuade myself that this 53d chapter, which has been justly styled the gospel abridged, was found in the Old Testament. After reading it, a Jew cannot doubt that Christ is the promised Messiah. Whence came so strong an impression? I had often read this same chapter; but this time I read it enlightened by the Spirit of God.

Whenever I had leisure in the morning, I retired to read the Bible; for I dared not read it before my uncle. One day I was particularly studying this passage of the 7th chapter of Isaiah; "Behold a virgin shall conceive and bear a son, and shall call his name Emanuel." I left the library, and found a Jewish physician, a friend of my uncle, waiting for him in the office. He was employed in publishing a new edition of the Bible. "See here," said he, "a difficult passage which we can hardly explain to Christians." It was the very passage of Isaiah upon which I had been meditating! My mind was deeply moved, and I here saw the finger of my God. "Ah! why," I replied to him, "should we not acknowledge the truth?" At this moment my uncle entered. It was the dinner hour. "What question are you discussing together?" he asked us. The doctor told him, and knowing how much my uncle had studied the writings of our teachers, he asked him what the Rabbins said of this passage. "Alas! a heap of nonsense," replied my uncle, rising; and we passed into another room, where dinner was ready. My heart beat strongly, and I blessed God inwardly, that I had heard these words from the mouth of a man whose Rabbinical learning gave him authority among the Jews.

I found, at last, Christ to be my life, the centre of all my affections and all my thoughts, the only object capable of filling the immense void in my heart, the key of all mysteries, the principle of all true philosophy, of all truth —the truth itself.

I every day felt more the necessity of making an open declaration of my sentiments. But my uncle,—that uncle who had loaded me with kindness, who had cherished me as the support of his old age,—O! how could I resolve to make an avowal to him, which, considering his choleric temper, would not fail to cause a shock, the consequences of which could not be foreseen?

Let me tell how the God of mercy listened to my cry, and heard the voice of my supplications. My uncle was in the habit after dinner of taking the public journals and reading them aloud. One day when I was, as usual, seated by him, in a state of deep dejection, I heard him read in an article from Hamburgh as follows:—"We have witnessed an interesting fact. A rabbin, after announcing to his brethren in the synagogue that an attentive examination of the prophecies had convinced him that the true Messiah was come, and after making confession of the Christian faith, was baptized in our city a few days ago, and received as a minister of the evangelical church." Upon which my uncle added these words, very striking to one in my situation:—"If this man took this step from any interested motive, he deserves contempt —if from conviction, he ought to be respected." Ye who have feeling souls, ye Christians, who can kindly sympathize with the strong affections of soul in others like yourselves, I am unable to describe what passed in my mind at this solemn moment! I felt the floor tremble under my feet, and in the transport of my joy, I fell upon the neck of this venerable old man, exclaiming, "My uncle, God gave you these sentiments! Know that he whom you love with the tenderness of a father, and whom you call by the name of son, is in the same case as this rabbin!" I uttered these words with such a tone of voice, and so much agitation, that my poor uncle, confounded and alarmed, believed that I had lost my senses. He made me sit upon his sofa, and after leaving me a moment, as if to let me recover myself, he returned and spoke on some other topic.

I resolved then, after encouraging myself in my God, to repeat to him the next day my declaration. We were at table alone, as usual. My uncle appeared to me a little reserved, but he was however very friendly to me. After dinner I spoke, but calmly and firmly, telling him I was sorry to see that my declaration yesterday was not understood, and therefore I was bound to repeat it, as in the presence of God, with the hope that he himself would one day acknowledge the truth. There was no more room for mistake, and an affecting scene followed. My uncle smote his breast, cursed his days, and exclaimed in the bitterness of his soul that I was bringing down his gray hairs with sorrow to the grave. These reproaches pierced my heart; but the Lord strengthened me, consoled me, and enabled me to show to this dear and venerable old man marks of love and tenderness, which calmed him a little. The next day he communicated the whole to my parents, and it seems there was an agreement among them to treat me with mildness.

But at last my uncle seeing that mildness was ineffectual to banish my religious impressions, and fearing I should make a public avowal of my faith, had recourse to other means, but which led to different results from what he expected. I had to bear from him continual sarcasms, scoffs and reproach: and although, alas! I more than once repelled them angrily, I may say, to the praise of God, that oftener I bore them in silence, and poured out my complaints in the bosom of my Saviour, from whom I already derived sweet consolations.

But one day, being alone with me, my unhappy uncle seemed to take particular pains to grieve me by his bitter and sharp irony. I was silent. Emboldened or irritated by my silence, he dared to utter a blasphemy against Him who was the object of my adoration, and the bountiful source of consolation to my soul. It was time to speak. I arose, and standing before him:—"Enough," I said to him. "Hitherto I only have been the butt of your scoffs and reproaches, and God has enabled me to bear them in silence; but now you begin to blaspheme what you know not. Beware, for I declare to you before God, who hears me, that if you continue to speak in this manner, though I possess nothing in the world, I will quit you in a moment, and will never more appear in your house." I felt resolved to keep my word. The firm and unusual tone with which I pronounced these words (for I may say that the Spirit of God moved me to speak thus) produced its effects. Whatever trials and tribulations I afterwards endured, never was the mouth of this unhappy old man opened to blaspheme the name of Christ. Help me to praise God, ye who read these lines, for He it was who on this occasion signally showed his faithfulness toward one of his poor children.

But my family were not easy to see me persevere in my resolution, in spite of all which had been tried to make me desist, and the cruelties exercised towards me increased. This was the time of greatest trial for my soul. Rarely did I meet one of my friends, either in my uncle's house or at my parents without having to suffer painful reproaches from them. One day at home my father, whose fiery temperament had often displayed itself against me, took me by the arm and led me to the chamber of my poor mother, whose chagrin had made her sick. I saw her seated in the corner, and absorbed in the greatest grief. "Thou seest her," said he to me, "it is thy work; thou art the murderer of thy mother!"

Conceive what I must have felt in this situation. Never had I experienced such an emotion, and I must say that what persecution could not do the tears and dreadful state of suffering in which I saw my poor mother might have effected. My faith began to shake, and I saw that the safest way for me was to fly. For a moment I was almost distracted. At last I hastily left the room and fled, as if frighted at myself, from my father's house. I ran into the street, without knowing where, and my steps led me to the gate of the city. Who knows how the day would have ended for me if the hand of the Lord had not arrested me? I had hardly set foot upon the bridge when a brilliant rainbow caught my eyes, moist with tears, and fixed my attention. Struck with this sign of the divine promise: "Behold," said I, "the God of the everlasting covenant." And instantly all my anguish was allayed, my faith became strong, and the Spirit of God poured consolating balm into my heart. Feeble in body, but inwardly sustained, I returned tranquil and submissive to my father's house.

It will be easily seen that this state of things could not last, and would strengthen the ardent desire I had publicly to confess my Saviour. Already my friend Dacosta and myself began to attract public attention. We had changed several of our habits: we no longer frequented our former society, and were rarely seen partaking the pleasures of our friends. The cause was at last suspected: it was a subject of great grief to those of our nation.

The moment for taking a decided resolution was come—I could defer it no longer. We set off for Leyden in the month of September, my friend, his interesting wife, who shared in our convictions, and myself. We were received with open arms, and with truly fatherly love, by the worthy Friends who had taken a lively interest in our struggles. Who more than they would share in the heavenly joy that now overwhelmed our souls?

The 20th October, 1822, was the wished for day, when we were received as members of the Christian church. By order of the pastor, a venerable old man, to whom we had made our confession of faith, there were placed before the pulpit, and in sight of the assembly, three cushions. There, kneeling before the God of our fathers, who is the true God, Father, Son, and Holy Spirit, we had the inexpressible joy, we unworthy and miserable sinners, of receiving on our foreheads the sign and seal of the covenant of grace, and of confessing in the Christian church the blessed name of the great God and Saviour, who came to seek us when we were lost! Glory to God!

The text selected by the pastor for the sermon of the day was: "Even so, then, at this present time also there is a remnant according to the election of grace."—(Rom. xi. 5.)

I will close here the extracts from the pamphlet of Dr. Capadose. This pious servant of Christ had still great struggles to endure, painful trials to surmount; but he remained firm in the profession of evangelical faith, and had the happiness to see another member of his family, his own brother, confess the name of Christ. Dr. Capadose is still a pillar and a light in the Reformed church of Holland.

Accept, &c.   G. DE F.

[Extract from an article in the Prairie Beacon.]

ILLINOIS PRAIRIES.

Prairie is a French word, signifying meadow, and is applied to any description of soil, destitute of timber, and clothed with grass. The great peculiarity of the prairies is the absence of timber, in other respects they present all the varieties of soil and surface that are found elsewhere; some are of inexhaustible fertility; others are of hopeless sterility; some spread out into the vast, unbounded plains, others are undulating or rolling, and perhaps broken by hills. In general, particularly in Illinois, they are covered with a luxuriant growth of grass.

Those strips of prairie that occur along the margins of water courses are commonly denominated alluvial or wet prairies. They are for the most part of a black, deep and very friable soil of exhaustless fertility, and contain evident marks of having been the most recent deposites of running water. A strip of land along the eastern bank of the Mississippi, below the mouth of the Missouri, known as the American bottom, is perhaps the most remarkable specimen of such a prairie. For most agricultural purposes, these are considered the best of soils; but are ordinarily too tender for the cultivated grasses. Yet the height and luxuriance of their native grass impress the beholder with astonishment.

Another kind of prairie, covered with hazel and a variety of flowering shrubbery, is commonly termed the healthy or bushy prairie. These present a broken and uneven surface, and abound in springs of water. They usually are met with along the skirts of timbered lands. In point of fertility, they are among the choicest portions of soil. No where are flowers of the gayest hue and sweetest fragrance to be found in richer profusion. Such tracts seem peculiarly adapted to the culture of the vine.

But by far the most extensive tracts are the dry or undulating prairie.

AN APT ILLUSTRATION.

In a little essay by E. Peabody, of New Bedford, on the subject of "Mystery, reason and faith," we find the following beautiful and apt illustration:

"Night comes down over a ship at sea, and a passenger lingers hour after hour alone on the deck. The waters plunge and glide away beneath the keel. Above, the sails tower up in the darkness, almost to the sky, and their shadow falls as it were a burden on the deck below. In the clouded night no star is to be seen, and as the ship changes her course, the passenger knows not which way is east, west, north or south. What islands, what sunken rocks may be on her course—or what that course is, or where they are, he knows not. All around, to him, is mystery. He bows down in the submission of utter ignorance.

"But men of science have read the laws of the sky. And the next day this passenger beholds the captain looking at a clock, and taking note of the place of the sun, and with the aid of a couple of books, composed of rules and mathematical tables, making calculations. And when he has completed them, he is able to point almost to within a hand's breadth to the place which, after unnumbered windings, he has arrived in the midst of the seas. Storms may have beat and currents drifted, but he knows where they are, and the precise point, where a hundred leagues over the water, lies his native shore. Here is reason appreciating and making use of the revelations (if we may so call them) of science.

"Night again shuts down over the waste of waves, and the passenger beholds a single seaman standing at the wheel, and watch, hour after hour, as it vibrates beneath a lamp, a little needle, which points ever, as it were a living finger, to the steady pole.

"This man knows nothing of the rules of navigation, nothing of the courses of the sky. But reason and experience have given him faith in the commanding officer of the ship—faith in the laws that control her course—faith in the unerring integrity of the little guide before him. And so without a single doubt he steers his ship on, according to a prescribed direction, through night and the waves. And that faith is not disappointed. With the morning sun, he beholds far away the summits of the gray and misty highlands, rising like a cloud on the horizon; and as he nears them, the hills appear, and the lighthouse at the entrance of the harbour, and sight of joy! the spires of the churches, and the shining roofs among which he strives to detect his own."

EVENING.

Dear is the shadowy close of day to me,
  The soul of silence, and the reign of rest,
Which brings the weary where they sigh to be,
  And sends the turtle to her downy nest,—
  Gives the fair infant to its mother's breast,
Lures home the wanderer, if a home he knows,
  Shuts up the busy world, and o'er the west
An iris-robe of dying glory throws,
Signal for toil to cease, and yield to calm repose!

But dearer far a Christian's trembling eye
  Deems of his sojourn here, the later hours;
When faith's refulgence, kindled from the sky,
  Her golden radiance o'er his sunset showers:
  What though the passing cloud a moment lowers,
Sweet is the thought of ceaseless rest in heaven;
  That land of fair and amaranthine bowers,
Where sin is sown not, and whence woe is driven,
And, of all sorrows past, forgetfulness is given.

              MATTHEW BRIDGES.

HAVERFORD SCHOOL.

WANTED, a Friend to act as Steward of this Institution. Apply to

        KIMBER & SHARPLESS,
        No. 8 South Fourth street.

The Origin and Object of Civil Government, according to the Views of the Society of Friends.

The enlightening influence of active faith, even in the conduct of the affairs of this life, has long been acknowledged. Is it not in the general want of this, that we may discover the cause why, notwithstanding so many generations have passed since the subject has claimed the attention of mankind, and so many volumes have been written about it; the true origin and legitimate object of government, seem still to be very imperfectly understood by the majority of men and legislators? All the existing governments of Christendom are guilty of many absurdities, follies, and even deeds of wickedness, and some of the leading principles of the policy which controls them are in direct contradiction to those of the Christian religion, and to the reasonable rights of men. But little progress in political knowledge appears to have been made since the days of Penn; and, indeed, if the frame of government established by him were to be taken as the standard of the times in which he lived, the movement, in practice at least, would seem to have been backward. We learn, however, that Penn was much in advance of his age, and that it was because a large proportion of the community which he founded, and upon which his government, under Divine Providence, depended for support, was greatly behind him in Christian knowledge and purity of purpose, that the noble political institutions to which he was instrumental in giving birth, were so soon violated, and in a great degree destroyed. A pure government can only be sustained by a pure people. This is a truth which mankind have continually forgotten. They have, in various ages, when the measures of government have become more oppressive than they were willing to bear, sought relief in violent remedies. Instead of going to the root of the evil, and attempting to destroy its grand though hidden and remote cause, which they might have found in their own moral deterioration, they have contented themselves with forcibly demolishing that which was but an effect of their own indirect agency—political oppression, the result of national corruption. The consequence has been a constant recurrence of the evil: for the bitter fountain will still continue to give forth bitter waters.

But such is the perversity of the human mind, when unenlightened by a higher influence than reason, that it resists the convictions which experience should force upon it, and ever seeks for the cure of the evils under which it suffers in some fallacious and insufficient expedient. History is filled with examples of this, and future times may witness yet more extraordinary fruits of the same kind, should the propagators of certain modern theories be permitted to succeed in the general diffusion of their anarchical opinions. They have observed that one form of government after another has failed in fulfilling the hopes of good men; that many unchristian practices and violations of the plain principles of justice and humanity are not only sanctioned, but

actively promoted by them, and have hence concluded most unreasonably, and irreligously too, that such abuses are inseparable from civil government, and that the only cure is in the extermination of every form of it.

And, strange to tell, on that continent, and in that very nation, where Penn so successfully carried into practice his enlightened views, the moral use, and the Divine authority of civil government are called in question. Some have even pretended to base these opinions on the acknowledged principles of the religious Society of which that wise legislator was so eminent a member. What a perversion of the orderly doctrines of that Society this is, would seem to be sufficiently obvious on the mere statement of the fact; but a very slight examination of their written testimonials on the subject, will suffice to settle the question as to what their sentiments really were, beyond dispute or cavil. And so just and consistent with the doctrines of the gospel were their ideas of civil government, it may, perhaps, not be altogether useless at this time to attempt, in a brief and simple way, to state them. They will be found to offer a wide contrast to the political theories now popular; and although the forms of government established in New Jersey and Pennsylvania by Friends may not have been, in all their details, adapted to the present needs of society, their prominent features, springing from immutable principles of truth, the same in all countries and in every age, might be profitably studied by the busy spirits of our day; and happy would it be for our countrymen were they more generally understood and appreciated.

As it may not be thought a satisfactory vindication of the Society to exhibit only the views of Penn, or of those colonists who followed him, or of those who before him planted a political community in New Jersey; let us begin with the official declarations of the Society, and with those of some of its approved writers. We shall learn from these sources, that the position taken by the original Friends was not merely that of a meek and resigned submission to government as an evil to be endured, as some of these wild speculators have ventured to assert was the case with them, and even with the apostles; but that it was a hearty approbation and support, so far as conscience permitted, of the authorities placed over them.

Probably the idea that Friends were inimical to government arose in part, formerly, as perhaps it may now, from the position they have ever maintained, that God alone is sovereign Lord of conscience, and that no earthly power can, of right, assume dominion over it. Yet, when the requisitions of law have contravened the dictates of conscience, they have always held themselves bound to bear the penalty; though not without the privilege of remonstrance, and the use of all peaceable and Christian methods to obtain relief. For want of appreciating the distinction they made between active and passive obedience, Christian and unchristian resistance, their opponents sometimes suspected and charged them with hostility to civil magistracy. But more fre-

quently they were accused of disloyalty to the ruling powers, arising from a supposed preference for other men or modes of government. The vindications which, from time to time, were drawn from them by such unjust and injurious imputations, furnish us with the materials for rebutting the repetition of them now.

It was with secret designs to substitute one form of government for another that they were most commonly accused, and it was to repel such charges, as well as to testify their allegiance, that they often addressed the supreme magistrate, either on a new accession to the throne, or on the occurrence of any event affecting its stability. In these addresses we find expressions exhibiting very distinctly the estimation in which they held civil government. Take, for example, some of early date recorded by Sewell and Gough. In that to Charles Second, on the discovery of the Rye House plot, which had excited the renewed suspicious and persecutions of their opponents, they assert, that "God Almighty had taught and engaged them to acknowledge, and actually to obey magistracy as his ordinance;" in that to James Second, in 1686, asking for relief from oppression, they declare themselves "in Christian duty bound to pray for the king's welfare;" and in 1687, on that monarch's declaration for liberty of conscience, they express, in decided terms, their attachment to government, and profess, that it "would be their endeavour, (with God's help,) always to approve themselves the king's faithful and loving subjects," and they "pray God to bless the king, and that, after a long and prosperous reign here, he may receive a better crown among the blessed."

They congratulated William Third on the treaty of Ryswick, which confirmed his throne; and in their address on that occasion, avowed their belief, "that it is the Most High who ruleth in the kingdoms of men, and appointeth over them whomsoever He will;" and, moreover, confessed it to be their "duty, gratefully to commemorate and acknowledge the favours 'of the government,' of which they had largely partaken."

In 1695, the representatives of the yearly meeting in England, when petitioning parliament for exemption from oaths, speak of "the just and good ends of law and government;" and in 1700, the yearly meeting, on the proclamation by the court of France of the pretender to the British throne, voluntarily offered to William Third a profession of allegiance, wherein they acknowledge him to be "a prince whom they believed God had promoted and principled for the good ends of government."

On the accession of Anne, they "sincerely declared that, with the assistance of the grace of God, they would always, according to their Christian duty, demonstrate their good affection, truth, and fidelity to the government." When the conspiracy of 1707, in favour of the pretender, was frustrated, they embraced that opportunity "to give them the, renewed assurance of their hearty affection to the established government."

To conclude: during the government of

George Second, they freely renewed the same professions, and expressed, emphatically, their desire "that those who were placed in authority might add vigour to the laws."

Such expressions as these, could have been adopted with sincerity by no people who held civil government to be an evil, only to be tolerated because it could not be shaken off by means consistent with their religious profession. Friends had good reason to know that much iniquity was practised in the name of government and under the sanction of law, but they no more thought of therefore desiring the abolition of government and law, than they did of desiring the destruction of mankind, because mankind had in all ages been prone to evil.

Edward Burrough, a contemporary of Fox, and a minister highly respected in the society, when addressing Richard Cromwell, the "protector of the commonwealth," declares in express terms, that, "as for magistracy, it was ordained of God, to be a dread and terror and limit to evil doers, and to be a defence and praise to all that do well; to condemn the guilty, and to justify the guiltless; but that the exercise thereof was degenerated, and some that were in authority did subvert the good laws of God and men to a wrong end and 'use;'" and he speaks of "how many of the Lord's servants do, and have suffered great injustice through the abuse of good government, and the degeneracy of magistracy from its perfect state, and place whereunto it was ordained of God in the beginning:" and in a book which he published in 1661, he goes on to say, that where any man's heresy do extend further than only against God and his own soul, even to outward wrongs, or evils, or violence, or visible mischiefs committed to the injury of others, then he forbids not punishment, to be inflicted upon the person and estate of such men."

But the deference paid by Friends to the authority of magistracy, is more fully exhibited in the remonstrance of Edward Pyot on behalf of himself, William Salt and George Fox, recorded in the journal of the latter, which was addressed "to John Glynne, Chief Justice of England," from the jail at Lancaster, where the above mentioned individuals were at that time, in the year 1656, imprisoned on account of their religious profession. He therein appeals to the law as "the one common guard or defence to property, liberty, and life;" as being established for the protection of those rights " so just and so equal," and which are of " the highest importance to the well-being of man." He demands of the chief justice, whether "they did not own authority and government oft times before the court;" and, says he, "didst thou not say in court, thou wast glad to hear so much from us of our owning magistracy." He tells him, that "pride, and fury, and passion, and rage, and reviling, and threatening are not the Lord's; these, and the principle out of which they spring, are for judgment, and must come under the award of the magistrate of God;" and, he adds, "the law seeks not for causes whereby to make the innocent suffer; but helpeth him to right who suffers wrong, relieveth the oppressed, and searcheth out the matter, whether that of which a man stands accused, be so, or not; seeking judgment, and hastening righteousness."

This remonstrance had the sanction of George Fox; but he expressed himself, in his own name, still more fully, on other occasions: as, for instance, in his address to Charles Second, from Worcester prison, wherein he asserts that "that spirit which leads people from all manner of sin and evil, is one with the magistrate's power, and with the righteous law; for the law being added because of transgression, that spirit which leads out of transgression, must needs be one with that law which is against transgressors. So the spirit which leads out of transgression is the good spirit of Christ, and is one with the magistrates in the higher power, and owns it and them; but that spirit which leads into transgression, is the bad spirit, is against the law, against the magistrates, and makes them a great deal of troublesome work." So that, according to George Fox, one office of civil government is to promote the good work of the Holy Spirit. He avowed the same sentiments at Houlker Hall before Sir George Middleton, Justice Preston and others, one of whom accused him of being "against the laws of the land." He answered, "nay; for I and my friends direct all people to the Spirit of God in them, to mortify the deeds of the flesh; this brings them into well-doing, and from that which the magistrate's sword is against, which eases the magistrates, who are for the punishment of evil-doers; people being turned to the Spirit of God, which brings them to mortify the deeds of the flesh from under the occasion for the magistrate's sword. This must needs be one with magistracy, and one with the law, which was added, because of transgression, and is for the praise of them that do well. In this we establish the law, are an ease to the magistrates, and are not against, but stand for all good government."

Robert Barclay, in the fourteenth proposition of his apology for the doctrines of Friends, announces their belief on this subject very distinctly, that it is not lawful for any whatsoever to undertake the government of conscience ; nevertheless, "that no man, under the pretence of conscience, shall prejudice his neighbour in his life or estate, or do any thing destructive to, or inconsistent with, human society ; in which case the law is for the transgressor, and justice is to be administered upon all, without respect of persons." And in his letter addressed to the ambassadors of the Christian states at Nimeguen, in the year 1677, "to consult the peace of Christendom," he makes a declaration which is exceedingly well adapted to our present purpose. He exhorts them not to be unwilling to hear one, that appeared among them for the interest of Christ his king and master, "not," said he, "as if thereby he denied the just authority of sovereign princes; or refused to acknowledge the subjection himself owes to his lawful prince and superior; or were any ways inclined to favour the dreams of such, as under the pretence of crying up King Jesus and the kingdom of Christ, either deny, or seek to overturn all civil government ; nay, not at all : but I am one, who do reverence and honour magistrates, and acknowledge subjection due unto them by their respective people in all things just and lawful ; knowing that magistracy is an ordinance of God, and that magistrates are his ministers, who bear not the sword in vain." Barclay gave the most conclusive proof of the sincerity of his belief, by accepting the appointment of governor for the colony of East Jersey, the duties of which office he exercised for two years by deputy.

That the Society of Friends were not averse to civil government, is evident, not only from the authorities already cited, but from the active part taken by many of its prominent and well esteemed members in the early settlement of New Jersey, nearly twenty years before the establishment of Penn's colony. Both East and West Jersey were under the control of Quaker proprietaries for a number of years; and their liberal political institutions have been a theme for the eulogy of historians; "there we lay a foundation," said the proprietaries of the latter colony, "for after ages to understand their liberty as men and Christians, that they may not be brought into bondage, but by their own consent : for we put the power in the people."

One of our most eloquent modern writers, who, while he has sadly mistaken some of the religious principles of our society, has done ample justice to its political influence, thus describes this community, associated upon principles, till then, practically, unknown to the administrators of government :—" The light of peace dawned upon West New Jersey ; and in the autumn of 1681, Jennings, acting as governor for the proprietaries, convened the first legislative assembly of the representatives of the men who said thee and thou to all the world, and wore their hats in the presence of beggar or king. Their first measures established their rights by an act of fundamental legislation, and in the spirit of 'the concessions,' they framed their government on the basis of humanity. Neither faith, nor wealth, nor race, was respected. They met in the wilderness as men, and founded society on equal rights. The formation of this little government of a few hundred souls, that soon increased to thousands, is one of the most beautiful incidents in the history of the age. The people rejoiced under the grace of God, confident that he would beautify the meek with salvation. A loving correspondence began with Friends in England, and from the fathers of the sect, frequent messages were received. 'Friends that are gone to make plantations in America; keep the plantations in your hearts, that your own vines and lilies be not hurt. You that are governors and judges, eyes you should be to the blind, feet to the lame, and fathers to the poor ; that you may gain the blessing of those who are ready to perish, and cause the widow's heart to sing with gladness. If you rejoice because your hand hath gotten much ; —if you say to fine gold, thou art my confidence,—you will have denied the God that is above. The Lord is ruler among nations; he will crown his people with dominion.' "

(To be continued.)

INSTITUTE FOR COLOURED YOUTH.

The annexed report was sent for insertion in "The Friend" early after its date, but was mislaid. It may now seem out of time, especially after the circular we lately published, announcing the purchase of a farm; yet we conclude to place it upon record, as part of the history of an institution which we trust will, under the smiles of a benignant Providence, in time become as a fruitful vine, abundantly rewarding the liberality bestowed upon it, by the good dispensed to the offspring of an afflicted, down-trodden people.

ANNUAL REPORT.

The board of managers of the Institute for Coloured Youth, in submitting their annual report required by the constitution, cannot but regret they have so little to communicate likely to prove interesting to the contributors.

Immediately after the organization of the board, a committee was appointed to look out for a suitable farm for the proposed institute, who entered on the duties of their appointment with much interest, being desirous of commencing operations; and although they have been industriously engaged in viewing such places as were offered for sale, and likely to prove suitable, they have not yet been able to meet with one upon which the board could fully unite. While they regret this circumstance, the managers are still encouraged to hope that at no distant period a suitable farm will be procured, and the interesting experiment carried out in accordance with the will of the kind donor, to whose benevolent feelings we are indebted for the design, as well as pecuniary aid to make a commencement, and also to the satisfaction of the contributors, and we trust the benefit of that oppressed portion of the human family for whom it is intended.

The experiment in which we have engaged is, in some respects, a novel one, and, as such, those who are conducting it, must expect to meet with difficulties, which arise from the want of that tact and knowledge which experience alone can impart. Unpopular with many, the cause we have espoused has not only to struggle with the opposition of those openly opposed to it, but also with the prejudices of its avowed friends. These circumstances, as may be readily conceived, have tended not a little to the difficulty of finding a suitable location for the intended establishment; and when we consider the present state of the public mind, excited as it is in relation to every thing connected with the cause of our coloured population; it is evident that it will require much care and wisdom properly to locate an institution of this character. Taking therefore these facts into view, together with the anxiety which the managers have always felt to proceed discreetly in this matter, it will not appear surprising that so much time has been suffered to pass away,

and so little has been effected towards accomplishing the design of the contributors. Two leading objects then still continue to engage the attention of the board, viz: the acquirement of a suitable farm, and a properly qualified superintendent to conduct it; and the managers would take this opportunity again to urge these two important subjects on the attention of every friend of this concern, believing that great assistance might be rendered by persons (knowing of suitable farms, or of a Friend qualified to conduct such an establishment) giving early notice thereof to the managers. It is confidently believed, were these two objects once attained, the institution would in a little time be able to commence its career of usefulness, and finally fulfil the expectations of its friends.

Although our means at present are limited, we believe them sufficient to warrant a commencement on a moderate scale, which we would earnestly recommend to our successors, doubting not that the sympathy which is felt by our religious society on behalf of this afflicted people, will produce a willingness to afford the necessary aid in the extension of its usefulness. When we consider the present degraded situation of our coloured population, the oppression and injustice to which they are subjected, and increasingly so at the present time, when the usual facilities of acquiring the knowledge of mechanical branches of business are not only withheld, but almost every avenue to them closed upon them, we cannot but sincerely hope that the day is not very remote, when the energies of this society will be availingly exerted in rendering them such assistance as will qualify them, under the blessing of Divine Providence, to take a more respectable station in society.

Since our last annual meeting the funds in the hands of the trustees of the late Richard Humphreys, bequeathed for the purpose, together with the donations of different individuals, have been paid to our treasurer, and are invested in good security, as will appear by the accompanying report of the treasurer.

Signed by order of the managers.

CASPAR WISTAR, Secretary.

4th month 9th, 1839.

LUTHER'S BOYHOOD.

The subjoined extract relative to this celebrated reformer possesses interest for most readers. The S. S. Journal from which we copy, credits it to "Luther and his Times," a fresh American work.

A poor miner, who wrought in the mines of Mansfield, and lived at Eisenach, took a journey to Eisleben, to attend the annual fair. His wife was too desirous to accompany her husband to be denied; and, on the night they arrived, she gave birth to a son. He was born on the 10th of November, in the year 1483, on the eve of St. Martin's day; and from this circumstance his parents named him Martin. The father strove to educate his son in virtuous habits; and, according to the spirit of the age, considered strict discipline a powerful aid to good conduct; to this the young

Martin was early subjected. As he grew older, he was placed in an institution at Eisenach, where he had access to the learning there taught; but was unprovided with funds, and had not money to procure food. In company with several other students, as poor as himself, he endeavoured to procure bread by singing at the doors of wealthy houses. On these occasions he sometimes sang his own compositions—at others the favourite ditties of the day—and sometimes he chanted forth the sufferings of the martyrs. All this he called bread music. It does not seem to have had the power " to soothe the savage breast;" for he was often taunted and reproached—accused of idleness and evil designs—and driven away by menials—though the only reward he asked for his musical exertions was a piece of bread. On one of those days, when his very soul was filled with shame and indignation for the hard language he received, he wandered to the humble dwelling of Conrad Cotta; and, throwing himself on a seat before it, overshadowed by ancient trees, he relieved his over-burdened heart by low, plaintive music. Whether moved by the melody of song, or the tenderness of a woman's soul, Louisa Cotta, the wife of Conrad, hastened to the door and invited him to enter. She then placed before him the simple fare her humble habitation afforded, bread and honey, with milk from the mountain goat. The honest, ardent gratitude of the youth, with his simple story, won not only her confidence, but her affection. She invited him to come every day and get his meals. He soon equally interested the husband, and they both continued their friendship to him. Many years after, when all Europe rung with the name of the reformer, they remembered the poor hungry boy they fed was Martin Luther!

In the year 1501, a thin, pale youth stood at the gate of the University at Erfurt, and petitioned for entrance. When asked if he was qualified to make such a request he replied: " He who prays as he ought, has already finished half his labours and his studies." This, too, was Martin Luther; but he did not now come unprovided with credentials; he brought undoubted testimony of his morals and good conduct, and was received with cordiality.

READING THE SCRIPTURES.

The scope of the sacred writers is of greater importance in understanding the Scriptures, than the most critical examination of terms, or the most laborious comparison of the use of them in different places. For want of attending to this, not only particular passages, but whole chapters are frequently misunderstood. The reasonings of both Christ and his apostles frequently proceed, not upon what is true in fact, but merely in the estimation of the parties addressed: that is to say, they reason with them on their own principles. It was not true that Simon the Pharisee was a little sinner, nor a forgiven sinner, nor that he loved Christ a little: but he thought thus of himself, and upon these principles Christ reasoned with him. It was

Pharisees were just men, epentance: but such we;e themselves, and Christ sug-;fore they had no need of came not to call the right-to repentance. Finally it t the Pharisees who mur-s receiving publicans and , like the ninety-nine sheep gone astray; nor that, like ' had served God, and never ;ressed his commandment; God had was theirs: but wn views, and Christ rea-cordingly. It is as if he so, that you are righteous hy should you murmur at ie poor sinners?" Now, to ple on which such reason-to lose all the benefit of nto many errors.

ter into the true meaning it is absolutely necessary) the spirit of the writers. knows by experience, that ne of mind, he can under-Scriptures in an hour, than nes, with the utmost appli-

It is by an unction from we know all things.

) of our own ignorance, and ndence upon God, has also n our coming at the true are few things which tend mind than a conceit of our nce we perceive the just-guage as the following: iothing.—He that thinketh ng, knoweth nothing as he " any man will be wise, let fool, that he may be wise. he Scriptures profitably, it conversant with them in ilix, not only faith, but the ith what we read. There nce between reading the ident, in order to find some-people, and reading them th a view to get good from soul. That which is gained i ways is, beyond all com-stest use, both to ourselves t which we communicate ir lips, unless we have first elves; or, to use the lan-a, tasted, felt, and handled Andrew Fuller.

FRIEND.

MONTH, 19, 1839.

!1st ult. contained a short Ohio Yearly Meeting, to on was made in the paper week. The annexed more subsequently forwarded by aber of that meeting, will table to many of our read-

continued its session until 7th; and with no material

falling off in the attendance of Friends. It was throughout favoured in a remarkable manner with the overshadowing of Divine good. The gospel of our Lord and Saviour Jesus Christ was preached in demonstration of the Spirit and of power.

"With much pertinency were our doctrines and testimonies upheld; and with equal clear-ness was our scriptural belief in the sensible influence of the Holy Spirit on the minds of the humble followers of Christ set forth. Such, indeed, was the baptizing power attend-ing the word in declaring these truths, that not a doubt, it would seem, could remain as to their divine origin; giving rise to the con-solatory assurance that the name and memo-rial of their early promulgators is not soon to be blotted out.

"Besides the ordinary care of the body over its branches, the meeting was feelingly introduced into sympathy with our fellow-men of the African race, both bond and free. No way, however, appeared to open with clear-ness to take any public step on behalf of the former class. But a memorial was prepared to be presented to our state legislature, solicit-ing the repeal of those laws which impose re-straints and disabilities on our free coloured population. A minute was also sent down to subordinate meetings, recommending such free persons of colour as may be found in our respective neighbourhoods to the Christian kindness of Friends. And in promoting the improvement of their general condition, to make way as much as possible for the educa-tion of their children, and as far as practicable to furnish the destitute with the Holy Scrip-tures and other suitable books. And in our efforts to serve the cause of this deeply in-jured portion of the human family, Friends were tenderly advised to move under religious concern, and thereby avoid the danger of vio-lating any of our peculiar testimonies by a free participation in the popular associations of the day.

"The meeting took a lively interest in the civilization and Christian instruction of the Indian natives; and a contribution was enter-ed into, both by men and women Friends, to be applied in supporting our establishment among the Shawnees west of the Mississippi, where we have a school for Indian children, in which the pupils are boarded and clothed.

"And, as connected with the prosperity of our religious Society, the more liberal and guarded education of our youth was felt to be of great importance. Our boarding school was reported to be in a prosperous condition, being well supplied with superintendents and teachers. And an increasing concern was evinced for the promotion and support of primary schools, under the care of, and taught by Friends.

"The plainness of speech and apparel into which the truth led the founders of our So-ciety, and which has since their day marked its consistent members, were adverted to in a feeling manner; and their propriety and supe-rior dignity persuasively held up to the view of all, but especially to our beloved youth.

"A holy solemnity was sensibly felt to overspread the meeting as it drew to a close,

wherein many present language of David, ' I not unto us, but unto for thy mercy, and for

—

The article, comme which treats of the ori government according t was recently prepared a under direction of the l sociation of Friends. V ed to exhibit concisely i ments of the Society or its publication at the p timed, especially in ref tions of our country.

—

James P. Espy's cou the Law of Storms, c made in our paper of mence on second day e at the Franklin Institu on successive evenings of a ticket, granting ad of himself and two fem dollars.

—

COMMUNI

The managers of Fr Insane, apprehending arise by constituting a receive applications for tients, have appointed t for that purpose, to wh applications are to be n

John G. Hoskins, N and No. 50, North Fo Edw. B. Garrigues, N street, and No. 153, Collins, No. 129, Filbe Commerce street; Ed west corner of Twelfth and No. 39, Market stre No. 73, North Tenth South Front street.

—

FRIENDS'

Visiting Managers ; Collins, No. 129, Fil Randolph, No. 122½, Charles Allen, No. 146

Superintendents. — J Redmond.

Attending Physician. No. 201, Arch street.

Resident Physician.-

—

MARRIED, at Friends' m 12th of ninth month, Mosa. to MARGARETTA, daughter maker.

—

DIED, at Wilmington, Del at the residence of her brot RACHEL, wife of George St. the 48th year of her age.

—

PRINTED BY A

Carpenter Street, below

THE FRIEND.

A RELIGIOUS AND LITERARY JOURNAL.

VOL. XIII.   SEVENTH DAY, TENTH MONTH, 26, 1839.   NO. 4.

EDITED BY ROBERT SMITH.

PUBLISHED WEEKLY.

Price two dollars per annum, payable in advance.

Subscriptions and Payments received by

GEORGE W. TAYLOR,

NO. 50, NORTH FOURTH STREET, UP STAIRS,

PHILADELPHIA.

SCENES IN SOUTHERN AFRICA.

(Continued from p. 18.)

On the 29th the party took the field, accompanied by the whole of the male inhabitants of three kraals, in addition to those that had accompanied them from the Mariqua river.

"The country here is generally undulating, extensive mimosa-groves occupying all the valleys, as well as the banks of the Tolaan river, which winds amongst them on its way to join the Mariqua. We had not proceeded many hundred yards before our progress was opposed by a rhinoceros, who looked defiance, but took the hints we gave him to get out of the way. Two fat elands had been pointed out at the edge of the grove the moment before, one of which Richardson disposed of with little difficulty, but the other led me through all the intricacies of the grove to a wide plain on the opposite side, immediately on emerging upon which the fugitive was prostrate at my feet in the middle of a troop of giraffes, who stooped their long necks, astounded at the intrusion, and in another moment were sailing away at their utmost speed. To have followed them upon my jaded horse would have been absurd, and I was afterwards unable to find them. Returning to the camp, after killing several elands and rhinoceroses, besides other game, which the savages quickly took charge of, I was furiously charged by a herd of horned cattle, and my horse being much exhausted, I had no small difficulty in escaping their persecution. Objecting, I presume, to my garb or complexion, they pertinaciously pursued me through thickets and other ravines, regardless of the loud whistle of the herdsman, to which they are usually very obedient. During the night, our camp was thrown into disorder by the intrusion of a rhinoceros, which actually stood some time between the wagons.

"Several hours' diligent search the next day brought us upon a herd of twelve camel-eopards. We pursued them a considerable distance, and repeatedly wounded the largest, a gigantic male, probably eighteen feet in height; but our famished horses falling repeatedly into the numerous holes with which the ground was covered, we at length became convinced of the impossibility of humbling the lofty head of the giraffe, until our steeds should have improved in condition upon the fine pasturage which now abounded. The day was sultry and the glare distressing. To the north eastward the distant prospect was bounded by a range of blue mountains which we visited some weeks afterwards; the whole of the extensive plain being sprinkled with huge mokaala trees, mat rushes and thistles. Large herds of elands were grazing amongst these, the host of savages by which we were attended quickly clearing away the carcasses of those we slew, and then quarrelling for the entrails. I hope my reader has understood that these barbarians generally devour the meat raw, although, when at leisure, they do not object to its being cooked. They usually seize a piece of the flesh by the teeth, cutting a large mouthful of it with the assagai close to the lips before masticating it, which they do with a loud sputter and noise. The meat being finished, they never fail to wipe their hands on their bodies, and then, being generally gorged, they lay themselves down to repose, previously relaxing their leathern girdles, which are so contrived as to be readily expanded according to their girth. As the sun was setting, our friend the rhinoceros imprudently appeared upon the bank of the river within pistol-shot. Five balls were immediately lodged in his body, with which he retreated, and was picked up the following morning. . . . . . Late in the afternoon we halted on the banks of the Simala-kate, a deep and tranquil stream, margined by reeds and rushes, affording a ready covert for lions, whose fresh marks were every where visible in the neighbourhood. The day had been very sultry, and our two dogs, nearly blind from thirst, ran down the steep bank to the water's edge into the very jaws of an enormous alligator. One of them returned immediately in a state of great alarm. Suddenly a splash was heard, and bubbles of blood, rising a minute after, too truly told what had been the fate of his unfortunate companion. Not contented with depriving us of our valued four-footed companion, the alligators quitted their watery homes during the night, and eat up a portion of the leather of the waggon furniture, besides the shoes of our followers. Those scaly monsters are very common in many of the African rivers, and this was not the only occasion on which we suffered from their ravages. We frequently killed some of an immense size.

"About sunset an unwieldy white rhinoceros approached the wagons, evidently with hostile intentions. There being neither bush nor hollow to conceal my advance, I crawled towards him amongst the grass, and within forty yards fired two balls into him. He started, looked around for some object on which to wreak his vengeance, and actually charged up with his eye flashing fire to within an arm's length of me. Crouching low, however, I fortunately eluded his vengeance, and he soon after dropped down dead."

The variety of game which now surrounded the party agreeably filled up the time of men panting to come to close quarters with elephants and giraffes. The conclusion of the following paragragh is a strong picture of the unsophisticated animal man in a state of savage indulgence.

"On the 5th November we followed the traces of elephants along the side of the mountains for miles, through stupendous forests, all the Hottentots excepting Piet dropping in the rear in succession, either to solace themselves with a pipe, or to expend their ammunition upon ignoble game. Time not permitting us to continue the search, we descended into a valley, bent upon the destruction of a roan antelope, a large herd of which rare animals were quietly grazing. A pair of white rhinoceroses opposed our descent, and, being unwilling to fire at them, we had some trouble in freeing ourselves from their company. A large herd of wild swine, or, as Indians term it, a *sounder* of hog, carrying their long whip-like tails erect, then passed in order of review, and immediately afterwards two bull buffaloes were observed within pistol-shot. It was a perfect panorama of game; I had with great difficulty restrained Piet from firing, and was almost within reach of the bucks, when a Hottentot suddenly discharging his gun put every thing to flight. The buffaloes passed me quite close on their way to the hills. I fractured the hind leg of the largest, and, mounting my horse, closed with him immediately, and, after two gallant charges performed upon three legs, he fell never to rise again. This was a noble specimen of the African buffalo, standing sixteen hands and a half at the shoulder. His ponderous horns measured four feet from tip to tip, and, like a mass of rock, overshadowing his small sinister gray eyes, imparted to his countenance the most cunning, gloomy, and vindictive expression. The savages instantly set to work upon the carcass, with their teeth and assegais, Piet providing himself with portions of the hide for shoe-soles, and of the flesh, which, though coarse, is a tolerable imitation of beef.

"From the summit of a hill which commanded an extensive prospect over a straggling forest, I shortly afterwards perceived a large herd of buffaloes, quietly chewing the cud beneath an umbrageous tree. Creeping close upon them, I killed a bull with a single ball, but the confused echo, reverberating among the mountains, alarming the survivors, about fifty in number, they dashed panic-stricken from their concealment, ignorant whence the sound proceeded, and, every thing yielding to their giant strength, I narrowly escaped being trampled under foot in their progress. We moved five miles to the eastward in the afternoon, stopping to take up the head of the buffalo, which Andries could with difficulty lift upon the wagon. Myriads of vultures, and the clouds of smoke which arose from the fires of the giant and his associates, directed us to the spot. In commemoration, I presume, of the exploit of Guy Fawkes, they had kindled a bonfire, which bid fair to destroy all the grass in the country, the flames fanned by the wind already beginning to ascend the hills. Nothing can be conceived more horribly disgusting than the appearance presented by the savages, who, gorged to the throat and besmeared with blood, grease, and filth from the entrails, sat nodding torpidly round the remains of the carcass, sucking marrow from the bones, whilst their lean famished curs were regaling themselves upon the garbage. Every bush was garnished with flaps of meat, and every man had turned beef-butcher, whilst swollen vultures were perched upon the adjacent trees, and others yet ungorged were inhaling the odours that arose."

The meritorious perseverance of these Nimrods was now about to be rewarded, for we shall presently find them in the very midst of an elephant preserve :

"Leaving the wagons to proceed to a spot agreed upon, we again took the field about ten o'clock, and pursued the track indefatigably for eight miles, over a country presenting every variety of feature. At one time we crossed bare stony ridges, at another threaded the intricacies of forests; now struggled through high fields of waving grass, and again emerged into open downs. At length we arrived amongst extensive groups of grassy hillocks, covered with loose stones, interspersed with streams and occasional patches of forest, in which the recent ravages of elephants were surprising. Here, to our expressible gratification, we descried a large herd of those long-sought animals, lazily browsing at the head of a distant valley, our attention having been first directed to it by the strong and not-to-be-mistaken effluvia with which the wind was impregnated. Never having before seen the noble elephant in his native jungles, we gazed on the sight before us with intense and indescribable interest. Our feelings on the occasion even extended to our followers. As for Andries he became so agitated that he could scarcely articulate. With open eyes and quivering lips he at length stuttered forth, 'Dar stand de oliphant.' Mohanycom and 'Lingap were immediately despatched to drive the herd back into the valley, up which we rode slowly, and without noise, against the wind; and, arriving within one hundred and fifty yards unperceived, we made our horses fast, and took up a commanding position in an old stone kraal. The shouting of the

savages, who now appeared on the b
tling their shields, caused the huge ¹
move unauspiciously towards us,
within ten yards of our ambush. ᵀ
consisted of nine, all females, with la
We selected the finest, and with p₁
liberation fired a volley of five balls
She stumbled, but, recovering herse¹
a shrill note of lamentation, when ¹
party threw their trunks above the
and instantly clambered up the adj₁
with incredible celerity, their huge
ears flapping in the ratio of their spe
instantly mounted our horses, and ¹
loose stones not suiting the feet of th
ed lady, soon closed with her. S
with blood, and infuriated with r
turned upon us with uplifted trunl
was not until after repeated discharg
ball took effect in her brain, and ᵗ
lifeless on the earth, which resou₁
the fall.

"Turning our attention from tho
scene I have described, we found ᵗ
cond valley had opened upon us, su
by bare stony hills, and traversed by
wooded ravine. Here a grand and
cent panorama was before us. Tʰ
face of the landscape was actually
with wild elephants. There could ı
been fewer than three hundred wⁱ
scope of our vision. Every height aᵛ
knoll was dotted over with groups
whilst the bottom of the glen exı
dense and sable living mass, their
forms being at one moment partial¹ʸ
ed by the trees which they were di
with giant strength, and at others ı
jestically emerging into the open
bearing in their trunks the branches
with which they indolently protecte
selves from the flies. The back-grₒ
filled by a limited peep of the blue n
ous range, which here assumed a ren
precipitous character, and completed ı
at once soul-stirring and sublime.

"Our approach, being still aga
wind, was unobserved, and created littl
until the herd that we had left beh
denly showed itself, recklessly th₁
down the side of the hill to join ¹
body, and passing so close to us that
not refrain from firing a broadside in
them, which, however, bravely wit
We secured our horses on the sumı
stony ridge, and then, stationing our
an opportune place on a ledge overloo
wooded defile, sent Andries to mancₑ
that as many of the elephants as
should pass before us in order of revⁱ
we might ascertain, by a close inₛ
whether there was not a male among
Filing sluggishly along, they occ₁
halted beneath an umbrageous tree w
teen yards of us, lazily fanning th₁
with their ample ears, blowing away
with their trunks, and uttering the fe
peculiar cry so familiar to Indians
all proved to be ladies, and most ᵗ
mothers, followed by their little old-fⁱ
calves, each trudging close to the hee
dam, and mimicking all her actions

and over, and every beholder seemed convinced that it was "a tremendous conflagration." The consternation in the metropolis was very great; thousands of persons were running in the direction of the supposed awful catastrophe. The engines belonging to the fire brigade stations in Baker street, Farringdon street, Watling street, Waterloo road, and likewise those belonging to the west of England station, in fact, every fire engine in London, were horsed and galloped after the supposed "scene of destruction" with more than ordinary energy, followed by carriages, horsemen, and vast mobs. Some of the engines proceeded as far as Highgate and Holloway before the error was discovered.

These appearances lasted for upwards of two hours, and towards morning the spectacle became one of more grandeur. At two o'clock this morning the phenomenon presented a most gorgeous scene, and one very difficult to describe. The whole of London was illuminated as light as noonday, and the atmosphere was remarkably clear. The southern hemisphere at the time mentioned, although unclouded, was very dark, but the stars, which were innumerable, shone beautifully. The opposite side of the heavens presented a singular but magnificent contrast; it was clear to the extreme, and the light was very vivid; there was a continual succession of meteors, which varied in splendour. They apparently formed in the centre of the heavens, and spread till they seemed to burst; the effect was electrical; myriads of small stars shot out over the horizon, and darted with that swiftness towards the earth, that the eye scarcely could follow the track; they seemed to burst also, and throw a dark crimson vapour over the entire hemisphere. The colours were the most magnificent that ever were seen. At half past two o'clock the spectacle changed to darkness, which, on dispersing, displayed a luminous rainbow in the zenith of the heavens, and round the ridge of darkness that overhung the southern portion of the country. Soon afterwards columns of silvery light radiated from it; they increased wonderfully, intermingled amongst crimson vapour, which formed at the same time, and when at the full height, the spectacle was beyond all imagination. Stars were darting about in all directions, and continued until four o'clock, when all died away. During the time that they lasted, a great many persons assembled on the bridges across the river Thames, where they had a commanding view of the heavens, and watched the progress of the phenomenon attentively.

From the Edinburgh Pilot.

The Aurora Borealis was remarkably vivid and magnificent in the firmament on Tuesday night, (September 3d,) presenting one vast shifting flame of light from the northern to the southern horizon.

Wire Shoe Thread.—It is stated in a French paper that M. Seller, in Paris, has secured a patent for using brass wire for attaching the upper leather to the welt of boots and shoes. The advantage of this metallic thread are said to be, that it allows neither moisture nor dust to enter the shoe, nor does it rip. The sewing is performed with as much ease as with waxed thread, nor is the work more costly.

The Norfolk Herald says, that during the fire in that town, a curious effect was produced by the bursting of a cask of oil on the wharf. "The oil being ignited, ran over the side of the wharf, and into the river, presenting the appearance of a cascade of fire, and spreading over the water, covered it with a sheet of brilliant flame."

Expenditure of the Precious Metals.—It is computed that at least fifty thousand pounds sterling worth of gold and silver are annually employed at Birmingham, England, for gilding and plating, and, therefore, for ever lost to the world as bullion.

MONETARY.

Money! money! is the cry on all sides. Give us money, or we perish! resounds from the right and the left. Money was pronounced to be the root of all evil, long since, by high authority; and it fully sustains that character to this day. It is the prolific root of tormenting desire, of anxious solicitude, of strifes and fightings, of almost every thing which goads, perplexes, and distresses mankind. It is all this, individually, and the same effect runs through communities and countries. The "state of the money market" is now one of foremost enquiry and solicitude. "Money is tight"—'money is easier"—are the terms which are eagerly caught and responded from one commercial point to another, ringing throughout the land. Every symptom of the system, whether of *tightness* or *relaxation*, is anxiously watched—every pulse is counted and computed with all that concern which men feel for their nearest and dearest friends. Men do not watch the changing signs of the vaulted heavens with half the vigilance they do the vaults of our money banks. The faces of the commercial community are walking thermometers, in which the minutest degrees, upward and downward, constantly affected by the pecuniary atmosphere which envelopes all, can be plainly read. The prices of labour and food implicitly obey this potent power. Finance is now the chief business of nations.

Notwithstanding the earth has been embowelled of its minerals, and banks have increased faster than the churches of the land—demonstrating that men care as much for their sales as their souls—still the scarcity of money is the burden of complaint; the crushing pressure extorts groans from one end of the land to the other. There is, and ever has been, of late years, a relative scarcity, and would be, were its amount increased ten fold. It results from the perfect madness for business which now characterises the commercial community of the age. All in this respect is on the high-pressure principle; and though it is productive of much good in promoting industry and feeding the hungry, it is the cause of the "panics" and the "crises" which constantly alarm and perplex the land.

This mania for business, prompted by restless activity and strong desire of gain, drives commercial transactions far ahead of the real wants of the world;—production and interchange become excessive, accumulate somewhere, and crush thousands beneath the ponderous loads they take upon themselves. It is this which causes the constant ebb and flow which is incessantly taking place between nations—this *golden* tide, now flowing one way, now another, back and forward, attracted and governed by the *lunatic* influence which reigns over the business world.—*Salem Observer.*

THE NEWFOUNDLAND DOG.

This powerful, intelligent, and docile animal, which in its unmixed state is certainly the noblest of the canine tribe, is a native of the country the name of which it bears, and may be considered as a distinct race. Its introduction into this country is of comparatively recent date; and the fine animal known to us by the name of Newfoundland dog is only half-bred, and of size inferior to the dog in its native state, when it measures about six feet and a half from the nose to the extremity of the tail, the length of which is two feet. In its own country it only barks when greatly irritated, and then with a manifestly painful effort, producing a sound which is described as particularly harsh. Its exemption from hydrophobia in Newfoundland appears to be well authenticated.

The dog is employed by the settlers as a beast of burthen in drawing wood from the interior to the coast. Three or four of them yoked to a sledge will draw two or three hundred weight of wood with great facility for several miles. In this service they are said to be so sagacious and willing as to need no driver or guide; but, having delivered their burthen, return, without delay, to the woods in the expectation of receiving some food in recompense for their labour. We see, indeed, in this country, that, from the activity of his disposition, the Newfoundland dog delights in being employed; and the pride of being useful makes him take uncommon pleasure in carrying in his mouth for miles baskets and other articles, of which, as well from that satisfaction as from the fidelity of his character, it would be dangerous for a stranger to dispute possession with him. In many respects he may be considered as a valuable substitute for the mastiff as a house dog.

The Newfoundland dog is easily satisfied in his food. He is fond of fish, whether fresh or dried; and salt meat or fish is more acceptable to him than to most other animals, as well as boiled potatoes and cabbage. When hungry, however, he has not very strong scruples about appropriating such flesh or fish as falls in his way, or even of destroying poultry or sheep. For the blood of the latter animal he has much appetite, and sucks it from the throat without feeding on the carcass.

It is well known that the Newfoundland

dog can swim very fast, dive with ease, and bring things up from the bottom of the water. Other dogs can swim, but not so willingly, or so well. This superiority he owes to the structure of the foot, which is semi-webbed between the toes; thus presenting an extended surface to press away the water from be-hind, and then collapsing when it is drawn forward, previous to making the stroke. This property, joined to much courage, and a generous disposition, enables this dog to render those important services in the preserva-tion of endangered life, of which such nu-merous instances are recorded.

The following anecdotes of the Newfound-land dog are taken from Captain Brown's in-teresting "Anecdotes of Dogs."

"A Newfoundland dog, kept at ferry-house at Worcester, was famous for having, at dif-ferent periods, saved three persons from drown-ing; and so fond was he of the water, that he seemed to consider any disinclination for it in other dogs as an insult on the species. If a dog was left on the bank by its master, and, in the idea that it would be obliged to follow the boat across the river, which is but nar-row, stood yelping at the bottom of the steps, unwilling to take the water, the Newfound-land veteran would go down to him, and with a satirical growl, as if in mockery, take him by the back of the neck and throw him into the stream."

"A native of Germany, fond of travelling, was pursuing his course through Holland, ac-companied by a large Newfoundland dog. Walking one evening on a high bank, which formed one side of a dike, or canal, so com-mon in that country, his foot slipped, and he was precipitated into the water, and, being unable to swim, he soon became senseless. When he recovered his recollection, he found himself in a cottage on the opposite side of the dike to that from which he had fallen, sur-rounded by peasants, who had been using the means so generally practised in that country for restoring animation. The account given by the peasants was, that one of them return-ing home from his labour, observed, at a con-siderable distance, a large dog in the water swimming and dragging, and sometimes push-ing, something which he seemed to have great difficulty in supporting, but which he at length succeeded in getting into a small creek on the opposite side to that on which the men were.

"When the animal had pulled what he had hitherto supported, as far out of the water as he was able, the peasant discovered that it was the body of a man. The dog, having shaken himself, began industriously to lick the hands and face of his master, while the rustic hastened across; and, having obtained assistance, the body was conveyed to a neigh-bouring house, where the usual means of re-suscitation soon restored him to sense and recollection. Two very considerable bruises, with the marks of teeth, appeared, one on his shoulder, the other on the nape of the neck; whence it was presumed that the faithful ani-mal first seized his master by the shoulder, and swam with him in this manner for some time; but that his sagacity had prompted

him to let go his hold, and shift his the neck, by which he had been (support the head out of the water. the latter position that the peasant the dog making his way along the di it appeared he had done for a di nearly a quarter of a mile. It is probable that this gentleman owed much to the sagacity as to the fide dog."—*Penny Magazine.*

THE SAPPHIRE GROT
From Dr. Hogg's Visit to Alexandria, Dama

The sapphire grot at the northern of the island of Capri having only b re-discovered, of course excites co attention. The sole entrance to thi able cavern is a small semicircular close to the edge of the water, at tl an almost perpendicular cliff, which a great height into the sea. In form resembles the mouth of an oven, wh ceeds but little in size; yet immedia in it enlarges into a grotto of coi dimensions, with an arched roof th like a dome, a placid expanse of wa deepest azure. A signal being mad narrow boat, specially constructed t visiters within the cave, pushes shore; but the entrance can only be when the weather is perfectly calu the favourable moment of the refl waves. The visiter now places hims the edge of the boat, which tw adroitly and speedily conduct thr narrow passage. He then finds hin spacious circular cavern, into whic rect rays of light only penetrate th aperture by which he has entered; not being more than four feet either or breadth, the space within would l gloomy and obscure recess, were it tinguished from all other known ca the peculiarity which has conferre the name of the Sapphire Grot. 7 stand that it must be remembered entrance to this singular cave is to dered as the apex of a subaquec springing on one side from the bott sea, and on the other from a ledge near the surface of the water. greater part of the light within i from the rays that pass through waters of the surrounding ocean. denser medium some of these rays a cepted and absorbed, while the re refracted by passing through the w then reflected upwards from the bo fuse a rich blue colour over the sides of this beautiful grotto, which varied in appearance by the direct pass through the entrance, as they f undulating surface of the waves wit

The singular effect of light thu through an aqueous medium is here illustrated by the shadow of the b thrown upon the roof of the cave, t by an experiment, easily made, of cl tirely the entrance of the grot, v creases the intensity of the rich ceru that so conspicuously distinguish

The Origin and Object of Civil Government, according to the Views of the Society of Friends.

(Continued from page 23.)

We will now proceed to notice, in a brief manner, the leading political principles of Penn, and his ideas of the object of civil government, and the method by which he made so happy an effort to realise them. William Penn was not a discoverer of new principles. He only endeavoured, under the influence of religious benevolence, and the guidance of that Holy Spirit by which he acknowledged himself to be led, to reduce to practice those sacred precepts which had, by divine revelation, long been made known to mankind, though the rulers of the nations had not heeded them, and worldly-minded politicians had only regarded them as pleasant but impracticable fancies. What was the pure and elevated influence under which Penn attempted this great and noble enterprise, may best be indicated by his own words. "Let the Lord guide me," said he, "by his wisdom, to honour his name, and serve his truth and people, that an example and a standard may be set up to the nations."—"God has given me an understanding of my duty, and an honest mind to do it uprightly."—"I shall not usurp the right of any, or oppress his person. God has furnished me with a better resolution, and has given me his grace to keep it."

Throughout the administration of the affairs of his colony, divested of all selfish and ambitious views, this was the high and holy Source to which he looked for wisdom to plan, and strength to persevere, and this was the secret of his unparalleled success. When the company of traders offered him a large sum of money and an annual revenue for a monopoly of the Indian traffic between the Delaware and Susquehanna, "which to the father of a family in straitened circumstances, was a great temptation," bound by his religion to equal laws, he rebuked the cupidity of monopoly. "I will not abuse the love of God," such was his decision; "nor act unworthy of his providence, by defiling what came to me clean." His was an example of civil government founded upon Christian principle; and a modern European writer, distinguished for the depth and extent of his researches into history, thus speaks of the success of his "Holy Experiment," as William Penn himself had termed it. "Of all the colonies that ever existed, none was established on so philanthropic a plan; none was more deeply impressed with the character of its founder; none displayed more, as it grew up, his principles of toleration, liberty, and peace, and none rose and flourished more rapidly than Pennsylvania. She was the last of the British colonies which was settled before the eighteenth century; but she soon exceeded most of her elder sisters in population, improvement, and general prosperity." His comprehensive design was, "not only to afford an asylum to his religious brethren against the persecutions with which they were still threatened, but also to establish a government adapted to his views and princi-ples,"—"a civil society of men enjoying the highest possible degree of freedom and happiness; and to restore to them those lost rights and privileges with which God had originally blessed the human race." "I propose," said he, "that, which is extraordinary—to leave myself and successors no power of doing mischief; that the will of one man may not hinder the good of a whole country." He trusted that a higher than human power would protect and guide the progress of his infant colony. "Our faith," he declared, "is for one another, that God will be our counsellor for ever."

Yet Penn was an advocate for the "divine right" of secular power, and totally rejected the notion that civil society might be maintained without its regulating influence; or that the divine law to which the heart of every man is required to bow, was intended to assume, the office designed to be fulfilled by a judicious system of legislation. In the preamble to the "Frame of Government of the province of Pennsylvania," he asserts this right to be "settled," on Scripture authority, "beyond exception, and, that for two ends: first, to terrify evil-doers; secondly, to cherish those that do well; which gives government a life beyond corruption, and makes it as durable in the world, as good men should be, so that government seems to me a part of religion itself, a thing sacred in its institution and end. For, if it does not directly remove the cause, it crushes the effects of evil, and is as such, (though a lower, yet) an emanation of the same Divine Power, that is both author and object of pure religion," &c. "They weakly err, that think there is no other use of government, than correction, which is the coarsest part of it: daily experience tells us, that the care and regulation of many other affairs, more soft, and daily necessary, make up much the greatest part of government; and which must have followed the peopling of the world, had Adam never fell, and will continue among men on earth, under the highest attainments they may arrive at, by the coming of the blessed second Adam, the Lord from heaven. Thus much," he says, "of government, as to its rise and end."

"For particular frames and models, it will become me to say little; and comparatively, I will say nothing. My reasons are:—

"First, that the age is too nice and difficult for it; there being nothing the wits of men are more busy and divided upon. It is true they seem to agree to the end, to wit, happiness; but in the means they differ as to divine, so to this human felicity; and the cause is much the same, not always want of light and knowledge, but want of using them rightly. Men side with their passions against their reason, and their sinister interests have so strong a bias upon their minds, that they lean to them against the good of the things they know.

"Secondly, I do not find a model in the world, that time, place, and some singular emergencies have not necessarily altered; nor is it easy to frame a civil government that shall serve all places alike.

"Thirdly, I know what is said by the several admirers of monarchy, aristocracy and democracy, which are the rule of one, a few, and many, and are the three common ideas of government, when men discourse on the subject. But I choose to solve the controversy with this small distinction, and it belongs to all three: any government is free to the people under it (whatever be the frame) where the laws rule, and the people are a party to those laws, and more than this is tyranny, oligarchy, or confusion.

"But, lastly: when all is said, there is hardly one frame of government in the world so ill designed by its first founders, that in good hands it would not do well enough; and history tells us, the best, in ill ones, can do nothing that is great or good; witness the Jewish and Roman states. Governments, like clocks, go from the motion men give them; and as governments are made and moved by men, so by them they are ruined too. Wherefore governments rather depend upon men, than men upon governments. Let men be good, and the government cannot be bad; if it be ill, they will cure it. But, if men be bad, let the government be never so good, they will endeavour to warp and spoil it to their turn.

"I know some say, let us have good laws, and no matter for the men that execute them but let them consider, that though good laws do well, good men do better: for good laws may want good men, and be abolished or evaded by ill men; but good men will never want good laws, nor suffer ill ones. It is true, good laws have some awo upon ill ministers, but that is where they have not power to escape or abolish them, and the people are generally wise and good: but a loose and depraved people (which is to the question) love laws and an administration like themselves. That, therefore, which makes a good constitution, must keep it, viz. men of wisdom and virtue, qualities that, because they descend not with worldly inheritances, must be carefully propagated by a virtuous education of youth; for which after ages will owe more to the care and prudence of founders, and the successive magistracy, than to their parents for their private patrimonies."

"We have (with reverence to God, and good conscience to men) to the best of our skill, contrived and composed the frame and laws of this government, to the great end of all government, viz. to support power in reverence with the people, and to secure the people from the abuse of power; that they may be free by their just obedience, and the magistrates honourable for their just administration; for liberty without obedience is confusion, and obedience without liberty is slavery."

To recite the code of laws enacted by Penn and his fellow labourers, would be tedious and foreign to our purpose. The principles involved in some of them, new in legislation then, especially those relating to equal rights, have since, at least so far as white men are concerned, been pretty generally adopted in this country; but others have been, and are greatly neglected or violated, to the serious detriment of good morals, the true welfare of the community, and to the great scandal of republican institutions. We will only notice a few of them.

First, with regard to electors, and candidates for election, it was provided, that "the elector that shall receive any reward or gift, in meat, drink, moneys, or otherwise, shall forfeit his right to elect; and such person as shall, directly or indirectly, give, promise, or bestow, any such reward as aforesaid, to be elected, shall forfeit his election.

"That all officers in the service of the government, and all members of assembly, and all that have a right to elect such members, shall be such as profess faith in Jesus Christ, and *that are not convicted of ill-fame*, or *unsober and dishonest conversation*, and that are of twenty-one years of age, at least." Nevertheless, "all persons living in this province, who confess and acknowledge the one Almighty and eternal God, to be the creator, upholder, and ruler of the world; and that hold themselves obliged in conscience to live peaceably and justly in civil society, shall, in no ways, be molested or prejudiced for their religious persuasion, or practice, in matters of faith and worship.

"That, according to the good example of the primitive Christians, and the ease of creation, every first day of the week, called the Lord's day, people shall abstain from their common daily labour, *that they may the better dispose themselves to worship God according to their understandings.*

"That all children, within this province, of the age of twelve years, shall be taught some useful trade or skill, to the end none may be idle, but the poor may work to live, and the rich, if they become poor, may not want.

"That *all* trials shall be by twelve men, and, as near as may be, peers or equals, and of the neighbourhood, and men without just exception.

"That as a careless and corrupt administration of justice draws the wrath of God upon magistrates, so the wildness and looseness of the people provoke the indignation of God against a country: therefore, that all such offences against God, as swearing, cursing, lying, profane talking, drunkenness,"—"and other uncleanness, (not to be repeated,) all treasons, rudeness,"—and "other violences, to the persons and estates of the inhabitants within this province; all prizes, stage-plays, cards, dice, May games, gamesters, masques, revels, bull-baitings, cock-fightings, bear-baitings, and the like, which excite the people to rudeness, cruelty, looseness, and irreligion, shall be respectively discouraged, and severely punished, according to the appointment of the governor and freemen in provincial council and general assembly."

But Penn did not content himself with guarding the rights and morals of his own people; the privileges of the feeble Indian were also carefully secured. In the conditions, or "concessions," as they were termed, agreed upon with the adventurers and purchasers in the province, it was provided,

"That no man shall, by any ways or means, in word or deed, affront, or wrong any Indian, but he shall incur the same penalty of the law, as if he had committed it against his fellow planter."

"That all differences, between the planter and the natives, shall be ended by twelve men, that is, by six planters and six natives; so that we may live friendly together, as much as in us lieth, preventing all occasions of heart-burnings and mischief."

"That the Indians shall have liberty to do all things relating to improvement of their ground, and providing sustenance for their families, that any of the planters shall enjoy."

These pledges were confirmed to the natives by treaty, and faithfully fulfilled under the administration of the proprietary. "Beneath a large elm-tree at Shakamaxon, on the northern edge of Philadelphia, William Penn, surrounded by a few Friends in the habiliments of peace, met the numerous delegation of the Lenni Lenape tribes—not for the purchase of lands, but, confirming what Penn had written, and Markham covenanted; his sublime purpose was the recognition of the equal rights of humanity. Under the shelter of the forest, now leafless by the frosts of autumn, Penn proclaimed to the men of the Algonquin race, the same simple message of peace and love which George Fox had professed before Cromwell, and Mary Fisher had borne to the Grand Turk."

"We meet"—such were the words of William Penn—"on the broad pathway of faith and good-will; no advantage shall be taken on either side, but all shall be openness and love. I will not call you children; for parents sometimes chide their children too severely; nor brothers only, for brothers differ. The friendship between me and you, I will not compare to a chain; for that the rains might rust or the falling tree might break. We are the same as if one man's body were to be divided into two parts; we are all one flesh and blood."

Such were the principles which lay at the foundation of the government of Penn. They were the result of his religious faith, which was, and continues to be, the faith of the Society of Friends; and is identical with that set forth in such plain and energetic language by the inspired writers of the New Testament; and how his colony was blessed under their influence, history attests in glowing terms.

In the autumn of 1683, "Philadelphia consisted of three or four little cottages; the colonies were yet undisturbed in their hereditary burrows; the deer fearlessly bounded past glazed trees, unconscious of foreboded streets; the stranger that wandered from the river bank was lost in the thickets of the interminable forest; and, two years afterwards, the place contained about six hundred houses, and the school-master and the printing press had begun their work. In three years from its foundation, Philadelphia gained more than New York had done in half a century. This was the happiest season in the public life of William Penn. 'I must without vanity, say' —such was his honest exultation—'I have

led the greatest colony into America that ever any man did upon a private credit, and the most prosperous beginnings that ever were in it, are to be found among us.'"

So much for the inspiring energy of Christianity applied to civil institutions. If the pretended political reformers of the present day would resort to that exhaustless fountain of healing and invigorating virtue, they would be more likely to bring back to us that reign of justice and mercy, and real prosperity, than by the wild and destructive measures they propose.

What saith the Scriptures? Let every soul be subject to the higher powers, for there is no power, but of God; the powers that be, are ordained of God; whosoever therefore resists the power, resists the ordinance of God; and they that resist, shall receive to themselves damnation. For rulers are not a terror to good works, but to the evil. Wilt thou then be afraid of the power? Do that which is good, and thou shalt have praise of the same; for he is the minister of God to thee for good. But if thou do that which is evil, be afraid; for he beareth not the sword in vain; for he is the minister of God; a revenger to execute wrath upon him that does evil. Wherefore ye must needs be subject, not only for wrath, but also for conscience sake. Submit yourselves to every ordinance of man for the Lord's sake, whether it be to the king as supreme, or unto governors, as unto them that are sent by him for the punishment of evil-doers, and for the praise of them that do well: for so is the will of God, that with well-doing ye may put to silence the ignorance of foolish men.

For "The Friend."

INDIANA YEARLY MEETING.

This body assembled at the appointed time at White Water meeting-house, near Richmond, in Wayne county, Indiana, on fifth day, the 3d of the present month. The meeting for sufferings had been held on second day, and the meeting for ministers and elders on third day preceding. A public meeting for worship had also been held on fourth day, before the opening of the yearly meeting for discipline. The meeting of this great body of Friends is always interesting; and in many respects peculiarly so. The territory represented by this yearly meeting is very large; and the coming together, in brotherly love and fellowship of so many, all holding the same faith, and aiming at the same thing, the glory of God and the salvation of their souls, but from points so distant from each other, and between which there may be little or no communication at any other time; the renewing of affectionate acquaintance which had been previously formed, and the new formation of such acquaintance with other individuals; the presence of messengers of the gospel from other lands, who come to us with the gladdening salutation of unity and peace and Christian fellowship; together with the evidence of the presence of the great Head of the church to protect and to bless us with his good spirit—all conspire to render the yearly meeting a season of peculiar interest. Here our bonds are strengthened; here our faith is renewed by confirmed; and here we are encouraged to persevere for the future in good works.

'The meeting the present year was not wanting in these several particulars. We had members with us from beyond Columbus, in Ohio, eastward; from the north, south, west, and middle of this state; from the state of Illinois; and even from the far distant Iowa; our eleven quarterly meetings were all represented; and we had some fifteen or twenty Friends from other yearly meetings, among whom was our beloved Jacob Greene, from Ireland. The number of members was as large as usual, if not larger; the house was filled, and many wanted room in it every day; the number seated was probably over three thousand, besides those on their feet in the aisles, and outside about the doors. From any eminence within view of the ground at the rise of the meeting the scene was truly impressive. The immense congregation of people, of horses and carriages, that swarmed like the bees from a hive, almost covering the ground for a considerable distance in every direction, with such a variety in appearance, from the rich dress of the city to that of the poor labourer in the woods—all combined to fill the mind with astonishment. In this view, the reflections must touch every feeling mind, that this generation must soon pass away; that the living multitudes now before us, and of which we form a part, must soon crumble into dust; and that "God has appointed a day in the which he will judge the world in righteousness," when all nations shall be assembled before him, of which this assembly is fitted to remind us; the awful condition of being called to it unprepared; and the inexpressible glory of being permitted to join "the general assembly and church of the first-born" in heaven.

On fifth day the epistles from other yearly meetings were read, among which stands conspicuous that excellent document called the London General Epistle, which was ordered to be reprinted for circulation; the appeals were considered, and several important matters were committed to large committees.

On sixth day the state of Society was considered, the queries and answers from the quarters being read. Much excellent admonition was communicated during the exercises of the meeting on this occasion. A remissness in the diligent attendance of our religious meetings, particularly those held in the middle of the week, and the lack of that love which becomes our Christian profession, were noticed to be corresponding deficiencies generally—the number of complaints this year was not, however, considered greater than usual. In regard to plainness of speech, &c., the departure in our Society of many from a correct use of the pronoun thou was particularly brought to view, and the inaccurate use of thee where thou should be used, was believed to arise more from the cross which the sound use of the word carries with it in the minds of many, than from any ignorance, real or imaginary, which may be supposed to exist. Secret closet prayer was pertinently recommended, in ac-

cordance with the instructions of our blessed Saviour, "Enter thou into thy closet, and when thou hast shut thy door, pray to thy Father which is in secret, and thy Father which seeth in secret shall reward thee openly."—Matthew vi. 6. Love to God and our neighbours, and a strict attention to the command of our Saviour, that we should do unto others as we would that they should do unto us, would effectually prompt us to a faithful and punctual fulfilment of contracts and engagements, which is our reasonable duty; and finally, Friends were advised to maintain their testimony against slavery, and against the use of the heathen names of the days and months. On seventh day morning a proposition was introduced, to consider the propriety of a division of the yearly meeting. This is a measure which, should it take place, must of course require to be thoroughly weighed, and much time to be allowed for mature consideration, and the ultimate pointing of the finger of Truth. There has been some talk among Friends of a new yearly meeting in the western part of Ohio; but there seems to be more reason to think, in reference to the growing population of Friends in the west, that if another should be set up, it will be in the western part of Indiana, or in Illinois. The subject was referred, for the present, to a large committee of men and women Friends, who are to report to the next yearly meeting.

The Indian committee reported in detail their proceedings. The attention of Indiana, Ohio, and Baltimore yearly meetings seems to be jointly turned to one small tribe, late resident in Ohio, now removed to the Kanzas, west of the state of Missouri. A small establishment has been maintained there, which conducts a farm, and a small school, which is hereafter to be enlarged. Ohio Yearly Meeting has sent on more than $300, and Indiana has appropriated $600 from the men's meeting and $100 from the women's meeting for its support the next year.

The subject of education has been made a yearly meeting concern for several years past. The reports were accordingly read thereon, by which it appeared, that there are more than 7,000 children in this yearly meeting of a suitable age to be sent to school. Several schools have been established under the care of monthly meetings. By the report of the boarding-school committee, which was not read until second day, it appears that the work has progressed, to the preparing of a considerable amount of materials, including bricks, lumber, &c., and that one of the out-buildings has been put up, and the cellar excavated, and the walls of it, together with the foundation walls of the main buildings, are nearly completed. The farm, nearly three hundred acres of valuable land, has been paid for, and seven or eight thousand dollars subscribed towards the school. But an unusual effort seems just now necessary, in order that the buildings may be raised and enclosed during the next season—which will require six or eight thousand more. The work could then, it is believed, be leisurely and easily finished. But in no case does the want of education more plainly appear than in the

difficulty of getting funds for this work; for although the school has many warm friends and supporters, yet it was evident, from the expressions of a number of others in the meeting, that their support would be withheld. The completion of this work is no doubt of great importance to the Society in the west, and the assistance of benevolent Friends of other parts would be very acceptable to the labourers in that cause in Indiana Yearly Meeting.

On first day two large meetings for worship were held; the concourse was great—hundreds, some say thousands, could not get into the meeting-house.

The committee on African concerns seem to be animated in the cause. It is hoped that their attention may be confined to the objects and duties of their appointment, which is the amelioration of the condition of the coloured man, without suffering their minds to be acted upon by the prevailing excitements of the day. Some attention seems to have been paid by them during the last year, to the education of some of the people of colour, as appeared by their report, which was read on third day.

The meeting closed on third day afternoon, after having transacted a great variety of business; a solemnity covered the close; at which many hearts felt thankful for the favour of the presence of the Lord by his good Spirit, giving evidence of his continued mercy and protection. * * *

For "The Friend."

GILES AND MAUD TYDMARSH.

I love to read and dwell upon the records of the days of our ancestors, and to contrast their simple habits—their plain and unsophisticated manners, with the boasted refinements and luxuries of these modern, and I fear, in many respects, less virtuous and less happy times. The following little scrap of history I met with on looking over a volume of The Friends' Monthly Magazine, published at Bristol, England, in 1830; which, while it is not destitute of attraction for readers in general, is calculated especially to interest the numerous descendants of at least one of the persons mentioned. Joseph and Sarah Lounds, or as the name is now written, Lownes, had eleven children, several of whom were still more remarkable instances of longevity than the elder Giles Tydmarsh and his wife, not only living to be very old, but retaining their mental faculties in brightness and vigour nearly to the last. Of the eleven children, Ann married Thomas Page, and lived to 60; Susannah married Thomas Lindley, and died aged 84; John died aged 84; Sarah married Jonathan Shoemaker, died aged 95; Joseph, age not ascertained; Hannah married Joshua Pancoast, died in her 83d year; William died aged about 79; Rebecca married Caleb Ash, and died in her 93d year; James died aged 91; Mary married Job Bacon, and died at about 60; Jane died young. Thus it appears that the ages of the seven oldest average eighty-seven.

The land on which William Tydmarsh settled was situated in the Neck below the city, part of which is yet in possession of some of the descendants, and Tydmarsh street, in the lower part of the city, thence derives its name.　　　　　　S. R.

John Audland and John Camm, in the course of their ministerial service, passing through Barton, in Oxfordshire, in the year 1654, stopped at the Cross, and exhorted the people to take heed to the light within them, after which they were walking along the street leading their horses, which a young woman named Maud Hierns, observing, went home and said, "Father, there have been two men preaching at the Cross, and nobody has asked them to eat or drink:" he replied, "Go, Maud, and ask them to come here, and bring their horses;" which they did and were hospitably received and entertained, continuing there till next day. During their visit they had much religious conversation with their host, Wm. Hierns, who was an ancient man, a baptist by profession. He assented to their doctrine, and said, "it is the truth, the very truth; but what would my brethren say to me were I to change my profession?" While they were in conversation, Maud placed herself behind John Audland's chair, listening attentively to their communications: her mind was opened to receive the principles they professed; and for her steady perseverance therein she suffered much bnkind treatment from her parents, notwithstanding their house was open to entertain travelling Friends: her going to meeting was much obstructed, particularly by her mother, who used to send her some distance into the fields to milk the cows, when she had several miles to walk to meeting. At length her diligent conduct in the family awakened tenderness in her father towards her, so that he said to his wife, "My dear, if Maud will be a Quaker, let her be a Quaker; she is best of all the children, and she shall have a horse to go to meeting on." Her situation now was rendered much easier: she attended Milton meeting, to which young Giles Tydmarsh used to go. He one day said to her, "Maud, I want to speak to thee;" she replied, "If thou hast any thing to say to me, Giles, come to my father's house;" he did so, and making matrimonial proposals, it met with the old man's approbation, who thereupon said to his wife, "My dear, if Maud will be a Quaker, a Quaker husband is best for her, and I like Giles well: I will go and speak to his father about it." Giles Tydmarsh the elder was then a prisoner in Oxford Castle, on an excommunication for not attending church. They met in the castle with "Ah! William, how dost do?" "How dost do, Giles? but to the matter in hand: thy son Giles has a mind to my daughter Maud; what wilt thou give thy son?" "I will give him the house in the Nether Row, at Chipping Norton." "That's enough, Giles." "And what wilt thou give thy daughter?" "I will give her seventy pounds." "That's enough, William." Matters being settled, they married, and lived in the said house. Old Giles Tydmarsh continued a prisoner seven years, and was then released, with about four hundred more in the nation, by

letters patent from King Charles, in the year 1672. During his confinement he used to make shoes, his wife or son going every two weeks with work, taking away what he had done. It does not appear, that after his release, he returned to his business again; but, with his wife, went and lived with his son and daughter, Giles and Maud Tydmarsh, at Chipping Norton. They both lived to be about ninety years of age, she surviving her husband only one day; they were interred in one grave at Milton. Some years previous to their death they were quite childish, and in that state were tenderly cherished by their daughter-in-law, Maud, who made it her daily practice, before any of the family were permitted to dine, to feed the old people, by placing herself on a stool between them, and giving first one, and then the other, a piece, till they were both satisfied. The above Giles and Maud Tydmarsh had four children: the eldest daughter married to Joseph French, who had surviving issue; Sarah married to Thomas Wagstaffe, of Banbury; Wm. Tydmarsh, their eldest son, removed with his family to Philadelphia; and his daughter Sarah married Joseph Lounds.

THE FRIEND.

TENTH MONTH, 26, 1839.

A respectable correspondent, a member of Indiana Yearly Meeting, has enabled us to place before our readers an account of their late annual solemnity, which will be found interesting.

The lectures of Dr. J. Bryan at Friends' Reading Rooms, so far as respects the first and second, already delivered, we believe have given general satisfaction. It ought to have been announced last week in "The Friend," that Nathan Kite intended to deliver two lectures, on the modes adopted and the materials employed in different ages to render knowledge permanent, with an outline sketch of the history of literature. The first lecture was delivered on third day evening last, to a crowded room of intently listening auditors, who, if we might infer from their countenances, were highly gratified. The other lecture is to take place on next third day evening, at half past seven o'clock.

COMMUNICATION.

Observing by the public papers that our gifted fellow townsman, Dr. Reynell Coates, is about to deliver a course of lectures on "The *History of Organic Development*, and the *Effects of Exercise upon Physical and Physico-Moral Faculties or Functions*," in the Hall of the Young Men's Institute, in Filbert above Eleventh street; it occurred to me that I should but render a service to the youthful portion of our religious Society, by calling their particular attention to these lectures.

There can be little doubt in the mind of any one acquainted with the ability of the lecturer, his general diversified acquirements in natural history, and the happy tact which he

possesses of
dience, that
a pleasing bu
tainment. I
younger me
spare an ho
to embrace t
intellectual r
will be open
next fourth
such of our
have an oppo
of the plan c
it is to be ho
10mo. 24

W
The wint
28th instant
extra carria,
Sixth street,
on the mor
Such of the
selves of th
names enter
that purpos
early on the
10th mo.

A stated
of the Auxi
will be held
P. M. in Fr
alley.
10th mo.

A stated
Association
Haddonfield
at Cropwel
the 4th of l
Na
10mo. 2

MARRIED,
meeting hous
England, ALI
RAH TAYLOR,

DIED, on th
Rochester, E
vanced age
highly esteem
was for a tim
New York, a
paid an acco
country. A
vious to his
faculties, and
that "it wa
bear testimon
nifying and
confidence o
glimpse, and
merited mer
his own to 1
died for him
deemed."
, on
York, CAROL
Charles W.
Hacker, of t

PRI
Carpenti

THE FRIEND.

A RELIGIOUS AND LITERARY JOURNAL.

VOL. XIII.   SEVENTH DAY, ELEVENTH MONTH, 2, 1839.   NO. 5.

EDITED BY ROBERT SMITH.

PUBLISHED WEEKLY.

Price two dollars per annum, payable in advance.

Subscriptions and Payments received by

GEORGE W. TAYLOR,

NO. 50, NORTH FOURTH STREET, UP STAIRS,

PHILADELPHIA.

MORAL MACHINERY SIMPLIFIED.

This is the title of a sermon delivered at Andover, Mass., on the 4th of seventh month last, by Parsons Cooke, a clergyman of Lynn, somewhat famous for his heroic assault upon the Grimkes during their anti-slavery labours in New England. It is by no means destitute of merit as a mere literary performance : but its tone and temper, its misrepresentations and superciliousness,—however adapted to the meridian of a theological seminary whose professors are remarkable for their ingenuity in reconciling slavery with Christianity,—will not commend it to the favourable regard of the honest lover of truth and justice.

We leave to others, who may attach more importance to it than we do, to deal with the assumption running through the entire discourse, that " ministers of the gospel," (by which we understand him to mean the gospel according to the Andover formula, or what is technically called " Evangelical,") are the only rightful instrumentalities of reform,—satisfied as we are that the common sense of not only the laity in general, but of a large proportion of the clergy themselves—the experience of the past—and the concurrent testimony of all history from the time when the " carpenter's son," the despised artisan of Nazareth, confuted the chief priests of the corrupt Jewish church, down to the present period, will prove a sufficient refutation of a doctrine at once absurd and arrogant. It is not in man to set metes and bounds to that duty of man towards his fellow man which our heavenly Father has made universal; nor to arrogate to himself the choice and appointment of the instruments whereby the benevolent designs of Providence are to be accomplished. The error into which the writer in question has fallen, is by no means an uncommon one. Human nature is the same now as it was in the days of the half-enlightened disciples :—" Master, we saw one casting out devils in thy name, and we rebuked him, *because he followed not us.*" We have seen the same thing in our own religious Society, and indeed in almost every sect and party, and even the sect of anti-sectarians are by no means exempt from it.

We wish to notice that portion of the pamphlet (pages 10 and 11) which virtually charges upon the Society of Friends, a desire to reap " advantages" to itself from anti-slavery organization. In other words, to promote its peculiar " policies" under the guise of abolitionism. Justice to ourselves, and such of our friends as are at the same time members of the anti-slavery society, and of the Society of Friends, compels us to declare that we know of no foundation whatever for this imputation. The " sectarian policies" to which the writer probably alludes, viz. the new views of the Rights of Women and non-allegiance to Human Government, &c. form no part of " *Quaker* sectarianism," as manifested from the days of George Fox to the present time. The views alluded to, may be sectarian ; but if so, they are not the sectarianism of the Society of Friends, and no one could regret more sincerely than ourselves that, whatever may be their intrinsic merits, there should be, either in fact or imagination, any connection between them and the anti-slavery association. They certainly have no necessary connection with it. The Society as such, has no theological or sectarian views whatever; it is simply and only anti-slavery.

The sermon condemns anti-slavery societies on the ground of their basis of combination—welcoming all who can subscribe to the one great principle of the association,—admitting the co-operation of infidels and *haters of the ministry !* For ourselves, from the origin of the anti-slavery society, we have cheerfully associated with persons of almost every religious denomination in the land, as well as with some whom common fame has charged with infidelity. From the fact that individuals of the latter class may be occasionally found in the anti-slavery societies, the writer of the Andover sermon infers that the whole organization is corrupt and defective ; and supposes, by way of a striking illustration, the infidel Thomas Paine, and the devoted missionary David Brainard, associated in the same anti-slavery society. It may perhaps edify him to know that Thomas Paine *was* an abolitionist—that his name now stands on record as the clerk of the house of representatives of Pennsylvania, appended to the glorious emancipation act of 1780 : and that, as *his* associates and coadjutors in the abolition societies of that day, were those whom even Andover delights to honour,—a Belknap, a Hopkins, an Edwards—the very guiding stars of New England orthodoxy! But, waving this point, we wish to say, that among those most endeared to us by their generous sacrifices,

their zeal, faithfulness and abundant labours in the cause of the slave, are members of the clerical profession. In prosecuting the cause, they have not interfered with our peculiar religious sentiments, nor have we with theirs; —and were we certain that they entertained towards " Quakerism," as a doctrine, a hatred as intense as that felt by Governor Endicott and the intolerant Puritan priests who scoffed at the body of Mary Dyer, hanging ghastly between earth and heaven, a martyr for that doctrine, we would still, for the promotion of the single object of emancipation, as cheerfully co-operate with them as we now do. Let them answer to God and their own consciences for their belief and practice on other subjects, and not to the anti-slavery society. As *abolitionists,* as men engaged, at the sacrifice of ease and influence, station and popularity, in the prosecution of measures for the deliverance of the slave, we love and honour them, not as clergymen, but as men who have hearts to feel for the woes of the oppressed, and moral courage to make that feeling manifest in the midst of timid time-servers and corrupt panderers to popular prejudice.

We have not been accustomed to expect more, in the cause of emancipation, from the clergy, than of lawyers, physicians, or other classes of the community ; and as a body of men, we do not conceive that they merit any *especial* censure from the abolitionists, unless, as in the case of the writer of the sermon in question, they seem disposed to arrogate to themselves the entire prerogative of reform. Then indeed do they pluck down upon themselves a mountain's weight of awful responsibility—every giant sin of the land clamours their unfaithfulness in the ear of heaven and earth,—every unrebuked iniquity publishes their shame; and the censures of the despised abolitionists, however severe, must be mild in comparison to those of the monitor within. If it be indeed true that to the professing church, through the clergy alone, is assigned the work of slave emancipation, let the latter bethink them of what account, at the final judgment, they shall render of their stewardship for the last six years.

We should like to know how the author of the sermon before us keeps his debt and credit account with conscience in this matter. Will he attempt to balance his especial and exclusive moral obligation as " a minister of the gospel," to plead the cause of the oppressed, by passing to his credit such items as his sermon, against the devoted daughters of South Carolina, the " Pastoral letter" of the Massachusetts Congregational Association, and the moral anomaly now under review, entitled " Moral Machinery Simplified!" —*Pennsylvania Freeman.*

COTTON AND SLAVERY.

We have before us the Charleston, S. C., Courier of the 12th inst., containing an article from the "South Carolinian," on the subject of the "Cotton Circular," of some of the planter politicians of the south and west. The plan proposed by the circular to effect a combination between the banking interest of the south and the great commercial cities and the cotton planter, whereby the former shall advance to the latter, to nearly the value of his cotton, so as to enable him to hold it until the market is favourable, the writer strongly objects to, as based upon the assumption that the cotton planters as a class are debtors. He admits that such is the fact to a great extent in regard to the planters of the southwest—but maintains that there is also a large class in the south who are not in debt, and stand in no need of bank advances to enable them to anticipate their annual income of cotton. He enquires somewhat significantly whether a combination to keep up the price of cotton would not almost necessarily produce combinations to keep it down, and suggests whether it might not make it the interest of consumers in France and Great Britain to encourage and foster the production of cotton out of the United States, and beyond the reach of such combinations of banks and planters as are contemplated in the "Cotton Circular."

The concluding portion of the article is worthy of attention, as it may furnish the friends of emancipation with some hints as to the great obstacle now in the way of their object.

"The southern planter, if he confines himself to planting, without speculation, asks no aid from banks—his cotton will be his passport through the commercial world. By the blessing of heaven, he is enabled to raise the noblest weed that was ever given for the comfort of the human family—a weed, destined to make a new era in modern commerce, if those who raise it have spirit and virtue enough to scorn and defy the banking and speculative quacks of the day. I have no idea that the slaveholding race could maintain their liberty or independence for five years without cotton. It is that which gives us our energy, our enterprise, our intelligence! and commands the respect of foreign powers. The Egyptian may look with devotion to his Nile, as the source of the power and wealth of Egypt; the pilgrim and inhabitant of the Holy Land may battle in sacred Jordan, and take comfort from washing his sins; the Hindoo may worship the Lotus, under an idea that Vishnu created Bramah from its unfolded flowers; but a genuine slaveholder in South Carolina, will ever look with reverence to the cotton plant, as the source of his power and his liberty. All the parchments upon earth could never protect him from the grasping avarice and fanatical fury of modern society. If he expects to preserve the peculiar institutions of his country, and transmit them to posterity, he must teach his children to hold the cotton plant in one hand, and the sword in the other, ever ready to defend it. A Cotton Planter."

We hope the above paragraph will [open] the eyes of British abolitionists. It [will] show them that they have a mighty responsibility in the question of the speedy termination or indefinite extension and perpetuation of American slavery. Cotton is now [a] great anti-abolition influence of this country. In whatever shape opposition to the cause of emancipation manifests itself—whether in church or the state—in a mercantile or ecclesiastical association—it may be traced directly back to the cotton-bale. Were English and French manufacturers supplied with Indian and Egyptian cotton, the demand for slaves as growers of men and women for the cotton planting region would find no market for their human staple—and, as a consequence, slavery would be unprofitable, and as a consequence, Virginia statesmen would begin to believe with Thomas Jefferson, "that men are created equal;" and Virginia divines—the Plummers and the Hills—would soon discover that slavery is incompatible with genuine Presbyterianism, whether of the old or the new school. Slavery now entrenched behind its cotton bags, like Jackson at New Orleans; and the efforts of British or even American abolitionists to dislodge it by moral suasion, we fear will prove as ineffectual as those of Gen. Packenham, to force the cotton barricades of the American camp, on the 8th of January, 1815. We call, then, upon the abolitionists of Great Britain, to urge their government to foster and promote, to the extent of its power, the cultivation of cotton in the Indies. By doing, they will promote the true interests of their own country—they will confer an incalculable benefit upon ours—they will lift the crushed millions of India from their degradation—and strike off the chains from the millions of American slaves.

The present annual product of cotton in Asia is estimated at 190,000,000 pounds, that in Egypt, at about 30,000,000. It is stated by Dr. Bowring, of England, that the slave trade which has heretofore desolated one of the finest cotton tracts in the world—the confluence of the Blue and White Nile—has been prohibited by Mehemet Ali; and that from henceforth the cultivation will go on without interruption. In this tract, finest cotton is found growing in the wild, uncultured by human hands. In the British possessions of the East, no longer weighed down by the monopoly of the East India Company, but open to enterprise, the cultivation must necessarily receive a favourable impulse. We confess that one of our main reliances, under God, for the bloodless termination of American slavery, is the increase of cotton cultivation in the Peninsula of British India.—Ibid.

Our Political Power and Responsibility.

What can the citizens of the United States do for the abolition of slavery? What constitutional power do they possess over slavery?

1. The people of the United States have the same power over slavery in the Di[strict]

of the first importance, the abolition of slavery wherever it is within their constitutional power.—*Ibid.*

SCENES IN SOUTHERN AFRICA.
(Continued from p. 25.)

Our author remarks that much has been said of the attachment of elephants to their young, but that on no occasion did he perceive that these animals evinced the smallest concern for the safety of their unwieldy infants; on the contrary, they left them to shift for themselves. That the converse of the proposition, however, does not hold, we have the captain's own evidence; nor do we think the worse of him for the compunction which the distressing conduct of the wretched little orphan elephant that followed its mother's murderers awakened:—

"Not an elephant was to be seen on the ground that was yesterday teeming with them; but, on reaching the glen which had been the scene of our exploits during the early part of the action, a calf about three and a half feet high walked forth from a bush, and saluted us with mournful piping notes. We had observed the unhappy little wretch hovering about its mother after she fell, and having probably been unable to overtake the herd, it had passed a dreary night in the wood. Entwining its little proboscis about our legs, the sagacious creature, after demonstrating its delight at our arrival by a thousand ungainly antics, accompanied the party to the body of its dam, which, swollen to an enormous size, was surrounded by an inquest of vultures. Seated in gaunt array, with their shoulders shrugged, these loathsome fowls were awaiting its decomposition with forced resignation; the tough hide having defied all the efforts of their beaks, with which the eyes and softer parts had been vigorously assailed. The conduct of the quaint little calf now became quite affecting, and elicited the sympathy of every one. It ran round its mother's corse with touching demonstrations of grief, piping sorrowfully, and vainly attempting to raise her with its tiny trunk. I confess that I had felt compunctions in committing the murder the day before, and now half resolved never to assist in another; for, in addition to the moving behaviour of the young elephant, I had been unable to divest myself of the idea that I was firing at my old favourite Mowla-Bukhsh, from whose gallant back I had vanquished so many of my feline foes in Guzerat, an impression, which however ridiculous it must appear, detracted considerably from the satisfaction I experienced.

"The operation of hewing out three pair of tusks occupied several hours, their roots, embedded in massy sockets, spreading over the greater portion of the face. My Indian friends will marvel when they hear of tusks being extracted from the jaws of a female elephant; but, with very few exceptions, all that we saw had these accessories, measuring from three to four feet in length. I have already stated my belief that the maximum height of the African male is twelve feet;

that of the female averages eight and a half; the enormous magnitude of the ears, which not only cover the whole of the shoulder, but overlap each other on the neck, to the complete exclusion of the *mahout* or driver, constituting another striking feature of difference between the two species. The forehead is remarkably large and prominent, and consists of two walls or tables, between which, a wide cellular space intervening, a ball, hardened with tin or quicksilver, readily penetrates to the brain, and proves instantaneously fatal.

"The barbarous tribes that people Southern Africa have never dreamt of the possibility of rendering this lordly quadruped serviceable in a domestic capacity; and even amongst the colonists there exists an unaccountable superstition that his subjugation is not to be accomplished. His capture, however, might readily be achieved; and, as he appears to possess all the aptitude of his Asiatic relative, the only difficulty that presents itself is the general absence, within our territories, of sufficient food for his support. Were he once domesticated, and arrayed against the beasts of the forest, Africa would realise the very *beau idéal* of magnificent sport. It is also worthy of remark that no attempt has ever been made on the part of the colonists to naturalise another most useful animal, the camel, although soil, climate, and productions appear alike to favour its introduction.

"We succeeded, after considerable labour, in extracting the ball which Andries pretended to have fired yesterday; and, the grooves of my rifle being conspicuous upon it, that worthy but unabashed squire was constrained not only to relinquish his claim to the merit of having slain the elephant, but also to forego his fancied right to the ivory. The miniature elephant, finding that its mother heeded not its caresses, voluntarily followed our party to the wagons, where it was received with shouts of welcome from the people, and a band of all sorts of melody from the cattle. It died, however, in spite of every care, in the course of a few days; as did two others, much older, that we subsequently captured."

But the rifle had yet to be tried upon a full-grown bull elephant, and an opportunity soon presented itself:—

"Although the ground was very heavy, we resolved upon shifting the camp a few miles to the eastward, in order to be within reach of the elephants. All the mountain-rills were full, but they were not of sufficient magnitude to obstruct the wagons. As we proceeded, several elephants were observed clambering with the agility of chamois to the very summit of the chain. Shortly after we had halted, I went out alone, and, ascending by a narrow path trodden by wild animals, entered a strip of forest occupying an extensive ravine. On the outside of this stood a mighty bull elephant, his trunk entwined around his tusk, and, but for the flapping of his huge ears, motionless as a statue. Securing my mare to a tree, I crept silently behind a block of stone, and levelled my rifle at his ample forehead. The earth trembled

under the weight of the enormous brute as he dropped heavily, uttering one deep groan, and expiring without a struggle. His height at the shoulder was eleven feet and a half, and his tusks measured more than seven in length. The echo of the shot reverberating through hill and dale caused the mare to break her tether and abscond, and brought large tribes of pig-faced baboons* from their sylvan haunts, to afford me any thing but sympathy. Their ridiculous grimaces, however, could not fail to elicit my mirth, whatever might have been my humour. It was long before I recovered my horse, and I did not regain the wagons till after nightfall. The new moon brought, if possible, a more abundant supply of rain than usual; nor did the lions fail to take advantage of the nocturnal tempest, having twice endeavoured to effect an entrance into the cattle-fold. It continued, until nine o'clock the next morning, to pour with such violence, that we were unable to open the canvass curtains of the wagon. Peeping out, however, to ascertain if there was any prospect of its clearing up, we perceived three lions squatted within an hundred yards in the open plain, attentively watching the oxen. Our rifles were hastily seized, but the dampness of the atmosphere prevented their exploding. One after another, too, the Hottentots sprang out of the pack-wagon, and snapped their guns at the unwelcome intruders, as they trotted sulkily away, and took up their position on a stony eminence at no great distance. Fresh caps and priming were applied, and a broadside was followed by the instantaneous demise of the largest, whose cranium was perforated by two bullets at the same instant. Swinging their tails over their backs, the survivors took warning by the fate of their companion, and dashed into the thicket with a roar. In another half hour the voice of *Leo* was again heard at the foot of the mountains, about a quarter of a mile from the camp; and from the wagon-top we could perceive a savage monster rampant, with his tail hoisted and whirling in a circle, charging furiously along the base of the range, and in desperate wrath making towards John April, who was tending

* *Cynocephalus porcarius.* Upon another occasion the captain fell in with a party of these animals while he was sitting at breakfast by a refreshing mountain rill, in their territory; and we must confess that we wish he had missed his mark for once:—

"A large colony of pig-faced baboons shortly made their appearance above us, some slowly advancing with an inquisitive look, others deliberately seating themselves on the rocks, as though debating on the propriety of our unceremonious trespass on their domains. Their inhospitable treatment at length obliging us to make an example, we fired two shots among them. Numbers assembled round the spot where the first had struck, scraping the lead with their nails, and scrutinizing it with ludicrous gestures and grimace. The second, however, knocked over one of their elders, an enormous fellow, who was strutting about erect, laying down the law, and who, judging from his venerable appearance, must have been at least a great-grandsire. This national calamity caused incredible consternation, and many affecting domestic scenes. The party dispersed in all directions, mothers snatching up their infants, and bearing them in their arms out of the reach of danger with an impulse and action perfectly human."

the sheep. Every one instinctively grasped his weapon and rushed to the rescue, calling loudly to warn the expected victim of his danger. Without taking the smallest notice of him, however, the infuriated monster dashed past, roaring and lashing his sides until concealed in the mist. Those who have seen the monarch of the forest in crippling captivity only, immured in a cage barely double his own length, with his sinews relaxed by confinement, have seen but the shadow of that animal, which ' clears the desert with his rolling eye.' "

But our captain has yet giraffes to slay, and African lions to roll in the dust, and we can afford no more than a glimpse of hippopotamus shooting.

"Our next movement brought us to the source of the Oori or Limpopo—the Gareep of Mosolekatse's dominions. Fed by many fine streams from the Cashan range, this enchanting river springs into existence as if by magic; and, rolling its deep and tranquil waters between tiers of weeping willows, through a passage in the mountain barrier, takes its course to the northward. Here we enjoyed the novel diversion of hippopotamus shooting—that animal abounding in the Limpopo, and dividing the empire with its amphibious neighbour the crocodile. Throughout the night, the unwieldy monsters might be heard snorting and blowing during their aquatic gambols, and we not unfrequently detected them in the act of sallying from their reed-grown coverts to graze by the serene light of the moon: never, however, venturing to any distance from the river, the stronghold to which they betake themselves on the smallest alarm. Occasionally during the day they were to be seen basking on the shore amid ooze and mud; but shots were more constantly to be had at their uncouth heads, when protruded from the water to draw breath, and, if killed, the body rose to the surface. Vulnerable only behind the ear, however, or in the eye, which is placed in a prominence, so as to resemble the garret-window of a Dutch house, they require the perfection of rifle practice, and after a few shots become exceedingly shy, exhibiting the snout only, and as instantly withdrawing it. The flesh is delicious, resembling pork in flavour, and abounding in fat, which in the colony is deservedly esteemed the greatest of delicacies. The hide is upwards of an inch and a half in thickness, and, being scarcely flexible, may be dragged from the ribs in strips like the planks from a ship's side. Of these are manufactured a superior description of sjambok, the elastic whip already noticed as being an indispensable piece of furniture to every boor proceeding on a journey. Our followers encumbered the wagons with a large investment of them, and of the canine teeth, the ivory of which is extremely profitable.

"Of all the mammalia, whose portraits, drawn from ill-stuffed specimens, have been foisted upon the world, behemoth has perhaps been the most ludicrously misrepresented. I sought in vain for that colossal head—for those cavern-like jaws, garnished with ele-

phantine tusk—or those pond which ' the formidable and . ruped' is wont ' to trample do of corn during a single nigh and inoffensive, his shapeless feebly supported upon short tioned legs, and his belly almo the ground, he may not inaptl an overgrown pig. The col brown, clouded and freckled tint. Of many that we shot, t sured less than five feet at the the reality falling so lamentab monstrous conception I had for horse,' or ' sea-cow,' was the the only South African quadru felt disappointed."

Dr. Andrew Smith's beautif figures of a female hippopot young one in his " Illustrati striking contrast to the moust mer draughtsmen, and fully b Harris in these observations.

The latter was now in a c ing literally, as he says, the a menagerie,—

" The hosts of rhinoceroses t bited themselves almost ex Whilst the camp was being fo head might be seen protrud bush, and the possession of t often stoutly disputed. In the mals lost no opportunity of r selves obnoxious, frequently cl elbow, when in the act of draw at some other object—and pur with indefatigable and ludicrou rying their noses close to th uttering a sound between a gr they would whistle. Irascible be quadrupeds, the African rhin subject even to unprovoked reckless fury; but the sphere exceedingly limited, that his at sudden and impetuous, are ea a shot behind the shoulder, di a distance of twenty or thirt rally proves fatal."

VISIT TO THE SANDWIC

Our last extracts from Tow tive left the party, having c journey across the Rocky Mou couvier, near the mouth of Soon after, the author and his concluded to embark in a bri for the Sandwich Islands. W ing a few extracts from this journal. After surmounting s and delays in reaching the mo the vessel at length gets fairl sea.

Dec. 14*th.*—There is to-da running, and we landsmen are merriment to the seasoned cre berly" manner of " fetching a tempts to walk the deck. I f that I must for the present c quish an erect and dignified adopt the less graceful, but

ing of an iridescent purple, with large oval spots of green and shining red; again, they were speckled and striped with all the colours of the rainbow, but without any one appearing predominant; and these changes were going on every minute while they remained near us, which was for the space of half an hour. When caught, and taken from the water, it is said that these changes occur precisely as when in their native element, with scarcely any diminution of brilliancy; and as vitality becomes less active, the variations are less frequent, until the colours finally settle into a dark greenish hue, and the animal is dead.

January 2d, 1835.—This evening, at five o'clock, we made distinctly the head land of three of the Sandwich group, Hawaii, Maui, and Morokai, being within about eighteen miles of the nearest. We have now light trade winds, and bear us at the rate of five knots, and an unusually smooth and placid sea. This, combined with a free, unwavering breeze, is considered by our mariners as a fortunate circumstance for us, particularly as we shall approach, and perhaps pass, the dangerous rocky coast of Maui in the night. It is much more common for vessels to feel the land breeze, as they near it, setting them off shore, while the trades, operating in a contrary direction, they become unmanageable, and not unfrequently founder upon the rocks. This has been the fate of a number of vessels, approaching as we are at present; and our skilful and careful captain, always on the alert and anxious in situations of apprehended danger, is at this moment pacing the quarter-deck, giving directions regarding the management of the vessel, in tones as firm, and with as decision as prompt as ever; but through it all he cannot conceal the anxiety under which he is evidently labouring. We passengers consider ourselves perfectly safe under such good guardianship, but cannot help feeling for the captain, who, to insure our safety, is losing the repose which he absolutely requires.

On the afternoon of the 4th we ran by several islands, and all within five miles. We could distinctly see the lofty and precipitous rocks of the coast, the deep ravines between them, and, by the assistance of our glasses, the green and rich-looking vegetation of the interrupted plains.

At noon next day we made the island of Oahu, our destination, distant about forty miles. In the evening we were enabled to run, the moon shining brightly, and the atmosphere being unusually free from haze. At 10 o'clock we were within a few miles of the island, so that we could distinctly see a number of lights from the huts on the beach; we let go our anchor off a point called Diamond Hill; and soon after the mountain ranges and the quiet valleys echoed the report of our pilot gun.

As I leaned over the rail this evening, gazing at the shore on our quarter, with its lofty peaks and lovely sleeping vales clearly defined by the light of the full-orbed moon, I thought I never had witnessed any thing so perfectly enchanting. The warm breeze, which came in gentle puffs from the land, seemed to bear fragrance on its wings, and to discourse of the

rich and sunny climes from which it came. The whole scene was to me like fairy land. I thought of Captain Cook, and fancied his having been here, and gazing with delighted eyes upon the very prospect before me, little dreaming that, after all he had endured, he should here be sacrificed by the very people to whom he hoped to prove a benefactor and friend. The noise and bustle on deck, sailors running to and fro making the ship "snug" for harbour, and all the preparations for an arrival, effectually banished my meditations, and I descended to my state-room, to sleep away the tedious hours, till the morrow should reveal all the new and strange features of the land to which we had come.

Early on the morning of the 5th, Mr. Reynolds, the deputy pilot, boarded us in a whale boat, manned by natives, and accompanied by two American gentlemen, residents of the town of Honoruru—Captain Wm. S. Hinckley and P. A. Brinsmade, Esq. Our anchor was soon weighed, and with a fine free wind we rounded Diamond Hill, and passed along a beautiful indentation in the shore, called Waititi Bay, within sight of a large coral reef, by which the whole island is surrounded. We very soon came in view of the lovely, sylvan-looking village of Honoruru. The shore below the town, from Waititi to a considerable distance above, is fringed with graceful cocoanut trees, with here and there a pretty little grass cottage reposing under their shade. As we approached the harbour these cottages became more numerous, until at last they appeared thickly grouped together, with occasionally a pretty garden dividing them. The fort, too, which fronts the ocean, with its clean, white-washed walls, and cannon frowning from the embrasures, adds very much to the effect of the scene; while behind, the noble hills and fertile valleys between, clothed with the richest verdure, soften down and mellow the whole, and render the prospect indescribably beautiful.

On nearing the shore, we observed some scores of curiously-formed canoes, with large outriggers, which had just put off, and were bound out on a fishing excursion. A number of these passed close to our vessel, and usually paused when opposite, that the denuded mariners might have an opportunity of surveying the strangers, and of bidding them welcome to their shores by a loud and gay *aroha*. Near the land a number of natives, of both sexes, were swimming and playing in the surf, and diving to the bottom, searching for *echinæ* and sea weeds, remaining under the water for a considerable time, while their heels were seen moving to and fro above the surface.

Our brig soon entered the narrow channel opposite the harbour, and with a light but steady breeze, stood in close to the town, and let go her anchor within a hundred yards of the shore. As we were about leaving the vessel, Captain Charlton, H. B. M. consul, and Captain W. Darby, of the H. B. Co.'s brig Eagle, came on board, and gave Mr. N. and myself a passage to the shore in their boat. They walked with us to the house of Mr. Jones, the American consul, to whom I had a letter from my friend Dr. M. Burrough,

of Philadelphia. We were received by this gentleman in a manner calculated to make us feel perfectly at home; a good and comfortable house was immediately provided for us, and every assistance was offered in forwarding our views. We dined at the sumptuous table of W. French, Esq., an American gentleman, and one of the most thriving merchants of the town, and were here introduced to several highly respectable foreign residents, Captain E. Grimes, Dr. Thomas, Dr. Rooke, Mr. Paty, and others. In the afternoon we strolled out with two or three gentlemen to view the village and its environs.

The town of Honoruru contains about three hundred houses, the great majority of which are composed of grass exclusively, and those occupied by the natives consist of a single room. Others, in which many of the foreigners reside, are partitioned with boards, and form as comfortable and agreeable residences as could be desired in a climate always warm. There are some few houses of frame, and several of coral rock, built by the resident merchants and missionaries; but they are certainly not superior, except in being more durable, to those of grass, and probably not so comfortable in the intensely hot seasons. The houses are scattered about without any regard to regularity, the hard clay passage-ways winding amongst them in every direction; but an air of neatness and simple elegance pervades the whole, which cannot fail to make a favourable impression on the stranger.

The natives are generally remarkably well formed, of a dark copper colour, with pleasant and rather intellectual countenances, and many of the women are handsome.

The dress of the men, not in the employment of the whites, consists of a large piece of native cloth, called a *tapa*, or a robe of calico thrown loosely round the body, somewhat like the Roman toga, and knotted on the left shoulder. The women wear a loose gown of calico, or native cloth, fastened tightly round the neck, but not bound at the waist, and often with the addition of several yards of cotton cloth tied round above the hips.

Their hair is generally of a beautiful glossy black, and of unusual fineness; it is folded around the back part of the head, very much in the manner common to our ladies at home, and splendid tortoise-shell combs, of their own manufacture, are used to confine it. They display much taste in the arrangement of wild flowers amongst their hair, and a common ornament for the forehead is the *re* of beautiful yellow feathers which is bound upon it. I have repeatedly seen women with hair of two, and, in some instance, of three distinct colours. Deep black and chestnut-brown, not promiscuously mingled throughout, but lying in separate masses; and in the rare instances of which I have spoken, they were black, brown, and a kind of ash colour, giving the head a most singular appearance. I had supposed that this party-coloured character of the hair was the effect of art, but was soon informed to the contrary, and perceived that by the natives themselves it was considered a deformity.

8th.—Mr. N. and myself are now fairly

domiciliated. We occupy a large and commodious room in a building called the Pagoda, which is in a central part of the town; from our front windows we have a fine view of the harbour and the shipping, and from a balcony in the rear we can see almost the entire length of the lovely valley of Nuano, with its bold and rugged rocks, and the luxuriant verdure on their sides; while nearer, the little square taro patches, crowded together over the intermediate plain, look like pretty garden plots, as the broad green leaves of the plant are tinted by the sunbeams.

10th.—This morning I saw the king for the first time. He is a very young man, only about twenty years of age, of ordinary size, and rather ordinary appearance. He was dressed in a little blue jacket, such as is worn by sailors when ashore, white pantaloons, and common black hat. He was walking in the street at a rapid and not very dignified gait, Some of these were rather fantastically dressed, with old naval coats and rusty epaulets, which had seen long service, and huge sabres with iron scabbards, which jingled on the ground as the wearer stalked majestically along. Others were habited plainly, like their master, and some few were of the true tatterdemalion school. I had the curiosity to follow the royal escort for a little way to see what would become of them all; they soon turned a corner and halted near a little wagon which had just stopped. The king approached the vehicle and handed from it an old and venerable-looking native, (who I afterwards learned was the chief *Kekeoena*, the former guardian of the king,) and they walked off arm in arm in a very affectionate manner, followed as before by the motley group of retainers.

The natives have very generally become acquainted with the pursuits of my companion and myself, and at almost all hours of the day, our mansion is besieged by men, women and children. Some bring shells, pearls, living birds, cocoanuts, bananas, &c., to sell, and others are attracted by curiosity to see us, which is no doubt much excited in regard to the use which we intend making of all the strange things they bring us.

Some good hints and wholesome truth may be picked out of the following article, beside the vein of pleasantry which recommends it.

THE INFANT KNOWLEDGE SYSTEM.

BY A MAN BORN OUT OF SEASON.

"Oh the sunny, sunny hours of childhood,
How soon—how soon they pass away!"

Very! There *was* a time when we had children.—The time is past, or is fast passing. The boys are premature mockeries of men—the girls, something between a doll and a stunted woman. The schoolmaster is abroad, also the schoolmistress, besides tutors and governesses.

Shortly after the children are weaned, they commence educating them. While the brain is yet in a soft pulpy state, they load it with heavy facts and hard names, to its serious detriment during the remainder of its mundane existence. The ancient Grecian commenced with carrying a calf upon his back a few hours every day, so that when the calf gradually grew into a bullock, he carried the bullock with as much ease as he had done the calf. This is now the education principle. They lay a few leaves of Cyclopædia or Encyclopædia on a child's tender brain, and keep adding thereunto day by day, expecting that when he is a man, he will carry the thirty volumes with perfect ease, without considering that in the attempt they may crush all sap and freshness out of that brain, rendering it as flat as a pancake, and " dry as the remainder of a biscuit."

Now is this wholesome—is it natural? Is it fair—is it humane, that a child should be cheated out of its childhood, and sent to learn the "use of the globes" before it has learned to play at marbles?—Or is it to be expected that this early forcing and hot bed system can produce as healthy plants as if they had been allowed to grow in the free air and open sunshine? Oh! in place of sending a child to school three or four years, let it enjoy three or four more years of healthy ignorance. Curb not its young freedom; abridge not its first holidays: cage not the pretty bird too soon! Change not the free air of heaven for the pent up atmosphere of the "seminary;" the gentle murmur of the winds for the dull hum of the prison house. We were children ourselves once. Let us have a fellow feeling for the young rogues. Let kind dame Nature nurse them a few years longer. There will be fewer rickety limbs and rickety intellects.

And does a child learn nothing because it has not its primer in its hand. Certainly it does. Every hour of its little life it is learning; it cannot help it. The flower that blows, the springing grass, the withered leaf, the running water, the birds that hop across its path, and the thousand sights of the fields and woods, or even the squares or suburbs of a city, cause it to think and to question. The wind as it blows, the falling rain, the fleecy snow, the sharp frost making firm the unstable water, the thunder peal, the sun that shines by day, and the moon that steals into the dark sky at night, all and each arouses its infantile wonder and young curiosity. Let it then have a few years of pleasant natural education before it commences its painful artificial one. Let it, as St. Paul says, when it *is* a child, "think as a child, and act as a child," and in due and proper season, no doubt of it, it will "put away childish things."

It makes one sad to see a fine little fellow sent to study Euclid at the age he should be reading Robinson Crusoe; and equally does a man good to see such a one enjoying his young existence in an appropriate manner. Few there are who cannot enter into the feeling so finely given in the very beautiful lines of an American poet, commencing—

" There's something in a noble boy,
A brave, free hearted, careless one,
With his unchecked, unbidden joy,
His dread of books and love of fun,
And in his clear and ready smile,
Unshaded by a thought of guile,

And unrepressed by sadness—
Which brings me to my childhood back,
As if I trod its very track,
And felt its very gladness."

Then let the children have their play out.—New York Mirror.

THOUGHTS ON EDUCATION.

BY DR. HUMPHREY.

The sensible remarks which follow we transfer from the last New York Observer, and they may fitly be placed here as a companion piece to the foregoing.

Were every parent capable of conducting the education of his children, in the elementary and popular branches, such as reading, spelling, writing and arithmetic; and could every one devote time enough to the task, it would be safer, and on some accounts better, to keep them at home, than to send them to school. But this we know is not the case. While a few parents are more competent to teach every thing which their children need to learn, than the ablest instructers they can employ, not one in a hundred, even of this class, can command the necessary leisure; and as for the great majority of heads of families, if they had nothing else to do, they are not qualified for the task.

I certainly think that more ought to be done by the domestic fire-side, than is commonly attempted. It is preposterous and cruel, to put a child into one of our primary schools, at the age of three or four years, to drawl out A B C, and sit whimpering and nodding in a close room, upon a high hard bench, six hours a day, and five or six days in a week. Thus to imprison and beat dulness into a poor little fellow, just from the arms of the nurse, is to deprive him of more than one of his "inalienable rights." The alphabet and some of the first lessons can be taught to much better advantage in the family than in the school-house; and I do not care how long the child is kept at home, provided that from the time he is old enough to have his mind tasked with letters and figures, his studies are judiciously directed. There is a great deal of force and truth in the remarks of a distinguished foreign writer, [*John Taylor*] upon the superior advantages of home education, though even he admits, that in the most favoured families, something is lost by shutting up children during their whole minority in the paternal mansion; and that the families of the middle and lower classes, if educated at all, must be sent to school. This is the conclusion to which, whether willingly or unwillingly, every one must come, who looks at things as they are. The time has not yet arrived in any country, and it probably never will arrive, when the school-house and the school-master can be dispensed with. The great majority of parents, (nineteen-twentieths at least,) have so much to do in feeding and clothing their offspring, or are so burdened with public cares and duties, that they cannot daily devote hour after hour either to the primary or higher branches of instruction. This is one of the thousand cases in which a division of labour is indispensable. They can and they ought to cooperate with the teachers, much more efficiently than they commonly do, as I shall have occasion to show in a subsequent paper; but they must have school-masters and school-mistresses, on whose abilities and fidelity they can rely, to discharge the duties of regular and thorough instruction.

Infant Schools.

In the whole history of education, I hardly know of a more sudden and remarkable revolution than the public mind has undergone, with reference to this class of primary schools. A few years ago they were hailed in every quarter—in the town and the country—by the educated and the uneducated, as among the most wonderful improvements of the age. There had been nothing like it. It had been "kept hid from the wise and the prudent for ages and generations," and was unquestionably the dawn of the long expected educational millenium. Every body was in raptures. Why had not the egg been made to stand up before? It was so delightful to think of mothers being relieved from rocking the cradle, and keeping their little ones out of the fire, and to see twenty or thirty of them transplanted into a common nursery, and furnished with pillows, and ginger-bread, and wooden alphabets, and pictures of lions, and tigers, and elephants, and eagles; to see them building miniature towns, and counting white and black balls; running, tottling, leaping, and going through all the tiny evolutions of their manual exercise; and then to hear them lisping, giggling, shouting, clapping their hands, spelling, reading—the whole scene was so novel and so taking that every body was carried away; and the general impression seemed to be, that to say nothing of the other great advantages of this most happy of all modern inventions or discoveries, it was a clear gain, of two or three years at least, in the education of our families.

Thus we were borne along by the popular current. Some hesitated, and some perhaps doubted. But an infant school there must be in almost every parish and village, if not in every district. Teachers were sent abroad to be trained for the business. Pictures, cards, and a great variety of showy and amusing toys and inventions were advertised, and sold, and brought in, to decorate the school-rooms; and at set times the doors were thrown open to parents and strangers, who eagerly pressed in to witness the exercises, and went away to circulate the marvels which they had seen. But only a few short years have rolled away, and now where are all these nonpariel infant seminaries? What a change! A few of them, I believe, are still left in some of the large

stilts, make their sand ovens, feed the chickens, and chase the butterflys, just as they used to do before infant schools were ever thought of.

How is this remarkable revolution in public sentiment to be accounted for? At first view, certainly, it seems to betray a fickleness of national character, which we should not esteem it very creditable to have fastened upon us. Were then our infant schools but the toys of older children which we have got tired of and thrown away, just as our little ones do their playthings in the nursery; or has experience taught us that, after all, the old way is better than the new! I am by no means sure that I can mention all the reasons which have led to the general abandonment of the infant school system, nor do I believe, that those who for a time were most enamoured of it, can tell exactly why they have changed their opinions; but I will venture to throw out two or three objections to it, which it appears to me, more than counterbalance the arguments which I have heard urged in its favour.

The first objection is, that it interferes with the freedom of nature. I know an infant school in this respect, is very different from any other. One of the leading objects is, to *amuse* and *divert* the children, and to give them plenty of air and exercise. But after all, it is a *school*, it is a *system*, it is a *confinement*. The exercises follow each other in a certain order. There are school hours, and the children must be kept to them, forenoon and afternoon. This is not natural. The infant wants its liberty—wants to lie down and get up just when it feels the impulse—wants to move, and act, and chatter, and laugh, without the least regard to system, or rule. Very young children may be amused and pleased, for a little while, with the novelty and variety of infant-school exercises; but I believe, that in a few months, at longest, they are apt to become irksome. The child learns a great many things sooner, no doubt, than it would be likely to learn at home; but it fails to learn others, which are quite as important, and altogether more after the order of nature.

Another, and perhaps the greatest objection to the infant school system is, that it ministers to the preternatural and unhealthy development of the intellectual faculties. Nothing is more delicate, more liable to injury, than the brain, during several of the first years of life. It needs repose. It must have time to grow, and is sure to suffer by every thing like artificial and unnatural excitement. This the more enlightened early advocates of infant schools were aware of, and they meant to guard against the danger, by the simplicity and variety of the exercises. They called it

poor little thing could bear, and the mis[
too often showed itself, in early and alarm[
if not fatal cerebral derangement. I feel
fectly satisfied, that in all the infant sch[
so far as my observation extends, too n[
was done and expected; and I doubt who[
many teachers ever realized, how very te[
and delicate the material is which they '[
daily employed in moulding and shaping.[
needs vastly more judgment and physiolo[
study, to conduct an infant school with sa[
than to carry a class of adults through
of the higher branches of a liberal educa[

A third objection to infant schools is,
they unfit children for all other sch[
When a child has been accustomed for y[
to do very much as he pleases in the sch[
house; to talk and laugh, and look at
tures, and repeat every thing by rote, it
almost, as a matter of course, be foun[
tremely difficult to bring him under pr[
subjection, and confine him down to st[
when he is old enough to be received
the common district school. His loose
sultory habits are too firmly fixed, to
changed without trouble. For myself, '[
I to return to the pedagogical chair,
which, by the way, I never used to si[
hour in a month,) I should rather under[
to manage *fifty* scholars *green from the st[*
than *thirty*, fresh and noisy and lawless, [
the infant school.

But while I am convinced, upon the w[
that infant schools have been discontinue[
good and sufficient reasons, and I hav[
wish to see them revived, I can conceive
they might do much of good, even in
country, by relieving hard-working mo[
from a great deal of care and anxiety, d[
school hours; and I should exceedingl[
gret to have them totally disbanded, in
large and populous towns. There are [
sands of very young children, in such a
as New York, or Philadelphia, whose pa[
cannot, or will not take that care of t[
which is indispensable for their health[
safety; and I can hardly conceive of a
benevolent employment than to find
out, gather them into schools, keep them
of harm's way, and bring them under a
social and moral influence. But in ge[
very young children are better off under
mother's eye, than any where else. Go[
distributed them into families, and he [
intended to release parents from the resp[
bility of taking care of them in their te[
years by devolving the task upon stran[
Show me a well ordered nursery and
ground, over which maternal love pre[
and where maternal smiles are daily an[
most hourly reflected from bright eyes
shining faces, and I will show you one o[
finest infant schools in the world.

manured planted
d, would yield
from the 1st of
May, should not
arrangements for
From our own
that this addi-
ted of the cows,
se of 2 lbs. each
from the first of
May, there are
ber of weeks at
give us 52 lbs.
riod named, or
if we set down
venty-five cents
ne hundred and
additional yield
with the product
s is not all—the
he spring would
ow that he had
the satisfaction
lition.—*Farmer*

for "The Friend."

time by my three
en.

ful voices
ear!
iices,
ear,
'aces,
sire be;
graces,
r m^n.

at presses
sk?
ond caresses
re speak?

ters,
ck!
lingers,
fluck.

anger,
ow,
iger,
eal and woe—

roses
way;
ses,—
en your stay.

uty,
life;
y—
wife.

rrow
ling heart,—
rrow
part.

ow unite us,
onds of love,
us
ve,

Father!
ree,—
gather
hee.
OSBORN.

eding is the best
e's ill-manners."

THE FRIEND.

ELEVENTH MONTH, 2, 1839.

Pennsylvania has been among the foremost, if indeed she has not led the way in the melioration of penal law, and the diminution of capital punishments. But it has long been a source of deep regret with a large portion of her citizens of various religious denominations, that the reformation had not been perfected, and that the punishment of death in all cases was not abolished. Under this impression a number of individuals have originated the memorial of which a copy is given below. It is very desirable that the movement be made as extensive and general through the state as practicable, and with this view printed copies have been prepared which it is intended shall be distributed for signatures throughout the respective counties. Yet as every locality may not thus be provided with copies, the deficiency can be supplied by transcribing from this or other papers in which the memorial may be inserted. It is hoped that all who take an interest in this important measure, especially our zealous and lively spirited young men, will be exertive and spare no pains in collecting all the signatures obtainable within their respective spheres of action, and in season to be forwarded to the legislature at an early period of its session.

To the Senate and House of Representatives, in General Assembly met:

The memorial of the subscribers, citizens of Pennsylvania, respectfully represents:—

That your memorialists, anxious to promote the substantial improvement of this great commonwealth, take the liberty of soliciting the attention of the legislature to that part of our penal code which relates to the punishment of death. It is deemed unnecessary to enter into any argument to prove, that the preservation of society from lawless depredations, and the reformation of criminals, are the great objects of the penal code in a Christian community. Now, so far as punishment operates as a preventive to crime, it is the certainty of its infliction, rather than its severity, that is effective: and experience sufficiently proves, that the aversion to the punishment of death, which many of the citizens of Pennsylvania entertain, renders the conviction of persons charged with the heinous crime of murder, much more difficult than it would be in case a less revolting punishment was the consequence. Hence, a criminal guilty of the atrocious crime of murder in the first degree, is more likely to escape with impunity, than an offender of a lower grade.

It is a consideration worthy the attention of the legislature, that there are many conscientious citizens of the state, who sincerely believe, that the infliction of capital punishment is not included within the authority which a Christian community can justly exercise upon its delinquent members; hence, they are necessarily averse to giving their testimony, or serving on juries, where the conviction of a culprit involving the punishment of death may be the probable result. The agents of the penal law, are, therefore, in great measure deprived of the aid of this valuable class, in the execution of their important trusts. And it is certainly desirable, that the examination of those charges which involve the lives or liberties of our citizens, should be entrusted to the most strictly conscientious among us.

The recent law of Pennsylvania which requires that the execution of criminals should be withdrawn from the public gaze, and performed within the precincts of the prison, was unquestionably founded upon a just conviction that such exhibitions are rather conducive to than preventive of crime. And we may reasonably question whether the private execution of a murderer ever operates as an example to prevent a similar offence. Indeed a little reflection upon the subject most lead to the conclusion, that murders are always committed under the influence of the most direful passion, which renders the actor regardless at the time of any consequences, immediate or remote, which may ensue.

For these, and other reasons, we earnestly request the legislature to revise this part of our penal code, and substitute a confinement for life in case of murder in the first degree, instead of the awful and irretrievable punishment of death.

A stated meeting of the Concord Auxiliary Bible Association of Friends, will be held at Middletown meeting house, on second day, the 11th day of the eleventh month, at 11 o'clock A. M. The female members are respectfully invited to attend.

HOWARD YARNALL, Sec'ry.
11th mo. 1st, 1839.

HAVERFORD SCHOOL.

WANTED, a Friend to act as Steward of this Institution. Apply to
KIMBER & SHARPLESS,
No. 8 South Fourth street.

MARRIED on third day, 10th mo. 1st, at Friends' meeting-house, Sixth street, JOSEPH W. HILYARD, of New York, to HANNAH A. THOMSON, of this city.
—— on fourth day, the 11th of 9th mo. last, at Friends' meeting, Lampeter, JOS WINDLE, Jr., of East Caln, to MARY EVANS, Jr., daughter of Isaac Evans, of the former place.
—— at Friends' meeting-house, London Grove, Pa., on the 23d ult., ALFRED COPE, of Philadelphia, to HANNAH, daughter of Thomas Edge, deceased, late of Downingtown.

DIED, at his residence near Camden, N. J., on sixth day, the 18th ult., after an illness of about a week, ISAAC JONES, in the 65th year of his age, a respectable member of Newton Particular, and Haddonfield Monthly Meeting. He appeared to be sensible that his dissolution was at hand, and, it is believed, that through the mercy of redeeming Love, he witnessed preparation for the awful change.
—— on the 22d of 10th month, at his residence in Hanover township, Burlington county, N. J., WILLIAM LETCHWORTH, aged about 77 years, a member of Burlington Monthly Meeting, and formerly of this city.
—— at his residence in Alexandria, D. C., on the 10th ult., ANDREW SCHOLFIELD, aged 78 years and 11 months. His disease was bilious fever, and he suffered the most excruciating pains during the whole of his illness, which lasted about a week. He appeared cheerful, and was sensible of his approaching end, —departed without a groan about 9 o'clock A. M., having left a consoling evidence that he has gone to dwell with the blessed in heaven.
—— at the residence of his son-in-law, Elisha Kirk, near Mount Pleasant, Ohio, on the 23d of fifth month, 1839, JESSE FOULKE, in the 78th year of his age, a member of Short Creek Monthly and Particular Meeting of Friends. Though his departure was sudden, and at a moment unlooked for by those with whom he lived, yet his mind had been evidently preparing for this solemn event. He expressed at different times that he believed his time here was near to a close, adding he had no desire it should be lengthened out, but felt willing to wait the appointed time. He delighted much in the reading of the Holy Scriptures and the writings of our worthy predecessors in the truth, and often spoke of the benefit of solemn quiet waiting and retirement of mind, that he experienced such to be some of his most profitable seasons. He was a diligent attender of our religious meetings, and for the last twelve months persevered in the performance of this duty under much bodily infirmity. Amidst all the difficulties with which the enemy has assailed the Society of Friends, his deep attachment to its ancient doctrines and testimonies remained, and his faith in the merits of his Redeemer was unshaken, and we doubt not he has been permitted to join the just of all generations.

PRINTED BY ADAM WALDIE,
Carpenter Street, below Seventh, Philadelphia.

THE FRIEND.

A RELIGIOUS AND LITERARY JOURNAL.

VOL. XIII.   SEVENTH DAY, ELEVENTH MONTH, 9, 1839.   **NO. 6.**

EDITED BY ROBERT SMITH.

———

PUBLISHED WEEKLY.

Price two dollars per annum, payable in advance.

Subscriptions and Payments received by

GEORGE W. TAYLOR,

NO. 50, NORTH FOURTH STREET, UP STAIRS,

PHILADELPHIA.

From Silliman's Journal.

On the Boracic Acid Lagoons of Tuscany; by JOHN BOWRING, LL. D.

The borax lagoons of Tuscany are entitled to a detailed description. They are unique in Europe, if not in the world; and their produce is become an article of equal importance to Great Britain as an import, and to Tuscany as an export. They are spread over a surface of about thirty miles, and exhibit from the distance columns of vapour, more or less according to the season of the year and state of the weather, which rise in large volumes among the recesses of the mountains.

As you approach the lagoons, the earth seems to pour out boiling water as if from volcanoes of various sizes, in a variety of soil, but principally of chalk and sand. The heat in the immediate adjacency is intolerable, and you are drenched by the vapour, which impregnates the atmosphere with a strong and somewhat sulphurous smell. The whole scene is one of terrible violence and confusion—the noisy outbreak of the boiling element—the rugged and agitated surface—the volumes of vapour—the impregnated atmosphere—the rush of waters—among bleak and solitary mountains.

The ground, which burns and shakes beneath your feet, is covered with beautiful crystallizations of sulphur and other minerals. Its character beneath the surface at Mount Cerbole is that of a black marl streaked with chalk, giving it, at a short distance, the appearance of variegated marble.

Formerly the place was regarded by the peasants as the entrance of hell, a superstition derived no doubt from very ancient times, for the principal of the lagoons and the neighbouring volcano still bear the name of Monte Cerboli (*Mons Cerberi*). The peasantry never passed by the spot without terror, counting their beads, and praying for the protection of the Virgin.

The borax lagoons have been brought into their present profitable action within a very few years. Scattered over an extensive district, they are become the property of an active individual, M. Larderel, to whom they are a source of wealth, more valuable perhaps, and certainly less capricious, than any mine of silver that Mexico or Peru possesses. The process of manufacture is simple, and is effected by those instruments which the localities themselves present. The soffioni, or vapours, break forth violently in different parts of the mountain recesses. They only produce boracic acid when they burst with a fierce explosion. In these spots artificial lagoons are formed by the introduction of the mountain streams. The hot vapour keeps the water perpetually in ebullition; and after it has received its impregnation during twenty-four hours at the most elevated lagoon, the contents are allowed to descend to the second lagoon, where a second impregnation takes place, and then to the third, and so forth, till it reaches the lowest receptacle; and having thus passed through from six to eight lagoons, it has gathered one half per cent. of the boracic acid. It is then transferred to the reservoirs, from whence, after a few hours' rest, it is conveyed to the evaporating pans, where the hot vapour concentrates the strength of the acid by passing under shallow leaden vessels from the boiling fountains above, which is quite at a heat of 80° of Reaumur,[*] and is discharged at a heat of 60°.[†] There are from ten to twenty pans, in each of which the concentration becomes greater at every descent till it passes to the crystallizing vessels, from whence it is carried to the drying rooms, where, after two or three hours, it becomes ready to be packed for exportation.

The number of establishments is nine. The whole amount produced varies from 7000 to 8000 pounds (of 12 ounces) per day. The produce does not appear susceptible of much extension, as the whole of the water is turned to account; the atmosphere has, however, some influence on the result. In bright and clear weather, whether in winter or summer, the vapours are less dense, but the depositions of boracic acid in the lagoons are infallible barometers to the neighbourhood, even at a great distance, serving to regulate the proceedings of the peasantry in their agricultural pursuits.

It had been long supposed that the boracic acid was not to be found in the vapours of the lagoons; and when it is seen how small the proportion of acid must originally be, it will not be wondered at that its presence should have escaped attention. In the lowest of the lagoons, after five, six, and in some cases a greater number of impregnations, the quantity of boracic acid given out does not exceed one half per cent.; thus if the produce

———

[*] The boiling point.   [†] 167° of Fahrenheit.

be estimated at 7500 pounds per day, the quantity of saturated water daily discharged is a million and a half of Tuscan pounds, or five hundred tons English.

The lagoons are ordinarily excavated by the mountaineers of Lombardy, who emigrate into Tuscany during the winter season, when snow. They gain about one Tuscan lira per day. But the works are conducted, when in operation, by natives, all of whom are married, and who occupy houses attached to the evaporating pans. They wear a common uniform, and their health is generally good.

A great improvement in the cultivation, and a great increase in the value of the neighbouring soil, has naturally followed the introduction of the manufacture of the boracic acid. A rise of wages has accompanied the new demand for labour; much land has been brought into cultivation by new directions given to the streams of smaller rivers. Before the boracic lakes were turned to profitable account, their fetid smell, their frightful appearance, agitating the earth around them by the ceaseless explosions of boiling water, and not less the terrors with which superstition invested them, made the lagoons themselves to be regarded as public nuisances, and gave to the surrounding country a character which alienated all attempts at improvement.

Nor were the lagoons without real and positive dangers, for the loss of life was certain where man or beast had the misfortune to fall into any of those boiling baths. Cases frequently occurred in which cattle perished; and one chemist, of considerable eminence, met with a horrible death by being precipitated into one of the lagoons. Legs were not unfrequently lost by a false step into the smaller pits (*putizze*), where, before the foot could be withdrawn, the flesh would be separated from the bone.

That these lagoons, now a source of immense revenue, should have remained for ages unproductive; that they should have been so frequently visited by scientific men, to none of whom (for ages at least) did the thought occur that they contained in them mines of wealth, is a curious phenomenon; nor is it less remarkable, that it was left for a man, whose name and occupation are wholly dissociated from science, to convert these fugitive vapours into substantial wealth.

Though to the present proprietor (the Chevalier Larderel) the merit attaches of having given to the boracic lagoons the immense importance they now possess, a succession of adventurers had made many experiments, and had produced a considerable quantity of boracic acid, but at a cost (from the expenditure of combustible) which left but little profit.

The small value that was attached to them may be seen in the fact, that the largest and most productive district of the lagoons, that of Monte Cerboli, was offered in perpetuity, so lately as 1818, at an annual ground-rent of £T. 200*l.* or 6*l.* 13*s.* 4*d.* per annum, though it now produces several thousand pounds sterling. The immense increase in their value arose from the simplest of improvements, the abandonment of the use of charcoal, and the application of the heat of the lagoons or soffioni to the evaporation of their own waters. Improvements, however, and very important ones, particularly by subjecting the waters to a succession of impregnations, had been gradually introduced by a Signor Ciaschi, and the importation of boracic acid from Tuscany into France, before 1817, had been between 7000 and 8000 pounds, of a quality gradually increasing in purity; but Ciaschi perished miserably, in consequence of falling into one of the lagoons which he himself had excavated, leaving his family in a state of extreme poverty. His death (which happened in 1816) naturally threw a damp upon adventure. The experiments were resumed in the following year, and in the midst of violent claims and controversies, M. Larderel has become the monopolist of the boracic productions of Tuscany.

With the increased productions of boracic acid has arisen an increased demand, growing out of the more extensive application of it to manufacturing purposes. In about four years the quantity has been quadrupled by superior modes of extraction, and by greater care employed in the collection of the boracic vapour. In 1833 about 650,000 Tuscan pounds were obtained, in 1836 two millions and a half.

But it appears to me that the powers and riches of these extraordinary districts remain yet to be fully developed. They exhibit an immense number of mighty steam-engines, furnished by nature at no cost, and applicable to the production of an infinite variety of objects. In the progress of time this vast machinery of heat and force will probably become the moving central point of extensive manufacturing establishments. The steam, which has been so ingeniously applied to the concentration and evaporation of the boracic acid, will probably hereafter, instead of wasting itself in the air, be employed to move huge engines, which will be directed to the infinite variety of production which engages the attention of labouring and intelligent artisans; and thus, in the course of time, there can be little doubt, that these lagoons, which were fled from as objects of danger and terror by uninstructed man, will gather round them a large intelligent population, and become sources of prosperity to innumerable individuals through countless generations.

It is common to overlook what is near by keeping the eye fixed on something remote. In the same manner present opportunities are neglected and attainable good is slighted by minds busied in extensive ranges, and intent upon future advantages.—*Johnson.*

VISIT TO THE SANDWICH
(Continued from page 38.)

11*th.*—Mr. Jones, the consul, ⸢ this morning, and we accompanied Seamen's chapel in our neighbo only church in the town in whi service is performed. The chap⸢ some building of *adobes*, or sun-⸢ lately erected, and, as its name in tended chiefly for the benefit of t who visit the island. It is surm⸢ handsome dome and belfry of which the bell was pealing out notes as we approached it. Joh⸢ pastor, officiated, to whom we wer at the conclusion of the service.

In the afternoon, Mr. N. and m⸢ with the consul to the native ch lower extremity of the town. enormous building, one hundred six feet in length by sixty in ⸢ capable of containing four thou⸢ It is built in the native style, of ⸢ bundles on a rude frame work of the ridge pole, which extends alo⸢ length of the apex of the roof wi ported by numerous roughly ⸢ driven into the ground. The nati⸢ numbers, were flocking to the c⸢ in every variety of costume, fro⸢ and dignified dress of the Euro⸢ man, to the simple and primiti⸢ native cloth; and women, from and feathers, silk gowns and stay life, to the light and much be robe of the country, with its i⸢ companiment, the *pau* or waist-fi⸢ calico. While we were standin⸢ the moving throng, we observed wheeled cart approach, drawn ⸢ in the native dress, in which sa⸢ great round beauties of the islar gay silk, with a large black hat⸢ drooped a magnificent ostrich fe⸢ was *Kinau*, the ex-queen, and wi *noa*, the commandante of the for⸢ called the colonel. At the door ⸢ she was assisted to dismount; swept along by us and entered t⸢ made us a low and graceful bow, her great head, and looking arou⸢ company assembled, with the air expected profound admiration a homage. In the church, we we⸢ Kekuanoa to take a seat on the ⸢ him and his wife; and when ⸢ commenced the service by read⸢ hymn, Kinau did me the honor⸢ me with her book, pointing to th⸢ a dignified and patronising air, knowledged with all suitable res⸢

The sermon, in the native ⸢ Mr. Bingham, was delivered in fluent manner, and in the whole concourse there was scarcely during the service. All seeme⸢ gaged in the business for which sembled; and as I looked arou⸢ quiet and attentive multitude, ⸢ with the wild and idolatrous ⸢ their assemblies exhibited in ti⸢ irresistibly forced upon me,

clean—a little pinch with the fingers is then taken of the fish which is perhaps floundering beside him, followed by a similar pinch of salt, to season the whole repast.

The principal beauty of the islanders, in their own estimation, consists in their being enormously fat, some of them weighing upwards of three hundred pounds, and measures are consequently resorted to, that will successfully and expeditiously produce this much desired result. With this view, the chiefs take but little exercise, and eat enormously of the nutritive paste before spoken of. After they have stuffed as much as their stomachs will contain, without the risk of positive suffocation, they roll over on their backs upon the ground, grunting like huge swine, when two attendants approach and place themselves on each side of the patient. One wields a *kahili*, or feather fly brush, to cool his master, and keep off the mosquitoes, while the other commences his operations by punching his fist violently into the stomach of the fallen man, who, with a great snort, acknowledges his consciousness, and the pleasure he derives from it. Soon the other fist of the serving man follows, and the regular *kneading* process is performed; at first, slowly and cautiously, but gradually increasing in quickness and severity until the attendant is forced to stop for breath, and the poor stupified lump of obesity forgets to grunt in unison with the rapidly descending blows. This is the operation called *rumi-rumi*, and is usually continued from ten to fifteen minutes, after which the patient rises, yawns, stretches his limbs, and calls loudly for another calabash of poe. This custom is followed almost exclusively by the chiefs, but is not confined to the male sex, the women enjoying the luxury equally with the men. The rumi-rumi is also practised in cases of abdominal pains, and in dyspeptic complaints. Even the foreigners sometimes resort to it, and find it beneficial.

17th.—Mr. N. and myself were invited to participate in a *lu-au* dinner, to be given in the valley of Nuano this afternoon. At about 2 o'clock, Mr. Jones called for us, and furnished us with good horses, upon which we mounted, and galloped off to the valley. After a delightful ride of about five miles, over a good, though rather stony road, between the hills which enclose the valley, we arrived at a pretty little temporary cottage, formed entirely of the broad green leaves of the ti plant, and perched on a picturesque hill, overlooking the whole extent of our ride. Here we found a number of the foreign gentlemen; others soon joined us, and our company consisted of fifty or sixty persons, the king, John Young, and several other distinguished natives being of the party.

As the collation was not yet ready to be served up, Mr. Jones, Captain Hinckley, Mr. N. and myself remounted our horses for a visit to the great *pari*, or precipice, two miles above. We found the road somewhat rough, and very hilly, in some places extremely narrow, and the path wound constantly through bushes and tall ferns to the elevated land which we were approaching. When within a few hundred yards of the precipice, we left our horses in charge of several native boys, who had followed us for the purpose, and ascended to the edge of the pari. The wind was blowing a gale, so that it was necessary to remove our hats and bind up our heads with handkerchiefs, and when we stood upon the cliff, some care was required to keep our footing, and to brace ourselves against the furious blast which was eddying around the summit.

The pari is an almost perpendicular precipice, of about six hundred feet, composed of basaltic rock, with occasional strata of hard white clay.

On the north is seen the fertile and beautiful valley of Kolau, with its neat little cottages, taro-patches and fields of sugar cane, spread out before you like a picture; and beyond, is the indented shore, with its high and pointed cliffs, margining the ocean as far as the eye can discern. Down this precipice, on the north side, is a sort of rude path, which the natives have constructed, and up this we saw a number of them toiling, clinging with their hands to the jutting crags above, to raise and support their bodies in the ascent. As they approached nearer to us, I was surprised to perceive that every man bore a burthen on his shoulder; some had large calabashes of poe, suspended one on each end of a long pole, and others carried living pigs, similarly suspended, by having their feet tied together, and the pole passed between them. The porkers, although hanging back downwards, in a position not the most comfortable, did not complain of the treatment, until they were deposited on the terra firma of the summit, when they tuned their pipes to a lusty squeal, and made amends for their former silence.

This spot is the scene of the last great battle of King Tamehameha, by which he acquired the sole and absolute sovereignty of the whole Sandwich group. The routed army of the petty island king was driven to take refuge among the wild crags of the pari, and hither it was followed by the conquering forces of the invader. No quarter was shown. The fugitives were hunted like savage beasts, and, almost to a man, were hurled from the giddy height and dashed to pieces on the frightful rocks below.

On returning to the cottage, we found that the dinner had been *dished* up, and that the guests were about taking their seats. Our table was the green grass, upon which had been arranged, with native taste, a circular *table cloth*, composed of ti leaves, placed one above another. On this the viands were laid. They consisted of fat pigs, and fat dogs, turkeys, chickens, boiled ham, and fish, with vegetables of various kinds, taro, sweet potatoes, &c.—all cooked in the native manner, in pits made in the ground, in which heated stones had been placed. Each pig and dog had such a stone within him, and around it had been wrapped a quantity of ti leaves, which were eaten as greens, and were excellent. The whole of the cookery was, in fact, very superior, and would have delighted the most fastidious epicure of our own enlightened land. We had also various liquors: Cham-

pagne, cherry, Madeira, and mountain dew, and were waited upon by native men and boys, with chaplets of green bound around their heads, and their persons profusely ornamented with the "fern and heather of their native valleys." Among the attendants, Mr. Mills, or *Deacon* Mills, as he is sometimes called, stood pre-eminent; he acted as purveyor and major domo; and showed, by his uniform conduct, that he was fully alive to the high responsibilities of his office.

Towards evening the whole party mounted their horses and galloped down the valley into the town. As we entered the precincts we formed ourselves into a battalion, and reined in our horses to a dignified trot, in order to pass a troop of gay native ladies who were returning from a visit to Waititi. At the head of this equestrian cavalcade, I was surprised to observe the large person of Madam Kinau, sitting astride upon a noble steed which evidently made an effort to curvet and appear proud of its queenly burthen.

While we were proceeding at this slow gait, a man suddenly sprang up behind my saddle and fixed his arms firmly around my waist. I was not more astonished than my horse at this intrusion; and the spirited animal which I rode, not being accustomed to carry double, and feeling unwilling to be so imposed upon, began kicking up his heels, and darting wildly about the road. I requested the intruder to dismount instantly, but the only attention which was paid to this was a reply, in the native language, which I did not understand. Supposing him to be one of the servants who had been heated by the refuse wine of the feast, and considering myself in real danger from the unruly conduct of my horse, I turned half round and dealt my merry companion a blow in the chest, which I intended should have unseated him. How was I astonished to hear the exclamation, "don't strike so hard, *hauri*," from him who occupied my crupper, and I was not long in discovering that the joker was the king, Kauikeaouli, himself. I apologized in the best manner I could, though out of breath with the exertion of restraining the fiery horse. His majesty did not seem in the least offended, but passing one arm each side of me, and taking the bridle in his hands, he guided the animal into one of the largest stores of the town, through which we went jumping and prancing, followed by all the king's train, and several white men of the party.

SCENES IN SOUTHERN AFRICA.

(Concluded from p. 36.)

"The most thrilling passage in my adventures is now to be recounted. In my own breast, it awakens a renewal of past impressions, more lively than any written description can render intelligible; and far abler pens than mine, dipped in more glowing tints, would still fall short of the reality, and leave much to be supplied by the imagination. Three hundred gigantic elephants, browsing in majestic tranquillity amidst the wild magnificence of an African landscape, and a wide-stretching plain, darkened as far as the eye can reach with a moving phalanx of gnobs and quaggas, whose numbers literally baffle computation, are sights but rarely to be witnessed ; but who amongst our brother Nimrods shall hear of riding familiarly by the side of a troop of colossal giraffes, and not feel his spirit stirred within him ? He that would behold so marvellous a sight must leave the haunts of man, and dive, as we did, into pathless wilds, traversed only by the brute creation, into wide wastes where the grim lion prowls, monarch of all he surveys, and where the gaunt hyæna and wild dog fearlessly pursue their prey.

" Many days had now elapsed since we had even seen the cameleopard, and then only in small numbers, and under the most unfavourable circumstances. The blood coursed through my veins like quicksilver, therefore, as on the morning of the 19th, from the back of *Breslar*, my most trusty steed, with a firm wooded plain before me, I counted thirty-two of these animals, industriously stretching their peacock necks to crop the tiny leaves which fluttered above their heads, in a mimosa-grove that beautified the scenery. They were within a hundred yards of me, but, having previously determined to try the *boarding* system, I reserved my fire. Although I had taken the field expressly to look for giraffes, and had put four of the Hottentots on horseback, all excepting Piet had as usual slipped off unperceived in pursuit of a troop of koodoos (*Strepsiceros Koodoo*.) Our stealthy approach was soon opposed by an ill-tempered rhinoceros, which, with her ugly calf, stood directly in the path ; and the twinkling of her bright little eyes, accompanied by a restless rolling of the body, giving earnest of her intention to charge, I directed Piet to salute her with a broadside, at the same moment putting spurs to my horse. At the report of the gun and the sudden clattering of hoofs, away bounded the giraffes in grotesque confusion, clearing the ground by a succession of frog-like hops, and soon leaving me far in the rear. Twice were their towering forms concealed from view by a park of trees, which we entered almost at the same instant ; and twice, on emerging from the labyrinth, did I perceive them tilting over an eminence immeasurably in advance. A white turban, that I wore round my hunting-cap, being dragged off by a projecting bough, was instantly charged by three rhinoceroses ; and, looking over my shoulder, I could see them long afterwards, fagging themselves to overtake me. In the course of five minutes the fugitives arrived at a small river, the treacherous sands of which receiving their long legs, their flight was greatly retarded ; and, after floundering to the opposite side and scrambling to the top of the bank, I perceived that their race was run. Patting the steaming neck of my good steed, I urged him again to his utmost, and instantly found myself by the side of the herd. The stately bull, being readily distinguishable from the rest by his dark chestnut robe and superior stature, I applied the muzzle of my rifle behind his dappled shoulder, with the right hand, and drew both triggers, but he still continued to shuffle

along, and being afraid of losing hin I dismount, among the extensive groves with which the landscape was scured, I sat in my saddle, loading a behind the elbow, and then placin; across his path, until, tho tears trick his full brilliant eye, his lofty frame totter, and at the seventeenth discha the deadly grooved bore, bowing his head from the skies, his proud form v trate in the dust.

" When I leisurely contemplated i sive frame before me, seeming as i had been cast in a mould of brass, tected by a hide of an inch and i thickness, it was no longer a matter nishment that a bullet, discharged fre tance of eighty or ninety yards, sho been attended with little effect up amazing strength. The extreme hei the crown of the elegantly moulded the hoof of this magnificent animal, v teen feet ; the whole being equally into neck, body, and leg. Two ho passed · in completing a drawing ; still not making his appearance, I c tail, which exceeded five feet in ler was measurelessly the most estimabl I had gained ; but proceeding to s horse, which I had left quietly grazi side of a running brook, my chagrin conceived, when I discovered that taken advantage of my occupation himself from his halter, and abscond ten miles from the wagons, and i fectly strange country, I felt convir tho only chance of recovering my pe following the trail, whilst doing wt infinite difficulty, the ground scarce ing to receive a foot-print, I had the tion of meeting Piet and Mohanyc had fortunately seen and recaptured ant. Returning to the giraffe, we al heartily upon the flesh, which, highly scented at this season, with Mokaala blossoms, was far from de; and, after losing our way in consec the twin-like resemblance of two hills, we regained the wagons after :

" The spell was now broken, and t of cameleopard hunting discovered. ' day Richardson and myself killed th: a female, slipping upon muddy gro falling with great violence, before been wounded, a shot in the head de; her as she lay. From this time v reckon confidently upon two out of er that we were fortunate enough to fin approaching as near as possible, in ensure a good start, galloping into th of them, *boarding* the largest, and rit him until he fell. The rapidity wit these awkwardly-formed animals car beyond all things surprising, our be: being unable to close with them u miles. Their gallop is a succession ing strides, the fore and hind leg on side moving together instead of diag in most other quadrupeds, the form kept close together, and the latter apart, that in riding by the animal's hoof may be seen striking on the c

appearance, he walked heavily off, expressing by a stifled growl his displeasure at being thus unceremoniously disturbed at dinner. It was not destined, however, that our acquaintance should cease here; for passing the scene of this introductory interview the following morning, Richardson and myself were suddenly made aware of the monster's presence by perceiving a pair of gooseberry eyes glaring upon us from beneath a shady bush; and instantly, upon reining up our horses, the grim savage bolted out with a roar, like thunder, and bounded across the plain with the agility of a greyhound. The luxuriant beauty of his shaggy black mane, which almost swept the ground, tempted us, contrary to established rule, to give him battle with the design of obtaining possession of his spoils; and he no sooner found himself hotly pursued than he faced about, and stood at bay in a mimosa grove, measuring the strength of his assailants with a port the most noble and imposing. Disliking our appearance, however, and not relishing the smell of gunpowder, he soon abandoned the grove, and took up his position on the summit of an adjacent stony hill, the base of which being thickly clothed with thorn trees, we could only obtain a view of him from the distance of three hundred yards. Crouched on this fortified pinnacle, like the sculptured figure at the entrance of a nobleman's park, the enemy disdainfully surveyed us for several minutes, daring us to approach, with an air of conscious power and pride, which well beseemed his grizzled form. As the rifle balls struck the ground nearer and nearer at each discharge, his wrath, as indicated by his glistening eyes, increased roar, and impatient switching of the tail, was clearly getting the mastery over his prudence. Presently a shot broke his leg. Down he came upon the other three, with reckless impetuosity, his tail straight out and whirling on its axis, his mane bristling on end, and his eye-balls flashing rage and vengeance. Unable, however, to overtake our horses, he shortly retreated under a heavy fire, limping and discomfited to his strong hold. Again we bombarded him, and again exasperated he rushed into the plain with headlong fury—the blood now streaming from his open jaws, and dying his mane with crimson. It was a gallant charge, but it was to be his last. A well-directed shot arrested him in full career; he pitched with violence upon his skull, and, throwing a complete somerset, subsided amid a cloud of dust."

MY FRUIT TREE.

Written by Dr. Isaac Watts to a female friend on the death of several young children.

I have a comely fruit tree in the summer season, with the branches of it promising plenteous fruit; the stalk was surrounded with seven or eight little shoots of different sizes, that grew up from the root at a small distance, and seemed to compose a beautiful defence and ornament for the mother tree: but the gardener, who espied their growth, knew the danger; he cut down those tender suckers one after another, and laid them in the dust. I pitied them in my heart, and said,

"How pretty were these young standards! How much like the parent! How elegantly clothed with the raiment of summer! And each of them might have grown to a fruitful tree;" but they stood so near as to endanger the stalk; they drew away the sap, the heart and strength of it, so far as to injure the fruit, and darken the hopeful prospects of autumn. The pruning-knife appeared unkind indeed, but the gardener was wise; for the tree flourished more sensibly, the fruit quickly grew fair and large, and the ingatherings at last were plenteous and joyful.

Will you give me leave, *Velina*, to persuade you into this parable? Shall I compare you to this tree in the garden of God? You have had many of these young suckers springing up around you; they stood awhile your sweet ornaments and your joy, and each of them might have grown up to a perfection of likeness, and each might have become a parent tree: but say, did they never draw your heart off from God? Did you never feel them stealing any of those seasons of devotion, or those warm affections that were first and supremely due to him that made you? Did they not stand a little too near the soul? And when they had been cut off successively, and laid one after another in the dust, have you not found your heart running out more towards God, and living more perpetually upon him? Are you not now devoting yourself more entirely to God every day, since the last was taken away? Are you not aiming at some greater fruitfulness and service than in times past? If so, then repine not at the pruning-knife; but adore the conduct of the heavenly husbandman, and say, "All his ways are wisdom and mercy."

When the granary was well stored with excellent fruit, and before winter came upon the tree, the gardener took it up by the roots, and it appeared as dead. But his design was not to destroy it utterly; for he removed it far away from the spot of earth where it had stood, and planted it in a hill of richer mould, which was sufficient to nourish it with all its attendants. The spring appeared, the tree budded into life again, and all those fair little standards that had been cut off, broke out of the ground afresh, and stood up around it (a sweet young grove) flourishing in beauty and immortal vigour.

You know not where you are, *Velina*, and that I have carried you to the hill of paradise, to the blessed hour of the resurrection. What an unknown joy it will be, when you have fulfilled all the fruits of righteousness in this lower world, to be transplanted to that heavenly mountain! What a divine rapture and surprise of blessedness, to see all your little offspring around you that day, springing out of the dust at once, making a fairer and brighter appearance in that upper garden of God, and rejoicing together, (a sweet company) all partakers with you of the same happy immortality; all fitted to bear heavenly fruit, without the need or danger of a pruning-knife. Look forward by faith to that glorious morning, and admire the whole scheme of providence and grace. Give cheer-

ful honours beforehand to your almighty and all-wise Governor, who by his unsearchable counsels has filled your best wishes, and secured your dear infants to you for ever, though not just in your own way; that blessed hand which made the painful separation on earth, shall join you and your babes together in his own heavenly habitation, never to be divided again, though the method may be painful to flesh and blood. Fathers shall not hope in vain, nor "mothers bring forth for trouble: they are the seed of the blessed of the Lord, and their offspring with them;" *Isaiah* lxv. 23. Then shall you say, "Lord, here am I, and the children that thou hast given me. For he is your God, and the God of your seed, in an everlasting covenant." *Amen.*

Lady Huntingdon once spoke to a workman who was repairing a garden wall and pressed him to take some thought concerning eternity and the state of his soul. Some years afterwards she was speaking to another on the same subject, and said to him, "Thomas, I fear you never pray, nor look to Christ for salvation." "Your ladyship is mistaken," answered the man. "I heard what passed between you and James at such a time, and the word you designed for him took effect on me." "How did you hear it?" inquired her ladyship. "I heard it," answered the man, "on the other side of the garden through a hole in the wall, and shall never forget the impression I received."—*Countess of Huntingdon's Life and Times*, vol. ii.

The late bishop Ravenscroft said, "I feel bound to record, that I owe much to the custom established in Scotland, of making the Scriptures a school book—a custom, I am grieved to say it, not only abandoned in the schools and academies among us, but denounced as improper, if not injurious. Although I was unconscious, at the time, of any power or influence over my thoughts and actions thence derived, yet what mere memory retained of the life-giving truths, proved of unspeakable advantage when I became awakened on the subject of religion; and I am constrained to believe that what was thus unconsciously sown in my heart, though smothered and choked by the levity of youth, and abused and perverted by the negligence and sinfulness of my riper years, was nevertheless a preparation of heaven's foresight and mercy to quicken me, a mighty help to my amazed and confounded soul, when brought to a just view of my actual condition as a sinner, both by nature and by practice."

THE KNOWLEDGE OF CHRIST.

BY SIR MATTHEW HALE.

Here is the privilege of the knowledge of Christ Jesus, that as it is of eminence and height, so it is of use and convenience, and that in the highest measure; as it is a pearl of beauty, so it is for value. This knowledge is a kind of catholicon, of universal use and convenience. It is so, in reference to this life. Am I in want, in contempt, in prison, in banishment, in sickness, in death? This knowledge gives me contentedness, patience, cheerfulness, resignation of myself to his will who hath sealed my peace with him, in the great covenant of his Son; and I can live upon this, though I were ready to starve. I am assured that if it be for my good and the glory of his name, I shall be delivered; if not, I can be contented, so that my jewel, the peace of God, and my own conscience by the blood of Christ, be safe. Am I in wealth, honour, power, greatness, esteem in the world? This knowledge teaches me humility, as knowing from whom I receive it; fidelity, as knowing to whom I must account for it; watchfulness, as knowing that the honour of my Lord is concerned in some measure in my conduct; and that the higher the employment is, the more obnoxious I am to temptation from without, from them that watch for my halting, and from within by a deceitful heart. And in all it teaches me not to over-value my condition; nor to value myself the more by it or for it, because the knowledge of Christ Jesus presents me with an object of a higher value, the price of the high calling of God in Christ. It teaches me to look upon the glory of the world as rust, in comparison of the glory that excelleth, and that the greatest of men is a worm in comparison with the great God. And as thus, in reference to the temporal condition of my life, this knowledge of Christ is of singular use, and makes a man a better philosopher than the best systems of morals, in reference thereunto; so it guides me in the management of all relations. First, to God; presenting him unto me as full of majesty, yet full of love, which teaches me to reverence and yet access with boldness, love, and obedience. Secondly, to man; enjoining justice, which is giving every man his due; mercy, to forgive; compassion, to pity; liberality, to relieve; sobriety, in the use of creatures, and yet comfort in the enjoyment of them; a right use of the world, and yet a contempt of its comparison of my hope. It makes death not terrible, because a most sure passage to life. I find a way to get all my sins pardoned, whereas, without this, all the world cannot contrive a satisfaction for one; I find a way to obtain such a righteousness as is valuable with God, and perfect before him, even the righteousness of God in Christ. And here I find the means, and only means, to avoid the wrath to come, the terror of the judgment of the great day, and to secure everlasting life unto all eternity with the blessed God and our Lord Jesus Christ, and all the blessed angels, and the spirits of just men made perfect. Thus this knowledge is useful for this life, and that which is to come, and that in the highest degree, which all other knowledge comes short of, and attains not to any one of the least of these ends.

Soil for the Sugar Beet.—A deep rich loom is the best; but any soil that can be made mellow will answer well. A very dry soil does not yield so large beets, but sweet and nutritious ones. The soil should be free from stones, and well pulverized to a good depth, that the root may pierce it freely and grow smooth and handsome. Plant in rows twenty-four or thirty inches apart, and leave the beets ten inches from each other in the rows. The ground should be thoroughly prepared and well manured.

For "The Friend."

MORAL MACHINERY SIMPLIFIED.

An article with the above caption, transferred from the columns of the Pennsylvania Freeman to the first page of the last number of "The Friend," contains some sentiments which appear to me very objectionable. In the first place, I cannot but reprobate the irreverent manner in which our blessed Saviour is spoken of, as "the carpenter's son," and "the despised artisan of Nazareth," epithets which are calculated, if not designed, to derogate from his divine character and degrade him to a level with fallible men. The expression "half enlightened disciples," is also highly objectionable. That the disciples of our Lord did not at once perceive the spiritual and peaceable nature of their Master's kingdom, and that the mysteries of the gospel were gradually unfolded to their minds as they were able to learn them, I readily admit. But to apply to them the term "half enlightened," with reference to the whole course of their religious lives, which the paragraph under consideration plainly does, is aiming a fatal blow at the authority of their examples, their preaching, and their writings. If the apostles of Christ were but "half enlightened"? It will be perceived at once, that the deference which we have been wont to pay to them and their writings, must quickly be lost where such an opinion is entertained. The sentiment savours to me of that levelling and disorganizing spirit which kicks against the authority of Holy Scripture, the restraints of religion and of government, and would make every thing yield to the proud but perverted reason of man!

Nor can I subscribe to the sentiment that Christians are at liberty to associate on terms of affability with infidels, even for the promotion of benevolent objects. We have abundant proofs of the dangers resulting from intercourse with "men of corrupt minds," and of their industry and plausibility in insinuating their poisonous notions into the minds of the unwary. With what hope of being heard can we put up the petition "Lead us not into temptation," if we voluntarily expose ourselves to its assaults? As we cannot preserve ourselves from evil, and our safety depends upon the merciful interposition and care of a watchful Providence, can we expect to receive the blessing from him, or to escape the snare, if we voluntarily place ourselves within its influence? These are serious considerations, and may well claim the calm and sober attention of all, but especially of the young and inexperienced who are, from various causes, more peculiarly exposed to danger.

"Be ye not unequally yoked together with unbelievers—for what fellowship hath righteousness with unrighteousness, and what communion hath light with darkness? And what concord hath Christ with Belial? Or *what part hath he that believeth with an infidel?*" Such are the pertinent exhortations of Holy Scripture, and I am old fashioned enough to think that they come from a mind divinely enlightened to a degree of which none in the present times can boast, and being penned under the immediate inspiration of the Holy Spirit, they claim, and ought to receive, our obedient attention.

To the righteous cause of negro emancipation we most heartily wish success. The wrongs and outrages inflicted on this persecuted class of our fellow men call loudly for the exercise of the tenderest sympathies of all who can feel—and the improvement of every proper and Christian means for their relief. But let us all remember that it is the benign spirit of the gospel only that can effectually counteract and subdue the selfish passions in which slavery originated, and by which it is sustained, and that our efforts to eradicate the evil will be availing in proportion as they are prompted and guided by the meek and quiet spirit of Him, who though he could have commanded legions of angels to destroy his persecutors and rescue himself from their hands, prayed for them in the hour of his greatest agony, "Father forgive them for they know not what they do."

R. T.

On the Value of Sun-flower Seeds for Oil.

To the Editor of the Farmer's Register.

ATHENS, August 25th, 1830.

Although a stranger to you, I take the liberty of addressing you upon the subject of the sun-flower plant; knowing that you take a deep interest in any and every thing connected with agriculture, &c. For the last five years my attention (mental I mean) has been at times occupied on the merits of this plant, as a valuable addition to, if not a supersedent of our oils, now in general and in avoidable use. I have used the term mental, because I have expended much more of thought than manual exercise upon the subject. From the limited trials made, however, both in the culture of the sun-flower, and the home-made extraction of the oil, and the results in its use for domestic purposes, I am compelled to believe, that the oil extracted is equal if not superior to any other now in use; answering the place of olive oil, for the table, and spermaceti, and all other kinds now in general use, for all the requirements of painting, lighting of lamps, &c. &c.

This may appear a very broad assertion to those who have for the first time had the subject brought to their view, and to others who have fallen into the received opinion, that the oils now in use are the best, because they answer the immediate wants and requirements; not reflecting that it takes two or more of these specific kinds and qualities of oil, to supply the necessary wants and uses—when this oil, if properly cultivated and prepared, will answer, if not take the place of all others put together.

A grand desideratum, and which ought not to be lost sight of, is, that for lamps, it burns us long, gives a clear and more brilliant light, exhales no disagreeable or unhealthy odour, no apparent smoke evaporates from the wicks, and consequently leaves none of those dark and unsightly features of soot attendant upon even our finest oils now in use. All of which, without the aid of philosophy, is apparent to even the most careless observer, to be detrimental to the health of families thus using them, and repugnant to the olfactory nerves.

These remarks hastily put to paper, are intended to draw from you any information or experience you may be possessed of in regard to the sun-flower plant, for the purposes here mentioned, or as food for stock or poultry; and you will confer a singular favour upon me, by letting me hear from you on the subject so soon as convenient.   With respect,
                                N. A. ADAMS.

We have no experimental knowledge on the subject of the foregoing letter; and request that any information possessed by others may be afforded through our pages. In the agricultural and other papers, sundry articles have appeared, within the last twenty years, recommending the oil of the seeds as a substitute for olive oil. But, so far as we know, there has been no statement of practical results, or of cost and profit.—*Ed. Farm. Reg.*

From the Cultivator.
A BIRD STORY.

MILTON, Ulster Co., N. Y. July, 1839.

Friend Buel—I would not have ventured to forward the following statement, were it not that the narrator of it, Edward Hallock, of the firm of William Hallock & Brother, of Milton, Ulster county, is known to thee, and known to be of unquestionable veracity. I have heard him before express his conviction, that if birds were protected and cherished by farmers and others, we should never be subjected to the loss of corn or other crops by grubs; and that other noxious insects would be sensibly diminished. There is a small kind of bird (the males nearly black, the females brown), that is noted for being around and following cattle in the field, as in the case I am about to detail. E. H. says, "on the 26th of the present month, I was ploughing for turnips, myself with one team, and my son with another; and observing that we were followed by a flock of the above little birds, I took it into my head to notice their motions, to ascertain what was the attraction, when I perceived that their object was grubs. We ploughed up plenty of a small white, and a large brown or gray grub, as well as some in a chrysalis state, and angle worms; all of them, *excepting angle worms*, appeared to be acceptable to them; and as the sequel will show, they were capable of devouring large quantities. I should think that one would make way with at least 100 per day. I cautioned my son against making any motion towards noticing them, in any way to intimidate them; as I found they grew more and

more bold in their honest avocation, and as the land diminished in width, they would remain in the opposite furrow when not more than three or four feet distant. At length my son spoke cautiously, and said there was one on his plough beam. I then stopped the teams and told the boy to pick up a grub and throw it to the bird that had distinguished itself by its tameness. He did so; and the bird immediately seized it. Encouraged by this, I told him to pick out the next white one and hold it out in his fingers near the ground; crawling down, he did so, and the bird came and picked it out of his fingers! Afterwards he stood up and held out one, and the bird lighted on his hand and picked out the worm. This was repeated until it lighted on my own hand; I raised it up and applied my cheek to its wing without frightening it away. The next day he was not slow in finding us, and practised the same familiarity, in presence of James Sherman, William Hallock, and others of the neighbours; it came into the corn field where the boys were weeding corn, and actually, without any special attraction, perched upon the head of one of the boys; it continued these visits until one of the boys in an adjoining field, could not repress his inclination to seize and hold it. This made him more wary, but he gradually recovered his confidence." I communicate these facts in the hope that they may contribute to produce an examination into the subject, of how far it would tend to the agricultural interests, to fall upon some method to tame and familiarize small birds, instead of frightening, maiming, or destroying them.   E. HULL.

From the New England Farmer.
BURYING BEES IN WINTER.

Our last swarm came off in June, and notwithstanding the old adage that "a swarm in June is not worth a spoon," we should refuse an offer of two spoons for this, and more, unless they were very nice and very heavy. True, the quantity of honey which they have gathered is not very great, but, with our way of managing such hives, we think amply sufficient for their supply. We propose burying them through the winter, a practice which we have adopted in two successive years, and had we continued it the third, our old colony, instead of coming to an untimely end, would probably have been in existence now through its descendants.

My method of burying bees is as follows. The operation is performed the last of November. The pit in which they are to be placed is dug considerably larger than the hives in every respect. On the bottom of the pit two sticks, say of scantling, four inches square, are so placed that a cavity may be left into which the water, if there is any, may settle, and run off without injury to the bees. On these blocks I lay my floor-board, which should be sound, and full an inch thick; if more, no matter. The top of the hive should be covered with a two-inch plank, or if more convenient, a piece of wide thick slab with the rounding side up, so that if the frost comes out, and heavy rains fall, it may serve as a

roof to carry the water from over the hive, and turn it into the pit below. Straw is then placed as compactly as may be around the hive, and the earth thrown on so as to form a cone above it, which again operates as a roof to turn the water as it falls. With regard to the depth of burying, we can only say, that in our former experiments, we never sunk the top of the hive below the surface. Whether it would be well to do so we cannot say. Some, when burying their bees, drive down a stake near the hive, as they say, to admit the air; but we do not see why a stake, drove with the earth compactly placed around it, can form an air hole more than the earth itself. And if it could, we do not see the necessity of it, for the object of burying bees is to put them as much as may be in a state of dormancy through the winter, by which their stock of provisions is lengthened out, to secure them from sudden and often fatal changes from heat and cold, and from storms and sunshine.

In selecting a place for burying, it is important that a *dry* one should be chosen, and *we* prefer one that is cold to a warm one, and could we regulate the condition of the earth around them, we would freeze it the night after their burial, and *keep it frozen* until time for their exhumation in the spring.

We, in both instances of our former burying, took them up some of the last days of March, and all the dead we found from the four hives thus kept would not half fill a person's hand, and on exposure to the sun and atmosphere, the living were as bright and lively as though they had known no winter, and they gave swarms earlier and more frequently than did the hives that were not buried, the ensuing summer.

THE WHEAT FLY.

Is an animal that has never attacked my grain. It has so happened that my neighbours' wheat and mine were in adjoining fields, separated only by a fence; that his wheat was nearly destroyed by the fly, and not one in mine. The only *solution* I can give to it, is as follows : My wheat *uniformly* is sowed late—never until there has been a hard frost, sufficiently so to kill insects of that kind. I cause a strong solution of salt and water to be made—strong enough to bear an egg, and my wheat is soaked about twenty-four hours in it, and then rolled in lime on the barn floor. When that rule has been followed, my crops have been about as good as my neighbours' when their wheat was not affected with the fly. Care should be taken not to soak the wheat more than about twenty-four hours, and then it should be rolled in lime, else the germinating quality of the wheat may be destroyed or injured.   A. DEY.
N. Y. July 23.   [*Poughkeepsie Tel.*

The March of Empire is West.—In a few more years the balance of political power will be transferred from the east to the west. This period is nearer at hand than is generally supposed. It cannot be procrastinated much beyond the next census. The population of the United States at the next census

: of 16,000,.
mate of the
uth western
:

t,500,000
900,000
700,000
350,000
150,000
400,000
400,000
200,000
400,000
·850,000
·950,000
500,000

7,300,000
·hin 640,000
ation of the
l not be sur-
if the actual
such is the
. in the west.

r.
·ng,

ew

brain,—
ain,—

o!

brought
o!

a

Cornwall.·

ID.

1839.

y comments
way into our
of the matter
with others,
ion, as is our
; to a closer
so happened,
ssed into the
the requisite
nts contained
posed to ap-
·ary, a more
us that they
concur in the

---

animadversions of R. T. Nevertheless, we
have no idea that the Freeman meant to be
"irreverent," or to give countenance to a
"leveling and disorganizing spirit," being inclined rather to ascribe the faulty expressions
to a want of that exact discrimination in the
use of terms consequent on rapid composition.

—

Our extracts from the Review in the
Edinburgh Quarterly of Harris' Travels in
Southern Africa, being now brought to a
close, we take occasion to remark in deference to hints from a worthy friend. First—
incredulity was expressed in regard to the
immense number of wild animals mentioned
in the narrative. In answer we may observe that the reviewer speaks of the author as one to be relied upon on the score
of veracity, and considering that he treats
of scenes in a wilderness country, remote
from the settlements of civilized man, we
do not see any good reason for doubt, especially if we recur to the countless herds
of buffaloes known to have ranged over our
western prairies. In the next place our
friend objected to the countenance given to
the spirit of sportsmanship and its attendant
cruelties. To this we can only say, that our
object was the interesting details in the natural history of a country, and respecting a
class of animals in their native haunts, comparatively but little known; and very far
from sympathy with, or in any degree ap-
proval of, the detestable enjoyments of the
professed sportsman. On that subject our
sentiments and feelings are much in unison
with the poet's:—

"The heart is hard in nature, and unfit
For human fellowship, as being void
Of sympathy, and therefore dead alike
To love and friendship both, that is not pleased
With sight of animals enjoying life,
Nor feels their happiness augment his own."

Again—

"I would not enter on my list of friends
(Tho' grac'd with polish'd manners and fine sense,
Yet wanting sensibility) the man
Who needlessly sets foot upon a worm."

"A necessary act incurs no blame.
Not so when, held within their proper bounds,
And guiltless of offence, they range the air,
Or take their pastime in the spacious field:
There they are privileged; and he that hunts
Or harms them there, is guilty of a wrong,
Disturbs th' economy of Nature's realm,
Who, when he form'd, design'd them an abode.
The sum is this—If man's convenience, health,
Or safety interfere, his rights and claims
Are paramount, and must extinguish theirs.
Else they are all—the meanest things that are—
As free to live, and to enjoy that life,
As God was free to form them at the first,
Who, in his sov'reign wisdom, made them all."
                                    Cowper.

A stated meeting of the Concord Auxiliary
Bible Association of Friends, will be held at
Middletown meeting house, on second day,
the 11th day of the eleventh month, at 11
o'clock A. M. The female members are respectfully invited to attend.

                    Howard Yarnall, Sec'ry.
11th mo. 1st, 1839.

Married at Friends' meeting, M
fifth day, the 7th inst, William M. (
aru C. Corn, daughter of Israel Cor
— on fifth day, the 10th, at :
house at Madison, Stephen Atwat
Atwater, of Lockport, in the state
Mary L., daughter of Zebulon Wea·
place.

Died at Amesbury, Mass., 24th of
a long and distressing illness, which.h
plary patience, David Edwin, only
and Ruth Challis, aged 12 years.
of this dear child his parents and frie
the loss of one of more than ordin
was of a mild and amiable temper, c
tionate to his parents, a strict obse·
honesty, accompanied with a spirit o
sensibility to the feelings of others,
deared him to all.
— at his residence in Zanesville
of 8th month last, Moses Dillon, in :
age. For more than sixty years th
member of the Society of Friends.
period in which he was engaged in
of husband, father, a member of reli
a useful citizen, his character was ma
integrity, liberality, and kindness.
years he passed in great serenity ·
delighting in reading the Scriptures,
journals, and other religious books
sight failed, he frequently requestec
be read to him. The meekness and
with which he bore the afflictions in
vanced age, were instructive, and a·
tion to those around him. He was
the doctrines of a crucified Saviour
tached to the religious society of whi
her; and as his close drew near he ·
signed, and said he "rejoiced that hi
leaving no doubt that the promises g
are realised, and his reward sure.

PRINTED BY ADAM W
Carpenter Street, below Seventh,

THE FRIEND.

A RELIGIOUS AND LITERARY JOURNAL.

VOL. XIII.   SEVENTH DAY, ELEVENTH MONTH, 16, 1839.   NO. 7.

EDITED BY ROBERT SMITH.

———

PUBLISHED WEEKLY.

Price two dollars per annum, payable in advance.

Subscriptions and Payments received by

GEORGE W. TAYLOR,

NO. 50, NORTH FOURTH STREET, UP STAIRS,

PHILADELPHIA.

For "The Friend."

THE CHINESE OPIUM TRADE.

Various statements have recently appeared in the public papers, tending more or less to develope the nature and extent of that contraband trade, which has been carried on for several years, at some of the ports of the Chinese empire; the object of which has been to introduce into that country immense quantities of opium, for the sake of pecuniary gain. It is also well known that the government of that empire has long opposed the introduction of this drug, and at length has come to the strong determination to put a stop to it, under the alarming consciousness that it was operating as a moral and physical poison, to a frightful extent, among their people. They have correctly considered themselves as greatly aggrieved by the pertinacity with which the merchants frequenting their chief commercial port have continued to smuggle this poison into the country; and have, after endeavouring for a long time to put a stop to it by earnest remonstrances, recently decreed capital punishment as the reward of any attempt to introduce the drug. The following abstract of a memorial, addressed to the privy council of Great Britain, by merchants engaged in this nefarious trade, will be read with melancholy interest, as its shows the enormous extent to which the trade has increased, and the manner in which the British government in Hindostan were implicated therein. It is lamentable that so many in our own country as well as in Great Britain, should be found capable of justifying this shameful business, and even of advocating a resort to force, to compel the poor injured Chinese to submit to the continuance of the deadly importations. The object of these petitioners was to obtain a guarantee from the British government, of reimbursement for the loss they had sustained by the late compulsory delivery of many thousand chests of opium to the Chinese authorities, in order to be destroyed. The whole subject is one worthy of the serious attention of the Christian community.

1st. The memorial states that the petition-ers are the parties interested in the opium trade between Calcutta and China, but asserts that the British authorities in Bengal are the producers of the drug, and have been most deeply interested in encouraging the trade; "which has been fostered into its recent magnitude by every means that ingenuity could devise on the part of the British government of India."

2d. That in six years upwards of 67,000 *chests* of opium were exported from Calcutta to China direct, with the express knowledge of the British Indian authorities; 16,297 *chests* being exported with that destination in the year 1837–8.

3d. "That the net profits of this trade have yielded to the Indian government an enormous revenue, varying from one to two millions sterling *per annum*; and that by this revenue have the proprietors of East India stock been enabled to receive the very high dividend guarantied by parliament in the new charter."

4th. That the bullion received in payment for the opium is of immense importance to British India, "has enormously extended the import of British manufactures throughout Hindostan," and "has paid in London the dividends of the proprietors of India stock, amounting to 630,000 pounds per annum."

5th. "That while the profits of opium shippers have seldom exceeded from 5 to 15 per cent. on the government sale price, those of the opium manufacturers, viz. the British government of India, have usually varied from 200 up to the enormous amount of 500 per cent. on the cost of manufacture."

Thus it appears that the British East India government is deeply implicated in this most shameful act of injustice to the people of that great empire, who may well look with a suspicious eye upon the ships of the "foreign barbarians," which approach their shores freighted with poison for a whole nation.

H.

From the London Literary Gazette of 9th mo.

THE ANTARCTIC EXPEDITION.

By the time this paper meets the public eye, this very interesting expedition will have left, or be leaving, the British shores. Had it been possible to complete the extensive philosophical and other equipments in shorter space of time, it would have been better, perhaps, had it been able to sail six weeks or two months earlier; but still its course is open, and the delay will lead to no other consequence than some slight alteration in the projected plan of operations.

On Tuesday the *Terror*, Captain Crozier, dropped down from off the dock-yard at Chatham to Gillingham, with all her white canvass spread, and looking like a bird of passage preparing to wing its way to another clime; and on Thursday, or as soon after as possible, her companion, the *Erebus*, Captain James Clark Ross, was appointed to follow, and then proceed on their voyage together. Having gone to take our farewell, a short description of the vessels, &c., cannot be unacceptable to our readers.

The Erebus and Terror seem to be twin ships, alike in build, in colours, in masts and rigging, and, indeed, in every external appearance. An inexperienced eye could not tell the one from the other. The Erebus is about 370 tons, the Terror 340. In each the full complement of officers and men is sixty-four; one hundred and twenty-eight in all. Nothing that the art of the shipwright could accomplish has been omitted to fit them for their perilous undertaking. Below, not only have the ribs been strengthened by transverse timbers, but these again have been interlaced by cross-beams at certain angles, so as to offer resistance to any invading body, such as ice, which would require a mighty force to overcome.

Thus, internally powerful beyond any former example, the outward hull has also been so shaped (curving from near the centre something like the turning-off edge of a glass or tea-cup,) as to throw the converging ice from the chain-plates, and thus protect the rigging from being crushed or invaded. The deck, too, is double; and the whole has a compactness and firmness which gives assurance of security from the worst elements which their gallant crews can ever be exposed to. A spare rudder, which could be shipped immediately in case of accident to the other, is safely stowed amidships; each vessel is provided with eight boats, two of them whalers, and framed to encounter rough seas and weather in separate expeditions, to explore passages and lands where the ships cannot penetrate. Six guns are borne in each; viz. four six-pounders and two salute guns. The apparatus for keeping the vessels at an equable temperature is admirable, and consists of a square iron tube, above a foot in diameter, running all around the sides, and distributing a comfortable warmth to every berth in the ship. The ventilation is not less attended to.

There are stoves in the captains' cabins, and the gun-room messes which adjoin; and the cooking conveniences are as ample and fit for every purpose as they could be on shore. There is a large kettle to dissolve ice into fresh water; another for dressing salt meat; another for fish; another for fresh meat; and ovens for baking. The mates' cabins are well constructed; and those for the officers to sleep in, though small, are arranged with all a seaman's skill and dexterity in making much of a little. The sick berths are forward, and so contrived that the invalids may be kept apart from the healthy, for their own sake, as well as for the general safety. Immense ice-saws are ranged along the lower deck; some of them thirty or more feet long, and looking like the jaws of sharks, competent to cut through any besetting adversary.

They are victualled with fresh provisions for three years; and pemmican and prepared meats in cases are stowed away in the least possible compass.

The provision of scientific instruments, under the superintendence of the Royal Society, is very complete; and double sets, to supply the loss of any which may be broken or rendered useless, seem almost to furnish the commander's cabin. In this respect the admiralty has been most liberal; and, indeed, we may say, that after the first official difficulties were got over, the government has taken up the expedition with the most commendable spirit, and done every thing that can contribute to its successful issue. The phenomena of terrestrial magnetism will be independently observed throughout the voyage, and also in connection with the new observatories about to be established, as already stated in the Literary Gazette, at St. Helena, the Cape, Van Dieman's Land, &c. The declination, inclination, and intensity of the magnet will thus form tables of the utmost importance toward solving this great problem. The declination instrument, the horizontal and the vertical force magnetometers, are constructed under the direction of Professor Lloyd, of Dublin; and there are, besides dip circles, transits with azimuth circles, and chronometers of the most approved construction.

There are also pendulums for ascertaining the true figure of the earth, thermometers for determining the temperature of the sea at given depths; other blackened thermometers to measure the atmospheric temperature in different latitudes; photometric sensitive paper for experiments on light; barometers to be observed during storms, white squalls, &c.; glasses for sideral observations; drawing utensils; repositories for geological, botanical, and natural history specimens; actinometers for finding the forces of solar and terrestrial radiation; hygrometers, Osler's anenometers, rain gauges, electrometers, skeleton registers of every needful kind; and, in short, such means to employ, and so much to be done, that there will be no great leisure for our enterprising countrymen when all these instruments are put in requisition, and their results are regularly chronicled for the information of the world.

In looking over the vessels about to depart on so deeply interesting an occasion, many slight matters and incidents touch the feelings. In almost every cabin and berth were tolerable collections of books; and Captain Ross's amounted to a fair library of the most useful description. In some were sweet remembrances of native land, in prints and pictures; and one engraving, conspicuous in the gallant commander's cabin, affected us much—it was of *our Saviour walking on the waters!*

Faith and hope could not have chosen a more beautiful illustration of the sailor's mind; the instruments of the soul, without the possession of which what were all that the philosophy and science of man could provide? In that engraving alone we read a more certain index of the success of the great work, than in the multitude of ingenious machines, and the volumes of wise instructions, by which our most estimable friend was surrounded.

Some kind heart had supplied a twelfth-cake, to be opened on the 6th of January, 1840! The diameter of the globe will then be between the giver and receiver.

Another pleasant circumstance to record, is the friendship subsisting between Captains Ross and Crozier. They have been messmates, and intimate together. Crozier was a midshipman in the ship where Ross was a lieutenant; he was a lieutenant where Ross was captain; and now he is captain where Ross is commodore of the expedition. They have served together, know and regard each other, and this is an auspicious promise for their mutual good understanding and cordial co-operation to the end; when bound together in their brave barks—

> "To reside
> In thrilling regions of thick-ribbed ice,
> To be imprisoned in the viewless winds,
> And blown [we trust not] with restless violence
>   about
> The pendant world."

The earlier proceedings of the voyage will lead them to St. Helena, where Lieutenant Eardley Wilmot, of the royal engineers, who goes out in the Erebus, will be left in charge of the new observatory. Next, at the Cape, will be landed for the like purpose another officer. The vessels then make their way across the ocean, touching at and examining Kerguelen's Land, Amsterdam, and other islands, either known or imperfectly reported in that vast expanse of water. Arrived at Van Dieman's Land, the instruments, &c., for the observatory will be sent ashore, and while it is erecting, they will cruise to various points where the scientific pursuits of the expedition are most likely to be advanced. On their return, they will start *de novo* in a direct southern course, between 120° and 160° east longitude, toward the antarctic pole; and it is a singular and fortunate thing that in this direction, during the present season, a ship of Mr. Enderby's has discovered land on both sides of the longitudes we have indicated, in about 65° and 68° south latitude.

These shores have been named Sabrina Land, seen March, 1839, and Balleny Isle, seen February, 1839; and between them, as well as upon them, the efforts of the Erebus and Terror will, in the first instance, be employed. How far they may penetrate is in the hands of Providence. They will afterward circumnavigate the pole, and try, in every quarter, to reach the highest point, whether near Enderby's Land, discovered in 1832, or by Captain Weddel's farthest reach, about 73°, in 1823.

It is between Sabrina Land and Balleny Isle, to the northward, in about latitude 50°, and east longitude 140°, that it is expected

the south magnetic pole will be found. Strange if he who discovered either that of the north, or so near an approach to it as Captain James Ross did, should also ascertain this long sought phenomenon. We had forgotten to mention that the vessels are constructed on the plan which divides them into three compartments; so that either extremity or the middle might be stove in, and yet the remainder be a safe hold for the crew.

Wherever the voyagers go, we have only to add, may God bless and prosper them, and return them in safety to a grateful country and their anxious relatives and friends!

Observations on some of the Domestic Instincts of Birds.[*]

Birds present in their habits an interesting feature which distinguishes them from almost all other animals, viz. that most of them not only live in monogamy, but in a union which ends only with the death of one of the parties. Moreover, the union of birds is distinguished by the circumstance, that the males of almost all the species living in monogamy interest themselves in their progeny; whereas in the *mammalia*, man alone excepted, it is only the female who takes charge of the young. This is partly a natural consequence of their being suckled by the female parent; but even after they have been weaned, the dam alone feeds or guides them, whereas the male does not even know or acknowledge his progeny.

It is the male that maintains, with great obstinacy, the place where the nest is to be constructed. This has been ascribed to the jealousy with which they assert their rights as legitimate husbands; and it is true that the male birds of many species do not tolerate any of their own species and sex within a certain district; but the females are never seen to contend for the building-place as the males do.

"A starling had this year built its nest in a box fixed on a tree near my house. The young had scarcely left it, when a couple of house-sparrows, who had before made several vain endeavours to build in the same box, took possession of it. A few days after, the young starlings being so far advanced that they no longer required the incessant attention of their parents, the latter appeared again, and dislodged the sparrows; but only the males fought. The male starling cleared the box of the feathers carried there by the sparrows, and by making use of both beak and wings, drove the vociferous cock sparrow to a good distance from the box. On the third morning the hen sparrow had laid an egg in the box; the male starling arrived, entered the box, brought out the egg in his beak, and dropped it. The cock sparrow now, for the first time, furiously attacked the starling, but was so ill received that it made a precipitate retreat. After this the starling no longer disputed the place with the sparrows, which built in the box and reared their young. In a similar

* By Dr. Brehm, of Renthendorf, in Saxony. Extracted from the Magazine of Natural History, No. 20, Vol. II.

manner are conducted all struggles for building places; the males fight it out, while the females remain passive spectators."

The great sea-eagles hover *in pairs* over their eyries, and both parents take a share in rearing their young. Nay, the male feeds and guides them, in common with the female, after they have left their nest, until they can provide for their own subsistence and safety. Buzzards, also, the male not only feeds the female while she is sitting, but takes care of the young with great kindness.

The male of the honey-buzzard presents the only instance known among birds of prey, of not only assisting the female in rearing the young, but *also in hatching.* They relieve each other regularly. Mr. Madel, of Gotha, shot a male upon its eyrie, and found that it had been sitting upon the eggs.

The male of both the russet and blackish-brown species of kite behave to their progeny like other birds of prey; but they show such caution in the exercise of their parental affection, that when they apprehend any danger, they will soar over the eyrie beyond the range of guns, and let the food fall into it from that height.

The males of the noble falcons evince about the same kind of affection for their young as the hawks. That of the peregrine falcon is but two thirds the size of the female, but he feeds her whilst she is sitting, and assists faithfully in rearing the young. He clings so much to the favourite rock on which the eyrie is built, as to remain there even after the female and young have been destroyed. There is another species of the falcon, called *Subbuteo,* that present peculiar features. "It feeds its sitting mate, but does not carry the food to the eyrie itself. When it has caught a bird, it flies round and round the nest, shouting glee, glee, glee. Upon this the female, uttering a similar cry, leaves her eggs or tender young, flies to meet the male, and takes the prey from him, carrying it to the eyrie, there to eat it in comfort. It is delightful to observe the affectionate meeting of these noble falcons. In feeding the young the same forms are observed; the male soars round the nest with his joyous call, until the female arrives to receive the prey and carry it to the young. It is only when the female has been killed that the male extends his functions, and carries the food to the eyrie, where he often feeds the young with insects from his craw. It is also very interesting to observe how the male trains the young to hunting.—At first they are taught to seize some prey which the male presents to them when both parties are on the wing. When they are able to do this with sufficient precision, they catch dead birds, &c. which the parent lets fall; and this instruction is continued until the young are skilful enough to catch living birds."

The behaviour of the Kestrel is very different. The males of this sub-genus are so much attached to their females, that they keep together even after the breeding season. They migrate with their respective mates to distant countries, and return with them. During the breeding season the attentions of the male become more marked, even before the first egg has been laid. When the female is resting near the newly-constructed eyrie, especially towards night-fall, the male will often carry to her a mouse, &c., and in arriving he utters a very tender call, which is returned by the female. When she has begun to sit, she may safely trust to the faithful care of her mate, who never fails to provide her with choice morsels. The food which he carries to her consists chiefly of mice. When he arrives he enters the eyrie with great eagerness, and appears to delight so much in seeing the female feasting, that he often stays a considerable time, during which the couple exchange many tender sounds. It is only after the female is duly provided for, that the male thinks about satisfying his own appetite; and this having been done, he perches on the pinnacle of an old tower, or a neighbouring tree, to keep watch over the female. He afterwards contributes his due share in rearing the young, to which he gives the food previously prepared in his craw. There is no eyrie where there is more bustle than about that of the kestrel.

Many are the peculiarities to be observed in the three species of sparrow-hawk, which are indigenous in Germany. "Even during the breeding season, the male perseveres in that stubborn and *insidious* disposition which is peculiar to the sub-genus, and which the female loses about that period. These species show a boldness when near their eggs or young, which is perfectly ridiculous. Instead of retreating when a man approaches the nest, they fly to meet him, perch before him in the most open place, and will even sometimes make a rush at the great enemy of all other creatures. On one occasion, a female sparrow-hawk would have taken my cap from my head, if I had not parried her off with my gun. The male does not act so openly. He supplies the female with food, as long as she is sitting or warming the young; but he proceeds in a very secret manner in performing the business. It is difficult to catch a glimpse of him when carrying food to his nest; and except at that time he is not to be seen at all. When the female of other birds of prey has been scared from her eyrie, and utters her anxious call, the male appears at once, joins her in her lamentations, and is ready to do all in his power to defend their progeny. The male of the sparrow-hawk behaves in a very different way. Let the female call ever so loudly and piteously, her mate will not make his appearance, at least so long as the young are not far advanced in growth. I am able to bear full testimony to the truth of this, having closely watched these birds near five different nests. It is only when the young are become larger, and the parents are obliged to make unusual exertions, that the male shows himself uncommonly active. He is then heard screaming about the eyrie, and seen carrying the prey to it. Four young ones, when nearly fledged, require a daily allowance of from sixteen to twenty small birds; and one or the other of the old birds arrives at the nest with food, at least once an hour, in case the neighbourhood abounds in such young birds as have lately left their nests; whereas before, the young were fed only once in two hours. Nay, if the female has been shot, the male makes double exertions, and will himself bring from twelve to fifteen birds daily."

"I know that the male of the reed-kite feeds his female whilst she is hatching, and assists her in rearing the young. This is also the case with the corn and meadow kite. It is remarkable how assiduously the females of the reed-kite are courted. I know an instance in which three males were shot near the same female in two days. The male of the corn-kite appears to take great delight in hovering over his sitting mate. If, in the month of June, we see a male of that species soaring much over one particular spot, we may be almost certain of finding the nest there, in corn, grass, or low bushes. While the young are being reared, the male of the kites hunts very eagerly and boldly, often till after sunset."

From the Genesee Farmer.

To cure Wounds on Horses and Cattle.

I became a subscriber at the commencement of the 3d volume of the Weekly Farmer, and in the first number of that volume, I found a recipe to cure wounds on horses and cattle, which alone has been worth more to me than ten years' subscription, and I think it would confer a favour on thy patrons to republish it in the present volume.

SILAS GAYLORD.

Skaneatcles, 7th mo. 26, 1839.

The following is the receipt alluded to in the above note of Mr. Gaylord:

As there are many useful receipts hidden from the public, for the sake of speculation in a small way, by many who would be thought something of in the world, I am induced to lay before the public a recipe for making *king of oil,* so called, which perhaps excels any other for cure of wounds on horses or cattle, and which has long been kept by a few only in the dark. Feeling a desire to contribute to the good of the public, but more especially to the farmers of Genesee, I send you the following very valuable recipe for publication:

1 oz. of green copperas, 2 do. white vitriol, 2 do. common salt, 2 do. linseed oil, 8 do. West India molasses.

Boil over a slow fire fifteen minutes in a pint of urine; when almost cold, add one ounce of oil of vitriol and four ounces spirits of turpentine.

Apply it to the wound with a quill or feather, which will immediately set the sore to running, and perform a perfect cure. Yours respectfully,

STEPHEN PALMER.

Middlebury, December 10, 1832.

London.—Population, including the environs attached, 1,610,868. Places of public worship 600, capable of seating 517,614 people. Three fifths of the seats only are ordinarily occupied, equal to 252,570.

For "The Friend."

MANUAL LABOUR SCHOOL.

Among the useful and valuable institutions to which the liberality and benevolence of our brethren on the other side of the Atlantic have given rise, the subjoined account of one in Ireland has interested me; and believing that institutions conducted on similar principles would be exceedingly valuable, in enabling Friends in many parts of this country to educate their children at a moderate cost, I send it for insertion in The Friend.

                                                                T. S.

In the year 1829, some Friends in Ireland, and a few from England, then on a religious visit to this country, were introduced into much feeling for the suffering and neglected condition of a large number of children, mostly residing in the province of Ulster, who were either the immediate or remote descendants of those who at various periods had forfeited their membership with the Society of Friends, chiefly by outgoing in marriage.

On attempting some enumeration of those who were thus circumstanced, there was found good reason to believe that there were not less than five hundred children, scattered over a pretty large district in Ulster, and a few in the other provinces, many of whose parents or relatives were either in indigence or in very low circumstances; and who, not being connected with any body of professing Christians, and very generally neglecting the attendance of any place of public worship, were both themselves and their offspring deprived of that oversight and care which most religious societies bestow in some measure upon their recognised members. In many cases their situation was found to be truly deplorable, and in several instances individuals had grown up to mature age in great ignorance. Families have been visited, no member of which could read, and many children were almost destitute of the very rudiments of learning. In some of these cases, notwithstanding that the claim to membership with Friends had long been forfeited, the parents still appeared desirous to be called by that name, and declined to unite with other professors.

To meet in some measure the immediate exigencies of this suffering class, subscriptions were raised for the purpose of providing clothing, and paying for the education at day schools of those whose cases were known, and whose necessities were considered most pressing; also for supplying their families with bibles and other religious books.

This partial measure of relief was found to be attended with benefit not only to the children, but to the parents, upon whose minds the friendly notice taken of their families had in some instances a favourable influence. It was evident however that there was necessity for much more to be done; and the fruits hitherto apparent furnished encouragement to pursue the object to a greater extent, and in a more complete manner, by providing an establishment wherein children of this class might be withdrawn from the hurtful association they were exposed to, and, together with

useful school learning, receive religious instruction, and be trained in habits of order and industry. The advantages of an agricultural school were so evident, that many Friends both in England and Ireland were disposed to contribute towards its foundation, which was further promoted by a liberal donation of £500 from Dr. Unthank, of Limerick. Sufficient funds were thus collected for the purchase of a small farm, called Brookfield, situated about five miles from Lisburn, on the road to Lurgan, containing about twenty-four English statute acres. An addition was built to the dwelling-house to fit it for the accommodation of about thirty children, and the Institution was opened in the Ninth month, 1836. A day school in addition was opened on the 1st of Fifth month, 1837.

The results of this undertaking, though still in its infancy, are highly satisfactory, and are calculated to encourage the extension of the present Institution, and to promote the foundation of similar establishments in other districts. It is thankfully believed that the Divine blessing has attended the persevering efforts of the superintendents and managers; the results of which are strikingly apparent in the conduct and deportment of the children. They regularly attend the meeting of Friends at Ballinderry, and are carefully brought up in a religious life and conversation. The boys receive with much readiness practical instruction in agriculture and gardening, and the girls in domestic and occasional out-door farming occupations; all are besides well taught in useful school learning. Their labour on the farm has materially contributed to the support of the Institution, the chief supply of provisions for the family being derived therefrom, besides which a considerable quantity of grain and other produce has been sold. The labour has been almost wholly performed by the boys during the past year. The culture of wheat by the spade has answered well, and they have also executed a considerable length of drains. A hired ploughman has occasionally been employed, but some of the boys have lately undertaken this service. The farm appears to have yielded a profit for the last twelve months of about £120, and the total average annual cost to the public for the maintenance, clothing, and education of the children does not appear much to exceed £5 each. The committee confidently expect that this cost may yet be reduced. For this purpose they are desirous to be put in a condition to purchase a further quantity of land, as the effective labour of the children, even at the present number, is considered fully competent to the management of a larger farm; hence there would be an obvious advantage, in point of the probable profit, if this object could be effected. Some funds are also required to provide suitable accommodation for the girls, whose present dormitory is quite too small. For these and some collateral objects, it is calculated that about £1000 may be wanted. But when it is considered that all which has hitherto been done only suffices to provide for a very small portion of the suffering class in question; that

on every vacancy which occurs many candidates for admission are necessarily disappointed; and that when once founded, a small annual sum will probably suffice for the maintenance and education of the pupils, it is hoped that way may open either for the extension of the present establishment, or the foundation of others in neighbouring districts; and that hence the liberality of those who may feel an interest in this concern will not be bounded by the immediate and pressing wants of the present Institution. There are not many objects to be assisted by a gift of money, which seem to promise more of good with so little mixture of any thing of a contrary nature.

In contrasting the present condition of the pupils at Brookfield with that in which they were before placed, there are many considerations gratifying to the philanthropist. The amount of individual good to the children is not to be undervalued, but even this appears only secondary to the important benefits to their families and connections; and it is hoped that the success of the plan, as demonstrating the value of combining agricultural labour with school instruction, both on moral and economical grounds, may have a salutary influence on society at large, by encouraging the application of the same principles in a more general way. Neither are we to overlook the advantage which may arise from a supply being provided of well trained young persons, qualified to enter into agricultural pursuits, either as farm servants or land stewards; or ultimately to undertake the management of land for themselves, applying it to the improved methods of modern husbandry, and the industry and skill which in some parts of Ireland are so lamentably wanting in the small landholders.

Fifth Month, 1839.

General Rules, for the government of Brookfield Agricultural School.

I. The object of this institution is to educate, in a manner consistent with the Christian principles of the Society of Friends, a number commensurate with its means, of children of persons in low circumstances, who may be descended from Friends though not in membership, and who are not brought up in connection with any other religious society; the boys to be instructed in husbandry or other handicraft employment, and the girls in domestic and out door labour suitable to their sex; in addition to such literary instruction as may contribute to their advantage and usefulness in after life. It is intended to be supported by donations and annual subscriptions, and by any sums of money paid for the education of the children, together with the profits arising from the farm and from the labour of the children.

II. It shall be under the control of the subscribers, and of thirty directors, members of the Society of Friends, ten of each quarterly meeting, six of whom, first named on the list, are to go out of office at the expiration of each year, and the vacancies thus caused, with any others that may occur by death or loss of membership, are to be filled up at the Annual General Meeting to be held as hereafter provided.

III. The directors and subscribers shall appoint six trustees, in whom the property of the Institution shall be vested.

IV. A general meeting of Directors and subscribers shall be annually held in Dublin, at some convenient time near the Yearly Meeting, by which vacancies in the list of Directors shall be filled up, and a committee of management, consisting of not less than twelve men and six women friends of the province of Ulster, shall be appointed, who shall be charged with the immediate care and management of the Institution for the ensuing year. The general meeting shall also appoint a treasurer and correspondents. A special general meeting may be convened at any time by the committee, or by any five of the directors.

V. A report of the state of the Institution, and a clear statement of its income, expenditure, and property shall be prepared by the committee, and laid before the general meeting every year.

VI. The committee shall meet at the school at stated times, as often as may be found necessary, and at such other times and places as they may appoint : three members shall be competent to transact business. They shall have power to appoint and dismiss the officers and servants of the Institution, and they shall draw on the treasurer for such sums of money as may be required for the current expenditure ; such orders to be signed by not less than two members of the committee. A record of their proceedings shall be kept, which is to be laid before each general meeting if called for.

VII. All applications for the admission of children shall be decided on by the committee, who may either grant admission gratuitously, or arrange with their parents or friends for the payment of such annual sum for their maintenance, clothing, and education, as under the circumstances of the case may in the judgment of the committee be proper.

VIII. The committee shall make such regulations as may appear necessary with regard to the manner in which children shall be recommended ; the ages at which they shall be eligible for admission and subject to removal ; the supplies of clothing, &c. with which they shall come provided ; and all other matters connected with the management of the Institution. They shall also frame a code of by-laws and advices, to regulate the conduct of the teachers and children, which shall be read or otherwise communicated to the members of the family, so as to put them fully in possession thereof ; and all by-laws and regulations of the committee, not inconsistent with the principles laid down in these General Rules, shall be valid unless disallowed by a general meeting of directors and subscribers duly convened.

IX. If any alteration in these rules be found necessary, such alteration shall be submitted to a general meeting of directors and subscribers duly convened, and shall be valid if approved thereby, and confirmed at a second

general meeting ; one of these general meetings to be the annual one.

X. If at any time hereafter the Yearly Meeting of Friends in Ireland shall think proper to assume the government and control of this Institution, it shall be surrendered thereto.

—

Report, &c.

At a general meeting of subscribers and friends to Brookfield Agricultural School, held in Dublin on the 4th of Fifth month, 1839.

A report from the managing committee and a statement of accounts were produced, which were highly satisfactory, and were directed to be printed and circulated, together with a statement of the origin and present prospects of the Institution, with the view of interesting Friends more generally in the object.

The subjects of increasing the accommodation for the girls, and of taking an additional quantity of land were considered, and both being fully approved of, the committee was authorised to have the required building erected, and land purchased as soon as there may be opportunity of doing so, and that the needful funds shall be placed at their disposal.

It is recommended that a liberal subscription be set on foot, in order to accomplish these objects, and to provide for the extension of the establishment, for which the success of the plan hitherto seems to offer much encouragement.

Report of the Committee.

The committee much pleasure in being able to give a satisfactory report of the state and progress of this institution during the past year.

Three boys and three girls have been admitted as boarders ; and two boys and three girls have left for situations in Friends' families. Twenty-five children (on an average) have attended as day scholars to receive instruction in school. James Mitten, one of the boys, has been bound an apprentice to the Institution, which will save a ploughman's wages.

The committee have to report the farm in good order, and much improved ; and the accounts will show a profit of £121 17 1½.

The committee request the particular attention of those interested in the welfare of this establishment to the absolute necessity of having more suitable accommodation for the girls, as that part of the old building which they now occupy is badly protected from the weather, and altogether unfit for the sleeping apartment of ten children. The opinion of an architect has been taken, who reports that it would be better and more economical to build an addition to the new house, than to make the necessary alteration in the old one; and that sufficient accommodation for the girls, with a dining hall, which is also much required, could be built for £300. The committee, however, having so small a sum in the hands of the treasurer, are reluctant to take any step further than to lay the subject before the general meeting.

The committee have every reason to believe that an addition to the farm would tend much to the increase of the funds, as the present number of boys in the school could cultivate considerably more ground.

Doctor Unthank has again kindly presented the school with £25, being the interest due on his donation, and also £25 for the express purpose of preparing a sleeping room for the girls.

The committee who were appointed to examine the children, report that their progress in the different branches of their education gave general satisfaction.

Signed on behalf of the committee,

JOHN G. RICHARDSON.

Belfast, 17th of Fourth Month, 1839.

Order of Occupation of the Children.

The children rise at five in the morning, and go to bed every night at nine, from the 1st of Third month to the 30th of Ninth month : in winter they do not rise so early. The family breakfast together about half past six, dine at half past twelve, and sup at half past seven in the evening. The children are allowed one hour in the morning for washing and recreation; at six o'clock they go into school, until called to breakfast; after breakfast a portion of Holy Scripture is read, and a time of silence ensues. They then return to school, and remain there till half past nine : the boys afterwards work in the fields until called to dinner. At one o'clock they go into school, and remain till four ; the day scholars are then dismissed, and the boys return to their field-work until seven, when they prepare for supper ; the rest of the evening is spent in recreation, or in gardening for their own amusement.

—

For "The Friend."

THOMAS RAYLTON.

Recently meeting with an interesting account of the early convictions of truth upon the mind of Thomas Raylton, of London, I send it to the editor of "The Friend." It was found after his decease in his own handwriting, and, though simple, exhibits the gradual openings of the good Shepherd to an honest heart, which as they are faithfully obeyed, prepare for the reception of greater light, and lead to an establishment in the truth as it is in Jesus.

"I was born on the 30th of the sixth month, 1671, at Bowes, in the north part of Yorkshire, and educated in the way of the church of England. In the year 1685, being about 14 years of age, and a scholar with the priest of the parish and teacher of the free school in Bowes, it providentially happened that by the invitation of one called a Quaker, at whose house a meeting was kept, about two miles from my abode, my mother went to a meeting there and took me to ride before her. John Bowron and George Rook, two ministers, being come to visit Friends thereaway, were at the meeting, by whose powerful ministry and lively prayer, it pleased God to open my heart, and to let me see the vanity of this present world, of which for my short time I had had some share, and for which I had often been secretly smitten by the just witness for God in my own heart. For all that I was pretty much a stranger to it and was not sensible from whence it came, until I was affected with the gospel, which I may say was glad tidings to me.

"From that day I joined in heart with that people who directed to Christ within, the hope of their glory. And although I have had many instructers in Christ since, yet I have not many fathers, for George Rook, who preached the gospel of Jesus Christ, was the instrument under the Lord of my convincement, for which I bow my knees and worship, and thank the Lord for his goodness hitherto.

"After I joined this people the word of God wrought more powerfully in me, and showed me that I was to alter the course of my conversation; that was, to leave the corrupt life and to shun evil company. For as I was bowed before the Lord, and had given up my name to serve him, I then saw that I must walk in the narrow way, and leave the vain compliments, the putting off the hat, and bowing the knee to man, &c. I was soon taken notice of and complaint made to my mother, for my neglecting to conform to these things, by the priest who was moved at my behaviour, and I suppose intended to have used the rod. Having made preparation he called me to him and said, I heard to-day thou wentest by Mr. Boonskell and didst not put off thy hat and bid good morrow. What is thy reason for so doing? Whether is it pride or religion? I told him it was not pride. Then, he said, it must be religion, and if so thou must not be religion, and laid down the rod. If for religion, he said, let me know why thou refusedst, and give me some precedent. I told him I had been reading in the Revelations, and there I found that an angel showed John many things; and John said, 'When I had heard and seen, I fell down to worship the angel that showed me these things.' But the angel said, 'See thou do it not, for I am of thy fellow servants, and of thy brethren the prophets, and of them which keep the sayings of this book; worship God.' And for this I told him I refused to do it unto men. But he endeavoured to persuade me, that what he requested of me, was no more than a civil respect between man and man, and from thence he thought I might the better conform to it. To make me the more willing to believe it was no worship, but respect, he referred me to the children of Heth and Abraham's bowing to each other, and also something of the like kind in the time of Moses and Joshua; but all these were to no purpose to me, for my eye was opened to see a more glorious dispensation than that of Moses or the prophets. For though by the Spirit of Christ in them, they foretold the coming and sufferings of Christ, yet they did not live to see those things come to pass which they spoke of; so that he had no force in his argument to make me use these things which might be used among the fathers and under the law. And since the New Testament is silent, and gives no account of either

Christ or his apostles bowing, I did not see why either knee or hat should be expected of me; therefore I stood to my principle, and kept to the light and understanding the Lord had given me through Jesus Christ my Saviour, who then was come to my house in spirit, and had brought salvation with him.

"That day I said to one of my schoolfellows, that what my master had shown me was out of the law and not the gospel, which he told my master, and I had a quiet day. This was but the beginning of further exercise, for he began to be more severe, and told me that unless I would make congees to him, as he called them, he would teach me no longer. I would gladly have learned a little more, yet perceiving it was in a way which I must bear testimony against, I forsook the school at that time and went home and told my mother the occasion of my return. Although she had taken me to the first meeting a few weeks before, she now repented it, and would not listen to me so as to give me any relief, upon which I left the house for a while. But I think I may say the arm of the Lord wrought for me, for my master soon sent word to my mother, that he had done what he could to persuade me to conform; but he saw it would not do; therefore he desired her to send me again to the school, and he would leave me to my liberty about religion. The tidings brought me while I was sitting under a hedge where I was retired, I received gladly, not then knowing what would become of me, nor with whom to lodge. I went to school again, and found it much as had been told me, and that the Lord pleaded my innocent cause, to whom be glory ascribed for ever."

The example of this lad in adhering faithfully to the testimony which the truth required of him, is worthy of the observation of young and old at this day. His obedience to his Saviour's command prepared him to bear further trial, and he was called on to manifest his sense of the emptiness of formal "closet prayer," and its incompatibility with the nature of that communion and worship which is only in "Spirit and in truth."

"Thus far I was got on my way and was still to go farther. My parents had taught us from our childhood, to ask of them to pray to God to bless us, and though it is true there is not an evil in the thing itself, yet the bringing of it into such a form, as to use it every night and morning, this also I found was my place to leave off; at which they were much offended, and began to beat me into a compliance with them, but that would not do, for I read that saying of our Lord, 'Whosoever loveth father or mother more than me, is not worthy of me.' So that in a holy resolution I went on, not doubting the Lord would help me over that as he had over other things before. The course I took, after much threatening and several beatings, was this: I left my father's house, and was kept privately about fifteen days. As Moses by the good providence of God, and care of his sister, who watched to see what would become of him, was ordered to his mother again to be his

nurse, so was I watched over by some of those people, to whom I was joined in fellowship, and invited by them to come to one of their meetings, being then remote from it, yet at their request I went. They were precious to me, having been at but two since the first, which was about three fourths of a year. A good meeting this proved, and some of the Friends undertook to go and offer me to my father. I went with them and they told him it was their desire he should take me home again as I was his son; if he would not accept me as a son, then as a servant in his house, but if he would do neither, then he becomes our care, forasmuch as he has become one of us. This proposition took such place with my parents, that the Friends were thanked for the care they had over me. I was now at home again and had free access to their presence morning and evening without insisting upon the ceremony, yet they were loath one of their children should leave their religion. After this I went to meetings with their knowledge, and in about seven weeks, went apprentice to a Friend, by the approbation of my parents, being conducted thither by my father.

"In my seven years' apprenticeship to the trade of a blacksmith, at leisure times, I often read the Scriptures of the Old and New Testaments, in which I found great benefit, being often broken into tears, especially when I met with places that mention the call of God to sinners, and their return to his call for their conversion and salvation. My delight was also in places which prophesied of the coming of the Just One and of the work of restoration which he should bring to pass. Though I delighted in these things, yet the crown of my rejoicing was, that I was counted worthy to know this blessed work begun. I did not only read in private, but in the family; we used to read much by candle-light, my master and mistress allowing it, and were in the practice themselves, being honest Friends who feared God, with all their children. These were dutiful to their parents, and kept very much out of the evil communication of the world, so that we were a comfort to one another, as we kept to that which was good. When I have been alone at my work the Lord did very often comfort me with his Holy Spirit, and gave me a sight, that he would give me a dispensation of the gospel to preach. For seven years the word of the Lord was often very powerful in my heart, not only to the fitting of me for so great a work, but growing upon me to the affecting of my heart, and during these years living breathings often ran through me to the Lord, that he would preserve me in his fear.

"After I had served my apprenticeship, I went to the place of my birth, and there followed my trade about a year. It was not long before the Lord brought nearer the work of the ministry which I had seen before me; and the nearer it came to me I still saw the more need to be weighty and solid, and much inward in spirit, often filled with the word of God, so that I could scarcely hold my peace in the assemblies of the people of God. Yet I was much inward and still, often remembering the building of Solomon's temple, where there was not the sound of a hammer or iron tool; and in this quietness in meetings I was greatly refreshed and filled with inward joy to the Lord, but could not yet utter by words what I felt. For, indeed, as the ministry is a great work, it made me the more cautious how I entered into it, remembering it was not approved that one of old laid hold of the ark when it was shaken. I found it safe not to appear in the ministry until I was fully satisfied of the Lord's requirings therein, although he had been often with me from meeting to meeting, and left his holy dew upon my spirit; thus was I filled with the odour of his ointment, with which I was anointed to preach the gospel, and thus led into the ministry."

How important it is that Friends should steadfastly keep to this ground in their appearances in the ministry, not only in the commencement, but as they advance in years. No man's talents or acquirements, no worldly distinction or reputation will serve as a substitute. However plausible the representation may be, it will not deceive nor satisfy the attentive, devoted soul, that hungers after the true bread which cometh down from heaven, and can alone nourish up into everlasting life. We may abound with doctrinal disquisitions, urged by the sagacity and contrivance of man, and apparently supported by the text of Holy Scripture; but if it is not afresh brought out of the treasury by him who only hath the key of David, it will be little better than the manna that bred worms, from which the quickened mind will turn with sorrow and disgust.

"In 1695, being at a meeting at John Bowron's, after a little time my soul was divinely touched with the power of God, and his word was again in my heart, as a burning fire in my bones, and I could then no longer contain; my tongue being loosed, my mouth was opened to speak of the Lord to his people in that meeting. I cannot but observe one thing, and that was the holy silence which was in the fore part of that meeting, before my mouth was opened, although several were there who had public testimonies; yet that power by which I was opened bound them to silence. But after I had spoken, there stood up a Friend, and he was like one who had a seal to set to the words I had delivered."

Thomas Raylton, after I had travelled much in the service of truth, settled in London about the year 1705, where he was very serviceable and edifying in his ministry, sound in his doctrine, mighty in the Holy Scriptures, zealous for the truth, and a faithful reprover of any undue liberty in the professors of it. In his last sickness he bore his pain with great patience and resignation. A few days before his death, he told a friend that he had settled his affairs, being satisfied that his departure was at hand, adding, in a humble manner, "Doubtless it will be a glorious change to me." To his wife he said, "My dear, be easy; let me go, and rejoice when I am gone to so great salvation." He departed the 6th of the 10th month, 1723, in the 53d year of his age, in peace and full assurance of endless happiness.

For "The Friend."

OPERA HOUSE MEETING.

I regret much to see it stated in the public papers that "a meeting of some of our *most respectable citizens* was held, to consider the project of erecting an opera house," and that "it will not be denied that a house devoted to operatic performances is much needed in this city." I feel no hesitation whatever in saying, that it is not only not needed, but that in proportion to the increase of such establishments, vice and immorality, and an increased laxity in relation to the obligations of worship and reverence to our Almighty Creator and Benefactor will be promoted by them. What can we expect from the exhibitions of play-actors, who are enemies of holiness and righteousness, but that licentiousness and depravity must be the results of their example, and the poisonous, debasing principles which their public shows inculcate. Was it necessary to say, that "some of our most respectable citizens" had originated this scheme of vice, to disguise the danger, and to lull the fears and apprehensions that might arise in the minds of the conscientiously scrupulous part of the community. I confess that my feelings are mournful at seeing connected with such a project the names of church-going individuals, who, I suppose, have either themselves made the vow, or for whom their sponsors have made it, that they will renounce "the pomps and vanities of this wicked world." They are surely objects for the care and discipline of their churches and their pastors. And an excellent employment would it be for Christians of all denominations to be looking after their own conduct and that of their respective church members, endeavouring to exert a salutary influence that would frown down vice and immorality, and every thing that gives birth to it. Were this really and generally the religious care and concern of all the active high-professing members of the different societies, Christians would no more think of erecting a play house, than they would a work shop for satan. Those who countenance this project are hostile to the Redeemer's kingdom, and the more conspicuous their characters as professors of religion, the more ground they give its enemies to vaunt over it, and encouragement to the young people to throw aside its restraints. Every religious periodical should protest against theatrical entertainments, and the feats of jugglers and mountebanks, exhibitions which are increasing in our city, and will degrade its character in the view of sober, religious persons, while they gradually, yet certainly deteriorate the manners and principles of its inhabitants. Z.

A VISIT TO PITCAIRN'S ISLAND.

The subjoined narrative is copied from a British periodical, the Mirror for 1838; in which it is given as an extract from "The Voyage of her Majesty's Ship Actæon, Capt. Lord W. Russel." The columns of "The Friend," it may be recollected, contain several notices relative to this interesting island;

—the present account applies to a period more recent by several years than our latest inserted in vol. xi.

We made Pitcairn's Island on the 10th, the weather squally, and the wind strong from the northward. This, and the following day, were so squally, and the sea ran so very high, that we were nearly bearing up for Valparaiso, as we could not work to windward: but fortunately on the 12th, the wind moderated, and our captain landed. Three canoes came off to the ship, through a very heavy surf. In these were Edward, John, Matthew, and Arthur Quintal, George Adams, and Charles Christian. Edward Quintal brought a note from Mr. Hill, which he delivered in due form. Mr. Hill was the man that had imposed upon the simple natives, by making them believe he was sent out by the English government to take charge of them, and look after their morals. They, never being accustomed to any deceits of this kind, placed implicit reliance in all he said. The consequence was that he became their ruler, and at length acquired such power over them, that he could make them do any thing he wished; although latterly they obeyed him more from fear than any admiration of his good qualities. We had heard of this man at Valparaiso, and consequently were very much prejudiced against him, and, as it turned out, most deservedly so. Mr. Buffett, whom Captain Beechey speaks of in his work, and to whom he gives an excellent character, was a passenger with us from Valparaiso. He had been long resident at Pitcairn's Island as a schoolmaster, and was much liked; but having a numerous family, was obliged to discontinue his services. This man was flogged by Edward Quintal, (Mr. Hill's right-hand man,) at his suggestion, for some trivial reason, and in consequence was obliged to leave, his wife and family remaining behind. His life even was considered unsafe. Things were in this state when we arrived, bringing back Mr. Buffett from his place of exile. We were heartily welcomed by all the island.

The inhabitants amount to ninety-two, the greater proportion of them being Quintals. Lord Edward Russell landed on the 12th; and having assembled all the people to hear the different causes of complaint, gave judgment against Mr. Hill, telling the natives who he was, and that he had no longer any power over them; also giving him to understand that he must leave the island by the first opportunity. Mr. Buffett was kindly received by his old friends, and found his family and children well. Mr. Hobbs, another Englishman, was elected schoolmaster, by the general voice.

Bounty Bay, so called from the place where the mutineers landed, and where the Bounty was destroyed, is where ships lay off and communicate with the shore. Canoes came off with stock and refreshments, it being impossible for boats to bring such things without much danger. The productions are cocoa-nuts, bananas, sweet potatoes, and yams, which are cultivated by the inhabitants, and of a superior quality ; also water melons, and excellent tobacco. Wild goats and poultry are pientiful, and the island is covered with verdure. They are obliged to work very hard at their yam beds, at certain seasons of the year, and, in consequence, are a strong, hardy race, well made, tall, and active, and very expert in the management of their canoes. The women are handsome, and above the common height, particularly strong and nimble. Their houses are well built, clean, and comfortable ; and, in every respect, this little community cannot but claim the admiration of every impartial and unprejudiced person, who, taking into consideration their fathers' crimes, would otherwise look upon them with no very favourable eye. We brought for their use a great quantity of kettles, fishing lines, and hooks, knives and forks, and clothing, all of which they were much in want of.

All the mutineers of the Bounty are dead. John Adams, the last survivor, died about five years ago. The wives of Christian and Adams alone remain out of the first generation. They are natives of Tahiti, and very old, being nearly eighty-seven, but still strong and active, which proves the salubrity of the climate. Mrs. Christian recollects Captain Cook in his first voyage, and showed a very great respect for him. There were several small remnants of the Bounty left, such as pieces of copper, and some parts of the different bulk-heads, also the keys of her store-rooms ; all of which were eagerly seized, and, as may be imagined, prized very much. We were astonished at the intelligence and quickness of the reply to any question we put to most of these people. They went through the kings of England without a mistake ; knew perfectly well all the reigning monarchs of Europe, and leading men of our own country, which made them doubly interesting to us. To find a race of men, inhabitants of one of the South Sea islands, speaking our own language, and following our customs, could not fail to interest us all ; and, when we see they have been brought up in every thing that is good and proper, that as yet no immorality has crept in among them, and every sin is abhorred, and they continue to live in all simplicity and truth, we are, at once, disarmed of every ill-feeling arising from a reflection on the manner in which they came thither, and forget the crimes of their fathers. No doubt appears to remain that Pitcairn's Island was inhabited a considerable time previous to the arrival of the Bounty. Stone hatchets, and other implements of war, have been found buried in the soil; also the remains of several morais, or burial places. This proves that people of some description once lived there, and were either driven away, or left it for some more convenient spot.

Familiarity with works of fiction; even such as are not exceptionable in themselves, relaxes the mind that wants hardening, dissolves the heart which wants fortifying, stirs the imagination which wants quieting, irritates the passions which want calming, and above all, disinclines and disqualifies for active virtues and for spiritual exercises.—*H. Moore.*

He that takes his full liberty in what he may, shall repent him: how much more in what he should not? I never read of Christian that repented him of too little worldly delight. The surest course I have still found in all earthly pleasures, to rise with an appetite, and to be satisfied with a little.—*Bishop Hall.*

They, who once engage in iniquitous designs, miserably deceive themselves, when they think that they will go so far, and no further ; one fault begets another; one crime renders another necessary ; and thus they are impelled, continually downward into a depth of guilt, which, at the commencement of their career, they would have died rather than have incurred.—*Southey.*

THE FRIEND.

ELEVENTH MONTH, 16, 1839.

From the limited nature of the information we have received respecting the late Yearly Meeting at Baltimore, our notice of it must necessarily be brief. It commenced on second day, the 28th ult., preceded, as usual, by the meeting of ministers and elders on seventh day, the 26th. A considerable number of Friends, including several in the ministry, were present from other Yearly Meetings. The deliberations upon the various interesting concerns which engaged attention, were conducted harmoniously and with brotherly love. Among these was that of the company of Indian natives, for many years under the care of this and the Yearly Meetings of Ohio and Indiana, and who have been removed to a location west of the Mississippi ; a further sum of money was directed to be raised in aid of the fund appropriated for their benefit. Another subject which occupied the meeting was the establishment of a new Quarterly Meeting at Dunning's creek, to be composed of the Monthly Meeting held at that place, and of that at Bellfont, and to be called Dunning's creek Quarterly Meeting. The proposition was agreed to, and a committee appointed to superintend the opening of the meeting. The Yearly Meeting concluded satisfactorily on the afternoon of fifth day, the 31st.

It is with pleasure we comply with a request to insert the following notice. The subject of the proposed lectures is of general interest, and susceptible of being rendered highly pleasing and instructive, and we therefore anticipate for our young people an intellectual treat.

FRIENDS' READING ROOMS.

A manager of the Reading Room Association will deliver two lectures on Carburetted Hydrogen Gas as it exists in nature and as prepared artificially for the purposes of illumination. The first on third day evening, the 19th instant, at 7½ o'clock.

J. G. W. did not reach us till the paper was made up. His communication will appear next week.

INSTITUTE FOR COLOURED YOUTH.

A suitably qualified Friend is wanted to take charge of the farm and family of this institution. Application may be made to
BENJAMIN COOPER, near Camden, N. J.
THOMAS WISTAR, Jr., Abington.
JOSEPH SCATTERGOOD, No. 14 Minor st. or
MARMADUKE C. COPE, 286 Filbert st.

A TEACHER WANTED,

At Newtown, N. J., to take charge of Friends' school. Apply to
BENJAMIN COOPER,
JOHN M. KAIGHN,
JOSEPH B. COOPER.

COAL.

Schuylkill, Lehigh, Hazleton, and Laurel Hill Coal for sale by George W. Taylor, at the office of " The Friend."

HAVERFORD SCHOOL.

WANTED, a Friend to act as Steward of this Institution. Apply to
KIMBER & SHARPLESS,
No. 8 South Fourth street.

Agency.

Nathan Breed, Weare, N. H., is appointed agent instead of Moses Gove, Jr., resigned.

DIED, on the 16th ult., in the 81st year of his age, JEREMIAH WILLITS, late a member and elder of Dansfield meeting, New Jersey. In the early part of life his mind was brought under religious exercise on account of his soul's salvation, and strong desires raised that he might so live as to be prepared for death. He was strengthened to put away many wrong things, and through divine assistance to walk with circumspection and care, and was early appointed to the offices of overseer and elder in the Society of Friends. He was a hospitable and cheerful entertainer of his friends, particularly of those who went forth on gospel errands, counting it a privilege to receive them under his roof. He was spared the affliction of much bodily pain, and in a very quiet and peaceful state of mind drew his last breath so gently, that his attendants were not aware when his immortal spirit took its flight to another and better world.

—— at his residence, Spiceland, Indiana, on the 24th of 9th month last, JOSEPH B. HUNT, in the 33d year of his age, after an illness of about four weeks, which he bore with a remarkable degree of patience and Christian resignation. He emigrated to this country from Bordentown, New Jersey, about the year 1828, and remained to the close of life, firmly attached to the doctrines and testimonies of the Society of Friends, as was evinced by the lively interest he manifested for their promotion. He died much lamented by his family and friends, who, notwithstanding their sorrow for the loss of so valuable a member of society, rejoice in believing that through the mercy and merits of Him whom he desired to serve, his spirit was sweetly prepared for the mansions of everlasting bliss.

PRINTED BY ADAM WALDIE,
Carpenter Street, below Seventh, Philadelphia.

THE FRIEND.

A RELIGIOUS AND LITERARY JOURNAL.

VOL. XIII.   SEVENTH DAY, ELEVENTH MONTH, 23, 1839.   **NO. 8.**

EDITED BY ROBERT SMITH.

PUBLISHED WEEKLY.

Price two dollars per annum, payable in advance.

Subscriptions and Payments received by

GEORGE W. TAYLOR,

NO. 50, NORTH FOURTH STREET, UP STAIRS,

PHILADELPHIA.

For "The Friend."

Remarks on the study of the Greek and Latin languages, suggested by the perusal of Dymond's Chapter on Intellectual Education.

Few persons, we are persuaded, entertain a more sincere respect for the author of the "Essays on the Principles of Morality" than ourselves. His writings as a whole, we think, possess no ordinary merit. Many, perhaps most of them, may be regarded as models of reasoning. His style is clear, free, and vigorous, and his logic, in general, remarkably correct. He appears, moreover, to have in rather an unusual degree the additional excellence of an earnest desire after truth. But as no man, however great may be his abilities, industry, and love of truth, can attain entire correctness in all his opinions, we ought not to be surprised to find that the mind of Dymond, though eminently judicious and enlightened on most subjects, is not always exempt from mistaken views. Some of these it is our intention to notice in the subsequent remarks. We are the more desirous to do so, because when a writer of high reputation adopts erroneous opinions, he does an injury to society proportioned to his influence, and therefore, the greater his celebrity, the greater is the importance of pointing out his errors. Before, however, proceeding to speak particularly of what we regard as the defects of the author before us, it is but justice to his memory to state, that a little before his death he considered no part of his writings fully prepared for publication. If indeed we take into view the disadvantages and difficulties under which he pursued his literary labours, we shall be led to wonder, not that he has sometimes fallen into errors, but that he has been, on the whole, so successful in avoiding them. But though his errors be few, it is not on that account the less needful to notice them, since, as has been already intimated, the general reputation which an author may possess for sound judgment and correct reasoning, can hardly fail to give authority to his views, even when erroneous.

In the commencement of his chapter on intellectual education, he observes, very justly, in the words of Playfair, that "education consists in learning what makes a man useful, respectable, and happy, in the line for which he is destined." He then asserts, we know not on what authority, that very little assistance can be derived from ancient learning towards discharging the duties of a parent or citizen of the state. It is much to be regretted that he has not stated more fully the reasons which led him to this conclusion. He says, indeed, in general terms, that the grounds on which he objects to the classics are, that they occupy time which might be more beneficially employed. But this is begging the question. It is asserting, without proof, the very point in dispute. And it is the very reverse position that we hope we shall be able to prove, viz.: that in obtaining such an education as is calculated to render a man useful, respectable, and happy, a portion of the time cannot be more beneficially employed, than by devoting it to the study of Greek and Latin.

It is a very prevalent idea, and one it would seem that Dymond himself entertained, that the chief advantage which can be derived from learning these languages, is merely to be able to read the ancient authors in the original, and translate those quotations which occur so frequently in the works of many of the English writers. But though this is a great convenience, and may be a source of much satisfaction and pleasure, it constitutes by no means the principal benefit which results from those studies when judiciously pursued. Their great utility, in our estimation, arises from the fact, *that by devoting a considerable share of our time to the Latin and Greek languages, we shall be able to acquire a thorough knowledge of our own more speedily, than if the latter should receive our exclusive attention.* This statement may, at first view, appear incredible, but we trust that an impartial and thorough examination of the subject, will convince every one that it is founded in truth. Let those who would satisfy themselves on this point, take up Webster's Dictionary, and observe what proportion of our words are derived from the Latin and Greek, either directly, or through the medium of some modern language. By carefully

looking over a few pages in different parts of the work, they will be enabled to form an estimate of the whole sufficiently accurate for their purpose, and they will find (if we are not mistaken) that the ancient tongues have given origin to about three fifths of our words. If they observe a little further, they will perceive that these include almost all the uncommon words of our language, and those which, on account of their length, are the most difficult to be remembered. As the greater part of these words are compound, an acquaintance with Latin and Greek is of the utmost advantage in giving a knowledge of their signification, since by learning the meaning of a comparatively few primitive words, we shall be enabled to determine that of an immense multitude of compound ones derived from these primitives. Thus when a scholar knows that CON, or COM, signifies *together*, DE, *down*, EX, *out*, or *forth*, RE, *back*, or *again*, and that *positum* signifies to *put*, or *act*, he readily learns that *compose*, means to *put together*, *depose*, to *put down*, *expose*, to *place out*, or *set forth*, and *reposite*, *to replace*, and that *composition is the act of putting together*, *exposition*, *that of setting forth*, or *explaining*, &c. Now if he learns one new word, for example *tractum*, *to draw*, he not only knows the meaning of *traction*, the act of drawing, but also the compounds formed with this word and the above particles, as *contract*, *to draw together*, *detract*, *to draw down*, (i. e. to *lower*) *extract*, *to draw out*, and *retract*, *to draw back*. In like manner from *pressum*, *to press*, he derives the words *compress*, *depress*, *express*, and *repress*. Examples of this kind might be multiplied almost infinitely, but we trust these will be sufficient to illustrate our meaning. It will readily be seen that the Latin student has but to learn the primitives, and he not only knows the English words derived from these primitives, (as *pressure*, from *pressum*, *position*, from *positum*,) but with scarcely burdening his memory any further, he becomes acquainted with all their compounds; while the mere English scholar is obliged to learn the compounds, as he learns the primitives; if there is any difference, he finds the former more difficult to remember, because they are composed of a greater number of syllables. So that, if we may be allowed the metaphor, the classical scholar can gather up his knowledge in the sheaf, while he who studies English alone, is doomed to the tedious labour of gleaning it ear by ear.

---

* It may be proper to call the reader's attention to the circumstance, that when several words from a common root occur together in the Dictionary, (the octave is referred to,) the principal one only is marked with an abreviation to indicate its origin, as L. for Latin, Gr. for Greek, &c. So that, were we to count none but those which are thus designated, we should probably omit four fifths. It may further be observed, that many words are given by Webster as coming from the French or Italian, when they might with equal or greater propriety be traced directly to the fountain-head—the Latin, or Greek. Thus he derives *generosity* from the French *générosité*, without mentioning the Latin *generositas*, the common origin of both the former words. Many similar examples might be adduced.

e correct-
st, that in
cessary to
re are no
y, that the
ways cor-
f the Latin
rived. In
y remark,
in the an-
one in our
h occur in
ldom, and
e common
any which
istantly to
ge. We
mmending
be under-
rticularly,
g a liberal
dge of the
necessary.
re peculiar
words in
st a slight
names of
ly adopted
alteration
es will in-
words from
derivatives
language
ing or dis-
sed in the
constitut-
language.
cessary nor
vords from
is not our
course of
ge; but as
zing mate-
hink it the
f it as we
naturalists
per to de-
Greek, and
ns is indis-
he question
ly formed,
convenient-
e of time,
swer, that
number of
distant re-
ion of the
ivative, we
ly rare in
ill not en-
he English
light upon
ence it is
y essential,
the syno-
moreover be
I does not
ent signifi-
prevailed
ory. Any
he writings
iled to ob-

serve this circumstance. The common translation of the Bible furnishes numerous examples of the same. Thus in the English version
of the New Testament, for the word "*honest,*"
we ought generally to understand *honourable,*
(see Phil. iv. 8. Acts vi. 3, &c.,) which
agrees with the original *honestus;* "*conversation,*" like the Latin *conversatio,* usually
signifies *intercourse,* or *manner of living in
relation to the world around us.* We may
instance the passage, "Let your conversation
be without covetousness" (Heb. xiii. 5. See
also, 1 Peter iii. 16.) Where the Psalmist
speaks of preventing the dawn with his prayer, (Psalm cxix. v.147,) the word "*prevent*"
evidently has a meaning nearly corresponding
with the Latin *præventum, to come before,* or
to anticipate.

(To be continued.)

For "The Friend."

PERSIA.

The researches of modern travellers have
disclosed to us along the course of the Euphrates and the Tigris, and in the deserted
regions beyond, the existence of mighty ruins
of the highest historical importance. The
grandeur of the Persian monarchy had scarcely faded at the time of its downfall; its wealth
and 'luxury were then at their height, and
Alexander held his riotous banquetings in the
royal palace of Persepolis, which had been
embellished by the labours of successive sovereigns, from the first to the last Darius,
until it had become the most magnificent in
all Asia. The Greeks, in a fit of drunken
delirium, gave this palace to the flames; and
though the conflagration took place nearly
2,200 years ago, the blasted ruins still remain, to tell the story of Persian grandeur,
and to guide the researches of the historian.

In the same parallel of latitude with the
head of the Persian Gulf, nearly 250 miles
east of the mouth of the Euphrates, and about
50 miles southeast of the city of Shiraz, the
traveller enters upon an extensive but somewhat winding plain, which bears the name of
Merdasht in its southern and of Mourghaub
in its northern portion, and which extends a
distance, from southwest to northeast, of between 50 and 60 miles. The whole extent of
this plain is strewed with the ruins of the first
and of the last of the Persian empires, and of
the caliphate. It is only in those of the ancient empire of Persia, however, that I wish
to interest the readers of "The Friend." The
remains which belong to that period consist
of an extensive palace, called Chehl Menar,
or the Forty Pillars, and two great sepulchral
monuments in the plain of Merdasht, at Persepolis, and of four sepulchres five miles distant to the northward, and of the ruins of Pa-
sargada in the plains of Mourghaub, about 45
miles still farther to the northeast.

The buildings at Chehl Menar are situated
at the foot of a crescent shaped chain of rocks
of the most beautiful gray marble, and are
constructed on a platform partly hewn out of
the rock, and facing the west, and partly
formed of enormous blocks of marble, so accurately fitted to each other, without lime or

cement, that it is often difficult to detect their
junctures. The platform which is thus constructed is 1425 feet long by 800 in depth.
It is thrown into three distinct terraces, the
main passages to which are by marble stair-
cases, of a grade and breadth that admit ten
horses to ascend them abreast. The main
platform must have been originally from 30
to 60 feet above the natural surface of the
ground beneath. The buildings which stood
upon this first terrace have disappeared, except four pilasters and four columns of a portico. The pilasters are sculptured with fabulous animals of a colossal size, that appear
like sentinels, and have no doubt a mythological meaning.

On the second terrace the first ruins that
meet the eye are four colonnades, consisting
of 72 fluted pillars, that must have formed a
columned hall with wings; they were from
45 to 50 feet high and 16 or 18 feet in circumference. A considerable number of them
still remain standing, and are altogether peculiar in the style of their architecture, which
is unlike any thing found in India, or Egypt,
or Greece. Their capitals are formed of the
heads of horses, placed back to back, so as to
form a hollow for the reception of the rafters
which supported the flat roof of the building.
These colonnades led to several edifices, portions of the walls and door-ways and windows
of which are still standing, so as to show that
the platform was the site of many separate
buildings of the utmost magnificence, forming
portions of one great plan.

The particular purpose of each is designated by the sculptures with which the walls of
the several terraces, with their stair-ways,
and the portals and windows, and huge blocks
of marble still standing, are decorated. These
represent all the strict and solemn ceremonials
of a Persian court with a fulness of circumstantial detail that renders the whole not only
intelligible, but highly instructive. On the principal stairway which conducts to the columned
hall of which I have spoken, are sculptured
the figures of the Median and Persian guards,
processions of ambassadors, deputies from the
various satrapies bringing their presents and
tributes; combats of monstrous animals, emblematic of the strength and power of the
Persian monarchy, and the sovereign seated
in state to receive the homage of his subjects.
In the wall itself there are marks around the
bases of certain of the columns which prove
that an elevated floor or dais occupied the
central space. There can be no doubt that
here was the great hall of audience of the
monarchs of the dynasty of Cyrus. The roof
was of wood, probably of cedar, and the
chamber of audience curtained round with
drapery, exactly as described in the book of
Esther, for there are no traces of a surrounding wall.

In the rear of this noble colonnade, at the
distance of 300 feet directly to the south, are
the remains of a building which was evidently the royal residence. It has numerous apartments surrounding a large central hall, and
walls covered with sculptures representing all
the various preparations for a banquet. On
another part of the terrace are the remains of

a large hall, more than 200 feet square, with a noble portico and portal at a distance, forming a grand approach, and constituting, if we may judge from the sculptures and decorations, the great hall of judgment. Between this and the royal residence stands a small building, evidently, from its sculptures and structure, appropriated to the private devotions of the monarch. Other buildings are scattered over various parts of the terraces in too ruinous a state to afford any clue to their destination. Between the hall of columns and the royal residence is a vacant space of 250 by 300 feet. This space is a confused mass of ruins that has assumed the appearance of grassy mounds, in which no trace of architectural form can be distinguished. There seems no reason to doubt that here stood the very banqueting room which the Macedonian in his drunken revels destroyed, and that in the efforts to extinguish the flames and save the surrounding buildings, the walls were battered in, and the whole left as it is to this day, a ruinous heap.

What reflections crowd upon the mind at this wonderful identification of the spot of some of the most interesting scenes in antiquity! It was on these platforms, or amidst these walls and columns, that Cyrus and Darius and Xerxes, Artaxerxes and Ahasuerus, received the homage of a subject world. It was here, perhaps, that Queen Esther triumphed over the enemies of her race; and from this spot went forth the decree for rebuilding the temple of the true God.

At the distance of 400 feet from the most eastern of these buildings, at a considerable height in the almost inaccessible side of the mountain, are two rock hewn edifices of a very remarkable character. They are exactly similar to four others which occur about five or six miles to the north of Persepolis, at the ruins called Nashti Roustam, or the mountain of Sepulchres. The face of the mountain at the latter place is an almost perpendicular cliff of white marble, nearly 900 feet high, in which have been excavated the tombs of the Persian monarchs. The lowest of them is at an elevation of not less than sixty feet. Its facade is two stories in height, the lower of which exhibits only a false entrance, while the upper, which is the entrance to the narrow chamber, designed for the coffin, is sculptured into columns, and ornamented with figures, evidently emblematic of the religious belief of the ancient Persians, and relating to the deceased monarch. There can be no doubt that they are the works of the age of Cyrus and Darius, and that one of them, probably that of Persepolis, is the tomb of Darius Hystaspes himself. Diodorus Siculus says, that about 400 feet eastward of the city of Persepolis is a mountain called the King's mountain, in which the graves of the kings are situated. "The rock there," says he, "is hewn into a multitude of chambers, which are not to be approached by any entrances made by art; but the coffins are wound up and introduced into the receptacle by means of machines." It is also related by Ctesias that Darius commanded a tomb to be prepared for himself, during his life-time,

in the double mountain, and that when he desired to see it, he was prevented by the Chaldeans. His parents having desired to ascend to see it, the priests who drew them up were seized with alarm and let go the ropes, and his parents fell down and were killed.

It was by being hauled up in this manner by ropes that Sir Robert Ker.Porter was enabled to examine these tombs.

(To be continued.)

Interesting Cases of Insanity.

A carpenter was admitted as a patient into the asylum at Wakefield. He had previously made several attempts at self-destruction, and was then in a very desponding state. After the diseased action had subsided, great dejection still remained; he was, however, placed under the care of the gardener, who was then constructing a kind of grotto or moss-house in the grounds. The contriving the building offered a scope for his taste and ingenuity. He was consulted on the arrangement of the floor, which was formed of pieces of wood of different kinds, set in various figures. He was furnished with tools, though he was of course most carefully watched. He took so great an interest in the little building, that the current of his thoughts was changed. All his miseries were forgotten, and his recovery took place at the end of a few months. He very justly attributed his restoration to the moss house. Many years ago, when the workmen were fitting up the asylum at Wakefield with gas-pipes, one of them carelessly left in one of the wards an iron chisel, more than three feet long. A very powerful and violent patient seized it, and threatened to kill any one that should go near him. Keepers and patients all got out of his way, and he alone was soon in possession of the gallery, no one daring to go near him. After waiting a little time, until he was at the further end of it, I went towards him quite alone. I opened the door, and balancing the key of the ward on the back of my hand, walked very slowly towards him, looking intently upon it. His attention was immediately attracted; he came towards me, and inquired what I was doing. I told him I was trying to balance the key, and said, at the same time, that he could not balance the chisel in the same way on the back of his hand. He immediately placed it there, and extending his hand with the chisel upon it, I took it off very quickly, and without making any comment. Though he seemed a little chagrined at having lost his weapon, he made no attempt to regain it, and in a short time the irritation passed away. It is impossible to account for the great effect occasionally produced in the minds of the insane by circumstances apparently most trivial. A practical illustration occurred at Wakefield. H. R., a female, about 40 years of age, had been insane for some years, when admitted. She was a very robust woman, and being usually in a state of great excitement, was the terror of all the patients in the ward, when not in confinement. If, at any time, a

softening influence could be produced upon her, and more gentle feelings called forth, it was by reference to the scenes of early life. In one of her most furious ebullitions of passion, she contrived to seize my wife, and to twist her hand in her hair at the back of her head, and she looked at her with a countenance expressive of the utmost rage, and told her that she could "twist her head round," which, from her great strength, was almost literally the truth; when my wife answered with perfect calmness, "Yes, ye could; but I know you would not hurt a single hair." This confident appeal pacified her, and she immediately let go her hold.—*Ellis on Insanity.*

For "The Friend."

A writer in "The Friend," over the signature of "R. T.," condemns some expressions in an article extracted from the Pennsylvania Freeman, and published in "The Friend." As the writer of that article, I trust I may be permitted to offer a word in explanation.

The charge of "irreverence" towards the Saviour of mankind, seems to me by no means warranted by the simple allusion to the language of those who could answer the sublime truths of his mission only by sneering at his lowly human station, as a Nazarene and a labourer. I intended nothing more than a simple recognition of this *fact*, as recorded in the Holy Scriptures, in illustration of the natural tendency to reject even truth itself, when the "rulers have not believed" it, and its propagator is, to appearance, of humble origin. The contemplation of this fact, it seems to me, can have no tendency to "*degrade*" the Great Teacher and Author of salvation. Inexpressibly tender and dear has ever seemed to me the beautiful and affecting union of the humblest form of our common humanity with the holy attributes of a Redeemer—this light of heaven shining through the depths of earthly humility—this vindication of man's relationship, even in his lowest estate, to his Creator and Preserver. It gives me a deeper sense of that unutterable condescension which prompted him to take upon himself the despised form of a servant—entering into the toils, the trials, the afflictions of our nature—"touched with a feeling of our infirmities"—enduring in his human character the wants, the necessities, the temptations of those whom he came to seek and to save. As the other charge in relation to his disciples is well answered by the admissions of "R. T." himself, I am free to leave it without comment ;—and while I highly respect the zeal for truth and sound doctrine manifested by "R. T.," and while I would do nothing to weaken the force of his communication, so far as it respects the authority of the Holy Scriptures and the divine character of the Redeemer, I would affectionately remind him that he can find abundant occasion for the exercise of that honest zeal without placing, as it seems to me, a forced construction upon the language of one whose opinions entirely coincide with his own.

J. G. W.

IMPORTANCE OF BREAD IN FRANCE.

Bread, which is really in France the "staff of life," is terribly dear. When bread is dear in England, it is undoubtedly an evil; but still the poor eat meat and potatoes, and fish and potatoes, and manage to rub on. This is not so here. The French poor live on bread, soup, fruit, and vegetables. The soup is made without meat in nine out of ten cases. It is made of vegetables, water, salt, and bread, and sometimes a little butter. A poor man who works his twelve hours per diem will eat a loaf of bread of two pounds, and perhaps a little sausage meat; but apples, either cooked or raw, vegetables and soup he will prefer. A poor labouring man in England could not believe that he would not sink with only such nourishment; and yet the French working classes are, on the whole, both healthy and vigorous. I mention all this in order that you may understand how the present enormous price of bread acts upon all classes, and especially on the mass of society in France. The four-pound loaf is now at 17½ sous, which is 8½d. in English money. The average price for years past has been 6½d. the four pound loaf, or at most 7d. British money. This great difference, then, has excited vast dissatisfaction, and has led already to very sad results. The labouring classes in this, as in every other country, are divided into two great categories—the honest, industrious, and worthy; and those who avail themselves of every excuse for pilfering, robbery, and even worse crimes. In France, where even the very best are noisy and turbulent to a certain extent, the working classes of the better sort have resorted in the provinces to emeutes and uproar against the exportation of grain; and to-day new troubles are announced as having taken place at Lille. Various incidental causes have led to the local insurrections in the French provinces during the last few weeks; but the great and capital source of all is the dearness of bread. A French workman who cannot afford to purchase bread enough for himself and his family on account of its high price, is literally half-starved. It is as necessary to his existence as are meat and potatoes to a London drayman. Besides bread, meat has also fearfully risen during the last twelve months. During seven years, the best joints of meat in Paris, of beef, mutton, and veal, taken together, one with the other, could always be had for 13 sous, or 6½d. per pound. Now the price is raised to 8d. English money, and the French are obliged to deprive themselves of their favourite pot au feu. What would Henry the Fourth say if he could now visit France? he who declared that it was his desire that on every Sunday all Frenchmen might be able to put a good fat capon into their pot au feu! Why, the French cannot now afford even a pot au feu of clods and stickings of beef, much more a good rump and a good fowl, as in former days. I admit that the dearness of meat is not so great an evil here as the dearness of bread, but together the evil is great indeed. The last two seasons, both for grass and grain, have not been favourable; pasturage have been alike dear, exportation of grain has increase[d] has followed that prices have rise[n] a forced scarcity prevails. Beside[s] ness of bread and meat, the stat[e of] commerce, and the money-marke[t] as to increase the evils to the lab[our] tion of the population. The dea[r] America are fewer. The trade has been knocked up. Belgium plies herself with multitudes of a used to import from France. A[t] sent very uncertain state of Europe as to the affairs of the East and I[t] ances, prevents speculation in mo[ney] and locks up large capitals. T[he] crisis in England, and the large the rate of discount, have also pr[o] effects. Not one, but many circ[umstances] have conspired to bring about t[he] wretched state of affairs here, and ed to prolong the commercial cris[is of] France.—*Paris Correspondent of* ard.

If the editor should consider th[is extract] taken from the United States Ga[zette of that] day, worthy a place in "The [Friend," it] would no doubt be acceptable [to the] friends of the temperance cause, [and] gratify   A SUB[SCRIBER.]

11th mo. 19th, 1839.

"*Execution of a Criminal.*—We [read with pleasure] the exertions of Governor Buchan[an of Libe-] ria for the suppression of the slave [trade. The] following fact shows the efforts w[hich he is] making for the prevention of inter[mperance.]

"*Execution of an Old Sentence.*—[A] member reading in America 'Th[e Judge and] Alcohol,' written by a celebrated [author, in] and the sentence which was pron[ounced by] his honour, Chief Justice Candou[r, had] never heard of the execution of th[is sentence] until lately, when it took place on [the beach] at Little Bassa, within the territo[ry] of the commonwealth of Liberia. [Governor] Buchanan finding this old offender [against the] law, secreted in the slave's facto[ry, to the] about twenty-five well-bound hogsh[eads, pro-] ceeded to inflict upon this universal [enemy of the] human family that condign puni[shment so] richly merited. In presence of a [numerous] course assembled to witness the [ceremony,] these twenty-five hogsheads were [brought and] severally rolled to the beach; the[n, by the] hands of several executioners, th[e] malefactor poured out into the wa[ves of the] Atlantic, until he was thoroughly [drowned.] May all his kindred spirits meet [as just and] awful fate!—*N. Y. Chris. Intel.*

"The above solemn proceeding [is a great] advancement of jurisprudence in Li[beria, and] what will some of our colonization [friends say] to the matter—those, we mean, wh[o are op-] posed to any punishment more se[vere than] protracted confinement. They sur[ely will] advocate the proceedings of Gover[nor]

Brief Memoir of the Life of John Croker.
Written by himself.

I was born on the eighth of the twelfth month, in the year 1673, in the town of Plymouth, in the county of Devon; my father was of the family of the Crokers of Lyneham, being by birth one called a gentleman; and he married Anstice, the daughter of Nicholas Tripe, a shopkeeper at Kingsbridge, in that county. They were both early convinced of the blessed truth, and stood boldly for it in the time of persecution, many times to the loss of their goods and imprisonment of their bodies, which they bore with patience, accounting it as nothing in comparison with the blessed truth, which God had revealed and made them sharers of.

Although I was then but young, yet I can remember their love and zeal for the way of truth professed by them: notwithstanding great was the rage of men against the professors of the light, which had discovered many of the dark ways of the professors of that time. My father and mother, with others, would not neglect the assembling of themselves together for divine worship, but frequently met together, and took their children with them; and sometimes they met in the open streets, because they were forcibly kept out of their meeting-house. Thus they were made a gazing-stock, and were mocked at by men of corrupt minds, who often ill-treated them, by pulling them down from their seats, and haling them before magistrates; who again often separated husband from wife, and parents from their children. This was the lot of my father, who was kept a prisoner some time at Exeter, forty-four miles from home, and my mother was at the same time a prisoner in the Bridewell at Plymouth. In all these trials I never heard or saw them uneasy; but they often encouraged their children to be sober and good, that they might come to be the servants of God, and to stand in *their* places when they might be called hence; believing, however it might fare with them as to these outward things, that God would be a portion to their children, as they kept in his fear, and the lot of their inheritance if they proved faithful; which would be the best of riches and the best of ornaments, far exceeding gold or silver, or any of the soft and shining raiments which they themselves had found a concern, in a great degree, to forsake and deny; accounting all things as nothing that they might win Christ, for whose sake they were made willing to be as the off-scourings of many people. They would not allow in us, their children, that which they found truth called them out of; but still showed us an example of self-denial, and constrained us, as much as in them lay, to refrain from all things that were not of a good savour, or seemed any thing like to the going back again into the rudiments of the world, or into that which they were brought to deny themselves of for Christ's sake.

Nevertheless, when I was young, I found there was an evil thing, stubbornness or rebellion, which grew in me; so that I often kicked at the reproofs of my parents, and alighted their tender counsel, and vainly spent my childish days to their, and since to my own, grief and sorrow; so that when they had brought me up to about twelve years of age, and educated me with some learning, as reading, writing, and arithmetic, and were earnest I should learn Latin, I was stubborn, and would not learn it.

In the year 1686, some Friends of Plymouth being about to remove to Pennsylvania, and I being willing to go with them, my father and mother concluded to bind me apprentice to a Friend, one John Shilson, by trade a serge-maker, but who also professed surgery; with whom I went to be instructed in the art of surgery. They had a good end in it; for I was sensible my mother was greatly exercised for my preservation, and that I might be brought to a sense of the power of God, to work me into a new lump; and by separating me from them and from my companions, I might be brought to a thoughtfulness how I had behaved myself towards them, and to a remembrance of my Creator in the days of my youth, before the strength of evil days came on. And truly this separation, and what I met with before I returned again, had a good effect upon me, as may be seen hereafter.

My parents' care for me was so great, that they sent in the same vessel with me a considerable parcel of goods, and appointed two Friends my overseers, who had the care of the said goods, and the care of me, if any thing might happen which should call for assistance, that I might not suffer too much the want of the things of this life; which proved very helpful. For soon after I came to Pennsylvania, my master put me with the rest of the servants into the woods, in order to clear land for a plantation; where I was made to work hard like the rest, for the space of about one year; in which time I often thought of my parents, and of their former care and advices, also of my stubborn rebellious behaviour towards them; which made me often say, "Lord forgive me, and look down in mercy upon me." Thus I mourned many times; yet I soon got over it, and at times grew wanton and foolish with the rest of my fellows, and got over the reproofs of instruction that were at work in my heart, which reproofs and chastisement I was not willing to bear; but the Lord intended good to me, and did not leave striving (at times) in my soul; and troubles outwardly followed one another, as the Lord saw good, for ends best known to himself. He soon took my master and mistress, their daughter and maid-servant, out of the world by the distemper of the country, which was then prevalent; then all our affairs in the country were shut up, and I was destitute, as well as others of the servants, some of whom soon went off.

I still remained in the country with one young man; we were like two pilgrims walking up and down the woods, making use of such provisions as were left in the house, and what we gathered in the woods; which being a solitary life, various considerations of different matters came before my mind, concerning times past and present, and how the Lord had hitherto preserved me by sea and land; and that I was not swallowed up by the one, neither was I taken away by the distemper that reigned on the other—being fearful of the latter, which was very mortal, having never had the seasoning of the country; but blessed be God I was never sick there. As the sense of these things grew on me, love to God increased in my bosom; and this drew me into tears, and solitary sittings with my Bible in my hand, reading oftener than I commonly used to do—desiring the Lord to open my understanding in what I read, and to show me my duty, for I was willing to serve him; and that he would be pleased to open a way for my return to my father's house, for now I was free from my apprenticeship by the death of my master;—then would I serve him, and then would I be obedient to my tender parents, and walk in awfulness before the Lord the remaining time I had to spend;—with some such breathings as honest Jacob had when he said to this effect—If God will be with me in the way that I go, so that I come again in peace to my father's house, then shall the Lord be my God, and I will serve him.

Now, although I did not suffer want as to food, not having spent what was left by the deceased, yet being fifteen miles from Philadelphia, those Friends to whom my father had committed the care of me, in case I should meet with any adversity, consulted each other what to do with me, until they could hear from my father, which they endeavoured to do with what speed they could; and in the mean time one of them (James Fox) took me to his house, where I remained a little while, doing such small business as I was set about, being still in the country about the same distance as before. At length they got me into the city, and put me to school to George Keith, who was then in esteem among Friends; but growing high and conceited in his arts and parts afterwards, he became troublesome to Friends and himself; so that at length, for the clearing of the truth, they were forced to deny him, and he became disesteemed, like unsavoury salt, as it were trodden under foot of men. Before they (the two Friends) heard from my father, I began to take liberty, and forsook my very frequent retirements, wherein I had been often tendered and broken before the Lord; and thus I became indifferent, and came to a loss as to my inward state and condition. But God having many ways of visiting his people, in order to bring them to a sense of their states, yet found me out, and another sore trial I had to pass through, whereby I might see the Lord could and would do as seemeth good in his sight; and that those who will not bow in mercy, he will make to bow in judgment, and they shall see the goodness of God in and through all—which was my lot; indeed, the great goodness of God to me I hope I shall never forget.

After a while I heard from my father, who was desirous of my return; and in order thereunto my friends made preparations, and got me a passage in a vessel to Newcastle upon Tyne, in England; in which vessel they put some effects which might be for my accommodation when I came to England, as well as to carry me to my father, who lived some hundreds of miles distance from Newcastle: and some other effects were put on board another vessel, which sunk in the sea, but being in company with other ships, the crew were saved by boat. So after having been four years in the province of Pennsylvania, I embarked for England, having taken leave of my friends in Pennsylvania, with hopes I should now see my native land, and my dear parents and relations.

Notwithstanding our vessel was alone, and it was war time, we were in hopes that the Lord would carry us safe: we were preserved on the boisterous seas, until, according to the opinion of the sailors, we were within one hundred leagues of England, when we met with three ships. The master of our vessel (who was a Friend) was willing to speak with those vessels, to know what news in England, though persuaded to the contrary by his mate, who feared what they might be; but to our great trouble and sorrow, they proved to be three French privateers, who soon bid us strike; and presently they hoisted out their boats, and came and stripped us almost naked, and dispersed us, some on board one ship, and some on board another, and afterwards they separated themselves; for one of those ships went for France with our vessel, and the other two were parted in a mist, so that they could not see each other, nor come together again. This fresh exercise brought more than a common fear upon me, (I being in one of those ships that remained at sea,) fearing how I should be dealt with, and what sufferings I should undergo. I was, in respect of clothes, almost naked, and destitute of relief, beyond what our enemies would be pleased to bestow; whose hearts God so far opened towards us, that we did not want for bread or water, and sometimes were allowed pork, beef, peas, and beverage, and at certain times a draught of sour wine; yet still I was in fear, not knowing whither we should be carried.

The ship in which we were, being a privateer of twenty-six guns, and out at sea on that account, she sailed far northward, until we fell in amongst islands of ice, and were forced to lie by in the night, for fear we should run amongst some of those islands, or great rocks of ice. For about six weeks I took my rest on the boards in the ship's hold, in which time they chased one vessel, which, when they came near to her, was thought to be too mighty for them, and the ship wherein we were being the better sailer, they let the said vessel pass without examining what she was; but soon after they took a Dutch ship bound for Newfoundland, which had little on board, only ballast and a few cheeses; which vessel and men they rifled, and took the vessel with them to Newfoundland; and as we drew near it, they put us on shore upon a small island or rock, (which lay between some other islands,) upon which there was no house, nor any fresh water or shelter. Being twenty-eight of us in number, they gave us a sail and some oars and poles, to make a tent; in which we all lay without any beds, having only some straw, which they brought us, and

stones for our pillows, with which we we forced to be contented: yet I found Go providence was over me, so that I was p served healthy and sound. Oh! the gre goodness of God is fresh in my mind, now the time of my writing this, and I hope t impression of it will remain as long as I liv so that I may never forget what I met with my youth, and how the Lord preserved r through it all.

The French used once or twice a week visit us, and bring us some spruce beer, wate pork, peas, and plenty of bread; of the bre we eat sparingly, laying some in store agair a time of scarcity, fearing such might com the bread we hid in some of the hollow rocl that it might not hinder or stop them fro bringing or supplying us with more as usu There were also about our rock, or litt island, plenty of lobsters, of which we caug some, and boiled, and ate, which were a gre help to us; and although we were not in ai great want considering our circumstances, y we were but thinly clothed, and the seas not very hot;—I having left me only o shirt, one pair of breeches, and a hat; un some taking compassion on me, gave me thin linsey-woolsey frock, one old shirt, a an old pair of stockings and shoes, for whi I was very thankful.

In this mean condition, I with the rest co tinued on this island about six weeks, which time we contrived our escape. The was an island at about half a mile distan from us, which was inhabited by the Fron for the fishing, whose boats went to and from by us almost every day; and there were al on our island some pieces of boards and woc which had been used, I suppose, by t Frenchmen, at times when they dried fi there, and were by them left; their boa were also lying at a wharf on the said inhab ed island, but guarded, as we afterwards u derstood, though then unknown to us. V one day took particular notice of one of the boats, which, with several others, lay ne the said wharf; and our men proposed in tl night by a float, to endeavour to swim out ar get the said boat. We, therefore, made raft, by tying together with rope-yarn sur wood and boards as we found on the islan and two of our men, notwithstanding sever privateers were lying by us as a guard, we so courageous, that they adventured in t night to stand on this raft we had made, a put off towards the boat which we had o served. Having got to her, they found n body in her, and the watch or guard being their huts very busy in discourse, those tv men cut the moorings of the boat, and let h fall off with the tide which was going ou and brought the boat towards us; by the help, we attained the same, which made rejoice.

There happened (far beyond expectatio to be in the boat, oars, sails, a compass, son pork and b$_{utte}$r, a tinder-box and candle, wi materials for striking fire; also some of tl Frenchmen's jerkins, made of lamb skin with the wool inward, and a pottage pot, i axe, and some fishing lines; all which we very needful and serviceable to us, and ga

meetings for worship, particularly those held in the middle of the week. We desire that such may be made so sensible of the value of the privileges of uniting with their friends in the public worship of the Almighty, that they may no longer refuse to participate in the blessings which attend upon it, but gladly embrace every opportunity for its performance. Some of us are bound to acknowledge that such seasons of quiet and reverence waiting upon the Lord have been among the happiest of our lives.

We crave too for our members more of that love to God which is incompatible with lukewarmness and the love of the world, under the influence of which we should serve him with fear, and rejoice with trembling. We should then maintain love towards each other becoming our Christian profession. It would show itself an active and operative principle in our hearts. We should be qualified to travail for and with each other, and thus be enabled to obey the apostolic injunction, " bear ye one another's burdens, and so fulfil the law of Christ." The unruly would be warned, the feeble-minded comforted, and the week supported : and when collected together we should know a being " baptized by one Spirit into one body," under a living sense of his presence, who has promised to be even with the two or the three who are assembled in his name.

Our hearts being thus enlisted in the dear Redeemer's cause, and for the welfare of the church, we should be made to see in the light of truth, the necessity and importance of consistency in our outward appearance, as well as in our walk and conversation. We have no doubt, dear friends, of the obligation resting upon our members to be good *examples* in these respects to their children, as well as to train *them* up in their observance. A hedge will thus be thrown around them, and they will gradually be prepared for usefulness in the church. Their guarded and religious education has also been brought very near to our hearts. We have earnestly desired that our friends may frequently and prayerfully consult the Holy Scriptures, both in their closet and before their collected families. We believe, if we were more diligent in our *private* exercises of this kind, that ability would be given more profitably to *unite together* in this religious duty. We desire to exhort and to encourage our dear friends not to neglect the daily practice of assembling their household for this purpose, believing that a blessing would attend upon its faithful performance both spiritually and temporally.

We desire too, that the hands of those upon whom the support of our discipline devolves may be strengthened, that they may not neglect its due and seasonable exercise in regard to those who have separated from the society and have not yet been disowned.

In conclusion, we beseech you to examine each one for himself how far he has been delinquent in any of those particulars, and if the unflattering witness for God in the soul, convict us of preferring the world and its transitory joys, to the love of God and the fellowship of saints—may the sense of our danger

and need, lead us to Him who can alone save us—unto Him, who will "take the stony heart out of our flesh, and give us a heart of flesh"—even unto " Jesus, the author and finisher of our faith, who for the joy set before him, endured the cross, despising the shame, and is set down at the right hand of the throne of God."

Signed on behalf of the meeting,
HUGH BALDERSTON, Clerk this year.

Report to said Meeting on Indiana Concerns.

To the Yearly Meeting now sitting :—Since the last report which we addressed to the Yearly Meeting, the committee having the charge of Indian concerns, have felt the same unabated solicitude as was then evinced for the interesting portion of their fellow-men, whose civilization and Christian instruction it is the object of their appointment to promote. They have not stood alone in this matter, but are glad to have it in their power to state, that our Friends in New York and Rhode Island appear to be renewedly impressed with the necessity of increased efforts to ameliorate the condition of the Indian natives: the former having taken measures to promote a general subscription, and the latter has already raised a considerable sum for that purpose. The committee on Indian concerns, of Indiana, invited us to attend a conference of delegates appointed by their meeting, and that of Ohio, at Mount Pleasant, at the period of the last Ohio Yearly Meeting, to take into consideration the peculiar condition of the Indian concerns at the present time, in regard to the limited state of the funds, &c. It was thought advisable to conform to this request, and accordingly a part of our number attended the meeting of the conference; a report to the Yearly Meeting of Ohio was prepared and adopted by it. Such a heartfelt interest pervaded that body, that measures were at once taken to raise a subscription, and $396 were collected, and such other schemes devised to obtain further pecuniary aid, and also clothing, in the subordinate meetings, as to satisfy the delegates to the conference, that Ohio Yearly Meeting was disposed to contribute liberally to the general fund. From the report of the committee on Indian concerns, of Indiana, to their last Yearly Meeting, it appears that meeting has directed its subordinate meetings to raise $600—and women Friends there have directed their treasurer to pay over for the same purpose, $100.

We think it would be of advantage to enter into some detail of the efforts made by Friends, to advance in civilization the Indian natives. At the time Friends commenced their labours amongst the Shawnese, at Waughpakonetta, Ohio, (at the Old Town, so named,) situated on the Oglaize river, their huts were made of poles, and covered with elm bark; they had cleared several acres of land adjoining, from which they raised a scanty supply of corn; the labour of planting it and its culture, were performed by the women; the men spent their time in idleness during the summer months, until their autumnal hunting season, when they packed up their cooking utensils, &c. and pitched their tents in a place where they

thought deer could be procured. In this situation, many of the women and children suffered extremely from cold, whilst in their open tents, lying on the ground, which induced diseases so malignant, that few survived unto the age of maturity. This is assigned as the reason that the nation dwindled to a mere remnant. In this desolate state, Friends found them, and advised them to leave their hovels, and locate themselves in different parts of their reserve, and thus have space to till separate farms, and raise grain and esculent roots for their support. The Indians having consented to Friends' proposal, labourers were provided to assist them to erect cabins, make rails, and fence their lands; and they were furnished with a sufficient portion of stocked plough irons; also, with hoes, axes, grubbing hoes, and cooking utensils; such was the progress they made, that in 1831, they had erected upwards of 100 hewn log-houses and cabins; they had wagons and gears, fruit-bearing orchards, and had raised considerable cattle and hogs, and a number of milch-cows —they also made a quantity of butter. In this comfortable condition, they were constrained to abandon their abodes, and seek a refuge in the remote west, on a portion of land appropriated to them on the Kanzas river, which they reached in the winter season. In the ensuing summer, they were visited by part of our committee from Indiana, who found them living in cabins; they had planted corn over a considerable extent of cleared ground; on this and their gardens they were busily engaged in tilling; within six months they had split upwards of 3000 fence rails. One of the same Friends visited them two years afterwards, and informed that their improvements had progressed beyond his expectation.

We have enlarged upon these interesting matters, so as to enable Friends to contrast the fruits of their beneficent labour, and their present condition, with that in which they were found at Waughpakonetta. But it will be presented to the mind of the genuine philanthropist, that much is to be done after provision is obtained for the body; efforts should be made to promote their intellectual culture, and to enforce the necessity of maintaining good moral habits; they should be watched over to prevent the introduction of spirituous liquors amongst them, and to guard them from the unjust impositions of speculators, and to extend over them a paternal care in preserving their rights and privileges as a nation. Having now nearly attained the object of enabling them to procure comfortable subsistence, our views should be directed to their acquiring religious and literary instruction. The salary of a teacher, and the cost of books and stationary, will be necessarily superadded to the compensation of the general supervisor or agent. The Indians have uniformly expressed their desire that Friends should take their children, and educate them in like manner as they would do their own. By information received within a few days from the committee on Indian concerns of Indiana Yearly Meeting, it appears that Elias Newbey was employed as teacher about one year since, and the school was re-opened on the first of first month last, and has been continued; 13 to 15 scholars have been regular in their attendance. The Ohio conference proposed that the executive committee of Indiana should employ a suitable family for two years to succeed those now engaged, whose term of service is about to expire, and that the number of scholars should be increased to 25.

We are informed by our superintendent, in a letter dated 8th month 8th last, that the progress of the children was encouraging; several can read short sentences, and they acquire the art of writing with a facility truly gratifying; and they all improve in the knowledge of the English language. The meetings for worship have been regularly held and attended (with one exception) twice a week. The Scriptures have been read in the family, and care has been taken to impart Christian instruction to the Indians as way has opened. The agent further informs, that they have 24 acres in corn, half an acre in potatoes, beans, pumpkins, broom-corn, &c.; 430 dozen of oats, and 370 dozen of wheat, one half of the latter will not yield any thing; the growth of all the rest is luxuriant; 50 bushels of old corn remain, flour for two months' supply, and enough of salt meat until autumn—10 head of cattle and 23 hogs belong to the establishment; 115 acres of prairie land are fenced in, one half of which is cultivated, the residue in pasture, which would sustain much more stock than there is in possession.

From an examination into the state of the treasury, it appears that after paying the arrears due the superintendent and teacher, and all the expenses up to the present time, there will remain at the disposal of the committee about $900, which, we apprehend, will be needed to defray the expenses of the current year, ending in the fifth month next.

It remains for us to suggest plans which have come under our consideration to raise the funds necessary to prosecute our benevolent undertaking: one mode is, to fix upon a sum which the yearly meeting can, with convenience, raise, and pay it out of its stock—enlarging our subscription in the subordinate meetings conformably. Another mode is, to raise voluntary subscriptions during the session of the yearly meeting, by a committee then appointed, who are to be continued to obtain money within the limits of the several monthly meetings, to be paid into the hands of Joseph King, Jr., treasurer to this committee.

Signed on behalf of the committee.
SAMUEL CAREY, Clerk.
10th month 28, 1839.

Early Rising.—The difference between rising every morning at six and at eight, in the course of forty years, amounts to twenty-nine thousand two hundred hours, or three years one hundred and twenty-one days and sixteen hours, which are equal to eight hours a-day for exactly ten years. So that rising at six will be the same as if ten years of life (a weighty consideration) were added, wherein we may command eight hours every day for the cultivation of our minds, and the despatch of business.

Sources of Social Happiness.—As regards public happiness, statesmen and politicians too often forget, that though good political institutions conduce to it, yet that they are but one means to the attainment of this end, and that more than these are requisite to make individuals and nations happy. The cultivation of good-will, kindness, humanity, and all the gentler affections, are far more influential in the promotion of private happiness than the justest balance of the political constitution can be; so that though the value of civil and religious liberty is great, and has a large influence on national well-being, still it alone does not constitute happiness; and therefore it seems to me that those writers who devote their energies to the task of endeavouring to soften and improve the social affections, do incomparably more to promote the benefit of communities than those who have only in view what is more strictly designated "the public weal."—*Curtis on Health.*

THE FRIEND.

ELEVENTH MONTH, 23, 1839.

The yearly meeting of Friends for North and South Carolina and Tennessee, held at New Garden, N. C., commenced on second day, the 4th instant. The following extract from a letter to a Friend in this city, is all that we have in our power at present to offer on the subject:—

"Our yearly meeting has closed its session this evening (8th inst.) Quite as large a number of Friends were in attendance as common, and the concerns of the meeting have been conducted in much brotherly feeling and condescension. Nothing out of the ordinary course was transacted; agreeably to a request from New York Yearly Meeting, the corresponding committee on Indian affairs was continued, to co-operate with like committees of other yearly meetings. No way seemed to open to enter into any thing for the benefit of the people of colour at this time. By the accounts from the quarterly meetings, it appears the state of society is rather improving, yet some acts of remissness continue to be brought forward. We have the company of our friends Jacob Green, of Ireland, Stephen Grellett, of your yearly meeting, and Daniel Williams, from Indiana, very acceptably with us."

In the notice last week concerning Baltimore Yearly Meeting, there was reference to an epistle of counsel addressed to its members, and a report on Indian concerns. This epistle and the report will be found on our pages of to-day.

Our obliging friend, Alexander R. Barclay, of London, has forwarded to us another volume, just completed, of the SELECT SERIES, edited by his late estimable brother, John Barclay. The volume consists of the respective Journals of William Caton and John Burnyeat, together with a brief memoir concerning John Croker, of Plymouth. Of the latter it is observed in the preface:—"The

concluding memoir, concerning John Croker, now first put in print, has remained in manuscript during several generations, in the possession of the Fox family, of the western counties of Devon and Cornwall, into which family a sister of the author married. It is hoped that this memoir will be perused with much interest and profit, especially by the youth amongst us." The memoir we have concluded to transfer to the columns of "The Friend," having commenced it to-day, and to be continued until completed.

INSTITUTE FOR COLOURED YOUTH.

A suitably qualified Friend is wanted to take charge of the farm and family of this institution. Application may be made to
BENJAMIN COOPER, near Camden, N. J.
THOMAS WISTAR, Jr., Abington.
JOSEPH SCATTERGOOD, No. 14 Minor st. or
MARMADUKE C. COPE, 286 Filbert st.

A TEACHER WANTED,

At Newtown, N. J., to take charge of Friends' school. Apply to
BENJAMIN COOPER,
JOHN M. KAIGHN,
JOSEPH B. COOPER.

HAVERFORD SCHOOL.

WANTED, a Friend to act as Steward of this Institution. Apply to
KIMBER & SHARPLESS,
No. 8 South Fourth street.

DIED, in this city, on the 8th instant, aged nearly 18 years, ALBAN KITE, son of Dr. John L. and Mary L. Kite. He had removed with his parents from Susquehanna county to reside here about four weeks, previous to his decease. He appeared to be then in good health, but a severe illness, of nearly two weeks' continuance, terminated in his death. He bore the sufferings with which his disease was attended with patience and fortitude, and appeared to look forward to the approaching solemn event in resignation to the Lord's will. As his life had been marked with great circumspection, so, it is believed, his end was peace.

——, at his residence, near Richmond, Indiana, on the 8th of 10th month, of congestive fever, WILLIAM POOT, aged 29, a member of White Water Monthly Meeting.

——, at the residence of his father, in Richmond, Indiana, on the 26th of seventh month, THOMAS POOT, at the age of 26, of dyspepsia, a member of White Water Monthly Meeting.

——, at the residence of his father, near Milton, Indiana, on the 25th of tenth month, CLARKSON MOORE, son of Thomas Moore, late of New Garden, North Carolina, in the 29th year of his age.

—— at his residence near Richmond, Indiana, on the 27th of 10th month, after a very short illness, JAMES PEGG, aged 71 years, an elder and member of White Water monthly meeting. He was of consistent and exemplary life and conversation, and long an active and useful member of our religious Society.

—— at his residence near Milton, Indiana, on the 4th of 11th month, of congestive fever, JOHN KINDLEY, a minister, of about 50 years of age, a member of Milford monthly meeting. He possessed much natural energy of mind, and was an active supporter of the views of Friends against those of the Hicksites in the separation.

—— at his residence, near the same place, of the same disease, on the 15th of 9th month, JOSEPH STUBBS, an active and useful member of Milford monthly meeting, and much respected in his neighbourhood.

PRINTED BY ADAM WALDIE,
Carpenter Street, below Seventh, Philadelphia.

THE FRIEND.

A RELIGIOUS AND LITERARY JOURNAL.

VOL. XIII.   **SEVENTH DAY, ELEVENTH MONTH, 30, 1839.**   **NO. 9.**

EDITED BY ROBERT SMITH.

PUBLISHED WEEKLY.

Price two dollars per annum; payable in advance.

Subscriptions and Payments received by

GEORGE W. TAYLOR,

NO. 50, NORTH FOURTH STREET, UP STAIRS,

PHILADELPHIA.

For "The Friend."

Remarks on the study of the Greek and Latin languages, suggested by the perusal of Dymond's Chapter on Intellectual Education.

(Continued from page 58.)

From what has been said above respecting derivation, it will be seen, that the study of Latin, so far from cultivating the memory exclusively, as some have asserted, actually requires much less exercise of the memory, in proportion to that of the other faculties, than the study of English alone. Indeed we are persuaded, that, among all the objects of knowledge which are offered for our selection, there is none which exercises the different intellectual powers more advantageously than the classics, when pursued in a proper manner. We wish not to be understood as *preferring* them to mathematics. We would only place them on a full equality with this noble science. We think that some knowledge of both is absolutely requisite, in forming a complete education. While we freely admit, that the mathematics contribute more highly to improve the mind in some respects, we hold that they are inferior to the classics in others. Were we asked to point out what faculties in particular these tend most to strengthen,—we might instance, besides the power of analysis, which is continually called into exercise in tracing derivations, that of the association of ideas, and of the classification of things by their general properties. —But of this we shall speak more fully hereafter.

While considering this part of our subject, it will be proper to notice an objection very commonly urged against the study of the languages, that it gives merely a knowledge of words, while it is said, that the mind might be more advantageously employed in becoming acquainted with facts or things. To this we answer, that in acquiring a language, much is learned besides mere words. At the same time we think that a thorough knowledge of the words of our language, is by no means to be despised. Few persons, perhaps,

are aware, to what extent correct views of things depend upon an accurate acquaintance with the meaning of words. Yet it is through them; that all our ideas which are derived from the wisdom or experience of others, must come to us. But if we know not their signification, how can we have a clear understanding of the thoughts which they are intended to convey? Hence it is absolutely impossible, by reasoning, to produce a correct impression on the minds of others, unless both the speaker and hearers, are thoroughly acquainted with the words employed. How often, indeed, do we see two persons argue vehemently about some point, each supposing the other to be egregiously stupid or perverse, when at last it is discovered that both are contending for exactly the same thing, the whole dispute having arisen from one or both being ignorant of some of the terms, which they have made use of.

The study of the ancient tongues not only contributes greatly towards obtaining a correct knowledge of the signification of English words, as has already been shown, but the process of translating from one language into another, often enables us to see the thoughts of an author in quite a new light. As we conceive this to be a point of no small importance, we hope we shall be excused for dwelling upon it somewhat at length. Most of our readers must be aware, how extremely common it is for ignorant and inexperienced persons to be captivated; and led astray; by some glowing speech, which they suppose to be replete with irresistible reasoning, when, if it were examined by a sensible and reflecting person, it would be found entirely destitute of valuable thought, and to contain little else than a multitude of high-sounding words. Now, an acquaintance with other tongues, as we shall endeavour to show, will often enable us to detect the imposition, which would palm upon us words instead of sense. Language is very justly termed the vehicle, or conveyer, of thought. Without this vehicle, it is impossible to carry our ideas properly to the minds of others. But great care must be used, or we shall often confound the conveyer with the thing conveyed; as some of our Indians are said to have done; when, seeing for the first time a man on horseback, they supposed the two to be but a single animal. Now, had they seen the man betake himself to some other conveyance, for example, an ordinary carriage; they would doubtless have soon discovered their mistake. In like manner, when we wish to scrutinize closely any idea, to ascertain whether its real is equal to its apparent value, we shall often find it useful to change the vehicle in which it is conveyed, that is, to express it in a new set of words,

which shall give as nearly as possible the same meaning.

To make this subject more fully understood, we may employ another illustration. Language may be properly regarded as the dress, as well as the vehicle of thought. Now in this, as in other cases, the clothes sometimes completely conceal, or disguise, the wearer. As by a change of dress, we may frequently discover, how much of the dignity and comeliness belongs to the person, and how much is owing to the attire; so, when we admire any piece of oratory or poetry, by clothing the ideas in another language, we can generally ascertain whether they are really excellent in themselves, or whether they do not owe much of their attraction to the specious ornaments with which they are arrayed.

While on this branch of our subject, it may not be improper to observe, that the practice of rendering the ancient authors into English, is highly beneficial in another point of view, viz. it teaches the art of composition. All who have attempted it must be aware how difficult it is to teach this art with success. When the pupil is directed to write a composition, he generally selects some hackneyed topic, and says what he is already perfectly familiar with, troubling himself but little to find out either original ideas, or appropriate words. But, in translating from Latin and Greek, the subject is generally new to him, (at least it ought to be so,) and he is obliged to use many words with which, as yet, he is but slightly acquainted. Hence he acquires a more extensive and perfect knowledge of the English tongue. As, moreover, a single word in the original has often several different significations, (which indeed is the case with every language,) his judgment and taste are continually exercised, in selecting those which are most appropriate. We own there is danger, lest he may employ the English words in an improper sense; but a reasonable care on the part of his preceptor, will be sufficient to prevent this.

The classics appear to us to furnish an intellectual exercise, which is peculiarly valuable, both because it is adapted to every stage of mental development, and because it calls into united exertion a great variety of faculties.

First, it is adapted to every stage of mental development. Most of our readers are doubtless aware, that before the reason is yet unfolded, the memory is quick and retentive, and can treasure up unconnected things or words, even more readily than in riper years. This is the season for accumulating those crude materials of thought, which the higher faculties afterwards reduce to shape and order. First of all, the young pupil becomes acquaint-

imple objects of sense, with which nded. It is evident that reason ittle service in obtaining a knowse. Reason, without sight, could an idea of colour; nor could it, sense of hearing, communicate ion of sound. To have a clear f the external properties of things, and they alone, are requisite. o ground for supposing, that an sight is perfect, has not as clear the colour or form of the bodies es, as he who is most highly enreason. But to understand the is demands something more than ense of hearing. It requires an etween the sound, and the object, sound is the representative. This rded as the earliest and simplest ason. The mind, however, beainted with things and words at e same time, that, for practical is perhaps needless to make any except in order to point out the tance of giving a knowledge of of sense, directly through the elves. If the word be learned upil is acquainted with the thing stands, it can suggest no idea to nd is therefore perfectly useless. tudy of things should always pref words, both for the reason just ecause, even in those cases where ceed in giving a tolerably correct ngs, by a verbal description, the will be far less distinct and duraen the things themselves are pretly to the senses.

int of no small consequence, to cercises of the mind, to its wants es. These are continually varye first dawn of perception, to the y of reason. To attempt to teach sciences to the infant mind, would hest degree irrational and absurd; be scarcely less so, after the def reason, to give the principal those pursuits, which tend to culsively the perceptive faculties. If t wisely, we must observe and co nature. First of all, the pupil r those subjects, which employ the ncipally or solely. As, however, e faculties are gradually unfolded, on of these must receive propor ion, till at length it becomes the ltimate aim of education. It has n said, that the study of things titute the earliest employment of as some previous knowledge of essary, to a proper understanding When, however, the pupil is soth the more common and simple erception, and the reason has be t itself, the ancient languages may ly be commenced. We do not set ar age for this, as much will dee capacity of the scholar, and on the convenience of circum t is, however, desirable that it e deferred until the memory has hness and susceptibility, as our

main reliance at the outset, must be on this faculty. But as soon as a sufficient number of words have been learned, to admit of comparing them together, and classifying them by some trait which they possess in common, the power of generalization is called into action. And here we may remark, that the construction of the Latin tongue is singularly favourable for cultivating this faculty, since, though very copious and complex, it is the most regular of human languages, and, in this respect, forms a striking contrast with that chaos of limited rules and boundless exceptions, of which the English is composed. The pupil is constantly obliged to generalize, in construing, and parsing, Latin or Greek. Thus, in tracing the agreement of the adjective with the substantive to which it belongs, a very simple kind of generalization (and therefore one which is well adapted to the young mind,) is continually practised. The referring of nouns or adjectives to their declensions, is an exertion of the same faculty, since a declension is but a class into which words are arranged in consequence of possessing certain general properties. The same remark will apply to the conjugation of verbs. As the classical student advances, the memory is less and less exercised, in proportion to the other intellectual powers; so that, when he has become acquainted with the greater part of the primitive words, the chief employment of his mind consists in analyzing derivatives, and in the learning and application of general principles. These mental operations may, without difficulty, be adapted to the various degrees of intellectual development, by employing, as occasion may require, the works of different authors; since, in the literature of Greece and Rome, is to be found not only every variety of subject, but an unlimited diversity of style. For, while one writer is characterized by the shortness and simplicity of his sentences, another seems to delight in constructing them of such a length and intricacy, that it requires the patient and united exertion of all the powers of the mind, to unravel them.

From the observations which were made on the subject of derivation, and from what has just been said, respecting the manner in which classical studies exercise the mind, it may be perceived, that they not only call into action, a great variety of faculties, but that they require the united operation of the different intellectual powers. In becoming acquainted with the objects of sense, we are obliged to exert little else than mere memory; in pursuing many parts of mathematics, we employ the reasoning powers almost exclusively; but in studying the classics, the memory, the reason, the taste, and the imagination, are exercised at the same moment.

(To be continued.)

For "The Friend."

PERSIA.

(Concluded from page 59.)

All these sculptures are accompanied by inscriptions in the unknown characters of an unknown tongue; characters so peculiar in their appearance as to excite to the utmost

the curiosity which they have effectually baffled. But the p Europe, which no obstacles ca difficulties dishearten, has seate to the task of decyphering th with a perseverance that ha attended with success.

These inscriptions have th peculiarity, that they consist o in size and position and groupi than two characters, the one wedge, or the head of a nall, o and the other consisting of two joined, so as to form an angle tirely from any known alphab city of their construction seen these characters an air of orig tiquity, as if they were an inven to the land in which they are are as peculiar, moreover, to th Euphrates, as the hieroglyphic to the valley of the Nile. stamped on the bricks of the lon, some of which perhaps ar cient fabrics in the world, an scribed on all the buildings Darius and Xerxes. A lea named Grotefend, obtained meaning of these characters fr inscription, by means of whic abled to indentify the several names of Cyrus, Darius, and language of the ancient Per Zend, in which language are the sacred books of the religio books which are probably (witl of the Hebrew Scriptures) th writings extant. These book to Europe and translated, du part of the last century by Ar ron, a learned Frenchman. in all probability, sufficient da us to arrive at the meaning o inscriptions, and it is by no ary expectation that the veil v erto hid them in impenetrabl ere long be lifted, and that w the lost histories of the Assyri and Persian empires, and resto fabulous monarchs to a place tic annals of the primitive seat

The fertile and well watered dasht and Mourghaub were th tions of the ancient Persians, region became covered witl temples, and cities, the ruins c present visible in all directi northern extremity of the plain is a platform of nearly 300 fe sisting of hewn blocks of marb size, and strewed over with d and blocks of marble, the ren cient and probably an unfinishe one of these columns is an em ture of a colossal human fig wings, representing one of th Persian religion, and decorate dress that is evidently Egypti head of this figure is an ins arrow-head character, which l by Grotefend, to be "Cyrus, King, the Ruler of the world

distance from these ruins, on an eminence that commands an extensive plain, is a very remarkable structure. This is a square pyramid, forty by forty-four feet at the base, and consisting of six steps, each being formed of enormous blocks of white marble, which recede as they rise, so as to form at the height of eighteen feet a platform about eighteen feet by twenty-two. This platform is surmounted by a marble building, twenty feet long by seventeen feet wide, built of stones five feet in thickness, so as to leave in the interior a chamber seven feet wide, ten feet long, and eight feet high. The door into this chamber is four feet in height, and the building is constructed of four layers of stones, the first being the sides of the door; the second its lintel; the third a projecting cornice, and the fourth the pediment and sloping roof. Nothing can exceed the simple and severe beauty of this pile of colossal stones. The floor of the chamber is composed of two slabs of marble, the surface of which is much broken, and which shows deep holes, from which it is plain that large fastenings of metal have been torn away. This tomb, for such it evidently is, is surrounded by a square colonnade, some of the pillars of which are still standing. It is situated in the midst of a beautiful and well watered plain, and corresponds so nearly with the description given by Arrian, from the testimony of one who had seen it, of the tomb of Cyrus, at Pasargeda, that there can be no doubt that it once contained the body of that renowned conqueror. The golden sarcophagus which was fastened by iron chains to the floor, the seat of gold, and the other ornaments have disappeared; but the building itself has withstood, uninjured, the winters of twenty-four centuries, and may last till the hills themselves decay.

On the road from Bagdad to Hamadan, the ancient Ecbatana, the capital of Bactriana, in northern Persia, are the remains of the ancient city of Baghistan, about 45 miles southwest from Hamadan. In the neighbourhood of these ruins is the mountain of Besitoon, exhibiting one of the most remarkable works of ancient art in Persia. The mountain is a huge mass of crags, that presents an almost perpendicular face of 1,500 feet in height. The lower part of this, to a breadth of 150 feet, and a height of 100 feet, has been smoothed by the chisel, and the ground below has been shaped into a platform, which the masses of hewn stones that are strewed around show to have been designed for a temple or a palace. According to Diodorus Siculus, it was on such a mountain, near Baghistan, in Media, that Semiramis caused her image to be carved, surrounded by a hundred of her guards, and an inscription commemorating the occasion to be written in Assyrian letters at a great height on the rock. Traces of sculpture, so defaced that it is almost impossible to make out any continued outline, are found on the rock of Besitoon, which may not improbably be regarded as that of which Diodorus speaks. But at an almost inaccessible point higher up on the same rock, are inscriptions and figures, evidently more recent than the other, yet exhibiting all the charac-

ters of the sculptures of Persepolis. They consist of fourteen figures, one of which is above the others, and represents the genius or spirit that is found in all the Persian sculptures of that age. The others consist of a royal personage, with two guards or attendants, and a file of captives. The king has his foot on a prostrate figure, and nine others tied together by their necks, with their hands tied behind them, stand before him in a row. The last of these wears a sort of pontifical cap. Over every figure is an inscription in the arrow-headed character; the dress of one of the captives contains another; two lines of characters extend along the rock beneath the whole length of the sculpture; while eight deep and closely written columns are seen still lower down. These inscriptions undoubtedly contain the history of the event represented by the sculpture, and we may hope, before many years, to see them copied and deciphered. Judging from the style of execution, they are probably of an earlier date than the figures at Persepolis, and refer to an earlier period of Asiatic history. The number of the captives, the pontifical cap of the last in the procession, the situation of the engraving on one of the great high roads of the Assyrian monarchs, give some colour to the conjecture which has been made, that it is designed to commemorate the conquest of the kingdom of Israel by Shalmanezer, and that it was executed at least 700 years before the Christian era.

The region between the Persian Gulf and the Caspian Sea, the original seat of mankind, is full of the remains of ancient grandeur, that have as yet only begun to be explored. We may regard it as a vast depository of historical fossils, which are destined to reveal to us the early history of our race; and which we may without presumption believe to have been providentially concealed and preserved in the solitude of the desert, and the darkness of superstition and ignorance, until in the fulness of time they should burst upon us with the force almost of a miracle, and drive from their last haunt of incredulity the disbelievers in the Sacred Volume.

For " The Friend."

Early Protest against Slavery in Georgia.

In an old pamphlet on the slave trade, which recently fell into my hands, are some extracts from an "Enquiry into the State and Utility of the Province of Georgia," printed in London in 1741, from which it appears that slavery was not established there without a decided a priori condemnation. Men who prized their own liberty, and who were taught to do as they would be done by, instinctively revolted at the proposition to enslave a portion of their fellow-men to gratify the demands of avarice. It is pleasing to find that some of the early settlers of that province gave utterance to their strong feelings of natural justice, in remonstrances to those in authority against the introduction of the "scourge." Forty-nine Salzburgers, settled at Ebenezer (25 miles from Savannah), with

their ministers, J. M. Bolzius and J. C. Gronau, "beseech the honourable trustees not to allow any negroes to be bro't to their place nor in their neighbourhood." "With respect to its being impossible and dangerous for white people to plant and manufacture rice in this climate, as being a work only for negroes and not for European people, having experience to the contrary, we laugh at such talking, seeing that several of us had a greater crop of rice last year than we wanted for our own consumption."

The inhabitants of Frederica also petitioned against slavery. Some Scotch settlers at New Inverness appear to have seen the end from the beginning, and to have looked at it as Christian freemen should. "Being informed that their neighbours of Savannah had petitioned for the liberty of having slaves," they say, in their remonstrance to Governor Oglethorpe, "We hope and earnestly entreat that before such proposals are hearkened unto, your Excellency will consider our situation, and of what dangerous and bad consequences such liberty would be of to us." Reciting some of these, they proceed: "It is shocking to human nature that any race of mankind and their posterity should be sentenced to perpetual slavery; nor in justice can we think otherwise of it than that they are thrown amongst us to be our scourge one day or other for our sins; and as freedom must be as dear to them as to us, what a scene of horror must it bring about! And the longer it is unexecuted, the bloody scene must be the greater. We therefore, for our own sakes, our wives, and children, and our posterity, beg your consideration, and entreat that, instead of introducing slaves, you will put us in the way to get some of our own countrymen, who, with their labour in time of peace, and our vigilance if we are invaded, (with the help of these), will render it a difficult thing to hurt us, or that part of the province we possess."

Dated Jan. 3d, 1788–9, and signed by 18 freeholders.

Well will it be for the inhabitants of Georgia, if, by what Jefferson has so happily called "the generous energy of their own minds," they avert "the bloody scene" which their prophet sires foresaw. VERUS.

The Learned Yankee Sea-Captain.

Some time since we gave an account of Elisha Burritt, a learned blacksmith in Worcester, Mass., who, while diligently and laboriously prosecuting his trade, had still found time to make himself master of many different languages. In the Journal of Commerce we find the following statement from a correspondent, respecting a sea-captain in this city, who seems to be equally worthy of admiration and praise:—

"We have in this city a captain of a ship, that has been trained to the sea from ten years of age until this day, who is not only acquainted with the popular languages of Europe, French, Spanish, German, Danish, and Dutch, with some other minor dialects, but is also a scholar in Latin, Greek, and Hebrew. Last winter "this inhabitant of the mountain billow' held a public debate, four different evenings, in the city of Rotterdam, in the French and German languages, with a learned (Jew) professor of languages, on the Divinity of the New Testament, and Jesus Christ the Messiah of God, 'the end of the law for righteousness. to all. that believe.' The Old Testament was read in its original language; the New Testament was read in Greek; while the fidelity of the protestant interpretation was shown from the prophecies in six different languages. The professor acknowledged. to the American captains, 'Your countryman, the captain, is better acquainted with the Old Testament than any man I ever conversed with; and his knowledge of the Books of Moses, and the customs of our people, is scarcely equalled by any Jew in Rotterdam. Really, there are some things that he is better acquainted with, having seen them practised on. the coast of Africa by the Jews, which the laws of Holland, indeed of all Christian Europe, and our sense of decency, will not permit us to practise.' It was the report with the common Jews that 'the captain was a Jew.' The captain weekly attends, including English and the synagogues, the worship of God in five different languages in this city. He says, 'I attend the synagogue to hear their new German Hebrew readers, as an American or Englishman cannot read Hebrew with any probable degree of its original pronunciation.' He was asked what induced him to attempt an acquaintance with Greek and Hebrew. He answered, 'When young, my mind was seriously impressed with the import and sublimity of the Christian religion; but my knowledge and delight in astronomy made me a sceptic in its reality and divinity, contrary to all the internal evidence that forced itself on my soul, in conviction of sin, or joy of redemption. My mind was continually crowded by—'It is impossible that God would take upon himself the likeness of human flesh to make an stonement for such a contemptible pebble as this, the most inferior of all planets, (except the moon,) when he is the adorable Creator of innumerable worlds of splendour, that excel in glory and magnitude our very sun.'' I doubted all interpretations, and external evidence of every kind I dare not venture upon. I was resolved to attempt the Greek. I surmounted its difficulties, to my peace and satisfaction. Then I grappled Hebrew as for life and death, until I understood it sufficiently, to the removal of all my doubts, and establishment in the fullest confidence and belief in the Divine Mission of Him that emphatically claims the appellation of Christ the Son of God, the Saviour of the world.''—*N. Y. Observer.*

CARE OF FARMING TOOLS.

We believe it may be safely asserted, that the farmer in a course of years sustains as much loss, or is put to as much expense in procuring tools, by their decay in consequence of needless exposure, as from their actual wear on the farm. How many are the instances in which the farming implements, the ploughs, harrows, roller, &c., instead of being carefully housed when their use for the year is over, are left in the fields, or peradventure drawn up in battle array in front of the house, occupying a goodly portion of the road, and when covered with snow, forming most convenient places for breaking horses' legs, tearing off shoes, &c. &c. Perhaps, in addition to these, are sundry wagons, carts, hay-racks, and other necessary things, like the former, exposed to the decay which must result from exposure to the rains, the freezings, thaws, and snows of winter. Now, one such season of exposure does more to weaken the wood of these implements, promote decay, and render new purchases needful, than their ordinary wear on the farm, with careful usage and protection from the weather. As a general rule, it may be remarked that no implement, tool, or carriage of any kind should be exposed when not in use. Those not wanted in the winter should be secured from the weather during that time; and so with those not required during the summer season, as sleighs, sleds, &c. The skilful, thrifty farmer is known by his attention to the minor points of agriculture, by his care to save, as well as to acquire; and he who neglects the lesser things cannot fail to find the drawback on his profits large and constant.—*Gen. Farmer.*

A Touching Incident.—Fidelity of a Dog.—The *St. Augustine News*, of a late date, mentions the following touching incident:

An Irish greyhound, owned by Colonel Harney, and which he had brought from Missouri, had formerly a very strong attachment to M; Dallam, the owner of the trading establishment at Caloosahatchie.' On the massacre of the men at that post, but little hopes were entertained by the survivors but that the dog had either been killed or captured by the Indians. Fourteen days after the occurrence, on the arrival of troops to give sepulture to these victims of Indian faithlessness, this faithful and attached animal was found, barely able to stand, emitting a feeble howl over the remains of his friend. The corses around were denuded by vultures; but Dallam was uninjured. This noble trait of fidelity was duly appreciated by the troops, and four carburretted hydrogen, and might be Romeo, the trusty guardian of a dead friend, is now sincerely and devoutly cherished by the garrison at Tampa Bay.

USEFUL DIRECTIONS.

Curtis, in his Treatise on the Eye, in regard to foreign bodies being forced into the eye by various causes, such as a gust of wind, mending a pen, &c., &c.; observes that the method taken to remove them is generally unsuited to the end. The eyelids are first rubbed with the hand, which always produces unpleasant sensations, and not unfrequently inflammation, there being danger of forcing the offending substance into the eye, whence it cannot, without considerable difficulty, be removed. The proper mode of proceeding in such cases is as follows:

"Let the head be leant forward, and the upper eyelid raised by the person suffering, who will be more gentle than another can be; by this means he will commonly succeed in expelling it. The natural consequence of raising the eyelid, and retaining it in that position, is a flow of tears, which bring with them the intruding body, or carry it towards the canthus of the eye next the nose, whence it may easily be removed. Should this, however, prove ineffectual, the finger may be gently passed over the eyelid, towards the nose, a few times, which seldom fails to cause the substance to descend to the lachrymal glands, and thus be dislodged.

But should he still be unsuccessful, then it will be advisable to let another person introduce, between the eyelid and the ball, a small hair-pencil dipped in cream, beginning at the outer corner, and proceeding towards the nose, which usually effects the desired object. Further from this I would warn unprofessional individuals from going; as a serious lasting injury may be done to so delicate an organ before they are aware of it.

When the eye has been stung by insects, such as wasps, bees, knats, &c., the first thing to be done is to ascertain if the sting is left behind, and if so, to extract it by means of a small pair of forceps. Beyond that, all friction is dangerous, and will produce inflammation. The following is a simple mode of dissipating any incipient swell caused by such accidents. Mix a small quantity of vinegar with water, and apply it to the part affected."

PROGRESS OF SCIENCE.

The following items are from recent London papers :

New Source of Light.—M. Seguin has communicated to the Académie des Sciences at Paris, a memoir of the distillation of animal substances, in which he states that he reduced the process to such a degree of simplicity as to render it profitable for the sake of the distillation. Thus from the carcass of a horse he obtained, by destructive distillation, 700 cubic feet of gas, suitable for illumination, 25 pounds of sal ammoniac, and 33 pounds of animal black. The gas obtained was found to be composed of one part of olefiant gas, and preserved four months, in contact with water, without being in any way injured, or its brilliancy, as a combustible, impaired. M. Seguin found that 3,234 cubic inches of this gas, when burnt for one hour, gave twice and a half as much light as a Carcel lamp.

White Lead.—A discovery has been made in the neighbourhood of Plymouth, of a mineral possessing, as a base for paint, all the properties of white lead. We understand that paints manufactured from the article, have been rigidly tested by exposure for a length of time to all weathers, and that the results have been so satisfactory as to lead to a conclusion that the future consumption of white lead must be very considerably reduced.

DIED, on seventh day, 16th inst., of bilious remittent fever, REBECCA RICHARDSON, widow of Joseph Richardson, late of Middletown, Bucks County, a member and esteemed minister of the Northern District Monthly Meeting.

Brief Memoir of the Life of John Croker.
Written by himself.

(Continued from page 62.)

In the morning we got into our boat again, and committed ourselves for direction to George Stidson, who was mate of our former ship, and had formerly been in these parts, and knew most of the places of fishery in Newfoundland. About the middle of the day we came to the entrance of a small fishing place, I think called Renuse. It being war time, the inhabitants (who were but few) were greatly surprised by reason of our number, fearing we were come to rob them; and with what men and arms they had, they appeared very furiously against us, to oppose our landing; so that we were afraid they would, without mercy, have fired on us and taken away our lives, before they knew what we were. At length, with signs and loud words, to let them know what we were, we stopped their intention; and they sent a single man to us in a small boat, who, finding we were all English, and had no arms, but were poor, ragged, and distressed men, they invited us kindly ashore, by the name of brothers! This I looked on as a fresh deliverance from the point of death; for if they had fired on us, no doubt but some of us had been killed. When we came on shore, they treated us with a good fire, spruce beer, and broiled fish; this was grateful to our hungry stomachs and weary bodies, and the best return we had to make them for the favours we received, was our thankful acknowledgments, and to give them an account of what we had met with; which so far opened their hearts, that they desired our stay awhile with them. The spruce-beer is what they make in those countries from the spruce tree.

We stayed with them two or three days, and then, with returns of thanks, took our leave of them, and went into our boat again, intending to keep along near the shore, until we came to some place where we might meet with shipping. So, like wayfaring men, we called at a place or two, and tarried a night; when the people hearing of us before we came, entertained us cheerfully, for which we were thankful. At length we came to a cove, called Todes Cove, where they had not heard of us before, and our coming surprised them, that they repaired to their arms; but they became soon sensible what we were, and let us come on shore. There was but one dwelling at that place, the master's name, as I remember, was Dier; he had many servants, and cured much fish: he entertained us with much civility, and we stayed and helped him about his fish several days. Here our mate (the chief amongst us) fell dangerously ill, which proved an exercise to us all, and to me in particular, for I had a kindness for him, he being always civil to me, both before we were taken by the French, and after, during the time we were together: so we took the best care of him we could, and wrapped him very warm, laid him on a hand-barrow, and carried him to the boat; and taking leave of our noble landlord, we made what haste we could to the Bay of Bulls, where he had an aunt, to whose care we left him, and hastened to a

place called St. Johns, (where we understood lay a fleet of ships,) hoping to meet with a passage for England: but when we came there we found they were bound to Cadiz and Bilboa.

Now my sorrow began afresh, and as great as ever; for I not being a sailor, and but about seventeen years of age, not any of the ships would admit me as a passenger, fearing they should not be paid for my passage; and a sailor they did not look upon me to be. My fellow-prisoners and companions dispersed themselves, some in one ship and some in another, and disposing of the boat and materials, turned all to their own use, leaving me destitute of friends, relations, acquaintances, and money, in a strange country,—having nothing wherewith to make friends, unless the Lord was pleased to raise some up for me. To Him, therefore, I made my complaint in secret: and I was willing to be as contented as I could, taking my walks amongst the inhabitants, who were generally kind, and gave me at their houses bread and fish, when I looked for it. When night came I lodged in an open boat, or in a hay-loft, such as I could most conveniently meet with. I was but very thinly clothed, and dirty for want of change: and the cold winter was coming on, which is grievously hard in those countries: the ships were hastening away for fear of the frost, and no more were expected that season: all these circumstances increased my sorrow, and my near approaches to God in these great straits,—that he would be pleased to spare me, and work a way for my deliverance out of that country; and I would serve him according to the abilities of strength and wisdom, which he might in his love be pleased to bestow on me: at which times I brought myself under promises, which I desire, at the writing of this, the Lord would please to bring to my remembrance,—that if I have not performed them, I may strive with all diligence to the performance of them; for he is good and worthy to be served by all who have received the least of his mercies and favours. "Lord, humble the hearts of the people;—bring them to see their own outgoings, and what any of us are without thee, who art the alone help of thy people;—then shall all men forsake them, thou hast worked a way for them unthought of, as thou didst for the least of many thousands."

Before the fleet sailed, I heard that there was one vessel that was bound for Bristol, with train oil and fish, one Barrister being owner or master: to him I made my application, laying before him my distressed condition, which, I believe, he was not insensible of; but, like one of a hard heart, he would not admit me a passage in his vessel, unless I paid him three pounds before I went, which I could not do, being not worth three farthings. This made me mourn to see him so hard, and with a heavy heart I went on shore; but still being earnest to try him the second time, I entreated him again for a passage, desiring him to consider my condition, and that he was sensible I had not then wherewith to pay him, but he should be faithfully paid when I came to England; all which seemingly made no

impression on him; so that my countenance began to show the sorrow of my heart, and tears began to fall from my heavy eyes; and I passed from his presence without any hope. But in an unexpected manner the Lord was pleased to order it thus:—there was a merchant on board with this Barrister, who, perceiving the sorrowfulness of my countenance, came after me with compassion, as one sensible of my grief, and desired to know my name and the place of my birth, which I really told him; he then inquired my father's name and trade, and in what part of the town of Plymouth he lived, which I told him likewise. It so struck him, that he said, "what, are you his son?—how came you in this condition? I am sorry to see you thus; for I know him," (meaning my father.) "Well, I would not have you trouble yourself, for you shall go for England, if I pay your passage; and my wife (said he,) is going in the same vessel, and whatever you want, apply to her, and she shall assist you."

This sudden alteration brought renewed thankfulness upon my heart to God, the author of all these favours and deliverances, that in such an unthought of way, when my expectations were laid aside, He should raise up a friend to make way for my returning to England. I have cause to remember these things; although I had another sharp season to pass through, before I set my feet in my native land, which was then hid from me, but was after the following manner:—After this my great friend, (whose name was Strong, a brother to one of the same name, a schoolmaster in Plymouth,) had made way for me, by promising payment for my passage, and I was got on board the ship; the master being a wicked base fellow, after we were out at sea, would not let me have a cabin, but I was forced to lie between two hogsheads of train oil. This was hard lodging,—yet necessity obliged me to be as contented as I could; and I can truly say, my lot was often made sweet to me; for the thoughts and meditations of my heart were very often upon the law of my God, and I had comfort and delighted myself therein. Yet having nothing but my wearing clothes day or night to keep me warm, which had not been washed or changed for two months; I need not relate how it was with me. But now to leave the reader without some charity towards the master, I may let him know that he afterwards dealt with me somewhat more favourably; for having lodged some nights in this condition, he gave me an old sail, to lay under me, or partly over me, as I pleased; for which I was thankful to God, being a favour I wanted, and also thankful to the master for showing me some good nature.

The sense of what I had met with, and the goodness of God which I had experienced in it, with the consideration of my former transgressions, drew me into tenderness of heart and brokenness of spirit, so that my very head and hair would be wet with tears; and the Lord was often near unto me in his goodness. Oh! that I may never forget that day!—but that it may be imprinted upon my mind, and engraven on my heart, as with a point of a diamond, that I may always have it in my view; that when I may meet with afflictions in my older years, I may look back to the days of my youth, like Job,—who desired it might be with him as in the days of his youth, when the secret of God was upon his tabernacle, and in whose light he walked through darkness; which dark ways the Lord hath in some measure now given me to see, by the lifting up the light of his countenance upon me. For I am not able to express the seasons that I had upon the mighty waters during that great affliction,—which makes me say, it was good for me that I was afflicted, or else I had gone astray: for now I know of thy judgment, O Lord,—and I can praise thee for thy manifold mercies, which are lengthened out beyond my deserts: and what shall I render to thee, O Lord, for them all, but holy praises and high renown for ever!

Now to proceed, after about ten or twelve days sail, having had pretty good weather and wind most of the time, we, unexpectedly in the night, fell in with the Land's End of Cornwall, on the north side of it; the wind increasing blew us in very near land, which put the seamen in a fright, believing they should all be drowned, and the vessel wrecked; for the wind rent our mainsail in pieces, which occasioned a great outcry and trouble to get another to the yard. During this I lay still, believing it not fit for me to appear amongst them at that time, their fury being great towards each other: so I lay as much retired as I could, with my mind freely given up to death, if the Lord did so please; at which time I thought I enjoyed abundance of sweetness in my heart, and the thought of death was nothing, the sting being taken away. I heard the master say, there was not a soul likely to be saved, and that he and another would get into the long boat, and the rest should shift for themselves:—this he said several times. But it pleased God, who commandeth both wind and sea, and sayeth—"thus far and no farther shalt thou come," that the wind began to turn easterly; so that with some nicety, as well as Providence, (day coming on,) we weathered the Land's End. Now there being some hopes, I was willing to see what danger we had been in, therefore I got upon the deck, and I think, had I thrown a stone, I might have struck the rock;—this I accounted another great deliverance.

The wind still continuing high, we came up the South Channel before Plymouth, my native town, as far as Dartmouth in Devon, and we ran in there. The wind being very strong, before we could come to an anchor, our foreyard arm broke, and we went a-head of all the ships which were then in that road. At length we dropped our anchor, but it did not hold, so that we drove until we were astern of all those ships, and no boats were able to come and help us, so that some cried out we must go; but at last the anchor held, and we weathered it that night, and the next morning the wind ceased, so that the boats came to us, and helped us in, where we lay safe, and seemed to be out of danger of the sea, and of the privateers which were on it.

Thus I was likely to put my feet again on English ground, and but about thirty miles from my father's house. Before this, my father had heard of my being taken, but could not understand where I was, and had sent several letters to France, and supplies were ordered for me there, but he could not hear of me; so he concluded I was not in the land of the living. This was cause of sorrow to my parents to think, if they had not sent me away, I might have been living; but, however, it all worked together for my good, and I believe God had a hand in it.

(To be continued.)

The Eighth Annual Report of the Executive Board of the Union Benevolent Association. Read at the Annual Meeting, October 15, 1839.

Whoso hath this world's good, and seeth his brother have need, and shutteth up his compassion from him, how dwelleth the love of God in him?

The close of another official year, of the Union Benevolent Association, suggests the propriety of again presenting an annual report of its proceedings to its numerous contributors and patrons. The year that has passed, like all preceding ones since the formation of our society, has brought its accustomed share of cares and duties. In a population as extensive as our own, the claims of the wretched and distressed for sympathy and charity, are ever earnest and pressing. To many the time of harvest affords no abundance, and though all is prosperity around them, they remain the sad victims of want and misery. The history of their condition is embraced in the same recital of accumulated and pressing misfortunes, or of the ruinous results entailed by a course of idleness and dissipation. Nor are the annals of benevolence less short and simple than those of the poor and afflicted. All demand relief—and whilst assistance is afforded, the drooping heart, borne down with many sorrows, is cheered with the soothing language of encouragement, whilst the vicious and depraved are warned of the pernicious results of their dissolute career. The work of benevolence is nevertheless arduous and difficult. To discharge the duty aright, domestic comfort and convenience must frequently be sacrificed—the abodes of wretchedness and misery visited and explored—and the case of each suffering member of society carefully investigated. Nor is less exertion demanded of the moral sympathies of our nature. The heart glowing with pure philanthropy will be made to bleed afresh at every new recital of disappointment and adversity, and be wrung with anguish at each renewed exhibition of the degradation inflicted by vice and immorality. Nor is this all. Even exertions such as these, are but ill repaid. By some the succour afforded is deemed a matter of right, for which no obligation is incurred —the well directed counsel is received with coldness and indifference, whilst base ingratitude frequently marks the after conduct of those, who, in moments of affliction and distress, were the most importunate supplicants at the hand of charity. All this must be en-

countered, and the board would shrink from the task of fulfilling the objects of this association, were they not sustained by the valuable and efficient labours of the board of lady-visiters. To their exertions on this as on every other occasion, they are desirous of giving the highest approbation, and of acknowledging the important and useful assistance afforded by them individually and as a body. As upon them is devolved a prominent and laborious station in the operations of our society, so the board of managers, feel happy in according to them, thus early in the detail of their proceedings for the past year, the commendation to which they are justly entitled.

Soon after the last annual meeting, the board commenced their preparations for the winter, which was rapidly approaching. Collectors were appointed for the various districts of the city and suburbs, and the annual report printed and distributed, in order that the citizens prior to their being called upon for their subscriptions, should be informed of the objects and proceedings of our society. The exertions of the collectors were not as successful as in some preceding years. The association for the last few years has been better supported by our citizens than in former ones —yet the supply afforded is but barely sufficient to meet the pressing calls constantly made for succour and relief. Our funds have been exhausted for some time, and the amount requisite for our operations has been advanced by the treasurer. Believing, as the board do, that no better plan than the one under which we are acting, could be devised for meliorating the condition of the poor, it is earnestly to be desired that we should be made the prominent channel for the distribution of whatever is given in charity, within the sphere of our operations. Although, in some instances, the really poor and deserving, may be found seeking their bread from house to house, yet in the great majority of cases, those thus employed, are utterly worthless, abandoned and depraved in their dispositions, and ready to pilfer and steal wherever an opportunity for so doing may occur. A reference to our office and agent would in such instances, be found efficient, by providing comfortably for the one class, and exposing the imposition practised by the other. Our visiters are frequently subjected to much discouragement by seeing the liberality of well meaning yet injudicious persons, secured by some plausible tale or affected propriety of demeanour, lavished upon those unworthy of it; which, if correctly employed, would have carried relief and comfort to others far better entitled to its reception, and thus have accomplished greater and more extensive good. The effect also upon the poor is injurious— they will be led to practise that which appears productive of the greatest benefit—and substitute the deceitful garb of hypocrisy for the simple vestment of truth.

The fund derived from collection and otherwise, a detailed statement of which will be exhibited in the treasurer's report, was distributed, as we believe, carefully and correctly. Each recipient of the public liberality was faithfully visited, and the mind of the visiter satisfied before the bounty was dispensed. In the account of our annual expenditures, the purchase and delivery of wood always constitutes a heavy item. Our winters are so long in their duration, and so frequently severe, that it is almost impossible for some, whose wages are but trifling, to encounter the expense required for providing fuel for themselves during an entire season. In very many instances, all the relief asked is a quarter of a cord of wood, and the individual furnished with this, is in all other respects able to provide comfortably for himself and his family. The number of cords purchased for the last season amounted to 300, at an expense of $2,796 32; and the quantity delivered to each proper applicant, except in urgent and extraordinary instances, was that which has just been specified. Such of the soup societies as were in operation, received as usual from our funds one hundred dollars each, in all $400, except the Spring Garden Society, from which no call was made; and these excellent institutions were again enabled to supply soup and bread to the poor during the season. Shoes and garments were also furnished by the lady-visiters; sometimes from the sums placed in their hands for disbursement, and sometimes from the Dorcas societies, with which many of them are connected. The system of visitation, it is believed, has been faithfully carried out, and the character, circumstances, and condition of every one under the care of the association duly investigated. The sewing department has been in operation during such periods as orders were furnished for work. It is to be regretted, however, that there has been a deficiency of such orders during the summer. The number of garments made during the past year is 2068, for which $710 was paid to the females employed in sewing. No branch of our operations is considered by the board as important as this—and it is to be hoped the time is not far distant, when some plan may be devised for furnishing constant employment to those standing in need of it, and thus every excuse for poverty be taken away from those who are physically able to earn a livelihood.

The board have long been impressed with the belief that intemperance, as it is the productive author of crime, so is it, also, the cause of much of the poverty and misery which we daily see around us. Statistics have so frequently been presented on this point, and tending to demonstrate this fact, that scarcely any can be found willing to contradict it; we fear, however, the public ear has become so used to recitals of this nature as to have grown almost callous. So many applications have been made, without success, in quarters from which alone permanent relief can come, as to discourage the efforts of such as are sensibly alive to the magnitude of the evil. Temperance societies have done much to arrest the progress of the destroyer, but there is a numerous class in the community who never come under their influence. No radical reformation can be expected until a complete and total revolution is effected in the nature of

our license laws, and until those laws are correctly and duly administered by our courts and judges. Our agent has collected some valuable information under this head. In his report to the board for September, 1839, he remarks—"In referring to my register of police reports, I find that 800 cases of drunkenness have been adjudicated by the mayor —of these 700 were fined at $1 50 each, amounting to $1050—probably near $1000 of this was paid by those who do not support their families without aid; in addition to this, there have been 157 cases of female drunkenness: about 50 of these were fined, and the rest committed to prison for different periods of time, according to their character. This does not include cases of riot, assault and battery, and other crimes originating from the same source. There are doubtless nearly as many more brought before the several magistrates, of which I can only judge by the weekly dismissals from prison, which amount to 450, all of which are for petty offences, riot, assault and battery, disorderly conduct, &c. I do not think I have more than one half of the cases. All these have occurred since January 1, 1839, less than ten months." Our courts of criminal sessions, quarter sessions, oyer and terminer, it may be literally said, are occupied with intoxication and its various consequences. Day after day their judges are employed in hearing and deciding cases, nine tenths of which have their origin in or are accompanied in their details by, the exhibition of this degrading vice. It is but a mockery of justice to invite to her temple for a proper license those who traffic in the poisonous draught, and then afterwards to drag before the same tribunal for correction and punishment, those who have been led to the commission of offences through the maddening influence of the stimulus afforded in the vile haunts of intoxication and vice. This subject should be one of interest to every citizen, for all are called upon, by the payment of taxes, to bear part of the penalty inflicted by the unrestrained granting of licenses. The courts to which we have adverted are sustained at an enormous expense. In a large number of cases, the individuals convicted of petty offences are unable to pay the costs of prosecution, and are consequently committed for thirty days, in the meantime their families are suffering for want of support, and public liberality is again called upon to save them from starvation. No evil is more serious in its character, or calls more loudly for redress, and your board feel confident that a reformation in this particular would be productive of great and permanent good—that it would diminish the ranks of the poor—be a saving of thousands in the public purse, and restore to society as good and virtuous citizens many who now are miserable and degraded outcasts.

It should ever be borne in mind that this society seeks to effect much of its good by moral means. It has ever protested against its being considered a mere alms-giving association. Its visiters have always made it a prominent point to reform, as well as to alleviate—to eradicate the evil, as well as to re-

move it for a season. One cheering fact is presented in their reports, by an enumeration of the number who, by their exertions, have been placed at week-day and Sunday schools. Education will ever be found a great preventive of pauperism. The mind well enlightened, or even but partially illuminated, is seldom content to remain in a dependent condition —the effort will be made to rise and assume an elevated station. Instruction, generally imparted, will prevent in this country what may be termed hereditary pauperism—a condition in which men have lived for successive generations in the same state of degradation, without a wish or desire to advance in the scale of civilization. An antidote so powerful as this, will tend to diminish the throngs of drunkards who infest our population, luring them from the bottle by exhibiting sources of more refined gratification, and furnishing that rational enjoyment which the mind requires in moments of relaxation from toil and labour, and which, when wanting, will be supplied by mere animal indulgence. The strong holds of vice and immorality may be successfully attacked with an instrument so productive of good as this. Let not then success be despaired of whilst the ability to resist is still in our possession.

Since our last meeting, the board in common with the rest of their fellow-citizens have been called to lament the decease of Matthew Carey, Esquire, who always evinced a lively interest in the operations of our association, and presided at various town meetings, under the authority of which collections were made from the citizens in our behalf.

It would be improper to close the record of our transactions for the past year without stating that the agent has attended to the duties of his office with his accustomed care and fidelity.

Another winter will soon be at hand, and from the present embarrassed condition of affairs throughout the community, much severe distress may be anticipated. The board, however, feel willing to persevere in their labours, nothing doubting, but that the same kind Providence which hitherto has prospered their efforts, will continue to crown with success all their endeavours in the cause of benevolence and philanthropy.

PHILIP GARRETT, President.
James W. Paul, Secretary.
October 15, 1839.

AMERICAN ABORIGINES.

The region assigned for the permanent location of all the Indians residing within the territories of the United States, is bounded as follows:

Beginning at the source of the Puncah river; thence down the same to the Missouri river; down the Missouri to its junction with the Kawzan river; thence south on the western line of the state of Missouri to the state of Arkansas; thence southwardly on the western line of that state to Red river; thence up Red river to a point two hundred miles west of the state of Arkansas; and thence northwardly to the beginning. Making a tract of little over six hundred miles long, from north to south, and two hundred miles wide from east to west.

So little is known of the remote tribes, that we cannot safely attempt to state either their names or their numbers. The estimate of their numbers, given below, has been made with much care by comparing the whole region inhabited by them with nearer districts, within which the numbers are well known, making allowances for climate, &c., &c.

Population of the tribes indigenous within the district, 21,660
Number of emigrants, is 73,200

Total within this district, 94,860
Within the territory, above described, which is designed for the permanent residence of the Indians, it is contemplated to accommodate all the tribes and remnants of tribes east of the Mississippi river, and the portion of the Sauks and Foxes west of that river, and north of the state of Missouri. When all shall be thus located the aggregate will be 140,682 souls.

Twenty-three tribes have already received assignments of land. These assignments are described by the surveying of the exterior boundaries of each tract. A large portion of these surveys have been made.

To each tribe a patent, in due form, signed by the President of the United States, will issue from the general land office. The Cherokee patent is the first ever given to an Indian tribe. Patents at once change the tenure by which Indians hold their lands. A patent secures to every individual of the tribe, an equal right in the land, and the right of one cannot be alienated by another.—*Baptist Advocate.*

For "The Friend."

The following Elegy was written on the death of Charles Heald, a young Friend, who expired, much lamented, on the 15th of 10th mo., 1839, and was interred in Friends' burying ground at Short Creek meeting-house, Mount Pleasant, Ohio. The communication is transmitted without a knowledge of the author by
A READER OF "THE FRIEND."

Loved spirit farewell; a lone pilgrim is here,
And his harp, strung to sorrow, strikes over thy bier.
When mild spring shall go forth, o'er the fields, thro' the bowers,
With her music of birds, and her garlands of flowers:
When summer rejoices in beauty again,
With its warmth and its greenness, its sun and its rain:
When the rich fruit is gathered, and garnered the sheaf,
And low o'er the plain rustles autumn's sere leaf:
And the sun has gone down from his pathway of light,
In the cool of the day and the quiet of night,—
To thy sad-silent grave I will sometimes repair,
And commune with my heart in its loneliness there.

For it has been my lot with earth's loved ones to part,
Whose affections were twined round the cords of my heart;
Like them, in their strength from the world they were torn,
To the house for all living lamentingly borne.

While my own mountain-sod is green over their dust,
With strangers, in sadness, I languish, and must;
Oh, how solemn the thought, my own lot it may be,
Those I loved will deplore as thy friends mourn for thee.

No brother, no sister was near to bestow
The sweet balm of affection, or soften thy wo;
Nor stood thy fond mother, for many a day,
O'er thy languishing couch while in sickness thou lay.

Alone thy sad father watched over his trust,
And alone went his heart down with thee to the dust.
Say, must he return, in his anguish, to share
The sorrows of those who will mourn for thee there?

And the tears that must fall when, alas, it is said—
"My son has gone down to the dust of the dead?"
Where waves the tall oak, where Ohio still flows,
Far-away from thy home, in thy silent repose.

And learning's loved haunts, where thy footsteps were free,
Are clothed in the garments of mourning for thee.
But we, too, may go down, in youth's strength and its pride,
By death's cruel archers laid low at thy side.

Since the all that we loved of thy mortal is borne
To the dark halls of death, o'er thy ashes we mourn;
Yet not without hope, and a faith-guiding prayer,
That our souls will, like thine, heaven's diadem wear.

Upon Jesus alone could'st thou trustful rely,
For in him thou had'st lived, and in him thou could'st die;
While as plain as the vesture all seamless he wore
Was the house that thy dust to its resting-place bore.

But a garment, as bright as the angels may wear,
It is thine with the ransomed of Jesus to share:
A mansion prepared, and a crown has been given,
Where, with angels, thou wavest the palm-branch in heaven.

Thro' the gushings of sorrow we hear a sweet voice,
"Rejoice with my spirit, rejoice, oh ! rejoice !
We parted a moment—I meet you again—
I died, and I live, with my Saviour to reign !"
L. T.

THE FRIEND.

ELEVENTH MONTH, 30, 1839.

We derive gratification in giving publicity to the following notice, and in the proof which it affords that the benevolent feelings of our citizens are thus early awake, and in activity in making timely provision for the destitute during the inclement months. That there will be much need for the exercise of liberality towards the labouring class cannot be doubted, when the circumstances of the times are considered; and these soup-house establishments, it seems to be on all hands agreed, are admirably adapted, as a cheap, safe, and efficient mode of administering relief. We trust, therefore, that the call for pecuniary support in the present case will meet with a cordial and generous reception.

WESTERN SOUP SOCIETY.

At the annual meeting of the Western Soup Society, it was decided to open the Soup-House, south east corner of Schuylkill Sixth and George streets, on the 16th proximo.

It is not deemed necessary, at present, to enter into detail respecting the operations of the society for the past season, a summary of which may be found in "The Friend" of the 27th, of the 4th month last; the necessitous condition of the poor still remains the same, except as it may be aggravated by a want of employment among the labouring classes, which, it is believed, is felt to an unusual extent.

Owing to the expenses necessarily attendant upon the removal to our present location, our wants are greater than usual: to feed the poor and hungry is a very obvious duty, and it is under a grateful remembrance of past kindness and liberality that we ask for the means to sustain the society during the coming winter season.

Donations in money will be thankfully received by the following persons, or in provisions at the Soup-House.
M. C. COPE, No. 286 Filbert st.
C. PEIRCE, No. 366 Chestnut st.
M. L. DAWSON, N. W. cor. Filbert & 10th.
LOYD BAILY, N. W. cor. 13th and Market.
AMOS JEANES & Co., corner Schuylkill Front and Market.
S. BETTLE, jr., No. 26 south Front street.

Another institution, differing in its mode of operation, but in harmony with the above, we have repeatedly adverted to, and should rejoice to see carried out co-extensive with its plan, and the capacity for good which it manifestly possesses. We allude to the Union Benevolent Institution. In the hope of doing something towards directing to it the attention it merits, we have inserted the last annual report of the managers.

In the editorial paragraph relating to the memoir of John Croker last week, instead of *Alexander* read *Abraham R. Barclay.*

JOURNAL OF DANIEL WHEELER.

It may be proper to state, that the editors of the *Friends' Library* do not expect to print in their series the Extracts from the Journal of our friend, Daniel Wheeler, during his religious visit to the isles of the Pacific; and as the publisher of the Extracts has commenced the work, he would be glad to have the subscription papers forwarded to him by the first of the coming year, or earlier if convenient. It is expected the work will be ready for delivery by the latter end of the first month next, of which due notice will be given.
Philadelphia, 11th mo. 26, 1839.

The committee to superintend the boarding-school at Westtown will meet in Philadelphia, on sixth day, the 13th of next month, at 3 o'clock, P. M.

The committee on teachers will meet on the same day, at 10 o'clock, A. M. And the visiting committee attend at the school on seventh day, the 7th of the month.
THOMAS KIMBER, *Clerk.*
Philadelphia, 11mo. 30th, 1839.

MARRIED at Friends' meeting on Twelfth street, the 23d ult., JOHN W. TATUM, of Wilmington, Delaware, to AMY Y. ELLIS, daughter of Ellis Yarnall, of this city.

DIED on the 20th of 7th mo. last, at his residence near Crosswicks, N. J., SAMUEL BUNTING, a much esteemed member and elder of Chesterfield Preparative Meeting, in the 71st year of his age.

THE FRIEND.

A RELIGIOUS AND LITERARY JOURNAL.

VOL. XIII. SEVENTH DAY, TWELFTH MONTH, 7, 1839. NO. 10.

EDITED BY ROBERT SMITH.

PUBLISHED WEEKLY.

Price two dollars per annum, payable in advance.

Subscriptions and Payments received by

GEORGE W. TAYLOR,

NO. 50, NORTH FOURTH STREET, UP-STAIRS,

PHILADELPHIA.

For "The Friend."

Remarks on the study of the Greek and Latin languages, suggested by the perusal of Dymond's Chapter on Intellectual Education.

(Concluded from page 66.)

While considering the question, whether a part of the time of education can be advantageously devoted to classical studies, we must not overlook their great utility, in cultivating a just and refined literary taste. That the Greek and Roman authors furnish models of composition more highly finished, than can be found in any modern language, is a point so generally conceded by those who are acquainted with the subject, that it would be superfluous to attempt to prove it here. But some may deny that this is a sufficient reason for studying these authors, and contend, that as the Greeks, who are acknowledged to have borne away the palm of literary excellence, confined their attention exclusively to their own tongue, we should follow their example, and leaving other languages to themselves, direct our undivided efforts to the cultivation of English literature. But those who reason thus, leave out of view a number of circumstances, which must be considered, if we would form a correct judgment of the point in question. It is to be borne in mind, that the Greek language is not, like, the English, chiefly derived from other nations, and therefore it was not necessary that Homer, Xenophon, or Demosthenes, should study other tongues, in order to become perfect masters of their own. Besides, the circumstances in which we are placed, are very different from those of the ancient Greeks. To them little was known of the useful sciences; hence they were not, like us, obliged to divide their attention among a thousand different pursuits. In time of peace, the labours of their most gifted men were, generally speaking, devoted to the exclusive cultivation of some one of the fine arts. It was thus, that in Architecture, Sculpture, Poetry, and Eloquence, they were enabled to bequeath to after ages, those monuments of transcendent skill,

which have never been and probably never will be equalled. Men, now, have not the time and attention to bestow, which are requisite, in order to attain the highest excellence in the works of art. With regard to composition, indeed, it may be doubted, whether the modern languages are capable of being wrought into such perfect models, even though men of genius should devote to this object, the undivided attention of a whole life. —We may, however, without envy, award the palm of superiority in the fine arts, to the ancients, since they possess the far more desirable and nobler distinction, which arises from an extended acquaintance with the natural and abstract sciences, and from more enlightened and elevated views of morality and religion. But while we set a just and high value upon those improvements, which are the peculiar glory of the modern world, we must not altogether withhold our attention from the fine arts, and least of all from that of composition.* The importance of cultivating literary taste, as connected with this art, is sufficiently enforced by considerations of utility alone, without urging the reasonableness and propriety of cherishing, on all occasions, that love of the just and beautiful, which the Creator has implanted in our minds, and which his works are so remarkably calculated to awaken. It is hardly necessary here to insist upon a point, which we trust few will be disposed to controvert. We would, however, briefly observe, that taste is absolutely essential to perspicuity and strength in writing. It not only selects those terms which are the most appropriate, and best calculated to convey the thoughts clearly and forcibly, but it also points out the most proper arrangement of words and ideas, and retrenches all superfluous expressions, which might obscure or encumber the writer's meaning. Even in those cases where, from the nature of the subject, or defect in the language, it is difficult or impossible to attain complete perspicuity, it will teach us to make the best of the circumstances in which we are placed. By avoiding, as far as possible, every thing which would unnecessarily discourage or disgust, it will often render a subject intelligible and interesting, which would otherwise be obscure or repulsive.

As there are so many things which claim the attention in a modern education, it is a point of no small moment, to pursue such a course as will most effectually form and refine the taste, with the least possible expenditure of time. In order to effect this object, it will

---

* Composition may properly be ranked among the fine arts, since it includes poetry, which is acknowledged to be one.

be important, to confine the attention of the pupil to the exclusive study of the most perfect models. The taste of no one is, by nature, sufficiently correct and constant, to enable him to contemplate deformity, or even imperfections, for a length of time, without in some degree impairing his sensibility to what is beautiful and true. Indeed in this, and some other respects, there exists a striking analogy between purity in taste, and purity in morals. Without making any comparison between the actual importance of these two qualities, it may be observed, that in order to the successful cultivation of either, the same general plan is necessary to be pursued; since before the mind has attained its full strength and maturity, they are alike impaired by vicious, and improved by excellent examples. But perhaps some, who may admit the justness of the preceding observations, will contend, that it is unnecessary to go far in search of models, since we have them at home of sufficient excellence: that, moreover, examples selected from our own writers, would be more easily imitated, and more useful, as making us familiarly acquainted with the English tongue. To this we answer, that while we freely admit the benefit, and even necessity, of studying our own authors attentively, in order to obtain a perfect knowledge of our language, we insist, that great advantage results from being conversant with the literature of other nations. We have not unfrequently remarked, that young persons, who have given particular attention to some of our most distinguished writers, have unintentionally copied their manner, and even their words, so exactly, that it was not difficult to say which passage was Addison's, or Blair's, or which should be ascribed to Johnson. To this fault every one is liable, who devotes himself to a few authors exclusively. It can only be avoided by practice in composition, and by extensive reading. But if we study the works of a great number of different English authors, we shall be forced to take some of an inferior character, which, as we have already intimated, must tend to vitiate the taste. This disadvantage is entirely obviated by having recourse to the writings of the ancients. On one account, indeed, these are especially to be preferred. In consequence of the wide difference in the idioms of our language and theirs, it is scarcely possible to imitate their style too closely, so that, while the student admires those beauties, and imbibes that spirit of exquisite taste, for which their works are so remarkable, his manner is left unconstrained and free.*

---

* It may not be improper here to say, that, in speaking, as we have done, of the great assistance to

We ought not to close these desultory remarks, without adverting to an objection not unfrequently made to the classics, on account of their supposed immoral tendency. That a few of them are liable to this charge, we pretend not to deny. Nor do we deny, that those which are read in many of the schools, have been selected with too little regard to the purity of their moral influence. But it must be recollected, that there is an almost endless diversity in the character, and subject, of the ancient writings. If from so various and ample materials, the evil parts have sometimes been chosen, the blame must rest chiefly on those who have made so improper a selection; at all events, it cannot justly attach to that far greater portion of the classics, against which no reasonable objection can be urged. We cannot perceive why it would not be as just, to proscribe all the distinguished works in our language, because among them are to be found those of a corrupting tendency, as to reject universally the authors of ancient Greece and Rome, because a few of them may contain immoral sentiments. Indeed, it may safely be affirmed, that of the extant writings of antiquity, there is a smaller proportion of an objectionable character, than among the more celebrated English authors, taken collectively. If, therefore, we would guard the minds of the young against every hurtful influence, it is quite as necessary to make selections from our own, as from the Greek and Roman literature. The promiscuous study of the latter, indeed, would be the less dangerous, for two reasons. First, an improper sentiment from a heathen is less likely to make an injurious impression, and the impression, if made, would be more easily effaced, than if such a sentiment were expressed by the writer of a more enlightened and Christian age. Secondly, the respect which a pupil feels for the ancient authors, depends in a great measure on the will of his instructors; if, therefore, he admires what is evil in their writings, the fault is, generally speaking, chargeable on those, who have abused the authority of their station, in order to instil injurious sentiments, or whose culpable indifference has omitted to draw the just distinction, between what is unworthy and what is deserving of admiration. But the influence of a corrupt English work, as it may be understood without the assistance of a parent or preceptor, cannot be so directly controlled. Here, the reader has easy and free access to every part, and may drink, without restraint, of its tempting but poisonous fountains.

be derived from the classics, in acquiring a knowledge of our own tongue, and in forming the taste, we are far from meaning to assert, that among persons unacquainted with Latin and Greek, there have not been those justly distinguished, as well for their admirable taste in literature, as for their skill in the use of English language. We freely admit, that genius will sometimes triumph over every disadvantage of circumstances.—But such instances are merely the exceptions to a general rule, and ought not to influence our decision, as to what system of instruction may be best adapted to the generality of persons. We believe, however, that even genius itself may be improved, by that training of its powers and multiplication of its resources, which would result from a judicious and liberal education.

But it may be said, that the classics are objected to, not because they are positively *immoral*, in the common acceptation of the word, but because many of them, which may be otherwise unexceptionable, are chiefly occupied with the history of wars, or in detailing the crimes of distinguished men, the contemplation of which must tend to excite in the young, a spirit adverse to that of genuine Christianity. To this we answer, that while we would earnestly recommend that care should be exercised in this respect,—whether the history be in English or Latin,—we may remark, that the reading of wars, and of the crimes of the great, does not necessarily cherish a martial spirit, or an admiration of what is criminal. It is true, young persons, who have read history, have sometimes manifested a warlike disposition, and a tendency to vice. But may not the same be observed in those who have never read a single page? Do we not, indeed, generally find the love of war most prevalent among the most illiterate classes?—On this point we are anxious not to be misunderstood. We are far from recommending that young persons should be habituated to the contemplation of vice and crime; on the contrary, we believe that great caution is required, lest they become too familiar with them, before their moral perceptions are sufficiently matured to make the just distinction between right and wrong. We maintain, however, that it is not necessary, or even desirable, that they should remain altogether ignorant of the melancholy fact, that wickedness abounds, and always has abounded in the world. We believe that a knowledge of history might be communicated in such a manner, that, instead of exerting an injurious influence on the mind, it would be productive of a twofold benefit;—it would enforce the solemn truth, that, sooner or later, sin must ever be followed by misery, as its inevitable reward; and, by exhibiting the wickedness which has so generally prevailed in every age and nation, it would impressively teach the weakness and depravity of human nature.

In conclusion, we propose to recapitulate, as briefly as possible, the arguments which have been presented to the reader in the foregoing remarks.—First, the study of Latin and Greek is strongly recommended by the fact, that by devoting to it a considerable portion of the time of education, the pupil will be enabled to obtain a thorough knowledge of English more speedily than if this language should receive his undivided attention.—Secondly, a knowledge of those tongues will assist greatly in distinguishing the substantial worth of an argument, or the intrinsic beauty of a poetic image, from the tinsel of words, with which it may be decorated. From our previous observations on this subject, the reader may perceive, that the knowledge of any language in addition to our own, would be useful in this respect. But we believe that the Latin and Greek are much to be preferred, because, in consequence of their idioms differing so widely from ours, the thought alone can be transferred from English into those tongues, or from them into English, as every attraction, which depends on mere language, is ne-

cessarily destroyed in the translation.—Thirdly, the practice of rendering the ancient authors into English, is an excellent mode—if not the very best—of teaching children the art of composition.—Fourthly, the study of the classics furnishes a most valuable exercise of the mind, both because it is adapted to every stage of education, and because it requires the combined efforts of many different faculties.—Lastly, the pursuit of Greek and Roman literature, affords the best means of forming a correct and refined taste in composition.

It is hardly necessary to observe, that in the expression of our views of the classics, which are contained in the foregoing pages, we have not aimed at producing a finished essay. Should the reader have remarked any considerable omissions, or should it appear to him that minor points have sometimes been dwelt upon, while those of more importance have been but slightly noticed,—we would here beg leave to say in our justification, that it was not our purpose to publish a full and elaborate disquisition on the study of the dead languages. Had we intended to do so, we certainly should not have chosen to insert in the columns of "The Friend," what might have furnished materials for an ample volume.—Had we not been limited as to space or time, we should have been strongly tempted to dwell upon a number of topics, which we have passed over hastily, or in absolute silence. We might have spoken of the satisfaction of being able fully to appreciate those exquisite passages from the ancient poets, which we find in every part of our literature,

" Thrown about like unstrung pearls."

We might have enlarged upon the pleasure and instruction, to be derived from conversing, in their own language, with men who lived near thirty centuries ago, and from being able to note all the various peculiarities, not only of expression, but of thought and feeling, which have prevailed at the different periods of Greek and Roman history. These, and many other subjects, might have been considered; but, for the reasons adverted to above, we were obliged to restrict ourselves. Leaving, therefore, several points which had already been treated at large by others, and some that we deemed too obvious to need comment, we thought it proper merely to call the attention of those, who might feel an interest in the subject, to a few arguments in vindication of the classics, which either had scarcely been noticed at all, or had not generally received that consideration, to which, in our judgment, they were justly entitled.

RESOURCES OF SWITZERLAND.

The following is taken from the London Mirror for 1838, in which it is stated to be extracted from a report made to Parliament on the commerce and manufactures of Switzerland, by Dr. Bowring.

The geographical position of Switzerland with regard to commerce (especially beyond seas) is the most unfortunate in Europe. The country being thickly studded with and surrounded by the highest mountains, offers the greatest obstacles even to ordinary communications, and scarcely permits any hopes of canals or railroads. Its soil is barren and unsuitable to a variety of cultivation. The mountains yield but little metal. It fetches from abroad the most of its food, metals raw and worked, machines and tools, all the raw material for its manufactures, even the coals used in the foundries. In every warehouse, in every shop in the land, English and French goods are exhibited by the side of theirs. The former have paid no duties; the latter have had no protection. Insignificant as were their early attempts, and confined as were their markets, their government denying them a helping hand, forcing the Swiss to shift for themselves; and in spite of the tremendous rivalry of British capital and French taste, this intelligent, virtuous, brave, and persevering people have succeeded. Despite every obstacle, weak as they are, without a single port or means of outlet, except such as are held at the good pleasure of their neighbours, their articles have found their way, and meet with a ready sale in the four quarters of the globe. Take the following history of

Watch-making in Switzerland.

One of the largest and most interesting branches of Swiss industry is the watch-making trade. It is carried on to an immense and still increasing extent in the mountainous districts of Neuchatel, in the French portion of the canton of Berne, and in the town and neighbourhood of Geneva. It has been a source of wealth and comfort to many thousands of the inhabitants, who, in the seldom-visited villages of the Jura, have gathered around them a large portion of the enjoyments of life. Switzerland has long furnished the markets of France; and, though the names of certain French-makers have obtained a European celebrity, yet I was informed by M. Arago, that an examination into this trade had elicited the fact, that not ten watches were made in Paris in the course of a year, the immense consumption of France being furnished from Switzerland, and the Swiss works being only examined and rectified (*repassés*) by the French manufacturers.

The Jura mountains have been the cradle of much celebrity in the mechanical arts, particularly in those more exquisite productions of which a minute complication is the peculiar character. During the winter, which lasts from six to seven months, the inhabitants are, as it were, imprisoned in their dwellings, and occupied in those works which require the utmost developement of skilful ingenuity. Nearly 120,000 watches are produced annually in the elevated regions of Neuchatel. In Switzerland, the most remarkable of the French watch-makers, and among them one who has lately obtained the gold medal at Paris, for his beautiful watch movements, had their birth and education; and a sort of honourable distinction attaches to the watch-making trade. The horologers consider themselves as belonging to a nobler profession than ordinary mechanics, and do not willingly allow their children to marry into what they consider the inferior classes.

As early as the seventeenth century, some workmen had constructed wooden clocks with weights, after the model of the parish clock which was placed in the church of Locle, in the year 1630. But no idea had been as yet conceived of making clocks with springs. It was only about the latter end of the same century that an inhabitant of these mountains, having returned from a long voyage, brought back with him a watch, an object which was till that time unknown in the country. Being obliged to have his watch repaired, he carried it to a mechanic named Richard, who had the reputation of being a skilful workman. Richard succeeded in repairing the watch, and, having attentively examined its mechanism, conceived the idea of constructing a similar article. By dint of labour and of perseverance he at length succeeded, though not without having had great difficulties to surmount, as he was compelled to construct all the different movements of the watch, and even to manufacture some ill-finished tools in order to assist him in his labours.

When this undertaking was completed, it created a great sensation in the country, and excited the emulation of several men of genius to imitate the example of their fellow-citizen, and thus, very fortunately, the art of watch-making was gradually introduced among our mountains, whose inhabitants had hitherto exercised no other trade or profession than those which were strictly necessary to their daily wants, their time being principally employed in cultivating an ungrateful and unproductive soil. Our mountaineers were frequently compelled, before the introduction of the above-named branch of industry, to seek for work during the summer months among the populations of the surrounding country. They rejoined their families in the winter, being enabled from their economical savings, the moderation of their wants, and the produce of a small portion of land, to supply themselves with the necessaries of life.

During the first forty or fifty years a few workmen only were employed in watch-making, and, owing to the numberless difficulties they had to surmount, to the slowness of execution, caused by the absence of convenient tools, the want of proper materials, &c., the productions and profits were inconsiderable. They began at length to procure the articles of which they stood in need from Geneva, and afterwards from England, but the high prices which these articles cost, induced many of our workmen to attempt to provide them for themselves. They not only thus succeeded in rivaling foreign tools, but they eventually introduced many superior ones, till then unknown.

It is not more than eighty or ninety years since a few merchants began to collect together small parcels of watches, in order to sell them in foreign markets. The success which attended these speculations induced and encouraged the population of these countries to devote themselves still more to the production of articles of ready sale; so much so, that very nearly the whole population has, with a very few exceptions, embraced the watch-

making trade. Meanwhile the population has increased three-fold, independently of the great number of workmen who are established in almost all the towns of Europe, in the United States of America, and even in the East Indies and China. It is from this period also that dates the change which has taken place in the country of Neuchatel, where, notwithstanding the barrenness of the soil, and the severity of the climate, beautiful and well-built villages are every where to be seen, connected by easy communications, together with a very considerable and industrious population, in the enjoyment, if not of great fortunes, at least of a happy and easy independence.

The number of watches manufactured annually in this canton may be calculated to be from 100,000 to 120,000, of which about 35,000 are in gold, and the rest in silver. Now supposing the first, on an average, to be worth 150 fr., and the others 20 fr., it would represent a capital of nearly seven millions, without taking into consideration the sale of clocks, and instruments for watch-making, the amount of which is very large.

The trade of clock and watch-making is of considerable antiquity in Geneva. In the ninth century clocks were first known there, and it is believed the art of manufacturing them was imported from Germany. The bell, or sounding part of the machine, was added some time after; and in the eleventh century clocks were not uncommon. Chimes were a later invention, and, as the machinery by which time is measured became more complete and minute, watches were the necessary result. In 1587, Charles Cusin, of Autun, in Burgundy, settled in Geneva, as a manufacturer of watches, which were then sold for their weight in gold. He had many scholars, and his success naturally drew labour from less profitable employment, and spread the watch-making trade very rapidly.

The manufacture of repeating-watches, led, as has been observed, to another species of industry. Attention to the various tones of the metal,—and it may be added, the education of the people in the science of harmony —soon connected music with machinery; and musical rings, seals, watches, and boxes, were produced in considerable numbers,—the first experiments having been costly, but practice so reduced the price as to create a large market, and still leave a considerable profit. Out of the success of this new branch of manufacture others grew—musical automata of various characters—some combining great perfection of motion with external beauty and perfect harmony, concentrated in an exceedingly small space.

The great advantage which the Swiss possess in competition with the watch-makers in England, is the low price at which they can produce the flat cylinder watches, which are at the present time much in request. The watch-makers of Great Britain buy largely both in Geneva and Neuchatel, and scarcely a single watch pays the duty of 25 per cent., because the risk of clandestine introduction is small. The average annual export to England is from 8,000 to 10,000 watches, and the average price about £10 sterling.

The watches of English manufacture do not come into competition with those of Swiss production, which are used for different purposes, and by a different class of persons. Notwithstanding all the risks and charges, the sale of Swiss watches is large, and it has not really injured the English watch-making trade. The English watches are far more solid in construction, fitter for service, and especially in countries where no good watch-makers are to be found, as the Swiss watches require delicate treatment.

English watches, therefore, are sold to the purchaser who can pay a high price; the Swiss watches supply the classes to whom a costly watch is inaccessible.

THE WEST.

Few persons thoroughly realize what are the capabilities of the valley of the Mississippi. A writer in the New York Review sets this matter in a most forcible light as follows:

"Look at it; in that valley there are one million four hundred thousand square miles, or eight hundred and ninety-six millions of acres, while Great Britain with all its islands, contains but eighty-eight thousand square miles, or fifty-six and a half million of acres. And what is the character of this vast region? One third of it, at least, is capable of cultivation, and thick settlement, and one third, four hundred and sixty-four thousand square miles in extent, about seven times as great an area as all the available land of England, Ireland, Scotland, Wales, and the islands. Look at it more minutely, and you find it, from the cleared fields of Ohio and Indiana, to the edge of the barren prairies of the Missouri, and from the wild rice swamps of the north to the cypress swamps of the south, fertile beyond example, almost level, or slightly undulating, and accessible in every direction. Never was there a finer country for the agriculturist: standing at his farm-house door, in the interior of Ohio, Indiana, or Illinois, a thousand miles from the salt water, he may see his produce afloat on its way to New York, or Europe; in a few years five complete lines of water and railway communication will exist between the interior of Ohio and the ocean; four are now in operation. Nor is that valley destined to be less eminently manufacturing than agricultural. The state of Ohio, if we may rely upon her geologist, Mr. Mather, contains as much bituminous coal of good quality and easy of access, as all England and Wales: and Ohio, in this respect, is, he thinks, no richer than Western Pennsylvania, Western Virginia, and Kentucky; judging from the little that is known, Indiana, Illinois, and Missouri are probably underlain to a considerable extent by this same great mineral treasure. Nor is it coal alone that abounds in the west; from the head waters to the Cumberland river across Kentucky and Ohio, extends a bed of iron ore twenty miles in width. Tennessee is filled with iron; immense beds were lately opened in Indiana—and who has not heard of the Missouri mountain of that most precious metal. Already do Pittsburg and Cincinnati,

yearly, manufacture seven or eight millions of dollars worth of iron articles for export to other points; and lead abounds also; salt is met with in inexhaustible quantities; lime is universally distributed; and the finest freestone found in the greatest profusion. Here then is a land, the soil and climate of which favour tillage in the highest degree; the interior of which is far more easy of access than the interior of any country in Europe, and filled with mineral wealth. Within its limits, grow maize, wheat, hemp, flax, tobacco, cotton, and sugar. It is a land which scarce needs foreign commerce; it is a world within itself; there is scarcely one considerable article of commerce, if we except coffee and some dye-stuffs, which the Mississippi valley cannot furnish. The first flint glass made in America was at Pittsburg; the porcelain earth within the limits of that region rivals that of China; the lake abounds in fish; and the burr stone of Ohio, may be compared with the best from France.

Now, what in the common course of things, must be the result of this wealth and capability? A dense population, a population of not less than one hundred and twenty millions of people; nay, if we base our calculations on the present population of France, of not less than one hundred and sixty millions, that is to say, a population greater than that now living in Great Britain, Ireland, France, Holland, Spain, Portugal, and all Germany.

THE ELDER SACRED POETS.

A late number of Fraser's Magazine has an article with the above title, the perusal of which has yielded us much gratification. It is in the form of a review of a work styled, "Lives of the Sacred Poets, by Robert Aris Wilmott, Esq., Trinity College, Cambridge." We have marked a portion, as forming a suitable contribution to the pages of "The Friend."

There is, perhaps, no field of research that more richly repays for the toil and trouble that accompany our survey of it, than that of sacred poetry. Its parentage and growth are alike interesting. It is one of the striking facts that arrest our notice at the very threshold of our enquiries, that the Reformation was the mother of the noblest poetry that has twined undying and amaranthine garlands around the brow of Europe. Notwithstanding the decorations which are studiously courted by the Roman Catholic communion, and the apparent scope she presents for the developement of poetic genius, it is yet true that the noblest poets prior to the Reformation put forth their most glorious inspirations, not when they tried to beautify, but when they ventured to expose, the "chambers of imagery" of that dark and desperate apostacy. Petrarch's most compressed and vigorous sonnets are those in which he rakes up and blasts, with withering words, the corruptions of Babylon. Dante never treads the burning plains of the Inferno with so majestic a step as when he puts the pope among its most meritorious inmates. The papal superstition

does not foster poetic genius; it depresses and destroys it. At the present day, the bright and the beautiful in modern poetry are not within the jurisdiction of the Vatican. The chains which the Roman superstition binds around the intellect of mankind; the suspiciousness with which it impregnates social intercourse; the pollutions which its confessionals at once originate, kindle, and canonise; the deference that must be given to the weakest, and often the worst of men; and the interdict fastened on free thought and mental expansion,—are all obvious reasons for the fact, that, within the precincts of popery, genius fades, and its offspring dwindles like flowers on the bleak heights of the Alps, or in the pestilential valley of Java.

Far otherwise has it been in Protestant lands. The Reformation unsealed those fountains more glorious than Helicon—the fountains of truth. It brought man back to a sense of his dignity and privileges; it taught Burns at the plough that it was his calling, if he would, to be the companion of God. It spread a holy and an ennobling atmosphere around the cottage and the palace. Immediately after the Reformation, and especially during the reign of Edward the Sixth, poetry burst forth from the cells in which it had too long been pent up, and circulated round the countries wherein it appeared in its primeval freshness; and though, as was to be expected, it languished during the papal and persecuting reign of Mary, yet, at her demise, the mantle of its most illustrious ones fell on Spenser, and originated, by its inspiration, *The Faëry Queene.*

Soon after Spenser, (on whom our remarks are, at this time of the world, supererogatory,) BARNABÉ BARNES, the son of a bishop of Durham, made his exit on Parnassus. He wrote a number of sonnets, terse and compressed, but shaped on the Procrustes' bed of Petrarch's prescriptions. The following is a very pleasing and not inappropriate specimen:—

"Benign Father, let my suits ascend,
 And please thy gracious ear, from my soul sent,
 Even as those sweet perfumes of incense went
 From our forefathers' altars, who didst lend
 Thy nostrils to that myrrh which they did send,
 Even as I now crave thine ears to be lent.
 My soul, my soul is wholly bent
 To do thee condign service, and amend;
 To flee for refuge to thy wounded breast,
 To suck the balm of my salvation, thence,
 In sweet repose, to take eternal rest,
 As thy child folded in thine arms' defence;
 But then my flesh, methought, by Satan fired,
 Said my proud, sinful soul in vain aspired."

FRANCIS DAVISON

Is another of the early poets, whose life includes a portion of the 16th and 17th centuries. His was the ordinary lot of great genius, if not its noblest attributes. He spent an obscure life, and found an early grave. His versions of the Psalms are very superior; many of them are models, and might be gathered into the National Selection, which many churchmen long to see in the Church of England. Sir Egerton Brydges has spoken in no ordinary terms of their poetic excellence. They are rather free, but still they are faithful to the original. We select a specimen in the twenty-third Psalm :—

" God, who the universe doth hold
    In his fold,
Is my shepherd, kind and heedful—
Is my shepherd, and doth keep
        Me, his sheep,
Still supplied with all things needful.

He feeds me in fields which have been
        Fresh and green,
Mottled with spring's flowery painting,
Through which creep, with murmuring crooks,
        Crystal brooks,
To refresh my spirits fainting.

When my soul from heaven's way
        Went astray,
With earth's varieties seduced ;
For his name's sake, kindly he
        Wandering me,
To his holy fold reduced.

Yea, though I stray through death's vale,
        Where his pale
Shades do on each side enfold me,
Dreadless, having thee for guide,
        Should I bide,
For thy rod and staff uphold me."

After the short epitaphs which R. A. Wilmott reverently writes on the tomb-stones of these departed poets, he refers briefly—more so than could have been wished—to the unfortunate Raleigh. He vindicates his " sere and closing days" from the charge of scepticism, too justly applicable to his youth. For this we refer to the pages before us. Wilmott quotes one solitary poetic specimen from the writings of Sir Walter, but it is a gem :—

" Rise, oh, my soul! with desires to heaven,
    And with divinest contemplation use
Thy time, where time's eternity is given ;
    And let vain thoughts no more thy thoughts abuse,
But down in darkness let them lie,
So live thy better, let thy worse thoughts die,

And thou, my soul, inspired with holy flame,
    View and review, with most regardful eye,
That holy cross, whence thy salvation came,
    On which thy Saviour and thy sin did die :
For in that sacred object is much pleasure,
And in that Saviour is my life and treasure.

To thee, O Jesu, I direct my eyes ;
    To thee my hands, to thee my humble knees ;
To thee my thoughts, who my thoughts only sees ;
    To thee myself, myself and all I give ;
To thee I die, to thee I only live."

With this extract our author winds up his introduction, or compendium of references to more obscure and early poets. His closing reflections on the short notices he was obliged to give, remind one of the sweetness and beauty of the preface of Bishop Horne to his *Commentary on the Psalms* :—

" I bring this hasty introduction," he adds, "to an end with regret. I have said little when my heart prompted me to say much. I have been compelled to pass over, without notice, many who left their *fame upon a harpstring*, and from whose antique leaves might be gathered thoughts of the serenest piety and peace. Of some of these I shall have an opportunity of speaking in the following pages. I have walked through the burial-ground of our elder poets with no irreverent footsteps, and I shall not have lingered there in vain, if I have renewed one obliterated inscription, or bound one flower upon their tomb."

GILES FLETCHER.

We have no hesitation in placing *Christ's Victorie*, Fletcher's most celebrated production, in a very high niche. His standing at the university, his duties at his rectory in Suffolk, and discontent with his parishioners, we pass by, and, in our present arrangement, regard him purely as a poet. The opening lines of Milton's *Paradise Lost* have been universally and justly admired, but we doubt if even these equal the splendid and massive invocation of Fletcher in the opening of *Christ's Victorie*.

Milton prays or sings—

" Of man's first disobedience, and the fruit
Of that forbidden tree, whose mortal taste
Brought death into the world, and all our wo,
With loss of Eden, till one greater Man
Restore us, and regain the blissful seat,
Sing, heavenly Muse !
              *   *   *   *
And chiefly thou, O Spirit, that dost prefer
Before all temples the upright heart and pure,
Instruct me, for thou know'st. Thou from the first
Wast present ; and, with mighty wings outspread
Dove-like, sat'st brooding on the vast abyss,
And mad'st it pregnant. What in me is dark
Illumine : what is low, raise and support ;
That to the height of this great argument
I may assert eternal Providence,
And justify the ways of God to men."

Fletcher begins,—

" O thou that didst this holy fire infuse,
And taught this breast, but late the grave of hell,
Wherein a blind and dead heart lived to swell
With better thoughts ; send down those lights that
      lend
Knowledge how to begin and how to end
The love that never was and never can be penned."

The following description of offended Justice, by Fletcher, is very 'magnificent :—

" She was a virgin of austere regard ;
    Not, as the world esteems her, deaf and blind,
But as the eagle, that hath oft compared
    Her eye with heaven's. So, and more brightly
        shined
    Her lamping sight ; for she the same could wind
Into the solid heart, and with her ears
The silence of the thought loud-speaking hears,
And in one hand a pair of even scales she bears.

No riot of affection revel kept
    Within her breast, but a still apathy
Possessed all her soul, which softly slept,
    Serenely, without tempest ; no sad cry
    Awakes her pity, but wronged poverty,
Sending her eyes to heaven, swimming in tears,
And hideous clamours ever struck her ears,
Whetting the blazing sword that in her hand she
      bears."

The following impressive portrait of the effects produced by the solemn appeal of Justice must have been read and recollected by Milton :—

" She ended ; and the heavenly hierarchies,
    Burning in zeal, thickly imbranded were,
Like to an army that alarum cries ;
    And every one shakes his ydreaded spear,
    And the Almighty's self, as he would tear
The earth and her firm basis quite in sunder,
Flamed all in just revenge and mighty thunder,
Heaven stole itself from earth by clouds that moisten-
      ed under."

Mercy is also exquisitely introduced in the midst of the tumultuous scene, like a rainbow in the storm :—

" As when the cheerful sun, slapping wide,
    Glads all the world with his uprising ray,
And woos the widow'd earth afresh to pride,

And paints her bosom with the flowery May,
    His silent sister steals him quite away ;
Wrapt in a sable cloud from mortal eyes,
The hasty stars at noon begin to rise,
And headlong to his early roost the sparrow flies.

But soon as he again deshadowed is,
    Restoring the blind world his blemish'd sight,
As though another day were newly his,
    The cozened birds busily take their flight,
    And wonder at the shortness of the night ;
So Mercy once again herself displays
Out from her sister's cloud, and open lays
Those sunshine looks, whose beams would dim a
      thousand days."

Remorse is thus strikingly depicted in the same poem :

" And first within the porch and jaws of hell,
    Sad deep remorse of conscience, all besprent
With tears ; and to herself oft would she tell
    Her wretchedness."

And again ;

" A flaming brand toss'd up from hell,
    Boiling her heart in her own lustful blood,
That oft for torment she would loudly yell ;
Now she would sighing sit, and now she fell,
    Crouching upon the ground in sackcloth trust ;
Early and late she prayed, and fast she must,
And all her hair hung full of ashes and of dust."

The description of a garden starting up in a dreary solitude in his account of the temptations of Christ, is very rich. It is much in the style of Milton, and shows that Fletcher was not destitute of glowing impressions of the beautiful, as well as of the terrific and sublime :

" Not lovely Ida might with this compare,
    Though many streams his banks besilvered ;
Though Xanthus, with his golden sands, he bare ;
    Nor Hylla, though his thyme depastured
    As fast again with honey blossom'd ;
Nor Rhodope's, nor Tempe's flowery plain ;
Adonis' garden was to this but vain,
Though Plato on his bed a flood of praise doth rain."

And again :

" The garden, like a ladie fair, was cut,
That lay as if the slumber'd in delight."

Advantages of Early Rising.—The habit of early rising is one which conduces much to health, and ought to be encouraged, by all proper means, among the denizens of schools, and the young generally. It tends to produce that cheerful, buoyant state of mind which exerts so beneficial an influence over the bodily condition, that whatever is calculated to promote it deserves to be practised and enforced. It is valuable, also inasmuch as it necessarily prevents the contrary habit of sitting up late ; one which is too frequently contracted at this period of life by the ardent-minded student.—*Curtis on Health.*

Knowledge of a God.—The Musselmen writers speak of an ignorant Arab, who, being asked how he knew any thing of the existence of a God? replied, " Just as I knew by the tracks in the sand whether a man or a beast has passed there ; so when I survey the heavens with its bright stars, and the earth with its productions, do I feel the existence and power of God."

Brief Memoir of the Life of John Croker.
Written by himself.

(Continued from page 70.)

Now, being come ashore, and having escaped from being imprest by reason of my being but a youth (for most of the men were imprest into the king's service, to help to man out the fleet, which lay then at Plymouth,) the master took me to one Lane, a merchant, at Dartmouth, to whom I gave a bill on my father for my passage. As soon as the merchant understood on whom I could draw the bill, he began to look at me, and compassion was opened in him towards me; and he offered me what money I would have, being sorry to see me in such a condition, for he said he knew my father well. So I took some money of him, and some of another man, who was going with me to Plymouth; at which place I now, indeed, longed to be, having called to mind my father's house, like a prodigal son now returning thither. Therefore, after I had bought a few things to shift me, which I soon did to my great refreshment, I, in company with the seamen that were imprest, set out and went for Plymouth, and unexpectedly came to my father's door; where I found my dear mother first, to whom there was not a quick discovery; but after some discourse, I made myself known to her, who with open arms received me, being as one that had been dead and was now alive again, and hoping this trial would work for my future good. This I am sensible it did;—for it so humbled me, that I was often thinking on what I had met with, and how the Lord had preserved me, which made me very humble and low in my mind, taking heed to the commands of my parents; and I feared to rebel against them, and minded what company I kept, being now willing to be as good as I could.

I spent some time in reading alone, and frequented meetings both abroad and at home, sometimes going ten miles to a meeting, and home again at night on foot, with much satisfaction.

My careful parents, who now began to take some comfort in me, being willing I should learn some trade, which I was myself free to do, gave me liberty to choose my trade, and in what city or town I pleased; and in order thereunto, my father put some money into my hand, and bid me try, by looking amongst tradesmen. So I rode to Exeter, and intended, if I could not please myself there, to go for London, it being about the time of the Yearly Meeting, and I between seventeen and eighteen years of age, as I suppose. When I came to Exeter, I thought a fuller or tucker was a good trade; so with the assistance of a Friend, I agreed with one who was of that business, and was accounted a civil man, but not one called a Quaker. He traded mostly to Holland; I was to serve him six years, and he was to have thirty pounds paid him at the time of sealing my indentures, and eighty pounds if he sent me to Holland the two last years. My father seemed to be pleased with it, and I went forward with my apprenticeship. But, alas! I found myself exposed to many temptations; for my master proved to

be an ill-company keeper, and a night-playing man; which caused me often to walk the streets in the night, to search the taverns and alehouses for him, or else I had no peace at home with my mistress. Sometimes he would come home with me pretty contentedly, and at other times would be in a passion, and sometimes keep me up with him all night, several times tempting me to play, offering to lay wagers on me, that I would worst the company at cards,—which I dared not meddle with, but always put him off with desires to go home, and urging that my mistress waited up for him. Sometimes I prevailed with him, and sometimes not; so that I have been forced to sleep in the chimney corner, and in the morning to take a nap and rise up to work. I am no way accused in myself, that I ever spent any idle time in his service; but I was as diligent as I could be, to serve both of them; and being conscientious, I believed I ought to serve them to the utmost I could, in what was lawful and not burthensome to my conscience.

My master, following this course of life, was, in about two years after I came to him, forced to put himself into the mint, (a prison so called,) and what he had left was seized, and the very goods of his house were carried away; so that his wife and children were forced to retire to her father's, and myself to seek fresh business, or another master. This brought fresh care upon me, for I was willing to attain to a business if it could be; but being a Quaker, few would be concerned with me: so I worked as a journeyman, and lodged at a Friend's house, boarding myself. At length, finding my stay was not likely to avail me much, I concluded to return to my father, who readily received me, and I set myself at work in my elder brother's trade, being a serge weaver; and to combing of wool I went, and earned six or seven shillings a week by my work, which brought me in money for a time. It was not long before my father bought an estate in money for a little he laid down all business, and retired into the country, and lived in a house with my elder sister, who was married to Francis Fox, a shopkeeper at Germains, where my father and mother remained until their death, and then my eldest brother went thither.

My father having left me a room at Plymouth, I continued there and lived retired, doing little for a livelihood in the world, spending most of my time in reading, and did some small matter in purse making, which I generally gave away. My desires often were to the Lord, that he would be pleased to open a way of some business for me, that I might be taken off from such inconvenience as did sometimes attend by reason of idleness, which often brought sorrow in calling over the actions of the day. For getting them in order before the judge of my conscience, those things which were done amiss brought trouble, which caused sorrow and tears, as well as prayers that the Lord would pass them by, and open of his wisdom more and more in my heart, and that I might not act contrary to his mind. For those, which some call small

things, and not worth minding, caused me sore exercise, so that I found a daily cross was to be kept to, in the management of words and conversation in this world: or else a good state might be soon lost, which I was under the fear of: and I found, when I had considered of those things which I had done, spoke, or acted in the fear of God, it always brought peace; and I took my rest with true content in the will of God, however he might be pleased to deal with me in the night season. The Lord preserve my dear children in this state, where they may often inquire within themselves, (for whose sake I am willing to leave these things,) and that they may learn obedience, and serve the God of their father, who wonderfully preserved him by sea and land, and brought him through many perils and straits of various kinds; for which I have reason to bless God, to whom be glory given for evermore!

Soon after this period, (viz. about the year 1695,) the Lord was pleased to deprive me of my dear and honourable mother, who was in her day a noble woman for truth, and who retained her integrity to God, and love to Friends to the end: I doubt not but she resteth in peace with the Lord. This was a trying time to me, and it made an impression on my very countenance. I then retired into the country to my father, who was soon after brought to his bed by reason of a sore distemper in his feet. So I waited on him, and to keep myself from idleness, and get a little money, I put forward some small business, which was spinning of tobacco, my father's former occupation.

My dear mother had always been a great help to me in my spiritual exercises, being sensible there was something at work in my heart which wanted to be perfected; and she would be very tender, and help me what she could. I had not courage to make my mind known to any after her decease, although my heart was many times loaded more heavily than I could bear, not knowing the reason of it; but in private places I sought relief by tears and prayers, which no mortal besides myself did know: it was this way by the alteration in my countenance and deportment, which might visibly appear: although I always behaved as cheerfully when in company as I could; but I am persuaded my dear mother had some sense of it, and that her prayers were heard on my behalf.

I now began to think of a settled life, and I had cast my eye on a virtuous young woman, the daughter of John and Margery Peters, of Minver, in the county of Cornwall. I was not hasty in proceeding, but well considered it, and laid the thing before the Lord in my heart, desiring, that if it were not the Lord's pleasure it should be so, he would remove it out of my mind, or else that he would increase my love towards her, which I found still continued with me. But when I was retired before the Lord, I could think of her with abundance of sweetness, although I had not seen her for some time, nor ever (that I remember) had been in her company above twice, she living at about twenty-six miles distance from me, and I had not been more than once at their house, although often invited by her parents.

While I was thus impressed, and none knew, it but myself and Him that knows the secrets of all hearts, I heard there was one of greater worth in the world than myself, endeavouring to gain her affections. Then I thought, if she did not answer him, after it was at an end, I would make known my feelings. Some time after I heard the other was put by, I then made my mind known to my father, and desired his thoughts: to which he did not seem very inclinable, saying, he did not know; "but," said he, "I love her parents, and would not have thee to be too hasty." So I waited some time longer, and then spoke to my father again, who said, if I could not be easy without it, I might go and see her, which I thought was sufficient. I therefore set forward; and when I came there, I opened my mind to her father and mother, who wanted to know if I had my father's consent in this matter. I told them I had, and that without their leave, I should not mention any thing to their daughter, whom I truly loved; so if they thought proper, I would leave the consideration of it with them and go home, or, by their leave, I would mention the same to my dear friend, their daughter. On this they were silent for a time, so I took the opportunity of walking in the fields a little while, and then came in and spent the evening in conversation with the father, mother, and daughter. Next day, I had the liberty to make known my mind to my dear friend Anne. So having an opportunity, after some little time, I let her know what had been in my mind, desiring her to take it into consideration; to which she said it was of great moment, and there was need of time, for she desired not to enter into any such engagements until she was well satisfied: so I went home to my father, and acquainted him how things were, and he hoped it would be well.

Now being come to the twenty-second year of my age, having in my time passed through various states, especially straits and great disappointments, and being about to enter into the state of marriage, I proposed to myself some comfort, believing I was going to be joined to a true help-mate, as well in relation to spiritual as temporal things, and that the Lord would favour us with his goodness and blessing together in this world. So in seasonable time we accomplished our intentions of marriage, to the good liking and well wishes of our relations and friends, being satisfied the Lord sanctioned our affections, and that by his Spirit we were united.*

* Respecting John Peters, the young woman's father, the following particulars, by way of testimony, are given by Thomas Gwin, of Falmouth, in a small volume printed 1709, entitled, "A Brief Narrative of the Life of John Peters."

"Mine acquaintance with him was of above thirty years' standing; in which time, having had frequently the benefit of his company, both at home and abroad, I never observed any carriage or deportment in him, but what was savoury, and becoming the gospel. He had a well ordered family, which he governed with discretion, bringing up his young ones in the fear of the Lord; though but one, and that a good son, survived him. He bore admirably and sweetly the sad providences that attended him, when it pleased the Lord to

We resided with our father and mother Peters, and carried on some business, which was blest, and we increased in this world's goods; for which we were greatly thankful to God, and the thoughts thereof often humbled our souls, so that we were not unmindful of praising God for it. Yet there remained something with me, which often led me into solitary walks and private retirements, sometimes into prayer, and sometimes I read, and sometimes I sat still, as one waiting to hear; the reason whereof I knew not,—for I was careful not to offend God in any thing which I knew he required of me: yet still it increased, insomuch that morning and evening it became my constant practice to retire; at which times I cried, and desired the Lord would be pleased to make known of his mind to me, that then I would obey him, if it were to the giving up of my natural life.

At last it was discovered to me;—but then I wanted signs and tokens, that I might be certain it was the Lord's requiring,—fearing, because the enemy, working many times in a mystery, had deceived many: and he was likely to have reasoned all good out of me, and made me prove disobedient to the call of God, though not without a desire of performing his will. However I thought if this or the other stranger would speak to my condition, or tell me what God required of me, I would not then consult with flesh and blood any longer. So it pleased God to answer my desire; for several spoke to me and bid me be faithful: and upon a time, on a First day morning, as I was walking alone, and more out of thought than usual, it opened in me like a voice, saying, "This day will I open thy mouth, if thou art faithful to me;" it seemed to surprise me, and being willing to be more

take away his tender children, not only those that died young, but those also who were grown up, and were very sober and hopeful. He laboured faithfully in the Lord's vineyard, both in doctrine and discipline; yet took great care, if possible, to give offence to none, so as to drive them further from the truth. He was of the mind of the husbandman in the parable, who would not presently have the fruitless tree cut down, but would dig about it, and try it one year longer. Yet he was very zealous against all enormities, and undue liberties; labouring, it possible, to reclaim such as wandered thereinto, and, if not, to testify against them, that the profession of the truth might be cleared. His ministry was sound and living, tending more to the reaching of the heart, than the tickling of the ear. And as his ministry was very intelligible, and attended with plainness, and demonstration, and power, to the piercing of many hearts, and the tendering the souls of those that heard him, and to the binding the broken hearted, and comforting the mourners; so his conversation and behaviour answered and came up to it,—being full of gravity and solidity; never unreproaching in his behaviour and carriage, what he delivered as doctrine. I have given but short touches concerning the life and labours of this servant of God; but in fine, his life was a life of diligence, and of faithfulness, and of much exercise, which he cheerfully underwent for the truth's sake. The love of God, the divine origin and well-spring of virtues, ruled in his heart; and in that love he lived, laboured, and passed the time of his sojourning here; and the sweet sense thereof did greatly adorn his languishing bed and last moments of time, and therein he had sweet peace under all his afflictions and sore distemper; in which love he finished his course, and concluded his days, and is fallen asleep in the Lord. His body was interred the thirteenth of the seventh month, 1708, at the burying ground of our Friends at Minver.

acquainted with this voice, I turned myself about, and walked further into the orchard, desiring the Lord to be wisdom and strength to me; and it rested with me that that was the day of the trial of my obedience. So I went home, and prepared for the meeting, to which most of our family went. I sat retired, until at last the word of the Lord was with me as a fire; my father and mother-in-law Peters, both took a little time in the meeting, —which I thought had relation to me, and my then present exercise; yet, I found it hard to give up: but being sensible it was my duty, at the latter part of the meeting I spake a few words; and, although it was a little out of my season, yet I was thereby, as one discharged of a great and heavy load, and comfort came into my soul; so that I found it was good to obey the Lord. Being faithful in the few things, he made me ruler over more; so that I found it often my place to speak a few words, and began to be concerned for the discipline of truth, that it might be kept up, and its first and primitive simplicity maintained amongst us; that we might not only profess the principles, but also be found like the first proselytes of truth in this island, in plainness of dress and fewness of words, as well as fearfulness, of running after the gain of riches, or too much frequenting the conversation of the people of the world; because there were many snares and dangers in it, which many incline after, respecting which, at times, I was concerned both to speak and write.

(To be continued.)

Emancipation in the West Indies.

A correspondent of the Commercial Advertiser, in a letter from Barbadoes, gives the following gratifying account of the results of emancipation in the West Indies.

Most of the afternoon I spent in the society of a merchant of Bridgetown, and of course the great subject engrossed our conversation. He not only spoke with confidence of the beneficial working of emancipation, but stated that all persons on the island were of the same opinion. "People in the United States," said, he, "may call emancipation an experiment; but here we do not call it so; the experiment is over, and the good results of emancipation are satisfactorily established." Like others with whom I had conversed, he alleged the great rise in the value of real estate, as ample proof of the pecuniary benefits of that great measure. One estate of 400 acres was lately rented for £2,000 per annum. Another plantation sold a few years since for £15,000, was lately purchased for £30,000. During the last two years, one estate has yielded the proprietor a net income of $120,000. The island, he concluded, is in a far better state than it ever has been.

In reply to my inquiries respecting Jamaica, and the difficulties said to exist there, he replied, "In that island many are raising clamours and fabricating rumours, from interested motives. A large number of the proprietors are non-residents. The resident attorneys and managers are naturally desirous of becoming owners of real estate, and of purchasing at the lowest rate. They hope that by fomenting or exaggerating difficulties, and scattering abroad rumours of trouble, disaster and loss, a panic will be created among the absentee proprietors, and thereby large quantities of real estate be thrown into the market. It is for their interest, therefore, to create trouble with the blacks where there is none; and to persuade the world that property in Jamaica is ruined or insecure. For this reason fabricated or exaggerated rumours are industriously circulated through every possible channel. Emancipation does not work so well in Jamaica as in Barbadoes, but the actual evils are far, very far, from being so many, or so great, as individuals there have represented. Even for those evils, such as they are, the planters and managers are responsible. By harshness and injustice they have alienated the minds of the blacks. During the system of apprenticeship, when the planter's interest could be promoted by it, he swore that the labour of each negro was worth about seventy-five cents per day. Now, when his interest lies in the opposite direction, he quarrels with his labourers if they demand more than twenty cents per day, and fills the world with clamour against the idleness and exorbitant demands of the slave."

Such were the statements of an intelligent merchant of Barbadoes. As corroborative of these remarks, I will here mention that on my voyage homeward, I was fellow-passenger with a gentleman who was himself the proprietor of an estate in Jamaica. He also, almost in the same language, stated the same facts, and ascribed to the same source the rumours of trouble, idleness and ruin, which have deluged the papers. Newspapers in Jamaica, as in some other parts of the world, can circulate gross and oft refuted falsehood.

My friend proceeded. " The first of August last was an interesting and wonderful day. I walked out in the morning, and found such solemn and awful stillness, that I was ashamed to be seen, and returned to my house. The churches were opened, and attended by crowded and attentive congregations. A we and sacredness seemed to pervade the atmosphere. Toward evening I rode out, and heard in many houses the voice of singing and praise to God. Many of the emancipated negroes I saw sitting by the road-side, reading the Testaments distributed among them by the British and Foreign Bible Society, which they highly value and preserve with great care. All of them appeared devoutly grateful to Almighty God for their freedom.

" Some whites feared violence and crime. But it is a remarkable fact, that not a solitary negro has lifted his finger against a white man since the act of emancipation. So far from exhibiting a disposition to violence, there have been some beautiful and striking instances of attachment to their former proprietors. One young man, whose parents had died, and left him in sickness and poverty, was received by one who had been his slave; that slave hired a room for the invalid, defrayed his expenses while ill, and after his decease, paid the cost of his funeral. Another family fell into poverty, and when the father

died, the daughters were supported with cheerfulness by negroes, who had once been their slaves."

Such was the substance of the information communicated in this and subsequent interviews with this intelligent merchant. At dinner, on the same day, I was in the society of another merchant of Bridgetown. From him also I received similar statements, in reply to my enquiries; corresponding indeed so nearly, that any account of the conversation would be little more than a repetition of the same words. Indeed, the unanimity of opinion on this subject is truly remarkable. Our passengers, twenty in number, have ridden much on the island; have visited numerous estates, and conversed with great numbers of people, of various classes on this subject. We have all found but one sentiment. None of us have found an individual who is not glad that emancipation has taken place, and fully satisfied that its results have been beneficial to master and slave; to the moral and pecuniary welfare of the whole population.

Cement for Mending Broken Vessels.—To half a pint of milk put an equal quantity of vinegar, in order to curdle it; separate the curd from the whey, and mix the whey with the whites of four or five eggs, beating the whole well together; when it is mixed, add a little quick lime through a sieve, until it has acquired the consistence of paste. With this cement, broken vessels or cracks of all kinds may be repaired. It dries quickly, and equally resists the action of fire and water.

No is a very useful word—be not afraid to use it. Many a man has pined in misery for many years by not having courage to pronounce that little monosyllable.

THE FRIEND.

TWELFTH MONTH, 7, 1839.

An almanac, however indispensable in every well-ordered household, and which, perhaps, is more universally read than any other publication, is, nevertheless, one of those articles in the choice of which people in general are the least scrupulous. Whereas, we have long thought that it is a matter of no inconsiderable importance, and in respect to which parents and heads of families should be very particular, and see before they purchase that the reading matter is well selected, and suitable in character for the perusal of those under their charge. Thus impressed, we deem it not beside our proper vocation once more to call the attention of our readers to " The Moral Almanac," published by the Tract Association of Friends in this city. The conscientious care exercised in the selection of the reading materials for it, entitles it to a decided preference among the members of our religious Society, and that for the year 1840 is especially worthy of all commendation.

Stanzas by " F. A." came too late for the present number,—will appear next week.

THE FRIEND.

A RELIGIOUS AND LITERARY JOURNAL.

VOL. XIII.   SEVENTH DAY, TWELFTH MONTH, 14, 1839.   **NO. 11.**

EDITED BY ROBERT SMITH.

PUBLISHED WEEKLY.

Price two dollars per annum, payable in advance.

Subscriptions and Payments received by

GEORGE W. TAYLOR,

NO. 50, NORTH FOURTH STREET, UP STAIRS,

PHILADELPHIA.

THE ELDER SACRED POETS.

(Concluded from page 77.)

The chief portion of the extracts we have given from Fletcher, are such as may lead our readers to presume that the terrible and the rugged are his sole excellences. This is not the case. He could pass from the fierce and awful to the most gentle. He was a poet of great range and versatility of genius. What can be more exquisitely beautiful in conception, or more expressively embodied, than the following view of heaven's joys:—

> "No sorrow now hangs clouding on their brow;
> No bloodless malady ever pales their face;
> No age drops on their hairs his silver snow;
> No nakedness their bodies doth embase;
> No poverty themselves and theirs disgrace;
> No fear of death the joy of life devours;
> No unchaste sleep their precious time defowers;
> No loss, no grief, no change, wait on their winged hours."

We have thus dwelt at some length on the excellences and beauties of this poet, and with our author tried to "revive the inscription on his tomb-stone," or, *Scotice*, to cast another stone to his *cairne*. There are fragments of unrivalled excellence, as well as defects and fallings off; but, as a whole, he has much merit, and will well repay perusal.

DRUMMOND OF HAWTHORNDEN.

The sonnets of this loyalist and lyrist are still loved and read. They were full of nature and of real feeling, notwithstanding the saucy description of Ben Jonson, that "they smelt too much of the schools." * * The following is a sweet sonnet, and exhales the fragrance of Hawthornden:—

> "My lute, be as thou wert when thou didst grow
> With thy green mother in some shady grove,
> When immelodious winds but made thee move,
> And birds their ramage did on thee bestow;
> Since that dear voice which did thy sounds approve,
> Which wont in such harmonious strains to flow,
> Is reft from earth to tune those spheres above—
> What art thou but a harbinger of wo?
> Thy pleasing notes be pleasing notes no more,
> But orphans' wailings to the fainting ear,
> Each strike a sigh, each sound draws forth a tear;

> For which be silent as in woods before:
> Or, if that any hand to touch thee deign,
> Like widowed turtle, still her loss complain."

QUARLES.

This is one of the leading eccentric and artificial writers of the seventeenth century. Many of that age were full of conceits and subtleties, and even despised great genius if it could not shape itself, or rather its offspring, to the Procrustes bed of a pyramid or hill, or an alliteration which made sense whether read backwards or forwards. They constituted the Chinese school of poetry. Their productions remind one of the trees that are occasionally observed, from the top of a stage-coach, on the roadside. The fantastic proprietors have cut them, living and green, into the shapes of eggs, sparrows, pyramids inverted, and similar chimeras. The writers of the age of Quarles would not be satisfied with nature—they must mend her; they would not read or admire the spontaneous effusions of genius, unless they could be diverted into certain channels, like the worm-pipes of a distillery. They murdered Nature by abortive attempts to mend her. They forced Poetry to walk like a Chinese woman, or to dress like a mandarin, before they would look at her. To this tortuous taste the naturally fine genius of Quarles cut and cramped its noblest children; on its altar he laid his poetry a holocaust. It is, therefore, the proof of great genius, that in his writings, labouring as they did under great disadvantages, are to be found passages that will bear comparison with those of any other poet. His genius broke out from the mass of crushing conceits, and by the beams it shot forth, gave token of an inner might and elasticity no pressure could keep down. The following verses, constructed primarily on the 139th Psalm, are full of rich and unutterable poetry:—

> "O whither shall I fly? What path untrod
> Shall I seek out to 'scape the flaming rod
> Of my offended, of my angry God?

> Where shall I sojourn? What kind sea will hide
> My head from thunder? Where shall I abide
> Until his flames be quenched or laid aside?

> What if my feet should take their hasty flight,
> And seek protection in the shades of night?
> Alas! no shades can blind the God of light!

> What if my soul should take the wings of day,
> And find some desert? If she springs away,
> The wings of vengeance clip as fast as they.

> What if some solid rock should entertain
> My frighted soul? Can solid rocks sustain
> The stroke of justice, and not cleave in twain?

> Nor sea, nor shade, nor night, nor rock, nor cave,
> Nor silent deserts, nor the sullen grave,
> Where flame-eyed Fury means to smite, can save.

> 'Tis vain to flee; till gentle Mercy show
> Her better eye, the further off we go
> The swing of Justice deals the mightier blow.

> The ingenuous child corrected doth not fly
> His angry mother's hand, but clings more nigh,
> And quenches with his tears her flaming eye.

> Great God! there is no safety here below;
> Thou art my fortress—thou that seem'st my foe;
> 'Tis thou that strik'st the stroke must guard the blow."

Fuller, the compiler of *Abel Redivivus*, has preserved several poems of Quarles's, two of which we extract:—

On Melancthon.

> "Would thy ingenious fancy soar and fly
> Beyond the pitch of modern poesy?
> Or wouldst thou learn to charm the conquered ear
> With rhetoric's oily magic? Wouldst thou hear
> The majesty of language? Wouldst thou pry
> Into the bowels of philosophy,
> Moral or natural? Or wouldst thou sound
> The truly depth, and touch the unfathom'd ground
> Of deep theology?
> Go search Melancthon's tomes."

The following sonnet, on the faithfulness of the martyr and reformer Ridley, compresses some of his most remarkable and powerful temptations:—

> "Read in the progress of this blessed story
> Rome's cursed cruelty and Ridley's glory,
> Rome's siren song: but Ridley's careless ear
> Was deaf: they charmed, but Ridley would not hear.
> Rome sung preferment; but brave Ridley's tongue
> Condemned that false preferment which Rome sung:
> Rome whispered wealth; but Ridley, whose great gain
> Was godliness, he waved it with disdain:
> Rome threatened durance; but great Ridley's mind
> Was too, too strong for threats or chains to bind:
> Rome thundered death; but Ridley's dauntless eye
> Stared in Death's face, and scorned Death standing by.
> In spite of Rome, for England's faith he stood,
> And in the flames he sealed it with his blood."

CRASHAW.

The writings of this poet are some of them remarkable for a power and vitality not excelled by any of our first poets. * * * We quote some exquisite gems, which are sufficient to reflect lasting glory on the poet's name: it is entitled the " Hymn of the Nativity:"—

> "Gloomy night embraced the place
> Where the noble infant lay;
> The babe looked up, and showed his face:
> In spite of darkness, it was day.

> We saw thee in thy balmy nest,
> Bright dawn of our eternal day;
> We saw thine eyes break from the east,
> And chase the trembling shades away.
> We saw thee, and we blessed the sight,—
> We saw thee by thy own sweet light.

> She sings thy tears asleep, and dips
> Her kisses in thy weeping eyes;
> She spreads the red leaves of thy lips,
> That in their buds yet blushing lie.

Yet, when young April's husband-showers
Shall bless the fruitful Maia's bed,
We'll bring the first-born of her flowers
To kiss thy feet and crown thy head,
To thee, dread Lamb! whose love must keep
The shepherds more than they their sheep.

To thee, meek majesty! soft king
Of simple graces and sweet loves,
Each of us his lamb will bring,
Each his pair of silver doves."

One of the Peculiarities of the Times.

The love of money has always indeed been a rank growth in man. Long has inspiration marked it as the " root of all evil." Eighteen centuries ago it was known, by sad experience, that, under its intoxicating power, Christians " erred from the faith, and pierced themselves through with many sorrows." But now especially, and in this new world, does that " root of bitterness" seem to have sprung up with unexampled strength, and in a soil especially favorable to its widest spread. The whole population seems literally " hasting to be rich"—" counting all things but loss for the excellency" of this prize—believing that a man's life *does* consist " in the abundance of the things which he possesseth." The mania has taken a most lamentable hold on many minds that once seemed looking for wealth, not in things which are seen and temporal, but those which are unseen and eternal. Many, every where, whose profession before God is to " seek *first* the kingdom of God and his righteousness," and to feel that their life and portion are " hid with Christ, in God," do yield themselves to this strife of gain, and lay themselves down to this race, and consume time, and strength, and heart, in pressing towards this mark to a degree exceedingly dishonourable to their " high calling of God in Christ Jesus," and utterly incompatible with the right discharge of any spiritual duty. Such, indeed, to an evil extent, has always been the case. But now, we apprehend, more than ever before in this land, is it a crying evil. The excitement is more general, more powerful, more engrossing, more unsparing. It stimulates the most languid—it enslaves the strongest minds. Men of regular business-habits, who love " the old paths" of honest, patient industry, complain with a thousand tongues, that " old things have passed away, and all things have become new." Old methods are too slow—old paths are too circuitous. The regular alternation of seed time and harvest has become antiquated. The farmer, the mechanic, the tradesman, is impatient " to reap where he has not sown ; to gather where he has not strewed"—not content unless he gain in a year, the prize which used to occupy a patient life-time. It is no less than the " covetousness which is idolatry." It is an excitement which is positive intoxication. We feel it in our schools and colleges. To form and discipline the mind, to train the morals, and endeavour the nurturing of youth in the fear of God—the very essence of sound education—is too slow and unworldly for the prevailing taste of the times. The science of

matter, not of mind ; the languages that open the doors of trade, instead of those which unlock the stores of classic or Scripture wealth ; these bear away the palm, in the judgment of the many. To suit their taste, education must be rapid, because business must be early. It must be all practical, because business is all its object. Its bearing upon the qualification of youth for money making, must be its test—because to make money, is thought the business of life.

But the Church feels it ; and when the present rising generation shall have risen to man's estate, she will feel it a great deal more, in her nurseries—in the domestic training of those innumerable little flocks within their family folds, to which she looks for the lambs of the sacrifice, and for the holy priesthood at her altars. This evil spirit, like one of the plagues of Egypt, *has come up into our houses, and into our bed chambers.* It has made the things of this life so prominent, and preparation for worldly business so important, that many parents, incapable of serving two masters, have grown lukewarm and formal, irregular and ineffective, in the training of their children for God and eternity. Prayer for their children, *prayer with* their children, it is much to be feared, has declined, or, with many, passed away. Instruction at home has, in many cases, become nearly silent and pointless, without earnestness and heart, or perhaps has been entirely laid aside ; the parent consoling himself that the Sunday School is an adequate substitute. Family worship, if continued, is cramped and hurried. The time is wanted for more stimulating concerns ; so that the morning and evening offering, instead of a living sacrifice, has become dead ; a form of godliness without the power. The influence of the father's daily society is withdrawn from his children ; they see him but at his hurried meals. Not only is the whole day given to business, but the evening to the same—at least to the gathering up of the fragments of business, that nothing be lost ; or else to such an engrossment of thought in " the course of this world," as leaves no liberty of mind or heart for the domestic duty of a Christian father, in charge of the souls of his children.—*Bishop M'Ilvaine.*

THE SALVATION OF YOUR CHILDREN.

It is not merely a very important object, deserving a high place of regard, and to be pursued with diligence, but it is comparatively *the only object,* in the interests of children. It is so great, that all others are hid under its shadow ; so precious, that whatever interferes with it must be sacrificed to it ; so engrossing, that if any thing in the domestic circle be really incompatible, it follows, necessarily, that it cannot deserve a place in the lowest regards of a rational mind. The place it occupies in the view of the Scriptures, and should hold in the estimate of the parent, is precisely that which is assigned to every one's own salvation. " What shall it profit a man if he gain the whole world and lose his own soul ; or what shall a man give in

exchange for his soul?" Every one sees in what a position of infinite consequence these words exhibit the interests of his soul. But let him repeat them for his children—" *What shall it profit me, or them, if they gain the whole world and lose their souls?*" Then what follows ? " Seek first the kingdom of God and his righteousness, and all these things shall be added unto you." This command, and this promise, are for " you and your children." They bid you, by all the infinite worth of your own and your children's souls, to seek, on their account as well as for your own, and to endeavour to have established in them, as well as in yourselves, " first the kingdom of God and his righteousness :" yea, to seek these as *first* in point of time, *first* in point of interest, *first* in point of our children or for ourselves, " is like unto a treasure hid in a field ; the which, when a man hath found, he hideth, and for joy thereof goeth and selleth all that he hath, and buyeth that field." In other words, he sacrifices every thing to get it, and does so cheerfully : not as suffering loss, but getting great gain. It is required of us, if we would enter into life, that we " count all things but loss for the excellency of the knowledge of Christ. " It is equally requisite that we set the same value upon the knowledge of Christ for our children ; that by whatever price or effort we may get for them that *hid treasure,* we be willing to give it, and feel it an unspeakable gift that a blessing so precious can be had at a rate so cheap.

Settle it, therefore, in your hearts, ye parents, that in the religious training of your children, houses and lands, and all worldly things, are to be despised, in comparison with the worth of their souls. " *This one thing*" you must do ; " Forgetting those things which (in point of importance) are behind," as if they were not, you must press towards the mark of the prize, by all judicious, all devout, all earnest, all tender and affectionate means, as *the one thing* in your children's welfare which, if gained, all things are theirs—if lost, *all* is lost.

How many have failed in the religious training of their children, because the *kingdom of God* was not the *first* thing, the *one* thing they sought for them !—*Bishop M'Ilvaine.*

For "The Friend."

Anti-Slavery and Colonization Society.

At this time, when there seems so much diversity of opinion and such erroneous sentiments respecting the plans and principles of the two important societies whose respective titles stand at the head of this article, I have thought the following just and unprejudiced character of these rival institutions would be interesting, and might tend in some degree to promote correct opinion in regard to them. It is believed to be copied verbatim, with one single exception, from the narrative of Reed and Matheson, and whether its publication at this time shall have the effect desired by the writers, of doing away prejudice and enlightening the readers of "The Friend," in relation to the deeply interesting and important subject of American slavery, or not, the graphic and masterly style in which the author has treated his subject cannot fail to gratify the intelligent reader. W.

11th mo. 25, 1839.

The more ostensible means for their relief, which have been created by the force of public opinion, are to be found in colonization and anti-slavery societies. The colonization society is the elder of the two, and originated in a pure motive of compassion for the slave. It proposes to establish a free colony on the coast of Africa, and by this means to confer a benefit on a country which has been wasted by our crimes, and to open a channel to the slave-holder to give freedom to his slaves. Its founders hoped that the movement thus made, while it brought the direct blessing of liberty to many, would indirectly, and without stimulating the prejudices of the planter, familiarize the common mind with the inherent evils of slavery, and thus contribute to ultimate emancipation. For many years this was the best and the only remedy offered to the public attention, and the benevolent, of course, took hold of it; and it has at present the concurrence of New England, and of the intelligent and influential in most places.

The anti-slavery society is of later formation. Without hesitation or condition, it demands immediate and complete abolition; and in doing this, it does not scruple to pit itself against the older society, and to denounce it as standing in its way, and as favourable to the perpetuation of slavery. This, as you may expect, has brought the two societies into a state of violent collision. Neither party has kept its temper; much personal abuse and bitter vituperation have been emitted; and both, in the heat of party conflict, have been in danger of losing sight of the slave, and affording a humiliating but acceptable spectacle to the slave-holder. Apart from these animosities, you seek an unprejudiced judgment on these societies. You shall have at least an honest opinion. The colonization society may have been well as a harbinger of something better; but it was never equal to the object of emancipation, and is now below the spirit and demands of the day. 1. It does not lay hold sufficiently on the public mind. What it proposes to do is indirect, and indefinite, and complicate; and bears no proportion to the pressure and extent of the evil with which it professes to deal. 2. It has lost a great measure of public confidence. Its founders and original friends are of unimpeached integrity; but it has now many devoted slave-holders among its chief supporters, and this awakens suspicion. Some of its agents, acting in difficult circumstances, and

wanting due discretion, to say the least, have commended it in the north as an anti-slavery society; while others in the south have laboured to show that it does not disturb slave property, and that its tendency is to secure and perpetuate it; and this has confirmed suspicion in distrust. The best friends of the society and the slave have protested against these conflicting and unworthy statements; but they have not been able to revive confidence. Then 3. As a remedy for slavery, it must be placed among the grossest of all delusions. In fifteen years it has transported less than three thousand persons to the African coast; while the increase on their numbers in the same period is about seven hundred thousand! By all means let this colonization society exist, if it will, as a missionary society for the benefit of Africa; but in the name of honesty and common sense, let it disabuse the public mind, by avowing that it does not pretend to be a remedy for slavery. 4. If this society could accomplish its object, and transport all the slaves to a foreign shore, it would inflict on America herself a most deadly wound. She wants the coloured people; she cannot do without them. She has hitherto depended, and does still depend, on the African or the Irish for every instance of consolidated labour; and she owes to the sweat of their brow a full moiety of her prosperity and wealth. If the Africans were removed to-morrow, one half of her territories would be a mere desolation. To wish to get rid of them is a mere prejudice—the most vulgar of all prejudices—the prejudice of colour. Only make them white, and America would know how to value them. It is quite evident, then, if benevolent opinion and effort in its improved state, was to be concentrated in favour of the slave, that some other association was indispensable. It is only to be lamented that the Anti-Slavery has shot at once as much in advance of the public mind as the older Society fell below it. By saying this, however, I would not be understood to complain of the great principle it adopts, but of the methods by which it has sought to give it predominance. Had it calmly and firmly announced, on religious grounds, that all slavery is a sin against God, as well as an offence against society, and that as such it requires, without delay, to be abolished; and had it refused to come down from the high vantage ground, to deal in personal invective and exaggerated statement, it would have won its way, unresisted, over the whole portion of the religious and philanthropic of the community, with surprising rapidity. But it has not done so. In looking to a noble issue, it has been impatient of means necessary to the end. In proposing to confer an inestimable good, it has not paused to ask how it may be granted with the least alloy of evil. It has allowed nothing to prejudice, nothing to interest, nothing to time. It has borne on its front defiance, and not conciliation, and this not merely against slavery, but against the slaveholder. Means leading to the result, and remuneration consequent on it, instead of being considerately discussed, are peremptorily denounced. If there be any thing that

has special power to shock existing prejudice, it has been called upon and placed in the foreground of the battle. It has been resolved on getting the wedge in, but in fulfilling this resolution, it seems to have been careless, whether it should be by the but-end or the fine one. As you might foresee, the effect has been that mostly those who would have been its best friends, have been afraid of it; and those who were pledged, from the truest benevolence, to the Colonization Society, have received offence; while in the slave states, its personality and want of prudence, apart from its devotion to a hated principle, has thrown back the cause to a lamentable distance. However, most of these evils, I believe, have originated with a limited portion of its agency, and are more or less in course of correction. It has, under forbidding circumstances, made to itself a host of friends; and if even now it shall recover its backward steps, and move to its great and holy object with ordinary wisdom and temper, it will soon collect all that is liberal in mind, and generous in affection, in its favour. Should its course be still repulsive and inauspicious, the cause will not be left in its hands. The public mind is in motion, and it will create some legitimate medium of action for itself. If the Colonization Society would renounce its pretensions to emancipation, and content itself with the work of a missionary to bless Africa by redeemed and pious Africans, there would be an end of all heart burnings between the institutions. If those who benevolently joined this society, as a means of emancipation, would unite with the wisest and best men in the Anti-Slavery Society, in the cause of abolition, the religions and generous energies of the nation would find a focus, from which they would fuse and dissolve every chain of every slave, and the world would be free.

THE CULTIVATION OF OPIUM.

In India, the extent of territory occupied with the poppy, and the amount of population and capital engaged in its cultivation, and in the preparation of opium, are far greater than in any other part of the world. Malwa, Benares, and Behar (Patna), are the chief localities; and nearly every chest of the drug exported from India bears one of their names, according to the part of the country in which it was produced. About one half of the whole product of India is obtained from Malwa. Though the chiefs of Malwa are under British protection, the management of the soil is entirely beyond the company's authority, and the cultivation of the poppy and the production of opium are free. The traffic in the drug is also free, excepting the "transit duties," which are levied upon it when passing through the British territories, as most of it does on its way to Bombay, from whence it is exported to China. But in Benares, Behar, and throughout all the territories within the company's jurisdiction, the cultivation of the poppy, the preparation of the drug, and the traffic in it, until it is brought to Calcutta, and sold by auction for exportation, are under a strict monopoly. Should an individual undertake the cultivation, without having " entered into engagements with the government to deliver the produce at the fixed rate," his property would be immediately attached, and the ryot[*] compelled either to destroy his poppies, or to give securities for the faithful delivery of the product. Nay, according to a late writer, " the growing of opium is compulsory on the part of the ryot." Advances are made by government, through its native servants, and if a ryot refuses the advance, " the simple plan of throwing the rupees into his house is adopted ; should he attempt to abscond, the peons seize him, tie the advance up in his clothes, and push him into his house. The business being now settled, and there being no remedy, he applies himself, as he may, to the fulfilment of his contract."

Vast tracts of land, formerly occupied with other articles, are now covered with poppies, which require a very superior soil in order to produce opium in perfection. Hence, its cultivation has not extended over waste and barren lands, but into those districts and villages best fitted for agricultural purposes, where other plants, "grown from time immemorial," have been driven out before it. But though poppies are now spread over a wide extent of territory, the cultivation is still, as it has long been, rapidly on the increase. In 1821, in the single district of Sarun, belonging to the province of Behar, there were, according to the testimony of Mr. Kennedy, (many years collector of land revenue and deputy opium agent in that district,) between 15,000 and 20,000 bighas of land, (about one third of an acre per bigah,) then under cultivation. In 1829, the amount was nearly, or quite doubled, and the produce, in the mean time, had increased in a still greater degree.

The mode of cultivation pursued in the "Patna district" may afford a good idea of that which obtains in other places. The ryot, having selected a piece of ground, always prefering (*cæteris paribus*) that which is nearest his house, encloses it with a fence. He then, by repeated ploughings, makes it completely fine, and removes all the weeds and grass. Next he divides the field into two or more divisions, by small dikes of mould, running lengthways and crossways, according to the slope and nature of the ground. He afterwards divides the field into smaller squares, by other dikes leading from the principal ones. A pit, or sort of well, is dug about ten feet deep at one end of the field, from which, by a leathern bucket, water is raised into one of the principal dikes, and in this way it is carried into every part of the field, as required.

This irrigation is necessary, because the cultivation is carried on in the dry weather. The seed is sown in November, and the juice is collected in February and March, during a period usually of about six weeks. Throughout the whole process, the ryot is assisted by his family and servants, both women and children. As soon as the plants spring up, the weeding and watering commence, and are

[*] The ryot is the immediate cultivator of the soil.

continued till the poppies come to maturity. Perpendicular cuts or scratches are then made in the rind of the bulbous heads, with a muscle shell, found in all the tanks of the country. From these cuts the juice exudes, and is daily collected and delivered to the local officers. This is a very tedious process, requiring constant attention. When the poppies are exhausted, their colour changes from green to white.

The seeds contain no opium, and the labours of the season are now closed. The cultivator receives about three and a half rupees (Sp. Dls. 1,65) for each seer[*] of the poppy juice, which is required to be of a specific consistency. This must be such that a gomastah can take it out of the vessel in which it is brought for delivery by the ryot, and turn it over without its dropping off his hand ; if it is not sufficiently dry to admit of this, it is either returned to the ryot for further evaporation, or an additional quantity must be delivered, to make up the deficiency.

The lands under cultivation are measured every year, and their boundaries fixed, in order to prevent collision among those to whom they are assigned. The government annually enters into an engagement with the cultivators, through an intermediate agency, constructed in the following manner :—There is first a collector, who is a European ; secondly, there are gomastahs, a superior class of men, both in education and caste ; thirdly, sudder mattus, a respectable class of land-holders ; fourthly, villagers mattus, the principal villagers, a little superior to the ryots ; and fifthly, the ryots, the chief labourers in the cultivation of poppies.

The "engagement" entered into with the government is this : when the poppy is ripe, and immediately before the period of extracting the juice, the gomastah and his establishment make a circuit of the country, and form, " by guess," a probable estimate of the produce of each field. He then makes the ryot enter into an engagement with him to deliver the quantity thus estimated, and as much more as the field will yield, at the price previously fixed ; if he fails to deliver the estimated quantity, and the collector has reason to suppose he has embezzled the deficiency, he is empowered by law to prosecute the ryot in the civil court for damages.

The product in India, for the last year, it is said, amounts to about 35,000 chests. The Malwa averages about 134 lbs. per chest ; the other, 116 lbs. The weight of a chest, however, varies, and is sometimes 140 lbs. In Turkey, the product may be 2000 or more chests, annually. In regard to China, we have only the testimony of the councillor Choo Tsun, respecting his native province, Yunnaw. The poppy, he says, is cultivated all over the hills and open campaign, and the quantity of opium annually produced there cannot be less than several thousand chests. From the foregoing statements, derived chiefly from official documents, the reader will be able to form some opinion as to the extent of territory, and the amount of popu-

[*] The seer = 1 lb. 13 oz.; 13,866 dr. avoirdupois.

lation and capital, now devoted to the production of opium. Taking into account the whole of Turkey, China, and India, it will be seen that many thousand acres, with millions of the inhabitants, are employed in the cultivation of poppies.—*Iniquities of the Opium Trade.*

For "The Friend."

STANZAS.

" And the far wandering of the soul in dreams,
  Calling up shrouded faces from the dead,
And with them bringing soft or solemn gleams,
  Familiar objects brightly to o'erspread,
And wakening buried love, or joy, to fear—
*These are night's mysteries—who shall make them
  clear ?*"

I roam once more thy forest wide,
  I see thee in my dreams ;
My childhood's home !—I hear again
  The murmur of thy streams.
I see thee in the sunny sheen
  Of thy departed hours,
And hear the glad song of thy birds,
  And gaze upon thy flowers.

Borne on the zephyrs through thy trees
  There is a sad, low tone,
A voice that telleth to my heart
  Of pleasant summers gone.
At stilly night, in visions sad
  I weep amid thy shade,
And sorrow o'er the shipwreck'd hopes
  Remorseless Time hath made.

Around that hearth, now desolate,
  What happy faces shone,
What cheerful voices mingled there,
  That far, far hence have gone.
Stern Time ! thou smitest upon the waste
  Of all our hearts hold dear,
And leavest thy withering trace on all
  We fondly cherish here !

I see a form, a stately form,
  Amid those green-wood bowers,
And calm that pale, high brow appears,
  As when in by-gone hours.
We wander where the clasping vines
  Adorn each brave old tree,
And list, as once we listened there
  The wild bird's minstrelsy.

My sire ! thy loving voice I hear,
  I see thee in my dreams !
Thine eye's bright spiritual glance,
  Ah ! too unearthly seems.
Methinks the howling storms of time
  Were all too rude for thee ;
Thou couldst not meet its chilling blast,
  Nor stem life's raging sea.

How can I e'er forget the hour
  I met thy last embrace,
And felt the clay-cold damps of death
  O'erspread thy saintly face.
But thy bark is safely anchor'd
  Where no tempest can molest,
" Where the wicked cease from troubling,
  And the weary are at rest."

I know thou'rt with the ransom'd,
  With their shining raiment on ;
But my sorrowing spirit mourneth
  To think that thou art gone.
O may thy household band at last
  Meet thee upon that shore,
Where tears of parting and of pain
  Shall cease for evermore.

Philadelphia, 11 mo. 1839.   F. A.

The late Duke of Bedford's rent roll was estimated at £250,000 per annum, or upwards of a *million* of dollars.

Brief Memoir of the Life of John Croker. Written by himself.

(Continued from p. 79.)

Thus, for about three years I passed my time, in the enjoyment of a tender and affectionate wife, who truly feared the Lord, and with whom I had great comfort; and we were a strength and rejoicing to each other. But at length it pleased the Lord to take from me my dear wife in child-bed, in the year 1699. What shall I say;—it was a near parting and a sharp exercise; yet I was made to say, Surely the Lord is good, let him do as it pleaseth him, and who dares to speak hardly, or say why doest thou so? Job said, the Lord gives and he takes away, blessed be the name of the Lord. God knows what is best for us, better than we ourselves; and therefore I will labour to be contented in his will, and to follow after that; hoping we may meet again where all disappointments are at an end: for all things here are uncertain, and man is born to trouble as the sparks fly upwards; there is no dependence on any thing below the sun, therefore my dependence shall be in the right arm of His salvation: hoping he will carry me through this vale of tears,—and how soon, the Lord only knoweth; I desire not length of days, but that I may at last finish my course in peace.

Now passing on in my widowhood, I found I had some way or other received hurt; for there seemed to come over me a cloud of thick darkness, so that my mouth was stopt for a time; and I was as in a wilderness, having no comfort in meetings nor in retirements, but great temptation followed me, and it was with me sleeping and waking, insomuch that I was not able to follow my business. At last I thought I would make my state and exercise known to my then father and mother-in-law Peters, who were then not only related to me by marriage, but were truly near in spirit. When they had the knowledge of it, I had their advice; and their prayers for me were not wanting, and I have reason to believe were answered; for in a little time the temptation began to grow weaker and weaker—strength began to increase—and light to shine out of darkness, which gave me to see the travail of my soul, and that it was good for me to be tried—for I should thus be better able to speak to such as might be under the like affliction. Then I had a word to speak again for God amongst his people, and cheerfulness increased; I also became fit for conversation with others, and followed my business, in which God blessed me, and I took delight in my friends. Although I lived four or five miles from our meeting, which was moveable, yet whatever I neglected, I attended that, if at home, on fourth days as well first days; God knew what inclined me so to do—it was my love to him and his truth, which was more to me than any thing in this world.

[It appears probable that it was during the prevalence of the afore-mentioned exercise of mind, that the following solemn language was committed to writing.]

"O Lord, in secret to thee do I appeal, knowing thou canst hear, and often dost reward openly; at this time I make my complaint, because dryness is over my soul, and thy comfortable presence is not known, as when thou with the shining of thy brightness ast pleased to arise. Yet in thee will I trust, having faith to believe, that in thy appointed time, and after thy wonted manner, thou wilt appear unto my waiting soul, which is breathing unto thee under a deep sense of the great want I at this time suffer—daily seeking thee and waiting for thy arisings; that so this cloud may be removed, which hath long remained. I doubt my confidence will fail, although there is a resolution that, if thou appear not again, I will trust in thee;—having tasted of thy loving-kindness, when thou wast pleased to appear, as a broad river sending forth pleasant streams of joy and consolation, by which my soul hath been refreshed. O my God, in judgment or in loving-kindness I pray thee appear, that my hungry soul may be filled: for I long after thee, O Lord, and I cannot find refreshment as in days past; yet I will not cease in secret to wait upon thee, or in silence to seek thee, because there it was thou didst appear to my soul, and then it was that I was made willing to make a covenant with thee—that if thou wouldst be with me, I would serve thee, my God, with a broken heart and an upright spirit; which I desired thou wouldest be pleased to place within me, that I might never more go from thee in heart or mind. I can speak to thy praise, thou hast often made me a shafer thereof, as in stillness I have waited upon thee. O Lord, I can crave from thee thy promise, that, for the cry of the poor (Lord, who so poor as I!) and for the sighing of the needy, thou wouldst arise: and who so needy as I! who at this time want thee, and by the want of thee want all things. Oh! how sad a thing it is to be overshadowed as by a thick cloud, wherein great difficulties, as the buffetings of Satan, and the suggestions of the enemy, are ready to prevail. Therefore, for the sake of the needy, arise; and let thy sun be seen to shine, whereby comfort may be conveyed to the soul. Lord, thou knowest it is my desire to be serviceable for thee and for thy truth; therefore I have been willing in secret before thee to offer up all into thy disposing hand, to do with that and me as seemed good in thy sight—who art an all-wise God, and knowest best what is best for the workmanship of thy hands. So, O my God, in patience will I wait, until my change shall come, for thou only knowest how it is with me at this time. In straits I have sought thee, and in difficult seasons I have waited in stillness upon thee, and thou hast never failed me; but according to thy good pleasure, hast broken in as a man of war, strong in power and excellent in might; for thou didst overcome, and set the prisoner at liberty, who, by reason of thy withdrawing, was ready to say thou hadst forsaken. What shall be said of thy loving-kindess and of thy tender mercies, but that thou art a never-failing God in the midst of difficulties; for although thou hidest thyself for a season, yet thou dost not wholly forsake, therefore what shall be said of thee? Open my mouth, and I will show forth thy praise;—speak but the word: thy fame is great in my soul, for my longing hath been great after thee. Oh! Lord, draw near as a counsellor to instruct me; for I will wait at thy footstool, that I may be filled with wisdom; for when I have enquired for the place of wisdom and of good understanding, I have turned into the centre of my soul, where thou, that art wiser than Solomon, art found teaching by thy Spirit. Here is wisdom and understanding, and thou art giving it freely without money or price; for nothing here, which thou hast bestowed as an outward blessing on man, is able to purchase it. Therefore, Lord, take all things here below that are thy blessings to me, rather than deprive me of the openings of wisdom to my soul; for it is that which I have desired, and through many difficulties have travelled to obtain. And now, Lord, seeing I have found thee, I desire a blessing from thy hand, that so I may never depart from thee more; be pleased to let thy presence still be with me, that I may for ever be encompassed therewith—that I may always be in sight of thee, whom I have chosen to be my leader. If thou wilt not let my soul be in the fulness of comfort, grant that my habitation may be always at the entrance of thy fulness, that whensoever thou openest, I may behold thy glory with delight, and that the sweetness that comes from thee may cause my heart to rejoice; which may be an evident token that as I hold out to the end, I shall receive an entrance into rest for evermore."

I spent two years a widower, and made not any motion towards marriage, but was willing to see my way clear, and often desired the Lord would incline my heart to a suitable companion and help-meet in all states. I did not see that the happiness of man consisted in what he might have as to portion, because the Lord is a portion to his, and those that put their trust in him, shall want nothing that is for their good—which I had faith to believe, as I kept here, I should certainly witness.

My honoured father Peters having a desire to visit some meetings in London, I accompanied him; and, as I found my heart engaged, I dropped a few words in meetings. So we went from Cornwall, through Devonshire, Somersetshire, and Hampshire, into Sussex; from whence we had the company of our friend, Elizabeth Gates, to London, whose company was very acceptable. We tarried the time of the yearly meeting, part of which was very comfortable: Friends seemed to have great affection for each other, and there appeared to be a regard to the worthy name of the Lord, which had been great in Zion for the strengthening of her, that she might not be divided, nor her mighty men confuted; but that her peace might be as a river, and her brightness as the morning sun without clouds—which was and is the travail of my soul. As to myself, I had a good and comfortable time there; and after the yearly meeting was ended, I returned with my father and friend Elizabeth Gates, to her father's at Horsham, and stayed thereabout a few days; then going to a marriage at Shipley, we passed without having any other meeting, to Ringwood, in Hampshire, being about seventy miles, and then to Poole, thence through Dorsetshire and Devonshire, and so home.

I was satisfied with my journey; my father showed a tender and fatherly care over me, as to the small gift I had, and my spiritual exercise, that I might grow therein.

[After his return home, his mind became engaged with a prospect of making proposals of marriage to his friend Elizabeth Gates, which was encouraged by his father and mother Peters, who loved his said friend E. G.]

In some reasonable time, I acquainted her parents with my intentions, had their consent, and then making my mind fully known to my said friend, prevailed with her to agree to my proposals; and in some time after I made it known to our monthly meeting.

The yearly meeting in 1702 approaching, I was desirous to bring things about before the beginning of that meeting, so that we might be married soon after, hoping several friends from Cornwall might be at our marriage; and accordingly there were, and also divers from London and other places; so that we had a large meeting, and greatly to the satisfaction of us and others; for the goodness of the Lord attended our solemnity to our great comfort, and was as a seal of his divine favour, in bringing us together, and uniting our hearts in affinity of love. And whatever troubles or disappointments may have since happened, they have no ways lessened our affections; and this has hitherto preserved us as true help-meets in the Lord, both in spirituals and temporals; for under any exercise either inward or outward, we have been as a succour and strength to each other; for, had it not been so, the many things we met with might have broken our union.

So we came down into Cornwall, took a house, and settled at Liskeard; and I found we had a service amongst Friends, and we were thankful to God for it, who never faileth them that put their trust in him. But after we had laboured under some difficulties, finding the things of this world did not answer, considering the increase of our family, and our willingness to be serviceable on Truth's account, not only to labour in word and doctrine for the promotion of the gospel, but also to entertain strangers and those of the household of faith—my wife inclined for her own country, hoping things might be better, and we more serviceable there; but I not seeing the way for our removal very clearly, and my good old father and mother Peters, with other Friends, being unwilling to part with us hastily, were not very willing at first to consent to our removing, but laboured some time to prevent the same. At length finding things rather grew worse—and the more so, because some unreasonable men had deprived me of that which was my chief income, I began to hearken to the request and desires of my wife; unto which Friends also now seemed a little to give way, fearing, I believe, lest they should be our hindrance, and so come under blame; and my father Gates happening to die about the same time, there seemed to be a want of some person in his room. So, after nine years,

having had four children, whereof three were living, we gave notice of a sale of our shop and household goods, and soon disposed of the same; then, taking leave of our sorrowful-hearted relations and friends, in a tender and broken frame of spirit, to the melting of many into tears, upon the bended knees of both body and soul, we recommended each other to God, and to the protection of his Divine Providence; desiring the Lord might go with us and preserve us in the way we were to go, and give us food and raiment, wherewith we hoped to be content. He who knows all, knew it was not great things which we longed after, but that we might be his servants, and be serviceable in our short space of time, for the good of souls; and we desired that he would be pleased to keep us in the remembrance of our friends, when tar separated outwardly, that so we might be as epistles written in one another's hearts—for the seasons which we had had together were tendering and often melting. More could I say of this, for it was a day of days, and not easily to be forgotten;—the Lord bring it often to our remembrance is what my soul desireth.

Having thus spent a little time together with Friends and other sober neighbours, with many embraces and hearty good wishes, we, with our little ones, and necessary conveniences, set forward, being accompanied by Friends and others to a place where we ate and drank together: then taking our farewell of them, being only myself, wife, and three children, a friend, J. S., (who in kindness came to assist us,) and our servant-maid. Being favoured with good horses, good roads, and fine weather, we met with very few disappointments for all which we were thankful to God, our great preserver.

Now, having made my observations during the passage of some part of my pilgrimage, I see that there is much trouble attends this life, and he that will live godly in Christ Jesus, must suffer much, and bear all things with patience, and press forward to the mark for the prize of the high calling in God; and I hope the Lord will preserve many in this labour, who will study peace with all men, and pursue it; which, that I may be found in during the remaining part of my pilgrimage, is what I desire.

(Conclusion next week.)

For "The Friend."

An Account of the Life of William Bennit.

When the apostle, in writing to the Hebrews, narrates various instances in which the holy ancients, through the "obedience of faith," had "pleased God," and become "heirs of righteousness," he does it to show how "great a cloud of witnesses" there was to the efficacy of that power which in all ages is present, to enable the humble believer to run with patience the race set before him. He strives to animate the spiritual feelings of the scattered descendants of the patriarchs and prophets by the consideration of their forefathers, who, through that faith which

"is the evidence of things hoped for," had been strengthened to triumph in the midst of varied calamities, intense sufferings, inhuman tortures, and cruel deaths. After thus inciting them to faithfulness, by the example of men of like passions with themselves,—who had obtained the victory over sin, and been made partakers of a "better resurrection,"—he crowns the appeal by bidding them to look unto Jesus, the author and finisher of the saints' faith. He exhorts them, in their afflictions and trials, to consider how even their glorious Master endured "the contradiction of sinners against himself." From the renewed recollection of the sufferings of the dear Son of God, and from the declaration that "whom the Lord loveth, he chasteneth," the apostle would strengthen them in patient endurance, that thus making straight paths for their feet, the lame of the flock for whom Christ died, might not be turned out of the way, through any misteppings of theirs. He warns them, by the unforgiven transgression of Esau, never for a morsel of meat, however tempting to their fleshly appetites, to sell their birth-right. Then, rejoicing in fellowship with the true Israel of God, he compares its present condition with the past. The outward signs and shadows of a typical dispensation, the mount that burned with fire, the blackness, the darkness, the tempest, the sound of the terrible trumpet, the unspeakably awful voice of words, appertained not to the spiritual kingdom into which the church was now brought. To each one of the baptized members of that body of which Christ Jesus is the living Head, the language of the apostle is applicable. "But ye are come unto Mount Sion, and unto the city of the living God, the heavenly Jerusalem, and to an innumerable company of angels; to the general assembly and church of the First-born, which are written in heaven, and to God, the judge of all, and to the spirits of just men made perfect, and to Jesus, the mediator of the new covenant, and to the blood of sprinkling, that speaketh better things than that of Abel."

The consideration of the sufferings, the tribulations, the triumphant victories over the temptations of sin, the trials of affliction and the terrors of death by saints in modern times, may well lead us to a train of similar reflections, and the enunciation of precepts and exhortations in accordance with those uttered by the apostle. Many of our early Friends, by faith in the spiritual manifestation of Christ Jesus as the "Light within," by obedience to its teachings, by submission to its sanctifying operations, were enabled to obtain a good report, and were entitled to be numbered amongst that company of whom it was declared the world was not worthy. The memorials of their meek constancy, and the Christian courage with which they bore an unflinching testimony for the truth as it is in Jesus, in the midst of multiplied trials and persecutions, add them to that cloud of witnesses which on every hand testify to the supporting, preserving and sanctifying power of the Holy Spirit, which, being that which teacheth what is to be known of God, is made manifest in man. Thus, whilst observing their innocent walking before men, we shall be at no loss to comprehend the principle by which they were directed, and whilst incited by their example, may we also seek for access to the only fountain-head of true wisdom and spiritual strength, " Christ in us the hope of glory." Through the operation of His Spirit, we may really profit by the record of their lives, whilst he is teaching us the same blessed doctrines, and instructing us to maintain them against every stratagem of the enemy. If we are faithful, he will preserve us from ever selling our spiritual birth-right, and enable us to stand in the union our forefathers were made partakers of, with the inhabitants of the city of the living God, the heavenly Jerusalem. O the spirituality, the holy security of such a state! It looks not abroad for Christ! It says not, " who shall ascend into heaven to bring Christ down from above, or into the deeps, to bring him up from the dead;" for those who have thus attained, have come to Christ, and know him to be nigh them, manifesting himself, in the secret of their souls, as their daily leader, their spiritual feeder, their watchful preserver and king.

William Bennit was one of those who, in the early times of our religious society, for their faithfulness to the requirings of the Holy Spirit, was persecuted by imprisonment to death. He was born in the year 1634, at Kirtly. From one of his publications, it appears that when very young in years, the visitations of the love of God were extended to him, through which, by the pure light in his conscience, he was frequently checked and reproved for sin. At times, when his evil doings were brought to his remembrance, he was introduced into much trouble of mind; but he knew not that that which reproved him was the light of Christ, nor that, by submission to its teachings, he might be delivered from the dominion of sin. He says, that when he was in the company of children who had not the fear of God, he ran with great delight and joy into sin and wickedness with them; but that, when he was alone in stillness and quietness, the pure witness of God arose with its reproofs, set his sins in order before him, and brought his evil doings to remembrance. Then trouble took hold upon him, and sin became his burden. But seeking for ease and liberty, he soon ran into sin and vanity again. Thus from year to year he went on in rebellion against the convictions of truth. Although even then the Lord, whose merciful regard was over him for good, sometimes strengthened him to refrain from speaking and acting the evil he had thought to say or do. When alone in the fields, he at times cried and prayed unto the Lord, earnestly desiring the knowledge of Him, his Way, and his Truth: But he says, " I prayed to a God I knew not; I imagined a God afar off, and did not then know it was the Lord that did search my heart, discovered unto me my thoughts, and judged me for sin. I knew not that it was the light, way and truth of God in my own heart, which sometimes raised desires in me to know the

truth, and to walk therein. My mind was abroad, as is the case with many in this day, who, having desires after truth and righteousness, are seeking them in carnal ordinances, forms, likenesses, beggarly elements, rudiments of the world, ceremonies and traditions of men."

At the age of fourteen, he was bound as an apprentice. At this time, he says, " It pleased the God of infinite loving kindness to visit me more than formerly, by his pure light and spirit, which increasingly strove with me, so that I scarce committed any evil but the Light would soon judge me for it. Yea! the Lord God, with his pure light and gift, did pursue me hard, and followed me closely, calling to me in my heart with his still voice, to come out of sin. But, like Samuel, I knew not that it was the Lord who did call. I went astray as a wandering sheep; yet I had desires to know the way to the fold; to know where the Lord feedeth his flock, and causeth them to lie down in peace, quietness and rest, where none can make afraid. It was rest my soul wanted, and true peace in God it many a time longed for and panted after. I was oftentimes wounded, because of sin, and, for want of the enjoyment of love and peace, I went bowed down in spirit day after day, with an aching mind and wounded conscience; with eyes full of tears and a heart full of sighing. Sometimes wishing and secretly saying, O that I were in a desert, solitary place, where no man inhabits, that I might mourn and weep my fill, pour out my tears unto the God of mercy, and spread my complaints before him whom my soul longs, thirsts and pants after, even as the hart panteth after the water brooks."

Whilst the light of Christ in his conscience thus broke his rest and peace in sin, and renewed in him true desires, and breathings and thirstings after righteousness, pity and compassion were raised in him for those who appeared under like exercise with himself. A tender love sprang up in him towards all whom he deemed the people of God. He was thus brought to feel with the travailing seed of Jacob, and brought into fellowship with those who were mournfully seeking an establishment in the truth. This feeling was strong with him through the whole course of his pilgrimage. His pity, love, compassion and tenderness, was still towards the seekers and mourners; he could not but sympathize with them; and his spirit was constrained to bear their burdens. He felt their sorrows in his bosom, and secret petitions were oftentimes raised in him to the Father of mercies on their behalf.

Being an apprentice at Yarmouth, he frequented the meetings of the Independent congregation there. At that time he deemed them the true people of God, although he saw much in the lives and conversations of some of the chief amongst them, which was not consistent with what they professed in words. He says that at times the pure witness of God in his own heart did, as it were, stop his mouth, that he could not sing with them, whilst he was frequently broken into tenderness, and brought to quake and tremble as a

leaf that is shaken by the wind. " I knew not," he continues, " that it was the power of God that brought such a trembling upon me, and that did in some measure let me see that it was not then a time of singing for me: I was in a strange land, in the land of captivity, and could not sing the songs of Sion, which they were ignorant of who were singing what others had prescribed and made ready for them. This I say without enmity towards that people, for my soul beareth love and good will towards all men, and desires to tender and own the least true appearance of God in any. But I desired the enjoyment of the love, joy, peace and sweet presence of God, which maketh glad the hearts of the righteous, and causeth the lowly, meek and upright to sing for joy, in the spirit with the understanding; not songs or psalms which men have invented by their human wisdom, from which the mysteries of God's kingdom are obscured and concealed, but the new and living song, which the dead cannot sing, nor any but the living who are raised, redeemed out of and from the earth; even the ransomed of the Lord, who are returned from Babylon to Mount Sion. These stand with the Lamb, whom they have followed through many tribulations. These have not loved their lives unto death—have washed their robes white in his blood, in and by whom they have gotten the victory over the beast and false prophet. In the heavenly dominion of the Lamb, by whom they are made more than conquerors, they stand on the sea of glass mingled with fire, with the harps of God, and can sing a new song of praise and thanksgiving unto him that was dead, but is alive and lives evermore."

In the time of his trouble and exercise of mind, he never made known his condition unto others. Although he would gladly have had some to have been acquainted with his state, he was straitened about communicating it. He found the spirit more and more working within him; but, amidst all its reproofs, unfoldings and directings, though strengthened thereby to resist many evils which others were overcome with, he was not sensible of its true character. He testifies that he knew not " that it was the light of Christ Jesus, or a measure of the spirit of truth; neither did I then know I should have taken heed thereto as unto a light shining in a dark place, until the day had more and more dawned, and until Christ the day-star had arisen in my heart. My mind was still gazing abroad, and imagining a God afar off. He was very nigh me, but I knew him not." " The pearl of great price was hid in my heart, but I knew it not; the kingdom of God was at hand, but I was gazing for it abroad, even whilst it was working in me like leaven hid in three measures of meal. The door into the fold, the entrance into rest was within, which I was seeking without. My Saviour was nigh, but I imagined him afar off; neither did any man in those days direct my mind unto the light and gift of Christ in my own heart."

N. E.

(To be continued.)

ANECDOTE OF WASHINGTON.

A correspondent of the New York Gazette relates the following anecdote of General Washington:

One Reuben Ronzy, of Virginia, owed the general about one thousand pounds. While President of the United States, one of his agents brought an action for the money—judgment was obtained, and an execution issued against the body of R., who was taken to jail. He had considerable landed estate, but this kind of property could not, at that time, be sold in Virginia, unless with the discretion of the person. He had a large family, and for the sake of his children, preferred lying in prison to selling his land. A friend hinted to him that probably General Washington did not know any thing of the proceeding, and it might be well to send him a petition, with a statement of the circumstances. He did so, and the very next mail from Philadelphia, after the arrival of his petition in that city, brought him an order for immediate release, together with a full discharge, and a *severe reprimand* to the agent for having acted in such a manner. Poor Ronzey was completely restored to his family, who never laid down their heads at night without presenting prayers to heaven for their beloved Washington. Providence smiled upon the labours of the grateful family, and in a few years he enjoyed the *exquisite pleasure* of being able to lay the money, with interest, at the feet of Washington. That truly great man reminded him that the debt was cancelled. Ronzy replied, that the debt of his family to the father of his country, and the preserver of their parent, could never be discharged; and the general, to avoid the pressing importunity of the grateful Virginian, who would not be denied, accepted the money only to divide it among Ronzy's children, which he did immediately.

Beautiful.—A deaf and dumb person being asked what was his idea of forgiveness, took the pencil and wrote—'tis the odour which flowers yield when trampled upon.

Swallowing a Farm.—A farmer in Connecticut who has occupied the same farm, on lease, for about thirty years past, was complaining that he had not been able to lay up any thing from his thirty years' labour. A neighbouring storekeeper offered to explain to him the reason, and proceeded as follows: "During the last thirty years that you have been on that farm, I have been trading in this store; and the distilled spirits I have sold you, with the interest of the money, would have made you the *owner* of the farm you *hire*.—Journal of Humanity.

The late Sir John Ramsden.—The property left by this baronet is prodigious. We have heard that his grandson, the young baronet, eleven or twelve years of age, succeeds to £120,000 per annum; £500,000 is divided among his three sons; £40,000 to each of his daughters; and to his widow the residence at Byron, with £8,000 per annum.—Leeds Intelligencer.

THE FRIEND.

TWELFTH MONTH, 14, 1839.

However matter of exultation with some, or whatever may be the feeling of the many, 'o us it is cause of sorrow,—of the deepest regret,—almost of despondency, that the opera-house project has really met with a formal reception, and is now before the public in all its length and breadth, its flattering but deceiving features, in the shape of an elaborate report by a committee of citizens. What say the watchmen on the walls of the different religious congregations, those who *should be* as shepherds of the flocks—"stewards of the manifold grace of God?" Will they not lift up the voice of warning? Can they do nothing to stay the threatening plague? We have already entered our protest against the scheme, utterly repugnant, as unquestionably it is, to the sobriety and holy circumspection of life, obligatory upon a professedly Christian community. At present, therefore, we shall content ourselves with copying from an exchange paper the paragraph below. Our humble little sheet finds its way to several places of concourse, and it may chance that some of the opera-folk may thus see what people abroad think and say on the subject, and possibly it may give rise to profitable reflections in the minds of some. It may also be pertinent to the case to refer to two extracts in another part of this sheet, from the writings of the amiable and pious, and, we suppose, popular Bishop M'Ilvaine. The sentiments therein inculcated, if carried out, would leave little place for the encouragement of such licentious modes of spending precious time.

"*Folly.*—Notwithstanding the 'hard times' in Philadelphia, a number of the leading men who cry out against the government are engaged in preparing to build an opera-house in that city, to cost nearly half a million of dollars! in which the 'extremely modest' Italian female dancers will display themselves, by twirling like a top on one foot, while the other is raised in the air. Honesty and morality will not be promoted by such a lavish expenditure, on such objects, at such a time as this."

A public examination of the Infant School, under the care of the Association of Friends for the Instruction of Poor Children, will take place on sixth day, 12th month, 20th, in the lower room of their school-house, on Wager street; at 10½ o'clock, A. M.

The first lecture on Instinct was listened to with much apparent interest by a crowded assemblage, of both sexes, at Friends' Reading room, on third-day evening last. The other lecture is to take place on third-day evening next.

HAVERFORD SCHOOL.

WANTED, a Friend to act as Steward of this Institution. Apply to
KIMBER & SHARPLESS,
No. 8 South Fourth street.

INSTITUTE FOR COLOURED YOUTH.

A suitably qualified Friend is wanted to take charge of the farm and family of this institution. Application may be made to
BENJAMIN COOPER, near Camden, N. J.
THOMAS WISTAR, Jr., Abington.
JOSEPH SCATTERGOOD, No. 14 Minor st. or
MARMADUKE C. COPE, 286 Filbert st.

MARRIED, at Friends' meeting house, Middleton, Col. co., Ohio, on 5th day, the 17th of 10th month, JOSEPH LYNCH, son of Joshua Lynch, of Upper Springfield, to REBECCA BEASON, daughter of Richard Beason, of the former place.

———, at Friends' meeting, Upper Springfield, Col. co., Ohio, on 5th day, the 28th of 11th month, WILLIAM CARSON, son of John Carson, to ELIZABETH MORRIS, daughter of Anthony and Hannah Morris.

———, at Friends' meeting, Salem, Col. co., Ohio, on 4th day, the 27th of 11th month, EDWARD BONSALL, son of Edward Bonsal, to HANNAH JONES, formerly of Philadelphia county, Pa., daughter of Joseph and Elizabeth Jones, both deceased.

———, same day, and same place, ELISHA STRATTON, son of Josiah Stratton, to ELIZABETH, daughter of David Painter.

DIED, at her residence in Wolfboro', N. H., on sixth day, the 29th of 11th month, of pulmonary consumption, HANNAH, wife of Joseph Varney, in the 58th year of her age. She was a member of Sandwich Monthly Meeting, and for several years has accordingly filled the stations of overseer and elder. She manifested from early life, an exemplary concern, in the attendance of meetings, taking great pains to attend her Monthly and Quarterly Meetings, the nearest of which was over twenty miles distant. For many years her health had been declining, and in the last autumn her complaints assumed a more alarming appearance; but she occasionally attended religious meetings until within three weeks of her dissolution. She bore her last illness with Christian patience, and imparted much salutary counsel to her children and friends about her. She frequently expressed an apprehension of her approaching change. And on one occasion, to a friend who came to visit her, she said; "I have no anxiety about recovering; I feel as though my day's work is nearly done; I have a comfortable assurance that I shall be received into my heavenly Father's kingdom." After a pause, she added, "It is not for any works of righteousness which I have done; I am a poor creature; it is all through the mercy and atonement of my dear Saviour." At another time, not having had any sleep for the night, it being a late hour, her daughter asked her if it was in consequence of pain that she could not sleep. She said "No; I am enjoying that that is better to me than sleep." At another time, in alluding to her past life, she said, "I have looked it over night after night, as I have been lying here, desiring that all my offences might be set in order before me. I see nothing in my way; I have received an unshaken evidence that all are passed by. It is through the unmerited mercy of my Redeemer." She was much engaged in prayer. Near her close, she prayed, "O heavenly Father, keep near me, and do not forsake me—to the end;" and much more, which could not be understood. Her physician observed to her, that he thought she was in great suffering, she replied, "No language can describe it—I am willing to suffer—my Redeemer suffered before me." A friend, in her hearing, mentioned, her suffering was nearly through; she said, "I am willing to suffer all that my Heavenly Father is pleased to lay upon me." Her understanding remained clear to the end; she quietly expired, without sigh or groan, an exemplification of the faithfulness of the heavenly voice, heard by John, "blessed are the dead which die in the Lord."

PRINTED BY ADAM WALDIE,
Carpenter Street, below Seventh, Philadelphia.

THE FRIEND.

A RELIGIOUS AND LITERARY JOURNAL.

VOL. XIII.   SEVENTH DAY, TWELFTH MONTH, 21, 1839.   **NO. 12.**

EDITED BY ROBERT SMITH.

PUBLISHED WEEKLY.

Price two dollars per annum, payable in advance.

Subscriptions and Payments received by

GEORGE W. TAYLOR,

NO. 50, NORTH FOURTH STREET, UP STAIRS,

PHILADELPHIA.

ABOLITION NOT IMPRACTICABLE.

Introduction to the Second Edition of "Jay's View of the Action of the Federal Government in behalf of Slavery."

The rapid sale of the first edition of this work, and the almost immediate call for another, afford gratifying evidence of the awakening attention of the public to the action of the federal government in behalf of slavery. That action is so iniquitous in itself, and so dangerous in its consequences to the liberties of the country, that it needs only to be fully known, to be restrained by the patriotism and moral sense of the community, within the limits prescribed by the constitution, and the obvious principles of humanity and justice. It is not easy, however, to enlighten those who prefer darkness to light, nor to persuade men to act in opposition to their supposed pecuniary or political interests. But there can be no triumph, where there is no struggle; that religion is worthless, which co-operates with human depravity, and that patriotism an empty name, which only echoes the shout of the multitude.

If the friends of human liberty have in this country much to cover them with grief and shame, they have also much to stimulate their exertions, and much to assure them of ultimate success. Their own rights—the virtue, happiness and liberty of their descendants, the honour, prosperity and freedom of their country, are all involved in the issue. Slavery is a perfidious, encroaching enemy, that must either conquer or be conquered. Let the warfare now waged against it be succeeded by a peace, and soon Texas, the valley of the Mississippi, and in time even the Atlantic States would be added to its dominions. Every dictate, therefore, of patriotism or religion, of personal interest, of paternal affection, unite in urging us to use all lawful means to stay the progress of the destroyer, and to teach our children after us to continue the contest.

But is not the struggle hopeless, and ought we not to sit down in utter despair at the prospect of desolation, misery and disgrace with which our country is threatened? So we are advised by high authority—PUBLIC OPINION, we are told, is against us. Indeed! and is it not also against every defeated candidate for office and every losing political party? But who hears our baffled politicians advising submission to the victors, because public opinion is against the vanquished? Public opinion is a mighty agent for good or for evil; but it is as fickle as it is powerful. It strewed the path of the Redeemer with palm branches, and afterwards nailed him to the cross. For ages it guarded and preserved the oppressions and cruelties of the feudal system; it is now gradually but surely destroying its every vestige. But a few years since, public opinion not merely sanctioned, but actually required, the use of intoxicating liquors. It is now their potent enemy.

But perhaps the most extraordinary change this mighty agent has undergone, is in relation to slavery itself; and the friends of emancipation will find in the history of this transformation one of the most powerful inducements to perseverance.

For more than two hundred years before its abolition, had the African slave trade been pursued by Christian nations, under the fostering protection of their rulers. No difference of religious faith, of government or of climate, offered any check to this accursed commerce. Catholics and Protestants, the subjects of monarchs and the citizens of republics, natives of the north and of the south, alike thirsted for the price of blood, alike participated in robbery and murder. In 1774, the British cabinet refused its assent to the imposition by the colonial legislatures of duties on the importation of slaves. "We cannot," said the secretary, Lord Dartmouth "allow the colonies to check or discourage, in *any degree*, a traffic so beneficial to the nation"! The feelings of humanity and the powers of conscience were on this subject almost universally and totally paralyzed. So late as 1783, in the trial of a civil cause in London, it appeared in evidence that one hundred and thirty-two Africans had been thrown into the sea by the captain of a slaver, to defraud the underwriters. Minutes of the evidence were submitted to the government; but the victims were only *negroes*, and the murderer was unmolested.

In 1786, the number of unhappy beings annually torn from Africa, was estimated at 100,000. Of those, it was admitted at least 20,000 perished on the voyage; and of those who survived to enter a state of hopeless bondage, 20,000 more exhausted by suffering and despair sunk into the grave within two years.

Individuals were occasionally found who protested against the traffic; but their voices were unheeded. For two centuries not a word in reprobation of the trade had been uttered within the walls of the British Senate. This long silence was first broken by Mr. David Hartley, who, in 1776, moved in the House of Commons that the slave trade was "contrary to the laws of God and the rights of man." But the moral sense of Great Britain, and indeed of the world, was then too obtuse to recognise these simple and now obvious truths; and the resolution was promptly rejected. Seven years after, a petition against the trade, the first ever offered, was presented by the Quaker Society to the House of Commons. But that body did not even condescend to consider it, the premier, Lord North, coolly observing that the traffic had, in a commercial view, become *necessary* to almost every nation in Europe.

On the 7th July, 1783, shortly after this official declaration, SIX Quakers* met in London, "to consider what steps they should take FOR THE RELIEF AND LIBERATION OF THE NEGRO SLAVES IN THE WEST INDIES, and FOR THE DISCOURAGEMENT OF THE SLAVE TRADE ON THE COAST OF AFRICA."

When we reflect on the peculiar circumstances under which these men assembled, we cannot but regard their meeting as one of the sublimest instances of Christian faith unrecorded in the sacred volume; a faith which, according to the promise, was effectual in removing mountains. At the moment of their meeting, the maritime powers of Europe were actively engaged in the trade—a trade, against which no petition had ever been presented except from the very sect to which they belonged, and which had within a few days, like certain petitions in modern times, been ordered to "*lie on the table*." They had, moreover, just witnessed the impunity of the wretch who had deliberately drowned one hundred and thirty-two of his fellow men—an impunity which warned them of the utter insensibility of the public to the sufferings of the miserable negroes.

And who were these six men who, under such circumstances, presumed to attempt the abolition of slavery and the slave trade—who aspired to move the moral world—to arrest the commerce of nations—to proclaim liberty to the captive, and the opening of the prison doors to them that were bound? Did they sway the councils or lead the armies of empires? Were they possessed of learning to

---

* William Dillwin, George Harrison, Samuel Hoare, Thomas Knowles, John Lloyd, and Joseph Woods. Their names are registered in heaven; let them not be forgotten on earth.

command the attention of the wise and great; or of eloquence to mould at their will the passions of multitudes? They were humble and obscure individuals, belonging to a small and despised sect, and precluded by their religious tenets and social condition from all political influence. But they had discovered from the Book of God, what had escaped many wise and good men, that the trade in question was opposed alike to the attributes and the precepts of the almighty Ruler of nations.

In labouring, therefore, for its suppression, they were assured of His approbation; and without regarding their own weakness, or the obstacles before them, they proceeded steadily in the path of duty, leaving the result to HIM with whom all things are possible.

They determined to hold frequent meetings, of which regular minutes were kept. Their first object was to enlighten and purify the public mind; and for this purpose they entered into negotiations with the proprietors of various newspapers, and secured a space in their columns for such articles respecting the trade as they might choose to insert. They likewise circulated books and pamphlets on the subject. The seeds thus scattered, germinated slowly, but ultimately yielded a glorious harvest. Within two years, a second petition was presented, and, like the first, was treated with neglect. The third year the six associates, with the aid of some friends, engaged the celebrated Clarkson as their agent; and so successful were his labours in exciting the sensibilities of the British public, that it was found expedient to divest the enterprise of its sectarian character, and the committee added six to their number from other denominations. This new committee soon became an important body, receiving and appropriating the pecuniary contributions to the cause, and directing and cheering the labours of its advocates. Gradually members of Parliament, dignitaries of the church, and political leaders subscribed to the funds of the committee, and avowed their hostility to the trade.

Petitions are multiplied, and the government so far condescended to notice the rising excitement, as to appoint a committee to enquire into the alleged atrocities of this branch of the British commerce. On the 9th of May, 1788, only five years after the first meeting of the committee, the House of Commons voted that they would at the next session take into consideration the complaints against the African slave trade.

It is unnecessary for our purpose to pursue the details of this instructive history. It has already taught us the possibility of rousing the public attention, however lethargic, by appeals to the conscience and understanding, and the influence which Christian zeal and faith, unaided by wealth and power, are capable of exerting. The few remaining facts we shall notice, convey the important lesson that no cause, however pure, no truth, however obvious, can shield their advocates from obloquy, when prejudice and selfishness find it expedient to assail them; and also, that constancy in maintaining and inculcating the great principles of justice and humanity, will finally be crowned with success.

No sooner did a parliamentary enquiry threaten to expose the abominations. and endanger the continuance of the traffic, than its advocates, reckless alike of truth and decency, vindicated its policy, and attacked with vindictive fury those who were labouring to destroy it. Abolition was denounced in parliament as "hypocritical, fanatic and methodistical." It would lead, it was asserted to "insurrection, massacre and ruin in the colonies; and in great Britain, to the reduction of her revenue, the decay of her naval strength, and the bankruptcy of her merchants and manufacturers." The trade was justified by the press, and even ministers of religion stepped forth to vindicate it on scriptural authority.* In 1791, a bill was brought in for the suppression of the trade. The opposition to it was malignant and successful. The measure was pronounced fit only for the bigotry of the 12th century. Lord John Russel termed it "visionary and delusive; a feeble attempt to serve the cause of humanity as other nations would pursue the trade, if abolished by Great Britain." Mr. Stanley insisted that it was the intention of Providence, from the beginning, *that one set of men should be slaves to another*; and he complained that the trade had been condemned from the pulpit!

The friends of abolition were ridiculed by Lord Chancellor Thurlow, from the woolsack and the Duke of Clarence, who afterwards, as WILLIAM THE FOURTH, gave his assent to the bill abolishing slavery throughout his dominions, regardless of parliamentary decorum declared in his place, in the House of Lords that the abolitionists were hypocrites and fanatics; and, in the application of these epithets, included Mr. Wilberforce by name.

Ten times did Mr. Wilberforce, in the House of Commons, endeavour to procure the suppression of the traffic, and ten times was he doomed to defeat. So late as 1807, Lord Castlereagh, in the British senate, vindicated the trade on scriptural grounds, and avowed that, in his opinion, the advantages resulting from it were so great, that were it not now existing, the trade ought forthwith to be established. But the triumph of justice, and the reward of faith and perseverance were nigh at hand. On the 25th of March, 1807 twenty-four years after the formation of the Quaker committee, the slave trade was abolished by act of parliament.

Splendid and glorious as was this triumph it was incomplete while shared by Great Britain alone. The whole of Christendom was yet to be brought to abjure a commerce condemned alike by reason and revelation. A long course of negotiation ensued, and treaty after treaty was made for the abandonment of the traffic, until, in 1830, every Christian

* As illustrative of public opinion at this time, we give the titles of two pamphlets published in London in 1788, viz.: "Slavery no Oppression," and Scripture Researches on the Licitness of the Slave Trade, 'showing its conformity with the principles of nature and revealed religion, delineated in the writings of the word of God."—BY THE REV. R. HARRIS.

their efforts to change public opinion, in order that a future Congress may grant what we know the next will refuse.

(Conclusion next week.)

For "The Friend."

THE CLASSICS.

The writer of "Remarks on the Study of the Greek and Latin languages, suggested by the perusal of Dymond's chapter on intellectual education," which have appeared in the three last numbers of "The Friend," commences his essay with strong expressions of respect for the author. His writings generally are acknowledged to be models of reasoning; his style is admitted to be clear, free, and vigorous; and his logic in general remarkably correct. The additional excellence of an earnest desire after truth is also conceded; and yet, in the opinion of the writer of the "Remarks," he has most unaccountably erred in his estimate of the value and importance of classical learning. And in order to obviate the injury which society is liable to suffer from the errors of an author of such deserved celebrity, he has kindly undertaken to expose and refute them.

After such an introduction we might reasonably expect that Dymond's views were doomed to undergo a thorough examination, and that the attempt at least would be made to show, that in this chapter of the work he was quite mistaken in his premises, or weak and illogical in his inferences. Yet, strange as it may seem, our writer does nothing more than refer to Dymond's assertions, that very little assistance can be derived from ancient learning towards discharging the duties of a parent or citizen of the state; that the classics occupy time which might be more beneficially employed:—and then charging him with begging the question, asserting without proof the very point in dispute, he proceeds to set forth at length the advantages of classical study, and we hear nothing more of Jonathan Dymond. From the manner in which the case is disposed of, one unacquainted with Dymond's writings would very naturally imagine that this was nearly all he had said upon the subject; he certainly would not suppose that the principal part of the chapter referred to was occupied with the consideration of the relative importance of classic lore, the cost of its acquisition, and its practical value compared with other branches of knowledge. It would be well for those who wish to form correct opinions upon a subject of some importance, and to understand what Dymond's views and arguments really were, to read the chapter on Intellectual Education, contained in his essays; and I apprehend they will generally be of the mind that his reasoning is as logical, and his conclusions as just and sound in reference to this matter, as they have been on any of the various topics which were subjected to the scrutiny of his lucid and powerful intellect. Let us, however, now follow the writer of the remarks, and see whether all the advantages claimed by him for the study of the Greek and Latin languages are well founded. It is asserted, and

the attempt is made to prove, "that by devoting a considerable share of our time to the Latin and Greek languages, we shall be able to acquire a thorough knowledge of our own more speedily, than if the latter should receive our exclusive attention." Now, abstractly considered, this may be true; but happily for us, we in fact acquire our principal knowledge of the English language, without making it an object of especial study at all. Words are but the signs of ideas, our acquaintance with them begins in early childhood, and keeps pace with our progress in knowledge, it is enlarged by conversation, by reading, by every proceeding which results in the enlargement of our stock of ideas.

If we must seek a correct knowledge of English through the Latin, on account of the large number of words derived from it, of much more consequence must be the study of the ancient Saxon language, as it forms the basis or ground-work of our mother tongue, and furnishes far the larger part of all the words employed in it, including a vast majority of those in common use. Indeed, the importance of the study of old Anglo-Saxon is much urged by some of our learned men, and a writer in the Princeton Review expresses the hope, that before many years an allotment of time for this purpose will be made in every college in America. Now, it will not be denied that all this may be necessary, in order to attain such a critical knowledge of the language as is aimed at by thorough scholars. What is contended is, that an acquaintance with our own language, sufficiently accurate and extensive to enable persons to communicate all their ideas with entire facility and correctness; and to read the best English writers with a perfect perception of their meaning, may be obtained without a resort to any such circuitous process. If this be doubted, I am quite willing to leave the question of fact to that portion of my readers whose experience qualifies them to judge in the case.

But we are also told that a knowledge of scientific terms is indispensable to the study of science, and that these are generally derived from the Greek or Latin. This is admitted. But is the knowledge of scientific terms to precede our study of science itself? The very supposition is absurd.

As we progress in the study of any branch of natural science, the various technical terms employed in it are learned almost without an effort. The name Oxygen is said to be derived from two Greek words signifying "acid" and "I generate." Now what classical student will pretend that his knowledge of the derivation of this term affords him any material aid in acquiring a knowledge of the properties of the substance to which it applies? Or will a merely English student of chemistry complain that the term is to him arbitrary and unmeaning? He understands perfectly well the substance to which it belongs, and when familiar with its properties and nature, finds no difficulty in remembering the word.

Another alleged benefit, and one which the writer of the "remarks" deems "of no small importance," is, that "the process of trans-

lating from one language into another often enables us to see the thoughts of an author in quite a new light;" and "that a knowledge of Greek and Latin will greatly assist in distinguishing the substantial worth of an argument, or the intrinsic beauty of a poetic image, from the tinsel of words with which it may be decorated." That an accurate knowledge of the meaning of words is essential to the correct understanding of an author or speaker is not to be disputed, and in so far as these languages help to fix shades of meaning, or decide between expressions of doubtful import, their usefulness is acknowledged. But this is all. If the ideas of a speaker or writer are once comprehended clearly, it is difficult to understand how any important difference can be effected in our appreciation of them by a change of the words in which they are conveyed. The writer refers, by way of illustration, to the case of ignorant and inexperienced persons, who, he says, are very apt to be led astray by some glowing speech which they suppose to be replete with irresistible reasoning, when it really is destitute of valuable thought, and contains little else than a multitude of high-sounding words. That some may commit such a mistake is probable, but the fact argues not merely want of learning on their part, but also great weakness or obliquity of intellect, since no person of good sense, however illiterate, could be so foolish as to suppose that an array of words, the meaning of which was beyond his comprehension; contained a chain of irresistible reasoning.

In the opinion of the writer, another very important advantage to be derived from classical study, is the intellectual exercise which it affords, requiring the combined efforts of many faculties. That some of the mental faculties are exercised, and probably strengthened, by such a course of study is doubtless true. But cannot they be as well exercised while acquiring knowledge of undoubted value?

Dymond very naturally observes that the employment of this argument by the advocates of the classics, is itself an indication of the questionable utility of the study. No one thinks it needful to adduce mental exercise as a reason for learning geography, arithmetic or natural philosophy. A farmer might find good exercise for a variety of his muscles by throwing stones or kicking a football; but we should probably think him wiser if he obtained the same invigorating exercise in tilling the soil or harvesting his crops.

It is urged, with considerable earnestness, that the practice of rendering the ancient authors into English, is an excellent mode of teaching children the art of composition. This is most likely true; but they may learn composition equally well without being obliged to seek it through the medium of dead languages. In the study of history, biography, &c., an opportunity would be presented for teaching this art, of which the judicious instructer would know how to avail himself. But lastly, and above all, it is contended that the pursuit of Greek and Roman literature affords the best means of forming a correct and refined taste in composition. The writer will here excuse me for quoting a passage from his essay, containing a statement of facts, calculated, if we draw our inferences wisely, to lead to a just view of the whole matter. "Besides, the circumstances in which we are placed, are very different from those of the ancient Greeks. To them, little was known of the useful sciences; hence they were not, like us, obliged to divide their attention among a thousand different pursuits. In time of peace, the labours of their most gifted men were, generally speaking, devoted to the exclusive cultivation of some one of the fine arts. It was thus that in architecture, sculpture, poetry and eloquence, they were enabled to bequeath to after ages, those monuments of transcendent skill which have never been, and probably never will be, equalled. Men now have not the time and attention to bestow, which are requisite, in order to attain the highest excellence in the works of art. With regard to composition, indeed, it may be doubted whether the modern languages are capable of being wrought into such perfect models, even though men of genius should devote to this object the undivided attention of a whole life. We may, however, without envy, award the palm of superiority in the fine arts to the ancients, since latter ages possess the far more desirable and nobler distinction which arises from an extended and accurate acquaintance with the natural sciences, and from more enlightened and elevated views of morality and religion." The observation with which the quotation concludes, is perfectly appropriate and just; it is indeed the natural sentiment of every reflecting mind. We do not rival the ancients in the vastness and splendour of their edifices, in the beauty and perfection of their statuary, or in the sublimity, genius and exquisite polish of their oratory and poetry; but what is better, we have substantial comfort instead of elegance and grandeur; science instead of literature; the knowledge of things, instead of the knowledge of words and graces of expression. Christianity and sound philosophy have given a better direction to the talents and energies of man. "Men now have not the time and attention to bestow which are requisite in order to attain the highest excellence in the works of art." Why? Because the field of useful knowledge is so immeasurably extended, its rich fruits surround us, and they better repay the toil of gathering. Our most highly gifted men perceive the folly of spending year after year of a short life, in the almost hopeless attempt to emulate Cicero's purity and elegance of style, when they have before them the example and the fame of Newton, Linnæus, Franklin, Davy, and a host of others, inviting them to explore the boundless field of scientific research, in which they were so successful. Let us, however, not utterly banish even mere literature. There are a few who possess great natural aptitude for the acquisition of language, with a mental constitution which inclines them strongly to literary pursuits; and that advantages may be realised by men of letters, from their acquaintance with the authors of Greece and Rome, will not be disputed. It may be well

enough that we should have some writers, even in this utilitarian age, who have formed their taste by "the pure models of antiquity." The superiority of their style, if real, will readily be appreciated, and may tend, in some degree, to elevate the standard of composition.

But, after all, the real question to be determined is not whether any benefits may be derived from an acquaintance with the Latin and Greek languages, and the study of ancient classics, but whether, in the education of the many, of the men who are to conduct the business of the world, they are worth the cost. The great majority of those youths who devote years of the time allotted for instruction to these studies, really make no valuable addition to their stock of knowledge, but on leaving their books to enter upon the duties of life, are compelled to look back with disgust upon the unavailing mental drudgery to which they have been subjected. In the words of Dymond, they have been obliged to "pore over rules and exercises, and syntax and quantities; but as to learning the language, in the same sense in which it may be said they learn English, there is not one in a hundred, nor probably in ten thousand, who does it. Yet unless a person does learn a language so as to read it at least with perfect facility, what becomes of the use of the study, as a means of elevating the taste? This is one of the advantages which are attributed to the classics. But without enquiring whether the taste might not be as well cultivated by other means, one short consideration is sufficient: that the taste is not cultivated by *studying* the classics, but by mastering them; by acquiring such a familiarity with these works as enables us to appreciate their excellences. This familiarity, or any thing which approaches to it, school boys do not acquire. Playfair makes a computation, from which he concludes that of ordinary boarding schools, not above one in a hundred learns to read even Latin decently well; that is, one good reader for every ten thousand pounds expended. As to speaking Latin, he adds: 'Perhaps one out of a thousand may learn that; so that there is a speaker for each sum of one hundred thousand pounds spent on the language.'"

But this great pecuniary expenditure is a trifling part of the cost. The time thus wasted might have been employed in acquiring useful knowledge, knowledge which would afford the most delightful and salutary exercise to all the intellectual faculties in its acquisition, and have a direct and practical bearing upon the business of life. The talents of children vary greatly in kind as well as in degree, and consequently, a judicious course of instruction will have reference to this mental diversity of its subjects. It was the opinion of Dymond that "education ought to convey to young persons some tolerable portion of the knowledge and the spirit of their age and country," and "that since human knowledge is so much more extensive than the opportunity of individuals for acquiring it, it becomes of the greatest importance, so to economise the opportunity as to make it subservient to the acquisition of as large and as

valuable a portion as ⟨...⟩ views, he considered, ⟨...⟩ struction even for ordi⟨...⟩ ought to embrace such ⟨...⟩ ing, viz. Natural histo⟨...⟩ botany, mineralogy, ⟨...⟩ kind, especially the hi⟨...⟩ Biography, natural ⟨...⟩ mechanics, pneumatic⟨...⟩ try, geology, land me⟨...⟩ metry, elements of po⟨...⟩ political economy. ⟨...⟩ certainly a wide ran⟨...⟩ wider than would be ⟨...⟩ were apportioned amo⟨...⟩ ing to their respective ⟨...⟩

The course of instru⟨...⟩ might also include the ⟨...⟩ and physiology, astron⟨...⟩ matical science gener⟨...⟩ Holy Scriptures aide⟨...⟩ Horne's Commentaries⟨...⟩ Moral and Mental Phi⟨...⟩ be expected, that boys ⟨...⟩ devoted to education, ⟨...⟩ foundly versed in any ⟨...⟩ ments of knowledge, ⟨...⟩ with improved method⟨...⟩ might make substantia⟨...⟩ all of them, and what i⟨...⟩ form habits of scientific⟨...⟩ servation, and philosop⟨...⟩ would tend to qualify t⟨...⟩ ties and responsibilities⟨...⟩ they are destined to fi⟨...⟩ greater degree than ⟨...⟩ we even concede the ⟨...⟩ for it by its advocates. ⟨...⟩ expect too much from ⟨...⟩ even if well devised ⟨...⟩ tered. It is well to rer⟨...⟩ science and learning, a⟨...⟩ balance, when placed i⟨...⟩ knowledge which is "⟨...⟩ our real happiness a⟨...⟩ much more upon the r⟨...⟩ nature, than upon the ⟨...⟩ tellect.

He that attempts to ⟨...⟩ a knife will fail in his ⟨...⟩ fingers. The same stre⟨...⟩ rightly applied, would ⟨...⟩ will, if misdirected, o⟨...⟩ rational beings may be ⟨...⟩ way, and those who mig⟨...⟩ rendered mischievous ⟨...⟩ their bad feelings and p⟨...⟩ best. If you want to ⟨...⟩ any good action, or to ⟨...⟩ in general, you are mu⟨...⟩ ceed by kindness than ⟨...⟩ viling. Even the worst ⟨...⟩ threatenings, terrors n⟨...⟩ due, have not been pro⟨...⟩ kindness.—*Anon.*

MARRIED, at Friends' ⟨...⟩ county, on fifth day, the 5 ⟨...⟩ LINGTON CORE, of Westche⟨...⟩ Enos and Hannah Thomas ⟨...⟩

the answer of "Well done," will be
[...],—and then we need not fear; for,
[...]e may be tried as to the things of
[...]t God will take care for us at last;
[...]e given glory and honour for ever-

[...]de with our true love to thee and
[...]n, hoping that, as they grow in
[...] may grow in the fear of the Lord.
be glad to hear of their welfare, not
[...]e things of this life, but in that
[...]urable, and will be lasting to them;
he sincere desire of thy affectionate

JOHN CROKER.

parent, he appeared to be closely
[...]for the welfare of his children:—
[...] writing the following advice, ad-
[...]re especially to his son Charles,
he eldest of the family :]

[...]ber thy Creator in the days of thy
[...]he more thou continuest thus to do,
[...]he Lord will love thee. And what
[...]ies thou hast, spend in serving of
[...]rivately walking and meditating on
[...] of God, and what relates to thy
[...]od. Keep to meetings, and when
[...]d thy mind to God, desiring him to
[...]thereunto; for in vain thoughts the
[...] no pleasure. Delight thyself in
[...]any of good honest Friends, dis-
[...]f good things, as thou hast oppor-
[...]it; be diligent to hear the ancient
[...]r elders, whose experience hath
[...] in the Lord; and let thy words be
[...]ned with grace, that those who
[...]ith thee may have cause to say,
[...]rt one who is careful to be a good
[...]both in words and actions. Flee
[...]d company as from a serpent; for
[...]t not a care, they will betray thy
[...]ring thee unto thraldom; for the
[...]h is to propagate and advance their
[...]kingdom, which is the devil, the
tonger of this world. But mind to
[...]s lest thou shouldest offend; and
[...]ire in thy heart of God the way
[...]s kingdom, that thou mayest not

wedge of Ophir;—there is nothing to be compared with it. Remember that I have told
thee, he that is the Giver is near unto thee,—
a measure or manifestation of his Spirit is in
the closet of thy heart; therefore, sink deep
there, for there the pearl is to be found. I
know, and am well satisfied, if thou keep near
to the Lord, it will be well with thee; and the
Lord, whom I desire to serve, will do great
things for thee, and thou wilt be honourable
in thy day.

Read not in dull foolish books, with which
the nation abounds; but read in the Holy
Scriptures, in which there is a great deal of
comfort: for by this wisdom which I would
have thee seek diligently after, they, the
Scriptures are able to make wise unto salvation: likewise read Friends' books, and others
which tend to edification.

If the Lord should think fit to give thee
years in this world, that thou dost grow to
the full stature of a man, and incline to marry,
mind these sayings of thy father. Let this
be thy principal concern, seek first the kingdom of God, and the righteousness thereof,
and all other things shall be added. This is
the first and principal thing; then as thou
findest freedom, thou mayest act farther, as
God shall direct; but ever mind to take the
advice of the ancient and honest Friends, and
weigh the affair well in thy own mind, lest by
fond affections and foolish inclinations, thou
be deceived. I have already informed thee
where thy counsellor is, therefore mind to
seek him; he will never fail thee. Let not
thy mind out too soon, whilst thou art young,
but rather tarry until the years of twenty-five
or thirty, and then thou wilt have consideration; and God, if sought unto, will so direct
thee, that thou mayest have a wife, who may
be suitable for thee, and helpful to thee in all
conditions, both spiritual and temporal; for
therein consisteth the great joy of a married
life. Therefore be sure choose one, who
cometh of an honest stock, and whose conversation is mostly with the well inclined;
for if any delight to be full of idle discourse,
the inclinations of such lead to vanity, and the

tion. And when troubles of this world happen, in which thou must expect to meet with a share, you will be a help and great rejoicing one to another; and happy will thy life be in such an one, for she will be contented with thee in all states. The abundance of the things of this life never made any happy, but it is godliness with content, that hath ever been the great gain of the righteous, which labour for more than for outward riches. Therefore, as I have said, seek the kingdom of God, and the righteousness thereof, and all other things shall be added; and if the Lord should be pleased to bless thee in the things of this life, set not thy heart thereon; but remember it is a blessing bestowed on thee, the more to humble thy soul; for the more God gives, the more humble he expects us to be. If losses and crosses come, be not dismayed nor discouraged; the Lord sees what is best for thee; and remember what a good man said in his day :—"I have been young, and now am old; yet have I not seen the righteous forsaken, nor his seed begging bread." And if things do abound, remember they are not for thyself alone; for "the earth is the Lord's, and the fulness thereof." Therefore be free, and desire God to open thy heart to those that stand in need, and be serviceable in thy day in doing good, and communicate to those who stand in need of outward things, with which God may have blest thee. Desire him to make thee serviceable in all things that will tend to the honour of his name, by opening thy mouth in wisdom, that thou mayest likewise charitably hand forth good advice to them that stand in need of it, for it is a charitable part to help the soul as well as the body. And if the Lord should see fit to give thee children, desire of him a blessing for them, that they may grow up in his favour, and that he may give thee wisdom to bring them up to his honour, towards which a good pattern of meekness and humility will be a great help. When thou chastisest them, do it not in anger, but in love and gentleness, and with mild words: seeking to reach the witness of God in them. Let it not be thy chiefest care to provide for them abundance in this world, but rather labour with the Lord, that He may be a portion to them; for it is He only that can make thee and them happy.

[The editor regrets that the biographical materials which have been preserved to this day, respecting John Croker, whose early life presented so much to interest the youthful reader more especially, should be found so limited. From the period of his removal to Horsham to his death, (which took place about sixteen years after,) but little has been left on record respecting him. Some few particulars of his expressions during his last illness, by his wife, now only remain to be brought forward.]

He was at our First day's meeting at Horsham, and the same night, he was taken with a violent pain. Sometime after, he signified his satisfaction that he had been at meeting that day: he had spoken in the meeting to his comfort, was much engaged in his testimony at that time, in advice to the young amongst us, (as very frequently he was at other times opened in the love of God to the youth,)—desiring that they might grow up in a sober, religious, righteous life, and conduct themselves agreeably to our holy profession; putting them in mind of our good elders, that trod the way for us through much sufferings, and great hardships. At this last meeting, he signified to us his desire to be clear; saying, the Lord knows whether ever I may be here again, which seemed as if he did somewhat question it.

In his illness, he many times prayed that the Lord would cut short his work in righteousness, his pain being great. At another time, that the Lord would send his angels, and carry him into Abraham's bosom: he also said, he had nothing to do but to die, and that he was easy and quiet in his mind; adding, that he did not fear death, hell, nor the grave; and at another time, that the accuser of the brethren was cast out. Several times he was free in advice and exhortations to Friends, as they came to visit him, that they might keep in the way of Truth, and mentioned the danger they would fall into, if they wandered out of it. He gave several cautions, which were very affecting and tendering to all present. He further said, he had much more on his mind to mention, if he could obtain ease; and he often advised to keep up our meetings, particularly our week-day meetings, and to live in love one with another, and not to let the world see to the contrary,—adding, he felt love and good will to all.

We had two sons at home, and he was frequent in advice to them, the substance of which was, that they might live in the true fear of the Lord, and be dutiful to their mother, and love the company of good Friends: he would often call for them, when out of his sight, with much love in his heart, for both them and me, and he manifested his love to me in many affectionate expressions.

Something more than a day before his end, either a Friend or myself saying his hands and legs were cold; his answer to us was, that we should rejoice and be exceeding glad; meaning that death was so near at hand to him; and sometimes when I said, "my dear, thou art cold," he would say, "not cold enough yet." He was sensible during most of his illness, and perceived the approach of death.

Although he had very little ease day or night, but was mostly in great pain: yet he gave us, who attended on him, not one hasty or unsavoury word; and he was very tenderly concerned for me, lest I should be over-much troubled for the loss of him; and said, " we came together in love, and had lived in love, and so should part ;"—with much more of this kind.

He was indeed a very tender, loving husband, and an affectionate father; yet not so blind in his affections, but that he could see the faults of his children; and he was not sparing in his reproofs. A considerable time before his distemper seized him, he often spoke of dying; and when night came, often said,—" one more day added to the rest," or to that effect.

He was one who numbered his days, and I may say, applied his heart to wisdom : of late years he slept but little, and at such times, when he failed of sleep, was very thoughtful of a future state, as I have found by discourse when I awoke. He dearly loved peace and unity, (and with his Friends a free conversation,) the contrary was a great trouble to him. He was also very ready and willing to do any service for such as did desire it, either Friends or others, as his neighbours can testify; and he was considerate and compassionate to the poor, both to strangers, and to those that were not, and relieved them sometimes with what we should otherwise have made use of.

As I lately lay on my bed, thinking on my dear husband, it came into my mind, with some comfort and satisfaction, that his memorial is blessed, and that his name shall be had in everlasting remembrance in the book of life : for he was an honest, innocent man, and prized the good in himself and in others, as some now in being are sensible of; encouraging them both by personal visits and advices, and also by writing to them.

As to my own part, my loss is very great in divers respects, I often think ; for he took a part with me in all the troubles and exercises in which he could be helpful to me, and I may say, he was to me a very faithful helpmeet.

Since it has pleased the Lord to remove my dear husband from me by death, it is my satisfaction that we lived in love and good agreement; and (I think) I may safely say, we performed the covenants we entered into before many witnesses; and I am satisfied he is entered into the glorious rest prepared for the people of God.

He was born in the year 1672, (by the Register,) the eighth of the twelfth month, in the town of Plymouth, in the county of Devon; and departed this life the twenty-ninth of the eleventh month, 1727, at Horsham, in the county of Sussex, aged very nearly fifty-five years; and was buried in Friends' burying ground at Horsham, the first day of the twelfth month.

For "The Friend."

An Account of the Life of William Bennit.

(Continued from page 87.)

The professed ministers and teachers in those days were wont to call that operation of the Spirit of Truth, by which men were brought under condemnation for sin, a temptation of Satan. In answer to such suggestions, William Bennit queries whether the devil would be as eager to judge, condemn, and trouble a man for sin, as to lull him to sleep in it ; to cry peace to him in his iniquities, and to keep him satisfied with the mere profession of Christianity, without the possession of the holy undefiled life. "Nay," he says, "it is the work of Christ to destroy the devil and his works: he is who brings trouble upon the transgressor; and ministers' judgment against the evil-doer. He kindles a fire in the earthly heart, and raiseth trouble, wars, a nd tribulations within, before he makes himself known there as the Prince of Peace, the Sabbath, the everlasting rest for the soul." When in after life William Bennit was brought to a more full acquaintance with the truth, he testifies, " Now I know infallibly that that which in those days did bring trouble upon me for my sins, and checked and judged me for evil, and begat good desires in me after the Lord, was the pure witness of God, the manifestation of his Spirit, the light of his Son Christ Jesus, a measure of his free grace and truth in my heart. If ten thousand should assert or affirm to the contrary, I know their testimony will be a lie."

After a long visitation of the love, goodness, and mercy of the Lord to his soul—after all the trouble of mind he had endured, the travail of his spirit, his continued seeking after the knowledge of the truth, he settled down in a false ease in the fleshly nature. Although he had been low, broken, and tender in heart, mourning under the load and burden of sin, with sincere desires to serve God in holiness of life—he now, having attained the form and likeness of that he had thirsted and hungered after, in a wrong liberty and false security, satisfied himself with feeding on the words of others, which were destitute of life and knowledge. He was at ease in the pride, fashions and vanities of the world, at ease in the flesh, and counting it freedom to do those things which once had been a burden and bondage. Through carelessness and disobedience he had almost quenched the strivings of the light of Christ. Sin was in dominion, but the sorrow and burden of it he now felt little of. He says,— " Through rebellion, I had almost murdered the just and holy one in me, and had so grieved and wounded the Spirit of the Lord that it had almost ceased striving with me." His face, which had been directed to Canaan, the land of light, and rest, was now turned back towards Egypt, the bondage-house of sin and corruption, a land of darkness and wickedness. Having got from under that secret power which had hitherto preserved him, he ran into the vanities and pleasures of the world, delighted in music and dancing, sporting and gaming. But although thus making merry over the witness for God, the patience and long-suffering of the Lord waited to be gracious, and in due time visited his poor soul once more.

In the year 1654, when he was about twenty years of age, it pleased the Father of mercies to remember the captive exile, and to deliver him from the hand of him who was too strong for him, lest he should die in the pit. At this time he says, "The everlasting gospel of light, life and peace I heard preached and declared by His precious servants in scorn called Quakers, and the pure witness of God in my own heart bore testimony to the truth declared by them. It was long after I was in some measure convinced of the truth, before I freely gave up my heart to obey it. But the Lord did in time so overcome me by the power of his love, his unspeakable love, and made me willing to resign up my heart in

obedience to him—to bow down to the yoke and to take up the daily cross. I learned by loving and taking heed to the light, to despise the shame, and to follow the Lord in that way which I knew not whilst my mind was abroad." He came to witness the Lord nigh of whom he said, he " now teacheth and guideth me by his light and spirit in the way of truth and righteousness, wherein I have found peace, rest, and true satisfaction of soul. Though it hath been my portion with many other brethren sometimes to eat the bread of adversity, and to drink the waters of affliction, yet my teacher and comforter can none remove from me. He is and hath been with me in the prison-house, and in the low dungeon. So that which now keeps me in peace and unity with the Lord, and in fellowship with his people,—the same thing and not another was that which did formerly check, reprove, and judge me for evil,—brought trouble upon me for my sins; and though I deny not but that I have now a greater measure of light and grace than I then had, yet in quality and nature it is the same. Although the seed of the kingdom be in the unbeliever and unconverted even as the least of all seeds, yet nevertheless where or in whomsoever it be received in the love and obedience of faith, in such it grows and increases until it become the greatest in them. Under its shadow they come to sit with delight, and its fruit is sweet to their taste. As a little leaven hid in three measures of meal, it worketh and operateth in the hearts and minds of those that believe in it, until it hath wrought out the old leaven of malice, sin and corruption, and hath brought all into its own nature, frame and quality. So the same light which did condemn me for sin, when I was in disobedience, doth now save me from sin, and justifies me as I am kept in faith and obedience. It now ministers peace and rest, whereas before it ministered trouble and condemnation. So this I assert and affirm experimentally for an invincible truth, that the light of Christ, even in the conscience of the man or woman who is in unbelief, is one in nature and quality with the light in that man or woman that is converted by it. The light in the conscience of the drunkard and swearer that doth check, judge, and reprove him for his sins, if believed in, loved and obeyed, is able to save him from them. But that man or woman that loveth evil and hateth the light, does not feel the saving, healing virtue, and the restoring, redeeming power—but it is only to such a judge and condemner. Those who receive it in faith and love have in and through it power to become the sons of God, and joint heirs with Christ of the kingdom of God, which endures for ever."

It would appear that William Bennit was convinced at meetings held by George Whitehead and Richard Hubberthorn. George Whitehead, in his journal, speaking of their united labours in 1654 and 1655 through the eastern part of Norfolk, says, " On that side the country were gathered a few Friends who were truly convinced and turned to the Lord, his light and spirit in their hearts; among whom was William Bennit, whom the Lord endued with a heavenly gift, so as he became

a living minister of the gospel of life and salvation, being also of an innocent life and holy conversation."

After his apprenticeship was completed, William Bennit removed to Woodbridge, in Suffolk, and soon after received a gift in the ministry of the gospel. As he was faithful in the exercise thereof, he witnessed an increase therein, and was drawn by the bonds of heavenly love and religious duty to visit the churches throughout various parts of England. Of the particulars of his earlier travels and imprisonments we meet with no account. The first record of his sufferings which has been preserved, commences early in the year 1660, when he was apprehended at a meeting in Leostaff, Suffolk, and committed to Blyborough jail. Here he appears to have been immured for more than a year. Whilst he continued in this imprisonment, he addressed a letter to his parents, dated the fifth month, 1661. In this, after expressing his tender love and affection for them, he exhorts them to be gathered into the spirit of holiness, in which is the unity of the faithful. Desiring that in that spirit they might wait to feel a growth, which stands not in words, but in life and power. He continues, " Obedience to the operation thereof is required by it of the creature,—for as it is to work upon the soul, so it worketh not without the soul's yielding obedience thereunto." " For though Christ is come a light into the world, and is the salvation of God, yet to those who believe not in him he is the condemnation. And yet he is the sufficient salvation to those who believe in and obey him. The light manifesteth evil, yet if the creature yield not obedience, he cannot have power over evil; but if he is obedient to the light, it gives him power, not of man, but that which, coming from God, bringeth forth the will and the deed also. The Lord requireth of every one a perfect obedience to the light, and a daily watch and wrestling against that which is condemned by it. So long as the creature knowingly lives in that, whether in words or deeds, that is reproved by the light, it cannot enjoy perfect peace with God. The peace of God is enjoyed in the light, and if that condemn, the Lord doth not justify. Many believe they are justified in the sight of God through Christ, although the witness of God lets them see that they are yet in their sins, and condemns them for it. This faith, or rather unbelief, leads them to think that they cannot be made free from sin on this side the grave, and yet they imagine that they are free from it in the sight of God. But beware of that faith, for it is not that which is the gift of God, which through Christ saveth from all sin. Where the wicked one hath seated this faith in the heart, (which admits of sin,) it is hard for such a one to come to live in the life of truth, which is holy. When the light doth let the soul see that it is in its sins, and brings trouble and condemnation for it, the wicked one who hath begot the persuasion that it cannot be freed from it, causes the creature to do despite to the Spirit of Grace, and to strive to quench its reproofs. Seeking to get at ease in that false faith, and in that wrong belief, and to set down short of the peace of God. So that which begot desires in the creature to be freed from sin, becomes veiled and slain. Many thousands are in this state who are boasting that they are justified by Christ, and that he hath done all for them. The apostle Paul saith, "If while we seek to be justified by Christ, we ourselves are found sinners, is Christ therefore the minister of sin? God forbid. Shall we continue in sin that grace may abound? God forbid; for how can we who are dead to sin live any longer therein?" William concludes his letter thus: "And, dear ones, one thing more I have to say unto you, beware and take heed of condemning one another for doing that evil which you see yourselves are addicted unto; but first see it subdued and mortified in yourselves, whether it be in word or action, before you condemn others for it, though they be a profane people. When you speak a word of reproof to any, beware of doing it in a light, frothy way, as many do, even in the light, airy spirit which bringeth forth the same things in themselves. But let it be done in the sober, solid, seasoned, savoury, holy spirit of the Lord, that it may reach to the witness in them unto whom you speak, and then it is profitable. So the Lord God Almighty, infinite and wise, preserve me, and you, and all his little ones, in his holy awe and dread, therein to pass the time of our pilgrimage here in fear and trembling." N. E.

(To be continued.)

A late voyager gives the following description of the North Cape, the most northern land in Europe, where the sun never sets:

"The North Cape is an enormous rock, which, projecting far into the ocean, and, being exposed to all the fury of the waves and the outrage of tempests, crumbles every year more and more into ruins. Here every thing is solitary, every thing is sterile, very sad and despondent. The shadowy forest no longer adorns the brow of the mountain; the singing of the birds, which enliven even the woods of Lapland, is no longer heard in this scene of desolation; the ruggedness of the dark gray rock is not covered by a single shrub; the only music is the hoarse murmuring of the waves, ever and anon renewing their assaults on the huge masses that oppose them. The northern sun, creeping at midnight, at the distance of five diameters along the horizon, and the immeasurable ocean in apparent contact with the skies, form the grand outlines in the sublime picture presented to the astonished spectator. The incessant cares and pursuits of anxious mortals are recollected as a dream; the various forms and energies of animated nature are forgotten; the earth is contemplated only in its elements, and as constituting a part of the solar system."

"Can't take care of themselves."—The following is an extract from a letter of a merchant in Middletown, Columbia county, Ohio, to an abolition friend in Pennsylvania; and was forwarded to this office for the disposal of the editor. We cannot do a better thing than to

publish it. Its own subject matter is a better comment than can be made.

"There are in this vicinity probably twenty families of blacks, many of whom were once in slavery. They have been treated as one Christian should treat another; and mark the effect of such treatment: of the twenty families, there is but one man who is not a good citizen; a moral, industrious, sober, and in every way respectable man. They are taught on first days at the Friends' school house, and are making rapid progress in school education. They have a regular organised temperance society among them, and in the several years they have been here, but two or three cases of intoxication have been known among them. They work for the farmers; and, besides clothing themselves and families in the best fashion, almost, of this country, many of them have considerable sums of money at interest, and add to the amount of their wages every year. Some of them are among my customers; and there are but few of them to whom I would refuse to sell goods on credit to the amount of $500 if they wished, and consider myself perfectly safe in so doing. And these men many of them were once in slavery, and not fit to take care of themselves.—Gen. Univ. Eman.

For "The Friend."

TO S. B.

Keep yourselves from idols. 1 John v. 21.

Thou'st seen, where Ganges' far famed waters flow,
Men worship idols—(idols of the clay
Beneath their feet) hast seen them slowly bow
E'en to the work of their own hands, and pray
To a frail image, the next moment may
Sweep from their view for ever. Didst thou then
Turn lightly from the piteous sight away,
Nor deem that ever, 'mid more gifted men,
'Twould be thy lot to mark worship like that again?

Like that?—nay, far more sorrowful: to us
What priceless, countless blessings have been given,—
Can we remember them, nor bow our souls
In humble, ceaseless gratitude to heaven?
Can we e'er turn from pure, "indwelling" light,
To phantoms that may lead to rayless night?

Yes, e'en where inspiration sheds
Its holy light around,
Is many an altar, many a shrine
Of idol worship found.

Sometimes we dream that from such shrine,
Beams a celestial ray,
Sometimes we know the image there,
Is but of painted clay;
And yet, alas! to it is given
Devotion only due to Heaven.

Oh, let us search our hearts, to find
The idols cherish'd there!
And seek for strength to banish them,
By penitence and prayer:—
More guilty far shall we be held,
Than they on Ganges' shore,
If for the "much" we have received,
We do not render more,—
More than those poor benighted men,
Whom we may pity, not condemn.

ELLA.

HAVERFORD SCHOOL.

WANTED, a Friend to act as Steward of this Institution. Apply to

KIMBER & SHARPLESS,
No. 8 South Fourth street.

THE FRIEND.

TWELFTH MONTH, 21, 1839.

Jay's View of the action of the Federal Government in behalf of Slavery, is one of those publications relative to the great topic so vitally connected with the happiness and prosperity of this country, which ought to be read and studied by every person desirous of being correctly informed on the subject in all its bearings. A cotemporary journal thus remarks respecting it:—

"The developements made by Judge Jay, in regard to the encroachments of slavery upon the rights of the free, and its control over the constitution and action of the federal government, are opening the eyes of abolitionists to a new aspect of our great struggle, and leading many to enquire whether there is any possibility of breaking the chains from our own feet, while the whole power of the national administration, and the organized strength of both political parties, are entirely pro-slavery."

It appears that a second edition, of this invaluable work has been issued, which is represented to be greatly improved by revision. We have been induced to transfer to our pages the introduction to this second edition, which contains a brief but forcible outline of the rise and progress of abolition, from the time the "Six Quakers" met in London, in 1783, to the abolition of the slave trade in 1787, and the emancipation in 1838.

We have been requested to state, that Dr. Kite has consented to give a short lecture upon the principles and means of happiness, next third day evening, at the Reading Rooms, Apple-tree alley, at half past seven o'clock.

INSTITUTE FOR COLOURED YOUTH.

A suitably qualified Friend is wanted to take charge of the farm and family of this institution. Application may be made to

BENJAMIN COOPER, near Camden, N. J.
THOMAS WISTAR, Jr., Abington.
JOSEPH SCATTERGOOD, No. 14 Minor st. or
MARMADUKE C. COPE, 286 Filbert st.

DIED, on the 10th of last month, in the 62d year of his age, at his residence near Moorestown, New Jersey, JOSEPH HOOTON, an esteemed member of Chester Monthly Meeting. The sufferings attendant on a lingering, painful disease, he was favoured to endure with patience and Christian resignation—quietly passing from the conflicts of time, we believe, to the fruition of peace and happiness.

—— at his residence in Burlington county, N. J., on the 29th of the eleventh month, 1839, JOHN AARONSON WOOLMAN, aged 83 years, a member of Burlington Monthly Meeting.

—— on the 8th day of eleventh month last, DUNCAN NEWLIN, aged 34 years eight months and twelve days, son of Nathaniel Newlin, formerly of Orange city, North Carolina, and a member of Spring Monthly Meeting, but for some years last past a citizen of Parke county, Ia., and a member of Bloomfield Monthly Meeting. The departure of this dear friend in the prime of life is much lamented by Friends, as a useful member of our Society, and by his acquaintance generally, as one beloved in the social circle.

—— on the 3d of twelfth month, 1839, at his residence in Dover, New Hampshire, of inflammation of the brain, ISA TUTTLE, aged 41 years. His loss will be sensibly felt in civil and religious society.

THE FRIEND.

A RELIGIOUS AND LITERARY JOURNAL.

VOL. XIII.   SEVENTH DAY, TWELFTH MONTH, 28, 1839.   **NO. 13.**

EDITED BY ROBERT SMITH.

PUBLISHED WEEKLY.

Price two dollars per annum, payable in advance.

Subscriptions and Payments received by

GEORGE W. TAYLOR,

NO. 50, NORTH FOURTH STREET, UP STAIRS,

PHILADELPHIA.

OUR OWN TONGUE.

[A late number of the Princeton Review contains an article full of interest and instruction, on Anglo-Saxon literature, founded on the great Dictionary of Dr. Bosworth, published last year in London. The subjoined observations and citations of the reviewer deserve the notice of American writers and readers.—*National Gazette.*]

Viewing our language as it now stands, we may observe that the great foundation of it is Teutonic. Almost all the verbs, particles, and other words which constitute the body, the frame-work of our discourse, are Saxon. Being more the language of the field and the fireside, they come home to our business and bosoms. While juvenile and late learned writers are enamoured of sesquipedalian terms of Roman origin, our best authors and others, our Websters,· and Southards, and Irvings, know the power of the racy Saxon roots. To this treasury they resort, as we must all do, for tender, gentle, comprehensive, as well as picturesque and powerful words. Turner, in his History of the Anglo-Saxons, has shown how many of our words are thus derived, by giving passages of the most eminent writers, both in poetry and prose, of different ages, with the words of Saxon origin printed in italics. Our learned fellow citizen, Mr. Duponceau, says: "So far as we are able to judge, from a superficial investigation of the subject, we are apt to believe that the English words of northern derivation are, to those derived from the ancient as well as the modern languages of southern Europe, in the proportion of something more than *three*, but not quite as much as *four to one*." An estimate somewhat different is made by Halbertsma. "My object," says he, "was to show the analogy between the two languages, (Friesic and English,) by translating them as literally as possible; and the cognate words in English, which do not perfectly agree with the Friesic in sense, I have explained by others in parentheses. In 1200 words, I have only had recourse to fifty which are not of

Saxon origin; a number which might be greatly diminished by a scholar thoroughly acquainted with the original stores of the English language. At this rate, about every twenty-fourth word of the original fund of the language is lost. In one hundred and twenty-five words in parentheses, I used fifty foreign words: here one word is lost out of every two and a half. The number of words was twelve hundred; add the words in parentheses, one hundred and twenty-five, it makes a total of thirteen hundred and twenty-five. The foreign words in twelve hundred were fifty, and in parentheses fifty, making the sum of one hundred. Then thirteen hundred and twenty-five, divided by one hundred, gives thirteen and a quarter, which shows that there is one foreign word for every thirteen English." The only remark which need be added is, that the passages by Halbertsma, as the subject of his investigation, were constructed on the plan of avoiding Latin terms in every possible case.

Every careful student of English literature has observed that if there exist two synonymous words, one of Latin and the other of Saxon origin, the latter is generally more expressive and poetical, and especially more available for reaching the common mind: for example, *fatherly, motherly, brotherly,* and *paternal, maternal, fraternal; happiness* and *felicity; faithfulness* and *fidelity; kindred* and *relation; witchcraft, necromancy; burst, rupture; strength, vigour; storm, tempest; tearful,* lachrymose; *offering,* oblation; *mirth,* hilarity; *hearty,* cordial; *dwell,* lodge; *bereave,* deprive. In Shakspeare and in the English version of the Bible, some of the most striking and tender passages owe these qualities, in a great degree, to the predominance of the Saxon element, and if the experiment be made of exchanging these for words of Roman or Latin derivation, the thoughts will be disparaged.

On such a topic, the judgment of so great a scholar as Mackintosh, will carry weight. "From the Anglo-Saxon," says he, "we derive the names of most of the ancient officers among us; of the greater part of the divisions of the kingdom, and of almost all our towns and villages. From them also we derive our language, of which the structure and a majority of its words—much greater than those who have not thought on the subject would at first easily believe—are Saxon. Of sixty-nine words which make up the Lord's prayer, there are only five not Saxon; the best example of the natural bent of our language, and of the words apt to be chosen by those who speak and write it without design. Of eighty-one words in the soliloquy of Hamlet, thirteen only are of Latin origin. Even

in a passage of ninety words in Milton, whose diction is more learned than that of any other poet, there are only sixteen Latin words. In four verses of the authorised translation of Genesis, which contains above one hundred and thirty words, there are no more than five Latin. In seventy-nine words of Addison, whose perfect taste preserved him from any pedantic or constrained preference for any portion of the language, we find only fifteen Latin. In later times, the language rebelled against the bad taste of those otherwise vigorous writers, who, instead of ennobling their style, like Milton, by the position and combination of words, have tried to raise it by unusual and far-fetched expressions. Dr. Johnson himself, from whose corruptions English style is only recovering, in eighty-seven words of his fine parallel between Dryden and Pope, has found means to introduce no more than twenty-one of Latin derivation. The language of familiar intercourse, the terms of jest and pleasantry, and those of necessary business, the idioms and peculiar phrases into which words naturally run; the proverbs, which are the condensed and pointed sense of the people; the particles on which our syntax depends, and which are of perpetual recurrence—all these foundations of a language are more decisive proofs of the Saxon origin of ours, than even the great majority of Saxon words in writing, and the still greater majority in speaking. In all cases where we have preserved a whole family of words, the superior significancy of a Saxon over a Latin term, is most remarkable. *Well being arises from well-doing,* is a Saxon phrase, which may be thus rendered into the Latin part of the language: *Felicity attends virtue;* but how inferior in force is the latter! In the Saxon phrase, the parts or roots of words being significant in our language, and familiar to our eyes and ears, throw their whole meaning into the compounds and derivations; while the Latin words of the same import, having their roots and elements in a foreign language, carry only a cold and conventional signification to an English ear."

To this we may add the opinion of one of the most harmonious and eloquent of modern English writers, the late Robert Hall. His biographer thus writes: "In one of my early interviews with Mr. Hall, I used the word *felicity* three or four times in rather quick succession. He asked, 'Why do you say *felicity,* sir? *Happiness* is a better word, more musical and genuine English, coming from the Saxon.' 'Not more musical, I think, sir.' 'Yes, more musical, and *no* are words derived from the Saxon generally. Listen, sir: *My heart is smitten and withered like grass;* there's plaintive music. Listen again, sir: *Under the shadow of thy wings will I rejoice*—there's cheerful music.' 'Yes, but *rejoice* is French?' 'True, but all the rest is Saxon, and rejoice is almost out of tune with the other words. Listen again: *Thou hast delivered my eyes from tears, my soul from death, and my feet from falling;* all Saxon, sir, except the *delivered.* Then, sir, for another specimen, and almost all good old Saxon English: *Surely goodness and mercy shall follow me all the days of my life, and I will dwell in the house of the Lord for ever.*' "

At the time of the Reformation, and during most of the sixteenth century, we observe in English writers a marked predominance of the Saxon ingredient, which makes the writers of that age peculiarly charming. The next age brought in many Latin and French words, so that the diction of that day was marred by an appearance of pedantry. This was especially the case in some writings of the time of Charles the Second. In the reign of Queen Anne, there was a return to the dignified purity of genuine English. The influence, however, of such writers as Johnson and Gibbon tended to burden and corrupt our language by needless importations from abroad. Of the latter, Hannah Moore said well, that if Gibbon had his will, the Christian religion and the English language would come to an end together. And at the present day, the wanton introduction of scientific terms from the Greek and Latin, and of phrases from the French, threatens to render our tongue still more piebald, heterogeneous, and unwieldy. Still, it may be observed in the citations just made, the suffrage of the most accomplished scholars and eloquent writers is wholly in favour of Saxon English. In our own country, indeed, the rage for what is sounding, pompous, swelling, and uncommon, leads our writers and speakers to deal much in words of Latin origin. In this respect the writers of our revolutionary period far surpass us.

The English of Franklin, Adams, and Ames is more chaste than that of our own day. Those, moreover, who most variegate their diction with uncommon, difficult, and polysyllabic phrases, are such as have come late and irregularly into the field of letters, and have least real acquaintance with the models of classical taste; just as we observe the greatest display of paste diamonds and jeweller's gold upon those whose wealth and credit are somewhat disputable. Still the current is evidently setting back in favour of pure English, and in proportion to the demand for this will be the avidity of scholars for the pristine literature of England. We hope to see, before many years, an allotment of time to Anglo-Saxon in every college in America; and in preparation for this, we earnestly wish that some of our learned men would prepare suitable elementary books for publication.

The ambition of a man of parts is very often disappointed for the want of some common quality, by the assistance of which men with very moderate abilities are capable of making a great figure.—*Armstrong.*

'For "The Friend."

Thinking the following article, from the Journal of the Franklin Institute for sixth month, 1838, likely to prove useful as well as interesting, I forward it for insertion, if thought worthy a place in the columns of "The Friend."

On the Cause, the Prevention, and the Cure of Cataract.

BY SIR DAVID BREWSTER.

Having submitted to the physical section of the British Association an account of a singular change of structure produced by the action of distilled water upon the crystalline lens after death, Sir D. Brewster was desirous of communicating to the medical section some views which this, and previous observations, have led him to entertain respecting the cause, the prevention, and the cure of cataract, he makes the following observations.

The change of structure to which I have referred consists in the developement of a negative polarizing band or ring between the two positive rings nearest the centre of the lens; the gradual encroachment of this new structure upon the original polarizing structure of the lens; and the final bursting of the lens after it had swelled to almost a globular form by the absorption of distilled water.

As the crystalline lens floats in its capsule, there can be no doubt that it is nourished by the absorption of the water and albumen of the aqueous humour, and that its healthy condition must depend on the relative proportion of these ingredients. When the water is in excess, the lens will grow soft, and may even burst by its over absorption; and when the supply of water is too scanty, the lens will, as it were, dry and indurate; the fibres and laminæ, formerly in optical contact, will separate, and the light being reflected at their surfaces, the lens will necessarily exhibit that white opacity which constitutes the common cataract.

This defect in the healthy secretion of the aqueous humour, as well as the disposition of the lens to soften or to indurate by the excess or defect of water, may occur at any period of life, and may arise from the general state of health of the patient; but it is most likely to occur between the ages of 40 and 60, when the lens is known to experience that change in its condition which requires the use of spectacles. At this period the eye requires to be carefully watched, and to be used with great caution; and if any symptoms appear of a separation of the fibres or laminæ, those means should be adopted which, by improving the general health, are most likely to restore the aqueous humour to its usual state. Nothing is more easy than to determine at any time the sound state of the crystalline lens; and by the examination of a small luminous image placed at a distance, and the interposition of minute apertures and minute opake bodies of a spherical form, it is easy to ascertain the exact point of the crystalline where the fibres and laminæ have begun to separate, and to observe, from day to day, whether the disease is gaining ground or disappearing.

In so far as I know, cataract in its early

stages, when it may be stopped or cur never been studied by medical men; a[n] when it is discovered, and exhibits i[ts] white opacity, the oculist does not atte[mpt] reunite the separating fibres, but wai[ts] patience till the lens is ready to be c[ut] or extracted.

Considering cataract, therefore, as ease which arises from the unhealthy tion of the aqueous humour, I have no tion in saying that it may be resisted early stages, and in proof of this I may the case of my own eye, in which the had made considerable progress. On[e] ing I happened to fix my eye on a very light, and was surprised to see rou flame a series of brightly coloured pr images, arranged symmetrically, and ference to the septa to which the fibre[s] lens are related. This phenomenon a me greatly, as I had observed the ver[y] images in looking through the lenses mals partially indurated, and in whi[ch] fibres had begun to separate. These became more distinct from day to d[ay] lines of white light, of an irregular tri[angular] form, afterwards made their appearance stopping out the bad parts of the lens, terposing a small opake body suffic[ient] prevent the light from falling upon vision becomes perfect, and by placi[ng] aperture of the same size in the sam[e] tion, so as to make the light fall on t[he] eased part of the lens, the vision e[ntirely] failed.

Being now quite aware of the natu[re] locality of the disease, though no opaci[ty] taken place so as to appear externally, the greatest attention to diet and re and abstained from reading at night, exposure of the eyes to fatigue or lights. These precautions did not produce any decided change in the appearances occasioned by the diseas[e] in about eight months from its com[mence] ment I saw the coloured images an luminous streaks disappear in a mom[ent] dicating, in the most unequivocal m[anner] that the vacant space between the fib[res] laminæ had been filled up with a flui[d] stance transmitted through the capsul[e] the aqueous humour. These change place at that period of life when the e[ye] dergoes that change of condition whi[ch] quires the use of glasses; and I have n[o doubt] that the incipient separation of the l[ens] would have terminated in confirmed ca[taract] had it not been observed in time, and i[ts pro]gress arrested by the means already tioned. Since that time, the eye, exposed to the hardest work, has pre[served] its strength, and is now as serviceable had ever been. If the cataract had greater progress, and resisted the treatment which was employed, I shou[ld not] have hesitated to puncture the cornea, expectation of changing the condition aqueous humour by its evacuation, or injecting distilled water, or an albu[minous] solution, into the aqueous cavity.

(OT IMPRACTICABLE.

e Second Edition of "Jay's
:tion of the Federal Govern-
of Slavery."

(uded from page 91.)

cts, the abolitionists of the
laced in circumstances simi-
ich their predecessors found
83. They, like us, had to
hostility of the government,
:a and prejudices of slave-
legislature,* with clerical
ielty and oppression, with
ity, and with heartless poli-
many other respects they
l than we are. They were
if the spirit of the age; we
with it. They were ad-
theories. We can point to
and South America for the
cessful operation of our doc-
ere striving to influence a
great degree independent of
re petitioning a government
creature of the popular will.
land despised. The hatred
we have experienced, attest
ttributed to us. They were
influence; where suffrage is
00 petitioners will not be
liticians. They could bring
rguments before the public
pace in the columns of a few
have numerous periodicals,
the largest size, exclusively
ropagation of our opinions,
gious and political journals
xhibiting the evils of slavery
es of emancipation. They
no official sanction of their
ncouraged and stimulated in
y the approving voice of the
the people.
ess to abolish slavery in the
prayer presumptuous or un-
If so, it becomes not the
entatives to rebuke us; for,
ary, 1829, that body " Re-
Committee on the District
directed to enquire into the

District of Columbia." In 1829, the Assembly of New York voted to direct the representatives from that State " to make every
proper exertion to effect the passage of a law
for the abolition of slavery in the District of
Columbia." In 1837, the Senate of Massachusetts " Resolved, That Congress, having
exclusive legislation in the District of Columbia, possess the right to abolish slavery and
the slave trade therein, and that the early
exercise of such right is demanded by the
enlightened sentiment of the civilized world,
by the principles of the revolution, and by
humanity." The other house, the same session, " Resolved, That Congress, having exclusive legislation in the District of Columbia,
possess the right to abolish slavery in said
District, and that its exercise should only be
restrained by a regard to the public good."
The next session, both branches of the legislature resolved " That the rights of justice,
the claims of humanity and the common good
alike demand the entire suppression of the
slave trade now carried on in the District of
Columbia." In 1838, the House of Representatives of the Legislature of Maine " Resolved that the continuance of slavery within
the sacred enclosure and chosen seat of the
National Government, is inconsistent with a
due regard to the enlightened judgment of
mankind, and with all just pretensions on our
part to the character of a free people, and is
adapted to bring into contempt republican
liberty, and render its influence powerless
throughout the world." The same year, the
Legislature of Vermont, without a dissenting
voice, instructed the representatives in Congress " to use their utmost efforts to procure
the abolition of slavery and the slave trade in
the District of Columbia." Yet there are
those who would fain paralyze all our efforts
by the assurance that public opinion is
against us !

But we are urged to desist, not only because our object is impracticable, but also
because it is *unlawful.* " When the people,"
we are told, " are bound by laws emanating
from a legislative assembly wherein they
have no representatives, *their will* must be
ascertained by manifestations from themselves." But why ought Congress to ascertain the will of the people of the District ?

sentatives in the legislatures, consented to be
thus placed under the authority of congress.
And shall we now be gravely told, after these
people have thus consented to be governed,
in all cases whatsoever, by the national legislature, and after the people of the United
States have, for this purpose, vested unlimited
and exclusive jurisdiction in congress, that it
is contrary to the principles of the Declaration of Independence, that this jurisdiction
should secure to each inhabitant of the District
the " inalienable rights of life, liberty and the
pursuit of happiness !" Again, if the declaration derives the powers of the government
from the consent of the governed, from what
representative majority, we would ask, are
we to infer the *consent* of six thousand of the
people of the District to be reduced to chat-
tels ; to be robbed of the rights of humanity ;
to be converted, with their wives and children,
into articles of merchandise ?

Surely the friends of emancipation will not,
after their past experience, look upon public
opinion as an *invincible* enemy ; still less will
they believe that the Declaration of Independence is the death-warrant of human rights
in the national domain. The principles for
which they are contending, are the principles
of the declaration ; the means they are using,
are those given them by the constitution—
freedom of speech and of the press—petition
and the elective franchise; and, by the blessing of God on these principles and means,
they will yet convert public opinion into an
ally, will yet purge the capital of the republic
of its loathsome plague, and restore the federal government to its legitimate functions, of
establishing justice and securing the blessings of liberty.

Bedford, September, 1839.

For "The Friend."

Discrimination in the Use of Means.

In looking, lately, over a copy of "Purver's
Translation of the Holy Scriptures," which
formerly belonged to that dignified minister
of the gospel, Abraham Gibbons, I found the
accompanying notes in his hand writing, and
they are believed to be his own reflections.
Perhaps the editor of " The Friend" will

work, and leave the event to God. I must neither be idle in the means, nor make an idol of the means. I will, therefore, henceforth lay my hands to the means as if they were all in all; and yet raise my eyes above the means as if they were nothing at all.

"Cicero spoke at random, when he said, *Ad decus and libertatem nati sumus;* we are born to liberty and honour. It is thou, O regenerate soul, that art born a child of love and heir of glory; thou art he, O excellent saint, that art clothed with the sun, crowded with the stars, and reckoned among the angels of God. O think upon thy dignity and consider: will an emperor live like a beggar? Is it a becoming thing for those that are clothed in scarlet to embrace a dunghill? Am I born of God, and shall I live like a man? Hath God raised my spirit with the highest excellencies, and shall I stain my nobleness with poor empty vanities? May I feed upon Christ, and shall I feed upon dust? Shall I sit to judge the world, and shall I be a drudge to the world? Hath Christ prepared for me a mansion in the heavens, and shall I be grovelling in the earth? Am I a child of light, and shall I commit the works of darkness? No; (as says Seneca) I am born to greater and higher things than to be a slave to lust, or a drudge to the world."

"Pure love runs clearly out of itself into the bosom of the object that is beloved. Heavenly love centres no lower than heaven itself; it is only God it loves, and it is only in God it lives. If love is a beam, it is only as it stands in reference to the sun; if it loves the creature, it is only as it is a step to advance it nearer God. Lord, I would not care for heaven, if it were not for thee; neither would I love myself, were I not in thee."

"Here the vessel is too capacious to be filled with all the pleasures and delights the world can lay together; but hereafter, our pleasures and delights shall be too full for the most capacious vessel to comprehend. Our glory shall be so great, that power, as well as goodness, shall come forth from God himself, to renew and enlarge these vessels, that so they may be capable to receive and retain that glory; and strength and love may go forth together with prepared and raised dispositions, suited to such a transcendent and high condition.

We are too weak for such a weight of glory; therefore God will bear us up, that we may bear up it: and because our joys cannot fully enter into us, we shall fully enter into them. Who would then set so large a vessel as the soul under a few drops of carnal pleasure, and neglect the springs and streams of everlasting joy? O my soul! what a glorious day is there coming, when the vessels of mercy shall be cast into the ocean of mercy, and be filled to the brim with mercy! when the sons of pleasure shall drink their fill at the torrents of pleasures, and be set for ever at rest in the rivers of pleasures! when the soul that is sick of love, shall lie in the bosom of love, and for ever take its fill of love! when the children of God shall have a full fruition of God, and be for ever satisfied

with the presence of God! The joy of which glorious presence, the fulness of which joy, the sweetness of which fulness, the eternity of which sweetness, the heart of man in its largest thoughts, cannot conceive.

Lord, let the thoughts of the joy and glory which thou hast prepared for me in the heavens, turn away my soul from the pleasures and delights which present themselves on earth; that, neglecting them, I may be pressing to thee, and breathing forth with thine, "O, when shall I come and appear before God!"

THE HUMAN EYE.

"But, of all the tracks of conveyance which God has been pleased to open up between the mind of man and the theatre by which he is surrounded, there is none by which he so multiplies his acquaintance with the rich and varied creation on every side of him, as by the organ of the eye. It is this which gives to him his loftiest command over the scenery of nature:—it is this by which so broad a range of observation is submitted to him;—it is this which enables him, by the act of a single moment, to send an exploring look over the surface of an ample territory, to crowd his mind with the whole assembly of its objects, and to fill his vision with those countless hues which diversify and adorn it;—it is this which carries him abroad, over all that is sublime in the immensity of distance; which sets him, as it were, on an elevated platform, from whence he may cast a surveying glance over the arena of innumerable worlds; which spreads before him so mighty a province of contemplation, that the earth he inhabits only appears to furnish him with the pedestal on which he may stand, and from which he may descry the wonders of all that magnificence, which the Divinity has poured so abundantly around him. It is by the narrow outlet of the eye that the mind of man takes its excursive flight over those golden tracks, where, in all the exhaustlessness of creative wealth, lie scattered the suns and the systems of astronomy. But, oh! how good a thing it is, and how becoming well for the philosopher to be humble, amid the proudest march of human discovery, and the sublimest triumphs of the human understanding, when he thinks of that unscaled barrier, beyond which no power, either of the eye or of the telescope, shall ever carry him; when he thinks that, on the other side of it, there is a height, and a depth, and a length, and a breadth, to which the whole of this concave and visible firmament dwindles into the insignificancy of an atom; and, above all, how ready should he be to cast his every lofty imagination away from him, when he thinks of the God who, on the simple foundation of his word, has reared the whole of this stately architecture, and, by the force of his preserving mind, continues to uphold it;—ay, and should the word again come out from him, that this earth shall pass away, and a portion of the heavens which are around it shall again fall back into the annihilation from which he at first summoned them,— what an impressive rebuke does it bring on

the swe
the who
prises
there re
teth on
which h
dours, a
hath ins
butes, in
manifes

It is
that cal
ing the
less fod
keep the
warm p
in a bar
can whi
weather
ments,
him con
while su
quantity
port life
But i
must no
as men,
ber of l
of this
tages of
ration, i
a few f
cattle,
close an

It is
should
both on
uncomfe
freeze
cattle
when th
a very
floor an
the boa
warm f
manure
to repai
than no
but the
boardin
as these
will sav
season.

At B
the Sto
wine h
1625.
francs.
pound i
worth i
a bottl
21,799,
2,723,0
lish.)

For "The Friend."
SAMUEL FOTHERGILL.

Samuel Fothergill, of Warrington, in Lancashire, England, was the sixth son of John Fothergill and Margaret his wife, both ministers of the gospel, the former of whom left a journal of his life, religious experience, and travels in the ministry. Although the father was religiously concerned to endeavour to lead the tender minds of his children to piety and virtue, yet his admonitions for a season seemed lost upon his son, who, being of an active, lively disposition, and mostly, during his apprenticeship, from under the watchful eye of his affectionate parent, gave way to his natural inclinations, indulged himself in the gratifications of folly and licentiousness, violating the repeated convictions of Divine Grace in his own mind, which had been mercifully extended from his early years, thus wounding the soul of his father, who beheld with grief his unsanctified career. Yet his faithful labours proved afterwards as bread cast upon the waters, which returned after many days; for about the twenty-first year of his age, the visitation of heavenly love was so powerfully renewed, that it proved effectual to turn his steps out of the paths of vanity; and as he afterwards expressed, with humble and awful gratitude to the Preserver of men, "It then appeared clear to his understanding, that would be the last call his heavenly Father would favour him with," he therefore consulted no longer with flesh and blood, but gave up to the holy visitation, experiencing repentance towards God, and faith in the Lord Jesus Christ, devoting his whole heart and affections to seek reconciliation with his Creator, through the mediation of his dear Son, and abiding in great humility under the purifying operation of the Holy Ghost and fire, he became thereby prepared for those services into which he was afterwards called.

But a few months elapsed after he was thus engaged to seek the way to Zion with his face thitherward, before he was engaged, by the constraining power and love of God, to open his mouth in public testimony to the sufficiency of that holy arm that had been made bare for his deliverance; a dispensation of the ministry being committed to his charge, he attended faithfully thereto, and moved therein at the requirings, and under the direction of Divine Wisdom, by which means he soon became an able minister of the gospel, called and qualified by the Holy Spirit. He laboured with diligence, and devoted much of his time and strength, when health permitted, to the service of his dear Lord and Master; for the continuance of whose favour, he counted nothing too near or too dear to part with, that he might be instrumental in gathering souls to God, which was the object he had in view in all his gospel labours. Being diligent himself, he endeavoured much to excite Friends to a due and constant attendance of meetings for religious worship, and those for the discipline of the church.

A communication is extant, addressed by him to the monthly meeting of which he was a member; as it is without date, the time of writing it can only be conjectured. It was probably composed soon after his first appearance in the ministry, and sets forth his humiliation under a sense of his former transgressions, his gratitude for deliverance from the thraldom of sin, and his fervent concern for his own preservation, and that of others; exhibiting, also, his state of mind under the prospects of religious duty gradually unfolding to his view, as follows:—

"Dear Friends,—It hath for some time lain heavy upon me to write a few lines to you, upon the following account. The Lord, in his everlasting kindness, (that long strove with my soul,) hath been pleased to unstop my deaf ears that I might hear him, the Shepherd of his flock, and to open my blind eyes and let me see my state as it really was, very desperate and lamentable. He hath shown me the dreadful precipice I was on the brink of, and hath breathed into me the breath of life, in order that I might arise from the dead and live; he has set my sins in order before me, and shown how far I had estranged myself from him, and raised strong desires in me to return to him, the Redeemer of my soul. The consideration of his kindness has raised in my soul a just abhorrence of my former practices, which induces me to make this public declaration of them in a few words; I know my sins are so many and obvious, that it is impossible and needless to recount and remark upon them, for I was then in the bond of iniquity, though it has pleased the Father of mercies to bring me since into the very gall of bitterness, and into anxiety of soul inexpressible, yea, not to be apprehended by any but those who have trod the same path, and drunk of the same cup; yet, blessed be the name of God, he that hath kindled breathings in my soul after him, would sometimes break in upon me, and though the waves of Jordan have gone over my head, his supporting arm was underneath, that I should not be discouraged. He, in his infinite love, has given me to understand, that the things which belong to my peace are not utterly hid from my eyes; that though I had drunk up iniquity as the ox drinketh up water; although I had exceeded others in sin, and long done despite to him, yet there was mercy with him that he might be feared.

"Now would I address myself to the youth amongst you, and in a certain sense of the divine extendings of that love wherewith he hath loved us, do I salute you with sincere desires, that that God which visited our fathers, while aliens and strangers to him, may be our God; that we may embrace the day of our visitation, and not turn our backs on so great a mercy as he, I am sensible, is daily extending. Oh! that we tasted of his love, I have had to celebrate his name, and though unfit for the work, I cannot be easy, or discharge my known duty, without calling upon you to forsake the vanities of the world, for the end thereof is unavoidable sorrow and endless torment; but happy are they who, by a timely application, are earnestly seeking the Lord, who will (I speak by blessed experience) be found of those who early and diligently seek him; for he has appeared to me when I was afraid I was forgotten, as a morning without clouds, to my exceeding great encouragement and consolation, and strengthened me in my resolutions to follow him who has done so much for my soul. Bear with me yet a little, for I write not my own words; that blessed Saviour has lain it upon me, who is willing that all should be saved, and come to him; let him, I intreat you, have his perfect work in you; he will wash you, or else you can have no share in him; I can truly say, that during the time of my first conviction, my lips quivered, and my belly trembled, that my soul might have rest in the day of trouble. I choose not to write this, but I cannot be easy, unless I call others to the like enjoyment; in bowels of tender love I again salute and take my leave of you, with strong desires that you who are advanced in years, and favoured with the Lord's goodness, may remember me when it is well with you, that I may be preserved, though beset with temptations on every hand. The Lord in mercy be with you, saith my soul. Farewell. SAMUEL FOTHERGILL."

Through the course of his gospel labours, both in public and private, animated by divine love, he expressed a strong and ardent affection for the rising youth, with whom he was frequently led to labour for their present and eternal welfare; and which concern was manifested towards this class of all denominations. The following extract from a letter, written by him to a serious young woman, the daughter of religious parents, exhibits this trait in his character, and is worthy of preservation for its solid and judicious counsel.

"Great hath been thy advantage, dear friend, in being descended from worthy parents, who, by example and precept, have sought thy nurture and growth in the things of God; the visitation of heavenly light and life have also been extended, and I hope in a great and good degree embraced, which has pointed out the means of help, or the terms of happiness, and inclined thy heart to seek it. Many are the besetments and probations of a mind awakened to seek an inheritance amongst the blessed, and of various kinds they are; but the mighty arm is revealed and made bare, for all those that refuse to be comforted without it. Many are the low places the righteous tread, and in the line of their experience deep answers deep; some are brought upon us through our inadvertency and negligence; let us, then, enquire the cause, and remove it; sometimes the heavens are made like brass to us, to teach us how to want, and like winter seasons, to strengthen our roots, that we grow not top-heavy; but in all things our Heavenly Father deals with us tenderly and for our good. Let, therefore, thy attention be steady to Him for counsel and guidance, and he will not forsake thee in the time of thy secret bewailings, but spread a table for thee in the desert. Oh! that our youth might thus awfully bow under the operation of the Lord's hand, that their minds might be subject to him, whom we are, and whom we ought to serve in the spirit of our minds. I feel in my mind the sympathy of the blessed covenant, and the spreading of the Father's wing theewards, and crave of the Almighty One to have thee in his keeping, and of thee never to forfeit it by any means. He is all sufficient to abide with thee continually. He is often with his people when they perceive it not; he dwells in the thick darkness often, and was as certainly the mighty help of Israel when they groaned in anguish in the land of Egypt, as when the glory of the Lord filled the temple at the feast of dedication. I commend thee to him; seek him diligently, serve him honestly, and follow on to know his requirings with full purpose of heart to be faithful thereto, and no weapon formed against thee will prosper, nor any place be allotted so low, in which the Omnipotent arm will not sustain."

(Conclusion next week.)

For "The Friend."

An Account of the Life of William Bennit.

(Continued from page 96.)

The precise time of William Bennit's release from the jail at Bliborough I cannot find, but about the middle of next year, 1662, he was, with many other Friends, apprehended in a meeting at Yarmouth, and sent to the prison in that place. Here eleven men and seven women were immured in one dungeon, without necessary conveniences for lodging, of suitable accommodation as to food. On application to the bailiffs of the town they were removed to an upper room, which furnished more comfortable quarters. On the seventeenth of the seventh month, the women were set at liberty by the sessions; and shortly after the recorder discharged the men also from confinement, on the ground that there was no regular process against them. The bailiffs, however, displeased at their release, framed a new mittimus, on which they were recommitted to the same prison. During this imprisonment, or shortly after, William found his mind engaged to address a tender and unfeigned salutation of love and good will to professors. His exercise was chiefly on account of those who, as poor scattered sheep without a shepherd, were wandering spiritually in deserts and waste wildernesses, hungry and thirsty, seeking diligently for food with souls unsatisfied. He addresses them as such, who running from mountain to mountain, and from hill to hill, cannot find that food which will satisfy, and who, turning from one broken cistern to another, are unable to procure one drop of water that will truly refresh their souls. To those who were seeking for the living amongst dead forms, searching for meat among shells, and substance in shadows, his mind was peculiarly drawn, and he earnestly desired that they might come to know where the Lord God, the good Shepherd of Israel, feeds his sheep and lambs, and there partake of refreshing streams, be strengthened by abundant pasture, and lie down in quietness and rest. He assures them that the mercy of the Lord was extended towards them, and that he was still seeking to gather the outcasts of Jacob, and the dispersed of Judah. He exhorts them to

leave outward husks, shells, and shadows, to come unto Jesus, the living Bread, which nourisheth up the soul unto eternal life. He tells them that thus they should witness the salvation of God, which is not to be had in any other than in Him, who is the Word of God. That Word which " was in the beginning, by whom all things were made, whether visible or invisible, and without whom was nothing made that was made. In whom was life, which life is the light of men. Who came unto his own, and his own received him not, but unto them that received him, he gave power to become the sons of God." " He who had a body prepared him, in which he suffered the will of him that sent him." Who was born of the Virgin Mary—whom King Herod sought to destroy, who was baptized by John the Baptist, eat the passover with his disciples, was betrayed by Judas, and being judged to die by Pontius Pilate, was crucified without the gates of Jerusalem. Who being laid in a sepulchre, rose again the third day, according to the Scriptures, ascended up into Heaven, and sitteth at the right hand of God, being glorified with the same glory that he had with the Father before the world began. Who came again to his disciples, according to his promises, " I will not leave you comfortless, I will come to you, I will send you a comforter that shall abide with you for ever, even the Spirit of Truth, whom the world cannot receive, because it seeth him not, neither knoweth him; but you know him, for he dwelleth with you, and shall be in you—yet a little while, and the world seeth me no more." Mark this, you who are so much gazing and looking for his coming without, that you know not his coming within you to be a comforter. Again he saith to his disciples, " But you see me, and because I live you shall live also. And in that day you shall know that I am in the Father, and you in me, and I in you. And he, the Spirit of Truth, shall lead you into all truth, and shall teach you all things, and shall shew you things to come, and bring all things to your remembrance that I have said unto you, and shall reprove the world of sin, of righteousness, and of judgment." His disciples, according to his command, waited at Jerusalem until they were endued with power from on high, and had received the promise of the Holy Ghost, the Spirit of Truth. They spake the wonderful things of God, as the Spirit gave them utterance. Then they came to witness his word fulfilled, when he said, " He dwelleth with you, and shall be in you." This is the Immortal Word which was in the beginning, which Paul (who had witnessed the Son of God revealed in him, and who was by the eternal Spirit made an able minister) preached, when he said, " None should need to ascend, that is, to bring Christ down from above, or to descend, that is, to bring Christ from beneath, but the word is nigh thee in the heart, and in the mouth, to be obeyed and done." This is the word of Faith that Paul preached nigh in the heart, even Christ in them the living hope, that was as an anchor to their souls, sure and steadfast, the hope of glory."

He shows them from Scripture that Christ was in them except they were reprobates; that they should not need that any man teach them, but as Christ the anointing teacheth; that in and through the operation of his Spirit the saints were born again, and witnessed reconciliation with God the Father. That those who had been as dead stones, were raised up living children unto Abraham; were made to taste that the Lord was good and gracious, —to handle the word of life, to feed on the bread of life and to drink of the cup of blessing. That thus all the faithful were baptized into one body, and were made to drink into one spirit, whereby they were brought to serve and worship the Lord in that fellowship which united their souls unto each other.

He tells them that a mere profession will not save them. That many who are still in the pride, covetousness, vanity, pomp and vain glory of the world, its vain customs, inventions and traditions, who are seeking and loving the praise of men more than the praise of God, are still professing that they are justified by Christ. That confessing that Christ died at Jerusalem for sinners would not sanctify the soul nor purge the conscience, until they should turn their minds inward to the pure light of Christ, which, discovering the sin and corruption of their own hearts, would also furnish them strength to resist and turn from it. He adds, " Then you will come to feel and find Him working out the old leaven of sin, iniquity and corruption, and working you into its nature, and so you will come to see, feel, and witness not only a talk of it, but your regeneration wrought in you by Christ, the immortal Word. Being born again of the incorruptible seed, which is known within to bruise the serpent's head,— the god of this world, the wicked spirit that leads man into sin, which hath been in his heart lord, head, and king."

After William's release from prison he seemed wholly given up in body and mind to serve the Lord. He spared no pains that he might forward the cause of truth, and his care was great over the church of Christ. He had the true qualifications of an elder and minister of Christ, and in his travels abroad in the work of the gospel, he walked in holiness, meekness and godly fear. As an example of humility, self-denial and meekness, he behaved himself towards the meanest. He was an incessant labourer in the gospel, and although very infirm in body, yet in his ministry he was carried forth with such fervency and zeal for the Lord, that there appeared no weakness in him.

About the commencement of the year 1664 he was again apprehended at a meeting, in Norfolk, and because of his faithfulness to the command of his Master, swear not at all, he was committed to the jail at Norwich. Here he remained most of the year. In the third month he addressed an epistle to Friends in the town of Yarmouth, exhorting them to bear a faithful testimony for the truth in that day of trial. He endeavours to encourage them not to flinch from the attendance of their religious meetings, either from the fear of man, or from a slothful careless spirit. He desires that in stillness, quietness, in peace, patience and contentedness, they might possess their soul, and know the dominion of truth over all the thoughts, reasonings, and consultings, which the enemy would seek· to infuse into their minds. He tells them if the Lord be for them, they need not matter who should be against them, and expresses his conviction, that everlasting mercy is still extended towards the poor and needy, and that, He who is a shadow from the heat, a deliverer out of trouble, will yet appear for the help of those who have no other helper but him. He concludes thus,

"So the Lord· be with you, and gird up your loins with courage, boldness, strength, and valour, and spread upon you the mantle of faithfulness, and cause you to persevere on in the perpetual patience, to abide in the continual content, and therein to run the race that is set before you, which you have begun. The Lord Almighty of heaven and of earth, for his own seed's sake, keep you from fainting by the way, and carry you through all you may meet with, either outwardly or inwardly, and preserve you to the end. That, dear lambs, we may lay down our heads together in the sweet bosom of the Lord God of everlasting rest, peace and quietness; in whose sweet, meek, heavenly, humbling, melting love, my soul dearly salutes you, and commits you all unto the Lord God Almighty."

N. É.

(To be continued.)

For "The Friend."

PHIPPS ON THE GOSPEL.

The gospel is a dispensation of the divine life, spirit and power of God, ushered into the world by his beloved Son, for the regeneration, sanctification and justification of fallen man. " I am not ashamed of the gospel of Christ," said Paul, "for it is the power of God unto salvation to every one that believes, to the Jew first, and also to the Greek. For therein is the righteousness of God revealed from faith to faith; as it is written, the just shall live by faith; for the *wrath* of God is revealed from heaven against *all ungodliness and unrighteousness* of men, who hold the truth in unrighteousness, *because* that which may be known of God is *manifest* in them, for *God* hath showed it unto them." To the Corinthians, he says, " But we preach Christ crucified, unto the Jews a stumbling block, and unto the Greeks foolishness, but unto them which are called, both Jews and Greeks, *Christ the power* of God, and the wisdom of God." The same Jesus Christ, who was crucified ·without the gate, was preached by the Apostles, as the power and wisdom of God for the salvation of sinners, both ·by· his outward coming ·in· the· flesh, as the ·propitiation· for all mankind, and· in his second appearance in·Spirit, as the light, life and power·, of God to root out sin, regenerate and sanctify and justify the soul.

." Search the Scriptures," said our Saviour, " for in *them* ye *think* ye have eternal life, and they are they that *testify* of me; but ye will not come unto *me* that ye· might· have

life." " I am the way, the truth, and the life; *no man* cometh to the Father but *by me*." Again, " no man cometh unto me, except the Father which sent me draw him." " I am come that they might have *life*, and that they might have it *more abundantly*." And the Apostle says, " The letter killeth, but the Spirit giveth *life*." This life and power is the distinguishing glory and excellency of the gospel dispensation. It is the grace of God which came by Jesus Christ that brings salvation, and hath appeared unto all men, and is the great agent in his hand in perfecting the redemption and salvation of mankind.

Joseph Phipps says, " without troubling myself with the unnecessary pedantry of etymologies, I shall say, we allow the word *gospel*, in an extended sense, may include both the mystery and the history, the inward and outward process of our Saviour, for the gospel came not in word only, but also in power and in the Holy Ghost. We believe this power of the Holy Ghost to be the internal essential part, and the words the exterior declarative, and occasional expression of it. We admit the history metonymically to a share of the title, but not to engross it; lest the power which is the life and reality of it should be excluded, and people be deceived into a belief, that the gospel essentially consists of nothing but words.

" We are far from denying that Paul, Peter, or any other true minister of Christ, preached the gospel, when by inspiration they preached concerning the historical process of Christ, but we cannot allow that this comprehends the whole of the gospel they preached. For we read in their writings, that the gospel is the power of God unto salvation, and that it shines as a light in the heart, to give the knowledge of the glory of God. The doctrines of the gospel are also called the gospel; but it is evident, neither the history nor the doctrines are the essential gospel intended in Galations i. For we find, after the Apostle had said, " If any man preach any other gospel unto you than that ye have received, let him be accursed;" he shows what he meant by the gospel they had received in the xi, xii, 15th and 16th verses. " I certify, you brethren, that the gospel which was preached of me, is not after man. For I neither received it of man, neither was I taught it, ·but by the revelation of Jesus Christ. But when it pleased God who separated me from my mother's womb, and called me by his grace, to *reveal his Son in me*, that I might preach him among the heathen, immediately I consulted not with flesh and blood. The gospel here intended, is plainly the immediate revelation of the Son of God within him, and neither an historical nor doctrinal relation of things without him. It is against the oppugners of this internal essential gospel, which is not of man, nor by man, but by the revelation of Jesus Christ within man, that the Apostle twice pronounces anathemas.

The opponent whom he is answering allows, that the gospel was attended by the power of the Holy Ghost, but asserts it was not that power. J. Phipps replies, the apostle

saith it is the power; then not we, but himself contradicts the apostle. In demonstration of this gospel spirit and power Paul preached, that the faith of his hearers might be fixed in this power of God, and not in the private interpretations of men's wisdom. His fellow believers preached under the influence of the same divine power which pricked their hearers *in their hearts*, and so must all that truly preach the gospel. For the kingdom of God is not *in word*, but in *power*. That everlasting power is the spirit of the gospel, wherein it mainly and most essentially consists; as the essentiality of the man doth of the rational soul; and the words and matters preached or written, are as the body or present outside. The apostle describes what kinds of men those would be, who having a form of godliness, would deny the power, and directs, "from such turn away."

His opponent supposes these two cases: "First, if I and some of my brethren were confined for rebellion, without any prospect but that of death, and a royal messenger brought a proclamation to the gate for our pardon and enlargement; or second, if we were actually brought to the place of execution, and the king's son in his father's name, there declared a free and full pardon to us, on practical conditions." Upon these suppositions he queries whether these declarations would not be gospel or glad tidings to us. I answer, yes, if the real fulfilment of them certainly ensues; but if not, they would prove sad tidings, and depress us the more upon a disappointment. Will he say that the whole is done by reading the proclamation? Is not the material part to follow? Are we delivered by hearing? Is it not necessary that we should fulfil the terms required, and then be unfettered and unbound, or the prison doors set open, to us? And· is this not the *essential* part? The words declare the kind offer and the good intent, but the *executive power* sets at liberty; and which is· preferable, if considered apart. Which would a man choose, to *hear* of liberty or to *enjoy* it? To resolve the whole of the gospel into mere tidings, and to reduce it into bare report, is to exclude the powerful reality which gives deliverance, from any share in the title, as though the report was the *Saviour*, and the notion, the *salvation*. This is what we cannot admit as an article in our creed. We know no Saviour but ·*Christ*, nor any salvation without his *power*.

Selected for "The Friend."

The Pursuit of Knowledge consistent with Religion.

Although human learning is not ·of itself sufficient to lead ·us to that knowledge which alone can make·wise unto salvation, I think there·may be almost as great a danger in despising it too much, as in giving it too high a place in our estimation; for in·studying the lives of the eminently good, we continually find fresh evidence to convince us, that learned and scientific pursuits are compatible with a life of holiness and dedication.

This opinion may be supported on very high authority. We read that " Moses was learned in all the wisdom of the Egyptians;" yet we know that he was preserved from all their abominations.

It was not either learning or science that became a snare to Solomon; although his " wisdom excelled the wisdom of all the children of the east country, and all the wisdom of Egypt." " And his fame was in all nations round about." And he spake of trees, from the cedar tree that is in Lebanon, even unto the hyssop that springeth out of the wall. He spake also of beasts and of fowl, and of creeping things, and of fishes;" none of these things had a tendency to lead him into idolatry. He continued to be the dedicated and highly favoured servant of the Lord, until the indulgence of sinful pleasures " turned away his heart after other gods."

When Paul became a chosen vessel, his learning and talents were sanctified, and all were evidently permitted to " work together for good" in his labours amongst the Gentiles. Numerous illustrations of the subject in question can be furnished by every age of the Christian church ; and our own society, in its rise and progress, is not without affording striking examples of it.

Robert Barclay, William Penn, Thomas Story, Anthony Purver, with many others of our early Friends, were men of deep learning, who, with Paul, were brought " to count all things but loss, for the excellency of the knowledge of Christ," and whose talents and attainments became subservient to the highest purposes. But it is not alone from accounts of the eminently religious that deep instruction is to be derived. The lives of literary and scientific men frequently bear testimony to the " truth as it is in Jesus," and it is often unspeakably edifying to find, that the gospel has been received with the simplicity of little children, by those whose talents and acquirements have excited universal admiration. Amongst such men, I know of none, the study of whose character affords more instruction than that of Herman Boerhaave. " So far was this truly eminent man from being made impious by his philosophy, or vain by his extraordinary genius, that he ascribed all his abilities to the bounty, and all his good qualities to the grace of God." It was his daily practice, through his whole life, as soon as he rose in the morning, which was generally very early, to retire for an hour to private prayer, and to meditate on some part of the Scriptures.

The following admirable observations of Lindley Murray are so much to the present purpose that I cannot forbear quoting them : " If in the acquisition of learning and knowledge, and in the enjoyments which they afford us, we perceive that the supreme love of God prevails in our hearts; that the interests and happiness of others are warmly and properly felt, and that our own well-being, hereafter, is the chief aim and concern of our lives; we may securely trust, that our studies and literary engagements are not only innocent and allowable, but conducive to the great ends of our existence."

OSTRICHES.

According to native testimony, the male ostrich sits on the nest (which is merely a hollow space scooped out in the sand) during the night, the better to defend the eggs from jackals and other nocturnal plunderers ; towards morning he *brummels*, or utters a grumbling sound, for the female to come and take his place ; she sits on the eggs during the cool of the morning and evening. In the middle of the day, the pair, leaving the eggs in charge of the sun, and " forgetting that the foot may crush them, or the wild beasts break them," employ themselves in feeding off the tops of bushes in the plain near their nest. Looking aloft at this time of day, a white Egyptian vulture may be seen soaring in mid air, with a large stone between his talons. Having carefully surveyed the ground below him, he suddenly lets fall the stone, and then follows it in rapid descent. Let the hunter run to the spot, and he will find a nest of probably a score of eggs (each equal in size to twenty-four hen's eggs), some of them broken by the vulture. The jackal is said to roll the eggs together to break them, whilst the hyena pushes them off with its nose to bury them at a distance.— *Alexander's Expedition of Discovery.*

From the Pennsylvania Freeman.
Suggested after reading lines by FRANCES K. BUTLER, *published in the Pennsylvania Freeman.*

Yes, in this world, all, all must share
One lot of sorrow, pain and care ;
Must early find in human life,
A weary path of toil and strife;
Waking within the aching breast
A longing for a place of rest.
Then gracious Saviour !—well to thee,
May all the heavy laden flee!
Thou, who our human grief didst share,
Thou who our throbbing flesh didst wear,
Thou knowest all. To Thee, to Thee,
Weary, oppressed, we bow the knee.
Sick of this world's corroding care,
Its gay delights proved false as fair,
We turn at last, and yield to Thee,
Our worn hearts, worthless tho' they be.
Oh ! when the peace of God is there,
What different aspect life doth wear!
Is the load heavy ? It is borne
Through weariness, and pain, and scorn,
Patiently, meekly—closer still
Cleaving to Him, whose holy will
In mercy gives the heart to know,
There is no rest for man below,
Save in His love.—Then seek ye there
The certain balm for earthly care,
And learn, when weary, tossed, distressed,
In Jesus only there is rest.

A wise man will desire no more than what he may get justly, use soberly, and distribute cheerfully, and live upon contentedly.

There is but one way of fortifying the soul against all gloomy presages and terrors of mind; and that is, by securing to ourselves the friendship and protection of that Being, who disposes of events, and governs futurity.

Flowers of rhetoric in sermons or serious discourses, are like the blue and red flowers in corn, pleasing to those who come only for amusement, but prejudicial to him who would reap the profit.

THE FRIEND.

TWELFTH MONTH, 28, 1839.

We have been requested to mention, that persons having charge of memorials to the legislature of this state, relating to the punishment of death, are desired to forward them early, by private conveyance, to George W. Taylor, No. 50 North Fourth street.

An article headed " The Classics," in answer to P. on the same subject, is necessarily postponed, but will have a place in our next. In his essay, P. refers to an article which appeared in the National Gazette, with the title " Our Own Tongue." This article we have deemed proper to transfer to our columns to-day, not only on account of its connection with the subject of controversy between our correspondents, but as possessing in itself a character which will commend it to readers of taste, and those who would duly estimate the riches and beauty of their mother tongue.

HAVERFORD SCHOOL.

WANTED, a Friend to act as Steward of this Institution. Apply to

KIMBER & SHARPLESS,
No. 8 South Fourth street.

DIED, on the 16th of tenth month last, in the 64th year of her age, REBECCA RICHARDSON, a minister and member of the Northern District Meeting in this city. During her illness her bodily sufferings were at times great, but she was enabled to endure them with patience and resignation, and appeared to have a prospect, from nearly the first attack, that she should not recover. She was frequently engaged in fervent supplication both on her own account and for others, and imparted much valuable counsel to those around her. At seasons she appeared wholly absorbed in devotional exercise, sometimes in silent communion, and at others pleading with her Maker in prayer or offering the tribute of adoration and praise. On one occasion she feelingly addressed some present on the right occupancy of the talent committed to them, and expressing the belief that if there was not more faithfulness and dedication, it would be taken away. Soon after lying down she prayed for a renewal of her patience, and with much fervency said, " Bow the heavens, O Lord, and come down and let the light of thy countenance shine upon us this evening, that our strength may be renewed in thee, O Lord, who art full of mercy and compassion." Speaking to a friend, with reference to being taken away at this time, she solemnly repeated that passage, " Blessed are the dead who die in the Lord ;" and we trust she has realised the truth of this precious declaration, and is now entered into the joy of her Lord.

— on third day evening, the 26th of eleventh month, 1839, at the residence of his son-in-law, JOS. D. Evernhim, of Blazing Star, New Jersey, JACOB FITZ RANDOLPH, in the 86th year of his age, a much esteemed member of Rahway and Plainfield Monthly Meeting of Friends.

PRINTED BY ADAM WALDIE,
Carpenter Street, below Seventh, Philadelphia.

THE FRIEND.

A RELIGIOUS AND LITERARY JOURNAL.

VOL. XIII.   SEVENTH DAY, FIRST MONTH, 4, 1840.   **NO. 14.**

EDITED BY ROBERT SMITH.

PUBLISHED WEEKLY.

Price two dollars per annum, payable in advance.

Subscriptions and Payments received by

GEORGE W. TAYLOR,

NO. 50, NORTH FOURTH STREET, UP STAIRS,

PHILADELPHIA.

For "The Friend."

THE CLASSICS.

In No. 12 of "The Friend," a writer under the signature of P. has made several objections to our Remarks on the study of the Greek and Latin languages. He seems to think that Dymond's views should have undergone a more thorough examination;—and that the manner, in which the subject has been treated by us, would lead the reader to suppose that he had said very little respecting the classics. We have already intimated that a full disquisition on the study of the ancient languages, could not with any propriety be published in the columns of "The Friend." But any thing short of such a disquisition would be insufficient to answer completely *all* of Dymond's objections to the classics. In order to a fair understanding of the subject at issue, we would invite our readers to an attentive perusal of the chapter on Intellectual Education. They will find, if we mistake not, that it contains a number of assertions for which the author adduces no sufficient authority. True, it would require no more space to contradict these assertions than to make them. But it is not sufficient merely to deny what we deem to be false, in order to make any impression on a reasonable mind we must give reason and authority for such denial. But an assertion may be made in a few words which would require pages for its complete refutation. This we trust will be esteemed a sufficient reason for our having omitted to notice several of Dymond's unimportant assertions, and confining ourselves chiefly to the consideration of his fundamental position, *that the classics occupy time which might be more advantageously employed.* But he shall speak for himself. The passage is as follows:

"The intelligent reader will perceive that the ground upon which these objections to classical studies are urged is that they occupy time which might be more beneficially employed. If the period of education were long enough to learn the ancient languages *in addition* to the more beneficial branches of knowledge, our enquiry would be of another kind. But the period is not long enough: a selection must be made; and that which it has been our endeavour to show is, that in selecting the classics we make an unwise selection."

If we understand him when he says "the *ground* on which these objections are urged, &c." he means the objections contained in this chapter, or at least the greater part of them, and we believe that no injustice is done him (we should be very sorry to do him any,) in terming this his fundamental position. Now, if it be proved that this ground is untenable, it is unnecessary to refute those objections which are based upon it. If it be shown that the foundation is unsound, it follows that the superstructure cannot be firm. That this has been shown we will not presume to assert. We leave the decision to those who may be willing to give our arguments an attentive and candid examination. Be this as it may, we can see no good reason why we should waste our time in lopping off the branches, when we have a fair opportunity of striking at the root, of an opponent's argument. As, however, this summary mode of proceeding has been objected to, we propose in a future number of "The Friend," to consider the views of Dymond more in detail. In the mean time we can assure P. that it was from no wish to misrepresent that author that we passed over his remarks so briefly. We have read the chapter in question repeatedly, with all the attention of which we are capable, without being able to form any other conclusion than that which has already been expressed;—but of this more particularly hereafter. If it be said, that we should have allowed Dymond to speak more fully for himself, that the reader might be able to judge how far our arguments against him were just; we reply, that to do him full justice it would have been necessary to quote almost the entire chapter. This we apprehended would be needless, since we had reason to believe that Dymond's "Essays" was not so scarce a work as not to be easily accessible to most of the readers of "The Friend." Indeed, it appears to us that nothing could be more idle than to make long quotations from writings which are in every body's reach or possession.

The want of acquaintance with his subject, which P. betrays when speaking of the importance of studying the ancient Saxon, would have been more excusable and less conspicuous, had it not been for the confident and unqualified manner in which he advances his assertions. He says, that "if we must seek a correct knowledge of English through the Latin, on account of the large number of words derived from it, of much more consequence must be the study of the ancient Saxon language, as

it forms the basis or groundwork of our mother tongue, and furnishes far the larger part of all the words employed in it, including a vast majority of those in common use." If the assertion that the Saxon tongue furnishes far the larger part of all the words employed in English has any meaning at all, it means that if a collection were made of all the different words of our language which are not obsolete, a large majority of these words would be found to derive their origin from the Saxon. This, we presume, is the substance of what the writer intended to say, and this, no doubt not, is the construction which every attentive reader would put upon this passage. That such a statement is very far from the truth, can be easily proved.[*]

---

[*] If the reader feels a curiosity, and will have the patience, to follow us, we will endeavour to explain the course which has been pursued in forming our estimate of the proportion of English words derived from Latin and Greek. Taking Webster's Dictionary we counted the words of the first half or column of every tenth page, placing the number of those which were obviously derived from Latin and Greek in one column, and in another the number of such as could not be directly traced to those languages;—setting also the number of obsolete words in two other columns. Each column was then added up separately. In this manner, taking the 1st, 11th, 21st, 31st pages, and so on, we proceeded through the first four letters of the alphabet, that is, to the end of D, counting in all twenty-nine pages. The results were as follow:—Total from Latin and Greek 565, obsolete 34. Total from Saxon, Welsh, French, &c. 580, obsolete 64. Commencing afterwards at page 5, the same course was pursued to near the end of D, twenty-eight pages being examined. Result: 577 from Latin and Greek, of which 52 were obsolete: from Saxon, &c. 511, of which, 33 were obsolete. Thinking, however, that objections might possibly be made to Webster's Dictionary, on account of its containing a great number of words seldom used, we had recourse to Walker's. Beginning at the first, and counting as before the first column of every tenth page, we went half through the dictionary, that is, to the 301st page inclusive. The following results were obtained: 361 from Latin and Greek; 399 from Saxon. These, added together, make 960. Now, 576 is three fifths of the last number, so that those from Latin and Greek wanted only fifteen of being three fifths of the whole number. It will be recollected that our former estimate was "about three fifths." That estimate was made in a manner similar to what has been stated above, though a smaller proportion of the words were counted. The examination was continued to the end of the letter M, the middle of the alphabet:—the minutiæ of the process have not been preserved. The number of those from the ancient languages was somewhat more than three fifths. It would seem, however, from comparing the results above given, that our first estimate was rather too high. But it cannot, we think, be far from the truth. In order to ascertain about what proportion of our words are from the Southern European and oriental languages, an examination conducted on the plan before described, was made through the first four letters of the alphabet, that is to page 381, inclusive. The result was 177 from French, Spanish, &c., which could not be directly derived from Latin and Greek. This deducted from the number of those from Saxon, &c., as given above, and added to

But even if it were true, it would not, we think, very materially affect our arguments on the importance of the study of Greek and Latin. We would here beg leave to refer the reader to what we have said respecting derivation, in the eighth number of "The Friend." From this it will be seen that the chief advantage of being acquainted with the original roots, is not that it gives a knowledge of the *simple* English words which are derived from these roots, but, that by learning a comparatively few primitives we shall be enabled to determine the signification of an immense multitude of compounds. Indeed, the knowledge of the original *positum* or *pressum*, could throw but little light on the English words *position* or *pressure*, though it might greatly assist the pupil in understanding and remembering their compounds, as *compression*, *exposition*, *reposition*, &c. This observation will, perhaps, be sufficient to show that a knowledge of the old Saxon,

the sum of those from the ancient tongues, will give the relative proportion of words from the northern and southern languages, 560—177=383; again, 565+177=742.

It may be proper to state, that in making the foregoing calculations, we have often placed words in the Latin list which Webster gives as coming from the French. In those cases where they evidently were of Latin origin, we thought that it was for the most part, not only allowable, but far preferable to go at once to the fountain head, for we often find that the stream is perfectly clear at its source, while below it is turbid and obscure. Webster derives the English *demand* from the French *demander*, to ask; but its derivation from Latin is to us much more satisfactory, as it gives clearly and forcibly the meaning of the word, *to order from*. Many instances of the same kind might be mentioned. It is to be borne in mind that P. does not merely assert that our words from Saxon origin are more numerous than those from Latin and Greek, he says they constitute "far the larger part of *all* those employed" in our language. How near the truth he is on this point we leave our readers to judge.—Allusion is made to an article in the Princeton Review—we suppose that which was noticed in the National Gazette a short time ago under the head of "Our Own Tongue." It *may* be that P. means to say what is said in that article, that Saxon words are, so common, and so often repeated, that in ordinary reading we meet with them far more frequently than those from the ancient tongues. If this should be his meaning, we cannot help regarding him as singularly unfortunate in his language, as we can hardly suppose it possible that any reader could have understood it, without having first read the article alluded to above. But if this be what he meant, what becomes of his assertion, that it is of more consequence to study the ancient Saxon than the Latin? Does the circumstance of words being common render it proportionally important to be acquainted with their origin? If so, an acquaintance with the Saxon word from which the article *the* is derived, must be of incalculable importance, as it occurs almost every line, and even sometimes much oftener. We are far from advocating the unnecessary employment of uncommon and sesquipedalian terms. On the contrary we think, that where there are two words not differing essentially in their meaning, good taste would generally lead to the choice of the more common and simple one, provided it be not vulgar. But by a term of several syllables we may sometimes express an idea clearly which could not otherwise be expressed without great circumlocution. Besides, it is certainly desirable to know the meaning of the words we meet with, even though we should not think proper to use them ourselves. It is hardly necessary to say, that in order to understand perfectly the writings of some of our most valuable authors, we must possess an acquaintance not merely with our words of every day use, but also with a great many which are rarely employed in conversation.

however interesting it might be to the philologist, must, in point of real utility, be far inferior to that of the Greek and Latin, since a large majority of our Saxon words are so perfectly simple, that their signification is easily understood and retained. The fact, moreover, that these are so extremely common renders it for the most part unnecessary to have recourse to the original, in order to determine their precise import.

What P. says respecting the word oxygen is doubtless true, but he should bear in mind that oxygen is one of those things which *can be presented directly to the senses.* Speaking of the course to be pursued in early education, we have strongly recommended that the study of the common and simple objects of sense should precede the study of words. (See the 9th No. of "The Friend.") But we may here remark, that analyzing the name, will often assist us greatly in remembering the properties and characteristics, even of the objects of sense, when these are not very common, or when we can only derive a knowledge of them from books. Who can doubt, that the pupil will recollect more readily both the situation and the name of Mesopotamia, when by having recourse to the original he finds that this word means *between the rivers?* Or, that he will remember more easily the use of the hygrometer (if he is not already familiar with this instrument) as well as the word itself, and the manner in which it is spelled, when he observes that it is composed of two simple and common Greek words which signify a *measurer of moisture.* A multitude of similar examples might readily be adduced, but these perhaps will suffice to illustrate our position.

If an acquaintance with the original roots is often very useful in enabling us to understand and retain even those words which are complex in their signification as well as in their construction, and especially such as express something which is not cognizable by the outward senses. In such cases an analysis of their parts is almost indispensable, in order to have a vivid and clear idea of their meaning.

Our writer says, that it is absurd to suppose that the knowledge of scientific terms should precede the study of science itself. This assertion is easily made, but we think it cannot be so easily proved. We appeal to all those who have given any considerable attention to the sciences, whether some previous knowledge of scientific terms is not highly useful, if not indispensable, in order to pursue their studies with advantage and success. We would ask why the definitions of several mathematical terms are thought necessary to be prefixed to Euclid's Elements? If it be replied that studying these definitions is in fact studying the science of mathematics, then learning the terms of any other science is studying that science. If it be said that nothing more was intended than that, it would be absurd to treasure up scientific terms in the memory without applying them, or understanding their application, to the objects of science, we freely admit the truth of the

position. But in this sense the statement could have no possible bearing on what we have formerly said with regard to this subject. He who acquires the ancient languages does not therefore get scientific terms by rote, but he becomes familiar with the elements of which these terms are composed. If afterwards in the pursuit of the sciences he meets with any long and difficult word, by analyzing it he will for the most part readily understand its signification, and, generally speaking, will comprehend it more perfectly than he could possibly do, were he unacquainted with those elements, by merely having recourse to the dictionary.

But P. seems to think that the various words of our language may be learned by observing how they are employed in reading and conversation, without resorting to what he calls the "circuitous process" of studying them through the medium of another language;—as if it was a more circuitous process to learn a few short and simple words, than a multitude of long and compound ones. (We would here again refer the reader to what is said on this subject in the 8th No. of "The Friend.") Notwithstanding what has been said by our writer on this point we cannot help believing, that the most *economical* mode of obtaining a thorough acquaintance with our tongue, is to pursue it in the way we have before pointed out. That an excellent knowledge of it may be acquired in the manner which he has mentioned, we cannot doubt, especially, when this acquisition is aided by the natural gifts of a strong discrimination and retentive memory. We think, indeed, that those, "who possess a great natural aptitude for the acquisition of language," least need the aids which classical studies afford, though *they* would derive great advantage from them.

While on this subject, we may further remark, that along with the convenience of learning our own language in the manner which P. proposes, (that is, without making it an object of especial study,) we believe there is no small disadvantage. For if, whenever we meet with a word that is new to us, we resort to the dictionary, the whole amount of time thus spent, would be more than sufficient for acquiring such a knowledge of Latin and Greek as would enable us to understand the greater part of our most difficult words. If, on the other hand, the reader should merely guess at the signification of the word, and neglect the dictionary, though he might at length come thoroughly to understand it, he could not so easily repair the loss sustained from not having clearly comprehended the subject of his reading. Add to this the still greater disadvantage of often receiving not merely a vague, but an erroneous impression, —an impression which may perhaps remain long after the verbal misapprehension which gave rise to it, has been corrected. This, we believe, is no uncommon thing. We appeal to our readers whether we are not correct in this belief.

It may not here be out of place to state that a friend of ours, in whose veracity and candour we repose entire confidence, has told us that he was sure the knowledge of Latin and Greek had saved him from the trouble of looking into the dictionary at least ten thousand times: (it was his practice always to refer to the dictionary whenever he met with a word which he thought he did not fully understand.) He added, that the assistance which he thence derived, was not valuable in relation to scientific works only, but also those of a lighter kind, and even some of the most common of the English classics. Many others, with whom we have conversed on this point, have expressed similar views.

Intimately connected with this subject, is the enquiry as to what education is proper for those whose circumstances will not allow them to devote any large portion of their time to literary and scientific pursuits. The full consideration of this question would require a separate essay; it will be sufficient, for our present purpose, to speak of it in so far as it is essentially connected with the study of the languages. First, however, we would say that we have never contended, nor advised, that every child in the community should become thoroughly conversant with the ancient classics. It was merely our object to state what we conceived to be their more prominent advantages, and leave parents to judge for themselves how much classical knowledge should be given to their children, or whether any at all. We are perfectly aware that some are so unfortunately circumstanced, that they can scarcely give attention to any thing else than procuring the means of subsistence. However, this ought not to affect our decision as to what plan of instruction is proper for those who can afford to be *well educated*. We assume that such should, at all events, have a thorough acquaintance with their own language, and with the groundwork of the more useful sciences. Now, in order to obtain the former, some knowledge of Latin, if not absolutely necessary, is at least expedient, as we trust we have already shown. The knowledge which would be sufficient for this purpose, we are persuaded, would not, if properly communicated, materially encroach on the time which should be allotted to a *good* education.* We shall be safe in saying that it need not occupy above one fourth of the period which is ordinarily allowed, in order to become well versed in the classics. If, however, it should be thought proper to confer a liberal education, and especially if the scholar should discover a decided taste or talent for the languages, we believe he may, not only without any waste of time, but with great advantage, continue this branch of study till he is able to enjoy and appreciate the beauties of the higher classical authors.

To P.'s criticism on what was said by us respecting the importance of an accurate knowledge of words, in order to reason forcibly; or judge correctly of the reasoning of others, &c. (See No. 9 of "The Friend," first page,) we have only to reply that we

* By this we mean such an education as those in the middle classes of society ought generally to receive—such a one as is calculated to "make a man useful, respectable, and happy."

cannot regard it as any positive evidence of "great obliquity or weakness of intellect," that inexperienced persons, and especially those in the hasty enthusiasm of youth, should sometimes consider that as sound reasoning, which a maturer examination would show to be entirely destitute of force; since we have so frequent occasion to remark, that persons of experience, and those by no means deficient in understanding, often, through haste or some other cause, form very erroneous conclusions, with regard to subjects, which a moderate share of candid attention would enable them to see in their true light.

Our writer says, that "Dymond very naturally observes," that adducing the intellectual exercise which the classics afford us an argument in their favour, "is itself an indication of the questionable utility of the study." We would here take the liberty of reminding him, that what is *natural* is not therefore *true.* When Copernicus first promulgated his new views of the system of the universe, many persons, not merely the weak and ignorant, but also those of understanding and experience, *very naturally* regarded them as wild and absurd. It has always been, and still is, perfectly *natural* for those who have not the time or inclination to investigate a subject thoroughly, to adopt erroneous or superficial views. We entirely agree with P. with respect to the wisdom of seeking exercise, whether physical or intellectual, in profitable pursuits. But if that which is highly useful in itself, should be also unusually well adapted to give vigour and health to body or mind, we should certainly regard it as a great additional recommendation.

Before leaving the subject entirely, we trust P. will excuse us for pointing out an error, into which he seems to have fallen, in regard to the importance which we attach to the classics on account of their tendency to elevate the taste. He says, "lastly, and above all," it is contended that the pursuit of ancient literature affords the best means of forming a correct taste, &c. The expression *above all* would, we think, give the impression that we regarded this as the chief recommendation of the classics. Now, we have expressly said, in speaking of the different advantages to be derived from them, that "their *great* utility, in our estimation, arises from the fact that by devoting a considerable share of our time to the Latin and Greek languages, we shall be able to acquire a thorough knowledge of our own more speedily, than if the latter should receive our exclusive attention." We may also notice here a trifling mistake in one of the quotations from our "Remarks." Alluding to the moderns, we have spoken of "their extended acquaintance with the natural *and abstract* sciences," and not of "their extended and *accurate* acquaintance with the natural sciences,"—we apprehend that the moderns have made far more valuable improvements in the abstract and mixed, than in the strictly natural sciences.

To what P. says respecting the relative value of natural and spiritual knowledge, we cordially respond. In case, therefore, after a candid and deliberate examination, it should

be found, that classical studies are necessarily adverse to this best of all knowledge, we would unhesitatingly recommend their entire proscription, since no intellectual treasure, however great, is to be placed in comparison with that pearl which can alone purchase the "crown of glory that fadeth not away."

THE WHIRLING DERVISHES.

From European Correspondence of the Massachusetts Spy.

CONSTANTINOPLE.

You have heard of that unique sect, called, from their peculiar religious ceremonies, the *Whirling Dervishes.* A description of this method of worship, as I have this day witnessed it, will constitute the subject of the present communication. The mosque in which they assemble, is in Pera, near the summit of the hill, upon which that city is situated. The yard, in front of it, is entered from the street, through a gateway in a gilded iron fence, at one extremity of which, beneath an appropriate shelter, a clock has been placed and a fountain constructed, for the public benefit. Between the gate and the mosque, beside the path leading to the latter, there is a small building, a mausoleum, containing the monuments of some of the deceased dervishes of rank. The monuments are composed of wood, their form being similar to that of a coffin. The top of each is shaped like the roof of a house, and, at one extremity, rises a standard which supports an accurate representation of the head-dress of the person to whose memory the monument is erected. Near the same extremity stands a splendid candelabrum. The floor of the mausoleum is richly carpeted, and the monuments are enveloped in green cloth. Similar edifices and monumental structures, commemorative of the dignitaries of the Mahometan faith, are seen adjacent to nearly all the mosques. In some of them, Cashmere shawls of the most exquisite richness and beauty, are laid, neatly folded upon the monuments, while the most elegant boxes, inlaid with pearl and gold, and other articles of equal richness, are placed in different parts of the room.

When we arrived at the mosque of the dervishes, the audience were rapidly gathering. Before entering, every person, whether Turk, Greek, Armenian, or Frank, was obliged to take off his boots. These, in some instances, were substituted by slippers, but many went in "in their stocking feet" and carrying their boots in their hands. An octogenarian dervish stood beside the door, to take charge of the boots of such as were disposed to leave them in his care. We left ours with him, taking a duplicate of the number which he placed upon them, and, putting on the slippers with which we had taken the precaution to furnish ourselves, mingled with the crowd and entered the place of worship. The audience were sitting cross-legged *à la Turque,* upon the floor. We followed the fashion, albeit unused to the favourite position of Turks and tailors. Being fairly, though not *comfortably* seated, I looked around to gain a knowledge of my whereabouts.

The mosque is octagonal. The audience

occupies a space of several feet in width, next the walls, throughout the whole circumference of the room. This is separated from the central portion, occupied by the Dervishes, by a balustrade. A gallery extends around the room, above the division devoted to the use of the audience. In this, and directly over the entrance, was the choir of musicians.

The Neapolitan had sought relief from a wearied limb, or a "foot asleep," by changing his position three or four times, when the Dervishes entered. Some of them were barefooted, and others wore sandals. A plain garment like a cloak, with neither cape or collar, was thrown over their other clothing, while their heads were covered by a peculiar drab hat, without any brim, and in shape, bearing a striking resemblance to a flower pot inverted. The cloaks were of various colours, some of them being scarlet, others drab, green, brown, purple, blue, or black. As the Dervishes entered, they proceeded nearly half way across the room, bowed low, before the extract from the Koran, inscribed in golden letters above the seat of the chief of their sect, and then stationed themselves, standing, beside the balustrade which separated them from the spectators. At length, the chief came in, supported, on either side, by a man next inferior to himself in rank. He was clad in a green robe, and a turban of the same colour surrounded his cap. The three advanced towards the centre of the floor, and made their low salaam. All the other Dervishes bowed at the same time. The chief and his attendants sat down upon the rich red cushion, beneath the inscription just mentioned, and on the side of the room opposite the door.

The ceremonies now commenced. One of the men in the orchestra chanted an extract from a book which he held, his voice being so nasal as to be exceedingly unpleasant. This was followed by a prayer from the chief of the sect, he and all the others kneeling the while, and occasionally bowing so as to bring the face in contact with the floor. Their appearance was that of sincere devotion, and I should have supposed them all deeply engaged in spirit, had not the gray old priest, or chief, stopped to gape when in the midst of a sentence. This ceremony completed, the chanting was recommenced and continued during several minutes. The whole band of music then began to play, while the Dervishes arose and walked, in single file, three times around the room, each one making three reverential bows every time that he passed the seat of the chief. Subsequently they kneeled and bowed their heads to the floor for a long time in silence. Meanwhile the strains of music became more plaintive than any I had ever previously heard. At one moment, they resembled the sweetest notes of the flute, at another, the softest and most plaintive melody of the Æolian harp. Suddenly, so suddenly that I started with surprise, the little drums began to be beat, every Dervish struck the floor with his hands, and sprung upon his feet. They threw their cloaks upon the balustrade, and each appeared in a loose garment similar to a frock or gown, and confined by a belt around the waist.

The most curious part of the ceremony now commenced. The man who stood nearest the chief walked forward, took his hand, kissed it, crossed his arms upon his breast, and moved off in the opposite direction, turning around pretty rapidly on his feet. His example was followed successively by the others, until seventeen of them were whirling like so many tops, upon the floor. Very soon after commencing, they released their hands from their breasts, and raised their arms to a direction nearly horizontal. They closed, or nearly closed their eyes, and partially reclined their heads upon their shoulders. As their motion became somewhat rapid, the skirts of their robes, made purposely very full, were thrown out as far as possible from their bodies, looking like a large umbrella, opened to its greatest extent. The music was continued, the chief and his two attendants remained standing, while another person walked about among those who were whirling, but never coming in contact with them. The space was so limited for the number who were whirling, that it seemed impossible that one could walk among them without being continually struck by their extended arms. After this rotary motion had been continued some fifteen minutes, sufficiently long to have made one unaccustomed to the business fall a dozen times, from giddiness, the Dervishes stopped, perhaps two minutes, and then kissing the hand of the chief, as before, went off again upon "their winding way." The ceremony was thus continued about thirty-five minutes, having another interval of about the same length as the first. The respiration of the whirlers seemed somewhat quickened towards the close, and a slight fatigue was evinced by a somewhat retarded motion.

One of the Dervishes, a man apparently thirty-five years of age, turned a little more rapidly than the others. I counted the number of his rotations per minute, soon after they commenced, and again near the close. At the former time it was *fifty-six*, and, at the latter, *fifty-one.*

The audience, at this singular religious performance, were, as might be expected, exclusively men. In that part of the house, however, in which I sat, there were several very close lattices in the wall, coming from behind which, we could occasionally hear the voices of women.

Thus situated, the females could see those engaged in the ceremonies, without being seen, either by them, or by the spectators.

AN ELECTRICAL LADY.

A respectable physician, in a late number of Silliman's *Journal,* relates the following curious account of an *Electrical Lady.* He states, that on the evening of Jan. 28th, during a somewhat extraordinary display of the nothern lights, the person in question became so highly charged with electricity, as to give out vivid electrical sparks from the end of each finger to the face of each of the company present. This did not cease with the heavenly phenomenon, but continued for several months, during which time she was constantly charged, and giving off electrical sparks to every conductor she approached. This was extremely vexatious, as she could not touch the stove or any metallic utensil, without first giving off an electrical spark, with the consequent twinge. The state most favourable to this phenomenon was an atmosphere of about 80 deg. Fah. moderate exercise and social enjoyment. It disappeared in any atmosphere approaching zero, and under the debilitating effects of fear. When seated by the stove, reading, with her feet upon the fender, she gave sparks at the rate of three or four a minute, and under the most favourable circumstances, a spark that could be seen, heard, or felt, passed every second! She could charge others in the same way when insulated, who could then give sparks to others. To make it satisfactory that her dress did not produce it, it was changed to cotton and woollen, without altering the phenomenon. The lady is about 30, of sedentary pursuits, and delicate state of health, having for two years previously suffered from acute rheumatism and neuralgic affections, with peculiar symptoms.

BRIDGE OF BOATS.

Some of the objects of interest to a traveller, in ascending or descending the Rhine, are the numerous bridges of boats with which he comes in contact, in crossing over the river from one town to another. Some of these bridges have from fifty to a hundred boats strung together. They are built of strong materials, in the firmest manner, flat bottoms, and both ends pointed, and are strongly chained together side by side, and to the bed of the river. To keep them in their place, they are attached to posts or sunken rocks. As the steamboat approaches them, they are loosened, and half a dozen or more gracefully curve round by the force of the current, to the right and left, and when the boat has passed, they are immediately drawn back by machinery, all of which is done in a very few minutes, in half the time that the drawbridges of our own rivers are raised and lowered.—*Mer. Journal.*

Habits.—Like flakes of snow that fall unperceived upon the earth, the seemingly unimportant actions of life succeed each other. As the snow gathers together, so are our habits formed. No single flake, that is added to the pile, produces a sensible change; no single action creates, however it may exhibit, man's character; but as the tempest hurls the avalanche down the mountain, and overwhelms the inhabitant and his habitation, so passion, acting upon the elements of mischief, which pernicious habits have brought together by imperceptible accumulation, may overthrow the edifice of truth and virtue.

A man should never be ashamed to own he has been in the wrong; which is but saying in other words, that he is wiser to-day than he was yesterday.

For "The Friend."

SAMUEL FOTHERGILL.

(Concluded from page 102.)

Samuel Fothergill travelled much in England and Scotland, several times in Ireland, and once very extensively in this land. He was singularly humbled in a sense of poverty, weakness and insufficiency on his first landing, but was afterwards remarkably strengthened, both in public and private, in gospel authority and love, to the awakening and comforting of many. Soon after his return from America he thus wrote to his friend John Churchman, to whom he was closely united in the bonds of the gospel, in allusion to the trials brought upon Friends at the time of the "French and Indian war." "I nearly sympathise with the living among you in this time of deep probation. Oh! that you may all stand fast, and quit yourselves like men, for that testimony and faith once delivered, and now revived to the saints. In this heavenly brotherhood I feel myself in spirit present with you in your land, not as having left aught undone which duty required, but in the sweet participation of the hope, patience and tribulation of the gospel and kingdom of our Lord. And if the church go into the wilderness, her place is prepared of God, whose eye looks towards, and his arm sustains every part of his extensive family, both in heaven and earth. The mourning of his heritage is as audible to his ear, as the hosannas of the fixed inhabitants of his holy mountain." Samuel Fothergill also wrote to his friend, James Wilson, about the same time, an interesting letter, in which he gives a lively description of the situation of Friends in the various provinces of this continent: as this letter has been inserted in "The Friend," vol. 3, page 191, the reader is referred to it, in the belief that it will amply repay an attentive perusal.

In the year 1762 he visited Ireland in company with Jonathan Raine, Isaac Wilson, and William Rathbone, it is believed, under appointment of the Yearly Meeting of London. From accounts preserved, his services were remarkably to the edification of the society in that country, labouring to strengthen its concerned members in their endeavours to support the testimonies of truth, and the discipline in divine wisdom, set as a hedge about us. In a select meeting, he spoke of a state which seemed to be much among Friends, even as among the royal tribes of Judah, which was a complaint, "that the bearers of burdens were like to fail, there is so much rubbish." He cautioned such not to give way to ineffectual bemoaning, but rather, be willing to arise and work to repair the breaches, and build up the walls, and they would find the King would be among them to help them. They would be furnished with a weapon of war in one hand, whilst they wrought with the other; so that he would not have such to be discouraged, or give way to that ineffectual bemoaning over the state of the church,. He endeavoured in a strong and moving manner to disengage the minds of the people from having their dependence on any mortal, even on such who might have la-

boured faithfully, as the Apostle did; reminding them that our minds are too apt to be drawn after what is visible, so as to worship that which is not God. One may say, "I am of Paul;" another, "I am of Apollos," and Satan, knowing this weakness, disputed formerly with the Archangel about the body of Moses, perhaps that he might deify it, and to delude this weak people, who before, whilst Moses was in the mount, made a calf to worship, and having such a veneration for Moses, it is probable they would have worshipped his body, had not the Almighty, in his wisdom, buried him himself where they could not find him.

In the early part of the year 1769, he visited most of the families of Friends, composing the Monthly Meeting of Grace Church Street, London, in which service he was divinely strengthened, and enabled to extend a helping hand to many, in close and necessary labour for their increasing care, to live and act consistently with our holy profession, to the comfort and help of divers, and to his own peace; and afterwards, at two different periods, he visited the families of Friends in Horsleydown and Westminster Monthly Meetings in that city, to the same good effect. He mostly attended the Yearly Meetings in London when of bodily ability, in which his gospel labours were very acceptable and edifying; being particularly careful, when called from home, to return to his family and friends with as much expedition as the nature of his service would admit.

Having acquired a moderate competency by his diligence and industry, he declined trade for several years before his decease, devoting his time and talents to the service of the churches. As a pillar in the Lord's house he was steadfast, being actuated by a Christian and manly zeal; in deportment grave; his private conversation was edifying, corresponding with his public ministry, which at times went forth as a flame, piercing the obdurate, yet descending like dew upon the tender plants of our Heavenly Father's planting, the true mourners in Zion, with whom he travelled in deep sympathy of spirit. In his appearances as a gospel minister he was free from affectation, in doctrine clear and sound, fervent in charity, being a minister and elder worthy of double honour, speaking whereof he knew, and what his own hands had handled of the good Word of life.

He endured a long and painful illness with much patience and resignation, and towards the close of his time, expressed himself to some of his relations when they took leave of him, previous to their setting out for the Yearly Meeting in London, to the following effect:

"Our health is no more at our command than length of days: mine seems drawing fast towards a conclusion; but I am content with every allotment of Providence, for they are all in wisdom, unerring wisdom." "There is one thing, which as an arm underneath, bears up and supports; and though the rolling tempestuous billows surround, yet my head is kept above them, and my feet are firmly established. O! seek it, press after it, lay

hold on it." "Though painful my nights, and wearisome my days, yet I am preserved in patience and resignation. Death has no terrors, nor will the grave have any victory. My soul triumphs over death, hell and the grave." "Husbands and wives, parents and children, health and riches, must all go; disappointment is another name for them." "I should have been thankful had I been able to have got to the ensuing Yearly Meeting in London, which you are now going to attend, where I have been so often refreshed with my brethren; but it is otherwise allotted. I shall remember them, and some of them will remember me. The Lord knows best what is best for us; I am content and resigned to his will." "I feel a foretaste of that joy that is to come; and who would wish to change such a state of mind?" "I should be glad if an easy channel could be found to inform the Yearly Meeting, that as I have lived, so I shall close, with the most unshaken assurance that we have not followed cunningly devised fables, but the pure, living, eternal substance." "Let the aged be strong, let the middle aged be animated, and the youth encouraged; for the Lord is still with Sion; the Lord will bless Sion." "If I be now removed out of his Church Militant, where I have endeavoured, in some measure, to fill up my duty, I have an evidence that I shall gain an admittance into his glorious Church Triumphant, far above the heavens." "My dear love is to all them that love the Lord Jesus."

He departed this life at his house, in Warrington, the 15th, and was buried the 19th day of the sixth month, 1772, at Penkeith, in the fifty-seventh year of his age, and the thirty-sixth of his ministry.

T. /:.

For "The Friend."

An Account of the Life of William Bennit.

(Continued from page 103.)

Whilst in outward bonds, William Bennit was often given to partake of spiritual freedom, and to rejoice in a sense of the tender love, and merciful regard of his Heavenly Father towards him. In the remembrance of that compassion which had been extended towards him all his life long, which had delivered him from his captivity under the god of this world, and had brought him to Zion even with a voice of thanksgiving and praise, he now found himself constrained to compose a song of deliverance. It was entitled, "God only exalted in his own work; or the work of God praiseth him in Zion." He commences by exhorting his soul to withdraw a little while to its secret chamber of rest and quietness, there to meditate on the loving kindness and tender compassion of the Lord: that from a consideration of mercies past and present, and in faith of these to come, it might be enabled to praise the name of the Lord. After rehearsing the various spiritual deliverances he had experienced, he closes with the ascription of glory, honour, thanksgiving and praise, to Him who is blessed for ever. He wrote many epistles to Friends, stirring them up to faithfulness; strengthening and encouraging them to bear with patience their varied trials. Those who were like himself in prison, seem in a peculiar manner to have claimed his sympathy.

About the close of the year 1664 he was released from bondage; but in a few months having returned to Norwich, he was again apprehended at a meeting there, and refusing to take an oath was committed to jail. He was soon set at liberty, and passing down into Suffolk, was arrested in Edmondsbury, and was committed to prison there, about the eighth month, 1665. Here he suffered a severe and distressing confinement for nearly eight years, during the greater part of which he scarcely ever set foot across the threshold.

In an address to the magistrates of Edmondsbury, which he wrote soon after his commitment, he informs them that he understands it is the desire and intention of some of them to proceed against him to banishment. He tells them that he is an innocent man, who had done nothing worthy of bonds, much less of banishment. On behalf of his suffering brethren, he testifies that they are a people who, being guided by a principle of love which they have received from God, the Fountain of Love, are constrained thereby to live peaceably with all men. Influenced by it, they cannot but desire and seek the good of all people, from the King on the throne, to the meanest inhabitant in the kingdom. Taught to love their enemies—to bless and not to curse, they were preserved from being led by the spirit of revenge, by which some were drawn into secret plots and conspiracies. He adds, "which spirit, with all its fruits, we deny and judge, and all those who are led by it to contrive and plot against any, or to seek the destruction of any people, through our enemies—such we disown, and their actions we defy, the Lord is our witness."

He informs them that by the operation of this principle of love in the heart the consciences of Friends were made very tender, inasmuch as they would not willingly sin,—and would rather suffer the loss of all external things, yea even of life itself than break their peace with God. He then proceeds to show them that it was because they were persuaded by the unerring Spirit of Truth, that they ought not to do certain things set up by law, and dare not forbear others prohibited by man, that he and his brethren had been made to suffer so much persecution, by stoning, whipping, fining and imprisonments. "And even at this day, our sufferings are greater than before,—and now we are even as sheep appointed for the slaughter,—and all is, because we endeavour to keep our consciences void of offence towards God; and because we dare not join with that idolatrous worship which he abhors; but must, as moved of the Lord, rather bear testimony against whatever we suffer.

"And because we dare not swear at all, knowing if we should swear we should then transgress the commands of Christ.

"And because we follow the practices of the primitive Christians, and dare not forsake the assembling of ourselves together; but must, as we are taught of the Lord, meet in the pure fear and dread of his name. Even for no other end, the Lord who knoweth the secrets of all hearts is our witness, but to wait upon Him, to pray to Him, and to build up, strengthen and edify one another in Him.

"It is not in rebellion and contempt to King Charles and his laws that we meet together to worship God, neither do we do it in a cross, stubborn, self-will, as by some we are charged—the Lord is our witness—but even in a cross to our own wills, and in obedience to the will of God; wherefore we have peace in the Lord, for whose sake we suffer, and stand justified in the sight of God, though by men and their laws accounted transgressors."

At this time the plague was raging at London, more than a thousand of its inhabitants were dying daily, and two hundred thousand were computed to have left the city. In allusion to this, William Bennet writes, "Oh, surely the Lord of pity, of mercy, of compassion and endless love, hath seen the sufferings of his people in this nation, and hath taken cognizance of their sore afflictions and the tribulations, burdens and grievous oppressions under which they have long groaned." Their cries the Lord "will answer, and will revenge their cause upon the head of their persecutors. He will oppress the oppressors, and devour the devourers of his people, even as stubble before the fire fully dry. They shall not be able to escape the stroke of this righteous judgment which he hath begun, to make manifest in the earth that the inhabitants might learn righteousness. The besom of his wrath is cleansing the land of evildoers; and many of those who desired to have banished the people of the Lord from their native country, and lawful habitations, are by the Lord banished from their houses; they have fled from their habitations, they run from his righteous judgments; but can man fly to hide himself from the Lord. The measure they meted out to others, is meted to them again. This is just with the Lord, who is equal in all his doings, and just in all his ways; he will not be mocked by any; such as men sow, such must they reap; according to their deeds they must receive a reward.

"Wherefore Friends, so far as ye have a hand in the sufferings of the innocent, you have cause to repent thereof, and to ease the burdened, and to set the imprisoned and the oppressed free." He warns them, as they desire mercy from the Lord, not in any wise to usurp authority over the consciences of the Lord's people. This he declares is Christ's seat, and the magistrates sword is not to rule there. He desires them to come and be obedient to the light in their own consciences, "and it will cause you to do unto all men as you would be done unto. In the light you must come to believe, and follow, and obey it, before your souls can enjoy true peace with the Lord. By it [you may] be enabled to deny all ungodliness and worldly lust—by it be taught to live soberly, righteously and godly in this present world, to lay your sword upon evil-doers, and to be a praise to them that do well; and rather tolerate and defend them in the exercise of their consciences towards God, in meeting together in his pure fear, to serve and worship him than to suppress them." He tells them that this light in them would teach them to exercise their power in breaking up the meetings of those, who gather to drink, swear, and to waste the good creatures of God upon their filthy lusts. He adds, "Suppress such, for that is the magistrates work. But as for those who fear the Lord, and live peaceably and honestly with all men, let such have free liberty to serve the Lord in his own way, and worship him in his own spirit, and do not compel them to a dead, dark, invented superstitious worship which is not of God. Then will the blessings of the Lord my God, be poured down upon you, and a good savour ye will be unto those that fear the Lord, from whom ye will be worthy of double honour."

William commends the moderation heretofore displayed by the magistrates, and alludes in connection therewith to the preservation Edmondsbury had experienced, whilst many of the neighbouring towns were enduring the visitation of this awful judgment from the Most High. N. E.

(To be continued.)   K

For "The Friend."

PHIPPS ON THE GOSPEL.

Joseph Phipps's opponent alleges that he insinuates, 1, That what the Apostles have spoken and written is not the gospel; 2, That the real meaning of their writings is only a dry theory; 3, That the gospel, in fact, is an inexplicable substance within all men, whether they know any thing of the character and redemption of Christ, as represented in the New Testament, or not; 4, That the whole of our salvation depends solely upon an inward power and virtue, without the inspired sentiments of the Book of God.

To which J. Phipps replies, If I may be allowed to speak my own sense, what I have asserted and do believe respecting these points, is,

1, That the evangelic and apostolic writings are descriptive and declarative of "the gospel, which therein is defined to be "the power of God unto salvation;" that Christ is the power of God, who spiritually and internally administers light and life to the souls of men, which spiritual and powerful administration is the essential gospel; and that both those parts of Scripture which bear testimony to the incarnation and outward process of Christ, and those that witness to his inward ministration in spirit, whether narrative or doctrinal, being the best and most eminent testifications of the gospel, are therefore, by a metonymy, usually called by its name.

2, In my observations, I fully made appear that the real meaning of the apostolic writings is not a dry theory, but a strong recommendation of the living and sensible operation of the power of God.

3, The reader may see in my answers, that I do not hold the gospel to be in fact an inexplicable substance; but that it is not to be truly and certainly known without Divine illumination; for "the things of God knoweth no man, but the spirit of God." We read that "life and immortality are brought to light by the gospel." But what is this life and immortality? Did not mankind believe in a future state before the incarnation of Christ? Yes, certainly; both Jews and Gentiles believed, and held the truth of it. What life and immortality, then, is that which is *peculiar to the gospel*, and which it is its particular property to unveil? It consists not wholly in the relation of the external procedure and doctrines of our Lord, but mainly in that spiritual gift he procured for us through his sufferings, which is the *life and power* that the immortal spirit of God manifests in the believing and obedient soul, that spirit which quickens those who have been dead in trespasses and sins, and therein alienated from the life of God. The very essence of the gospel is that spirit, which is issuing forth of this spirit of life to the hearts of men. "Keep thy heart with all diligence," saith the wise man, "for out of it are the issues of life." This teaches that these living issues arise *in* the heart of man, but not *from* the heart itself. Was it so, the heart would be its own quickener and Saviour, and Christ would be excluded as such; but he alone is the way, the truth, and the life; therefore the issuings of life to the heart are from the spirit, and in and through it by his spirit.

The divine influence of it is the life of the soul, that which renders it living, and void of this it cannot be, in a gospel sense, a *living* soul. It may endure to eternity, but mere duration is not this divine life. To exist without this life, is to be scripturally dead. It is therefore requisite for the soul to wait for, feel after, and find this immortal life, and also to keep to it with all diligence, that it may experience the daily issues thereof to its comfort and preservation, and to be as "a well of water springing up into everlasting life."

4, The pretence that I assert, the salvation of those who have the privilege of perusing the Scriptures, depends *solely* upon an inward power and virtue, without these as a means, is no assertion of mine. Page 14, I say "we do not pretend, that the internal motion of the spirit is the *only* means of reformation and religion to those who are likewise favoured with the Scriptures; but highly prize, thankfully accept, and use them as the *best secondary means extant*." I also understand the propitiatory sacrifice of our Saviour; by which he opens the door of reconciliation for us, to be the initiatory part of man's salvation, and the internal work of regeneration by his spirit, to be its actual completion; for thereby an entrance is administered into the heavenly kingdom.

Lastly, no man can have "the influence of the inspired sentiments of the Book of God," without receiving those inspired sentiments, which I have sufficiently shown no man hath, who reads without the inspiring power. Every reader hath only his own conceptions about the sentiments inspired of God, and not those *real* sentiments, without a degree of inspiration from Him, which the manifest mistakes and contradictions of many demonstrate they are strangers to.

His opponent cites this remark of J. P.—"The confidence of a true Christian is not in what he hears or reads, but in what he feels of the Holy Spirit." Hereupon he says, "Now this sets aside the real use and importance of a written revelation to all intents and purposes, for its contents cannot now be known but by either reading or hearing." To which J. Phipps replies, The real use of the Scriptures is to afford instruction and comfort, and their *chief* importance is to recommend to the spirit of Christ, from whence they came, that his people may be enabled rightly to put their trust in him. The apostle declares, God had given them the earnest of the spirit; therefore they were always confident. Was not their confidence, then, grounded in the earnest of the spirit given them of God? And is a trust in this spirit, and a belief of the contents of Scripture, incompatible with each other? Or is a Christian to have no confidence in the spirit and power of the Saviour himself, but all in his own notions of what he reads in Scripture, and will his own efforts, according to these notions, save him? Cannot he follow those scriptural exhortations and doctrines which plainly teach us to pray for the spirit, to live and walk in the spirit, without setting the Scriptures aside, and treating them with contempt?

Those who have experienced a living sense of the spirit, instead of dividing from the Scriptures, and depreciating their service, are, by the divine influence, more closely united to them, read them with a better understanding, and more to their comfort and advantage, than ever—are altogether as fervently concerned to press the frequent perusal of them, as any of those who so unjustly accuse them; and who are so inexperienced in the truth, as it is in Jesus, as to place their whole confidence in the opinions they gather from reading the Scriptures, and remain strangers to the necessary knowledge of Christ within, the hope of glory.

SALVATION.

What news so welcome to the prisoner, as that there is a hand stretched forth to break his chains? What intelligence so cheering to the sick, as that the physician has a remedy for his disease? And what tidings so delightful to the startled and trembling sinner, as that there is One who "shall save his people from their sins?" He shall *save* us—he shall translate us from misery to happiness; from pollution to purity, from the depths of perdition to the seats of eternal tranquillity and joy. He shall save us from our *sins*—from their guilt, and their terrible dominion; from their power in this world, and their penalties in another. He shall save *his people* from their *sins*—not the careless or cold, the worldly or the inconsistent; not those who openly submit to the dominion of other lords; who have a name only to live, and are dead; who say they are his, and are not; who call

him, Lord, Lord, and do not the things which he says: but those alone who are the faithful sheep of his flock; who "hear his voice," and "follow" it, and who hear not the "voice of strangers." Such individuals may be poor, may be forsaken, may be persecuted; but they shall be "saved" with an "everlasting salvation;" and when the '. day of the Lord shall come," "in the which the heavens shall pass away with a great noise, and the earth also, and the works that are therein, shall be burnt up," they, like the bush amidst the sacred fire, shall remain unhurt even amidst the elements of destruction. Lord Jesus, may we practically know Thee as this great Deliverer! Save us from the world; save us from the devil; save us from the awful flame which is kindled for the unholy and impenitent; save us from our worst enemy, ourselves.—*Cunningham.*

CARBONIC ACID GAS.

Dr. Webster repeated his lecture on the solidification of carbonic acid gas on Saturday evening, before a large and highly gratified audience. Before the process of the solidification, he explained the nature of several different gases, and made some experiments in illustrating. In all his attempts, he was perfectly successful. By the aid of the air-pump, he exhibited the pressure of atmospheric air by some very interesting experiments. After this, he proceeded to show the method of solidifying carbonic acid gas. This discovery has been lately made in France, and soon after the accounts reached this country, Dr. Webster succeeded in bringing about the same result. He first formed the gas in large quantities, which, after being subjected to a very great pressure in a strong vessel, was taken out, and exhibited in a solidified form. This solidified substance is somewhat like snow, though more compact. It is excessively cold, so much so, that when held in the hand, it produces the same effect as excessive heat, and soon raises a blister. After being a short time exposed to the air, it disappears, melting, as it were, returning to its original state as a gas. Dr. Webster repeated the operation several times, and handed round to the audience the freshly made substance. By being wrapped in cotton wool, and kept from the air, this could be preserved for some time.—*Boston Daily Advertiser.*

Dr. J. Mitchell has already performed here these experiments with perfect success.

Boundaries of the British Empire in the East.

Among the greatest phenomena in the history of the world may, undoubtedly, be reckoned the British empire in the East Indies.

This empire has, within a single century, risen from the humble rank of a trading factory to an *imperium* of more than 100,000,000 of inhabitants, with an equal number (100,-000,000) who, though under their own princes, still obey the British power, extends over 1,250,000 *English square miles* of the most fertile part of the surface of the earth (from 8° latitude to 35°, and from 68° longitude to 92°), and consequently contains a polar altitude the same as from *Messina* to *Tornea*, and a breadth as from *Lisbon* to *Smolensk*, which shows that it cannot be compared to any thing in Europe, either as to size or population, any more than in difference of climate and temperature, but that it must be compared with *Europe itself*. This empire has within its boundaries, the *Gauts* and *Himalay* mountains, always covered with ice, which rise, the former 15,000, the latter 27,000 feet above the level of the sea; it is intersected by rivers, each of which, like the Indus, Jumna, Sutledge, Ganges, and Brahmapootra, offers a navigation of not less than 1,200 English miles, and the two last-mentioned during certain months pour into the Bay of Bengal a mass of water containing more than 1,000,000,000 cubic feet in an hour. It has for its defence a standing army excellently disciplined, and considerably greater than that of Austria, and a revenue half as large again as Russia. Within its boundaries there are towns which, like *Calcutta*, have a population of a million; others which, like *Delhi*, *Agra*, *Benares*, *Luckno*, and *Poona*, reckon from 300,000 to 500,000 inhabitants; and others again—Madras and Bombay, which carry on a trade greater than that of ancient *Carthage*, *Venice*, or *Genoa*, during their most flourishing periods. It has kings as vassals, with a greater number of subjects than Naples; of dynasties older than the Bourbons; and the emperor in Hindoostan, the descendant of Tamerlane (Thimur Khan), the great Moghul, still sits on his golden throne, in Delhi, surrounded by all the grandeur of the East, himself only a prisoner in the power of the British.

For "The Friend."

THE DEPARTED YEAR.

Departed year! the voice is hushed
　That charmed thee on thy winged way,
And hearts with joy and pleasure flushed
　Have seen thee wasting in decay,
And felt a sadness o'er them steal
Which the lone soul is wont to feel.

The young, the gay, the buoyant heart
　Checks its free lightness at this hour,
And memory's sacred visions start,
　With an ungovernable power,
Before the spirit; man looks back
To trace life's ever-changeful track.

Since rosy spring came forth in flowers,
　With gladness beaming on her brow,
Time has rushed swiftly on, the hours
　Unheeded flown; where are they now?
Seek ye an answer? look upon
The desolation they have done.

The well-beloved and beautiful,
　For whom it were a joy to weep,
Are laid where sighing winds shall lull
　The rank grass o'er their couch of sleep,
Where naught of earth shall e'er destroy
The quietude which they enjoy.

Earth has released her lovely; they
　Have gone, like flowers, to their repose;
Pale, chill disease, and cold decay
　Have stolen, as o'er the summer rose,
Upon them, and their kindred turn
To weep above the mouldering urn.

Earth has given up her young; like dew
　They shone in life's first morning ray,
Then, like that exhalation, flew
　To climes as pure and bright as they,
Before the world's corrupting things
Had stained the soul or checked its wings.

The aged, too, are gone, whose locks
　Were whitened by the snows of years,
Whose hearts had long sustained the shocks
　Of human woe, and grief, and tears;
Yes, they have gone, the good, the blest,
To mansions of eternal rest.

Such is our lot; though man may boast
　Gems rich and beautiful to-day,
Ere dawns to-morrow they are lost,
　Like summer glories pass'd away;
The fair, the lovely bend the knee,
And all acknowledge Death's decree.

And what is man? to-day he hath
　A place upon the page of story,
And thousands join to strew his path
　With flowers of fame, and wreaths of glory;
The laurel decks his lordly brow,
And mortals at his presence bow.

To-morrow dawns; the trump of Fame
　Has hushed the sound with which it rung;
His worshippers are changed, his name
　Dies, like an echo, on the tongue,
Forgotten; but it shall not be
Thus changeful is eternity.

No: in the world beyond the tomb
　Eternal joy, eternal love,
Eternal bliss for ever bloom—
　The flowers of paradise above:
Change has not found that region fair,
Mutation hath not wandered there.　　P. E.

19th mo. 31st, 1839.

A more glorious victory cannot be gained over another man, than this, that when the injury began on his part, the kindness should begin on ours.

The coin that is most current among mankind is flattery; the only benefit of which is, that by hearing what we are not, we may be instructed what we ought to be.

Shining characters are not always the most agreeable ones; the mild radiance of an emerald, is by no means less pleasing than the glare of the ruby.

Although men are accused for not knowing their own weakness, yet perhaps as few know their own strength. It is in men as in soils, where sometimes there is a vein of gold which the owner knows not of.

THE FRIEND.

FIRST MONTH, 4, 1840.

It has not been our practice to deal in what are termed *the compliments of the season*, nor, indeed, in mere compliments of any description, but we present our readers to-day

with that which is much better; we mean the beautiful requiem to the parting year by P. E.—to whom we would say for ourselves and others interested, that we should be glad of other touches upon the same sweet chords.

The keen, searching blasts from the northwest within the last few days—the mercury in Fahrenheit nearly at zero, naturally turn one's thoughts to the condition of the poor, and while we draw round our comfortable fire-sides, or partake of the delicacies of a well supplied table, we cannot in recurrence to the Source whence all our blessings come, but remember with commiseration, the hundreds who are destitute of those indulgences, and even of the means of obtaining the common necessaries of life. At such moments there is consolation in the reflection that expedients are provided against positive suffering for the want of food, in those excellent establishments the "Soup Houses." We have already given notice of the opening of the Western Soup House, at the southeast corner of Schuylkill Sixth and George streets, and we insert below a notice of the similar establishment for the southern portion of our population. The intimation relative to the low state of the funds, we trust, will receive a ready and liberal response. A one, three, five or ten dollar bill contributed "not grudgingly, or of necessity," but willingly, to one of these charitable funds, cannot well be placed to a better interest, especially in reference to the principle sanctioned by high authority, that "he which soweth bountifully, shall reap also bountifully." The Northern Soup Society, whose location is at No. 181 Coates street, has not, as we understand, yet been opened the present season, but will be, it is expected, shortly.

SOUTHERN SOUP HOUSE.

The Southern Soup House was opened on fifth day, the second instant, at No. 16 Green street, (running from Spruce to Pine, between Fourth and Fifth streets,) where soup will be delivered to the poor every day between the hours of eleven and one.

The low state of the funds, and the destitute situation of many deserving poor, who are unable to obtain employment at this inclement season, induce the society to make an earnest appeal to the benevolent in behalf of this useful charity, and to solicit contributions in money, provisions, &c., which will be gratefully received at the Soup House, by Thomas Evans, No. 129 south Third street. Jno. J. Smith, Jr., Philadelphia Library. Isaiah Hacker, 32 Chestnut street, or any other of the members.

Married at Friends' meeting-house, on Mulberry street, on fifth day the 2d instant, John F. Sheppard, of Greenwich, N. J., to Margaret Garret, daughter of Philip Garret, of this city.

PRINTED BY ADAM WALDIE,

Carpenter Street, below Seventh, Philadelphia.

THE FRIEND.

A RELIGIOUS AND LITERARY JOURNAL.

VOL. XIII.   SEVENTH DAY, FIRST MONTH, 11, 1840.   **NO. 15.**

EDITED BY ROBERT SMITH.

PUBLISHED WEEKLY.

Price two dollars per annum, payable in advance.

Subscriptions and Payments received by

GEORGE W. TAYLOR,

NO. 50, NORTH FOURTH STREET, UP STAIRS,

PHILADELPHIA.

SCHOOL BOOKS.

The following remarks on the importance of a scrupulous regard to the character of school books, well merit the close attention of all interested in the proper training of youth. They are extracted from Thoughts on Education, by Dr. Humphrey, published in the New York Observer.

Without claiming for school books an equal influence with family education, in moulding the intellectual and moral character of children, it is perfectly safe to say, that few other causes operate so steadily, or extend their influence so far. From eight to ten years is the average period of common school education in this country; and during all this time, the class books in the schools are silently, but almost indelibly imprinting their image, as it were, upon the young and ductile mind. What an influence for good or for evil! Give to any class of men the exclusive writing and selection of school books, for one generation, and by the aid of teachers of kindred views and aims, they will do more to form the character of that generation, than every body else out of the domestic circle.

Such being the mighty influence of books, it is no very difficult task to point out in general terms what kinds ought to be excluded from our schools. No book should ever be used which is erroneous or superficial in its elementary principles. It sometimes takes a child a great while to unlearn what is wrong in his class book, and to get rid of the bad habits which it has helped him to form. The ruling passion just now is extreme *simplification*. What used to be called the rudiments of learning, are well nigh exploded, by abecedarian reformers, as quite too abstruse for young beginners. The elements of popular education must be rendered still more elementary by new analytical processes. Hence it comes to pass that some of the most admired lessons for infant minds are truly *simple*, in more senses than one. It requires rare talents to write a child's primer. It demands a highly discriminating and cultivated

intellect, brought down to the child's level; but so brought down as to lure him on to harder lessons, as fast as his strength will enable him to bear it.

I remark in the next place that no school book should be tolerated for a moment which has the slightest stain of impurity upon its pages, or, in other words, which is not as chaste in thought and expression as the driven snow—no book which has so much as one profane word or vulgar dash from beginning to end—which contains the remotest insinuation against the truth or inspiration of the Holy Scriptures; or which seems to sanction a hair's-breadth deviation from any one of the great principles of Christian morality. We send our children to school to be *taught*, not to be *contaminated*,—to be *nurtured*, not to be *poisoned;* and it were infinitely less dangerous daily to put just arsenic enough into their bread and milk, secretly to undermine the citadel of life, than to expose them to such deleterious moral influences.

Again, I observe, in the *third* place, at the risk of being called illiberal, that in compiling reading books, for the use of common schools and academies, no selections should be made from popular authors, whose works cannot safely be put into the hands of our children. It would be easy, no doubt, to find passages in some of the most *skeptical* writers, which do not militate at all against the Bible, as it would be to make selections from *profligate* writers, which would not raise a blush upon the cheek of modesty. But if admired and elegant extracts are taken from these classes of authors, and incorporated into our school books, what will be the consequence? Will precocious boys and romantic girls content themselves with the few paragraphs which they have received from a cautious compiler? Will they not want to see the heavy octavos from which these charming, these bewitching extracts were taken? And can you hinder them? Will they not, in one way or another, find access to Shelley, Moore, Byron, and other writers of splendid genius, but of debauched and infidel principles, at the most perilous age, if their admiration is early excited by the dazzling coruscations of such baleful meteors in the pages of their class books? Even were we to allow that nothing equally finished and beautiful can be found in other writers, how small is the advantage compared with the danger. But in compiling a reading book of the very highest literary character, there is no need of having recourse to infidels and libertines to help fill out the pages. It would be easy to select from perfectly unexceptionable authors, specimens enough of the finest writing to fill twenty volumes, if so many were wanted; and in this

way, while the taste of the scholars would be improved, they would be led early to enquire for the writers themselves, whom they had learned so much to admire.

I add in the *fourth* place, that in my view, no reading book, containing garbled, or altered extracts from distinguished Christian writers, whether in prose, or poetry, ought to be sanctioned by committees, parents or teachers, whatever other claims it may have to popular favour. I will explain my meaning. Whenever a compiler borrows one of his chapters, or sections, from Jeremy Taylor, or Robert Hall; from Cowper or Pollok, he is bound to take it just as it is, and neither to leave out what happens not to suit his fancy, or to harmonize with his creed, nor to substitute phrases and sentiments which he likes better. It is due to great and good men, who have charmed and instructed mankind by their writings, to let them speak their own sentiments, whenever they speak at all. If a compiler thinks the elegant, or sublime passage, which he would be glad to extract, too theological to suit his purpose, he can let it alone; but I maintain, that he has no right, for the sake of making his book popular with the religious part of the community, to transfer honoured and illustrious names to his pages, and then draw off, what those departed worthies regarded as the life blood of their writings. The opinions which they held were their own. They had as much right to hold and express them, as we have ours; and whoever takes liberties with the finest effusions of their genius and piety, does them a great wrong, which no school committee, or district ought ever to sanction.

Nor is this the only ground of remonstrance, against such unwarrantable liberties, in getting up school books. If an author whom we ourselves admire, and whom we wish our children to revere, as a holy man of God, is allowed to be stripped of the ephod by sacrilegious hands in their presence, and turned over to the companionship of pretty essayists and frozen moralists, how much will it derogate from the sacredness of his character, in their inexperienced estimation. The admirers of Watts, or Hall; of Mason, or Dwight, or of any other distinguished Christian author, have a right to insist, that he shall not be shorn of his glory, in the school books which they purchase for their children. If I put a reading book into the hands of my child, which either by omissions, or additions, does injustice to an eloquent and pious writer, I thereby virtually sanction the wrong, and lead the boy to infer, that I have no great partiality after all, either for the piety, or the principles, which he may have heard me often and highly extol.

FASHION.

From Sketches and Essays, by William Hazlitt.

Fashion constantly begins and ends in the two things it abhors most, singularity and vulgarity. It is the perpetual setting up and then disowning a certain standard of taste, elegance, and refinement, which has no other formation or authority than that it is the prevailing distraction of the moment; which was yesterday ridiculous from its being new, and to-morrow will be odious from its being common. It is one of the most slight and insignificant of all things. It cannot be lasting, for it depends on the constant change and shifting of its own harlequin disguises; it cannot be sterling, for, if it were, it could not depend on the breath of caprice; it must be superficial, to produce its immediate effect on the gaping crowd; and frivolous, to admit of its being assumed at pleasure, by the numbers of those who affect, by being in the fashion, to be distinguished from the rest of the world. It is not any thing in itself, nor the sign of any thing, but the folly and vanity of those who rely upon it as their greatest pride and ornament. It takes the firmest hold of weak, flimsy, and narrow minds, of those whose emptiness conceives of nothing excellent but what is thought so by others, and whose self-conceit makes them willing to confine the opinion of all excellence to themselves, and those like them. That which is true or beautiful in itself, is not the less so for standing alone. That which is good for any thing, is the better for being more widely diffused. But fashion is the abortive issue of vain ostentation and exclusive egotism: it is haughty, trifling, affected, servile, despotic, mean, and ambitious, precise and fantastical, all in a breath—tied to no rule, and bound to conform to every whim of the minute.

"The fashion of an hour marks the wearer."

ON TASTE.

From the same.

Genius is the power of producing excellence: taste is the power of perceiving the excellence thus produced in its several sorts and degrees, with all their force, refinement, distinctness, and connections. In other words, taste (as it relates to the productions of art) is strictly the power of being properly affected by works of genius. It is the proportioning admiration to power, pleasure to beauty: it is entire sympathy with the finest impulses of the imagination, not antipathy, not indifference to them. The eye of taste may be said to reflect the impressions of real genius, as the even mirror reflects the objects of nature in all their clearness and lustre, instead of distorting or diminishing them;

"Or, like a gate of steel,
Fronting the sun, receives and renders back
His figure and his heat."

Instead of making a disposition to find fault a proof of taste, I would reverse the rule, and estimate every one's pretentions to taste by the degree of their sensibility to the highest and most various excellence. An indifference to less degrees of excellence is only excusable as it arises from a knowledge and admiration of higher ones; and a readiness in the detection of faults should pass for refinement only as it is owing to a quick sense and impatient love of beauties. In a word, fine taste consists in sympathy, and not in antipathy; and the rejecting of what is bad is only to be accounted a virtue when it implies a preference of, and attachment to what is better.

Third Annual Report of the New York Association for the Benefit of Coloured Orphans.

The Board of Managers of the Association for the Benefit of Coloured Orphans, in presenting their third annual report, would once more renew the expression of grateful praise to the Author and Giver of all good. While they call upon the friends of the coloured orphan to join their solemn thanksgiving in the review of the past year, they feel how eloquent is the rebuke which its varied mercies have conveyed to the unbelief that fears to lean upon the promises of God, or trust in the boundless resources of his providence. The same beneficent hand that has led them through all their vicissitudes, has now brought them to the close of another year; has enabled them to sustain their orphan family, has blessed them with faithful and competent fellow labourers in the heads of the household and the school, and has relieved them from pecuniary difficulties in a manner equally opportune and unexpected. Under all these encouragements they are impelled to the cheerful prosecution of their undertaking, and although they feel that in relation to the children of their charge they have assumed one of the highest responsibilities ever committed to human hands, they cannot doubt that if faithfully discharged, it will bring with it a sweet and sure reward.

It is a subject for gratitude that the board is enabled to report great improvement in the health of the orphans. During the first six months of the year, it was their painful duty to witness the decline and death of six children from consumptive disease. Since that period there has been neither a death nor a case of severe illness, and with the exception of some local affections, the household has been entirely exempt from sickness. Among the causes of this pleasing change may justly be assigned the sedulous and judicious manner in which the laws of health, as dependent on diet, exercise, clothing and ventilation, have been carried into effect by their excellent matron, to whose attention and good management the house owes many of its comforts. It must, however, be observed that greater discrimination has latterly been employed in regard to the constitutions of children admitted; and also that of those received at an earlier period, nearly all of the more feeble subjects of their charity have died. The best method of promoting the health of the Institution will, however, as the managers believe, be found in removal to a more spacious and appropriate building. The conviction that the house was too small for the number of occupants induced the managers to bind out several of the orphans during the summer, and to place four, who were in feeble health, at board in the country. The latter course was evidently highly beneficial to those who enjoyed a change of air, and the diminution of their number was no doubt serviceable to all. Their physician is of opinion that not more than fifty children can prudently be allowed to occupy the present habitation.

Among the deaths which have occurred, was that of a little girl about three years of age, whose playfulness and intelligence had rendered her an object of much interest to the managers, and had drawn forth the most pleasing demonstrations of affection from the older children. She had been abandoned by a vicious mother, and thrown on the care of an aged and destitute coloured woman, whose " deep poverty abounded" towards the deserted infant, until reluctantly and with many tears she relinquished her to the protection of the managers. Another death was that of the little boy mentioned in the last report, who had been cruelly beaten and turned out of doors in the depth of winter. He was naturally a feeble child, and the exposure to which he was at that time subjected probably prepared the way for the pulmonary affection which terminated his life.

One case deserves to be noticed as affording an interesting instance of the kind and grateful dispositions, which the managers have had many opportunities of observing in the children, who have been brought under their notice. A worthy coloured woman, who died while at service in a respectable family, had requested on her death-bed that her only child, a little boy, should be placed in the Asylum. His health began to decline shortly after his admission, and he evidently pined after the home which he had left. For some time it was believed that his indisposition arose from a feeling not uncommon among children, when removed from scenes to which they are strongly attached, and although it soon became apparent that he was labouring under incurable scrofulous disease, he continued to manifest the strongest affection towards the family by whom he had been formerly protected. When asked if there was any thing he wished, he almost invariably answered, "only to see Miss——." The desires of the little invalid were gratified, and the kind and frequent visits of his friends always seemed for the time to impart animation and hope, and never ceased to be expected and welcomed until the close of life.

Another case which made a deep impression on the feelings of the managers, was that of J—— T—— an orphan boy, born in slavery in the West Indies. He was brought by his mistress from Havana to this city, and here voluntarily emancipated. When admitted, he was suffering from disease of the spine, and to those who saw him for the first time, his sadly expressive countenance and the distressing infirmity under which he laboured, made a most touching appeal. It was hoped that the spinal affection might be arrested, but the approach of cold weather developed consumptive symptoms, which proved ultimately fatal. His disposition was grateful and uncomplaining, and always readily responsive to the slightest expression of interest or sympathy. During the last few painful hours which preceded his death he was frequently heard to exclaim in mournful tones, " *no father, no mother.*" He had learned nothing of the English language except a few broken sentences, but a lady familiar with the Spanish endeavoured to ascertain the nature of his feelings on religious subjects. Little could be learned, except that he knew there was a God, and that he had sought him in prayer. And surely, for this child of ignorance and sorrow, it is not presumptuous to indulge a hope, founded on the assurance that there is acceptance with God " according to that which a man hath, and not according to that which he hath not."

The school continues to be the object of great interest and attention, and the board have pleasure in assuring their friends that the children are receiving a course of solid and practical instruction, with reference not only to their welfare and usefulness in this life, but to the momentous subject of fitting them for a world of perfect knowledge and enduring happiness.* The necessity for securing teachers, who should be inmates of the house, rendered it the duty of the managers to make arrangements, which deprived them of the services of their former instructress, whose character and qualifications were highly valued. The school has been conducted, during the last six months, by two ladies whose principles and abilities have secured the confidence and approbation of the board. Great advantages have resulted from the domestication of two efficient teachers with the children. There are now distinct sections for the younger and older scholars, an arrangement which has evidently facilitated the efforts both of the preceptors and pupils.

As an instance of the success which has crowned this most important department, they would cite the case of a boy about eight years of age, who was ignorant of his letters when admitted, but began to read *six weeks* afterwards. This is a child not only of great aptness, but of very promising habits and dispositions, a fact the more interesting, as he is the son of a depraved mother. As objections have sometimes been made to the charity that

grateful feeling, that a benignant Providence has rescued them from a probable career of ignorance and infamy. It should also be remembered that coloured children are excluded from the Long Island Farms, and that out of the Asylum they have no refuge but the Alms House, where they are placed in circumstances unfavourable to moral and mental culture.

In connection with the subject of education, the Managers are happy to report that the Sabbath school is in a flourishing state, and highly interesting to the children. They would also mention with gratitude the faithful and most acceptable services of an association of local preachers of the Methodist Episcopal Church, who hold two meetings for religious worship every Sabbath in the Asylum, and by accommodating their instruction to the capacities of their youthful audience, make the duties of that day pleasing as well as improving.

The statistics of the institution are as follows:—

Admitted since the opening of the Asylum, 84.

No. of children at date of last report,	50
Admitted during the present year,	23
	—
	73
	—
Present number, . . .	50
Indentured, ...	6
Returned to surviving parents, .	9
*Transferred to the Alms House,	2
Deaths, ...	6
	—
	73
	—

The Board feel that acknowledgments are due to their advisers for the continuance of their efficient and seasonable assistance and counsel. They would also record their obligations to their physician for his professional services, as well as to Dr. Alfred C. Post, who officiated during Dr. Macdonald's absence from the country.

The gift of five hundred dollars from a "Friend to the Institution," was received at a time when an accumulating debt and general commercial embarrassments had subjected the Board to a greater degree of anxiety than had been felt at any period since its or-

quim; thus completing a circle of upwards of two thousand miles, a great part of which was through a country hitherto almost unknown. In the course of this journey, Mr. Schomburgh collected many rare specimens in natural history, among others the *sudis gigas*, one of the largest fresh water fish, besides several other kinds, which will probably be new to ichthyologists; in birds, the Helmeted Chatterer, the Cock of the Rock, &c.; a large collection of insects, and numerous plants from the Rio Negro and the mountainous region of Roraima. Mr. Schomburgh is accompanied by three Indians of different tribes, from the interior, and has brought specimens of their arms, implements, and utensils.—*London Courier.*

THE LATE DR. ROBERT MORRISON.

The great Chinese scholar and missionary, the founder of the Anglo-Chinese College, the author of the great Anglo-Chinese Dictionary, (a stupendous monument of human ingenuity, labour, and perseverance,) and the first translator of the beauties and blessings of Scripture into a language spoken by upwards of four hundred millions of the human race—had to struggle against all the supposed obstacles of low birth and unlucky fortune. The son of a poor last and hoot-tree maker in the town of Newcastle-on-Tyne, he was himself an apprentice and industrious workman at the same humble trade. But a passion for knowledge and intellectual attainment—originating in his case, it would seem, in an over-mastering religious sentiment—seized him in early life, and every incident in his after career only proved what surpassing purity and enduring strength belong to such a passion· Excellence was with him, as with other great scholars who have equally proved their easy superiority to adverse circumstances, the simple and natural result of a strong determination to excel. A good memory and a lively sensibility to external impressions, are the only advantages we take him to have been at this period in possession of, besides the strength of resolution we have named. The last had its origin, as we have intimated, in a peculiar religious fervour, which though scarcely at that time so discreet in expression as it was always sincere and devout in feeling, yet animated him then, and to the latest moment of his life, with an unselfish desire to benefit his fellow-creatures.

Nothing can conquer a desire which originates in such a motive, and proposes as its object the acquisition of knowledge. The love of knowledge is, in itself, the attainment of knowledge. Poverty or toil discourage it in vain. It supplies the scarcity of time by the concentration of attention, and replaces comfort by self-denial. No man proved this better than the subject of this biography. No one ever proved more satisfactorily that the privileges and delights of intellectual cultivation depend upon the man himself, and not upon his external fortunes. The learned Dr. Morrison, surrounded by all the accommodations of study in his library, and learned leisure at Canton, was not a more laborious

or successful student than the last-maker's apprentice, who stole his leisure from toil-purchased sleep in the poor workshop of Newcastle.

From the New York Mercury.

SLAVERY IN CUBA.

From a gentleman long residing in Cuba, we have recently obtained the following statements:—

The population of Cuba is now about one million. Forty estates belong to resident Americans, and were lately purchased. Some of the Spaniards think our countrymen are emigrating to Cuba with a view to take ultimate possession, à la Texas.

Up to 1835, Bozal negroes, that is, Africans recently imported, to the number of fifteen thousand, were delivered over to the Spanish authorities, to be instructed in some trade, agreeably to the arrangement between the Spanish and British governments; but most of them were publicly sold in the market, the same as other slaves—that is, their *services* were sold for five to ten years; some of them being sent to the mines, and some to the other side of the island. Very few of them will ever probably recover their liberty. It is the practice, when a slave dies, to put one of the Bozals in his place, and thus his identity is lost. Since 1835, the Mixed Court turn the Bozals over to the British islands. In that year, considerable numbers of slaves were shipped from Cuba to Texas. There is not a slave on the island legally educated.

The mortality of slaves in Cuba is very great, owing chiefly to their being excessively overworked. In the towns, the yearly mortality is about 3 per cent.; on the breeding farms, 5; on the coffee plantations, 6 to 7; and on the *sugar* plantations, 10 to 15 per cent. There is no increase by births on the plantations. In fifteen years the slave population would be swept away, except for the foreign slave trade. The slaves on sugar plantations, from December to May, have only four hours for sleep. On the coffee plantations they work moonlight nights. The proportion of sexes on the sugar plantations, is thirty females to seventy males. The proportion of females is larger on coffee plantations. Of the Africans imported contrary to the treaties and to law, the proportion of females is from 30 to 35 per cent.

Slaves are badly fed in Cuba. They have no ground to cultivate for themselves. They are shut up at night promiscuously in large enclosures called baracoons, having no roofs. Much of the whipping is for scaling the walls.

General Tacon was Governor General for four years. He took away twenty-eight thousand doubloons, perquisites of office. He received ten dollars a head on all persons brought into the Havana district from Africa. And yet the importations are contrary to law.

For nearly a year no cargo of negroes has been brought to Cuba under the Spanish flag—but they are brought under the flags of Portugal and the United States.

Dr. Channing's publications on slavery have found their way to Cuba, and their contents are privately circulated in Spanish manuscripts. Many of the young professional men are abolitionists, and the literature of the island is becoming more and more favourable to the doctrine of human rights.

A small volume of literary articles, by a man who was a slave in Cuba, has been printed in London.

THE 'NARAS, A NEW FRUIT.

The 'naras was growing on little knolls of sand; the bushes were about four or five feet high, without leaves, and with apposite thorns on the light and dark green striped branches. The fruit has a coreaceous rind, rough with prickles, is twice the size of an orange, or fifteen or eighteen inches in circumference, and inside it resembles a melon, as to seed and pulp. I seized a half-ripe one, and sucked it eagerly for the moisture it contained; but it burned my tongue and palate exceedingly, which does not happen when this most valuable fruit is ripe; it has then a luscious sub-acid taste.

Some plants of 'naras are now growing in England, (March, 1839,) from seeds which I brought home; they are a foot high, and beginning to branch, having two thorns at each articulation, and a stipule scarcely to be called a leaf between them, on the axis of which is the bud, but no leaves.—*Alexander's Expedition of Discovery.*

According to a statistical account drawn up by M. Hericart de Thury, the ground in the environs of Paris, cultivated as market-gardens, produces 30,000,000 fr. annually, and affords employment for 50,000 persons. The cultivation of flowers and fruits also makes a return of several millions of francs. About 200 florists of Paris and the neighbourhood supply the markets. The sale of flowers on the eve of great fetes is of incredible extent; on the 14th of August last, the eve of the Assumption, flowers were sold in Paris to the amount of 50,000 fr., and M. Hericart de Thury calculates that during the full winter season, these sales vary from 5,000 to 20,000 fr. a day.

TO THE MORNING STAR,

Seen rising, 5 A. M., 16th of October, 1839.

BY JOHN QUINCY ADAMS.

Bright star of morning! welcome to mine eyes!
More lovely than at eventide's decay,
For now thou comest with the dawning ray,
And soon the glorious lord of light shall rise.
Anon, his splendour shall emblaze the skies,
And in his flame thy own shall melt away;
But, mingled with his radiance, thine shall play,
With lustre, though unseen, that never dies.
Rise! Morning Star of man's immortal soul!
Rise! let thy beams irradiate the pole,
Redeeming earth from midnight's ebon sway!
Dispel the gloom of Slavery's deadly shade;
Turn to the ploughshare, War's ensanguined blade,
And glow with promise of unclouded day!
Quincy, Mass.

Observations on the Commencement and Progress of the work of Vital Religion in the Soul; on Divine Worship; and on the Partaking of the Flesh and Blood of our Lord Jesus Christ. By Samuel Rundell.

INTRODUCTION.

When we look around us, and observe how many conflicting creeds and systems of religion are sedulously propagated in the present day, our reflections on the subject should lead us to appreciate duly the privileges with which, through divine love and mercy, we are favoured,—the light of Christ being given to illuminate our minds, and the Holy Scriptures being placed within our reach, to which we can refer for instruction. In the Sacred Record, the doctrine preached by our Lord and Saviour Jesus, on the subject of the redemption and salvation of man, is clearly exhibited. As no other subject of equal interest and importance can be presented to us, may these few pages, designed to point out from this high authority the way by which all mankind may come to the knowledge of the truth, and be saved, prove the means, under the divine blessing, not only of convincing the merely nominal Christian of the imminent danger he is in; but also of encouraging the weak yet sincere believer, to hold fast the " grain" of living faith; (Matt. xvii. 20;) that so, amid all the conflicts with which he may be proved, his confidence may be steadily fixed on Him, who is the " Wisdom of God, and the Power of God." 1 Cor. i. 24. By submission to his command, "Take my yoke upon you, and learn of me;" and by the consequent fulfilment of his gracious promise, " ye shall find rest unto your souls," (Matt. xi. 29,) the sincere believer will be enabled eventually to adopt the ancient language, " The Lord is my light, and my salvation; whom shall I fear? The Lord is the strength

lest his deeds should be reproved. (21st.) But he that doeth truth, cometh to the light, that his deeds may be made manifest, that they are wrought in God."*

By this highly important declaration of our holy Redeemer, it appears, that the salvation of God through him, is not limited to any particular class or portion of mankind; for God so loved the world, that he gave his only begotten Son, " that the world, through him, might be saved." The Son of God " tasted death for every man;" (Heb. ii. 9;) and his salvation is partaken of by every one who truly and availingly *believes in his name.* Now the name of the Son of God, in this and in many other places of the New Testament, appears to signify, or have reference to, his divine attributes, viz. his power, life, light, &c. ;† and this light being " the life" of " the Word," or Son of God, is that " true light, which lighteth every man that cometh into the world." (John i. 4—9.)

By this light, shining in the hearts of all the children of men, they are, at seasons, reproved and convicted of sin; " for all have sinned, and come short of the glory of God." (Rom. iii. 23.) They who do not reject this light, are enabled to see the miserable state they are in while unregenerate, being in bondage under the power of sin, and defiled by its pollution. Deeply humbled by this view of their own real condition, their hearts

* In the 16th verse of the above quotation, faith in the Son of God is set forth as necessary to the obtaining everlasting life. In the 18th verse, condemnation is represented as the result of unbelief in his name. In the 19th and 20th verses, the cause of condemnation is more particularly described, being declared to consist in the not loving, but hating, which of course includes the not believing in, the light. Hence it appears, that in this very important passage of Scripture, *the light* should be regarded as the spiritual manifestation of the Son of God in the soul of man; " I, (said Christ) am the light of the world." John, viii. 12. The light

are contrited,—
nnce ;—and the
ciful to me a
Abiding in pati
ration of the div
for the receptio
tion of the ligh
Christ, whereby
which in some
exercised,) is
Thus the work
those who do n
the light, which
of God. (Titu
of his power, th
are in degree
bility is impart
brought to feel
value of a Sav
faith, through
God,* they are
baptism of his
sion of their p
who is " the pr
whole world."
thus walk in th
dience of faith
lievers formerl
our Lord Jesu
ceive " the ator
God. (Rom. v.
tism of the Spi
gresses in the
secret springs
alloy of sin, ho
which it lurks.
tive language of
fire." (Luke,

The soul-sat
these have four
and obeying, t
engage them s
tions; they sub

riches or pleasures,—but breaking off from and avoiding every thing which the light discovers to be evil, they gradually witness the advancement of *the new birth* in their souls:—old things pass away, and all things become new. (2 Cor. v. 17.) The floor of the heart, figuratively speaking, becomes cleansed; and the chaff burnt up "with unquenchable fire." (Matt. iii. 12.) Having thus received Christ Jesus the Lord, he giveth them "power to become the sons of God, (this grace being dispensed) to them that believe on *his name.*" (John, i. 12.)

The preceding description of the commencement, and progress of conversion, is not put forth as an exact delineation of the steps, by which *every one* is conducted, in whom this important work has been accomplished. The degree of depravity, by which the human character is marked, previously to conversion, is much greater in some cases, than in others. The repugnance, also, of the natural disposition, to submit to the control and guidance of the light of Christ, and thus to come under his yoke, varies greatly in different persons; and consequently a corresponding variation may be requisite, in the duration, and in the intensity, of "the refiner's fire." And when individuals of a serious disposition have embraced doctrines, which, by leading them to place an undue stress on outward forms and ceremonies, do really obstruct their coming to Christ, their prejudices are not easily overcome; these have to pass through a time of stripping—of breaking to pieces all those things, however highly esteemed, the tendency of which is to prevent their receiving Christ in the simplicity and humility of little children. (Matt. xviii. 3.) It may be expected, therefore, under this great diversity of character, that in the process of conversion, there would be "diversities of operations:—but it is the same God, which worketh all in all." (1 Cor. xii. 6.)

The foregoing view of faith in the name of the Son of God appears to have been *set forth by Him* in the latter part of that memorable portion of Scripture, with which this chapter commences. When our holy Redeemer had declared, "He that believeth not, is condemned already; because he hath not believed in the name of the only begotten Son of God; (John, iii. 18:) he proceeded, as already observed, still more particularly to point out *the cause* of condemnation: for he immediately added, "And this is the condemnation, that light is come into the world, and men loved darkness rather than light, because their deeds were evil. For every one that doeth evil hateth the light, neither cometh to the light, lest his deeds should be reproved. But he that doeth truth, cometh to the light, that his deeds may be made manifest, that they are wrought in God." From these words of our blessed Saviour, it may be inferred, that although professed Christians may be very assiduous, in acquiring the literal knowledge of the doctrines contained in the Holy Scriptures, and may profess an unlimited confidence in the benefits resulting from the sufferings and death of our Lord Jesus Christ; yet if they persist in disregarding and rejecting the

admonitions of the light, which at seasons shines in their hearts, in order to their being delivered from the power of sin, and cleansed from its pollution; they do not, according to his doctrine, truly *believe in his name,* and consequently they are in a state of condemnation. For such persons to conclude, while they remain in this state of unbelief and disobedience, that because they profess a faith in the personal appearance, sufferings, and death of Christ, therefore they are cleansed from their sins in his blood and are justified in his sight, would be indeed a lamentable and dangerous delusion.

In the texts before quoted from the sacred record, the Saviour of the world briefly, yet in clear and emphatic language, *preached the doctrine of the light;* showing, that this divine gift is embraced and adhered to, by every one who "doeth" or walketh in the path of "truth;" and that it is hated by all who do evil; who reject it, in order to escape from its convictions. Now, these two classes comprehend all mankind; and therefore it is clear, that this divine gift is dispensed unto all. Evil men could not hate or reject the light, if it did not in some degree illuminate their minds, reproving them on account of their evil deeds. Their not believing in, nor loving the light—refusing to hearken unto, and to obey its admonitions—gratifying their corrupt propensities by continuing in their evil ways,—*this* is the ground of their condemnation—the cause of their exclusion from that salvation, which is by and through Jesus Christ. On the other hand, they who walk in the paths of "truth" and righteousness, in the obedience of faith, following the guidance of the light, ordering their conduct and conversation according to its dictates,—all who take this course and persevere therein, are brought out from the darkness and death of our fallen nature, and are made partakers of the salvation of God, through Jesus Christ their Redeemer. (See 1 John, i. 7.)

But although all mankind may be comprised in these two classes, yet it is a truth clearly deducible from the doctrines of Scripture, that individuals may pass from either of these classes into the other. Those who have begun to walk in the paths of truth and righteousness, and even such as have made considerable advancement in a religious life, may, by not abiding in the fear of God, and in obedience to his holy will, fall into temptation, and be overcome thereby, and thus become evil doers. (Ezek. xxxiii. 18. 1 Cor. ix. 27.) So also, if individuals of the latter description, before the day of mercy passes away, happily embrace the renewed visitations of a long-suffering and gracious God, they may undoubtedly, through sincere repentance and faith in his Son Jesus Christ, be cleansed from the pollution of sin, and be brought into a state of reconciliation and favour with God. Thus the declaration of the apostle to the Corinthians will be applicable to them; when describing various kinds of evil doers, he adds, "And such were some of you; but ye are washed, but ye are sanctified, but ye are justified, in the name of the Lord Jesus, and by the Spirit of our God." (1 Cor. vi. 11.)

An Account of the Life of
[Continued from p]

The plague having rea Colchester, he found hims gospel love to visit his frie epistle of consolation and dresses them as brethren de having tasted of the good and the sweetness of the u had witnessed their souls liberty from the bondage c tion. He rehearses to the the Lord who, by his powe from the dust, made them his name and truth, and them to bear testimony the care and dealings towards y than I can demonstrate by you, then, but still trust upon his arm, depend upor and hope in his tender m same yesterday, to-day, a hath been with you when passed you round, to keep in the midst of perplexity, being distressed; and in p cour and cherish you, and r as with new wine. Surel is with you still, to comf nourish, and strengthen yc support, to keep and defe never leave you nor forsak sake him not. As you clea cleave to you." "Oh, dea loveth you, and I often ren cially since the Lord hat visit that place with such to give it to drink so dee his righteous judgments. that the Lord may keep s hollow of his hand, whate come upon your bodies. enable you to wade throug all with patience and conte not that he cares not for may permit the besom of l ments, which he hath se away the wicked, to swee your bodies from off the strange soever his doings nal reasoning, fleshy part, intends good in all his de the honest, simple, innocen ones. It is inwardly well ever outwardly is suffered t it shall be we well with the whatever the Lord perm their bodies. The sense know doth cause joy to s

of outward sorrow; is comfort in
rest in the time of trouble, content
ction in affliction, and enableth the
r all with patience. Such can say,
God be done. It is the Lord that
t thus to be, and why should I
gainst him, seeing he knoweth
est for me, and will not suffer any
fall me, but what, through his love
y, shall work for my good, as I
and am faithful unto him. Though
n vessel may be broken to pieces,
ned to the dust, and be taken away
cked are, who know not God, yet
ss I know it shall not be with my
shall be with theirs. It shall go
em that die and are cut off in their
: is, and shall be, well with my soul,
ll never die."

istle from which the above extracts
n, although addressed to Friends in
, was sent to various places in
d Norfolk, to which the pestilence
pread.

one of the little works which he
ng this long confinement, we learn
s the tenth imprisonment he had
r the truth. In his various epistles,
litations, and letters, there is much
t is most excellent, and well worthy
ntion of Friends of the present day.
roduce extracts from all, would ex-
memoir to an unreasonable length.
erefore pass on to his release from
sonment, This happened in 1672.
at time he married, we have no
out it was probably soon after his
nt. He was now again drawn
i the work of the ministry, and

to prison, where he remained for half a
year.

After this, he does not appear to have been
molested for several years. But in 1683,
Edmond Brume, priest of Woodbridge, began
again to stir up the magistrates against
Friends. At his instigation, the town officers
came on the 12th day of the sixth month to
the meeting in that place, and William being
on his knees at prayer, he was forcibly taken
from the house, and was, with several other
Friends, committed to Melton jail. The
charge in his mittimus was that he had been
at a Quaker meeting, which was contrary to
law.

William greatly rejoiced that the Lord
had seen meet that he should bear his testimony in this time of suffering with his friends
and brethren at home. He was kept a close
prisoner at Melton until the time of the next
sessions at Woodbridge. Here he was in-
dicted for having been at a riotous assembly,
the charge not agreeing with the tenor of
his mittimus. In answer to the indictment,
William testified that the meetings of Friends
were with no other design than that they
might wait on and worship the Lord their
God. They therefore could not be dangerous
to the government, or hurtful to the peace of
the community. He then pleaded "not
guilty."

The court then demanded that he should
give bail for his appearance at the next quarter sessions, and for his good behaviour in the
mean time. William knew that attending
religious meetings, or exercising his gift in
the ministry, would be considered a violation
of good behaviour, and he could not therefore
enter into such bonds. By direction of the

Se
There is a Calm
That softens sorr
There is a Peace
When all withou
There is a Light
When dangers th
That Calm to fai
That Peace rema
That Light shine

" Sometime
we have to un
to a great bun
us to lilt; bu
carry the who
the bundle, an
we are to ca
which we are
This we mig
only take the
day; but we c
by carrying y
day, and addi
lond, before v
Newton.

" The reli
pillars, namel
flesh, and wh
Spirit. Most
to separate th

" There ar
great service
should stand
David, Solom
Satan is a foo
a man in goin
with his neck

globe as equal to 196,836,658 square mile-, and as the land is to the water in the proportion of nearly 265,734, it follows that the whole land occupies a surface of 52,263,231 square miles, and the ocean has an area of 144,473,427 square miles."

The whole surface of the dry land is elevated more or less above the general level of the ocean, with some remarkable exceptions, which have only of late years been detected by barometical measurements, which have shown that a vast area of central Asia. "no less than 18,000 square leagues, is considerably below the level of the ocean," including the Caspian Sea and Lake of Aral, the surfaces of which have recently been shown to be 101·2 feet lower than the surface of the Black Sea. Therefore, should any convulsion of nature, like those which earthquakes are known to produce, depress the low sandy tract which now separates the sea of Asoph and the Caspian, the waters of the Euxine, and also of the Mediterranean and the Atlantic, would inundate an enormous extent of the sandy steppes of Asia, and entirely change the climate and face of that portion of the globe.

It has also lately been proved, by the experiments of G. Moore, Beck, and Professor Shubert, that the surface of the Dead Sea is 598 feet below the level of the Mediterranean, and the surface of the lake of Tiberias, from which the river Jordan runs into the Dead Sea, is 500 feet below the surface of the same sea. The Lake of Genesareth is also considerably below the level of the Mediterranean, so that, should any disruption of the land take place which separates the latter from the former, a tremendous deluge must be the consequence in Palestine and Arabia.—*London Mirror.*

THE FRIEND.

FIRST MONTH, 11, 1840.

We cheerfully comply with the supposed design in forwarding to our address the annexed circular, by giving to it a conspicuous place.

CIRCULAR

OF MOUNT PLEASANT BOARDING SCHOOL.

Inquiry having been frequently made, concerning the Mount Pleasant Boarding School, by distant Friends, the committee and officers of the institution have thought proper to issue the following circular for their information.

COURSE OF STUDY.

Elementary Branches—Spelling and Dictation; Reading, Writing, and Mental Arithmetic, and Conversations on Philosophy and Common Things.

English Language and Literature—History, Ancient and Modern, Grammar, Rhetoric, Criticism, Composition and Rhetorical Reading.

Mathematical Sciences—Arithmetic, Mental and Written, Algebra, Geometry, Mensuration and Surveying.

Natural Sciences—Geography, Natural Philosophy, Chemistry, Botany, Mineralogy, Geology and Natural History.

Intellectual and Moral Sciences—Mental and Moral Philosophy, Evidences of Christianity, and Recitations of Scripture.

☞Instruction will be given in the Latin and Greek Languages, if desired.

☞*Lectures* on Chemistry, Natural Philosophy, Astronomy, Natural History, Anatomy, Physiology, Intellectual and moral Science, &c. will be given twice or oftener each week.

☞The Institution has been lately furnished with Philosophical and Chemical apparatus, which will render the subjects they are intended to illustrate more pleasing, and more easily comprehended.

☞The friends of the school, in different parts of our country can render it great service, by contributions of Natural Curiosities, Apparatus, Books, &c. as such collections are calculated to create an increased desire for knowledge, as well as to familiarize the mind with the wonders and beauties of nature.

The school is divided into two sessions a year winter session of 28 weeks, and a summer session of 18 weeks. The winter session commences the second day after the 1st first day in the ninth month and closes about the last of third month. Two weeks vacation will be given at the end of the winter sess and four weeks at the close of the summer sess The price of board and tuition is $76.00 per year $46.50 for the winter session, and $29.50 for the summer session; one half to be paid in advance and remainder at the middle of the session. Books stationary are furnished at the Institution, at the low retail prices.

The house is open for the reception of students any time during the session, when not filled; but it very desirable that all should be present at the beginning and not leave until the end of the session. No reduction is made for absence, during the session time entered, unless sickness, or a similar emergency shall be the cause.

The regulations of the school, require the pupils use the plain language, and appear in a garb consistent with our profession. Boys will not be allowed to wear caps, double-breasted coats, or coats and waistcoats with falling collars. All that is merely ornamental to be omitted, and objectionable clothing will be turned, or altered, at the pupil's expense. Each article of clothing is to be marked with the owner's name. Outside garments should be of a dark colour, firm texture,—preference being given to worsted light woollen stuff—and the summer dress of the pupil should be of plain dark calico, gingham, or other suitable articles. Each boy should bring four shirts with collars attached, omitting loose collars and shirts; avoid unnecessary washing; and each pupil should be furnished with three towels—three dark coloured handkerchiefs—three pairs of stockings with strong pieces of tape sewed to them for tying to wash. Woollen stockings will not be allowed in summer unless the health of the pupil require it, and each student should be provided with cloth and yarn for repairing.

Pupils are not to bring, or circulate in the school any literary productions of an objectionable character and parents and others should not visit the school or bring students, on the First day of the week.

It will be the primary object of the committee and officers, to make the instruction imparted, bear upon the duties of life—to combine theory with practice and secure the moral and religious instructions of the pupils.

During the week, as well as on First days, occasions are taken for reading Friend's Journals, and appropriate doctrinal writings, and for otherwise acquainting the students with the history of our society, and the character of its founders. By order of the acting committee.   JOHN C. HILL, Clerk

G. G. Plummer, Jane M. Plummer, Superintendents. Barnabas C. Hobbs, Louis Taber, Moses D. G. Teachers—Male Department.

Delaroh B. Smith, Susan M. Thomas, Teachers Female Department.

12th month, 2d, 1839.

On our fifth page of to-day, we have commenced a republication of a pamphlet, known to few in this country, the author Samuel Rundell, which, divided into convenient portions, will probably extend into five or six numbers. We print from the second edition issued in London, 1838, and having given it a careful reading, feel safe in commending it to the attention of our readers, both young

THE FRIEN[

A RELIGIOUS AND LITERARY JOURNAL

VOL. XIII. SEVENTH DAY, FIRST MONTH, 18, 1840.

EDITED BY ROBERT SMITH.

PUBLISHED WEEKLY.

Price two dollars per annum, payable in advance.

Subscriptions and Payments received by

GEORGE W. TAYLOR,

NO. 50, NORTH FOURTH STREET, UP STAIRS,

PHILADELPHIA.

For " The Friend."

EDUCATION IN GREECE.

BY PLINY EARLE, M. D.

Among the nations of the earth holding, in respect to extent and population, a subordinate rank, there is no one which, whether we consider the degree of perfection to which its arts and sciences attained in the early ages of the world, or the position held by it in modern times, in relation to surrounding nations, has awakened a greater or more general interest than Greece. But a few years have elapsed since the sympathies of the Americans were awakened in behalf of the natives of that country, and liberal contributions were elicited, for the purpose of relieving them from some of the evils, at all times more or less attendant upon a protracted war, and, in their case, existing to an almost unparalleled extent. But, as the Greeks have established a sovereignty which is nominally, if not actually, independent, and as this new government has been in operation several years, doing something, at least, if it has not done all that it might have effected, towards the melioration of the condition of the people, it may not be uninteresting to some to take a glance at the results of the policy of that government in regard to education, one of the best criteria by which to estimate the utility of the political institutions of any country.

Six or seven years since, the Grecian government adopted a system of education and established institutions differing in grade ac-

of this kind for boys, but none for girls. The number of pupils in these is about three hundred. There are Hellenic schools and Gymnasia at Athens, Syra, Patrass, Missolonghi and Napoli di Romana. I believe that in most of these places the two institutions have hitherto been united into one. This is not true, however, in respect to Athens. The pupils of the Hellenic school at Patrass are divided into five classes, according to their intellectual acquirements. Those of the first class study reading, writing, the ancient Greek grammar, the catechism and mythology; the second class, arithmetic, analytical grammar, technology and Grecian history; the third class, geography, syntax, general history, mythology, Latin, and the higher mathematics; fourth class, geography, general history, mythology, prosody, Latin, and the higher mathematics; fifth class, ancient Greek authors, psychology, logic, Latin, the higher mathematics and natural philosophy.

As recently as the commencement of the year 1839, the three branches last mentioned had not been taught, from the want, as was said, of a suitable teacher. It is altogether probable that a deficiency of attainments, in the other branches, had prevented any exertions to obtain a teacher with the requisite qualifications for teaching these.

In the Hellenic school at Athens, the common branches are taught, together with the ancient Greek, geometry, and the elements of drawing. This school has eight teachers, and the number of pupils varies from 250 to 300. In the Gymnasium of the same city, where every thing taught is inculcated by lectures, the following branches are studied, viz. algebra, geometry, mathematical and political geography, modern history, ancient history, both sacred and profane, natural philosophy, and the French, English, German, and Latin languages. This institution has nine professors, and about three hundred students. The university includes four departments, literature and science, law, physic, and divinity. In the four there are about twenty professors.

The buildings of this institution occupy a

school, at tl
eight. Of
were borne
allowed to t
has not been
every one w
government
the public sc
ing adequate
or to refund
which has l
especial bon
school takes
cording to
first, or low
and write w
mental rules
tained some
the catechis
dition to the
must have a
Greece, the
arithmetic,
Greek langu
rank require
included in t
culture, ge
modern, dra
of the Gree
one had yet
leaving the
ers, those o
pensation of
the governm
month from
piques, or al
Those of th
90, and thos
month from
above menti

The Lanc
trass, is tau
building ere
Capo d'Istri
as well org
pline as som
United State
little in com
It is supplie

on the list but 142 answered to their names. The law is severe against such neglect, but its requisitions never being enforced it has become a nullity. It imposes a fine of six lepta for the first absence, and for subsequent ones, a gradual increase up to fifty drachmas. The teacher is required to keep a list of attendance, and, at the end of each month, to make a computation of the number of offences, in respect to absence, and present it to a magistrate, whose duty it shall be to adjudge the fine and require its payment.

There is a school for girls in Patrass. It was founded by an English lady, a member of the Society of Friends, who for several years forwarded ten pounds sterling, per annum, to contribute towards its support. It was continued under the care of the English, and became very flourishing, when a delegation from the government came to the persons entrusted with its management, thanked them for their labours and informed them that their assistance was no longer required. The school was, in fact, *seized* and placed under the care of Greeks. It is now taught by a young woman from Corfu, under the supervision of a priest of the Greek church. The number of its pupils is about 150. They study the same branches as the boys in the Lancasterian school, except that needlework is substituted in the place of drawing. We saw their writing books, and think they will compare with those of almost any school of the same grade. Some handsomely wrought samplers, lace veils and handkerchiefs, the work of the pupils, were also exhibited. One rarely sees a collection of more intelligent faces than we saw in this school. The girls are mostly dressed in the costume of western Europe, with the addition of the red cap worn by the men of both Greece and Turkey.

Cephas Pasco, one of the American missionaries resident at Patrass, accompanied me to the several schools in that city. He remarked that the Greek children have a remarkable facility of committing to memory, but are little disposed to reflect upon the knowledge thus obtained. I know not whether the government has made provision, in respect to schools, for such villages as have a population less than two hundred. There are, however, small schools in various places, some of which are private. The others may or may not be so. One of these is in the suburbs of a village between Athens and Marathon. It is kept in a building containing but one apartment, and that is unprovided with a floor. It serves the double purpose of grog-shop and school-house. When I visited it there were, in one extremity of the room, some half-dozen casks of wine, and in one other, a "bar," situated between the fire place, on one hand, and the school on the other. The pupils, eight or ten in number, were sitting cross-legged, some upon boards laid upon the ground, and others upon the ground itself. They formed a circle, in the midst of which there was a small fire kindled upon the ground. The old man who acted in the twofold capacity of teacher and bartender, was leaning against a bench smoking a pipe, the stem of which was three or four

feet in length. The boys were reading in concert and with loud voices. As they crossed themselves repeatedly, I suspected that they were reading either a prayer or a portion of the church-service. This proved to be the case. The old man patted their heads in approbation, chuckled over them and talked very rapidly in praise of the intelligence and proficiency of his pupils.

In connection with the foregoing remarks, it may be proper to refer to the efforts of Americans in the cause of the intellectual renovation of the benighted Greeks. The exertions of J. H. Hill, one of the American missionaries at Athens, are very generally known in this country. The school which, under the auspices of the society in whose name he acts, he has established and continued in active and serviceable operation, is now in a flourishing condition. It is taught in a large building, three stories in height, including the basement, erected for the purpose and situated very near one of the most interesting relics of ancient Athens, the gate of the new Agora. In its organisation it is divided into several departments, the number of pupils in each, of which, is stated below. They were furnished me by my friend, J. H. Hill.

Infant school,	.	.	.	.	250
Girls' superior school,			.	.	75
Boys' lower department,		.	.	150
Boys' upper department,		.	.	41
School of industry, for girls,			.	50
			Total,	.	.	426

In the upper department for boys, the subjects taught are reading, writing, orthography, geography, mental and practical arithmetic, ancient Greek grammar, sacred history, elements of natural history, the history of Greece, and the Greek catechism. The school of industry is intended to qualify poor girls for obtaining a livelihood by the use of the needle. A flourishing Sabbath school is taught in the same building, under the superintendence of J. H. Hill and his wife.

One of the most important institutions in Athens, whether we regard its rank or the ultimate effects which may be anticipated as its results, is the boarding and day school, under the special charge of the wife of J. H. Hill. It is now a little more than three years since this school was established, and, so long ago as the commencement of the year 1839, it had succeeded beyond the most sanguine expectations of its friends. The accommodations had already been increased, and, at that time, the number of pupils was 70. Of these, 25 were boarders, ten of whom were Greek girls from Constantinople. Twelve of the pupils are in part supported by the government of Greece, fifty dollars per annum being paid for each, from the public treasury. Ten of them are taught gratuitously, their expenses being defrayed by the association of ladies in this country, under whose auspices the school was established. They are being qualified for teachers. Already had this institution furnished teachers for a school at the Pyræus, and another at the island of

Crete, a[...]
under th[...]
Having [...]
tioned, I [...]
and day [...]
stated, is [...]
efficientl[...]
well in [...]
quiremer[...]
of a sim[...]
There w[...]
and thre[...]
the Fren[...]
branches [...]
for teach[...]
ral histor[...]
but one r[...]
ing from [...]
with an i[...]
From 4 [...]
in singir[...]
reading r[...]
This i[...]
thus far,[...]
fluence f[...]
The sen[...]
women i[...]
the Gree[...]
of knowl[...]
Prejudic[...]
come, th[...]
persed, r[...]
from its [...]
in these [...]
lustre w[...]
beauty, i[...]

s[...]

It has [...]
son and [...]
boundary[...]
pose the.[...]
of cours[...]
claim ou[...]
for their [...]
bered th[...]
cipated r[...]
limits fr[...]
tardy mi[...]
wented th[...]
law of I[...]
operatio[...]
the cens[...]
THOUSAr[...]
slaves! l[...]
under 1(...]
24; 823 [...]
and 55 ;[...]
upward r[...]
these we[...]
Somerse[...]

It ma[...]
should h[...]
years of [...]
attention [...]
feature r[...]
pealed, r[...]
very in t[...]
in 1798,[...]
settled r[...]

and retain them for life, and "foreigners and others having only a temporary residence in the state" may bring, employ, and take away their slaves, but not sell them. The mere statement of these laws is, I trust, sufficient to insure their reprobation, and if proper effort is made, their immediate abrogation. It cannot be that the *people* of New Jersey are willing to lure from the unhealthy, and, at times, insurrectionary south, slaveholders and their "gangs," and insuring them protection from those whom they defraud, induce them to take a "settled residence" in our state. That the law is not a dead letter the census shows, thirty-four slaves under twenty-four years of age having been introduced; how many above that number we cannot tell. A few in the vicinity of Trenton were brought from Georgia.

As to the treatment of slaves in New Jersey I know nothing; but human nature is the same every where. Where irresponsible power exists passion and avarice will induce abuses. There is little probability of a slave obtaining legal redress for harsh treatment, as in our courts slaves can only be witnesses *against each other*. We reprobate the similar law of South Carolina, &c., forgetting that our own statute book sanctions the enormity. Even the evidence of a *free* coloured person cannot be received, unless he can *prove* his freedom. A black skin being held presumptive evidence of slavery!!! Is New Jersey a *free state?* VERUS.

EFFECTS OF COLD.

The following is given in an English periodical, as part of an interesting paper on the Effects of Cold, which was read at the Royal College of Physicians, by the president, Sir Henry Halford.

In Dr. Hawkesworth's account of Captain Cooke's voyage round the world, we find it stated that Sir Joseph Banks and Dr. Solander landed on Tierra del Fuego, and determined to pass the night there in a wood, with a very meager and inadequate stock of provisions; and the unhappy result of the expedition was, that a black servant and two others of the party were left behind, dead in the snow.

You may remember, perhaps, that Xenophon, in his modest and beautiful narrative of the return of the ten thousand Greeks, after their invasion of Persia, under the younger Cyrus, whose death in the battle of Cunaxa (near the site of the modern Bagdad) rendered their retreat necessary, encountered some unusually severe weather in Armenia, which proved fatal to a part of the army. It had marched three successive days in the snow, and on the last a strong north wind having arisen, which blew in the faces of the men, thirty soldiers died in one night, seared as if burned, and stiffened by cold. We have also the same effect of cold described by Livy, in speaking of its influence on the animals passing over the Alps—

"Torrida membra gelu;"
and Milton has it—
"And frost performs the effect of fire."

I know that some philosophers, who are familiar with the operation of freezing mercury, have lost the skin of their fingers by touching the metal in its frozen state; and it is remarkable that Captain Back, in the interesting detail of his northern expedition, relates that the Indians compared the sensation imparted to their hands by the triggers of their guns, under extreme cold, to the effect of a red-hot iron.

When Charles XII., of Sweden, was killed at the siege of Frederickshall, in Norway, General Ahrenfield, who lay before Drontheim, resolved immediately to withdraw his army to Sweden. It had been reduced by casualities and by desertion to 7,300 men, and his enemies—the Danes and Norwegians—were in possession of all the principal roads which led to Sweden. He was compelled, therefore, to make his retreat over a desert, at Donnaschuntz, in Sweden. In short, the number of those who perished in this march amounted to 5,200, out of an army which mustered 7,800 when they broke up from Drontheim.

But the disastrous effect of cold on a retreating army was never more remarkably exemplified than in the return of Buonaparte from Moscow. You remember the insolent triumph with which, after having captured several of the capitals of the continent of Europe, he marched to invade the Russian empire at the head of an army of nearly half a million of soldiers. He did, indeed, possess himself of the ancient capital of that empire also. *Sed qualis rediit?* The determination of the Russians to resist the aggressor to the utmost, and at the expense of any sacrifice, even the voluntary burning of their ancient beloved city, compelled him to remeasure his steps over a country which he himself had laid waste, at a period of the year when frost and snow, co-operating with the strenuous efforts of his enemies, so harassed and discomfited him, that, out of that immense army, not more than 10,000 Frenchman and 25,000 auxiliaries lived to return to their native country; and, notwithstanding repeated desperate efforts, made in vain, for a while afterwards,

"He left the name at which the world grew pale,
To point a moral, or adorn a tale."

The emperor of the French left Moscow on the 19th of October, when he had ascertained the extent to which the fire had destroyed the resources on which he had depended for the subsistence of his army during the winter, and by the time that he had reached Smolensko, the frost had become intense; and although he had left Moscow with 120,000 men, and the fragments of various divisions besides had assembled here, it was with great difficulty that 40,000 men could now be brought together in fighting order. The troops often performed their march by night, by the light of torches, in the hopes of escaping their mer-

abridged where despondency, privation, and fatigue—all of which are likely to be the fate of a retreating army—combine with cold. The unhappy, benumbed being feels quite easy; he complains that he cannot move, in answer to solicitation to exert himself, and only desires to be left quiet. Insensibility steals softly over all his system, as the pressure upon the brain increases, and death, at length, sets his imprisoned spirit free.

When the cold has not been severe enough to destroy life entirely, it mutilates the extremities, and mortification ensues from a want of circulation. The Lascars who arrive in this country from India, in the winter season, are very prone to this effect of a climate so much colder than their native one, as the records of the hospitals in the city abundantly prove.

Analogous to this is the mortification which sometimes occurs to elderly persons from ossification of the arteries of the extremities. The blood-vessels having become impervious, the vital principle no longer pervades the feet and the toes, and they perish in consequence.

In confirmation of this opinion of the effect of cold in a severe degree upon the human frame under depression of spirits, and privation, and fatigue, and of its influence, also, short of fatality, I have an unpublished narrative of the misfortunes encountered by four English gentlemen in a pedestrian expedition from Contamine to Col de Bonhomme, in Switzerland. The walk is one of about three hours, in common circumstances. One of the party was a clergyman, who had lately lost his wife, and had been recommended to travel, in order to dissipate his sorrows. He set out with his companions, and a guide, on the 12th of September, 1830, at six o'clock in the morning, after a light breakfast. It had snowed in the night, and was raining a little when they started; but in a short time it began to snow again, and continued to snow during the whole of their passage. The path was soon obliterated, and they lost their way. After walking seven hours, the clergyman complained of his inability to proceed further. He said he could not move his legs. The danger of stopping, however, was pointed out. He was encouraged to go on, and was supported, assisted, carried; but at length he entreated that he might be left, adding that he was quite easy, ready to fall asleep, and must stay where he was. They then wrapped him up in his cloak, and left him, and proceeded as well as they were able; but at the end of eight hours, when they had at last regained the path, and had arrived within a quarter of an hour's walk of the place of their destination, another of the gentlemen failed in his strength, and could go on no longer. The other two, and the guide, attempted to carry him, but they fell headlong continually into the snow, and further exertions to assist him appearing vain, and only to endanger their own safety, he, too, was left wrapped up, as well as they could wrap him, and seated upon two knapsacks; and they redoubled their efforts to reach the Col de Bonhomme, in order to send assistance to him. They soon reached it, and instantly despatched seven

men to bring him in. He was brought in, in the course of an hour, alive, it is true, but he died the next day. A third lost three of his fingers soon after at Geneva; and the fourth escaped unhurt. I need not add that the poor clergyman was found a corpse.

Yet a cold climate, with the appliances of art, is not insalubrious, nor even incompatible with long life. The proportion of deaths annually in Switzerland is one in fifty-nine. The proportion in this country is one in sixty; though in the metropolis and in Birmingham, it is one in forty, if we may believe the latest statistical accounts. In France, throughout the whole of it, it is said to be one in forty; in Italy, one in thirty-three; in Rome, one in twenty-eight; owing, perhaps, to a malaria there. But what shall we say of Russia? I was informed by the late Russian ambassador, that there was a level country about 100 leagues square, sloping to the south, on the borders of Siberia, where a year rarely passed in the course of which some person did not die at the age of 130. The question one asked, of course, was—"Can you depend upon your registers there?" To which the reply was—"Any body who knows the practices of the Greek church will tell you that the bishops are more careful of their registration there, if possible, than your parochial clergy are in Great Britain.* Is it, then, that these people are longer in coming to their maturity than the inhabitants of southern latitudes, and proportionably slower in their decline and decay, as the oaks of the forest are compared with other trees? Or are they the Hyperborei of the ancients? of whose happiness we read in the Choephori of Æschylus, as if it were proverbial. We must presume that these people have the power of counteracting the effects of great cold by artificial resources, as experience and modern ingenuity contrive to provide for the safety of our mariners who have been exposed frequently of late years, almost with impunity, to the rigours of a winter even at the pole.

At one period arose geology from the earth's depths, and entered into mortal combat with a revelation which, pillared on the evidence of history, has withstood the assault. At another from the altitudes of the upper firmament was astronomy brought down, and arrayed in hostile altitude against the records of our faith; and this attack has also proved powerless as the former. Then, from the mysteries of the human spirit, an attempt has been industriously made to educe some discovery of wondrous spell, by which to disenchant the world of its confidence in the gospel of Jesus Christ. From lecture-rooms of anatomy, both in London and elsewhere, the lessons of materialism have been inculcated, and that for the purpose of putting a mockery on all religion, and driving it, if possible, from the face of the earth. But the most

* It is stated in a late number of the French Moniteur, that in the year 1835, there died in the Russian empire 416 persons of 100 years of age, and upwards —that the oldest was 135 years, and that there were 111 above 110 years old.

singular attempt to graft infidelity on any thing purporting to be a science has been made by those who associate the doctrines of phrenology with their denial of the Christian Revelation, as if there were any earthly connection between the form of the human skull and the truth or falsehood of our religion. The science of theology has been made a sort of play-ground for all manner of inroads in regard to human speculation; but it is not without a peculiar evidence of its own, unassailable and beyond the reach of external violence. It is not the hammer of the mineralogist that can break this evidence. It is not the telescope of the astronomer that can enable us to descry in it any character of falsehood. It is not by the knife of the anatomist that we can find our way to the alleged rottenness which lies at its core. It is not by a dissecting of metaphysics that the mental philosopher can probe his way to the secret of its insufficiency, and make exposure to the world of the yet unknown flaw, which vitiates the proofs of Christian faith. All these sciences have, at one period or other, cast their missiles at the stately fabric of our Christian philosophy and erudition; but they have dropt harmless and impotent at its base.—*Chalmers.*

TENDER-HEARTED LANDLORD.

"James," said a worthy merchant on Main street to his clerk the other morning, "go down to Water street, to Mr. ——'s and tell him his rent must be paid to-day; I can't wait any longer, as he's already two quarters in arrear."

The clerk obeyed the direction, and soon came back with great appearances of milkiness about the eyes.

"Mrs. —— wants to see you, sir, about that rent, very much, sir."

The merchant happily was at leisure, and went at once to visit his tenant. He found him extended upon a coarse bed, in an insensible stage of a dangerous malady. His wife was busy over a scanty fire; apparently preparing some simple aliment for her sick husband. Three little children sat shivering in the corner. His approach was unnoticed.

"Ma," said one of the little urchins, "when be you going to get breakfast?"

"Breakfast, my child, that is more than I can tell."

The merchant advanced.

"My good woman—my good woman—ahem—that is,"—and the worthy man felt very much like choking. He grasped his pocket-book convulsively, and laid some bills upon the table—he opened the door and disappeared.

"James," said he again to his clerk, "take this order to Mr. ——, and tell him to have the provisions delivered immediately."

The merchant felt much better' than he would have done, if he had got his rent. There is something in a good action that makes one's heart feel lighter—warmer—better. We would publish the good man's name, but we know he would dislike it, and we would not for all the world offend him.—*Massachusetts Spy.*

Observations on the Commencement and Progress of the work of Vital Religion in the Soul; on Divine Worship; and on the Partaking of the Flesh and Blood of our Lord Jesus Christ. By Samuel Rundell.

(Continued from page 118.)

Among other declarations of Christ, in accordance with the foregoing, are these: "I am the Light of the world; he that followeth me, shall not walk in darkness, but shall have the light of life." (John, viii. 12.) To some of the Jews, who through unbelief, were in danger of having this divine gift taken from them, he said, "Walk while ye have the light, lest darkness come upon you." "While ye have light, believe in the light, that ye may be the children of light." (John, xii. 35, 36.) These declarations of Christ, in which he represents himself under the character of "the Light," appear to have reference to him, principally as that divine Word, the life of which, as the apostle declares, is "the light of men." (John, i. 4.) By the operation of this Word, the work of regeneration is effected in them who believe, and walk in its light. They are "born again, not of corruptible seed, but of incorruptible, by the Word of God which liveth and abideth for ever." (1 Pet. i. 23.) Thus they become children of light—in other words, true Christians.

It may further be observed, that all who believe in the light of Christ, and walk in obedience to its manifestations from day to day, fully participate in the benefits procured by the sufferings and death of the Redeemer. "*If we walk in the light*," said the apostle, "as he is in the light, we have fellowship one with another, and *the blood of Jesus Christ his Son cleanseth us from all sin.*" (1 John, i. 7.) Hence it appears that the being cleansed from all sin, by the blood of Christ, is the blessed privilege of those who walk in the light.

Christ is the gift of God unto mankind, not only in respect of his outward, or personal appearance sufferings, and death, but also in respect of his spiritual manifestation in their hearts. The Almighty declares, "I will give thee for a light to the Gentiles, that thou mayst be my salvation to the end of the earth. (Isa. xlix. 6.) His salvation is freely offered unto all; but it is partaken of by those only, who in humility of mind receive and obey this manifestation of his holy light or Spirit; and embracing the faith, which is its fruit, are baptized in or into the name—the life and power, of the Father, Son, and Holy Spirit: —as it is written, "He that believeth and is baptized, shall be saved." (Mark, xvi. 16.) The faith of these will necessarily embrace the testimony of the Holy Scriptures, if they have access to this invaluable record, respecting the birth, life, doctrine, miracles, death, resurrection, and ascension of our holy Redeemer; for the gift of the light or Spirit of Christ, (especially with respect to the increased measure, in which it is vouchsafed under the Christian dispensation,) is altogether to be ascribed to the efficacy of that which Christ, in his appearance in the flesh,

did and suffered for the human race. Thus the benefits of the "one offering," are not depreciated, but are more *completely* exalted by the doctrine of the manifestation of the Spirit, or universal saving light and grace.

It is evidently the practice of the wicked one, to endeavour by various stratagems, to induce the children of men to shut up their hearts against the influence of the light, or Spirit of Christ; and as far as he succeeds in this design, so far he maintains his evil power and dominion in the world. If, for instance, the subtle adversary, in order to effect his purpose, can so far beguile any of the professors of Christianity, as to instil into their minds, a secret aversion to the heart-searching manifestation of the light of Christ; and if, by following up the advantage he has gained, he can induce them to affix on this doctrine, the stigma of enthusiasm, or fanaticism, it then becomes easy for him to persuade them to disregard and to reject altogether, the admonitory dictates of this divine Teacher in their own minds, in order that he may without restraint bring forth his own works of darkness in their hearts. But he who was manifested "to take away our sins," was also "manifested to destroy" these "works of the devil." When this blessed light of Christ is believed in and allowed freely to shine in our hearts, the works of the adversary at their very origin are clearly detected; and if its warnings and requisitions are observed, we are enabled, through the power which it imparts, to "overcome the wicked one" in his various devices,—"to deny ungodliness and worldly lusts, and to live soberly, righteously, and godly in this present world." (Titus, ii. 11, 12.)

The great importance of this divine gift unto mankind appears very evident, in the account given of it, by our Lord Jesus Christ, in the texts which have been already quoted. The apostolic epistles also, furnish corroborating testimony, by the designations under which they describe it, and by the effects which they attribute to it. In the epistle to the Corinthians, it is declared, that "God, who commanded the light to shine out of darkness, *hath shined in our hearts*, to give the light of the knowledge of the glory of God, in the face (or manifestation) of Jesus Christ. But we have this treasure in earthen vessels, that the excellency of the power may be of God, and not of us." (2 Cor. iv. 6, 7.) The same apostle describes this divine gift, also as "The grace of God, that bringeth salvation, and hath appeared unto all men." (Titus, ii. 11, 12.) He also represents it as the Spirit of God" or "of Christ." (Rom. viii. 9.) "A manifestation whereof, is given to every man to profit withal." (1 Cor. xii. 7.) It is also called "the Anointing" which "teacheth of all things." (1 John, ii. 27.) "Christ in you the hope of glory." (Col. i. 27.) The 5th verse in the 13th chap. 2 Cor. is very emphatic: "Examine yourselves whether ye be in the faith, prove your own selves, how that Jesus Christ is in you, except ye be reprobates."* "All things that

* "Reprobates," that is, not approved.

are reproved, are made manifest by the light, &c." (Eph. v. 13.)

In addition to the above, the following texts are adduced, as having reference to the same divine gift, under the character of "the Word," or the "Word of God." There are some professed Christians, however, who suppose, that these texts should be understood as referring to the Scriptures: the impropriety of this supposition, it is apprehended, will be now be quoted, be duly considered. It will be found to embrace attributes, which, it is conceived, are ascribable, not to the Scriptures, but to Christ, who is "the Word," by whom the world, and all things in it, were created. (Heb. xi. 3.)—The apostle Paul declares, that the righteousness which is of faith, speaketh on this wise, "Say not in thine heart, who shall ascend into heaven, that is, to bring down Christ from above; or who shall descend into the deep, that is, to bring up Christ again from the dead. But what saith it? The word is nigh thee, even in thy mouth, and in thine heart, *that* is the word of faith which we preach." (Rom. x. 8.) The apostle James exhorts, "Receive with meekness the engrafted word, which is able to save your souls." (James, i. 21.) The apostle Peter addresses the believers as "Being born again, not of corruptible seed, but of incorruptible, by the word of God, which liveth and abideth for ever." "All flesh is as grass," &c., but "the Word of the Lord endureth for ever." (1 Pet. i. 23, 24, 25.) In the Epistle to the Hebrews, we have a very particular description of this divine word. The apostle declares that "the Word of God is quick, and powerful, and sharper than any two-edged sword, piercing even to the dividing asunder of soul and spirit, and of the joints and marrow, and is a discerner of the thoughts, and intents of the heart. Neither is there any creature that is not manifest in his sight; but all things are naked, and opened unto the eyes of him, with whom we have to do." (Heb. iv. 12, 13.) Here this eminent apostle ascribes the divine attribute of omniscience to the Word of God. Now they who say the "Word of God," described in this text, is the Scriptures, must of course ascribe this attribute (omniscience) to them; but in doing this, they should consider whether they are not subjecting themselves to the serious imputation of *idolising the Scriptures.*

The apostle Paul teaches us that the Holy Scriptures were given by divine inspiration; and are "profitable for doctrine, for reproof, for correction, for instruction in righteousness, that the man of God may be perfect, thoroughly furnished unto all good works;" and they "are able to make wise unto salvation, through faith which is in Christ Jesus." (2 Tim. iii. 15, 16, 17.) They bear testimony to Christ, as the Saviour of the world; setting forth the doctrine which he preached, when personally on earth, and describing what he did and suffered for mankind. They also hold forth very clear declarations respecting his spiritual appearance in their souls, in order to effect their regeneration and sanctification. But in the various dispensations of "his grace and truth," unto mankind, the Lord Jesus Christ "the High Priest of our profession," (Heb. iii. 1,) works immediately or by outward means, as he pleases. Indeed one of the distinguishing excellencies of the Christian dispensation, is, that it leads to a communion with the Father and the Son, which is not dependent on any external medium. Through Christ we have "access by one Spirit unto the Father." (Eph. ii. 18.) While we highly estimate the benefit to be derived from the sacred record, we should not forget, that we shall abuse this precious gift, if we exalt it, so as to put it in the place of Him, who is thus described : " In the beginning was the Word; and the Word was with God; and the Word was God.—All things were made by him.—In him was life, and the life was the light of men." (John, i. 1, 3, 4.) Let us then, in ascribing to the Bible, all the honour which the inspired writers themselves attribute to it, be careful, not to exalt it above, nor to place it on an equality with, Christ or the Holy Spirit, from whom its authority is derived.*

In publishing this concise view of the commencement and progress of vital religion in the soul, the writer wishes to observe, that probably it may fall into the hands of religiously disposed persons of different denominations; some of whom may be ready to say, " this doctrine does not accord with that which we have been accustomed to hear from our ministers; it is a doctrine, which, in many material points, as far as our observation has extended, is seldom heard from the pulpit in the present day." Should objections of this kind be excited in the minds of any persons, who in sincerity of heart are seeking that knowledge which " is life eternal," (John, xvii. 3,) the writer entreats them to consider, that this doctrine was promulgated by our Lord Jesus Christ himself; and that his apostles preached substantially the same truths; of which assertion, abundant proof may be found, by reference to the various texts quoted in the preceding paragraphs.

While the reader is engaged in the investigation of this momentous subject, he is also earnestly entreated to recur to his own experience, in past seasons of serious reflection. Hast thou not witnessed, at least in some degree, the truth of the declarations of Scripture, to which, in the preceding pages, thy attention has been directed?—*Has not the light of Christ shone in thy heart?*—Has it not awakened thee from a state of carnal security, and placed thy transgressions in order before thee,—soliciting thee to break off from thy sins by repentance and amendment of life?—Thou mayst be well assured of this truth, that it is not the work of thy soul's

---

* Such, however, is the deference that is due to this authority, that the Scriptures are to be considered as the only fit outward test, by which controversies among Christians on religious subjects are to be decided; so that whatsoever doctrine is contrary to their testimony, may therefore justly be rejected as false; and whatsoever any persons, pretending to the Spirit, may do, which is contrary to the Scriptures, should be considered as the effect of delusion. See R. Barclay's Apology, Prop. 3.

---

enemy, thus *to detect*, and to *lay open* his own devices; he seeks to deceive, to cover up, and to darken, his own ways and baits, that their real nature and tendency may not be discovered. It is the light of Christ Jesus our adorable Redeemer that detects, and makes known the workings of the grand deceiver. If then thou art now convinced, by the concurrent testimony of the light or Spirit of Christ, and of Holy Scripture, that the doctrine preached by men (whom thou hast esteemed as ministers of the gospel,) is not in full accordance with that which Jesus Christ, and his apostles preached; surely eternal happiness is involved, in thy faithfully embracing the latter. And should this course of inward conviction and renovation of heart, prove very contrary to thy natural inclination, so as to be indeed a cross difficult to be endured; yet, remember, who it is that said, " Whosoever doth not bear his cross, and come after me, cannot be my disciple." (Luke, xiv. 27.) Be encouraged, then, *to bear this cross*, and faithfully to follow Christ, in the path of self-denial. It is one of the greatest privileges held out to thee by the Christian dispensation, that *He is given, to be thy " Leader," thy spiritual Guide* : (Isai. lv. 4:) and if, in humility of mind, thou obey the monitions of his holy light revealed in thy heart, *thou herein followest Christ.*

As this is an important point of Christian doctrine, the writer is inclined to repeat the assertion, that he, who truly believes in, and follows the light of Christ, is virtually a believer in, and follower of Christ; and therefore, a partaker of the benefits resulting from his sufferings and death.* On the contrary, he who practically disregards and rejects this light, disregards and rejects Christ; and thus deprives himself of that salvation, which those who believe in and follow Christ, partake of. These positions are supported by the texts quoted in the beginning of this chapter, taken in connection with John, viii. 12, and 1 John, i. 7: corroborating testimony appears also, in the following gracious declaration of the Almighty concerning Christ, already quoted: " *I will give thee for a light to the Gentiles:†*
that thou mayest be my salvation to the ends of the earth." (Isai. xlii. 6.) They who believe in, and follow this divine Light, are favoured with access to the fountain of wisdom and strength. Through faith, they receive power to fulfil its requisitions; and the obedient are rewarded with peace and joy. " Thanks be unto God for his unspeakable gift !"

May the attention of the sincere seekers

---

* This assertion is not invalidated by the fact, that some persons who have professed (although falsely) a belief in the light or Spirit of Christ, have disregarded and rejected the Holy Scriptures. As the Sacred Record was written under the inspiration of the Holy Spirit, and as this divine Teacher, in itself is unchangeable, it evidently follows that its influence never can lead any one to contemn that which it has dictated for our instruction. Therefore they who disregard and reject the Holy Scriptures, do plainly show, whatever they may profess, that their minds instead of being under the influence of the light or Spirit of Christ, are involved in gross darkness and delusion.
† The word " Gentiles," in the language of Scripture, appears to signify all mankind excepting the Jews.

---

after truth be turned, day by day, to this inward monitor, the true spiritual Guide. It will not lead you in the least degree to disregard the Holy Scriptures; on the contrary, it will enable you to understand them more truly in the sense in which they were written, than the best unassisted faculties of man can do, and to apply them most effectually to your individual instruction and comfort: moreover, the harmony which you will witness, as you advance in your religious progress, between the law of the Spirit written on the heart, and the precepts and doctrines contained in the Bible, as far as the latter apply to your individual states respectively, will not fail to afford you much satisfaction and encouragement. That you may then be kept from falling into any temptation, by which the enemy may strive to mar the Lord's work in your souls, may your secret aspirations, under the influence of the Spirit of Christ, frequently ascend unto your heavenly Father, with fervent desires, that his kingdom may come, and be set up in your hearts, and that his holy will may be done, in and by you, even in all things: and when the light of Christ points out what he requires of you, as individuals, both in doing that which is right in his sight, and in avoiding that which is evil, may the language of each soul be,— " Not my will, O Lord, but thine be done!" By thus endeavouring in all things to follow your Redeemer, through that divine aid, which will assuredly be granted unto every one, who seeks it in sincerity of heart; his gracious declaration, already quoted, will be fulfilled in your experience;—" I am the light of the world; he that followeth me, shall not walk in darkness, but shall have the light of life."

The apostle Paul made this observation respecting the Jews:—" When Moses is read," (who wrote of Christ, John, i. 45,) " the vail is upon their heart; nevertheless when it shall turn to the Lord, the vail shall be taken away." (2 Cor. iii. 15, 16.) So also it may be said now, of very many professed Christians,—that when they read the New Testament, the vail is, in some measure upon their heart: for although they receive the doctrine held forth in the Scriptures, concerning the outward, or personal appearance of Christ, his sufferings and death for mankind, which doctrine the Christian faith fully embraces; yet they are deficient in respect of that important article of the same faith, which the apostle enforces in this emphatic language,— " Examine yourselves, whether ye be in the faith; prove your own selves; know ye not your own selves, how that Jesus Christ is in you, except ye be reprobates?" (2 Cor. xiii. 5.) He also declares that, " If any man have not the Spirit of Christ, he is none of his." (Rom. viii. 9.) We may, however, confidently entertain the same assurance, concerning the professed Christians now adverted to, as the apostle expressed respecting the Jews; viz., that when their heart " shall turn to the Lord, the vail shall be taken away." When this change takes place, (*O that it may be speedily effected!*)—they will then be prepared to receive the light, or Spirit of Christ, for their "Leader;" (Isa. lv. 4,) and by submitting to his heart-purifying baptism, and following him in the path of regeneration and sanctification, they will bring forth the fruit of the Spirit, through its quickening, life-giving influence. This fruit, the apostle declares, is " Love, joy, peace, long-suffering, gentleness, goodness, faith, meekness, temperance. (Gal. v. 22, 23.) Again, "The fruit of the Spirit is in all goodness, and righteousness, and truth." (Eph. v. 9.) What greater blessing can the most enlightened philanthropist desire for the whole human race, than this,— that the fruit of the Spirit, as above described, may be universally brought forth? moral evil would then be driven from the face of the earth ; " The kingdoms of this world [would] become the kingdoms of our Lord, and of his Christ ; [who] shall reign for ever and ever." (Rev. xi. 15.)

(To be continued.)

For " The Friend."

An Account of the Life of William Bennit.
(Concluded from page 112.)

When William was brought again to trial, he plead his own cause before the jury, and that with so much effect, that they returned a verdict of " not guilty." The court were very much displeased at this, and persuaded the jury at the bar, to alter their verdict. They now returned " guilty of an unlawful assembly." Upon this it was ordered that William should be removed to Ipswich to be fined. The day was exceedingly cold, and it snowed much, but no remonstrance availed to delay the execution of the sentence. Being very feeble as to his bodily powers, he felt that it would be more than he could endure. As they were hurrying him away he said, "If it lay in my freedom to go or not, although I might gain much as to the outward, I could not [go,] my weakness is such ; yet for the truth's sake I am freely given up, though it prove the dissolution of my body." His death, indeed, appeared to be accelerated by the exposure he that day and night endured. Before he arrived at the prison in Ipswich, it was late in the evening, and there being many there and no timely notice given to the jailer, there were no beds for them to lie down on. Thus was this tender Friend, who had been thoroughly wet and chilled by the snow, obliged to sit up all night in that condition.

Being brought up at the ensuing sessions at Ipswich, he was fined twenty pounds, and committed until the fine should be paid. Being unwilling to answer some unreasonable demands from the jailer, he met with hard usage which aggravated the closeness of his confinement. At the next sessions he was again called into court, but no reference was made to the cause of his original commitment, or to the fine already set upon him ; he was told, however, that they had a particular order from the king to deal with him, and the oath of allegiance was proffered. But though declining in body, he was strong in spirit, and bore a clear and faithful testimony against oaths. Being sent back to prison, his weak-

ness increased, and signifying that his departure was at hand, his wife and several of his friends were permitted to visit him.

During the confinement of the sufferer, we learn from William Peart's testimony concerning him, that he was frequent in prayer with the Lord for the good of all, especially for those of the household of faith. The afflicted of all sorts were remembered in his petitions, particularly those who for the testimony of a good conscience were suffering bonds and imprisonments. He prayed that through the incomes of the Lord's heavenly life and blessed presence in and to their souls, their prisons might be made as palaces to them. He desired that God would be the comfort of those who were laid upon the bed of sickness and pain. That to such as were travelling by sea or land in his work and service, he would be a support, by his living power make their service effectual, and enable them with cheerfulness to bear whatever it might please him to appoint or suffer to befall them. Having learned to love his enemies, he often interceded for them, that the Lord might be pleased to turn their hearts to his fear, and to open their eyes to behold against whom they were striving. That they might look to the Lord Jesus, whom by their sins they had pierced, and whom in his members they had persecuted.

As at the very hour of his departure his wife with several other friends were sitting by the corpse, very sorrowful for their great loss, the love and life of God broke in upon them in an abundant manner, to their great refreshment and satisfaction. From this they were instructed, that although the servant had been taken from them, yet that the life of the Master would remain for all those who walked worthy of it.

It was on the twenty-third day of the fourth month, 1684, about three in the morning, that he laid down his head in peace with God, and died as a faithful sufferer for the testimony of the Lord Jesus. The outward walking of this valiant soldier in the Lamb's army was as becometh the gospel of Christ. It was as a light set on a candlestick, clearly apparent to all in the household of faith. His very enemies were forced to confess that he was a man of an honest, godly and upright life. In the town of Woodbridge, where he dwelt, the truth was honoured by the lustre which the world could see in his conduct and conversation. His life preached ; his behaviour was innocent, his words were very savoury, and ministered to his hearers.

He was very faithful to the testimony which God had given him to bear in word and doctrine ; and was often drawn to travel in the love of the gospel when in great weakness and infirmness of body. The feebleness of his body towards the last was great, yet the strength and vigour of his inner man would oftentimes seem to swallow up all external appearance of weakness. He would frequently go to meeting when his friends thought he had more need to be in bed. The love which drew him forth to attend meetings in times of great weakness and illness, was with him therein to strengthen him to serve the Lord

his God, in ministering to his people. Oh, the sweet streams that at such seasons flowed from him as from a pleasant fountain ; truly they were to the refreshment and consolation of the right seed and the true birth. He would often appear filled with the strength of life, and such heavenly courage that he would seem as a giant refreshed with new wine, and ready to run a race. Yet, when his testimony was ended, and his service for that time over, he would be almost ready to die away.

Oh, could the children of the family in this day be but stirred up to the faithful dedication of their time, and their talents, to the cause of their Lord and Master, they would witness preservation through all the trials and sufferings of time, and be enabled at last to lay down their heads in the same quiet peace and serenity of mind which crowned the close of William Bennit. He was a simple, honest-hearted member of our religious Society, brought experimentally to witness the saving sanctifying operation of the light of Christ, and prepared to uphold it in the face of the world, as a principle of life and salvation. That which made him a proficient in the school of Christ is present to teach us the same lessons which he learned ; to impart the same doctrines which he received, and to bless us with the same sanctified graces which adorned his conversation in this world. But we shall never find them in theory, or in study ; biblical commentators cannot give them ; learning and science cannot of themselves attain them. Come then, let us go to the only true fountain spring of spiritual knowledge in the obedience of faith, and there we shall receive them. Let us trust in the revelations of the Spirit of Christ, take him for our teacher, and following in the path which he opens before us, time shall witness our sanctified probation, and eternity our measureless reward.   N. E.

THE VAIN SHOW.
From Leighton's Lectures on the 39th Psalm.

They are happy persons, (but few are they in number,) who are truly weaned from all those images and fancies the world dotes so much upon. If many of the children of men would turn their own thoughts backwards in the evening but of one day, what would they find for the most part, but that they have been walking among these pictures, and passing from one vanity to another, and back again to and fro, to as little purpose as the running up and down of children at their play! He who runs after honour, pleasure, popular esteem—what do you think ? Does not that man walk in an image, pursuing after that which hath no other being than what the opinion and fancy of men give to it ?—especially the last, which is a thing so fluctuating, uncertain and inconsistent, that while he hath it, he hath nothing ? The other image that man follows and worships, is that in the text; that wretched madness of *heaping up riches*. This is the great foolishness and disease especially of old age, that the less way a man has to go, he makes the greater provision for .

it. When the hands are stiff, and fit for no other labour, they are fitted and composed for scraping together. But for what end dost thou take all this pains? If for thyself, a little sober care will do thy turn, if thy desires be sober; and if not so, thy diligence were better bestowed in impairing and diminishing of these; that is the easier way a great deal. And if it be for others, why dost thou take a certain unease to thyself, for the uncertain ease of others? And who these are thou dost not know; may be, such as thou didst never intend them for. It were good we used more easy and undistracting diligence for the increasing of those treasures which we cannot deny are far better, and whosoever hath them may abound therein with increase: he knows well for whom he gathers them; he himself shall possess them through all eternity.

If there were not a hope beyond this life, there were reason for that passionate word in Psal. lxxxix. 47; *Why hast thou made all men in vain?* To what purpose were it for poor wretched man to have been all his days tossed upon the waves of vanity, and then to lie down in the grave, and be no more heard of? But it is not so: he is made capable of a noble and blessed life beyond this; and our forgetfulness of this is the cause of all our misery and vanity here.

It is a great folly to complain of the shortness of our life, and yet to lavish it out so prodigally on trifles and shadows. If it were well managed, it would be sufficient for all we have to do. The only way to live indeed, is to be doing service to God, and good to men: this is to live much in a little time. But when we play the fool in mispending our time, it may be indeed a sad thought to us, when we find it gone, and we are benighted in the dark so far from our home. But those that have their souls untied from this world and knit to God, they need not complain of the shortness of it, having laid hold on eternal life. For this life is flying away, there is no laying hold on it; and it is no matter how soon it goes away; the sooner the better, for to such persons it seems rather to go too slow.

DULL BOYS.

We are not to conclude that those who are at first exceedingly dull, will never make great proficiency in learning. The examples are numerous of persons who were unpromising in childhood, but were distinguished in manhood for their great acquirements.

Adam Clarke, D. D., was taught the alphabet with great difficulty. He was often chastised for his dulness; it was seriously feared by his parents that he never would learn; he was eight years old before he could spell words of three letters. He was distinguished for nothing but rolling large stones. At the age of eight, he was placed under a new teacher, who, by the kindness of his manner, and by suitable encouragement, aroused the slumbering energies of his mind, and elicited a desire for improvement. It is well known that he became even more distinguished for his various and extensive ac-

quirements, than he had ever bee stones.

Isaac Barrow, D. D., for tw years after he commenced goin was distinguished only for qua rude sports. This seemed to b passion. His father considered l for usefulness or respectability a he often said, if either child wa hoped it would be Isaac. But wards became the pride of his fat and an honour to his country. pointed master of Trinity Colle, time the king said, "he had giv to the best scholar in England."

The Rev. Thomas Halyburton Professor of Divinity at St. Ar until he was twelve years old, a sion to learning. I might me other examples to illustrate the —*Davis's Teacher.*

REVIEW OF THE D

An ancient said, "The reflec night are deepest." And it has be that David, in the nineteenth Psa speech to the day, and wisdom t night. It is an excellent advice of and the verses that contain it, do serve to be called *golden*, "The not allow ourselves to go to s have seriously revolved the ac day, and asked ourselves, "What amiss? What good have I done, to do? that so we may reprove what has been wrong, and take of what has been as it ought."

Rowe's translation and paral follows:—

Let not the stealing god of sleep surl
Nor creep in slumbers on the weary
Ere ev'ry action of the former day
Strictly thou dost and righteously su
With reverence at thy own tribunal
And answer justly to thy own demar
Where have I been? In what have I
What good or ill has this day's life e
Where have I fail'd in what I ought
In what to God, to man, or to mysel
Inquire severe, whate'er from first to
From morning's dawn till ev'ning's .
If evil were thy deeds, repenting mo
And let thy soul with strong remors
If good, the good with peace of mind
And to thy secret self with pleasure
Rejoice, my heart, for all went well

THE FRIEN

FIRST MONTH, 18,

Our Jersey friends we hope gard the short, but pithy and pu many, perhaps, startling artic entitled Slavery in New Jersey. lature of the state, if we misthi in session, and perhaps it may late for an energetic attempt to the removal of the evil complain it has been suffered to sleep lon

We refer our readers to the the present number for an artic Education in Greece, which

THE FRIEND.

A RELIGIOUS AND LITERARY JOURNAL.

VOL. XIII.   SEVENTH DAY, FIRST MONTH, 25, 1840.   **NO. 17.**

EDITED BY ROBERT SMITH.

PUBLISHED WEEKLY.

Price two dollars per annum, payable in advance.

Subscriptions and Payments received by

GEORGE W. TAYLOR,

NO. 50, NORTH FOURTH STREET, UP STAIRS,

PHILADELPHIA.

From Silliman's American Journal of Science and Arts.

Account of a Journey to the Côteau des Prairies, with a description of the Red Pipe Stone quarry and Granite boulders found there; by George Catlin, *in a letter to Dr. Charles T. Jackson.*

Read in the Boston Society of Natural History, Sept. 4, 1839, and communicated for this Journal.

Dear Sir—In the summer of 1835, whilst visiting the tribes of Indians on the Upper Mississippi, I spent some months at and in the vicinity of the Falls of St. Anthony. Whilst there, I resolved to pay a visit to the "Red Pipe Stone quarry," (as it is called,) on the "*Côteau des Prairies,*" the place where the Indians procure the stone for their red pipes; of which place I had already learned many very curious and interesting traditions from the Upper Missouri tribes. From the exceedingly strange nature of these traditions and the great estimation in which this place is held by the savages, as well as from a full conviction in my own mind, that this pipe stone, differing in itself from all other known minerals, might be a subject of great interest to science, I determined to see it *in situ*, and not only to understand its position and relations, but also to enable myself to give to the world, with more confidence, the strange and almost incredible traditions and legends which I have drawn from the different tribes, who have visited that place.

For this purpose I had made all the necessary preparations, and was to start in a day or two, accompanied by several officers and men of the garrison, whom Major Bliss, then in command, had allowed to accompany me. Just at this time, however, we got news by a steamer which arrived from below, that Mr. Featherstonhaugh, was near the fort with fifteen men, in a bark canoe, on his way up the St. Peter's, having been sent by government to explore the Côteau des Prairies. At this intelligence, I immediately abandoned the journey, and taking a corporal with me from the garrison, descended the Mississippi in a bark canoe, to Prairie du Chien, and afterwards to Rock Island and St. Louis. In that city I learned on the return of Mr. Featherstonhaugh, that he did not go to the Pipe Stone Quarry, and I returned to New York in the fall, and in the succeeding spring, made a journey from that city, by the way of Buffalo, Detroit, Green Bay, Prairie du Chien, and Falls of St. Anthony, to the Côteau des Prairies, and the Red Pipe Stone Quarry, a distance of 2,400 miles, for which purpose I devoted eight months, travelling at a considerable expense, and for a great part of the way with much fatigue and exhaustion. At Buffalo I was joined by a young gentleman from England, of fine taste and education, who accompanied me the whole way, and proved to be a pleasant and amusing companion.

From the Falls of St. Anthony we started on horseback with an Indian guide, tracing the southern shore of the St. Peter's river about eighty miles, crossing it at a place called "Traverse de Sioux," and recrossing it at another point about thirty miles above the mouth of "Terre Bleue," from whence we steered in a direction a little north of west, for the "Côteau des Prairies," leaving the St. Peter's river, and crossing one of the most beautiful prairie countries in the world, for the distance of one hundred and twenty or one hundred and thirty miles, which brought us to the base of the Côteau. This immense tract of country which we had passed over, as well as that along the St. Peter's river, is every where covered with the richest soil, and furnishes an abundance of good water, which flows from a thousand living springs. For many miles in the distance before us we had the Côteau in view, which looked like a blue cloud settling down in the horizon; and when we had arrived at its base, we were scarcely sensible of the fact from the graceful and almost imperceptible swells with which it commences its elevation above the country about it. Over these swells or terraces, gently rising one above the other, we travelled for the distance of forty or fifty miles, when we at length reached the summit, and also the Pipe Stone Quarry, the object of our campaign. From the base of this magic mound to its top, a distance of forty or fifty miles, there was not a tree or a bush to be seen in any direction; the ground was every where covered with a green turf of grass about five or six inches high; and we were assured by our Indian guide that it descended to the west, towards the Missouri, with a similar inclination, and for an equal distance, divested of every thing save the grass that grows and the animals that walk upon it.

On the very top of this mound or ridge, we found the far famed quarry or fountain of the Red Pipe, which is truly an anomaly in nature. The principal and most striking feature of this place is a perpendicular wall of close grained, compact quartz, of twenty-five or thirty feet in elevation, running nearly north and south with its face to the west, exhibiting a front of nearly two miles in length, then to disappears at both ends by running under the prairie, which becomes there a little more elevated, and probably covers it for many miles, both to the north and the south. The depression of the brow of the ridge at this place has been caused by the wash of a little stream produced by several springs on the top of the ridge, a little back from the wall, which has gradually carried away the superincumbent earth, and having bared the wall for the distance of two miles, is now left to glide for some distance over a perfectly level surface of quartz rock, and then to leap from the top of the wall into a deep basin below, and from thence seek its course to the Missouri, forming the extreme source of a noted and powerful tributary, called the "Big Sioux."

This beautiful wall is perfectly stratified in several distinct horizontal layers of light gray and rose or flesh coloured quartz; and through the greater part of the way, both on the front of the wall and over acres of its horizontal surface, it is highly polished or glazed, as if by ignition.

At the base of this wall and running parallel to it there is a level prairie of half a mile in width, in any and all parts of which the Indians procure the red stone for their pipes by digging through the soil and several slaty layers of the red stone to the depth of four or five feet. From the very numerous marks of ancient and modern diggings or excavations, it would appear that this place has been, for many centuries, resorted to for the red stone, and from the great number of graves and remains of ancient fortifications in its vicinity, (as well as from their actual traditions,) it would seem that the Indian tribes have long held this place in high superstitious estimation, and also that it has been the resort of different tribes, who have made their regular pilgrimage here to renew their pipes.

It is evident that these people set an extraordinary value on the red stone, independently of the fact that it is more easily carved and makes a better pipe than any other stone; for whenever an Indian presents a pipe made of it, he gives it as something from the Great Spirit; and some of the tribes have a tradition that the red men were all created from the red stone, and that it thereby is "a part of their flesh." Such was the superstition of the Sioux on this subject, that we had great difficulty in approaching it, being stopped by several hundred of them, who ordered us back and threatened us very hard, saying "that no white man had ever been to it, and that none should ever go." :

In my notes on Manners and Customs of North American Indians, which will shortly appear, I shall give a very novel and curious account of their traditions and superstitious forms about this great medicine or mystery place.

The red pipe stone will, I suppose, take its place amongst interesting minerals; and the "Côteau des Prairies" will become hereafter an important theme for geologists, not only from the fact that it is the only known locality of that mineral, but from other phenomena relating to it. The single fact of such a table of quartz, resting in perfectly horizontal strata on this elevated plateau, is of itself, as I conceive, a very interesting subject for investigation, and one which calls up on the scientific world for a correct theory with regard to the time when, and the manner in which, this formation was produced. That it is a secondary and sedimentary deposit, seems evident; and that it has withstood the force of the diluvial current, while the great valley of the Missouri from this very wall of rocks to the Rocky Mountains has been excavated and its debris carried to the ocean, I confidently infer from the following remarkable fact.

At the base of the wall and within a few rods of it, and on the very ground where the Indians dig for the red stone, rests a group of five stupendous b wlders of gneiss leaning against each other, the smallest of which is twelve or fifteen feet, and the largest twenty-five feet in diameter, weighing, unquestionably, several hundred tons. These blocks are composed chiefly of feldspar and mica, of an exceedingly coarse grain, (the feldspar often occurring in crystals of an inch in diameter.) The surface of these bowlders is in every part covered with a gray moss, which gives them an extremely ancient and venerable appearance, while their sides and angles are rounded by attrition to the shape and character of most other erratic stones which are found throughout the country.

That these five immense blocks, of precisely the same character, and differing materially from all other specimens of bowlders which I have seen in the great valleys of the Mississippi and Missouri, should have been hurled some hundreds of miles from their native bed and lodged in so singular a group on this elevated ridge, is truly matter of surprise for the scientific world, as well as for the poor Indian, whose superstitious veneration of them is such that not a spear of grass is broken or bent by his feet, within three or four rods of the group; where he stops and in humble supplication, by throwing plugs of tobacco to them, solicits their permission (as the guardian spirit of the place) to dig and carry away the red stone for his pipe. The surface of these bowlders I found in every part entire and unscratched by any thing, and even the moss was every where unbroken, which undoubtedly remains so at this time, except where I applied the hammer to obtain

some small specimens, which I brought away with me.*

The fact alone that these blocks differ in character from all other specimens which I have seen in my travels, amongst the thousands of bowlders which are strewed over the great valley of the Missouri and Mississippi, from the Yellowstone almost to the Gulf of Mexico, raises in my mind an unanswerable question as regards the location of their native bed, and the means by which they have reached their isolated position, like five brothers, leaning against and supporting each other, without the existence of another bowlder of any description within fifty miles of them. There are thousands and tens of thousands of bowlders scattered over the prairies at the base of the Côteau on either side, and so throughout the valley of the St. Peter's and the Mississippi, which are also subjects of very great interest and importance to science, inasmuch as they present to the world a vast variety of characters, and each one, although strayed away from its original position, bears incontestible proof of the character of its native bed. The tract of country lying between the St. Peter's river and the Côteau, over which we passed, presents innumerable specimens of the kind, and near the base of the Côteau, they are strewed over the prairie in countless numbers, presenting almost an incredible variety of rich and beautiful colours, and undoubtedly traceable, (if they can be traced) to separate and distinct beds. Amongst these beautiful groups, it was sometimes a very easy matter to sit on my horse and count within my sight, some twenty or thirty different varieties of quartz and granite in rounded bowlders, of every hue and colour, from snow white to intense red and yellow and blue, and almost to a jet black, each one well characterised and evidently from a distinct quarry. With the beautiful hues and almost endless characters of these blocks, I became completely surprised and charmed, and I resolved to procure specimens of every variety, which I did with success, by dismounting from my horse and breaking small bits from them with my hammer, until I had something like an hundred different varieties containing all the tints and colours of a painter's pallet. These I at length threw away, as I had on several former occasions, other minerals and fossils, which I had collected and lugged along from day to day, and sometimes from week to week.

Whether these varieties of quartz and granite can all be traced to their native beds, or whether they all have originals at this time exposed above the earth's surface, are generally matters of much doubt in my mind. I believe that the geologist may take the different varieties which he may gather at the base of the Côteau in one hour, and traced to the continent of North America all over, without being enabled to put them all in place; coming

* In a specimen with which we are favoured by Mr. Catlin, the feldspar is in distinct crystals, is tinted red and greatly abounds; the quartz is gray and white, and the mica black, while the moss covers nearly half the mass.—Ed.

at last to the unavoidable conclusion, that numerous chains or beds of primitive rocks have reared their heads on this continent, the summits of which have been swept away by the force of the diluvial currents, and their fragments jostled together and strewed about, like foreigners in a strange land, over the great valleys of the Mississippi and Missouri, where they will ever remain and be gazed upon by the traveller, as the only remaining evidence of their native ledges, which have been again submerged or covered with diluvial deposits.

There seems not to be, either on the Côteau or in the great valleys on either side, so far as I have travelled, any slaty or other formation exposed above the surface, on which grooves or scratches can be seen, to establish the direction of the diluvial currents in those regions; yet I think the fact is pretty clearly established by the general shapes of the valleys, and the courses of the mountain ridges which wall them in on their sides.

The Côteau des Prairies is the dividing ridge between the St. Peter's and the Missouri rivers; its southern termination or slope is about in the latitude of the Falls of St. Anthony, and it stands equidistant between the two rivers, its general course bearing two or three degrees west of north, for the distance of two or three hundred miles, when it gradually slopes again to the north, throwing out from its base the head waters and tributaries of the St. Peter's on the coast; the Red river and other streams which empty into the Hudson's Bay on the north; "La Riviere Jaques" and several other tributaries to the Missouri on the west; and the Red Cedar, the Ioway and the De Moines on the south.

This wonderful anomaly in nature, which is several hundred miles in length, and varying from fifty to an hundred in width, is undoubtedly the noblest mound of its kind in the world: it gradually and gracefully rises on each side, by swell after swell, without tree, or bush, or rocks, (save what are to be seen at the Pipe Stone Quarry,) and is every where covered with green grass, affording the traveller, from its highest elevations, the most unbounded and sublime views—nothing at all,—save the blue and boundless ocean of prairies that lie beneath and all around him, vanishing into azure in the distance, without a speck or spot to break their softness.

The direction of this ridge clearly establishes the course of the diluvial current in this region, and the erratic stones which are distributed along the base I attribute to an origin several hundred miles northwest from the Côteau. I have not myself traced the Côteau to its highest points, nor to its northern extremity, but on this subject I have closely questioned a number of travellers who have traversed every mile of it with their carts, and from thence to Lake Winnepec on the north, who uniformly tell me that there is no range of primitive rocks to be crossed—in travelling the whole distance, which is one connected and continuous prairie.

The surface of the top and the sides of the Côteau is every where strewed over with granitic sand and pebbles, which together

ive bowlders resting at
rry, show clearly, that
ge has been subject to
rrents, which could not
it, without having dis-
ts beautiful symmetry.
olished surface of the
pe Stone Quarry I con-
g subject, and one which
e a variety of theories,
hich it has been formed,
have led to such singu-
rtz is of a close grain
l, eliciting the most bril-
ol; and in most places,
o the sun and the air, its
lish, entirely beyond any
aave been produced by
perfectly glazed as if by
sufficiently particular in
ascertain whether any
of these rocks under the
ed to the action of the
d, which would afford an
in forming a correct
o it: and it may also be
ortance, that this polish
the whole wall or area,
r it in parts and sections,
ddenly, and re-appearing
e character and exposure
ame, and unbroken. In
l points most projecting
e highest polish, which
he case whether it was
or by the action of the

For "The Friend."

SLAVERY IN NEW JERSEY.

NO. II.

The act of 1804, designed to prevent the
future enslavement of infants, was considered
at the time of its passage as terminating the
struggle for freedom in our state. The claims
of nearly 12,000 persons to the inalienable
rights of men seem to have been lost sight of.
During the period which has since elapsed,
a large proportion of these individuals have
gone to "that far clime" where colour is
neither a crime nor a misfortune. Held until
death as slaves by the stern vigour of the law,
scarcely a voice has been heard to plead before the legislature for the rights of the dumb
—our down-trodden brothers and sisters. But
the remnant which still remain in bondage,
have, in their long-forgotten humanity, claims
to the unobstructed exercise of human rights.
The merely adventitious circumstance of their
birth being prior to the "4th of July, 1804,"
offers to the mind of the inquirer slender
ground for depriving them by legislative
enactment of freedom for life. Nor is the
claim founded upon the condition of their ancestors more valid, as wrongs inflicted upon a
parent can scarcely be alleged as sufficient
reason for inflicting them upon his children.
The case then stands thus. A considerable number of persons in New Jersey, many
of them in the prime of life, are the slaves of
other men; unable to acquire property or
freedom; not permitted to testify of injuries
inflicted upon themselves or others; liable to

TRAITS OF

The following
OF INDIAN CHA
cable to the Ab
Drawn from v
personal observa
TURNER, memb
Philosophical S
on." Publishec
Perhaps they wi
ers of "The F
proper to insert

I,

At certain se
meet, in order t
new their ideas
pum. On suc
around the place
and, taking out
another, hand th
and, that they r
ing, repeat the
livery, in their
means they we
premises recipr
boys related to
became early ac
al concerns. T
wampum docum
terity. The fo
how well this
swers the purpe
A gentleman

the preceding season, and the Pottowatomies had made the usual demand for his surrender. On a representation, however, that he was deeply in debt, and that his immediate death would cause much injustice to some of the traders, the injured tribe at length agreed to postpone his execution till another season; so that the products of his winter's hunt might be applied to the discharge of his debts. He had been successful in his exertions, and had paid the claims against him. He was about to leave his friends, and to receive, with the fortitude of a warrior, the doom which awaited him. He was now, for the last time, enjoying the society of all who were dear to him. No man doubted his resolution—no man doubted his fate. Instructions, however, were given to the proper officer to redeem his life, at the expense of the United States.

Indian Reminiscence, or a Tribute to Worth.

One of the prettiest touches of feeling, of which we have ever heard, (says a Philadelphia periodical,) was witnessed in the conduct of certain Indians from the interior, who some years ago visited our city.

When the statue in the hospital yard was pointed out to them as the figure of Miquon, or WILLIAM PENN, they all, with one consent, fell down on their knees before it; thus testifying, in the strongest manner in their power, their reverence for the character of one of the few white men who had treated their race with humanity.

It was not an exhibition got up for effect—it was the spontaneous result of a burst of feeling—of a deeply implanted feeling, which neither time nor distance had been able to eradicate. It had descended from father to son—had been cherished in the western wilds, and evinced itself in the midst of civilized society, by the strongest of natural signs—REVERENCE ON THE KNEE!

Sensibility.

A certain town of Maine once exhibited a striking display of Indian character. One of the Kennebec tribe, remarkable for his orderly demeanour, received from the state a grant of land, and settled himself in a new township, where several families had already been settled. Although not ill-treated, yet the common prejudice against Indians prevented any sympathy with him. This was made manifest at the death of his only child, while none of his neighbours came near him to join in the obsequies of burial.

Shortly afterwards he called on some of the inhabitants—"when white man's child die," said he, "Indian man be sorry;—he help bury him. When my child die, no one speak to me,—I make his grave alone—I can no live here." He gave up his farm, dug up the body of his child, and carried it with him two hundred miles, through the forest, to join the Canadian Indians.

Reminiscence of Times gone by. First Settlement of New York.

In the city of New York, 1789, General Knox, then secretary at war, gave a dinner to a number of Indians, who had come on a mission from their nation to the President of the United States. A little before dinner was served up, two or three of the Sachems, with their chief, or principal man, ascended to a balcony, which commanded a view of the city, the harbour, and Long Island. They remained but a short time, and returned apparently dejected—and especially the chief. This was noticed by the secretary; who said to him, "Brother! what has happened? This was noticed by the secretary; who said to him, "Brother! what has happened? You look sorry. Is there any thing to distress you?" "I'll tell you, brother," said the chief. "I have been looking at your beautiful city—the great water—your fine country—and I see how you are situated. But I could not help reflecting, that this fine country, and that great water, were once ours. Our forefathers lived here; they enjoyed it as their own domain. It was a gift from the Great Spirit to them and their children. At length, the white people (meaning the Dutch) came in a great canoe, and only requested permission to tie it to a tree, lest the waters should carry it away. We consented. They next said, that some of their people were sick, and they were desirous to land them under the shade of the trees. Their desire was granted. The ice now came, and they could not go away; so they begged for a piece of ground on which to build wigwams, to shelter against the cold and storms of winter. This was also granted. They next asked for some corn—they promising to go away when the ice was gone. The corn was given. And, when the ice was gone, our fathers told them they must go away with their big canoe. But they pointed to their big guns around their wigwams, and said they would stay there, and we could not make them go away.

Afterwards more came. They brought with them strong and maddening drink, of which the red people became very fond. They persuaded the red people to sell them some land. Finally, they drove them back, time after time, into the wilderness, far from the water, and fish, and oysters. They have destroyed the game; our people have wasted away; and now we live miserably and wretched; while you are enjoying our fine and beautiful country. This makes me sorry, brother, and I cannot help it."

The following anecdote shows forcibly the enfeebling and enervating influence of ardent spirits; and its utter impotency in enabling the body to resist extreme cold.

In the winter of 1829, the ship Tuscarora, captain Serrill, of Philadelphia, on her homeward voyage from Liverpool, was caught in the river Delaware, by a heavy northeast snow storm, and obliged to put into Chester piers for safety; at which place a considerable fleet of vessels had already taken shelter. As the storm was violent, and the weather very cold, it was a matter of no small difficulty to secure the vessels properly. The men were long exposed, and suffered so severely, that of all the crews then collected there, not one escaped without some of the men being frost-bitten, except the crew of the Tuscarora. This was remarkable, and naturally occasioned some inquiry into the cause of her exemption from the common lot. Her men had been as much exposed as the others, they were not better clothed, and having just got in from a winter's passage across the stormy Atlantic, may be supposed to be somewhat exhausted from previous fatigue, and therefore, rather more liable to suffer than some of the rest. Yet there was one individual on board of her who did suffer. He was not, however, one of the crew, had not just returned from a boisterous voyage with strength impaired, nor did his station require him to be nearly so much exposed to the weather as the sailors were,—for he was the pilot. It appeared on inquiry that the crew of the Tuscarora had refrained during the homeward passage from the use of ardent spirits,—that the crews of the other vessels had not so refrained,—and that the pilot of the Tuscarora was a drinking man. This at once explained the mystery, and was a most striking proof of the advantage of abstaining from the use of ardent spirits even when exposed to labour in severe cold.—Burlington Gazette.

The disinterested spirit of Paul did not appear only in his readiness to renounce every pecuniary claim. He was prepared, and stood always ready, to make a sacrifice of his ease, his health, his strength, his reputation, his life, in prosecution of his high calling, and for the advancement of the spiritual welfare of those among whom he laboured; nor could their ingratitude and insensibility to his services cool the ardour of his generous determination to do them good: "I will very gladly spend and be spent for you; though the more abundantly I love you, the less I be loved." Nor was this disinterested benevolence confined to "those who were Christians." If the maxim be just, "out of the abundance of the heart the mouth speaketh," then his unpremeditated reply to King Agrippa is a convincing proof of this. Struck with his fervent appeal to him, and with the character of his whole appearance and defence, the king could not refrain from exclaiming, "Almost thou persuadest me to be a Christian." "I would to God that not only thou, but also all that hear me this day, were both almost and altogether such as I am, except these bonds." O how gladly would Paul have continued to wear "these bonds;" how gladly would he have withdrawn his "appeal to Cæsar," and consented to "go up to Jerusalem, and there be judged," provided he could have obtained but half his pious wish! My brethren, if that sentiment, instead of lying in this despised book, had occurred in a Greek tragedy or a Roman story, or had it proceeded from the mouth of a Socrates or a Cicero, instead of that of an apostle, it would have been quoted an hundred times in the writings of the age as an effusion of the sublimest and purest benevolence. But, alas! our wits have taste and feeling on every point but one.—M'Crie's Sermons on the character of Paul.

Observations on the Commencement and Progress of the work of Vital Religion in the Soul; on Divine Worship; and on the Partaking of the Flesh and Blood of our Lord Jesus Christ. By Samuel Rundell.

(Continued from page 127.)

CHAPTER II.

THE WORSHIP WHICH, UNDER THE CHRISTIAN DISPENSATION, IS ORDAINED OF GOD.

In the coversation which our Lord condescended to hold with the woman of Samaria, he declared, "The hour cometh, and now is, when the true worshippers shall worship the Father in spirit and in truth; for the Father seeketh such to worship him. God is a spirit, and they that worship him, must worship him in spirit and in truth." (John, iv. 23, 24.) On other occasions he said, "No man cometh unto the Father, but by me." (John, xiv. 6.) "Without me, ye can do nothing." (John, xv. 5.) These declarations plainly indicate, that the worship of God, under the Christian dispensation, is of a spiritual character, and must be offered in truth;—that we cannot come unto the Father, and offer unto him this true worship, but by Jesus Christ, who is "*the way, the truth, and the life.*" Now, his assistance is communicated to us by the quickening influence of his Holy Spirit, without which the important duty of worship cannot be acceptably performed. This appears to have been the sentiment of the apostle Paul, for he declares, that "No man can say (or acknowledge) that Jesus is the Lord, but by the Holy Ghost," or Spirit. Hence it is apparent, that all worship, having a different origin, and which is of the kind designated by the apostle "will-worship," (Col. ii. 23,) being merely the act of self—the mere product of the will and wisdom of man—whether or not it be adorned with eloquence of speech, or accompanied with vocal or instrumental music, is not the true worship of God. Even if this worship be supported by human authority, and sanctioned by it as orthodox, still the declaration of Jesus Christ is applicable unto it: "In vain they do worship me, teaching *for* doctrines the commandments of men." (Matt. xv. 9.)

It may be said of merely nominal Christians in the present day, that, although in many instances, supineness respecting religion is the prominent feature of their character; yet in many other cases, they are zealous in supporting the creeds of the religious communities to which they are individually attached. But they refuse to submit to the convictions of the Spirit of Christ—they will not come to his baptism—they refuse to walk in the path of self-denial;—and the consequence is, that their hearts are not cleansed —the chaff is not burnt up—they remain carnally minded. Now while they continue in this state of resistance against the Spirit of Christ, there is cause for them to fear, that the worship which they offer to Almighty God, is not more acceptable in his sight, than was that of the Pharisees formerly. The Pharisees rejected Christ in his outward, or personal appearance; the merely nominal Christians above described, reject Christ in

his inward or spiritual appearance in their hearts. Like the Pharisees, they think they "have eternal life" in the Scriptures; and like them also, they will not come to Christ, that they "might have life." (See John, v. 39, 40.)

But it is much to be lamented, that the adversary of mankind so much prevails, not only in diverting the merely nominal Christian from even entering on the true spiritual course, but also in impeding the progress of many serious persons, who have *begun* to walk in it; and who, loving the Lord Jesus in a good degree of sincerity, have so far followed his holy guidance, as to be redeemed from many evil customs and vanities of the world. Yet, not patiently and humbly submitting to the operation of that power, by which "old things are" made to "pass away," and "all things to become new, and all things" to be "of God" (2 Cor. v. 17, 18;) their growth in the divine life is obstructed; and their strong attachment to human prescriptions relative to forms of worship, and ceremonial observances, prevents them from attaining that clearness of spiritual discernment, into which they would have been introduced, if, in childlike simplicity, they had been passive in the Lord's hand, like clay in the hand of the potter. In this state of defective submission to the divine will, they are not in a capacity duly to appreciate the benefits resulting from a practical faith in *the name* of the Son of God. Their views and dependence being outwardly directed, are limited to a merely literal explanation of this holy name; they do not therefore clearly perceive the necessity of seeking and waiting for divine influence, to effect the needful preparation of heart before him, previous to the offering of their prayers at the throne of grace. And if in their assemblies for divine worship they are not gathered together in the name of Christ, can it be expected that he will be in the midst of them? (See Matt. xviii. 20.)

The necessity of the influence of the Spirit of Christ in this solemn engagement of worship, is fully acknowledged by the apostle Paul; for notwithstanding his extraordinary gifts, and large experience in the ministry of the gospel, he declares, respecting himself and his fellow-believers, "Likewise the Spirit also helpeth our infirmities: for we know not what we should pray for as we ought; but the Spirit itself maketh intercession for us, with groanings which cannot be uttered;" (Rom. viii. 26,) that is, as a late writer* observes, "with fervent internal aspirations, the sensible effect of that powerful cause,— even the silent operation of the Spirit of truth; showing unto man, from time to time, his real condition; and teaching him immediately, both what to pray for, and how to pray aright."

By Him, Jesus Christ, let us then worship and serve God "in newness of spirit, and not in the oldness of the letter," (Rom. vii. 6,) believing in *his name*,—even in that name, which God hath exalted above every name,

"that at," or in* "the name of Jesus, every knee should bow, of *things* in heaven, and *things* in earth, and *things* under the earth; and *that* every tongue should confess, that Jesus Christ is Lord, to the glory of God the Father." (Phil. ii. 10, 11.) Were the true *bowing at the name of Jesus* understood, and witnessed in our hearts,—were we so humbled by his power, as to submit to his government, however contrary to our former views and practices, the performance of our religious, as well as of our moral duties, being brought under his holy influence and control, we should be Christians indeed; we should be able *in truth* to address Jesus Christ as our Lord;— his holy light being our leader, and his holy will, made known to us thereby, being done in and by us in all things. *Thus* would the name of Jesus be "exalted above every" other "name, to the glory of God the Father."

In the opening of this chapter, reference is made to those merely nominal Christians, who, rejecting the admonitions of the light of Christ, refuse to enter the path of self-denial, and are consequently disqualified; while they persist in their disobedience, for the performance of that worship which is in spirit and in truth. In pursuing this subject, it is designed to show the necessity, not only of entering, "in at the strait gate," but also of *continuing* "to walk in the narrow way," bearing the cross daily, and following Christ; that the Christian traveller may be preserved from taking up a rest in his own works, confiding in a form of godliness, without its life and power. May a sense of this danger, deeply impress the minds of such religiously disposed persons, as have been addressed in several preceding paragraphs of this chapter. In order to place the subject before them in a clear point of view, their attention is solicited to the following observations, founded principally on the precept of our Redeemer —of Him, let us ever remember, whom our heavenly Father has commanded us to hear: (Matt. xvii. 5:) "If any man will come after me,"—in other words, if any man will be a Christian indeed,—"let him deny himself, and take up his cross daily, and follow me." (Luke, ix. 23.) The effects which result from faithfully persevering in this course, which, we must acknowledge, our Saviour himself has pointed out to us, are thus briefly described by the apostle Paul: "I am crucified with Christ; nevertheless I live; yet not I, but Christ liveth in me: and the life which I now live in the flesh, I live by the faith of the Son of God, who loved me, and gave himself for me." (Gal. ii. 20.) This eminent minister of Christ not only witnessed the mortification of the flesh in his own person; but also enforced it on those among whom he laboured, in the following emphatic language: "This I say then, walk in the Spirit, and ye shall not fulfil the lusts of the flesh; for the flesh lusteth," or striveth "against the Spirit, and the Spirit against the flesh; and these are contrary the one to the other." (Gal. v. 16, 17.) And in order to convince us, that walking in the Spirit and bearing the

* Priscilla H. Gurney.

* J. G. Bevan's Life of Paul, note, page 363.

daily cross, are absolutely necessary to our becoming true Christians, he declares, "They that are Christ's, have crucified the flesh, with the affections and lusts." (Gal. v. 24.)

This observation of the apostle, respecting the conflict which takes place between the Spirit and the flesh, may be considered applicable to all mankind, however diversified as to religious profession. "Now whichsoever of these, (the Spirit or the flesh) we join with and obey, by this are we influenced and governed,—" His servants ye are to whom ye obey, whether of sin unto death, or of obedience unto righteousness." (Rom. vi. 16.) The Spirit prompts us to deny self, to crucify the flesh by taking up our cross daily, and to follow Christ; its purifying effects in our hearts being evinced, by our living soberly, righteously, and godly in this present world." And if this divine instructer in its further manifestations in our hearts be obeyed, through the ability which it imparts, it will enable us "to worship the Father in Spirit and in truth." But the tempter, through the medium of the flesh, strives in various ways to obstruct and prevent these most desirable results. When his efforts are ineffectual to draw awakened minds back again into their former habits of gross irreligion and sin, he then employs a more insidious snare, by assuming a religious character, and making a specious show of piety and devotion; but still opposing the Holy Spirit, by endeavouring through deceptive insinuations to prevent its salutary admonitions from being listened to and obeyed. In particular, he strives to excite, and to foster in the minds of many professed Christians, an aversion to the duty of "watching." (Eph. vi. 18; Mark, xiii. 37; —xiv. 38; Col. iv. 2;) under which, that of patient waiting for the Lord, in the exercise of faith and love, appear to be included; (see Hosea, xii. 6; Isai. xl. 31; Psalm xl. 1;) a duty mercifully designed as the means by which, in stillness,* (weak and feeble and liable to be misled as we all are of ourselves,) the sincere in heart may hear the voice of the "good Shepherd," and may receive from him instruction to perceive, and strength to avoid temptation, and ability also to offer up their prayers in His holy name, to their heavenly Father. But the enemy, through the carnal mind, suggests doubts, whether this duty of watching be really obligatory; and it may be apprehended, that in order effectually to divert the professors of religion from the practice of it, he prompts them to place their dependence on *their own* wisdom and activity, rather than to submit to so self-denying an exercise of mind. In all cases, in which these insinuations are embraced and followed, the secret monitions of the Spirit of Christ become gradually disregarded; darkness then ensues; and of course, the great work of purification of heart is obstructed. They seek, and soon find, a way to walk in, that is more agreeable to the natural will and the pride of the human heart, than that in which the denial of self, and the patient bearing of the daily cross are required. Their faith

* "Be still and know that I am God." (Ps. xlvi. 10.)

standing not in the power of God, but in the wisdom of men, (1 Cor. ii. 5,) they are frequently running after this or the other eloquent minister, not regarding the declaration of Christ—" the kingdom of God is within you," nor seeking (the manifestation of) this kingdom and the righteousness of God according to his command: (Matt. vi. 33:)—as they go on in this course, they become, in very many instances, strongly attached to forms and ceremonies, set up and enjoined by human wisdom and authority; and thus they are led into the practice of will-worship.

Alas! how greatly is the brightness of genuine Christianity obscured in the present day, among very many professors of it; through their not duly watching against and avoiding the influence and efforts of the carnal mind, in every form, under which it opposes, and strives against the Spirit of Christ. They will probably admit that watchfulness is requisite, as a preservative from the violation of the precepts of morality, in their general conduct and conversation; but they appear not to be sufficiently aware, that it is especially necessary in regard to the worship which they offer to Almighty God: for in this solemn engagement, as far as they are led by the activity of self or the flesh, so far are their minds disqualified for the reception of the life-giving influence of the Spirit of Christ, through which alone the acceptable worship, which is in spirit and in truth, can be offered. So that, however ardent their zeal may be in devotional exercises, and however delightful the animation it excites, yet, if the influence by which they are actuated in their worship, be not that of the Spirit of Christ, the conclusion seems inevitable, that it proceeds from self or the carnal mind.

How needful then is it, for professed Christians of every denomination, under a conviction of the great danger in which a mistake in this important concern would involve them, to lay open their hearts, in all humility and sincerity, to the discriminating ray of the light of Christ,—to that standard, to which the apostle directs our attention;—"All things that are reproved, are made manifest by the light, for whatsoever doth make manifest is light;" (Eph. v. 13;) that, under its direction, they may be enabled to form a true judgment, as to the influence which hath obtained the government in their minds. The sad consequences of continuing to act under the influence of that which opposes the Spirit of Christ, may be inferred from these words of the same apostle: "To be carnally minded is death, but to be spiritually minded is life and peace; because the carnal mind is enmity against God, for it is not subject to the law of God, neither indeed can be; so then they that are in the flesh" (they in whom the carnal mind predominates) "cannot please God:" (Rom. viii. 6, 7, 8;) to which it may be added, that however highly they may characterise their religious attainments, yet while they remain in this state, they are incapable of participating in that fellowship, which is "with the Father and with his Son Jesus Christ." (1 John, i. 3.)

In reverting to the description which the

apostle gives of his own experience already quoted, let us take into view what he says in another place, on the same important subject: "Know ye not, that so many of us as were baptized into Jesus Christ, were baptized into his death; therefore we are buried with him by baptism into death; that like as Christ was raised up from the dead by the glory of the Father, even so we also should walk in newness of life: knowing this, that our old man is crucified with him, that the body of sin might be destroyed, that henceforth we should not serve sin." (Rom. vi. 3, 4, 5.) By thus conforming to the doctrine of his Lord, in bearing the daily cross, and by submitting to the baptism of the Holy Spirit, the apostle was enabled to say, "I am crucified with Christ, nevertheless I live, yet not I, but Christ liveth in me."

May all professed Christians be stimulated and encouraged to press forward to the attainment of this state,* according to the measure of divine light or grace severally dispensed to them. May they be so humbled by the power of God, as to become willing to "deny self," "the flesh," or "the carnal mind;" in other words; to "put off *the old man* with his deeds;" (Col. iii. 9;) not only *his* grossly corrupt and sinful practices, but also *his* acts of devotion, *his* praying and singing, and (in respect to ministry) *his* preaching too. Then will they be enabled, by following Christ in the regeneration, (Matt. xix. 28,) to "put on the new man; which after God is created in righteousness and true holiness." (Eph. iv. 24.) They will become true worshippers, like the believers formerly, *worshipping God in Spirit, rejoicing in Christ Jesus, and having no confidence in the flesh.* (Phil. iii. 3.)

The Scriptures declare, that " as many as are led by the Spirit of God, they are the sons of God;" (Rom. viii. 14;) and that "the manifestation of the Spirit is given to every man to profit withal." (1 Cor. xii. 7.) How desirable, how indispensable then is it, that all, and especially those who call themselves ministers of Christ, should follow the puttings forth and leadings of his spirit in their own minds. The teaching of the Spirit of Christ is always in accordance with his doctrines and precepts, which are presented to us in the Scriptures; so that those who are in office, as ministers of Christ, if they be truly such, and be indeed led by his Spirit, will evince, not only in their conduct and conversation, but also *in their ministry,* a faithful adherence to that portion of his doctrine already adverted to, enjoining the denial

* Let it not be supposed that the high privileges which the Christian dispensation holds out to mankind, do not comprise the attainment of this state. Our Lord Jesus Christ prayed to the Father not only on behalf of his immediate followers, but for them also which should believe on him through their word,— "That they all may be one, as thou, Father, art in me, and I in thee, that they may be one in us. *I in them, and thou in me.*" &c.—concluding his supplication (which should be read with reverence and awe) in these words: "I have declared unto them *thy name,* and will declare it; that the love wherewith thou hast loved me, may be in them, and *I in them.*" (John, xvii. 20, 21, 23, 26.)

of self, the taking up the daily cross, and the following of him.

But, if any who undertake the office of a Christian minister, evince in their general deportment, a disposition to evade the denial of self, to shrink from bearing the cross, and from putting " off the old man with his deeds;" (Col. iii. 9;)—if, instead of following the Spirit of Christ, in their ministry, they follow the suggestions of their own " fleshly wisdom," (2 Cor. i. 12,) " teaching for doctrines the commandments of men," (Matt. xv. 9,) his own declaration seems to authorise the conclusion, that their worship is " in vain." And when any of those, who, declining the use of the modes and forms of worship prescribed by human authority, profess to depend on the direction of the Spirit of Truth, do not wait in humility of mind for its lifegiving influence, but in their self-will under the impulse of creaturely zeal, undertake to preach or to pray in their public assemblies, these performances, like the offering of strange fire under the Mosaic dispensation, (Levit. x. 1,) may be considered to be in an especial manner offensive in the divine sight. In all these cases, unless they submit to that divine word, which is said to be " like a hammer that breaketh the rock in pieces," (Jer. xxiii. 29,) and unless by its effectual operation they are brought to the experience of true humiliation and contrition, and through repentance witness purification of heart from pride and exaltation of self, they are in danger of becoming like unto some formerly, of whom we read,—that they " shut up the kingdom of heaven against men;" neither going in themselves, nor suffering " them that are entering to go in." (Matt. xxiii. 13.) And if they persist in this course, disregarding the convictions of the Spirit of Christ, which, from the time when they began to reject its admonitions in their own consciences, it may be presumed, has not failed at seasons still to reprove them, they will become more and more " laden with iniquity;" and by thus continuing in the transgression of the law written on the table of the heart, there will be much ground for them to fear, however successful they may esteem their ministerial labours, that ultimately their portion will be with those, concerning whom our holy Redeemer has declared, " Many will say to me in that day, Lord, Lord, have we not prophesied (or preached) in thy name? and in thy name have cast out devils? and in thy name done many wonderful works? And then will I profess unto them, I never knew you: depart from me, ye that work iniquity." (Matt. vii. 22, 23.)

(To be continued.)

For " The Friend."

Deceptive Editions of Religious Books.

I wish, through the columns of " The Friend," to make public what I conceive to be an act of duplicity and injustice.

There are few deviations from honesty held in greater abhorrence among men than that of wilfully defaming the character of the dead, or the helpless; and in no way is this odious practice more mischievously effected than by imputing to them, sentiments and language which they never held. A little book has just been published in this city, purporting to be a reprint of the " Guide to True Peace," &c.; but which, on comparison with that excellent work, will be found to consist of little more than a garbled and mutilated compilation of extracts from it. The author or publisher of this spurious edition, seems to me, guilty in no small degree of moral turpitude, in so changing the language, and misrepresenting the meaning of the eminently pious authors, from whose works " The Guide to True Peace" was originally compiled, as, in some instances, completely to alter their sense; and, in others, to confuse and mystify their meaning so as to render them almost unintelligible.

The chief aim of the publisher in this dishonest attempt seems to be, an endeavour to palm upon his readers his own infidel opinions, under the sanction of the names of the highly esteemed and Christian authors whom he has thus misrepresented, and endeavoured to make particeps criminis, or partakers in his insidious attempt to detract from the Divine character and holy offices of Jesus Christ, as the adorable Saviour and Redeemer of men.

In the accomplishment of this purpose, the publisher has not scrupled to resort to the old and oft-tried expedient of subterfuge and cunning. Instead of manfully avowing his difference of opinion in a preface, or in foot notes to his edition, and endeavouring to rebut with argument the sentiments of these excellent writers, and showing their contrast with his own views, as, in duty bound, a sincere lover and single-eyed searcher after truth alone should have done, he seems to have been solely intent on carrying his point by deception, and thus to lead astray the ignorant or unwary reader.

The awful, holy and scriptural name of the Most High, to which all true Christians love to bow in reverence and awe, seems to be particularly ungrateful to our publisher, and hence, in almost every instance, where it can be made to suit his purpose, the term God, as the name of the great Jehovah, is omitted in the reprint, and the name of some of his divine attributes adopted in its place, as for instance, almighty power, divine goodness, infinite purity, &c. &c.

In other instances, whole sentences or paragraphs are altered, or altogether omitted, especially where such sentences are inculcatory of the doctrine of the fallen and corrupt nature of man, and of his redemption through the atoning blood and mediation of Jesus Christ. Great pains also appear to be taken, though in an insidious manner, to divide Christ, and separate him that was made flesh, and was, and is, God, from the oneness and identity of the blessed Jesus of Nazareth. Thus, when the term Jesus Christ occurs in the original, one or the other title is dropped; and frequently the latter appellative is alone adhered to, as may be deemed most accordant with the confused and sublimated mysticism of modern deism.

Now, our object is not to restrict any man, or set of men, in their opinions on religious or any other subjects. We would concede to all entire freedom in this regard, and we claim the same privilege for ourselves. We freely accord to others the right to propagate and defend their sentiments in any fair and honourable manner, provided always, in so doing they adhere strictly to the regulations of propriety and truth.

When, however, we find one supporting his cause by a resort to dissimulation, as we conceive to be the case with the authors of the reprint before us, we not only lament the deep delusion of their sentiments, but are obliged to turn away in disgust from their recklessness of truth, and the utter want of sincerity and good faith which they evince.

With the view then of counteracting, as much as in us lies, the intended mischief, as well as for the sake of truth and justice, we have felt it incumbent on us thus to expose this insidious effort to disseminate, under the guise of distinguished and esteemed names, anti-christian sentiments.

Of the author or authors of this undertaking we have no knowledge, we do not even desire to know who they are, although we truly grieve that any one can be found willing to undertake so pitiful a task. We are told, however, that it is the work of a female of some respectability of character; if so, it will only furnish another instance of the sad and demoralizing effect on the mind of imbibing unsound and deistical opinions.

It will be right to say, before closing this article, that in using the term publisher in the above observations, we mean it to apply only to the person or persons who have prepared, and caused to be published this spurious reprint, and not to the publisher, technically speaking. We hope we have now said enough to put our young Friends on their guard, and to prevent any one who may read these remarks from being deceived, and induced to purchase this distorted edition of one of the most estimable little books in the English language.   C.

Communicated for " The Friend."

At the annual meeting of the Philadelphia Association of Friends for the Instruction of Poor Children, held first month 6th, 1840, the following persons were appointed officers for the ensuing year:

Clerk—JOSEPH KITE.
Treasurer—BENJAMIN H. WARDER.
Managers—Samuel Mason, Jr., Benjamin H. Warder, M. C. Cope, Geo. M. Haverstick, John M. Whitall, Joel Cadbury, Joseph Kite, James Kite, Samuel Randolph, Elihu Roberts, Samuel Scattergood, Loyd Bailey.

Extracts from the Report of the Managers to the Association.

The school for coloured infants has been under charge of the same teacher reported last year, and has been regularly visited by committees. It has been satisfactory to observe the attendance of the scholars, which evidence a continued disposition on the part of their parents or guardians to embrace the opportunity of placing their children under our care. The improvement in learning, and orderly conduct of the children, generally merit commendation. There have been 74 admitted during the year.

The school for coloured girls has also been visited by committees of the board. The class list is now 50, and the number admitted since the opening of the school is 84.

In the fifth month last, a committee previously appointed to take into consideration the method of instruction pursued in the girls' school, made a report, in which, after recommending a plan, they also suggest whether advantage might not arise from occasional exhibitions of suitable objects by means of the solar microscope, &c., not as a part of the regular system of education, but rather as a reward of good behaviour, those only to be allowed to participate who the teacher may say deserve such a privilege. Such exhibitions, while they may be made opportunities of conveying useful ideas, and thereby expanding and elevating their minds, would, we apprehend, afford a stimulus for them to obey the requisition of their teacher, and in this way have a salutary influence in advancing them in their usual studies.

The report of this committee was adopted, and some efforts have been made to carry their suggestions into effect. A solar microscope has been procured, the exhibition of which it is hoped will act as a stimulant and reward of application and good behaviour.

On the 20th of the twelfth month, a public examination of the scholars in the infant school took place, which was to the satisfaction of a considerable number of Friends who had assembled on the occasion. There were nearly 80 scholars present. The different questions proposed were promptly responded to by the children in conjunction, and all the exercises exhibited the care and ability of the scholars;—while the general neatness of the children's appearance was the subject of remark by many of the spectators, whose sympathies seemed awakened for the objects before them. The managers are of the judgment that examinations of this nature have a salutary influence on the teachers and the children, as well as on the parents and care-takers of the scholars, awakening a desire in all to be found fulfilling their respective duties in this course of education.

The library belonging to the school consists of 326 volumes, most of them small, and many of a character peculiarly calculated to interest the scholars.

Some years having elapsed since the publication of any narrative of the origin and proceedings of this institution, the board considered it advisable to reprint in pamphlet form a former edition, with some alterations and additions, including the constitution, by-laws, &c.—a portion of which have been distributed.

By order of the Board of Managers,
JOEL CADBURY, *Clerk.*

Philadelphia, 12th mo. 26th, 1839.

EMIGRATION.
THE RISING VILLAGE.

[Written by Oliver Goldsmith, a descendant of the author of "The Deserted Village," and published in 1820, with a Preface by the Bishop of Nova Scotia; and in imitation of his much-admired namesake, addressed to the author's brother:—]

When looking round, the lonely settler sees .
His home amid a wilderness of trees;
How sinks his heart in those deep solitudes,
Where not a voice upon his ear intrudes—
Where solemn silence all the waste pervades,
Heightening the darkness of its gloomy shades;
Save where the sturdy woodman's strokes resound
That strew the fallen forest on the ground.
See from their heights the lofty pines descend,
And, crackling down, their ponderous lengths extend;
Soon from their boughs the curling flames arise,
Mount into air and redden all the skies;
And where the forest late its foliage spread,
The golden corn triumphant waves its head.
His perils vanquished and his fears o'ercome,
Sweet hope portrays a happy, peaceful home;
On every side fair prospects charm his eyes,
And future joys in every thought arise.
His humble cot, built from the neighbouring trees,
Affords protection from each chilling breeze;
His rising crops, with rich luxuriance crowned,
In waving softness shed their freshness round:
By nature nourished, by her bounty bless'd,
He looks to Heaven and lulls his cares to rest.
Where the broad fire once sheltered from the storm,
Soon, by degrees, a neighbourhood they form;
And as its bounds each circling year increase,
In social life, prosperity, and peace,
New prospects rise, new objects too appear,
To add more comfort to its humble sphere.
Now in the peaceful arts of culture skilled,
See his wide barns with ample treasures filled;
Now see his dwelling, as the year goes round,
Beyond his hopes with joy and plenty crowned.
London Mirror.

THE FRIEND.

FIRST MONTH, 25, 1840.

The interesting case of the Amistad and the native African prisoners, which has so extensively been the object of public sympathy, has at length, it appears, been decided in favour of justice and humanity. We give the substance of the decision as contained in the Emancipator.

AMISTAD TRIAL—TERMINATION.

On Monday, Jan. 13th, the judge read an elaborate opinion, in which he decided:

1. That the District Court for Connecticut has jurisdiction, the schooner having been taken possession of, in a legal sense, on the "high seas."

2. That the libel of Thomas R. Godney and others is properly filed in the District Court of Connecticut.

3. That the seizors are entitled to salvage, and an appraisement will be ordered, and one third of that amount and cost will be decreed just and reasonable.

4. That Green and Fordham, of Sag Harbour, who claim to have taken original possession of vessel and cargo, cannot sustain their claim, and therefore that their libels be dismissed.

5. That Ruiz and Montez, through the Spanish minister, have established no title to the Africans, as they were undoubtedly Bozel negroes, or negroes recently imported from Africa, in violation of the laws of Spain.

6. That the demand of restitution, to have the question tried in Cuba, made by the Spanish minister, cannot be complied with, as by their own laws, it is certain they cannot enslave these Africans, and therefore cannot properly demand them for trial.

7. That Antoine, being a creole, and legally a slave, and expressing a strong wish to be returned to Havana, restoration will be decreed under the treaty of 1795.

8. That these Africans be delivered to the President of the United States, under the 2d section of the act of March 3d, 1819, and the 1st section of the law of 1818, still in force, to be transported to Africa, there to be delivered to the agents appointed to receive and conduct them home.

The court stands adjourned to meet at Hartford on the 23d inst., and meantime, the decree will not be entered, to give opportunity to the parties to appeal if they see fit.

A letter from H. G. Ludlow to one of the editors of the Journal of Commerce, dated January 13, gives the following particulars, which will be read with much interest:

"If ever men were inspired to present with sunbeam clearness the claims of righteousness, to the mind of a court, the counsel of the poor Africans were thus assisted. Messrs. Staples and Sedgwick, of your city, and R. S. Baldwin, of New Haven, "with thoughts that breathed and words that burned," stood up as their champions—and I speak not my own opinion only, but that of our community, who hung upon their lips spell-bound —when I say that for argumentation, and for eloquence too, their appeals to the court were irresistible. At times the feelings of the audience were inexpressible, and they showed their sympathy by external demonstrations of pleasure. The cause on the other side was conducted as well perhaps as its badness permitted.

The judge decided the case this morning, and in a masterly manner—showing an enlightened head and a warm heart. I do hope his decision will be given to the public at full length.

It was my happy lot to communicate this decision to Cinquez and his companions, and the scene is indescribable. No sooner was it communicated, than with hearts overflowing with gratitude, they rose and fell down at my feet. Words cannot express the joy they felt. They long to go back to their father-land. All of them but one belong to the Mendi tribe or nation. He sat still, not knowing what was meant; but through one of the others who can converse with him, our interpreter communicated the decision to him. He instantly prostrated himself at my feet at full length, clapping his hands for gladness of heart.

A stated meeting of the "Female Branch" of the Auxiliary Bible Association of Friends in Philadelphia Quarterly Meeting, will be held on the 30th instant, at 3 o'clock P. M. in Friends' Reading Room, Apple-tree alley. 1st mo. 25th, 1840.

THE FRIEND.

A RELIGIOUS AND LITERARY JOURNAL.

VOL. XIII.   **SEVENTH DAY, SECOND MONTH, 1, 1840.**   **NO. 18.**

EDITED BY ROBERT SMITH.

PUBLISHED WEEKLY.

Price two dollars per annum, payable in advance.

Subscriptions and Payments received by

GEORGE W. TAYLOR,

NO. 50, NORTH FOURTH STREET, UP STAIRS,

PHILADELPHIA.

Harrison on the Aborigines of Ohio.

The following is part of an article in the New York Review, and which in the National Gazette is attributed to our townsman Job R. Tyson. The article is in the nature of a critical notice or review of a Discourse on the Aborigines of the Valley of Ohio, &c. by William Henry Harrison, of North Bend.

The most interesting portions of this address, to us, relate to the ancient remains of the Indians which are scattered over the western country. No labour bestowed upon the subject of these antiquities, can be too great. They are intimately connected with the early history of the so called aboriginal inhabitants, and the curious question of their extraction. The late Doctor M'Culloch of Baltimore, laboriously compiled, some years ago, a very learned work upon these monuments of the past. Caleb Atwater, of Circleville, has added to our knowledge of the mounds and fortifications of the west, by his contributions to the Archæologia Americana. But there is a desideratum beyond what these performances supply. We want a thorough and ardent investigator, enthusiastic in the pursuit of some latent treasure—some concealed evidences of a higher civilization than we have yet had the good fortune to discover. How long hidden from the observation of travellers, were the Mexican or Tultecan antiquities, which, rivalling in elegance and skill the renowned glories of Egypt, are become the wonders of the world! We do not anticipate such trophies to the gallant antiquary who may explore the vast wilds of the Ohio and Mississippi, but we have no doubt that a species of knowledge would be gained of the greatest value, as connected with the antiquities of our land.

General Harrison ventures the opinion that the Indian remains on the Ohio river and at Circleville, are the works of a superior and different race of Indians from the present, and conjectures the line of their retreat from the country. In regard to the latter, he says:

"Taking into consideration all the circumstances which can be collected from the works they have left on the ground, I have come to the conclusion that these people were assailed both from their northern and southern frontier; made to recede from both directions, and their last efforts at resistance were made on the banks of the Ohio. I have adopted this opinion, from the different character of their works, which are there found, from those in the interior. Great as some of the latter are, and laborious as was the construction, particularly those of Circleville and Newark, I am persuaded they never were intended for military defences. On the contrary, those upon the Ohio river, were evidently designed for that purpose. The three I have examined, those of Marietta, Cincinnati, and the mouth of the great Miami, particularly the latter, have a military character stamped upon them which cannot be mistaken. The latter work, and that at Circleville, never could have been erected by the same people if intended for military purposes. The square, at the latter place, has such a number of gateways, as seem intended to facilitate the entrance of those who would attack it. And both it, and the circle, were completely commanded by the mound, rendering it an easier task to take than to defend it. The engineers, on the contrary, who directed the execution of the Miami work, appear to have known the importance of flank defences. And if their bastions are not as perfect, as to form, as those which are in use in modern engineering, their position, as well as that of the two long lines of curtains, are precisely as they should be. I have another conjecture as to this Miami fortress. If the people of whom we have been speaking, were really the Astecks, the direct course which that mode of retreat would afford, seems to point out a descent of the Ohio as the line of that retreat."

Other writers are of opinion that these works—those of Circleville especially—were intended and employed for military purposes. But upon this subject, Gen. Harrison speaks with the voice of authority. The writers on these remains lean upon one another, and the opinion of each is quoted by his immediate successor, without judgment and with little examination. Our author, on the contrary, under the guidance of an independent, cultivated, and vigorous intellect, has scanned these mounds and fortifications with the eye of an experienced and scientific soldier.

That these works were constructed by Indians of higher civilization than the present savages of North America, is manifest. The fortress at Marietta, with its subterranean communication to the river, exhibits no ordinary intelligence and skill. The fortification

at the mouth of the Great Miami, with its flank defences, shows a superior address to what the Indians supplanted by the white inhabitant could have accomplished. Dr. M'Culloch speaks of mounds on the Cahokia, opposite St. Louis, whose great magnitude must have required a thousand persons, employed for years, to construct them. The Indians on the Ohio were untutored savages, unacquainted with the useful arts, except those of the simplest manufacture and rudest necessity. But though unequal themselves to the fabrication of these remains, it does not follow that they were a different race of men from their architects. History proves that nations, like families, may undergo an injurious change. The present and former state of Egypt and Greece presents a humiliating contrast. The ancient Britons, as described by Cæsar, who so valiantly opposed the Roman legions, seem to have lost their identity when contending with the barbarians.

But whoever may be the authors of these works, nothing can be plainer than that the works themselves are of a high antiquity. Our author's well informed and luminous views upon this subject can with no propriety be withheld:

"The sites of the ancient works on the Ohio," says he, "present precisely the same appearance as the circumjacent forest. You find on them all that beautiful variety of trees, which gives such unrivalled richness to our forests. This is particularly the case, on the fifteen acres included within the walls of the work at the mouth of the Great Miami, and the relative proportions of the different kinds of timber are about the same. The first growth, on the same kind of land, once clear, ed, and then abandoned to nature, on the contrary, is more homogeneous—often stinted to one or two, or at most, three kinds of timber. If the ground has been cultivated, yellow locust, in many places, will spring up as thick as garden peas. If it has not been cultivated, the black and white walnut will be the prevailing growth. The rapidity with which these trees grow, for a time smothers the attempt of other kinds to vegetate and grow in their shade. The more thrifty individuals soon overtop the weaker of their own kind, which sicken and die. In this way there is soon only as many left as the earth will well support to maturity. All this time the squirrels may plant the seed of those trees which serve them for food, and by neglect suffer them to remain,—it will be in vain, the birds may drop the kernels, the external pulp of which has contributed to their nourishment, and divested of which they are in the best state for germinating,—still it will be of no avail; the winds of heaven may waft the winged seeds of the sycamore, cotton-wood, and maple, and a friendly shower may bury them to the necessary depth in the loose and fertile soil,—but still without success. The roots below rob them of moisture, and the canopy of limbs and leaves above, intercepts the rays of the sun and the dews of heaven; the young giants in possession, like another kind of aristocracy, absorb the whole means of subsistence, and leave the mass to perish at their feet. This state of things will not, however, always continue. If the process of nature is slow and circuitous, in putting down usurpation and establishing the equality which she loves, and which is the great characteristic of her principles, it is sure and effectual. The preference of the soil for the first growth, ceases with its maturity. It admits of no succession, upon the principle of legitimacy. The long undisputed masters of the forest may be thinned by the lightning, the tempest, or by diseases peculiar to themselves; and whenever this is the case, one of the oft rejected of another family will find between its decaying roots shelter and appropriate food, and springing into vigorous growth, will soon push its green foliage to the skies, through the decayed and withered limbs of its blasted and dying adversary,—the soil itself yielding it a more liberal support than any scion from the former occupant. It will easily be conceived what a length of time it will require for a denuded tract of land, by a process so slow, again to clothe itself with the amazing variety of foliage which is the characteristic of the forests of this region. Of what immense age, then, must be those works, so often referred to—covered, as has been supposed, by those who have the best opportunity of examining them, with the second growth after the ancient forest had been regained."

The character of the North American Indian has been so differently represented by different writers—the accounts of him have been so various and contradictory—that an honest inquirer will hereafter be at a loss how to form his conclusions. Old Burton, in his Anatomy of Melancholy, puts him down as a cannibal, and depicts him, in the quaint rhetoric of his time, as a monster in the human shape. The Spaniards, on the other hand, who followed the chivalrous but unfortunate De Soto to Florida—with a view, perhaps, to mitigate the ignominy of defeat—represent him as a magnanimous enemy, and almost superhuman in valour, agility, address, and the power of physical endurance. Though the portraits drawn at the present day, have not the extravagance of either of these pictures, they are equally unlike each other. The Puritans of New England describe the Indians of that region as children of the Devil, and only fit for carnage or servitude. The Friends of Pennsylvania, by pursuing a different policy, were able to give them a different character. They were proved to be capable of being mollified, by acts of good neighbourhood, into the most disinterested of friends, and the most faithful of adherents.

It need not be concealed, that recent occurrences have had a tendency to strengthen the animosity which has been fostered towards the Indians, and accelerated their removal to the inhospitable residence selected for them, beyond the Mississippi. Our author expresses a very favourable opinion of the endowments and native qualities of the Indians, and bears his testimony to the high susceptibilities of their moral and intellectual nature. We do not intend to open anew those wounds which are yet bleeding, by a particular reference to the hardships in the case of the civilized Cherokees, but we may be permitted to advert to the celebrated letter of John Ross to a gentleman of Philadelphia, in confirmation of the sentiments expressed by General Harrison in the discourse before us. We leave the fate of the Indians under Providence, in the hands of those who are able to control it, believing that for every violation of engagement which we commit—for every wrong and oppression and outrage which we inflict—there is a retribution in store, which will fall, one day, upon our devoted country. General Harrison's opinion of the Indian character, as we have said, is favourable. He pays a deserved tribute to many of the sachems, or chiefs, for high talents and elevated moral worth. As he acted in the capacity of agent for the United States at the treaty of Grenville, in the year 1795, and has had extensive intercourse with them in his military expeditions and as governor of the northwestern territory, his opinion is of intrinsic value. He uses the following pointed language in regard to the good faith of the government of the United States, during the administration of Jefferson and Madison, under whose successive appointments, we believe, he acted.

"I am satisfied that this is not the proper time to inquire how far the United States have fulfilled the obligations imposed upon them, by their assuming, at the treaty of Grenville, the character of the sole protectors of the tribes who were parties to it, a stipulation often repeated in subsequent treaties. But I will take this opportunity of declaring, that if the duties it imposed were not faithfully executed, during the administrations of Mr. Jefferson and Mr. Madison, as far as the powers vested by the laws in the executive would permit, the immediate agents of the government are responsible, as the directions given to them were clear and explicit, not only to fulfil with scrupulous fidelity all the treaty obligations, but upon all occasions, to promote the happiness of these dependent people, as far as attention and the expenditure of money could effect these objects."

We take leave, with regret, of this able and instructive discourse, premising the consciousness that we feel of not having done justice to its merits. It evinces, in an eminent degree, great patience of research, combined with high powers of historical and philosophical analysis, while the literary execution of the paper reflects great credit upon the distinguished author.

It is generally better to deal by speech than by letter; and by a man himself, than by the mediation of a third.—Bacon.

From the Library of Health.

Sleeping with the Head Covered.

Before the danger of sleeping with the head covered can be rendered sufficiently plain, it will be necessary to state one fact in physiology to which we have not yet adverted.

The same change of blood from bad to good—from pure to impure—which is effected in the lungs, is effected also, in some degree, on the whole surface of the body. Some insects or worms may be said to breathe entirely on the surface of the body. They have no lungs whatever. As we rise in the scale of existences, to snakes, &c., we begin to find lungs, or gills, in which a part of the change of blood to which we allude is effected. Rising still further in the scale of being, we find the lungs larger, and the skin less and less concerned in the change, till we come to man, and some few other animals, in whom the change is almost wholly accomplished by the lungs. Still we repeat it, the skin, even in man, has some share of the work of renovating the blood to perform, as may be shown by a very simple experiment, like the following:

When a person has lain several hours in a bed, closely covered to the neck with thick covering—say with the modern article called a comfortable—let a candle or lamp be introduced under the clothing, and it will soon be extinguished. The oxygen is so much diminished, and the carbonic acid gas so much increased, as to be incapable of supporting combustion; and by the same rule unfit for respiration. Let it be also distinctly understood, that this change is wholly effected without the agency of the breath; though, when the head is covered, it is, of course, accomplished much faster.

The fact, that we breathe, as it were, that is to say, purify the blood and poison the air with the whole surface of our body, as well as by means of the lungs, is of the utmost practical importance. It is of importance to be understood by those on whom we urge the duty of keeping the skin clean; for how can a foul skin—a skin varnished over with dust, or dirt—perform its delicate and important functions? It is of importance to be understood in order to know how to clothe ourselves; for all those forms and circumstances of our clothing which tend to embarrass or interrupt the action of the skin, in its work of assisting the lungs to purify the blood, are, of course, objectionable. It is, however, of still higher importance that it should be well understood by mothers in the management of their infants, not only in regard to cleanliness and dress, but particularly in regard to sleep.

For, in the first place, the bed-clothing ought to be as loose and porous as it can be, and yet, at the same time, retain a sufficient amount of heat, in order that the carbonic acid gas may have opportunity to escape, and the purer air find its way through it. Secondly, the clothes ought to be often thrown open, and the air under them thus exchanged for better. Thirdly, the child ought never to be allowed to sleep with its head under the clothing. Immense is the mischief done in this way, as we have already said, by ignorant parents, and even by those whose fault is more that of carelessness than of ignorance. Fourthly. He should sleep alone as much as possible, either in a bed or a crib, rather than with parents, brothers, sisters, &c. Fifthly. He should never be permitted to have domestic animals, as favourite dogs, or cats, sleep in the bed with him—a practice quite too common in our country—especially that of having a puppy in the bed. The child's body poisons the imprisoned air quite fast enough without any aid from dogs and cats, or from other human bodies; and, above all, without being aided by his own breath.

What has been said in relation to the management of infants will be generally applicable—the principles which it involves will at least be so—in the management of childhood and youth, and manhood, and old age. Fires without flues, lamps, candles, breathing, and the action of the skin, and many more causes, will continue to operate, to deteriorate the atmosphere at every period of existence. There will be no moment of our lives when we shall not need the whole active force of a free, vigorous pair of lungs, and a healthy skin to form and reform the blood, and to cast off the poisonous carbonic acid gas which is formed in these important processes.

A HINT TO MOTHERS.

A correspondent of the Cincinnati Chronicle has commenced in that paper the publication of a series of " Cases from the Note Book of a Physician," with a view of illustrating the evil effects of a great variety of medicines used in families, that should never be taken without the advice of a physician. We copy the first "case" on account of the interest which parents and nurses have in it.

January 19, 183-.—Early this morning I was called by Mr. ——, on Fourth street, to see an only child, said to be extremely ill of croup. Upon arriving at the house, I found the little patient, a beautiful and well-formed boy of sixteen months of age, upon the lap of a nurse, an elderly matron, apparently insensible, his countenance blue, face swelled or bloated, and his breathing deep, long, irregular, and stertorous. The nurse informed me that when she first awoke, she found him rubbing his nose, and hence she concluded he might have worms as well as croup.

Upon examining the case, it appeared that the mother of the child had gone to a party at 8 o'clock on the previous evening, leaving her child playful and well, and that when she returned, which was, at a late hour, she retired without inquiring into its condition. It was asleep with the nurse, and hence she supposed that all was well, until she was aroused in the morning by its deep and difficult respiration. Its parents, as well as the visiters, thought it now in the last stage of croup. The nurse had seen many in the same situation, and could not therefore be mistaken. To me, however, it was apparent there was no inflammation in the case. The child had

evidently taken a powerful narcotic, and from the time which had elapsed since it was administered, as well as from the deep congestion of the lungs and brain, it was probably beyond the possibility of cure.

As the nurse appeared to be extremely alarmed for the safety of the child, inquiring most anxiously whether it could recover, I came to the conclusion that she was not entirely ignorant of the cause of its present situation. I therefore took her aside, and informed her that it had taken a large portion of either opium or laudanum, and that it could only be relieved by a full knowledge of all the facts in the case. At first she declared, in the most solemn manner, that she had not given it any thing; but, when informed that the truth could be easily ascertained by an examination after death, she admitted she had at first given it a small portion of paregoric—all that was in the vial—an hour or two after the departure of the mother, in order to keep it quiet, as it cried continually for her return. As this did not have the desired effect, she gave it a small pill of opium, after which they both fell asleep. I inquired where she got the opium. She replied she always kept it with her, as paregoric or Godfrey's cordial had little or no effect upon some children, who were so very cross that she could not sleep without its aid. When questioned as to the size of the pill, she said it was not larger than a pea. I then informed her that the child must die, but agreed not to expose her, if she would promise never to administer opium again, in any form, without the advice of a physician. To this proposition she readily assented, and called heaven to witness that her promise should never be violated. She evidently did not intend to injure the child. She only wished to keep it quiet with as little trouble as possible.

All the means of cure known to physicians in such cases were immediately resorted to, but the poison had taken too deep a hold upon the nervous system. All my efforts to rescue it from an untimely grave, proved abortive, and in twenty minutes it ceased to breathe.

On the following day, the Gazette contained a notice of its death, and an invitation to the funeral, commencing with "Died of Croup." Thus perished a beautiful and healthy child. The cause of its death was never known to its parents. Neither of these can now be affected by its publication, as the mother has since followed her babe, and the father is absent from the city. The loss of her infant continued to prey upon her spirits, until her remains were conveyed to the churchyard, and placed beside those of her offspring. The nurse still remains. She may be assured that the cause of the death of her victim remains known only to her and myself. I am assured, however, that she has not seen so many in the same "condition" since that event, as before.

The above case is not one of fiction. It is strictly true, without a single exaggeration; and were I to give the names of the parties, the principal circumstances would readily be

remembered by those now living in the neighbourhood.

From the New York Observer.

NEWS FROM IRELAND.

70,000 JOINED THE TEMPERANCE SOCIETY.

Letter from Richard Allen, Esq., Cor. Sec. of the Irish Temperance Union, to E. Delavan, Esq.

DUBLIN, Nov. 19, 1839.
To E. C. Delavan, Esq.

Dear Friend,—Truly, we live in an age of wonders. The days of weakness are past; what was a little taper, kept alive by the greatest care of a few, has now burst into a mighty flame. The principles of total abstinence are now spreading with a rapidity which their warmest friends never dared to hope for. The weekly Royal Exchange meeting in Dublin has been so immensely crowded, that it has been found necessary to make a double charge for admission. But it is in the south that wonderful progress is making, under the labours of Theobald Matthew, a Roman Catholic clergyman. Here the people are joining by thousands, (9000 in two days lately;) Cork, Yonsel, Limerick, Clommel, Dungarvon, seem to vie with each other in the extent and vigour of their movements. In Limerick alone, 10,000 have taken the pledge. Dungarvon, recently the most drunken place in Ireland, seems to be taken by storm. A thousand and more have signed the pledge. In Drogheda are a thousand teetotallers, and during a space of nine months, since the reform commenced, there were two special, two quarter, and nineteen petty sessions, there was not a single person before it for any misdemeanor. In Belfast are 5000 members. Here workmen have formed themselves into anti-usage associations, with excellent effect. All the Dublin associations are in an active state, and in Culow, Acklow, Westford, Ennerserthy, Shillelagh, good societies are active in their operations; 70,000 have been added to us. Till liberty has been given to Sir E. Blakery, commander of the force in Ireland, to hold temperance meetings in the barracks, upwards of 2000 soldiers have been addressed; the meetings are to be held fortnightly.

We have now, for a few weeks, been assiduously feeding the press with small and valuable documents. In our leading Dublin paper, (daily,) the News Letter, we have had temperance matter five days out of six, and many others, both Dublin and provincial, have copied our articles. But a great and powerful ally has lately joined in the Dublin Evening Post, the Irish government organ, the editor and proprietor of which has fully entered into the cause, and states that he will leave no stone unturned, until he carries this great reformation through the length and breadth of the land. You may judge of the influence this new ally is likely to exert, when I inform you that it numbers 300 Roman Catholic clergymen among its subscribers; that it incessantly calls on them to follow in the footsteps of Father Matthew;

and that every paper (tri-weekly) has from one to two columns of temperance matter.

The morning press has last week sent an intimation that its columns were open to temperance; so that, with one exception, all the Dublin press is with us.

The Roman-Catholic clergy of Dublin, with Dr. Murray, the archbishop, at their head, held a meeting this week, for the purpose of taking up the question of temperance. There was some difference respecting the giving pledges and medals, free of charge. Theobald Matthew is doing wonders. From all accounts, he is a noble character. Of his worth, and the simplicity and openness of his measures, I have this day a very strong testimony, borne by the Church of England clergyman. Two Dublin Roman Catholic clergymen, Mr. O'Connell, and Dr. Yole, vicar-general, have taken a very active part. The latter recently got one hundred members at a meeting. Our former opponents now repeat to us our arguments in favour of temperance. It is undoubtedly owing to the Roman Catholic clergy having taken up the cause, that it prospers so greatly. Truly we live in an age of wonders, and we know not what effects, as regards the spread of temperance, the next month may bring forth. I must add, the Union have employed themselves a good deal in watching public movements, and have succeeded in two important points; one, in suppressing Donnybrook fair, which was a ruinous nuisance to our city population; another, for preventing, by an application to a peer, the passage of a bill, allowing grocers to retail spirits, which they had succeeded in carrying through the house.

Yours in the great work,
RICHARD ALLEN.

Soiling Cattle.—Soiling cattle is feeding cattle, either in barn or yard, through the summer, with new mown grass or roots. The following are some of its advantages over pasturing: 1. A spot of ground, which, when pastured upon, will yield sufficient for only two head, will maintain five head of cattle in one stable, if the vegetables be given in proper order. 2. The stall-feeding yields at least three times the quantity of manure from the same number of cattle. 3. The cattle used to stall-feeding will yield a much greater quantity of milk, and fatten faster than when they go to the field. 4. They are less subject to accidents—do not suffer so much from heat, flies, and insects; on the contrary, if every thing be properly managed, they will remain in a state of constant health and vigour.—*Von Thayer.*

And he Died.—It is reported of one, that, bearing the fifth chapter of Genesis read, so long lives, and yet, the burden still, *they died*—Seth lived nine hundred and twelve years, *and he died;* Enos lived nine hundred and five years, *and he died;* Methuselah, nine hundred and sixty-nine years, *and he died;*—he took so deeply the thought of death and eternity, that it changed his whole frame,

and turned him from a voluptuous, to a most strict and pious course of life. How small a word will do much, when God sets it into the heart! But surely this one thing would make the soul more calm and sober in the pursuit of present things, if their term were truly computed and considered. How soon shall youth, and health, and carnal delights, be at an end. How soon shall state-craft and king-craft, and all the great projects of the highest wits and spirits, be lain in the dust! This casts a damp upon all those fine things. But to a soul acquainted with God, and in affection removed hence already, no thought so sweet as this. It helps much to carry it cheerfully through wrestlings and difficulties, through better and worse; they see land near, and shall quickly be at home: that is the way. *The end of all things is at hand;* an end of a few poor delights and the many vexations of this wretched life, an end of temptations and sins, the worst of all evils; yea, an end of the imperfect fashion of our best things here, an end of prayer itself, to which succeeds that new song of endless praises.

PERICLES.

Plato in his writings, teaches that the end of education and of the instruction of youth is to make them better; not simply more intellectual, but more moral. He says of Pericles, he "filled Athens with temples, theatres, statues, and public buildings, beautified it with the most famous monuments, and set it off with ornaments of gold; but can any one name the man, native or foreigner, old or young, that he made wiser or better?" From the time of Pericles, the Athenians began to degenerate; they became idle, effeminate, babblers, and busy-bodies, fond of extravagance and vain superfluity.

For "The Friend."

VANITIES OF LIFE.

In early years our hopes run high,
On meteor wings our moments fly,
In future years we can descry
    Some fanciful felicity.

We vainly hope or fondly cling
To some imaginary thing,
Which can at best but sorrow bring
    With clouds of dark adversity.

Some trifling toy desire endears,
Seen through the mist of future years,
To our enchanted mind appears
    A gem of true reality.

We fly to catch the gaudy prize,
Whose glittering rays enchant our eyes;
But, Oh! the airy vision dies,
    And proves a vain uncertainty.

'Tis thus from youth to hoary age,
Some trifling toys our hearts engage,
But when on life's remotest stage
    We find that "all is vanity."

Since then each earthly joy is vain,
We may one lasting hope retain,
Whose kindly influence will remain
    To comfort frail humanity.

Then let us quit this lower sphere,
Nor longer cling with ardour here,
For earthly joys must ever wear
    The impress of mortality.

DIED, on the 25th RICHARD SMITH, of th England. He was an in the pursuit of busin and gratitude in a v about twenty years h late venerable Frienc two dollars per week. years, he was entirely has acknowledged, th have so good a place. his employer, he enter retailing of books and tal was very limited, an entire contentment. avoided running into so scrupulously upri, "honest Richard." and utility he was a and his voluntary offe disproportioned to hi times hesitated to ca every more than was married, and for many alone—and in reviewi that a kind and gra watched over and car nothing; for which fav His last illness was a it, he felt great povert that he "had nothir trust to, but the merc also said, that he was for him—his help mu he desired to settle do he might experience his illness advanced, h calm and quiet, which another occasion, he settling—and being a "settling away to a the last day, he app though, from the ind few words could be question, "how he fel and peaceful, and tha Saviour with him." Sl away, we believe, to a undefiled." "Mark upright, for the end o —— on the 11th o dence near St. Clairs THOMAS THOMASSON, J ing first the kingdom he was preserved in a fessed by our religiou of his departure drev granted to him, a we tance into that rest wl —— on the 11th o dence near Mount Ple JOHN HALL, aged 59 y ber of years an elder ing. Appointed to th evident he became own growth in the tru the flock so as to hele "follow me as I follov to which our religious exposed in this part c to stand as a faithfu earned that the min that ground on which when he first gathere people, that it might i man's wisdom, but in of power. As his ol with much solemnity i able expressions, evinc ness was peace, and th ness and assurance fr the Lord, in that he w the trying affliction h his hope of salvation Christ Jesus, on a re taken, he said, "I h vised fables," but subt

Observations on the Commencement and Progress of the work of Vital Religion in the Soul; on Divine Worship; and on the Partaking of the Flesh and Blood of our Lord Jesus Christ. By Samuel Rundell.

(Continued from page 135.)

CHAPTER III.

ON BAPTISM—CONTINUATION OF THE SUBJECT OF DIVINE WORSHIP, IN CONNECTION WITH OBSERVATIONS ON THE PARTAKING OF THE FLESH AND BLOOD OF CHRIST.

The qualifications requisite for admission into the church of Christ, do not comprise the observance of any of the types, ceremonies, and carnal ordinances, of the Mosaic dispensation, or of that of John the Baptist; which were fulfilled, and abrogated by the Son of God, in his personal appearance and death on the cross. But the apostle Paul plainly declares, that, "if any man have not the Spirit of Christ, he is none of his;" (Rom. viii. 9;) that is, if any man have not accepted the Spirit of Christ for his teacher, his baptizer, and his sanctifier, but on the contrary, in respect of these offices, have disregarded and rejected him, this man is not Christ's. Whatever may be his profession or performances, as to religion, whether he be a member of the established church, or a dissenter from it, he is not a member of the spiritual body or church, of which Christ is the Head. For according to the doctrine of the same apostle, the baptism, by which believers are introduced into this church, is the baptism of the Spirit; (1 Cor. xii. 13;) consequently it is not that of water, applied either by sprinkling or immersion. The baptism of the Spirit is an inward work; and it should never be forgotten, that it is not the body, but the soul of man, that is the subject of it.

John the Baptist makes a very clear distinction between his baptism with water, and the baptism of Christ: " I indeed (said he) baptize you with water unto repentance; but he that cometh after me is mightier than I, whose shoes I am not worthy to bear, he shall baptize you with the Holy Ghost and with fire:" (Matt. iii. 11.) and a similar and equally clear description of the two baptisms is given by our Lord himself. (Acts i. 5.) This baptism with the Holy Ghost, is that which has been already adverted to in the first chapter of this pamphlet. It is the work of the Spirit of Christ operating in the soul of man, principally immediately, but sometimes also instrumentally by the ministry of the gospel. This baptizing ministry appears to have been instituted by Jesus Christ himself; we do not find that he gave any commission to his disciples to baptize with water, or that he so baptized any one himself. We read that after his resurrection, he declared to them, " All power is given unto me in heaven and in earth," adding " Go ye therefore and teach all nations, baptizing them in the name (the divine power and life) of the Father, and of the Son, and of the Holy Ghost." (Matt. xxviii. 18, 19.) Of this baptizing ministry, we have an instance in the account which the apostle Peter gives of his visit to the family of Cornelius : " As I began to speak," said he, " the Holy Ghost fell on them as on us at the beginning : then remembered I the word of the Lord ; John indeed baptized with water, but ye shall be baptized with the Holy Ghost." To this the apostle added, " God gave them the like gift as he did unto us." (Acts, xi. 15, 16, 17.)

Thus the gift of the Holy Spirit appears to have accompanied the preaching of Peter, and was communicated *independently of water-baptism;* although this apostle was not then fully weaned from an attachment to this typical ordinance; for it appears that in this case of early Gentile conversion, he directed it to be administered to them, who had previously received the Holy Spirit ; (Acts, x. 47, 48,) although under a doubt, which the inquiry " Can any man forbid water," &c. seems to imply. In process of time, however, this eminent apostle's views on the subject of baptism appear to have been enlarged; for we find, that in his general epistle, describing the baptism by which believers are now saved, he declares, it is " not the putting away the filth of the flesh," (which is the proper effect of baptism, or washing in water,) " but the answer of a good conscience toward God, by the resurrection of Jesus Christ." (1 Peter, iii. 21.) Now this is a description of the effect of Christ's baptism with the Holy Spirit, and with fire; by which a death unto sin, and a new birth unto righteousness, through faith in that divine power, by which Christ rose from the dead, are witnessed ; and thus the answer or testimony of a good conscience is produced. The apostle Paul's language on this subject is also very instructive: having adverted to the mystery which hath been hid from ages and generations, but now is made manifest to the saints, which (saith he) " is Christ in you, the hope of glory; whom we preach, warning every man, and teaching every man in all wisdom, that we may present every man perfect in Christ Jesus;" he then proceeds, " As ye have therefore received Christ Jesus the Lord, so walk ye in him ;"—" and ye are complete in him, which is the head of all principality and power;"— " buried with him in baptism, wherein also ye are risen with him, through the faith of the operation of God, who hath raised him from the dead." (Col. i. 26, 27, 28; Col. ii. 6, 10, 12.) " Therefore we are buried with him by baptism into death; that like as Christ was raised up from the dead by the glory of the Father, even so we also should walk in newness of life." (Rom. vi. 4.) This is that one baptism of which the apostle speaks, Eph. iv. 5: " There is one body and one Spirit, one Lord, one faith, one baptism;" and describing the agent in this important work, (whether commenced through the medium of instrumental ministry, or not,) he declares, " By one Spirit are we all baptized into one body," or Church of Christ; " and have been all made to drink into one Spirit." (1 Cor. xii. 13.)

The terms " water" and " fire" are used in the New Testament, in reference to the baptism of Christ, and to the new birth, which is the effect of this baptism. It is said of Christ, " He shall baptize you with the Holy Ghost and with fire." (Matt. iii. 11.) Again we read, " Except a man be born of water and of the Spirit, he cannot enter into the kingdom of God." (John, iii. 5.) But these terms, in the texts quoted, are not to be understood literally, but figuratively. As the property of water is to cleanse, and that of fire to refine, so the baptism of Christ cleanses and refines the soul, which submits to it, from the stains and dross of sin.

In the apostolic age, although the baptism of Christ, when administered instrumentally, by the preaching of the gospel, was in many instances accompanied by miraculous gifts; yet we have no ground to conclude now, in the absence of such gifts, that a measure of the same baptizing influence of the Spirit does not still accompany the ministry of those, whom he calls, qualifies and employs in his service; and who act therein, only under his ministration and guidance, in an humble dependence on his wisdom, life and power. Through the gracious continuance of divine mercy and love, this influence is yet witnessed, in a greater or less degree, when the word, thus preached, is " mixed with faith" in them that hear it. (Heb. iv. 2.)

Some of the advocates of water-baptism lay much stress on those instances which are recorded in the New Testament, in which some of the apostles appear to have used, or to have directed the use of, this typical ordinance. But when it is considered that some of the apostles for a while after the crucifixion and ascension of our holy Redeemer, were in the practice not only of water-baptism, but also of some other typical ordinances, viz., circumcision, &c., there appears no valid reason why their practice with respect to water-baptism, should be considered more obligatory on the Christian church at the present day, than their practice with respect to circumcision and some other Mosaic rites. On a view of the whole matter, there appears sufficient ground for the conclusion, that it was permitted by divine wisdom, that the typical ordinances of the preceding dispensations, (of Moses and of John,) although virtually abrogated by the death of Christ on the cross, should not in the infantile state of the church be laid aside suddenly, but gradually, as the minds of the Christian converts became capable of more clearly comprehending the spiritual character of the Christian dispensation. It is therefore earnestly recommended to all those, whose minds are so far enlightened as to see clearly that something more than the mere name or outward profession of Christianity is absolutely necessary, that in seeking to become in reality members of the church of Christ and sheep of his fold, they do not endeavour to climb up through the ways which human wisdom may uphold, by a recurrence to the use of any of the types or ordinances of former dispensations, which were fulfilled and abrogated by the coming and death of Christ, as the Scripture declares: (Heb. ix. 8—11; Col. ii. 14, 16, 17:) for Christ is the door of the true sheep-fold, or church; (John, x. 9;) and they who become members of it, must enter in by faith in him, and by submission to the baptism of his Holy Spirit. (1 Cor. xii. 13.)

They who thus become members of the true church of Christ, are permitted to witness its blessed privileges. They partake of that divine food, which he describes as his flesh and blood; and this food is so necessary for their preservation and growth in true religion, that he declared, "Except ye eat the flesh of the Son of Man, and drink his blood, ye have no life in you." (John, vi. 53.) Some who heard him speak these words, thought then, as many professed Christians appear to think in the present day, that this declaration should be understood as relating to the flesh and blood of his outward or material body. Our Lord, however, graciously condescended to correct this mistake:—may every one, who has adopted this, or any other outward signification of the words of Christ now under notice, very seriously reflect upon and accept the explanation which *He* gave, on this highly important subject. After it had been queried, "How can this man give us his flesh to eat?" this was his reply: "*It is the Spirit that quickeneth.*" Surely, then, if it be the Spirit that quickeneth, or giveth life, it should be concluded, that it was the partaking of the quickening, life-giving influences of his Holy Spirit, diffused in the soul;—He dwelling in us and we in him, (v. 56,) which he designed to represent under the terms, eating his flesh and drinking his blood, without which we have no life in us. And it seems, as if it were in order to place this important point beyond the risk of mistake or doubt, that after he had said, "*It is the Spirit that quickeneth,*" he immediately added, "*the flesh profiteth nothing; the words that I speak unto you, they are Spirit and they are life.* (John, vi. 63.) The doctrine of the apostle Paul on this very important subject, is in perfect unison with that of his divine Master. In his epistle to the Corinthians, he declares, that "the Spirit giveth life." (2 Cor. iii. 6.) It also appears, from his first epistle to the same church, that long before the incarnation of Christ, some of the Israelites partook of that spiritual meat and drink, which are derived from him; for the apostle declares, "they did all eat the same spiritual meat, and did all drink the same spiritual drink; for they drank of that spiritual rock that followed them, and that rock was Christ." (1 Cor. x. 3, 4.)

If the followers of Jesus Christ could have been permitted to eat the flesh of his material body, it is evident, from his own words, that it would have profited them nothing. It was the life-giving influence of his Holy Spirit, by which alone those who believed on him in that day, were made alive, and preserved "alive unto God." (Rom. vi. 11.) And in the present day the same divine influence produces similar effects, in the souls of all those, who, believing in the light, life, and power of Christ, receive him for their Teacher, Saviour, Priest, and King; believing also, if they have access to the Holy Scriptures, all that those sacred records declare, respecting the sufferings and death of Christ, and the benefits resulting therefrom to mankind. These partake of the true supper of the Lord; as it is written, "Behold, I stand at the door" (*of the heart*) "and knock; if any man hear my voice, and open the door, I will come in to him, and will sup with him, and he with me." (Rev. iii. 20.) This divine food is essentially the same as that which our holy Redeemer described under other figurative terms; viz. as the bread which cometh down from heaven, and giveth life unto the world; (John, vi. 33;) as "living water," which, in them who drink of it, should be as a "well of water, springing up into everlasting life." (John, iv. 10, 14.)

Amidst the manifold mercies which they partake of, who, through divine grace, witness an advancement in the work of regeneration, this communication of spiritual food to their souls should ever be gratefully acknowledged. Like the sap, that enables the branches which abide in the vine to bring forth fruit, so the quickening, life-giving influence of the Spirit of Christ, who is the "true vine," (John, xv. 1,) enables those who, as branches, abide in Him, to bring forth the fruits of the Spirit, which are, "in all goodness, and righteousness, and truth." (Eph. v. 9.) For under his holy influence, they are incited and strengthened from day to day to maintain, even in their temporal concerns, a strict adherence to justice, truth, and equity, doing unto others, as they would that others should do unto them. Their words and actions being leavened by Christian purity, sincerity, humility, and love, they exemplify, as their growth in the divine life progresses, not only in their own families, but amongst all with whom they associate, the powerful efficacy of that holy name, in which they have believed, and into which they have been baptized.

If we seriously recur to those solemn declarations of our Lord Jesus Christ, "Except ye eat the flesh of the Son of Man, and drink his blood, ye have no life in you;" "He that eateth my flesh, and drinketh my blood, dwelleth in me and I in him;" (John, vi. 53, 56;) and if we keep in view the clear explanation which he condescended to give of these words, the conclusion must surely be admitted, on the highest authority, that whatever may be our religious profession,—however largely our minds may be furnished with the literal knowledge of the doctrines and precepts of the Holy Scriptures, or our memories charged with the recorded experience of good men of ancient and modern times,—and however highly we may think of ourselves, or be esteemed by others, on this, or on any other account; yet, *if we do not partake of the quickening influences of the Spirit of Christ, we have no life in us;—we dwell not in him, nor he in us;*—and consequently we are more or less in a state of spiritual darkness and death. A conviction of the vast importance of this subject, induces the writer, under, he trusts, some degree of the constraining love of Christ, to press it upon the close attention of those, with whom he is connected in religious profession, as upon Christians of every other denomination.

Having endeavoured, in the preceding pages, to point out the means whereby the soul, through the obedience of faith, may attain to a capacity of partaking of this divine food, and to show the necessity and benefit thereof, it may be proper in the next place to make some further observations, with respect to its communication and effects.

The great Head, of the church dispenses this heavenly sustenance to the living members of his body, in their religious assemblies, sometimes by the instrumental ministry of the gospel, at other times by the immediate effusion of his Holy Spirit upon their minds, when, it may be, the assembly is in a state of solemn silence, and reverent waiting before him. They are also permitted to enjoy this privilege from time to time, in seasons of private retirement; and even day by day, whilst engaged in their lawful occupations, if, feeling the want of the enlivening influence of the Spirit of Christ, they humbly seek it. It is pre-eminently for this divine nourishment —for this bread "that cometh down from heaven," that our blessed Saviour teaches us to pray to our heavenly Father,—"*Give us this day our daily bread.*" When favoured in their public assemblies to witness the gracious promises fulfilled, that, "They that wait upon the Lord shall renew their strength," (Isai. xl. 31,) and that where even two or three are gathered together in His name, there, *He, who is "a quickening Spirit,"* (1 Cor. xv. 45,) *even the Lord Jesus Christ, is in the midst of them;* (Matt. xviii. 20;) they can thankfully acknowledge, that, although the baptizing ministry of the gospel is a great blessing to the church of Christ, and should be received with feelings of gratitude to the Source of all good; yet it is a higher privilege to be fed immediately by *Himself,* the holy Head of the church and Bishop of souls, than through the instrumentality of their fellow-members.

The solemn declaration of our holy Redeemer to the woman of Samaria on the subject of worship, should indeed make a deep and awful impression upon the minds of all who profess to prostrate themselves before the Most High! "God is a Spirit, and they that worship him, must worship him in Spirit and in truth." And again he said, "No man cometh unto the Father but by me;"—and "without me ye can do nothing." How needful then must it be, in order to perform this worship, that the mind be brought into a state of entire humiliation,—bowed down under a true sense of its great weakness,—of its many wants, and utter unworthiness,—accompanied with a conviction of the perfect purity of that Almighty Being, whose sacred presence is unapproachable, except through our holy Mediator, the Lord Jesus Christ. Perhaps it may be said, that there is no other engagement in which the religiously exercised mind is so fully penetrated by these feelings, as in that of silent waiting upon God in assemblies for public worship.

But although Christ is always in some measure present with those, who, through the baptism of his Holy Spirit, are members of his church; yet, according to the experience of many who are of this description, he is frequently pleased to withhold from them, for a season, in their religious assemblies, as well as at other times, that increased communication of his power and life, which is needful to qualify them for the performance of the solemn act of divine worship. Yea, for a wise and gracious purpose, he oftentimes permits them to feel how weak they are of themselves,—how utterly insufficient by their own strength, to resist the efforts of their soul's adversary; who, by exciting the natural propensity to be occupied with terrestrial objects, or by presenting to the imagination creaturely ideas relative to worship ,or doctrine, often endeavours to draw off their minds from that denial of self—that subjugation of their own will and wisdom—which are requisite in order to wait patiently upon God in the exercise of faith and love. But although He, the good " Shepherd and Bishop of souls," (1 Pet. ii. 25,) may permit those humble believers in him to be thus tried and proved, yet he does not forsake them:—in his own time, (for which with fervent desire they reverently wait,) the enlivening, purifying influence of his Holy Spirit imparts fresh vigour to their souls: thus strengthened, they surmount those impediments, of what kind soever, which had obstructed their access " unto the throne of grace;" (Heb. iv. 16;) and they are enabled to " draw near in full assurance of faith." (Heb. x. 22.) The worship thus offered in religious assemblies, whether it be accompanied with vocal ministry, prayer or praise, in obedience to the will of the great Head of the church, immediately communicated to such of its members as he may see meet to employ in his service,—or whether in obedience to the same holy will, it wholly consists in silent* aspirations, arising from quickened souls, in a state of reverent prostration before the throne of grace,—in either case, this worship does not fail to meet the divine acceptance.

Although many individuals, in whom the work of regeneration has been begun, and who are in the practice of waiting upon God in assemblies for public worship, may not always receive such a supply of spiritual food, as the apprehension of their own need leads them to expect; yet may these not be discouraged: may they duly consider, that the Lord knows better than they do, what is best for them. He knows what will conduce to the progress of that great work, which he has begun in their souls. For a wise and benign purpose, he introduces his children into a state of poverty of spirit; the tendency of this discipline being to increase their faith, and to establish them more firmly on Himself, the " sure foundation,"—" the Rock of ages." Therefore, ye who hunger and thirst for the bread and water of life, be not dismayed on account of the apparent smallness of the portion sometimes, yea frequently, dispensed unto you. Should it be no more, figuratively speaking, than a crumb of this bread, or a drop of " living water," yet, if received with thankfulness, it will be found sufficient for the present need,—sufficient to strengthen you still to trust in the Lord,—still to wait upon him in faith, and with a lively hope in his goodness and mercy ; and whenever these effects are witnessed, they should be considered as an evidence, that, through the gracious regard of your heavenly Father, a portion of divine aid and sustenance has been dispensed unto you. The revival of this faith and hope, when felt, after much mental labour and conflict, whether in religious assemblies, or in private retirement, how precious is it to the tribulated soul! The Lord's holy name be praised for all his mercies partaken of by those, who are engaged, although frequently under a feeling of many discouragements and infirmities, to seek for ability to worship him in Spirit and in truth !

(To be continued.)

From the New Haven Palladium.

DECISION OF THE COURT.

His honour, Judge Judson, has kindly permitted us to publish his very able decision, in the case of the Africans, from his own manuscript.

DISTRICT COURT OF THE U. S. DISTRICT OF CONNECTICUT, Jan. 7, 1840.

Thos. R. Gedney and others, vs. The schooner L'Amistad. } Libel for salvage.

On the 26th of August, 1839, Lieutenant Gedney, commanding the brig Washington, of the U. S. Navy, seized and brought into the port of New London, in this district, the schooner L'Amistad, with a cargo of goods, and 49 Africans, then claimed as slaves by Don Pedro Montez and Don Jose Ruiz, subjects of her Catholic Majesty the Queen of Spain—the said Montez and Ruiz also being on board the schooner. On the arrival of the schooner within this district, New London, being the first port into which the schooner was brought after her seizure, a libel was filed here by Lieutenant Gedney, the officers and crew of the brig Washington, claiming salvage.

At a special District Court, held on the 19th of September, other libels were also filed in the following order:

That of Jose Ruiz.
That of Pedro Montez.
That of Henry Green and Peletiah Fordham.

A libel in behalf of the United States by the district attorney—first, claiming that the vessel, cargo and slaves be restored to the owners, being Spanish subjects—and, secondly, demanding that the negroes be delivered up to the president to be transported to Africa.

That of the Spanish Consul claiming Antonio.

And on the 19th day of November another libel was also filed, by the district attorney, in favour of the United States, alleging that the Spanish minister had, in pursuance of the treaty between the United States and Spain, demanded of the government of the United States, the restoration of the schooner L'Amistad, her cargo, and the slaves on board for the owners thereof, being subjects of Spain.

The ordinary process of attachment issued, and the schooner, goods, and Africans so alleged to be slaves were taken into custody by the marshal of this district, for adjudication upon these various libels and claims.

At the District Court in November, a part of these Africans, by their counsel, filed a plea to the jurisdiction of this court, alleging that they were free; and that they were seized within the territorial jurisdiction of the state of New York, claiming to be set at liberty.

This plea is now withdrawn, and an answer is filed alleging, substantially, as follows :—That Cinquez, Banna 1st, Damma, Fawni 1st, Phumah, Connoma, Choday, Bunnah 2d, Bash, Cebha, Pooma, Kimbo, Peeah, Bangyah, Saah, Coclee, Parte, Mona, Nahquoi, Quato, Jesse, Con, Fawni 2d, Kenna, Laumamee, Fajana, Jebboy, Fauguanah, Bewnu, Fawnu, Cherkenall, Gubbo, Curre, Seme, Kene, Majera, are all Africans, entitled to their freedom ; that the said schooner was at anchor near Culloden Point, within the territorial jurisdiction of the state of New York, and that part of said Africans, as named in said plea and answer, were on shore on Long Island, within the jurisdictional limits of the state of New York; whereupon they say that this court had no jurisdiction over their persons, and pray to be discharged.

Lieutenant Gedney now appears and pursues his claim for salvage. Henry Green and Mr. Fordham appear and pursue their claim for salvage. The district attorney of Connecticut pursues the libels filed by him in behalf of the minister of Spain, for a restoration of the ship, cargo, and slaves, under the treaty between Spain and the United States.

In the discussion of this case have been involved numerous questions, of great importance, requiring, as we have seen, industrious examination and patient deliberation. It has been my endeavour to afford ample time for this investigation; and the ability with which these questions have been discussed at the bar, must satisfy all, that every thing which talent and learning could accomplish, has been done.

It devolves upon the court to dispose of these various and complicated questions, in such manner as will seem to be demanded by the laws of the land; and of this the responsibility rests on me. That responsibility will be met, and when discharged, according to the dictates of my own conscience, I shall be relieved from its further perplexities.

It will be a satisfaction, while doing this, that neither party or claimant can be prejudiced by my determination, because the law secures an appeal to the highest tribunal in

---

* It must not be supposed, that all, who are in the practice of sitting in silence, in assemblies for public worship, are benefited in the manner above described. It is only the awakened mind,—the mind in which the work of regeneration is in some degree begun, that is capable of truly waiting upon God in silence, under an exercise of faith and love towards him. Yet there is ground to believe, that in numerous instances, persons who have previously evinced little or no concern about their soul's salvation, being induced, some of them probably by mere curiosity, to enter a silent religious assembly, have been awakened; and their minds greatly contrited by the divine power; although not a word has been spoken in the assembly. And this visitation of the love of the Redeemer, has proved the commencement of the effectual working of his grace in their souls.

144   THE FRIEND.

this country, where my decision may be both reviewed, and, if wrong, corrected.

It is then of little importance to the persons in interest, what may be the determination of this court, for a case like this will not and should not rest upon a single trial, without review before the Supreme Court, in whose decision all would be satisfied.

The case is not only important to those immediately interested, but there are involved principles important to the nation and the world. If a few months have elapsed since this cause has been pending, it has been owing to circumstances beyond my control, but this surely has produced no inconvenience or suffering to those in custody. They have all been humanely treated; liberally fed and clothed by the government, into whose hands they have been providentially cast. Whatever may be the final result of this case, so far, it may be safely said, that no one step has been taken which could have been avoided.

I do not say that it is my wish to escape the responsibilities which devolve upon me, neither would it be just to myself to say, that I have not been deeply anxious to investigate this case, and decide it according to its true merits.

[The judge then proceeds to discuss, as the first in order, the question of jurisdiction, which he does at considerable length, and with much ability; and arrives at the conclusion, that the jurisdiction of the District Court of Connecticut attaches to the whole subject matter.]

We approach now the merits of the case, and the facts involved may be stated in a few words; and about these facts there is little diversity of thought. A Spanish vessel owned in Cuba, proceeded from thence to the coast of Africa, and having procured a cargo of native Africans, returned and landed them near Havana, where they were put into a slave mart for sale. Within fifteen days from the time of landing, Jose Ruiz and Pedro Montez, subjects of the Queen of Spain, and residents of Guanaja, in the province of Puerto Principee, on the island of Cuba, being at Havana, purchased fifty-four of these Africans. The schooner L'Amistad, then lying in the port of Havana, possessing rightfully the national character of a Spanish vessel, owned and commanded by one Raymond Ferrer, master, and regularly and lawfully licensed in the coasting trade, between the ports of Havana and Guanaja, and being laden with Spanish goods for the latter port, the said Ruiz and Montez put on board thereof the said fifty-four Africans, with permits from the governor of the island of Cuba, to be transported as freight to the said port of Guanaja; and the said Ruiz and Montez took passage in said schooner. All grounds of suspicion that the L'Amistad had been any wise connected with the original importation of these Africans, is wholly excluded from the case.

Three days from Havana, the negroes rose upon the vessel, and killed the master and cook, and by force took command, and after being sixty-three days upon the ocean, she came into the waters of the United States, in

a condition perilous to the vessel and the lives of Ruiz and Montez, and all others on board. Being found as heretofore stated, the schooner and all belonging to her were seized by the brig Washington, and from thence was first brought into the port of New London, within the district of Connecticut; and the schooner, cargo, and Africans, now claimed as slaves, are here libelled for salvage, by Lieutenant Gedney, &c.

Having stated these various claims, and the circumstances of the seizure, I will now proceed to the consideration of each claim, somewhat in the order in which they stand upon the record.

1. The claim of the officers of the brig Washington.

In considering and disposing of this claim, it may not be improper to divide it into two parts.

1st. The vessel and goods.

2d. The Africans alleged to have been the slaves of Messrs. Ruiz and Montez.

1st. The claims to salvage for the *vessel* and *goods*, stands upon ground, almost beyond question. The services rendered by Lieutenant Gedney were not only meritorious, but highly praiseworthy. They were such, as would entitle the seizor to his proper allowance. The vessel was at the mercy of the winds and waves. She was in the possession and under the command of those negroes, who were utterly ignorant of the science of navigation—without law or order—without commission or any lawful authority, guided alone by their ignorance or caprice—just on the point of sailing for the coast of Africa, and yet without the possibility of conducting the vessel in safety for a single day. The seizure, under such circumstances, was meritorious, and will entitle the seizors to an adequate compensation, unless something shall be found in the case, to oust them of this right. In opposition to this claim, Pedro Montez and Jose Ruiz, allege that they, each of them, own a part of these goods, and the minister of her catholic majesty, in behalf of the owners of the schooner, and the residue of the goods on board, alleges that the whole were owned by subjects of the queen of Spain, and that under the treaty, between Spain and the United States, a restoration, entire, should be decreed.

Here it may be remarked that Montez and Ruiz have ceased to prosecute their claims in person, and the Spanish minister comes in the name of his government, basing himself on the treaty of 1795, for them and in their stead, claims the restoration entire of the vessel, the cargo and slaves. There are two articles in the treaty of 1795, which have some bearing on this question.

(Remainder next week.)

From an intimation by a friend it would seem proper to mention, that the compiler or publisher of the book purporting to be a reprint of "Guide to True Peace," &c., respecting which were inserted last week some critical remarks by C., was not a member of the Society of Friends.

THE FRIEND.

A RELIGIOUS AND LITERARY JOURNAL.

VOL. XIII.   SEVENTH DAY, SECOND MONTH, 8, 1840.   NO. 19.

EDITED BY ROBERT SMITH.

PUBLISHED WEEKLY.

Price two dollars per annum, payable in advance.

Subscriptions and Payments received by

GEORGE W. TAYLOR,

NO. 50, NORTH FOURTH STREET, UP STAIRS,

PHILADELPHIA.

From the Methodist Magazine for 1791.

On the Motto of a Seal—Believe! Love! Obey!

This motto is indeed a very short one; but surely it contains much in little. It is replete with every instruction necessary to teach us how to be happy both in time and in eternity. Let us then examine a little into each of its particulars, beginning with the first:—

BELIEVE!

When the jailer asked of the apostle, What he should do to be saved? he was answered, "Believe on the Lord Jesus Christ, and thou shalt be saved." This answer is what remains to be given to every one who shall make the same inquiry, to the end of the world. This being the case, let us next inquire, What it is to believe in Jesus Christ? Our Saviour tells us, John, iii. 16, that "God so loved the world, that he gave his only begotten Son, that whosoever believeth in him should not perish, but have everlasting life." Now the whole tenor of the Old Testament teaches us, that Christ should come to be a sacrifice, and a propitiation for the sins of the world; to make reconciliation for iniquity, and to bring in everlasting righteousness. All which he has done, according to the Scriptures; being raised from the dead, and ascended on high; for when he had by himself purged our sins he sat down on the right hand of the Majesty on high, to give eternal life to all that should come unto him. In consequence of this, remission of sins is preached in his name to all that believe. "To him give all the prophets witness, that through his name, whosoever shall believe in him shall receive remission of sins." Acts x. 23. Now, as Christ's blood was shed for the remission of sins, so faith in his blood receives the remission of sins; and "being justified by faith, we have peace with God, through our Lord Jesus Christ." Every true believer experiences the same thing in his own soul, whereof the Holy Ghost is the witness. "He that believeth, hath the witness in himself." And we are all called; we are all invited; we are all commanded, to "believe in him whom

God hath sent." May we all accept this great salvation, and by faith receive the atonement! Now let us proceed to the next particular,

LOVE!

This can never be separated from true faith; for faith, when it is real, always works by love. How is it possible that we can really believe that God hath loved us, and forgiven us our sins, without loving him again? It can never be. For, as St. John says, "We love him, because he first loved us." And he that says he believes in Jesus Christ, and does not find love to God, may be assured he deceives himself with only a notion of faith. A picture of fire is without heat; but a real fire cannot be without it. A notional faith is without love, but a real one is never without it. But to you who are indeed believers, "Christ is precious;" yea, more precious than all things. Love then, and walk in love; increase in love; and let love be your element, your business, your every thing. But remember the flower withers when cut off from the stalk; so your love will wither, unless you stand fast, and grow in the faith. Without you abide in the faith, the fire of love will go out. If this is the case with any, let them believe again, and love will come again; for they always come and go together. Do we profess to believe? and do we profess to love? Say, my friends, is our faith unfeigned? And is our love without dissimulation? If so, let us proceed to the third particular, which is,

OBEY!

As a heart-felt faith in Jesus Christ produces a heart-felt love to him; so obedience to his commands will follow as the opening flowers and ripening fruits follow the genial heat of the sun. Christ saith, "If ye love me, keep my commandments." What are his commandments? Love to God, and love to one another: the first shows itself in doing what we know is our duty, and patiently suffering; yea, and resigning ourselves to his disposal in all things. The second shows itself in doing to others as we would be done by. In all loving and kind offices, in forgiving injuries; in all things being just and true; also in patience, long-suffering, and forbearance, and all other duties mentioned in the law. Also loving our enemies, returning good for evil, and praying for our persecutors. Obedience to God is showing the reality of our love to him, in following the example of Christ in all his imitable perfections. And this obedience is the result of having his Spirit dwelling in us, inclining us to walk in all the ways of holiness; summed up in loving God with all our hearts, and our neighbour

as ourselves: in which are contained all the precepts of the moral law, which law is written in the hearts of all true believers. See I Cor. xiii.

Thus we see in these particulars—Believe—love—obey! are contained the very essentials of all true religion. What then remains, my friends, but that we give all diligence to be found *believing, loving, obedient followers* of the Lamb of God? If so, let us not quarrel about other matters. Let us keep the unity of the spirit in the bond of peace, and bear with one another's different opinions and forms that do not clash with true faith, true love, and true obedience. Let us not wrangle about circumcision or uncircumcision, but let us contend for the faith which worketh by love. Let the strong bear with the weak, and let the weak not be offended with the strong. May the motto of the seal be engraven in all our hearts; and may our sober, godly, and righteous lives and conversations, demonstrate to all the world that it is really so!

In a word: may we all believe—may we all love—and may we all obey! So prays, from his very heart, one who is a lover of all the true Church of Christ—one who is for Christ's sake their truly affectionate servant in the ministry of the gospel of peace and salvation.

Decision of the District Court in the case of the Africans of the Amistad.
(Concluded from page 144.)

[The judge next quotes the articles of the treaty relating to the question, which, and his reasoning upon them, for the sake of brevity we pass over. He then continues.]

It results then, that the seizors are entitled to salvage. This lien is placed upon the vessel and her effects by the laws of all nations. It is founded on the broad principles of justice acknowledged by all, and the treaty stipulation is entered into, with this lien, which can not be considered as inconsistent with the treaty. The decree will be, that the schooner and her effects be delivered up to the Spanish government, upon the payment, at a *reasonable rate*, for the services in saving this property from entire loss.

An appraisement will be ordered, and one third of that amount, and cost will be deemed just and reasonable.

2d. The next question is, can salvage be allowed upon the slaves?

There are insuperable objections to this portion of the claim. There is no foundation here laid for a decree in personam. The decree, if at all, must operate in rem. That is, the salvage must be considered as a lien upon the slaves themselves, and the amount to be decreed must be raised out of them, as out of other property.

Here then I find this claim hedged about by fixed and known laws, over which it would be impossible for me to leap. I have heretofore decided, in the very outset of this case, that these alleged slaves cannot be sold. There is no law of the United States or of the state of Connecticut by which title can be given to them under any decree of this court. I am still confirmed in that opinion. It is impossible! Can a decree be predicated upon a supposed valuation to be ascertained by an appraisal? There is no authority in this court to cause such an appraisal. Who can appoint these appraisers? Who can administer to them an oath? And above all, by what rule could their estimate be formed?

Are they to be estimated by their value in the district of Connecticut? That is not one cent. The laws which I am bound to administer can recognize no value in them. Can the appraisers travel into other states or countries to seek their value? Surely not. If a decree should be made, it would be wholly nugatory, inoperative and void. This the court is never called upon to do. When a decree is made, it always presupposes that the court making it, possesses the power of enforcing it. This part of the claim, therefore, will be passed over.

[The court then decides against the claim of Green and Fordham, as not being sustained by the facts proved,—and thus proceeds.]

The two great questions still remain to be settled. Shall these Africans, by a decree of this court, be delivered over to the government of Spain, upon the demand of her minister, as the property of Don Pedro Montez and Don Jose Ruiz? But if not, what ultimate disposition shall the government of the United States make of them?

The other questions, in importance, cannot be compared with these. Here we have, her majesty the queen of Spain to her resident minister, at the court of the United States, unequivocally demanding for her subjects these Africans as their property, in the fulfilment, as he says, of treaty stipulations, solemnly entered into by this nation. These Africans come in person, as our law permits them to do, denying this right. They say that they are not the slaves of Spanish subjects—and are not amenable to Spanish laws. We have also, the humanity of our own laws, ready to embrace them, provided we are not compelled by these treaty stipulations to deliver them up.

Upon the first of these questions, all absorbing as it is, I am called upon to pronounce an opinion. And what I have now to say applies to Jingua and others, who have filed their answer to the claim, on record, not including Antonio.

Shall these Africans be decreed to the Spanish government?

What is the object of the demand made upon the president by the Spanish minister? Not to have them transported to Cuba for punishment, but because they are the property of Spanish subjects—their effects, or

merchandise—their property. I begin here by finding certain facts, which necessarily must be part of my decree, and upon which it must be based.

These are the facts that I find proved in this case.

In Cuba there are three classes of negroes, well known and distinguished: Creoles, who were born within Spanish dominion; Ladinos, who have been long domiciliated on the island, or sufficiently so, that the laws of Spain operate upon them—or in other words, embracing those who owe Spain their allegiance; and lastly, Bozals, embracing all such as have but recently been imported from Africa.

The negroes now in question were all born in Africa—they were imported to Cuba by the slave traffic, about which Montez and Ruiz had nothing to do—they were put into a baracoon near Havana, and after remaining there not exceeding fifteen days, Montez and Ruiz brought them to the schooner Amistad as their slaves, and put them on board for Guanaja. Consequently, I find these negroes to be Bozals: they were so at the time of the shipment.

The demand of the Spanish government, is for these Bozals to be restored to them, that Montez and Ruiz may have them as their property. To justify this demand, and require this government to restore them under the treaty, these negroes must not only be property, but Spanish subjects must have a title to that property. In other words, Spanish subjects must own them—must come lawfully by them—they must have lawful right to hold them as their own. Suppose a slave should be demanded of us, by the Portuguese government, and it should appear in evidence that the slave in fact belonged to a citizen of South Carolina, we could not give him up to Portugal. Although he may be a slave, the Portuguese have no title in him. They cannot demand, nor we surrender. The right of demand and the necessity of surrender rests on the title to the property. Property and title both are to be made out.

In all cases where property and title are proved to be in Spanish subjects, the treaty is imperative, and at all hazards it must be surrendered. The obligations are solemn, and war might be the consequence of a breach of this duty on our part. I go up to the letter and spirit of the treaty both, but I do not step over it, merely because the demand is made by a high contracting power. The demand must be lawful. The minister has demanded the schooner, and suppose in point of fact it should turn out that the schooner belonged to a subject of France, instead of Spain, can we deliver it to Spain? Surely not. How stands the case here. The government of Spain demand of us, under their treaty, a restoration of these negroes, and we ask them for their title. It is a very well settled principle, here and elsewhere, that the party demanding restoration, must show his title—the onus probandi lies on him. Aware of this rule of the law, the Spanish claimants send to me their evidence or title. And what is that document. A deed—a bill of sale—a transfer? No. It is a permit—a license—a

pass—signed by the governor-general of Cuba for Don Pedro Montez and Don Jose Ruiz to transport 54 Ladinos to Guanaja, and this is all! This embraces the whole evidence of property and title both. In point of fact they are not Ladinos. They might be lawfully sold and carried to Guanaja. These negroes are Bozals and not Ladinos. Here then is the point—the point upon which this great controversy must turn!

To show that it is so, I shall be obliged to recur to the laws of Spain, as the same are here proved, because those laws make a part of the case itself. They are to be proved in the courts of the United States as matters of fact. This has been done on this inquiry, and this court is just as competent to judge of the effect of a foreign law, when thus proved, as of a law of the United States.

I find them as a matter of fact, that in the month of June, 1839, the law of Spain did prohibit under severe penalty the importation into Cuba of negroes from Africa. These negroes were imported in violation of that law, and be it remembered, that by the same law of Spain, such imported negroes are declared to be free in Spain. This accounts for the declaration of the Spanish consul, "that if these negroes should be returned to Cuba, some of the leaders might be punished, but none of them could be made slaves." This declaration is in exact conformity with the law of Spain, so far as the matter of slavery is concerned. They could not be free slaves there, because the law declares them free. They were bozals, and not slaves. This declaration is from a government functionary of Spain. Why then should the law be doubted by me? I do not doubt it. I do expressly find it to be such. If there has been any doubt as to what the law of Spain is, I ask, would not the Spanish minister resident at Washington, have communicated the law to this government, so that it might have been sent here?

We are bound to believe, that the minister of every foreign country brings with him the laws of his sovereign, and is able, on the shortest notice, to make those laws known to us, when questions may arise. Between nations, it is not required that every matter of form should be strictly complied with. In the intercourse of friendly nations, the substance is all that is required. Why has not the Spanish minister told us that a law exists, by which bozal negroes are slaves in Cuba? Why has he not sent us that law with his claim! Ample time has been afforded. He should turn the burden of proof lies with him, and still withholds the law, if it does exist! How can he expect an American court to decree that these negroes are property, while he omits to produce the evidence which makes them such. In reply it may be said they were in possession of Spanish subjects. But possession is only one indicium of property, and that has been rebutted by the proof that these are Bozal negroes, and cannot be made property, by any machinery of sale, or transportation.

This brings me to the question of title in Montez and Ruiz, who now claim them through their government. Though they do not come into court in person, yet they do come in the majesty of their sovereign. They need not come in person, and if they do, they may stand aside and put forward the shield of regal authority, as they do in this case. But this establishes no title to property. Suppose I admit that slaves are property, yet Montez and Ruiz must possess the title in themselves. They have furnished no proof of payment,—they have shown no bill of sale,—no witness has sworn that he was present when these negroes were sold. They have not shown us from whom they derive their title. It is the naked possession on which they rely. When the right is disputed this is not enough.

Shall these Bozals be given up under the treaty? And if so, for what purpose? To have the question tried *there*, whether they are slaves by the laws of Spain!! The Spanish law declares they are not slaves; it would be utterly useless, then, to send them back to Cuba. It would only be a work of supererogation. If by *their own* laws, they cannot enslave them, then it follows of necessity, they cannot be demanded. When these facts are known by the Spanish minister, he cannot but discover, that the subjects of his queen have acquired no rights in these men—they are not the *property* of Spain. His demand must be withdrawn. The very essence of his demand consists in the supposed Spanish right of property in the thing demanded. That being removed, *by his own law*, there can no longer be cause of complaint.

At all events, this cannot be expected at my hands, because the supreme court have always refused to surrender property, unless *there was proof of title in the claimants*. The same rule applies equally to foreign and domestic claimants. Title *must* be shown in the property claimed, as belonging to the claimant, or it cannot be surrendered. The positions I have laid down here are fully recognised in the Antelope 10, Wheaton 66. The argument of the attorney general in that case, sanctioned as it is by the able opinion of the chief justice, affords me full confidence that I am right.

The strongest case which can possibly be adduced for the surrender, is the La Jeune Eugenie in the 2d of Mason. There, a French ship, engaged in the slave trade, was brought into the Massachusetts district and libelled. The French minister made a demand of the vessel, and she was surrendered by Judge Story. But in that case the *property* was admitted to be in *French citizens*. They themselves were claimants against their own government, and both sides agreed that it was French property. The judge did right in surrendering it. But there is a great distinction between the two cases. *Here* the right of property is not only the principal contest, but I find clearly that the right of property is not in any Spanish subject whatever. The cases then are dissimilar in principle. Had *this* case, as in *that*, found the right of property in the claimant, I should have gone the whole length and breadth of that decision, and restored the property. . . . . .

This case is ample authority to that extent;

and to show that I abide by the treaty, and that authority, I take another branch of this case. Antonio is demanded, and the proof from him is, that he is a Creole—born, as he believes, in Spain; he *was*, at the time his master was murdered by Jingua, a slave, so recognised and known by the laws of Spain. The property in him was in Rayman Ferrer, a Spanish subject, at the time of his death on board the schooner, and now is in *his* legal heirs. Here is both property and right of property in Spanish subjects. I shall decree a restoration of this slave, under the treaty of 1795. For this likewise I find authority in the cases adjudged by the supreme court, from which I have neither power nor inclination to depart.

The question remains: What disposition shall be made of these negroes by the government of the United States?

There is a law of congress, passed the 3d of March, 1819, which renders it essential that all such Africans as these should be transported, under the direction of the President of the United States, to Africa. The humane and excellent provisions of this act characterize the period when it was adopted. Among the prominent provisions of congress to meliorate the condition of Africans brought away from their homes in this traffic, which is spoken of and believed to be odious, is this act of 1819. Considering the object embraced within these provisions, the statute itself must receive the most liberal and generous construction. Those technicalities of construction, which pertain to another class of acts, do not belong to this act. Those rules which govern courts in deciding on *penal acts*, are to find no place by the side of this statute. They must govern no mind employed in carrying out the noble intentions of the framers of this law. What is the spirit of that act? It is to return to the land of their nativity all such Africans as may have been brought from thence wrongfully. This being the spirit of that act, I stop not in the mere forms of legislation. I do not wait to consider whether every letter and syllable of that act has been followed by the officers of the law. When the spirit of goodness is hovering over us, just descending to bless, it is immaterial in what garments we are clad to receive the blessing.

'I do not maintain this construction upon my own mere suggestion, but I shall be able to show, by a recent determination of the supreme court of the United States, that the door has already been opened, and the passage already provided, to send these men back to their own Africa. That if the aspirations of these unfortunate beings have been heard to rise for Sierra Leone, the law of that country into which they have been cast, has provided the means, and already the supreme court have, in their profoundest wisdom, given a construction to that law which bids them God speed.

[The quotations from the act of March 3d, 1819, &c. and the reasoning of the judge thereon, we here omit, and proceed to his conclusion.]

Cinquez and Grabeau shall not sigh for

Africa in vain. Bloody as may be their hands, they shall yet embrace their kindred. I shall put in form a decree of this court, that these Africans, excepting Antonio, be delivered to the President of the United States, to be transported to Africa, there to be delivered to the agent, appointed to receive and conduct them home. To do it we have ample authority, and ample means. What American can object to this decree? No one, surely, when the case is correctly understood. It will indeed require the executive arm to carry out this decree. This may well be anticipated, because the facts which I have found and shall put upon the record, will carry conviction to every mind.

Antonio, falling clearly within the other principle, and in the presence of the court, expressing a strong wish to be returned, will be decreed to the government of Spain, with the vessel and goods, the vessel and goods being alone subject to the lien which the necessity of the case has thrown upon them, for the salvage service and the cost.

COMMERCE OF THE UNION.

In a note appended to the late report of the secretary of the treasury, we find some interesting statements presenting general results concerning the past imports and exports of the United States, drawn from official tables in the department. These results are expressed in round numbers, without aiming at fractional accuracy.

It is stated, and we presume the statement will cause some surprise, that the whole imports of the country have not more than doubled since the first four years of the government, while the exports of domestic produce have quite quadrupled. The consumption of foreign merchandize in the United States during the same period, has increased not much over a hundred per cent. while our population has increased fully four hundred per cent.

In regard to some of our chief articles of export, the great southern staple, cotton, has been augmented in value from a thousand dollars to sixty or seventy millions. Tobacco has remained nearly stationary, ranging in value from six to seven millions; flour, about four millions; lumber, from two to three millions; rice, from one to three millions; pork, at a million and a half; and furs, at about three quarters of a million. The exports of domestic manufactures were estimated to be worth in 1793, one million; in 1838, they were reckoned at eight millions. In the state of Massachusetts, the manufactures of leather alone, which is mentioned as an example to show how great has been the tendency towards an increase of manufacturing industry in the country, have reached in value an amount exceeding that of any of the great articles of production in that state, and nearly equal to one fourth of the immense exports of raw cotton from the whole Union.

The imports of cotton fabric into the country, amounted, in 1836, to seventeen millions; during the last three years, the average has been about eleven millions. The silks imported were estimated, in 1821 and 1822, at a sum ranging from four to six millions yearly. 1836, the imports of these goods increased to twenty-two millions; during the last three years, they have been, on an average, equal in value to twelve millions and a half annually.

The imports of specie have been enlarged from three and five millions to about twelve millions yearly; and those of coffee from four and five millions to eight millions, though considerable portions of these are, as formerly, re-exported. The imports of woolens, for the last twenty years, continued at about seven millions annually; in 1836, they rose to twelve millions.

It is stated, as a matter worthy of special notice, that with a population augmented, since 1821, quite seventy-five per cent., the great imports of cotton and woolen goods have augmented but little. Those of silk have increased three or four fold in amount.

With regard to imports, New Orleans has increased nearly four fold in the last twenty years, and presents an aggregate of fourteen or fifteen millions annually; yet she is only the third, in this respect in the Union. The imports into New York constitute nearly three-fifths of the whole importations into the United States. In 1802, they were a little more than one fourth of the whole; in 1821, they had enlarged to twenty-three millions; in 1836 they reached the aggregate of *one hundred and eighteen millions of dollars.* In the reduced business of 1838, they were nearly eighty-nine millions. Among the older cities of the Union, the imports of Boston alone, leaving out New York, have indicated a continuance proportionate to what they were in 1802.

Among the foreign nations with which our commerce has been most extensive, in the way of exports, England held the chief place during our colonial state; but in consequence of the revolution and other causes, it increased to France during the first ten years of the government, to about twenty millions annually; nearly double the amount of our export trade with England. Since that period, our exports to England have risen to about sixty millions annually, without much change in our trade with France. To Spain, our exports are next in value, having increased from four millions to eight, without including any part of Spanish America.

In the foregoing statements, wherever the average of the last three years is spoken of, the estimate should be taken in connection with the embarrassed condition of the country during that period. Imports fell off very considerably, while exports of cotton increased largely. Thus the importations into New York alone in 1836, amounted in the aggregate to one hundred and eighteen millions—much more than for any year since. So on the other hand, New Orleans exported in 1838, when the country was labouring to pay foreign debts, commodities worth thirty-three millions, and other southern cities in similar proportion.—*Balt. Amer.*

From the Methodist Magazine for 1792.

ON ETERNITY.

What is eternity? Can aught
Point its duration to the thought?
Tell every beam the sun emits,
When in sublimest noon he sits;
Tell every light-winged thought that strays
Within his ample round of rays;
Tell all the leaves, and all the buds,
That crown the gardens, and the woods;
Tell all the spires of grass the meads
Produce, when spring propitious leads
The new-born year; tell all the drops
The night upon their bended tops
Sheds in soft silence, to display
Their beauties to the rising day;
Tell all the sands the ocean laves,
Tell all its changes, all its waves:
Or tell, with more laborious pains,
The drops its mighty mass contains:
Be this astonishing account
Augmented with the full amount
Of all the drops the clouds have shed,
Where'er their watery fleeces spread,
Through all time's long-continued tour
From *Adam* to the present hour,—
Still short the sum—nor can it vie
With the more numerous years that lie
Embosomed in *eternity.*

Was there a belt that could contain
In its vast orb the earth and main;
With figures were it clustered o'er,
Without one cypher in the score;
And could your labouring thought assign
The total of the crowded line—
How scant the amount! The attempt how vain,
To reach duration's endless chain!
For, when as many years are run,
Unbounded age is but begun.

Then hear, Oh men! with awe divine,
For this *eternity* is thine!

For "The Friend."

We are gratified to learn that Dr. Reynall Coates has agreed to repeat his interesting course of physiological lectures at the Masonic Hall, in Chesnut street, on the evenings of 2d and 5th days. Having attended the previous course of Dr. Coates, we can bear testimony to the value and interesting character of these lectures. And we cheerfully recommend them to the notice of the younger portion of our religious society of either sex, as opportunities of rational enjoyment and instruction. A thorough acquaintance with his subject, and an admirable command of language, together with various well adapted drawings and anatomical preparations, enables the lecturer so clearly to illustrate his subject, that there is little difficulty in comprehending it even in those who have previously paid little or no attention to anatomical studies.

The first lecture will be delivered on 2d day evening next, at half past seven o'clock, and will be continued through a series of 16 or 18 lectures.

W.

From the North American.

THE BLOOD-HOUNDS.

The employment of these ferocious animals, to hunt down and destroy the Seminole Indians, is a circumstance so utterly abhorrent to every feeling of humanity, that when the design was first announced, but few of our citizens could credit it. We are now, however, gravely told in the newspapers, that Colonel Fitzpatrick has arrived from Cuba, with thirty-three blood-hounds, and six Spaniards, their trainers; and a Tallahassee paper, noticing this fact, says there is now some hope that the war may be brought to a close. In another paper, it is stated that on the voyage, the cook of the vessel in which these dogs were embarked, having killed a pig, the savage creatures became so excited by the smell of the blood as to be unmanageable, and drove the crew from the deck into the shrouds. It is to the fury of these merciless beasts, that our fellow beings are to be exposed; men, women, and children. to be ferreted out, pursued, overtaken, and torn to pieces, to satisfy their blood-thirsty appetites! And will a *civilized* people, a people professing the benign principles of the gospel, silently look on and see such an outrage committed in their name, and by the rulers whom they elect, and not lift up the voice of reprobation? I earnestly hope they will not—but that means will be promptly taken, to prepare and circulate for signature, remonstrances or petitions, imploring congress to interpose its authority, to save our country from this "*darkest, foulest blot.*" Every citizen who loves his country, and who values the national character, should be aroused to action, and exert himself and his influence to avert this horrible calamity.

CHATHAM.

IMMENSITY OF CREATION.

Some astronomers have computed that there are not less than 75 millions of suns in the universe. The fixed stars are all suns, having, like our sun, numerous planets revolving around them. The solar system, or that to which we belong, has about thirty planets, primary and secondary, belonging to it. The circular field of space which it occupies is in diameter 3600 millions of miles, and that which it controls much greater. The sun which is nearest neighbour to ours, is called Sirius, distant from our sun about 852 millions of miles. Now, if all the fixed stars are as distant from each other as Sirius is from our sun, or if our solar system be the average magnitude of all the 75 millions of suns, what imagination can grasp the immensity of creation! Who can survey a plantation containing 75 millions of circular fields, each 10 millions of miles in diameter? Such, however, is one of the plantations of Him who has measured the waters in the hollow of his hand—meted out heaven with a span—comprehended the dust in a measure—and weighed the mountains in scales, and hills in a balance. He who, "sitting upon the orbit of the earth, stretches out the heavens as a curtain, and spreadeth them out as a tent to dwell in.—Nations to Him are as a drop of a bucket, and are counted as the small dust of the balance;" and yet, overwhelming thought! He says, "Though I dwell in the high and holy place, with him also will I dwell who is of an humble and contrite spirit, and trembles at my word!—*Christian Almanac.*

Observations on the Commencement and Progress of the work of Vital Religion in the Soul; on Divine Worship; and on the Partaking of the Flesh and Blood of our Lord Jesus Christ. By Samuel Rundell.

(Concluded from page 143.)

CONCLUDING OBSERVATIONS.

In reviewing the subjects adverted to in these pages, the writer is inclined to say a little more on some of them, especially on that very important one, the benefits resulting to mankind from the sufferings and death of our blessed Saviour Jesus Christ on the cross: this is followed by some additional remarks respecting worship and ministry, with an exhortation to professed Christians.

The Scriptures declare, that the "Word which was in the beginning with God, and was God, was made (or took) flesh." (John, i. 1—14.) "As the children are partakers of flesh and blood, he also himself likewise took part of the same; that through death he might destroy him who had the power of death, that is the devil." (Heb. ii. 14.) "He is the propitiation for our sins, and not for ours only, but also for the sins of the whole world." (1 John, ii. 2.) He suffered death on the cross, and was buried. On the third day he rose from the dead and ascended into heaven, where, glorified with the Father, he is our Mediator and Intercessor with him.

In proceeding to describe more particularly the benefits which result to mankind from the death of Christ, the sentiments of the writer on this subject being well expressed in R. Barclay's "Apology for the true Christian Divinity," he inserts the following selection from that work.

"We consider our redemption in a twofold respect or state; both which, in their own nature are perfect; though in their application to us, the one is not, nor can be, without respect to the other.

"The first is, the redemption performed and accomplished *by Christ for us, in his crucified body, without us:* the other is the redemption wrought *by Christ in us;* which no less properly is called and accounted a redemption than the former. The first, then, is that whereby a man, as he stands in the fall, is put into a capacity of salvation; and bath conveyed unto him a measure of that power, virtue, spirit, life, and grace, that was in Christ Jesus; which, as the free gift of God, is able to counterbalance, overcome, and root out the evil seed, wherewith we are naturally, as in the fall, leavened. The second is that, whereby we witness and know this pure and perfect redemption in ourselves, purifying, cleansing, and redeeming us from the power of corruption; and bringing us into unity, favour, and friendship with God.

"By the first of these two, we that were lost in Adam, plunged into the bitter and corrupt seed, unable of ourselves to do any good thing, but naturally joined and united to evil; forward and propense to all iniquity, servants and slaves to the power and spirit of darkness, are, notwithstanding all this, so far reconciled to God, by the death of his Son, while enemies, that we are put into a capacity of salva-tion, having the glad tidings of the gospel of peace offered unto us; and God is reconciled unto us in Christ, calls and invites us to himself. In which respect we understand these Scriptures: 'He slew the enmity in himself. He loved us first.—He who did no sin, his own self bare our sins in his own body on the tree. And he died for our sins, the just for the unjust.' (Eph. ii. 15; 1 John, iv. 10; 1 Peter, ii. 22, 24, and iii. 18.)

"By the second, we witness this capacity brought into act, whereby receiving and not resisting the purchase of his death, to wit, the light, Spirit, and grace of Christ revealed in us, we witness and possess a real, true and inward redemption from the power and prevalency of sin, and so come to be truly and really redeemed, justified, and made righteous, and to a sensible union and friendship with God. Thus, 'he gave himself for us, that he might redeem us from all iniquity;' and thus, 'we know him, and the power of his resurrection, and the fellowship of his sufferings, being made conformable to his death.' (Tit. ii. 14; Phil. iii. 10.) This last follows the first in order, and is a consequence of it, proceeding from it as an effect from its cause; for as none could have enjoyed the last without the first had been, (such being the will of God,) so also can none now partake of the first, but as he witnesseth the last. Wherefore as to us, they are both causes of our justification; the first the procuring, efficient, the other the formal, cause." Apology, prop. 7, sec. 3.

As it is evident from Scripture testimony, that it is absolutely requisite to our complete redemption, that we should individually believe in the divine light or Spirit of Christ, and by submission to his baptism, witness the work of regeneration in our souls, how desirable is it, that among all professed Christians, (as hath been already hinted,) no doctrines should be embraced, nor any ordinance or institution relative to ministry and worship set up, and practised, the tendency of which is, to divert their attention from this internal teacher, or in any degree to obstruct or restrain its influence and operation in the soul. An attentive perusal of the New Testament, will show, that one of the principal objects of the ministry of Jesus Christ, and also of his apostles, was, to turn the attention of -the people to this divine gift, as their teacher and guide, in the way to everlasting happiness. And surely this should be a principal object, in the view of every professed minister of Christ *in the present day;* for the Christian religion is, in itself, the same now as it was in the apostolic age; yet, alas! great is the degeneracy from its original purity, among many of its professors, not only in regard to conduct and conversation, but also respecting doctrine and worship.

True believers in Christ, after their conversion, and the remission of their past sins through his blood, are still liable in their intercourse with the world, when the daily watching unto prayer is not fully maintained, to contract contamination from its spirit, and also from the flesh and the devil; which contamination when received, however minute it may be, cannot escape the detection of Him who seeth all things. In the degree in which this has prevailed, it tends to obstruct the access of the soul unto God, who is a Being of infinite purity and holiness. Now the great Head of the church, the High-priest and Bishop of souls, beholds the state of every individual in religious assemblies, and does not fail, when he sees meet, to dispense unto every one according to his need, who in the exercise of faith and love comes to him. He breaks the bread of life unto the pure in heart, and in his abundant mercy he gives repentance and contrition of soul unto those, who, through unwatchfulness have contracted any degree of defilement, cleansing their hearts from an evil conscience by the blood of sprinkling: (Heb. x. 22;) thus the gracious declaration of our Lord is verified, "Where two or three are gathered together in my name, (and consequently when a larger number is so gathered,) there am I in the midst of them;" (Matt. xviii. 20;) for these words of our holy Redeemer are not unmeaning sounds: they are definite and most certain truths. What a blessed privilege then is it, that a religious assembly may witness the life-giving presence of Christ revealed in and among them! But it should ever be borne in mind, that this high privilege is held out to those, and to those only, who are gathered in his name; which, as already observed, signifies or has reference to his divine attributes, viz. his power, life, light, &c. That we may participate in this high privilege, the command of our holy Redeemer to his disciples, "What I say unto you I say unto all, watch," and again, "Watch and pray, that ye enter not into temptation, (Mark, xiii. 37; Matt. xxvi. 41,) should never be forgotten: it is indeed a duty very needful to be observed in the course of our daily conduct and conversation, among men; but on no occasion is the practice of it more necessary, than in assemblies for public worship. For there is ground to believe, that the enemy of all good, strives, by every means in his power, to prevent the worshipping of Almighty God in spirit and in truth; and the human mind by its own strength is entirely incompetent to withstand his efforts. As, therefore, the declaration of Jesus Christ on this important subject, "The hour cometh, and now is, when the true worshippers shall worship the Father in spirit and in truth; for the Father seeketh such to worship him," (John, iv. 23,) affords sufficient ground for the conclusion, that it is consistent with the will of our heavenly Father that this pure spiritual worship should every where prevail, —how indispensable to the being preserved from opposition to the divine will, in this particular, when assembled for the purpose of divine worship, is a uniform, implicit adherence to the injunction of our Lord,—even that "all," of every denomination in his militant church, should "watch;" that so, under the influence of his Holy Spirit, the supplications of their souls may ascend unto him, that they may not enter into any of the temptations of the enemy, including the temptation to preach, or vocally to pray or sing, before the quickening influence of the Spirit of

Christ is felt distinctly to lead unto any one of these acts.

In the duty of watching, that of waiting upon God may be considered to be included; and if this duty be patiently persevered in, there is a gracious assurance that the result will be a renewal of strength. (Isai. xl. 31.) Thus invigorated, true believers, through the loving kindness and strength of the Lord, will surmount the temptations of their souls' adversary; and will be enabled to worship the Father of spirits, in spirit and in truth—in solemn reverential silence;—followed, as often as the great Head of the church shall be pleased to direct, by vocal ministry, prayer, and praise. And this direction, communicated by the immediate influence of his Holy Spirit, when, and as he seeth meet to give it, in religious assemblies, will be clearly understood by those individuals, (if duly watchful and attentive,) whom he may be pleased to entrust with a gift of the ministry; and he will also furnish them with the needful supplies of that "wisdom, which is from above," for the edification of his church. Then their dependence being placed *on this wisdom and not on their own*, the apostolic direction will be thoroughly complied with; "If any man speak, let him speak as the oracles of God; if any man minister, let him do it as of the ability which God giveth; that God in all things may be glorified through Jesus Christ." (1 Pet. iv. 11.)

In divine worship, agreeably with various texts of Holy Scripture bearing on this subject, the life-giving influence of the Spirit of Christ should be regarded as the only true spring to action. The will and wisdom of man should not be suffered to predominate, or take the lead, but should be kept in entire subserviency. The general tenor of those declarations and promises which the Scriptures hold forth, relative to Christ and his Holy Spirit, describes him as given to mankind for *their Lord—their Leader—their Guide—their Shepherd—their High Priest, &c.* (John, xiii. 13; Isai. lv. 4; John, x. 14, and xvi. 13; Heb. ii. 17.) Now these characters convey the idea of *precedence—of direction—of going before*—but not of *following*. Accordingly we find that when our Lord described himself as "the good Shepherd," he said, "When he *putteth forth* his own sheep, he goeth before them, and the sheep follow him; for they know his voice." (John, x. 4.) "The good Shepherd" then "putteth forth his own sheep" *in all their religious services*, in public assemblies, and on other occasions. If therefore it be admitted, that the worship which is in spirit and in truth, is performed only under the quickening influence, and guidance of the Spirit of Christ,—it behoves the professors of Christianity in general, very seriously to consider, whether they are performing this worship, when in their public assemblies they begin their religious services according to a previously prescribed form,—and when their ministers depend on their own wisdom, for a supply of matter for their sermons and prayers. If, on the contrary, their worship commences in the manner, and is performed under the circumstances now described,—or, in respect to those professed Christians who do not use any prescribed forms of worship, *if any of their ministers* be not careful reverently to wait for that "ability which God giveth," (1 Peter, iv. 11,) and if without this essential qualification they presume to preach or to pray in their assemblies; it should be a subject of grave consideration, whether in all these cases they are not proceeding without the only sure Guide and Leader, and substituting another leader, human wisdom, in its stead? For, indeed we have no ground from the testimony of Holy Scripture to expect, that the Spirit of Christ *will follow us with its life-giving influence*, when in our religious assemblies we put ourselves under the direction of our own will and wisdom, by beginning to preach, or to pray, or to sing, before the quickening influence of the Spirit of Christ is felt to put forth and lead in the performance of any one of these acts.

Far be it, however, from the writer, to assign any limits to the love and mercy of our Lord Jesus Christ. He fully believes that in very many instances, where uprightness and sincerity of heart are found, our holy Redeemer graciously condescends to render religious services, which are in some degree of the character now described, effectual to the awakening of the unconverted, to the convincing them of the danger of living in forgetfulness of God, and to the exciting in their hearts a lively feeling of their want of a Saviour. How greatly is it to be desired, that this gracious condescension of infinite goodness, may not be held up as an argument to obstruct their reception of, and obedience to, such further manifestations of divine light, as the great Head of the church may be pleased to dispense; in order to enable them more clearly to discriminate between that worship which is in spirit and in truth, and those performances to which the appellation of will-worship is in any degree applicable.

When it is considered that the well-being in this life, and the eternal happiness hereafter of every individual, depends on his becoming not merely a nominal, but a real Christian; the subject appears evidently one of the greatest importance: for, as said our blessed Saviour, "What shall it profit a man if he gain the whole world, and lose his own soul." Let then every professed Christian be stimulated, not to place his dependence on his being a member of any religious community, or on his being in the practice of uniting in any external form of worship, or ceremonial observance; but let him, with an anxiety in some degree adequate to the importance of the subject, seek an experimental knowledge of the power of God inwardly revealed; that by submission to its humbling operation, "every mountain and hill (of self-exaltation, may) be brought low;" (Luke, iii. 5;) that so every obstacle to his coming unto Christ, and his partaking of the salvation which is by him, may be effectually removed.

With this important object in view, let us apply to ourselves a portion of the doctrine adverted to in the preceding pages. God, in his infinite love to mankind, has declared respecting Christ : "I will give thee for a light to the Gentiles, that thou mayest be my salvation to the ends of the earth; (Isai. xlix. 6;) and our holy Redeemer referring to this divine gift, and describing the cause of the condemnation of those who perish, said "This is the condemnation, that light is come into the world, and men loved darkness rather than light, because their deeds were evil;" therefore, that we may not bring on ourselves this condemnation, by our not loving, but disregarding and rejecting Christ, under the manifestation of the light, let a heart-searching examination take place individually, by our conscientious application to ourselves of the following questions : *Dost thou believe in Christ, in reference to his spiritual appearance in thy own soul ?* (2 Cor. xiii. 5.) *Hast thou, in the metaphorical language of Scripture, opened the door of the heart unto him, when, by the secret convictions of his holy light or Spirit, he has knocked there for admission ?* (Rev. iii. 20.) *Hast thou thus received Christ for thy leader,* (Isaiah, lv. 4,) *thy baptizer,* (Matt. iii. 11,) *thy high-priest and thy king ?* (Heb. ii. 17. Isaiah, xxxiii. 22.) *Is it become thy daily concern to obey him in all things, avoiding that in every part of thy conduct and conversation, which the light manifests to be evil,* (John, iii. 20, 21,) *denying thyself and taking up the cross, in respect to every pursuit and gratification, which this divine Monitor does not allow, however earnestly pleaded for by thy natural inclination and desires ?* (Luke, ix. 23.) And finally, *dost thou witness, through submission to the baptizing operation of his Holy Spirit, the work of regeneration begun, and gradually progressing in thy soul ?* (John, iii. 3.)

To promote this great work of reformation among professing Christians of every denomination, is the object which the writer has in view: he fervently desires that the awakening visitations of divine love and mercy may be extensively embraced,—that great may be the number of those, who, feeling the burthen of sin, and their need of a Saviour, and under the conviction that the form of godliness without the power cannot save them, will be prepared to accept the gracious invitation, "Come unto me all ye that labour and are heavy laden, and I will give you rest. Take my yoke upon you, and learn of me, for I am meek and lowly in heart; and ye shall find rest unto your souls." As a general solicitude prevails thus to come unto Christ, to submit to his yoke, and to learn of and to be baptized by him, the fruit of his Holy Spirit will be abundantly produced; genuine Christianity will again shine forth in her ancient beauty; the name of Almighty God will be glorified by the consistent conduct and conversation of professed Christians; and in their religious assemblies, the will and wisdom of man being no longer suffered to predominate, but being kept in due subserviency, the eternal light, love, power and wisdom of our God will be exalted in dominion over all.

"*Even so, holy Father, thy kingdom come, thy will be done on earth, as it is done in heaven.*"

For "The Friend."

Account by George Fox of the "Spreading of Truth."

I have been induced to copy the following "Narrative of the spreading of truth, and of the opposition from the powers which then were, written by George Fox in the year 1676," in the hope that it may animate some amongst us to greater dedication of heart, to that blessed cause which was dearer to our honourable predecessors than life, liberty, or the good things of this world.   A. H.

—

. The truth sprang up first to us, so as to be a people to the Lord, in Leicestershire in 1644, in Warwickshire in 1645, in Nottinghamshire in 1646, in Derbyshire in 1647, and in the adjacent counties in 1648, 1649 and 1650, in Yorkshire in 1651, in Lancashire and Westmoreland in 1653, in London, and most of the other parts of England, Scotland, and Ireland, in 1654. In 1655, many went beyond sea, where truth also sprang up, and in 1656 it broke forth in America, and many other places. In the authority of this divine truth, Friends stood all the cruelties and sufferings that were inflicted upon them by the long parliament; to the spoiling of goods, imprisonment and death, and over all reproaches, lies, and slanders; as well as those in Oliver Cromwell's time, and all the acts made by him and his parliament; his son Richard after him, and the committee of safety; and after withstood and outlasted all the acts and proclamations since 1660, that the king came in. Friends never feared their acts, prisons, jails, houses of correction, banishment, nor spoiling of goods, nay, nor the loss of life itself; nor was there ever any persecution that came, but we saw in the event it would be productive of good; nor were there ever any prisons that I was in, or sufferings, but it was for the bringing multitudes out of prison; though they who imprisoned the truth, and quenched the Spirit in themselves, would imprison and quench it without them; so that there was a time when so many were in prison, that it became as a by-word, "truth is scarce any where to be found but in jails." And after the king came in, divers Friends suffered much, because they would not drink his health, and say, "God bless the king;" so that many Friends were in danger of their lives from rude persons, who were ready to run them through with their swords for refusing it, until the king gave forth a proclamation against drinking healths; for we were and are against drinking any healths, and all excess, both before his coming in and after; and we desire the king's good, and that the blessing of God might come upon him and all his subjects, and all people upon the face of the earth; but we did desire people, not to drink the king's health, but to let him have his health, and all people else; and to drink for their own health and necessity only, for that way of drinking healths and to excess, was not for the king's health, nor their own nor any others; which excess often brought forth quarrelling and destroying one another, and this was not for the king's wealth, nor health, nor honour, but

might grieve him to have the creatures and his subjects destroyed; and so the Lord's power gave us dominion over that also, and all our other sufferings. But oh! the number of sufferers in the commonwealth's and Oliver Cromwell's days, and since; especially those who were haled before the courts for not paying tithes, refusing to swear on their juries, not putting off their hats, and for going to meetings on the first days; under pretence of breaking the Sabbath, and to meetings on other days of the week; who were abused both in meetings and on the highways. Oh! how great were the sufferings we then sustained on these accounts! for some times they would drive Friends by droves into the prison houses like penfolds, confine them on the first days, and take their horses from them and keep them for pretended breach of their Sabbath, though they would ride in their coaches and upon their fat horses to the steeple houses themselves, and yet punish others. And many Friends were turned out of their copyholds and customary tenements, because in obedience to the command of Christ and his apostle they could not swear; and as they went to meetings, they have been stoned through the streets, and otherwise cruelly abused. Many were fined with great fines, and lay long in prison for not putting off their hats, which fines Friends could never pay, though they kept them in prison till they had satisfied their own wills, and at last turned them out, after keeping them a year or more in prison. Many books I gave forth against tithes, showing how the priesthood was changed that took them; and that Christ sent forth his twelve and afterwards seventy disciples, saying unto them, "Freely ye have received, freely give." So all who do not obey the doctrine and command of Christ therein, we cannot receive them. I was also moved to give forth several books against swearing, and that our yea and nay might be taken instead of an oath, which if we broke, let us suffer the same punishment as they who broke their oaths. And in Jamaica, the governor and the assembly granted the thing; it is also granted in some other places, and several of the parliament-men in England have acknowledged the reasonableness thereof. The magistrates, after some time, when they saw our faithfulness in yea and nay, they who were moderate, both before and since the king came in, would put Friends into offices without an oath, but the cruel and envious would fine Friends to get money of them, though they could not pay them any.

Thus the Lord's power hath carried us through all, and over all, to his everlasting glory and praise, for God's power hath been our hedge, our wall, and our keeper, (the preserver of his plants and vineyard) who have not had the magistrate's sword and staff to help us, nor ever trusted in the arm of flesh, but have gone without these, or Judas' bag, to preach the word of life, which was in the beginning before they were; which word reconciles to God. And thousands have received this word of reconciliation, and are born again of the immortal Seed by the word of God; and are feeding upon the milk of the

word which lives and abides for ever. Many have suffered death for their testimony, in England, and beyond the seas, both before and since the king came in, which may be seen in an account given to the king and both houses of parliament, being a brief, plain, and true relation of the late and sad sufferings of the people of God, in scorn called Quakers, for worshipping and exercising a good conscience towards God and man. By reason whereof eighty-nine have suffered till death, thirty-two of which died before the king came into England, and fifty-seven since, by hard imprisonment and cruel usage. Forty-three have died in the city of London and Southwark, since the act made against meetings, &c., about 1661, of which a more particular account was given, with the names of the sufferers, to the king and parliament about 1663. And though divers laws were designed against us, yet never could any of them justly touch us, being wrested and misapplied in their execution by our adversaries, which some have been made to confess. All those laws that were made, and the oath which they imprisoned us for, because, in obedience to the command of Christ Jesus, we could not swear us; and yet we suffered by the several powers, and their laws, both spoiling of goods and imprisonment, even to death. And the governor of Dover castle, when the king asked him if he had dispersed all the sectaries' meetings? said that he had, but the Quakers, the devil himself could not; for if he did imprison them, and break up their meetings, they would meet again; and if he should beat them or knock them down, or kill some of them, all was one, they would meet and not resist again. Thus the Lord's power did support and keep them over their persecutors, and make them to justify our patient and lamb-like nature. This was about 1671.

Since the king came in, three acts have been made against us, besides the proclamations, by which many have suffered imprisonment and banishment, and many to death. And yet for all these acts and proclamations, persecutions, sufferings, banishments, faithful Friends are as fresh as ever in the Lord's power, and valiant for his name and truth. Some weak ones there were, when the king came in, who did take the oath; but after they had so done, they were sore troubled for disobeying the command of Christ and the apostle, and went to the magistrates condemned themselves, and offered to go to prison.

Thus the Lord in his everlasting power, hath been the stay and support of his people; and still his Seed reigns, his truth is over all and exceedingly spreads unto this year 1676.

———

For "The Friend."

CIRCULAR.

In again calling the attention of Auxiliaries to the annual queries subjoined, the committee of correspondence of the Bible Association of Friends in America, earnestly request that answers may be forwarded early in the *third* month from *all* the auxiliaries. Where it is not practicable, from the scattered situation of the members in many country places or from other causes, to institute new inquiries, so as to answer all the queries with accuracy for the current year, it is desirable that such information as can be given relative to the state of the respective associations, may not be withheld; for, though full reports would better enable the managers of the parent institution to look after and provide for the various wants of Friends as far as ability may be furnished, a general account of each auxiliary, such as their committee of correspondence or secretary may be able to give, would be more satisfactory than no answer at all. As funds are much needed to enable the managers to meet their various engagements, it is hoped that the auxiliaries will afford such pecuniary aid as their circumstances and condition will admit of, towards the promotion of the good causes in which we have embarked; and especially where there is any thing due, on account, to the depository, such balances as can be conveniently paid would be acceptable and opportune.

JOHN PAUL,
THOMAS EVANS,
ISAAC COLLINS.

1. What number of families or individuals have been gratuitously furnished with the Holy Scriptures by the Association, since its establishment, and how many during the past year?

2. What number of Bibles and Testaments have been sold by the Association, since its commencement, and how many within the past year?

3. How many members, male and female, are there belonging to the Association, and what number of families of Friends reside within its limits?

4. Are there any families of Friends within your limits not duly supplied with the Holy Scriptures; and if so, how many?

5. How many members of our Society, capable of reading the Bible, do not own a copy?

6. How many Bibles or Testaments may probably be disposed of by sale or otherwise to Friends within your limits?

7. Is the income of the auxiliary sufficient to supply those within its limits who are not duly furnished with the Holy Scriptures?

THE FRIEND.

SECOND MONTH, 8, 1840.

To bring the decision in the Amistad case within the space convenient to appropriate to it, we have been obliged to curtail to a larger extent than at first intended. It is proper to mention, that since our last we have learned an appeal has been prepared to the circuit court by the representative of the Spanish authorities.

The newspaper paragraphs relative to BLOOD-HOUNDS had not escaped our attention, but a project of such glaring atrocity and barbarism seemed to us so totally incredible, that we waited for stronger proof. The truth of the reports, however, would appear to be now fully confirmed, and we trust there will be no lack of zeal and promptitude on the part of our young men and others, both here and elsewhere, in effecting the objects of the annexed communication.

For "The Friend."

THE BLOOD-HOUNDS.

Several months ago one of the newspapers in this city published an article, stating that it was the intention of those who had the direction of the war, which the government is waging with the Seminole Indians in Florida, to procure from the West Indies a number of blood-hounds, to be employed against those natives. The idea was so repulsive to every humane and noble principle, that few persons could credit it. A general impression appeared to prevail, that in the nineteenth century the rulers of a free, high-minded and enlightened people, would not dare to blacken the national character by so foul a stain, and that the notion must have originated in the heated imagination of some zealous partizan. But in a while after, a New Orleans paper announced that five thousand dollars had been appropriated for accomplishing this object, and that Colonel Fitzpatrick had sailed to Cuba to purchase the animals. Still people were reluctant to credit the statement, or to believe it could be intended to use those ferocious brutes against our fellow men—the workmanship of our common Creator and Father. More recently, however, a southern paper states that "Colonel Fitzpatrick has arrived with thirty-three blood-hounds and six Spaniards, their trainers;" and a Tallahassee paper states, that "now there is some hope of bringing the war to a close" through the aid of these animals. The Globe, a newspaper published at Washington, and the official organ of the government, at first denied that this savage proceeding had the sanction of the heads of department there—but recently it has lowered its tone, and seems to admit the fact, and plead necessity for the measure. There is no doubt whatever that the whole matter is well known. to the officers of government at Washington, and that they have so far sanctioned it, as not to exercise their power and authority in forbidding it. The war is carried on by authority and at the expense of the general government. Florida is a territory, and therefore subject to its control, and if our rulers do not put a stop to this diabolical measure, the guilt of it must rest, not on Florida merely, but on the nation at large. War is fraught with wickedness and cruelty even in the mildest forms in which it can be viewed, but to aggravate its horrors and its crimes by a measure so repugnant to humanity and civilization, to say nothing of an appeal to the benign spirit of the Gospel, is retrograding to the darkest ages of the Spanish barbarity.

The following remonstrance is circulating for signatures among our fellow-citizens; and we hope our friends through the country will endeavour to get it extensively circulated and signed. Printed copies of the remonstrance may be had at the office of "The Friend." It is necessary each person should sign two—one for the senate, and the other for the house of representatives.

To the Senate and House of Representatives of the United States of America, in Congress assembled.

The memorial and remonstrance of the undersigned citizens of the United States—respectfully showeth—

That your memorialists have learned with deep regret and abhorrence, that a number of blood-hounds have recently been imported from the island of Cuba, for the purpose of employing them against the Seminole Indians, with whom the government is now carrying on a war in the territory of Florida. Dreadful as are the evils attendant on a state of warfare, even in its most mitigated form—to aggravate them by the introduction of so barbarous and inhuman a measure, we view as an outrage upon every feeling of humanity, against which we are bound solemnly to protest. As a territory of the United States, Florida is subject to the control of the general government; and we earnestly beseech congress to interpose its authority to arrest this attempt, and preserve our country from the deep and lasting disgrace which must be inflicted by so foul a blot upon the national character.

The annual meeting of the Auxiliary Bible Association of Friends in Philadelphia Quarterly Meeting, will be held on the evening of second day, the 10th instant, at half past seven o'clock, in the Committee Room, Arch street. The members of both branches are invited to attend.

NATHAN KITE, Sec'ry.
Philadelphia, 2d mo. 4th, 1840.

FRIENDS' ASYLUM.

Committee on Admissions.—John G. Hoskins, No. 60 Franklin street, and No. 50 North Fourth street, up stairs; E. B. Garrigues, No. 185 North Seventh street, and No. 41 Market street, up stairs; Isaac Collins, No. 129 Filbert street, and No. 50 Commerce street; Edward Yarnall, southwest corner of Twelfth and George streets, and No. 39 Market street; Samuel Bettle, Jr., No. 73 North Tenth street, and No. 26 South Front street.

Visiting Managers for the Month.—Joel Woolman, near Frankford; Lindzey Nicholson, No. 24 South Twelfth street; George R. Smith, No. 467 Arch street.

Superintendents. — John C. and Lætitia Redmond.

Attending Physician.—Dr. Charles Evans, No. 201 Arch street.

Resident Physician.—Dr. Thomas Wood.

DIED, at his residence in Smyrna, Chenango county, N. Y., on the 29th of twelfth month, in the 79th year of his age, JAMES PEARDE, late of Norwich, England, after a painful illness, which he bore with Christian patience and fortitude, showing to those near him, the truth of that passage of Scripture, which saith," Blessed are those who die in the Lord."

—— on the 7th of last month, in the 54th year of her age, ANNA JONES, daughter of Stephen and Eunice Jones, of Brunswick, Maine.

PRINTED BY ADAM WALDIE,
Carpenter Street, below Seventh, Philadelphia.

THE FRIEND.

A RELIGIOUS AND LITERARY JOURNAL.

VOL. XIII.   **SEVENTH DAY, SECOND MONTH, 15, 1840.**   **NO. 20.**

EDITED BY ROBERT SMITH.

PUBLISHED WEEKLY.

Price two dollars per annum, payable in advance.

Subscriptions and Payments received by

GEORGE W. TAYLOR,

NO. 50, NORTH FOURTH STREET, UP STAIRS,

PHILADELPHIA.

From Silliman's Journal.

ON THE TAILS OF COMETS.

BY WILLIAM MITCHELL, OF NANTUCKET.

There is perhaps no department of astronomical science, connected with the solar system, of a nature more interesting than that of comets, and certainly no one which has so nearly defied the researches and the reasonings of the astronomer. Aside from these bodies, if such they may be called, the greater and the lesser lights have been subjected to rigorous weight and measure, and the solar system is emphatically the beaten way of the astronomer. Comets, however, have presented difficulties so insuperable, that in latter times, the subject seems to have been nearly abandoned in despair; and armed as the present age may be against the horrors of superstition, a cometary appearance as imposing as that of 1680, or even of the less threatening aspect of that of 1744, would create no small degree of uneasiness in some hearts of the stoutest mould. When Dr. Olbers announced that a portion of the earth's orbit would be involved in the nebulous atmosphere of Biela's comet in 1832, one half at least of the civilised world quaked with fear. Notwithstanding the alluring promise held out to the modern student by the glories of sidereal astronomy, nothing can justify a neglect of phenomena, which, by a close investigation, might result in contributing so much to the tranquillity of the world. Impressed forcibly in my youth by the beautiful appearance of the comet of 1807, and, at a riper age, with those of 1811, 1819, 1825, and 1835, visible to the naked eye, and with others, seen at various periods by telescopic aid, I have been led frequently to reflect on the probable nature and physical properties of these erratic objects, and especially on that distinguishing appendage, which by common consent is denominated the *tail*. In looking over the history of comets, and noting the explanation of the trains (with which they are for the most part attended,) as given by many distinguished astronomers, at periods very remote from each other, I am constrained to acknowledge, high as the authority unquestionably is, that no one has afforded to my mind the slightest satisfaction.

Notwithstanding the great number of writers on this subject, and the diversity of opinions that have been promulgated, there appear to have been only two prevailing theories. The more ancient of these supposed the tails to be formed by the lighter parts being thrown off by the resistance of the ether through which the comet passed. The modern and the more generally prevailing theory is, that these particles are driven off by the impulsive force of the sun's rays. In each of these theories, the tails are supposed to consist of *matter*. With regard to the former theory, the simple fact that the tail precedes the comet in its course through a portion of its elliptical journey, is a sufficient refutation; and to afford weight or plausibility to the latter, it is necessary to assume that the sun "blows heat and cold with the same breath"—in other words, that it attracts and repels with the same *modus operandi*. If we have no evidence of a repulsive force in the sun, to say nothing of a force sufficient to repel the lighter particles of these bodies to a distance from the head of the comet, equal to and sometimes exceeding a hundred millions of miles, this theory, to say the least of it, is laboured and unsatisfactory. The length of these trains is far from being exaggerated. Referring to my minutes of the late return of Halley's comet, I find that, at one period, the tail, by direct vision, subtended an angle of twenty degrees, and on some occasions, by oblique vision, more than forty degrees. The tail of the comet of 1089, is said to exceed sixty-eight degrees, and that of the comet of 1680, ninety degrees. Making a proper allowance for the faintness of the extremity of the tail, and the obstruction of the view by the atmosphere of the earth, it is by no means unsafe to conclude that many of them extend some hundreds of millions of miles from the nucleus of the comet.

In view, then, of the last mentioned theory, it is by no means a matter of surprise, that Newton, and with him La Place and Sir J. Herschel, should entertain the opinion that the more remote particles, could never be recalled by the gravitation of the nucleus, and that portions of the tails were at each revolution scattered in space, and hence that comets were continually wasting.

Arago, in speaking of the then anticipated return of Halley's comet in 1835, makes the following remark:—"It appears probable that in describing their immense orbits, comets, at each revolution, dissipate in space all the matter, which, when they are near the perihelion, is detached from the envelope forming the tail; it is therefore very possible that in time, some of them may be entirely dissipated." But these views were not confirmed by the appearance

of Halley's comet in 1835, and Arago has with a very becoming candour acknowledged this fact. "If the reader," says he, "will take the trouble to compare what I record of the comet of 1835, with the circumstances of its former apparition, he certainly will not find in this collection of phenomena, the proof that Halley's comet is gradually diminishing. I will even say that if, in a matter so delicate, the observations made at very different periods of the year, will authorise any positive deduction, that which would most distinctly result from the two passages of 1759 and 1835, would be that the comet had increased in size during that interval. I ought to seize with more eagerness, this occasion to combat an error extensively accredited (a belief in the constant wasting away of comets) because I believe I have somewhat contributed to its dissemination."

The truth is, as I apprehend, that the data on which this conjecture was based, are probably false, and the tails of comets, if the subject is properly investigated, will not be found to consist of matter at all that has the least connection with the comet, but formed by the sun's rays slightly refracted by the comet, and uniting in an infinite number of points beyond it, throwing a stronger than ordinary light on the ethereal medium, near to or more remote from the comet, as the ray from its relative position and direction is more or less refracted.

It is not important to the truth of this hypothesis whether the nucleus be a solid mass or not, so that it be more dense than the surrounding nebulosity, nor yet that the tail be projected in an exact line with the radius vector of the sun and comet, so that it be nearly so. It is, however, important to its truth, that an etherial medium should exist, otherwise the reflection of these points of light would be impossible; also, that the comet should *assume* the tail as it approaches the sun, and that it should progressively increase in strength and brilliancy, the light of the sun increasing in the proportion of the square of the diminution of distance;—again, that the tail should have a cylindrical and hollow appearance, the rays of light being at least partially obstructed by the nucleus; moreover, that the tail should be curved, by the necessary effect of aberration. I apprehend it will be acknowledged that the weight of testimony is decidedly favourable to the fact that the nuclei of comets, though they generally resemble planets in form and brilliancy, may not be solid or opaque, inasmuch as some are unquestionably transparent, and the quantity of matter in all is exceedingly inconsiderable.

evidence of its existence, in its effect upon the duration of the revolution of the Encke comet. Professor Encke, in a dissertation on this subject, after giving the minutiæ of his observations, very modestly remarks—"If I may be permitted to express my opinion on a subject which for twelve years has incessantly occupied me, in treating which I have avoided no method, however circuitous, no kind of verification, in order to reach the truth, so far as it lay in my power, I cannot consider it otherwise than completely established, that an extraordinary connection is necessary for Pon's* comet, and equally certain that the principal part of it consists in the increase of the mean motion proportionate to the time."

Professor Airy, in an appendix to a translation of Encke's memoir, adds—"I cannot but express my belief, that the principal part of the theory, namely, an effect exactly similar to that which a resisting medium would produce, is perfectly established by the reasoning of Professor Encke." Arago, in speaking of the discrepancy between the result of calculation and observation on the period of the Encke comet, states that the cause " can be nothing but the resistance of the ether." And Dr. Bowditch, distinguished as he was for cautiousness, fully recognised the effect of an ethereal medium, in the translation of the Mécanique Celeste. The fact, however, that Halley's comet, at its late return, reached its perihelion *later* rather than *earlier* than the calculated time, independent of an allowance for a resisting medium, seems to have created some doubts in reference to the doctrine of resistance; but of the three comets whose periods are certainly known, those of Biela and Encke only can be relied upon as indicating resistance, inasmuch as that of Halley has its aphelion in a region beyond the scan of human power, and the influence of planetary bodies which may exist there, is now, and will perhaps for ever remain unknown to us. These facts, then, and the concurring opinions of the high authority above quoted, render it nearly unquestionable that there is diffused through the celestial regions, an ethereal and exceedingly elastic medium; nor would it be unreasonable to suppose that this very medium constitutes the solar atmosphere, of which the zodiacal light may be a denser region.

When an opportunity is offered to observe a comet nearer from the sun, it is generally

light are more obstructed by t the rarer portions of the comet

That there is, in these tails, a considerable length, a slight to that portion of the orbit wh has left, there is ample testim the light is progressive, a p must elapse while the rays of ing from the head of the comet of union, and during that per moves onward in its course, t necessarily is a gentle or sligh tail, the effect being greater o portion as the union of the ra less distant from the comet. that if a ray of light could be its entire course from the sun would present a similar phenom degree if the motion of a plane that of a comet. The comets Encke have no tails, nor is speaking a nucleus in either. T during the long period in 1828, tion was so favourable to observ appearance of a mere film of circular, but not well defined, a stellar point could be detected scopic power which I employed sion. In fact, all the phenomer of comets appear to be so well this theory that I cannot doubt though nothing like demonstra nies it.

There are, indeed, optical dif I have been unable to overc however, which may not be fa to our ignorance of the partic constitution of these bodies. confirmation of the truth of th of the tails of comets, that th slightest evidence, worthy of c the earth which we inhabit b sensibly affected by a visitatic enormous appendages, while t collision between the earth and a comet, properly so called, i small; yet when we reflect upo of comets belonging to our sys dreds that range within the ear their paths have every possible the ecliptic, that these immer trains projected in a direction describe an inconceivable swe are encompassing the sun in their perihelion;—I say, in vie cumstances, it is difficult to av

Let me ask those who have a sort of instinctive dread of religious instruction in our common schools, to consider what it is; and what kind of influence it will have over our children, provided they can be made to understand, embrace and practise it. Is it a friend, or an enemy to their highest welfare? Does it not, in its most comprehensive sense, include a belief in the being and perfections of God; in the revelation of his will to man; in a state of rewards and punishments; in piety of heart, and in the practice of all moral duties? And what is there here to be afraid of? Suppose, now, that every child in every common school throughout the length and breadth of the United States, could not only be *taught*, every day, but *induced*, to " fear God and keep his commandments ?" Would there be any more lying, swearing, quarrelling, cheating or stealing; any more youthful dissipation; any more gray hairs brought down to the grave by filial ingratitude? Would not every school be more orderly, studious and flourishing; and every family more happy? Would not all these millions of children, as they come forward into life, make better husbands and wives, fathers and mothers, neighbours and friends, rulers and citizens? Would not the whole face of society be changed, and changed infinitely for the better, in a single generation; and could the same influence be perpetuated in the school, from generation to generation; would not every living soul have reason to rejoice in the mighty change? Would it not produce just such a state of society as one would wish to live in, and to leave his dearest friends in, when removed himself by the stroke of death?

The truth is, and it cannot be too earnestly insisted on, that education ought to be conducted on strictly *Christian principles*, through every stage of its progress, from the primary school room, up to the college and university. Nothing short of this, is worthy of an enlightened and professedly Christian people. Every common school *ought* to be made a nursery of piety, as well as of elementary learning; and certainly will be, in that coming day of millennial glory, when " all shall know the Lord from the least even to the greatest." Religion should be so wrought into all our systems of education, as to give them a decidedly Christian character, and to let the world know, that so far from being ashamed of our faith, we glory in it; and that in leaving our institutions as a legacy to our children, to be handed down in turn to theirs, it may be seen to have been our main concern, to teach them " the fear of the Lord which is the beginning of wisdom, and to depart from evil which is understanding." The sanctions and principles of the gospel, ought to be just as familiar in the school room, as the rules of reading and spelling; and if they were made so, it would obviate the objection which many now feel to religious instruction, by making it easy and natural; and in that way, *interesting*, rather than *repulsive*, to the scholars. If you dress up religion in black crape, and toll the bell, and put on a funeral countenance, every time it is introduced, they will dread it as they do passing by a graveyard in the dark; and it may do them more harm than good; but if you represent it as it is, full of light, and love, and mercy; of joy and peace to all who cordially embrace it, it cannot fail of commending itself to their reason and consciences; and of early bringing thousands, under the blessing of heaven, to the saving knowledge of the truth.

I have not the school laws of any other state before me; but in what light the early settlers of Massachusetts regarded the religious education of their children, will be seen in the following extract from one of their statutes, passed in 1683.

" Forasmuch as it greatly concerns the welfare of this country, that the youth thereof be educated, not only in good literature, but in sound doctrine :—this court doth therefore commend it to the serious consideration and special care of the overseers of the college, and of the selectmen in the several towns, not to admit, or suffer any such to be continued in the office or place of teaching, educating and instructing youth, or children in the college, or schools, that have manifested themselves unsound in the faith, or scandalous in their lives, and have not given satisfaction, according to the rules of Christ."

In agreement with the design and spirit of this ancient statute, is the *seventh section* of the law entitled Public Instruction, now in force.

" It shall be the duty of the president, professors and tutors at Cambridge, and of the several colleges, and of all preceptors and teachers of academies, and all other instructors of youth, to exert their best endeavours, to impress on the minds of children and youth committed to their care and instruction the principles of *piety*, *justice*, and a sacred regard to truth; love to their country, humanity and universal benevolence; sobriety, industry and frugality; chastity, moderation and temperance; and those other virtues, which are the ornament of human society, and the basis upon which a republican constitution is founded; and it shall be the duty of such instructors, to endeavour to lead their pupils, as their ages and capacities will admit, into a clear understanding of the tendency of the above mentioned virtues, to preserve and perfect a republican constitution, and secure the blessings of liberty, as well as to promote their future happiness, and also to point out to them the evil tendency of the opposite vices." Revised Statutes, chap. 23.

How deeply indebted Massachusetts is, to this wise and sound legislation, in connection with the other equally wise provisions of her school laws, for the virtue and intelligence of all classes of her citizens, scarcely admits of calculation; and the more firmly she adheres to this enlightened policy, in the management of her common schools and higher seminaries of learning, the brighter will her prospects be of a still nobler destiny.

For "The Friend."

SLAVERY IN NEW JERSEY.

NO. III.

The right to hold human beings as slaves, and the non-right of the legislature to interfere and prevent it, is asserted by some of our citizens, and I have even heard the position maintained, that our legislature has no more right to emancipate the slaves in the state than it has to take the horses from our farmers' stables.

Let us examine this subject. In a time of darkness, New Jersey, through her constituted agents, agreed with her slaveholders that they might retain their slaves for life, and that the children of slave-mothers should follow their condition. Acting upon the principle that " what the law declares to be property *is* property," the holders of slaves made their arrangements, and purchased and sold bondmen with the faith of the state pledged to continue the relation. But the sun of liberty arose, and as it dispelled the vapours of the night, our legislators partially discovering the wrong they had committed upon an unfortunate class of their fellow men, made some reparation, by decreeing that all born after a certain date should be free. In the further progress of the day, motives of justice and humanity induce an application for the liberation of the remaining thousands in bondage, and the question arises, " Can the legislature rightfully liberate?" There can be no doubt that they are bound to the fulfilment of all contracts which do not violate the moral law; but no agreement or contract, public or private, which is subversive of that law can rightfully be executed. The general assembly had no right to legislate away the claim of any man to his own moral and physical powers, unless guilt or insanity made his freedom dangerous. Our right to liberty does not depend upon any constitutional or legal arrangement of our fellow men. It is in its origin antecedent to all human government, being derived from the relation in which we stand to our great Creator, whose high moral purposes concerning us are frustrated if we are degraded into mere beasts of burden. Man in society must relinquish some of his natural freedom, but in a recognition from himself and his children—still less can other men alienate from him, those rights and powers the possession of which are necessary to the proper fulfilment of his duties as a moral and accountable being—the expansion of his intellectual faculties and the purification of his moral nature. In the declaration of the indestructibility of human rights, the old American congress appealed successfully to the sympathies of the Christian world, and the golden rule of the Redeemer can only be observed in a recognition of the universal brotherhood and equality of man.

We come, then, to the conclusion that the legislature, having violated the moral law in reducing man to the condition of slaves, not only *may* rightfully liberate, but *are bound* by the simplest principles of justice " to proclaim liberty to the captive."

Legislators, however, are sometimes unmindful of their duties. Who will plead before them for the slave?　　VERUS.

THE LEXINGTON.

Verdict of the Coroner's Jury.

The evidence on the investigation of the coroner's jury terminated on Thursday of last week. The coroner in his address to the jury before they retired, observed, " Never, perhaps, did there go forth to this community, a coroner's inquest, the consequences of which were likely to affect so many public and private interests. The words of this inquest will reach the bosoms of those whose relatives have perished by this melancholy calamity, and may dispose them to resignation, or aggravate their grief, according as your verdict tells them that their loss was owing to unavoidable accident, or the negligence of those in whose hands they entrusted their lives. Your verdict may also, in a pecuniary point of view, affect materially not only the interests of the company most immediately concerned in it, but also of several others; and hence, gentlemen, the necessity of great caution in determining on your verdict."

The jury delivered the following opinion and verdict:

From the testimony adduced before the court of inquiry by the coroner's inquest to investigate the causes which led to the destruction by fire of the steamboat Lexington, the inquest are of opinion, that the fire was communicated to the promenade deck by the intense heat of the smoke pipe, or from sparks from the space between the smoke pipe and steam chamber, as the fire was first seen near the casing of the steam chimney, on the promenade deck. They are further of opinion, that the Lexington was a first rate boat, with an excellent steam engine, and a boiler suitable for burning wood, but not coal, with the blowers attached. Furthermore, it is our opinion, that had the buckets been manned at the commencement of the fire, it would have been immediately extinguished. Also, that inasmuch as the engine could not be stopped, from the rapid progress of the fire, —with presence of mind of the officer, and a strict discipline of the crew, the boats could have been launched, and a large portion of the passengers and crew, if not the whole, might have been saved.

It is the opinion of this jury that the present inspectors of steamboats, either from ignorance or neglect, have suffered the steamboat Lexington to navigate the Sound at the imminent risk of the lives and property of the passengers, giving a certificate, stating a full compliance with the laws of the United States, while in our opinion such was not the case.

That the system adopted on board the Lexington, of using blowers on board of boats, is dangerous; which has been proved to this jury by competent witnesses. And that the conduct of the officers of the steamboat Lexington, on the night of the 12th of January, when said steamboat was on fire, deserves the severest censure of this community; from the facts proved before this jury, that the captain and pilot, in the greatest hour of danger, left the steamboat to her own guidance, and sought their own safety, regardless of the fate of the passengers. Instead of the captain or pilot retreating to the tiller, aft, when driven from the wheel-house, forward, and the ropes there being burned off, there being at the same time a communication to the same tiller, there appeared to be no other thought but self-preservation. And it further appears to this jury, that the odious practice of carrying cotton, in any quantities, on board of passenger boats, in a manner in which it is

liable to take fire, from sparks or heat, from any smoke pipe or other means, deserves public censure.

Signed by James Goadby, Thomas E. Burlew, S. H. Harriott, Teunis Fokkes, James Green, P. M. P. Durands, Junrs. Edmund B. McVeagh, A. S. Chase, Abraham Crevelin, Robert Buttle, Richard M. Hoe, Henry V. Davids.

We, composing part of the jury in the case of the loss of the Lexington, fully exonerate and exculpate Captain Stephen Manchester from any blame or censure after the breaking out of the fire on board.

(Signed,)   BENJ. VINCENT, Foreman.
             JOSEPH E. MOUNT.

January 31st, 1840.

AN ORIENTAL OPIUM EATER.

An English ambassador, lately sent to a Mahomedan prince, was conducted upon his arrival at the palace through several richly decorated and spacious apartments, crowded with officers arrayed in superb dresses, to a room, small in dimensions, but ornamented with the most costly and splendid furniture. The attendants withdrew. After a short interval, two persons of superior mien entered the saloon, followed by state bearers, carrying under a lofty canopy a litter covered with delicate silk and the richest Cashmere shawls, upon which lay a human form to all appearance dead, except that its head was dangling loosely from side to side as the bearers moved into the room. Two officers, holding rich filagree salvers, carried each a chalice and a vial containing a black fluid. The ambassador considered the spectacle to be connected with some court ceremony of mourning, and endeavoured to retire; but he was soon undeceived by seeing the officers holding up the head of the apparent corpse, and after gently chafing the throat and returning the tongue, which hung from the mouth relaxed and gaping, pouring some black liquor into the throat, and closing the jaws, until it sank down the passage; after six or seven times repeating the ceremony, the figure opened its eyes and shut its mouth voluntarily; it then swallowed a large portion of the black fluid, and within an hour an animated being sat upon the couch with blood returning into its lips, and a feeble power of articulation. In the Persian language he addressed his visiter, and inquired the particulars of his mission. Within two hours this extraordinary person became altered, and his mind capable of arduous business. The ambassador, after apologising for the liberty, ventured to inquire into the cause of the scene he had just witnessed. "Sir," said he, "I am an inveterate opium-taker, and I have by slow degrees fallen into this melancholy excess. But of the diurnal twenty-four periods of time, I continually pass eighteen in this reverie, unable to move or speak; I am yet conscious, and the time passes away amid pleasing fancies, nor should I ever awake from the wanderings of this state had I not the most faithful and attached attendants, whose regard and religious duty impel them to watch my pulse.

As soon as my heart begins to falter, and my breathing is imperceptible except on a mirror, they immediately pour the solution of opium into my throat, and restore me as you have seen. Within four hours I shall have swallowed many ounces, and much time will not pass away ere I shall relapse into my ordinary torpor."—*Dublin University Magazine.*

PROFITABLE FARMING.

The following facts are stated in the last number of Governor Hill's Monthly Visitor:

James Hill, of West Cambridge, has taken, in ninety successive days, five thousand dollars in cash, in Boston market, for articles raised on his farm.

Isaac Locke, of the same town, has raised the present year, 30 bbls. of quinces, which sold on the ground for seven dollars a barrel; he has also sold in the present autumn, several barrels of Baldwin apples at three dollars per barrel.

The value of the strawberries raised in West Cambridge and sold in the Boston market, is more than was taken thirty years ago for all the agricultural products of the town put together.

The apple orchards of this town are extensive. Two hundred, three hundred, five hundred, and sometimes a thousand barrels of carefully picked apples are produced in a single year by one farmer.

George Pierce of the same town, cultivates only *seven* acres, and yet he has taken in the market for produce, the present season, as by memorandum kept, *nearly or quite* four thousand dollars.

This season, very early, among his articles for market, was about one third of an acre of the dandelion, which grows spontaneously in many mowing fields—these he with some difficulty obtains from the seed; but the crops turn out very profitable. He had about an acre of strawberries, from which upwards of two thousand boxes of that fruit were picked last summer; these at 37½ to 50 cents a box, for which they readily sold in the market, produced not a small profit on a single acre.

G. Pierce also cultivated the raspberry, which thrives with great luxuriance. He thinks he could make of the *blackberry,* which grows in the hedges and amongst piles of decayed wood or rocks in neglected fields, a profitable article.

CONVENIENCES.

Some people seem to think that economy pertains only to the necessaries, and not to the conveniences of life. This is not always, if it be often true. The necessaries of life we must have at any rate, and where the attainment of them is not rendered easy by convenient means, the labour of procuring them is often great, besides there being not a little time lost in the acquisition. Whatever saves time, saves money to an industrious man, and conveniences often save very much of time. Consequently they subserve the cause of economy. In the construction of buildings, farm-yards, and plantations, many steps and much hard labour may be saved by having every thing planned in reference to the greatest convenience. Better have your water in a well at your door, than to have it a quarter of a mile off in a natural stream or spring. It is better to draw it with a pump than a windlass, and better still to have it brought into your kitchen or sinkroom by a lead pipe and house pump, than to have to trot out of doors in cold and heat, wind and rain, for every pailful or draught which you or any member of the family may require. If a well is situated near the house, ordinarily the expense of letting a lead tube down to the water and then extending the pipe under ground to your premises, with a small pump attached from the sink, would cost but little more than an old-fashioned wooden pump at the well. By this means many steps would be saved, health would be less exposed in severe weather, and your house would be kept warmer by the doing away of the necessity of frequently throwing open the back door and leaving it open for a rush of cold air into the house, whilst a pail of water can be drawn. A good housekeeper knows how to economise by securing all such conveniences about his premises. His water he will have drawn in his house. His wood he will have under cover, nearly connected with his kitchen; nor will he neglect to have water in his barnyard or stable for the convenience of his horses and cattle. Those who go only for necessaries and but little for convenience, are poor husbandmen, and will seldom thrive in the world.

But it is said these conveniences cost too much; and we must get along without them. Well then, get along without them and fret your life out with your hard fortune; but this course will cost you more. An ingenious and an industrious man can add a great many conveniences to his premises without much cost in the sense that he has to pay out money to secure them. He is never idle. His leisure hours are always busy ones; that is to say, he devotes them to fixing this thing, that thing, and the other to his mind, till in the course of years he has secured an amount of conveniences which make his premises worth to the purchaser, should he be disposed to sell, vastly more than the cost of them to the seller.—*Maine Cultivator.*

Musk.—Of all odours, the most intolerable to those who do not use it, is musk. Many persons are inconvenienced by it to such a degree, that they could not stay for five minutes in a room containing the minutest quantity of it. It is also the odour which adheres the longest. A coat upon which musk has been thrown will smell of it at the end of two years, though it may have been during the whole time exposed to the open air; but in apartments it will endure almost for ever. The late Empress Josephine was very fond of perfumes, and, above all, of. musk. Her dressing room at Malmaison was filled with it, in spite of Napoleon's frequent remonstrances. Twenty-five years have elapsed since her death, and the present owner of

Malmaison, M. Hagerman, has had the walls repeatedly washed and painted; but neither scrubbing, aquafortis, nor paint, has been able to remove the smell of the musk, which continues as strong as if the bottle which contained it had been but yesterday removed.

THE GOOD WIFE.

She commandeth her husband in any equal matter, by constantly obeying him. She never crosseth her husband in the spring-tide of his anger, but stays till it be ebbing water. Surely men, contrary to iron, are worse to be wrought upon when they are hot. Her clothes are rather comely than costly, and she makes plain cloth to be velvet by her handsome wearing it. Her husband's secrets she will not divulge; especially she is careful to conceal his infirmities. In her husband's absence she is wife and deputy husband, which makes her double the files of her diligence. At his return, he finds all things so well that he wonders to see himself at home when he was abroad. Her children, though many in number, are none in noise, steering them with a look whither she listeth.—*Thomas Fuller.*

THE LATE JULIUS R. FRIEDLANDER.

The following short notice of the late Principal of the Pennsylvania Institution for the Instruction of the Blind, was prepared, as will be seen below, in obedience to a resolution of the board of managers, by one of their number, and was published in the "Student's Magazine," which, it may be recollected, is the title of the periodical printed in raised characters at the institution, principally for the use of this unfortunate class of our fellow-beings. Its republication in "The Friend" would probably gratify many of its readers, among whom are some that have been witnesses to the pure philanthropy and disinterested zeal that ever characterised the subject of the memoir, and who can join with its author in declaring, that "all that he was and all that he possessed he consecrated to a holy purpose."   · K.

Biographical Memoir of Julius R. Friedlander. Written by Benjamin W. Richards, Esq., in compliance with a resolution of the Board of Managers of the Pennsylvania Institution for the Instruction of the Blind.

Julius R. Friedlander was born in Upper Silesia, in the year 1803, of Jewish parentage. He received instruction in a private school at Breslau; and in 1821, was sent to the academy at Dresden. He afterwards repaired to Leipsic, for the benefits of the university of that city. While at Leipsic, he entered the Christian church, became occupied in private tuition, and not long after appears to have directed his mind to a preparation for the object to which he subsequently devoted himself.

The principal occupation in which he appears to have been engaged, was that of tutor and instructor in the family of the Prince of Furstenburg, whose confidence and respect he

seems to have entirely secured. Of the early life of J. R. Friedlander, no important incidents are known to the writer; and it is mainly with reference to his efficient and benevolent action since he came amongst us, that an attempt is made to record some memento of his merit. The effectual relief which he saw afforded to the apparently hopeless and helpless destitution of the blind, through the systems invented and adopted in Europe, seems to have concentrated his benevolent impulses, and directed them to that class of sufferers, as demanding his peculiar solicitude and exertion. He therefore selected our country as unoccupied ground, and addressed himself to our city as the field upon which to develope his object, and execute his plans. It was as fortunate for the cause that impelled him hither, as it was creditable to himself, that he came with the single and exclusive design of establishing a school for the instruction of the blind. His was not the spirit of the adventurer, nor did he adopt this scheme because he found other modes of occupation or personal advancement difficult of access; but actuated by a true and practical philanthropy, he came to carry out a plan which he had carefully considered, maturely weighed, and deliberately determined on, before he left Europe. Accordingly, he had visited many of the institutions for the blind in Europe, and resided for a considerable time in the school at Paris. He was therefore qualified for his undertaking, prepared to avail himself of all essential aids, and entitled to demand in advance the confidence and reliance of those whose support was important to the cause. His personal integrity, his intellectual attainments, his moral and social habits, and his direct preparation for the work, were all presented in proper relief at the outset. His position thus fortified, gave assurance of success, while it illustrated the character of the man, and the genuine nature of his philanthropy. There is an ephemeral and irregular sensibility, a hasty and unstable impulse of benevolence sometimes exhibited in similar undertakings, the result of which is too often a deep wound to the friends whom it has embarked in. His was happily a zeal guided by knowledge, and an ardour tempered by sound discretion. Accordingly, no attraction withdrew him for a moment from his purpose, no obstacle dismayed him; nor did he falter because notoriety or celebrity did not attend his early efforts. He commenced with a single pupil; and in the seclusion of his own chamber, with admirable patience, he devoted laborious hours by day and night to his instruction. His success with this pupil was so. rapid and so remarkable, as to attract the lively interest and animated support of those who witnessed it. From that moment our venerable president, whose heart had been devoted to a school for the blind was secured. Upon the opening of the school, this aptitude of Friedlander was evinced by the rapid improvement of the pupils, the exact discipline of the school, and the apparent contentment of all the inmates. A rare excellence of this teacher was, his quick apprehension of the characters and temperaments of his several pupils; to which he added an intelligent and discriminating sympathy with their peculiar embarrassments, and a patient and affectionate forbearance. His authority was eminently that of affection, powerful and prevailing for all purposes of order and obedience; and rarely, if ever, calling to its aid even the most moderate physical force. This spirit, the spirit of Christian charity, "which suffereth long and is kind," bore abundantly its happy fruits. He secured in a remarkable degree the filial or fraternal confidence and attachment of all the pupils; and was enabled to exhibit a family, originally of rude, untutored, and discordant members, animated by a pervading spirit of fraternal kindness, of cheerful sensibilities, and of striking intellectual activity. He has left the impress of his government upon the school; and those who would contrast the Pennsylvania Institution with other similar institutions, may mark, in addition to its scholastic merits, an active cheerfulness, a real contentment, and a confiding temper, influencing the pupils toward each other, and towards their teachers and governors, in a peculiar manner. It is the impress of its first teacher, of his own kind and gentle spirit; and long may it endure, as the guardian and protector of the blind.

J. R. Friedlander was not negligent of the useful arts and occupations, so essential as a branch of instruction to the future welfare of the blind. With great assiduity, he secured their instruction in music, and guided their employment in a variety of mechanical occupations; and was always solicitous that each should acquire some art, that might prove available to support and benefit in after life.

Having been thus led and sustained to the accomplishment of his original design, the foundation under the auspices and support of the benevolent in this city, of a well-organized and endowed institution for the blind, he was not long permitted to contemplate the work of his hands. A hopeless malady seized upon his feeble frame, defied the skill of his physicians, and the action of the most genial climates. After a voyage, fruitless of benefit to his sinking body, he returned to the bosom of his adopted and cherished family at the Institution. Denied the intercourse of early friends and kindred, the most careful solicitude and attentions were not wanting in his declining hour. He lingered for a few days, his spirit greeted by grateful voices, and solaced by the sound of melodies which himself had tuned. On the 17th of March, 1839, he sank tranquilly to death, not unwept or unhonoured. Sightless eyes shed tears of unbidden and ingenuous sorrow over a parent and a brother; and the benevolent of a philanthropic city felt and acknowledged that a good spirit had departed.

J. R. Friedlander was a man of education, of courteous manners, of extensive reading, and of cultivated taste in letters and the arts. All that he was and all that he possessed he consecrated to a holy purpose.

In the centre of a spot in a neighbouring cemetery, devoted as a burial-place for the Institution for the Blind, there rises in simple and unornamented beauty a lofty shaft, inscribed with the name of "Friedlander:" and as the stranger visits the spot, he will rejoice that, amidst the monuments that are commanded to rise in commemoration of wealth, of science, of social and of public merit, the cal philanthropist are not forgotten: and if he should visit the Pennsylvania Institution for the Blind, he will there witness, in its efficiency and success, the more enduring monument, which is destined to embalm and perpetuate the memory of Friedlander.

LIFE OF WILLIAM CATON.

The latest published volume of the Select Series, edited by the late John Barclay, consists in part of a Journal of the Life and Gospel labours of William Caton, written by himself. It bears on the face of it throughout evidences of that singleness of purpose, unaffected simplicity, and devotedness to apprehended duty, which characterize generally these autobiographical accounts of our early Friends. We propose to insert the first and second chapters entire, which, perhaps, will hereafter be followed by some additional selected passages. The interest of the narrative is enhanced from the intimate connection which it has with George Fox and the family of Judge Fell of Swarthmore Hall.

CHAPTER I.

The God of my salvation hath been pleased of his infinite love, to show mercy unto me from my very infancy unto this present day, and hath through a secret hand kept and preserved me from many of the evils in the world, which befall the children of men, and with which many of them are overcome; yea, from my very childhood hath he dealt exceeding gently, bountifully, and mercifully with me, and especially since he was pleased to make known his heavenly truth in me, and his eternal salvation unto me. How should I therefore forbear to show forth his praise, and to declare his wonderful works! to the end that others may learn to fear and know him, to serve and obey him, that their souls may receive mercy from him as I have done, and that they may praise and magnify him in the land of the living—who is God over all, the Creator of all things; to whom be glory, honour, and dominion for ever and ever.

When I was a child, I was nurtured and tutored with such a fatherly care and motherly affection, as my parents at that day were endued with. While I was yet very young, my heart was inclining to wisdom and understanding: and being inspired with a divine principle, I did in those days sometimes feel the power of it overcoming my heart, and begetting tenderness in it towards my Creator, when I have stood musing upon his handiwork: and through this divine principle, I was much restrained from some evil vices which children are prone and incident to. But, alas, I knew not that that which restrained me was within me, though I had a dread and fear upon me when I was liable to sin against my Creator; which now I know right well, came through the aforesaid divine principle. Howbeit, I had also a fear upon me of reproof and chastisement from my parents, who, according to their knowledge, endeavoured to educate me in virtue and godliness; and therefore did they instruct me to pray morning and evening, to read often, and to go frequently to hear that which they called the Word of God. And great was their care to bring me up in the fear of the Lord, according to their ability and understanding, as also in good fashion (as they called it) in the world; therefore did they educate me in such schools as the country there did afford, and that for many years.

When I was about fourteen years of age, my father took me to Judge Fell's, there to learn with a kinsman (a priest) who was preceptor to the aforesaid judge's son; and thereby I came to have an opportunity to be conversant with them that were great in the world. And through the mercy of the Lord, I behaved myself so well among them as to the outward, that I found favour among the whole family, even from the greatest to the least of them; and was in due time promoted to be a companion night and day to the judge's son, and did eat as he did eat, and lodged as he lodged, and went after the same pleasure which he went unto, as to fishing, hunting, shooting, &c. In that day my heart was affected with my condition; forasmuch as Providence had cast me into such a noble family, where there were such sweet children, with whose company I was more than a little affected; and in much pleasure, ease and fulness, I lived with them as my heart could well desire. In those days there remained an integrity in my heart towards God, and often did I call upon his name; to that end, I would linger in the chamber until the judge's son, with whom I lodged, was gone down, that afterwards I might go to prayer alone; for my soul desired to have the blessing and favour of the Lord, in which there was satisfaction to be found, but not in the pleasures which I followed, nor yet in the ease and fulness in which I then lived.

After we had learnt some time together in the judge's family, we were removed to a school in the country, at a place called Hawkshead; where I met with many temptations, and seldom good company, but such as were given to folly and wantonness. But the Lord was wonderfully gracious to me; and many times when I have deserved nothing but stripes from him, hath he broken and overcome my heart with his divine love; so that I have often stood admiring his wonderful mercy, his long-suffering, forbearance, and infinite goodness; for truly had his compassion failed, I might have been destroyed in the sins of my youth; but blessed be his name for ever, he had mercy on me. And as Providence ordered it, we did not stay long at that school, but returned to Judge Fell's, where it was with me as before mentioned, so that I began to see pretty far into the depth of what the world could afford.

Being then about fifteen years of age, my

pretty much inclined after wisdom, seek after knowledge; for in that ere was a great profession, and such speak of the Scripture, and could etitions of sermons, and paraphrase , were held in esteem: therefore I red much to retain the heads there- hen my memory would not serve me some did in that particular, I used write much after the priests: but h I reaped thereby could not give on to my soul, which at times hun- ch after the Lord.

CHAPTER II.

George Fox's first visit to Swarth- the tendency of his doctrine—W. C. school, and becomes an inmate in the family, as teacher and writer; the love and refreshment prevalent at them—Is moved to go into steeple- , markets, &c.—Quits Swarthmore.

year 1652, about the middle of the month, was that faithful messenger ant of the Most High, by name Fox, cast among us, who declared he way of life and peace. Of those mily who believed his report, I was came finally to be affected with his though at the first I did as much t his non-conformity to our fashions, and salutations, as strangers at this re at our non-conformity unto them; thing in me did love him, and own ony. And I began to find the truth he spoke in myself; for his doctrine ery much to the bringing of us to , *which Christ Jesus had enlightened t, which shined in our hearts, and I us of sin and evil;* and into love , and obedience to that, he sought us, that thereby through the Son we brought into unity and covenant Lord.

n due time the witness of God was l in me, whereby my sins came to be ler before me; and it brought judg- condemnation upon me by reason of at I, being as the wild heifer which stomed to the yoke, sought to get ler it, as I often did, until I came to

folly. Sometimes I would separate myself from the rest of my school-fellows, and get retired into some place, where I might wait upon the Lord, and ponder upon his marvel- lous works. When I was thus retired, and in singleness of heart waited upon the Lord, I received refreshment from him; but when I was drawn aside through the provocation of my companion, or the temptations of the wicked one in myself, then was I troubled and disquieted in my own heart.

In process of time my study become my burden; for when I was so much in trouble through the condemnation that was upon me, I was so much the more incapable of making themes, Latin verses, &c., neither could I well give unto the master the trivial compli- ment of the hat, for I was then convinced in my conscience of the vanity of it. My special friend Margaret Fell (the judge's wife) taking notice of my condition, was not willing to suffer me to go longer to the school than I was free, but caused me to stay at home to teach her children, and to go with her when she went abroad, and to write for her, &c., which was a happy time for me; for after that I left the school, I was also much exer- cised in writing of precious and wholesome things pertaining to the truth; whereby I came to have good opportunities to be con- versant with Friends, in whom the life of righteousness began to bud and spring forth, and who grew in love and unity, with which my soul was exceedingly affected; and I de- sired very much to be one with them in it, that I might share with them therein, for my soul was delighted with it and in it, far be- yond the pleasures and delights of this tran- sitory world.

When I was about seventeen years of age, the power of the Lord God did work mightily and effectually in me, to the purging, cleans- ing, and sanctifying of me; and then I began to see something of the gloriousness of the ministration of condemnation, and of the goodness of the word of life, which was be- come *as a fire in my bones,* and *as a sword and hammer in my heart.* And then I began to be broken, melted, and overcome with the love of God, which sprang up in my heart, and with the divine and precious promises that were confirmed to my soul. Oh! the

volume by much, than now I am intending; but, my very heart is affected with the re- membrance of them at this very day.

In those days were meetings exceeding precious to us, insomuch that some few of us did commonly spend some time every night in waiting upon the Lord; yea, often after the rest of the family were gone to bed: and, oh! the comfort and refreshment which we had together, and the benefit which we reaped thereby, how shall I declare it! For if we had suffered loss in the day-time, when we had been abroad about our business or the like, then we came, in a great measure, thus to be restored again, through the love, power, and mercy of our God, which abounded very much unto us: howbeit, sometimes I was de- prived of that sweet society (when my heart was with them) through my going to bed so early with the judge's son, with whom I then did lodge; who for a season was tender and hopeful; but afterwards meeting with many temptations, his heart was drawn aside from the truth, and his mind ran after the delights and pleasures of this present world. When he was removed to another school, we came to be separated, which was at that time no disadvantage to me in one respect, though I looked upon by some to be a disadvantage to me as to my outward preferment: but in that day I could have chosen much rather to have done any kind of labour pertaining to the house, with the servants that were in the truth, than to have enjoyed the delights of this world with this son, or any one else, for a season. For my delight was not then, so much as it had been, in the vain, perishing, and transitory things of the world, but my delight was then in the Lord, in his mercy and loving-kindness, and to be with his peo- ple; for the sake of whose company I could have exposed myself to some pretty hard em- ployment; neither was it then too contempti- ble for me to become as Amos, a keeper of cattle, or as Elisha, to follow the plough; for indeed in those days I did enjoy and possess that which made all things easy and light to me. And oh! the abundance of living re- freshment, which I received from the Lord! it is hard for me to utter or declare the same to the utmost: for I was often overcome with the love of my Father, which did exceedingly

came to be filled with love to their souls, and with zeal for God and his truth. And about that time I began to know the motion of his power and the command of his spirit; by which I came to be moved to go to the places of public worship, to declare against the deceit of the priests, and the sins of the people, and to warn all to repent: for I testified to them that the day of the Lord was coming. But oh! the weakness, the fear and trembling in which I went upon this message,—who shall declare it? and how did I plead with the Lord concerning this matter: for I looked upon my own weakness and insufficiency, and how unfit I was in my own apprehension, to encounter with gainsayers, who I knew would also despise my youth. Howbeit, whatsoever I alleged by way of reasoning against the Lord concerning this weighty matter, I could not be excused; but I must go, and declare what he should give me to speak; and his promise was, he would be with me.

(To be continued.)

The following touching lines were written by a late teacher in the New York Institution for the Deaf and Dumb, and presented to one of the pupils:—

A SONG FOR ONE WHO NEVER SUNG.

My harp, a tuneless, shattered thing,
    That knows no song,
Swings silently without a string,
    On willows hung.
The weeping boughs have gently shed,
Their tears upon my drooping head,
And drenched my dewy, grassy bed,
    The flowers among:
But Flora wastes her gayest bloom,
Her choicest hues, and her perfume,—
She cannot dissipate my gloom,—
    My harp's unstrung

The little birds that flutter so
    From tree to tree,
Sing merrily, but never know
    'Tis naught to me!
The fragrant zephyrs pass me by
In *silence*, as I sadly lie,
And never *hear* their breathing sigh:
    What's that to me?

door means much; it m
only nonsense, but busir
company abroad, but the
it means—let thy poor so
and refreshment; and Go
to speak to thee in a still
will speak to thee in thun

THE FR

SECOND MONTI

It is satisfactory to perc
dence that the public min
on the subject of the bloo
newspapers abounding in
sive of indignant feeling
relation to it. The me
which our paper of last w
been extensively circulate
promptly signed by thos
called upon, of all classes
with but very few excepti
copies with numerous sign
been forwarded and preset
the house of representativ
was accompanied, or follo
appropriate remarks in su
rial by Wise, the distingui
gate, and we also learn th
debate of considerable int
reading of the memorial t
quite evident that a con
has been the effect of
Washington of these m
should serve as an addit
diligence and perseveranc
ers. In this remark we
only our Friends here, bu
in other parts of the U
journal circulates—in
York, the New England
and in the west. Let all
made to increase the nu
In the words of a cotemp
from those engrossing top
mediately affect our inter

THE FRIEND.

A RELIGIOUS AND LITERARY JOURNAL.

VOL. XIII.   **SEVENTH DAY, SECOND MONTH, 22, 1840.**   **NO. 21.**

EDITED BY ROBERT SMITH.

PUBLISHED WEEKLY.

Price two dollars per annum, payable in advance.

Subscriptions and Payments received by

GEORGE W. TAYLOR,

NO. 50, NORTH FOURTH STREET, UP STAIRS,

PHILADELPHIA.

Geneva and its neighbouring Scenery.

The Alps have so frequently been the theme of description by tourists, that novelty in any new attempt seems scarcely to be looked for. We think, however, it will not be denied, that the following possesses more than common claim to graphic force and beauty. It is from Cheever's letters from Switzerland, in course of publication in the New York Observer.

In its central situation, its society, and its scenery, Geneva presents attractions for the sojourn of a stranger, especially during the milder half of the year, such as scarcely any other place in Europe can command. Brussels and Geneva are compared; the first, larger and more fashionable, more of a European capital, but less delightful to a lover of nature, as well as of society and literature, and far less central in its position. Nothing can rival the deliciousness and convenience of Geneva as a European traveller's home, his point of departure and return, his favourite resting-place. He may pass from winter into summer, from summer to the spring, may reverse the seasons, or take them in their course, and, almost at his pleasure, turn the varying face of nature to their sweetest aspects. From the heart of the Alps, even in the dead of winter, he may step across the Simplon, and sun himself in Italy, amidst the soft gales of the Mediterranean and the South; or, in the summer, ranging from lake to lake, from mountain to mountain, may enjoy, in pedestrian independence, alone, or with a friend, vicissitudes of sublimity and beauty in climate and scenery, whether in the Swiss or the Tyrol Alps, of such perpetual novelty and magnificence, that even a lifetime so spent would scarce tire.

The canton of Geneva is the smallest in the Swiss confederation, composed of the territory of the ancient republic of Geneva, together with some districts detached from Savoy, and the French territory of Gex, by the congress of Vienna, in 1815. The whole canton speak the French language, and, with the exception of about 20,000 catholics, and 100 Jews, the whole population, nearly sixty thousand in all, are protestant. The sovereign power of the canton is in a representative council, composed of 278 members. Four syndics preside over this body. A council of state, twenty-eight in number, are chosen for eight years, invested with administrative and executive powers; the four presiding syndics also belong to this body. The population of Geneva, the capital of the canton, is numbered at 31,000; about 5,000 of whom are catholics. The arts of agriculture have no where else in Switzerland been carried to such perfection as in this small and delightful territory; the suburbs of the capital are a series of country seats and gardens, of English richness and refinement, and of a beauty of situation unrivalled in the world. The Genevese artisans are not less industrious, nor less skilful, in their business, than the cultivators of the soil in theirs. Geneva is, in some sort, the city clock of Europe. Seventy thousand watches are fabricated annually. Its central position, with all its advantages, is brought as forcibly to the mind by a glance at the post-office department, as by any thing else. The hours of departure and arrivals of mails are designated from France, England, Holland, Belgium, the French and English colonies, United States, Spain, Portugal, Germany, the North, Turkey, Greece, Malta, the Ionian Isles, Savoy, Piedmont, Milan, the Lombard Venitian kingdom, Lower Italy, and the several Swiss cantons.

The market-place in Geneva, on a Saturday morning, is a scene of great picturesque interest to a stranger. Of a Saturday morning in November, it reminded me more of New England, the day or two before thanksgiving, than any other similar scene I have encountered. The women and the men, the peasants and the husbandmen, are in from the country with all the produce of the harvest, and every sort of merchandise; stores of eatables of every kind, meats and fruits, salads and vegetables, butter, cheese, eggs, and poultry; all the abundance of a hardy and bountiful soil and climate, inferior only in richness and luxuriousness even to a market of the south of Spain. The squares are crowded with buyers and sellers, frank, smiling, animated; for there is something in the bright, fresh, clear autumnal morning, that invigorates and inspirits every body. See the multitudes of wrinkled industrious old women, in immense straw hats, seated by their benches of vegetables, or heaps of provisions, or stalls of fruits and viands. Here are women with scales in their hands, selling apples by the pound, a universal custom. A stranger will be amused at the indignation with which an old dame will refuse to sell you a single one, if you want no more, to eat. Here are a parcel of stalls for shoes and moccasins, and the women tending; and here, thrown together in the square, are heaps of defences for the feet and legs against Alpine snows and precipices, leathern, wooden, and woollen, apparently of Titanian origin and architecture, if size and cumbrousness may be taken as antediluvian indications. Here are ribbons and trinkets, clothes, books, and medicines. Here are loads of corded wood, like a New England winter. Here are enormous pumpkins, enough to supply the whole state of Massachusetts. Here are milk and cream, grapes and honey. Here are chestnuts roasted and boiled, and loaves of bread, and cheeses which none but à Swiss mountaineer would dare lay siege to. You can hardly conceive the vivacity and variety of the scene. If there were a little more wickedness in it, a little more seductive allurement, and a little less of broad, honest, Swiss utility, one might easily imagine himself walking with John Bunyan, in the wilderness of this world, through " Vanity Fair." Here they are packing up their baskets, having already disposed of their stores. Here a fellow is selling pictures by a walking lottery. He carries a bag of counters, with a certain numeral upon each of them, and every person willing to pay a sou puts his hand into the bag and draws at hazard. See that little bright-eyed boy in the plaid frock and cap; his sou is gone, and you can see by his countenance that he has drawn a blank. The frank contentedness and industrious look of the market people cannot fail to strike you, and if your thoughts happen to be turned to the subject of temperance, you will not fail to notice the apparent deliverance from the curse of liquors and intoxication. In German Switzerland the people drink more than in the cantons further south. I witnessed but little intemperance in Geneva.

The region in and around Geneva one might fancy to have been laid out on purpose for its varied and almost unlimited command of rich views of the glory of the Alps; it is full of standing points that you might deem built to gaze upon Mont Blanc; as, in the panorama around the cataract of Niagara, it seems as if the same omnipotence, that poured the torrent from its hollow hand, had raised those perspective heights, on purpose for its just appreciation and admiration in the distance. I shall give you simply my first impressions, and afterwards may possibly take you with me in a pedestrian excursion to the Vale of Chamouny and the roots of Mont Blanc. Visiting with a friend, almost the first day of our arrival in Geneva, we passed to the northern side of the lake and of the Rhone, outside the town, in a region which commands on a vast scale, an uprising series of views of the Alpine ranges in the opposite horizon, with Mont Blanc midway between them. When we entered the house, the clouds around the mountains prevented our enjoying a perfect prospect, but when we came out, a change had passed upon the scene, and "the Monarch of Mountains," with his regal compeers, was distinctly visible. How shall I give you the least idea of the magnificence of the view? Descending a little towards the lake, we came to a prominent bastion and station on the city fortifications near its borders, where a sort of metrical dial of observation of the mountains has been erected, it being perhaps the best spot upon the land, which could have been chosen for this purpose. There is a pillar of stone, with a broad, circular, bronze tablet on the top, having a point in the middle, towards which lines are drawn from the circumference, in such directions, that the eye may command along them the various summits of the mountains, with the accurate statement of their names and different elevations above the level of the sea. At this hour, the whole eastern and southern ranges, with all their eminences, were distinctly visible from the Dents du Midi along the points of the Needles, the Jorasses, the Mole, Mont Blanc, the Grand and Petit Saleve, with all the intermediate summits. No mere description in words can convey to the mind any adequate idea of their beauty and splendour—so varied, so glittering, so shafted and pinnacled, in crags and ridges, spires, points and pyramids. The pile called the Mole, from its nearness to the city, being only four leagues distant, is especially magnificent, robed with the new-fallen snow of the storm in which we crossed the Jura. It seems one entire, majestic pyramid of spotless snow, so soft and yet so definite and perfect in its outlines, that the mind is quite filled with its unity of beauty. In the summer it is covered from the bottom to the top with rich verdure, and I have seen it as dark vast mass of living green, against the bright autumnal sky, in as pure and perfect a pyramidal outline of soft foliage, as it now were of purest virgin snow.

In the evening of this day the setting sun poured upon the eastern ranges of the Alps with an effect of almost inconceivable loveliness and glory. Behind the stupendous ridges of the Grand and Petit Saleve, farther towards the north, rise the pyramidal white apexes of Mont Blanc and the neighbouring summits, reflecting the splendour of the sun, as if it were thrown back from the towering battlements of a city in heaven. The flashing brightness of the vast quantities of new-fallen snow, the shadows thrown from one summit to another, the sun pouring upon the pyramidal and shafted tops, while their bases were in the shade, the crimson, purple, delicate and changing hues upon the whiteness of the snow, the majestic stillness, distance, and repose; all circumstances combined to fill the soul with an impression of the very extreme of loveliness and sublimity, and might well prepare it for an act of evening worship before such a vast material altar to God's praise. That majestic pyramid of snow just

before us,—so near and yet so distant,—it seems, in its relief against the sky, as if chiselled out from the blue profound of ether by the hand of Omnipotence.

As the sun is sinking behind the Jura mountains, the range of the Saleve becomes crimsoned with light, and the perpendicular rocky ravines of its sides are like the half transparent edges of rocks of jasper. The sheets and piles of snow, contrasted with such reflections of the light, make all the mountain ridges that environ the plain, the city, and the lake, a circle of flashing splendour; a circle glorious in itself, and striking in its contrast with the dark ground of the foliage and the verdure of the mountain bases, and the sloping plains, with their clustering and girdling woods. The city and the lake, thus surrounded by mountain ridges and pyramids, gigantic cliffs and pinnacles, with their robes of new-fallen snow, like rocks, battlements, and spires of purest alabaster piercing the heavens, form a panorama of sunset magnificence, the like of which you cannot find in the world.

Then, too, the borders of the Lake Leman, so lovely, so romantic, so rich with verdure, so picturesque with villas and villages! The waters of the lake itself so blue, so spiritually clear, to reflect the sky, the trees, the towers, the clouds, the mountains! The Rhone, the arrowy Rhone, running from the lake through the city, to join the turbid Arve, from Mont Blanc; the beauty of the bridge thrown across it, and of the receding ranges of buildings on either side; the openings to the south and west, out upon the mountains beyond; the variety, the interest, the mingled sublimity and picturesque loveliness of the scene, even in the month of November, that dreariest month of all the year, defy description. There were some lovely mornings and evenings in that month while we were there, in which the season seemed to have renewed its youth, and that being the first of our acquaintance with Geneva and the Alps, I have chosen to sketch the first impressions of the scenery as then exhibited, rather than to draw a picture in those more verdant and lovely hues in the decline of summer, and the brightness of September and October, with which I afterwards became familiar; but which, though more beautiful, could not possess the untold power of a first sight or a first love over the mind.

The two finest points of view are that to which I have referred above as containing the geometrical tablet, and a higher elevation on the southwest bastion of the city, commanding at once the long stupendous ridge of the Jura on the northwest, the beautiful valley of Carouge, the southern opening in the direction of Mont Cenis into Italy, the sunny perspective where the Jura ends and the Rhone hastens to the south of France, the sublime ranges of Mont Blanc on the east and south, and the great and little Saleve nearer to the city. Here you have the most splendid view of the Jura ranges in the morning, and the Alpine ranges in the evening. The stupendous ridge of Jura is so near, and runs along so perpendicularly with

its vast sheets of snow, and dark ridges of soil intermingled (I speak still of the month of November), and such rich, dark, verdant plains at its base, in a girdle round the city, that it seems, as you lift your eye towards it, like the sudden flashing vision of an army of supernatural intelligences, with banners floating in the sun, or like the instantaneous revelation of the golden and alabaster crags, that might have been piled up to hide and defend the paradise of an unpolluted world, in the happy dawn of its creation. The scene on the other side, towards Mont Blanc, is yet more sublime, more exciting. One can hardly refrain from tears of admiration in the presence of such awful forms of nature. How is it that they have such power over the mind? Is it because they are so much more than any thing we daily meet with like the symbols of those ideas, with which the soul is to be conversant as realities in the eternal world—the furniture of the soul's birth-place and its home—the scenery of its redeemed possession, its heavenly inheritance? How often I am reminded of Wordsworth's remarkable ode on the Intimations of Immortality from the recollections of early childhood.

Both the moral and intellectual power of Swiss scenery is very great. A man's mind feels it vividly on first acquaintance; nor need its power be lost in familiarity, but it may become an enduring discipline both to the mind and heart. Sometimes it brings God very near to the soul. A Christian accustomed to pray among those mountain tops, will often find their climbing ridges, as they lose themselves in heaven, conducting him there also, and greatly aiding his spiritual intercourse with God. The finest passage in Wordsworth's Excursion, towards the close of the last book in that poem, a passage worthy to be put, even for its Christian sentiment, by the side of Cowper's "One song employs all nations," commences with a few lines so remarkably expressive of feelings, which every mind of Christian sensibility must often experience among the Alps of Switzerland, that I need make no apology for closing this letter with them:

Eternal Spirit! Universal God!
Power inaccessible to human thought,
Save by degrees and steps, which Thou hast deigned
To furnish; for this image of thyself,
To the infirmity of mortal sense
Vouchsafed; this local, transitory type
Of thy paternal splendour, and the pomp
Of those who fill thy courts in highest heaven,
The radiant cherubim;—accept the thanks
Which we, thy humble creatures, here convened,
Presume to offer; we, who from the breast
Of the frail earth, permitted to behold
The faint reflections only of thy face,
Are yet exalted, and in soul adore!
Such as they are, who in thy presence stand,
Unsullied, incorruptible, and drink
Imperishable majesty streamed forth
From thy empyreal throne, the elect of earth
Shall be:—divested, at the appointed hour,
Of all dishonour—cleansed from mortal stain!

Ministers should not preach sounding words, so much as sound words, lest sound preaching should be turned into a sound of preaching.— *From Venning's "Milk and Honey."*

The Fourth Annual Report of the Association for the Care of Coloured Orphans. Adopted twelfth month 6th, 1839.

The "Association for the care of Coloured Orphans" now presents, with renewed feelings of gratitude and encouragement, the following brief statement of its situation. Believing that the sympathy excited for the parentless child, and the aid which has been so liberally bestowed by the patrons of this institution, will be more than compensated by the reflection, that through the continued blessing of the Father of the fatherless, and their bounty, many a solitary orphan has been sheltered, clothed, fed, and rescued, no doubt, from scenes of vice and immorality, and a foundation laid for future usefulness in the minds of this injured and helpless class of our fellow-beings.

The Shelter remains under the care of the same matron, who is tender and affectionate in the management of the little flock committed to her care; exercising an equal system of control over them, without prejudice or partiality. The older children are, at stated periods, employed in services adapted to their strength or capacity, with a view of training them into habits of industry; and care is also particularly extended over their religious and moral instruction.

The matron has been assisted by the association and many of its friends in making up garments, &c., for the children; which has been a saving of considerable expense to the institution.

The friend who has for many years been engaged as teacher, continues her unabated interest in the school; and the children give evidence of her care, by the propriety of their conduct and their improvement in the useful branches taught by her. A portion of their time is devoted to sewing, and they give proof that this part of their education is not neglected.

For professional aid we are still indebted to Dr. Casper Wistar.

From the monthly reports of the superintending committee it appears, that the domestic arrangements of the house have been highly satisfactory; and that order and economy have been strictly adhered to. The general health of the family has been good, and the comfort of the children greatly increased by the change in their residence, having the advantage of well-ventilated apartments, and sufficient ground for recreation and exercise, with a large play-room in the basement story, for their accommodation in wet weather.

The association acknowledges the timely liberality of its friends, in enabling it to meet the current expenses of the year, which have been much increased by the size of the family, and the additional aid consequently requisite. But it will be obvious, from the account of the treasurer, that continued assistance will be necessary for the support of this interesting institution. But one death has occurred during the past year, and that by pulmonary consumption.

Donations of dry-goods, vegetables, &c.,

will be particularly acceptable and thankfully received at the Shelter, on Thirteenth and Willow streets.

Annual subscriptions are also earnestly solicited, as a means calculated to place the institution on a firmer basis.

We are still indebted to Peter Christian for his fees for binding the children.

When the former report was adopted, there were in the house,

Children	36
Since admitted . . .	26
Apprenticed . . 1	
Deceased . . 1	
Returned to their friends 5	
Now in the house . 55	
	62
	62

Abstract of the Treasurer's Account for 1839.

Dr.

Paid for printing report . .	$25 00
" Water rent . . .	12 00
" Wages	423 48
" Milk	269 62
" Marketing . . .	198 26
" Washing . . .	48 00
" Flour and corn meal .	347 94
" Groceries . . .	170 92
" Sundries . . .	54 62
" Wood . . .	70 25
" Coal . . .	27 50
" Potatoes . . .	39 53
" Boots and shoes .	65 00
" Dry goods . .	95 76
" Furniture . .	17 25
" Carpenter work and materials	116 74
Repaid loan	103 00
Lehigh loan and stock . .	1838 87
Balance in the hands of the treasurer	63 73
	$3987 27

Cr.

Balance received from the late treasurer, including the annual subscriptions for 1839 . .	$1530 11
Board of orphans . . .	149 66
Interest on bonds . . .	315 00
" on Lehigh loan . .	30 00
Bank dividends . . .	20 00
Instalment on house in Race street	500 00
Bequest of John G. Mason, late of Salem, N. J. . . .	300 00
Donations	1142 50
	$3987 27

The Annual Report of the Board of Directors of the Pennsylvania Institution for the Deaf and Dumb, for 1839.

To the Senate and House of Representatives of the Commonwealth of Pennsylvania, and to the Directors of the Pennsylvania Institution for the Deaf and Dumb.

In presenting to the general assembly and to the contributors their report of the present condition of the Pennsylvania Institution for the Deaf and Dumb, the directors may be indulged in giving a brief sketch of its past history.

Instituted in the year 1820, by the zeal

and philanthropy of a number of citizens of Philadelphia, it was, on the 17th day of April, in the following year, incorporated by the legislature; which, at the same time, granted the institution the sum of eight thousand dollars, and made provision for the education of the indigent deaf mutes of the commonwealth. The term of tuition was limited to three years, each the sum of one hundred and sixty dollars allowed for each pupil educated, clothed and supported at the expense of the commonwealth. The annual appropriation was to continue for five years, and was not, in any one year, to exceed $8000.

The school was first opened in a house on the south side of High street, west of Broad. Finding this building unsuitable, more appropriate accommodations were procured and the establishment was removed to the southeast corner of High and Eleventh streets. It was however deemed advisable to erect a convenient and commodious edifice. After much serious reflection and consultation, a lot at the northwest corner of Pine and Broad streets was selected as the most eligible, and the plan of a building, neat and convenient, adopted. In November 1825, the board were enabled to occupy their own buildings. They consisted of a centre building on Broad street, forty-six feet front by fifty deep, and two wings, each twenty-five feet front and ninety-eight feet deep, containing school-rooms, dormitories, and other apartments, sufficient for the number of pupils at that time. As the number of pupils increased, it became expedient to erect a school-house, which was completed in 1832. It was ninety-six feet front by thirty deep, three stories high, and contained eight school-rooms, twenty-six by eighteen feet in the clear, and three other rooms in the basement story.

The advantages of such an institution to the community soon became apparent, and it has been ever cherished by the people and their representatives. The annual appropriation has been from time to time continued, and as experience proved the propriety, the term of tuition extended.

In the winter of 1836, the board were gratified by a visit from a committee of the legislature. This committee, after a full examination of the institution, were satisfied, that from the increased number of mutes in this and the neighbouring states, further accommodations were requisite. On the 11th of March, 1837, the sum of twenty thousand dollars was appropriated to enable the board to accomplish this desirable object.

Measures were immediately adopted by the board to carry the benevolent design of the legislature into effect: eighty-two feet were added to each of the wings, and thirty-four feet to the centre building.

On the 4th of April, 1838, the legislature granted the further sum of eight thousand dollars, to enable the directors to complete their improvements.

By this act, the legislature enlarged the term of the state pupils to six years, and extended the benefits of the institution to all indigent mutes in the commonwealth between the ages of ten and twenty years. This annuity granted is to continue for six years from the 1st of April, 1838. During that year the additions commenced the preceding were finished, and a story added to the school-house.

The cost of these additions has very considerably exceeded the grants of the legislature; to meet this excess, the directors were obliged to rely on the resources of the institution. The treasurer's account will exhibit the receipts and payments for the past year.

Measures have been adopted to introduce the gas.

While it is a subject of gratulation that so many of those who were active in the foundation of this noble charity, are still left to promote its welfare by their continued and acceptable services and counsel, the directors have to lament the deaths of several of the early and steadfast friends of the deaf and dumb. With these is now to be numbered their beloved colleague, Thomas Astley, Esq. He departed this life on the 15th day of October last. To a spotless integrity of character was joined an undeviating suavity of manner, which endeared him to his associates;— his virtues will long be held in affectionate remembrance by them.

It is hoped that in this enlightened and philanthropic community, the number of contributors to the Pennsylvania Institution for the Deaf and Dumb will not be diminished. No charity can have stronger claims on our sympathies—none more deeply interest our feelings. By it have the blessings of education already been enjoyed by hundreds; and by it, through Divine Providence, will these blessings be extended to thousands.

Of the whole number of pupils admitted into the institution—four hundred and twenty-eight—two hundred and twenty are stated to have been born deaf; one hundred and one to have lost their hearing by disease or accident. Of thirty-four it was not ascertained from what cause the sense of hearing was destroyed. With regard to the remainder, no satisfactory information has been obtained —whether they were deaf at their birth, or subsequently lost their hearing.

On the 1st of January, 1839, there were one hundred and seven pupils in the Asylum. During that year thirty-five were admitted, viz.—(twenty-three boys and twelve girls)— twenty-six from Pennsylvania, one from New Jersey, five from Maryland, two from Delaware, and one from North Carolina.

During the same period twenty-four left the institution.

Of those now under charge of the board, 72 are supported by the state of Pennsylvania

9	do	do	New Jersey
2	do	do	Maryland
25	do	do	By the Institution or by their friends
118			

Those supported by Pennsylvania are from the following counties:

1	from Adams.	1	from Huntingdon.
3	Allegheny.	1	Jefferson.
1	Armstrong.	2	Juniata.
3	from Beaver.	4	from Lancaster.
8	Berks.	1	Lebanon.
2	Bucks.	3	Montgomery.
1	Centre.	2	Northampton.
5	Chester.	12	Philadelphia.
2	Columbia.	1	Pike.
1	Cumberland.	2	Schuylkill.
3	Delaware.	2	Susquehanna.
1	Fayette.	1	Union.
1	Franklin.	1	Wayne.
2	Green.	5	York.
	Total, 72.		

It affords the directors unfeigned gratification to bear testimony to the flourishing condition of the establishment, and the ability and zeal of their valued principal and his assistants.

No alteration has been made in the studies of their pupils. They have, with few exceptions, enjoyed uninterrupted health. Only three cases of serious indisposition occurred; one of these, the board are concerned to say, terminated fatally.

The best feelings exist among the scholars. Every proper attention is paid to their comforts; and on every fair day they have abundant opportunity of enjoying the fresh air in the exercising yards, which are spacious. While due care is bestowed on their physical training, the most unremitting attention is paid to their mental improvement and moral culture.

Divine worship is regularly held on each Lord's day. In imparting religious instruction, care is taken to impress on the minds of the pupils the great truths of Christianity, without sectarian bias, and to train up the child in the way he should go.

The discipline observed is entirely parental; and the excellent order and cheerfulness which reign throughout our large household, are highly gratifying proofs of its success.

The institution continues to enjoy the valued services of Drs. George B. Wood, Jacob Randolph, and Joseph Pancoast.

All which is respectfully submitted.

By order of the board of directors.

PHILIP F. MAYER, Vice President.

Attested—*James J. Barclay*, Secretary.

Philadelphia, January 1, 1840.

On the proper management of Posts, with reference to their durability.

Perhaps there is no subject connected with agriculture, on which a greater diversity of opinion prevails, than the question, whether with reference to their durability, posts should be put into the ground green or seasoned? When I first settled, I took considerable pains to inform myself on this point, by consultation with those whose experience should constitute them proper fountains of information. The diversity to which I have alluded, impaired greatly the acquisition of decisive results. Thomas Thweatt, of Dinwiddie, a gentleman of great judgment and observation on all agricultural subjects, related to me a circumstance which contributed much to the attainment of my object. He stated, (if my memory be correct,) that in the erection of his garden, a number of posts, as he supposed, were prepared and suffered to remain until they were thoroughly seasoned. Its completion, however, required one in addition, which was taken from an adjacent tree and immediately put in the ground. Seventeen years had elapsed, and every post had rotted down, except that one, which remained sound. In the progress of my investigation, another instance was related, in which an entire side of a garden exhibited the same results. My own limited experience furnishes an incident worthy of being mentioned. My garden enclosure was erected of posts while green. Several pieces remained exposed until they were completely seasoned. Out of these a horse-rack was constructed, which was entirely rotted down, while every post in the garden remains firm. From these facts, I deduce the belief, that a post planted when green will last longer than when previously seasoned; and for the reason that the operation of seasoning produces cracks in the timber, which admitting the moisture from the ground, cause its decay. I recollect to have read the account of an experiment proving that the inversion of posts from the direction in which they grew, operated beneficially. Two gate-posts were hewn from the same tree—one was planted in the manner in which it grew, the other inverted. The former rotted, while the latter was sound. It was accounted for in this way—that nature had formed valves for the ascension of the sap, which allowed the moisture from the ground to penetrate through the same channel; but that the inversion of these valves interposed a barrier to its admission. This theory corroborates the idea previously expressed, that the moisture of the ground, alternately penetrating within the timber, and in drowths, measurably receding, causes its decay. Whether the posts should be cut while the sap is up or down, I am unable to determine. A writer in some of the numbers of the American Farmer, states that oak timber should be cut while the sap is up, because it is glutinous, and forms a cement, or substance which acts as a preservative.

I have ventured to express these hasty and imperfect reflections, with the hope that, although they may not impart any useful information, they may elicit some from others. These are controverted subjects, in which every person who erects a gate or encloses a garden, is deeply interested, and their further discussion will be valuable, at least to S. —*Farmer's Reg.*

CROTON WATER WORKS.

It appears from the semiannual report of the Water Commissioners, just published, that they had paid, prior to 1st of January last, towards the construction of the Croton Aqueduct, 3,947,859 dollars 52 cents. The entire cost of the work, when completed, it is now calculated, will reach the sum of 9,000,000 dollars, being double the original estimates; and it will be fortunate if it be not found at last, that a still further sum is necessary. A committee of the legislature, we perceive, estimate the entire cost of the work at about 12,000,000 dollars. So much for "pure and wholesome water," for the city of New York.—*Journal of Commerce.*

LIFE OF WILLIAM CATON.

(Continued from page 162.)

Wherefore when I saw it must be so, I put on courage in the name of the Lord; and having faith in him, which stood in his power, I next gave up to his will, and went in obedience to his motion. And when I came to the place, behold, the consultations which before I had had, were gone, and the fear of man was departed from me; and strength, and courage, and boldness, and utterance were given me, so that I became, through him that strengthened me, rather as a potent man than as a stripling, and that even in the face of the congregations. Howbeit, my testimony was by many little regarded, neither did they lay to heart what I declared among them; but some as brute beasts fell upon me, and did much abuse me; others pitied me and were much troubled for me; and sometimes they were much divided among themselves, for some were for me, and others against me; but in the midst of them the Lord was with me, and his mighty power did preserve me; and when I had cleared my conscience among them, I returned in much peace and joy in the Holy Ghost, for my reward was with me.

After that the Lord had fitted me for his work as aforesaid, I was much exercised in going to steeple-houses, insomuch that there seldom passed a first day of the week, but I was at one or another; and I was also often in markets, where I was moved to declare God's eternal truth, which through his infinite mercy I was become a witness of. And though when I went to such places as aforesaid, I seldom knew what I should say till I came there; yet behold when I was to speak I never wanted words or utterance, to declare that which the Lord gave me to publish; but oftentimes on the contrary I had fulness to my great admiration. And the beating, buffeting, stocking, stoning, with the many reproaches which I went through in those days, were little to me; nay, not to be compared to the refreshment which I had through the enjoyment of the life, power, and love, which the Father had revealed in me, and by which I was carried through them and over them all. By how much the more the Lord tried me in those days, by so much the more I came to experience his loving-kindness to me.

And after that the Lord came to honour me with bearing his name, and accounted me worthy to bear my testimony, both in public and in private, to his eternal truth, I had much favour and respect from and among his people, whose love abounded much to me; and I being sensible thereof, was very much supported and strengthened thereby, in that service which God appointed for me, and called me unto in those days. When such service was over I returned again to the place of my residence, where I was diligent in my employment, until the Lord ordered me to other service again, either to meetings abroad on the first days of the week, or else to steeple-houses: and the Lord was with me, and his word of life did often pass powerfully through me, and never did I go about any service for the Lord, in which I was

faithful, but I had always my reward with me.

When I returned again unto that honourable family, the place of my external abode, (I mean Judge Fell's at Swarthmore in Lancashire,) then was our refreshment very great together in the Lord, and with rejoicing did we speak together of his wonderful works, which were very marvellous in our eyes. And after I had had many glorious days there, and seen many of the wonderful works of the Lord, in the fulness of time, according to the will of God, I was called out from among them, the Lord having other service for me abroad elsewhere. When it was the will of the Lord that I should go, the judge was much against it, being then very unwilling to part with me; but his dear wife, who could not well give me up before, was then made willing freely to resign me to the will of the Lord, especially upon so honourable an account; for I left not them to go to serve other men, but to publish the name of the Lord, and to declare his eternal truth abroad.

CHAPTER III.

It was in the year 1654, in the eleventh month, when I was about eighteen years of age, that I took my leave of that renowned family at Swarthmore. But, oh! the tears that were shed among us at our parting;— oh! the prayers and intercessions that were made to the Lord; and what deep impression our parting had upon our hearts, who can declare the same! So exceedingly were we united and bound up together, that it was very hard for us to part one with another. Howbeit, when we considered upon what account it was, and that notwithstanding our then external parting, we should enjoy one another in the Lord, &c. then could we give up to the will of the Lord so much the better in the thing. Therefore according to the will of the Lord, in his name and power, I set my face southwards; and visited Friends in Lancashire, and in some parts of Yorkshire and Derbyshire, which counties I passed through into Warwickshire, to a place called Badgley; where I met with many of the brethren, who did dearly own the power, and the motion of it, by which I was drawn forth into that glorious work: and being very sweetly refreshed together, and confirmed in the faith and power of God, and encouraged to go on in that glorious and honourable service, I took my leave of them, and went on in the name and power of the Lord towards Norwich in Norfolk, (being accompanied with another Friend;) and coming to Wellingbo-rough in Northamptonshire, we found several there newly convinced of the Lord's truth, with whom we were much refreshed. And being there the first day of the week, it was upon me to go to their steeple-house, where I had some liberty (and but little) to declare the everlasting truth of God. After that I returned to the meeting of Friends, where the power and presence of the Lord God was with us; so that a very sweet, comfortable, and refreshing meeting we had. Howbeit, that day I and my companion were appre-hended, and kept that night in custody; but

the next day, as Providence ordered it, while the priest and some with him (as we were informed) were gone to get a warrant to bring us before a justice, we were by a certain officer released.

After that we travelled towards Cambridge, where we had a very good opportunity to visit Friends; which having done, we passed on our journey towards Norwich. It being in the depth of winter, and we travelling altogether on foot, it was something hard to the outward man; but the Lord was with us, and his mighty power upheld us, and carried us through all, and through mercy we got finally well to Norwich; where there were several of our north country Friends in prison, whom we visited, and with whom we were sweetly refreshed.

In this city we had a very large meeting, unto which many people resorted; and the Lord was with me, and gave me a mouth and wisdom freely and powerfully to declare his living truth: at that time we were also in much jeopardy of being taken, but the Lord preserved us out of the hands of unreasonable men. At that city my companion left me, and returned towards the north; and after I had visited Friends and the brethren there, I went into the country, and had very good service for the Lord; and in a short time after I went to London, where I was very kindly received by Friends there, and we were refreshed together in the Lord.

Not long after, came several of the brethren to the city out of the north and other parts; and the mighty power of the Lord God was with us, and very much we were exercised, sometimes in steeple-houses, and sometimes in the meetings of separatists: upon one first day I was at two of their steeple-houses in the forepart of the day, and at one of them I had large liberty to speak; and in the afternoon I was at a meeting of professors, where there were six that spoke one after another; and afterwards I had liberty to speak freely among them without opposition or contradiction from any of them, and afterwards I departed in peace.

About that time, the word of the Lord grew mightily in that city, and many were added to the faith; and many steeple-houses, and most of the meetings in the city were visited by some of the brethren; for at one time there were ten or twelve of us (the ministering brethren) in the city, most of us come out of the north, even plain, honest, upright men, such as the Lord was pleased to make use of in that day; and very diligent we were in his work night and day, labouring faithfully so much as in us lay, to exalt his name over all, and to make his truth and salvation known even unto all.

Many meetings we had about that time in the city, and I began to experience much of the faithfulness of the Lord to me, who furnished me according to necessity, and was pleased to give that which was suitable to the condition of the people, unto whom I was to communicate it.

About that time, I met with my dear brother John Stubbs, who was also come up to London out of the north; and though at that time we had little outward knowledge one of another, yet Providence did so order it, that we became companions and fellow-travellers together. And it was upon us to go into the country, partly towards Uxbridge; and at a certain place within a few miles of Uxbridge, we had very good service both in the steeple-house, and also at a meeting, which was ordered upon our coming to that place; and the Lord was with us, in whom we were strong; and our word powerful, though in our own eye we were weak, and contemptible in the eyes of many. And the priest being moved with envy, did stir up the people against us, so that through his means we were apprehended, and carried before a justice; but he being a moderate man, reasoned moderately with us, and perceiving our innocency, discharged us. Afterwards we returned to London again with joy and rejoicing, when we saw how the Lord had been with us, and how eminently he had appeared, (through us weak and contemptible vessels;) which we made known to the brethren at our return, who when they understood it, rejoiced with us.

[In the further extracts we may make, it is not proposed to follow consecutively the narrative in the order of the chapters, but to select some of the more striking passages. These faithful labourers in the gospel vineyard, William Caton and John Stubbs, leaving London, proceed into Kent towards Dover; from thence to Falkestone, and so on to Hythe.]

In that town the baptists allowed us the use of their meeting-room, and at the first were pretty moderate and civil to us, but afterwards they became (or some of them) our great opposers; howbeit some there were in that place who believed and received our testimony.

Then we went from that town further into the country, and were at Romney and Lydd, where there were many high professors, and among the rest one Samuel Fisher, a very eminent and able pastor among the baptists; and it was upon me to go to the meeting of the independents, and upon my dear brother, to go to the meeting of the baptists, where he had good liberty; the aforesaid S. F. had been speaking among them, but (as it appeared) was so much affected with John's doctrine, that after John had done, Samuel began with his wisdom to paraphrase upon it with excellency of speech, thereby to set it forth in his apprehension beyond what John had done: at the meeting where I was, they would scarce allow me any liberty to clear my conscience among them. After that, we had meetings in both places; and being one time at a meeting in the street at Lydd, (for the Friends' house would not contain the multitude,) the magistrates, or some of them, sent to the aforesaid Samuel Fisher, (who was also present at the meeting,) to tell him that we might have the church-door (as they called it) opened to go in thither, but we refused to accept of it, and chose rather to continue our meeting in the street. The aforesaid S. F. believed our report, with several more in those two towns, who were convinced of the

truth of God, which had not in those parts been declared by any Friend before.

We were also up in the country about Ashford and Tenterden, and had great meetings, and strong contests with professors, who did much oppose us, especially in those two towns; howbeit some we found who were simple and tender-hearted in most places where we got meetings. We were also at Cranbrook and Stapleburst, where we found a very open people, who were very ready to receive, and to embrace the everlasting truth, which we freely and powerfully (according to our measures received) administered unto them, in the power and demonstration of the eternal Spirit; and several large and precious meetings we had among them, and the power and presence of the Lord God were much with us, in which we rejoiced together, freely distributing of the word of life unto them, which at that time dwelt richly and plenteously in our hearts; and as we had received it freely, so we did dispense the same freely. For though there were those that would have given us both gold and money, which some would even have forced upon us, yet we had not freedom to receive one penny of them; for we told them it was not theirs but them which were sought: and many were convinced and much affected with the truth, which with joy and gladness they received. And among them, as at other places, we sought to settle and establish meetings, and to bring those that were convinced to wait upon the Lord in silence, in that light of life in themselves, which we turned them unto; to the end that they might enjoy the substance of what they had professed. And accordingly meetings came to be settled in most of the places before-mentioned, which they that were convinced kept up after our departure.*

After that, we were moved to go to a great town called Maidstone; and it being on a first day of the week, we were in the fore part of the day at a meeting of the people called baptists in the country; and after we had declared the way of salvation among them, we left them and went to the meeting aforesaid. When we came there, it was upon my dear brother J. S. to go to their public place of worship, and it was upon me to go to the meeting of the independents, which accordingly we did; and John was taken at their steeple-house, and I the day following at my inn, and were both sent to the house

* [Dover Friends were among the first that set this noble example of gathering in the name of Him, who promised to be in the midst of them, and who was found to be the faithful and true witness unto them.
"I may also acquaint you a little how things were with us in our first convincement and meetings, after we came to sit down to wait upon the Lord in silence; which was our practice for some years, except some travelling Friend came amongst us. I can truly say, the Lord was our teacher, and his presence and power were manifested amongst us, when no words have been sounded in our outward ears: for several of us, at several times, in these meetings, have felt the power of the Lord, that hath made our outward bodies tremble as well as our hearts; and great fear and reverence took hold of my heart; and the Lord confirmed his truth in me from day to day, and answered my doubts, and settled my faith by and in his power." —Luke Howard's Collection of Writings, 1704, p. 29.]

of correction, (so called,) where we were searched, and had our money, and our ink-horns, and Bible, &c. taken from us; and afterwards we were stripped, and had our necks and arms put in the stocks, and in that condition were desperately whipped; and afterwards we had irons and great clogs of wood laid upon us, and in that condition they would have compelled us to have wrought, saying, he that would not work should not eat, &c. Forasmuch as they had dealt so wickedly with us, and that without any just cause, neither could they justly charge us with the breach of any law, we were not free to consent so far unto their cruel wills as to do their work; and therefore did they keep us without victuals for some days, only a little water once a day we had allowed us: he that committed us, and was the chief agent in cruelty against us, was a noted presbyterian. And though the malefactors that were there, would have given us of their bread, yes, the women of the house being moved with compassion towards us, would have given us something privately, but we were not free at that time to accept of either, until that they (by whose order provision was kept from us,) did give consent that it should be brought in to us; which finally he or they did; many in the town began to be offended at their cruelty, which they manifested towards us. And when they, who sought to bow us to their wills, were made to bow by the power of God, we were free to receive victuals for our money, and did eat and were refreshed.

The next day following, (after their cruelty seemed to be abated,) they sent an officer, who did make restitution of some of our things again which they had taken from us, but burned several good wholesome papers and letters; afterwards they parted us, and with officers conveyed us out of the town, one at the one end of it, and the other at the other, which was no small trial to us to be so separated. Afterwards we were conveyed from one officer to another in the country, and in that manner sent towards our habitations in the north; but when I had been in the hands of about twelve of them, they began to grow careless of their order, and finally suffered me to travel alone, which accordingly I did towards London.

The day following I got well up to London, where I was more than a little refreshed with the brethren; and there I met with my dear companion J. S. again to our great refreshment. And behold it came presently upon us to return to the town of Maidstone again, and into that country, which was no small trial to us; however to the will of the Lord we gave up, and returned again within two or three days. When our grand persecutor at Maidstone heard of our return again, he sent a hue and cry after us, and it being gotten eight miles into the country, the officer came into a Friend's house where we had lodged, but were then at another place; and it being on a first day in the morning we went to their steeple-house, but the officer was not then there; so Providence did so order it, at that time we were preserved out of their hands. Afterwards we passed through the country, visiting the brethren that had received the gospel, who were confirmed in the faith, and the more so through our patient suffering. We were also at Canterbury where we had exceeding good service, especially among the baptists and independents so called; for we were at their meetings, and had pretty good liberty to declare the truth of God amongst them, and some there were that received our testimony in that place also, who were convinced of the truth, so that there came to be a meeting settled there.

(To be continued.)

From "*A brief Sketch of the Life of the learned and excellent James Usher, late Archbishop of Armagh, Ireland.*

This extract is offered for insertion on a page of "The Friend," if the editor should deem it sufficiently interesting.

A Reader.

" The year before this learned and holy primate, Archbishop Usher, died, I went to him and earnestly desired him to give me in writing, his apprehensions concerning justification and sanctification by Christ; because I had formerly heard him preach upon those points, wherein he seemed to make those great mysteries more intelligible to my mean capacity than any thing I had ever heard from any other; but because I had but an imperfect and confused remembrance of the particulars, I took the boldness to importune him that he would please to give a brief account of them in writing, whereby I might the better imprint them on my memory; of which he would willingly have excused himself, by declaring his intention of not writing any more, adding, that if he did write any thing it should not exceed above a sheet or two; but upon my continued importunity, I at last obtained his promise. He coming to town some time after, was pleased to give me a visit at my own house, where I failed not to challenge the benefit of the promise he had made me; he replied that he had not writ, and yet he could not charge himself with any breach of promise. For (said he) ' I did begin to write, but when I came to write of sanctification, that is, of the new creature which God formed by his Spirit in every soul which he doth truly regenerate, I found so little of it wrought in myself, that I could speak of it only as parrots by rote, and without the knowledge and understanding of what I might have expressed, and therefore I durst not presume to proceed any further upon it.' And when I seemed to stand amazed, to hear such an humble confession from so great and experienced a Christian, he added, ' I must tell you, we do not well understand what sanctification and the new creature are, it is no less than for a man to be brought to an entire resignation of his will to the will of God, and to live in the offering up of his soul continually in the flames of love as a whole burnt offering to Christ; and how little (says he) are many of those who profess Christianity experimentally acquainted with this work on their souls.'

" By this discourse, I conceived he had very excellently and clearly discovered to me that part of sanctification which he was unwilling to write."

MEMORIAL OF FRIENDS OF NEW YORK ON SLAVERY.

The following memorial addressed to Congress by the Meeting for Sufferings, of New York, was forwarded for insertion by a friend of that city.

To the Senate and House of Representatives of the United States of America, in Congress assembled—

The memorial of the representatives of the religious Society of Friends in the state of New York, and parts adjacent, at a meeting held in the city of New York the 31st day of the 12th month, 1839.

Respectfully showeth—

That your memorialists highly appreciate the magnanimous sentiment put forth in that important and justly celebrated state paper, the Declaration of American Independence, which, by its adoption, has become the language of the nation.

" We hold these truths to be self evident, that all men are created equal, that they are endowed by their Creator with certain inalienable rights; that among these, are life, liberty, and the pursuit of happiness." When your memorialists reflect that the language of inspiration is in full confirmation of this generous and noble view; that this blessed and holy Creator " hath made of one blood all nations of men to dwell on all the face of the earth;" that all the human family, without distinction of caste or colour, are the objects of Divine mercy, through the atoning blood of Christ, " who, by the grace of God, tasted death for every man," they are constrained, by a sense of religious duty, to present themselves before Congress, on behalf of a large number of our fellow creatures of the African race, who are held in unconditional bondage in the United States.

The portion of the Christian church to which we belong, have given unequivocal evidence, that they consider slavery in all its parts to be utterly at variance with the Gospel precept :—" All things whatsoever ye would that men should do to you, do ye even so to them:" and indeed with that inflexible justice that is uniformly enjoined by the holy religion we all profess, the religion of Jesus Christ.

That the Society of Friends has been steady, honest and conscientious, in its uniform opposition to slavery, that philanthropy and humanity constitute the basis upon which it has always advocated the cause of freedom, was recently conceded in the Senate of the United States, in a courteous manner, by a distinguished member of that body. It is upon the same humane and peaceable principles that your memorialists now act.

If then the solemn declarations already quoted are true, the whole system of slavery must be a fearful violation of the Divine law, a palpable infringement of human liberty and of human rights, and, of course, sinful in the

sight of Heaven; that it has been so considered, we confidently infer from the various humane enactments made by Congress for the suppression of the foreign slave trade, which by several of the Christian nations, including our own, has been adjudged to be piracy. Your memorialists deeply regret, however, that notwithstanding the existing laws, penal as they are, the unjust and cruel traffic in the inhabitants of Africa is at this day carried on (in which it is understood our own citizens largely participate) to an extent unparalleled in the history of slavery. A fact that cannot fail to awaken painful feelings in the heart of the Christian philanthropist, and indeed the solemn inquiry, " how can we expect that the blessings of Heaven will be continued to our beloved country, with such a weight of guilt resting upon it ?"

Your memorialists would therefore most respectfully but earnestly beseech Congress to make such further provision, as in its wisdom may be deemed effectual to protect the unoffending inhabitants of Africa from the grasp of unprincipled men, who, for the lust of gain, are wresting her children from her, and consigning them to hopeless bondage.

Your memorialists would also state their deep conviction of the sin and degradation that rest upon our country, by the internal traffic in the persons of our fellow-men by this iniquitous and disgraceful trade, scarcely second to the foreign trade itself; the most tender connections are severed with impunity in a manner shocking to the feelings of humanity—while slavery is steadily spreading its blighting influence over our widely extended domain; to an extent calculated to excite very serious anticipations for the future, demanding, as your memorialists most solemnly believe, the full exercise of all the constitutional powers Congress is in possession of, to put an effectual check to this accumulating evil, by which the stain upon our national character is also made more indelible.

Well might a popular statesman of our own times exclaim in consideration of the enormity of slavery, " I tremble for my country when I consider that God is just, that his justice cannot sleep forever, and that an exchange of circumstances is among probable events—the Almighty has no attribute that can take sides with us in such a conflict."

In conclusion, your memorialists feel deeply on this great and exciting subject, they have no wish to increase excitement—they have the good of the master, the slave, and the whole country at heart—but believing as they do, that the captive must be permitted to go free, " and every yoke be broken," either by the timely application of humane and virtuous means, or in default of these, by the operation of those laws of Providence that can break in pieces the manacles of the oppressed, as a reed is broken.

They desire to unite with all true Christians every where, in humble and reverent prayer, to that Almighty being in whose hand is the destiny of nations, that he may so influence the councils of the nation, and so imbue the hearts of the people with his love, and an abiding sense of his omnipotence, that by a united and generous energy of mind, the great object of our solicitude may be attained —the solemn duty that we owe to the descendants of Africa be performed, and our beloved country be blessed with peace, quiet, and the smiles of indulgent Heaven.

Signed, on behalf and by direction of the meeting. SAMUEL PARSONS, Clerk.

The watchmen in Germany amuse themselves during the night by singing their national songs, as well as those of a more devotional character. Of the latter the following is a specimen, taken from that very interesting work "The Autumn on the Rhine." When their voices are good, which is frequently the case, the effect is solemn and pleasing.

Hark ye neighbours and hear me tell
Ten now strikes on the belfry bell!
Ten are the holy commandments given
To man below—from God in heaven.
  Human watch from harm can't ward us,
  God will watch, and God will guard us,
  May he through eternal might,
  Give us all a blessed night.

Hark ye neighbours and hear me tell
Eleven sounds on the belfry bell;
Eleven apostles of holy mind
Taught the gospel to mankind.
  Human watch, &c.

Hark ye neighbours and hear me tell
Twelve resounds on the belfry bell,
Twelve disciples to Jesus came,
Who suffered rebuke for their Saviour's name.
  Human watch, &c.

Hark ye neighbours and hear me tell
One has peeled on the belfry bell,
One God above, one Lord indeed,
Who bears us up in the time of need.
  Human watch, &c.

Hark ye neighbours and hear me tell
Two resounds on the belfry bell,
Two paths before mankind are free,
Neighbour choose the best for thee.
  Human watch, &c.

Hark ye neighbours and hear me tell
Three now falls on the belfry bell,
Threefold reigns the heavenly Host,
Father, Son, and Holy Ghost.
  Human watch from harm can't ward us,
  God will watch, and God will guard us,
  May he through eternal might,
  Give us all a blessed night.

For "The Friend."

INSTRUCTION TO COLOURED PEOPLE.

As abolition is the prevailing topic of the day, and who that has a heart of flesh does not feel, deeply feel for the poor and down-trodden? I would call the attention of the readers of "The Friend," and in particular the young, to the improvement of the coloured people at home, in your own domestic circle; whether children or adults, whether bound or free servants, strive to elevate them all in your power; give them what instruction they will take, and you can bestow, grudge not the pains it may cost, mind not the trouble, nor the exercise of patience to teach the stupid and the dull. Ye pity the poor slave! ye sigh, and sighing say, "I wish I could do something for them!" But it is your favoured lot not to be surrounded by slaves. There is

much meaning couched in the anecdote of the celebrated John Randolph; when on a visit to some of his female friends, he found them assembled to sew for the poor Greeks! "Ladies," said he, "there are Greeks at your door;" and on their rushing out to see, he archly pointed, and with peculiar force, to their naked and neglected slaves. O consistency, thou art a jewel! how many who profess abolition principles, will not labour and persevere in teaching those who are living in the same house. Think of this, dear young Friends, and "be not ye weary in well doing," and ye may exclaim with the amiable poetess,

"I know indeed, I cannot free
The countless slaves who round me pine,
But yet to be one negro's friend
Might, blessed chance, might now be mine!"
          W.

HUMILITY.

It is recorded of one of the ablest and best of men of the age in which he lived, that when he heard of a criminal condemned to die, he used to think, and often to say, "Who can tell whether this man is not better than I? Or, if I am better, it is not to be ascribed to myself, but to the goodness of God." It is the advice of an apostle, that, "in lowliness of mind each should esteem others better than themselves;" and if we seriously reflect upon the many sinful passions and desires which lurk in our bosoms, the many evil thoughts which sometimes arise in our minds, our many omissions of duty, our many unguarded expressions—there probably is not one of us but will find reason humbly to acknowledge, that he knows more harm of himself than he knows of any one else.

ICELAND DEVOTION.

There is a sweet and simple custom prevalent in Iceland, which marks the habitual devotion of its inhabitants. Whenever they leave home, though for a short journey, they uncover their heads, and for the space of five minutes silently implore the protection and favour of the Almighty. Dr. Henderson, from whom the fact is derived, and who observed it in the Icelanders who often attended him on his excursions, also remarked it in the humblest fisherman when going forth to procure food for their families. After having put out upon the sea, they row into quiet water, at a short distance from the shore, and bowing their uncovered heads, solicit the blessing of their Father in heaven. Even at passing a stream, which in their country of precipices is often an operation fraught with danger, they observe the same sacred custom. This affecting habit of devotion has been imputed to the fact, that, from their isolated situation and mode of life, the mother is almost the only teacher, and her instruction seems to have become incorporated with their very elements of being.

DIED, at his residence in this city, on seventh day morning, the 15th instant, in the 75th year of his age, THOMAS LOVD, a respected member of Twelfth street meeting.

THE FRIEND.

SECOND MONTH, 22' 1840.

We have given part of our space in the present number to interesting documents, relating to two of the many benevolent associations of this city, which we especially regard with partiality, and take pleasure in embracing occasions to bring into notice. That pertaining to the institution for the deaf and dumb, may indeed be safely left to speak for itself; —a charity so truly benign, so successful and beneficial in its results, and so prominently an object of favour in the public estimation, will surely not be permitted to languish through deficiency of patronage. The other, the Association for the care of Coloured Orphans, familiarly known as The Shelter, more humble in pretension, and inferior in point of notoriety, is nevertheless not less in accordance with the spirit of Christian philanthropy, which is limited by no invidious distinction either of nation or condition, or colour. It moreover has claims upon our attention as an institution exclusively our own; its members (female altogether) are also members, all of them, of our religious Society, as are likewise nearly all the contributors to its funds. The establishment is conducted upon the most economical plan, but so large a family necessarily involves considerable expenditure, the annual disbursements amounting to about $2000. To meet this, the income from money at interest is about $500, the annual subscription is about as much more,—thus leaving a deficiency of one thousand dollars, for which the association is dependent upon the liberality of its friends. The yearly resort to a call upon the benevolent for the supply of this deficiency, however prevalent the disposition to liberality may be, it is desirable should be provided against, and one step in effecting this would be, to use strenuous endeavours to increase the number of annual contributions. It scarcely can be admitted as doubtful, that many would be willing to enter their names on a personal appeal for that purpose. We may also take the liberty to intimate, that persons about to make their wills, might do well to consider, whether the Shelter might not properly come in for a share of their substance.

FRIENDS' READING ROOMS.

Dr. Pliny Earle will deliver a lecture on "Malta," on third day evening next, the 25th instant, at 7½ o'clock.

A qualified female Friend is desirous of a school; if chiefly of the children of Friends it would be most acceptable.

Should such a teacher be wanted, application may be made to Ann Taiem, Woodbury, N. J., Elizabeth Passmore, Willis town, Pa., or Ann Williams, No. 71 North Seventh street, Philadelphia.

PRINTED BY ADAM WALDIE,
Carpenter Street, below Seventh, Philadelphia.

THE FRIEND.

A RELIGIOUS AND LITERARY JOURNAL.

VOL. XIII.　　　　SEVENTH DAY, SECOND MONTH, 29, 1840.　　　　NO. 22.

EDITED BY ROBERT SMITH.

———

PUBLISHED WEEKLY.

Price two dollars per annum, payable in advance.

Subscriptions and Payments received by

GEORGE W. TAYLOR,

NO. 50, NORTH FOURTH STREET, UP STAIRS,

PHILADELPHIA.

Ancient City of Palenque in Mexico.

A late number of the Richmond Compiler contains an article under the above heading, in the introduction to which it is stated, that the editor of that paper sent a letter last autumn to a young citizen of Richmond, then in the city of Mexico, for the purpose of eliciting information respecting the result of an expedition to Palenque by Waldeck, a German, with the view of exploring the remarkable ruins of that supposed ancient city of this sometimes called *New World*, but which would seem to be in a fair way of being proved a misnomer by these and other remains of somewhat similar character. The letter received in answer, dated Mexico, Dec. 2d, 1839, details several particulars relative to the subject of inquiry, and holds out the expectation that at some future period the writer would be enabled to comply more fully with his friend's wishes. In the mean time, (he remarks) perhaps the following description may prove interesting to you. I translate from a Mexican periodical called "El Mosaico."

Extract from the "Tour of Don Antonio del Rio to the Ruins of Palenque, in 1787."

"On the 3d of May, 1787, Captain Antonio del Rio, by order of the king of Spain, arrived at the Ruins of Palenque, accompanied by some Indians, to facilitate his exploration. The following are the details of his relation:

Under the name of Stone Houses are known certain ruins situated at the distance of five leagues from New Palenque, the last settlement to the north in the district of Carmen, province of the Royal City of Chiapas. At two leagues from a chain of mountains which separates the republic of Guatamela from the department of Yucatan, runs the little river Micol in a westerly direction to join the great river Tulija, whose waters wash the side of the province of Tobasco. From Micol you commence to ascend to these ruins, and at the distance of about half a league, at the point where it receives a little river called Otolum, you encounter great ridges of rocks, which render the pass difficult for another half league. On reaching the extreme height you perceive

fourteen edifices of stone, of which some are in a worse condition than others; but, notwithstanding, there are many apartments or habitations which may be distinctly seen in a good state of preservation.

At the foot of one of the highest mountains of the great chain of which I have above spoken, you observe a plane or rectangular superficies of three hundred varas long by the half in breadth, in the centre of which, and upon a base twenty varas high, you find the greatest of the constructions which have been discovered there: this is surrounded by five other edifices on the north, four on the south, one on the southeast, and three on the east. Remains of other edifices extend also to the east and west along the mountains, to the distance of three or four leagues in a right line drawn from the centre; which induces me to suppose this city comprehends an extension of seven or eight leagues—but it diminishes considerably at a little less than half a league towards the point situated near the river Micol, where the ruins terminate.

The situation is most beautiful, the climate delicious, and the soil fertile.

The interior of the great edifice is of a style of architecture approaching to the Gothic; its construction rude and compact—the assurance of great duration. You enter on the eastern side by a portico or piazza thirty-six varas long, and by a door three varas high. This is supported by polished pillars of a rectangular form without pedestal or base, over which are four stones, joined together, more than one third of a vara in thickness, and which form an architrave with two kinds of shields, as exterior ornaments, in stucco; lastly, upon these stones there is another rectangular piece of a vara and two thirds in width, by two in length, which rests upon two pillars. Some medalions or reliefs in stucco, representing different figures, appear to have served as decorations to the dwellings; and it is presumed from the other heads which are yet distinguishable, that these figures were the busts of a series of the kings or lords of the country. Between the medalions you observe a range of windows resembling niches, which extends from one extremity to the other of the wall. Some are square, others have the form of a Greek cross, and others again, which complete the range, are two thirds of a vara in height by eight inches in depth.

Beyond this piazza there is a square court, to which you descend by a stair of seven steps. The part towards the north is entirely destroyed; but you can see in other times it had a portico and hall similar to those of the eastern part. To the south there are four small rooms, with only one or two small windows each—such as before described. The western side is equal in all respects to its pa-

rallel, except the ornaments of stucco, which are much coarser. The figures form a kind of grotesque masquerade, each person wearing a crown and a long beard like a goat, and having at his side a Greek cross.

Advancing in the same direction, you find another court of the same width as the former, but not so long, and a narrow passage communicating with the opposite side. Here are two chambers similar to those before spoken of, and an interior gallery, one side of which looks into the court, and the other into the country. In this part of the edifice you yet see the remains of several pillars, with bass-reliefs, which represent, as is believed, the sacrifice of some unfortunate Indian.

Returning to the south side, there is a tower sixteen varas high, which contains another interior tower, with windows, to give light to the stair that conducts to the top.

After the four chambers already mentioned, there are two others, of greater dimensions, very well ornamented, at least according to the rude manner of the Indians, and which might have served them as oratories. Among the ornaments, there are some enamelled stuccoes: the Greek heads representing sacred objects. Beyond the oratories there are rooms which extend from north to south, twenty-seven varas long, by seven wide; but which do not contain any object worthy of note unless it be a stone, of an elliptical form, whose greatest diameter is a vara and a quarter, and its least, one vara; this stone is incrusted to the height of near a vara from the pavement. Under this stone there is a rectangular piece, two varas wide, by one vara and four inches long, and seven inches thick, placed upon four feet like a table, with a figure in bass-relief, which appears to sustain it. On the borders of this table, as well as upon many stones and stuccoes, there are characters or symbols, whose signification is unknown.

At the extremity of the last room, and on a level with the floor, there is an opening, two varas wide, by one long, which leads by means of a stair, to another subterraneous passage, in which you discover other openings. Along this stair, at regular distances, there are resting places, each one with a door; at the second one you are obliged to use lighted torches, in order to continue descending by an easy declivity. This stair, which turns at right angles, terminates at another door, which communicates with a room seventy-four varas wide, and perhaps the same in length as those anterior to it. There is another similar apartment illuminated by windows, which receive the light from a corridor that looks to the south, and leads to the interior of the edifice. The only objects worthy of being noticed, are some polished stones, two varas and a half long, by one inch and a half wide, placed upon four

n their arms, all of
-reliefs are executed
s are without heads.
ary, and on each side
to the saloon, there
square, covered with
-relief.

e edifice, and travers-
ers, which were per-
to the principal edi-
all uncovered valley,
here you find as in
saloon, on the door
nent in stucco, whose
ppear the superstition
east of this edifice,
ill ones forming a tri-
forms a square room
leven broad, on the
first; but they have
f turrets, three varas
ents and devices in
of the first of these
mity of the gallery,
destroyed, there is a
room at each end;
of these, there is an
e varas square, pre-
the entrance, a stone
ich is represented a
e frontispiece of the
ree stones, on which
tions. The exterior
moulding of small
overed with bass-re-
l united, and is eight
ng dug to the depth
able-vase of earthen-
lismeter, was found
nother of the same
pth of one third of a
r a stone of circular
re discovered in a
, armed with a point
l pyramids, and the
a crystallized stone,
country by the name
rs, with their covers,
ones and a piece of
jects were found in
where you discover
the interior angles

are similar in their
ly in the allegorical
ss-reliefs. The fron-
ory consists of three
n excavation having
were found beneath
ok place in the third.

From the Raleigh Register.
SIGHT TO THE BLIND.

An interesting letter was handed us some days ago from Mary A. Smith, of Stokes county, containing a request that it should be published in the Register. In it, she says that she was born blind, and remained in that condition till she was eighteen years of age, when she was brought to her sight by an operation performed upon her by Dr. John Beckwith, of this city. Having recently heard through this paper of several similar operations, she says she is reminded forcibly of her remissness in having so long neglected, what she considers a sort of religious duty, towards those whom Providence may have placed in a similar affliction—and she requests us to supply any deficiencies in the history of her case, by inquiries of Dr. B. who has related to us substantially the following:

He was requested to visit the family of General P. some miles from town. As he was about to leave the next morning, the general remarked that he was one of the wardens of the poor of the county, and as it was not much out of the way, would join him in the ride as far as the poor-house, and show him the comfortable arrangements of the establishment. It was a warm morning in August, and they started early, and had not been long seated in the shade before the door, when a finely formed and rosy young woman approached them, bearing a pail in her hand. The general addressed her with, "good morning Mary, how do you do; can you see your way to the spring?" "I thank you general, I know the way." The doctor then learned that she had been blind from her birth—that her parents died while she was young, and having no near relations who felt much interest in watching over her helplessness, she was thrown upon the "world's cold charity," and she finally found her way there, where she received whatever of kindness and comfort the place afforded.

Among other inquiries, she was asked if she would be willing to submit to an operation upon her eyes to obtain her sight? She replied, "I don't know—it would be a great blessing—but as it has pleased God to bring me into this world blind, I am not sure it would be right to try to alter his will—I am not unhappy,† but would be thankful to be like other people." "But Mary, though God has been pleased to afflict us with many infir-

* * A vara is equal to 33½ inches.
† It is a remarkable fact, that blindness is almost invariably accompanied by cheerfulness.

tion of this sort, she
whatever they though
cordingly removed to
be conveniently attend

Her eyes were in co
had no control over
of chalky whiteness, y
ception of light, could
large objects, and d
colours, in a clear li
useful, purpose. Th
surgeons call capsular
ed and very dense.),
with perfect calmness
said she suffered no p
known that the needle
not told of it; havin
against the ball. On
adhesions, it became
operation several time
accomplished at once
yet she never betrays
alarm.

It would be hardly t
the minute circumstan
cure, as they could be i
cal men. Her eyes w
ed," and she saw as v
cases ever do. A new
her—she looked upon
and all was new, yet k
nor could she determin
was much perplexed
yard, on comparing the
shadow upon the grou
step high over the sha
against it. There were
a small dog, and a larg
—they had early came
Mary, and she knew t
to distinguish them by
ceedingly, and she oft
others by her attempts
Some interesting and
tween Mary and othe
class occurred at the do
were restored, particul
20, from Iredell county
several years, and a yo
Cabarrus county, who
Hiram Blackwelder.
benevolence of feeling
make one enjoy their n
and their method of co
several discoveries, if
paring, where all tal
were almost tumultuo
of joy, yet in Mary's
often be observed a si
of piety; that showed

humble instruments of her relief, to Him who first "gave sight to the blind."

Her progress in acquiring an accurate knowledge of objects by sight, was at first rather slow, but by frequent repetitions of comparison, and a good deal of natural sprightliness of mind, she at length became "like other people," and could discharge all the ordinary duties of life with comfort to herself and usefulness to others. She returned no more to the poor-house, but became the inmate of a respectable family, where she has ever since resided.

A FEARFUL CONTEST

With a grizzly bear is thus graphically described in the New Orleans Picayune, in one of a series of interesting papers entitled "Rocky Mountain Sketches:"

The following anecdote we had from a young fellow who spent five years among the mountains. He told us the story by our camp fire at night, when the winds were shrieking over our heads among the clefts of mountains, and darkness hung around us like a funeral pall. With a single companion he had been five days away from his party, searching for some new stream on which to trap beaver. As the sun was sinking, on the fifth day, they stopped at a spot where wild berries were growing very plentifully, and a little mountain spring was trickling over the rocks. They alighted, unsaddled their horses, and placed their rifles leaning against a tree. Our hero then turned toward the bushes to pick some berries, and being well pleased with their flavour, and withal somewhat hungry, he did not at first notice that there was a rustling among the bushes. When he did, however, he sprung for his rifle, and had scarcely turned again before an enormous grizzly bear broke through the bushes, and dashed directly at him. His own rifle had a single trigger, that of his companion's a double, and in his confusion he had seized his companion's instead of his own, so that when he attempted to fire, the trigger not being properly set, his effort was useless. A deadly faintness thrilled him, and an instant and terrible death stared him in the face. The furious animal was crouched to spring upon him; his companion was too far from the spot to render him any assistance, and bewildered with terror, unable to account for the state of his rifle, and faint with fear, destruction seemed inevitable. The animal sprung, and despair proved the poor trapper's salvation, for with the motion his strength returned, the strength of desperation wrought up by the last extremity of peril, and giving his rifle one wide swing, he struck the infuriated beast upon the head with the heavy barrel, while in the very act of descending upon him. The bear was stunned; one of his fore paws fastened on the shoulder of the trapper as he fell, and they both came to the ground together. The trapper described his sensations at this moment as having undergone the most wonderful change.

All fear had vanished, and a savage delight seemed to have taken possession of his soul. He felt a consciousness of strength equal to that of the enormous brute with which he was struggling; and as the grizzly beast opened its huge jaws to fasten his tusks upon him, uttering most appalling growls, and while he inhaling its strong, sickening breath, he plunged the barrel of his rifle down his throat, and springing to his feet, endeavoured to force the gun completely into the animal's stomach. His arm had been dreadfully lacerated, and his deer-skin coat entirely torn from his body by the sharp fangs of the bear, which now rose to his feet, and gripping the rifle barrel firmly in its teeth, endeavoured to wring it out of the trapper's grasp. The bear had been stunned and hurt, and in a high phrensy of rage. The trapper clung for life to his rifle, and the next instant, by a furious effort of the enraged beast, he was lifted from his feet and dashed to the ground at the distance of some four yards from the spot. The fall bereft him of power to move, and here his fate would have been sealed for ever, but for his companion, who, the instant he saw the separation, discharged the other rifle, and broke one of the bear's shoulder bones. The shot would have been more effectual, but he also having the wrong rifle, and not being aware of the mistake, had fired when he thought he was only setting the hair trigger. The bear fell, however, still holding the rifle fast in its teeth, close to where the first trapper was lying, who had barely strength to seize the butt end of the rifle once more, set the trigger, and fire the contents down the animal's throat. The grizzly bear was then soon despatched, and the unfortunate rifle is now to be seen in the museum at Chihuahua with the heavy barrel bent, and the marks of the bear's teeth distinctly visible.

For "The Friend."

THE HUMAN VOICE.

We are all sensible of the varieties of the human voice; we distinguish our acquaintances by its tones, as unerringly as by the features of the face; and in speaking of each other, we refer to its qualities as constituting a most essential point in our descriptions. Yet, how few of us have any distinct consciousness of the immense influence which the *tones of the voice* exercise—not only in qualifying the import of our words, but in communicating, almost independent of them, the most delicate sensations, as well as the most violent emotions, and in disclosing the deepest and most hidden traits of the "concealed heart."

Every one feels how many physiognomical peculiarities are indissolubly connected with certain moral and intellectual qualities; but this connection is far less extensive and fixed, than that between peculiar tones and these qualities.

From the first to the last breath of our existence, the voice takes its character from the mind and the heart. Education, as it modifies our other attributes, may modify this, and even bestow command over some of its powers: still its *tones* will remain the index of the soul. The various changes, from the angelic innocence of the little child, through the joys of childhood, the hopes of youth, and the designs of maturity, down to the indifference of old age, continually produce their corresponding changes in the tones of the voice.

What description of the purity, the innocence, the helplessness of an infant, could move our hearts towards the little being, like its sweet and wordless tones—what call of distress so irresistibly draws assistance, as the cries of its wants and pains? Nature has given to these tones a peculiar power commensurate with its entire dependence upon us, and we are its servitors. Then is there on earth any thing like the playful and joyous tones through which after childhood pours out its unchained spirit? Nothing—no wit, no humour, no exhilaration of the mature man has power over our sympathies like the bursts from the spotless hearts of laughing children.

In youth, that state between the artless child and artful adult, when the bosom is in perpetual commotion, its hopes and its passions assuming new positions, and new combinations, at every new incident that agitates the mind—how impotent are mere words—how meagre would be the pictures of the heart, without the *tones of the voice* peculiar to that age.

In manhood, when the mind directs every act and every speech according to design, good or bad, and attempts to bend every incident to its purposes, we acquire the art, ofttimes, of appearing what we wish to be thought, instead of what we really are. Every thing yields to the cunning devices of the mind, except the voice. The tones which belong to particular emotions cannot be altogether suppressed—nor can the most consummate hypocrisy perfectly imitate those tones where the emotions do not exist. Hence it is that the pure, the simple, the upright, the sincere, need no vouchers; they have only to speak, and the tones of their voice beget at once implicit faith. Deception may practise her wiles in every other way; she may force the eye to weep, the lips to smile, the tongue to utter false words; but she essays in vain to subdue entirely the tones of the voice. At every moment they rebel in favour of truth.

From old age we need no declarations of decayed sensibilities, of indifference to the excitements of the younger world, of loved repose; this state of mortality has its own tones, which convey the sad truth of decay, in despite of all the treasured phrases of former and more vigorous habits.

Between friends, lovers, parents, and children, in all the dearer relationships of life, mere words are as the "idle wind" that passes by unheeded; it is to the tones of the voice that they listen—those ever true messengers between mind and mind, and heart and heart. Even in our slighter intercourse with the world, the attractions and aversions which we feel towards particular persons depend, more than upon any thing else, perhaps, on the impressions received from the tones of the voice.

That eloquence which rivets every eye of the immense assembly on the speaker, and makes every bosom swell with his own—which hushes an audience into stillness, and bathes almost every eye in tears, does not depend so much upon the mere words, the attitudes, and gesticulations—but upon the voice. These are the mere outlines—the orator's impassioned tones perfect the figures, put on the colouring and shadow, and give the picture its life and beauty.

At every stage of life,—under the influence of every passion,—amidst all the various scenes of business, of love, of hate, of enjoyment, and of misery, *the tones of the voice,* and they only, denote us truly.

For "The Friend."

"Yea, the stork in the heaven knoweth her appointed times," &c.—*Jer.* viii. 7.

Warbler! what evil star hath led thee
   From southern woods, where sports the balmy breeze
'Mid fragrant blooms—what impulse sped thee
   To our bleak snowy hills, and leafless trees?—
Now, let me read a lesson in thy story—
   Thou comest duly, at the time ordained
Of Him, who guides the planets in their glory,
   And e'en thy humble path, hath not disdained.
Obedience then I learn—not reasoning
   With carnal ease—*Faith,* in the love and power
Of Israel's Lord, right on to stretch the wing,
   Though clouds arise, and fearful tempests lour,
Thou lookest not *below* thee, where the snow
   Lies spread abroad, in cold and sparkling sheen,
But *upward,* for the sun a spring-like glow
   At noon-day hath—tho' loud the blast, and keen—
And hark! thou triest the song—'tis spring's *own* lay,
   (Though tremulous the notes) for on the breeze
   Are spicy odours, that foretell a day
When leaves and blossoms bright shall clothe the trees.
So 'mid Time's cold and gloom, a genial ray
   From Zion's sun, oft cheers her mourner's breast,
Kindles his fading hopes, and lights the way:—
   Then rouse my soul and seek *thy* glorious rest,
And should thy quickened sense, on sorrow's gale
Like perfumes blest, the promise sweet inhale—
Nor wintry storms—nor earth's vain glitter heed,
But sing Immanuel's grace, and onward speed.

2d mo. 1840.

EARTHQUAKE IN BURMAH.

The following account of the earthquake in Burmah in March last, is from the pen of Eugene Kincaid, a baptist missionary who has resided several years in that country. It is from a letter addressed to Dr. Paine, of Albion, New York.

On the 23d of March, between three and four in the morning, Ava was visited with one of the most terrible earthquakes ever known in this part of the world. A loud rumbling noise, like the roar of distant thunder, was heard, and in an instant the earth began to reel from east to west with motions so rapid and violent, that people were thrown out of their beds, and obliged to support themselves by laying hold of posts. Boxes and furniture were thrown from side to side, with a violence similar to what takes place on board a ship in a severe storm at sea. The waters of the river rose, and rolled back for some time with great impetuosity, strewing the shores with the wrecks of boats and buildings. The plains between Umerapora and the river were rent into vast yawning caverns, running from north to south, and from ten to twenty feet in width. Vast quantities of water and black sand were thrown upon the surface, emitting at the same time a strong sulphurous smell. As you will suppose, the three cities of Ava, Umerapora, and Sagaing, are vast piles of ruins, burying in their fall great numbers of unfortunate people who were asleep at the awful moment. The destruction of life, however, is not so great as might have been expected from the entire overthrow of three large and populous cities,

The reason is, the great mass of the people lived in wood and bamboo houses. Had the houses in these cities been built of bricks and stone, as cities are built in America, the entire population must have perished. Every thing built of bricks—houses, monasteries, temples, pagodas, and the city walls are all crumbled down. Of all the immense numbers of pagodas in Ava, Umerapora, and Sagaing, and on the Sagaing hills opposite to Ava, not one is standing. The labour and wealth of ages, the pride and glory of Boodhism has been laid low in the dust in one awful moment. To me this is a deeply afflicting thought; for in great numbers of those proud temples of idolatry, I have preached the gospel; and while hundreds were bowing down before huge idols, I have proclaimed the power, majesty, and glory of that Almighty Being who sits enthroned in the highest heavens; that the day was at hand when God would vindicate the honour of his name; and that all these proud monuments of heathenism would fall into hopeless ruin, and be forgotten by succeeding generations. Some were convinced, some had their confidence in idols shaken, but the great multitude were quite indifferent. Some few would zealously defend their religion. Little did I then think that the hour of God's vengeance was at the door, and that so soon these enormous idols and lofty temples, the labour of thirty generations, were to become a frightful mass of ruins.

Letters from Ava up to the 11th of April, inform us that the rumbling noise, like distant thunder, had not yet ceased; and shocks, often considerably violent, were felt day and night, with seldom as much as one hour's intermission. The extent of the great shock, or rather the succession of great shocks, on the morning of the 23d of March, is not yet fully ascertained. It was felt so severely at Maulmain, that many sprang out of bed, supposing a gang of thieves had broken into the house; yet it was not violent enough to do any damage. As far as is now ascertained, Prome to the south, and Bomee to the north of Ava, were entirely overthrown by the earthquake; so that from Prome to the borders of China, more than six hundred miles north and south, embracing the most populous part of the empire, not a single pagoda, temple, or brick building, is left standing. The earthquake was severe in Arracan, and an old volcano on the island of Bromree, was re-opened, and the long-concealed fires, mingled with smoke and ashes, rose to a fearful height. It remains to be ascertained yet, how far this great earthquake extended into China; but as there are several volcanoes among the mountains between Burmah and China, it is more than probable to me, that there are subterranean communications between these volcanoes of the north, and the volcanoes of the south, as among the mountains between Arracan and Burmah, and in the island of Bromree, and also on the Andaman islands in the Martiban-gulf. The two extremes are more than one thousand miles apart, in a direct line north and south. But the fact that the whole intermediate country was shaken at the same moment, and a prodigious subterranean noise was heard, resembling the rolling of thunder, is, I think, satisfactory evidence that there are subterra-

nean communications between these widely separated volcanoes. How else can we account for so terrible an earthquake over so vast an extent of country?

The coincidence of volcanic eruptions and earthquakes, is not remarkable, but that several hundred miles of territory, with all its mountains and rivers, should be thrust up, and thrown into undulating motions at the same moment of time, accompanied by sounds from the centre of the earth, like the rolling of thunder, are phenomena which cannot be accounted for on any other supposition than that of vast subterranean lines of communication between volcanic mountains.—*Baptist Register.*

A gentleman in this city has received a letter from Paris, in which it is stated, that a chemist has obtained from the French government a patent, for the discovery of a process by which whale oil is perfectly purified and disinfected. Some of this oil, thus purified and disinfected, has been tried by several manufacturers of cloth and soap, with complete success. By these experiments it has been proved, that whale oil, thus purified by the process in question, can be employed with equal success as olive oil, in all kinds of manufactures, as well as for lamps, being superior to all other oil hitherto used for this purpose.—*Augusta Constitutionalist.*

Cloth made without Spinning or Weaving.—An American has procured a patent in England, and several other countries of Europe, for an invention for making broad or narrow woollen cloths, without spinning or weaving. Leeds Mercury says, "After an inspection of patterns of the cloth, we should say there is every probability of this fabric superseding the usual mode of making cloth by spinning and weaving. The abridgement of labour will be very great.

A New York paper states that a grocer in that city in closing his store one evening lately, accidentally cast his eyes on a shelf where some loco foco matches were deposited, and there beheld a mouse nibbling at the pasted end of one of the boxes. The mouse was allowed to proceed with his meal undisturbed, till he was observed to spring back in alarm, and in an instant the whole contents of the box was ignited. The friction produced by the teeth of the animal had kindled a blaze which would probably have destroyed the store, and perhaps the adjoining buildings, had the grocer left the store without observing the little incendiary.

One hundred and ninety-five towns in France are provided with public libraries, containing altogether 2,500,000 volumes. At Paris there are five great public libraries, containing 1,378,000 volumes.—*Late paper.*

Twelve tin packets of preserved French beans, in a wooden box, have been brought up from the Royal George, stamped "Conserve Artichens de Catron, Marseilles." Neither vinegar nor pickle had been used; they had been boiled, and placed in air-tight vessels, and were as fresh and fit for use as when first enclosed. They have been 57 years under water.—*Kentish Observer.*

LIFE OF WILLIAM CATON.

(Continued from page 167.)

In the spring of 1665, W. Caton visits Calais, in France—returns to Dover—travels to Yarmouth, and afterwards into the north.—With John Stubbs sails to Holland—soon after his return to England, with the same fellow labourer he visits Scotland, passing through Northumberland—has good service for the Lord at Edinburgh and Glasgow—returns to Swarthmore, and proceeds to Cheshire. He attends a general meeting in Leicestershire, unto which, he says, "many of the brethren resorted, and among the rest there was dear George Fox, whom I much desired to see: and a very precious meeting it was; and afterwards I had some precious time with the brethren, and took my leave of them, and returned into Lancashire." He again visits Scotland; has good meetings at Edinburgh, Leith, Stirling, &c. Returns to Swarthmore, and proceeds to Bristol and into Cornwall.—Visits George Fox in Launceston jail, in respect to which he remarks, "where my refreshment was so much, that my cup was even made to overflow,—there being at that time dear G. F. and several other Friends prisoners there: of whom in due time I took my leave, even in the fulness of endeared love, and returned again out of those parts."

At the date mentioned in the commencement of our next extract, W. Caton was but about twenty years old, and less than two years had elapsed since his first entering into the ministry. That in this brief time he should have travelled so extensively and performed so much service as the above summary and the preceding extracts indicate, is truly surprising; and yet perhaps it is no more than a fair sample of the industry and devotedness characteristic of early Friends.

—

About the latter end of the fifth month, or the beginning of the sixth, 1656, I was at Plymouth, where I visited Friends; and after I had had a meeting among them, I travelled into the country, and being refreshed with Friends in Plymouth as also in the country, I came to a place called Totness in Devonshire; where upon my coming into the town I was apprehended, and carried before the mayor, who threatened to have the whip laid upon my back, (though without cause;) but Providence did order it otherwise, for others of the magistrates were more moderate; and when they examined me the priest was present, and a very gallant opportunity I had, to bear a large and faithful testimony unto the truth, which accordingly I did; for indeed the Lord was much with me, and it was given me in that very hour what I was to speak. That night they kept me prisoner, and the next day they sent me away with a pass from tithing-man to tithing-man, or from constable to constable; and thereby I had a fine opportunity to declare the truth to the people in the country as I travelled. For when I had come into a town, and was in the officer's hand, many people that heard of it came out of their houses to see the Quaker, as I was called; and some were pretty tender and loving, and others were otherwise: however, I freely declared the truth among them as I was moved;

and in due time I was freed from that entanglement by a countryman that would trouble himself no further with me, but gave me the pass, and let me depart in peace.

Afterwards I got well to Taunton in Somersetshire, where I visited Friends, as elsewhere in the aforesaid shire; and, in due time I got well to Bristol, where I found several of the brethren, as Francis Howgill, John Audland, &c., with whom I was more than a little comforted; for the Lord's presence was with us, and his heavenly power was amongst us, so that we were not only a refreshment one unto another in the Lord, but many were refreshed through us, and we all in the Lord, whom our souls did magnify and praise.

And when we had been sweetly refreshed together among Friends at Bristol, we went into Wiltshire, and were together at a great general meeting: after which we parted in abundance of love and unity; for I was to go into Kent, and they elsewhere.

And when I came to a place called Basingstoke, there did I happily meet with my dear brother and former companion, John Stubbs; and another dear brother called William Ames was with him, who had been together in Holland; but they being travelling westwards, and I eastward, we had but little time together; howbeit, in that little time we were together, we were truly comforted one in another; and afterwards, in the ancient brotherly love, we parted again. And I travelled along my journey being much as alone, but indeed the Lord's heavenly presence was with me; and several good and precious meetings I had in my journey, to mine and Friends' great refreshment in the Lord: and finally through mercy I came well into Kent, where I went from place to place, and visited such (especially) as before had received our testimony. Many precious and large meetings I had in the county, and the Lord was very much with me, who furnished me plenteously with his word and power; insomuch that I stood admiring at sundry times, from whence I had that fulness, (and this was not only the case with me, but with many more,) who looking with the eye of reason upon my earthly tabernacle or outward man, could not expect any great thing from myself, being then but about twenty years of age;—neither ever had I been in much profession, until I was convinced of the truth of God; yet plenty of heavenly things the Lord was pleased to open in me and through me, to the end that I might communicate the same to the multitude, which sometimes being great, I was ready to say within myself, whence shall I have wherewithal to satisfy all these? And when I looked out at my own weakness and insufficiency as of myself, I was ready to faint within myself; but when I looked only at the Lord, and put my confidence entirely in him, I was strong and courageous. For the Lord showed me by his eternal light, at a time when I was even bemoaning my own weakness, and groaning under the sense of the weight of the service and work of the Lord; saying or thinking within myself, Oh! such and such (meaning the ablest and wisest of the brethren) are so and so fitted and furnished, that they need not care what service they are called unto,—but

as for me, I am so simple,—I am so weak,—and I never have any thing beforehand,—neither do scarce ever know, when I go into a meeting of several hundreds, what I shall say, or whether any thing or nothing; and even when I was full of those and such like reasonings, the Lord showed me (I say,) how they that had much had nothing over, and they that had little, had no lack: even as it was with the Israelites of old. For the brethren that were wise and eminent, who had received much from the Lord, behold there was so much the more required of them: so that of all they had, they had nothing over, but what they were to employ in the work and service of God. As for my own part, I, who was so little in my own eyes, and so mean and contemptible in the eyes of others, had no cause to complain; for though I was often in the state that I knew not what I should say when I went into a meeting, yet even in such a meeting, hath the Lord been pleased to give me his word so plentifully, that through him I was enabled to speak two or three, yea, sometimes four hours in a meeting with little or no intermission: and often it hath been with me, that as I knew not before the meeting what I should speak in the meeting, so neither could I well remember after the meeting what I had spoken in it; and yet had plenty and fulness, though I was often daily at meetings; and not only so, but in the evenings also; and the Lord gave a fresh supply always out of that good treasury, which affords things both new and old.

Now these things I rehearse not for my own praise, but do say, *not unto me, not unto me*, (who have nothing but what I have received,) *be the praise*; but only that I may show who is the giver of every good and perfect gift. And I can truly say, that which I received from him, I delivered unto his people: and no small favour, love, and esteem, I had from them and among them; so that the Lord (whom I faithfully served,) was pleased to give me even what my heart and soul desired; and an exceeding glorious day I had of it, and did much rejoice in the Lord, notwithstanding my great travails and sufferings; all which, through him, were made easy to me: neither were they much to me, with all the perils and dangers I went through both by sea and land, in comparison of the power and presence of the Almighty, which did so sweetly and eminently accompany me in those days.

After I had had exceeding good service in Kent and elsewhere in the country where I had travelled, I went up to London.

About the beginning of the seventh month, 1656, I being at London, with several of the brethren, we had at that time pretty much disturbance in our meetings in the city by some troublesome and unruly spirits, who were gone from the truth into extremes; and though we suffered by them, yet we were refreshed together in the Lord, and one in another.

About that time it was upon me to go over for Holland, unto which I was given up in the will of the Lord. I was then but weak in body, having gotten a surfeit through heats and colds in my travels, as it was judged; nevertheless I was in readiness (though in that weak condition) to take the first oppor-

ance were in pretty much danger. And at that time great was the fear and anguish that came upon those that were so wicked: and even then did the Lord raise me up, in whom my faith and confidence was. It was upon me to speak to them in their distress, and then the witness of God was near and ready to answer to the truth of what I spoke: and the goodness and mercy of the Lord to me in that storm was very great; through whose hand we were preserved, and finally (through his mercy) brought well to our desired haven; blessed and magnified be his name for ever and ever.

When I landed at Dort, I do not know that I could speak three words of their language, and so was much pressed in spirit, and sorely laden with the weight of iniquity, which fell upon me; and seeing I wanted an interpreter, therefore was my burthen the greater. From Dort I sailed to Rotterdam, where I found some few that had heard the truth, and who, in some measure, received it; howbeit, I staid not long there neither, for my drawings were pretty much to Amsterdam. And through the good hand of the Lord I got finally well thither, where John Stubbs and William Ames (my dear brethren) had been before with another Friend; and very good service they had had among the professors there: some had received their testimony, and the truth in the love of it; and such with gladness and joy of heart received me. And the Lord made my service effectual among them for the establishing and confirming them in that living truth, which they had heard and believed. There were some among them that could understand me, and interpret that which I spoke to the rest; so that very good service I had among them, for that little time I staid among them, which was not long, till it was upon me to return to Rotterdam again. In the mean time, a young man came over from England, who went with me, and could understand both English and Dutch; but when I was at Rotterdam he left me for a while; and in the meantime, I was much straitened for want of an interpreter; but there being one that could speak some Latin, I spoke some time in that language to him, and he did interpret it to the rest. But oh! my sufferings at that time were exceeding great in that country, and that in divers respects; and they were augmented through some forward and unruly spirits that were convinced, but who run out into extremes both in words and writing; whereby both the truth, and they that lived in it, came to suffer much: for my part, I had fainted through weakness and sufferings, had not the Lord by his mighty power upheld and preserved me.

At that time few or none of the priest's proselytes came to our meetings; but several high conceited professors both at Amsterdam and Rotterdam attended, and several of them were more apt to take upon them to teach

after their worship was ended, I a Friend had some pretty good s some of them in one of their house a very hard, obstinate, and conceite their way. When I had staid so Rotterdam, it was upon me to go t which accordingly I did, about the of the eighth month, 1656, and th young man went along with me. we had been some days at Middl aforesaid young man went to son meeting places in that city, and hended; which I finally understan to visit him, and they, perceiving his companion, secured me also. we were examined very late in the after our examination we had thr soldiers to guard us, and a place ap us where we might lie. But quick were laid down, we were called t great haste, and were carried from the prison, about the eleventh or tw at night, and put in two distin which caused my sufferings to be t and that the more, because I could or none of their language. There some days, (being weak in body,) cess of time, we were brought befor cil, and were severally examined, b to prison again.

It seems they ordered (by what that we should be sent for England after, a coach-wagon was brought t to carry us to the water side, a soldiers were also provided to guar the city seemed to be as in an upro rude multitude did rage exceedingly would have torn us to pieces; bu was with us, who was our chi though there were some in the w us, and some that went on foot alo wagon. And according to their o brought us on board of a ship of v we were kept prisoners, near upon t being confined to an open cold roor men were so hard-hearted toward they would not allow us so much sailcloth to lie under us, or above t the most part of that time we lay up boards in very cold stormy weath our sufferings were great both in and outward man.

But oh! how is the goodness an the Lord to be admired, for even while I was in prison, when I was used, even then I say, did my str much, and I recovered: my health measure again, even to my own a admiration; and thereby I came to h experience of the goodness and m God, for which my soul hath cau and magnify his name for ever.

About the middle of the ninth m through mercy, we got well to Er about the same time came up to Lo

being but young, and having had a pretty sore storm, were somewhat scattered and scattering, being discouraged and frightened through the indignation and wrath of the magistrates and priests, which was somewhat kindled against them: I made it my work to gather them together again, and to establish them so much as was possible in the eternal truth. And besides what they had met with from the magistrates, &c., there had been a bad instrument among them, who had bred much discord and dissension among them; but through the mercy and goodness of the Lord, they came in due time to be restored again into faith and confidence, peace and tranquillity, in which they kept their meetings. But as for the professors, they were high and conceited, and would scarce believe that a greater light was sprung up in any part of the world, than what was arisen among them; neither could they well endure to receive instruction from such as would not or need not be instructed by them. There were also at that time many stumbling-blocks laid in the way of the simple, and many obstructions the truth met withal in that place; and therefore were my burthens the more, and my sufferings the greater; but the Lord was with me, and the right hand of his righteousness upheld me,—glory be to his holy name for ever and ever!

(To be continued.)

THE OPIUM TRADE IN CHINA.
Extracted for "The Friend," from "Malcolm's Travels in India."

The great blot on foreigners at Canton, though not on all, is the opium trade. That men of correct moral sensibilities, and enlightened minds should be so blinded by custom, or desire of gain, as to engage in this business is amazing. A smuggler in Canton is no more honourable than a smuggler on any other coast; in some respects less so. There is less chivalry, hardihood, fatigue, exposure, and inducement, than in the case of a poor man, who braves both the war of elements and legal penalty to obtain subsistence for his family. Here among a peaceable and perhaps timid people, they incur no personal hazards, and set at defiance edicts and officers. No other smuggling introduces an article so deadly and demoralising. The victims of it daily meet the smuggler's eyes, and are among the patients resorting to the hospital he helps to support. So well do they know the moral and physical evils of opium, that not one of them ventures on the habit of using it himself. In this as in other cases, magnitude gives dignity and sanction to the operation. No other smuggling is on so grand a scale. The annual sale amounts to a sum equal to the entire revenue of the United States, and to the whole value of teas, exported to England and America. At this very time, (1837,) though efforts so extraordinary and persevering have been put forth by the Chinese government to stop this infernal traffic, there are twenty-four opium ships on the coast. We have little reason to wonder at the reluctance of China to extend her intercourse with foreigners. Nearly the whole of such intercourse brings upon her pestilence, poverty, crime and disturbance.

No person can describe the horrors of the opium trade. The drug is produced by compulsion, accompanied with miseries to the cultivators, as great as slaves endure in any part of the earth. The prices paid to the producer scarcely sustain life, and are many per cent. less than the article produces in China. The whole process of carrying and vending is an enormous infringement of the laws of nations, and such as would immediately produce a declaration of war by any European power—the grandest and grossest smuggling trade on the globe. The influence of the drug on China is more awful and extensive than that of rum in any country, and worse to its victims than any outward slavery. That the government of British India should be the prime abettors of this abominable traffic, is one of the grand wonders of the nineteenth century. The proud escutcheon of the nation which declaims against the slave trade, is thus made to bear a blot broader and darker than any other in the Christian world.

Note by the Editor.—The above powerful extract was forwarded and received some time since, but its insertion has been accidentally delayed.

From the Albany Argus.
Temperance Reform in Ireland.
BALLSTOWN CENTRE, Feb. 5, 1840.
To the editors of the Albany Argus:

Gentlemen—I enclose you a letter I received a short time since from Dublin, alluding to the commencement of a mighty moral revolution in progress in Ireland. In your paper of the 3d instant, you gave your readers the wonderful results of the effort in Limerick, by which, in three days 150 to 200,000 individuals, solemnly pledged themselves to total abstinence from all that can intoxicate. I have now before me Irish papers by the late arrival, filled with continued triumphs. After the efforts of Father Matthew at Limerick, we find him at Waterford. The account of his visit there I now enclose you. It is long, but I do not see how it can be shortened, and give a correct view of the case. As you have kindly opened your paper to this important reform now in progress in Ireland, I trust you will continue to publish the accounts as they reach us. I feel assured there is not an individual in our land, having a heart to feel, but must rejoice in the prospect of seeing the Irish people abandoning the use of alcohol, which has heretofore occasioned a great proportion of all their misery. Yours respectfully,
EDWARD C. DELAVAN.

From Waterford, Ireland.

Glorious Revolution.—Never did we witness any thing comparable to the enthusiasm of the people, with respect to the glorious cause whose progress we have been for some time noticing, and the scenes connected with which, in this city, we have endeavoured to convey some faint idea of below. It is impossible for pen to do it justice, and beyond the reach of imagination to conceive any thing its parallel. To those at a distance, the details we have endeavoured to collect and embody

may appear exaggerated, and the work more of fancy than of fact; but we can only assert, that we pledge ourselves to the literal accuracy of every circumstance we furnish, and that we find ourselves unable to paint the picture as it presented itself to our eyes. We have seen the masses excited by political causes—assembling in their numbers and strength to vindicate themselves from the rod of the oppressor—hanging on the lips of their great champion and leader, and apparently prepared to rush on destruction itself, did he tell them to do so. At the period that the unanimous voice of the nation arose in full swell against the giant iniquity of tithes, we were present on many soul-stirring occasions, and beheld many memorable scenes; but all previous reminiscences and experience fade into utter insignificance, as mere dust in the balance, compared to the achievements of yesterday. We confess that we were prepared for something extraordinary in consequence of our accounts from Limerick; but we candidly admit that we received these accounts cum grano salis—and entertained serious doubts of their implicit fidelity. But we avow ourselves mistaken in the estimate we formed of them, and believe that the whole truth remains to be told. To see thousands and thousands of human beings, whose days had been much devoted to a fascinating, but perilous habit, coming from a far distance, amid the rain and the storm—braving the hostility of the elements and of poverty and destitution—committing themselves to the slender chance of secular commiseration for the means of support during their absence from a humble home—doing this, not because of a worldly prospective advantage, but attracted by the fame of an unpretending priest, whose time is given up to the cause of charity and the poor—to see this is indeed marvellous, and to account for it without acknowledging the intervention of a special Providence, is out of the question. But so it is. An intense feeling appears to have taken hold of the popular mind—a feeling widely spread and deeply rooted—planted, we verily believe, in a religious soil, and promising to bring forth the fruits of joy and happiness, social as well as physical, in good season. We are not philosophers enough to explain why it is, that, strictly catholic though Ireland has been, since Christianity first dawned upon her, no movement of this description has been hitherto made. But even the sceptic has learned that a great—an unexpected movement has at length set in, and he scarcely doubts any longer, from what he has seen, that it will stop before it embraces the entire of the land.

The great apostle of the glorious cause, which is making such triumphant—such miraculous headway through the south of Ireland, despite the sinister influences combined to arrest its onward career, arrived unexpectedly in this city, by the Cork mail, on the evening of Tuesday. His advent was not looked for until the following morning; and hence he "stole a march," anxious as he is, and as he always has been, to avoid the gaze and applause of the multitude, which are an inevitable concomitant of his footsteps. He was set down at the Commercial Buildings, where, in a few

y were holding one of their usual meetings. appeared somewhat fatigued after his long rney, and after addressing the meeting in nguage expressive of thankfulness for their warm reception, accompanied by Mr. Murphy and a few other gentlemen, he left there for residence of our venerable bishop. On esday evening and throughout that night nbers continued to pour into town from the rounding country. From the dress and account of many, it was apparent that they had ne from a far distance. Their demeanour, are happy in being enabled to remark, was efly, and partook, in no instance that came ler our notice, of the "whiskey leaving" esses which have stigmatised the proceeds of other localities. The majority were of humbler classes, and came provided with necessaries for travelling in their situation, uring their kit, after the fashion of soldiers. ring the whole of the night the bridge, the at thoroughfare to and from the Lienster nties continued open, a circumstance hitherrarely remembered, whilst all the avenues ling from the west and south contributed a tinuous tide of human beings of all ages, of each sex—of every description, from affluent to the destitute—from the person rarely sacrificed reason at the demoralizsbrine of intemperance, to the habitual and dless drunkard.

(Remainder next week.)

The Mastodon in Texas.—The remarkable il quadruped, it appears, existed also in xas, as well as in almost every latitude of United States south of 45 degrees. A late xas paper says, General Demyss has succeded in disinterring nearly all the bones of Mastodon, found two miles below Bastrop, r the Colorado.—*Late paper.*

THE FRIEND.

SECOND MONTH, 29, 1840.

We acknowledge our obligations to the kinds of some unknown friend for the transmisn at different times of several numbers of British Emancipator published in London. om one just come to hand of twelfth month h, we extract the following. This conned account of the testimony borne by the worthy governor of Jamaica to the good duct of the emancipated in that island, is to truly gratifying, and is a sufficient counterse to the various adverse statements of fish and interested persons.

of their sense of the benefits which have resulted from his humane and enlightened policy while administering the government of Jamaica. The deputation were most courteously and cordially received, and were deeply interested by the information his excellency, with much candour and kindness, was pleased to give them in respect to the existing state of things in Jamaica. His excellency's observations relative to the good conduct of the recently emancipated bondsmen, confirmed to the fullest extent the statements to the same effect which have been received from other authentic sources. There appears to be no want of labour on the estates where the labourer is properly treated and fairly remunerated. And his excellency's testimony to the exemplary behaviour of the coloured population, in their obedience to the laws, their observance of religious and moral duties, and their gratitude to their benefactors, was extremely pleasing to the members of the deputation. His excellency stated that he should most willingly receive the proposed address from the committee of the British and Foreign Anti-Slavery Society. The noble and disinterested line of conduct pursued by Sir Lionel Smith in his benevolent endeavours to protect the oppressed, during his late government, claims for him the esteem and gratitude of every Christian philanthropist.

Some weeks past notice was taken in this paper, perhaps more than once, of a scheme at that time in agitation, and defended with much plausible but deceptive argument by persons of no inconsiderable standing in the community, to erect at an expense of several thousand dollars, an OPERA HOUSE in a conspicuous part of this city. We now learn through a source which we deem authoritative, that this more than foolish and profligate project has not been sustained, in other words, has been abandoned. We do not take credit to ourselves for much, if any effect in producing this result by the protest we put forth against it, but rather would infer the conclusion that the moral sense and religious feeling of the body of citizens was opposed to it.

Two or three weeks since we inserted, under the head of News from Ireland, a letter giving some account of the remarkable success of Theobald Mathew, a Roman catholic clergyman, in promoting the cause of temperance among the people of that island. A friend has put into our hands a later and more extended account, cut from the Albany Argus, which we have concluded to give to our readers without curtailment as we find it, not doubting that it will be read with lively interest.

Ca

THE FRIEND.

A RELIGIOUS AND LITERARY JOURNAL.

VOL. XIII.   **SEVENTH DAY, THIRD MONTH, 7, 1840.**   **NO. 23.**

EDITED BY ROBERT SMITH.

PUBLISHED WEEKLY.

Price two dollars per annum, payable in advance.

Subscriptions and Payments received by

GEORGE W. TAYLOR,

NO. 50, NORTH FOURTH STREET, UP STAIRS,

PHILADELPHIA.

For " The Friend."

THOUGHTS ON THE TIMES.

NO. I.

As people are apt to think the last spell of very cold or hot, or wet or dry weather, the most so within their memory, so we can scarcely help believing the difficulties of the present time to exceed all former embarrassments. Without undertaking to affirm this conclusion to be true, it may safely be said, that the fit or paroxysm of distress under which the country is groaning is a sort of ague which attacks us every few years after regular intervals, like the chill of an intermittent fever. And as the doctor cannot be sure that the patient is well, until he sees whether the chill returns, so the mere absence of distress, a demand for goods, and plenty of money, cannot of themselves be looked upon as signs of sound health in the commercial body. The man who suffers under a tertian ague will not rest till he has taken the doctor's prescription. He will be much less anxious about it, if the chill comes but once in two weeks; and will scarcely think himself sick, though it should attack him regularly every quarter. Yet the last case may be as clearly an intermittent as the first, and it may seriously affect his health and strength during the whole interval of ease between the chills.

It is worth while therefore to try if we can find out whether these paroxysms of distress are accidental, or whether they are the cold fits of a disease under which the body politic is labouring. If it should prove that the intervals of prosperity between them, so far from being a mark of sound health, are but the hot stages and the intermissions which alternate with the chills, we may be inclined to try other remedies than those which a false notion of the nature of our case would prescribe. We shall be more likely to listen to any advice which may bear the stamp of good sense and of a knowledge of our ailment, now that we are in the paroxysm of the chill, than when the distress is lessened and we think we can do without the doctor. I am of the mind too that the disease has taken a very strong hold of our system, that the patient is much worse than he himself thinks; in fact, that his constitution is fast breaking down under the excesses of high living and intoxicating drinks to which he has enslaved himself.

Now, if it were a real tertian, or even three monthly ague, there would be no difficulty in the case. Blood-letting and dieting, and quinine, with perhaps a little calomel, if the liver were affected, would soon put all to rights.

But it will not do to let blood in the body politic, and then, who will take the remedies? Be that as it may, I have a mind to offer my advice, and to submit to the readers of "The Friend," a few thoughts on the present distress. If their patience to read and mine to write should hold out, I propose to inquire into the causes of the existing difficulties, and to seek to know how far those causes are influencing our own religious community.

If in this inquiry I should seem to put forth trite and familiar maxims, it will not be that I think them new or original, but because the nature of the evils under which we suffer, is only to be thoroughly understood by going back to their original and elementary causes. The chief thing which must strike every observer of the present times, is the frequent and almost regular recurrence of these periods of disaster and embarrassment. If, as is clearly the case, their causes must be deeply seated in the frame work of modern society. What then are the facts? a few years of prosperous commerce induces a blind confidence in the continuance of prosperity; extravagant schemes of speculation find eager adventurers and dupes; the impulse which has been given to business and enterprise becomes at last a giddy whirl, which intoxicates all who fall within its vortex. The prices of most kinds of produce are steady, the demand is brisk, rents advance, till the tenant can scarcely stagger beneath them—real estate rises, and money is loaned freely at low rates, and in large sums.

It is not possible, under any favourable circumstances, that these things should long remain stationary, and a slow and steady advance in prices, is on all accounts desirable. But the peculiarity of our situation is that the rate of advance continually accelerates, until our fancied prosperity goes off like a rocket, with a transient blaze that ends in smoke and darkness.

What is there in the constitution of society that subjects us to these constantly returning disasters?

How barren a tree is he that lives, and spreads, and cumbers the ground, yet leaves not one seed, not one good work to generate after him. I know all cannot leave alike; yet all may leave something answering their proportion, their kinds.—*Owen Feltham.*

From the Albany Argus.

Temperance Reform in Ireland.

(Concluded from page 179.)

Wednesday, nine o'clock, A. M.—This morning from an early hour the city was the scene of busy animation. Notwithstanding that the rain fell in vast quantities, the avenues to the city continued to present a dense mass of living beings wending their way to the apostle. Several hundred arrived from the county Wexford in market boats, whilst the river steamers, which ply between the counties of Waterford and Wexford, were thronged far beyond their usual fare. At nine o'clock the Very Rev. T. Matthew, accompanied by the Right Rev. Dr. Foran, our beloved and apostolic bishop, Major Gahan, Sir Benjamin Morris, Mr. P. J. Murphy, and other gentlemen, left King street for Ballybricken, in the midst of whose large area a temporary husting was erected. The ground had already been occupied by Alderman H. Alcock, mayor, *pro tempore*, Colonel Manners, and two companies of the 37th depot, with the city police under the command of Captain Wright, and the members of the Local Temperance Society, with medals displayed. The military and police formed a cordon around the hustings, and the members exerted themselves with zeal for the preservation of order. But it was unavailing; the torrent of human beings bore down every obstacle—the hustings, after the pledge was administered to about two thousand individuals of both sexes, were besieged, despite the efforts of those engaged to restrain the multitude. It was found to be impossible to persevere, and after much exertion, the reverend gentleman with difficulty adjourned to the court-house. Here we are able to say that Mr. Matthew and his friends were comparatively comfortable, and the postulants better off than they were in the area of Ballybricken. The court-house steps were occupied by a file of the 37th and the police, and not more than two hundred at a time were permitted to enter. Some individuals were severely crushed in consequence of their anxiety to rush forward; but we are happy to say that no serious accident took place. As each batch entered the court-house hall, they knelt, in humility and devotion, took the pledge at the hand of the great administrator, and passing out by a different door from that which they went in, gave sufficient room to their followers. This plan was admirable, and tended very considerably to the convenience of the reverend gentleman and the people. As each batch rose up after repeating the words of the pledge, brightness glowed in their countenances, such expressions as, " Thank God, we are happy now!"—" Heaven bless you, Father Matthew," issued from the lips of the regenerated. We were happy to observe that many of the police knelt before the apostle, and plighted their vow never to drink intoxicating liquors more. And this we are sure, will render them objects of especial favour to their commanders. Alderman Alcock introduced the commanding officer of the garrison, Colonel Manners, to Father Matthew, in the hall of the court-house. Colonel Manners, we should observe, is a decided friend of the cause.

Twelve o'clock.—Thousands continue to arrive. The exemplary catholic pastors of Tramore, Kill, and Newton, &c., with their indefatigable curates, have come into town at the head of imposing cavalcades. Mr. Carr, of Ross, has also appeared with upwards of a thousand men and women from that town. We perceived some highly respectable persons among this group. The court-house externally presents at this moment a fearful sight. Crowds rush up the steps despite the military and police, whose conduct is exemplary in the highest degree. The doors have been forced in and the hall is thronged. The apostle is surrounded by Alderman Poole, the Rev. Nicholas Cantwell, P. P. Tramore; the Rev. James Vaile; P. P. Newtown; the Revs. Messrs. Dixon, Morrissey, Fitzgerald, J. Power, N. T. Dowley, J. Clarke, Heffernan. It is said that ten thousand persons have been already received; but they are not missed from the myriads who await to take the pledge. We regret that some of the postulants appear to labour under the effects of fatigue—arising from the circumstance of having travelled all night through the rain. An instance of magisterial petulance has occurred which we shall notice. Captain Newport has called upon some of his brother magistrates to advise Mr. Matthew to withdraw, as personal danger may ensue. But the gallant captain's remonstrances are not heeded, for the very good reason, that no danger is as yet seen by the most experienced persons. "Talk of the victories of the Duke of Wellington," said Alderman Poole, as he regarded the mighty mass of human beings rapidly approaching to take the pledge, "they are nothing to those of Mr. Matthew. He has done more for the Irish people than any man who has as yet appeared, or perhaps, who ever will appear in Ireland."

Two o'clock.—Crowds on crowds continue to pour in, in apparently exhaustless abundance. It is computed that the reverend gentleman has received twenty thousand at least since morning. Each batch, amounting on an average, to 170 persons, is disposed of in about two minutes, and instantly succeeded by another. Mr. Matthew, on being asked was he not tired, and would he not take some refreshments, replied, "I feel no fatigue in the world. Oh, how rejoiced I am to see them pour in, in this way." And well may he rejoice, for never was man made an instrument in the hands of an all-wise and gracious Providence for the achievement of such incalculable benefit to society! Several country gentlemen have arrived to witness the proceedings, amongst whom we perceived Andrew Sherlock, Esq., Killaspey; Richard Duckett, Esq., Tramore; Wm. Peet, Esq., &c. There are many protestants and Quakers in the hall looking with wonderment at what is passing. Some

accidents of a slight nature have taken place—one woman is bruised and two men are cut Mr. Ryan, the worthy governor of the county jail, had them removed to the prison, attended to and nourished.

This being the dinner hour of the working classes, we noticed the bacon-cutters of many establishments, and other description of labourers, taking the pledge. In Patrick stree the crowd is so dense that a passage through it is quite difficult, whilst thousands occupy the ground opposite the court-house and throughout Ballybricken. The rain continued to fal with unabated velocity. The military police and people are drenched. Sir Benjamin Morris and Alderman Alcock, persevere with the same activity as usual in the preservation of order.

Twenty minutes to four o'clock.—The reverend gentleman has continued without intermission to receive postulants up to this moment; and thousands yet throng the streets despite "the pitiless pelting of the storm," and even from a great distance. The employers were anxious that their servants should not go forward to-day, in order that an opportunity should be afforded strangers to take the pledge without any unnecessary delay. But it is expected that there shall be few servants in Waterford who will not have become members of the total abstinence society by to-morrow evening. It is thought that one hundred thousand (and we speak within limits when we say so) shall have been received in this city, previous to the departure of the apostle.

Mr. Matthew and his friends left the court-house at the hour above named, for the bishop's, where he continued to receive postulants up to dinner hour. Vast numbers surrounded the Right Rev. Dr. Foran's residence, anxious to take the pledge at once. After dinner Father Matthew continued to receive postulants to a late hour. Several very respectable parties took the pledge. Many ludicrous scenes occurred during the day, exhibitive of the enthusiasm and devotion of the people. A Carrick woman on arriving at this side of the bridge was heard to exclaim, after turning towards the west, "Joy be with you, Carrick, and all the whiskey I ever drank. I'll never drink more." Nearly all the fishermen of Tramore, Islands o'Kane, and the coast around to Bamahon, took the pledge. The bathing men of Tramore, a peculiarly moist sort of people, were the foremost in enrolling themselves under the standard. Hundreds were present from the farthest extremity of Wexford, Carlow, Wicklow, Kildare, Queen and King's counties. As proof of the great excitement prevalent, it may be observed that the High street Loan Fund Society, (to which we have so frequently called attention,) which receives upwards of twenty applications *per diem*, and is a bitter pill to the pawnbrokers, received but one application to-day. It was observed with pleasure that females outnumbered males by about twenty-five per cent. This has not, we believe, been the fact elsewhere. The virtuous, as well as the most debased and forlorn of the community, have taken the pledge. Several of the unfortunates, who have lived on the wages of sin, renounced

bribed to run the risk of being bit by a mad dog. In consequence of this universal applicability of money as the measure of value, it comes to stand for the things which it measures. We look with complacency on the key which unlocks our treasures; and gaze on a dirty bank-note, which is only a rag.

In Pitcairn's island, at the latest account, there was no money, nor any need of it. But does it follow that there can be no avarice there? I think not. The passion may look beyond the medium to the end in view, but it is still the same. The dislike to part with our cash, when reduced to its principles, is a mode of selfishness. It is only one aspect of our love of the things which money will buy. If any man would guaranty to us all these things for life, we would freely give him the money. Hence the moral evils of avarice. But for this the love of gold would be as innocent as the love of roses and lilies.

But even on the selfish principle, I have sometimes thought that a more refined and profound view of the matter would loosen our hold on the purse. By pinching hard we hurt nobody but ourselves. Every one sees that if a man spends none of his money, he is wretched; hence the name *miser*, which is only the Latin for a wretch. But many make it the business of their lives to come as near this as they can. They sail as near the wind as is possible. Sound economy will teach a man that a liberal outlay of money is in some cases no more a loss, than a liberal sowing of wheat. STOLIDO has adopted the saving maxim never to cut a packthread of a parcel, but always to untie it: he therefore fumbles at a hard knot for ten minutes, in which he could have earned the worth of ten such packthreads. BASSO grudges sixpence for a dose of physic, and in the end loses six weeks. We all agree that *time is money*. Why so? Because time will procure us money, or, what is the same, money's worth. But we are not so ready to admit, though it is equally true, that health is money—that temperance is money—that good habits are money—that character is money. Nay, I go further than this: if we must value every thing by this mercenary standard, then I say, *ease is money*, because it is worth money, and we labour all of our life to earn it. Comfort is money, and happiness is money.

These remarks are certainly not intended to foster the disposition to estimate every thing by pounds, shillings, and pence. God forbid! Our money-making nation need no spur in their race: we are already pointed at by the finger of nations. But as the world's ready reckoners insist on gauging human bliss by this rule, I wish to show that on their own principles a man may be too saving. Even the rule of the usurer in the old play, which was short enough to be engraven on his ring, and which is engraven on many a heart, *Tu tibi cura*, "Take care of number one," is often violated by unwise parsimony. We may be sparing to our damage. There are better things than money. O that I could ring it through every shop, factory, and counting-house of my country! There is good which gold cannot buy, and which to barter for gold were ruin. It cannot buy the kindly affections of the fireside. It cannot buy the blessings of friendship. It cannot buy the serene comforts of virtue, the quiet of conscience, the joys of religion. This lesson should be inculcated on the young. It is idle to fear that such a lesson will make them careless or profuse. It is a lesson opposed not to frugality, but to parsimony. Those who learn it will not hoard, but neither will they squander. They will look on money, not as an ultimate good, but as the representative of purchasable advantages; and they will count it as nothing when put in the opposite scale to moral and eternal things, which are above all price.

THE HONEY BEE—A NEW HIVE.

The following communication, although more particularly intended for the agriculturist, can scarcely fail to interest and please the dwellers in the city. It is copied from Ex-Governor Hill's Monthly Visiter, and was written by S. Keith, of Oxford, Me.

The bee possesses the united skill of the mason, the architect, the geometrician, and the civilian. Many naturalists of this and other countries have devoted much time in searching out their habits, admiring their sagacity, and giving to the world the result of their researches. They have learned much and there is much more yet to be learned of this wonderful insect. I have myself kept bees for thirteen or fourteen years: I long since felt the necessity of preserving these little creatures from the barbarous custom of annual suffocation. For a while I tried the box hive, but found my bees unwilling to enter it, and I lost several swarms in trying to force them into it. I abandoned this kind of hive, and finished a room in my garret, dark and tight, with a communication through the external wall of the house, through which to give them a passage way. I placed a hive of bees in this room, their entrance into the hive being on a level with this communication and near to it. To this room I have a door from my garret, never accessible to children or intruders. The room should be made impervious to rats and mice, which are very fond of bees, fearing not even their weapons of defence. This young swarm soon filled their hive, and then commenced their operations beneath, above and around the hive, filling in the white virgin comb, without the aid of bars, slats or cross pieces to build to, from the roof of the house to the floor of their room. At times, I stole into this apiary, and by the aid of a light, viewed the progress they were making, and the splendid columns of comb they were erecting. They had the benefit of the labour of all their increase—all their progeny; there was no swarming, no colonizing from their numerous family. Give bees room and they never swarm. Who ever heard of bees swarming from a hollow tree, till the space within it was filled? After the second year of their operations, and during the coldest of the winter, while the bees all lay dormant at the centre of their *nectarine pile*, I took my family stores from the external layers, which always contain the whitest and purest in the store house, and is the only portion which can be taken without injury to the residue. For many years my table was supplied from this room with the choicest of sweets, from which many a friend has enjoyed a treat, and lingered to admire this simple contrivance for the preservation of the bee, and the store house so well adapted to receive the fruits of his labour.

For "The Friend."

ELIZA RUMPFF.

I recently met with a memoir of Eliza Rumpff, which so beautifully exemplified the transforming and preserving nature of that grace, which when yielded to, bringeth salvation, that I have made some extracts from it for the pages of "The Friend," if the editor should deem them suitable.   H. L.

"Eliza Rumpff, the subject of this memoir, was the daughter of John Jacob Astor, of the city of New York. Her childhood and early youth was spent under the paternal roof. Her character, during that interesting period of life, was chiefly distinguished by a sweet, amiable, retiring, benevolent disposition. In the year 1823, she accompanied her father to Europe, and spent two years in France, Switzerland and Germany. It was during this visit that she became acquainted with the gentleman to whom she was married in 1825, at Paris: —A union of uninterrupted happiness, until it was dissolved by her death, after thirteen years duration. With her marriage commenced her permanent residence in Europe; with the exception of two visits made to the United States. Her winters she spent in Paris, where the official duties of her husband (who was then, and still is the minister resident at the court of the Tuileries, for the Hanseatic towns of Germany) required his presence during that part of the year; whilst her summers were passed in Switzerland, near the lake of Geneva, at a delightful country residence given her by her father. For several years after her marriage, she tried what happiness the splendid scenes of the palace of the Tuileries, the music and amusements of the opera and theatre, and the excitement and fascinations of Parisian saloons could afford. Although she attended a place of worship, with greater or less regularity, and evinced a respect for religion, was charitable to the poor—and in her deportment there was much that was interesting. But she had not yet experienced that 'grace of God which bringeth salvation.' And every thing short of this ever fails of giving the happiness which we so earnestly desire, and so fruitlessly seek in the enjoyment of this world.

"But at length the time arrived when her attention was effectually awakened to the great subject of religion. The means by which this was accomplished were very simple, and such perhaps as will seem to those who know nothing of the various ways which God employs to call mankind to himself, quite improbable. There resided in her family for some time a pious and excellent woman, in the capacity of nurse; to her she devoted many leisure hours in reading from the sacred Scriptures, and other religious books, and the simple and judicious remarks, which her humble friend occasionally made, led her mind in the most gradual manner, to realise the transcendent importance of religion as a personal concern. The good work thus commenced did not cease to make progress. A severe attack of cholera was greatly sanctified to her in the increase of her religious impressions. She also made and greatly enjoyed the acquaintance of several Christians in Paris, who proved to be very useful to her, in promoting her growth in religious knowledge, and who encouraged her in every step of that divine life which she was striving to pursue.

"As the work of religion gradually advanced in her heart, she relinquished more and more every thing which she learned to be incongenial with true piety. The theatres, the operas, the balls, and every worldly amusement inconsistent with a strictly religious and spiritual life were all abandoned. But she did not become a recluse, or disagreeable in any way in her manners, and in her intercourse with society; on the contrary, religion seemed, as it did in reality, to devolope and strengthen every lovely feature in her naturally amiable and benevolent character. It elevated and ennobled every sentiment—it added new charms to every trait.

"Although her husband was affluent, and she had the prospect of a princely inheritance, no one could discover in her the slightest tribute to their relief. Nor was she content merely to give money, but was often seen visiting the abodes of poverty, and by the bedside of the sick and dying, alleviating their distresses. She gave large sums for the promotion of religious and charitable objects; and studied economy in her dress, and in her style of living, that she might have means for doing good. She was a woman of uncommon system, and strictly pursued order in every thing.

"In the early part of last summer she accompanied her husband to their quiet retreat in Switzerland. The first two or three months passed pleasantly away in the prosecution of her various benevolent labours. It was in the midst of these occupations she was seized with sickness, the malady soon assumed an extraordinary character, and its malignity manifested itself by severe sufferings; yet, during the eight weeks it continued, no murmuring word escaped her lips. Having asked the physician if he still had any hopes of a cure, and receiving an affirmative answer, she said, 'Oh! it is impossible; it cannot last long; I suffer too much; but no, it is not too much, since God does not think it too much. But it is very sad. Oh God, have pity upon me, according to the greatness of thy mercy.'

"A few days before her death, she addressed some exhortations to one of her domestics, and among other things said, 'O seek the Lord Jesus whilst you are in health and have strength, for if God should take away your health, and you should be laid on a bed of suffering as you see me, you could not always think and pray.' At another time, addressing herself to the person who watched by her side, she said, 'I do not fear death, I shall be happier with God; may the Lord render me entirely submissive to his will.' She conversed also with her husband on the arrangements to be made for her funeral, requesting that she might be buried with the greatest possible simplicity. She also spoke of the continuance of her schools after her death.

"The last day of her life, the 25th of October, 1838, she appeared exhausted, and incapable of any effort; about mid-day her forehead and hands became cold, and the dews of death were upon them—her mouth seemed as if it could not articulate one word more. What then was the emotion of those who surrounded her, when she distinctly asked who were around her, for her sight was gone, and when named in order, she addressed to each some affectionate and pressing exhortations, suited to their conditions. But it was no longer the voice of a feeble woman. It was a voice which spoke under the powerful influence of the spirit of God. She added, 'I die happy, I die in Christ; I have been a stranger on the earth, I return to my true country.'

"Her husband said to her, "Dear Eliza, it will not be long until I shall join you; I will try to walk in your footsteps.' She responded, 'Amen! amen !' An expression of joy diffused itself over her countenance; and she added, 'Now Lord give deliverance, amen !' These were her last words. Thus, in the 37th year of her age, she sweetly entered into the joy of her Lord."

---

religious knowledge, and who encouraged her in way in her manners, and in her intercourse with society; on the contrary, religion seemed, as it did in reality, to devolope and strengthen every lovely feature in her naturally amiable and benevolent character. It elevated and ennobled every sentiment—it added new charms to every trait.

And yet there was no unbecoming levity; there was no trifling conduct. Her conversation was always such as became a woman 'professing godliness.' Her piety was deep, mature, and active. Religion was, in her estimation, emphatically, the 'one thing needful.' She daily applied herself with diligence to its maintenance in her own heart, and she was also constantly solicitous to see others embrace it. She was not one of those who think it an easy thing to be a Christian, or to live a Christian life. Her's was a life of watchfulness, of self-distrust, of prayer; she read the Scriptures not only daily, but much every day. Thus she maintained, amid the great temptations and allurements of Paris, her steadfast course towards that 'city which hath foundations, whose builder and maker is God.' In her delightful abode in the vale of lake Leman, surrounded by the grandeur and beauty of nature, she did not pass her time in luxurious idleness. No; her heart was ever planning, and her hands ever executing some labour of love. She and her husband established, and maintained at their own expense, three schools in the villages around them for small and poor children, and finding that several poor families could not enjoy the advantages which her schools afforded, on account of the long distance their children had to go, she employed, daily, a servant, who went from village to village in the morning, with a sort of infant omnibus, and gathering up the children, carried them to the schools; and in the evening going round again, he carried them home to their parents. The sick and the poor were not forgotten by her. She felt sincerely for the destitute, and was ready to con-

SWISS HUSBANDRY.

The Alpine pasturages are elevated in heights of two, three, or more ranges, according to the season—the herdsmen ascending with their cows and goats, and often with sheep, as the heat increases from early spring to the high temperature of July and August, and then descending as autumn declines into winter. These pastures form the principal source of maintenance and opulence to the inhabitants of the greater part of Switzerland, Savoy, the Voralberg, and the Tyrol. Each pasture elevation has its particular *chalets* for the herdsmen. The butter and cheese afterwards carried down to market are made in these tiny habitations. Below in the valleys, or often in sheltered nooks on the brow of the mountains, are the winter houses for the cattle, which are then fed with the hay gathered by great industry even in spots to which the goats can scarcely resort. * * * The intrepidity of the *mâlier* (mower) of the Alps is scarcely less than that of the chamois hunters. Whether he be gathering grass for the cows, blue melilot to mix with the cheese, or medicinal herbs for the druggist, he starts forth provided with food, kirchwasser, and tobacco; the soles of his shoes fortified with pointed nails, and with hay inside to soften his fall when he leaps from rock to rock; his gaiters unbuttoned below to leave him free at the ancles, and a whetstone stuck under his belt to sharpen the little scythe or sickle carried over his shoulder. He thus ascends to the hollows and crests of rocks on the brows and summits of mountains, and ties the hay he cuts in firm bundles, which he then pitches downwards from the heights. In this perilous way he in summer gains a scanty living. In winter he may be seen suspended by ropes over precipices and gorges, to reach fallen trees, which he contrives to displace and slide downwards for fuel. If he succeeds in saving by these daring pursuits enough to justify his demanding the hand of the maiden he loves, and whose father often has no more fortune than a little chalet, an Alpine pasture, and the milk of three or four cows, which the pretty peasant maid carries to sell in the valley where he has probably first met her, he marries, takes a chalet, and becomes, in his turn, a herdsman, and in time the proprietor of a few cows, and the father of a family.—"*My Note Book*," *by John Macgregor.*

FRIENDS' READING ROOM.

Dr. Joseph Warrington intends to deliver a lecture at Friends' Reading Room,—on the Right Employment of our Time and Talents, —on second day evening, the 9th instant, at 7½ o'clock.

FRIENDS' READING ROOM ASSOCIATION.

The annual meeting of Friends' Reading Room Association, will be held at 8 o'clock, on third day evening, the 10th instant, in the lower room occupied by the association, on Appletree alley.

JOSEPH SCATTERGOOD, Sec'ry.

3d mo. 1840.

Correction.—In the announcement last week of the failure of the opera house scheme, the word *hundred* was inadvertently omitted before *thousand.*

LIFE OF WILLIAM CATON.

(Continued from page 175.)

[At this part of the narrative the following epistle is introduced, dated "Amsterdam, in Holland, 15th of third month, 1657." It has an endorsement which the editor believes to be in the handwriting of George Fox, thus: "W. Caton to Friends, 1657." It is rich in matter tending to edification, and with simplicity, combines no small degree of beauty in style.]

To all my dearly beloved Friends that be elected of God, sanctified through the Word of his grace to be vessels of honour, to the praise and glory of his name everlasting; mercy, grace and peace be multiplied amongst you, from God, the Father of our Lord Jesus Christ, the fountain of love and life, from whom all goodness doth come; who hath distributed of the riches of his grace unto you, and manifested his living power amongst you; by which he hath quickened some of you who were dead in trespasses and sins, and given you a sight of the entrance into the eternal inheritance, which never fades away: yea, light is sprung up unto you who walked in darkness, and upon you who dwelt in the land of the shadow of death, hath the light shined; and your understandings hath the Lord opened, and hath given you to see *that* in yourselves, which separated you from him; and some of you are come to distinguish betwixt the precious and the vile, betwixt that which entereth into God's kingdom, and that which is shut out. And so that which once you esteemed highly, which did appear beautiful and glorious in your eyes, comes now to be accounted dross and dung in comparison of that pearl, which some have found, and many are digging for; which is not purchased by all that seek it, because they are not willing to part with the whole substance for it. But I know that many of you have forsaken much; and yet something remains which must be also offered, (even that which would save its life, and would not come to judgment,) must be brought to light and tendered, if it be as dear unto you as your right eye or right hand; and those I say, who keep nothing back, but are willing to part with all for the truth's sake, shall receive an hundred fold, and in the life to come life everlasting. For I do assure you, that none are ever made losers for parting with any thing for the Lord, neither need they repent thereof: and that which you lose and have lost for the truth, the time is at hand when you shall account it gain. And though the world may account you fools, because of the loss of your reputation; when your honour and dignity comes to be laid in the dust it matters not; for it is better to be reproached by the world, and to suffer persecution of the world for righteousness' sake, than it is to revile them whom the Lord hath chosen out of the world. Therefore eye his mercy to you, that are reproached and not reproachers, persecuted and not persecutors; yea, I say, rejoice that you are accounted worthy, not only to believe, but also to suffer for his name's sake. Therefore be ye comforted, in the midst of your deepest sufferings and tribulations, with the consideration and hope of the joy and glory that shall be revealed unto you, which your present suf-

ferings (which are but for a moment) are not worthy to be compared unto. For the night is far spent in which the sorrows are; and the day is at hand when sorrow and sighing shall fly away: then shall you that mourn be comforted, and receive beauty for ashes, the oil of joy for mourning, the garment of praise for the spirit of heaviness; that ye may be called the trees of righteousness, the planting of the Lord; although for the present you be in pain and sorrow, groaning to be delivered from the bondage of corruption into the glorious liberty of the children of God. Be patient therefore and hope to the end, for he that shall come will come, and will not tarry; whose arm is already stretched out, in which he carries his babes and lambs, who are born again of the incorruptible seed, nourished and fed with the sincere milk of the living word, by which they grow from strength to strength. And the Lord will not lay any more upon any of them than they are able to bear; but he strengthens the weak, comforts the feeble, binds up the broken-hearted, fills the hungry, clothes the naked, satisfies the weary and the thirsty soul; whose everlasting treasury is always full, and his banqueting-house ever well stored with durable riches; where the distressed are relieved, and every one's necessity supplied, that hungers after righteousness. For he is a Father to the fatherless, and he increaseth the strength of such as have no might: so unto him you may come, as unto a living fountain, from whence none are sent empty away, who thirst and pant after the Lord. Oh! blessed are all they that come to drink here of this fountain of living waters; their souls shall never thirst more: and you, whose souls are thirsting and longing to participate of it, you shall be satisfied. For I know that no visible created thing can satisfy that which longeth to be refreshed with the living streams which issue out from this fountain, which watereth and refresheth the whole city of God,—the streams whereof make glad the hearts of the righteous, whose souls come therewith to be everlastingly satisfied. So come hither, all you that thirst, "come ye to the waters, and he that hath no money, come ye, buy and eat, yea, come and buy wine and milk without money and without price;" yea, eat, O Friends, eat abundantly and be satisfied; for a living fountain hath the Lord set open, for Judah and Jerusalem; and all that are bathed and washed in it come to enter into the holy city, which hath no need of the sun nor of the moon to shine in it; —for the glory of the Lord God doth enlighten it, and the Lamb is the light thereof;—the gates of which are not shut at all by day, for there is no night there;—neither can any thing enter into it that defileth, neither whatsoever worketh abomination, or maketh a lie; but they whose names are written in the Lamb's book of life. And towards this your faces are turned, and your feet are guided into the way that leads to it.

But woe to them that take up their rest by the way, and so come short; they shall inherit sorrow and vexation, and trouble shall be their portion; and with terror and great fear shall they inherit their possessions; and poverty and distress shall be their garments, by reason of the drought, scarcity, and famine,

that shall be in their inheritance. But with the righteous and them that fear the Lord it shall not be so;—for the Lord is their shepherd, and they shall not want any good thing; —they shall eat in plenty;—feed in pastures which are green and large, and their souls shall delight themselves in fatness. There shall no devourer nor venomous beast come within their liberty to make them afraid; neither shall there be scarcity nor desolation in their land; for the dew from heaven shall fall upon it, which shall cause it to bring forth more abundantly, by which its increase shall be watered and refreshed; for the Lord hath blessed their inheritance, and the curse shall no more come upon it, neither shall the unclean enter into it,—but showers of mercy shall descend upon it:—because the Lord hath blessed it,—yea, and will bless it, and all their posterity, that doth inherit it for ever and ever.

So, my dear Friends, know the seed of God in yourselves, and dwell in the living power of God, which will overturn and dispossess that which by violence hath kept the seed of God in bondage; that that which hath led captive may go into captivity, and that which hath suffered violence under the violent oppressor, may come to be set free. Then will you see your deliverer come forth of Sion, who purchased your redemption, and will make you free from that which hath held you in thraldom and bondage: then shall you return unto Sion with the ransomed of the Lord, with everlasting joy upon your heads,— being made inheritors amongst them that are sanctified and crowned with victory. So, the everlasting powerful God, who is strong and mighty, bless, preserve, and keep you;—that you may multiply, increase, and prosper, and bring forth some an hundred, some sixty, some thirty fold, to the praise and glory of our God—to whose custody and protection I commend you: his grace and peace be with you for ever and ever, amen. Your dear brother in the living truth,

WILL. CATON.

The journal then proceeds:—

When I had staid there for the most part of seven weeks, I left Friends for a season, having had very good service in that place, not only at meetings, or the like, but about getting books printed and published, which were of very good service in that country.

Afterwards I went with my dear brother William Ames through some of the principal cities in Gilderland; howbeit our movings were especially to a place called Zutphen, a city out of which W. A. had been banished before: and when we came there we went to the meeting-place of the Mennonists, (otherwise baptists;) but when we would have gone in, they bolted the door to us, and would not suffer us to enter in among them: and William being pretty well known in the city, the rude multitude gathered about us; but to avoid the occasion of a tumult, we withdrew out of the streets to the walls of the city, and very many people followed us. As we were moved and allowed of God, so we spoke in his power, to the making known of his eternal truth; and a very good opportunity we had thereunto upon the walls of the city, from which we withdrew, when we were free; howbeit, the baser sort of people were very rude in throwing stones and clods at us; but the Lord did so preserve us, that we received little harm thereby. In the afternoon there came very many people to us out of the city to our lodging, where we had also a very good opportunity to declare the everlasting truth freely among them, and to disperse many books in their own language, which we had bought along with us; and several there were that received pretty good satisfaction. My dear companion had proposed to have staid there some time, but the magistrates being moved with envy, would not suffer the people to entertain him; besides they took it as a great presumption in him, that he should dare to return again thither, after he was banished from thence. Moreover, they threatened that if the baptists came at us they should be served in like manner; which threatenings, together with what they had done before, did keep the people much in fear and slavery, so that they durst not appear to vindicate that which they were convinced of.

After we had such good service there, and in those parts, I returned again to Amsterdam, where my service consisted much in keeping things in as good order as was possible; and likewise in getting books printed and published, and in several other respects.

In this year (1657) I was at the Hague, the place at which the head court is kept for the Seven Provinces: but little entrance there was for the truth, though some good service I had with some in that city. I was also at the city of Dort (when the plague was pretty much there,) where I found some two or three that were somewhat loving; howbeit, there was also little entertainment for the truth in the place, and therefore was my suffering the greater.

I went also some time to the city of Utretcht to visit them that were convinced, where I had now and then good service, and pretty fine meetings; but in those days I spoke mostly by an interpreter. And when the magistrates and priests came to understand how that the truth seemed to get some entrance in that place, their enmity began to increase against it; and they gave forth an order, that those that entertained us, and had meetings at their houses, should from henceforth neither entertain us, nor have any more meetings in their houses, in pain of being turned out of the city, or of being arbitrarily punished; which threatenings did terrify some, and caused some to draw back, but not all.

I was also at the city of Leyden, where their great university is; there a baptist woman received me into her house, whose husband was a papist, at whose house I was allowed to have a meeting, unto which many sorts of people resorted. The truth being there a new thing and very strange, I met with no small opposition, especially from the papists and baptists, both which sorts were stirred and offended; and more so, because the man and woman of the house came both to be convinced. A meeting was in due time settled and established in that city, where oftentimes (as also in other places) I had good service for the Lord and his truth. And most

commonly, when my service was over in the country, I returned again to the city of Amsterdam, which was a place of great concernment, and where there was a more constant service than in other parts in that country; in due time there was an addition to Friends, and the number of them increased; their meetings were kept in very good order, and for the most part were pretty peaceable; and the goodness and mercy of the Lord abounded much to the remnant that were there gathered. Howbeit, sometimes the rude multitude was tumultuous and troublesome at our meetings: once especially there were many rude people gathered together, who doubtless had much wickedness in their hearts, and some of the worst of them came into our meeting, and sought presently to lay violent hands on me, and to have done much mischief to me and others; but the Lord's power prevented them, and preserved me and Friends, even to our admiration; for I was through Providence cast into a house in the presence of the rude multitude, who if they had not been, as it were, smitten with blindness, and restrained through the power of God, they might have executed their fury upon me and the rest; but he that was in us, and by his power preserved us, was greater than he that was in them, who in their madness would have devoured us at once: but blessed be the Lord our God, who very often showed mercy unto us, and did very plenteously, at sundry times, with his heavenly presence and infinite loving-kindness, refresh and comfort our souls and spirits;—infinite praises be to his name for ever and ever!

When I had spent above a year in the service of the Lord in the Low Countries, especially in Holland, (in which time I had also written two or three books at the least,) I was free in the Lord to return for England, which accordingly I did, through Zealand; where I wrote the book called, *The Moderate Inquirer*, &c.: and in due time I got well to London, through the mercy and goodness of the Lord, where I found many of the brethren; and several precious meetings we had in and about the city, even to our great refreshment; for about that time the truth did multiply, grow, and spread, and many were added to the church, and came to receive the gospel. For in those days the Lord endued his servants and handmaids with very much power and wisdom from above, and they went on in his name, preaching the word of life, both in season and out of season, not only in the meetings which they were moved to appoint, and which Friends duly kept, but also in steeple-houses and markets, in streets and highways, or elsewhere, wheresoever or whensoever any was moved of the Lord to publish and declare his living truth.

(To be continued.)

From Bache's Report on Education in Europe.

Institute of Agriculture and Forestry at Hohenheim, near Stuttgard.

This is the most complete agricultural school in Europe, and extends its usefulness not only throughout, but beyond Wurtemberg. It was established in 1817 by the Agricultural Society of Wurtemberg, under the patronage of

the king, who devoted a royal seat, with extensive buildings, to the purposes of the institution. The farm includes nearly one thousand acres, exclusively appropriated to the support of the school, or the practical instruction of the pupils. In 1820 the school of forestry was united with this, and the pupils now follow, in part, the same courses.

The entire institution is divided into two departments, one of which is intended to give a higher, general and practical education than the other. In the higher, the object is less the acquisition of manual dexterity in the operations of agriculture, than the knowledge required to superintend them; while in the lower, the practice is the principal end. The latter department ranks with the rural schools of Switzerland, and the agricultural school of Templemoyle, in Ireland, already described. In the higher school, all the pupils are expected to pay for their education. In the lower, natives of Wurtemberg are admitted gratis, if their circumstances require it. Foreigners may be admitted to either; their payments being, however, on a much higher scale than those of natives.[*]

The direction of the establishment is delegated by the Agricultural Society to a director and treasurer, the former of whom has the general superintendence of all the concerns of the institution, while the latter is responsible for its financial state to the society and to the royal exchequer. The director is also an instructor. There are, besides, four regular or ordinary professors, and four extraordinary professors, besides an overseer and steward, for the management of the farm and domestic economy. The treasurer has a book-keeper and an assistant in his department.

Pupils are admitted at seventeen years of age, and are expected to possess elementary attainments necessary to the prosecution of the courses of the school. Between 1820 and 1836, one hundred and eighty natives, and one hundred and eighty-two foreigners have been educated in agriculture, and one hundred and forty-seven natives, and one hundred and seventy-seven foreigners in forestry, making a total of five hundred and thirty-nine in the institution. The number of pupils in the higher school in 1836, was seventy-two. That in the lower school is limited to twenty-seven.

The pupils of the *lower school*, in general, come under obligations to remain three years at the institution, in consideration of which their payments for instruction are diminished, in part, in the second year, and cease in the third. They are engaged in the operations of the farm, the garden, and other parts of the establishment, which will be hereafter enumerated, under the direction of the workmen, and under the superintendence of the steward, their time being so distributed that they may acquire practice in the various operations of farming. They are also required to attend certain of the lectures given to the higher classes, and receive instruction at times when

* For the yearly courses at the higher school natives pay forty dollars, and foreigners one hundred and twenty dollars. For instruction in forestry only, a native pays twenty-four dollars, and a stranger seventy-two dollars. For the three years instruction in the lower school, natives pay forty dollars.

hey are not engaged in agricultural labour. They receive regular wages for work done, from which they are expected to pay for their maintenance and clothing. Premiums are given to those who display great skill and industry. While in the house, the younger pupils are under the charge of the elder ones, and all are under the general superintendence of the overseer. The same superintendence exists in the refectory and dormitories. It subserves the double purpose of economy, and of training the elder pupils in the management of men, which is one object of their education. The institution undertakes to find places for those pupils who have given satisfaction while in the school, on their completing its courses.

The agricultural course of the *higher school* may be accomplished in one year, if the preliminary studies of the pupil have been directed with a view to his entering, but, in general, it requires two years. The same period of two years is required for that of forestry. Each scholastic year has two sessions, the one from the first of November to Palm-Sunday, and the other from two weeks after Palm-Sunday to the 1st of October. The intermediate periods are vacations.

The branches of special theoretical instruction are as follows :

First—*Agriculture.* General principles of farming and horticulture, including the culture of the vine. The breeding of cattle. Growing of wool. Raising of horses. Rearing of silk-worms. Arrangement and direction of farms. Estimation of the value of farms. Book-keeping.

Second—*Forestry.* Encyclopedia of Forestry. Botany of forests. Culture and superintendence of forests. Guard of forests. Hunting. Taxation. Uses of forests. Technology. Laws and regulations, accounts and technical correspondence relating to forests.

Third—*Accessory branches.* Veterinary art. Agricultural technology, especially the manufacture of beet sugar, brewing, vinegar making, and distilling. The construction of roads and hydraulic works.

Besides these special branches, the following general courses are pursued :

First—*The Natural Sciences.* Geology. Physiology of plants. Botany, as applied to agriculture and forestry. Natural history of animals, beneficial or noxious to plants and trees. General chemistry, and its applications to agriculture. Physics and meteorology.

Second—*Mathematics.* Theoretical and practical. Geometry. Elements of trigonometry. Arithmetic. Elements of algebra.

The institution possesses the most ample means for the illustration of those courses in its farm and collections. The farm is divided into arable land, about five hundred and one acres ; meadow land, two hundred and forty-two acres ; fields set apart for experiments, thirty-three acres ; woodland, thirteen acres ; nursery, sixty-seven acres ; plantation of hops, two acres ; botanical garden, fourteen acres ; ground for exercising the pupils in ploughing, two acres ; garden, one acre ; the remainder, eighty-five acres. Total, nine hundred and sixty acres. The arable land is cultivated according to five different rotations of crops, that the pupils may have specimens of the varieties of system. The botanical garden, nursery, and experimental farm, are prominent parts of the establishment. There is a large stock of cattle of different kinds, foreign and domestic, and of sheep, that the pupils may acquire practical knowledge of the relative advantages of different breeds, the mode of taking care of the stock generally, and of rearing them for different purposes. Horses are kept for a riding-school, as well as for the purposes of the farm. The institution has a large collection of agricultural implements in use in Wurtemberg, and of models of the varieties of foreign and new implements. These are made in a workshop attached to the school, and afford practice in the manufacture to the pupils, as well as instruction by their use or inspection, with the explanations of the professors. The sale of these implements and models also contributes to the support of the establishment. There are two collections of seeds and grain—one as specimens for illustrating the lectures, the other in quantities for sale. The pupils learn the mode of preserving them, and useful seeds are distributed through the country. There is a collection of soils of all kinds for the lectures on terraculture, and the analysis of soils, with specimens of the means of melioration used in different cases. The collections of natural history, though small, are interesting, from the precise adaptation of the specimens to the objects of the school. They consist of birds, beasts, and insects, and of plants, woods, and rocks. The woods are arranged in the form of a library, the separate specimens having the forms of books given to them, and being covered in part with the bark. The name is inscribed upon the back. Cross and longitudinal sections are usually found in the same book, forming the covers. Between the covers is a box containing the seeds and flowers of the tree, the parasites, &c., and a description. There is a small collection of physical apparatus, a library, and a laboratory. The following farming and technological establishments are connected with the school, and worked by the pupils, under the charge of the teachers ; namely, a cider-press and appertenances ; a beet-sugar manufactory, a brewery, a distillery, and a vinegar manufactory. Though I saw better individual collections than these, the whole suit stands unrivalled, as far as my examination extended.

Examinations take place every year, which are obligatory upon those forestry pupils who intend to enter the service of the government ; strangers are not required to be examined. Persons wishing to learn the details of the institution, may be received as visiters for a period not exceeding a month, living with the pupils.

Each pupil in the higher school has his own sleeping-room ; or, at most, two rooms together. They bring their supplies of clothing, &c. at entrance. The rooms are kept in order by the servants, who receive a small compensation from the pupil. They take their dinner and supper in a common hall, and order what they please for breakfast from the steward's assistant.* This institution has supported

* The dinner and supper costs four dollars a month, which is paid in advance to the steward.—*Venning.*

itself for several years, which is readily to be understood from the scale of its farming operations. The success of the farm does not depend exclusively upon the productive manual labour of the pupils. It is analogous to the support of a family on a large estate, the members of the family aiding in the work, and contributing also in money to their own support, but the working of the farm not depending entirely upon their manual exertions.

House of Refuge, Philadelphia.

On the first of January, 1839, there were one hundred and fifty-eight inmates under the guardianship of the board, viz., one hundred and five boys, and fifty-three girls ; and during that year one hundred and twenty-seven were received—seventy-three boys, and fifty-four girls ; and one hundred and fourteen left the institution—seventy-one boys, and forty-three girls. Of those discharged,

65 were indentured, viz.,			42 boys, 23 girls.	
15	sent to sea,		15 "	
19	returned to their friends,	13 "	6 "	
5	unsuitable subjects,	0 "	5 "	
6	18 years of age,	0 "	6 "	
3	sent the Almshouse,	0 "	3 "	
1 escaped,			1 "	

The accounts received of the children who are placed out under indentures, still continue, in a great majority of cases, to be highly favourable. The numerous applications for apprentices, enable the indenturing committee to select good places. Those in the country are generally preferred.

Experience confirms the opinion heretofore expressed, of the great importance of having children sent to the institution before habits of vice are confirmed. At an early age, evil propensities, by careful training, may, in most instances, under Divine providence, be eradicated, and virtuous dispositions implanted and cultivated, and habits of regularity and industry fixed.

But where there has been a long continuance of depravity, and the period during which the discipline of the house can be exerted is short, the hope of reformation is greatly diminished.

The most painful duty the board have to discharge, is that of declining to receive into the Refuge. those whose age and previous course of life render them unfit associates for the members of our family. Yet if these unfortunates had been placed under the parental discipline of the institution when they first manifested a disposition to deviate from the paths of rectitude, they would, in all probability, have been reclaimed, and rendered virtuous and happy members of the community.

The library is still a useful auxiliary to our plan, affording the means of instruction and pleasure. It is regularly resorted to by the inmates. The state of the funds has not warranted any considerable appropriation towards its support. Many of the books which were first placed in it by the generosity of the booksellers of Philadelphia, are now considerably worn. The board indulge the hope that they again may receive further aid from the same liberal body.

For "The Friend."

The following was written upwards of twenty years ago, and communicated to a village newspaper, but so misprinted in its publication that I have often wished to see it in a correct form. In that form it is now placed at the disposal of the editor of "The Friend."

"THE BROOK."

'Twas a beautiful brook, and serenely it flowed
O'er the white polished pebbles, that shine in its breast,
And its banks seemed to promise a charming abode,
Where the pensive could muse, or the weary might rest.

Yet, in spring, I had seen it, when loudly it roared,
And rushed, like a mountain stream, proudly along,
And its wave, now so gentle, so angrily poured,
That the birds fled affrighted, and hushed was their song.

And again I had seen it, when summer was high,
And the sun, in meridian altitude, shone,
And the flowers had faded, its channel was dry,
Scarce a drop trickled over its bosom of stone.

And now, when the mildness of autumn prevails,
In sadness the stream seems to murmur along,
On its bosom the sear yellow leaf slowly sails,
And its borders, no longer, are vocal with song.

Too soon in his sternness, will winter appear,
In his fetters of ice, chain this beautiful stream,
Arrest, with his rigours, its gentle career,
And its breast reflect only his pale languid beam.

And such is the lot of poor mortals, I sighed,
As the seasons of life, as of nature prevail;
Spring's impetuosity, anger, and pride,
When the stream is a torrent, and high is the gale.

How barren! how feeble! ere summer has flown,
When care or ambition has dried up the stream,
When life's early flowers are withered and gone,
And manhood awakens from youth's charming dream.

My spring-time is past, and my summer is high,
My spring's swollen current flows proudly no more,
My flowers have faded; my channel is dry,
Nor can autumn, their bloom, or its fulness, restore.

Oh, God! ere the winter of death shall arrive,
Ere its coldness shall wrap this frail fabric of clay,
May thy presence, like mildness autumnal, revive
The purified spirit of life's early day.

Or at least, be thou pleased, that the sear yellow leaf
May admonish my heart that the winter is near,
To prepare, but in rather submission than grief,
For the end of my autumn, the close of the year.
                                    ORROHN.

Philadelphia, Feb. 28, 1840.

MOUNTAIN COTTAGES.

They are scattered over the valleys, and under the hill sides, and on the rocks; and even to this day, in the more retired dales, without any intrusion of more assuming buildings:

Cluster'd like stars some few, but single most,
And lurking dimly in their shy retreats,
Or glancing on each other cheerful looks,
Like separated stars with clouds between.

The dwelling-houses and contiguous out-houses are, in many instances, of the colour of the native rock, out of which they have been built; but frequently the dwelling or fire-house, as it is ordinarily called, has been distinguished from the barn and byer by rough-cast and white-wash, which, as the inhabitants are not hasty in renewing it, in a few years acquires, by the influence of weather, a tint at once sober and variegated. As these houses have been, from father to son, inhabited by persons engaged in the same occupations, yet necessarily with changes in their circumstances, they have received without incongruity additions and accommodations adapted to the needs of each successive occupant, who, being for the most part proprietor, was at liberty to follow his own fancy; so that these humble dwellings remind the contemplative spectator of a production of nature, and may (using a strong expression) rather be said to have grown than to have been erected;—to have risen, by an instinct of their own, out of the native rock, so little is there in them of formality, such is their wildness and beauty. Among the numerous recesses and projections in the walls and in the different stages of their roofs, are seen bold and harmonious effects of contrasted sunshine and shadow. It is a favourable circumstance that the strong winds which sweep down the valleys, induced the inhabitants, at a time when the materials for building were easily procured, to furnish many of these dwellings with substantial porches; and such as have not this defence are seldom unprovided with a projection of two large slates over their thresholds. Nor will the singular beauty of the chimneys escape the eye of the attentive traveller. Sometimes a low chimney, almost upon a level with the roof, is overlaid with a slate, supported upon four slender pillars to prevent the wind from driving the smoke down the chimney. Others are of a quadrangular shape, rising one or two feet above the roof; which low square is often surmounted by a tall cylinder, giving to the cottage chimney the most beautiful shape in which it is ever seen. Nor will it be too fanciful or refined to remark, that there is a pleasing harmony between a tall chimney of this circular form, and the living column of smoke ascending from it through the still air. These dwellings, mostly built, as has been said, of rough unhewn stone, are roofed with slates, which were rudely taken from the quarry before the present art of splitting them was understood, and are, therefore, rough and uneven in their surfaces, so that both the coverings and sides of the houses have furnished places of rest for the seeds of lichens, mosses, ferns, and flowers. Hence buildings, which in their very form call to mind the processes of nature, do thus, clothed with this vegetable garb, appear to be received into the bosom of the living principle of things, as it acts and exists among the woods and fields; and, by their colour and their shape, affectingly direct the thoughts to that tranquil course of nature and simplicity, along which the humble-minded inhabitants have, through so many generations, been led. Add the little garden with its shed for bee-hives, its small beds of pot-herbs, and its borders and patches of flowers for Sunday posies, with sometimes a choice few too much prized to be plucked; an orchard of proportioned size; a cheese-press, often supported by some tree near the door; a cluster of embowering sycamores for summer shade; with a tall Scotch fir, through which the winds sing when other trees are leafless; the little rill or household spout murmuring in all seasons; combine these incidents and images together, and you have the representative idea of a mountain cottage in this country so beautifully formed in itself, and so richly adorned by the hand of nature.—*From Wordsworth's Description of the Scenery of the Lakes.*

THE FRIEND.

THIRD MONTH, 7, 1840.

We had observed in several of the papers a paragraph relative to a decree or bull of the pope of Rome, Gregory XVI., against slavery and the slave trade. In the Pennsylvania Freeman of the present week, we have this remarkable document in full, translated and forwarded by an American at Paris. If the pope is really in earnest in this matter, the effect of the exertion of his influence and authority must be very great. The bull appears to have been issued at Rome, December 10th, 1839. We insert an extract which contains the most important part. After a cursory history of the previous action of the "Holy See" upon the subject, the document proceeds:—

"But, although this barbarous trade is in part abolished, yet that the Holy See may rejoice in the full success of its efforts and of its zeal to remove the foul opprobrium from all Christian countries, after having maturely consulted with our venerable brothers, the cardinals of the holy Roman church in council assembled, and following the footsteps of our predecessors, in virtue of apostolic authority, we do advertise and admonish, in the power of the Lord, all Christians, however strong their condition may be, that hereafter they cease from the cruel traffic in Indians, negroes, and other human beings, by which they have been treated as if they were not men, but bought, sold, and doomed to the most severe labour, like mere brutes, fomenting in their own country incessant wars, by a thirst for gain, first instigated by their own despoilers. It is on this account, and in virtue of the apostolic authority, that we prohibit these things as absolutely unworthy the Christian name, and by the same authority we do solemnly interdict all ecclesiastics or laity from receiving any support which is the produce of trade in human beings, or from preaching or teaching, in public or in private, or in any manner whatever, contrary to these apostolic letters.

"And that these letters may be more publicly known, and that no person plead ignorance, we direct and ordain that they be published and affixed, according to usage, before the door of the Prince of the Apostles, the Chancelry Apostolic, the Palace of Justice of Monte Citorio, and at the Champ de Flore."

The account of the Institute at Hohenheim, contained in the extract inserted from Bache's report, possesses matter of interest to those of our readers, at least, who are partial to the manual labour plan of instruction.

A stated annual meeting of "The Contributors to the Asylum for the relief of persons deprived of the use of their reason," will be held at Mulberry street meeting house, on fourth day, third month 18th, at three o'clock P. M.

SAMUEL MASON, Jr., *Clerk.*

2d mo. 29th, 1840.

PRINTED BY ADAM WALDIE,
Carpenter Street, below Seventh, Philadelphia.

THE FRIEND.

A RELIGIOUS AND LITERARY JOURNAL.

VOL. XIII.   **SEVENTH DAY, THIRD MONTH, 14, 1840.**   **NO. 24.**

EDITED BY ROBERT SMITH.

PUBLISHED WEEKLY.

Price two dollars per annum, payable in advance.

Subscriptions and Payments received by

GEORGE W. TAYLOR,

NO. 50, NORTH FOURTH STREET, UP STAIRS,

PHILADELPHIA.

For "The Friend."

THOUGHTS ON THE TIMES.

NO. II.

It is evident that the system of credit upon which every department of business is conducted, is intimately connected, even if it be not one of their causes, with these embarrassments of the times. Can that system be abandoned to advantage or with safety? I think it requires little skill in human affairs to answer that it cannot. For it is the natural, nay, the inevitable consequence of a state of prosperous industry and tranquil order. It is the result of one of those social instincts which act with a wisdom higher than that of man, for they are the beneficent arrangements of Providence. It is one of the great levellers of the inequalities of fortune, by which the capital of the rich is distributed through a thousand channels that fertilize the fields and minister to the necessities of the poor.

The higher price which the labouring weaver can give for yarn, if he is not to pay for it till the cloth into which he weaves it is sold, will be reason enough for the capitalist who sells it, to allow him a convenient credit. Once introduced, the practice must necessarily spread, till it extends to the larger portions of the bargains made in every community. The system of giving credit is brought to its highest pitch of refinement by the modern invention of banks of discount. As these are generally formed by the junction of small subscriptions, they bring into activity an amount of capital which would otherwise remain unemployed. They enable the trader to turn his promissory notes into money, and thus to realise all the advantages of a cash business with all the accommodation to his customers of selling on credit. If, as is now generally the case, these banks of discount are also banks of circulation, they issue their own notes to a certain extent in place of coin, and thus increase the circulating medium of the country.

In prosperous times nothing can work more smoothly and beautifully than this machinery. It imparts to all the operations of business an energy and punctuality which are the great elements of success. By slowly increasing the quantity of the circulating medium, it gradually raises prices and infuses as it were the glow of health into the commercial system. It administers a constant stimulant in the shape of loans, to industry and enterprise, and it is itself rewarded for the aid which it furnishes to commerce, by the profits which it returns to its proprietors. Advantageously as all this machinery of credit may work when skilfully managed, it is difficult to restrain its movements within the limits of prudence. For the profit and convenience with which the system of credit and banking is attended has caused the multiplication of banks beyond any demand of prudence or advantage. It becomes a favour to borrow instead of to lend, and men without capital, and without experience, obtain the means of engaging in the business of speculation. The rise of prices consequent upon the temporary increase of the circulating medium, tempts them to play a desperate game, while the brilliant success of a few, draws crowds in their train. This deceitful prosperity has its appointed time. The excessive issues of paper are returned upon the banks, the inflated currency collapses, and an explosion takes place scarcely less disastrous than that of the fines in a crowded steamboat. A period of exhaustion and depression succeeds, a new generation of traders repairs the losses of the past; a few years of prosperous commerce follow; success inspires confidence and blinds the judgment; the same temptations again present, attended with the same disastrous consequences; and the commercial world seems destined to a constantly revolving cycle of blind confidence in the future, of rash speculation and ruinous disappointment.

Are then the banks of circulation and discount the cause of all this confusion, and shall we rid ourselves of the one by getting rid of the other? We may answer confidently, that they are not. The cause, it must be admitted, lies deeper in the frame-work of society; for although the banks have had an influence in shaping the form of the evil, they have but shared in common with the public at large in prevailing opinions, and have been swept along by a current which few have the power, even if they have the disposition, to resist.

We must look for the real cause to that great feature of modern civilisation, the vast and rapid developement of the mechanic arts, the infusion into society of a new element of power before unheard of. These new interests have arisen with a suddenness which has altogether disturbed the old balance of the social power. They have invaded as it were the ancient and settled order of society; and being unchecked in their course, have given an ascendency to the desire for wealth, which not only renders it at this moment, the great controlling influence of the civilised world, but imparts to it an unnatural energy which is in imminent danger of overwhelming freedom and morality, and religion, in one common destruction.

THE AGE OF THE EARTH.

BY WILLIAM PATRICK.

Egypt, like India, has been long a field in which the infidel has catered for materials to overturn the truths of revelation. In that country of wonders and antiquities, it was vainly hoped that some lucky fact would ultimately turn up to prove the great antiquity of the earth, and thus disprove the record of Moses, and free the world for ever from the dominion of ignorance and superstition. It was not, however, till the invasion of that country by Napoleon, that sufficient opportunities were afforded for the exploring of its antiquities, and in this highly curious and interesting undertaking, the *savans* of France were encouraged by their republican leader. Among the many relics of antiquity then dragged to light, were the famous Egyptian zodiacs, which for some time occupied almost the entire attention of the antiquaries, and of learned men in most parts of Europe. There were two of these zodiacs, one in the ceiling of a temple at Dendera, in Upper Egypt, and another in a corresponding position in a temple at Esire, the ancient Satapolis. These works were eagerly seized upon by the atheistical disciples of the French school of philosophy, and were supposed to afford the most conclusive evidence, that no history yet known had recorded the true epoch of the creation of man; and not a few writers exulted in the belief, that at last reason and science had triumphed, and that now the minds of men were no longer to be held in religious bondage. The zodiac mania for some time went a great length in France, and infected with the same leprosy not a few in other countries. But to let the reader understand the meaning of this phrenzy, for it seemed to be little else, it is necessary to state, that the zodiac is the path in the heavens in which the sun, moon, and planets seem to move, and is formed of the Greek word signifying *animal*, because the constellations in the zodiac have the forms of animals given them. In that at Dendera, the same figures are employed that are chosen to represent the constellations at the present day. Here the sign of the lion is made to head the band. He is directing his course towards the north (the temple faces the north) and his feet towards the eastern wall. Then follow the other figures of the constellations in succession. Now the force of the argument for the antiquity of this monument, lies in the supposition that the peculiar distribution of these figures represented the exact state, or relative positions of the constellations, with respect to each other, at the time when it was constructed; and that, by astronomical calculations made backward, from the present state of the constellations, it could be ascertained at what period they were actually in the position represented by this zodiac, and thus the period of its construction would be known. Figures of the zodiacs were first published by Denon in his work on Egypt; and it appears that the subject excited the most intense interest among learned men of Europe, and particularly of France. Science struck out into systems very bold; and the spirit of infidelity, seizing upon the discovery, flattered itself with the hope of drawing from it new support. In the midst of this apparent triumph of infidelity, a circumstance happened which gave a new excitement to the subject of the zodiacs. This was no less than the arrival of the planisphere of Dendera at Paris. M. Leloraine, an enterprising young traveller, in spite of many obstacles, was the means of detaching this celebrated monument from the ceiling of the temple, and of transporting it to the sea, whence it was shipped, and finally reached Paris in 1821. M. Greppo describes the intense interest it there excited: "An object of interest," he says, "to educated men, and of vanity to those who thought themselves such, it could not remain unnoticed by the multitude; and classes of society, who knew not even the signification of the term zodiac, rushed in crowds to behold it. In the journals, in the saloons, the zodiac was the only topic of discussion. Have you seen the zodiac? What do you think of the zodiac? were questions to which every one was seemingly compelled to give a well-informed answer, or to be degraded from a place in polished society." It was pretended, that the zodiac exhibited the state of the heavens at a very remote date; but how far back, philosophers could not agree among themselves. M. Burkhard pretended to demonstrate, that the temple of Esire had stood seven thousand years; while M. Mouet, from the same data, proved that this temple was built four thousand six hundred years before the Christian era, or six hundred years nearly before the creation, according to the Mosaic chronology. M. Dupuis, taking a still different view of the subject, and making his demonstrations from some peculiar data, which his learning and sagacity had discovered, shows, by calculations through which few could follow him, that these temples must have stood at least fifteen thousand years. The figures of the zodiac, be it known, were engraved on wood; so that the sight of a piece of timber fifteen thousand years old, must of itself have been an object of great curiosity. A man of ordinary sense would at once have said, that the existence and entire preservation of an organic piece of matter for such a length of time was an impossibility. But infidelity is easily deluded; and although it would not believe in the record of Moses, yet it would believe in the existence of a carved piece of timber at least eight thousand years older than the surface of the earth on which it grew. At the very height of the discussion of the zodiac system of infidelity, a circumstance arose, which gave a new turn to the arguments of the philosophers; who, it would seem, had no correct

notions as to the actual age of the temples in which the zodiacs were found, and far less of the zodiacs themselves. This was the arrival of no less a personage than M. Champollion the younger, the celebrated antiquary, from a visit to Egypt. This youthful philosopher, in the course of his peregrinations, had contrived, like our countryman Dr. Young, to master the Egyptian hieroglyphics. He had visited the zodiac before its removal from Dendera, and had there decyphered not only the inscriptions which it contained, but also several others, inscribed on various parts of the temple itself. It was reserved for him to show, that the following letters AOTKPTP, with certain letters interspersed, which are written on the zodiac, form the Greek word for Emperor. He also discovered in the temple of Dendera, the names, titles, and surnames of the Emperors Tiberius, Claudius, Nero, and Domitian; and upon the portico of Esire, whose zodiac has been judged many centuries older than that of Dendera, he read the names of Claudius and Antonius Pius! In this simple circumstance, the entire substratum of the "zodiacal system" of infidelity," so carefully concocted, so zealously fostered and propped up by its fanatical friends and abettors, is at once and for ever annihilated; and, like the hopes of those by whom it was fabricated, flies off in smoke like the mists from the summits of the mountains on the approach of the "lord of day." In proof of its utter want of foundation or stability, it is only necessary to state, that it is now demonstrated, beyond a doubt, that the Egyptian zodiacs can boast of no greater antiquity than the Roman dominion in Egypt, which commenced one or two centuries after the Christian era; and that these signs do not, in any respect, relate to astronomy, but are connected with the idle phantasies of judicial astrology! The figures, therefore, which were so lately and confidently expected to revolutionize the Christian world, and reduce it to heathenism, are nothing more than what adepts in the pretended science of astrology call themes of nativity!

I shall only allude to one other notorious piece of jugglery respecting the lava beds of Etna, which has been practised upon the too ready susceptibilities of the infidel, by an individual of our own country, the well known Brydone, author of a volume of travels in Sicily. Brydone, in the present instance, is cautious enough not to publish his own opinions, but those of the canon Recupero, who lived in the neighbourhood of Etna, and who, it is stated, was a competent judge in such matters. This man of undoubted piety, of great simplicity of life, and well known for his hospitality, is made by Brydone to say that, in his opinion, a bed of lava requires two thousand years' exposure to the weather, in order to undergo sufficient decomposition to form a soil of a certain thickness. On examination, it was found that Etna afforded seven beds of lava, with a thickness of soil between each equal to that which the canon had said could only have been formed in two thousand years. By this mode of calculation, it was therefore proved that the first eruption in this series must have been fourteen thousand years ago; and there would, of course, be reason to

suppose that the mountain itself might be much older than the first bed of lava. This pretended discovery was, as usual, instantly seized upon by the infidel press, and was at once set down as an undeniable proof that the world is much older than the record of Moses supposes it to be. But before yielding our judgments to the theory of Brydone, and his lava currents, let us see upon what grounds the assertion is made, and how far he and the canon are trustworthy on such a subject. In the first place, supposing Brydone's statement to be correct; that no estimate of time can be obtained from any such circumstances, is proved by observations on other beds of lava. M. Daubuisson shows that some of the lavas of Auvergne have maintained an entire surface, all over blistered, and bristling with asperities, whose edges and angles are still sharp and well preserved. We might even imagine these lava streams to have just flowed from the bowels of the earth, and that they had hardly had time to cool. It is, however, probable that these lavas have lain on the soil of Auvergne for three thousand years, exposed to the action of the elements, so that here Brydone's theory is evidently at fault. But, on the other hand, Sir William Hamilton has shown that over the matter which buried Herculaneum, there are six streams of lava, with veins of good soil between them. Now, Herculaneum was destroyed about one thousand eight hundred years ago, which shows that veins of good soil have there been formed in three hundred years instead of two thousand; so that Brydone's theory is here also at fault. For, on the one hand, we have seen that lava may lie exposed to the sun and air for three thousand years without assuming a vegetable covering, and that, in other instances, this effect may be accomplished in three hundred years. But worse than all this (if M. Daubeny is to be believed) Brydone's statements respecting the lava beds of Etna are not true,—they are not according to fact. This able and philosophical traveller lately visited the famous pit at Acé Réale, on which the Scottish traveller made this canon to speculate without his consent; and, after discussing the subject at some length, remarks; "at all events, Brydone has been greatly deceived in imagining that the seven beds of lava, lying the one above the other, near the spot, have been sufficiently decomposed into vegetable mould; the substance which really interferes between the beds being nothing more than a sort of ferruginous tuff, just similar to what would be produced by a shower of volcanic ashes, such as naturally precedes, or follows, an eruption of lava mixed up with mud, or consolidated by rain;" so that Brydone's pretended vegetable soil between the lavas might be deposited in a few hours instead of two thousand years. But Brydone has not only misstated facts, but, if Dolomieu, the celebrated mineralogist, be right, he has also greatly injured the canon Recupero. Of this subject Dolomieu says, "The canon Recupero deserves neither the praises which have been bestowed on his science, nor the doubts which have been raised concerning his orthodoxy. He died without any other affliction than that which was caused to him by the work of Brydone. This simple man, very religious," and attached to the faith of his forefathers, was far from admitting, as an evidence against the book of Genesis, pretended facts which are false, but from which, even if they had been true, nothing could have been concluded." Dolomieu then goes on to show, as Daubeny has already done, that Brydone was mistaken in his observations, that there are no layers of vegetable soil between the beds of lava—that which he believed, or pretended to believe, was decomposed lava, was only what geologists call *volcanic tufa*, or *volcanic ashes*, either of which, as we have seen, might, under ordinary circumstances, cover the surface of a lava current a foot or two deep, in a few hours, instead of two thousand years, as he makes the cannon to suppose.

Another portion of philosophical speculators try to prove the antiquity of the globe by its internal heat, discovered by those scratches on its upper crust termed mines and artesian wells : and also by the saltness of the sea : but the arguments furnished up for the occasion, are too childish, and too superficial, to require notice.

It must be gratifying to the Christian to know, that the bulwarks of his holy religion are proof against the united attacks of its ablest and most powerful enemies. It is also a singular circumstance, that most of these attacks have, under the providence of God, been refuted by infidels themselves ; and thus all idea of collusion, on the part of the friends of religion, is precluded. At the present moment, it is not the fashion for philosophers generally to attack the truths of revealed religion ; they have been so often beaten off, that they are at length ashamed of their own futile attempts. We have the testimony of the chairman of the British Association, that philosophers are now rather favourable to the truths of religion. Comparing this statement with former statements, from the same class, especially in infidel France, we may truly say, " This is the doing of the Lord, and it is wondrous in our eyes."

HAZARDOUS ADVENTURE.

A correspondent of the Madras Herald gives the following account of an adventure with a *cobra di capello*, which occurred to a gentleman who was reposing under a tamarind tree alone, after a day of shooting :

" I was aroused by the furious baying of my dogs ; on turning round, I beheld a snake of the *cobra di capello* species, directing its course to a point that would approximate very close to my position. In an instant I was upon my feet. The moment the reptile became aware of my presence, in nautical phraseology, it boldly brought to, with expanded hood, eyes sparkling, neck beautifully arched, the head raised nearly two feet from the ground, and oscillating from side to side, in a manner plainly indicative of a resentful foe. I seized a short bamboo, left by one of the bearers, and hurled it at my opponent's head. I was fortunate enough to hit it beneath the eye. The reptile immediately fell from his imposing attitude, and lay apparently lifeless. Without a moment's reflection, I seized it a little below the head, hauling it beneath the shelter of the

tree, and very coolly sat down to examine the mouth for the poisoned fangs of which naturalists speak so much. While in the act of forcing the mouth open with a stalk, I felt the head sliding through my hand ; and to my utter astonishment, became aware that I had now to contend against the most deadly of reptiles, in its full strength and vigour. Indeed, I was in a moment convinced of it ; for as I tightened my hold of its throat, its body became wreathed around my neck and arm. I raised myself from my sitting position to one knee ; my right arm, to enable me to exert my strength, was extended. I must in such an attitude have appeared horrified enough to represent a deity in the Hindoo mythology, such as we see rudely emblazoned on the portals of their native temples. It now became a matter of self-defence. To retain my hold, it required my utmost strength to prevent the head from escaping, as my neck became a purchase for the animal to pull upon. If the reader is aware of the universal dread in which the *cobra di capello* is held throughout India, and the almost certain death which invariably follows its bite, he will, in some degree, be able to imagine what my feelings were at that moment ; a shudder, a faint kind of disgusting sickness pervaded my whole frame, as I felt the cold clammy fold of the reptile's body tightening round my neck. To attempt any delineation of my sensations would be absurd : let it suffice, they were most horrible. I had now almost resolved to resign my hold. Had I done so, this tale would never have been written ; so no doubt the head would have been brought to the extreme circumvolution to inflict the deadly wound.

Even in the agony of such a moment, I could picture to myself the fierce glowing of the eyes, and the intimidating expansion of the hood, ere it fastened its venomous and fatal hold upon my face and neck. To hold it much longer would be impossible. Immediately beneath my grasp there was an inward working and creeping of the skin, which seemed to be assisted by the firmness with which I held it ; my hand was gloved. Finding, in defiance of all my efforts, that my hand was each instant forced closer to my face, I was anxiously considering how to act in this horrible dilemma, when an idea struck me, that if it was in my power to transfix the mouth with some sharp instrument, it would prevent the reptile from using its fangs, should it escape my hold. My gun lay at my feet ; the ramrod appeared to be the very thing required, which, with some difficulty, I succeeded in drawing out, having only one hand disengaged. My right arm was now trembling from over exertion, my hold becoming less firm, when I happily succeeded in passing the rod through the lower jaw up to its centre. It was not without considerable hesitation that I suddenly let go my hold of the throat, and seized the rod in both hands, at the same time bringing them over my head with a sudden jerk, discharging the fold from my neck, which had latterly become almost tight enough to produce strangulation. There was then little difficulty in freeing my right arm, and ultimately throwing the reptile from me to the earth, where it continued to twist and writhe

into a thousand contortions of rage and agony. To run to a neighbouring stream to lave my neck, hands and face in its cold waters, was my first act after despatching my formidable enemy."

From the Boston Mercantile Journal.

DOMESTIC SLAVE TRADE.

But few persons, comparatively, are aware of the great extent to which the traffic in slaves is carried on, and has been carried on for years between the northern slave-holding states and the states at the far south. This domestic traffic in slaves presents a serious impediment to the abolition of slavery in the middle states —and it ought to be suppressed. We see that by a decision of the federal court for the district of Mississippi, declaring that under the constitution of that state, as amended in 1832-3, forbidding the introduction of slaves into that state for sale, all contracts for slaves since May, 1833, are void ! This is a tremendous blow to the slave speculators—as will be seen by the following article from the New York Whig, containing a number of interesting facts in connection with this subject :

" In the last four months of 1833, several thousands of slaves were carried to Mississippi for sale, and the success of their enterprises induced many to embark in the abominable traffic in the following year, and to triple the number of slaves thus transported. The first were sold for cash, and the second for bills on New Orleans at four months. Stimulated by this success, the speculators of Virginia, Kentucky, Tennessee, the Carolinas, Georgia, Missouri, and Maryland, neglected every thing for this domestic slave trade, and, in 1835, carried to Mississippi four times the number of any previous year ; the competition among these traders forcing them to give the planters a credit of 12 and 15 months, at 10 per cent. of interest, upon prices varying from $700 to $1200. The planters, paying in bills on New Orleans at a long time, did not object to these prices, and bought extensively. The traders returned with their accepted bills, cashed them at the banks, embarked still deeper in the trade, and persuaded others to follow, the example ; and every corner of the slave states was ransacked for slaves. In the autumn of 1836, the number in the market of Mississippi exceeded 40,000, and its public highways were filled with these droves, and its towns and villages were surrounded with their tents. The traders, greatly alarmed, waited for purchasers in vain, and as the winter of 1837 approached, advertised that they would give a credit of one or two years for bills on New Orleans at 10 per cent. The terms were accepted, and many planters purchased a second, and some a third supply, at prices varying from $1200 to $1800. By this time, the merchants who had accepted these bills began to fail ; and all drawn in the autumn of 1835, and spring of 1836, at 12 and 15 months, were protested for non-payment, and all drawn in the winter and spring of 1837, for non-acceptance. The speculators, alarmed, secured their debts by mortgages and deeds of trust upon nearly all the property in the state. Under this system, the slave population of Mississippi had increased from 70,000 to 160,000, and its debts for slaves, at the average cost of $1000 each, was $90,000,000!

" From 1833 to 1837, the high prices of cotton stimulated the planters to its excessive cultivation, and the neglect of every thing else ; and besides purchasing, on credit, more horses, mules, and agricultural implements, they neglected to raise corn and pork for their slaves, and purchased these supplies of the merchants, whom they neglected to pay. When the *revulsion* came in the spring of 1838, nearly all the paper held by the merchants against the planters was sued, the courts were delayed by the pressure of business, and the judgments when recovered, were worthless for want of property to levy upon, every thing being covered by the mortgages of the slave dealers. The merchants were ruined ; their creditors, the banks, were ruined in turn ; and the remorseless slave dealers, exulting in their own security, beheld with indifference the decay of plantations and the depopulation of towns. But their turn came in due time. In a suit by one of them upon one of these mortgages, the Federal court, sitting at Jackson, decided that the introduction of slaves into the state being prohibited by the constitution, as amended in 1832-3, all contracts for slaves made since May, 1833, are *void*. Two-thirds of the present debt, having been contracted for slaves, is thus extinguished ; and the property covered by the liens of the slave dealers is liberated, and ready for the second liens of the banks and the merchants, of much less amount. The planters, instead of surrendering all to the slave dealers, are now striving to pay the more meritorious demands of the banks and the merchants ; and when the crop of 1841 shall be sold, the state will be redeemed from ruin, and the balance turned in her favour."

From the Metropolitan Magazine.

THE UNION OF EXTREMES.

Sir Isaac Newton, in the severe abstraction and abstruseness of his studies, seems to have had none of the " gentler elements" of poetry " mixed in him," yet what poet has said any thing more beautiful than his remark about his own discoveries, as recorded by Spence ? The saying, too, has a resemblance to a passage in Milton. " Sir Isaac Newton," says Spence, " a little before he died, said, ' I don't know what I may seem to the world, but as to myself I seem to have been only like a boy playing on the sea shore, and diverting myself in now and then finding a smoother pebble or a prettier shell than ordinary, while the great ocean of truth lay all undiscovered before me.' "

" Who reads
Incessantly, and to his reading brings not
A spirit and judgment equal or superior,
(And what he brings, what need he elsewhere seek ?)
Uncertain and unsettled still remains,
Deep versed in books, and shallow in himself,
Crude or intoxicate, collecting toys
And trifles for choice matters, with a sponge,
As children gathering pebbles on the shore."
Par. Regained Book IV.

Since the late earthquake which extended over most of Scotland, and was felt also in va-rious parts of the continent, seve springs of water in the neighbou verness have been dry. On th land, or elevated flat, between t Inverness, there are a number of were never without three or four in the most sultry season, but all o now dried up. The same has oc vicinity of Rosebank, and the pe sort to Aultnaskiasch Burn for su ter. The concussion probably clo horizontal strata of rock throug water had its course.—*Inverness*

EARTH'S CHANGE

BY L. H. SIGOURNEY.

As waves the grass upon the field to-da
Which soon the wasting scythe shall sw
As smiles the flowret in the morning d
Which eve's chill blast upon the winds
Thus, in brief glory, boast the sons of d
Thus bloom awhile, then wither and de

Dust tends to dust—with ashes, ashes b
The senseless turf conceals the buried i
A few may sigh upon the grave's dark i
A few soft tears the broken soil may di
A few sad hearts in lonely sorrow blee
And pay that tribute which they soon i

I saw the infant in its robe of white,
Its doating mother's ever dear delight ;
It clapped its hands when tones of mirt
And nature's gladness glistened in its e
Again I came: an empty crib was ther
A little coffin, and a funeral prayer !

I saw the ruddy boy, of vigour bold,
Who feared not summer's heat nor win
With dexterous heel he skimmed the fi
His laugh rang loudest 'mid his mates
Again I sought him: but his name wa
On the low stone that marks you churc

O, boasted joys of earth! how swift ye
Rent from the hand, or hidden from th
So through the web the weaver's shuttl
So speeds the vessel o'er the billowy tid
So cleaves the bird the liquid fields of li
And leaves no furrow of its trackless fli

But we, frail beings, shrinking from the
We love those skies that glittering clou
Though wounded oft, as oft renew our
To rear a fabric on this sand-swept soil
And still we strive, forgetful of the grav
To fix our anchor on the tossing wave.

Yet He who marks us in our vain care
Oft shows how frail is what we hold mo
Spreads o'er some face beloved the dest
Or hides a parent in the lonely tomb;
Arrests the thoughtless, bids the world li
Wounds to admonish, and afflicts to hea

Look to that world where every pain sh
Grief turn to joy, and labour end in pea
O! seek that world, by penitence and p
Sow the seed here, and reap the fruitag
Where shadowy joys no longer cheat th
But one unclouded year in changeless li

Destructive Hurricane at Mao mendous hurricane, with an inun sea, occurred on the 16th of N Coringa, on the coast northward Some particulars of the devastatio are given in the Madras Spectator thority of letters written on the s water from the sea rushed in wi lence, that the houses at Coringa, large house, and three or four othe houses—all the rest they say hav ried away. I have had two and a

LIFE OF WILLIAM CATON.
(Continued from page 182.)

[In the fourth month, 1659, W. C. for the third time went on a visit to Holland, with which part of the journal our next extract commences.]

In due time through the good hand of God I got well over to Rotterdam, where I visited Friends, as also elsewhere in the country. I found things pretty well in reference to the truth, and meetings pretty peaceable; and about that time strangers did come more frequently to our meetings than formerly: and if things had not been carried in much wisdom, we might have been often in tumults, for there were those who watched for iniquity, and were ready to do mischief, thinking that if the magistrates would not meddle with us, as we then were, yet if they could but procure an uproar or tumult at or about our meeting-places, that then we should be punished as uproar-makers. Yet notwithstanding the evil conspiracies of the wicked, the Lord was exceeding good to Friends, and very gently and compassionately he dealt with them; and they grew bold and valiant, and the truth got dominion among them: so that whereas my suffering before had been great in that country, (especially before I could speak their language,) yet the Lord refreshed me much among that small remnant which were called by his name, and which walked in his eternal truth: and having gotten their language, and being able to minister in it, I could much better ease and free myself of the weights and burdens than before. When I had staid about two months in that country, and seeing things in a pretty good posture as to the truth, Friends and their meetings kept in good order, it was upon me again to return for England, where there was such an effectual door open: in order thereunto I took my leave of Friends in Hollands, whom I committed to the custody and protection of the Almighty, and so left them.

In the latter end of the fifth month, 1659, I took shipping for England, partly intending for London. When we had been about twenty-fours at sea, we saw another ship which proved to be a pirate or robber, which chased us; when the master perceived it, he caused all to be made in readiness to fight, and the passengers that were aboard they were furnished with arms as well as the rest, but for my own part I could not touch any of their weapons, as to shed blood with them, but stood simply given up to the will of the Lord. But as Providence ordered it, when they were almost within shot of us, their hearts failed them, and they were not suffered to come up to us, so that there was no blood shed, nor harm done to each other; wherein the Lord even answered my desire, and for which mercy my soul did even bless, praise, and magnify his holy name.

But after we were delivered through the good hand of God from the hands of the aforesaid pirate, we were in pretty imminent danger through a very violent storm, which upon us when we were near the coast of England; and coming to cast anchor we left both anchor and cable, and had our boat split in pieces; one great ship that rode by us was swallowed up

of the raging sea, (a sad sight to behold,) there not being one man saved alive in her; yet nevertheless, the same God that delivered us from the hands of the aforesaid pirate, did also deliver us out of that violent storm; through whose mercy we got finally into harbour at Yarmouth, though it was near upon a hundred miles from the place for which we partly intended.

When I was put so far to the northward as Yarmouth, I determined to go from thence by shipping into the north; which accordingly I did, with a Friend to Sunderland, where I found two of the ancient ministering brethren, (viz.) Francis Howgill, and John Audland; with whom I was much refreshed, as also with the rest of Friends. And when the first day came, we went together unto a general meeting in the country, where there were abundance of Friends and others; and the power and presence of the Lord was much with us, through which we were much refreshed together.

After that meeting I visited pretty many Friends in the bishoprick, and in some short time after I passed westwards towards Lancashire through Westmoreland, visiting Friends in my journey, as my manner was: and in due time I got well to Swarthmore, where I was received in the same ancient and entire love, with which we were usually favoured together, through the infinite mercy of the Most High, which even abounded much to us and among us in those days.

When I had staid some weeks there, and thereabouts, I went into Cumberland, to visit the flock of God there again, among whom I had many precious meetings; for indeed the power and presence of the Lord did accompany me, and his word of life run freely and powerfully through me, to the strengthening of the weak, to the comforting of the feeble, and to the satisfying of the thirsty soul. And when I had been through a great part of the county, and had visited most of the Friends in it, I returned again into Lancashire; where I could not stay long at that time, because it was much upon me to go into Scotland to visit Friends there. In order thereunto I took my leave, even in an extraordinary manner, of my dear and near relations (in the eternal truth) at Swarthmore, where we spent several hours in waiting upon the Lord, and in pouring forth our supplications before him, and in being refreshed abundantly together, after we seemed to be perfectly clear and ready to part one from another; which finally we did, in exceeding much love and unity.

Being accompanied by two dear brethren, (Leonard Fell, and Robert Salthouse,) I went back again into Cumberland, and visited Friends in my journey thither, where I heard much of the troubles that were in that nation, and of the likelihood of their increasing; yet nevertheless I could not be freed of the journey, but must go on (like as I did,) in the name and power of the Lord: and presently after our coming into that nation, the aforesaid brethren took their leave of me and I of them, in the fulness of our Father's love, in much brokenness of heart; committing one another unto the protection and custody of the Almighty; and afterwards I and another Friend

travelled towards Edinburgh, where in due time through the mercy of God we arrived, after some hard travel.

The next day after our arrival there, we went to a general meeting at Linlithgow, about twelve miles from Edinburgh; where we found Friends at their meeting by the highway side, unto which many people resorted, and a good service we had at it; howbeit the people of the town were so incensed against us, that we could scarce get any entertainment among them for our money; but the wife of the governor of the castle being at the meeting, her heart was opened and filled with love towards us and the truth, and she constrained us to turn in with her, and to take up our lodging in the castle; which we were free in the Lord to do. Afterwards we had some more good service in the town, which when it was over, I returned back again towards Edinburgh and Leith, where I had some good service.

[He concludes the account of this journey thus:]

Upon my return from Scotland, I visited Friends again in Cumberland, and with some difficulty, (it being in the winter season and very tempestuous weather,) I got back again into Lancashire, and so to Swarthmore, which was always a place of refreshment to me.

[The extract which follows is interesting as referring to some of the circumstances of that eventful period in English history, the coming in of Charles the Second.]

When I had continued at Swarthmore some time, it was upon me to go down into the south of Lancashire, to visit Friends and their meetings; which accordingly I did, and several good and serviceable meetings I had in divers of the great towns in Lancashire, as at Garstang, Preston, Wigan, Liverpool, and Warrington, &c.

Being at a meeting in Warrington, the 7th of the twelfth month, 1659, there came several rude soldiers of the baser sort, who did much abuse Friends; and after they had done much violence to us, they broke up our meeting, and forced us out of the town: but near unto the town upon the road-side we gathered together again, and had a sweet and precious meeting; but it was not long before the soldiers came thither also, and as I was speaking they took me violently from among the rest, and beat me, some with their muskets, and others with their spears, in the sight of Friends, to the breaking of the hearts of many. And when they had satisfied their wills with abusing of me, they suffered me to return into the meeting again, which afterwards we kept a certain time to our great refreshment in the Lord, whose power and presence did exceedingly appear amongst us; for as our suffering at that time was greater than ordinary, even so was our refreshment in the Lord. After that I visited Friends in some parts of Cheshire and elsewhere; and when I had had exceeding good service in those parts, I returned again to Swarthmore, where I always found refreshment in the fulness of the Father's love, which abounded much among us in that blessed family.

I had not been long there, and with my own dear mother, (who about that time laid down the body, when I was with her,) but it was upon me to go southwards, first towards a general meeting of the brethren from several parts of the nation, which was at Balby in Yorkshire, and afterwards towards London; and it was so ordered that Thomas Salthouse (my dear companion and fellow-servant) together with Bridget and Isabel Fell did accompany me. When the time of our departure from Swarthmore was come, our very hearts were sad and broken within us, as they used to be at such seasons; and when with prayers and supplications unto the Lord we had earnestly interceded one for another, and had committed one another to his custody and protection, as our manner was at such times, we took leave one of another in the fulness and virtue of love and unity; and then set forwards on our journey, in the name and power of the Lord.

When we came into Yorkshire, we had some meetings before we got to the aforesaid Balby; and when we got thither we found many of the ancient brethren there, and Friends that were come from several parts of the nation: so that the meeting consisted of many hundreds: when it was about the height, there came a part of a troop of horse to break it up, and to dismiss Friends, but they were moderate, and Friends did continue their meeting until they had freedom in the Lord to break it up. The next day we had a very large and precious meeting, not far from that place; and when we were abundantly refreshed together in the Lord, through the supreme abounding of his mercy and goodness to us, we took leave one of another in much love and unity, and every one went in peace towards his respective place where the Lord had a service for him. And as for me, and the aforesaid Thomas Salthouse, (my dear brother,) we travelled southwards towards London, and visited Friends in our journey: and as we were travelling in Nottinghamshire, some stoops met us upon the road and apprehended us, and carried us before some of their commanders, who sent us to the commissioners at Nottingham, where we were further examined by them, or some of them, and being found innocent were discharged, and suffered to pass on our journey in peace.

Coming into Northamptonshire we visited Friends at Wellingborough and thereabouts, and being sweetly refreshed among them, we took our leave of them, and travelled along until we came well, through the mercy of the Lord, unto London; where we had several precious meetings, and were more than a little comforted with the flock of God there, as oftentimes my soul had been before in that city: where I staid about two weeks, and afterwards parted with my dear brother Thomas Salthouse.

[The following letter, descriptive of the state of things in London at this period, may be here inserted; it is taken from the Swarthmore Collection.]

LONDON, 7th of 3d mo. 1660.

To THOMAS WILLAN.

Dear Friend,—Our dear and unfeigned love reacheth unto thee, and to the brethren with thee, whom we dearly salute in the living Truth. We rejoice in the Lord, who lifteth up our heads above the wickedness of wicked and ungodly men, which indeed is grown to an exceeding great height in this city; which doth exceedingly abound in pride, fulness, excess, and in all manner of superfluity of naughtiness, to the grieving of the spirits of just men, and to the making of their hearts sad, who fear the Lord and work righteousness. Yet, nevertheless, this we would have the brethren to know, that as yet we see scarce any stop at all put to the work of the Lord in the city or country. For several precious meetings we had, as we came through the country, as a letter that is coming by the carrier makes mention of more at large than at this time we shall do. And as for the meetings, in general, in and nigh unto the city, they were, the last first day, as full, large and peaceable, even almost as Friends have at any time known them; and abundance of sober people resorted to them and were generally quiet. The guard of soldiers which for a season were kept at the Bull and Mouth, is now from thence removed; and several quiet, large and precious meetings we have had there of late, since the guard was removed, which is not only removed from thence, but also from several parts of the city; and it is reported that the citizens would have all the soldiers of the old army removed out of the city forty miles, or rather disbanded; and they would undertake to guard and to protect both the king and parliament. The old soldiers are come in exceeding great contempt, and with the most of men they are holden in derision, and dreaded them are now become a dread unto them. And, indeed, now is anguish and distress come and coming upon many, whose hearts have been nourished, and exalted, and puffed up without the fear of God; who have not regarded the cries of the oppressed, nor stood in God's counsel; but have ever boasted themselves against [those] that hewed with them once; and, therefore, is it just with the Lord to give them for a prey unto their enemies, who were a prey unto them, while they stood in God's counsel; from which many of them have departed, and therefore are they fallen, snared and taken, &c. Friends in the city are almost generally well, as far as we know. John Stubbs is gone into Kent, Richard Hubberthorne is yet in the city. The chiefest discourse among the people here is, about the king and the parliament's proceedings; who are speedily preparing the way for his coming, which is suddenly expected: but blessed be the Lord for ever, in whose power we can testify, that our King is come, who reigns in power and great glory; and therefore need not we look for another.

W. CATON, THOMAS SALTHOUSE.

London, 8th of 3d mo.—This very day the king hath been proclaimed in an extraordinary manner; the concourse of people that have been in the streets this day have been innumerable; the shouting for joy hath been so exceeding great among the people here is, that the sound of many trumpets could scarce be heard, nay the bells themselves could not sometimes be heard, but the noise hath been exceedingly confused, like unto the noise of many waters. Time would fail me to relate the fantastical ceremonies that this day have been used, and the extraordinary pomp, the mayor and aldermen with the gentry have appeared in. And oh! the vanity and superfluity of wickedness which this day hath appeared in the city, my pen could not declare it in several hours' time to the utmost. But at present I have not much time, being about to go to a meeting, not knowing certainly whether this day they will or no suffer us to keep any of our meetings; for they would not suffer that at Westminster to be kept this day. This wickedness, which is now at an extraordinary height, will have an end in the Lord's time. Let this be sent to Swarthmore, after Friends have seen it at Kendal; my entire love is unto all the faithful there and elsewhere. Farewell.

W. C.

My dear love in that which is our life, is unto you all, and if G. F. be there I would gladly hear from him, as he is free.

RICHARD HUBBERTHORNE.

As for the sufferings of Friends, which G. F. said should be given to this parliament, it is not yet a convenient time to present them, because they do not act any thing till Charles come, but what is in order to the bringing of him in, and so they were but lost to be given to them at present.

London, 8th of 3d mo. 1660.]

[Also in R. H.'s handwriting apparently.]

(To be continued.)

For "The Friend."

HAVERFORD SCHOOL.

Inquiry has frequently been made for more exact information in relation to the course of study at this institution; the following report from the teachers to a committee of the board of managers, shows the occupations of the students during a part of the present term, and furnishes more accurate knowledge of the manner in which the school is conducted than can be otherwise obtained by those who have not the opportunity of being present at the exercises.

TO THE COMMITTEE ON INSTRUCTION.

The council of teachers at Haverford submit the following report on the studies pursued at that institution during the present term.

Classical Department.

The first-junior department each of the classes has recited five times a week, and has pursued the study of the Greek and Latin languages alternately by weeks. Since the commencement of the present term, the Third Junior Class have read the second book of the Æneid, and part of the third, making 996 lines; have recited such parts of the Latin grammar as are commonly committed to memory, and have written an exercise from the Latin Tutor, weekly. They have read twenty-four pages of Jacob's Greek Reader, and recited the Greek Grammar from the beginning through the regular verb.

The Second Junior Class have read the first, third, and fourth of Cicero's orations against Cataline, that for Archias, and six sections of that for the Manilian law; in the Græca Majora they have read thirty-seven pages of the extracts from the Cyropædia of Xenophon, and a small portion of those from Herodotus. During the greater part of the term, they have written an exercise from the Latin Tutor weekly, and recited once a week from the Manual of Classical Literature, in all 110 sections of the Mythology.

The *Junior Class* have read thirty-three sections from the first book of Cicero de Officiis, and the whole of the treatise De Senectute. In the Græca Majora they have read seven pages of the extracts from Thucydides; eleven pages of those from Xenophon's Memorabilia of Socrates; eleven pages from the Crito of Plato, and five pages from the Phædo of the same author. They have recited weekly from the Manual of Classical Literature, in all, 144 sections on Grecian and Roman antiquities.

The *Senior Class* have read the first book of the History of Tacitus entire, being 90 sections; the Medea of Euripides entire, being 1416 lines, and the Hymn of Cleanthes. They have reviewed the most of the Latin Grammar, and have recited weekly from the Manual of Classical Literature, in all; 194 sections, viz. 69 sections on Grecian literature, 72 sections from the Archæology of Art, and 53 from the Archæology of Grecian Literature.

Department of Mathematics and Natural Philosophy.

The *Third Junior Class* have recited five lessons weekly to the teacher of mathematics. They have studied Bridge's Algebra through Quadratic Equations, and more than half the first book of Davies' edition of Le Gendre's Geometry as translated by Brewster. One student has been learning Lewis's Arithmetic. The class has been exercised weekly in the practice of arithmetical rules.

The *Second Junior Class* have studied Gummere's Surveying with the teacher of mathematics and natural philosophy, reciting five times a week. On third-day afternoon an hour is occupied in practical exercises in arithmetic, and on seventh day morning they hear an experimental lecture on natural philosophy.

The *Junior Class* have studied Le Gendre's Spherical Trigonometry and Davies' Analytical Geometry, with the same teacher, reciting four times in the week. They have also had a weekly lecture and recitation on the principles of the rules of arithmetic. They have recited three times a week to the teacher of English literature, from the Principles of Chemistry, prepared for the use of the school, and during the review will recite five times weekly from the same treatise.

The *Senior Class* have recited five times in the week to the teacher of mathematics. They have gone over Davies' Differential Calculus, and the theoretical part of Gummere's Astronomy.

Department of General Literature.

The *Third Junior Class* have learned the history of America and France, and first four sections of the history of England, from Worcester's History, reciting twice in the week. They have learned the syntax, and corrected the examples in Murray's Exercises; as far as the nineteenth rule, and have written composition every two weeks. They have also read four times weekly.

The *Second Junior Class* have been occupied with investigating the etymology of the English language, tracing words to their origin, and discriminating the shades of their meaning. Oswald's Etymological Dictionary has been used as the basis of this course, which has occupied two recitations in the week. The class have gone over Parker's Exercises in the English Language, reciting two lessons weekly. They have also written English composition every two weeks.

The *Junior Class* have pursued the course of English etymology mentioned above, having one recitation weekly, and have written exercises in English composition nearly every week, that is, whenever not occupied with chemistry.

The *Senior Class* have recited four times a week from Whately's Rhetoric and Dymond's Essays. They have attended every week a lecture and recitation on physiology and comparative anatomy, and one on geology.

An hour is devoted every seventh day morning to writing from dictation for the sake of improvement in spelling. In this exercise all the students in the large room participate, except those who make no mistake during a trial of several weeks, and these are only occasionally exercised.

The whole school recites twice every week from the Scriptures, viz: on fifth day, before meeting; and on first day afternoon. The third junior class recites from the historical part of the Old Testament, having learned as far as the book of Joshua. The other students use the Scripture Lessons, printed by the board of managers. At the close of the recitation on first day afternoon, a lecture is given. Those of the present term have been biographical sketches of the Reformers, and of early Friends.

The classes are now all engaged in reviewing the studies of the present term.

In conclusion, the council bear their testimony to the general good conduct and docility of the pupils, which have at no former time been more satisfactory and encouraging.

All of which is respectfully submitted.

WM. DENNIS, Sec'ry.

Haverford, 2d mo. 19th, 1840.

CIRCULAR.

The managers of Haverford School Association, desiring to extend more widely the benefits of the institution, have reduced the price for board and tuition to $200 per annum; payable as follows, $80 at the opening of the summer term; $60 at the opening and $60 in the middle of the winter term.

The rule which requires every student to pursue all the studies of his class, having in some instances prevented the admission of those who were desirous of studying certain branches of learning, but from want of time, or a deficiency in their previous acquirements could not so profitably apply themselves to others, the board have determined to receive applications from such as may wish to pursue a part of the studies of the course only. The course of instruction which has heretofore been pursued is maintained, and the board can with great confidence recommend the

school to parents who desire to have their sons instructed in the higher branches of learning, under circumstances conducive to the preservation of sound morals, and to an acquaintance with, and regard for the principles of our religious Society.

By direction of the Managers,
CHARLES YARNALL, Sec'ry.

Philada., 2d mo. 15th, 1840.

Communicated for "The Friend."

A SERIOUS MEDITATION,
OR
A CHRISTIAN'S DUTY, BRIEFLY SET FORTH.

Supposed to have been written by Rachel, wife of David Barclay.

There is nothing I ought to wish for so much as to have my heart clean in the sight of God; so that after I die, my soul may be happy for ever. But how may I secure to myself this blessing? By performing, with the assistance of his grace, my duty to him, my duty to my neighbour, and my duty to myself. My duty to God, is to love, honour, and fear him, as my Maker, my Governor, and my Judge—remembering that he knows all my thoughts, and sees all my most secret actions. I must accept every dispensation of his providence, with thankfulness; I must also keep his commandments, and pray to him to pardon and bless me, for the sake of Jesus Christ, who died to save the souls of all men, upon condition that they sincerely turn unto him, in faith, and endeavour, by obedience to his will, to live a virtuous and holy life. My duty to my neighbour is, to love him as myself, and to take care that all my actions be just, and honest, and words true and sincere; and all my thoughts charitable, and kind, so that I may, in every respect, do to all others, as I would they should do unto me.

My duty to myself, is to be sober, chaste, and temperate. To spend my time prudently, and profitably; to carefully examine the designs of my heart, and to keep my conscience free from offence, in the sight of God, and man.

If I sincerely apply my heart to these duties, I may humbly hope, that the Almighty will continue unto me the assistance of his grace, and thereby enable me to perform them. And then I shall be made happy in his life, and eternally happy hereafter.

For "The Friend."

Ventilation of Meeting and School Houses.

As pure, wholesome air is necessary to comfort and health, so it is indispensable to the possession of an unclouded and vigorous intellect. Who has not remarked that in studying in a warm close room, he sometimes finds it impossible to pursue even the simplest train of reasoning, when after breathing the fresh air for a few minutes, he can understand clearly, and without effort, what before was perfectly unintelligible. Familiar as this fact must be to almost every one, it seems to be but little attended to, at least it seldom receives that full share of attention which its importance deserves. How can it be expected that children can pursue their studies with advantage, when crowded, as they not unfrequently are, into small, close school-rooms! This is sometimes done from mistaken views of economy, but oftener, probably, from thoughtlessness, or ignorance. True, in some parts of the country where the number of scholars is small, and the means of those who support the school limited, very large school-houses are neither necessary nor proper. Still, they should be large enough to render the inmates comfortable; otherwise, the loss of time which the pupil will sustain from attempting to study, where he can with difficulty breathe, will overbalance whatever may be gained from such economy; to say nothing of the loss of health and enjoyment, or of the disgust of intellectual pursuits which must almost inevitably follow.

The proper ventilation of meeting houses is perhaps even more neglected than that of school-rooms. People seem to think, that an inconvenience which occurs only once or twice a week, and then lasts but a short time, may easily be borne. But it has been already intimated, that when the body is oppressed for want of air, the mind must suffer with it. Now all will admit, that in order to pursue our studies advantageously, it is of the utmost consequence that our mental faculties be unclouded and fresh;—should they not be so, in order to engage in the most important work which can possibly claim our attention—devotion, "watching unto prayer?" Independently, however, of the above considerations, care should be taken, I think, to make our meeting houses comfortable, that as little excuse as possible may be afforded to those who neglect our meetings. Not that I would at all exculpate as absent themselves for every trifling cause. But though we cannot justify, we may be allowed to pity them; and perhaps we ought to use every innocent means of inducing them to be more faithful. As it is very desirable that our younger members should be in the habit of regularly attending our assemblies for public worship, it appears to me, a point of no small moment, to avoid exciting in their minds an aversion to this duty, before experience has taught them its inestimable value. But there are many who, by weakness, or by an inability to breathe in a close and crowded room, are often prevented from attending our meetings, yet are anxious to do so, whenever health and strength permit. These might frequently be able to sit a meeting of an hour and a half, without any great inconvenience, if refreshed by a reasonable allowance of wholesome air; whereas they would be entirely overcome in half the time by such an atmosphere as we too often find in many of our meeting houses. It may perhaps be said, that among the great disunity of inclinations and infirmities, which prevail in a large assembly, it is scarcely possible to provide perfectly for the comfort and satisfaction of all. Thus, if a room be kept cool and airy to accommodate a part, others will be liable to take cold. But it does not follow, that because air is pure, it must therefore be uncomfortably cool. It would not be difficult, I think, certainly not impossible, to have a liberal supply of air from out of doors, heated before or while entering the room. It is especially important that there should be some contrivance of this kind where the room is small. At all events, however, let it be borne in mind that, generally, it is far more easy to provide against the inconveniences of too cool, than of too warm a house. In the former case, one can have recourse to foot-stoves, or to warmer clothing, but in the latter, to abandon the house is the only refuge. Perhaps some additional remarks on this subject may be offered in another number of "The Friend," T. X.

THE FRIEND.

THIRD MONTH, 14, 1840.

Were the people of the south only disposed to listen with soberness to reason and truth, instead of closing every avenue to enlightened investigation on the subject which so nearly interests them, they might soon have their eyes opened to the true remedy for their worn-out fields and wasting population. The following simple statement, as it seems to us, suggests the line of policy for them to pursue —in connection with the aid of their coloured people, not as slaves, but in the capacity of free labourers.

From the Carolina Planter.

Mr. Editor—I have experienced much pleasure in perusing the Carolina Planter, and I do believe that it should be circulated with special industry among the small planters and farmers, which may be done, as the low price of the paper puts it in the reach of every man who can read. No farmer can read such a paper with care, and not be benefited infinitely beyond the small amount he pays for it.

Poor men are especially to be benefited by learning how to revive worn-out land, increase the produce of their land, and improve their stock of cattle.

A German came to Pendleton with a wife and five or six children, very poor, so that they had to labour at wages for subsistence. The next year he hired a farm, on which he made a crop. The following year he bought a place adjoining, on which he commenced his work of improvement. He made baskets of willow, which he did at such times as he could not work on his farm—and with the proceeds of their sale began to get a stock of cattle about him, both for family comfort and manure. He has increased his stock, and by their manure, and the industry of his sons, has improved his land so much that I was assured that he would gather at least fifteen bags of cotton, besides a crop of provisions, a large portion of which would be sold. He has now no time to spare from his farm to make baskets. He has been about five years in this country, and with his skill and industry has already paid two thirds of the purchase money of his land, while at the same time he has doubled its productiveness.

Such examples are worthy of notice to encourage others to improve their old lands, and save the leaves of their wood lands for manure. How little value do some people set on manure, when they allow their cattle to lie in the road till you have to walk with care, lest you get your feet soiled. Our German does not so. Every particle of manure is counted as gold, and not a particle permitted to be wasted.

Should you think the above of any value, you are at liberty to use it in any way you please. S. B.

The paper from which we copy, the Emancipator, thus remarks upon the article: "It shows how easily the worn-out soil from which the planters are fleeing through sheer starvation, may be reclaimed by free labour. There are, no doubt, large sections of that state, where extensive tracts of land might be bought at a very low rate, which, if divided into small farms, say of 50 to 200 acres, and cultivated by the diligent and careful hand of the owner of the freehold, would be easily restored to fertility, and reward the labourer with progressive comfort and ultimate independence. It is a good opening for emigrants, particularly from the milder portions of Europe. An influx of such settlers as would till their own acres, and tend their own farm-yards, would soon place the haughty aristocracy in a minority at the elections, and prepare the way for a removal of Carolina's deepest stain. So long as a large portion of the state shall be occupied by planters, the free labouring farmers will probably find a home market for the most of their produce, as may be seen by the following estimate on a single article of consumption.

From the Carolina Planter.

For a rough estimate, let us suppose one half of the pork and bacon consumed in the state is purchased from other states. It will be readily perceived this is not too high an estimate. When "laying in" our meat for the year, the planters in the middle and upper parts of the state, generally calculate a hog for each member of their families, (white and black.) This, we suppose, is not the case in the lower country. But we may safely estimate 100 lbs. of pork as the average amount used yearly by each inhabitant of the state. According to the latest census, the population exceeds a half million. Suppose then 500,000 lbs. of pork to be the quantity consumed, one half of which is purchased at $6 per cwt. The cost will be one million and a half dollars! This we expend annually for meat! !

At the expense of washing away her lands under the culture of cotton, leaving a scanty opportunity for their future improvement, and, in fact, without any good or valuable consideration, ought the state to give annually for pork the enormous sum of $1,500,000! To a condition of affairs so ruinous, how long are we to submit? J. D.

A stated annual meeting of "The Contributors to the Asylum for the relief of persons deprived of the use of their reason," will be held at Mulberry street meeting house, on fourth day, third month 18th, at three o'clock P. M.

SAMUEL MASON, Jr., Clerk.
2d mo. 29th, 1840.

DIED, on the 25th ult., ANN S. wife of Robert Pearsall, of this city, in the 43d year of her age.

PRINTED BY ADAM WALDIE,
Carpenter Street, below Seventh, Philadelphia.

THE FRIEND.

A RELIGIOUS AND LITERARY JOURNAL.

VOL. XIII.   **SEVENTH DAY, THIRD MONTH, 21, 1840.**   **NO. 25.**

EDITED BY ROBERT SMITH.

PUBLISHED WEEKLY.

Price two dollars per annum, payable in advance.

Subscriptions and Payments received by

GEORGE W. TAYLOR,

NO. 50, NORTH FOURTH STREET, UP STAIRS,

PHILADELPHIA.

For "The Friend."

THOUGHTS ON THE TIMES.

NO. III.

The remote causes of the evils which we suffer, I have supposed to be the sudden and prodigious improvement of the mechanic arts, and the unchecked expansion, under the peculiar circumstances of the age, of the system of dealing upon credit. The former of these causes, which have virtually created millions of unresisting and obedient slaves to perform the labour of human hands; slaves who neither eat, nor drink, nor sleep, nor grow weary, nor die, has released large numbers from the servile occupations, and created a corresponding demand for hands to perform the exchanges necessary to circulate this vast accumulation of products.

The extraordinary profits which often reward successful discoveries or contrivances in the mechanic arts have stimulated to the utmost the ingenuity of the age; and by devoting to their improvement a far larger amount of inventive genius than at any former period, has prodigiously accelerated their progress. While these causes have preternaturally quickened the industry of the age and given to it a speculative and bargaining turn, the eager desire for wealth which they have fostered has found new means of gratification in the refinements of the credit system through the agency of monied institutions. For as these can increase the circulating medium of the country, and therewith the general rate of prices, by the simple process of exchanging their notes for those of eager borrowers, they swell its amount, without being able to measure with accuracy the effects of their own agency in raising prices, in spreading the spirit of speculation, and giving impulse to the train of events I have before alluded to.

Unfriendly as are all those results to the monied prosperity of the state, they are far more so to its virtue and morality. The constant fluctuation in prices which is by these means created, holds out a continued inducement to forsake the pursuit of steady business, the profits of which are regular and moderate, and to grasp after sudden wealth in some bold and lucky adventure. The spirit of gambling with all its attendant temptations and vices is thus infused into the operations of trade; the humbler and more laborious occupations, which are the true foundations of national prosperity, are neglected and despised, and a general rush takes place after the chances in each new lottery of speculation.

The inevitable consequence of these undue expansions of the circulating medium which occasion the rise of prices and of the over-wrought excitement of the spirit of adventure, being the rapid collapse of both, it is an equally certain effect of the frequent reverses which thus ensue that the public notions of commercial honesty become greatly relaxed. The magnitude of the engagements which have been entered into, shut out in many cases of bankruptcy the possibility of such a change of circumstances as will enable the bankrupt to pay his debts.

So intimately are the engagements and interests of the merchants blended by the credit system, so closely does the power of each to meet his engagements depend upon the punctuality of all to him, that a large bankruptcy never takes place without involving others in its train. Those periods of collapse, of which I have spoken, overwhelm in the general ruin which ensues, hundreds who have been but indirectly and remotely affected with the spirit of the times. The frequency of these bankruptcies takes away their disgrace. Men come to consider them as the mere chances of a game. The unfortunate adventurers regard themselves in no worse light than as the drawers of a blank instead of a prize. They have only to take their chance in the next adventure, and the next, till a turn in the luck of the game shall bring them in as winners. The close of each unlucky adventure is supposed to close all its obligations, and they begin anew, as we say, clear of the world. It cannot be but that these selfish and dishonest maxims of conduct must in the end corrupt the virtue and integrity of the community to its very core.

And yet success in this career of speculation is scarcely less injurious than failure, to the public morals. The intoxication of sudden wealth is almost always fatal to virtue and moderation, and it is greater when it overtakes the young and presumptuous than when it comes upon those who are more advanced in life and of a cooler temperament. They plunge into a wilder career of extravagance and folly, and seek to acquire distinction by surpassing those around them in the display, as they have outstripped them in the pursuit of wealth. The effects of this extravagance of speculation and expense are felt in a greater or less degree throughout every rank in life. A certain style of living altogether disproportioned to the means of men in moderate circumstances comes to be regarded as essential to respectability, and a heavy tax is thus entailed upon them, which, while it may be said to keep one half the world poor, stimulates the other half to a course of wild enterprise, of which the issue in the greater number of cases is disastrous either to the circumstances or to the morals, or to both.

It is thus, by its tendency to render the slow and humble rewards of honest industry despicable, to convert commercial transactions into a gambling speculation, by the alternations of deceitful prosperity and universal panic; by the extravagance of expense which success engenders; by the desperate expedients and dishonest maxims to which men in the convulsive struggles against impending ruin resort; by the chains which it throws over the spirit, and the subjection of all the other interests of the state and all the other desires of the individual at its feet, that the love of wealth has acquired in our own times a strength which it never before possessed.

A new power, as I have said, has arisen in the state, which has outgrown the other elements of the social system, and which threatens to stifle all those which it cannot render its pliant instruments.

J. D.

For "The Friend."

SKETCHES OF SUPERSTITIONS.

If we want a striking illustration of the weakness of the human intellect, of the gross absurdities it is capable of receiving for truth, of the moral degradation which may, and will be associated with high intellectual refinement and great progress in those arts, which are commonly asserted to have a peculiarly elevating and moralising influence upon society—poetry, music, painting, and sculpture; let us look upon the religious system of the polished Greeks—a people pre-eminent among the nations of antiquity in all these respects, nevertheless, to whose *sage* philosophers and *profound* metaphysicians, reputed to be such deep inquirers into the secrets of nature and Providence, the simple system, taught by the fishermen and tent-makers of barbarian Judea, was foolishness.

The following sketch of the results of their wisdom, is somewhat abridged from a late number of Chambers' Edinburgh Journal.

Let us learn, from so instructive and humiliating a picture, that the most brilliant intellect, without the guidance of divine revelation, has no other superiority, in its attempts to unravel the sacred mysteries, over the dullest, than this; that it is more ingenious in the construction of its errors, and is able to throw a lustre around them which may blind the beholder and effectually prevent their author himself from perceiving their absurdity, how gross soever it may be.

GREEK SUPERSTITIONS.

Mankind have in all ages been prone to the most lamentable superstitions. The enlightened nations of antiquity were subject to them as well as the most ignorant. The Jews, as we are repeatedly informed in Scripture, could with difficulty be restrained from idolatrous and superstitious practices, and confined to the worship and service of the only true God. This remarkable tendency of the Hebrew nation was in all likelihood caused by their sojourn for the space of four hundred years among the Egyptians, whose whole system of religion was a mass of idolatrous observance. They had a number of ideal gods, to whom they erected temples of prodigious size and architectural splendour; the principal of these deities were Osiris and Isis, which are thought to have been typical of the sun and moon. But they also offered worship to various animals, as the ox or bull, (hence the golden calf of the Hebrews), to which they gave the name of Apis; the dog, the wolf, the hawk, the ibis or stork, the cat, and other creatures; they likewise paid adoration to the Nile, personifying it in the crocodile, to which temples were erected, and priests set apart for its service. The Egyptians, notwithstanding their learning, also believed in dreams, lucky and unlucky days, omens, charms, and magic. In a word, they were grossly superstitious, and seem to have had but a feeble conception, if any, of the laws which regulate the ordinary phenomena of nature.

The absurdities of Egyptian superstition formed a basis for what followed in Greece and Rome. The colonisation of the Grecian states occurred about the period that Moses led forth the Jewish host from the land of the Pharaohs (1490 years before Christ), and Egypt at that period was at the height of its civilisation and superstition. The mythology and superstitious observances of the Greeks deserve to be particularly noticed, both as a matter of amusement and instruction. In the first place, they had no idea of an omnipresent and omnipotent God, the creator and ruler of the universe. Their notions of divinity, like those of other pagans, were grovelling and contemptible. The gods whom they adored were imagined to have been at one period rulers or heroes on earth, and still had their habitation somewhere within the Grecian territory, or at no great distance from it. It may be premised that we should have known little of this monstrous system of belief but for the numerous allusions to the gods, their character and pursuits, in the works of the Greek and Roman poets, and also the various sculptured figures and representations which have been brought to light in modern times. Of the innumerable imaginary beings who were thus held in religious reverence, Jupiter was the chief. According to the stories told of him, Jupiter was the son of Saturn, a god who had been compelled by a powerful and tyrannical brother, named Titan, to promise that he would destroy all his male children. This promise Saturn for some time fulfilled, by devouring his sons as soon as they were born; but, at last, Rhea, his wife, contrived to conceal the birth of Jupiter, Neptune, and Pluto, who thus escaped the fate of their brethren. On discovering that Saturn had male offspring alive in contravention of his engagement, Titan deposed him from his authority, and cast him into prison. But Jupiter, having grown up to manhood, overcame Titan in turn, and restored Saturn to his throne. These vicissitudes, it is to be observed, and others that befell the early divinities, were the result of the decrees of Fate; a power over which the heathen gods are represented as having no control. Notwithstanding this filial conduct of Jupiter, he afterwards quarrelled with his father, whom he dethroned and chased into Italy, where Saturn is said to have passed his time in a quiet and useful manner, occupied solely in teaching the rude inhabitants to cultivate and improve the soil. He was afterwards known (under the name of Chronos) as the god of Time, and was usually represented under the figure of an old man holding in one hand a scythe, and in the other a serpent with its tail in its mouth, in allusion to the destructive influence of time, and the endless succession of the seasons. The rule of Saturn in Italy was productive of so much happiness, that the period ever afterwards was called the golden age. After Saturn had been driven into exile, his three sons divided his dominions amongst them. Jupiter reserved to himself the sovereignty of the heavens and the earth. Neptune obtained the empire of the sea, and Pluto received as his share the sceptre of the infernal regions. Jupiter did not, however, enjoy unmolested his supreme dignity, for the offspring of Titan, a race of terrible giants, set the new deity at defiance, and by piling the mountains named Pelion and Ossa on the top of one another, endeavoured to ascend into heaven to pluck him from his throne. The gods, in great alarm, fled from their divine abode on Mount Olympus into Egypt, where they concealed their true character, by assuming the forms of various animals; but Jupiter, assisted by Hercules, at last succeeded in destroying the giants, and reasserting his sovereign sway. Jupiter is always represented on a throne, with thunderbolts in his right hand, and an eagle by his side.

Jupiter took in marriage his sister Juno, who is described as a beautiful but ill-tempered goddess. Nine of the most important of the heathen deities were considered as the children of Jupiter.

Apollo was the god of music, poetry, painting, and medicine. Mars, the god of war, is drawn as an armed man in a car, with an inferior female deity, named Bellona, by his side. Bacchus was the god of wine. His name has given rise to many phrases in our language, expressive of circumstances connected with drinking. Mercury was the messenger of Jupiter, and the god of oratory, of merchandise, and of thieving; Minerva, the goddess of wisdom; Venus, the goddess of beauty and love; Diana, the goddess of hunting and of chastity; Hebe, the goddess of youth; she took the form of a blooming young girl, and was said to bear the cup of Jupiter. Another of the children of Jupiter was Vulcan, who, being of ungainly form and disagreeable in the eyes of his father, was cruelly thrust by him out of heaven, so that he fell on the isle of Lesbos, and, breaking a limb, was lame ever after. On earth Vulcan employed himself as an artificer in iron, and hence he has been assumed as the patron of blacksmiths. Jupiter is said to have employed him in fabricating his thunderbolts. The gay goddess Venus is represented as married to this homely deity, to whom she occasioned much uneasiness by the levity of her conduct. The workshop of Vulcan was believed to be under the burning mountain, Ætna, in Sicily; and the term volcano is derived from that circumstance.

Besides the other attributes and avocations of Apollo, he was the deity of the sun, having the task confided to him of guiding that luminary in its diurnal course through the heavens. His sister, Diana, had a similar charge over the moon. Apollo, or Phœbus, as he was also named, had a son called Phæthon, who, being, like many other young people, self-confident and rash, took advantage of the indulgent disposition of his father to obtain from him the charge of the chariot of the sun for one day. Phæthon had not travelled far on his journey up the heavens, when his fiery steeds became unmanageable, and, running away with the sun, they descended so close to the earth, that that body was set on fire. Jupiter perceived what had happened, and fearing that the whole universe would be consumed, he struck Phæthon dead with a thunderbolt; then, after a good deal of trouble, he extinguished the dangerous conflagration, and set the sun once more in its usual course. Notwithstanding Apollo's care of the sun, that luminary, on its rising, was the special charge of Aurora, who was called the goddess of the morning or dawn—hence the common flowery expression, "the beams of Aurora rising in the east, tipping the distant hills with their golden hues." None of the heathen deities is more frequently referred to than Cupid, the god of love. He was the son of Venus, and though he bore the aspect of a beautiful boy, so great was his power, that he could tame the most ferocious animals, and break in pieces the thunderbolts of Jupiter.

There was a number of minor deities. Hymen, the god of marriage; Æolus, the god of the winds, which he kept in caverns, and, when he chose let them loose; Pan, the god of the country, flat-nosed and horned, with legs, feet, and tail, like those of a goat; Ceres, the goddess of agriculture, whose beautiful daughter, named Proserpine, was carried off by Pluto, and installed as queen of the infernal regions. Ceres, in despair at the loss of her daughter, and uncertain as to her fate, lighted a torch at mount Ætna, and sought for her over the whole earth. In the course of her wanderings she arrived in Attica, and, finding its inhabitants ignorant of husbandry, furnished them with grain, and taught them how to cultivate their fields. She at length learned the fate of her daughter, and immediately demanded redress from Jupiter, who promised to compel Pluto to restore Proserpine, provided she had eaten nothing since her descent into hell. On inquiry it was ascertained that she had eaten some pomegranates, so that her return to the upper world was, according to the laws of the infernal regions, impracticable. But Jupiter, compassionating her disconsolate parent, ordained that Proserpine should divide her time between her mother and her husband, residing six months with each, alternately.

Inexorable destiny, was personified by three sisters, called *the Fates*, who represented the Past, the Present, and the Future. They were poetically described as constantly employed in spinning the thread of human life. One held the distaff, another spun, and the third cut the thread when it had reached its appointed length. To the decrees of these stern sisters even Jupiter himself, it was said, must yield, and his thunders, which affrighted all the other divinities, were heard by them undisturbed. To the three *Furies* belonged the task of punishing the guilty both on earth and in hell. Instead of hair, their heads were covered with serpents, and their looks were fierce and terrible; wars, famine, and pestilence, proceeded from them, and *g,ief*, *terror*, and *madness*, were painted as their inseparable followers.

These avengers form a striking contrast to another sisterly trio, to whom the ancients gave the name of the Graces. The Graces were named Aglaia, Thalia, and Euphrosyne, and their aspect and attributes corresponded with the common name they bore. They were the daughters of Bacchus and Venus, and were usually represented as unattired, and linked in each other's arms. The nine Muses were named Thalia, Melpomene, Calliope, Clio, Erato, Euterpe, Polyhymnia, Terpsichore, and Urania. They were the patronesses of literature and the fine arts, and resided on Parnassus, a lofty mountain in the district of Phocis. Thalia presided over comedy; Melpomene over tragedy; Erato over amatory poetry; Polyhymnia over lyric poetry; Calliope over heroic or epic poetry and eloquence; Clio over history; Euterpe over music; Terpsichore over dancing; and Urania over the study of astronomy.

(To be continued.)

THE WHITE STORK.

This tall and stately bird (*Ciconia alba*), although a visiter of the continent of Europe, from the north of Spain to Prussia, and particularly common in Holland, is only seen in this country as exhibited in menageries. It was once, however, common; and its almost complete extinction here is one of the many evidences of the changes which man produces by the operations of his industry. The marshy grounds, which formerly existed to a great extent in England, have been drained and cultivated. One or two solitary storks have been shot in this country during the present century. The bird generally stands from three and a half to four feet high, including the long neck. The feet are webbed, and the legs are exceedingly long, and do not appear of a thickness commensurate to the bulk they sustain. The neck is also of great length; and the beak is straight, long, pointed, and compressed. The stork walks slowly, and with measured steps; but its flight is powerful and long continued, and it is accustomed to traverse the higher regions of the air.

Storks are birds of passage. They spend the winter in the deserts of Africa and Arabia, and in summer return to towns and villages in

colder latitudes, where they build their nests on the summits of old towers and belfries, on the chimnies of the highest houses, and sometimes in dead trees. In marshy districts, where the services of the bird in destroying reptiles are of peculiar value, the people frequently fix an old cart-wheel, by the nave, in an horizontal position, to the extremity of a strong perpendicular pole;—an accommodation which seems so very eligible to the birds, that they rarely fail to construct their capacious habitations on such platforms. The nest is a large cylindrical structure, built very strongly and durably with sticks, twigs, and strong reeds; and lined on the inside with fine dry herbs, mosses, and down gathered from the bushes. These fabrics last many years, and to them the faithful couples yearly direct their unerring course, from far distant regions, to deposit their eggs, and rear their young.

The eggs in a nest vary in number; not less than two, and seldom exceeding four. The female covers these with the most tender solicitude. Instances are recorded in which she has rather chosen to die than resign her charge. An affecting incident of this nature occurred on the day of the "memorable battle of Friedland," as related by M. Bory de St. Vincent, in an article of the "Encyclopédie Moderne." A farm in the neighbourhood of the city was set on fire by the falling of a bomb, and the conflagration extended to an old tree on which a pair of storks had built their nest. It was then the season of incubation, and the mother would not quit the nest until it was completely enveloped in flame. She then flew up perpendicularly; and, when she had attained to a great height, dashed down into the midst of the fire, as if endeavouring to rescue the precious deposit from destruction. In one of these descents, enveloped in fire and smoke, she fell into the midst of the burning embers, and perished.

This constancy during the period of incubation is succeeded by the most assiduous care in the rearing of the young. The parents never lose sight of them. While one of the two is abroad in search of serpents, lizards, frogs, or snails, the other remains in charge of the nest. When the young have acquired strength and vigour, it is highly interesting to observe the tender couple assist them in their first career through the air. The progency are said to repay this care and kindness, when the parents are old and feeble, by supporting their wings, when weary, in the long flights of their migration. But though it be true that the weak and old are thus assisted by the vigorous and young, we have no means of knowing that the assistants are the progeny of the assisted. The parents and the young continue to live together until the season of migration. For about a fortnight previous to that event, all the storks of the district assemble frequently in some neighbouring plain, and appear to hold a council to determine the destination, and the time of departure.

When they at length take their departure, the flocks are generally of great extent, and vary much in compactness. They are sometimes, according to Dr. Shaw, half a mile in breadth, and take three hours in passing. As they have no voice, their course is usually un-

attended by any noise but that of their wings; but, when any thing occurs to startle them, or engage their attention, they make an extraordinary clattering noise, which may be heard to a great distance, by striking the mandibles quickly and forcibly together. By their migrations, they enjoy at all times a nearly equal temperature; avoiding those severe seasons in which the reptiles that form their food remain hid and torpid during a considerable part of the year.

There is a peculiar interest attached to this bird, from the efficient protection which, in all ages and countries, it has received from man. In ancient Egypt it was a capital crime to kill a stork; and there, and elsewhere, its safety and existence are still defended by penal laws. Indeed, there is, perhaps, no country which it is accustomed to visit where its death would not be avenged, either by legal penalties or popular indignation. This protection is, doubtless, in some measure owing to the amiable dispositions it exhibits; but must chiefly be attributed to the importance of its services in destroying the reptiles which abound in the districts that it usually frequents. The protection it receives is returned by the confidence with which the stork constructs its domicile in the midst of the most densely populated cities, and views from it the near approach of man without alarm.

In Bagdad, and some other of the more remote cities of Asiatic Turkey, the nests of storks present a very remarkable appearance. The *minars*, or towers of the mosques, at Constantinople, and most other parts of Turkey, are tall, round pillars, surmounted by a very pointed cone; but at Bagdad, the absence of this cone enables these birds to build their nests upon the summit; and as the diameter of the nest generally corresponds with that of the minar, it appears as a part of it, and a regular termination to it. The curious effect is not a little increased by the appearance of the bird itself in the nest, which thus, as part of the body and its long neck are seen above the edge, appears the crowning object of the pillar. The Turks hold the bird in more than even the usual esteem, which may be partly attributed to its gesticulations, which they suppose to resemble some of their own attitudes of devotion. Their name for the stork is *Hadji lug-lug*; the former word, which is the honorary title of a pilgrim, it owes to its annual migrations, and its apparent attachment to their sacred edifices. The latter portion of the denomination, " lug-lug," is an attempt to imitate the noise which the bird makes. The regard of the Turks is so far understood and returned by the intelligent stork, that, in cities of mixed population, it rarely or never builds its nest on any other than a Turkish house. J. Hartley, in his " Researches in Greece and the Levant," remarks:—" The Greeks have carried their antipathy to the Turks to such a pitch, that they have destroyed all the storks in the country. On inquiring the reason, I was informed 'The stork is a Turkish bird: it never used to build its nest on the house of a Greek, but always on that of a Turk!' The tenderness which the Turks display towards the feathered tribe is indeed a pleasing trait; in their character."—*Penny Mag.*

The National Gazette remarks, in reference to the following poem, it "is from the pen of William Pitt Palmer. It enriches the last number of the Knickerbocker magazine, and we transfer it to our columns as a poetic effusion of rare excellence in thought and diction."

LIGHT.

"Bright effluence of bright essence increate!
Before the sun, before the heavens, thou wert."—Milton.

I.

From the quickened womb of the primal gloom
The sun rolled black and bare,
Till I wove him a vest for his Ethiop breast,
Of the threads of my golden hair;
And when the broad tent of the firmament
Arose on his airy spars,
I pencilled the hue of its matchless blue,
And spangled it round with stars.

II.

I painted the flowers of the Eden bowers,
And their leaves of living green,
And mine were the dyes in the sinless eyes
Of Eden's virgin queen;
And when the Fiend's art on her trustful heart
Had fastened its moral spell,
In the silvery sphere of the first born tear
To the trembling earth I fell.

III.

When the waves that burst o'er a world accursed
Their work of wrath had sped,
And the Ark's lone few, the tried and true,
Came forth among the dead,
With the wondrous gleams of my braided beams,
I bade their terrors cease,
As I wrote on the roll of the storm's dark scroll
God's covenant of peace.

IV.

Like a pall at rest on a pulseless breast,
Night's funeral shadow slept,
Where shepherd swains on the Bethlehem plains
Their lonely vigils kept;
When I flashed on their sight the heralds bright
Of heaven's redeeming plan,
As they chanted the morn of a Saviour born—
Joy, joy, to the outcast Man!

V.

Equal favour I show to the lofty and low,
On the just and unjust I descend;
E'en the blind, whose vain spheres roll in darkness and tears,
Feel my smile the blest smile of a friend;
Nay, the flower of the waste by my love is embraced,
As the rose in the garden of kings;
At the chrysalis bier of the worm I appear,
And lo! the gay butterfly's wings!

VI.

The desolate Morn, like a mourner forlorn,
Conceals all the pride of her charms,
Till I bid the bright Hours chase the Night from her bowers,
And lead the young Day to her arms;
And when the gay rover seeks Eve for his lover,
And sinks to her balmy repose,
I wrap their soft rest by the zephyr-fanned west,
In curtains of amber and rose.

VII.

From my sentinel steep, by the night-brooded deep,
I gazed with unslumbering eye,
When the cynosure star of the mariner
Is blotted from the sky;
And guided by me through the merciless sea,
Though sped by the hurricane's wings,
His compassless bark, lone, weltering, dark,
To the haven-home safely he brings.

VIII.

I waken the flowers in their dew-spangled bowers,
The birds in their chambers of green,
And mountain and plain glow with beauty again,
As they bask in my matinal sheen.
O if such the glad worth of my presence to earth,
Though fitful and fleeting the while,
What glories must rest on the home of the blest,
Ever bright with the Deity's smile!

W. P. P.

From the Farmers' Cabinet.

QUINCE TREES.

Those who love good fruit should aid in its cultivation.

The cultivation of the quince is much neglected, though it may be justly ranked among our most valuable fruits. For preserves it has long maintained a distinguished rank, and the fruit either in a green or dried state, is not surpassed by any other article for communicating a pleasant and agreeable flavour to pies made of apples. It is easily propagated by layers, and also by cuttings, and any approved kinds may be perpetuated by grafting in the usual manner.

It produces the finest, fairest fruit when planted in a soft, moist soil, in a rather shady or sheltered situation. It keeps well if properly managed, and always sells for a very high price; the markets never being overstocked with them, as is the case with many other fruits in plentiful seasons.

The quince derives its name of Cydonia, from the town of Cydon, in the Isle of Crete, whence it was originally brought. There are four kinds of the quince; the pear quince, from the resemblance of its shape; the apple quince; the Portugal quince, which is less harsh and more juicy than the two preceding kinds; and the eatable quince, which is less astringent and milder than either of the other kinds enumerated. The trees being small, they can be planted ten or twelve feet apart along fences, or in places where they won't interfere with other trees, or the business of agriculture.

It is hoped that the present season will not be permitted to pass over without the cultivation of this valuable fruit being considerably extended among our farmers and gardeners. Put some cuttings in a suitable soil and situation, and see how they will grow and flourish; this would be an interesting amusement for the boys and girls who love good pies, and would occupy but a few minutes of their time.

PHILIP.

Change of Soil Effecting a Change in Plants.

A change of soil may be effected either by removing a plant from one spot of earth to another, differing from it in fertility, or by the addition of manure, producing a change in the character of the soil in which the plant grows, without changing the location of the plant. The effect of removing a plant from a comparatively barren to a more fertile soil, is to increase the size of all its parts, and often to convert its organs of one kind into those of another. Experience has taught us, that it is advantageous to supply food to plants artificially. Where increase in the size of vegetables, without reference to their number, is desired, it can almost always be accomplished by affording an increased supply of all the ingredients of the food of plants, distributed in a well pulverised soil, in such a manner that the roots of the plants can easily reach it. The effect thus produced can be greatly increased by additional heat and moisture, and by a partial exclusion of the direct rays of the sun, so as to modify the evaporation of fluids from the plant. Experience alone can determine to what extent this may profitably be carried in the case of such species of vegetable. The results which have been produced in some instances, are truly remarkable. Loudon states, that cabbages have been produced, weighing half a hundred weight, apples a pound and a half, and cabbage-roses of four inches in diameter, or more than a foot in circumference. By cultivation and a change of soil, the appearance of many trees has been entirely altered. The wild crab-apple, the original stock from which all our vast variety of apples have sprung, has its stem and branches set thick with thorns. On removing it to a more fertile soil and more favourable circumstances, all these thorns have disappeared, and their place has been supplied by fruit-bearing branches. Yet all the distinctive characteristics of the tree, the structure of its wood and bark, the shape and arrangement of its leaves, the form and aggregation of its flowers—indeed, all that a botanist would consider characteristic of the plant, have remained unchanged.

Perhaps the most remarkable changes which result from a change of soil, are those of organs of one kind into those of another. It is by such changes that all our double flowers have been obtained. The organs which are most commonly converted into others, are the stamens, and next to them the pistils. In the hundred-leafed rose, and some other double roses, almost all the stamens have been converted into petals: in the flowering cherry, the pistils have been converted into green leaves—in the double columbine, a part of the stamens have been converted into petals, another part into nectaries, whilst a third part have retained their original form. The perfect regularity with which the changes have taken place in the last mentioned flower, is worthy of notice. Wherever one stamen has been converted into a petal, a corresponding one has always been converted into a nectary; and so regularly have these changes proceeded, that by careful dissection, you may separate one of these double flowers into several single ones, each perfect in itself, and destitute of none of its appropriate parts. Where flowers have been doubled by art, the only sure way of propagating them, is by some means by which the new plant should be nothing more than a continuation of the old one, as by slips or cuttings. Whenever the seed is resorted to, there is danger that the plant will revert to its original type, and the flowers appear single again. A change of colour also frequently results from a change of soil. Respecting the nature of this change, no fixed laws have been yet discovered. As a general thing, however, the brightness of the colours of a flower is injured by enriching the soil in which it grows; and hence florists, when they wish to procure tulips of very bright colours, prefer planting the bulbs in a light sandy soil, which is rather poor than otherwise.—*Farmer's Register.*

LIFE OF WILLIAM CATON.

(Continued from page 192.)

[In the autumn of 1660 this indefatigable servant of Jesus Christ found his mind engaged, for the fourth time, in the love of the Gospel, to visit Holland, &c.]

I passed towards Dover, where I took shipping for Zealand, in order to my going for Holland; and after some hardship sustained at sea, (the more by reason of tempestuous weather and contrary winds,) through the providence of the Lord I got to Flushing, where I staid but little, and passed for Middleburgh, where I visited the very few Friends that were in the city; and afterwards I went to Treveare, where I found a vessel almost ready to sail for Dort in Holland. And truly in my journey I was exceedingly filled with the Lord's love, and the power of his might, though I was as alone, not having any Friend in company with me, but many passengers; and among the rest a Catholic, who was filled with much envy and wickedness, and uttered desperate threatening words against me, giving some to understand what a small matter it was in their account, to do a man a mischief who spoke against their religion. In the height of his wickedness he boasted of a pardon which he had in his pocket, not only for the sins he had committed, but also for what he should commit: but before we parted, the power of the Lord reached to his own witness in the man, whereby he was smitten in himself for his folly, and his fury against me was much turned into friendship towards me. Thus do we often see the Lord changing the hearts of our enemies, and restraining them from the evil they intend against us; which we must needs acknowledge to be the Lord's doing, which is and often hath been marvellous in our eyes; to him therefore be glory, honour, and dominion, for ever and ever.

Afterwards I got well to Rotterdam (through mercy,) where I found Friends very well in the Lord. And after we had been sweetly comforted, together, I took leave of them, and went to the city of Leyden, where I also visited that little flock, with whom my soul at that time was comforted. From thence I passed to the city of Amsterdam, where my refreshment was augmented in the Lord among his babes in that place, at which I arrived the sixth of the Tenth month, 1660.

Afterwards it was upon me with another Friend (called Peter Hendrix) to go into Friesland, which accordingly we did; and in due time (through mercy) we arrived well upon a First day in the morning, at a place called Dockham, where we went into the meeting of the Doopsgesinds, (i. e. Baptists so called,) which was indeed very large. When he that spoke had done, I stood up and began to declare the everlasting truth in their own language; but they were much divided among themselves, for some would gladly have had me, others would not suffer me; but one of the chiefest of their teachers was very moderate, and spoke to this purpose, that if I had a nearer way to God to declare, than that which they knew, or one that was more excellent than theirs, they would willingly hear me. And in order thereunto many of them came together in the afternoon, and heard me declare that way

which I preferred before theirs, and affirmed it to be nearer to God, and more excellent than theirs; and little they had at that time to object against it. Before we parted they were so far satisfied, that by their great silence (in which they sat as if they had been Friends,) they seemed not to have anything further to object. After the meeting was done, the aforesaid teacher invited us to his house, and to take up our lodging there, which (for several reasons) we were free to accept of. When we got to his house at night, many people followed us, so that we had a very good meeting in his house that night. And when we had continued there some time in very good service, we left that place and returned to Leewarden, the metropolitan city of that province: there we found some in whom there were desires after the truth, with whom we had some meeting or meetings. Afterwards we passed to a place called Mackham, where there were also many of the aforesaid Doopsgesinds, and there we were entertained by an old man, who had been a preacher among them for many years.

When the First day came, it was upon us to go to their place of worship, which accordingly we did; and there we waited until he that was speaking had done: afterwards I began to speak, but he would not suffer me, (to wit, he that had preached,) but became presently very angry, though the people would gladly have heard me; but he would not suffer them; and he became finally so uncivil, that he put the people out of the meeting-place with his own hands; at which some being much offended, a skipper or master of a vessel, stood up and said, *Wilt ghy hem alhier niet toelaeten om te spreechen, dan sall hy tot mynents spreechen*; that is, If they would not suffer me to speak there, then I should speak at his house; and the same man came and took us to his house, where afterwards we had a pretty good meeting, and such as had desires to hear the truth (which the aforesaid angry man would not suffer me to declare in their meeting-place) those came thither, so that some very good service I had there for the Lord.

When we were free of that place, we went to Worchum, where we also had a meeting or meetings. When we were pretty clear of those parts, we returned again for Amsterdam, where we were received with joy and gladness by Friends there, who rejoiced with us in the good service which we had had; and blessed be the Lord for our preservation.

[From this city W. C. addressed a letter to Friends in England, (as is supposed,) from which the following extracts are selected.

"O! my beloved Friends,—It is delightful to me to meditate upon the Lord's love to you, and it is a comfort and a refreshment to my soul to feel you in the unity of the eternal Spirit, wherein I have daily communion with you, though I am necessitated, for the scattered seed's sake, to be much as without the camp, where the reproach is borne, with many weights and burdens, by reason of which my soul is sometimes bowed down: yet O! my friends, I share with you of that joy and peace, love and life, which abound in your tents; and

therein can I rejoice with you in the midst of our trials and sufferings, though as to the outward I am far separate from you; yet know that I have no more want and scarcity than I had when I was with you; for my heart is full of love, my mouth with praise, and mine eyes with tears, when I behold your integrity and innocency, your faithfulness and constancy, under your trials and burdens. Often is my soul poured forth unto my Father on your behalf;—unto whom a child is born, unto whom a Son is given; whose name is called the Prince of Peace, and of the increase of whose government there shall be no end. And this is He, of whom I bare testimony to the nations, though they abhor Him, and say within themselves,—"we will not have Him to rule over us, or we will not suffer any of His messengers and servants to dwell among us, but we will imprison them, and put them to death," &c. And thus the Lord may suffer them to do, until they have filled up the measure of their iniquities, as the Amorites did; and then shall his iron rod be stretched over them, by which they shall be broken to pieces like a potter's vessel, who have abhorred Him, and hated Him without a cause; but in that day will he spare you, who have followed Him through great tribulation.—In the meantime, O! beloved, he will try your faith and patience; but be ye not therefore troubled, for he knows what is good for you, in whom he has chosen in these latter days to manifest his power and glory, to the families of the earth, whose glory and dignity must be stained and brought to nothing.'

'—The sudden and violent storm which ye have had in England,[*] hath also stirred the waters very much here, so that they rage and swell, as if they would prevail beyond the bounds which are set for them : and much mire and dirt they cast up, vending part of it forth in their currents or weekly intelligence, and part in ballads, wherein they seem to lay that chiefly to the charge of Friends which at late happened in London, as if they had conspired together to do much more than what was done: and the vulgar sort of people that have no feeling of the witness of God in themselves, they believe it; but some sober, and honest-hearted men slight it, and do not much regard it: but the baser sort hath taken a mighty occasion hereby against us, and they rage and tear as if they would swallow us up quick. And we are credibly informed that fifty of the wildest men here have combined together, not only to break our meeting, but also to pull down the house to the ground, where we have often met: so that ye may understand, that we are here daily in as great jeopardy as they in England, that are not yet cast into prison. The last First day there were some very wicked men at our meeting, who were exceeding desperate and violent; but blessed be the Lord! they were not suffered to do much harm, and that which they did, was more to the house than to Friends, who are given up to the will of the Lord, as well to suffer with you for the Truth, as to rejoice with you in the Truth.

[*] See the Histories of England, concerning the troubles consequent upon the return of Charles II.

"Now friends, ye know this day hath been long foreseen, and often have ye been told that it would come: and seeing it is come, think not these fiery trials strange which attend, though for the present they may not seem joyous; yet without all controversy, good will be brought forth by them to some, and these things shall not be in vain; for it appears to me that they work together for the hastening of that work, which the Lord is determined to cut short in righteousness for the elect's sake. Therefore, let that reasoning part be kept under, that would say, this would hinder the work: for who art thou that reasonest with the Lord? is not the work his? and knowest thou better than he, what would be for the furtherance of it? If not, be still, patient, and content; and let him work for his Truth with us, or without us, according to the good pleasure of his will; who hath all power in his hand; and this is he in whom we have believed, who commands the winds and the seas to be still, and they obey him; have we not seen it, and are not we his witnesses? if so, let us be patient a little, and we shall see the Lord work wonderfully. Though I have writ thus large to you at present, yet my heart is as full of love as it was when I began to set pen to paper; so in the fulness, do I most dearly salute you, and in it do I leave you, and commit you unto Him, who is of power to establish all your hearts in the living Truth, in which I remain, your dear brother in the fellowship of sufferings, in the Gospel of Peace,

WILLIAM CATON."

Amsterdam, 25th of 11th mo. 1660.

[*From the Swarthmore Collection.*]

After that I continued several months in Holland, having a very good service, sometimes at Atkmore, sometimes at Haarlem, sometimes at Leyden, sometimes at Rotterdam, but mostly at Amsterdam; and I was much alone, especially about that time, for William Ames who had had very good service in those parts, was sometime in Germany, and sometime at Hamburgh: and once he travelled through Bohemia, and to Dantzie, and from thence to Poland; and John Higgins who had been much in Holland, was seldom with me neither; so that (I say) I was much alone in the country: but indeed the mercy and goodness of the Lord abounded very much towards me, for which my soul hath cause for ever to praise and magnify his name.

About the time called Whitsuntide, in the year 1661, it was upon me to come over to London, chiefly to visit Friends there and thereabouts, after their great suffering. And the Lord gave me an opportunity, with two other Friends, (viz. William Welch, and Benjamin Furly;) and in due time, through the mercy of the Lord, we got well over to Harwich, and from thence to Colchester, and so to London; where I was at several precious meetings, and was more than a little refreshed with the brethren, not only at London but also at Kingston. But being pretty much pressed in spirit to return for Holland again (where there was some needful service for me, which required my hasting,) I took my leave of friends and brethren, in much love and unity at London, with whom my refreshment at that time was so great, that the remembrance of it

afterwards was a great comfort to me. Afterwards we got well back to Colchester, where we had a very large and precious meeting, to our own and Friends' strength in the Lord. We then went to Harwich, from whence we passed over to Holland again, and had a prosperous and successful journey of it (blessed be the Lord,) which tended much to our encouragement.

At that time I had in hand the book, called, An Abridgement,* which I printed at Rotterdam; and after I had finished it, I visited Friends in most places of that country, and had several good meetings among them, to their and my refreshment in the Lord.

About that time it was upon me to go into Germany, partly to visit Friends, and partly to speak with the Prince Palatine, and some else in that country: in order thereunto I took my leave of Friends in Holland with much tenderness of heart, committing them to the custody and protection of the Almighty. And about the tenth of the seventh month 1661, I with my dear brother William Ames set forwards on our journey towards Germany, and in due time we got well to Cologne; from thence we travelled towards the Grave de Whitt's country, who had promised large liberty to all sorts of people, that would come and inhabit in his dominion. When we came there, we went to his house, and had an opportunity to speak with him; and he reasoned very moderately with us a pretty while, and we endeavoured to inform ourselves as much as we could from his own mouth, of the certainty of what was published in his name concerning liberty. But in the end, we perceived clearly from him, that his invitation, though promising liberty or toleration, was not so much out of love to tender consciences, as out of covetousness for what was theirs, as since hath more evidently appeared.*

After we had had a very good time with him, and had informed ourselves sufficiently, and tried the ground from whence such things had proceeded, we parted from him, and went up into the country, and had some good opportunity to speak with some of the priests and people; and after we had satisfied and cleared ourselves, we left those parts, and travelled on our journey towards the Palz or Palatinate; where in due time we arrived, through the mercy of the Lord, at a place called Kriesheim, where we found a small remnant of Friends, that bore their testimony to the truth; with whom we were refreshed, after our long and pretty tedious journey. There we continued some time, helping them to gather their grapes, it being the time of their vintage; and when we had had a time of refreshment among them, we travelled towards Heidleberg, the place of the prince's residence. Soon after we came at Heidleberg, we went to the captain of the prince's life-guard, and made known our desires to him as concerning speaking with the prince; and he was willing to procure us access to him: so that soon after, the prince sent for us to his palace, and he be-

ing at dinner, caused us to stand by him; and withal he heard very moderately what we had to say to him. Afterwards we presented several books to him, all which he kindly received from us, and was indeed very courteous to us, and reasoned very familiarly with us in the presence of the great ones that were with him; and after we had had a favourable opportunity with him, we returned again to our lodging.

In a short time after, we went up to the prince's palace again, having some further occasion to speak with him; and having free access to him, we found him very moderate and courteous to us as before. He spoke to his captain to cause us to sit down at the table with his attendants, which we found freedom in the Lord to do; for he seemed to be somewhat troubled before, when he had observed our unfreeness in that thing. After dinner we had much private discourse with him, (the governor of Manheim being only present,) and we found him to be pretty courteously affected towards us; and therefore we were the more free to declare the truth in much plainness to him, and zealous in pleading Friends' cause with him, who had suffered by the priests about their tithe in his dominion. After we had spent some hours with him that day, we returned to our lodging again.

(To be continued.)

From the Hampshire Gazette.

ANTIDOTES FOR POISONS.

The following communication from Dr. Hall will be read with interest at this time. Every family should keep the antidotes named by Dr. Hall, laid up where they can be instantly obtained, in any case of emergency. When an active poison is taken, the only safety of the sufferer is in the *immediate* application of an antidote. A short delay is fatal.

"Every bitter hath its sweet, every poison its antidote."

The repeated cases of poisoning which have recently occurred in this village, have induced me to make public some of the most efficient antidotes for poisons, especially for those which are found in the domestic department of almost every family. I am induced to make these "antidotes to poisons" public, because in instances of poisoning, from accident or otherwise, the urgency of the case does not allow us to wait for medical assistance, which is scarcely ever obtained without some delay, and consequently of comparatively little or no avail when it is, and the life of an individual is often lost by waiting, when by prompt interference it might have been saved.

I have confined myself to mentioning those antidotes which are the most simple and the most easily obtained; and it is worthy of notice, that *those* are the very articles that are most effectual. The practice of forcing down large doses of powerful and irritating emetics, which in themselves are almost sufficient to destroy life, cannot be too strongly reprehended. When emetics are necessary, as they sometimes are, especially in those cases of poisoning by substances which produce great torpor of the system, (such as opium and all the narcotics,) the safety of the patient requires that the dormant energies of the stomach be

* * "An Abridgement or Compendious Commemoration of the remarkable Chronologies which are contained in that celebrated Ecclesiastical History of Eusebius," &c. 1661. Reprinted 1689. Whiting's Catalogue.

aroused. In these cases nothing is better to be given than ground black mustard, a large tea spoonful of which may be mixed with water and swallowed at once. It operates very promptly—it is perfectly safe, and nothing can be more effectual.

As a general rule, the effects of poisons are better counteracted by articles, which, being taken into the stomach *immediately* after the poison is swallowed, enter into combination with the poison, and form with it a new substance, either harmless in itself, or incapable of being acted on by the fluids of the stomach.

For *Oil of Vitriol*, the best antidote is large doses of magnesia and water, or what is still better, equal parts of soft soap and water.

For *Aqua Fortis*, same remedy as the last.

For *Oxalic acid*—(This resembles Epsom salts, and is often used for bed-bug poison.) Chalk and water renders it perfectly inert, forming an insoluble salt of lime. Magnesia is also a good antidote.

For *Tartar emetic* in poisonous doses, Peruvian bark and water renders it harmless; if that cannot be procured, use a strong decoction of tea until it can.

For *Saltpetre*, (which is also sometimes mistaken for salts) a prompt emetic of mustard and water—afterwards mucilages and small doses of laudanum.

For *Opium* or *Laudanum* in over doses, an emetic of mustard, constant motion in a wagon or otherwise, and the stomach pump, where it can be obtained.

For *Lunar Caustic*, (the principal ingredient in indelible ink,) common salt forms an insoluble substance which is harmless.

For *Corrosive Sublimate*.—(This is the most common bed-bug poison, but it has probably destroyed as many persons as bed-bugs.) The whites of eggs mixed with water is the best and most effectual remedy. This should be given until free vomiting takes place. (Albumen renders this poison harmless, the whites of eggs are mostly albumen.)

For *any of the Salts of Copper*.—The same remedy as the last.

For *Arsenic*.—Three or four cases are reported as having been cured by doses of magnesia. But the only sure antidote is the *freshly prepared* hydrated per oxide of iron. This is not always at hand, and cannot well be prepared except by a physician, or an apothecary.

From the Farmers' Cabinet.

Benevolence in Birds—their usefulness, &c.

The communication of H. C, in the Farmer of the 5th inst., relative to the canker-worm, in which he says the only effectual remedy against these insects known to him is " the encouragement of birds," brings fresh to our recollection some reminiscences respecting this persecuted, interesting, and useful race, which we think will be pleasing to our readers, particularly to the younger ones. We can hardly say with the writer of the article, that " killing a small bird should be placed in our penal code next to killing a child ;" but we do say that it ought to be met with a punishment sufficient to prevent the destruction which annually takes place, in mere wantonness or sport, among the innocent songsters of our groves and orchards. We have been almost disposed in times past to bring the boys before Judge Lynch, and might probably have done it could we have put our hands upon them.

While residing in Lancaster a few years since, we were located near the river which runs through the town, whose banks and intervals are ornamented with numerous fine elms and other trees, which add much to the beauty of this pleasant village : in these trees the birds congregate in great numbers, and rear their young. A gigantic elm, the admiration of travellers and the pride of the village, threw out its wide-spreading branches over the cottage in which we dwelt, and while it shielded us from the scorching sun, afforded in its ample head, (a forest almost in itself,) a secure retreat for a great variety of birds, whose movements afforded much amusement for the family. Among these birds were a pair of crow black-birds, who had selected the fork of a partly decayed limb very high in the tree, as a place to build their nest and rear their young. Having in my juvenile days some prejudice against this bird, as I was taught, that with the crow it would dig up the newly sprouted corn, and commit sundry other depredations, I therefore viewed them with a suspicious eye as I saw them in company from day to day upon my newly planted grounds, busily engaged in helping themselves to what they liked best. I satisfied myself soon, however, that they had been vilely slandered, and that they were friends and not enemies : it was evident they were clearing my grounds of grubs and worms at a great rate. They soon found that I was no enemy to them, and consequently became quite tame and familiar, following the plough or harrow with nearly as much confidence as the domestic fowls. It appeared that there was a good state of feeling among the numerous tribes that inhabited the tree, consisting as they did of so many families, embracing the robin, blue-bird, sparrow, golden robin, and a variety of others, and things seemed to prosper among them and go on well, until the night before old fashioned "'lection," (a fatal day to the feathered tribe :) during that night there was a very high wind : early in the morning I was awakened by an unusual clamour among the birds, and rose to ascertain the cause—I found that the decayed limb, on the fork of which was the crow black-bird's nest, had been broken off by the wind, and the nest and contents, (five young ones,) precipitated to the ground, and that four of them were dead or dying. The surviving one was nearly fledged, and could fly a little. I picked it up from the grass, and placed it in a secure situation, supposing the distressed parents would take care of it. The old one continued their clamour all the morning, which, with the sympathising cries of the other birds, formed a melancholy concert.

While the black-birds had perched upon a neighbouring tree near the road, still giving vent to their sorrow, a boy passed with his gun, fired, and brought them both to the ground and carried them away in triumph : luckily for the boy, I did not witness the barbarous deed, but it was noted by one of the family and soon reported to me. As I had become somewhat interested in the unfortunate orphan, I proposed to my children that they should feed it with worms until it could take care of itself, and accordingly placed it in a pen under the tree and returned to my work near by. It was not long before I heard from the young bird its peculiar note which it uttered when its parent brought food, and on looking up, saw that it had hopped up on to a joist to which the board fence was fastened, and to my great delight and surprise, beheld a blue-bird in the act of feeding it. That beautiful passage of scripture flashed upon my mind—"Are not five sparrows sold for two farthings ? and not one of them is forgotten before God." My curiosity was now raised to see what would be the issue, and I soon found that any further care on my part would be superfluous, for the young chap had fallen into better hands. It was with the deepest interest I watched the movements of this devoted pair of blue-birds to their adopted one, for it appeared that both male and female had taken part in this work of disinterested benevolence, and devoted themselves with unremitting attention to its wants, until it was able to take care of itself. For a couple of days it remained near the spot where I first saw the birds feeding it, and being near a window, had a good opportunity to see how things went on between them. It appeared that the young one kept his benefactors pretty busy ; for their incessant labours could hardly satisfy the young gormandiser, as upon an estimate, after much attention, he received a portion of food every two and a half minutes during the day, which appeared to consist of worms and grubs. The black-bird probably weighed twice as much as both blue-birds, and when it opened its capacious mouth to receive the food, it seemed as though its kind friends were in imminent danger of being swallowed whole. The blue-birds appeared alternately with the food and lit down a few feet in front of the bird on the fence, and viewed with apparent astonishment, the extended mouth of the young one for a second, then hopping up, deposited the food, then as quick back to the first position, regarding for another second with marks of satisfaction, the object of charity, and then away for a new supply.

In a few days the young bird found the use of its wings, and was followed from tree to tree upon the premises by its faithful providers, for nearly a week : it had by that time learned to find its own food ; and soon it fell in company with some of its own kith and kin, and I could recognise it no more. Whether it ever returned to express its gratitude to its foster parents, we have never learned.

Many of my neighbours could testify to the above facts, as some of them called daily to see for themselves. J. B.

—

To take a rancid taste from butter.—Melt and simmer it ; then dip into it a crust of bread well toasted on both sides. Bad butter may be cured by melting it in a considerable quantity of hot water, skimming it off, and working it again in a churn, with the addition of salt and fine sugar.

For "The Friend."

To Friends' Reading Room Association.

The managers report, that the rooms have been kept regularly open during the past year, and visited by committees appointed monthly as heretofore.

In consequence of the low state of the funds, but two volumes of books have been purchased; the binding of periodicals has added a few more to the library; while thirty-nine volumes deposited by a friend, since deceased, have been reclaimed by the heir, leaving a less number on the shelves than was reported last year.

The periodicals mentioned in the last annual report continue to be received at the rooms.

The cabinet has not been materially increased. The collection of natural productions is, however, quite respectable, and many of them are rare and valuable. It would be well if the attention of visiters were more frequently directed to them as objects for illustrating various branches of natural science.

The Association having recommended an increased attention to the subject of lectures, efforts were made to procure the delivery of such as were compatible with the character of the institution. A course of sixteen on Physiology were delivered, for which a compensation was paid: and by the kindness of several friends, twelve have been delivered gratuitously; three of these were on the modes adopted and materials employed in different ages to render knowledge permanent, with an outline sketch of the history of literature; two were on carburetted hydrogen gas as it exists in nature, and as prepared artificially for the purposes of illumination; two on instinct; one on the principles and means of happiness; three on history, as developing an overruling Providence, and two on Greece and Malta, making twenty-eight; and one remains to be delivered on the right employment of our time and talents. The variety of the subjects added much to the interest; and all of them were well attended, and most of them gave general satisfaction.

It would afford the managers much gratification if they were able to make as favourable a statement as regards the primary object of the Association, the attendance of those at the reading room for whose benefit it was designed. From some cause, this, and the conversation room is not as much frequented as would be desirable; and we deem it a matter of sufficient importance to engage the attention of every member of the Association, as well as of every manager, and that they endeavour by all the means in their power to forward the original views of Friends in forming the institution, that the benefits it is susceptible of conferring may be more generally diffused.

The number who frequented the rooms the past year, is, as nearly as we can ascertain, about 100: yet at certain seasons the attendance is very small.

The treasurer's account, herewith presented, shows the state of the finances. From the balance of $754 21 in his hands on the 5th instant, there is to be deducted orders for bills passed since, amounting to $78 40, and reducing the balance to $675 81.

From the account it appears that donations have been received to promote the objects of the Association, amounting to $1086 50, most of which it is intended to invest so as to form, with the legacy of the late Beulah Sansom, a permanent fund, to which we hope other gifts and legacies will be added, that the institution may, under the blessing of Providence, eventually be placed on a more durable basis.

By direction and on behalf of the Board of Managers.

JOSIAH H. NEWBOLD, *Clerk pro tem.*
Philada. 3d mo. 9th, 1840.

God's promises are not intended to slacken or supersede, but to quicken and encourage our own endeavours.—*Henry.*

THE FRIEND.

THIRD MONTH, 21, 1840.

The exigencies of the case to which it relates are so well stated in the following communication, that little addition is needful on our part by way of enforcing the appeal to the generous impulses of our readers; and such addition, perhaps, cannot better be made than in the words of the note which accompanied the communication. "From E. Greenfield we have nothing more to expect, and our helpless little ones must be abandoned, and they returned to their miserable homes, or become wanderers in the street. Already have we seen coloured children of the tenderest age confined to the lonely cell of Moyamensing prison; for *them* there exists no 'House of Refuge.' What must we expect if these schools are now closed in a neighbourhood where evils of the most degrading character surround them, without a counteracting influence to prepare their minds for the dangers that inevitably await them."

COMMUNICATION.

The managers of the Gaskill street School for coloured infants have more than once made application through the medium of "The Friend," for funds to enable them to continue this valuable institution—which, but for the aid rendered by Friends, would long since have languished. It is, therefore, with reluctance that the subject is again presented; but the situation of this and the other school under their care, renders it imperative on the managers to make unusual exertions at this time: the funds of both being now exhausted.

In the spring of 1837 a donation of $1000 from Elizabeth Greenfield enabled the society to open a coloured school in a destitute part of the district of Moyamensing. Subsequent receipts from the same benevolent individual, with a few donations from other sources have defrayed its expenses for nearly three years, and it was understood to be the intention of E. Greenfield to render this support permanent. Owing to changes in affairs which have affected even the most wealthy, this support has been discontinued, and the managers are reduced to the alternative of closing the school or seeking aid from citizens as for similar establishments. It is a prosperous and valuable school, and for the sum of $450 per annum, afforde the advantages of a good elementary English and religious education to from 80 to 100 poor children—many of whom would otherwise be roaming the streets in idleness and vice. The question which the managers are now compelled to consider is, shall this school be disbanded? Encouragement to continue its salutary influence is respectfully and earnestly solicited.

The school is held in a brick meeting-house back of Eighth, between Christian and Carpenter streets, and is open daily to visiters. The friends of education are invited to call and judge for themselves of its utility before contributing.

Donations to either school will be thankfully received by Sarah H. Yarnell, No. 22 South Twelfth street, or Cornelia Davidson, No. 268 Walnut street.

March 16th, 1840.

The article " *Sketches of Superstitions,*" commenced to-day, and which will extend into several numbers, the presentation of a valued correspondent, whose contributions have before enriched our columns, we predict will be read with more than ordinary interest. We have not seen the subject of the heathen mythology, with its splendid figments and cumbrous load of absurdities, exhibited in a form more instructive, combined with condensation and perspicuity.

WANTED, at the Coloured Orphan Asylum, New York, a person qualified for the situation of Matron. Unexceptionable references will be required. Apply at No. 283 East Broadway, or address Robt. J. Murray, Fourteenth street.

Haddonfield Boarding School for Girls.

Under the care of Amy Eastlack, will be vacated from the 9th of 4th month to the 7th of the 5th—when it will again be ready for the reception of pupils. The course of instruction embraces most of the branches of an English education. Terms are thirty dollars per quarter, of twelve weeks, payable in advance, washing included. The age of pupils is not limited, and they can be admitted at any time for a quarter or more. Each pupil is to be furnished with wash-basin and towels, and have all things distinctly marked. The scholars all attend the religious meetings of the Society of Friends. No deduction made for absence, except from indisposition. Application may be made at the school, or to

WILLIAM EVANS, No. 134 south Front st.
THOMAS KITE, No. 32 north Fifth st.
HARKER & SHIVERS, No. 45 Arch st.
JOSEPH B. COOPER, Newton, New Jersey.
HENRY WARRINGTON, Westfield, New Jersey.

Those who wish their children to commence at the opening of the school, please apply early in the 4th month.

DIED, at his residence in East Bradford, Chester county, on third day the 3d instant, JOHN FORSYTHE, in the eighty-sixth year of his age, a member of Birmingham Monthly Meeting.

PRINTED BY ADAM WALDIE,
Carpenter Street, below Seventh, Philadelphia.

THE FRIEND.

A RELIGIOUS AND LITERARY JOURNAL.

VOL. XIII.   SEVENTH DAY, THIRD MONTH, 28, 1840.   **NO. 26.**

EDITED BY ROBERT SMITH.

PUBLISHED WEEKLY.

Price two dollars per annum, payable in advance.

Subscriptions and Payments received by

GEORGE W. TAYLOR,

NO. 50, NORTH FOURTH STREET, UP STAIRS,

PHILADELPHIA.

For "The Friend."

SKETCHES OF SUPERSTITIONS.

[Continued from page 195.]

There was a class of demi-gods also, who filled every corner of earth and sea. The shady groves and flowery vales were peopled by Dryads or wood-nymphs, and Satyrs, a species of rural deities, who, like Pan, had the horns, legs, and feet of a goat. Mountains and streams possessed their guardian gods and goddesses, and every fountain had its Naïad or water-nymph. The lively imagination of the Greeks made them consider the thunder as the voice of Jupiter; the soft breezes of summer were to them the movement of the wing of Æolus; the echo of the forest was the voice of a goddess, and the gentle murmur of the streamlet sounded as the tones of its presiding deity. In short, wherever sound or sight in nature charmed their fancy, the Greeks ascribed the pleasure to the agency of unseen, but beautiful and immortal beings. Even the meanest things and offices had their presiding deities; there was a goddess of common-sewers and sinks. Beyond this it would be impossible to go. Petronius humorously said of their chief city, Athens, that " it was easier to find a god there than a man.'

These beings were believed to mingle invisibly in the affairs of mortals, and frequently to lend their assistance in the promotion of schemes of vice and villany. They were animated by envy, malice, and all the evil passions to which men are subject, and they did not hesitate to adopt any measures, however base, to gratify their nefarious purposes. Even Jupiter, the king of heaven, is described as having acted a very profligate part. A belief in immortality, and of a future state of rewards and punishments, formed a part of the Greek religion. Immortality was figured in their temples by a butterfly (called Psyche,) that a, may by its transformations, being, as they thought, typical of the changes which the human being must undergo. They imagined that, after death, the souls of men descended to the shores of a dismal and pestilential stream, called the Styx, where Charon, a grim-looking personage, acted as ferryman, and rowed the spirits of the dead across the melancholy river,

the boundary of the dominions of Pluto. To obtain a passage in Charon's boat, it was necessary that the deceased should have been buried. Those who were drowned at sea, or who were in any other manner deprived of the rites of sepulture, were compelled to wander about on the banks of the Styx for a hundred years, before being permitted to cross it. After quitting the vessel of Charon, the trembling shades advanced to the palace of Pluto, the gate of which was guarded by a monstrous dog, named Cerberus, which had three heads, and a body covered with snakes instead of hair. They then appeared before Minos, Rhadamanthus, and Æanthus, the three judges of the infernal regions, by whom the wicked were condemned to torments, and the good rewarded with heavenly pleasures.

The Greeks were pre-eminently an imaginative people, and, accordingly, both their mythology and their religious rites were calculated rather to amuse the fancy than to interest or improve the understanding. Their public worship was altogether ceremonial. In magnificent temples they invoked and offered sacrifices to the gods, and the solemn festivals of their religion consisted of pompous processions, public games, dramatic entertainments, feasting, and masquerading. To these were added in the worship of Bacchus, drunkenness, indecency, uproar, and every species of licentiousness. It was no business of the priests to inculcate lessons of morality; the only doctrine taught by them was, that the gods demanded slavish adulation, and an outward show of reverence from their worshippers, who would be rewarded with the divine favour in proportion to the abundance and costliness of their offerings. Besides the public services of religion, there were certain secret rites, performed only by the initiated, in honour of particular divinities. The most remarkable of these mystical observances were the feasts celebrated at Eleusis, in Attica, in honour of the goddess Ceres. They were called, by way of eminence, the Mysteries; and all who were initiated in them, were bound by the most solemn oaths never to reveal them. The Athenians alone were admissible to the Eleusinian rites, and they were very careful to avail themselves of their peculiar privileges, believing that those who died without initiation would be condemned to wallow for ever in mud and filth in the infernal regions. The penalty of death was denounced against all who should divulge these mysteries, or who should witness them without being regularly initiated; but, notwithstanding the rigorous manner in which this law was enforced, sufficient disclosures have been made concerning them, to prove that they consisted principally of such mystical ceremonies, and optical delusions, as were fitted to excite the superstitious

veneration and dread of the bewildered votaries. Processions, gymnastic contests, music, and dancing, constituted an indispensable part of this religious festival as of others, and the nocturnal orgies of the devotees were scarcely less extravagant and immoral than those of the Bacchanalians.

The Greeks believed in the possibility of foretelling future events. The wisest among them were in this respect not more advanced in intelligence than those ignorant beings in the present day who put faith in fortune-tellers. The practice of divining what would be the result of important enterprises, was connected with the religion of the country, and therefore countenanced and supported by the state. In all matters of importance, the desired knowledge of futurity was sought for from certain oracles, or as we should now call them, fortune-telling establishments. By far the most celebrated of the Grecian oracles was that of Apollo at Delphi, a city built on the slopes of Mount Parnassus, in Phocis. At a very remote period it had been discovered, that from a deep cavern in the side of that mountain an intoxicating vapour issued, the effect of which was so powerful as to throw into convulsions both men and cattle. The rude inhabitants of the surrounding district, unable to account for this phenomenon, conceived that it must be produced by supernatural agency, and regarded the incoherent ravings of those who had inhaled the noxious vapour as prophecies uttered under the inspiration of some god. As the stupifying exhalation ascended out of the ground, it was at first conjectured that the newly discovered oracle must be that of the very ancient goddess *Earth*, but Neptune was afterwards associated with this divinity, as an auxiliary agent in the mystery. Finally, the whole credit of the oracle was transferred to Apollo. A temple was soon built on the hallowed spot, and a priestess, named the *Pythoness*, was appointed, whose office it was to inhale, at stated intervals, the prophetic vapour. To enable her to do so without the risk of falling into the cavern, as several persons had previously done, a seat, called a tripod, from its having three feet, was erected for her accommodation directly over the mouth of the chasm. Still, however, the Pythoness held an office which was neither safe nor agreeable. The convulsions into which she was thrown by the unwholesome vapours of the cavern, were in some instances so violent, as to cause immediate death, and were at all times so painful that force was often necessary to bring the official to the prophetic seat. The unconnected words which the Pythoness screamed out in her madness, were arranged into sentences by the attendant priests, who could easily place them in such an order, and fill up the breaks in such a way, as to make them express whatever was most suitable to the interests of the *shrine*, which was the main object. Lest the oracle should be brought into discredit, care was, in general, taken to couch the response in language so obscure and enigmatical that, whatever course events should take, the prediction might not be falsified, or rather might appear to be verified. It may be observed that, in the course of time, the plan of simulating convulsions was most probably adopted by the chief agent in these impositions.

The fame of the Delphic oracles soon became very extensive, and no enterprise of importance was undertaken in any part of Greece or of its numerous colonies, without a consultation of the Pythoness. The presents received from those who resorted to it for counsel, not only afforded the officiating priests a comfortable maintenance, but furnished also the means of erecting a splendid temple instead of the rude edifice which had been originally constructed; and the high veneration in which the oracle was held, gave its directors a large share of influence in public affairs.

It is understood that the Greeks derived their belief in oracles from the Egyptians. In the deserts of Lybia was situated the temple of Jupiter Ammon, one of the most magnificent structures in the world. Alexander, on the occasion of his conquest of Egypt, consulted the oracle there respecting the fortunes of his family. Romans, as well as Greeks, reverenced the distant fortune-telling establishment. After the battle of Pharsalia, Labrenus besought Cato to consult so celebrated an oracle, but that great man made the following memorable reply:—"On what account, Labrenus, would you have me consult Jupiter? Shall I ask him whether it be better to lose life than liberty? Whether life be a real good? We have within us, Labrenus, an oracle that can answer all these questions. Nothing happens but by the order of God. Let us not require of him to repeat to us what he has sufficiently engraven on our hearts. Truth has not withdrawn into these deserts; it is not engraven on the sands of Lybia. The abode of God is in heaven, in the earth, in the sea, and in virtuous hearts. God speaks to us by all that we see, by all that surrounds us. Let the inconstant, and those that are subject to waver according to events, have recourse to oracles. For my part, I find in nature every thing that can inspire the most constant resolution. The coward, as well as the brave, cannot escape death. Jupiter can tell us no more."

The oracles of Greece, like those every where else, in time fell into disrepute; their predictions were laughed at, and exposed either as equivocal or false; and, finally, as the light of Christianity spread over the Roman provinces, they became altogether dumb.

(To be continued.)

Novel News-carrier.—Copied from a shipping report at St. Helena—

"The brig Memnon, belonging to Nantz, when off Cape Good Hope, caught an Albatross, having a ribbon around its neck, with a quill, sealed at both ends, containing a slip of paper with the following words, viz: 'Ship Leonidas, of Salem, bound to New Zealand, 74 days out, latitude 40 south, longitude 26 east.'"

The Leonidas sailed from Salem on the 9th of Aug. last, and this is the first intelligence from her.

For "The Friend."

The following notice of a valuable work on a subject of vast concernment to the people of the United States, will probably be interesting to the readers of "The Friend." It is extracted from the pages of the Journal of the Franklin Institute,—a scientific periodical, not only highly creditable to its founders and supporters, but for the extent and value of the information it contains, one of the cheapest works of that character with which we are acquainted in the English language.

N. M.

Report on Education in Europe, to the Trustees of the Girard College for Orphans; by Alex. Dallas Bache, LL. D., *President of the College.*

It is probably known to most of the readers of this Journal, that soon after the appointment of Professor Bache to the presidency of the Girard College, he was deputed by the trustees to visit those parts of Europe in which it was known that education had made the greatest progress, for the purpose not only of making the system of instruction therein pursued better known to his countrymen, but especially that he might have more abundant materials and a broader foundation for a plan of education for the magnificent institution over which he is to preside. He was engaged about two years in his visitations and inquiries, and no reader, we are persuaded, will venture to say, that his time was not most industriously and judiciously occupied. We have read the report with the deepest interest—albeit an octavo volume of 666 pages—and we make the unqualified acknowledgment that in our estimation Dr. B. has performed the task assigned him, thus far, with sound discrimination, and in the exercise of a judgment and good taste which will redound to his credit on both sides of the Atlantic.

It was necessary in such an expansive survey of the educational institutions of different nations, to classify the objects of his investigation; not only to consider education in its threefold relation to the physical, the intellectual, and the moral nature of man, but to regard it in its aptitudes to the different classes into which human society is, in every civilized country, inevitably arranged, by age and condition in life. The importance of such a distinction was at once perceived by the author, and instead of giving a geographical detail of the schools and systems which he examined, he first describes the institutions for the education of orphans and destitute children in England, Scotland, Germany, Prussia and Holland; then the schools for infant instruction—primary or elementary schools in France, England, and other countries—schools of agriculture and industry—seminaries for the preparation of teachers, including the normal schools of France—secondary schools; and finally superior schools, embracing all that is most worthy of notice under each of these heads in the different countries which he visited.

The report is indeed voluminous, but we could not easily point to the chapter or even the page that could well have been spared, considering that the task was assigned him of

making a faithful exhibition of the most important institutions of Europe. We rather indeed regret that its needful limitations precluded the author from reporting upon the universities of Great Britain and Ireland, and the older institutions of the Continent, appropriated to the higher grades of classical literature and science.

"They had their origin (says the author) in the wants of an early period of civilization, and have continued to be as necessary in its progress, requiring great changes, however, to enable them to keep pace with the times. Schools of arts, or polytechnic schools, have originated in the requirements of modern times, in which occupations have risen in standing and importance, or have been actually created, by the progress of science and the arts. Considered as special schools, the universities have very different objects from those which the founder of the Girard College intended as the aim of his institution, while the purposes of the polytechnic schools are strictly in accordance with those which his will points out for the highest department of his college. This being the case, a description of foreign university systems of different countries, especially so from the amount of talent arrayed in favour of, and even positively against, different systems, and I should make no pretensions to offer such a judgment, the institutions are by no means difficult to describe, so that a reader may conceive the form of the system, and endow that form with spirit, in proportion to the force of his own natural powers and his experience. The differences between the university systems of Great Britain, France, and Germany, afford interesting subjects of reflection to those whose pursuits and dispositions lead them to efforts for the improvement of 'superior education.' Considering these different systems as so many experiments made under different circumstances, the study of their results, and the modifying effect of circumstances, is no less interesting than useful. The field is, however, vast; the varieties in Great Britain alone would require much space for due description, as a few words will suffice to show. The Scotch and English universities differ very much in their organization, discipline, and instruction, and even the several Scotch universities are not alike. At Glasgow, and the academical institution at Belfast, founded upon its model, the pupils enter, in general, in very early youth. The lectures are, therefore, mixed with recitations held by the professors, which, however, the large classes at Glasgow prevent from being efficacious. The students do not reside in either of these institutions. At Edinburgh, the average age of the student is greater, and the medical department assumes, relatively to that of letters, an importance which modifies the character of the school. The lesser universities of St. Andrews and Aberdeen differ more from the others in the arrangement of discipline, resulting from the residence of a part of the students in the colleges composing them, than in the character of the instruction. In the larger English universities of Cambridge and Oxford, composed of colleges and halls, in the buildings of which the students generally reside, the discipline of each college may be said to be its own, with a general conformity to that of the university." The same is true in regard to the instruction, with this difference, that as all the courses tend towards the preparation for university degrees and university honours, there is a general conformity in the several colleges in the subjects taught and methods of teaching. The instruction given by the tutors in the colleges is upon the same general plan, a mixture of lecture and recitation; and as the attendance upon the lectures of the university professors is not obligatory, forms the real basis of the intellectual part of the university education. The inducements held out to exertion in these schools by the rewards which the fellowships and the stations to which they may lead hold forth, and which bring into them the greater part of the best talent of England, produce results which are of the highest order, but which cannot fairly be considered as depending mainly upon the system of instruction and discipline. It must require a very accurate knowledge of facts, with an entire absence of prejudice, to reason as to the general results of the various parts of the complex system, which has grown with the growth of these institutions themselves, and is, therefore, now very deeply rooted.

" I consider the opportunity which I enjoyed of witnessing some of the written examinations at Cambridge as of the highest value, and am no longer surprised at the attachment to this method which is there felt. It is accurate and expeditious in its results, removes all possibility of, or temptation to, show, and even the suspicion of partiality, in the distribution of important places. While I am not yet persuaded that it can supersede the viva voce method, or be employed to such an extent as to sink the use of the latter into comparative insignificance, yet, if the choice lay between the use of the one or other method extensively, I should now prefer the former.

" At the university of Dublin (Trinity College,) the advantages of the tutorial system are combined with that of the lectures by professors, which the students are enjoined to attend, and the same is the case at the recently erected university of Durham. This university has set the example of adding instruction in civil engineering to its literary courses, and has admitted the modern languages into the latter. King's College and London University College have hardly yet taken the form which time must impress upon them in their new connection with the London University; the enactments of this recent corporation, in regard to the requirements for degrees, must

* A very accurate account of the universities of Cambridge and Oxford is to be found in the report to the Board of Trustees of the University of Pennsylvania, by Philip H. Nicklin, Esq., one of its members.

ultimately regulate the higher studies of these and other institutions, presenting candidates for them. This bare enumeration will serve to show, that to give any thing like an idea of institutions so various in their character, would require much time and more space than could properly be bestowed in a report, to the purpose of which the greater part of the particulars would be found inappropriate. No doubt useful hints might be gathered, but by far the greater part of the matter would be entirely inapplicable to our purpose. For example, the system of university degrees, by which encouragement is given to general effort, and of the privilege to teach, or of stations without actual duty, by which, in many establishments, individual exertion is stimulated and rewarded, are entirely inapplicable to the circumstances of our institution. Again; the tone and modes of discipline, both in those institutions where the pupils reside and in those where they merely come at stated times to receive instruction, are inapplicable to our case, and the general organization and government are not less so. Further, the instruction, as far as it is of a special character, qualifying for admission to the learned professions, as in the continental system, has, of course, no bearing upon our arrangements, and leaves for profitable study the subjects of at most two faculties. In these the titles of the branches themselves would be all that could serve us ; for the mode of lecturing being universally adopted, the treatment of the subject depends upon the individual professor."

We hope that the author may be induced, at some future time, to furnish, either in a supplementary report, or in some other form, the result of his visits to the universities. A detail of their organisations, various and dissimilar as they are, and complicated as some of them by long usage have become, would be highly interesting to the scholars of this country.

However disposed some of the readers of this volume may be to complain of repetition in the statistical accounts of institutions, similar in their objects, we do not see how the reporter could have omitted any of his tabular illustrations, or individual statements, without furnishing grounds of complaint to those who will look to his volume for a specific statement of each or any of the prominent institutions relative to which they may wish information. It is by a minute comparison of means and results that we arrive at the most valuable truths in practical science; and certain it is that in the great science of education there is still much to be learnt, and to no people is this knowledge more important than to the inhabitants of our republic.

The state of popular education in the different parts of our extended territory is perhaps as various as in the different countries of Europe visited by Dr. Bache. However we may be disposed to congratulate ourselves on the provision made in most of the states for supporting schools, a strict examination would, we fear, demonstrate in many parts of our country, as great a destitution of all literary instruction as could be found in almost any part of Europe. In particular sections of the United States the most laudable efforts are un-

questionably in operation to elevate the standard of common schools and academies to the highest point of philanthropic ambition ; but whoever reads attentively the volume before us must make the acknowledgement, however painful to his amor patriæ, that in no part of our favoured land is the science of education fully understood, and its precepts carried into practical operation. The main reason is that little or nothing has been done to educate those who are to become the educators of the people. The means have not been provided for opening the arena of competition for the display of genius and talent in the highest of all practical arts—the discovery of the most efficient means of evolving the powers of the mind in connection with the virtuous energies of the heart and affections. Until the business of the educator is raised to a rank correspondent in respectability with any other professional pursuit, it is not be imagined that skill will be shown in the management of schools to a degree which the wants and faculties of the men, while " yet in the gristle," absolutely require.

This subject we know is beginning to claim attention in several of the states, and we regard it as the earnest of a spirit of higher importance to the welfare of the country, than any thing within the whole range of politics, trade, or other matters relating to mere physical improvement. It is in this point of view especially, that we could wish the Report of President Bache placed in the hands of every teacher and manager of schools throughout the country. It will show them at what an unimagined distance we are still behind in spirit and advancement, the educational institutions of some parts of Europe ; and yet with what an accelerated motion, with the means and appliances in our possession, we may follow on in the track of a noble rivalship, and the acquirement of a distinction as flattering to the moral strength of the nation as its ships, factories, and rail roads are to its intellectual and physical energies.

(To be continued.)

ADVENTURE ON THE CLYDE.

After an agreeable residence of a few weeks on the sea-shore near Gourock, which may be styled the Margate or Ramsgate of Glasgow, I went one day on board a steamer to re-ascend the Clyde. The weather was fine, and the deck of the boat was crowded with passengers of all kinds, from the portly manufacturer of the western capital, returning like myself from a little pleasurable rustication, to the poor shattered invalid, whom the beautiful day and the low fare had tempted to take a sail down the river and back again. Many were the vessels passing to and fro that day on the Clyde, but one only of these drew any particular attention from our company. This was a large Irish steamer, which shot past us just as we were opposite to Dumbarton, being probably on its way to Belfast or Dublin. Perhaps it was the number of genuine and unmistaken Milesians on the deck, all returning, ragged as they came, to their native soil, that made myself and others fix our gaze for a minute or two on this vessel. While doing so, we heard a loud cry emitted by some one on board, and saw a great bustle take place on the deck, all the passengers running to one side. Almost immediately the steam was let off, and the vessel brought to a stop. Our captain, on seeing these movements, said, "Surely there is some one overboard!" But the distance was every moment increasing, and we failed to satisfy ourselves that such was the cause of the stir. In a little while, the passengers, one after another, turned loungingly and indifferently away, and the Irish steamer was soon alike out of sight and out of mind.

Our own vessel moved on. We passed the terminus of the Roman wall and site of Henry Bell's well-deserved monument. As we were approaching Erskine ferry, a female voice was heard exclaiming, "My bairn! my bairn! Where is my bairn?" and, on turning round, I found that the words proceeded from a young woman of six or seven and twenty, who bore one child in her arms, and led another in her hand. Her countenance was turned anxiously and imploringly to the captain, as she uttered the words just mentioned. The captain was close behind me. "My good woman," said he, "don't distress yourself. If you have missed one of your children, it cannot be far away." "Oh, sir," returned the mother, "I missed it but shortsyne; but I looked every where about the deck before I spoke. Oh, where is my bairn?" The passengers had assembled around the spot, and the poor woman's appealing eyes were cast on the circle, as she gave vent to the last exclamation. "Some of the men may have taken the child below for amusement," said the captain, soothingly, and away he went to ascertain the truth of his own conjecture. The young wife followed him. The result, however, was, that the child could not be seen or heard of in the ship. The captain began to look gloomy, and the company on board the steamer were again in a buzz of sympathising curiosity. Conjecture once more was busy, though it could only tend to one single point—that the child was overboard. But how it had got overboard was the question. Being but five years of age (the eldest of the three who had been with the mother), he could scarcely be supposed to have climbed the side of the vessel, even if he had been desirous of looking over into the water. How then could the thing have happened?

One man only could throw a single ray of even conjectural light on the fate of the child. This passenger stated, that, while he had been seated by the side of the vessel occupied in reading, and in such a position that his eye could see the water nearly to the side of the boat, he had at one time got a momentary glance of what seemed to him a piece of paper or rag on the water; but, through the motion of the vessel, the object had been but an instant before his sight, and could scarcely be said to have occupied his thoughts for a second's duration, if at all. Shortly afterwards, he observed another circumstance which he did not then suppose to have any connection with what he had previously seen. This was the open state of the gangway door, or that portion of the bulwark which is so constructed as to open for the admission of passengers and goods. On observing it open, he had risen to shut it, but thought no more of the matter.

Both incidents were so trifling that he could not say at what period of the voyage they had taken place.

The passengers and captain proceeded to the gangway door. The bolt was examined, and it was found on trial, that the wood beneath the staple, and the staple itself, were so much worn away, as to cause the door to burst open to the outside, on the instant that any force was applied to it from the deck or inside. Every face looked sad, and yet satisfied, at this discovery. Here was, in all human probability, the place and the cause of the child's unhappy disappearance; and the object seen on the water by the reading passenger confirmed the supposition. We remember feeling pleased with the conduct of an Englishman present on the occasion. With the straightforward and fearless candour of his country, he openly administered a severe reprimand to the captain for his carelessness in permitting the gangway door to remain in such a condition. "It is nothing less," said the rebuker, "than a direct *trap* for children! Where can they think themselves safe, when agitated by natural fears at finding themselves for the first time in a ship, if not when they seat themselves on deck, and lean for firm support against the vessel's sides? This child has entertained the thought, and has fallen a victim to it."

Who can describe the state of the poor mother all this while? When the discoveries just related had been made, hope seemed to take flight for the first time. Her exclamations went to the heart of all on board. She was the wife of a humble tradesman in Glasgow, and her children having been attacked by an epidemic, she had been sent by her husband to take a trip down the Clyde and up again, in order to speed their convalescence. "Oh! what will their father say!" was her constant cry; "I took *three* away, and bring hame but two! What will *its* father say!" The prospective distress of her husband seemed to pain her more than any thing else, yet, ever and anon, all feelings but the mother's departed, and she shed the agonising tears of a "Rachel weeping for her children." While glancing now and then at her grief-steeped countenance, which was naturally a comely and interesting one, every person on board that vessel would have given much to have been able to alleviate her distress, and when the boat landed at the Broomielaw, many were eager to assist her on her course homewards. But she was accompanied by a friend of her own sex, who precluded the necessity of any such aid. With this person, then, she wended her way to the home, which, for the first time, probably, she felt reluctant to enter. What were the feelings of the father on hearing of the accident, can only be imagined.

I afterwards learned that the distress of the honest pair lasted but one night. Joy came to them with the morning—and the Greenock coach; for in that vehicle, before breakfast-time, arrived the missing boy. He had, it appeared, fallen backwards through the treacherous gangway door, and been precipitated into the water. The receding tide had carried him rapidly down the river for a short space. Luckily he was observed from the

Irish steamer, the captain of which instantly stopped to pick him up. This was the cause of the bustle we had observed in that vessel; and I now wondered that no one had thought of the possibility of such being the case when the mother was wailing for a lost son. By using the proper exertions life had been restored to the poor child, and when they reached Greenock, the parties on board left him to be sent back to his parents, each contributing a trifle to pay the necessary expenses. I could not help thinking it almost worth while to have a son thus endangered, and suffering the acutest pain on his account for a night, in order to draw forth so much good feeling from one's fellow-creatures, and experience so joyful a relief from temporary sorrow.—*Chambers's Edinburgh Journal.*

Cabbage, as Food for Hogs.

A gentleman remarked, in our hearing, a few days since, that cabbage was a valuable food for store hogs. The idea was new to us, and we inquired the manner of feeding. In reply, he gave us the following as the result of his experience, the last summer. Having a fine patch of plants, and observing the bottom leaves beginning to decay, he directed his farmer to procure a water-tight cask, and gather a bushel of the lower leaves from the cabbage plants, and deposit them in the barrel, with a handful of salt, and one quart of corn meal. On this was poured the contents of the kitchen swill-pail, and the whole was suffered to stand undisturbed for twenty-four hours, when the process was repeated, with the exception of the salt—and so, every day, until the cask was filled with a mass of wilted leaves, about six quarts of corn meal, potatoe peelings, crumbs of bread, &c. from the kitchen; all in a state of partial fermentation. He now commenced feeding it to the hogs, and they ate with greediness, leaving other food for this. They were evidently as fond of this kind of mush, as ever "Mynheer" was of *sour-krout.*

While the hogs were consuming the contents of the first barrel, a second was in course of being filled, and so alternately, till the stock of leaves was exhausted, which was about four weeks.

This gentleman gave his opinion, that he could not have prepared any other kind of food for his hogs, known to him, at double the expense, that would have produced results so decidedly beneficial. An increase of appetite, improvement in their appearance, and better heart, was the result of this method. The cabbages, he thinks, were greatly improved by plucking the redundant foliage; and he intends to plant a large patch of cabbages, the coming season, more fully to test the advantages of this kind of food for hogs. We invite him, and others who may "experiment" in the business, to give us the results for publication.—*Farmers' Cabinet.*

Among the passengers of the British Queen just arrived at New York, it is stated, is the famous giant of Belgium, who is eight feet six inches high, with a body in proportion. He has gained great notoriety in Europe, by his astonishing feats of strength.

LIFE OF WILLIAM CATON.

(Continued from page 198.)

About that time we were very busy in answering several books that were extant in High Dutch against the truth and Friends; the answers to which we had intended to have printed here, but the printers fearing the reproof of the clergy, durst not print them for us in this city. We then departed from thence, and returned again to Friends at Kriesheim; and when we had staid some time with them, W. A. determined to return again to Amsterdam, there to get the aforesaid books printed; and in due time he took his leave of Friends, and I went along with him to a place called Alstone, where the governor of those parts lived. It was upon us to go to him, to lay some abuses before him that were sustained by Friends. He was moderate towards us, and a good service we had with him; and after that he gave me an order for the officer of the place where Friends lived, for him to take care that the rude multitude did not abuse Friends. After we had been with him, we took leave of each other in the endearedness of our Father's love, and he [W. A.] went for Holland, and I returned to Kriesheim again; there I staid with Friends some certain time, and afterwards went to Heidleberg again, for I was not clear of that city. When I came there I hired a lodging in a goldsmith's house, and sometimes I went up to the prince's palace, and had good service there; and sometimes I was with some of the great ones of the city, with whom I had also very good service, and some of them were very courteous and respective to me: and more love did appear in some of them towards me than others could well bear. Then began the enmity in the clergy to get up against me; and through the means of some that were envious against me, I with another young man, (who were all the Friends that were in that city,) were ordered to appear before the council, as also the man that entertained us; which accordingly we did, and a very good service we had, for never had there been any Friend there before: so that they had many things to query of me; and the Lord was pleased at that very time to give me enough wherewith to answer them, as also utterance, boldness, and dominion, even to the admiration of some. They were moderate towards us, and suffered me to speak pretty freely and largely among them; but in the end (that they might appear to do something,) they would have me depart out of their city, though they had nothing to lay to my charge, except for declaring the truth, and dispersing some books which testified of the truth; nevertheless, they suffered us then to depart from their judgment-seat in peace.

Afterwards the prince came to hear of it, at which (as we were informed,) he was very highly displeased with the council for troubling us, when we had given them no just occasion. After that I went to the president's house, who had examined me before the council; and after a little discourse with him, he became pretty moderate, and did reason very familiarly with me, and asked me many things concerning our Friends in England; as also concerning the magistrates' proceeding towards them; and I was very free to give him a full account there-

of for his information. Before we parted he seemed to be very loving to me, and thanked me for the present I had given him, which was some Friends' books; and yet before the council, my giving of such books to people was the greatest crime they had to lay to my charge, though both the prince and he did receive them from me, and accept of them.

I was several months (yea half a year) in that country, where I had very good service for the Lord, some time in one place, some time in another. I was several times at a city called Manheim, where there were a sort of baptists, who lived together as one family, and had their goods common; with whom I was several times, and did bear my testimony among them to the truth of God, though few of them received it. I was several times with the governor of that city at his own house; and he was very courteous to me (at least seemingly,) and desired me as often as I came to the city, to come to his house. I was also in the country with a countess (so called,) who was very loving to me, and pretty open to hear the truth; and at her house I found a great lord (so called) who formerly had been general of the emperor's army, (as I was informed;) and a great conference I had with him in the countess' presence, who was rather one with me in her judgment than with the great man before mentioned; and after I had had some very good service with them, I left them.

I was also at Frankfort, and endeavoured to get some book or books printed there, but could not prevail with the stationers; for the books that were to be printed there, were first to be viewed by some of the clergy. When I saw I could not prevail there, I went (with a Friend) to another city called Hannau, where we got our business done; and afterwards returned again to Frankfort, one of the chief (if not the chiefest) city in Germany. And upon a certain time, I went into their chief monastery or temple, where the emperors are usually crowned; and the priests were gathering to their devotion: they were exceedingly offended with me, because I did not stand uncovered in that (they call) sacred, (though it be an idolatrous) place. Some of the priests did speak to me, and one especially was exceeding angry; and when we had spoke but a little together in Latin, he turned from me in a fury, and another that was with him fell upon me, and did beat me sorely, and there he left me bleeding in the temple, where I left pretty much of my blood behind me, as a testimony against the idolatry of that idolatrous place.

I was also in the synagogue of the Jews, of that city, where I reasoned pretty much with them, and had a good opportunity to bear a faithful testimony of the eternal truth; though they could apprehend little of it with their dark minds, which were blinded with the god of this world, like as their forefathers were. I had also some books to dispose of among them, which for novelty's sake they coveted much after: and when I had cleared myself of them, I left them; and in due time returned again into the Palz.

I was also at the city of Worms; and it was upon me to go to the Jesuits' college, to

reason with them, or some of them, concerning the truth of God, and their traditions, which accordingly I did. And when I came there, one that was eminent among them did soon enter into discourse with me, and spoke very feignedly to me for some time; for at the first he seemed to have hopes (as it appeared to me) to have won or gained me to his religion; and therefore did he seem to be the more ready and willing to resolve me in whatsoever I propounded, so far as (I believe) he well could. But when he saw I did notwithstanding lay open their apostacy, and boldly gave my testimony against their inventions, superstitions, and traditions, he could scarcely contain himself from breaking out into a pasion. I had spent some hours in dispute with him, in the presence of several that belonged to the college, for whom he was as the mouth for the whole. When I had cleared my conscience, and borne a faithful testimony unto the truth among them, I left them, and returned again to Kriesheim, where our Friends inhabited; for sometimes I was there, sometimes at Heidleberg, and sometimes elsewhere, where I saw the Lord had a service for me.

[Extract from an Epistle addressed to Friends in London, by William Caton, dated Kriesheim, near Worms, in Germany, 30th of 11th mo., 1661. This instructive Epistle is printed at large in Besse's Sufferings, vol. ii. p. 451.

"We have cause to praise and magnify the Lord God omnipotent for ever, who doth not only comfort and refresh us in our tribulations, through the consolations of his eternal Spirit, but also hath prepared a refuge for us, which we have truly found in his eternal light and pure power. And now if no storm had come, then I believe there would not have been such flocking and flying to this refuge, as there hath been, and as there is, and as, I hope, there will be; therefore, if the storm of persecution do drive such as were neither cold nor hot from under their green trees of specious pretences and fair shows of religion and reformation, to this sure hiding place or refuge, which is in the eternal light, life, and power, which you have now made manifest, then will it be good in its season. Therefore let none be afraid of it who are faithful in their measures; for indeed our heavenly Father is so abundant in mercy and goodness to his people, that if he suffers storms and tempests to arise, he doth not only still them, but even in the very time of them he covereth his dear babes with the banner of his everlasting love, so that truly they need not to fear, though sometimes they that are tender and young among them may be too much afraid. And forasmuch as I know that the refuge before mentioned is known to you, and the covering of the Lord's eternal Spirit manifested in you, (which is the banner of his love spread over you,) therefore I beseech you to be of good courage in the Lord: for to what end should you fear? to what end should you be troubled? to what end should you take thought? You know that neither fear of heart, trouble of mind, nor yet taking of thought, can in anywise avert these things. And if it be the good pleasure of the Almighty to purge and refine you in the furnace of persecution, (as heretofore he hath done with many of his witnesses in the world,) think it not strange that it should be so with you: but rather think it strange that the Lord hath so long dealt so gently with you, and that he hath so remarkably restrained the violence of the mighty, who have risen up against you, as if they would have devoured you at once. But behold, how have they been abased, brought down from their seats, and overturned; and though they have, as it were, bruised your heel, yet they have not prevailed against the Lamb, the captain of your salvation; neither have they overcome you, whose faith hath stood in the power of the Most High, through which you have overcome, and not by the force of arms, nor by might of princes, nor by the greatness of your multitude. Remember, therefore, these things; and strengthen ye one another in the faith and in the patience; and look ye alone unto the Lord, and hearken and hear what his Spirit saith in you and to you.

" When the spirit of enmity rules in a dominion, there is not much liberty to be expected by us to be enjoyed in matters of religion; for it is well known to you, how through that spirit we have suffered from the beginning, which hath wrought mightily against us in our native country. In these countries here are three sects tolerated, viz. the papists, the Lutherans, and the Calvinists; and all these have their particular government in their particular cities and villages; and all of them are addicted to persecute those that are not of their sect. But above all others they seem to be bent against us, as the most offensive, irregular, and perturbations people that are of any sect; and notwithstanding the great variance that is and hath been among themselves, yet they can, as it were, join hand in hand against the truth and us. As for the papists, they hate us as new upstarted heretics, whom they account worthy of death: and the protestants, they revile us and upbraid us, as if we were the pope's emissaries; and many of them esteem us as not fit to live upon the earth: so that as much as in them lies, they seek to toss us to and again, as a ship upon a troubled sea. But thanks be to God, our anchor holds; so that they, with all their hard threatening, which proceed from their rocky hearts, cannot split our confidence, nor make shipwreck of our faith; which is in the Lord Jehovah, who is over all, blessed for evermore!'']

Upon a certain time when I was at Heidelberg, there came two of my dear brethren to the city, viz., John Stubbs and Henry Fell, who had been at Alexandria in Egypt, and in Italy, &c. The postmaster of the place seeing them, did bring them to my lodging, (for he knew me well,) for they had no knowledge of my being in the city; presently after, came the captain of the prince's life-guard, having seen them in the street; and he being a very courteous man to us, discoursed very friendly and familiarly with us, and afterwards told the prince of the aforesaid Friends being in the city. Soon after, the prince sent his secretary to my loding to desire us to come up to the castle to speak with him, which accordingly we did; and when we came there, he began to speak friendly and familiarly to us, as his manner was, and did ask them much concern-

ing their travels, and how it had been with them, &c. And a very gallant opportunity we had with him in the presence of the nobles, (so called,) that were conversant with him. After he had discoursed long with us, he parted very lovingly from us, and soon after we went out of the city.

When the aforesaid brethren were with me, I received some letters out of Holland, whereby I was informed of the death of Niesie Dirrix, of Amsterdam, who had been a dear, extraordinary, and special friend of mine, and a true and faithful servant to the flock of God in the Low Countries; of whose love and virtue, faithfulness, and good service which she did in her day, a volume might be writ: so that when I heard of her departure, my heart was very much saddened, and broken within me; and indeed it was more than I could well bear; but the aforesaid brethren being with me, they bore with me; and the Lord he supported me in that heaviness, and comforted me with the promise and assurance which I had from him, of his raising and bringing her sister Anneken Dirrix (with some else) into her love, life and spirit, to perform that or the like service for the Lord which she had done.

In process of time, something came before me and upon me, as from the Lord (which afterwards did more fully appear,) concerning my taking Anneken Dirrix to wife; unto which I took little heed at first, but sought rather totally to expel all such cogitations out of my mind; yet, behold, by how much the more I seemed to extinguish the appearance of such a thing, by so much the more did it prevail in me, and came to be clearer and clearer to me; which when I observed, I began to weigh the thing more seriously, and to hearken more diligently, to see what the Lord would require of me concerning it, and what the effects of it might be. And many things the Lord was pleased to show me concerning it; as in reference to the service that there might be in it as to the truth and Friends; and how helpful I might be to her, in assisting her in effecting that service which I saw in the light of the Lord would be required of her after the removal of her dear sister, who had been to her as her right hand; together with several other things which for the present I may omit to mention.

Thus did the thing for a pretty long time remain very fresh in me, both night and day, and abundance of objections came in my mind in many respects concerning it; but withal matter sufficient wherewith to answer them. And after I had very much tried and discussed the thing in the light of the Lord in my own heart, and in due time found it to be of the Lord, I began to acquiesce and to rest satisfied in myself, through giving up to the will of the Lord in the matter; but did not once open my mouth of it to any for the space of many weeks, (I might say months,) nay, not while I remained in Germany.

And withal it was about that time shown me how I should proceed in the matter, viz.: I was to keep it secret until I came into Holland, and then I should motion it to some of the brethren, before I should once mention it to her either by word or writing; and if they did own it and approve of it, I should thereby

be so much the more assured that it was of the Lord.

When I had been about half a year in Germany, and had had very good service, especially in the Palatinate, it was upon me to return again for Holland, which accordingly I did.

When (through the mercy of the Lord) I was gotten well thither, I visited Friends, (as my manner was,) and we were sweetly refreshed together. And as for the aforesaid Anneken upon it, and weighed it in the light of the Lord, they made known to me the unity they had with the thing, and how their hearts were affected with it, and what service there might be in the thing, as to the truth and Friends in those parts; by all which I was the more confirmed in the matter, and further satisfied concerning its being of the Lord. And in some certain time when I had a convenient opportunity to speak with her about it, I began to tell her in much humility and fear, (as before the Lord) what was entered into my heart in Germany: and how it was upon me at that time to acquaint her with it; and then I did open the very ground of the matter to her, and told her at large how it had been with me in the thing: and that I desired her to consider of it, and that except she did also see and feel something of it, as from the Lord, she should let it cease, and speak no further of it. And withal I had three things to propound to her, which I was to leave to her consideration, and unto which I desired in due time to have her answer: The first was, in case she was to give her to understand, that as for matter of estate, mine was not like unto hers, for I had not much as to the outward: and she was to consider whether she could notwithstanding consent unto the thing. Secondly, she was to consider how I was to expect my liberty (which was more to me than the treasures of Egypt) to go abroad in the service of the Lord, as I had done before, whether it was to visit Friends, or upon any other service for the Lord, or upon the truth's account; this she was also to consider beforehand, that when the thing came to pass, it might not seem strange to her. Thirdly, she was to consider how if the thing should come to pass, there might peradventure follow some trouble, either from the magistrates, or from some of her relations, or other discontented spirits, who might be dissatisfied with the thing; and therefore she was to consider whether she could bear that or no.

(To be continued.)

Those persons who creep into the hearts of most people—who are chosen as the companions of their softer hours, and their reliefs from care and anxiety—are never persons of shining qualities nor strong virtues. It is rather the soft green of the soul on which we rest our eyes, that are fatigued with beholding more glaring objects.—*Burke.*

For "The Friend."

It is not needful, we apprehend, to remind the editor of "The Friend" of the influence which the sheet over which he presides exerts among the members of our widely scattered society, in the most remote settlements of which, we presume, it is more or less to be found. The object of the present remarks, from a constant reader, is not to be censorious, but to offer a few suggestions with respect to some features in its character which are not altogether agreeable to some thorough-going old fashioned Quakers. If the writer is plain, it must be attributed to his love for the truth; he is fully aware of the difficulty of providing matter for a publication of this kind, and is willing, so far as is proper, to appreciate the plea sometimes held up in relation to the various *tastes* of the readers of "The Friend." Will it be too severe to say that we think this taste has sometimes been improperly gratified, and that matter has been introduced calculated to strengthen in a love for, and an allowance of what truth forbids? It is not our present purpose to mark out many of the particulars which have excited these feelings, but in a gentle way to remind the editor that the influence of "The Friend" should be altogether *good*, to say the least, altogether *consistent*. Its sentiments, although not official, are yet esteemed in some sort as oracular, and having its origin among those who are as authority in the society at large, makes the power, which it exerts among all classes, great, either for good or evil. The offence (if such it may be called) which has been given, arises not so much from original articles as from those selected from other papers, and the recording upon the pages of "The Friend" expressions as used by others, which we should be unwilling to use were we writing ourselves. As illustrative of this matter, we will refer to some passages in two or three articles in a late number, (of third month, 7,) which seem to be obnoxious, at the same time observing that our feelings have often been affected with the sight of similar unguarded language passed by without reprehension. Such expressions as "Thank God," and "God forbid," used upon ordinary occasions, and by those whose reverence for their Creator is at best vague and undefined, and who use his sacred name in a loose and vain manner, are not fit (excuse our zeal) to be placed upon the pages of a periodical which is to go to our children under the guise of *spiritual food* for them. True, these are not words which the editor or his coadjutors would use or recommend; they are such as without hesitation they would condemn; they are given as the language of others, and the force of the extract might be in some measure destroyed by their omission. But shall considerations of this kind weigh against the danger of distinguishing, in any degree, that holy reverence which we endeavour to inculcate in our families for the name of the Most High, shall we, for the sake of *ofttimes unimportant* intelligence, or to turn a period, admit them to our pages as matters of little moment? We trust not.

In Exodus xxiii, verse 13, we read the children of Israel were commanded in *all things* to "be circumspect, and make *no mention* of the name of other gods, neither let it be heard out of thy mouth." Will not this prohibition and warning apply with double force to a people professing as we do? How shall we answer its close requisition not to "let it be *heard out of our mouth*," if we adopt upon our editorial page "the Holy See," and set forth the decrees of Antichrist as given in the "power of the Lord," and with "apostolic authority?" If in our notices of passing events we set down, apparently without repugnance, those flattering titles of adulation which worldly minded men give to one another? See editorial notice, second month, 29th.

We are not insensible of the defence which may be set up, that in thus extracting passages from other publications, the editor is not accountable for the language or sentiments used. It is fully granted that difficulties of this kind will sometimes occur in the transmission to its readers of highly interesting intelligence; but would not wisdom dictate that articles of this kind should by re-written to suit them to a people of pure language? The labour required would be small compared to the evil effects which may be produced upon the minds of children and young persons by the reading, without comment, of such sentiments in the columns of "The Friend." When we meet with them in an ordinary newspaper we pass them by as what may be expected from the conduct of it—but when transferred to these pages, they assume a different character, and may be the means of insidiously undermining our esteem for some of those blessed testimonies which our forefathers set forth to the world, and which we are bound by our profession to maintain.

We will not at present pursue this matter further, trusting that "a word to the wise is sufficient," and that in catering for his readers the editor will see the propriety of giving no offence either to Jew or Gentile, or to the church. Our habits of thinking as a society have become, if we may use the expression, *loose* of latter years in relation to the subjects animadverted upon; and liable as "The Friend" is to contributions from all quarters, it is not unlikely that, although prominently responsible, the editor may not be strictly accountable for what may have been at times admitted to its pages. These remarks, therefore, may extend themselves to such as, mingling much with the busy world around them, become leavened into its spirit, and before they are aware their eyes become dim, and things which in the tenderness of early visitation were set before them as wrong become reconciled. We become habituated to passing over as unimportant some seemingly little things, which have their origin in that which is at enmity with the simplicity of the truth, and it too often happens that "we first endure, then pity, then embrace."

"The Friend," is undoubtedly calculated, if rightly conducted, to convey much instruction of various kinds to families living in remote situations, and to furnish them with *reading* which seems to have become an *essential* in these days; esteeming it as such, we have contributed to its support from its commencement, and have felt much interested in its being properly maintained—but also desire that its pages may be preserved from perpetuating sentiments which are in *any degree* inconsistent with our holy Christian profession. If thus freed from any pernicious tendency, it may continue to be supported by the Society as a Society affair; but if it connive at what is improper, we must be permitted to say that it is in danger of becoming a burden to the right minded.　　A. V.

For "The Friend."

QUEEN'S MARRIAGE.

The accompanying address, which I find copied from the London Court Circular, I think is not unworthy of a vacant corner in "The Friend."

The address evidences that the Society of Friends in England, notwithstanding the persecutions to which they have been too often subjected, are still not only among the most loyal subjects, but that they always uncompromisingly put prominently forward the true foundation of royal and national prosperity.

ALPHA.

From the London Court Circular of Feb. 20.

The queen held a court yesterday afternoon at Buckingham palace, for the reception of addresses, on the throne.

The members of the religious Society of Friends having, according to ancient custom, been uncovered by the yeomen of the guard, were then introduced to the presence of her majesty on the throne and presented to her majesty the following address;—

To Victoria, Queen of the United Kingdom of Great Britain and Ireland and the dominions thereunto belonging.

The respectful address of the undersigned, members of a meeting appointed to represent the religious Society of Friends in Great Britain and Ireland.

May it please the Queen:

As a Christian and loyal body, permit us on the important and deeply interesting occasion of thy marriage, to convey to thee the renewed assurance of our cordial attachment to thy person and government.

The institution of marriage we have ever regarded as a Divine ordinance, and it is our prayer to God that his blessing may richly crown thy union and render it conducive alike to thy own happiness and the welfare of thy people.

It is with heartfelt satisfaction that we anticipate thy future happiness in this union, and earnest are our desires for thee and for thy consort, that, walking in the fear of the Lord, your example may be so ordered in all things by that wisdom which is from above, as powerfully to promote the course of true religion and virtue throughout the land.

The real prosperity of our beloved country is an object dear to our hearts, and under this feeling we would express our belief that in proportion as pure practical Christianity is permitted to sway thy counsels and is promoted among thy subjects, will the prosperity be most effectually advanced, social order maintained, and thy throne established in the affections of thy people.

May He, by whom kings reign and princes

decree justice, bless thee, O Queen, and increasingly make thee a blessing to thy own and to surrounding nations, and mayest thou at the end of thy days, through the mercy of God in Christ Jesus our Saviour, be received into everlasting glory.

Her majesty returned the following most gracious answer:

I earnestly join in your prayers for the welfare of my people, and acknowledge with thanks your interest for my own happiness, which is inseparably connected with the subject of your congratulations.

I feel with you that the prosperity of nations is most effectually secured by observing the precepts and cherishing the benevolent spirit of the Christian religion.

From the Irish Friend.

LINES

" On seeing the Blind Asylum at Edinburgh,"

BY LORD FRANCIS EGERTON.

The following verses, although, I apprehend, not much known, appear to me truly poetical and expressive of Christian sentiments, both in sympathy for the afflicted blind, and sound advice to those who are favoured with their outward sight. The beautiful allusions which they contain, have forcibly reminded me of the warning words of our blessed Lord to those who seemed to query with him whether those Galileans were not sinners above all the Galileans, because calamities had been permitted to befall them. "I tell you," said he, " Nay ; but except ye repent, ye shall all likewise perish."—Luke xiii. 1—5.

Islington, 1840.   J. P.

Children, whom Heaven, in seeming denial,
Has reft of the light which to us it secures,
Unproved in our patience exempt from your trial,
Shall we give you our pity or ask you for yours?

Ill would it beseem us, your darkness deriding,
To deem the false beacons we steer by, are true ;
Many a proud vessel of ours lacketh guiding,
And many among us are blinder than you.

Though we bask in the light of this world, we may
borrow
Through the depth of your darkness a ray from
above,
A rebuke for our pride, and a balm for our sorrow,
A lesson of warning, of comfort, and love.

Though it bloom in concealment, yet sweet is the
flower;
And the harp that is hid still enraptures the ear ;
And Heaven, in its mercy, has left you the power,
The Word which was preached to blind nations, to
hear.

The star which conducted the Magian stranger,
In vain on your pathway, its lustre has thrown ;
But the song of the angels to Bethlehem's manger
Has led you as surely through regions unknown.

That song is not silent : around us, and o'er us,
The ear of the spirit still traces the sound,
Swelling on, till the full host of Heaven in chorus
Proclaims, with hosannas, the threshold is found.

Though veil'd for a season, that star's culmination
O'er the portal of Eden has still to aspire,
When the cherub who guards it, released from his
station,
Shall sheath, at that signal, his weapon of fire.

The steps to that portal, by Jacob, in slumber
Once seen, but too many and glorious to count,
Your eyes, re-awakened, shall measure and number—
Your footsteps, assisted by angels, shall mount.

Await, then, in patience, His second descending,
Who came the dark fetters of sin to unbind,
And to cancel the sentence on mortal offending,
With words to the speechless, and sight to the blind.

And, perhaps, the bright vision of splendour unbounded
Shall burst on your long-darkened eyes more sublime,
Than those which the world with its glare has confounded,
Or dimm'd with the mists of corruption and crime.

Bee moth.—James Thatcher, author of the " American Orchardist," &c. &c., in a communication to the New England Farmer, says : " I will embrace this opportunity to communicate for the benefit of the cultivator, what I believe to be an infallible remedy against the bee moth, which has proved so destructive to bees throughout our country of late years. The remedy is simple and easily applied. It consists merely of covering the floor board on which the hive stands, with common earth about an inch thick. A hive set on earth will never be infested with worms, for the bee moth will not deposit her eggs where the earth will come in contact. She naturally resorts to a dry board as her element. The remedy has been employed by a number of persons in this vicinity for several years, with the most complete success."

Break not your promise, unless it be unlawful or impossible ; either out of your natural, or out of your civil power.—*Taylor.*

THE FRIEND.

THIRD MONTH, 28, 1840.

It has been our desire from the first, in conducting this journal, to preserve a disposition docile and teachable ; not only to hold ourselves open to reproof and correction, when offered in the spirit of kindness, but even to invite the watchful supervision of those, who from age and experience are best entitled to exercise it. We have therefore not hesitated to insert to-day the sensible animadversions by a writer under the signature A. V., having a bearing of considerable severity upon ourselves, yet couched in terms both courteous and friendly. An additional motive for giving the article a place, is to be found in the latter portion of the remarks, which have a more general application, and are worthy of all acceptation. But while we admit for the most part the soundness and pertinency of those remarks, and hope to derive improvement from them in the future exercise of our editorial functions, we may be allowed, in justice to ourselves, to allude to the hundreds of cases of which the writer of the article may not, nay cannot be aware, wherein we have carried out into practice the scrutiny and vigilance recommended, by curtailment, revision, and the substitution of one word or phrase for another, in order to maintain consistency of character with the name we bear, and to avoid all occasion of wounding the tender feelings of the most scrupulous. It ought also to be remembered, that such is the frailty of our nature, the most circumspect and watchful are liable to occasional lapses, and that in filling out the periodical sheet, additional matter is called for by the printer, time presses, and articles will sometimes inadvertently slip in, without having been subjected to that strict examination which is always necessary.

WESTTOWN SCHOOL.

The committee to superintend the boarding school at Westtown, will meet there on fifth day the 9th of next month, at 3 o'clock, P. M.

The committee on teachers, is to meet on the same day at 1 o'clock, P. M.—and the visiting committee to attend at the school on seventh day the 4th of the month.

THOMAS KIMBER, Clerk.

Philadelphia, 3d mo. 28th, 1840.

DANIEL WHEELER'S LETTERS

Are now ready for delivery to subscribers. Those who left their subscriptions at the office of " *The Friend,*" can receive the work there—where also the work will be kept for sale. Any subscription papers not yet sent in had better be forwarded without further delay.

FRIENDS' ASYLUM.

Committee on Admissions.—John G. Hoskins, No. 60 Franklin street, and No. 50 North Fourth street, up stairs ; E. B. Garrigues, No, 185 North Seventh street, and No. 41 Market street, up stairs ; Isaac Collins, No. 129 Filbert street, and No. 50 Commerce street; Edward Yarnall, southwest corner of Twelfth and George streets, and No. 39 Market street ; Samuel Bettle, jr., No. 73 North Tenth street, and 26 South Front street.

Visiting Managers for the Month.—Geo. R. Smith, No. 487 Arch street ; Lindsey Nicholson, No. 24 South Twelfth street ; George G. Williams, No. 61 Marshall street.

Superintendents.—John C. and Lætitia Redmond.

Attending Physician.—Dr. Charles Evans, No. 201 Arch street.

Resident Physician.—Dr. Thomas Wood.

Apprentice wanted, to the retail Drug and Apothecary business, by a Friend of this city —apply at this office.

MARRIED, at Friends' meeting, New Garden, Chester county, on fourth day, the 11th inst., PENNOCK HOOVES, of New Garden, to HARRIET B. daughter of Issachar Hoopes, of Kennett Square.

——— at Friends' meeting house, Cropwell, New Jersey, on fifth day, the 19th inst., JOHN S. LOWRY, of Philadelphia, to ELIZABETH C. daughter of Isaac Stokes, of the-former place.

——— at Friends' meeting house, Deep River, N. C. on the 19th of third month, 1840, THOMAS M'CRACKIN, of Randolph county, to JANE H. daughter of Nathan Mendenhall, of Guilford.

DIED, on the 21st of twelfth month last, at her residence in Fayette county, Ohio, in the 85th year of her age, ELEANOR TODHUNTER, widow of our late esteemed friend, Isaac Todhunter. They were early settlers within the limits of Indiana Yearly Meeting, while the natives of the land were still hunting game in the surrounding woods. They were members of Fairfield Monthly Meeting, and the principal location of the meeting on Walnut Creek, near their residence. At their house the weary traveller in the service of Truth found a welcome resting place. Near the close of her advanced life she enjoyed the satisfaction of seeing an enlargement of the little meeting which she had so long laboured to sustain, and having faithfully lived her day and generation, she is, we have not a doubt, gathered to the fold of rest.

PRINTED BY ADAM WALDIE,

Carpenter Street, below Seventh, Philadelphia.

THE FRIEND.

A RELIGIOUS AND LITERARY JOURNAL.

VOL. XIII.   SEVENTH DAY, FOURTH MONTH, 4, 1840.   **NO. 27.**

EDITED BY ROBERT SMITH.

PUBLISHED WEEKLY.

Price two dollars per annum, payable in advance.

Subscriptions and Payments received by

GEORGE W. TAYLOR,

NO. 50, NORTH FOURTH STREET, UP STAIRS,

PHILADELPHIA.

LAURA BRIDGMAN.

The last number of the Annual Report of the Trustees of the Perkins Institution and Asylum for the Blind, contains some further interesting intelligence respecting this little girl, who is deaf, dumb, and blind. She is also deprived of the sense of smell, and enjoys taste but imperfectly—the *touch*, alone, being the medium of communication between her and the outer world. The following account of the progress of this little girl in intellectual knowledge, is furnished by the report:

"There is one whose situation is so peculiar, and whose case is so interesting in a philosophical point of view, that we cannot forbear making particular mention of it; we allude to Laura Bridgman, the deaf, dumb, and blind girl, mentioned in the two last reports.

"The intellectual improvement of this interesting being, and the progress she has made in expressing her ideas, is truly gratifying.

"She uses the manual alphabet of the deaf mutes with great facility and great rapidity, she has increased her vocabulary so as to comprehend the names of all common objects; she uses adjectives expressive of positive qualities, such as hard, soft, sweet, sour, &c. verbs expressive of action—as give, take, ride, run, &c. in the present, past and future tense; she connects adjectives with nouns to express their qualities; she introduces verbs into sentences, and connects them by conjunctions: for instance, a gentleman having given her an apple, she said, *man, give Laura sweet apple.*

"She can count to high numbers; she can add and subtract small numbers.

"But the most gratifying acquirement which she has made, and the one which has given her the most delight, is the power of *writing a legible hand*, and expressing her thoughts upon paper. She writes with a pencil in a grooved line, and makes her letters clear and distinct.

"She was sadly puzzled at first to know the meaning of the process to which she was subjected, but when the idea dawned upon her mind, that by means of it she could convey intelligence to her mother, her delight was unbounded. She applied herself with great diligence, and in a few months actually wrote a legible letter to her mother; in which she conveyed information of her being well, and of her coming home in ten weeks. It was, indeed, only the skeleton of a letter; but still it expressed in legible characters, a vague outline of the ideas which were passing in her mind. She was very impatient to have *the man* carry this letter—for she supposed that the utmost limit of the Post Office Department was to employ a man to run backward and forward between our institution and the different towns where the pupils live, to fetch and carry letters. We subjoin to this report an exact *fac simile* of Laura's writing—observing that she was not prompted to the matter, and that her hand was not held in the execution. The matter is quite original, and the chirography is entirely her own.

"She has improved very much in personal appearance, as well as in intellect—her countenance beams with intelligence—she is always active at study, work, or play—she never repines, and most of the time is gay and frolicksome.

"She is now very expert with her needle; she knits very easily, and can make twine bags and various fancy articles very prettily. She is very docile—has a quick sense of propriety—dresses herself with great neatness, and is always correct in her deportment. In short, it would be difficult to find a child in the possession of all her senses, and the enjoyment of advantages that wealth and parental love can bestow, who is more contented and cheerful, or to whom existence seems a greater blessing than it does to this bereaved creature, for whom the sun has no light, the air no sound, and the flowers no colour or smell."

In the appendix, a more elaborate description is given of the case and acquirements of this little girl—thus shut out in a great degree from communication with her fellow beings. It must be gratifying to those who are interested in the study of the operations of the human mind, to know that careful observations continue to be made, with a view of ascertaining the order of developements, and the peculiar character of her intellectual faculties. The following extracts from the appendix will be found interesting:

"Having mastered the manual alphabet of the deaf mutes, and learned to spell readily the names of every thing within her reach, she was then taught words expressive of positive qualities, as hardness, softness; and she readily learned to express the quality, by connecting the adjective hard or soft with the substantive; though she generally followed what one would suppose to be the natural order in the succession of ideas, placing the substantive first.

"No definite course of instruction can be marked out; for her inquisitiveness is so great, that she is very much disconcerted if any question which occurs to her is deferred until the lesson is over. It is deemed best to gratify her, if her inquiry has any bearing on the lesson; and often she leads her teacher far away from the objects he commenced with.

"For instance, picking up a nail in one of her lessons, she instantly asked its name—and it being spelled, she was dissatisfied, and thought the teacher had made a mistake; for she knew *n a i l* stood for her finger nail—and she was very anxious to go to head quarters, to be sure the teacher was right.

"She often asks questions which unfortunately cannot be satisfactorily answered to her; for it is painful to excite such a vivid curiosity as now exists in her mind, and then baulk it. For instance, she once asked with much eagerness, why one arrangement of letters was not as good as another, to express the name of a thing; as why *t a c* should not express the idea of the animal as well as *c a t.* This she expressed partly by signs, and partly by words, but her meaning was perfectly clear; she was puzzled, and wished an explanation.

"In her eagerness to advance her knowledge of words, and to communicate her ideas, she coined words, and is always guided by analogy. Sometimes her process of *word making* is very interesting; for instance, after some time spent in giving her an idea of the abstract meaning of *alone*, she seemed to obtain it, and understanding that being by *one's self* was to be alone, or *al-one*; she was told to go to her chamber, or to school, or elsewhere, and return *alone*;—she did so, but soon after, wishing to go with one of the little girls, she strove to express her meaning thus. Laura go *al-two.*

"Having acquired the use of substantives, adjectives, verbs, prepositions, and conjunctions, it was deemed time to make the experiment of trying to teach her to *write*, and to show her that she might communicate her ideas to persons not in contact with her.

"It was amusing to witness the mute amazement with which she submitted to the process—the docility with which she imitated every motion, and the perseverance with which she moved her pencil over and over again in the same track, until she could form the letter. But when at last the idea dawned upon her, that by this mysterious process she could make other people understand what she thought, her joy was boundless.

"Never did a child apply more eagerly and joyfully to any task than she did to this, and in a few months she could make every letter distinctly, and separate words from each other.

"The following anecdote will give an idea of her fondness for teazing, or innocent fun, or mischief.—Her teacher, looking one day unobserved into the girls' play-room, saw three blind girls playing with a rocking-horse. Laura was on the crupper, another in the saddle, and a third clinging on the neck, and they were all in high glee, swinging backward and forward as far as the rockers would roll. There was a peculiarly arch look in Laura's countenance—the natural language of sly fun. She seemed prepared to give a spring, and suddenly when her end was lowest, and the others were perched high in the air, she sidled quickly off on to the floor, and down went the other end so swiftly as to throw the girls off the horse.

"This Laura evidently expected, for she stood a moment convulsed with laughter, then ran eagerly forward with outstretched hands to find the girls, almost screaming with joy. As soon, however, as she got hold of one of them, she perceived that she was hurt, and instantly her countenance changed, she seemed shocked and grieved, and after caressing and comforting her playmate, she found the other, and seemed to apologise by spelling the word *wrong*, and caressing her.

"When she can puzzle her teacher she is pleased, and often purposely spells a word wrong, with a playful look; and if she can catch her teacher in a mistake, she bursts into an ecstacy of laughter.

"When her teacher had been at work, giving her an idea of the words carpenter, chairmaker, painter, &c. in a generic sense, and told her that blacksmith made *nails*, she instantly held up her fingers, and asked if blacksmith made them, though she knew well he did not.

"With little girls of her own age she is full of frolic and fun, and no one enjoys a game at *romps* more than Laura.

"She has the same fondness for a dress, for ribbons, and for finery, as any other girls of her age, and as a proof that it arises from the same amiable desire of pleasing others, it may be remarked that whenever she has a new bonnet, or any new article of dress, she is particularly desirous to go to meeting, or to go out with it. If people do not notice it, she directs their attention by placing their hand upon it.

"Generally she indicates her preference for such visitors as are the best dressed.

"She seems to have a perception of character, and to have no esteem for those who have little intellect. The following anecdote is significant of her perception of character, and shows that from her friends she requires something more than good-natured indulgence:

"A new scholar entered school—a little girl about Laura's age. She was very helpless, and laura took great pride and great pains in showing her the way about the house, assisting her to dress and undress, and doing for her many things which she could not do herself.

"In a few weeks it began to be apparent, even to Laura, that the child was not only helpless, but naturally very stupid, being almost an idiot. Then Laura gave her up in despair, and avoided her, and has ever since had an aversion to being with her, passing her by as if in contempt. By a natural association of ideas, she attributes to this child all those countless deeds which Mr. *Nobody* does in every house—if a chair is broken, or any thing is misplaced, and no one knows who did it, Laura attributes it at once to this child.

"It has been observed before that she is familiar with the processes of addition and subtraction in small numbers. Subtracting one number from another puzzled her for a time, but by help of objects she accomplished it. She can count and conceive objects to about one hundred in number—to express an indefinitely great number, or more than she can count, says, *hundred*. If she thought a friend was to be absent many years, she would say—will come hundred *Sundays*—meaning weeks. She is pretty accurate in measuring time, and seems to have an intuitive tendency to do it. Unaided by the changes of night and day, by the light, or the sound of any timepiece, she nevertheless divides time accurately.

"With regard to the sense of touch it is very acute—even for a blind person. It is shown remarkably in the readiness with which she distinguishes persons: there are forty inmates in the female wing, with all of whom of course Laura is acquainted; whenever she is walking through the passage ways, she perceives by the jar of the floor, or the agitation of the air, that some one is near her, and it is exceedingly difficult to pass her without being recognised. Her little arms are stretched out, and the instant she grasps a hand, a sleeve, or even part of the dress, she knows the person and lets them pass on with some sign of recognition.

"The innate desire for knowledge, and the instinctive efforts which the human faculties make to exercise their functions, is shown most remarkably in Laura. Her tiny fingers are to her eyes, and ears, and nose, and most deftly and incessantly does she keep them in motion: like the feelers of some insects which are continually agitated, and which touch every grain of sand in the path, so Laura's arms and hands are continually in play; and when she is walking with a person she not only recognises every thing she passes within touching distance, but by continually touching her companion's hands she ascertains what he is doing. A person walking across the room while she had hold on his left arm, would find it hard to take a pencil out of his waistcoat pocket with his right hand, without her perceiving it.

"Her judgment of distances and of relations of place is very accurate; she will rise from her seat, go straight towards a door, put out her hand just at the right time, and grasp the handle with precision.

"When she runs against a door which is shut, but which she expected to find open, she does not fret, but rubs her head and laughs, as though she perceived the ludicrous position of a person flat against a door trying to walk through it.

"The constant and tireless exercise of her feelers gives her a very accurate knowledge of every thing about the house; so that if a new article, a bundle, bandbox, or even a new book, is laid any where in the apartments which she frequents, it would be but a short time before in her ceaseless rounds she would find it, and from something about it she would generally discover to whom it belonged.

"She perceives the approach of persons by the undulations of the air striking her face;

and she can distinguish the step of those who tread hard, and jar the floor.

"At table, if told to be still, she sits and conducts herself with propriety; handles her cup, spoon, and fork, like other children; so that a stranger looking at her would take her for a very pretty child with a green ribbon over her eyes.

"But when at liberty to do as she chooses, she is continually feeling of things, and ascertaining their size, shape, density, and use—asking their names and their purposes, going on with insatiable curiosity, step by step, towards knowledge.

"Thus doth her active mind, though all silent and darkling within, commune by means of her one sense with things external, and gratify its innate craving for knowledge by close and ceaseless attention.

"Qualities and appearances, unappreciable or unheeded by others, are to her of great significance and value; and by means of these her knowledge of external nature and physical relations will in time become extensive."

For "The Friend."
SKETCHES OF SUPERSTITIONS.
(Continued from page 202.)

While the oracles continued to act the part of public and accredited prophets, there were various other means of looking into futurity, and procuring tokens of good or bad fortune. Of these, the most remarkable were certain signs, or marks in the intestines of victims, slain as sacrifices at the altars. The mode of sacrificing is worthy of explanation. Bulls, goats, sheep, pigeons, cocks, and other creatures were immolated to the gods of the country. Sometimes there was a hecatomb or sacrifice of a hundred animals at a time, to appease the manes or restless spirits of the deceased. A notion prevailed that the animals to be sacrificed would show signs of satisfaction on being brought to the altars, if the gods to whom they were offered felt pleased with the oblation. On bringing forward a bull or goat, the officiating priest drew a knife from the forehead to the tail, at which, if the victim struggled, it was rejected as not acceptable to the gods; but if it stood quietly at the altar, then they thought the gods were pleased with it; yet a bare non-resistance was not thought sufficient, unless it gave its assent, by a gracious nod; to try if it would nod, they poured water or barley into its ear. We should imagine that these tests seldom failed in making the animal plunge with its head. Being satisfied with the sign, the priest proceeded to pour wine, and sometimes fruits or frankincense, between the horns of the victim, and afterwards struck it down and bled it to death. Great dexterity was requisite in striking down and bleeding a victim; for if it did not fall at once upon the ground, or stamped or kicked, or struggled to be loose, or did not bleed freely, or seemed to die with pain, it was thought unacceptable to the gods.

The sacrifice being ended, the priest had his share, and another portion was given as a due to the magistrates; the remainder was usually carried home by the offering party for the sake of good luck and the preservation of health. Sometimes portions were sent as presents to absent friends; and sometimes they were exposed for sale at the public shambles. It was against partaking of the latter that the primitive christian church warned the disciples.

Besides the sacrifices, there were also other offerings to the gods, either to pacify them when angry, or to obtain some benefit, or as an acknowledgment of past favour. These consisted of crowns and garlands, garments, cups of gold, or any other thing that conduced to the ornament or the enriching of the temples. When any person changed his employment or way of life, it was customary to dedicate the instruments belonging to it as a grateful commemoration of the divine favour and protection. Thus, a fisherman dedicated his nets to the nymphs of the sea; shepherds hung up pipes to Pan, or some other of the country deities; and a lady, decayed with age, dedicated her mirror to Venus.

Divination by inspection of the intestines of the animals slain as sacrifices, was a business of a very grave kind, calling for the most earnest attention on the part of its professors. If there were any appearance of disease or injury, or any discoloration in the entrails, if the liver was dry, or if the heart palpitated, or was shrivelled, the sacrifice was unpropitious, and bad luck was to attend the proposed enterprise; if the gall was large and ready to burst there were to be bloody wars or fights. It was also a very unlucky omen when the fire applied to the victim did not ascend calmly and in a straight line, or when the smoke curled and spread abroad. There was also a mode of divination by dreaming. Its professors threw themselves at will into a trance, during which, it was pretended, they visited in spirit the celestial regions, whence they returned with supernatural knowledge. *In Athens a professed dreamer was kept at the public expense.*

Divination by watching the cries and motions of birds was a superstition of great antiquity. It was observed that certain kinds of these animals disappeared in flights at particular seasons, and again returned, in a manner equally mysterious and incomprehensible, to their wonted haunts. When they left the land toward the approach of winter, to seek warmer skies, they were believed to retire from our earthly sphere, and to visit the heavenly regions, there to enter into communication with the gods, and to receive from them a knowledge of future events; as birds could not disclose their information by language, it was customary to watch their flight, and also to kill them, for the sake of omens. If an eagle wheeled in its flight, or flew upwards, or perched on the ground, or if a flock of smaller birds settled on a temple, or was seen flying in a particular manner or direction, *something,* either good or evil was betokened. There were also lucky and unlucky birds. Both Aristotle and Pliny, two great men of antiquity, reckoned vultures to be very unlucky, because they were generally seen before any great slaughter. Owls were, for the most part, looked upon as unlucky birds, but at Athens were omens of victory and success, being sacred to Minerva, the peculiar tutelary

goddess of that city. The dove was thought to be lucky; so also was the swan, especially to mariners, being an omen of fair weather. Ravens were believed to receive a power of foretelling future events from Apollo. When they appeared about an army it was a bad omen; if they came croaking upon the right hand, it was a tolerably good omen: if on the left, a very bad one; the appearance and chattering of magpies were unlucky omens. Pliny affirms that the worst omens were given by ravens when they made a harsh sort of noise, rattling in their throats, as if they were choked. Cocks were also accounted prophetical, especially in matters of war, and their crowing was an auspicious omen: wherefore, Themistocles, after his victory over the Persians, instituted an annual feast, which was celebrated with exhibitions of fighting cocks. It was thought to be a token of a dreadful judgment, if a hen was heard to crow.

The superstitious beliefs of the Greeks and Romans were without number. Bees, ants, and various reptiles and beasts, were imagined to have the power of giving omens of good or bad fortune. It is related, that before Pompey's defeat, a swarm of bees settled upon the altar. This was a dreadful omen. Yet bees were not unlucky in all circumstances. When Plato was an infant in the cradle, bees are said to have come and sat upon his lips, whereupon the augurs foretold that he should be famous for sweetness of language and delightful eloquence. The death of Cimon, a Greek warrior, was reported to have been presaged by a swarm of ants, which, on the occasion of a sacrifice, crept in a cluster round his great toe. Toads were accounted unlucky omens, and snakes were likewise ominous. To meet a boar was reckoned very unlucky; and when a hare appeared to an army in time of war, it signified defeat and running away.

The phenomena of the atmosphere and planetary bodies were likewise a fertile source of superstitious delusions. Nieras, the Athenian general, being surrounded by his enemies, was struck with such consternation by an eclipse of the moon, that he commanded his soldiers to lay down their arms, and so with a numerous army tamely yielded himself up to slaughter. Lightning and thunder, if seen or heard on the right hand, were believed to be good omens, and if on the left, the reverse. It was a common belief that danger from lightning might be averted by hissing or whistling to it. When a thunder-storm commenced, all Athens fell to whistling. At Rome, places struck by lightning were held sacred, and enclosed from ordinary use. Not a wind could blow, but it was attributed to Æolus; nor a meteor could appear in the sky, but was imagined to be ominous of approaching good or evil. When two meteors appeared together, they were fancied to be torches held out by Castor and Pollux to light the mariner to port, and to forebode good weather; but if a third meteor happened to appear, it was declared to be Helena with a fiery dart chasing away Castor and Pollux. Among a people so superstitious as the Greeks and Romans, it will readily be conceived that earthquakes were ominous of signal national evils. Neptune, the subterranean deity, was believed

on these occasions to be so wrathful, that nothing short of the most valuable offerings, thrown into the gap caused by the earthquake, would appease his anger. Thus, Midas, king of Phrygia, on one occasion cast valuable jewels, and also his own son, into such a chasm; and when a gulf opened in Rome from a similar cause, Curtius leaped into it on horseback, as a voluntary sacrifice to Neptune, who was supposed to be gratified with the offering, for the gulf immediately closed upon and swallowed its heroic victim.

It will have been observed from the preceding sketches, that neither the Greeks nor Romans, two of the most refined nations of antiquity, had any just idea of the operations or works of nature, as arising from a train of immutable laws established and supported by an all-wise Providence, for the government of the universe. In this respect they stood exactly on a parallel with those uneducated persons of the present day who believe that the winds can be raised by incantation, and that bodily illness is an effect of the evil eye. The Greeks and Romans, however, excelled the ignorant of modern times, for they had formed a regular code of superstition, which was applicable to every circumstance, event, or condition, either in nature or art. Never, perhaps, was there such a laboured and complex mass of superstition, never such a complete bewilderment of the human faculties as that which lately existed in Rome, and all to account for what could be explained by an appeal to the most simple laws of nature.

In those days of mental hallucination, occupying many centuries of the world's history, the human being was handed over from deity to deity from the moment he came into life, and before he had seen the light, till he was at last consigned to the grave or the funeral pile. According to the improved and extended mythology of the Romans, Deverra presided over his destiny before birth, Janus and Ops helped him into the world, whilst Egeria took care of the mother, Lucina watched over his cradle, Vegetanus had the charge of him when he cried, Rumina was his guardian when he suckled, Edura presided over his food, and Stelinus instructed him in walking. As he grew in stature, he came successively under the charge of gods and goddesses who watched over his youth and manhood. When he married, both he and his bride became. the peculiar charge of five different deities: and when he died, his funeral was duly presided over by Libitina, the deity of burial ceremonies. Besides all this, every meal in the day, every kind of apparel, every transaction of business or amusement, every distinct part of the body had its tutelary deity, on whom the blame fell if any thing was amiss. The enormity of the superstition is overpowering; yet all that we have related as respects the belief in ideal gods, oricles, dreamers, sacrifices, omens from birds and entrails of beasts, also omens from natural phenomena, formed scarcely a moiety of the superstitious delusions of this ancient people.

Their belief in omens and divination of future events seems to have been absolutely boundless. Any perturbation of mind was supposed to be ominous of evil, but the evil was greatly aggravated if a number of persons at the same time felt an unaccountable emotion of dread. When such was the case, the fears were ascribed to the wicked influence of the god Pan, and hence the common phrase *panic*, or panic fears. The dread of approaching evil was also felt if the left eyelid quivered, or the left ear rang; the quivering of the right eyelid, or the ringing of the right ear, portended good. The latter is a superstition which has come down to our own day. Moles or other marks on the person meant something of importance, and were carefully noted. All kinds of internal pains or emotions were likewise the subject of superstitious dread, and a book was written to explain the precise extent of evil of which they were the premonitory warnings. No sudden involuntary motion in body or mind was so much the object of remark as sneezing. Both Greeks and Romans of the highest rank paid extraordinary attention to sneezing. A sneeze was accounted fortunate or unfortunate, according to the manner or period in which it occurred. When Xenophon was persuading his soldiers to encounter the enemy, some one sneezed, and it was accounted so dangerous an omen, that public prayers were appointed to expiate it. To sneeze between midnight and the following noon was lucky, but to sneeze between noon and midnight was unlucky. Aristotle talks very gravely on the difference between sneezing during these two periods of the day. If, in undertaking any business two or four sneezes happened, it was a lucky omen, and gave encouragement to prodeed; if more than four, the omen was neither good nor bad; if one or three, it was unlucky. If two persons were deliberating about any business, and both of them chanced to sneeze together, the omen was prosperous.

(To be continued.)

For "The Friend."

THOUGHTS ON THE TIMES.

NO. IV.

The sentiments which I have expressed may sound strange in the ears of the mere political economist, the professor of a science which investigates the causes of the prosperity, meaning thereby the wealth, of nations, without reference to its morals. But the Christian who applies himself to these investigations can never lose sight of the great fact, which is so carefully shut out from the prevailing systems of philosophy, that, namely, of the fallen condition of our race, and the inability of the human mind itself, to do any good thing. Let us then, at the risk of being tedious, trace those laws of our nature which the Creator has ordained for the social improvement and physical well-being of the species, and the influence of the sense of duty in rendering them subservient to the higher interests of religion and morality. It will be found that those desires, the unchecked predominance of which is so fatal to virtue, are the very principle of life, of social improvement, and when maintained in their just subordination to the higher authority of duty, exert an influence altogether unmixed with evil upon individuals and communities.

That it is the divine will that man should labour for the support of his bodily frame, is clear, from the sentence pronounced upon our first parents; from the circumstances with which the Creator has surrounded us, and from the indissoluble connection which He has established between labour and the attainment of most of the objects of desire.

The Christian law respecting this duty is contained in the sermon upon the mount; and the doctrine which is there inculcated is, that if we resign ourselves to be the disciples of Christ, and seek first the kingdom of heaven, the necessary provision for the wants of the body will follow upon the performance of those duties. The true interpretation of our Saviour's language is, that the taking care of the body and the providing for its sustenance being essential duties of man, they will find their proper though subordinate place in the mind that seeks first the kingdom of heaven. They will thereby be preserved from engendering the sin of covetousness, and from occupying an undue portion of our time and thoughts. No rule can be more simple, and comprehensive, and practical, than that which is here laid down. It is a rule which adapts itself to the circumstances and social duties of every individual in all the various conditions of civilized life. If we seek first the kingdom of heaven, keep in view in all our thoughts and actions the great ends of our existence, every other interest and pursuit will naturally assume their just level, and occupy no more than their proper space in our affections.

We cannot doubt that it is lawful and commendable to explore the works of the Deity, and that our capacities for enjoyment were meant to be gratified. There is nothing in the severest interpretation of the law of self-denial to forbid our sharing moderately of those fruits with which the bounty of Providence has surrounded us; to restrain us from employing those processes in the preparation of our food, which not only render it more palatable, but without which a large portion of the destined nutriment of man would be even unwholesome; nothing to condemn that attention to the selection of raiment which regards the usefulness or healthiness or convenience of the fabric and its fashion; or to prevent us from seeking, amidst the lavish variety of nature, new and more wholesome and more agreeable materials for food and clothing.

The first discovery that men make in entering upon this pursuit after the means of sustenance, is that of the advantages of the division of labour. At so early a period do men distribute themselves into particular occupations, that it seems almost like the operation of a social instinct. Not only does a far less amount of labour thereby produce the same results, but it accomplishes its purposes with more skill and sagacity. The continued application of human ingenuity to the means for accomplishing a certain end, must necessarily create improvements therein. These improvements do not perish with the individual, but are thrown into the common stock of the community. There is, therefore, a necessary tendency to improvement in the shape and texture, and materials, for example, of our clothing, which is continually bringing about changes

in the habits of the community, and in the direction of its industry. This tendency is the very principle of life of the industrious arts; for they could not survive without it, and it has invigorated and sustained until they have filled the world with their wonders. If we examine the manner in which the sense of Christian duty operates, we shall see that it is not hostile to this improvement. The Christian, as well as other men, has his inducements to cultivate the arts of industry, for the time which he can gain from servile labour and the earnings of that labour beyond his reasonable wants, are due to the service of his Maker. He enters upon life, like all other men, possessed of arts and knowledge according to the age and community in which he lives. Luxury and abstinence, riches and poverty, self-indulgence and self-denial, are terms in a great measure relative. What constitutes the luxury of the few in one age, becomes the conveniences or the necessaries of life to the many in another. As communities advance in intelligence and civilization, new arts almost spontaneously arise, for new wants are felt which give a new direction to industry.

He who seeks first the kingdom of heaven will maintain the desires and interests which are thus incessantly modified by a changing civilization, subordinate to his higher duties. But he is part of that community, he feels its wants and shares its attainments, and he is to be measured, and he must judge of his duties and regulate his occupations, by the standard of his own time, and not by that of another. He is born likewise in a particular station, and is entrusted with gifts of mind as well as with advantages of condition by his Maker.

The duties and the occupations of each one of us vary with the lot in which Providence has placed us, and no wise moralist will estimate by the same inventory of things forbidden and things allowable, the virtues and the duties of widely different circumstances in the social condition. The Christian, therefore, in giving the necessary attention to the provision for his bodily wants, cannot but be influenced by the circumstances to which he is born, by the competition of industry in his particular avocation, and by the incentives to improvement which are thus carrying forward the arts of life to perfection.

The desire of accumulating wealth on the one hand, and that for new pleasures on the other, are the two great powers which give to the mechanism of the industrious arts, its intense and unceasing energy. Uncontrolled by the spirit of religion, they extend the dominion and increase the power of the passions, until, being mainly directed to the gratification of sensual indulgence; they place sin and pride and sensuality, in the seat of truth and virtue and conscience, as the governors of the world. The power. which is thus imparted to the spirit of improvement in the arts, becomes at length a diseased and vicious power, perverted from the true ends of industry, hostile to the true interests of man. Those energies of the human mind which are thus absorbed by the arts that minister to the evil and sensual passions; the industry, for example, that is expended in perfecting the arts of war and destruction, or the attractions of vain amusements, are due to the intellectual and moral improvement of our race and to the service of our Creator ; and reason condemns and religion forbids this perversion of our powers.

The great end in view of those who labour is to gain the means of leisurely enjoyment. So far as the inclinations of mankind lead them to seek their satisfaction in sensual delights, example and emulation are continually increasing the costliness of these pleasures, and the difficulty of obtaining the means of enjoyment. The temptations to engage in the pursuit, augment with the estimate that is formed of the prize in view. The number of those who rashly and improvidently partake of these luxurious pleasures, and who are thereby plunged into an imbecile poverty, is thus continually increasing with this increase of vicious luxury and splendour. An almost universal consequence of this has been, that the wealth of nations is collected in the hands of a comparatively few, while the many are doomed to a hopeless struggle after those pleasures which are spread before them, yet placed beyond their reach. The industry of the whole is intense, yet the rich have too often been able to bring the influence of political institutions to keep down the poor and reduce the wages of industry to the minimum of subsistence.

The spirit of religion modifies these evil influences in many ways. It moderates the desires of all, and changes the objects of desire from sensual and vicious to intellectual and virtuous enjoyments. It teaches us to regard the interests and to minister to the wants of our fellow creatures ; it banishes the pleasures of vice, and forbids the occupations that are devoted to the service of the fierce and sensual passions.

After all our exultation over the advancement of the arts, we must admit that they are valuable as means rather than as ends ; that beyond the points of actual subsistence and homely comfort, if they do not add to our moral strength and intellectual dignity, they are but encumbrances to the soul.

The conclusions to which these reasonings lead are, that the influence of religion and duty in retarding the advance of the industrious arts, by moderating our desires, is more than compensated by narrowing the field of labour, and cutting off all those occupations which minister to vice and folly ; that the restrictions which they impose upon our love of sensual indulgence convert narrow circumstances into independence ; and that they thus enable us to appropriate to intellectual and religious improvement the time which the sordid and sensual devote to anxious labour and to dissipation. All the great ends of existence are thus gained. The individual lives to God, and in thus living performs all his duties to society. The improvement of the race in all the arts that minister to lawful enjoyment, is steadily advancing. There is no progress made that is at the same time a downward progress in morals ; and although particular societies and classes of society will not so speedily attain an extraordinary height of cultivation, virtue, independence, intelligence, industry and contentment will be far more widely and advantageously diffused.

Report on Education in Europe, to the Trustees of the Girard College for Orphans ; by ALEX. DALLAS BACHE, LL. D., President of the College.

(Continued from p. 203.)

As an example, appropriate to the pages of our journal, of the style and descriptive talent of the reporter, so long an efficient *colaborateur* in the concerns of the Franklin Institute, we quote his account of the " School of Arts of Berlin."

" *Institute of Arts of Berlin.*"*

" This institution is intended to impart the theoretical knowledge essential to improvement in the arts, and such practical knowledge as can be acquired to advantage in a school. It is supported by the government, and has also a legacy, to be expended in bursaries at the school, from Baron Von Seydlitz. The institution is under the charge of a director,† who has the entire control of the funds, of the admissions and dismissions, and the superintendence of the instruction. The professors and pupils do not reside in the establishment, so that the superintendence is confined to study hours. There are assistant professors, who prepare the lectures, and conduct a part of the exercises, in some cases reviewing the lessons of the professors with the pupils. Besides these officers, there are others, who have charge of the admirable collections of the institution, and of the workshops, offices, &c. The number of professors is eight, and of repeaters, two. The discipline is of the most simple character, for no pupil is allowed to remain in connection with the institution unless his conduct and progress are satisfactory. There is but one punishment recognised, namely, dismission ; and even a want of punctuality is visited thus severely.

" In the spring of every year the regencies advertise that applications will be received for admission into the institute, and the testimonials of the candidates who present the best claims are forwarded to the director at Berlin, who decides finally upon the several nominations. The pupils from the provincial schools have, in general, the preference over other applicants. At the same time notice is given by the president of the Society for the Promotion of National Industry, in relation to the bursaries vacant upon the Seydlitz foundation. The qualifications essential to admission are —to read and write the German language with correctness and facility, and to be thoroughly acquainted with arithmetic in all its branches. The candidate must, besides, be at least seventeen years of age. Certain of the pupils,

* Gewerbinstitut, literally, trade institute. I am indebted to the director, privy counsellor Beuth, for a lithographic outline and programme of this institution, and to Henry Wheaton, minister of the United States at Berlin, for an account of the industrial schools of Prussia, by Captain Beaulieu, Belgian chargé d'affaires at Berlin. Beuth gave me every facility in visiting the institution.

† The director, Beuth, is also president of the Royal Technical Commission of Prussia, and has the distribution of the funds for the encouragement of industry, amounting to about seventy-five thousand dollars annually. He is also a privy counsellor, and is president of the Society for the Encouragement of National Industry in Prussia.

as will be hereafter more fully stated, require to have served an apprenticeship to a trade. The Seydlitz bursars must, in addition, show —1st. That their parents were not artisans,* relatives of the founder having the preference over other applicants. 2d. That they have been apprenticed to a trade, if they intend to follow one not taught in the institution. 3d. They must enter into an engagement that if they leave the mechanical career they will pay back the amount of their bursaries. There are sixty or seventy gratuitous pupils in the school, of whom eighteen are upon the Seydlitz foundation. Forty are admitted annually, this number having been adopted because it is found that, in the course of the first month, about a fourth of the newly admitted pupils fall away from the institution. Each bursar receives two hundred and twenty-five dollars per annum for maintenance. The education is gratuitous. The regular pupils enter on the first of October ; but the director is authorised to admit, at his pleasure, applicants who do not desire to become bursars, but who support themselves, receiving gratuitously, however, the instruction afforded by the institution.

" The education of the pupils is either solely theoretical, or combines theory and practice, according to the calling which they intend to follow. The first division is composed of students, who receive theoretical instruction only, and who are preparing to become masons, carpenters, and joiners. They are supposed to have become acquainted with the practice of their trade before entering the institution, being required to have served previously, a part of their apprenticeship. An excellent reason is assigned for this rule, namely, that on leaving the school such pupils are too old to begin their apprenticeship to these callings, and would, if they attempted to do so, find the first beginnings so irksome as to induce them to seek other employments, and thus their special education would be lost, and the object of the school defeated. The second division embraces both theoretical and practical instruction, and consists of three classes. First, the stone-cutters, engravers, lapidaries, glass-cutters, carvers in wood and ivory, and brass-founders. Second, dyers and manufacturers of chemical products. Third, machine-makers and mechanicians. The practical instruction is different for each of these three classes.

" The general course of studies lasts two years, and the pupils are divided into two corresponding classes. The first class is, besides, subdivided into two sections. The lower or second class is taught first ; mechanical drawing, subdivided into decorative drawing, including designs for architectural ornaments, utensils, vases, patterns for weaving, &c. and linear drawing, applied to civil works, to handicrafts, and to machines. Second, modelling in clay, plaster, and wax. Third, practical arithmetic. Fourth, geometry. Fifth, natural philosophy. Sixth, chemistry. Seventh, technology, or a knowledge of the materials,

* The object of Von Seydlitz appears to have been to counteract, to the extent of his power, the tendency to the increase of the learned professions, at the expense of the mechanic arts, by an inducement to a course exactly contrary to the usual one.

processes, and products of the arts. The studies of the lower section of the first class are general, while those of the first section turn more particularly upon the applications of science to the arts. In the lower section, the drawing, modelling, natural philosophy, and chemistry, of the first year, are continued; and, in addition, descriptive geometry, trigonometry, stereometry, mixed mathematics, mineralogy, and the art of construction are studied. In the upper or first section, perspective, stonecutting, carpentry, and mechanics applied to the arts, are taught, and the making of plans and estimates for buildings, workshops, manufactories, machines, &c. These courses are common to all pupils, whatever may be their future destination; but beside them, the machinists study, during the latter part of their stay at the institution, a continuation of the course of mechanics and mathematical analysis. The examples accompanying the instruction in regard to plans and estimates are adapted to the intended pursuits of the pupils.

"The courses of practice are begun by the pupils already enumerated as taking part in them, at different periods of their stay in the institution. The future chemists and mechanics must have completed the whole range of studies above mentioned, as common to all the pupils, while the others begin their practice after having completed the first year's course. There are workshops for each class of pupils, where they are taught the practice of their proposed calling, under competent workmen. There are two foundries for bronze castings, one for small, the other for large castings, and the work turned out of both bears a high character. A specimen of this work is retained by the institution in a beautiful fountain, which ornaments one of the courts of the building. The models for castings are made in the establishment. In the first division of pupils, in reference to their callings, there are usually some whose art is connected with the fine arts in some of its branches, and these have an opportunity during part of the week to attend the courses of the Berlin Academy. The future chemists work for half the year in the laboratory. They are chiefly employed in chemical analysis, being furnished with the requisite materials for practice by the institution. In the shops for the instruction of mechanics are machines, for working in wood and the metals, a steam-engine of four horses' power, a forge, tools in great variety, lathes, &c. The pupils have the use of all the necessary implements, according to their progress, and are gradually taught, as if serving a regular apprenticeship. When capable, they are enabled to construct machines which may be useful to them subsequently, as a lathe, or machine for cutting screws, or the teeth of wheels, &c. and are furnished with all the materials for the purpose, the machine becoming their own property. In these workshops, also, the models for the cabinet of the school are made. This is by far the most complete establishment for practice which I met with in any institution, and I believe the practice is both real and effectual. It involves, however, an expenditure which in other cases it has not been practicable to command. The scale of

the whole institution is, in the particular of expenditure, most generous.

"This is one specimen of the various plans which have been devised to give practical knowledge of an art in connection with theory in a school. It is first most judiciously laid down that certain trades cannot be taught to advantage in a similar connection, but that the practical knowledge must be acquired by an apprenticeship antecedent to the theoretical studies. There are besides, however, a large number of trades, the practice of which is to be taught in the institution, and requiring a very considerable expenditure to carry out the design properly. This could not be attempted in a school less munificently endowed, and requires very strict regulations to carry it through even here. The habits of a school workshop are, in general, not those of a real manufactory, where the same articles are made to be sold as a source of profit; hence, though the practical knowledge may be acquired, the habits of work are not, and the mechanic may be well taught but not well trained. At the private school of Charonne, workshops were established, giving a variety of occupation to the pupils; but the disposition to play rather than to work, rendered these establishments too costly to be supported by a private institution, and the plan adopted instead of this, was to make the pupils enter a regular workshop for a stated number of hours, to work for the proprietor or lessee. This plan remedies one evil, but introduces another, that as the machinist takes orders, with a view to profit, the work may have so little variety as only to benefit a small class of the pupils. The pupils at Charonne are, however, under different circumstances from those at Berlin; they are generally younger, and being independent of the school, where they pay for their education, are not under the same restraint as in the other institution; hence the experience of the one school does not apply in full force to the other. At Dresden, in a school somewhat similar to that of Berlin, a different mode from either of those just mentioned has been adopted. An arrangement is made with a number of mechanics, of different occupations, to receive pupils from the schools as apprentices, allowing them the privilege of attending, during certain specified hours of the day, upon the theoretical exercises of the institution. Where such an arrangement can be made, the results are unexceptionable, and the advantages likely to accrue to the mechanic arts, from the union of theory with practice, will offer a strong inducement to liberally disposed mechanics to take apprentices upon these terms. Small workshops, connected with an institution, must necessarily offer inferior advantages, even if closely regulated, so as to procure the greatest possible amount of work from the pupils; this should be done for the sake of the profit, but to give him genuinely good habits.

"The difficulties in giving practical instruction in the chemical arts are not to be compared with those under discussion, and will be found to have been satisfactorily obviated in several schools. This subject will receive its more appropriate discussion in connection with the polytechnic institution of Vienna, where the chemical department, at least as far as

manufacturing chemistry is concerned, is generally recognised as having produced the best results of any yet established.

"Returning to the subject of the theoretical instruction in the Berlin institute of arts, the following statement will serve to show the succession of the courses, with the time devoted to each:—

"Winter Course.

"*Second day of the week.*—*First Class.* First division—drawing and sketching machines, eight A. M. to twelve o'clock. Discussion of machines, estimates of power, &c. two P. M. to five P. M. Second division—machine drawing, eight to ten. Modelling in clay, ten to twelve. Physics, two to five. *Second Class.* Machine-drawing, eight to ten. Modelling, ten to twelve. Elements of geometry, two to four. Repetition of the lecture, four to five.

"*Third day.*—*First Class.* First division —architectural plans and estimates, eight to twelve. Practical instruction in machinery, two to five. Second division—ornamental and architectural drawing, eight to twelve. Trigonometry, two to five. *Second Class.* Ornamental and architectural drawing, eight to twelve. Physics, two to four. Repetition of the lecture, four to five.

"*Fourth day.*—*First Class.* First division —original designs, eight to twelve. Discussion of machinery. Second division—mineralogy, eight to nine. Machine-drawing, nine to twelve. Trigonometry, two to five. *Second Class.* Machine-drawing, eight to twelve. Practical arithmetic, two to five.

"*Fifth day.*—*First Class.* First division —drawing and sketching machines, eight to twelve. Architectural instruction, estimates, two to five. Second division—decorative and architectural drawing, eight to ten. Modelling in clay, ten to twelve. Trigonometry, two to five. *Second Class.* Decorative and architectural drawing, eight to ten. Modelling in clay, ten to twelve. Physics, two to four. Repetition of the lecture, four to five.

"*Sixth day.*—*First Class.* First division —architectural plans, eight to twelve. Practical instruction in machinery, two to five. Second division—machine-drawing, eight to twelve. Physics, two to five. *Second Class.* Machine-drawing, eight to twelve. Elementary mathematics, two to four. Repetition of the lesson, four to five.

"*Seventh day.*—*First Class.* First division —perspective and stone-cutting, eight to twelve. Original designs, two to five. Second division—mineralogy, eight to nine. Decorative and architectural drawing, nine to twelve. Trigonometry, two to five. *Second Class.* Decorative and architectural drawing, eight to twelve. Practical arithmetic, two to five.

"The summer term, which follows this, embraces the practical instruction.

[The summer term is also given, which we omit.]

"The chemical division of the practical classes is engaged every day in the laboratory from eight, P. M. on two days of the week.

"The collections for carrying out the various branches of instruction are upon the same liberal scale with the other parts of the institution. There is a library of works on architecture, mechanics, technology, the various arts, archeology, &c. in German, French and English. This library is open twice a week, from five to eight in the evening, to the pupils of the first class of the school, and to such mechanics as apply for the use of it.

"There is a rich collection of drawings of new and useful machines, and of illustrations of the different courses, belonging to the institution. Among them is a splendid work, published under the direction of Mr. Beuth, entitled Models for Manufacturers and Artisans (Vorlegeblatter fur Fabricanten und Handwerker), containing engravings by the best artists of Germany, and some even from France and England, applicable to the different arts and to architecture and engineering. Among the drawings are many from original designs by Shenckel, of Berlin. There is a second useful but more ordinary series of engravings, on similar subjects, also executed for the use of the school. These works are distributed to the provincial trade schools, and presented to such of the mechanics of Prussia as have especially distinguished themselves in their vocations. The collection of models of machinery belonging to the school probably ranks next in extent and value to that at the Conservatory of Arts of Paris. It contains models of such machines as are not readily comprehended by drawings. Most of them are working models, and many were made in the workshops of the school. They are constructed, as far as possible, to a uniform scale, and the parts of the models are of the same materials as in the actual machine. There is an extensive collection of casts, consisting of copies of statues, basso-relievos, utensils, bronzes, and vases of the museums of Naples, Rome, and Florence, and of the British Museum, and of the models of architectural monuments of Greece, Rome, Pompeii, &c. and copies of models, cameos, and similar objects; those specimens only have been selected which are not in the collection of the Academy of Fine Arts of Berlin, to which the pupils of the Institute of Arts have access. There are good collections of physical and chemical apparatus, of minerals, of geological and technological specimens.

"The instruction is afforded in part by the lectures of the professors, aided by text-books especially intended for the school, and in part by the interrogations of the professors and of the assistants and repeaters. At the close of the first year there is an examination to determine which of the pupils shall be permitted to go forward, and at the close of the second year to determine which shall receive the certificate of the institute. Although the pupils who come from the provinces are admitted to the first class of the institute, upon their presenting a testimonial that they have gone through the courses of the provincial schools satisfactorily, it frequently happens that they are obliged to retire to the second, especially from defective knowledge of chemistry.

"The cost of this school to the government is about twelve thousand dollars annually, exclusive of the amount expended upon the practical courses, and upon the collections—a very trifling sum, if the good which it is calculated to do throughout the country is considered. The comparatively recent existence of the institution does not admit of appealing to decided results which have flowed to the mechanic arts in Prussia from its establishment, but there can be no doubt of its tendency, and its pupils are already known to be making their way successfully, in consequence of the advantages which they have here enjoyed."

We trust it will not be very long before the institution of seminaries, analogous in principle to the one above described, will become an object of legislative regard, in some, at least, of the United States. Schools for the blind, and for deaf mutes, have taken root effectually in the philanthropy of the country, and it is scarcely to be questioned that the tendency of our civism is to the adoption of every useful discovery, whether in mechanical or moral science, as soon as its character of utility and beneficence has received the sanction of an evident demonstration.

G.

LIFE OF WILLIAM CATON.

(Concluded from page 206.)

These three things I left to her consideration, and when she was free, she was to return me an answer thereunto, which in several weeks after she did. As to the first she said, it was not means that she looked after, but virtue: and as to the second she said, that when I was moved of the Lord to go upon any service on account of the truth, whether to visit Friends or otherwise, she hoped that she should not be the woman that would hinder me upon such an account. And as to the last, she said, that if the Lord did once bring the thing so far as to be effected, she hoped to bear what people without should say, (when we were perfectly clear in the thing before the Lord,) for that would be one of the least crosses.

[W. C. then notes other circumstances confirming to his mind in the important step he was about to take, and proceeds:]

In the mean time I wrote of it to several of the brethren in England, whose answers in due time I received, and compared them together, and behold I found them unanimously agree in their mutual approbation of the step, which also was a further confirmation to me of its being of the Lord; yet in all this time we did not certainly know whether it would come to pass or no. We also were determined to keep clear from binding ourselves by promise; as some that are unwise have done, yes, and have resolved to accomplish the thing, though Friends should be against it; nevertheless will they ask advice, and that when it is too late. But this we resolved to avoid, to the end that we might be the better example; for it lay upon me that if the affair came to pass, it should be carried on in such wisdom, as that it should not only be of good report among the brethren, but that it should also be exemplary to them that should afterwards follow us in things of that nature; for it was the first marriage in those parts that was according to the approved manner and practice among Friends.

[He further remarks, "after we had waited long in the affair, and when several months were expired, and I had imparted it to several Friends in Holland, by word of mouth, and did not meet with any opposition"—and concludes his account of the matrimonial connection as follows:]

In the fulness of love and unity in the everlasting covenant did I receive her as the Lord's gift unto me. And oh! how were our hearts and souls overcome and refreshed through the infinite love of God; for as we had desired that our joining together might be entirely by the Lord, that we might have the evident testimony of his eternal spirit in ourselves, even so it came to pass, to our great comfort in the Lord.

After we were thus joined together by the Lord, and in his presence, it was upon me to write of it into the north of England, to have it published in that honourable meeting at Swarthmore, unto which I belonged, which accordingly was done, to Friends' great satisfaction. In the mean time I proceeded to the publishing of it in our meeting at Amsterdam, which I did three times one after another, without any opposition; but on the contrary public testimonies were given of it by Friends in the public meeting. Finally when the time was come that the marriage should be perfected, there was a general meeting at Amsterdam of Friends from several parts of that country, who were eye-witnesses of our accomplishing of it in the fear and wisdom of the Lord, and in the unity of his spirit, the last day of the 8th mo. 1662. When it was accomplished as aforesaid, all the men Friends that were then and there present at the meeting, did subscribe their names to a certificate, which for the future was for such as might desire to have an account of the matter for their satisfaction and information.

[His marriage, it appears, produced no relaxation of dedication in his Master's service; from the period of its consummation, to the time when the journal closes, less than two years, there was but little intermission in his labours. At the conclusion of the journal the editor has introduced several interesting epistles, which, he remarks, "will serve to carry on the narrative." With one of these we close our extracts from the volume.]

WILLIAM CATON TO FRIENDS.

"Yarmouth Common Gaol, 9th of 8th mo. 1663.

"Dear and affectionately beloved Friends—In the everlasting fellowship of the gospel of peace (into which we are brought through the arm of God's eternal power) do I dearly and tenderly salute you; who are dear and near unto me in the truth of God, which he hath made known unto us, to the comfort of our souls; whereby he hath engaged us above all the families of the earth to love and to serve him with reverence and godly fear. And though they that are without, do judge we are losers through our knowledge of the Truth, yet we find that we are become gainers through it; for if we lose the love and peace and liberty, which the world in times past hath afforded us, we have gained the peace of God and liberty in his eternal spirit; if we lose that honour and treasure which was of the world, and which we have had in the world, we are honoured of our God with bearing his name, and we are become sharers, with the rest of his sanctified ones, of heavenly treasure, which the world cannot give us, neither can it take away from us. So that whosoever deem or imagine we are losers through our coming to be of this way, or by our coming to the knowledge of this eternal truth, I say, nay; for the things that we have lost by reason of it (being but as dross and dung,) are not worthy to be compared to what we have gained through it. Shall not we therefore love the truth! and shall not we be willing to suffer the loss of all this world can afford us for its sake! For can we have a better cause to suffer for than the truth! can we suffer upon a more honourable account, than upon the truth's account, upon the account of which all the righteous men, who have suffered in all ages, have suffered! And who are we that we should be called to this high and honourable calling!— or that we should be accounted worthy to become witnesses of this ancient truth in this generation, to bear our testimony unto it, with the rest of the faithful witnesses, servants and handmaids of the Most High! The consideration of these things I confess might even be enough to break and overcome our hearts, and to engage us, as it were, afresh unto our God, who hath chosen us and loved us, before we loved him or made choice of him to be our Lord and God; and whom we have found to be so exceeding gracious and merciful to usward. Let our souls and spirits therefore praise and magnify him for ever and ever!

"And now, Friends, you may hereby understand, how that after I had had a very precious opportunity with many of you in the north, to my great refreshment in the Lord, I was clear in myself to return again for Holland; and in order thereunto, I passed towards the seacoasts; and when I came there, I heard of ships that were near ready to go for Holland, both at Newcastle and Sunderland; but the wind being out of the way or contrary, and I being desirous to improve my time to the utmost, and withal being very desirous to see as many Friends as I could before I took shipping, I travelled therefore along the coasts towards Whitby and Scarborough, and had some very good and precious meetings among Friends by the sea-side. And finding a ship ready at Scarborough, and the wind being good, I went aboard her; but the wind came contrary again; howbeit we kept out at sea and that for the space of nine days, whereas if the wind had been good we might have sailed it in two days. But finally a tempestuous storm came upon us, of which I had had some sight before, and told the master of it, and would have had him return again for England; and indeed it was so violent that as to outward appearance we were in very imminent danger; and the more so because our ship had gotten a sore leak, or rather more than one, and sometimes the pump was so out of order that it would do them no service, and besides they had lost the use of their helm, even in the very height of the storm. And in the mean time the ship was in no small danger of being foundered or overset; and as for the poor men they were as if they had been plunged into

the sea, and by reason of their continual pumping, besides the extraordinary toil they had with the sails, they were so exceedingly wearied out, that their courage and strength were very much departed from them. In which time I did much intercede with the Lord, and did with much fervency of spirit wrestle with him, that if it was his will their lives might be spared, and we preserved out of that extreme danger; though as for my own part I found myself exceeding freely given up to bequeath my soul into his bosom of everlasting love, indeed I confess I could sometimes expect little else. At that time I could have bid you all farewell, and all that in this world I do enjoy, and could have gone unto my everlasting home in peace with my God; who even then beheld my meditations and intercessions; and because he loved me, was he prevailed withal, even for his mercy's sake, who was determined, as appeared, to show mercy unto us. For when we were near unto the sands (where dear Hugh Tickhil's wife and another Friend were cast away, as I am informed, in their passing for Holland,) the Lord was pleased to cast us betwixt two sands, which if our ship had come to strike upon either, she must in an instant have become a wreck. But blessed be the name of the Lord who preserved us out of that imminent danger, whereby he hath exceedingly engaged me unto him, and his unspeakable mercy I hope shall be held in a perpetual remembrance by me his servant; who at this time do make mention of this remarkable deliverance unto you, to the end that you may know how good the Lord hath been to me, and that you with me may return thanks unto him; not only for his mercies in general to us-ward, but for this to me in particular; the consideration and sense of which hath more than a little broken my heart, which hath been filled with praises unto the Most High.

Moreover, Friends, I would have you understand, that the Lord having delivered me out of the storm before mentioned by sea, he hath suffered me to come into another by land among unreasonable men, who are even like unto the waves of the sea; but he that limits the one, limits the other; and I am confident that he that hath preserved me in the one, will in due time deliver me out of the other. By contrary winds, after we had been nine days at sea or thereabouts, we put in here at Yarmouth; and I being here on a first day did go to the meeting of Friends, which was a precious peaceable meeting: at the end of it, when we were standing up to depart, came their officers and many soldiers, and carried eight of us away prisoners to the main guard, where they kept us that night among the soldiers; and the next day we were carried before the magistrates of the town, who presently tendered the oath unto us. For my part I told them I had never sworn an oath in my life but one that I knew of, and that was when I was a boy; and I had known the terrors of the Lord against the thing, and therefore I durst not swear again. But without any respect to my or our tender consciences, they committed us to the common gaol; and so much confidence they had that we would be true to our principle, that they had made out our mittimus before-

hand, yea, before they examined us; wherein the only thing charged against us was for refusing to swear. We were all strangers to the town, come occasionally and accidentally to it; for five of the Friends belonged to one vessel in the town, who were come hither to load with herrings for the Straits, one of them was the merchant, another the master, another his mate, and the other two seamen; the others are Friends out of the country; and there are warrants out for the apprehending of Friends in the town also. And very high they are (as the sea was for a season;) and they keep Friends from us, and would force us to have what we have occasion for of the gaoler, which we cannot consent unto, though we suffer five times more than we do at present. But notwithstanding their fury and rage against us, it is well with us,—blessed be the Lord; and resolved we are in his name and power, to bear our testimony for the Lord in this place, as many of our brethren have done elsewhere."

A very important discovery in Paris is spoken of. A gentleman has succeeded in making very excellent bread from beet-root, mixed with a small portion of potato-flour. It is said that this bread is of very excellent quality, and can be sold to the public as low a price as two sous per lb.—*Late Paris paper.*

THE FRIEND.

FOURTH MONTH, 4, 1840.

It will be in the recollection of many of our readers, that in vol. 12, pp. 76 & 224, of "The Friend," some account was given of Laura Bridgman, the blind, deaf, and dumb girl. We have copied into the present number, extracted from the late Annual Report of the Trustees of the Perkins Institution and Asylum for the Blind, a more detailed statement, with additional circumstances relative to the wonderful attainments and mental developement of this interesting being, restricted, as she appears to be, in the perception of external objects, almost singly to the sense of touch.

HAVERFORD SCHOOL.

The semi-annual examination of the students of this institution will be continued on second and third day next, and close on fourth day, the 8th inst. The attendance of those who take an interest in the school, is respectfully invited. Copies of the order of examination may be had at this office.

4th mo. 2d.

WESTTOWN SCHOOL.

The committee to superintend the boarding school at Westtown, will meet there on fifth day the 9th of next month, at 3 o'clock, P. M.

The committee on teachers is to meet on the same day at 1 o'clock, P. M.—and the visiting committee to attend at the school on seventh day the 4th of the month.

THOMAS KIMBER, Clerk.

Philadelphia, 3d mo. 28th, 1840.

THE FRIEND.

A RELIGIOUS AND LITERARY JOURNAL.

VOL. XIII.   **SEVENTH DAY, FOURTH MONTH, 11, 1840.**   **NO. 28.**

EDITED BY ROBERT SMITH.

PUBLISHED WEEKLY.

Price two dollars per annum, payable in advance.

Subscriptions and Payments received by

GEORGE W. TAYLOR,

NO. 50, NORTH FOURTH STREET, UP STAIRS,

PHILADELPHIA.

For " The Friend."

SKETCHES OF SUPERSTITIONS.

(Concluded from page 212.)

The falling of any object in the temples, the slamming of doors, the cracking of furniture, unexpected gusts of wind or deluges, a black dog coming into a house, the appearing of a snake on the house-top, the spilling of salt, water, honey, or wine, a sudden silence, the putting on of the left side of the garment first, were all unlucky omens. Augustus Cæsar, it is said, one day put on his left shoe first, and a mutiny of his soldiers immediately after broke out. This famous general, who is usually called the greatest of the Roman emperors, and in whose time learning was at its climax, would not perform certain duties on particular days, in this respect not being more intelligent than the most ignorant peasants of the present age. It was no uncommon thing to postpone an important public meeting because a weasel or a mouse was seen to cross the path. Thus the fisherman in our own day, who will not put to sea because he has met a woman with a pair of particularly broad thumbs, is not more justly a subject of ridicule than the grave legislators of Athens, eighteen hundred years ago. All bodily ailments, as will naturally be supposed, were ascribed by the Greeks to the malignity of some of the presiding deities; the idea of an illness being caused by physical derangement was totally out of the question. Being in this manner made ill by a god, it was presumed they could get well only by appealing to another god, who could beat the enemy from his position. Æsculapius was generally esteemed the god of healing, or of medicine, and was appealed to on most occasions of illness. According to the Greek writers, Æsculapius was the son of Apollo, and studied medicine under a supernatural instructor in the form of a centaur; being very successful in his cures, Pluto became alarmed for the diminution of his customers in the nether regions, and complaining to Jupiter, the doctor was killed by a thunderbolt. Such is the fable told by the Greeks of Æsculapius and his genealogy. The true source of the Æsculapian superstition was in Egypt, where a symbol, consisting of the figure of a man, with a dog's head, carrying a pole with serpents twisting around it, was periodically exhibited to mark the recession of the Nile. This symbol of preservation was called Æscaleph, from Æish, signifying man, and Caleph, dog, and hence the sonorous Greek term Æsculapius. The Æsculapius of the Greek mythology was ministered to by a numerous body of priests, who offered sacrifices to him in his temples, and communicated his prescriptions for medicines and modes of cure to the attending worshippers. These priests, according to all accounts, were a set of worthless impostors. They pretended that Æsculapius only made known his prescriptions through the medium of dreams or visions, and that to enjoy these oracular communications, it was necessary to pass the night, or even several days and nights at a time, in perfect darkness, in one of the chambers of the temple. Those who were disinclined to perform this trying ceremony, employed the priests to dream and receive responses for them, and paid them accordingly for their trouble. Crowds of sick persons repaired to the great temple of Æsculapius at Epidaurus, and to another at Cos, to seek relief in these ridiculous mummeries; and as the priests were able to work successfully on their imaginations, or to prescribe the use of some suitable kind of medicine for their ailments, the number of cures performed at both places was very great. With the hope of bespeaking the favour of the oracle, the afflicted brought votive offerings of great value, which were hung on the walls round the altar, and there remained a certain length of time before they became the perquisite of the officiating priests. The pillars, likewise, were inscribed with narrations of the wonderful cures which had been already performed, accompanied with the oracularly delivered prescriptions of the god. A few of these votive tablets, discovered amidst the ruin of fallen edifices, have come down to the present day. We copy the four following from the work of an intelligent author.

1. " In these latter days, a certain blind man, by name Caius, had this oracle vouchsafed to him:—' That he should draw near to the altar after the manner of one who could see; then walk from right to left, lay the five fingers of his right hand on the altar, then raise up his hand and place it on his eyes.' And behold! the multitude saw the blind man open his eyes, and they rejoiced that such splendid miracles should signalise the reign of our Emperor Antonius."

2. " To Lucius, who was so wasted away by pains in his side, that all doubted of his recovery, the god gave this response:—' Approach thou the altar: take ashes from it, mix them up with wine, and then lay thyself on thy sore side.' And the man recovered, and openly returned thanks to the god, amidst the congratulations of the people."

3. " To Julian, who spitted blood, and was given over by every one, the god granted this response:—' Draw near, take pine apples from off the altar, and eat them with wine for three days.' And the man got well, and came and gave thanks in the presence of the people."

4. " A blind soldier, Valerius Asper by name, received this answer from the god:—' that he should mix the blood of a white cock with milk, make an eye ointment therewith, and rub his eyes with it for three days.' And lo! the blind recovered his sight, and came, and publicly gave thanks to the god."

The magistrates of Greece and Rome sanctioned and applauded these absurdities. We do not read of a single philosopher, or man of learning condemning them. Socrates, who was unquestionably the most enlightened moralist of his time, requested at his death that a cock should be sacrificed to Æsculapius. When we find so great a man sanctioning by his express orders such a gross superstition, we can easily conceive how widely the delusion was spread among the people.

There was another superstition common with the Greeks and Romans, namely, that of divination by *sortes* or lots. The practice of casting lots, to determine intricate questions, was of remote antiquity, having been in use in the oldest eastern nations before it made its appearance in Greece. The divination was performed in many different ways. One consisted in erecting two sticks on the ground, and determining the question by the direction, left or right, in which they fell. This ancient practice, which resembled our tossing of a halfpenny, was resorted to by the Israelites, who, for it, and other follies, were justly reproved: " My people ask counsel at their stocks, and their staff declareth unto them." Hosea iv. 12. Among both the Greeks and Romans, lots were cast by dice or by inscribed pebbles, but more commonly by verses, which were drawn from a jug, or by the chance opening of a poem. Appeals to Homer, or the Sortes Homericæ, formed the most respectable mode of divination by lot. The Iliad was opened, and the first lines to which the eye was directed, told the fortune or answered the desire of the questioner. Virgil was the accredited Roman oracle for this kind of divination. Sometimes single letters or words were written, and put into an urn; after being well shaken, they were poured out on the ground, and any sentences that could be made from the promiscuous heap, were believed to be oracular or prophetic; this was called the *Sortes Prenestinæ*. Another kind of sortes consisted in rushing along the street with a handful of verses on small tablets, and bidding the first boy that was met with to draw one;

if the tablet or scrap so drawn contained words agreeing with the previous conception half formed in the mind, it was taken as an infallible advice or prophecy, and followed accordingly. The early Christians were not exempted from these delusions. In matters of difficulty and doubt, they dipped their hand into the sacred books, or into the Psalter, and sought for direction and assistance according to the principle pursued in the Sortes Virgilianæ. St. Augustine in his epistle to the Januarins, sanctions the practice, if performed for spiritual ends. The superstition survived the middle ages, and was in some degree fashionable and in force in the seventeenth century, when all other appeals of a magical nature had been given up as unwarrantable. The occasional truthfulness of the responses helped to sustain the credit of the superstition. A striking instance of random truth in one of these prophetic sortes occurred to Charles I. Having in the course of his troubles retired to Oxford, he was taken one day by Lord Falkland to see the public library, and was there shown among other books a Virgil finely printed and exquisitely bound. Lord Falkland, to amuse the king, proposed that he should make trial of his fortune by the Sortes Virgilianæ. Charles consented, and opening the book, the passage that struck his eye was part of Dido's imprecation against Æneas:—

"Oppress'd with numbers in the unequal field,
His men discouraged, and himself expell'd;
Let him for succour sue from place to place,
Torn from his subjects, and his son's embrace."

The king being somewhat concerned at this untoward prophecy, his companion, to relieve his mind, and hoping to fall on some passage bearing no allusion to either his own or his master's condition, opened the book, and the following passage was disclosed:—

"O Pallas! thou hast fail'd thy plighted word,
To fight with caution, not to tempt the sword,
I warn'd thee, but in vain; for well I knew
What perils youthful ardour will pursue;
That boiling blood would carry thee too far,
Young as thou wert in dangers, and to war.
O curst essay of arms, disastrous doom,
Prelude of bloody fields, and fights to come!"

This unfortunate attempt at fortune-telling disconcerted both Charles and his attendant, and was remembered afterwards, when Falkland fell at the battle of Newberry, and the king had perished on the scaffold. Had the fate of both been otherwise, we should, of course, never have heard of the prophecy.

It is certainly a very remarkable circumstance, and one which it would puzzle the infidel to explain, that in an age when classic Greece was involved in such confusion and darkness on all that related to religion, and the mysteries of the spiritual and mental world, the Jews, a rude, agricultural people—barbarians, as they were styled, by their self-complacent cotemporaries—should, not only then, but from the earliest period of their history, have been in possession of those just and sublime sentiments which have been handed down to us through the medium of the Scriptures—which have stood the test of ages, and which promise one day to supplant all others the world over: for they rest upon those immutable principles of truth, which, as the hu-

man mind advances in virtue and, consequently, in its ability to appreciate them, must become predominant. Verily, it was the true God who spake, in time past, unto our fathers by the prophets.

For "The Friend."

Interesting information from Jamaica.

In the eleventh month, 1839, a Friend, accompanied by his wife, left England, as agent to the Society of Friends in that country, to ascertain the present state of the negro population in Jamaica. From a letter written to his brother in Baltimore, dated Kingston, second month 18th, 1840, the following is extracted.

"Among the persons who have called on us, and invited us to their houses and plantations, we may number seven magistrates, and two members of the house of assembly; and we have been received with great kindness both here and in Spanish-town, by the authorities; and by many of the planters, who seem disposed to be open and candid, and to conceal nothing from our observation; in some instances, not even their overseers' books, or ledger accounts. When Sir Charles Metcalfe, the governor, held his levee in this city, I attended it, and asked him whether he would be pleased to know the object of my visit to Jamaica, and to hear the instructions which my friends in England had given me; he said he should. On my reading them he bowed assent to every one of them, said the object was very praiseworthy, and that he should be glad to assist me in the inquiries to be made; and that I might freely write to him, and visit him at the government-house. I then left, and have since received from him two special invitations by post; one to meet a party at a public ball, which, I need not say, was declined; and one to dine with him on a given day, which did not reach me in time, as I did not send to the office for letters till the day was over.

"It is the wish of the Society in England to spend money,—some thousands of pounds if needed,—in assisting to promote the moral and religious welfare of the black and coloured late slave population. It is not for me to say at present, what I would recommend to be done with this view, as we have gone hitherto so little among the sugar plantations, and have not visited a fourth of the island in extent; but I may say, generally, that the labourers have such ample means of providing for all their wants of every kind, that it would be very unwise to make them, under the plea of kindness and benevolence, dependents on the bounty of any class of men. They are very well able to feed and clothe themselves, and to change their cabins into comfortable cottages. They can very well afford to educate their children, and even to build chapels and school-houses, which they are indeed doing to a great extent. So far as simply concerns the means of living, and providing themselves temporal comforts, there is probably no peasantry in the world so well off, as that of Jamaica and some others of our West India colonies; and were it not that some of the laws are harsh and unjust, and the administration of them by local magistrates worse than the laws themselves, and that it is only within a few years past that the people

have had free access to schools and public worship, and are therefore, many of them, degraded in morals and ignorant, they might be called a happy peasantry.

"The planters are endeavouring to confound right and wrong, both in morals and political economy, by using their power as landlords to coerce wages and compel labour. They charge extravagant rents for provision grounds, in the manner of a capitation tax; and often, if the labourers who live on their estates intermit labour, or go for higher wages to a neighbouring proprietor, they charge them double rent, and harass them with a summons to some local court. This question of rent is now the great vexation here; but the labourers will soon have the best of it, for labour is much wanted, and the tendency of wages is to rise; so that the planter cannot long successfully contend to keep them down, and resist the rising freedom, as the very means they pursue to get labour at a cheap rate, tends to drive it farther from them.

"I know of one parish in the island in which the negroes, since freedom came, have purchased 800 acres of land, in small portions of from one rood, to two or three acres, which they cultivate as their own freeholds, and on which they build themselves habitations, selling their surplus labour where and to whom they please.

"There is in the negroes of the West Indies an air of independence which has astonished us:—no servility, no crouching, scarcely a touch of the hat; in short, no trace of slavery left: they would do well for American republicans. * * * * *

"If our health should be continued,—and it is thus far, I am thankful to say, excellent,—we intend, on leaving Kingston to take apartments in Spanish-town, and afterwards at other stations in different parts of the island; branch out from them, and visit the plantations in their respective neighbourhoods, call on missionaries, and inspect schools. It is our intention to visit every parish in Jamaica, and obtain, if we can, the moral and religious statistics of the whole island, for the information and government of our friends at home. This work will engage us, probably, something like a year in all, after which we purpose going to Hayti, on a tour in that island; and after accomplishing that, visiting the United States on our way back to England."

From the New York Observer.

MISSION TO SIAM.

The missionaries of the American Board in Siam are rendering essential service to the king of that country in carrying into effect two important measures, viz., the eradication of the small-pox, and the suppression of the opium trade. The Missionary Herald for the present month gives the particulars. We have room only for the following summary notices condensed from the Herald for the Boston Mercantile Journal.

Revolution in Siam.

It appears from the March number of the Missionary Herald, by recent advices from Siam, that the missionary physician at Bankok,

Dr. Bradley, has accomplished a revolution of the most extraordinary character, affecting the social and economical interests of the whole of the kingdom of Siam. This has occurred by his knowledge of vaccination, and through the medium of his friend the king.

It appeared that *he* had been informed of the successful inoculation of the children of the missionaries and several of the Siamese, and had thus had his hopes excited, that inoculation might afford some important relief from the smallpox, which disease, among this people, exceeds all others in fatality. It rages among them four or five months in every year. The season of its reign is November, December, January and March. It is almost impossible to find a family of some years standing in the kingdom, that has not suffered from this terrible disease, the loss of some two or three, or more lives; so that a large majority of the Siamese are pitted—and very many have either lost their eyes, or had them greatly injured, by the same disease.

Dr. Bradley's Letters and Journal convey full information respecting the progress of this innovation. These are deeply interesting, and we should gladly cite the whole account, did our limits permit. In one place he writes:

"Paw Maw called again for further information. He informed me that *more than a thousand persons* had already been inoculated by the king's personal physicians, and innumerable others by the physicians of the common people—and that not one untoward circumstance has occurred among them all.

"Have spent a large portion of this week in inoculating the families of the rulers, princes, nobles, &c. &c., and in instructing Siamese physicians on this subject. My hopes are greatly raised that the Lord will make this work the occasion of vast good to this people. Inoculation is now the all-engrossing topic of conversation in Bankok and the country, from the king to the beggar. Several thousand have been inoculated with perfect success. As yet, not one death has been heard of from inoculation, while smallpox in the natural way is very mortal."

In a word, Siam, so far as this dreadful disorder is concerned, may be said to be completely revolutionised. These benefits may be called secondary, but they are of incalculable importance.

Opium in Siam.

We have referred to the medical revolution effected by the missionaries in Siam. It appears from the same despatches that the government of that country is adopting measures like those of the Chinese, to get rid of the opium trade. The Herald recognises it as a remarkable fact in the providence of God, that such a movement as this for the promotion of temperance, and that in China, should be made at the same time, in two great adjacent but independent nations, like those of China and Siam, embracing, perhaps, half of the heathen population of the globe, and that the effort should be made by the heathen rulers, to save their people from the destructive effects of intoxicating drugs, at the very time when the most civilised and Christian nations of the earth are engaged in a similar struggle to save themselves from a similar evil.

The king had issued a proclamation on the subject, it seems. Of this he got the missionaries to strike off 10,000 copies. The setting up of the type and the printing of this number was done in six days. *This is the first official document, of any kind, that was ever printed in Siam.* Dr. Bradley regards it as forming an interesting era in Siamese history. "It bespeaks a people fast rising in the scale of civilisation, who are desirous to avail themselves of improvements that are clearly made known to them. It also shows that the king of Siam, and his highest and most experienced officers, regard the Siamese as a *reading people*, or they would not have thought of asking for ten thousand copies of such a document. It shows that the king and his ministers are in earnest."

We are farther told that the king has recently had several large public burnings of large quantities of opium, on the famous site of all the royal funeral piles. His object was not to mourn over its loss, but to triumph over its capture, and to show his subjects that he would not take advantage of the opportunity to enrich himself by its sale, even in a foreign country. One of the nobles has recently had a ship return from Singapore, having on board twenty-three chests of opium, which was shipped for him before the reform commenced. On the arrival of the vessel on the bar, he hastened to her and cast the whole overboard.

All this looks well; and the coincidence above-mentioned is indeed remarkable. It would seem that the Great East is indeed moved and moving, at length.

From the New York Observer.

Hints upon the Mental Education of the Young.

From the German of Zollikofer.

Learn them to be always observing. Observation is the mother of all the fundamental sciences. Habituate them, in its exercise, not to pass too hastily from one thing to another, but to contemplate an object from several, and if possible, from all sides; and to look not only upon the whole, but also upon its individual parts. It were not desirable, however, that you should weary their attentiveness of observation in the first years of their education, by compelling them to fix their minds too long upon one and the same thing, but that you should gradually convince them of the great benefit of a closer observation in general. This may be done on the most trivial occurrences. If they admire and delight in the beautiful tints and the pleasing odour of a flower, then teach them what evidences of skill and wisdom the experienced eye of the connoisseur discovers in the structure of that flower, in the form of its leaves, and in the peculiarities of its staminal. Show them often how much more they might have observed from this or that thing, had they considered it less hastily, or devoted more time to its contemplation. This manner of exercising and refreshing their observation, will be far more effectual with them, than the most earnest admonitions to duty, and the severest reproofs for its neglect.

Another rule which should be observed, is

this: Be careful not to give them a false or too indefinite idea of anything, however small it may be. It were far better that they should remain entirely ignorant of a hundred different things, than they should entertain erroneous perceptions of them; far better, that you should wholly decline answering their questions, than that you should answer them ambiguously or unintelligibly. In the first case, they know that they are still ignorant upon the subject of inquiry, but that their want of information may be remedied by time In the other case, on the contrary, they think themselves sufficiently instructed upon the subject, while they still remain in ignorance with regard to it. Hence it comes that the first impressions which we receive, of natural or moral things, are, as it were, the groundwork of all subsequent ones. If the first are indefinite or false, their baneful influence will extend to the latter. Some persons think that any answer is good enough for the inquiry of the child or youth. Some make no scruple at all in employing misrepresentations, so that they can only bring their children to silence; thinking that, with time, they will become better acquainted with things. But this hope is exceedingly delusive. First-impressions endure the longest, and they may either guide us to truth, or lead us into error. If a man impresses his child with the idea, that the thunder and the lightning are the effects and tokens of divine indignation against man, and are only designed to frighten and punish the inhabitants of the earth, what a deep root will such a sentiment take in his soul! How difficult will it be for him in riper years, to contemplate a thing as the effect of divine wisdom and goodness, which he has so long considered as a palpable evidence of the Almighty's anger! And if the youth or man confounds these errors and truths, how often will the impressions which remain on his mind from his first mode of conception, seduce his will and understanding to false conclusions, or fill him with fear and apprehension! Are not these very defects of education the reason why certain species of superstition are so difficult to be eradicated, and why they often follow men themselves through their whole life?

E. B.

A Chinese Map of the World.—It is two feet wide by three and a half high, and is almost covered with China! In the left hand corner, at the top, is a sea, three inches square, in which are delineated, as small islands, Europe, England, France, Holland, Portugal, and Africa. Holland is as large as all the rest, and Africa is not so big as the end of one's little finger! The northern frontier is Russia, very large. The left corner, at the bottom, is occupied by "the western ocean," as it is called, containing the Malay peninsula pretty well defined. Along the bottom are Camboja, Cochin China, &c., represented as moderate-sized islands, and on the right is Formosa, larger than all the rest put together. Various other countries are shown as small islands. I should have given an engraving of this curious map, but that a true reduction to the size of a page would have left out most of these countries altogether! The surrounding ocean is represented as huge waves, with smooth passages, or highways branching off to the different countries, or islands, as they represent them. They suppose that ships which keep along these highways go safely; but if they, through ignorance or stress of weather, diverge, they soon get among these awful billows, and are lost!—*Malcom's Travels.*

THE HEATHEN.

From Howard Malcom.

"Idolatry tends steadily downward, and eighteen centuries have served to degrade the heathen far below the latest and most corrupt Greeks and Romans. When mankind began to fall away from the living God, there remained some knowledge of the proper attributes of Deity, and a comparative nobleness and purity in the human mind. But the object of worship, the rites enjoined, and the character of the people, steadily sunk lower and, lower. Hence all nations refer to past ages, as having greater purity and happiness than the present. Iniquitous oracles, abused asylums, horrid bacchanalia, and human sacrifices, were known, even in Greece and Rome, only to later generations. With all these abominations, they possessed no contemptible amount of arts, sciences, literature, and poetry. Syria, Macedonia, Greece, Italy, and Northern Africa, were the centre of civilisation and intelligence. The wide intercommunication maintained by travelling philosophers and marching armies, gave impulse to intellect, and disseminated knowledge.

For a long period before the birth of Christ, a leaven of contempt for pagan rites had been diffused by Pythagoras, Socrates, Lycurgus, Demosthenes, and others. Every century brought forth some such writers, and increased the effect of the former works. Socrates, Lycurgus, Demosthenes, and others, had by their orations stirred the public mind. Euclid, Zeno, Epicurius, Apollonius, Archimedes, and Erastothenes, led the select few to a noble expansion and activity of the intellectual powers. Afterwards came the satires and exposures of Horace, Lucian, and Juvenal, turning a strong tide of ridicule upon the prevailing mythology. To quote some names might seem pedantic; but there was scarcely a department of learning without writers which, to this very day, maintain not only a place among our studies, but admiration and utility. Poetry, philosophy, history, eloquence, tragedy, mathematics, geography, botany, medicine, and morals, were all cultivated. Such was the state of mankind when Christ came; and while it would have allowed a new system of superstition or error little chance of prevalence, it made a happy preparation for Christianity. Not indeed, that any of the philosophy agreed with it, or that any of the philosophers adopted it. 'The wisdom of this world,' then, as now, deemed the cross 'foolishness.' But the people were trained to think, and both, Jews and pagans were capable of examining, and disposed to understand, the nature of the new religion.

The nations among whom missions are now conducted, are, in general, the reverse of all

this. With them the human intellect has for ages been at a stand. Improvements in any thing are not imagined. Without valuable books, without a knowledge of other countries, without foreign commerce, without distant conquest, without the strife of theology, without political freedom, without public spirit, what is left for them but listlessness, ignorance, and pride? Such of them as attempt to study, learn only falsehood and folly; so that the more they learn, the less they know. Their history, chronology, geography, physics, astronomy, medicine, and theology, are so utterly wrong, that to fill the mind with them is worse than vacuity. This is true of the *most civilised* heathen of this day; and of many of them a much stronger picture might be drawn. Such indurated ignorance is incomparably worse to deal with than fine reasonings and false philosophy. What can argument do if not understood? The edge of truth itself is turned by impenetrable dulness.

The depreciation of morals is as great as that of intellect. We look in vain even for Spartan or Roman virtue. Except, perhaps, among the Cretans, it is hardly probable that the first preachers any where encountered such a spirit of falsehood and deceit as distinguish the heathen now. Truth is utterly wanting. Man has no confidence in man. The morality is not only defective, it is perverted. Killing a cow or an insect, is more shocking than the murder of an enemy: lying for a brahmin is a virtue; stealing for real want is no sin: a few ceremonies or offerings expiate all crimes. Transmigration abolishes identity; for, if perfectly unconscious in one state of existence, of all that transpired in previous ones, identity is virtually lost. Sin is reduced to a trifle, the conscience rendered invulnerable, generous sentiments extinguished, and the very presence and exhortations of the missionary engender a suspicion destructive to his success. His reasons for coming are not credited; and the fear of political treachery is added to a detestation of his creed. The best supposition they can make, is that he is seeking religious *merit*, according to their own system, and careful not so much for their conversion, as for his personal benefit in a future state."

Malcom's remarks have especial reference to South Eastern Asia. The unsophisticated North American Indian was a much more promising subject for the missionary, than the bewildered and besotted Asiatic; yet, alas! how have his better qualities been appreciated and made use of?

From the Irish Friend.

A Dreadful Imprecation Awfully Fulfilled.

About the year 1777, some men were engaged together in collecting "Christmas Boxes" in the parish of Luton, Bedfordshire. In their rounds they had forgotten to call at one house, which one of them recollecting, went thither by himself, asked, and obtained the gift. In a day or two afterwards they resumed their engagement, and called at the same house, the man who had been there before and received the money not being then with them. On asking the person of the

house for a "Christmas Box," he said he had already given one, and mentioned the name of the absent man as the person who had received it. The party then called upon this man, and on his being asked about it, he declared he had *not* received it; on its being repeatedly urged that he had certainly got the money, he denied it with vehemence, at the same time making use of an oath, he wished his hand might drop off if he had taken it! In this state of uncertainty his companions left him, each one forming his own opinion as to where the truth lay. The same night, when the man went to bed, he felt his hand and arm benumbed, and in the morning he had little use in either. His hand continued to get worse the next day, and towards the evening, it was observed to have changed its colour, and he had but little feeling in it. The hand continued growing blacker until he rose from his bed on the third morning, when, awful to relate, it had separated from his arm and lay by his side.

The manuscript from which this extraordinary and awful case is extracted, concludes thus:—

"The writer of the above saw the hand with the flesh dried on the bone, not long after this striking event took place, and there are persons now living at Luton who can bear testimony to the truth of it."   J. P.

Islington, 1839.

LOCUSTS AT SEA.

A letter from the mate of the brig Levant, of Boston, to his friends in Beverly, dated Montevideo, Jan. 17, 1840, states that after having encountered a very severe gale, on the 13th September, when in latitude of about 18 degrees north, and the nearest land being over 450 miles distant, they were surrounded for two days by large swarms of locusts, of a large size—and in the afternoon of the second day, in a squall from the N. W. the sky was completely black with them. They covered every part of the brig immediately, sails, rigging, cabin, &c. It is a little singular how they came there, and how they could have supported themselves in the air so long, as there was no land to the N. W. for several thousand miles. Two days afterwards, the weather being moderate, the brig sailed through swarms of them floating dead upon the waters.—*Salem Register.*

Apprehended Loss of the Sea Gull.

We learn that there is too much reason to apprehend that the pilot boat Sea Gull, attached to the exploring expedition, as tender to the U. S. sloop of war Vincennes, has been lost, and that all on board have perished. She has not been heard of since the month of June last. Then she left Orange, Terra del Fuego, in company with the Flying Fish. A gale soon after arose, and the latter succeeded in beating off the shore. This was the last seen of the Sea Gull. Lieutenants Reed and Bacon, two promising young officers, were on board. The Porpoise had been twice in search of her without success.— *Courier.*

For "The Friend."

EXHORTATION TO BROTHERLY LOVE

The excellent spirit, and apostolic soundness of principle which breathes through the following extract, induces the belief that its revival at the present time may be of use. It forms the concluding part of "An Epistle of tender Counsel and Advice to all that have believed in the Truth every where," by Stephen Crisp. W. J.

"And, Friends, let the brotherly love that was sown in your hearts, as a precious seed in your first convincement, continue and increase daily, that as ye are made partakers of one hope of salvation in Christ Jesus, so ye may continue of one mind and heart, according to the working of his Spirit in you, having a tender respect one for another, as children of one father, and as such as feed at one table; for Christ hath ordained, and doth ordain in all his churches, that we should love one another, that we should shun all occasions of offence and grief, that we should walk orderly, and as becomes his holy gospel, that we may be an honour thereunto, and a strength and comfort to one another: this is our great ordinance, our new commandment, which was also from the beginning, and will always abide the same through all generations. Therefore, my Friends and brethren, let the fruits of sincere and brotherly love abound amongst you both in word and deed, and let none be wanting in fulfilling the law of charity, without which all profession will be but like sounding brass, or tinkling cymbal.

But if this law be kept to, the life of religion will be felt, and each one will thereby be taught their duty and charge concerning another, and know how to comfort in charity, to admonish in charity, to reprove in charity, and also to receive all these in charity; and this will exclude for ever all whispering and talebearing, and bring every one to deal plainly and uprightly with every one, not suffering sin to rest upon the soul of thy brother, but to deal with him quickly, plainly and tenderly, even as thou thyself wouldst be dealt withal; and however this kind of dealing be taken, thou shalt not miss of thy reward, but thy peace will remain with thee. For while Friends' eyes are fixed upon the power of God, as their guide and leader in all these things, and their design is simply God's glory, the clearing their own consciences, and the good of their brother, they will not be discouraged in their undertakings; for they know the power will certainly come over whatsoever opposeth it, and this will keep your minds quiet and free from disturbances, when you see men, and things, and parties arise against the power, knowing that the power is an everlasting rock. But as for those things that appear against it, they are but for a season, in which season patience must be exercised, and the counsel of wisdom stood in, and then you will be kept from staggering, or from scattering by all the fair shows the spirit of opposition can make.

For they that do enjoy the life and substance, and feed daily of the bread that comes down from heaven, have a quick sense and discerning of things that are presented to them, and do know them that are of the earth earthly, by their earthly savour, from those that are of the heavenly with their heavenly savour; they know what feeds the head and the wit, and carnal reason, and what will nourish the immortal soul, and so come to be fixed, and are not ready to feed upon unsavoury food, nor to be easily tossed, nor to be troubled at evil tidings; nor can they be drawn after one thing or man by an affection, nor set against another man nor thing by a prejudice, but the true balance of a sound judgment, settled in the divine knowledge, according to the measure that the Father hath bestowed, keeps such steady in their way, both in respect to their own testimony and conversation, and also in respect to their dealing with others. Oh, my dear Friends, in such doth the truth shine, and such are the true followers of Christ, and they are worthy to be followed, because their way is as a shining light, shining on towards the perfect day. And in this sure and steady way, my soul's desire is, you and I may walk, and continue walking, unto the end of our days, in all sobriety, truth, justice, righteousness and charity, as good examples in our day, and comfortable precedents in our end, to them that shall remain, that so we may deliver over all the testimonies of our Lord Jesus unto the succeeding generations, as pure, as certain, and as innocent as we received them in the beginning; and in the end of all our labours, travels, trials and exercises, may lay down our heads in that sabbath of rest that remains always for the Lord's people.

This is the breathing desire that lives in me, for all you who have believed in our Lord Jesus Christ, in whose name, and in the sense of his power, and of the life he hath revealed in every member of his whole body, I salute you all, and bid you farewell."

Two Addresses to the Prisoners in the House of Correction at Spandau, in Prussia; delivered by Thomas Shillitoe, of London.

INTRODUCTION.

Some interesting particulars relative to the visit at the prison of Spandau, are contained in the journal of Thomas Shillitoe, published during the last year; the two addresses now printed, were taken down at the time of their delivery, and were preserved in German manuscript for about ten years, when they were printed in the form of a tract; a copy of this tract was sent to England and was translated into our language; those who feel interested in the engagements of the Christian soldier, whose liberality of mind, unceasing labours, and entire devotedness, remind us of the preachers of truth during the earliest ages of the church, will probably be gratified by perusing them. This tract is intended to be simply a faithful and literal translation from the German, with the exception of this page.
Chelmsford, 9th month, 1839.

PREFACE.

The two following Addresses, delivered in the principal jail at Spandau, in the summer of the year 1824, were taken down by a competent short-hand writer, and have been preserved until the present time. They found a universally good reception, even among the prisoners, and, especially upon several, appeared to make a very lively impression; and as they not only made an impression at the time, but the advantage was found to continue afterwards, it is hoped that a wider diffusion of them in other places, may also have a beneficial influence upon the minds of those unhappy persons, who, whilst they are justly punished for their crimes, are nevertheless objects of compassion to those, who have feeling, sympathizing hearts, and who are solicitous for the advancement of the happiness of all their fellow men.

FIRST ADDRESS.

It is a sense of my duty towards God, and a sincere love to you as my fellow men, who have immortal souls, which are of as much value in the sight of the Lord as my own soul; it is unfeigned gospel love which has disposed me, and made me willing to pay you this visit, and now it is my fervent desire, that I may serve as an instrument in leading you into a very weighty inquiry.

I wish that you may examine and inquire, what it is that has brought you into this sorrowful condition, in which you must be deprived of that precious privilege, your freedom, and endure the painful separation by which husbands are removed from their wives, parents from their children, and children from their parents; which, as I am convinced, is not the will of our heavenly Father, who certainly has no pleasure in our misery. He wills much more our happiness, as well in this world, as in the world to come. And in order that every man may attain thereto, and that he might fulfil his gracious design, he has written in the heart, and placed in the soul of every one, his divine law, which shows us what we are to do, and what we must avoid and leave undone, if we would walk acceptably in the sight of God, and secure for ourselves the enjoyment of his present and everlasting peace, which he has appointed for each one of us. When you enter into this inquiry, and examine yourselves and ask, what was it then which brought me into my present sorrowful condition, I am convinced that every one will find, that for want of attention to the divine voice in his conscience, and from disobedience thereunto, he has fallen into such extreme wretchedness. For this voice (which gently speaks to us in the secret of our hearts) clearly shows us and all men, what is good, and what is evil; so that each one of us may know and distinguish what we should choose and do, or avoid and leave undone, as we are concerned to walk conformably to the will of God.

It appears then very plain, that from want of attention to this inward witness in your breast, and from disobedience to its secret admonitions, you have been brought down to the unhappy state in which you now are; that I can with truth say, it is the prayer of my heart for you, that the time past, in which you have not been concerned to regard the reproofs and chastisements of the Holy Ghost in your heart, that this time that is gone by, I say, may be sufficient; and that in future it may be your earnest endeavour to listen with greater attention and obedience, to the inward voice of the divine law in your hearts.

This remains to be the means to obtain pardon for your sins and transgressions, which in truth is of the greatest importance for each one of us, that at a future time the precious soul may come from the troubles of this life into the land of eternal rest.

But you can only secure this pardon when you turn with sincerity to Jesus, the Saviour and Redeemer of man, who has endured the cross for your sins, that he might produce in your hearts a true sorrow, which works a blessed repentance, not to be repented of. Now the first step which you have to make under a sense of this godly sorrow, is this, that you implore Almighty God, that he would be pleased to grant you pardon, so that you may forgive from the bottom of your hearts, those who were the cause of your imprisonment, and may cherish no hatred against the court of justice which has passed sentence upon you. This is in truth a hard sacrifice to flesh and blood; but you must remember it is the express declaration of our Saviour Jesus Christ himself, that we must forgive if we would obtain forgiveness.

But hard as the sacrifice may be to you, I am notwithstanding convinced, that as you keep near to the holy help and mighty power of our Lord Jesus Christ, you would, like myself, come to the experience, that he would strengthen and enable you to do all things through him.

Let it be far from you to cherish a feeling of dissatisfaction towards the law of your land. For, as you examine yourselves impartially, you will find, that the cause of your misery is not in the law, but that it lies in your having given way to the temptations of the enemy of your souls, by which he has beguiled you into your past transgressions.

Let it therefore be much more your endeavour, through the co-operating power of the Holy Ghost, to show forth a grateful disposition to your superiors, and consider it a great privilege that you live under a mild government.

I am by no means disposed, and do not desire, that you should regard what I say to you as if I would reproach you; no, I can truly say, that were it possible that the heart, of man should bleed, my heart indeed would bleed, whilst I seriously consider your condition.

O! then, yet once more I say, consider it a great privilege that your lot has been cast in this land; for had you been in my native country, (England,) and had been punished according to the law of that land, it is very probable that it would have cost several of you your natural lives, and then you might have been obliged, in a very unprepared state, to appear before the Lord in judgment.

I do not then give any of you any temptation to say;—" It were perhaps better for me to have lost my life, than to be deprived of my liberty and separated from my friends." Here I can perhaps unite with you in this opinion, or explain it when I say,—Yes, indeed if I were not to consider, that after this life yet another life follows, of eternal duration. When we rightly consider this, it must

appear clear to us what a privilege it is, to live under a government which knows how to estimate the precious life of man.

That it is now the supplication of my heart, that you may be disposed from what you suffer at the present time, to listen in future more attentively to the law which God the Lord has written upon the tablet of your heart. Then your afflictions will become from day to day more easy to bear; and then will the godly sorrow which you are sensible of, produce in you a blessed repentance, not to be repented of, and which can make you acceptable in the sight of a gracious God.

Perhaps you are at times tempted to make use of unbecoming expressions, or frivolous and wicked words. O! then, seek the divine aid of your Redeemer to withstand them. By this means, as you obey his voice in your souls, you would be enabled to go forward, and so to conduct yourselves, that through your good behaviour, you would commend yourselves to your governors and superiors. Then you would occasion no more uneasiness to them, and the care and trouble which they have to endure on your account, would be much easier to bear;—and when your hours of labour are finished, do not give way to unprofitable conversation, but rather read in the Holy Scriptures; for these serve us " for doctrine, for reproof, for correction, for instruction in righteousness." I cannot in words fully describe of what importance to mankind these holy records are; but I am convinced that they can greatly contribute to your welfare; for if after your work is finished you read therein with quiet attention, you will undoubtedly find greater peace in your souls, and will not feel so uneasy as when you spend your leisure time in unprofitable or frivolous conversation; —and in this manner, as it is your earnest endeavour always to seek to God for divine aid, and to walk in humility before him, you will daily experience his assistance, and thereby will become more able patiently to endure the severe trial of separation from your dear relatives.

O! then, be kindly disposed one to another, and regard not one another for evil!

I believe that when God, who searches the heart, beholds your sincere desire and earnest endeavour to become acceptable to him, he will be pleased to effect for you an earlier deliverance than you perhaps expect; for he is a God who has the hearts of all men in his power, and can turn them like a waterbrook.

Obedience to his holy law, which he has written in your heart, is the means to become acceptable to him.

Therefore, let no one think or say, that his condition is a hopeless one; for all that will be required on your part, is a willingness to endeavour to preserve in your hearts the fear of the Lord, and to keep his commandments. He will give you the ability to do this; and as you follow his instructions, you will find that your state is by no means hopeless.

And now I commend you to God, and the word of his grace, which, as you attend thereunto, is able to make you acceptable to him; for thereby you will also show, that a godly sorrow has truly taken place in your hearts. And that this may be your blessed experience,

is my fervent prayer for every individual of you, who is now present.

Note.—It will not be useless to observe, that at his first visit at Spandau, Thomas Shillitoe could not see all the prisoners at that place, because they would not venture to admit with the others, a certain number of vicious characters among them, from whom they feared disturbance and interruption. In the mean time, he found that that visit did not entirely relieve his spirit of its duty. He believed a word of exhortation and encouragement to improvement, to rest upon his mind, and to be required of him towards those unhappy persons, whom he had not seen before; and therefore sought permission for the same, which was granted him with great kindness. The result thereof was very different to what they had expected.

The men hitherto so wild and formidable, and who had already occasioned much harm, demeaned themselves during the time that the discourse was spoken to them, so quietly, silently, and attentively, that a noisy, foolish, or offensive gesture was not observed in any one, but they expressed with evident emotion, their gratitude for the communication they had heard, and gave their calm resolve for the improvement of their lives and behaviour.

(Second address next week.)

From the Irish Friend.
" *If any man be in Christ Jesus, he is a new creature.*"

The remembrance of this important language has led me seriously to reflect on the total change which must take place in the soul, before a man can be truly in Christ Jesus. It is a very possible thing to make a profession of religion, to be in appearance a consistent Friend, to attend meetings for worship and discipline with great regularity, to appear to the eye of the outward observer, a Christian—and yet to know nothing of being " created anew in Christ Jesus."

May not an humble individual, a member of our highly professing and greatly favoured society be excused, therefore, if she attempt to draw the attention of her fellow professors to the important declaration, " If any man be in Christ Jesus he is a new creature." It is the earnest desire of the writer that her own heart may be deeply and daily sensible, that it is not an outward profession,—not a conformity to rules, however excellent,—not a putting on of an appearance of Christianity —not a fasting as it were twice in the week, and giving alms of all that is possessed, not the performance of any or every external duty, which constitutes the real Christian. The poor publican who smote upon his breast and would not lift so much as his eyes unto heaven, but cried under a sense of his lost condition— " Lord, have mercy on me a sinner," was justified, rather than he whose regularity in the performance of every outward duty was so complacently viewed by himself—as though his strict adherence to these was likely to render him acceptable to God.

My dear Friends and fellow professors, is there not occasion for many of us deeply to search and try our ways and turn with full purpose of heart to the Lord. Have we not from education and from habit, rather than from conviction, performed many of these duties which the true disciple will never omit, and is there not a danger of our having a name to live whilst we are really dead? What do the words of our blessed redeemer to Nicodemus signify? " Except a man be born again, he cannot see the kingdom of God"—and again, "except ye be converted and become as little children, ye shall in no wise enter into the kingdom of Heaven." Those who know any thing of the natural state of their own hearts, must be deeply sensible of the corruption and depravity which exist there.

They must feel, that in us, that is, in our flesh, dwelleth no good thing, and cannot but acknowledge the absolute need of a change of heart before an entrance can be gained into the everlasting kingdom of our Lord and Saviour, Jesus Christ. Let us not, my friends, be satisfied with this acknowledgement only, but earnestly seek unto Him who has said, ye "shall seek me and find me when ye shall search for me with your whole heart."

Surely the aspect of things in our society would greatly brighten were there a general laying of these things to heart—those points which are called minor would not be left undone, while these weightier matters of the law claimed the first place in our hearts—we should be as the real disciples of the Saviour always are—Lights to the world; and again through us as a people would glory be given to God. Amongst ourselves would once more be known judges as at the first, and counsellors as at the beginning—fathers and mothers who would invite to the true fold, and babes and sucklings who would perfect the praise of the Shepherd of Israel.

For "The Friend."
FRIENDS' READING ROOMS.

It must have been gratifying to other friends of this interesting concern equally with myself, to learn from the managers' report recently published, that the different courses of lectures were so well attended, and so generally satisfactory—amid the increasing variety of them, with which Philadelphia may be said to abound (some certainly objectionable) it is not a small matter to know that the attentive care of the managers has been thus successful in procuring the delivery of such at this institution, as were consistent with its character.

The reading and conversation rooms, the report states, have been frequented by about one hundred visiters. A considerable number of these are probably members of our religious Society, far separated from the homes of their youth, and the kindnesses they have enjoyed around the parental hearth. Whether we retrospect with interested feelings upon their former days, or whether we look to the future course of their lives, it is pleasant to regard the reading rooms as extending something like a welcome to those who might otherwise feel more as strangers among us,—and in some measure at least, as placing guards around them, and giving a proper tone and impulse to their present character; yet, it is not to those alone its benefits are confined; the young men of our own families who have enjoyed the advantages of a guarded education in the different institutions established among us with so great care, and at so large an expenditure, at the reading rooms are provided with opportunities to extend their researches in the various departments of useful learning. It may be too, that among the visiters are interesting young men, who have to mourn the bereavement of fathers who would have watched, counselled, and guided them, and of mothers who would have loved and cherished them; to these classes we may trust are frequently added Friends of matured years and acquirements, who have leisure to avail themselves of the facilities to literary pursuits seldom to be met with but in the retirement of literary institutions,—which here must certainly be considerable—both in the cabinet of natural history, in the selected periodicals of the day, and in the library, which, if I recollect aright, by a former report appears to have comprised between sixteen and seventeen hundred well chosen volumes.

My attention, however, has been particularly arrested by a remark of the managers, that "for some cause the reading and conversation rooms are not so much frequented as would be desirable." In this sentiment, whilst I freely concur, yet I cannot but consider the extending the privileges of these rooms to one hundred individuals, in addition to the numerous classes who attended the various lectures, as circumstances which ought to afford much encouragement both to the managers, and to the other friends of the institution; and I may express my belief that the great and principal causes which have impeded its greater resort, and more extended usefulness, may be readily found in the want of a more central, and more inviting situation. In this opinion I think I am sustained by the experience of our select schools, which languished until central situations were provided; upon this being effected in one instance, or arranged for in the other, their numbers almost immediately increased beyond expectation—but an especial difficulty, as I apprehend, under which the reading rooms now labour, is the need of more commodious apartments, which would afford to the visitants an inducement to frequent them, by a greater appearance of comfort; and being to them more of a home feeling. I therefore cannot but cherish the hope, if the managers who have evinced so much care toward the trust confided to them, would, at a suitable period, deem it well to consider the whole subject, they might see a propriety in endeavouring to procure more eligible accommodations; and that it would be reasonable to trust, if this should incur increased expenditure, that it would be fully sustained by those who enjoyed the benefit, as well as from others; thus more extensively realising the advantages which we may expect will result from this institution.

A PARENT.

The following article from the New York Morning Chronicle deserves to be read and reflected on.

THE LEXINGTON AND WAR.

The sacrifice of human life by the destruction of the ill-starred Lexington has sent a thrill of horror throughout this vast republic; and even at this very hour, the name of the Lexington cannot be mentioned without producing the most painful sensations. Each one feels that he might have been a victim of that dreadful catastrophe; or that he is liable to a similar fate whenever he journeys in a steamboat. The press has rung the changes on this appalling event; the pulpit has teemed with solemn warnings; the people in masses have given utterance in strong terms to the intensity of their feelings; and the halls of congress, even, have rung with the eloquence of the most gifted in relation thereto. In a word, the whole nation seems agitated in consequence of so mournful a disaster. It is well it should be so; for human life, precious life has been sacrificed on no trivial scale—recklessly sacrificed by negligence and cupidity. Who can remain unmoved under circumstances so appalling? Who, who that has not a heart of adamant, can think of the horrors of that night, when men, women and children, frantic with despair, huddled confusedly together on the deck of the blazing steamer, and plunged by scores into the cold and boisterous deep, to buffet for a few moments the friendless billows, and then to go down to a watery grave.

Yet, after all, what is the burning of the Lexington, what the destruction of her passengers and crew, compared with the horrors of war! What, compared with some great naval battle, in which ships are blown up and sunk, and the decks of those that are left afloat and flowing with blood, and bestrewed with the limbs and the mangled bodies of the victims of the fray! What, compared with the battle field of a Borodino, where eighty thousand men bit the dust! where, for the space of a square league, not a spot was uncovered with the wounded and the dead! where lie those wounded, piled in heaps, rending the air with their shrieks of agony, and invoking death in vain! where the scene of misery was so appalling, as to move even the iron soul of Napoleon to compassion and grief! What, compared with the retreat from Moscow, in which vast multitudes perished with cold and starvation; from whose eyes gushed tears of blood; whose hair and beards were frozen into solid masses; who, rendered delirious by their intolerable sufferings, rushed with horrid laughter like fiends into the flames of burning habitations; and whose half-naked bodies their famished companions drew from the flames to appease their ravenous appetites!

Such, such is "glorious war." Such the scenes which render conquerors immortal, and fill mankind with admiration! How strange a being is man! A single steamboat may be destroyed by accident or carelessness, and a nation assumes the weeds of wo. But human ambition may marshal its myriads in battle, and strew the field with the slain; and lo! your church bells send forth their loudest peals, your artillery pours forth its most deafening thunders, your bonfires blaze with the most intense brightness, and your sacred temples ring with the loudest hosannas, in testimony of your joy. Where now is your regard for human life? your shuddering at untimely death? your consternation at wholesale destruction? Is death the less terrible, when inflicted by the sword? Are men no longer men, when they perish in the field? You do not, indeed, rejoice for the sacrifice of life, but for victory. But where is your sympathy for the mangled and the slain—for the mangled and the slain in your own ranks; nay, in the ranks of the foe! Human nature is equally the sufferer, whether an American or a Briton bleeds; whether the victory crowns the Eagle or the Lion. Where, then, are philanthropy's tears for the horrors of victory—for the miseries of war? Again, we are constrained to exclaim:—How strange a creature is man! Nations, for the merest trifle, for a word, nay, for a straw, will rush into a war, deluging the world with tears and blood; while they mourn over a trifling casualty, or a slight visitation of the judgments of God! Once more we repeat, and let the whole universe join in the exclamation:—How strange a creature is man!

From the Irish Friend.

THE LAW OF LOVE.

BY R. C. FRENCH.

Pour forth the oil—pour boldly forth;
  It will not fail *until*
Thou fullest vessels to provide,
  Which it may largely fill.

But, soon as such are found no more,
  Though flowing broad and free,
'Till then, and nourished from on high,
  It straightway staunched will be.

Dig channels for the streams of love,
  Where they may broadly run;
For LOVE has ever-flowing streams
  To fill them every one.

But if, at any time thou cease
  Such channels to provide,
The very founts of love for thee
  Will soon be parch'd and dried.

For we must share, if we would keep
  That good thing from above—
Ceasing to give, we cease to have,
  Such is the law of love.

The above beautiful and descriptive lines, very forcibly illustrate a principle which lies at the very foundation of that religion which our Lord exemplified in his conduct and enforced by his precepts when he was upon the earth, and which will always continue to be a true characteristic of Christianity, under whatever name it may be exhibited.

The reader will not fail to be reminded of the beautiful but simple record of the miracle of the widow and her cruise of oil—2 Kings, iv. 6.—"And it came to pass, when the vessels were full, that she said unto her son, Bring me yet a vessel, and he said unto her, There is not a vessel more. And the oil was stayed."

The way to receive the blessing must be in keeping the hand open.   J. P

Islington.

From the Manchester Times of January 11, 1840.

A letter not exceeding half an ounce in weight may now be sent from any part of the United Kingdom to any other part, for one penny, if paid when posted, or for two pence if paid when delivered. It depends then, upon the people themselves, whether they shall introduce an uniform rate of a penny or not. If all prepay, the whole boon will be enjoyed at once. If none prepay, the rate will be doubled. A resolution should be come to by every body to receive no letter that is not paid, and to send none that is not paid. The Bishop of Lincoln, we observe, has given notice to the clergy of his diocese that, as he means to pay all the letters he sends, he expects that all sent to him should be paid. His example should be universally followed. It would be very unreasonable and shabby in a writer to save a penny at the expense of twopence to the person to whom he writes.

THE FRIEND.

FOURTH MONTH, 11, 1840.

To our kind friend A. R. Barclay, of London, we are indebted for the transmission of a small tract, containing two addresses delivered in the summer of 1824 by Thomas Shillitoe, to the prisoners at Spandau, in Prussia. The first of these is inserted to-day, and the other is intended for next week. Making the proper allowance for the disadvantages attendant upon a transfer from one language to another, the simple energy and straightforwardness of manner, characteristic of T. Shillitoe, are at once apparent. His own account of these visits to the prisoners at Spandau, is exceedingly interesting and instructive, wherein allusion is made to the fact of the addresses being taken down in short-hand, though unknown to himself at the time. See Friends' Library, vol. iii. p. 292.

An obliging friend, of Baltimore, has enabled us to place before our readers an extract of a letter of recent date, from Jamaica, containing highly interesting information respecting the coloured people in that island, and the effects of the free labour system, and which is the more to be valued as its character for authenticity is unquestionable. In the "Irish Friend" of first month 1st last, is a paragraph relating to the two Friends from whom this letter comes, which says: "Their object in going to the West Indies is, to promote the education of the people of colour, and the improvement of their religious, moral, and social condition. They took with them a liberal supply of suitable books, including many of the writings of Friends, and a large quantity of school materials, kindly furnished, gratuitously, by the British Foreign School Society."

FRIENDS' ASYLUM.

Committee on Admissions.—John G. Hoskins, No. 60 Franklin street, and No. 50 North Fourth street, up stairs; E. B. Garrigues, No. 185 North Seventh street, and No. 41 Market street, up stairs; Isaac Collins, No. 129 Filbert street, and No. 50 Commerce street; Edward Yarnall, southwest corner of Twelfth and George streets, and No. 39 Market street; Samuel Bettle, jr., No. 73 North Tenth street, and 26 South Front street.

Visiting Managers for the Month.—Geo. G. Williams, No. 61 Marshall street; John Richardson, No. 77 North Tenth street; Mordecai L. Dawson, No. 332 Arch street.

Superintendents.—John C. and Lætitia Redmond.

Attending Physician.—Dr. Charles Evans, No. 201 Arch street.

Resident Physician.—Dr. Thomas Wood.

TRACT ASSOCIATION OF FRIENDS.

The annual meeting of the Tract Association, will be held on the evening of third day, the 21st of fourth month, at 8 o'clock, in the Committee Room, Mulberry street.

JOHN CARTER, Clerk.

A stated annual meeting of "The Institute for Coloured Youth," will be held at the Committee Room, Arch street meeting house, on the evening of fourth day, the 22d instant, at 8 o'clock.

SAMUEL MASON, Jr., Clerk.
4th mo. 11th, 1840.

Haddonfield Boarding School for Girls.

Under the care of Amy Eastlack, will be vacated from the 9th of 4th month to the 7th of the 5th—when it will again be ready for the reception of pupils. The course of instruction embraces most of the branches of an English education. Terms are thirty dollars per quarter, of twelve weeks, payable in advance, washing included. The age of pupils is not limited, and they can be admitted at any time for a quarter or more. Each pupil is to be furnished with wash-basin and towels, and have all things distinctly marked. The scholars all attend the religious meetings of the Society of Friends. No deduction made for absence, except from indisposition. Application may be made at the school, or to WILLIAM EVANS, No. 134 south Front st. THOMAS KITE, No. 32 north Fifth st. HARKER & SHIVERS, No. 45 Arch st. JOSEPH B. COOPER, Newton, New Jersey. HENRY WARRINGTON, Westfield, New Jersey. Those who wish their children to commence at the opening of the school, please apply early in the 4th month.

WANTED, by a Dry Goods House, a lad of 16 to 18 years of age, who is disposed to make himself generally useful. A member of our Society will be preferred. Address in handwriting of applicant A. & O. box 706 Philadelphia Post Office.

DIED, on fifth day morning, the 26th ultimo, in the 34th year of his age, EDWARD C. MARSHALL, of this city. His gentle and unassuming manners, the kindness of his disposition, and circumspect deportment, endeared him to a large circle of friends and acquaintance.

Departed this life, at Burlington, N. J., the 26th of third month, 1840, EDITH LAWRIE, Jun'r., daughter of Joseph M. Lawrie, in the 36th year of her age. Her disease was pulmonary consumption, which, after seven months' confinement, removed her from the trials and sufferings of time, we thankfully believe, to the joys of a happy eternity. She was during her sickness an example of meek, and uncomplaining submission to the divine will; and in the full possession of her mental faculties, calmly resigned herself into the hands of her dear Redeemer, in humble, but steady hope, that he would be with her through "the valley of the shadow of death,"—saying a few minutes before the vital spark fled, that "her entire dependence was on her blessed Saviour, who felt very precious to her."

PRINTED BY ADAM WALDIE,
Carpenter Street, below Seventh, Philadelphia.

THE FRIEND.

A RELIGIOUS AND LITERARY JOURNAL.

VOL. XIII.   SEVENTH DAY, FOURTH MONTH, 18, 1840.   NO. 29.

EDITED BY ROBERT SMITH.

PUBLISHED WEEKLY.

Price two dollars per annum, payable in advance.

Subscriptions and Payments received by

GEORGE W. TAYLOR,

NO. 50, NORTH FOURTH STREET, UP STAIRS,

PHILADELPHIA.

For "The Friend."

ON THE TAILS OF COMETS.

It is not without some hesitation, that I presume to offer the following remarks, on a subject which has engaged the time, talents, and ingenuity of many of the greatest men who have adorned the scientific world. But on looking over an article on this subject, which appeared some weeks since in the columns of "The Friend,"* several objections to the theory there proposed presented themselves to my mind, which to me appeared inseparable. I therefore felt inclined briefly to state my objections, hoping that if they should prove unfounded, my error might be pointed out, and the whole subject fully explained.

The theory proposed by the writer of the article alluded to, appears to be similar to that of Tycho-Brahe, and others, who supposed that the sun's rays, in passing through the transparent head of the comet, were refracted so as to form a beam of light behind it; but they did not explain in what manner this light was rendered visible. This difficulty W. Mitchell endeavours to overcome, by supposing the rays thus refracted to be reflected by the ethereal medium, which is conceived to pervade the planetary space. Now, the great objection to this supposition is, that there cannot be any substance pervading space sufficiently dense to reflect the light thus cast upon it so as to be perceptible. Even supposing the light to be very much concentrated by the refraction produced by the nucleus or its surrounding atmosphere, no one can imagine that the exceedingly subtile vapour, (if any there be) which may pervade the planetary space, can perceptibly reflect the strongest light which can be cast upon it; for if such were the case, the light coming from the fixed stars would also be partly (if not entirely) reflected, and in consequence, it would be barely possible for a sufficient quantity of light to escape reflection to render them visible, considering their immense distances, and the vast extent of the supposed ethereal medium. We cannot suppose that if all the light cast upon a comet at that distance from the sun at which the tail begins to be formed, was concentrated into one

* See No. 20 of the present volume.

point, its intensity would be nearly so great as that of the light received directly from the sun in the space immediately surrounding him. If therefore the theory proposed were correct, we should expect to find the sun enveloped in a luminous vapour, which would extend at least many thousands, if not millions of miles; for if the light received on a comet when concentrated into *one point* is greater than the *unconcentrated* light in the immediate vicinity of the sun, and if the light of the comet when united in "*an infinite number of points,*" is sufficiently intense to be partly reflected by the ether in the neighbourhood of the comet, how much more would the stronger light near the sun be reflected by the surrounding ether, particularly when we consider the greater density of that ether.

Another objection to this theory is, that if the rays of the sun are refracted by the vapour of the comets, so as to form a luminous train, the same thing should occur to the planets, at least to the two inferior planets. If it be said that it is doubtful whether these have any atmosphere capable of perceptibly refracting the rays of light, I answer, that to suppose them devoid of an atmosphere seems contrary to the hypothesis upon which this theory is based, that of the existence of an ethereal medium; for, granting the existence of such a medium, (and I think it by no means improbable,) it must necessarily be increased in density, the nearer it approaches to any body capable of attracting it. Now, at the surface of the planets this increase in density would be very considerable, and thus would constitute an atmosphere. If we suppose the atmospheres of the planets to be nothing more than a condensed state of the ethereal medium, their densities would be proportionable to the quantity of matter in the planet; hence the planetary atmospheres would possess far greater refracting powers than those of the largest comets.

There is one feature in the tails of comets which the proposed theory seems insufficient to explain, and that is the occasional appearance of *two or more* tails attached to a single comet. Such appearances were observed in the comets of 1744, 1823, and 1835. To the former there were seen *six divergent streams of light* each nearly 30° in length. (*See Professor Joslin's Observations on the Tails of Halley's Comet. Silliman's Journal, vol. xxxi. page 142.*)

Further objections to this theory might be adduced, but from those already given the conclusion seems irresistible, that William Mitchell's method of accounting for the tails of comets is not only insufficient, but also incompatible with sound philosophical principles. Indeed, a strict examination of the various theories that have been invented to explain these phenomena, must, I think, result in the

conviction, that they are all wholly unsatisfactory. If, therefore, the objections here offered should prove well grounded, W. Mitchell may derive some consolation from the reflection that *his* theory is ranked with those of Newton, Tycho, and other renowned philosophers.

While stating my conviction that the various theories on this subject are *all wholly* unsatisfactory, I should have made one exception, for Dr. Hamilton, of Dublin, in a small treatise entitled "Conjectures on the nature of the Aurora Borealis, and on the tails of Comets," attributes both these phenomena to electricity, and supposes them to be produced in precisely the same manner. This hypothesis, although by no means *entirely* satisfactory, appears to me to approach nearer to the truth than any other with which I am acquainted. That the tails of comets are of an electrical nature, or at least that they are produced by some fluid very similar to electricity, appears extremely probable; for, from the considerations above given, it is evident that they cannot be caused by reflected light, unless there be some medium of very considerable density to produce the reflection. But if such a medium were thrown out from the comet to so great a distance, a large portion of it would reach beyond the sphere of the comet's attraction, and thus a rapid waste would take place: but facts seem to justify the assertion that this waste is not perceptibly going on. Hence we naturally conclude that the tails of comets shine by their own light. Their similarity to the Aurora Borealis has been noticed by several astronomers. Dr. Halley, in his description of the Aurora of 1716, says, "The streams of light so much resemble the long tails of comets that at first sight they might well be taken for such." D. de Marian styles the train of a comet the *Aurora Borealis* of the comet. Dr. Hamilton remarks, that to a spectator at some distance from the earth the Aurora Borealis would appear as a tail opposite the sun, as the tail of a comet lies. That it would not also be seen on the side of the earth towards the sun, appears from the fact that it has only been observed during the night, although its brightness is sometimes such as to render it visible, if it were ever actually formed in the day time. As a further confirmation of this theory, Vince, in his astronomy, observes that "the comet in 1607 appeared to shoot out at the end of its tail. Le P. Cysat, remarked the undulations of the tail of the comet in 1618. Hevelius observed the same in the tails of the comets in 1652 and 1661. M. Pingré took notice of the same appearance in the comet of 1769. These are circumstances exactly similar to the Aurora Borealis."

From these views of the subject, it must be acknowledged, that the arguments in favour of

which may be proved to exist, and which must of necessity produce the effects which we are endeavouring to explain.

It is with the hope that this may be the case with the subject under consideration, that I desire to see more attention given to it, believing that an investigation of these phenomena may contribute to the suppression of superstition and error, as well as to the advancement of science and truth.   L. L. N.

For " The Friend."

VENTILATION.

In order that air may be wholesome, three things are necessary. It must be pure; it must contain the requisite proportion of moisture; and it must be of a comfortable temperature.

First, it must be pure: it should not only be free from all exhalations and extraneous gases, but it should contain the same relative proportion of oxygen and nitrogen, as would be found *out of doors*, in a healthy region of the country. It is a fact familiar, doubtless, to most of my readers, that at every breath we draw a certain quantity of oxygen (the life-supporting principle of our atmosphere) is consumed, and in its place carbonic acid gas is produced, which is not useless merely, but positively detrimental; in other words, its influence on the lungs, is directly poisonous. Hence, the greater the number of persons assembled in a room, the more indispensable it is to change the air thoroughly and often. It is not, however, sufficient merely to *change* it, the place of the impure must be supplied by that which is pure. Obvious as this point may appear, it is often entirely neglected. In cold weather, we frequently see rooms ventilated by admitting air from an adjoining apartment, which itself needs ventilation, quite as much as the former. Many people seem to think, that if air is cool enough, little more is required. This is a great mistake. Impure air is not indeed so oppressive when cool, as when uncomfortably warm; but its effects in the former case are perhaps more dangerous, because less likely to attract attention; while in the latter, the immediate distress, which is felt, excites us to remove the cause. When persons breathe air containing a large proportion of carbonic acid gas, for any length of time, disease, often of a malignant character, is the inevitable result; and even when the proportion is very small, it is more than probable that it frequently lays

necessary for their subsistence; without able to provide sufficient clothing or against the inclemencies of the season order, therefore, to defend themselves a the cold of the winter, their small apar was closely shut up, and the air exclude every possible means. They did not re long in this situation, before the air beca vitiated as to affect their health, and prod fever, in one of the miserable family. fever was not violent at first, but gen crept on gradually; and the sickness of c the family became an additional reason fo more effectually excluding the fresh ai was also a means of keeping a greater p tion of the family in the apartment durin day-time; for the sick person was neces confined, and another as a nurse. Soon the first, a second was seized with the and in a few days more, the whole famil haps were attacked, one after another, the same distemper."

He adds, " I have more than once see of a family ill at one time, and sometim lying on the same bed. The fever app sooner or later as the winter was more o inclement; as the family was greater or sr as they were worse or better provided clothes for their persons and beds, and fuel; and as their apartment was more o confined." The fever here alluded to typhus.

The second condition necessary, in that air may be wholesome, is that it b ther too moist nor too dry. It may b from all impurities, and it may be of a fectly agreeable temperature, and yet s as to be wholly unfit for respiration. It seem, that a certain quantity of moisture dispensable, in order that the lungs ma form their office properly. Perhaps air, is extremely dry, may effect such a cha the lining membrane of the air-cells, i vents the oxygen from being absorbed thus nearly the same result may be prod as when we are compelled to breathe atmosphere, which contains a very smal portion of oxygen. I must leave, hov the consideration of this, and similar ques to the physiologist. But whatever ex tion may be given, the fact is indispu that excessively dry air does not affec skin merely, but sometimes produces the serious and distressing effects upon the s

* See Good's Study of Medicine, vol. ii. page

warmth, or the closeness of our meeting houses. He has been induced to write on this subject by the earnest request of those, who, though not deficient in amiableness in other respects, have not that interesting weakness which has been alluded to; and who, he feels sure, would utter no complaint without just cause. He is, however, fully aware that it is much easier to complain than to avoid all occasion of complaint: he is not ignorant that the proper regulation of the air of our meeting houses might be attended with some trouble and expense. Nevertheless he feels persuaded, that if those who have the charge of such affairs, could fully appreciate the amount of annoyance and suffering which it is in their power to relieve, they would not refuse to make the needful sacrifice. T. X.

CIRCULAR.

Philadelphia.

Esteemed Friend,—It has long been a subject of deep concern to many friends, that the people of colour who are amongst us, are deprived of so many of the advantages partaken of by other members of the community. The Managers of the "Institute for Coloured Youth," impressed with these views, have the satisfaction to state they have purchased a farm, which is considered very eligible for the purposes of the proposed institute, being about seven miles north of the city, on the Willow Grove or Old York Turnpike Road. On this place it is intended to receive a limited number of coloured children, who will be instructed in farming, some of the useful arts, and the elementary branches of an English education; in the hope that if the young be thus prepared to enter on the duties of life, they will be qualified to take their station as useful members in the community.

In taking this preliminary step towards carrying out the wishes of the benevolent individuals to whose liberal bequest, in connection with the contributions of other friends, we are indebted for the means of making a commencement in this effort, the funds have been nearly exhausted; but trusting that the sympathies of the members of our Religious Society will be increasingly awakened in behalf of the oppressed portion of the human family, for whose benefit this fund is intended, we are encouraged to hope that an appeal will not be made in vain, but that ample means will be afforded to carry on this important work. We respectfully request thy pecuniary assistance for this desirable object, as well as thy influence and exertion in procuring the aid of others.

Signed by direction and on behalf of the Board of Managers.

CASPAR WISTAR, *Secretary.*

Donations or subscriptions will be gratefully received by either of the undersigned managers :

Benjamin Cooper, near Camden, New Jersey.—George Williams, No. 71 North Seventh street.—Philip Garrett, Noble above Sixth street.—Blakely Sharpless, No. 8 South Fourth street.—Thomas Evans, No. 129 South Third street.—John G. Hoskins, No. 50 North Fourth street.—Saml. Mason, Jr.

No. 68 North Seventh street.—John Elliott, Race above Seventh street.—Thomas Wistar, Jr. Abington.—Caspar Wistar, No. 184 Arch street.—Mordecai L. Dawson, N. W. cor. Tenth and Filbert streets.—Marmaduke C. Cope, No. 286 Filbert street.—Stephen P. Morris, N. E cor. Eighth and Spruce streets. —Joseph Scattergood, No. 14 Minor street. —Wm. Biddle, N. W. cor. Eleventh and Arch streets.

From the Boston Recorder.

THE BEST COAT.

Most people have some choice articles of apparel. There is the best hat, the best coat, the best bonnet, the best shawl, &c. These are not for every day use. They have some place of quiet retirement until they are called for by some special exigency. No one can object to this.

We are sorry that so good a thing as the best coat should furnish so striking an illustration of the nature of some people's religion. There are certain exigencies only that call for the best coat. So we have seen righteousness that seemingly could not be used every day, but must be put on and put off with varying circumstances. Jehu put the best coat on when he said, "Come and see my zeal for the Lord." But it was only for an occasion. For he had no such coat on when it was soon after written concerning him, "But Jehu took no heed to walk in the law of the Lord God of Israel with all his heart, for he departed not from the sins of Jeroboam which made Israel to sin." Judas wore the best coat for a long period. But it was thrown off at last. Ananias, Sapphira, and Simon Magus, belong to the same class. We wish there had been no such cases since their day.

But the best-coat-religion has flourished in every generation. There have always been some that have had goodness at hand, like a garment, ready to put on as the occasion called for it. There is a good deal of Sabbath-day goodness. There is a serious deportment, careful regard for public worship, serious remarks upon serious things, &c. &c. The best coat is on, and it sets well and looks well. We are glad to see it. And the man looks so well in it, we wish he would keep it on through the week. We do not see why one should not be devout, prayerful, spiritually-minded on a week day as well as on the Sabbath day. "Always abounding in the work of the Lord," we suppose, does not mean for one day in seven only. *Always* covers the whole week, and every day of it. And if a man enters into the full spirit of that injunction, he will not pull the best coat off, and hanging it up, say, "There is my religion; I shall have no use for it till next Sabbath."

"But did you ever hear such a speech as that?" No, never; but we have seen just such things though. We have seen very excellent Sabbath-day goodness, and poor, very poor week-day goodness in the same person. And it leads us to suppose that the person in question had conceived that religion was an affair for times and seasons only, like the best

coat; that he was a Jehu sort of disciple, or a relative, morally, of him that betrayed his Master.

Well, religion is rather an inconvenient thing for some people to carry with them through the week. It would place a heavy burden on the heart of him that should make "the ephah small and the shekel great." It would thump terribly, and with intelligible rebukes upon the rum cask of him that draws the spigot. It would be inconvenient to have present such a witness of a fraudulent bargain, of violated contracts and broken promises. It would be a grim and frowning spectre to the doer of many kinds of evils. He must relax his grasp from many a precious coin, and see passing out of his reach many an anticipated victim of fraud and deceit.

It is no great affair to be religious of a Sabbath day. You have not any thing else to do, unless you are a very vagabond, and defy all religious obligations. It requires no great self-denial. You are not mingling with the busy world in the high career and powerful excitement of business. Good influences of all kinds form a healthful atmosphere around you. Put on the best coat, then, and see that it be a spiritual garment, "a robe of righteousness." Such apparel, unlike the best coat, looks better the more you wear it. It never becomes threadbare. Wear it every day and every where. It never can be injured by use. It is pulling it off that injures it. Keeping it on is essential to its beauty and preservation. You cannot die in better apparel. And it will clothe you with salvation in the day that you are judged.

JEWS IN EUROPE.

The delegation which the church of Scotland sent last year to Palestine, have given a very encouraging report of the facilities of access to the Jews in Europe and Asia. The statement as given in the English papers is too long for our columns, but the Boston Recorder gives the following summary of them.

Tuscany is the most free of all the countries of Italy, and Leghorn, its principal city, is a free port; yet there it is not allowed to preach the gospel to Roman catholics. But in the same place you may go freely to the lost sheep of the house of Israel. Thus the door is shut to the Gentiles, but open to the Jews.

In Egypt and Palestine you cannot preach the gospel to the deluded followers of Mahomet, except on penalty of instant banishment or death; yet you may preach freely the gospel to the Jews, in every place—in the bazaars, the market-places, and the synagogues. The same is true in ancient Sidon, Tyre, Sychar, Tiberias, and Acre. In Constantinople, where are 80,000 Jews, you may go freely to them, and though converts to the faith among them may meet persecution from their brethren, they meet none from the government.

In Moldavia, and Wallachia, where the established religion is that of the Greek church, an attempt to convert an adherent to that church would be fatal to the missionary; but he may preach to the Jews without hazard, at any time and in all places, under the very eye of government. No man will forbid him.

228

THE FRIEND.

Austria will suffer no missionaries, and no distribution of Bibles in English, Hebrew or German. There, it is out of the question, as yet, to carry the gospel to the people—even to the Jews, who are themselves willing to hear it.

At Cracow in Poland, are 22,000 Jews living in a separate quarter of the city—and they have among them a single missionary, whose labours are of the most interesting kind. He is not allowed to preach openly in the congregation, but he goes to a bookseller's shop, where he opens the book of life, and the unsearchable riches of Christ.

In the Grand Duchy of Posen, though under the government of the emperor of Russia, a protestant prince, a Christian missionary could not preach the gospel to the people at large; but the door is open for the missionary to the Jews—and a missionary actually labouring there, has from 200 to 400 collected in his church, out of the 74,000 living in the country.—*S. S. Journal.*

THE FRIEND.

FOURTH MONTH, 18, 1840.

The attention of the readers of "The Friend," is again earnestly called to the situation of the "Institute for Coloured Youth." The circular of its managers setting forth the objects and wants of this institution, and calling for the aid of its friends, will be found in another part of this sheet. This concern is founded on the mutual labour principle, and the managers have struggled along through many difficulties, until at length they have so far attained their object as to be able, it is hoped, in a short time to open the establishment for the reception of pupils. In doing this, however, their funds have been nearly exhausted, and they are now obliged to look to the friends of the coloured man for the necessary means of consummating this truly benevolent design. It is particularly desired that such of our country friends as shall be in attendance at our approaching annual meeting, and are able so to do, will liberally contribute their aid to this deeply interesting experiment. Thus far the burden and expense of carrying out the design has rested on comparatively a small number of Friends, but it is now hoped, as the managers have procured a suitable farm with the necessary appertenances, that our members generally will feel sufficient interest to attend the annual meeting of the institute to be held on fourth day evening next, at Arch street meeting house.

Through the kind attention of a Friend of Rhode Island, we have received two pamphlets:—the first entitled "Views of the Society of Friends in relation to Civil Government;" the other, "A Declaration of the Society of Friends in relation to Church Government;" both having recently been issued by a meeting of the representatives of New England Yearly Meeting, and addressed to the Quarterly, Monthly, and Preparative Meetings, within the boundaries of that division of our religious society. Believing, however, the matter which they contain to be

calculated for more extensive service, we have concluded to insert them in our pages. That on civil government occupies a place in the present number; and the other, on church government, which is of considerably greater length, will be divided into convenient portions, and follow in successive numbers.

A Stated Annual Meeting of "The Bible Association of Friends in America," will be held on the evening of second day, the 20th instant, in the east room, Mulberry street Meeting House, at 8 o'clock.

SAMUEL MASON, JR. *Clerk.*

4th mo. 18th.

TRACT ASSOCIATION OF FRIENDS.

The annual meeting of the Tract Association, will be held on the evening of third day, the 21st of fourth month, at 8 o'clock, in the Committee Room, Mulberry street.

JOHN CARTER, *Clerk.*

A stated annual meeting of "The Institute for Coloured Youth," will be held at the Committee Room, Arch street meeting house, on the evening of fourth day, the 22d instant, at 8 o'clock.

SAMUEL MASON, Jr., *Clerk.*

4th mo. 11th, 1840.

MARRIED, on the 8th instant, at Friends' Meeting House, in Orchard street, New York, HENRY WOOD to ELIZABETH KING, daughter of the late John King.

DIED, on the morning of the 13th instant, in the 67th year of her age, JANE BETTLE, wife of Samuel Bettle, a member and elder of the Monthly Meeting of Friends of Philadelphia. After having devoted many years of her life to the service of the Society, and the promotion of the cause of Truth, in the year 1832, she was attacked with a painful disorder which confined her wholly to the house for the remainder of her days, and, during a considerable part of the time, to her chamber. Throughout this protracted season of privation and of suffering, the Christian virtues shone conspicuously in her example, and rendered her society truly pleasant and profitable. She evinced a cheerful and patient resignation to the ordering of Divine Providence, and a humble yet steadfast reliance on the supporting arm of her dear Redeemer, which were edifying and instructive. Nothing like a disposition to repine at her lot was ever manifest, but on the contrary a frequent and grateful acknowledgement of the gracious dealings of the Lord with her, and of his goodness to her soul. The sense of her own sufferings, great as they appeared to those about her, seemed much absorbed by her affectionate concern for others; and when her mind was drawn to dwell in reverent contemplation on what the blessed Son of God endured for the sins of a guilty world, they seemed to sink into insignificance. At one time being in a very weak and suffering state, something was proposed for her relief, when she answered, "It seems hardly worth while, considering the short time I shall want these accommodations;" and after a little pause, she continued, "When I consider the blameless Lamb of God, who bore our sins in his own body on the tree, our own light afflictions seem not worthy to be spoken of." She was often engaged to speak a word in season, by way of affectionate admonition, encouragement, or caution, to those who visited her, and though prevented from mingling with her friends in the performance of public worship, she was frequent in reverent, silent, waiting upon God, being sensible that all her supplies were in him, and that from his bountiful hand, "the strength to suffer and the will to serve," must be daily received. Her interest in the concerns of the Society and the prosperity of the cause of true religion continued unabated; and she observed, "I have sometimes almost

wondered at my long continuance in my present feeble condition, very much shut out, as it seems to me, from opportunities of usefulness; but I think I may say that my prayers are very often offered up on behalf of my own family and of the church." Thus as a faithful servant, waiting for the coming of her Lord, she was concerned to have her loins girded and her light burning, and when the solemn summons arrived, it brought with it no alarm. For some weeks previous to her close, she was sensible of the near approach of death, and intimated it to those around her, expressing her apprehension that she should be taken when they were not looking for it, which proved the case. On the 26th of third month, being asked how she was, she replied, "I am as well as I expect to be—I think I shall not be long with you—but it is not best for us to be too anxious about the time of our being called home; seeing we have a merciful High Priest, who is touched with a feeling of every infirmity." After a quiet pause, she proceeded: "I do not think it is best to be too gloomy —but as our day's work goes on, to wear the aspect of cheerfulness. I have very many outward blessings; a kind husband, and children and family, and much to love and enjoy; but my concern is, so to live and watch that when summoned to leave them, I may render in my account with joy and not with grief. But in order to attain this state, we must experience many deep baptisms, and much of the searching and purifying operation, must be submitted to. I think I may say that even in my lowest moments, when the billows have seemed to rise, and the storm to beat, I have never entirely lost my hold upon the anchor—the hope in Jesus—finding it even in such seasons, both sure and steadfast." Dwelling in humble contemplation on the greatness and majesty of the High and Holy One, and her own unworthiness, she was deeply bowed under a sense of his matchless condescension, in regarding his dependent children; and on one occasion remarked, "When we consider the greatness of Him, without whom not a sparrow falls, what cause for thankfulness have we for his care over us, unworthy as we are—that he who feedeth the ravens, careth for us also." On the 6th of this month, in the course of a serious conversation with her husband, she said, "I have for some time felt as if the period of my continuing here was drawing to a close, and this feeling increases. I have been endeavouring to give up all, and lay every thing at the feet of my merciful and blessed Saviour; and poor as I am, and at times low in faith and patience, I have never had my trust and confidence in him removed." And after a solemn pause, as if in the fresh renewing of that precious faith and confidence which he is pleased to grant to his believing disciples, she added, "He will be with me, I feel assured, through the valley and shadow of death." Her bodily weakness increased, while the progress of disease, and the urgency of some of her symptoms, added much to her sufferings, but her patience and resignation failed not. He who had graciously sustained and comforted her during her long illness, was now mercifully near, calming and supporting her departing spirit, and enabling her to evince, even amid the decay of expiring nature, that there is a blessed reality in the Christian's belief. On the evening of the 12th, her mind was remarkably calm and unclouded, and her husband observing to her that it was a favour, she replied, "I esteem it as a very great favour indeed. I have loved the Lord Jesus from an early period of my life until the present day, and he has not forsaken me; and notwithstanding my short comings, I have hope in him. But it is not by any acts of righteousness that we have done, but of his mere mercy that he saveth us." After this she said but little, except on one occasion when her pain seemed to be more severe than usual, she sweetly remarked, with a pleasant countenance, "these light afflictions are but for a moment." About four o'clock on the morning of the 13th, she slept quietly for half an hour, and on waking was permitted gently to pass away without any struggle, about 5 o'clock, and we have the consoling belief that her redeemed and purified spirit, through the mercy of God in Christ Jesus, has joined the just of all generations in the unceasing song, of "Worthy—worthy—worthy is the Lamb that was slain."

Quietly departed this life, on the evening of the 2d instant, at his residence in Little Britain, Lancaster county, Pa., JOSEPH BALLANCE, aged eighty-four years, six months and twenty-one days.

Two Addresses to the Prisoners in the House of Correction at Spandau, in Prussia; delivered by Thomas Shillitoe, of London.

(Concluded from page 222.)

SECOND ADDRESS.

King Solomon says, "The lamp (or the light) of the wicked shall be put out." This important truth, together with many others, is preserved to us in the records of Holy Writ, for doctrine, for reproof, and for instruction in righteousness, and we dare not therefore esteem lightly, or consider as fables any of the admonitions which concern our spiritual condition. But let us first consider what is to be understood in this place, by the lamp, or the light of which the king speaks. I hope we shall easily see that this expression does not refer to an outward object, but contains for our comprehension, a spiritual idea, or points out a spiritual light whereof the Scripture says, that it is "as a lamp to our feet and as a light to our path;" whilst it proves itself a sure means of preserving us from the destructive path of the enemy of our souls. Now if this light of the soul is often put out, it must also be often lighted up again; and this is the case with all men, who strive against the divine light, and whom a merciful God always visits again and again with the light of his grace (so long as the day of their visitation continues, and they are susceptible of the convictions of his grace and truth.) But what may now be the reason that God has withdrawn so very far from you, this light of his love, which makes manifest and reproves the evil in every man, and discovers to him his duty towards him, his beneficent Creator, and also towards his fellow-men, that you have fallen into the perverse paths which have led you on into your present condition.

Was it not a want of disposition on your side, to direct yourselves into the paths of divine love? Was it not disobedience to the convictions of this pure light, which searches into and makes known the depths of the human heart? Truly these were the reasons, my dear fellow-men, why you, who were created for freedom, at present find yourselves in imprisonment and separated from your dear relatives. But let me pray you not to regard what I say, as if I were come to reproach you,—No,—this is by no means my design; I will rather willingly confess, that I also am not without fault;—that I can be secure from falling only so long as I continue in inward watchfulness and prayer, and further, that I have nothing whereon I can rely with greater confidence, than upon the mercy of God in Christ Jesus my Redeemer. I can with truth say, I pity your condition whilst I speak to you, and it is the supplication of my heart to the gracious and Almighty God, that the time which is past, in which you have not yielded obedience to the visitations of his love, may now be sufficient, and that you may be strengthened in future to observe a greater watchfulness over your hearts; to evince more obedience towards the divine law in your souls, and to behave yourselves better to your superiors and one towards another. And O! do not allow yourselves by wicked and frivolous conversation, to take delight in provoking one another to

sins. Consider, that under the mild government under which you live, you have it in your power, by good behaviour continually to be making your condition even more easy. May you know how rightly to estimate what a blessing it is for you that you live under so good a regent, and under so mild a law, where time and opportunity are allowed you for improvement, and for the advancement of your happiness. I have often thought, and already have also expressed, that indeed some among you, if they had committed in my land the crimes of which they have made themselves guilty, it would have cost them their natural lives; and O! how awful must that condition be, in which I often know my fellow-countrymen, who without proper, or not sufficient preparation, are hurried into eternity, to appear before the judgment seat of Christ, where every one will receive the recompense of his deeds, whether they be good or evil. Therefore it is the fervent supplication of my heart, and my prayer for you, my dear fellow-men, that you may rightly estimate and value the past prolongation of the term of your lives, and the time for the attainment of true repentance and conversion, which is so graciously afforded you. Consider, what a serious and weighty matter it is, to be called from works to rewards! But would we at any time experience true repentance and conversion, it must come to pass here;—here in time, when we receive and experience the gracious visitation of God. This is a work which every one must experience for himself; for no man can appear for his friend or brother, or redeem him; but every one must give account for his own works. And if this necessary work make a just progress, it must come to pass through our Lord Jesus Christ, who is "the Author and Finisher" of true faith. He must awaken the souls out of the dead sleep of their trespasses and sins, purify them therefrom, redeem them, and prepare them for a blessed eternal life. O! how great is my desire that your thoughts, all your expectations, yea, your whole souls may be directed to this most important subject! Then, however great your temptations may be, however corrupt your natural dispositions, and however strong their provocations to evil—all the temptations of the enemy will nevertheless avail nothing towards him, in whose conquering and redeeming power you believe. Yea, if you then must also confess, that sin has become exceedingly powerful in you, and that evil still cleaves to you continually, and hinders you from good; you will nevertheless experience that the grace and power of Jesus is still much mightier than the power of sin and of the tempter, if you hold fast by Him, "who has all power in heaven and upon earth." Now if you are earnestly endeavouring in this manner to become other creatures, you will not only experience, that the Lord can strengthen you by his grace, to overcome all temptations to evil; but you will also attain, that you will no more murmur or trouble yourselves about your hard lot; yea, you will endure with more patient submission, the chastisements which the Lord permits to overtake you. Then your very afflictions will serve to advance your sanctification, purification and justification.

It is still further my fervent desire that you

may rightly comprehend and estimate the great blessing of being allowed to assemble for the worship of Almighty God, for this is a Christian privilege which is not granted to all men. Now when you assemble together for this weighty and sublime object, so conduct yourselves that your hearts may be prepared to approach the Holy God, who sees the heart, and who knows our true inward condition—to approach him in an acceptable manner, viz: with broken and contrite hearts and sorrowful spirits. As you thus appear before him, and address yourselves to him with prayer and supplication in spirit, your meeting together will truly be blessed, and will conduce to your best interest. Then also will the instruction, which is thereby imparted, serve you for encouragement and strength to withstand, in the course of the week, the temptations to sin, and so will your seasons of divine worship be also the means to sweeten the bitter cup, which many among you have to drink. That this may now be your experience, is the sincere prayer of my soul! I do not believe that any one among you has reason to consider his condition as a lost, or a hopeless one; and should any of you be buffeted with such thoughts, I can tell you that this is a work of the wicked enemy of your souls, who, I have already often proved, never ceases to be a cruel deceitful enemy, whilst he at first tempts us and provokes us do evil, and then, when we behold with pain how we have erred and committed sin in the pure sight of God, and with truly sorrowful spirits implore him for pardon—he appears as our accuser of the evil, to the commission of which he has seduced us and urged us on; he accuses us harshly and seldom fails to represent our sins so great that we may despair of their pardon; in order that we may give up, or be hindered from calling upon God for help and preservation, and may not obtain pardon for our sins, through sincere repentance and conversion. Therefore, I beseech you, that you watch over the false representations of the enemy in your spirits, that no one may be thereby disappointed or deceived; and that you may not only be informed, but may also believe that with God, "there is plenteous redemption." Then I trust you will truly experience that he is a God nigh at hand, and not a God afar off; a present helper in every time of trouble and affliction. It is from entertaining continued love to you, that I am come here once more for the purpose of seeing you; and it is my sincere desire, that if we shall not see each other again in this world, it may be our lot to meet together again at a future time in heaven, where all trouble will be at an end, and all tears be wiped from our eyes; where we shall be employed throughout the whole of a boundless eternity, in the worship, adoration, and glorification of God, and his beloved Son Jesus Christ, who, by his salutary chastisements and corrections, has guided us into the narrow path of life. But before all, let me once more beseech you to be especially grateful that you enjoy the permission of taking part in the worship and adoration of God. For I can tell you, that the neglect of this sacred duty has already brought many in my native land, to a premature and an unprepared-for death. I wish therefore that you, as I also do, may accept this privilege with deeper gratitude from the hand of the Lord, from whom we receive all temporal and spiritual blessings. When you come together in such a temper of mind, for the purpose of divine worship, you will thereby obtain substantial advantage, then, also you will not pass the remainder of the day in useless and sinful conversation, but will much rather be endeavouring to promote the welfare one of another.

Views of the Society of Friends in relation to Civil Government.

The representatives of the Yearly Meeting of the Society of Friends for New England, being impressed with the importance of diffusing among their own members and in the Christian community corréct information on some points of our faith and practice, have believed it right for them at this time to issue this address, to the end that the principles that we have ever maintained in relation thereto, since our origin as a people, may be faithfully supported by us, and clearly understood by others.

It is a time of much excitement in civil and religious society, and we are earnestly desirous that our members may individually seek to manifest on all occasions a meek and quiet spirit, ever demeaning themselves as good citizens, prompt in the support of right order, and in all things adorning the doctrines we profess. This has at all times been the concern of our Society. Acknowledging God as the alone Supreme Ruler of the conscience, they have been ever ready cheerfully to submit to all the laws and ordinances of men that did not conflict therewith, and to contribute to the support of well-ordered civil government.

We do indeed believe that war and fighting are contrary to the Divine Will, and unlawful for us as Christians—and we cannot, therefore, in any way, countenance or contribute to military operations.

We believe that, under the government of the Prince of Peace, swords are to be beaten into ploughshares and spears into pruning-hooks, and men are to learn war no more. The nature of the Christian dispensation, in contrast with the fierce passions of man, is beautifully portrayed by the evangelical prophet—' Every battle of the warrior is with confused noise, and garments rolled in blood; but this shall be with burning and fuel of fire. For unto us a child is born, unto us a son is given; and the government shall be upon his shoulder; and his name shall be called Wonderful, Counsellor, The Mighty God, The Everlasting Father, The Prince of Peace. Of the increase of his government and peace there shall be no end.'' Isa. ix. 5, 6, 7.

When our Saviour walked among men, he inculcated the principles of peace in clear and emphatic language, and by his own shining example. " Ye have heard that it hath been said, an eye for an eye, and a tooth for a tooth —but I say unto you, that ye resist not evil." " Ye have heard that it hath been said, thou shalt love thy neighbour and hate thine enemy —but I say unto you, love your enemies, bless them that curse you, do good to them that hate you, and pray for them that despitefully use you and persecute you, that ye may

be the children of your Father which is in heaven." And in his own example, when he could have summoned twelve legions of angels to his rescue, he quietly submitted to his persecutors, and in the end offered the intercession, " Father forgive them, for they know not what they do." The apostle James in allusion to this subject queries, " From whence come wars and fightings among you? Come they not hence, even of your lusts that war in your members?"

Believing, then, that under the Christian dispensation, which was ushered in with the annunciation of " Peace on earth, good will toward men," we cannot in any way be engaged in war or contribute to its support, every faithful member of our body has felt bound conscientiously to abstain from all participation in it;—and in our earlier existence as a people, were subjected to the spoiling of goods, imprisonment and much suffering, on account of our religious scruples in this respect—but we dare not in the Divine sight do otherwise than steadfastly maintain our testimony, based as it is on the precepts of Him who was emphatically the Prince of Peace, and consonant with the doctrines and practice of his apostles and early followers.

Nor can we for conscience sake agree to any commutation for military requisitions; for hereby should we be consenting to the justness and propriety of the exaction. And in this we trust that those who view this subject differently from us, will discover no disposition to screen ourselves from onerous duties, but will do us the justice to believe that it is for the answer of a pure conscience unto God, which is dearer to us than our natural lives. And for the sincerity of our motives we may appeal to the history of our Society, in which no instance will be found where a consistent member has ever borne arms, or voluntarily paid a fine or tax as an equivalent; but has chosen rather patiently to suffer whatever might be inflicted upon him for the support of his religious belief.

Within the limits of New England our scruples as to bearing arms have generally received the favourable consideration of the different state legislatures, and we trust that our members will continue to act so consistently with their Christian profession as that they may still be deemed worthy of the immunity which has been heretofore extended.

But while we have thus felt bound uncompromisingly to maintain our belief of the peaceable nature of the Christian dispensation, we have ever acknowledged the propriety and necessity of human government in conducting the affairs of men, and have since our origin, from time to time, declared our views in this respect, manifesting our fidelity to whatever government an overruling Providence might place us under. Nor do we believe that in this way our peaceable principles are at all infringed upon.

We find in the New Testament clear and undeniable evidence that civil government was fully recognized by Christ himself, and his apostles; and we have ever considered it to be essential to the preservation of good order and the promotion of the happiness of men—nor

have we as a Society any unity with the views of those who deny the necessity of human governments.

When the apostle Peter was inquired of, " Does not your master pay tribute?" he replied in the affirmative, and Christ upon the occasion wrought a miracle to obtain money to pay for himself and the apostle. Here the authority of civil government in exacting tribute is acknowledged by our Lord, and practically complied with; and in no instance do we find that he refused to conform to it, but expressly commanded to " render unto Cæsar the things that are Cæsar's."

We may now introduce several injunctions and conclusions of the apostles respecting governments in their own words. " Let every soul be subject unto the higher powers; for there is no power but of God. The powers that be are ordained of God: whosoever, therefore, resisteth the power, resisteth the ordinance of God; for rulers are not a terror to good works, but to the evil. Wilt thou, then, not be afraid of the power? do that which is good, and thou shalt have praise of the same; for he is the minister of God to thee for good. But if thou do that which is evil, be afraid; for he beareth not the sword in vain: for he is the minister of God, a revenger to execute wrath upon him that doeth evil. Wherefore ye must needs be subject, not only for wrath but also for conscience sake: For, for this cause pay ye tribute also; for they are God's ministers, attending continually upon this very thing." Rom. xiii. 1 to 6. " Submit yourselves to every ordinance of man for the Lord's sake; whether it be to the king as supreme, or unto governors as unto them that are sent by him for the punishment of evil doers, and for the praise of them that do well: For so is the will of God, that with well doing ye may put to silence the ignorance of foolish men." Peter, 1st Epistle, ii. 13, 15. " Put them in mind to be subject to principalities and powers, to obey magistrates, to be ready to every good work." Titus, iii. 1. The apostle Paul acknowledges and practically submits to the authority of human governments, when he declared unto Festus that if he had " committed any thing worthy of death he refused not to die," and then appealed unto Cæsar to be judged by him.

These citations from Holy Scripture we think sufficiently establish the position that civil government was recognized and sustained by the author of Christianity and his apostles, and we now proceed to show that the Society of Friends has always acknowledged its authority and contributed to its support; and to prove this, we shall quote from various writers of standard authority in the Society. And, firstly, we adduce the testimony of George Fox on this point.

In his address to Charles II., from the prison in Worcester, he asserts that " the spirit which leads people from all manner of sin and evil is one with the magistrate's power and with the righteous law; for the law being added because of transgression, so the spirit which leads out of transgression is the good spirit of Christ, and is one with the magistrates' in the higher powers, and owns it and them;" and he expressly declares that he and his

Friends "are not against, but stand for all good government."

He sometimes called upon the civil authority to interpose its sheltering power to protect his person, and in an Epistle to Friends in some of the West India islands, when the governor had desired them to take a part in keeping up a watch to protect from incursions, and had granted them the privilege of doing so without carrying arms, he enters into an argument to show the propriety of their complying; and enjoins them faithfully to perform this service, and report to the magistrates all cases of offence that they may discover, in order that the offender may be arrested in his course and punished—and thus proceeds: "For rulers are not to be a terror to the good workers, but to the evil; and wilt thou, then, not be afraid of the power? do that which is good, and thou shalt have praise of the same; for he is a minister of God to thee for good, for he should keep down the evil; but if thou doest that which is evil, be afraid; for he beareth not the sword* in vain; for he is a minister of God to revenge and execute wrath upon him that doeth evil. So he is the revenger and executioner of the wrath upon the evil doer, as God hath placed him—on him that steals, or kills, or bears false witness," &c. "And to that power that executes the revenge, and brings the sword upon the murderer, thief, false witness and other evil doers, we must be subject to that power, and own that power, not only for wrath, but for conscience sake; which is for the punishment of the evil doers, and the praise for them that do well."

In his letter to Charles II., George Fox thus addresses him: "Thou earnest not into this nation by sword, or victory of war; but by the power of the Lord; now, if thou dost not live in it, thou wilt not prosper."

Robert Barclay, in his letter addressed to the ambassadors of the Christian states, assembled at Nimeguen, in the year 1677, to consult the peace of Christendom, exhorts them "not to be unwilling to hear one that appeared among them for the interest of Christ, his King and Master—not as if thereby he denied the just authority of sovereign princes, or refused to acknowledge the subjection himself owes to his lawful prince and superior; or were any ways inclined to favour the dreams of such as, under the pretence of crying up King Jesus and the kingdom of Christ, either deny or seek to overturn all civil government;—nay, not at all, but I am one who do reverence and honour magistrates, and acknowledge subjection due unto them by their respective people in all things just and lawful; knowing that magistracy is an ordinance of God, and that magistrates are his ministers, who bear not the sword in vain."

When Edward Pyott, William Salt and George Fox were imprisoned in the jail at Lancaster in 1656, on account of their religious profession, the former addressed a remonstrance to John Glyn, chief justice of England, on behalf of himself and his companions, in which their deference to the authority of magistracy is fully exhibited by their appealing to the law as "the one common guard or defence to property, liberty and life;" as being established for the protection of those rights "so just and so equal," and which, as to the outward, are of "the highest importance to the well being of man." He adds, "the law seeks not for causes whereby to make the innocent suffer; but helpeth him to right who suffers wrong, relieveth the oppressed, and searcheth out the matter, whether that of which a man stands accused be so or no; seeking judgment and hastening righteousness."

Edward Burrough, a contemporary of Fox, and an eminent minister in our Society, when addressing Richard Cromwell, "the protector of the commonwealth," expressly declares that, "as for magistracy it was ordained of God, to be a dread and terror and limit to evil doers, and to be a defence and praise to all that do well; to condemn the guilty and justify the guiltless,"—and in a book which he published in 1661, he says, that where any man's "heresy do extend further than only against God and his own soul, even to outward wrongs or evils, or violence, or visible mischiefs committed to the injury of others, then he forbids not punishment to be inflicted upon the person and estate of such man."

In a conversation between Charles II. and Richard Hubberthorn, the respect of Friends for civil government is plainly declared.

Question by the king.—"How do you own magistrates or magistracy?" Answ.—"Thus we do own magistrates: whosoever is set up by God, whether king as supreme, or any set in authority by him, who are for the punishment of evil doers, and the praise of them that do well, such we shall submit unto, and assist in righteous and civil things, both by body and estate; and if any magistrates do that which is unrighteous, we must declare against it; only submit under it by a patient suffering, and not rebel against any by insurrections, plots and contrivances." To which the king replied, "that is enough."

Again, in an address to the king, entitled "The humble address of the people commonly called Quakers," the following language is used: "O king, we do further declare, that God Almighty hath taught and engaged us to acknowledge and actually to obey magistracy as his ordinance, in all things not repugnant to his law and light in our consciences, which is certainly agreeable to the Holy Scriptures," &c.

On the restoration of peace they addressed an acknowledgment to William III. over England, &c., king, after this manner: "May it please the king, seeing the Most High God, who ruleth in the kingdoms of men, and appointeth over them whomsoever he will, hath by his over-ruling power and providence placed thee in dominion and dignity over these realms, and by his divine favour hath signally preserved and delivered thee from many great and imminent dangers, and graciously turned the calamity of war into the desired mercy of peace."

On the accession to the throne of Queen Anne, the people called Quakers thought themselves no less obliged than others to express to the queen their condolence on account of the king's death, and to testify their affection and fidelity to her, and therefore drew up an address, in which they declare their sorrow and sense of great loss sustained in the death of their late king, William III., whom God made the instrument of much good to these nations," and assure the queen of their loyalty to her government. "We sincerely declare that with the assistance of the grace of God, we will always, according to our Christian duty, demonstrate our good affection, truth and fidelity to the queen and her government, and heartily pray that his wisdom may direct and his blessings be upon the queen and her great councils to the suppressing of vice and immorality, and the promoting of piety, peace and charity to the glory of God and the benefit of these nations. May the King of kings make thy reign long and glorious, to which temporal blessings we shall pray for thy eternal happiness."

Were it necessary to our purpose, these extracts from the writings of Friends might be greatly extended, but we think that sufficient has been adduced to show that they did not view civil government as an evil, but as an ordinance of God; nor on account of its maladministration were they willing to throw off its salutary restraints; on the contrary they availed themselves of legal assistance for the redress of wrongs. It is stated on unquestionable authority, that "during the height of the persecution which Friends suffered, when the prisons were crowded, and many illegally arrested, it was found necessary to make frequent application to persons in authority, for the redress of grievances. Though Friends cheerfully endured the penalty of the laws, rather than violate their consciences, yet they promptly availed themselves of the means of relief which the illegality of the proceedings against them offered. Many of these cases involved legal questions of intricacy and moment, requiring the advice of the most experienced and judicious Friends; and not unfrequently the judgment of able counsel was necessary to guard them from injury." The more effectually to attain this end, certain Friends in the city of London were appointed, who met weekly, "to whom the accounts of sufferings could be forwarded for examination and proper arrangement, and on whom the duty of applications to the different branches of the government might devolve, as well as that of advising country meetings in difficult and important cases."

If we trace the history of the Society, we shall find that whenever a change in the ruling sovereign of England has taken place, Friends have ever been ready to acknowledge the authority of the government, and to declare their fealty to the throne. And in our own country, when a change of government was effected by the war of the revolution, we find Friends, on the restoration of peace, manifesting their allegiance to the government then established. Nor can we omit to refer to the example of William Penn, who, as governor of Pennsylvania, in the administration of his laws, and in his treaties and dealings with the natives, illustrated the truth, which we firmly believe, that civil government may be efficiently administered without the aid of military power —moral influence being, as we apprehend,

* The term sword is used by Friends figuratively, as emblematical of the power vested in the civil magistrate.

that which mainly supports the fabric of civil order; its " great bulwarks resting on a firmer foundation than any outward visible means of defence."

It being then undeniable from what we have cited, and from abundant other testimony that might be given, that our forefathers in religious profession and their successors to the present day, have respected and supported human governments as essential to the peace, the safety and the happiness of communities, we would earnestly exhort every individual bearing our name to be careful that the speculative views advanced by some at the present time, do not lead him off from the substantial and practical ground, which our Society has hitherto maintained in relation thereto.

May it be remembered by us as a warning, that among the first evidences of defection manifested by George Keith, who early departed from the faith of the Society, was the imbibing of " notions subversive of all social order, which led him to conduct himself with great disrespect towards the civil authorities in the state; and rendered him dissatisfied also with those wholesome restraints which the Society in its church discipline enjoins upon its members."—*Diary of Alexander Jaffray, by John Barclay.*

Believing that the minds of our early Friends were divinely illuminated to understand the teachings of Christ and his apostles—that they were led to discover the truth and to walk in it—we cannot safely attempt to find for ourselves any other way. The truth is immutable —it changeth not—it is the same yesterday, to-day, and for ever—and hazardous, we are persuaded, will it be for him, who, confiding in some supposed greater illumination which he has received, ventures to call in question the plain practical doctrines of Holy Scripture, and the practices of those who acted in conformity to them. Rather let us in humility and meekness, and with that help which may be graciously afforded us, seek to imitate the virtues and walk in the footsteps of those who, having fought the good fight and kept the faith, have finished their course, and through adorable mercy, have been permitted to enter into everlasting rest.

Signed on behalf and by direction of a meeting of the Representatives aforesaid, held at Providence, Rhode Island, the 3d of third month, 1840.

THOMAS HOWLAND, *Clerk.*

For "The Friend."

FIRST DAY MEDITATIONS.

Our blessed Redeemer, when he declared that where two or three were gathered together in his name, there He was in the midst of them, abundantly set forth the advantages which result to his disciples and dependent children from meeting together either in public assemblies or in a more private way, which, if rightly considered, is calculated to incite us to a diligent attention to this important duty. In order, however, rightly to profit by this exercise, it is manifest that we must come together *in the name of Jesus.* The promise is not extended to any promiscuous assembly of indifferent and careless persons, who, either through habit, education, or a desire to maintain something of the appearance of religion, meet periodically under the name of worshipping the Creator of heaven and earth. It is to those who meet in his *name,* and the inquiry very naturally arises, in what does this qualification consist? There are, perhaps, few who commonly frequent religious meetings but would say they came to them as Christian people, believing in the name of the Lord Jesus, and with some desire to partake of his blessing. Few, perhaps, there are who would not be grieved, were they told that they had no part or lot in the matter, and hardly any but profess, in some degree, to be followers of the crucified Redeemer. It is well for us, if we have been brought up in this practice, and are diligent in the pursuit of it, to ponder deeply whether we reap the benefit of it, and whether we experience, in our assembling together, the presence of the Head of the Church, strengthening, confirming, and satisfying our souls with living bread from his table, and causing the word which he speaks unto us to be as a well of water springing up into everlasting life. If we are thus participating in the joys of his salvation, then it is well with our souls, and we are of the number who meet in his name; but if we do not reap these fruits, if we find in our going to meeting that our minds are occupied pretty much as they are out of meeting, and the world and worldly thoughts have the preponderance, that we do not experience refreshment, and strength to pursue the path of rectitude, or if we have swerved from it, resolved not to do better, then we have need to see to our standing, for all our profession of religion or of worshipping our Creator in spirit and in truth will avail us nothing, and we shall find in the day of reckoning that we have " sown the wind and shall reap the whirlwind."

There were some of old who swore " The Lord liveth," and they swore falsely:—Are there not some of us in the present day who are declaring that the Lord liveth, and yet say it falsely? We make an outside profession of acknowledging his existence, and that he is worthy of worship and praise, and yet in our hearts the living spring has not arisen; we attend religious meetings because we have been accustomed to do it, perhaps, from our childhood, or we are unwilling to have the name of being altogether regardless of what is good, and may esteem it a respectable thing to be in such a practice; but how can we expect, if these be our motives, to find in those meetings the promise realised to those who meet in the name of the Lord? We know that with respect to outward food, the real enjoyment of it must be in an appetite for it, and that when the stomach is diseased, there is no satisfaction in it. So it is in the inward. Our Saviour declared that he was the living bread which came down from heaven, and of which, if a man eat, he should live forever; if, then, we have no appetite for this kind of food, we can have no true satisfaction in seeking it; even when it is communicated either instrumentally or immediately in our meetings, unless this earnest desire has been raised we may miss the benefit intended by it. The end, therefore, and design of our religious assemblies is not likely to be answered where those met are deficient in an inward engagement to be found watching and waiting, where they are not *earnest* in seeking that in every meeting the Lord's presence may be known among them for their help and refreshment. This frame of mind cannot, however, be put on for the occasion; we cannot pursue our worldly and sensual desires in our every-day life, and put on this seeking fervency of spirit as we clothe ourselves with our outward garments: it must be a daily hunger and a daily thirst; it must be an increasing appetite; one that grows with our growth, and strengthens with our strength; we must have a *life* to be nourished by it, just as the outward body is sustained by the satisfied desire for outward Jacob.

If all those who make a profession of diligently assembling for divine worship were thus engaged to struggle and beg for the opening of the living spring, how would the Master of Assemblies bless us at times in our gatherings, even in remote and lonely situations; how should we be encouraged, though in very small companies, to meet together for this solemn engagement. Whatever difficulties we might have to encounter, the language of our hearts would be, " I was *glad* when they said unto me, let us go up to the mountain of the Lord, to the house of the God of Jacob." The fervent breathing of our spirits would be towards the Lord and the remembrance of his name, and we should esteem his favour and the sense of his consoling presence as better than many earthly riches.

May this fervent concern increase and abound amongst us as a religious society, and may we learn to enjoy *silent* meetings and benefit by them. As we experience this to be our condition, there will be raised in our hearts living praises, and with the voice of thanksgiving shall we be at times enabled, through qualified instruments, vocally to acknowledge, that " the Lord is good to Israel, even to all such as be upright in heart."

From the Episcopal Recorder.

I AM WEARY.

I am weary of straying—oh fain would I rest
In that far distant land of the pure and the blest,
Where sin can no longer her blandishments spread,
And tears and temptations for ever are fled.

I am weary of hoping—where hope is untrue,
As fair, but as fleeting, as morning's bright dew;
I long for that land whose blest promise alone,
Is changeless and sure as eternity's throne.

I am weary of sighing, o'er sorrows of earth,
O'er joy's glowing visions, that fade at their birth;
O'er the pangs of the loved, which we cannot assuage,
O'er the blightings of youth, and the weakness of age.

I am weary of loving what passes away—
The sweetest, the dearest, alas, may not stay!
I long for that land where those partings are o'er,
And death and the tomb can divide hearts no more.

I am weary of sighing, o'er sorrows of earth,
Oh! joy's glowing visions, that fade at their birth;
I am weary—but oh, let me never repine,
While thy word, and thy love, and thy promise are mine.

PRINTED BY ADAM WALDIE,

Carpenter Street, below Seventh, Philadelphia.

THE FRIEND.

A RELIGIOUS AND LITERARY JOURNAL.

VOL. XIII.　　　　　SEVENTH DAY, FOURTH MONTH, 25, 1840.　　　　　NO. 30.

EDITED BY ROBERT SMITH.

PUBLISHED WEEKLY.

Price two dollars per annum, payable in advance.

Subscriptions and Payments received by

GEORGE W. TAYLOR,

NO. 50, NORTH FOURTH STREET, UP STAIRS,

PHILADELPHIA.

For "The Friend."

THOUGHTS ON THE TIMES.

NO. V.

The due care of the body implies the providing of wholesome articles of food and of clothing, and this, not merely from day to day and for the individual who labours, but such an excess over the daily consumption as shall meet the ordinary casualties of life, such as sickness, infirmity and old age; and be sufficient not only for ourselves, but for those who are dependent upon us for support.

Of the measure of quantity and quality in these particulars there is, as I have said, no invariable standard. In the ordering of an all-wise Providence, we are each born to a certain inheritance and condition in society; and the habits, the tastes, and the wants of the man are formed for him almost without any agency of his own, by the circumstances with which he is surrounded from his birth. The individual is thus a being of a *double nature,* not merely with the capacities and propensities common to the species, but superadded to these a *second nature,* as habit is aptly termed, the creature of artificial circumstances.

The child of the humblest day-labourer, for example, is educated to feel certain wants and require certain conveniences and gratifications. These are necessarily few and simple, and accurately graduated to the amount of luxuries which the ordinary rate of wages will purchase. The necessity which limits the indulgences of the day labourer, narrows also the means of educating his offspring, so that in many countries the race is doomed from generation to generation to the same condition of servile labour. Notwithstanding their limited means, it is the duty of all who are thus situated to support their families, to provide against the casualties and infirmities of life, to train up their children in the maxims of virtue, and, to the duties of religion, and to give them all the useful knowledge in their power. All this can be done only by the exercise of the strictest frugality, which becomes therefore the cardinal virtue of him who is placed by the allotment of Providence in this humblest station of society. If he "walk his narrow

round," and fulfil his simple duties, in the fear of his Maker, he will receive the same reward in the moral elevation of his character as if he filled a larger space in the public eye. Hard as his lot may seem, it has many compensations for its hardships. The stern necessity which binds him to severe and almost incessant labour removes him from all the enervating indulgences. The toil which bends the body leaves the spirit free. The all-beautiful creation is around him, the holy ties of kindred, the consolations and hopes of the gospel may be his; and he can feel that no outward circumstances are able to impair this true equality of man.

It is the same with every condition in life. The education which a child receives is generally such as to fit him for entering upon the race of competition with those with whom he is most nearly connected, and the particulars which make up the sum of his enjoyments become, by the desire of possessing and enjoying them which they inspire, a spur to the industry of every class in life. That this industry, however liable to excess, is in itself allowable and proper, we cannot doubt, and the safest rule by which to estimate its lawfulness where the things pursued are honest in themselves, is its effect upon the mind. Whoever finds it to absorb his attention with the things of sense, to indispose him for self-examination and watching unto prayer, to render him selfish, indifferent to the rights, or the distresses of others, luxurious and self-indulgent, or slavishly sordid, may be certain that it occupies too great a share of his attention, and exerts an evil influence on his character.

Yet all the rules of conduct which can be framed respecting indulgences and pursuits in themselves allowable, are of a general nature, or they are conditional applications of general maxims; and after we have laid them down with the utmost care, the great and all important question of how do they apply to the present case, to thee and to me? still remains. It is a question which can only be answered by the inspeaking voice of the Holy Spirit in each one of us: and the immeasurable superiority of Christianity over all systems of morality, is in nothing more evident than in the manner in which it guides the conduct of believers in this respect. That no set of abstract general principles of morality can enable us to determine this point with any degree of certainty, is evident; because the facts respecting which we are to form our judgment, are beheld through the medium of the feelings and inclinations and opinions of the individual himself. According to the temptations, to the habits, to the prejudices, and temperament of the person, therefore, will the decision vary, and the uncertainty of our fallible and changing nature will therefore perplex the con-

clusions which we draw from abstract immutable principles.

It is not so with the spiritual believer and follower of Christ. Accustomed to the severe discipline of the cross, to watch over the avenues of temptation, to listen in humility, and in the silence of all flesh to the intimations of the divine monitor within; his primary law of conduct is obedience to those intimations. He knows that they will conduce to his temporal and eternal happiness, and that they are most useful to mankind at large. But these considerations, however they may settle and confirm his confidence in the wisdom and beneficence of the Almighty, are not his motives to obedience. He obeys because it is fit and proper that a humble finite creature should submit to the will of his Almighty Creator, because it is his first and paramount duty to love and to serve the Lord his God, with all his heart. He knows that all the requisitions of that Infinite Being are dictated by infinite goodness, and he follows them with unquestioning alacrity. He who thus hears behind him the word saying, this is the way walk thou in it, will at times be led by his divine Master, in a way that seems inexplicable to the natural powers of the understanding. He does not wait to calculate the consequences of particular actions, of the remote and general expediency of the course he pursues; but, confident that the guide of life is unerring, he implicitly obeys its leadings.

There are few cases in which the value of these truths is more strikingly shown than in the restraints which they place on our worldly pursuits. Wealth seems so necessary as a security against the unforeseen misfortunes of life; so useful in securing an advantageous position in the social relations for one's descendants; so invaluable as a means of Christian benevolence; that he who is disposed to pursue it, can be at no loss for reasons to vindicate his conduct. It is moreover true that there is no inventory of particulars by which we can determine what is and what is not allowable wealth in a Christian, and therefore the question must ever be indeterminable on general and abstract grounds. So that when, instead of referring the decision to the unerring guide of life, we make the reasoning powers the umpire in the case, they are almost certain to be biassed by the temptations of wealth. There are so many innocent indulgences, so many luxuries that have become conveniences, and, in popular estimation, even necessaries of life; so many splendid schemes of beneficence are afloat; so much power and influence seem added by wealth to virtue, that the human mind is absolutely unable to determine with accuracy the proper point of self-restraint, but will of necessity be governed, in the absence of a higher rule of conduct, by its love of pleasure or of activity, by ambition or by indolence. The tendency of the pursuit of wealth to engross the affections; the influence of the luxuries attendant upon wealth in robbing the spirit of its watchfulness and in relaxing its self-denial; its gradual overcasting with the clouds of sense and sensuality, the mental horizon; all these sufficiently prove that there is a point at which it becomes an evil; while the peculiar nature of its temptations renders it a thing impossible for any but the divine monitor to protect us from their snares. The gentle yet clear intimations of duty are therefore the only guides which we can safely follow.

For " The Friend."

BOODHISM AND BRAHMINISM.

Budhism, or, as it is pronounced, Boodhism, is a system of religion which far outnumbers Christianity in the multitude of its prosylites, and extends over a larger portion of the surface of the globe. Hindustan is pervaded by it, and there it stands by the side of, but not in union with, another system equally dark, with which it has been in some degree confounded; —the religion of Brahma. Both these systems, though irreconcilable in many particulars, embrace notions which, in various forms, have, at different periods, been entertained by mankind. They seem to be the common result of that natural religion which springs up in the dark and unregenerate mind of the observant, but ignorant, and superstitious man.

The phenomena of the creation by which he is surrounded, teach him that there is a powerful invisible intelligence constantly at work about him; the changes which take place in his own body, and the very emotions of his mind bespeak a superior agency, whose influence is universal, and can by no means be evaded. He seeks then, to conciliate this mighty power;—he strives to do so by sacrifices, by inflictions on his body, by the mortification of his senses, and by acts which he fancies will render him meritorious in the sight of that being or beings, and an object worthy of favour.

One method of effecting this, is by endeavouring to separate existence here, from the ordinary conditions of humanity, under the idea that such an approximation, as he supposes it to be, to the spiritual life, would be agreeable to a spiritual being. Hence the abstinence from flesh, from the pleasant things which the bounty of the Creator has provided for the gratification of man, and even from the enjoyments of society. Such sentiments as these have, according to the state of civilization and religious light, assumed, in different ages, various garbs, and among many others that of Christianity itself. Papacy includes a number of the doctrines and usages of Boodhism and Brahminism.

It is interesting to us, then, to know particularly what these systems are which exert so fascinating and unhappy an influence upon the nations of mankind, from pagan Japan to superstitious Rome, or rather, in a modified form, to every country reached by the papal arm, even including our own.

Howard Malcom has traced in a forcible manner their prominent features, and shown how much they differ, although a origin has been claimed for them.

Boodhism is, probably, at this time been for many centuries, the most form of religion upon earth. Half of lation of China, Lao, Cochin-china, lon; all of Camboja, Siam, Burmah Tartary, Loo-chôo, and a great part and most of the other islands of the seas, are of this faith.

Chinese accounts make its introdu that empire to have occurred about Marshman supposes the Siamese and have received the system about three before Christ. A very great increas Boodhist faith is known to have occ China early in the sixth century, wh have resulted from the flight of pries that time, from the persecution of t minists.

Boodh is a general term for divi not the name of any particular god. have been innumerable Boodhs, in ages, among different worlds, say the ists, but in no world more than five some not any. In this world there h four; the last, named Guadama. O to come.

It has been said, that Guadama wa for one of the incarnations of Brahm Vishnu. This idea has probably o with the Hindus, and is advanced to their assertion, that this religion is a l theirs. But no two systems bear less of one being derived from the other minism has incarnations, but Boodhis of none, for it has no permanent god. Hinduism teaches one eternal deity, B has now no god. That has a host this only one. That enjoins bloody s this forbids all killing. That requires self-tortures; this inculcates fewer a than even popery. That makes lyi cation, and theft, sometimes commend describes the gods as excelling in thes ties; this never confounds right and w never excuses any sin. That makes al into deity the supreme good; this ann None of the Brahminical books are by the Boodhists as authoritative, and tices seem to be derived from them.

There are some reasons for co Boodhism, if not the parent system, ably more ancient than Brahminism. rious parts of Hindustan are found mo indications, of great antiquity, that I was once the prevailing faith. The Budo, or Bud'ho, is in the Javanese synonymous with " ancient" or ' The history of Guadama is this—He son of the king of Ma-ge-deh, (now c har) in Hindustan. He was born al years before Christ.

He had previously lived in four millions of worlds, and passed throu merable conditions in each. In this had been almost every sort of worm, fish or animal, and almost every grad dition of human life. Having in the these transitions attained immense was at length born the son of a kii moment he was born he jumped upon and, spreading out his arms, exclaime

infinite number of systems, called sak-yas. These systems touch each other at the circumference, and the angular spaces between them are filled up with very cold water. Each side of these spaces is three thousand uzenas long.

Of these innumerable systems, some are constantly becoming chaotic, and reproduce themselves in course of time. Of these formations and dissolutions there was never a beginning, and will never be an end.

Each system consists of a great central mountain surrounded by seas, and four great islands, each surrounded by five hundred smaller ones, and with celestial and infernal regions. Of this great mountain, the eastern side is of silver, the western of glass, the northern of gold, and the southern of dark ruby. It is called *myenmo*, and is eighty-four thousand uzenas high. Its base is equally deep.

The four great islands have each a different shape. Ours is oval, another is semi-lunar. The inhabitants have the shape of their faces conformed to that of their island. Those of the eastern and western islands practise agriculture and the arts, much as we of the southern do; but those of the northern have no such employments. A tree is there which yields all manner of garments, meats, fish, &c. They have no sorrows or pains, and every individual lives just a thousand years.

The earth is a convex plane, supported on water, which, again, is supported on a stratum of air, which is supported by internal explosions: beneath is vacuum.

At first, man lived as many years as there would be drops of rain, if it rained three years incessantly. In a Siamese version of the same book, it is given as a period of years, embracing one hundred and sixty-eight ciphers. Falling off in virtue and correct habits, the term gradually contracted, in the course of myriads of ages, to ten years. Then mankind was led to reflect and reform, and the period gradually enlarged, as they became more temperate and correct, till it rose even to the primitive duration. By succeeding degeneracy, it gradually contracted again to ten. Of these increases and diminutions there have been eleven. At this time, the period of life is contracting.

When, by the power of fate, a system is to be destroyed, it occurs either by fire, water, or wind. The process of renovation is exemplified by our own world. After lying in chaos many ages, the crust of the earth recovered firmness, and was covered with a thin crust of sweet butter. The grateful fragrance ascending to the heavens, celestial beings were filled with desire to eat it, and, assuming human shape, came down in large numbers. Their bodies were luminous, and they needed no other light. Becoming quarrelsome and corrupt, the delicious crust disappears, and their bodies become dark. In their distress, the sun appears, and afterward, the moon and stars. The race degenerating still more, chose a king. Quarrels, multiplied, and men were dispersed. Climate, water, and food, then produced the diversities of nations.

There are twenty-six heavens. The aim of mortals is to attain to one of these, whose

king, Thig-ya-men, possesses a huge white elephant, fifty uzenas high, and with seven heads; each head has seven tusks, and each tusk seven tanks. In each of these tanks grow seven lilies; each lily has seven blossoms; each blossom seven petals; each petal bears up seven palaces, and in each palace are seven wives of the king.

The description given of the twenty-four places of punishment are quite as absurd and very horrible. For killing a parent or a priest, a man will suffer in one of these, the whole period of a sak-ya system. To deny or disbelieve the doctrines of Guadama, incurs *eternal* suffering. Killing men or animals, causing criminals to be executed, insulting women, old men, or priests, cheating, receiving bribes, selling any intoxicating liquor, and parricide, are punished in the worst hells. In some books a regular scale is made out for estimating the gradation of guilt in all these crimes.

Merit may be gained by good conduct in any of these hells, so that except the criminality has incurred eternal torment, the sufferers may rise again to become insects, beasts, men, &c.

Many pages might be filled with similar matter; thus much has been quoted, as part of the history of the human mind, and as necessary to a proper estimate of the Boodhist religion.

(To be continued.)

Twenty-third Annual Report of Friends' Asylum for the Insane, near Philadelphia.

In presenting their annual report to the contributors, it is gratifying to the managers to state, that at no former period has the Asylum been in a more prosperous condition, or the proportion of restorations larger than during the past year.

From the detailed and interesting report of the physicians to the institution it will be seen that the whole number of patients that have been under care since last report is one hundred and nineteen—of this number fifty-four have been admitted during the last year, and sixty discharged, four having died; of those discharged twenty-five were restored, five much improved, nine improved, and seventeen without improvement. Of the fifty-nine patients remaining in the house, ten are restored, three convalescent, four improved, and forty-three without any improvement. The average number of patients who have partaken of the benefit of the institution during the year is sixty-two.

From the annual report of the committee on accounts, which is herewith submitted to the contributors, it will appear that the whole balance remaining in the hands of the treasurer on the 1st inst. is $680 28, including the special bequests of the late Anna Guest and Beulah Sansom, deceased, and that the amount which has accrued for board of patients is $18,267 45. Contributions and donations, $5 00. The disbursements for all purposes amount to $16,392 32, including interest on the loan and annuities. A legacy of $2000 00, less the collateral inheritance tax of $50 00, has been received from the executors of Abra-

ham Hillyard, deceased, and $1,531 15, the proceeds of property conveyed on annuity by Victor Ehrman. The funds accruing from these two sources have been in part applied by the managers towards the liquidation of the debt of the institution, of which $2,500 00, has been paid.

The farm has produced 34 wagon loads of hay; 158 bushels of oats; 127 bushels of wheat; 112 bushels of corn; 450 bushels of potatoes; 55 bushels of ruta-baga; 10 cart loads of pumpkins; 10 hogs weighing 2,306 pounds, in addition to an ample supply of garden vegetables during the season. It is believed that some change may be advantageously made in this department the coming season, which will afford greater opportunity for the employment of the patients in out door labour.

Important alterations have been made in the mode of warming the house, in addition to a complete repair of the furnaces in the basement of the wings, and lodges; Olmstead's stoves have been placed in each wing, and also in two of the parlours in the centre building; those in the wings are enclosed by iron railings, to prevent the patients from injuring themselves.

The carpenter's shop having been found too small, has been enlarged and furnished with additional tools and materials, and placed under the care of a competent person, who has the oversight of the patients who are employed there:—the experiment thus far has been safely and successfully pursued; in the room in the lower story a number of patients have been employed in basket making, under the instruction of a person temporarily employed for that purpose: it has been gratifying to the managers to witness the proficiency and skill of some of the patients, in an employment, new to most of them.

Many of the patients of both sexes spend a portion of each day in the library, which is situated some distance from the main building, and furnished with a small selection of books, periodicals and specimens in natural history:—the managers are desirous of increasing the number and variety of books, and the cabinet of natural history, and trust it will be borne in mind by the friends of the institution, believing that it would tend greatly to increase the interest and utility of this department.

The use of the circular railroad is advantageously continued, and carriage riding daily resorted to in pleasant weather, and exertion is made to induce the patients to combine amusement, with healthful exercise in walking and assisting in the business of the farm and garden:—the experience of the past year has confirmed the board in the opinion heretofore expressed, that useful and amusing occupation is a most essential auxiliary in the treatment of the insane, and they have endeavoured to avail themselves of the experience of other institutions, in augmenting as far as practicable the facilities for useful employment.

The managers continue to be impressed with the advantages resulting to the funds of the institution from the admission of patients unconnected with Friends, and recommend the continuance of that privilege for the ensuing year.

Our friends John C. Redmond and wife

sponsible trust reposed in them by the contributors, the managers desire to acknowledge their gratitude to a Beneficent Providence for the success which under his blessing has attended their efforts to restore, and alleviate the sufferings of, an afflicted class of our fellow beings.

Signed on behalf and by direction of the Board of Managers.

EDWARD YARNALL, *Clerk.*

Philada. 3d mo. 9th, 1840.

From Tait's Magazine.

TO A ROBIN.

Thou, sweet one, that so lonely
    Pourest thy simple song,
Thou lingerest, and thou only,
    Of all the vocal throng.
The merle hath hushed her wailing,
    The thrush, his mellow thrill ;
But thou, with love unfailing,
    In music greet'st us still.
Tho' chilling snows surround thee,
    And all looks dread and drear,
Another year has found thee
    Unchanged, still warbling near.

The gay lark carrols lightly ;
    But 'neath a warm spring sky,
When the sun he meets shines brightly,
    And all breathes harmony.
From the general joy he borrows
    The brilliance of his tone :
For each breast leaves its sorrows,
    And is buoyant as his own.
His song is like the gladness
    From the untried heart that springs,
Ere the first cloud of sadness
    Its dark'ning shadow brings.

When a summer moonlight glistens,
    And a south-wind fans his wings,
And when his own rose listens,
    Then the sweet night-bird sings.
But, ah ! when roses wither,
    When south-winds die away,
Depart they not together,
    That heavenly strain and they ?
Like passion's witching, lending
    A charm, to lure us thro'
Youth's gilded hours, but ending
    With life's short summer, too.

But thou !—what different feeling
    Thy liquid notes impart—
In wintry weather stealing
    Thro' cold air to the heart.
They tell—tho' Care has bound us
    In his chain, of trials wrought—
Our friend still hovers round us :
    We bless them for the thought.
They are like the love we cherish
    When youth's vain dreams are o'er,
Which sees all beauty perish,
    Yet clings to us the more !

THEOBOLD MATTHEW.

This extraordinary man ; this Whitefield, or rather Peter the Hermit of Temperance, seems destined under Providence to effect the most extraordinary changes which have been witnessed in modern times. There must be a rare fascination in his eloquence. The crowds of people which press to hear him ; the readiness of the unnumbered multitude to sign the total abstinence pledge offered ; (for 20,000

enthusiasm of the people to spread the almost without a parallel in works of r

Of its value, should it be perman O'Connell says it will be, we, in this (can have faint conceptions. The expe of the Irish for strong drink, and thei quent degradation and suffering, far e those of any other nation. If the c broken, and we see not but it will Emerald Isle may become one of the t spots on our earth. We wish a deep could be awakened for the Irish in th try. They have been and still are exec great sufferers from intemperance. Ir cities, on our canals and railroads, th wasted away before strong drink as th before the warm beams of the vert Our friend Keener of the Maryland rance Gazette, well asks, Is there no Matthew to be found among the pri in this country, whose heart, glowing v pure benevolence of the gospel of Christ, is willing to exert that in which his clerical authority will exer rightly attempted—who will visit o roads and canals, our streets, and lar alleys, where large masses of our fell congregate, and where this influence felt and owned to an extent hardly to gined, and seek to reclaim them to the lies and to society ?

At a meeting of our City Tempera ciety, at which the interesting intelliger first communicated, it was inquired v Father Matthew might not be induced v himself to this country, and perform i mage among his suffering brethren great cities. The suggestion has alreac communicated in a letter we have forv In the mean time let no pains be spare terest the Irish in all our great cities subject. Let them be approached kin made to understand the great work of at home, and we have no doubt that, v blessing of God, we may see great resu

The pledge, and the only pledge Father Matthew offers is,

"I solemnly promise to abstain from toxicating liquors, and by my advice a ample, to persuade others to abstain al *Temperance Jour.*

A Bottomless Lake in Sussex Cou

A writer in the Troy Morning Mai the following notice of a remarkable p Sussex county in New Jersey :

White Lake is situated about one mi of the Paulis Kill, in the town of Stil It is nearly circular, and about one thir mile in diameter. It has no visible in its outlet is a never-failing stream of co able magnitude. The name is derive its appearance. Viewed from a little di it seems of a milky whiteness, excep rods in the centre, which, by the c appears perfectly black. The appear self is singular enough, but the cause more remarkable.

An Address to the Society of Friends on Complimentary Titles.

BY GEORGE RICHARDSON.

"Let me not, I pray you, accept any man's person, neither let me give flattering titles unto man."

"For I know not to give flattering titles, in so doing my Maker would soon take me away."—ELIHU.

ADVERTISEMENT TO THE READER.

In submitting the following pages to the serious attention of my fellow professors, it is not my desire to place any one point, either of faith or practice, in a more prominent position than it is fairly entitled to, on Scriptural grounds. But we may remember our blessed Lord declared, " Whosoever therefore shall break one of these least commandments, and shall teach men so, he shall be called the least in the kingdom of heaven." Matt. v. 19. The following *Inquiry into the Reasons which induced the early Members of the Society of Friends to decline the use of the customary modes of Salutation and Address, and how far the practice continues to be obligatory on their descendants in Religious Profession,* is hoped may operate in confirming the minds of some of the wavering, and induce them to hesitate before they forsake the good old paths.

Newcastle upon Tyne, 3d month 28th, 1833.

AN INQUIRY, &c.

The fear of the Lord is the beginning of wisdom. Psalm iii. v. 10. The degree in which this holy filial fear presided in the minds of many of our worthy predecessors, is a remarkable trait in the history of their lives. So afraid were they, after they were brought to the knowledge of the truth as it is in Jesus, of grieving or offending Almighty God, that when they were once favoured with a clear and satisfactory discovery of his will, in what way soever it was made manifest unto them, they appear to have endeavoured to yield faithful and unreserved obedience to it; and thus it was that their minds became further enlightened, agreeably to our blessed Lord's declaration, " If any man will do his (the Father's) will, he shall know of the doctrine whether it be of God." John vii. 13.

As disobedience and rebellion against the known will of God, tend to harden the heart and to darken the understanding, so the obedience of faith brings into closer fellowship and communion with the Father, and with the Son, and to the blessed experience of that more constant indwelling of the Holy Spirit, which our Lord promised to his followers, whereby the true disciple may come to be immediately taught and led into all truth. John xvi. 13. Thus the eyes of the understanding become gradually more and more illuminated to discover the difference between good and evil, and even to see their more remote ramifications and tendencies.

In the manner of the dealings of a gracious God with his creature man, in order to rescue him from under the power and dominion of sin and Satan, we find great diversity. Various are the means and ways by which the important and essential work of regeneration is effected. But according to the experience of many, it is the grosser sins of which he is first and most powerfully convicted, by the inshining of the light of the Holy Spirit in the conscience; but most especially does he stand convicted of enmity against God, alienation from him, and rebellion against his holy law. This state of mind is the source from which evil thoughts and evil actions have their spring and growth. Therefore in the awakened soul, the wrath of God is felt to burn as an oven, at times, against this state. Thus he is led to mourn over his fallen lost condition, and is drawn to look up to him for deliverance. His affliction is seen, and in the exercise of the small grain of living faith, with which he is favoured, he cries unto God for help, and his cry is heard. " Without faith it is impossible to please God, for he that cometh to God must believe that he is, and that he is a rewarder of them that diligently seek him."

In this the time of the visitation of the Day Spring from on high, the tribulated soul may have a season, and in some cases a long and dreary season of deep mourning. But when the blood of sprinkling is revealed, " which speaketh better things than that of Abel;" when the mind is turned in living faith to him who is the appointed Mediator between God and man; and who has, by his Spirit, been graciously striving with him, even when he knew him not; then is the living fountain opened, for cleansing and for refreshment. Thus the enmity is subdued, the heart is humbled and contrited; reconciliation with God is experienced through our Lord Jesus Christ.

The Messenger of the new covenant being received into the temple of the heart, there to sit as a refiner with fire, not only is sin seen and felt to be exceeding sinful, not only is the dross and the tin to be removed, but even that which is comparable to the reprobate silver. The transgressing nature is consumed, and the heart purified by this true and saving baptism. New affections and new desires spring up; the sincere milk of the living word is earnestly desired and fed upon; yea the sense of the manifold mercies of God, so predominates, that the body, or whole man, is ready to be presented as a living sacrifice. There is no longer a liberty to conform to this world, in what is seen to be contrary to the Divine will. The Holy Scriptures are read with diligence, and meditated upon with comfort and instruction; with desires that the Divine will may be more clearly discovered. The conscience thus further enlightened, becomes very tender, and the Divine law more legibly written upon the softened heart.

We find by the records of the lives of several of the early Friends, that it was after having passed through dispensations of the character attempted to be delineated above, that their minds were opened to see how inconsistent many of the customs which prevail in the world are with the pure precepts of Christ and his apostles. They felt a necessity laid upon them to devote themselves freely to the Lord's service, and were made willing to endure hardness, as good soldiers of Jesus Christ. They patiently submitted to be led in the narrow path of self-denial, by what they believed to be the secret influences of the Holy Spirit, out of various practices which, by many around them, were accounted harmless. They found that they must really renounce the pomps and vanities of this sinful world if they would enjoy true peace of mind. They could no longer conform themselves to the foolish and changeable fashions in their apparel, in which so many are entangled; but must rather seek that adorning, which in the sight of God, is of great price; nor were they at liberty to use language which had its origin in idolatry, or in a desire to foster the pride of the human heart, and which they now saw to be inconsistent with the simplicity which is in Christ. Thus they became singular in their garb and manners; but it was the love of purity, and of gospel simplicity, which made them so. It was after they had become experimentally acquainted with the substance of true religion, by repentance towards God, and faith in our Lord Jesus Christ, that it became the earnest desire of many of them to be cleansed " from all filthiness of flesh and spirit, perfecting holiness in the fear of God," speaking the truth in love without respect of persons.

Hence it appears to me that the candid reader, in perusing the history of the lives of many of our worthy predecessors, will see that in the course of their Christian progress, they became very devoted followers of the Lord Jesus Christ, and that they accepted his precepts and instructions, and those of his apostles, as recorded in the New Testament, more simply and with less endeavour to reason away their plain obvious import than was common with other religious professors; and that following the guidance of the Spirit of Truth in singleness of heart, they were favoured with more clear views of the purity and spirituality of the gospel dispensation, than was the case with many of those good and eminently useful men, who had been their precursors in the work of reformation; although it appears from the history of those times, that some of these excellent men saw the need of a reformation in various respects, which, possibly from their peculiar circumstances, they were not able fully to effect, and which it was afterwards laid upon Friends, as they apprehended, to carry out in practice.

The great distinction appears to have been, that they were *more resigned to suffer* in support of their testimony than was the case with most others. They observed that much had crept into use amongst those called Christians, during the long dark night of ignorance, superstition, and apostacy, which was of corrupt or heathen origin, and which yet had been permitted to remain. They believed themselves called to come out of such corruptions, and to bear a faithful testimony against them.

Thus it was that they were brought to believe that He, who commanded his disciples to love their enemies, did thereby virtually forbid them to avenge themselves, or be engaged in wars and fightings. That when he said, " Swear not at all," he forbade all oaths; that, in commanding them to give the gospel message freely, seeing they had received it freely, he prohibited them from preaching for money, or using their ministry as a trade. In like manner they believed, that when our blessed Lord rebuked the Scribes and Pharisees for seeking and receiving honour one of another, instead of desiring that honour which cometh from God only, and points out that thereby

ages. They saw that the spirit of world exhibited itself amongst many professing Christians, in a variety of and usages, which were completely ace with the tenor of our Lord's pre- and with the pure spirit of genuine unity. Hence they could no longer attering titles unto men, merely because ccupied certain stations or offices in civil ious society, such as reverend, right d, father in God, &c., to such as were ed bishops or ministers of religion; or f gracious, or noble, or excellent, to were in exalted civil stations; unless lieved that such appellations were in ace with truth, and strictly applicable ersons in question; nor even then, if w it would partake of the character of n or flattery. In reference to the terms or mistress, with the customary abbre- of these terms, when used to persons not actually stand in those relations to conceived that their use is prohibited Lord Jesus Christ in the passage in v xxiii. 5—12, when, speaking of the and Pharisees, he says, "All their hey do to be seen of men; they make eir phylacteries, and enlarge the bor- their garments; they love the upper- oms at feasts, and the chief seats in the rues, and greetings in the markets; and lled of men rabbi, rabbi; but be not ye rabbi; for one is your Master, even and all ye are brethren. And call no ur father upon the earth, for one is ather which is in heaven: neither be ed masters, for one is your Master, arist. But he that is greatest among all be your servant. And whosoever alt himself shall be abased, and he that mble himself shall be exalted." ne injunction in the ninth verse, our aim appears to have been, to turn the f his disciples to a reliance on the Su- Source of all our blessings, whether d or spiritual, even of life itself: "One Father, which is in heaven." ke manner must the other portion of be understood. We cannot conceive blessed Lord meant to forbid the use f the term father, or master, to those ictly stand in those relative stations; he meant to prohibit the compliment- false use of them is manifest, from eral tenor of the passage before us. our Lord meant also to reprove that use of mind which led the Pharisees to in being thus addressed, and to warn his rs against it. "He that is greatest you shall be your servant: and whoso- all exalt himself shall be abased." And y remember, that on another occasion to his disciples, "Ye know that the of the Gentiles exercise dominion over und they that are great exercise authority em. But it shall not be so among you; osoever will be great among you let him minister; and whosoever will be chief you, let him be your servant." Matt. —27.

count of their violation of truth, when thus used, and also of the practice originating in an unprofitable love of distinction on the one hand, and of their character of flattery on the other. Therefore, in a tender conscientious desire to obey our Lord's precepts, according to their real meaning and import; and in accordance with that lowliness, meekness, and humility, which his spirit, precepts, and example, lead into, they felt that they could not gratify the disposition of such as seek to receive honour one of another, and seek not the honour which cometh from God only, without endangering their own peace of mind. They therefore re- frained from the practice in question, though thereby they subjected themselves to much scorn and reproach.

The apostle Paul, addressing the early be- lievers, says "Let no corrupt communication proceed out of your mouth, but that which is good, to the use of edifying. Wherefore, put- ting away lying, speak every man truth with his neighbour." Again, "I beseech you that ye walk worthy of the vocation wherewith ye are called." He desires for them, "That speaking the truth in love, they may grow up into him in all things, which is the head, even Christ." Eph. iv. 1—25. And to the Colos- sians he says, "Lie not one to another, seeing ye have put off the old man with his deeds, and have put on the new man, which is re- newed in knowledge, after the image of him that created him." iii. 9, 10.

Is it not evident that the usages in question are *a corruption of language;* that they do not edify, do not build up in newness of life; that they are inconsistent with our high and holy vocation, with Christian integrity and uprightness, with the purity and simplicity of the gospel, for this plain and obvious reason, amongst others, that they flatter the vain mind, and are inconsistent with truth.

Let me entreat my dear friends and fellow members to consider, that whilst letting fall and trampling upon, as many do, those precious testimonies to gospel purity, which, as a reli- gious society, we are called to bear, against many of the corruptions which have so lament- ably spread amongst the professors of the Christian name, whether it does not increase the danger of descending further in this down- ward course than many of them have hitherto done. For after having adopted the customary forms of address, Mr., Mrs., &c., will they not be expected to go a step farther, and conclude with the usual subscription of, "Your most obedient, humble servant," &c.? Are they pre- pared to go on in such a course of falsehood and dissimulation, "after the traditions of men, after the rudiments of the world, and not after Christ?" Will they pollute their minds with writing so palpable an untruth, as this, in many cases, would most undoubtedly be felt to be?

Perhaps some would be ready to query what they are to do when they are not ac- quainted with the names of the persons whom they have to address. We would answer, be willing to appear among your fellow-mortals as fools for Christ's sake—confess plainly that

matter diency plicity what who, f thus c their a culty, brance deemed me bef my Fa The latter c a pure name c sent. T conven for this hoods, purity spirit c It is inconsi address the cus bly th claimed the gen impose upon t course, quite o duct of what v adhere

The amiss i these i pray t earth a our du withou on pur that "
they m ment."
worse.
tion, "
and by Matt. our me tongue of iniq the hec and bre and be glory c is holy versati

My ters in that th going t this va measur coming bondag which, many

tinues to lead the faithful amongst us down to the present day. My own mind was, in early life, deeply penetrated with the truths set forth in this paper; being brought under strong conviction, until I was made willing to take up the cross in these respects, and to yield implicit obedience to the manifestations of the divine will. Therefore, whereunto any of us may have attained in the narrow path which leads to eternal life, let us, in true humility and abasedness of self, endeavour to walk by the same rule; let us all mind the same thing—pressing onward toward the mark for the prize of our high calling of God in Christ Jesus, and let us not rest satisfied with *any other* rule, but *the will of God*, in what way soever he may be pleased to manifest it unto us.

Persuaded I am, notwithstanding the terrible shaking which, as a Society, we have had to endure, when, at times, it may have appeared to some as though the very foundations were about to be removed, that, even now, we may be comforted in remembering the promise, which was spoken by the Lord's prophet to his people formerly, "I will leave in the midst of thee an afflicted and poor people, and they shall trust in the name of the Lord. The remnant of Israel shall not do iniquity, nor speak lies; neither shall a deceitful tongue be found in their mouth; for they shall feed, and lie down, and none shall make them afraid." Zeph. iii. 12, 13.

A Declaration of the Views of the Society of Friends in relation to Church Government: By the Meeting for Sufferings of New England Yearly Meeting. Compiled principally from the writings of George Fox, Stephen Crisp, Robert Barclay and William Penn.

To the Quarterly, Monthly, and Preparative Meetings and individual members of New England Yearly Meeting of Friends.

It is, we trust, under a feeling of religious concern and in gospel love that we are engaged to address you, and to express our earnest desire for your preservation and growth in the unchangeable truth.—We would thankfully commemorate the name of Him who, for purposes of His wisdom, and by the fresh outpourings of His own Holy Spirit, first called and gathered us as a people, and who hath hitherto been pleased to preserve us—to Him be the praise.

But, dear friends, it is not for us to expect the continuance of this preservation and gracious help unless we abide faithful unto Him —looking unto him as our leader, our bishop, and adorable high priest, who is head over all things unto his church.

It was, we believe, by the direct, immediate visitations of his spirit, and by a remarkable manifestation of his power, that our forefathers were led to take that spiritual view of the gospel dispensation, and to sustain it under much persecution, which we doubt not was designed by its author, and embraced by his immediate followers, and the primitive believers; and it is only as we are made partakers of the same divine influence and abide under it, as we acknowledge it as they acknowledged it—as we yield unto it even as

they did, that we shall be walking faithfully in the footsteps of those who were our predecessors and fathers in the truth. And it is with a view to encourage in faithful dedication and consistent walking as members of our religious society, that we are now concerned briefly to revive some of the measures that were taken by our early Friends, under the guidance, as we fully believe, of best wisdom, for the maintenance of right order in the church, in the establishment of our Christian discipline, and in the inculcation of that subordination which is due from inferior to superior meetings, and from individual members to the body.

From the history of our society, it appears that at a very early period, George Fox was actively engaged to promote the establishment of men's and women's meetings for discipline, and the power and authority in which he was concerned that they should be maintained, may be gathered from the emphatic words often repeated in his epistles :—" Let all your men's and women's meetings be held in the power of the Lord." And it should be instructively remembered that this concern of George Fox and other Friends for the introduction of a system of church discipline, was the cause of much disturbance to some, who claimed for themselves an extent of individual liberty inconsistent with that subordination which is essential to the prosperity of the body. It is thus noticed in the Book of Discipline and Advices of London Yearly Meeting :—" The persevering efforts of George Fox to establish a regular discipline, a work in which he was assisted by nearly all those who had been instrumental in gathering the society, proved a great trial of spirits : to a large proportion of the members the arrangements appear to have been quite satisfactory; there was, however, a considerable number of objectors—the self-willed and lawless opposed it with vehemence; and it must be admitted that not a few of a very different class were drawn aside by specious arguments, to oppose what was represented as an encroachment upon individual spiritual liberty. Certain it is that a schism to some extent took place on this occasion; which, however, there is reason to believe, left the society in a more healthy state than it found it. The general meeting of 1677 issued a strong declaration on the subject. Robert Barclay wrote upon this occasion his "Anarchy of the Ranters;" William Penn his "Liberty Spiritual," and Stephen Crisp an excellent tract; all of them endeavouring to prove the necessity of established order and discipline in the church of Christ. This very conflict, and the close examination to which it led of the true limits of church authority, tended, there is reason to believe, under divine direction, to establish the discipline at once more firmly and safely throughout the society than might otherwise have been the case.

Thus was a system of order and government, in conformity with the spirit of Christianity and the practice of the primitive churches, established amongst us in early times; and thus a field was opened for the exercise of the various gifts by which the church, the body of Christ, is edified. It is very observable in

the history of our society, that the declension or revival of religious zeal has ever been accompanied by a corresponding relaxation or increase of care in the exercise of the discipline."

Stephen Crisp thus describes the concern he early felt after his convincement and the state of mind he believed necessary in order to the right discharge of his duty to others :—" The more," says he, " I came to feel and perceive the love of God and his goodness to me, the more was I humbled and bowed in my mind to serve him, and to serve the least of his people among whom I walked; and as the word of wisdom begun to spring in me, and the knowledge of God grew, so I became a counsellor of those that were tempted in like manner as I had been ; yet was kept so low that I waited to receive counsel daily from God, and from those that were over me in the Lord, and were in Christ before me, against whom I never rebelled, nor was stubborn; but the more I was kept in subjection myself, the more I was enabled to help the weak and feeble ones."

In our weak and erring condition as men and creatures, " it must needs be that offence will come," and among the ends aimed at in the institution of disciplinary regulations, are the preservation of the individual members of the society, and the reformation and restoration of offenders, or where this is impracticable, a separation of them from the body; that thus the blessed truth may be preserved from reproach. Our Lord has not left us without directions as to the course to be pursued with such as depart from the right way, and the discipline of our society is designed to be, and we believe is, in conformity to these divine instructions. "If," says he, " thy brother shall trespass against thee, go and tell him his fault between thee and him alone. If he shall hear thee, thou hast gained thy brother. But if he will not hear thee, then take with thee one or two more, that in the mouth of two or three witnesses every word may be established. And if he shall neglect to hear them, tell it unto the church ; but if he neglect to hear the church, let him be unto thee as an heathen man and a publican." And the promise given to the church in the performance of its duties is calculated to sustain every dependent member. " Again I say unto you, that if two of you shall agree on earth as touching any thing that they shall ask, it shall be done for them of my Father who is in Heaven; for where two or three are gathered together in my name, there am I in the midst of them."

In order to experience this divine blessing, it is indispensably necessary that we should be really gathered in the name and power of the Lord Jesus, whether for the purpose of worship, or for the transaction of the affairs of the church, and the necessity of the immediate direction and presence of the one Great Head is essential to the right performance of the latter as well as of the former duty. And this doctrine has always been religiously held by our society. But let us constantly bear in mind, it is not every one who is a member of *the society*, who is really a member of *the true church*. It is those only who have submitted to and abide under his baptizing power, who wait to know his puttings forth, who hear his voice and follow him, who are truly of the fold of Christ, and qualified to sustain the authority and execute the discipline of his church.

Among these there may be different degrees of experience, but each living member has his allotted station, and thus they "grow up into him in all things, which is the head even Christ; from whom the whole body fitly joined together and compacted by that which every joint supplieth, according to the effectual working in the measure of every part, maketh increase of the body unto the edifying of itself in love." And may we remember, the *body* is constituted of those members, whether few or many, who manifest their obedience and conformity to Christ, the one eternal head.

While by the salutary provisions of the discipline, our dear children are members of the society, and as such are desired and expected to attend our meetings for the transaction of the affairs of the church, believing they may prove to them seasons of instruction, yet, may it be borne in mind, it is only as they come to experience that *change of heart* which *every living member must know*, that they can be qualified usefully to act in such meetings. And those, of whatever age, who have witnessed this blessed change, will manifest it by fruits of righteousness; they will not only be consistent in their daily walks before men, and in faithfully maintaining our Christian testimonies, according to our discipline, but they will give evidence of a meek, quiet, and teachable spirit, which will ever listen to the reproofs of instruction and the counsel of Friends. It is these that can hopefully seek to restore a brother, agreeably to the apostolic injunction—"Brethren, if a man be overtaken in a fault, *ye who are spiritual*, restore such an one in the spirit of meekness, considering thyself lest thou also be tempted." This doctrine, that those who walk conformably to the requirings of truth—who may be justly denominated *spiritual*—are to direct in the government of the church, has ever been religiously acknowledged by Friends. It was never the view of the church that all, of whatever religious growth or age, were equally entitled to influence and deference—nothing like the determining of questions by majorities has ever been admitted, or can at all be received, while we stand on the ancient foundation of the society.

There are fathers and elders in the church who "are worthy of double honour." The injunction of the apostle Peter should never be forgotten: "Likewise ye younger submit yourselves unto the elder, yea, all of you be subject one to another, and be clothed with humility." And the elders he exhorts to "feed the flock of God, taking the oversight thereof, not by constraint but willingly, not for filthy lucre but of a ready mind, neither as being lords over God's heritage, but ensamples to the flock"—and adds the consolatory assurance that, "when the chief shepherd shall appear, they shall receive a crown of glory that fadeth not away."

Among the provisions of our discipline which we would now revive, and especially

to the consideration of our younger friends, is that in relation to the care that is to be maintained with respect to the ministry. While the solemn and important service of preaching the gospel is not to be exercised by any, except under the immediate direction and anointing of the Holy Ghost, neither is it to be *judged of*, but by those who have been dipped, in measure, into the same spirit, and have received a qualification therefor from the same source. A disposition to cavil and to criticise, or in any way to speak lightly of the ministry, is dangerous to him who indulges it, as tending to self-exaltation, and to the lessening of his regard for sacred things, as well as the source from whence they spring. And it is to preserve the right order and harmony of the church that elders are appointed, whose delegated duty it is to judge in these matters, and to extend assistance or caution as it is required; and let none, in the forwardness of their spirits, presume to assume to themselves this office, or attempt to exercise its duties.

(To be continued.)

THE FRIEND.

FOURTH MONTH, 25, 1840.

Reserving for another number a more circumstantial notice, we shall at present very briefly refer to the interesting event of our yearly meeting, which commenced its sittings in this city, on second day, the 20th instant,—the meeting of ministers and elders, as usual, convening on the seventh day preceding. In regard to the number in attendance, we consider ourselves safe in stating, that it is greater than on any similar occasion within the last dozen years. The several subjects which have claimed attention, have been discussed and determined, in much brotherly harmony and quietude, and the serious, and orderly deportment of a very large number of young persons present, is not the least among the causes of encouragement and hope. We have had the acceptable company of Thomas and Elizabeth Robson from England, and of Jacob Green from Ireland;—also, of a number of Friends from other yearly meetings on this continent, several of them ministers.

The twenty-third annual report relative to the Asylum near Frankford, placed on another page, is an interesting document. At a meeting of the contributors which took place on the 18th of the past month, the following officers were chosen:

Clerk of the Contributors.—Samuel Mason, Jr., No. 68 North Seventh street.

Treasurer.—Isaiah Hacker, No. 112 South Third street.

Clerk of the Board of Managers.—Edward Yarnall, No. 39 High street.

Attending Physician.—Dr. Charles Evans, No. 201 Arch street.

Resident Physician.—Dr. Pliny Earle.

Superintendents.—John C. and Lætitia Redmond.

Managers.—Charles Allen, Joel Woolman, Joseph R. Jenks, Isaiah Hacker, John G. Hoskins, Lindzey Nicholson, Edward B. Garrigues, William Hillis, Edward Yarnall, Sam. B. Morris, George R. Smith, Isaac Collins,

John Richardson, Mordecai L. Dawson, John Farnum, George G. Williams, Samuel Bettle, Jr., Thomas P. Cope, William Jones, Clayton Newbold.

Edward B. Garrigues, No. 41 High street, is authorised to receive the money for the board of patients, from those persons to whom it is inconvenient to call on the superintendent.

WESTTOWN SCHOOL.

The Summer Term will commence on second day, the 4th of next month: on which day the stage, and other suitable conveyances, will leave the office (at James Douglass' in Sixth below Arch street) at 7 o'clock in the morning.

Those who wish to avail themselves of this opportunity of sending their children out, are requested to have their names entered on or before the 2d of the month, in a book left at the stage office for that purpose.

Phia. 4th mo. 25th, 1840.

The annual meeting of the Ladies' Liberia School Association of this city, will be held in the lecture room of the First Presbyterian Meeting House, (Washington Square,) on third day evening, the 5th of fifth month at 8 o'clock. The annual report will be read. All persons favourable to the promotion of education in Africa are invited to attend.

WANTED, an apprentice to the Wholesale Drug and Paint Business. A Friend, about 16 years of age, would be preferred. Inquire at the office of "The Friend."

DIED, at Dartmouth, Massachusetts, on the 23d ult., SARAH TUCKER, wife of James Tucker, aged 61 years. She had long been suffering under infirm health, when a severe attack of lung fever proved too much for her feeble frame, and in a few days terminated in death. She was a much esteemed minister of the Society of Friends; sound in doctrine, and looking with a single eye to the Divine aid in all her movements, she was enabled rightly to divide the word—whether of reproof, encouragement, consolation, or instruction. Nor was her usefulness confined to the public exercise of her gift in the ministry; with a mind very much redeemed from the world and its spirit, she was peculiarly exemplary in all her deportment; a sympathetic friend; a judicious counsellor; a peace-maker in families and in the church. Her loss is greatly felt, not only by her immediate family and friends, but by Society at large. Yet they do not mourn as those without hope. She has doubtless become united, through infinite mercy, to the innumerable company of those whom the beloved disciple was permitted to behold in the visions of light, who had come out of great tribulation, and had washed their robes, and made them white in the blood of the Lamb.

—— on the 7th of twelfth month, 1839, in the 79th year of his age, ENOCH PEARSON, a minister and member of Millcreek Monthly Meeting of Friends, Miami county, Ohio.

—— on 10th of 7th month, 1839, in the 39th year of her age, REBECCA KESTER, daughter of Samuel and Sarah Kester. Her disorder was pulmonary consumption, which she suffered under for several years, being taken to her bed about two weeks before her final close. She was a believer in the doctrines of the gospel as professed by the Society of Friends, and a frequent attender of our meetings when ability of body permitted; her mind appeared impressed with a feeling sense of that purity that is needful for an admittance within the pearl gates, and she was favoured to be fervent in prayer to the alone Helper of his people, not only for herself, but also for the family. After much suffering of body she quietly, and, we believe, peacefully expired. She was a member of Greenwood Particular Meeting, and Muncy Monthly Meeting.

THE FRIEND.

A RELIGIOUS AND LITERARY JOURNAL.

VOL. XIII.   SEVENTH DAY, FIFTH MONTH, 2, 1840.   **NO. 31.**

EDITED BY ROBERT SMITH.

PUBLISHED WEEKLY.

Price two dollars per annum, payable in advance.

Subscriptions and Payments received by

GEORGE W. TAYLOR,

NO. 50, NORTH FOURTH STREET, UP STAIRS,

PHILADELPHIA.

For "The Friend."

BOODHISM AND BRAHMINISM.

(Continued from page 235.)

Of any supreme God, or any eternal, self-existent being, Boodhism affords no intimation; nor of any creation or providence. From the annihilation of one Boodh till the developement of another, there is literally no God. Intervening generations must worship his image, law, and priests, and for their rules of life keep the sayings of the last Boodh.

Not only has the universe existed from eternity, according to this system, but also the souls of all the inhabitants, whether animals, men, or celestials. These souls have from eternity been transmigrating from one body to another, rising or falling in the scale of existence and enjoyment, according to the degree of merit at each birth. This rise or fall is not ordered by any intelligent judge, but is decided by immutable fate. In passing through these various forms of existence, the amount of sorrow endured by each soul is incalculable. The Bedagat declares that the tears shed by any one soul, in its various changes from eternity, are so numerous, that the ocean is but as a drop in comparison. Existence and sorrow are declared to be necessary concomitants; and therefore " the chief end of man" is to finish this eternal round of changes, and be annihilated.

The great doctrines of this faith are five, viz. 1, The eternity of existence. 2, Transmigration. 3, Annihilation. 4, The appearance, at distant periods, of beings who obtain deification and subsequent annihilation.' 5, The obtaining of merit.

Merit consists in avoiding sins, and performing virtues; and the degree of it is the sole hope of the Boodhist. The forgiveness of sins, and the receipt of favour through the merit of another, are doctrines unknown. That suffering can be in any way regarded as a blessing, is to him absurd. His moral code consists of five principal laws:—I', Thou shalt not kill. 2, Thou shalt not steal. 3, Thou shalt not commit adultery. 4, Thou shalt not lie. 5, Thou shalt not drink any intoxicating liquor. These are made to include all sins. The first is extended to the killing of animals for food. The very religious will

not kill vermin. War and capital punishments are considered forbidden by it.

In the sacred books, men are urged to avoid excessive perfumes, ornaments, laughter, vain joy, strong drink, smoking opium, wandering about the streets in the night, excessive fondness for amusements, frequenting bad company, and idleness. Those who aspire to annihilation are cautioned to abhor sorcery, not to credit dreams, nor to be angry when abused, nor elated when approved, not to flatter benefactors, nor to indulge in scorn or biting jests, and most carefully to avoid enkindling strife. The best state is that in which neither good things gratify us, nor evil things distress; we are then rapidly preparing for annihilation.

Some of their illustrations are good; such as, that he who runs into sinful enjoyments is like a butterfly, who flutters round a candle till it falls in; or one who, by licking honey from a knife, cuts his tongue with the edge.

Merit is of three kinds:—1, The observance of the five laws, and the duties deducible from them; such as beneficence, gentleness, integrity, veneration to parents, &c. 2, Giving alms and offerings. This includes feeding priests, building monasteries, temples, and shelters for pilgrims, placing bells at pagodas, making public roads, tanks, and wells, planting trees for shade or fruit, keeping pots of cool water by the way-side for the use of travellers, feeding criminals, birds, animals, &c. 3, Repeating prayers, and reading religious books. Of this last there are three degrees or sorts; the first consisting in merely reciting prayers, or reading thoughtlessly; the second, and more meritorious, is praying or reading, a mind attentive to the exercise; the third, and most excellent, is the performing these exercises with strong desire and awakened feelings. He who neglects to lay up merit, is compared to a man who sets out on a journey through an uninhabited country, beset with wild beasts, and provides himself neither with food nor weapons.

Alms-deeds are considered meritorious according to the objects on which they are bestowed:—1. Animals. 2. Common labourers, fishermen, &c. 3. Merchants and the upper classes, when in necessity. 4. Priests. For the first, the rewards are long life, beauty, strength, knowledge, and prosperity, during a hundred transmigrations; for the second, the same, during a thousand transmigrations; for the third, the same, during ten thousand; for the fourth, a vastly greater number, but indefinite, being graduated according to the degree of sanctity the particular priests may possess. Alms given by a poor man are declared to be incomparably more meritorious than those given by the rich. The *most* meritorious deed is to make an idol, and this in proportion to its size and value. He who does any deed of alms

or offering receives a title of honour. Such titles are in common use, and are regarded with the same respect as squire, captain, colonel, &c. are with us.

In attaining the third sort of merit, a prominent exercise, is the frequent repetition of three words, the first of which implies our liability to outward injuries and evils; the second, our exposure to mental sufferings; the third, our entire inability to escape these evils. The repetition of this prayer or soliloquy is of far greater merit than even alms-giving. To keep some reckoning in this most important particular, the votary commonly uses a string of beads, and passes one through his fingers at each repetition, according to the practice of the members of the church of Rome.

Many discourses said to have been delivered by Guadama, are given in the Bedagat. In these the duties of parents, children, husbands, wives, teachers, scholars, masters, slaves, &c. are drawn out and urged, in a manner which would do honour to any casuist.

The following precepts were addressed to a distinguished personage:—

" Know thou, that to keep from the company of the ignorant, and choose that of learned men; to give honour to whom it is due; to choose a residence proper to our station, and adapted for procuring the common wants of life; and to maintain a prudent carriage,—are means of preserving a man from evil things.

" Docility in receiving the admonitions of good men; frequent visits to priests; spiritual conferences on the divine laws; patience, frugality, modesty; the literal observance of the law; keeping before our eyes the four states into which living creatures pass after death; and meditation on the happy repose of annihilation;—these are distinguished rules for preserving man from wickedness.

" That intrepidity and serenity which good men preserve amid the eight evils of life, (abundance and want, joy and sorrow, popularity and abandonment, censure and praise;) their freedom from fear and inquietude; and, finally, their insensibility to suffering; these are four rare gifts, that remove men far from evil."

Images and sacred edifices pass through no form of consecration; and an intelligent Burman, when pressed in argument, strenuously denies that he worships these things. He claims to use them as papists do. He places no trust in them, but uses them to remind him of Guadama. Hence he feels no horror at beholding them decayed, and the country is full of such as have gone to ruin. That the common people do really and truly worship the very pagodas and images, is most evident. Indeed, such seldom obey it. Few would dare to strike or deface one.

Worship is not performed collectively, though crowds assemble at the same time on set days. Each one makes his offerings, and recites his prayers alone. No priests officiate; no union of voices is attempted. On arriving at the pagoda or image, the worshipper walks reverently to within a convenient distance, and laying his offering on the ground, sits down behind it, on his knees and heels, and, placing the palms of his hands together, raises them to his forehead, and perhaps leans forward till his head touches the ground. He then utters his prayers in a low tone, occasionally bowing as before, and having finished, rises and carries forward his gift, laying it somewhere near the idol or pagoda.

Old people, who cannot remember the forms, and persons who are diffident of their ability in this exercise, get some priest to write them a few sentences, which they carry before the pagoda or idol, and, fastening it in one end of a stick, stick the other end in the ground, and put themselves for a time into the posture of prayer behind it.

Frequently a worshipper spends an entire day or night at the pagoda, reclining in some of the zayats, or shelters for pilgrims. When the night is chosen, he takes his bed and some refreshments, candles, &c. These are so light that the most aged persons carry them on a pole. They remind one of our Saviour's command, "take up thy bed and walk." The beds consist of a clean mat, which weighs but three or four pounds, and a short, round pillow, with sometimes a cloth or sheet.

None but priests go to the pagoda without some offering, though it be but a flower, or a few sprigs plucked from a bush, in passing. A tasteful nosegay is the common gift, but those who can afford it, carry, once a week, articles of food and raiment. The former is always cooked in the nicest manner, and delicately arranged in saucers made of the fresh plantain leaf. Women carry their gifts in shallow baskets on their heads, and men in their hands, or suspended from the ends of a shoulder-pole. They proceed in groups, gossiping and gay, and display their piety with exuberant self-complacency.

The observance of a sabbath is not required, though held to be meritorious; and the number of worshippers on that day, is always sufficient to produce a large amount of offerings. The slaves of the pagoda divide such as are useful among themselves. On other days, dogs and crows consume the offerings, often attacking a gift the moment the worshipper quits it, and devouring it without the slightest molestation. I used to supply myself sometimes with a handsome bouquet from before the idol, walking unmolested among prostrate worshippers. Whatever remains next morning is swept out like common dirt.

Many of the people worship gnats—beings said to inhabit the six lower heavens, and to be possessed of great power in human affairs. In honour of these, little huts, resembling a common dog-house, are erected on a post, and on another, of the same height, in front, is fastened a flat board, on which the offerings are placed. Feasts are often made to them, to avert calamity, or to be healed from sickness.

But this worship forms no part of Boodhism, and is in fact heterodox.

Priests are not hereditary. Any one may become a priest, and any priest may return to secular life, at pleasure. Thousands do, in fact, thus return every year, without the least reproach. The far greater number enter with the avowed purpose of remaining only a few months, or years, for the acquisition of learning and merit.

(To be continued.)

SPEECH OF AMBROSE H. SEVIER,
OF ARKANSAS.

In U. S. Senate, March 17, 1840.—In Executive session, on the treaty with the New York Indians.

A. H. Sevier addressed the senate as follows:

Mr. President: The treaty now under consideration is a complicated affair, and on that account, as well as on account of its importance to the Seneca Indians, to the state of New York, to the grantees of the state of Massachusetts, and to the United States, I hope, while I endeavour, in discharge of my public duty as chairman of the Committee on Indian Affairs, to explain it, that I shall be indulged with the patient attention of the senate.

This is a treaty of much more importance than is generally supposed. It is one about which the Senecas and their friends feel, as they have felt for upwards of two years, (during all of which time it has been before the country, in one form or another,) a deep, intense, and an all-absorbing interest. The written appeals of a large majority of this tribe to the president, and to the secretary of war; to the senate, and to individual senators, earnestly imploring a rejection of this treaty; the immense mass of testimony with which they have furnished us respecting it; the constant attendance of their delegates here, upon their own expenses, at a great distance from their homes, and at the sacrifice of an utter abandonment of their private pursuits, at all times, when this treaty was before the senate; and their daily attendance in our galleries, to observe and to gather, if possible, something from our proceedings; show most abundantly the light in which this treaty is viewed by them.

On the other hand, the citizens of New York, and especially those residing about Buffalo, have their wishes and hopes and fears respecting its fate with the senate. They have furnished us, also, with testimony and memorials, and sage suggestions, upon the subject of Indian policy and Indian welfare. They, too, have had their lobby members and ambassadors here, consisting of both red and pale faces, for the purpose of urging this treaty through this body. Nor are these the only interested parties. Massachusetts seems to have, in this treaty, something more than a general interest; she seems to have an interest somewhat particular and identical, which I deem important first to consider and explain, that we may fully understand it in all its bearings.

Prior to 1786, Massachusetts claimed, as properly belonging to her, a portion of the state of New York. This claim New York contested; and this somewhat angry controversy was not finally settled, as we learn from the public journals of that day, until 1786. This dispute was then settled, by Massachusetts ceding to New York all her right and title to the *government, sovereignty,* and

jurisdiction ov[...] in consideratio[...] New York ced[...] grantees, and t[...] grantees, *the ri*[...] *of her native I*[...] in this comproi[...] pying the ter[...] thus acquired[...] then, as now, t[...] New York.

It was furthe[...] by New York, [...] any time, by p[...] for that purpos[...] with these Indi[...] *lands.* And fur[...] have the right [...] right to any pe[...] mise was appr[...] gress in 1787.[...] this contract is[...] of Journals of[...] page 788, to [...] honourable sen[...]

The right of [...] to her, as well[...] Massachusetts[...] this right of pr[...] company, and [...] and Ogden to[...] present claima[...] presentatives o[...] putable right tc[...] with the native[...] chasing out th[...] and in exercisi[...] might *seem* to[...] under no obli[...] York or the U.[...] able to lay my[...] tween Massacl[...] therefore ignor[...] But, judging fi[...] chusetts invari[...] of the acquisit[...] seeing her rep[...] tendent, at ev[...] cluded that she[...] contract to eith[...] and probably t[...] superintendenc[...] this matter sta[...] information be[...] I presume the c[...] York and Mas[...]

Mr. Preside[...] interests invol[...] of the Senecas[...] and of the g[...] committee hav[...] der, in connect[...] terest of a four[...] United States.[...] this complicate[...] deavoured to t[...] Nations of Ne[...] ment up to tl[...] Senecas are co[...] covering if the[...] *charged obliga*[...] terested in the[...] The first treaty[...]

with the Six Nations of New York, was concluded in 1784. That was a treaty of peace; a relinquishment of territory on their part, and a definition of their boundary lines on ours. In 1789, five years thereafter, a second treaty was made, which is, so far as I have been able to discover, but little more, if any thing, than a recapitulation of the former one.

The third and last treaty ever made by us with the Six Nations of New York, in their confederated character, (unless the one we are now considering should constitute a single exception,) was made in 1794. This was an important treaty, and has governed us in all our intercourse with them ever since. In that treaty, we acknowledged *separately* to each of the tribes composing the Six Nations, their individual right and title to certain specific reservations of land; and we guarantied to them *separately* the possession and enjoyment of their respective reservations; and conferred upon them the right to dispose of their reservations respectively, in whole or in part, to any citizen or citizens of the United States, whenever and however they might choose; and for these rights, the Indians, on their part, engaged, in the same treaty, never to set up any claim to any other lands in the boundaries of the U. States, than those granted in that treaty.

This was the last treaty ever made by us with those Indians, collectively or separately, from 1794 up to 1838; a period of more than forty years. From that time onward, to 1838, we acted in good faith, and permitted those Indians, according to the terms of the treaty of 1794, so far at least as the Senecas were concerned, to dispose of their New York lands as they chose. Since 1794, the Senecas have disposed of their lands on several occasions. In 1797, they were permitted to sell to Robert Morris of Philadelphia, a portion of their reservations. Afterward, in 1802, the same Senecas were permitted to sell another portion of their lands to Phelps, Bronson, and Jones; and again, in the same year, to Wilhelm Willick and others; and again, in 1823, to Grigg and Gibson. Each and all of those sales were made openly, freely, and voluntarily, and under the guardian care *only* of the United States on the one hand, and of the agent, or superintendent of the state of Massachusetts on the other. These lands were transferred by the Indians to their grantors, *not by treaty*, but by the ordinary deeds of conveyance; nor does the transfer of those lands to Ogden and Fellows, in 1838, vary in any degree, but in the prefixture of a preamble to it, from all the other deeds of conveyance which have been made by them subsequent to 1794.

Having then, as we have seen by the treaty of 1794, such ample power to dispose of these lands—a power so often and so satisfactorily exercised by them; and the United States having no interest whatever in these lands, and being constitutionally incapable of having any, and not being bound by compact, as in the case of Georgia, to extinguish the Indian title to those lands, it may well be asked, why have we interfered in this affair? Why have we attempted, with unabated assiduity, for more than two years, with our influence, with our agents, and means, and money, to barter with those Indians for their New York reservations?

I will endeavour, sir, to unravel this mystery; it is a curious piece of intrigue and history, which should never be forgotten, as it may be of some service to the country hereafter.

As early as 1818, we find the agents of two small bands of New York Indians applying to Mr. Monroe, then president of the United States, for permission to purchase, *with their own means and upon their own account*, of the Menomonees of Green Bay, a portion of their lands. The files of the war department will show that the grantees of Massachusetts were at the bottom of this simple, unpretending, and modest application; and, among other reasons, we find that religion, which is so often prostituted by the designing to cover up intrigue and sinister motives, was the argument used on that occasion to obtain this permission. It will be recollected that the United States will permit no Indian tribe, which they have any thing to do with, to dispose of their lands except to the United States. The authority, therefore, of the United States was indispensable to enable the missionaries, Williams and Hendricks, to make a valid purchase of the Menomonees. Mr. Monroe, not foreseeing the objects in view, and understanding distinctly, as their memorial expressly stated, that these two bands were to pay out of their own means for all the land they purchased of the Menomonees; and further, that they were to acquire, by such purchase, no other or better right than that held by the Menomonees—so understanding it, Mr. Monroe gave his assent to such a purchase. The assent of congress, or of the senate, to such an unusual arrangement, was neither asked nor obtained. It seems to have been looked upon by Mr. Monroe as quite a small affair. Under his authority, thus obtained, the agents of these two small tribes, as *they alleged*, made a purchase, and paid for it, as they informed us, the sum of $12,000. This purchase, however, has ever been strenuously denied by the Menomonees, and the contract made between those Indians, whatever it was —if, indeed, there ever was any—is not now to be found where, surely, if in existence, it ought to be found—in either the Indian bureau or in the war department. As matters now stand, however, it is but of little consequence for us to know, (unless for the purpose of seeing in what manner we have been imposed upon,) whether such a contract ever existed or not. We all know there was a controversy about it between the parties, and that we were drawn into it. This controversy was settled by us in a treaty with the Menomonees in 1832. Thus we see that this small affair, which originally was to be confined to two small tribes, and which, on our part, was to have been nothing more than a mere naked assent, now loses its insignificance, and begins to swell into a matter of considerable importance. Here we find ourselves placed in a dilemma, which was brought about, as they doubtless anticipated, by the early intrigue of this land company. These small bands, under Mr. Monroe's permission, moved to Green Bay, and as the title to the lands they claimed by purchase was controverted, we were called upon to interfere, and, as we supposed, to benefit the Indians, did interfere and bought out the Menomonees for them, and gave them the

lands. And there they are yet. This treaty does not disturb them. This is not all. We have paid back to them, not only the $12,000 they allege to have paid the Menomonees, but we have given them a great deal more. We have given them, besides the lands they claim to have purchased of the Menomonees, for their $12,000, the sum of $40,000; $5,000 to the St. Regis tribe, and $35,000 to the Oneidas, *as a remuneration to them for their purchase of*, and *removal to, the Green Bay lands*, under Mr. Monroe's permission. Now, let me ask, if it be not too late, why have we submitted to such imposition? Why have we bought land for these New York Indians, over whom we had no control or jurisdiction? Why have we made large advances to them, without any consideration? We have done so, for the double purpose of gratifying New York and this overgrown and grasping land company. We have thus seen Mr. Monroe's permission, of which I have spoken, first leading to an Indian controversy, and then ending in a settlement of it, by which we have had to buy land and advance thousands of dollars as a remuneration (as it is falsely called) to these New York Indians, and all without the pretext of an obligation or consideration on our part.

(To be continued.)

For "The Friend."

YEARLY MEETING.

It is one of the wise as well as beautiful features in the admirable organisation of our religious Society, that once in each year the members from all the little meetings are assembled and embodied in the examination of the state of the church, and the transaction of the concerns of the discipline. No one can attend one of these annual assemblies in a proper disposition of mind, without being sensible that, when rightly held, they contribute to the health and preservation of the body, and are the means of a renewal of strength and encouragement to the members to persevere in their several stations and allotments, in the faithful maintenance of our Christian principles and testimonies. Through the condescension of our Holy Head, the yearly meeting which has just passed, was one of these refreshing seasons, being favoured with the overshadowing of his ancient goodness, contriting and comforting the hearts of many, and uniting them more closely in a living engagement for the advancement of the precious cause and kingdom of our dear Redeemer.

The meeting was the largest held since the separation, the number of men being about 1200, and the number of women about 1600.

The epistles received from our brethren of other yearly meetings, were generally lively and instructive, and fresh evidence was afforded that this interchange of exercise and concern for each other, tends to bind together the different portions of the Society as brethren of one family, holding to the same precious faith, and speaking the same language; and desires were felt that the correspondence might be maintained in the fresh feeling of divine love and life.

The minutes of the Meeting for Sufferings were deeply interesting, unfolding among other matters, a condensed view of the evidence they had collected respecting the extent and horrors of the African slave trade, as now carried on, and in which American citizens and capital are deeply involved. It appears that the number of persons annually devoted to the barbarities of this abominable traffic, exceeds all former experience; being computed, from indisputable data, to be considerably more than *one thousand every day*, about two thirds of whom perish by cruel and unnatural deaths before they reach the places where the survivors are destined to linger out a miserable existence in bitter and hopeless bondage. A memorial has been prepared by that meeting to be presented to congress, asking the interference of government to arrest this awfully devastating scourge.

The state of Society was as usual brought up by reading the queries and answers, and elicited much pertinent admonition and counsel. The want of more love and devotedness to our heavenly Father, manifested by the negleet of attending religious meetings, especially on week days, was painfully felt, and tender exhortation and encouragement extended to the delinquent, to labour after more redemption from the spirit and love of the world, and to seek a qualification for the performance of all their religious duties. The excellency and preciousness of that love and unity which are in Christ Jesus, the living Vine, and circulate from him through the different branches, were held up, and all invited to press after an increased experience thereof.

The important duty of endeavouring to bring up children in the nurture and admonition of the Lord, and to labour more for their growth in piety and virtue, than to secure them outward accomplishments or temporal riches, was also recommended to the solid attention of parents and guardians—as was also the necessity of more vigilant care, in this book making age, respecting the character and tendency of the works admitted into the families of Friends—that thus not only the trash, and loose and unprofitable reading, contained in many of the periodicals and other publications of the day, might be carefully excluded, but the susceptible minds of children preserved from the injurious effects of works which, though they contained much that is valuable, advocated sentiments incompatible with our Christian principles and testimonies.

The practice of looking into the grave at funerals, after the remains were deposited there, was cautioned against, as useless, and producing unsettlement and excitement, and disturbing that quietude and solemnity which it has always been the concern of the Society to promote on that serious occasion.

The report of the state of the boarding school at Westtown was very satisfactory, affording the encouraging belief that the religious watchful care exercised over the pupils, is blessed to many, and that under divine favour, it is in good degree answering the design of the yearly meeting in its establishment.

The committee who have charge of the concern for the civilization, &c. of the Indian nations, made a painfully interesting report, from which it appears that a treaty, unfairly obtained, has been ratified by the senate and proclaimed by the president, and that these defenceless people are to be driven from their homes and improvements to seek a precarious subsistence in an uncultivated country west of the Mississippi. A deep feeling of tender sympathy with them pervaded the meeting, and the committee were encouraged to persevere in their efforts to soothe their sorrows and mitigate their sufferings.

The appalling evils of the slave trade and slavery were feelingly spread before Friends, and all were affectionately encouraged to enter into a serious and impartial examination how far their trade, or business, or habits, were affording direct or relative encouragement to these fruitful sources of calamity to the human race; and that where uneasiness with any part of their proceedings in those respects, was awakened, they might carefully attend thereto, and yield obedience to the pointings of duty, so that the members of our Society might thoroughly cleanse themselves of all encouragement to the abominable traffic and system.

On sixth day afternoon, under a covering of precious solemnity, and with feelings of increased love to each other, and gratitude to Him, who had condescended to enable the meeting to transact the business, in his fear, and with an humble regard to his honour, Friends separated from each other; and many we believe could sincerely adopt the language "It is good for us that we have been here."

For "The Friend."

The annual meeting of "The Institute for Coloured Youth," was held on the 22d of 4th month, and attended by a considerable number of Friends from various parts of our Yearly Meeting.

Much interest was manifested in the objects of the institution, and with the view of carrying them into effect at an early period, several Friends were named in each Quarterly Meeting to endeavour to procure the necessary funds.

The following officers were appointed for the ensuing year.

Secretary.—Saml. Mason, Jr.

Treasurer.—John Elliott.

Managers.—Benjn. Cooper, Mordecai L. Dawson, Thomas Evans, Jno. G. Hoskins, Stephen P. Morris, Blakely Sharpless, George Williams, Caspar Wistar, Thomas Wistar, Jr. Wm. Biddle, Philip Garrett, Joseph Scattergood, M. C. Cope.

Extracts from the annual report of the managers :—

"Soon after the last annual meeting, an opportunity presented to obtain a farm for the purposes of the institution, which, after examination, being deemed eligible, we concluded to purchase, as being, in our judgment, the best adapted of any within our knowledge. It is located at the 7 mile stone on the Willow Grove Turnpike, in Bristol Township, Philadelphia County. It contains about 133½ acres, nearly 25 of which are woodland, a small portion is meadow, the balance, good arable land, in tolerable condition. It has several fine springs, and is well watered by small streams passing through it.

The buildings consist of a large farm house and two small tenements, with the usual out houses. These, with the fences, not being in good repair, we have commenced placing them in order, and expect soon to have them in such condition as will fit them for our purposes.

After deliberate consideration, it was deemed best to let the farm for one year, from 4th month 1st, to Isaac Jones, Jr. a member of our religious society. He has taken it partly on the shares, we reserving accommodations in the buildings, and 5 acres of land as a garden and nursery for the uses of the institute, and stipulating for the board of such children and their caretakers as we may place there.

The subject of receiving coloured children, and the manner of holding and educating them, early engaged the serious consideration of the board, and after mature deliberation upon the difficulties likely to attend their management by an unincorporated institution, we have come to the conclusion that it will much facilitate our successful operation if an act of incorporation can be obtained. We therefore recommend this measure.

The low state of our funds, and condition of the farm and buildings, with our want of practical knowledge, seem to render it inexpedient to undertake the control of many children for some time. We hope, however, after an act of incorporation shall be obtained, circumstances will warrant us in receiving a small number of children of suitable age, and placing them under the care of a competent teacher. By commencing in this manner, an opportunity will be afforded of gaining experience in the details of this interesting concern, which, we trust, may confirm our most favourable anticipations of its ultimate usefulness.

It would render the success of our undertaking much more certain, however, if we could obtain the services of one who, with the requisite qualifications of a teacher, combined such an interest in the concern as would induce an engagement in it mainly to promote the welfare of the interesting objects of our solicitude: and we entertain the hope that a friend of this description will be found.

It will be obvious to all, that to enable us to succeed in carrying out the designs of the institute without embarrassment, and to the extent desired, large additions must be made to our funds. Although this has been deemed of primary importance, and has taken up the attention of the managers, yet from various causes no other effort has been adopted to accomplish, than by issuing a circular on the subject. The time has now, however, arrived, when it will be necessary to take such measures as will insure a sufficient annual income to meet the expenses which will be incurred in taking even a very small number. We trust that a concern which, we believe, with the Divine blessing, is calculated to produce an excellent influence over the minds and morals of this neglected class of our fellow beings, and one in which Friends can so freely participate, will not be allowed to languish for the want of an ample endowment. From the report of the treasurer, herewith transmitted, it will be seen that he has in his hands a cash balance of $178.16.

(Signed) CASPAR WISTAR, *Secretary.*
4th mo. 13, 1840.

A Declaration of the Views of the Society of Friends in relation to Church Government: By the Meeting for Sufferings of New England Yearly Meeting.

(Continued from p. 240.)

The following extracts from the writings of worthy and experienced Friends, expressive of their concern for the preservation of the church, we deem pertinent and instructive, and commend them to the careful consideration of all. We commence with some extracts from the advices of George Fox, of whom William Penn testifies that "he was a man that God endowed with a clear and wonderful depth, a discerner of others' spirits, and very much a master of his own."

"Friends, live in the power of the Lord God, and in his truth, light and life, that by it you may all, with one heart and mind, keep dominion and do true judgment and justice, truth and righteousness in all your men and women's meetings, without favour or affection to relations, kindred or acquaintances, or any respect of persons.

For if you do not so, judgment will come on you from God, to put you down from your places. For the power of God, his light and truth, respects not any, but justice, truth, righteousness and equity.

Let mercy overshadow the judgment-seat, and let mercy be mixed with judgment.

Take heed of foolish pity; and if you be not diligent against all profaneness, sin, iniquity and uncleanness, looseness and debauchery, and that which dishonoureth God, then you let those things come upon you, which you should be a top of and subdue and keep down, with righteousness and the truth and power of God.

And in all your men and women's meetings let all things be done in love, which doth edify the body; and let nothing be done in strife and vain glory; but keep in the unity of the spirit, which is the bond of peace; and let all things be done in the wisdom of God, which is pure and gentle from above, above the earthly, which is sensual and devilish."—1668.

"Now, dear Friends, let there be no strife in your meetings, nor vain janglings, nor disputings, but let all that tends to strife be ended out of your meetings, that they may be kept peaceable, so that you may be at peace among yourselves, and the God of peace and love may fill all your hearts; whose love edifies the church."—1683.

"Let all your meetings be preserved by the wisdom of God, in the unity of the spirit, the bond of peace, and in the fellowship of the Holy Ghost;—that, being ordered by the pure, gentle, heavenly, peaceable wisdom, easy to be entreated, they may be holy and virtuous examples to all others. Let all be careful to speak shortly and pertinently to matters, in a Christian spirit, and despatch business quickly, and keep out of long debates and heats, and with the help of the Spirit of God, keep that down which is floating about questions and strife of words, and tends to parties and contention. In the church of God, no such custom is to be allowed. Let not more than one speak at a time, nor any in a fierce way, but as the apostle saith, ' Be swift to hear and slow

to speak, and let it be in the grace which seasons all words.'

"And if any one should speak or talk any thing out of your monthly or quarterly meetings, to the blemishing or defaming of any person, or of the meeting, such are to be brought to judgment and condemnation; for it breaks the privilege and order of Christian society in your meetings; so that all may be kept and preserved in the power of the Lord, and in his spirit in love and unity."—1669.

"And be it known unto all, we cast out none from among us; for if they go from the light, and spirit and power in which our unity is, they cast out themselves. And it has been our way to admonish them, that they may come to that sPirit and light of God which they are gone from, and to come into the unity again. For our fellowship stands in the light that the world hates, and in the spirit which the world grieves, vexes and quenches; and if they will not hear our admonition, as before, the light condemns them, and then the testimony of truth goes out against them."

"And, dear Friends, you who are gathered in the power of the Lord God, which is the authority of your men's and women's meetings; in the power of the Lord Jesus, see that all things be well amongst you, and that all walk in the truth, and as becometh the gospel of Christ, and his glorious light and life, so that all may stand up for God's glory, and be valiant for his truth and grow up in it. Admonish, exhort and encourage such as are young and tender, to keep and preserve them in the way of life; and watch over one another for good."

"Dear Friends, do all that you do in peace and love and in the fear of God, condescending one unto another in the simplicity and innocency of truth, and in the wisdom of God, that this may be every one's crown, that nothing may be done in strife to occasion words; for you are called to peace and holiness, in which the kingdom stands, and to serve one another in love."

"And in the Lord's power and spirit meet together, and keep your meetings in the name of Jesus Christ, who hath all power in heaven and earth given to him, that you may feel his living and divine presence among you, and in his pure, gentle, heavenly love and wisdom, may be valiant for his name and truth upon the earth. Be not ashamed of Christ your Teacher and Prophet, whom God hath raised up in his new covenant and testament, whom you are to hear; neither be ashamed of Christ your Shepherd, who hath laid down his life for his sheep, whose voice you are to hear, who feedeth his sheep and giveth them life eternal, and none is able to pluck them out of his hand. Neither be ashamed of your High Priest, who hath offered up himself for you and doth sanctify you, who is a priest made higher than the heavens: neither be ashamed of your Bishop, the Chief Shepherd of your souls, to whom ye are now returned by his grace and truth, who oversees you with his heavenly eye, that you do not go astray from God. In him let your faith stand, who is the author and finisher of it, the Lord Jesus Christ, who is your Sanctuary, in whom you have life, peace, rest and salvation—who is the Amen."

That ancient, faithful minister of the gospel, Stephen Crisp, thus speaks of the course pursued by some in his day when the discipline was introduced and established among Friends:

"And when some exalted spirits came to see unto what this work would tend, they took offence thereat, and sought to weaken the hands of faithful Friends in this good work, under pretence, that all must be left to the witness of God; and if people did not find judgment in themselves for what they did, they must not be judged by others, being themselves gone from Truth's judgment and hardened; then they cried out innovation and imposition, and such like."

"And hereupon were many again seduced and subverted, and drawn away from their steadfastness in the truth, and began to appear against the good order of the Lord's people, and to reflect upon the godly care that lay upon them, with unhandsome and unsavory speeches and writings, until a secret root of bitterness and enmity got into several that had been convinced. In this root the enemy wrought with great craft and subtlety to draw them from the blessed unity that is in Christ Jesus, the true Head of the true church, and begat them into many jealousies and groundless fears of an apostacy, while in the meantime he drew *them* so far to apostatize from their first love and first works, that they proceeded to expose Friends, both in particular and in general, to the reproach and scorn of the world, as much as in them lay."

He proceeds to exhort Friends as follows:

"Let all beware of their own spirits and natural tempers, and keep in a gracious temper, then ye are fit for the service of the house of God, whose house ye are, as ye keep upon the foundation that God hath laid, and he will build you up and teach you how to build up one another in him. As every member must feel life in himself, and all from one head, this life will not hurt itself in any, but be tender of the life in all; for by this one life of the word, ye were begotten, and by it are nourished, and made to grow into your several services in the church of God. It is no man's learning or artificial acquirements; it is no man's riches or greatness in this world; it is no man's eloquence and natural wisdom, that makes him fit for government in the church of Christ; all his endowments must be seasoned with the heavenly salt, and his spirit subjected, and his gifts pass through the fire of God's altar, a sacrifice to his praise and honour, that so self may be crucified and baptized into death, and the gifts made use of in the power of the resurrection of the life of Jesus in him. When this great work is wrought in a man, then all his gifts and qualifications are sanctified, and made use of for the good of the body which is the church, and are as ornaments and jewels, which serve for the joy and comfort of all who are partakers of the same divine fellowship of life, in Christ Jesus our Lord. Thus many come to be fitted and furnished to good works, which are brought forth in their due seasons, for edification and building up the weak, and for repairing the decayed places, and also for defence of them that are feeble, that hurtful things may not come near them."

"It was a good saying, he that judgeth

among men judgeth for the Lord, and he will repay it. Therefore let all be done as unto the Lord, and as ye are willing to answer it in his presence, and although some may for a time be discontented thereat, yet in time God shall clear up your innocency as the sun at noonday. They that kick at sound judgment will find hard work of it; they do but kick against that which will prick them; and however such through their wilfulness, and their abounding in their own sense, may hurt themselves, yet you will be preserved and enjoy your peace and satisfaction in the discharge of your consciences in the sight of God."

"Dearly beloved, keep upon your watch, keep on your spiritual armour, keep your feet shod with the preparation of the gospel of peace, and the God of peace will be with you and crown your endeavours with good success, to your joy and comfort. He will bring his power over your adversaries and opposers, more and more, to which many shall bow and bend in your sight; and will bring shame and confusion upon the rebellious, who harden their hearts and stiffen their necks, against the Lord, and his Christ and kingdom, which he will exalt in the earth, notwithstanding all that Satan and his evil instruments can do, to hinder the growth and progress of his blessed truth; for of the increase of the government and of the peace of the kingdom of Christ, there shall be no end."

The following extracts from the writings of Robert Barclay, in which church order and government are asserted, we deem appropriate to our present purpose.

"Some," says he, "are so great pretenders to inward motions and revelations of the spirit, that there are no extravagancies so wild, which they will not cloak with them; and so much are they for every one's following their own mind, as can admit of no Christian fellowship and community, nor of that good order and discipline which the church of Christ never was nor can be without. This gives an open door to all libertinism, and brings great reproach to the Christian faith." He alludes to the other extreme of receiving the Scripture as the only means through which God's will is manifested, and declares, that it is and hath been the work of Friends to avoid both of these extremes, "and to be found in that even and good path of the primitive church, where all were (no doubt) led and acted by the Holy Spirit; and might all have prophesied one by one; and yet there was a subjection of the prophets to the spirits of the prophets. There was an authority some had in the church, and yet it was for edification and not for destruction; there was an obedience in the Lord to such as were set over, and a being taught by such, and yet a knowing of the inward anointing, by which each individual was to be led into all truth. The work and testimony the Lord hath given us is to restore this again, and to set both these in their right place, without causing them to destroy one another."

"The ground of all schisms, divisions or rents in the body is, when as any member assumes another place than is allotted it; or being gone from the life and unity of the body, and losing the sense of it, lets in the murmurer, the eye that watches for evil, and not in holy care over its fellow members; and then instead of coming down to judgment in itself, will stand up and judge its fellow members, yea, the whole body, or those whom God has set in a more honourable and eminent place in the body than itself. Such suffer not the word of exhortation; and term the reproofs of instruction, (which is the way of life,) imposition and oppression, and are not aware how far they are in the things they condemn others for; while they spare not to reprove and revile all their fellow members; yet if they be but admonished themselves, they cry out as if their great charter of gospel liberty were broken. Now, though such and the spirit by which they are acted, be sufficiently seen and felt by thousands, whose hearts God has so established, as they are out of danger of being entangled in that snare; and who have power and strength in themselves to judge that spirit, even in its most subtle appearances; yet there are who cannot so well withstand the subtlety and seeming sincerity some such pretend to, though in measure they have a sight of them, and others that cannot so rightly distinguish between the precious and the vile; and some there are that, through weakness and want of true discerning, may be deceived, and the simplicity in them betrayed for a season, as it is written, 'with fair speeches and smooth words they deceive the hearts of the simple.'"

"He hath not gathered us to be as sheep scattered without a shepherd, that every one may run his own way, and every one follow his own will, and so to be as a confused mass or chaos without any order; but he, even the Lord, hath also gathered and is gathering us, into the good order, discipline and government of his own son, the Lord Jesus Christ; therefore he hath laid care upon some beyond others, who watch for the souls of their brethren as they that must give account."

He proceeds to describe a certain class that gave the church trouble in his day, who, "not keeping low in their own habitations, but being puffed up, and giving way to the restless imaginations of their exalted and wondering minds, fall out with their brethren; cause divisions; begin to find fault with every thing, and to look at others more than at themselves; with swelling words to talk of, and preach up, a higher dispensation, while they are far from living up to the life and perfection of this present; like unto such who said, 'we will not have this man to rule over us:' cry out of formality and apostasy, because they are not followed in all things; and if they be reproved for their unruliness, according to the good order of the church of Christ, then they cry out, 'breach of liberty, oppression, persecution! we will have none of your order and government; we are taught to follow the light in our consciences, and not the orders of men.'"

After fully establishing, from scripture, that "Christ did appoint and ordain that there should be order and government in the church, and that any one refusing to hear the judgment of the church, or whole assembly, he doth thereby exclude himself, and shut out himself from being a member, and is justly judged by his brethren as an heathen and a publican," Robert Barclay proceeds:

"The church, gathering or assembly of God's people, has power to examine and call to account such as appearing, to be among them, or owning the same faith with them, do transgress; and in case of their refusing to hear or repent, to exclude them from their fellowship; and that God hath a special regard to the judgment and sense of his people thus orderly proceeding, so as to hold such bound in heaven whom they bind on earth, and such loosed in heaven whom they loose on earth; and if there should be any so unreasonable as to deny it, I could prove it by inevitable consequences; which, at present, us taking it for granted, I forbear to do. If it be reckoned so great a crime to offend one of the little ones, that it were better for him than so to do, that a millstone were hanged about his neck, and he were drowned in the depth of the sea; without question, to offend and gainsay the whole flock, must be more criminal, and must draw after it a far deeper judgment."

"And seeing, in case of difference, the Lord hath, and doth, and will reveal his will to his people; and hath and doth raise up members of his body, to whom he gives a discerning, and power, and authority, to instruct, reprove, yea, and command, in some cases, those that are faithful and low in their minds, keeping their own places and minding the Lord, and the interest and good of his truth in the general over all, shut out the murmurer; and the spirit of God leads them to have unity, and concur with their brethren. But such as are heady and high-minded, are inwardly vexed that any should lead or rule but themselves; and so it is the high thing in themselves that leads them to quarrel with others for taking so much upon them; pretending a liberty, not sinking down in the seed, to be willing to be of no reputation for its sake. Such, rather than give up their own wills, will study to make rents and divisions, not sparing the flock—but prostrating the reputation and honour of the truth even to the world." After various scripture quotations, he cites 2d Thess. iii. 40.—"And we have confidence in the Lord touching you, that ye both do, and will do the things which we command you"—verse 6: "Now we command you brethren, in the name of our Lord Jesus Christ, that ye withdraw yourselves from every brother that walketh disorderly, and not after the tradition which he received of us." What more positive than this? And yet the apostle was not here any imposer. And yet further, verse 14: "And if any man obey not our word by this epistle, note that man and have no company with him, that he may be ashamed." Thus, Heb. xiii. 7: "Remember them which have the rule over you, who have spoken unto you the word of God; whose faith follow, considering the end of their conversation"—verse 17: "Obey them that have the rule over you and submit yourselves; for they watch for your souls as they that must give account, that they may do it with joy and not with grief, for that is unprofitable for you."

(To be concluded.)

The Eleventh Annual Report of the Bible Association of Friends in America: read at the annual meeting, held on the evening of the twentieth of fourth month, 1840.

To the Bible Association of Friends in America.

The Board of Managers submit their eleventh Annual Report.

There have been issued from the Depository, since the last report, 1238 Bibles, and 441 Testaments; of which 481 Bibles and 184 Testaments were sold to auxiliaries.

The fifth edition of 1000 copies of the 24mo. Bible, which was in press at the time of the last Annual Report, was completed soon after.

The stock of books on hand consists of—

In Sheets.

396 copies of 8vo. Bible without references,
704 "   "   " with   "
610 "   24mo. "
1399 "   " Testaments,
75 "   12mo. "

Bound.

27 Bibles 8vo. without references,
213 "   " with   "
768 "   24mo.
453 Test's. "
143 "   12mo.

The Biblical Library has received a small addition during the past year.

From the annual report of the treasurer, it appears that including the balance on hand, fourth month, 1839, he has received the sum of $2984.39, from the following sources, viz:—

Balance on hand 4th mo. 6th, 1839, $506.89
From auxiliaries in payment and on
account, ...   838.79
      "   donations, .   .   58.75
Sales of Bibles and Testaments, .   1261.96
Annual subscriptions,   .   .   .   153.00
Other   "   .   .   .   160.00
Donation from an individual,   .   5.00
                                    ————
                                 $2984.39

The payments during the same period, including $500 borrowed money, have amounted to $2228.34, leaving a balance in his hands, on the 3d inst. of $756.05.

Reports have been received from eleven auxiliaries, viz :—Philadelphia, New York, Purchase, N. Y., Cornwall, N. Y., Concord, Pa., Burlington, N. J., Salem, N. J., Springfield, Indiana, Westfield, Indiana, White Lick, Indiana, and Western, Indiana.*

* In addition, reports have been received from three auxiliaries, viz :—Haddonfield, N. J., White Water and Spiceland, Indiana.

These state they have distributed 69 Bibles and 6 Testaments during the past year.

One of them reports, " There are about 200 families not duly supplied, and one family destitute of a copy of the Holy Scriptures. The number of members of our society capable of reading, who do not own a copy of the Holy Scriptures, is 521.

Another,—" There are about 290 families within our limits, we know of none of them who are not supplied with a copy of the Holy Scriptures. There are about 280 Friends capable of reading the Bible who do not own a copy. The income of the auxiliary is not sufficient to supply those within our limits who have not a copy of the Holy Scriptures."

Nine of these state the number of Bibles and Testaments distributed by them during the past year, being 273 Bibles and 160 Testaments, some of which were gratuitously disposed of. But few have given particular answers to the queries. The following extracts have been taken from these reports, as exhibiting the best account of their condition.

One auxiliary states that, " Our distribution, although greater than in some former years, it will be perceived, is still small. But conscious that our duties do not depend on the great amount of good which appears to result from their performance, we desire to encourage one another to a steady, patient continuance in our quiet and unobtrusive field of action. For we often find individuals engage in labours of love with zeal and energy, under the excitement produced by new prospects of benevolent action, who soon permit or allow their interest to abate.' The motive to action in the Christian disciple should be stable, springing from a sense of duty, and neither dependent on novelty, excitement, nor success."

Another, that " We continue to be persuaded, that our association, although small, is still useful; and that the Bibles and Testaments printed by the Parent Association, are preferred to all others. We are desirous that parents and heads of families should supply the younger members with a copy of the small Bible. This has been encouraged at our annual meeting, and we hope it will be more generally attended to."

From the report of an auxiliary we make the following extract : " The number of families within the limits of this Quarterly Meeting is about eighty. None of these are destitute of a copy of the Holy Scriptures, and most of them have more than one. We cannot give the precise number of members within our limits, capable of reading, who are not furnished with a Bible, but there are several young persons of an age suitable to possess a copy, who are not yet supplied. It affords us satisfaction to state, that we have the addition of several new subscribers. The whole number the present year is forty-four, of whom ten are females. No books have been sold the present year, but all that were received (16 in number) have been gratuitously disposed of.

" The whole number of Bibles procured by this auxiliary since its formation, is about 113. The number of Testaments, 126—very few of these have been sold ;—some have been placed in schools belonging to the society. The remainder have been gratuitously distributed among members of our religious society, with the exception of a few, that have been bestowed upon those who were not in membership with us."

A report from an auxiliary in a remote district, that ceased to correspond for several years, states, that " It is but lately that an attempt was made to revive the concern. We are now again organised, though our numbers are small and our means limited. Within our limits we have five Preparative Meetings, mostly small, composed of 180 families and parts of families, the greater part of whom are in more limited circumstances than is usual for members of our society in this part of the country to be. They contain 600

readers, who have but 228 Bibles, and 66 Testaments amongst them; no family destitute of a copy of the Bible. Our greatest need is school Bibles and Testaments."

An auxiliary states, that " Although our labours have been very much circumscribed in relation to distributing the Holy Scriptures, in consequence of there being but few amongst us who are destitute thereof; yet we entertain a hope, that the original objects for which the parent as well as this auxiliary were formed, are advancing; and if we properly appreciate the many blessings a kind Providence has been pleased to bestow upon us, and among them, and not the least, that of having the opportunity of perusing the sacred pages, it ought to stimulate us to renewed exertions to endeavour to place them within the reach of all our members.

" In conclusion we would remark, as in a former report, that we think the time not very distant, when it will be right for Friends to turn their attention to supplying those not in membership with us, with copies of the Holy Scriptures."

One remarks, " that in attempting to offer you our annual report, we feel that we have but little to contribute that will be likely to edify or encourage you in your very laudable, and, as we conceive, Christian labour, for the diffusing the beneficial reading of the Holy Scriptures ; which we believe all Christians will unite in, with the great apostle Paul, that ' they are able to make wise unto salvation, through faith in Christ.' We have felt, in our small and scattered situation, a weight of discouragement, but when convened in our small meetings for the purpose of the concerns of the auxiliary, we have been favoured to feel uniting strength of encouragement, to persevere in doing the little that we may have the ability to do, to help and encourage a work so good and desirable. We have been so happy as to be able to supply all suffering cases that have been known in our Quarterly Meeting ; but in consequence of the general pressure of the times, we are not able to do much ; but we are comforted and encouraged to perseverance, by the evidence that the concern is owned by the great head of the church. We believe Friends are increasingly concerned, that the Scriptures should be more used, in all schools of literature, than they have been.—There is no doubt a very considerable number of Bibles and Testaments needed, to supply all wants for that purpose."

Another auxiliary in the West, states, " that no family is destitute of the Holy Scriptures, though some are not in possession of more than one full copy, while the greater part are more fully supplied. A considerable number of our youth who are capable of reading, remain yet unfurnished with separate copies. Our schools are pretty well supplied. It has been our practice nearly from the commencement, to offer the Scriptures for sale at low prices, in order to induce a more general diffusion amongst Friends and others ; which practice, we think, is in some degree having the desired effect. They have generally been offered a little below cost, though in several cases, varied (to Friends) according to circumstances ; and a few Bibles and Testaments to some coloured people within our limits. But we acknowledge that a more lively feeling in promoting a greater diffusion and a more diligent and serious perusal of the Holy Scriptures, would produce more beneficial effects than have been heretofore manifest amongst us."

One report says, "we are induced to believe, that many among us still continue to evince a lively interest in the concern, which gave rise to the formation of the association, and are engaged to promote the objects of the parent institution. Notwithstanding the field in which we are destined to labour is very extensive, (being over three hundred miles from east to west,) we apprehend that much good has, and still more may be done, by merely keeping on hand a supply of the Holy Scriptures, suitable for families and schools, of a durable kind. Our funds being limited, we have not done much as yet towards furnishing destitute families and individuals with the Holy Scriptures.

"There are eleven families of Friends residing within our limits not duly supplied with a copy, and about four hundred and five members of our society, capable of reading the Bible, who do not own a copy of it. The income of the auxiliary is not sufficient to supply those within our limits with a copy of the Holy Scriptures, who are not duly supplied."

Another, that "one family of Friends within our limits appears to be destitute of a copy of the Holy Scriptures; and about four hundred members of our society capable of reading the Bible, who do not own a copy. The income of the auxiliary is insufficient to supply those within our limits who are not duly furnished with the Holy Scriptures. Five dollars and twenty-five cents is the amount of annual subscription during the past year."

In conformity with the directions of the last annual meeting of the association the managers purchased the lot and building at the corner of Fourth street and Apple-tree alley, for the stipulated price, twenty-two thousand nine hundred dollars; of which seven thousand nine hundred dollars was paid, and a mortgage given for the balance. The estate is held, for the use of the association, by three Friends, appointed trustees for the purpose.

Towards meeting the payment for this mortgage, there exists the sinking fund, which, on the 2d of the third month last, amounted to four thousand eight hundred and ninety-seven dollars and ninety-one cents, chiefly invested in safe securities, though not immediately available.

In consequence of the embarrassed situation of the currency of the country, and the depression attendant thereon, it was not deemed advisable to solicit subscriptions and donations to make up the deficiency of the funds, to complete the entire payment for the property; the same cause operated to prevent the use, to a greater extent, of the securities in which the sinking fund was invested. It is to be hoped a more favourable opportunity will occur for accomplishing these objects, and enable the managers to pay the debt and free the income, for the purpose of distributing Bibles.

Although we have not any very great amount of business to report this year, we feel encouraged to look forward to a time of revival and greater usefulness. The association is possessed of an eligible property, well rented, and not very heavily encumbered. They are also the owners of stereotype plates of excellent copies of Bibles and Testaments. The cause in which we have embarked, is one of great importance. The benefit that may be conferred by spreading the Holy Scriptures in a proper manner, is beyond estimation. Let us then continue our endeavours in this good work, that the treasures contained in those sacred records may be more generally diffused.

By direction and on behalf of the managers.

BENJAMIN H. WARDER, Secretary.
Philad. 4th month 11th, 1840.

THE FRIEND.

FIFTH MONTH, 2, 1840.

The promise expressed or implied in our notice last week, of a more detailed account respecting the late yearly meeting, has been, our readers will perceive, well complied with by another hand.

We commend to the attention of readers, two articles in the present number, each having strong claims to their regard as members of our religious Society:—the proceedings of the annual meeting of "The Institute for Coloured Youth," and the eleventh annual report of the "Bible Association of Friends in America." The officers appointed by the latter, at the annual meeting held on the evening of the 20th ult. are:—

Secretary.—Samuel Mason, Jr.
Treasurer.—Henry Cope.
Corresponding Members.—John Paul, Thomas Evans, Thomas Kimber.
Managers.—Thomas Stewardson, Thomas P. Cope, Joseph Snowdon, Thomas Wood, John Richardson, Benjamin H. Warder, John G. Hoskins, George Williams, Blakely Sharpless, Mordecai L. Dawson, Jeremiah Hacker, John Elliott, Joseph Rakestraw, Isaiah Hacker, Stephen P. Morris, William Thomas, Samuel Bettle, Jr., Townsend Sharpless, Lloyd Mifflin, Uriah Hunt, George M. Haverstick, John Carter, George G. Williams, William M. Collins.

The report in pamphlet form is now at the Depository ready for delivery. Auxiliary associations who have opportunity, are requested to send there for their proportions. The packages for the auxiliaries within the limits of New York and New England yearly meetings will be found at the book store of Mahlon Day & Co., New York.

A meeting of the Concord Auxiliary Bible Association of Friends, will be held at Friends' Meeting House, Concord, on second day, the 11th of 5th month, at 11 o'clock A. M. The female members are respectfully invited to attend.

HOWARD YARNALL, Secretary.
4th mo. 27th, 1840.

WESTTOWN SCHOOL.

The Summer Term will commence on second day, the 4th of next month: on which day the stage, and other suitable conveyances, will leave the office (at James Douglass' in Sixth below Arch street) at 7 o'clock in the morning.

Those who wish to avail themselves of this opportunity of sending their children out, are requested to have their names entered on or before the 2d of the month, in a book left at the stage office for that purpose.

Phia. 4th mo. 25th, 1840.

WANTED, an apprentice to the Wholesale Drug and Paint Business. A Friend, about 16 years of age, would be preferred. Inquire at the office of "The Friend."

DIED, in this city, on the morning of the 15th ult., after a protracted illness, borne with Christian patience, MARGARET SMITH, eldest daughter of the late Thomas Smith, in the 55th year of her age.

—— on first day, the 26th ult., at her residence in Burlington, N. J., HANNAH SMITH, widow of the late Richard S. Smith, in her 85th year.

—— at the residence of her son, Samuel Newbold, on the morning of the 23d ult. REBECCA NEWBOLD, relict of the late Joshua Newbold, of Trenton, in the 82d year of her age, a member and elder of the Monthly Meeting of Friends of Chesterfield, New Jersey. The bodily sufferings of this dear Friend, which were very great during the last few days of her life, were borne with that patience and resignation which is the result of a long life spent in acts of Christian love and benevolence, and a cheerful dedication to the service of her Divine Master. At times when her sufferings were the most intense, she expressed a wish that she might be released, but desired to wait in humble submission to her Heavenly Father's will. She quietly departed without sigh or groan, and having done her day's work in the day-time, has, we doubt not, entered into that rest prepared for the just of all generations.

—— at the residence of her brother, Paul Upton, in Stanford, Duchess county, N. Y., the 26th of third month, 1840, MARY MARRIOTT, widow of Henry Marriott, Jun'r. She endured the pains of a protracted illness with patience and resignation to the Divine will, and gave satisfactory evidence that her end was peace.

—— on the 23d of first month, 1840, at his residence in Pine Plains, Duchess county, N. Y., CHARLES HOAG, an elder of Stanford Monthly Meeting: Being a man of sound judgment and strict integrity, he was not only a useful member of our religious Society, but discharged with fidelity the duties of the various trusts committed to his care by the general community.

—— at her residence, on the 21st of tenth month last, near Pennsville, Morgan county, Ohio, SARAH HOLLINGSWORTH, wife of Elisha Hollingsworth, in the 38th year of her age, a minister and member of Pennsville Monthly and Particular Meeting. Having a short time previous to her last illness paid a visit to the meetings of Salem and Springfield Quarterly Meetings, to the peace of her own mind and the satisfaction of Friends, soon after her return home she was taken ill of congestive fever, which in thirteen days closed her useful life. She evinced to those around her, by Christian patience and resignation, that her confidence was in that arm of Divine Power which had been her support through life, and we doubt not her purified spirit has entered into that rest which is prepared for the righteous.

PRINTED BY ADAM WALDIE,
Carpenter Street, below Seventh, Philadelphia.

THE FRIEND.

A RELIGIOUS AND LITERARY JOURNAL.

VOL. XIII.   **SEVENTH DAY, FIFTH MONTH, 9, 1840.**   **NO. 32.**

EDITED BY ROBERT SMITH.

PUBLISHED WEEKLY.

Price two dollars per annum, payable in advance.

Subscriptions and Payments received by

GEORGE W. TAYLOR,

NO. 50, NORTH FOURTH STREET, UP STAIRS,

PHILADELPHIA.

For "The Friend."

If the writer of an article, on the *Tails of Comets*, which appeared in "The Friend" of the 18th instant, and which has just met my eye, will make his communication under his proper signature to the "American Journal of Science," whence my essay was transferred to the columns of "The Friend," without my agency, I will endeavour, by the permission of the editors, to show that the *single* seeming objection to my theory which he has adduced, by the plurality of tails attached to the comet of 1744 (the anomalies of the comet of 1823 and of 1835 being exceedingly unlike a tail) has by no means escaped my attention. We shall then reason together on equal ground, and if he should still remain confident that my "*method*," as he is pleased to term it, "of accounting for the tails of comets, is incompatible with sound philosophical principles," *he* "may derive some consolation from the reflection" that he has combatted error openly.

WM. MITCHELL.

Nantucket, 4th mo. 21, 1840.

SPEECH OF AMBROSE H. SEVIER,
OF ARKANSAS.

In U. S. Senate, March 17, 1840.—In Executive session, on the treaty with the New York Indians.

(Continued from page 243.)

I will now, Mr. President, take my leave of the Green Bay Indians, and return to the treaty of 1832. In that treaty, concluded in this city with a delegation from the Menomonees of Wiskonsin, we obtained of them, for the sum of $20,000, 500,000 acres of their lands, near Green Bay, for the future residence, not only of those small bands who emigrated under Mr. Monroe's permission, but for *all* of the New York Indians, then residing in New York. We obtained this land, so far as we were concerned, as a mere *gratuity*, and without any other consideration, so far as appears to me, than the wishes of New York and this land company that we should do so. New York desired this land secured, not so much for the residence of those then residing in Wiskonsin, for their welfare had ceased to interest her, but

for the New York Indians then within her borders, in the hope that her Indians could be induced to move to them, and, in that event, that she would be rid of an Indian population at the expense of the United States, she was most anxious to get clear of; and that the land company would be able, for little or nothing on their part, to get of them their New York lands, mainly, but indirectly, at the expense of the United States also. These were the calculations; and hence we find that, in that treaty, the New York Indians, although apparently so deeply interested, were not parties to it. And why were they not? I will endeavour to inform you, sir.

In the treaty of 1794, the New York Indians engaged to claim no other land within the boundaries of the United States than that particularly described in that treaty. They had modesty and honesty enough to know that there was no treaty ever afterwards made, by which we were pledged or bound to purchase land for them at Green Bay, or any where else. They knew they had no claim of any character upon us; and not desiring any other lands than those they were possessed of, and seeing no necessity for a treaty, they stood aloof, and had no participation in it. And in this same treaty the Menomonees disclaim any right or just claim of the New York Indians to the Green Bay lands. And this is not the only disclaimer. We find, in the printed documents now before us, at page 127, that the Senecas say that "the Senecas have no right or title to that country, (Green Bay,) as we have never accepted or paid for any interest there, nor do we at this time have any claim to that country whatever." And I will add, that in a letter received last night, I am informed that the Senecas are now holding a council for the purpose of *retransferring* to you *this gratuity*, which, given to them in 1832, without their knowledge or consent, you seem determined to force upon them, and which they, on their part, seem disposed just as decidedly to reject —with a full knowledge that the New York Indians, then residing in New York, had no claims upon us for lands any where, and, on the contrary, when we knew they had solemnly engaged, in their treaty of 1794, to set up no claim for any other within the boundaries of the United States than those particularly described in that treaty, yet, with a full knowledge of all this, we made the treaty of 1832.

In that treaty, in which the New York Indians were not parties, it was stipulated, without their consent or knowledge, that they should remove to the lands we purchased for them at Green Bay, within three years thereafter, or else that their right to this 500,000 acres of land should be forfeited, and revert to the United States. This penalty was inserted, under a belief that it would not be disregarded

by the Indians, but, on the contrary, would be considered of such consequence as to induce their emigration. If it was not so designed, why was a time fixed for their emigration at all? Of what consequence was it to us, whether those Indians emigrated this year or next year, or never? Sir, the Indians looked upon the whole of these proceedings, in which they had had no participation, with a provoking indifference and nonchalance. They cared nothing for these lands, or the forfeiture thereof. They considered they had comfortable homes in New York, and there they determined to remain. This temper of the Indians was soon found out by those desiring their emigration; and it was, therefore, necessary to get the time for their removal extended, so that the company could have time to apply the *proper remedies*, and bring about a conversion of the Indians to an acquiescence in their desired policy. Governed by such considerations as these, we were applied to, to change this provision in the treaty; and, as usual, we permitted ourselves, like a nose of wax, to be twisted about by this company, and, to gratify them, did modify this provision, by a supplementary article to the treaty, so as to leave the time for their removal to the discretion of the president of the United States. So it stands now. Eight years have elapsed since that treaty was made, and yet the president has not required those Indians to move to their Green Bay lands, according to the terms of the treaty, by a given time, that he should exact the penalty, according to the terms of the treaty. The reasons of the president for permitting those Indians to remain upon their New York lands, without exacting the penalty, are doubtless benevolent, humane, and praiseworthy. His forbearance upon this subject, thus far at least, is not considered by me just cause of censure. Yet I should consider it his duty, before a great while, to close up this contingent claim. I think if these Indians do not, within a reasonable time, move to these lands, that they should revert to the United States; and in this reversion they can have no just cause of complaint. Their title to these lands is *conditional*—*dependent entirely upon their removal to them*. It was a mere gratuity on our part, and cost them nothing, not even solicitation, or empty thanks; and now, if they will not accept of our proffered gratuity, if they will not occupy those lands, voluntarily tendered to them *on that condition*, there can be no injustice in exacting their forfeiture, on their failure to comply with the condition.

Mr. President, we purchased, as before observed, in 1832, 500,000 acres of land at Green Bay, for the future residence of the New York Indians. This purchase being on our part, as before stated, a mere gratuity, and, so far as appears from our records, without the knowledge or solicitation of the Indians, five years thereafter, in the year 1837, for what reasons, or at whose promptings, we are left to conjecture, it seems to have become suddenly, and all at once, a matter of vital importance for us to purchase out this gratuity, a gratuity which the Indians considered of so little consequence or value to them, that they would neither move to it, nor have it. But no matter for that: we determined to buy back from them what we had given them as a present five years before; and in furtherance of these views, in 1837 we appointed a commissioner to accomplish for us this all-important object.

A purchase of this Green Bay land was the *ostensible* object of this mission. The *real* object, as I shall show you in the progress of this discussion, was to obtain our influence, and our means and money, to *assist* a dozen or so of land speculators to purchase of the New York Indians their New York lands, for which they held, under Massachusetts, the pre-emption right. And, sir, we have already done so, to some extent. We have purchased out for this company, and for New York, five of the six tribes—all of the New York Indians, except the Senecas, and we have attempted to buy them out also, whether successfully or not, remains to be seen by a decision upon the question now before us.

In 1837, as before observed, we appointed a commissioner, with the ostensible object of purchasing of the New York Indians their Green Bay lands. So soon as this was known, we found much excitement and agitation among the Indians, growing out of their attachment for, and reluctance to leave, their native land. They understood very fully the object of the negotiation. They knew the Green Bay land was but a *pretext*, and not the *real* object of the commissioner. They understood all this. They knew the object of the treaty was to get from them, for the land company, their New York lands. To overcome these scruples, and to reconcile them to the measure, the agents of the land company went to work, and I will now show you, sir, in what manner.

"Articles of agreement, made and concluded this 29th day of July, 1837, between Hemeh B. Potter, of the city of Buffalo, of the first part, and John Snow, a Seneca chief, of the Buffalo Creek reservation, in the county of Erie, of the second part.

"Whereas, in conformity with the declared policy of the government of the United States, the proprietors of the pre-emptive title of and in the four several tracts of land, reserved by the Seneca tribe of Indians, within the said state of New York, are desirous to induce the abovementioned tribe of Indians to accept, for their future and permanent residence, a tract of country in the territory west of the river Mississippi, appropriated for Indians inhabiting the Atlantic and other neighbouring states, and are, also, desirous, by fair purchase, to extinguish the right of the said Indians in and to the lands in this state, so reserved by them:

"And whereas, in furtherance of these objects, and in order to a future treaty by which to effect the same, the said proprietors have authorised negotiations to be opened with the chiefs and other leading men of the said tribe of Indians, and certain offers to be made to them in money as a permanent fund for the nation, and a compensation for their improvements; and have also deemed it advisable and necessary to employ the aid, co-operation, and services of certain individuals who are able to influence the said Indians to accept the offers so to be made to them:

"And whereas, the said Hemeh B. Potter, the party of the first part, is empowered to act on behalf of the said proprietors, and to contract with any individuals whose co-operation and agency may be necessary and efficient, in accomplishing the abovementioned object; and the said John Snow, the party of the second part, has agreed to contribute his influence and services in the premises; and in case of the extinguishment of the said Indian title to the said reserved lands as aforesaid, to sell to the said proprietors all and singular his improvements, of, in, and to the same:

"Now, therefore, it is mutually agreed by and between the parties hereto, as follows:

"First. The party of the second part undertakes and agrees to use his best exertions and endeavours to dispose and induce the said Indians to adopt and pursue the advice and recommendations of the government of the United States, in respect to their removal and future location; and on such said terms as the party of the first part, and his associates, in the name of the said proprietors, shall propose to sell and release, by treaty, their said reserved lands; and on all occasions to co-operate with and aid the said party of the first part, and his associates, as he may be, from time to time, advised, in talks and negotiations with the chiefs and other influential men of the said tribe; and in the active application of his whole influence at councils, and confidential interviews, for the purpose of effecting a treaty between the said tribe and the said proprietors, for the extinguishment of the Indian title to the said reserved lands.

"Second. The said party of the second part hath sold, and hereby doth sell, to the said proprietors, all and singular his buildings and improvements on the lands so to be released by treaty, and agrees to accept compensation therefor in the manner hereinafter mentioned; said buildings and improvements in the meantime not to be leased, or in any manner disposed of by said party of the second part.

"Third. In consideration of such efforts, co-operation, and services on the part of the said John Snow, faithfully bestowed in the premises, and of the sale and release of all and singular his said buildings and improvements upon any of the lands aforesaid, without leasing or otherwise disposing of the same, as hereinabove stipulated, the said Heman B. Potter, on his part, and that of his associates, agrees to pay, or cause to be paid, to the said John Snow, the sum of two thousand dollars, within three months after notice of the ratification, by the senate of the United States, of a valid treaty between the said tribes and the owners of the said pre-emptive title, or their trustees, by which the right and title of the said Indians shall be effectually released and extinguished, in and to the said reserved lands; subject, however, to the following qualification and understanding : that in case the said treaty shall provide for the payment to individual Indians for their buildings and improvements, then and in that case the said party of the second part shall accept and receive, as part payment of the aforementioned sum of two thousand dollars, such sum or compensation as he shall or may be entitled to, by and under the provisions of such treaty, for his said buildings and improvements, and the balance of the said two thousand dollars which shall remain, after deducting therefrom such compensation as aforesaid, and that only to be paid by the said party of the first part, as above specified, within the time abovementioned, or as soon thereafter as the said balance can be ascertained; and in case said party of the second part shall be entitled, by and under the provision of said treaty, to the sum of two thousand dollars and upward, he shall receive the same as may be therein provided, and the said party of the first part shall be discharged from paying any part of said two thousand dollars.

"And the said John Snow shall also be entitled, at a nominal rent, to a lease from the owners of the pre-emptive title, or their trustees, of and for the lot of land actually improved and occupied by him, called the Whipple farm, near the old council house, on the Buffalo reservation, for and during his own natural life, determinable when and as soon as he shall cease to live on and occupy the same; said lease to be executed by the lessors as soon after said treaty as said lands shall have been surveyed and allotted, said lease having reference to said survey.

"This agreement on the part of said party of the first part, being expressly dependent upon a treaty, to be made and ratified upon terms, conditions, and stipu-

lations, to be proposed and offe[...] the first part, and his associate[...]

H.
JC

Witness:
his
GEORGE x JIMESON,
mark.

True copy :
*F. S. Marius B. Pierce, abo[...] chiefs who signed the Buffalo t[...]

"Articles of agreement made [...] day of August, 1837, betwee[...] the city of Buffalo, of the [...] Gordon, a Seneca Indian, o[...] servation, in the county of E[...]

"Whereas, in conformity wi[...] of the government of the Unite[...] of the pre-emptive title of, an[...] tracts of land reserved by the S[...] within the said state of New Y[...] duce the abovementioned tribe [...] their future and permanent resi[...] propriated for Indians inhabit[...] other neighbouring states, and [...] fair purchase, to extinguish the [...] dians in and to the lands in thi[...] them :

"And whereas, in furtheranc[...] in order to a future treaty by w[...] the said proprietors have author[...] opened with the chiefs and oth[...] said tribe of Indians, and certai[...] them in money, as a permanen[...] and a compensation for their in[...] also deemed it advisable and ne[...] aid, co-operation, and services [...] who are able to influence the sa[...] the offers so to be made to ther[...]

"And whereas the said Hem[...] of the first part, is empowered t[...] said proprietors, and to contrac[...] whose co-operation and agency [...] efficient in accomplishing the a[...] and the said Samuel Gordon, tl[...] part, has agreed to contribute hi[...] in the premises:

"Now, therefore, it is mutus[...] tween the parties hereto, as foll[...]

"First. The party of the seco[...] agrees to use his best exertions [...] pose and induce the said Indian[...] the advice and recommendation[...] the United States in respect to t[...] location; and on such fair ter[...] first part and his associates, in [...] proprietors, shall propose, to se[...] their said reserved lands, and [...] operate with and aid the said pa[...] his associates, as he may be fro[...] in talks and negotiations with t[...] fluential men of the said tribe; [...] plication of his whole influence [...] dential interviews, for the purpo[...] between the said tribe and the r[...] extinguishment of the Indian ti[...] lands.

"Second. In consideration of [...] tion, and services, on the part o[...] don, faithfully bestowed in the [...] man B. Potter, on his part and [...] agrees to pay, or cause to be pa[...] Gordon, the sum of five thousa[...] months after notice of the ratifi[...] the United States, of a valid t[...] tribe and the owners of the sa[...] Indians shall be effectually rele[...] in and to the said reserved land[...]

"This agreement, on the pa[...] first part, being expressly depen[...] be made and ratified upon term[...]

lations to be proposed and offered by the said party of the first part and his associates.

H. R. POTTER, [L. S.]
SAMUEL GORDON, [L. S.]

Witness: O. ALLEN.

"It is understood and agreed that the sum of one thousand dollars is to be added to the within contract.

September 29, 1838.

O. ALLEN,
H. P. WILLCOX.

There are six other contracts of a similar character, which I will not take up the time of the senate to read. These eight have lately come to light. How many are yet behind, undisclosed, time will tell.

Here, Mr. President, we have a few illustrations, most liberal and honest and patriotic illustrations, of the means used by the agents of this land company, and under the authority of the proprietors, to induce the leading and influential chiefs to sell the lands of their unwilling constituents. Here we see, under the very nose of our commissioner, and at the moment of commencing his negotiation, *ostensibly* for the purchase of their Green Bay lands, the sum of *twenty-one thousand, six hundred dollars* in cash, besides leases, some for a term of years, some for life, some during occupancy, and one grant in fee simple, offered and promised in writing to eight leading and influential chiefs, by this land company, as rewards, or rather as *bribes* for serving this company *faithfully*, with their influence *in council, and in confidential interviews with the other Indians, so as to effect a treaty with the government for their Green Bay lands, and so as to effect a release and relinquishment of the Indian title to the proprietors of their reserved lands in the state of New York; and in case of success in these double negotiations, and in the event of their ratification by the senate of the United States, then these bribes were to be consummated, and not otherwise.*

By these dark and midnight transactions, the order of things was to be curiously reversed. The *emigrating party* were to stay in New York upon their leases, and the *non-emigrating party* were to be transported beyond the Mississippi. And are these contracts denied? No, sir; they are unblushingly and shamelessly admitted and justified! They are admitted and justified by Seneca White, one of the chiefs, in favour of the treaty and of emigration, in his speech to the secretary of war last August. They are admitted and justified by N. Strong, another chief in favour of the treaty and of emigration, in his letter to the president, of the 9th of last March. They are admitted by Orlando Allen, a white man, and one of the active agents of the land company, and justified, in his letter to the president, of the 11th of last March. And pray what is the justification?

Mr. Allen tells us, in his testimony, which he communicated to the president last spring, "that he *has understood* (and believes the attempt was never made to conceal it) that provision was made for some of the chiefs, in accordance with all former usages among the Senecas." Yes, sir, Mr. Allen may well say *he has understood* that provision was made for some of the chiefs; for I find this same Orlando Allen, who under oath, speaks so *doubtingly,* as though by hearsay only, is a subscribing

witness to at least two of these contracts. But, as to his *belief* that there were no attempts made to conceal these contracts—contracts which were for *secret* influence and *confidential services*—we of the committee, who have travelled through this whole mass of testimony, will believe just as much of this part of his testimony as we please, and that is precious little of it, if any. While voluntarily furnishing a part of his testimony for the benefit of the president, he would have done but an act of justice if he had given him, in addition, that part of his testimony, taken on the same occasion, which was, that he was an agent of the company, and *directly interested* in the success of the treaty—Mr. Allen assimilates these rewards, promised and given to these chiefs, in this underhanded and clandestine manner, to the annuity given to Red Jacket, Corn Planter, and others. Sir, there is no similitude in these cases. What was given to Red Jacket, Corn Planter, and to the others he has named, was given in open day, in the presence of the nation, and with the knowledge and approbation of their tribes. But enough of all this, for the present at least.

(To be continued.)

For "The Friend."

BOODHISM AND BRAHMINISM.

(Concluded from page 242.)

When a youth assumes the yellow robe, it is an occasion of considerable ceremony, and of emolument to the monastery. The candidate, richly clad, is led forth, on a horse, handsomely caparisoned, attended by a train of friends and relations, and passes in pomp through the principal streets. Before him go women, bearing on their heads his *future* robes of profession, and the customary utensils of a priest, with rice, fruit, cloth, china, cups, &c., intended as presents to the monastery and its superior.

This splendour of array bears a striking similarity to the display of dress, &c., made by a nun when about to renounce the world. Henceforth, at least while he remains a priest, the youth is no more to wear ornaments, ride on horseback, or even carry an umbrella. Priests are bound to celibacy and chastity; and if married before their initiation, the bond is dissolved. They must not so much as touch a woman, or even a female infant, or any female animal. They must never sleep under the same roof, or travel in the same carriage, or boat, with a woman, or touch any thing which a woman has worn. If a priest's own mother fall into the water or into a pit, he must not help her out, except no one else is nigh, and then he must only reach her a stick or a rope. He is not to recognise any relations. He must not have, or even touch, money; nor eat after the noon of the day; nor drink without straining the water; nor build a fire in any new place, lest some insect be killed; nor spit in water, or on grass, lest some creature be defiled. He must not dance, sing, or play upon musical instruments, nor stand in conspicuous places, nor wear long hair, nor have a turban, or shoes; and his raiment must be made of rags and fragments gathered in the streets. As the burning sun makes some

shelter absolutely necessary for a shorn head, he is allowed to carry a huge fan for this purpose. He must hold no secular office, nor interfere in the least with government. Seclusion, poverty, contemplation, and indifference to all worldly good or evil, are henceforth to distinguish him.

In eating, a priest must say, "I eat this rice, not to please my palate, but to support life." In dressing himself, he must say, "I put on these robes, not to be vain of them, but to conceal my nakedness." And in taking medicine, he must say, "I desire recovery from this indisposition only that I may be more diligent in devotion and virtuous pursuits."

All this strictness, though required in the books, is by no means exemplified in the conduct of the priests. They wear sandals, carry umbrellas, live luxuriously, and handle money. They not only wear the finest and best cotton cloth, but some of them the most excellent silks. They, however, preserve a shadow of obedience, by having the cloth first cut into pieces, and then neatly sewed together. They even look at women without much reserve. The huge fan, peculiar to priests, is intended partly to prevent the necessity of their seeing women when preaching, &c.; but the manner in which they are represented in native pictures, as looking over them, is more amusing than true.

Their office may be called a sinecure. Few of them preach, and those but seldom, and only on special request; after which donations of clothing, &c., are always made to them. On these occasions, though only one preaches, there are generally several present. They sit cross-legged, in a row, on a raised seat, and each holds up before him his fan, to prevent distraction by looking on the audience, and especially by gazing at the women. At funerals, they attend only when desired, and after reciting the prayers, retire, with liberal gifts, borne on the shoulders of boys. Marriage being utterly unholy, they have no services to render there. [It was some time before the Christian converts, under charge of the missionary Judson, could be reconciled to his performing the marriage ceremony, or being present.] Deeming it wholly unprofessional to do any work, most of them spend their time in sheer idleness.

It is the rule that each priest perambulate the street every morning, till he receive boiled rice, &c., enough for the day. From the dawn of day till an hour after sunrise, they are seen, passing to and fro, in groups, and singly, carrying on their arm the *thabike*, which is often sustained by a strap passing over the shoulder. They walk on briskly, without looking to the right or left, stopping when any one comes out with a gift, and passing on without the least token of thanks, or even looking at the giver.

The thabike is a black earthen pot, containing about a peck, with a lid of tin or lackered ware, which is made to fit, when inverted, so as to hold little cups of curry, meat, or fruits. The more dignified priests omit the morning perambulations, and either depend on a share of what their juniors receive, or have their own servants, and supply their private table from the bazar, and from offerings which are brought to them by the devout. Except in times of scarcity, the daily supply is superabundant, and the surplus is given to day scholars, poor persons, and adherents, who perform various services round the monastery. These retainers are very convenient to the priests in many ways. They receive money, which the priest may not openly touch; go to market for such little luxuries as may be wanted; sell the superabundant gifts of clothing, mats, boxes, betel-nut, &c. Some of the priests are known thus to have become rich. Father Sangermano, who spent many years among them, declares, that they make no scruple of receiving even large sums, and that "they are insatiable after riches, and do little else than ask for them."

The daily gift of food is supposed to be entirely voluntary, and doubtless generally is so. But I have often seen the priest make a full stop before a house, for some time. A gift was generally brought at length; but if not, he moved on without remark. If any family is noticed constantly to neglect giving, complaint is lodged with the ruler, and fines are sure to follow.

No false religion, ancient or modern, is comparable to this. Its philosophy is not exceeded in folly by any other; but its doctrines and practical piety bear a strong resemblance to those of Holy Scripture. Did the people but act up to its principles of peace and love, oppression and injury would be no more known within their borders. It has no mythology of obscene and ferocious deities; no sanguinary or impure observances; no self-inflicted tortures; no tyrannising priesthood; no confounding of right and wrong, by making certain iniquities laudable in worship. In its moral code, its descriptions of the purity and peace of the first ages, of the shortening of man's life because of his sins, &c., it seems to have followed genuine traditions. In almost every respect it seems to be the best religion which man has invented.

Yet, we must regard Boodhism with unmeasured reprobation, if we compare it, not with other false religions, but with truth. Its entire base is false. It is built, not on love to God, nor even love to man, but on personal merit. It is a system of religion without a God. It is literally atheism. Instead of a Heavenly Father forgiving sin,—and filial service from a pure heart, as the effect of love, it presents nothing to love, for its deity is dead; nothing as the ultimate object of action but self; and nothing for man's highest and holiest ambition but annihilation.

The system of merit corrupts and perverts to evil the very precepts whose prototypes are found in the Bible, and causes an injurious effect on the heart, from the very duties which have a salutary effect on society. Thus, to say nothing of its doctrines of eternal transmigration, and of uncontrollable fate, we may see, in this single doctrine of merit, the utter destruction of all excellence. It leaves no place for true holiness; for every thing is done for the single purpose of obtaining advantage.

Sympathy, tenderness, and all benevolence, would become extinct, had not Jehovah planted their rudiments in the human constitution. If his neighbour's boat be upset, or his house be on fire, why should the Boodhist assist? He supposes such events to be the unavoidable consequences of demerit in a former existence; and, if this suffering be averted, there must be another of equal magnitude. He even fears that by his interfering to prevent or assuage his neighbour's calamity, he is resisting established fate, and bringing evil on his own head.

The same doctrine of merit destroys gratitude, either to God or man. If he is well-off, it is because he deserves to be. If you do him a kindness, he cannot be persuaded that you have any other object or reason than to get merit; and feels that he compensates your generosity by furnishing the occasion. If the kindness be uncommon, he always suspects you of sinister designs. In asking a favour, at least of an equal, he does it peremptorily, and often haughtily, on the presumption that you will embrace the opportunity of getting merit; and, when his request is granted, retires without the slightest expression of gratitude. In fact, there is no phrase in his language that corresponds with our "I thank you."

The doctrine of fate is maintained with the obstinacy and devotedness of a Turk. While it accounts to them for every event, it creates doggedness under misfortune, and makes forethought useless.

Boodhism allows evil to be balanced with good, by a scale, which reduces sin to the shadow of a trifle. To pray before a pagoda, or offer a flower to the idol, or feed the priests, or set a pot of cool water by the way-side, is supposed to cancel a multitude of sins. The building of a monastery, or pagoda, will outweigh enormous crimes, and secure prosperity for ages to come. Vice is thus robbed of its terrors; for it can be overbalanced by easy virtues. Instances are not rare of robbery, and even murder, being committed, to obtain the means of buying merit. All the terrors, therefore, with which hell is represented, do but serve to excite to the observance of frivolous rites. The making of an idol, an offering, or some such act, is substituted for repentance and reparation, for all inward excellence, and every outward charity.

It ministers also to the most extravagant pride. The Boodhist presumes that incalculable merit, in previous incarnations, has been gained, to give him the honour of now wearing human nature. He considers his condition far superior to that of the inhabitants of the other islands of this system, and his chance of exaltation to be of the most animating character. Conceit, therefore, betrays itself in all his ways. The lowest man in society carries himself like the "twice born" Brahmin of Hindustan.

The spread of Matthewism has seriously affected the revenue in those parts of Ireland where it has been introduced. The excise collection in Cork district is 23,000l. deficient compared with the corresponding quarter of last year; and the Fermoy collection shows a deficiency of 11,000l. for the same period.

The Rotary Power Stocking Loom.

A correspondent of the Boston Courier gives the following description of the powers and capacities of this machine, a notice of which was given a few days since.

It is a beautiful piece of machinery, occupying but about twenty inches square space, with motions quick and regular, with very little friction, so that it must be durable. It is easily worked by hand, and is, therefore, well calculated for domestic purposes, as also for steam or water power.

The loom is superior to any apparatus for hosiery now known in this country or Europe, inasmuch as it knits, with equal facility, hard or soft twisted woollen yarn, cotton, or silk, and will; with less hand power, produce four feet of hosiery for every one foot that can be produced by any other loom, and of a superior quality of fabric. It costs forty per cent. less than an English loom, is much less complicated, less liable to get out of order, and it will cost fifty per cent. less to keep it in repair.

The proper motion for the machine is forty revolutions per minute, although it may be driven fifty, without risk. Forty revolutions, of one hundred strokes each, make three inches of stocking in length, in a minute, or fifteen feet per hour, so that each day of ten hours, gives fifty yards of beautifully executed stocking-web. But apply power to the loom, and allow one girl to attend four only, although she may as well attend to six, and we have, from one hand, six hundred and fifty feet of web per day, being four hundred and fifty feet more than four hands can produce upon four of the best English looms, within the same time.

An official return recently made to the Austrian government shows that there are 56 manufactories of beet-root sugar in Austria, producing annually 650,000 quintals of sugar, or nearly one third of the quantity consumed within the Austrian dominions.

M. Huzard has presented to the Société d'Encouragement a proposition for granting prizes for the best methods of preserving and increasing the number of leeches in France. He states that about 25,000,000 of these useful animals annually consumed in France, but their price is raised to an enormous rate on account of the difficulty of keeping them alive. The objects of the proposed prizes are—the stocking of such pieces of water and streams as are fit for the propagation of leeches, but at present have none in them; for the best means of making them disgorge after an operation without injuring them or diminishing their powers; and introducing a new and effective species hitherto unknown in France.

No man that considers the promiscuous dispensations of God's providence in this world, can think it unreasonable to conclude, that after this life good men shall be rewarded, and sinners punished.—*Tillotson.*

A Declaration of the Views of the Society of Friends in relation to Church Government; By the Meeting for Sufferings of New England Yearly Meeting.

(Concluded from p. 245.)

"I might at length enlarge, (continues Barclay,) if needful, upon these passages, any of which is sufficient to prove the matter in hand, but that what is said may satisfy such as are not wilfully blind and obstinate. For there can be nothing more plain from these testimonies than that the ancient apostles and primitive Christians practised order and government in the church; that some did appoint and ordain certain things, condemn and approve certain practices, as well as doctrines, by the Spirit of God; that there lay an obligation in point of duty upon others to obey and submit; that this was no encroachment nor imposition upon their Christian liberty, nor any ways contradictory to their being inwardly and immediately led by the Spirit of God in their hearts; and lastly, that each as are in the true feeling and sense, will find it in their places to obey and be one with the church of Christ in such like cases; and that it is such as have lost their sense and feeling of the life of the body, that dissent and are disobedient, under the false pretence of liberty."

Robert Barclay, in the course of the instructive work from which we are quoting, all of which may be profitably read, fails not to condemn such as, claiming the privilege of immediate revelation, say, "that they, being moved to do such and such things, though contrary to the mind and sense of the brethren, are not to be judged for it, (they) adding, why may it not be so that God hath moved them to it?" Now, if this be a sufficient reason (says he) for them to suppose as to *one* or *two*, I may without absurdity suppose it as well to the *whole body*. He declares, "that ordinarily God hath, in the communicating of his will under his gospel, employed such whom he had made use of in the gathering of his church, and in feeding and watching over them, though not excluding others;" and goes on to say, "And indeed I mind not where, under the gospel, Christ hath used any other method; but that he always, in revealing his will, hath made use of such as he himself had before appointed elders and officers in his church; though it be far from us to limit the Lord, so as to exclude any from this privilege; nor yet on the other hand, will the possibility hereof be a sufficient warrant to allow every obscure member to stand up, and offer to rule, judge and condemn the whole body; nor yet is it without cause, that such an one's message is jealousied and called in question, unless it have very great evidence, and be bottomed upon some very weighty and solid foundation."

From William Penn's "Brief Examination and State of Liberty Spiritual," we make the following extracts. He commences:— "Dear Friends and Brethren, it hath of long time rested with some pressure upon my spirit, for Zion's sake and the peace of Jerusalem, to write something of the nature of true spiritual liberty. Liberty, one of the most glorious words and things in the world, but little understood, and frequently abused by many. I beseech Almighty God to preserve you his people, in the right knowledge and use of that liberty, which Jesus Christ the Captain of our salvation, hath purchased for us and is redeeming us into." He queries—" But must I conform to things whether I can receive them or not? Ought I not to be left to the grace and spirit of God in my own heart?" This he fully answers, and says: —" It is a dangerous principle and pernicious to true religion, and which is worse, it is the root of ranterism to assert, that nothing is a duty incumbent upon thee, but what thou art persuaded is thy duty; for the *seared* conscience pleads his liberty against all duty, the *dark* conscience is here unconcerned, the *dead* conscience is here uncondemned. As to the second part of the question—" Ought I not to be left to the grace of God in my own heart?" he answers—" That is of all things the most desirable, since they are well left, that *are* there left, for there is no fear of want of unity; where all are left with the one spirit of truth, they must be of one mind, they cannot be otherwise; so that to plead this against unity, is to abuse the very plea, and to commit the greatest contradiction to that very doctrine of Scripture, viz : "That all should be guided by the grace and spirit of God in themselves," for the end of that doctrine is certainty, "They shall all know me, saith the Lord, from the least to the greatest, and I will give them one heart," &c. "Therefore I must say to thee, Friend, what if thou wilt not be left with the grace and spirit of God in thyself, nor wait for its mind, nor be watchful to its revelations, nor humble and quiet, till thou hast received such necessary manifestations; but pleadest against the counsel of the Spirit of the Lord in other faithful persons, under the pretence of being left to his Spirit in thyself; by which means, thou opposest the Spirit to the Spirit, and pleadest for disunity under the name of liberty."

"Since the Spirit of the Lord is one in all, it ought to be obeyed through another as well as in one's self; and this I affirm to you, that the same lowly frame of mind that receives and answers the mind of the Spirit of the Lord in a man's self, will receive and have unity with the mind of the same Spirit through another; and the reason is plain; because the same self-evidencing power and virtue that ariseth from the measure of the spirit of truth in one's self, and that convinceth a man in his own heart, doth also attend the discovery of the mind of the same spirit when delivered by another; for the words of the 'second Adam, the quickening spirit,' through another are spirit and life, as well as in thy own particular; this is discerned by the spiritual man that judgeth all things, although the carnal man pleadeth being left to his *freedom*, and it may be, talks of being left to the *spirit* in himself too; the better to escape the sense and judgment of the spiritual man. It is my earnest desire that all that have any knowledge of the Lord, would have a tender care how they use that plea against their faithful brethren, that God put into their mouths against the persecuting priests and railings of the world, namely, 'I must mind the spirit of God in myself;' for though it be a great truth that all are to be left thereunto, yet it is as true, that he whose soul is left with the spirit of truth in himself, differs not from his brethren that are in the same spirit, and as true it is that those who err from the spirit of truth, may plead being left to the *spirit* in *themselves*, against the motion and command of the spirit through another, when it pleaseth not his or her high mind and perverse will; for a saying may be true or false according to the subject matter it is spoken upon or applied to; we own the assertion—we deny the application—there lies the snare."

Query—"But though this be true, which hath been alleged for heavenly concord, yet what if I do not presently see that service in a thing that the rest of my brethren agree in? In this case, what is my duty and theirs?

"Answer—It is thy duty to wait upon God in *silence* and patience, out of all fleshly consultations; and as thou abidest in the simplicity of the truth, thou wilt receive an understanding with the rest of thy brethren about the thing doubted. And it is their duty, whilst thou behavest thyself in meekness and humility, to bear with thee, and carry themselves tenderly and lovingly towards thee; but if on the contrary thou disturbest their godly care and practice, and growest contentious, and exaltest thy judgment against them, they have power from God to exhort, admonish and reprove thee; and (if thou perseverest therein) in his name to refuse any further fellowship with thee, till thou repentest of thy evil."

A little farther on, William Penn remarks: "This I affirm from the understanding I have received of God, not only that the enemy is at work to scatter the minds of Friends by that loose plea, 'What hast thou to do with me? Leave me to my freedom and the grace of God in myself;' and the like; but this proposition and expression as now understood and alleged, is a deviation from, and a perversion of, the ancient principle of truth." After reasoning closely on the impropriety of an individual's urging the measure of his own light to justify him in courses and practices not approved by Friends, he goes on to say : "This is that very rock both professors and profane would long since have run us upon, namely, 'That a way is hereby opened to all the world's libertines, to plead the light within for their excesses;' which indeed grieves the Spirit of God, and was severely judged by our friends in the beginning, and is still reproved by them that keep their habitation, though some are become as wandering stars, through their own pride, and the prevalency of the hour of temptation that hath overtaken them; whereas had they kept in the channel of love and life, in the orb and order of the celestial power, they had shined as fixed stars in the firmament of God forever. And from the deep sense that I have of the working of the enemy of Zion's peace, to rend and divide the heritage of God, who under the pretence of crying down *man*, forms and prescriptions, is crying down the heavenly man Christ Jesus, his blessed order and government, which he hath brought forth, by his own revelation and power through his faithful witnesses, this I further testify, that the enemy by these fair pretences, strikes at the godly care and travail that dwell upon the spirits of many faithful brethren, that all things might be

l sweet, comely, virtuous and of good the church of God."

the Lord God of heaven and earth, sent his son Jesus Christ a light in- arts and consciences, to whose search ment all ought to (and must) bring eds, and render up their accounts, toly record, that for this end hath he pon the spirits of his servants, and good end only have his servants th, recommended and put in practice, ngs that are now in godly use among le, whether in this or other nations, to men's and women's meetings, and ers and weighty services. And fur- he fear of the Almighty God I shall heavenly peace and prosperity dwell se who are found in an holy and practice of them; wherefore I warn hey take heed of a slighting and ob- ind, and that they have a care how way to the outcry of some falsely ' Liberty of conscience against impo- &c., for the end thereof is to lead in and give ease to the carnal mind, last, will bring death again upon the God, and the living society of his

an epistle written by that experienced hy elder in the church, Joseph Pike, e the following pertinent extract: are," says he, "and always will be, degrees of growth in the members of h of Christ;—yes, as all are growing and drawing one way, and aiming at thing, namely, the honour of the prosperity of his Holy Truth, there general condescension and submission other; but more especially to godly d overseers; here the strong and self- an is kept out, and the unity of spirit, venly harmony, maintained in those as well as among the whole body or 'Christ."

ght continue our quotations from the of Friends much farther; all show- propriety and necessity of subordina- government in conducting the affairs urch, but we will conclude them by ph from the writings of our friend, iffith: "None have a right to ap- such a self-sufficiency as to be inde- of other members." "It likewise hat every member entered as such, her voluntary consent, is strictly keep and maintain the established hat body; the breach of which not lers him or her guilty in God's sight, accountable to the body.—It also be- is body immediately upon the trans- of its rules and orders, to exert itself g with transgressors, and to admi- und judgment in order to restore on failure of success in that, to dis- fuse to have unity with such; and to vorld know they are not of their

ow, beloved Friends, in conclusion, end the advices that we have revived erious attention, and solid considera- ay they be received by you in love urefully remembered; and prove as a the inexperienced and self-confident,

an incentive to the retiring and timid, and a strength and encouragement to those who, under a feeling of religious duty, are concern- ed to contend for the faith once delivered to the saints and for the order of the gospel. May the word of the Lord, through the mouth of his prophet, be received by us all for our good. "Stand ye in the ways, and see, and ask for the old paths, where is the good way, and walk therein, and ye shall find rest for your souls." Jer. ch. vi: 16.

Signed on behalf and by direction of a Meeting for Sufferings, held at Providence, the 3d of 3d month, 1840.

THOMAS HOWLAND, Clerk.

Communicated for "The Friend."
COLOURED SCHOOLS.

At an annual meeting of the Association of Friends for the free instruction of adult co- loured persons, held fourth month 2d, 1840, the following Friends were appointed to serve as officers for the ensuing year:

William H. Brown, Secretary.
John C. Allen, Treasurer.
James Kite, Josiah H. Newbold, Israel H. Johnson, Nathaniel H. Brown, William L. Edwards, Executive Committee.

To the Association of Friends for the free in- struction of Adult Coloured Persons.

In accordance with the duties assigned to it, the executive committee opened a school for coloured men on the 1st of the tenth month last, in the Willing's alley school-house. Joseph Whitall, Jr., who had for several years accept- ably filled the station, was re-engaged as teacher, and Samuel Allen employed to assist him.

At the commencement of the session, a much larger number of scholars than usual were in attendance, and the school filled up with a rapidity unprecedented; so that we were soon obliged to decline entering the names of any more applicants for admission. This was done with very great reluctance, but the crowded condition of the room rendered it unavoidable. It is believed that about forty persons applied after this measure was adopt- ed, ten of whom were afterwards admitted, when it was found that the irregular attendance of some of the scholars, would warrant an increase in the number. The rest of the appli- cants, however, had no opportunity of partici- pating in the benefits of the school; as through- out most of the winter it continued uncomfort- ably crowded.

The orderly behaviour, and close attention of the scholars have afforded us great satisfac- tion, and the general improvement manifested, has surpassed that of any former session of the school. A few who were particularly dili- gent made very remarkable progress, while a decided improvement was perceptible in all.

It is due to the members of the association who have assisted in the school, to mention, that some of them have laboured with great faithfulness; and their exertions largely con- tributed to the improvement of the scholars.

One hundred and sixty-one names were en- tered on the roll, and the average attendance was about forty-eight.

acceptable, will continue to prosper the work in which we are engaged.

Signed by direction and on behalf of the Executive Committee.

ISRAEL H. JOHNSON, *Clerk.*

Philada., 3d mo. 16, 1840.

The Association of Friends for the free instruction of Coloured Women, report,

That having obtained the use of the schoolhouse on Willing's alley, they opened their school on the 1st of tenth month, and continued it till the 28th of second month.

The entire number who have, in a greater or less degree, availed themselves of the advantages thus afforded, during the past season, is 181. The average attendance thirty-eight. Many of these being in the very rudiments of learning, require almost constant attention, in order that they may reap as much benefit as possible from the limited opportunity furnished them. Being sensible of this, we believed it best to avail ourselves of the services of two teachers; and the experience of the winter has proved the advantage and necessity of it, as the location of the school prevents many of the friends of this interesting concern from rendering it much assistance.

Considerable advancement appears to have been made by many of the women in spelling, reading, and writing, and the desire to learn, industry and application manifested, have been gratifying. Such of them as can read have been encouraged to learn portions of Scripture to repeat weekly.

We believe this school continues to be a benefit to many of those for whose good it is designed, and we desire, that, while there appears to be an increase of feeling in favour of the coloured population of the south, we may not overlook those around us, but, remembering that "Charity begins at home," that we may be willing to give up a portion of our time to the instruction of these; and it is encouraging to reflect, that by thus enabling them to occupy their leisure time with interesting and instructive reading, the temptation to idleness and unprofitable company will be greatly diminished.

Philada., 2d mo. 29th, 1840.

EPISTLE BY JOHN BURNYEAT.

On looking into the Journal of John Burnyeat (edition of the late John Barclay) my attention was arrested with an epistle appended thereto written by him, which, for the excellent spirit which pervades it, and its salutary counsel and warning, I thought would justly entitle it to a place in "The Friend." Annexed to it is the following note. "Let copies of this be sent to New England, Virginia, Maryland, and Barbadoes." Q.

TO FRIENDS.

London, 10th of third month, 1677.

Dear and well beloved,—Unto you, who are the called of God in those parts, unto whom the visitation of his day hath reached, and upon whose hearts the heavenly light thereof hath shined in its pure spiritual breakings forth, so that you are become the children thereof, and do walk therein; unto you all doth the tender salutation of my soul reach in the love of God, and in the fellowship, which is a mystery, which is held in a pure conscience, and continued, as we walk and abide in the light. In this light we have fellowship with the Father, and with the Son, and also one with another, and so are of one family and household, partakers of that one bread, which the sanctified in all ages did feed upon; which is that which we are to wait for in this day, that we may live thereby unto God, and grow through the divine nourishment thereof into his nature, and into his strength; wherein we may triumph over the adversary, as the ancients did of old, and rejoice in the God of our salvation, who is our strength and tower of safety for ever.

Dear Friends, great and large hath the love and kindness of our God been unto us (who were strangers, aliens, and enemies in our minds unto him) in this, that he hath called and chosen us to be his people, and to bear witness unto his appearance, and the shinings forth of his light, and of the glory of his presence, whereby he hath richly comforted our souls, and lifted up our heads above all sorrow, even when the enemy hath thought to sink us down into the pit. Thus hath the Lord dealt bountifully with our souls, and been a ready help in the needful time; to him be the honour and glory for ever and ever! So that now it behoves all, after so many deliverances, favours, and mercies, to [cleave] close unto the Lord, and seek his glory above all, and that with all their strength; that so he who is the good husbandman, may be glorified through every one's bringing forth fruit,—according to Christ's command.

Now, my Friends, this all observe, that none can bring forth fruit unto God's glory, but as they abide in Christ the living vine; for from him is the life received, by which every one lives unto God; and it is by the virtue of that life, that every one must act to his praise. And therefore, see that you all retain it in its own purity, and live in subjection thereunto through your whole day; that you may be as fruitful branches, abiding in the right nature, and bearing holy fruit: and then will you feel the holy dew abide upon your spirits, throughout your age, which will preserve you from withering, your leaf from fading; and so your fruit shall be ripe in due season, and not be untimely brought forth in that which will not endure: for that in which we have believed, will endure for ever. The heavenly power which God hath revealed in our hearts, and made manifest for a standing foundation, is sure for ever; upon which, as you all abide steadfast, the gates of hell, with all the power of darkness, shall not prevail against you; but you shall be able to withstand him, and keep your habitations in the dominion thereof, and dwell in peace upon the rock of safety, in the midst of all storms; and sing for joy of heart, when those that forsake this rock, shall howl and lament for vexation of spirit. For the Lord God will bring his day and his power over all, and upon all that fly to any shelter, or seek any other defence, who have once known his truth; and he will be unto such as a moth, and as rottenness, and their strength he will waste, and their garment and clothing he will destroy, and their beauty and glory he will cause to fade; though they have been as a beautiful flower in the head of the fat valley, yet will fading come upon them, even dryness at the root, and withering and decaying upon the beauty of their blossoms. Therefore let all keep unto that, and in that, which will not decay, come to nothing, nor ever be turned into darkness; but abide in its virtue and glory, in and by which the Lord hath visited you, and through which his day hath dawned upon your souls, the morning whereof you have known bright and clear, as without clouds, in which you have seen the Son in his glory to appear unto your souls, with his heavenly healing, warmness, and virtue. Now Friends, this is that which for ever is to be kept to, that the day may be known to increase in the light and glory of it, in its own clearness, without mixture; not mixing with it your own wisdom, thoughts, or carnal imaginations, which do prove such clouds, where they are suffered to arise, that they bring darkness over the understanding, and make the day cloudy and dark, and so occasion wandering, and to some turn the very eyelids of the morning into the shadow of death. And through such things hath the enemy so prevailed over some, that he hath brought them again into the night of everlasting darkness and confusion, ere they have been aware whither he would lead.——

Dear Friends, that which preserves from these dangers, is that arm and power which God revealed in the beginning, by which (as we are witnesses) he redeemed our souls out of many afflictions. And therefore, let it be every one's care, to wait for a clear and sensible feeling of this same power in its own pure nature, to spring up in all your hearts every day; and then will your delight be so in it, and your acquaintance (in a clear understanding) will be so with it, that you will never be deceived, so as to take any other for it. Then to your comfort, will your heavenly peace spring, under the power and government of him, who is the Prince of true peace; and so will your hearts be made truly glad, and weighty, and ponderous, and not be carried about with every wind: for in this is the true and sure establishment of the soul with grace in the covenant of life for ever; and these are they whose peace is of a standing nature, who are not given to change. But this I have always observed, that where there is an uncertain spirit or mind, though in some states into which at times they may come, they may have peace, and feel some refreshment, yet for want of constancy and steadfastness (which is preserved through a true, watchful, and diligent attendance upon that which doth not change, which is sure for ever,) they lose their habitation, and their state of peace, and come to be tossed in their minds, and afflicted in their spirits, and also are the occasion of tossing, affliction, and distress unto others, who not being aware, may sometimes be in danger to suffer with them, when they fly from the word, that should uphold, as it was with Jonah in the days of old. And therefore it is good for every one, to have their hearts established with grace, and in the grace to wait for a settlement; that under the pure teachings thereof, they may be preserved from going into those things that will procure woe:

and so shall every one's state in that which is good, be more and more constant, and then will there be a growing, and going forward and not backward. For that which doth occasion any to linger, or draw back, is carelessness, unbelief, and disobedience; and in such the Lord's soul doth take no pleasure. Therefore in that which doth not change let all live, by which all changeable and mutable thoughts, and imaginations, and desires will be judged down, and the spring of life over all will flow: and the first will be last; for in that the beauty and glory doth stand for ever. And all that abide not in it, and grow in the virtue thereof, whatever they have been, at the best will be but as a fading flower in the head of the fat valley, as it was with Ephraim; the Lord will take no delight in them, but reject them, and cast them out, as such whose beauty is gone, whose gold is become dim, and whose wine is mixed with water: and so as reprobate silver shall they be esteemed even of men, because the Lord hath rejected them.

So the Lord God keep and preserve you all in that which was from the beginning, and will endure unto the end; that therein ye may flourish and grow, as the lilly of the valley, and the tree by the rivers of water. This is the desire of my soul for you all, who truly loves you in the love of God; wherein I remain one with you, and am your brother in the truth.   J. B.

TO MY SOUL.

WRITTEN IN SICKNESS.

Be patient yet, my soul, thou hast not long
To groan beneath accumulated wrong :
Soon, very soon; I trust, the galling yoke
That clogs thee now, for ever shall be broke.
It comes, thy freedom comes; from grief arise;
Prepare, exulting, for thy native skies :
Soon, very soon, this world's unholy dreams,
Its poor possessor', and their trifling schemes
Shall worthless seem to thee as leaves embrown'd
That blasts autumnal scatter o'er the ground.
O then, from all of earthly taint made free,
What scenes unthought thy blessed eyes may see !
Perhaps, commission'd thou shalt bend thy flight,
Where worlds and suns roll far from mortal sight,
And, half'd by beings pure, who know no care,
Thy gracious Master's high behests declare:
Or raptur'd bend, amid the seraph band,
That round the throne of light attending stand,
To golden harps their dulcet voices raise,
And ceaseless hymn the great Creator's praise.
O while such hopes await, can aught on earth,
My conscious soul, to one sad sigh give birth?
Be far each anxious thought, no more repine,
Soon shall the crown of amaranth be thine.
                                    DAVENPORT.

THE FRIEND.

FIFTH MONTH, 9, 1840.

With respect to the short communication on our first page, it may be well to remark, that in transferring the article from the "American Journal of Science" to our pages, we had no intention to espouse the theory which it puts forth, or any other, on a subject in regard to which we confess ourselves totally incompetent to judge. With the style in which it was written we were pleased, and the argument seemed at least ingenious. When the com-

munication in reply presented i appeared to be in it no depart rules of courtesy, we deemed permit its insertion, expecting would there end. We do thi that the proposition of our res tucket friend is perfectly reason not but hope that the writer of the Tails of Comets, in the F ult. will see it in the same l that be the case, and he be wi himself of our agency, probabl in our way to render some servi the object.

—

The annual meeting of Hav Association, will be held in th Room, Friends' meeting house, on second day, the 11th instant, P. M.

CHARLES EVA

—

A meeting of the Concord A Association of Friends, will be h Meeting House, Concord, on se 11th of 5th month, at 11 o'clock female members are respectful attend.

HOWARD YARNALL,

4th mo. 27th, 1840

—

FRIENDS' ASYLU

Committee on Admissions.—
kins, No. 60 Franklin street,
North Fourth street, up stairs ;
gues, No. 185 North Seventh st
41 Market street, up stairs ; 1
No. 129 Filbert street, and No.
street; Edward Yarnall, southv
Twelfth and George streets, and
ket street ; Samuel Bettle, jr.,
Tenth street, and 26 South Fror

Visiting Managers for the 1
decai L. Dawson, No. 332 Arel
Richardson, No. 76 North Tenth
Bettle, Jr., No. 73 North Tenth

Superintendents.—John C.
Redmond.

Attending Physician.—Dr. C
No. 201 Arch street.

Resident Physician.—Dr. Pl

—

MARRIED, on the 23d of 4th mo
Meeting House, in Au Sable, (former
county, New York, SENECA HAZARD,
Hazard, of Ferrisburgh, Vermont, t
daughter of David and Elizabeth Hoa
——, at Friends' Meeting House, N
Carolina, on fifth day, the 23d of
DUNN L. CHAMNESS, of Randolph cou
daughter of Joseph McCollum, of the

—

DIED, of consumption, in Lynn, M
12th mo., 1839, at the residence of her
HANNAH B. DOW, wife of Franklin Do
Maine, in the 25th year of her age. F
previous to her illness, she was impres
that her time was short, and by her
deportment, evinced that she was end
pare for her final change; and althou
ture of her disease she passed throu

THE FRIEND.

A RELIGIOUS AND LITERARY JOURNAL.

VOL. XIII.   SEVENTH DAY, FIFTH MONTH, 16, 1840.   **NO. 33.**

EDITED BY ROBERT SMITH.

PUBLISHED WEEKLY.

Price two dollars per annum, payable in advance.

Subscriptions and Payments received by

GEORGE W. TAYLOR,

NO. 50, NORTH FOURTH STREET, UP STAIRS,

PHILADELPHIA.

SPEECH OF AMBROSE H. SEVIER,

OF ARKANSAS.

In U. S. Senate, March 17, 1840.—In Executive session, on the treaty with the New York Indians.

(Continued from page 251.)

Sir, the Indians being thus tampered with, and prepared by bribes, in advance, for the occasion, our commissioner entered upon the stage for the performance of his part of the drama. And, sir, not to be tedious, to pass over a thousand details, and to come at once to the result, I will inform the senate that our commissioner, after a protracted negotiation, did actually succeed in purchasing for us, the Green Bay lands. And he got these lands for us for the very trifling and frivolous consideration of $400,000 in cash, and 1,800,000 acres of land, west of and adjoining the state of Missouri. Here is a negotiator for you, which I am satisfied that nothing but patience and perseverance and skill and dexterity and adroitness, aided with good friends to " back his suit withal," ever could have achieved. This $400,000 in cash, 1,800,000 acres of land, is all that our commissioner agreed to give for 435,000 acres of land at Green Bay, which five years previously we gave these Indians gratuitously, and which gratuity they would neither move to, nor accept of us as a present!

Appended to this treaty we find an ordinary deed of conveyance from the Tuscaroras to Ogden and Fellows, of all their title to nineteen hundred and twenty acres of land; and from the Senecas, a similar deed of conveyance to Ogden and Fellows of all their title to one hundred and sixteen thousand acres of land, all lying in the state of New York, and some of it in the neighbourhood of Buffalo, and making altogether, from both tribes, in round numbers, about 118,000 acres of land, for which Ogden and Fellows agreed to pay the sum of about two hundred and eleven thousand dollars—not quite two dollars an acre. These deeds are honoured with a preamble, and recite the important fact that a treaty had been concluded between our commissioner and these Indians. These deeds are otherwise distinguished, by being *approved*, not by the superintendent of Massachusetts,

whose duty it probably was to approve them, but they were also approved of by our commissioner, not as a witness, but in his official capacity—and what is still more remarkable, when this treaty came to the senate, in 1838, for ratification, these deeds came with it.

Well, sir, what next occurred? The treaty was read in the senate, was properly referred, and then your committee went to work upon it. They found it so *essentially defective*, that it was out of their power to recommend its ratification. The objections to it were communicated, among others, to the senators from New York. Some alterations in it were suggested by the war department, and all agreed, without a dissenting voice in any quarter, so far as I recollect, that it could not be ratified in the form in which it was excented. We amended it, and so thoroughly, as to make nearly a new treaty out of it; and in these amendments the senate concurred, and I believe with unanimity.

While this treaty was before the committee, we heard many complaints from the Indians and others, against the treaty. Fraud, unfairness, and bribery, of which, *at that time*, we had no evidence, were charged; and it was stated that a majority of the chiefs neither approved of nor had signed the treaty, although from the preamble it purported to have been executed in council, and properly assented to. To guard these charges, the senate adopted the resolution of the 11th of June, 1838, which was recommended by the committee on Indian affairs, and which is as follows:

" *Provided always, and be it further resolved, two thirds of the senate present concurring,* That the treaty shall have no force or effect whatever, as it relates to any of said tribes, nations, or bands of New York Indians, nor shall it be understood that the senate have assented to any of the contracts connected with it, until the same, with the amendments herein proposed, is submitted, and fully and fairly explained, by a commissioner of the United States, to each of said tribes, or bands, separately assembled in council, and they have given their free and voluntary assent thereto; and if one or more of said tribes or bands, when consulted as aforesaid, shall freely assent to said treaty as amended, and to their contract connected therewith, it shall be binding and obligatory upon those so assenting, although other or others of said bands or tribes may not give their assent, and thereby cease to be parties thereto. *Provided, further,* That if any portion or part of said Indians do not emigrate, the president shall retain a proper proportion of said sum of four hundred thousand dollars, and shall also deduct from the quantity of land allowed west of the Mississippi, such number of acres as will leave to each emigrant three hundred and twenty acres only."

Thus it appears that we sanctioned the treaty of the 15th of January, 1838, on the *express condition* that the treaty, as amended by us, should be approved of by a majority of the chiefs of each tribe, separately assembled in open council, and after it had been, by our commissioner, fairly and fully explained *in*

open council, and by a majority of them freely and voluntarily assented to in open council.

Well, sir, what next? With the treaty, as amended, our commissioner was once more despatched to his red brethren, with whom he had previously been so very successful, to obtain their assent to the treaty in its amended form. He received his instructions on the 9th of July, 1838, and was at his post in the month of August following. He succeeded in obtaining the assent of all the tribes but *the Senecas.* These he found, as usual, a little refractory. He met them in council on the 17th of August, in a council house he had built for the purpose; and as many of the chiefs were absent, he, at the request of the Indians, adjourned the council for three days. On his return on the 20th, he found his council house *burnt down*—the work of an incendiary. He built him another, and then fully and fairly explained the treaty and the amendments made to it by the senate. He found the Senecas decided, not upon the subject of selling us the Green Bay lands, but upon the subject of *emigration,* which to us was a matter of no consequence. He gives us the decisions in the tribe, in a very minute and satisfactory manner. He then tells us that

" It will be recollected that at the time of making the original treaty, providing new homes for these Indians at the west, and the means of removing and subsisting them, that another treaty was signed between this tribe and the pre-emption owners, under the supervision of a superintendent from Massachusetts, conveying the Indian rights to their several reservations in New York. That treaty of sale was ratified by the governor and council of Massachusetts. At the late council, it was the sale under this treaty, and not the advantages secured under the one negotiated by me, that formed the principal subject of consideration. The government treaty was generally conceded to be liberal and advantageous; still there appeared to be a settled purpose on the part of some to misrepresent the value of the advantages secured under it, as one means of defeating the other."

Here, Mr. President, we have the whole story, fresh, full, and complete, from the lips of our frank and candid commissioner. *It was the sale to the land company,* brought about, as I have shown you, by bribery and corruption, that has occasioned the failure of our commissioner in perfecting, from this tribe, the purchase of their Green Bay land. Our treaty, he tells us, was considered liberal and advantageous, and with it no fault was found, and, I confess, it would have been passingly strange to me, if there had been any objections to it.

And now let me ask, if our *real* object had been to purchase the Green Bay land, why was our treaty embarrassed by negotiating with them for their removal beyond the Mississippi? Why not let them remain? they are not in our way. We are not bound, in any manner that I know of, to purchase their lands for these pre-emptioners. What have they done for "the state" that we should give them a million or so of dollars, in cash and land, to aid them in their speculations. Sir, our commissioner desired honour, and glory, and promotion; and he was taught to believe, and no doubt truly, that if, by negotiation, he could succeed in getting those Indians out of New York and over the Mississippi, at the expense of the United States, that glory, and honour, and promotion would be his reward.

Sir, the Green Bay lands, if ever the subject of *serious* discussion at any time, were all along considered but a trifling matter with either the Indians or our negotiator. But I proceed, for I have yet, sir, a good deal of ground to travel over.

The commissioner tells us, that, "at an early period of the council, that Marius B. Pierce, then an opponent of the treaty, in public council proposed to me the following questions:"

"1. If the amendments of the treaty were not now assented to, whether I could adjourn the council; and whether, if not adjourned, it could be again convened?

"2. Whether the senate could recede from its amendments?

"I was also asked, at about the same time, by others in council, whether the deed to the pre-emptive purchasers, being ratified by the governor and council of Massachusetts, was obligatory upon the nation, without further action on the part of the nation? Also, whether the senate of the United States had any legal jurisdiction over the subject?"

To these questions the commissioner declined giving any answer; and as he has not condescended to tell us why these questions were asked, I will endeavour to supply his omissions as I feel myself able to do, from the testimony before us. The first question was asked because the opponents of the treaty then had a majority in council against the treaty, and were able to vote it down, and he was apprehensive that the commissioner might keep adjourning the council from day to day, until a majority might be got *in some way or other* to assent to the treaty. He and his friends were then neglecting their private affairs; were poor, without money, and depended for their bread upon their daily labour. They wanted to see the council closed, that they might go home; they were unwilling that the council should be kept open any longer, or convened again, after it was closed. These were Pierce's reasons for asking the first question.

He asked the second, because he had been told, as an inducement for their agreeing to the treaty, that the senate would, *if necessary*, recede from its amendments, and that the treaty would be ratified as originally made, and then, in that event, they would lose the *rewards* and *life-leases*, &c. which they then had it within their power to obtain from their friends, the generous and liberal minded pre-emptioners.

The third question was asked, because they were told the New York land was gone at any rate—that their deeds had been approved by the governor and council of Massachusetts. The commissioner also declined answering this question; but afterwards, "learning that General Dearborn had expressed a 'different opinion,'" (from that expressed by the head of the Indian bureau, and by Mr. Ward, a clerk of that bureau,) "I informed the council of it,

and General Dearborn gave Governor Everett's reasons for his opinions. The Indians were then left to form their own conclusions on the question of title and probable action of the senate. *I then informed the Indians, that if the interests of the Indians required it,* I believed I had the right, and should adjourn the council to some future day." Yes, sir; and he did adjourn the council. The opinions of Governor Everett, respecting the validity of the sale, produced this result. The pre-emptioners could no longer frighten them "with the scarecrow" that their lands were gone. This being the case, it became necessary for the pre-emptioners to change their mode of attack; and time was necessary to agree upon the *modus operandi;* and therefore the council was adjourned.

The next entertainment we have of the commissioner is as follows:

"Learning from the discussions in council, that many desired to remain longer than five years on their reservations, I induced the agent of the pre-emptive owners, on the 26th of September last, to authorise me in writing, to say to the council that he would, on behalf of the pre-emptive purchasers, agree to allow them to occupy their farming lands ten, instead of five years. His proposition is marked No. 30. This offer did not, as *was anticipated*, produce unanimity of feeling. Some said it was their desire to remain for their lives; but that they were willing others might remove if they chose to do so. In connection with General Dearborn, I requested the agent to offer life leases, free of rent, to all who chose to remain. His offer to do so is marked No. 31. Without consulting with a single individual, a chief in the opposition, by the name of Israel Jemison, rose and stated that he was authorised to say that the opposition *unanimously* declined the proposition. Knowing that no one had authorised him to speak on a subject but that moment named in council, I did not consider his statement entitled to any respect. No one of the opposition rising to set him right in such a case of palpable falsehood, I became satisfied of the truth of the allegation so often made, that many *dare* not speak their minds in council, and that compulsion was used to prevent chiefs from signing."

He talks of *fear* and *compulsion!* Why should they fear? Why should Indian warriors manifest a timidity which, in a virtuous cause, would disgrace even their squaws? They fear because they are in a minority, and know they are doing, *from base and mercenary considerations,* what a majority of their people disapprove of. Their fear is but the palpable evidence of a guilty heart! An honest man, red or white, fears nothing! Cowardice and trembling are the attributes of a guilty conscience!

He tells us that—

"Immediately after communicating and explaining the offer of life leases to all who desired them, I presented the manuscript copy of the amended treaty, to which I had attached a written assent. I informed the council that those who chose to do so could sign. It there, and those who, *from fear, or other cause,* preferred signing at my room in presence of myself, the superintendent from Massachusetts, the agent, and such other persons as might be present, might do so. I then received sixteen signatures, and subsequently at my room, in presence of General Dearborn, thirteen, and two other signatures at the rooms of chiefs who were too unwell to attend council, making in all thirty-one chiefs."

Yes, sir, with all the bribery I have previously alluded to, with *life leases, free of rent, for all who chose to stay,* embracing the *whole tribe,* we yet find the commissioner unable to get, in *open council,* as he was required

to do by the resolution but *sixteen signatures* one, to the amended to these sixteen, he obt council, but at his pri natures of assent of thi *own residence* the sig making, in all, but thir fore stated, out of eigh to the Seneca nation. case, he then, on the bouring, if not prayin wards of forty days in heathens, he informed tioners, *(not the India negotiating,)*

He adjourned the c November.

"On adjourning the co which is marked No. 39. posed to emigration did not and, in making it, I did w and *to the purchasers.* If t signed, it may be done at a gration party, who have li government, may be saved would otherwise await then tures sufficient to meet your turn out that the legal titl the condition of the Senecas would be without a home, t offered to them."

Poor Senecas! how s ed they are! Why will pathetic advice of the go ly delivered, and save tl sion? Why will they so happen that the title in the purchasers, how condition? Why will one else but the commi that if the treaty should they would be without their Green Bay lands sell us? What insanity they are in desiring to homes and firesides! hearted they are, in refi mane and benevolent, God-serving pre-empti Senecas!! How you headed fathers of the se

Mr. President, we sioner laying aside his tions, and talking math ing the number of chiefi and their *manner of si* the question to the secr it be necessary to have chiefs upon the reserva

"If so [he says] it was n presence. [And he might sufficiently in open council, done by the Senate's reso signed by more than a majo attended the council. [He we would not otherwise pro

this is what is usually required in legislative bodies, and reasoning from analogy, the assent is sufficiently signed. If it requires a majority of all who may have been from time to time, for short periods, at council, it is not in my power to give you the necessary facts whereon to decide."

Now, sir, our most worthy commissioner, (who is an ex-member of congress, and who, on that account, should be presumed to be familiar with the proceedings of deliberative bodies,) has lost sight of one very important point in his analogy, which is, that the official acts of members of congress, out of their respective houses, (alias, the councils,) are nugatory. Does he not know that if members of congress were to sign their assent to the passage of bills, or if senators to the ratification of treaties, at their private rooms or lodgings, as this Indian assent (in part) was signed, that it would be nugatory, nonsensical, and unconstitutional? I leave the question to himself to answer. Speaking of analogies, I will go a little farther, and as he has said it better than I can say it, I will avail myself of the remarks of Gov. Everett upon this subject:

"The treaty making power [says the governor] is granted by the constitution in general terms. No modification of its exercise, in reference to Indian tribes, is recognised, as it would certainly be unconstitutional for the president of the United States to attempt to treat with individual members of any foreign state or government, (not duly authorised to represent such body,) or to attempt to obtain the ratification of a treaty by means of the assent of individuals of the senate, not duly assembled and acting as such." "I remain of opinion that the constitutionality of attempting to obtain the assent of individual Indian chiefs to the amended treaty, in the manner in question, is doubtful."

Sir, were ever these old, safe, rational, and salutary rules dispensed with by our government, in treating with any nation, foreign or domestic, civilised or savage? I know of no dispensation of those time-honoured and customary forms in any case whatever. I hold, that if it be necessary to treat at all, that we should treat according to the ordinary and constitutional forms.

The commissioner concludes his report by telling us, what we could well have imagined, that all the expenses of the amended treaty had been defrayed by the United States; and thinks if any further expenses are to be incurred, that the pre-emption purchasers should pay *their part of it*. He ought to have said the *whole of it*, as it would all be for their private benefit.

The report of General Dearborn to Governor Everett corresponds, in the main, with that of Mr. Gillett, and therefore I shall not be considered, I hope, as treating that able state paper with disrespect, if I dispose of it very briefly. General Dearborn tells us that,

"Among the numerous and very cogent reasons which were urged by the commissioner for inducing the Indians to assent to the amended treaty, during the progress of the long protracted deliberations, he observed that he had been directed by the officer at the head of the bureau of the Indian department, to state, as his opinion, that the contract of the Indians for the sale of their right of possession to the Ogden company was complete, and might be carried into effect, whether the treaty with the United States was ratified or not.

"As this was the only statement made by the commissioner to which I did not fully concur, I informed the chiefs it became my duty to announce to them that the governor of Massachusetts entertained a different view of the subject; and was authorised to state, that unless the amendments made to the treaty were assented to, he considered the contracts, for the sale of their right of possession, null and void; but that he did not undertake, peremptorily, to decide a question of such great importance; that it was one which required the most grave and deliberate consideration, and must ultimately be referred to the highest judicial tribunals of the country, if it should be insisted on by the pre-emptioners.

"It was, therefore, for the chiefs to determine how far their decision was to be influenced by the doubtful position in which the subject was placed, from these conflicting opinions; for if they should reject the treaty, and the contracts for the sale of their reservations were declared binding, they would be left without a home."

This disclosure needs no comment. The unfairness and reprehensibility, on the part of the commissioner, of the use of such terrible and unsound arguments to the ignorant Senecas, is obvious to all. The general also tells us, that

"The commissioner was induced to afford the last named accommodation, in consequence of having been informed that there were several chiefs who were in favour of emigration, but were afraid to sign the treaty publicly, as they had been threatened with fatal consequences if they did. Intimidation has been extensively used by the leaders and their partisans in the opposition, for the purpose of defeating the wishes of those who are desirous of removing to the west. The commissioner was informed by the chiefs of the Tuscaroras, that threats had been sent to them from the Tonawanda reservation, to deter them from ratifying the treaty.

"It had been repeatedly represented, during the last council and the present, that there were a number of Indians, and especially among the aged, who were desirous to remain here, and who often observed: 'Let the young go to the new country, beyond the great river, if they wish, but we are too old to begin new establishments; we had rather live and die where we have so long resided, on the land of our fathers.' To obviate this objection to the ratification of the treaty, the commissioner recommended to the pre-emptioners that they should offer to give leases for life, free of rent, to such Indians as were anxious to remain, and I concurred in opinion as to the propriety of that measure, believing that it would not only be just towards the Indians, but considered as beneficent, magnanimous, and liberal on their part, let the result be what it may; that I considered it important it should be done in open council, and made general in its operation, to preclude every ground of complaint or misrepresentation.

"The pre-emptive agents having been finally induced to adopt that measure, a communication was made to the commissioner, for carrying it into effect, which he laid before the assembled chiefs immediately after he had concluded his remarks on the method in which the assent was to be given to the treaty.

"One of the chiefs, in behalf of those in the opposition, then rose and stated, that they did not desire to avail themselves of the offer which had just been made by the pre-emptive owners; and observed that they wished the council might be kept open, after those had signed the treaty who were present, as they desired to execute, in the presence of the commissioner of the United States and superintendent of Massachusetts, a written declaration of their dissent. The commissioner replied that he was not authorised to authenticate any document other than such as he had been specially directed to submit for their consideration, and therefore could not with propriety keep the council open for the purpose which had been stated.

"I was then reminded by another chief of the opposition party, that I had informed them on the opening of the council, although I was not instructed to advise them either to remain where they were or to emigrate to the Indian territory in the west, I had been sent there by the governor of Massachusetts to see that impartial justice was done to the Seneca nation of Indians, and that I had observed, on another occasion, I should not be deterred by the flash of the tomahawk or the crack of the rifle in the independent and honest discharge of my duty; and as I should be a witness to such of the chiefs as were in favour of emigration, who signed the treaty, 'MY HEAD WOULD NOT BE STRAIGHT' unless I also verified their proceedings; and then asked me if I would remain for that purpose.

"I answered, that I considered it my duty to comply with all proper requests, from any portion of the Seneca Indians, so far as it was in my power to do so; that I should, with great pleasure, remain and witness the signatures to the declaration which it was proposed to execute, after the commissioner of the United States retired from the council house.

"As many of the emigration chiefs were absent, only sixteen names were affixed to the treaty, in council, on the 28th ult.; and immediately after the adjournment, the written declaration of the chiefs opposed to emigration was produced and signed in my presence."

Here we find that our commissioner refused to receive the list of the names of the dissenting chiefs, or what they called their protest, which was tendered him *in open council*. But General Dearborn, who is a military man—a man of mettle—who is not, as he informs us, to be "deterred from a faithful discharge of his duty by the flash of the tomahawk or the crack of the rifle," did receive and witness this dissent, or protest; and he forwarded it, according to the request of the Senecas, to Governor Everett. This protest contained the names of *sixty chiefs*, out of eighty-one, and is to be found in our printed document, at page 174. Here ends my review of the reports of Messrs. Gillett and Dearborn, upon their first embassy. They had another, which I will briefly dispose of; but, before doing so, it will be necessary to notice the official action of the head of the Indian bureau, upon our commissioner's report. Let us now see how Mr. Crawford viewed this matter. Mr. Crawford says, in his letter to the secretary of war, of the 29th of October, 1838:

"The only difficulty in the way of regarding the acts of the Indians as meeting the resolution of the senate, that appears to me insuperable, concerns the assent reported to have been given by the Senecas. There are in this band seventy-eight chiefs. The assent of sixteen was obtained in council, of thirteen at the room of the commissioner, and of two others at their own quarters, making thirty-one; and, since the arrival of Mr. Gillett in Washington, he has received the written assents of five more, properly authenticated, making an aggregate of thirty-six. The commissioner reports that not more than sixty-one chiefs attended the council at one time, and that thirty-six is more than one half of the number of chiefs that probably gave their attendance in council at all the meetings; two of the chiefs, it is said, hold a questionable authority, and two have removed from the country. Is this an assent of the tribe by the chiefs? The authority of the band resides in *all* the chiefs; and although uniformity in their views can scarcely be expected, at least a majority of the chiefs, not of those who appeared in council, but of all upon the reservation, it strikes me should consent to constitute the 'free and voluntary assent' *of the tribe*. Deduct the two who, it is represented, exercise a doubtful authority, and the two who have removed, and seventy-four chiefs of the Senecas remain, of whom, including the five whose assents were not attached to the modified treaty, but transmitted by mail, and we have thirty-six only. The last five, in my opinion, cannot be reckoned; but I have not noted more particularly the defective manner of their assenting, because it was, in the view taken, unimportant. Perhaps, too, it *was intended by the senate that they should consent in council*. Mr. Gillett states in his report that a printed copy of the treaty and amendments was handed him, to which was affixed the signatures of thirty-five chiefs and one hundred and seventeen warriors, declaring their assent thereto. *This writing is dated six days before the assent in council was obtained, preceded, as I presume, the full explanations of the commissioner, and, although witnessed by James Stryker, United States sub-agent, and H. P. Wilcox, and no doubt fairly obtained ; (for it embraces the names affixed to the assent prepared by Mr. Gillett, and four additional ones,) can scarcely, it seems to me, be considered as within the intent of the senate. If, however, you should think differently, the four chiefs added to the whole 'number first mentioned, would 'give forty assenting chiefs out of seventy-eight. Even if the legal right was as clear the one way as it appears to be the other, would it be expedient to act upon it ? The Senecas are evidently divided into two very nearly equal parties, the one for and the other against the treaty, splitting on the subject of emigration, which is much to be regretted. Their own true interest and the liberal views of the government they do not comprehend, and however desirable it is that they should leave New York, which would be the probable, but not the necessary consequence of the ratification of the treaty, one half of them appear to be otherwise determined for the present. The report and accompanying papers show that much excitement prevails among them on the subject, and makes it so certain that but for bad advice they would accede to the proposed terms, which perhaps a renewed application might find them willing to do. For this last purpose the door is still open, as the council was adjourned to the 15th of November next."*

(Remainder next week.)

On the Habits and Instincts of Animals. By William Swainson, A. C. G., Fellow of the Royal Society, and of several Foreign Academies.

The above is the title of a volume proceeding from the London press within the current year. It is divided into eleven chapters, chiefly made up of interesting facts, illustrative of the subjects treated of in each respectively, viz :—On the instincts of the animal world, as different from human reason—on the senses, the passions, the motions of animals—the means of defence possessed by them, and the injuries, direct and indirect, inflicted by them—on their hybernation, torpidity, and migration—on imperfect and perfect societies of animals, and on luminous animals.

Upon the complicated and much discussed question relative to the nature of instinct, the author takes the ground that it is clearly distinct from the superior gift of reason, the latter exclusively pertaining to man.

His reasoning in support of this position, appears to us lucid and fully satisfactory. We commence with citing a considerable portion of this, and in subsequent numbers propose to offer a selection from the instructive and entertaining facts with which the volume abounds.

We shall not repeat all that has been said on the nature of instinct ; but a few remarks may, perhaps, strengthen our position, that MIND is totally distinct from this lower faculty, both in its intention, its operation, and its ultimate result. The *intention* of instinct is simply to fulfil those functions of volition which each particular species is peculiarly organised to perform. The lowest development of instinct is probably seen in those molluscous animals, which are fixed to rocks, and merely open their mouth, or their shelly covering—as does the oyster—for the purpose of imbibing nourishment ; the instinct of the parent having prompted it to deposit its eggs, or spawn, in such a locality, rather than upon a soft muddy or sandy beach. The woodpecker is

led to alight upon the perpendicular bole of a tree, rather than on the ground, because, in one situation, its scansorial feet enable it to climb with rapidity, while, upon the other, it could scarcely walk. Ascending by such progressive steps as these, we may come to the elephant, the honey-guide, and the bee—the most apparently rational of the three most perfect orders of animals ; and yet in their ordinary habits, the same principle holds good. There are, indeed, instances upon record, of such extraordinary actions performed by animals, as to induce the suspicion that a higher power of discrimination, of judgment, or of forethought, had been given to them, than what is ordinarily implied by the term instinct ; yet, before we can confound such high developements of this faculty with *mind* or reason, we must well consider the perfections of these latter, and the necessary consequences which result from their possession. We know not, indeed, the limits of *instinct ;* but we know full well, inductively, by natural religion, and assuredly, by revealed, that man, an accountable being : and no theorist will go so far as to suppose, that the same may be said of a bee, or an oyster !

The *operations* of instinct are limited to those circumstances which tend only to keep the species in the same state of intelligence (so to speak) in which it was born. There is no progressive advancement, in succeeding generations, by which a higher advance is made either by the communication of experience, or the effects of example, in higher animals. Each species has its own limited range, and there its powers cease. The ox, which "knows his master's crib," and followed the patriarchs in their journeys, four thousand years ago, was not less intelligent than those of the present day ; and the dogs of Nimrod were, probably, as far advanced in civilisation as those possessed by our modern hunters. The wild ass of Scripture—which was probably the zebra—is still the same untameable inhabitant of the desert ; and all the efforts of man to make him obedient to the curb have been utterly fruitless. The hen does not discriminate between a real and an artificial egg ; and the tomtit will still go on building her nest in the same hole, after it has been destroyed four or five times. These, and a thousand similar instances, may be cited to illustrate what we have just advanced.

But, it may be said, instinct is improvable by what is called domestication. And when we hear of learned pigs, birds firing cannon, and tigers becoming tame as kittens, who shall determine how far such intelligence may be carried ? True ; but we may ask, again, are these acquired faculties, unnatural as they certainly are, transmitted ? Are they not the effect of a long, and often inhuman, training ? and do they not perish with the possessor ? The extent of cultivated instinct, as we may properly term all these acquired habits, is only to be known by experiments ; and these have been carried sufficiently far, as to convince us that the faculties thus called forth, do not touch upon any one of those prerogatives which, we shall hereafter shew, belong to REASON. In a former volume, we established

the fact, that a uniform aptitude for domestication is not spread over the whole of the higher animals ; but that, on the contrary, it has been more especially granted to such as Infinite Wisdom has set apart for the service, or the sustenance, of MAN. He may, indeed, arrogantly vaunt that, in training such to his use, he conquers nature ; but the boast is not only idle, but absolutely groundless. He does no more than bring out latent qualities, planted by another and an Almighty Hand. One might be tempted, therefore, to imagine that those animals would always exhibit the nearest approach to reason, which had been domesticated from time immemorial. But this, if we except, perhaps, the elephant, is assuredly not the case. The ants and the bees, as we shall hereafter show, possess an instinct far above all other known animals ; yet they have never been domesticated, nor can we conceive how their admirable economy could be improved. The operations of their instincts appear to carry them no further than what is necessary to the well-being of each particular species, which every naturalist knows is more or less dissimilar. There are, indeed, a few anecdotes, which occasionally appear in our natural history and other periodicals, of such a marvellous nature, as to indicate reasoning faculties among brutes ; but we look on these statements with the same degree of scepticism as those which vouch for living toads being inclosed in solid marble ; for no real naturalist, scrupulously jealous of the greatest possible accuracy, has put them forward. Such, then, are the *operations* of instinct. In defining them, we have also given their *ultimate results.* They tend to nothing more than the economy of the present life : they have no relation to the improvement of existing communities, or the transmission of knowledge to succeeding generations : each individual, however highly gifted by nature, or improved by art, passes away, and is forgotten. The end of its creation, in the economy of nature, is fulfilled : it has had all the enjoyment of animal life, which, from its very nature, it was alone capable of receiving ; it followed its own appetites, its own wishes, and its own will. No consciousness of moral obligation or responsibility was given to it when alive, therefore there remains no ultimate object to be accomplished after its death.

Let us now turn to that higher species of volition, to which *we assign the term reason ;* and in like manner consider its intention, its operation, and its ultimate results. We are free to confess that the higher and the lower faculties, viewed merely in some of their operations, appear so intimately blended, that it becomes impossible to mark their limits, by the naked facts they unfold. Man, it is true, is guided by instinct, more or less, in every stage of his existence—from the moment when he turns to the maternal breast, to that at which he expires. The economy of a state of probation renders it absolutely necessary that he should be subject to the animal instincts and passions of the brute creation ; for, were it otherwise, there would have been no occasion for his being peculiarly gifted with a higher and a controlling power. This power is REASON: and with this intent, in a primary sense, has it been granted to us—and to us only. Reason, in fact, is almost but another name for *mind*, or that principle which guides our volition, whether for the better or the worse, in all such cases as come not within the scope of animal instinct. Reason is superadded to instinct, as a distinct faculty, and is not a mere expansion of the same power. The history of the world, unfortunately, exhibits too many instances of men—particularly among the ancients—endowed with the noblest developement of this power, who, yet, have given themselves up to the most gross and brutish sensualities; thus exhibiting the animal propensities of the one faculty in its most pitiable force—since it was accompanied by a total prostration of the other —one hour a philosopher, the next a debauchee.

The operations of reason, again, are very different from those of instinct; it commences not, like the latter, in early infancy—but is of slow growth. There is nothing to contradict the hypothesis—that all the powers of instinct an animal will ever possess, are given to it so soon as it quits the sustenance it may derive from the parent, and begins to provide for itself. It will be observed, that a kitten is just as wary and cunning at catching such birds and mice as it can conquer, as is its mother; and a young duckling will swim, dive, and procure its food, with the same ease and expertness as its parents. But the operation of reason, as every one knows, is quite different. It is dormant at an age when the animal instincts have long begun to show themselves; and only awakens, and asserts its claim to be heard, when the passions and the inclinations of advanced youth require the discretion and control which it was intended to exercise. But, although it comes slowly into being, and is afterwards always liable to be affected by the infirmities of the body, its growth is not for time, but for eternity. It may be clouded by anxiety, dimmed by sickness, or perverted by evil; but still it does not, of necessity, permanently lose its force, as do several of the animal instincts, in proportion to the decay of the body. We pretend not to frame any hypothesis by which to account for the apparent extinction of right-mindedness, or reason, in maniacs, further than to suppose that causes, moral or physical, have operated to the total or partial derangement of a faculty which, nevertheless, exists in full force, although in a perverted state. But this is certain—that the powers of reason, in sane and well regulated minds, are in their full vigour and expansion, long after the animal functions of the body have begun to decay; and that innumerable instances might be quoted, of the reasoning mind preserving all its depth, and acuteness, and discrimination, when the animal man is fast approaching that age which the Psalmist has measured out. To all but the Christian philosopher, who inwardly feels that *mind* is indestructible, and therefore immortal, nothing can be more depressing, inconsistent, and unaccountable, than to see those favoured beings, who have been gifted with a high developement of this faculty—and which they are employing for the good of others—gradually

sinking into old age and decrepitude, at a time when their mind, although clouded by a diseased body, is still sending forth rays of genius and of wisdom—the accumulated results of thoughtful experience and calm deliberation.

One would imagine that such a picture as this—and they are thickly dispersed in the pages of human history—would force upon the conviction of every unbeliever, the immortality of mind, and of the reasoning faculty. If these were the same as instinct, where would be the necessity of preserving them in vigour, when all the rest of the human economy is hastening to decay? The whole of the animal races show us that every thing is perfection in its kind; that, so soon as one part of the animal frame begins to decay, all the others evince the same propensity; and that no one creature exhibits a deviation from this rule, but that which has been pronounced the most perfect —Man. Old age deadens all the animal faculties, but leaves the mental sound, hale, and even in a yet expanding progress; the oil burns with brightness, while the earthen lamp that contains it is fast mouldering to its parent dust. Why is this inconsistency? Clearly, because the one is indestructible, and the other perishable. The former is still to grow on in another and a brighter world, unshackled by a companionship with animal instinct. The time of its probation, uninfluenced by the state of the body, arrives—and it is then to receive its reward or its punishment, according as it has been exercised to control the animal instincts, or to become their slave.

The ultimate objects of reason are clearly those pointed to in the last paragraph; but the right use of it can only be learned by revelation. The past and present history of the human race shows us, that, without this guide, the most perverted uses have been, and are now, daily made of this faculty. The savage, indeed, reasons with himself according to the degree of developement which this power has attained in his mind; and we know, by daily experience, in others, if not in ourselves, how much the faculty may be enlarged. Nevertheless, the usages, the customs, and the prejudices of every nation oppose insuperable obstacles to a right and unperverted exercise of reason, which nothing but a divine standard of laws can possibly clear away. The gospel was ushered into the world at a time when human reason in the polished schools of Greece, may be said to have attained its height—on purpose to show how utterly incompetent that wisdom was, to instruct mankind in the true intentions of this faculty. In perusing the works of the sages of that age, we find the most noble, and even godlike sentiments, and the most profound reflections, mixed up with others of a completely opposite character—reasoning so perverted, as to sanction, in the first intellectual nation that ever existed, acts which would disgrace savages, and from which even the lowest of civilised beings would instinctively turn with disgust. The heathen, indeed, has a law written in his mind, which he is bound to fulfil—and, if he walk by this, he is in the hands of a merciful judge; but with the Christian it is otherwise. His Maker has given him, in revelation, a

guide both for his moral and religious duties; the right use of reason is, to diffuse those principles into all his actions; and he has the exclusive power of communicating to his cotemporaries, and of leaving to his successors, the fruits of his own experience ;—faculties which belong not to that animal intelligence we term instinct.

(To be continued.)

ANECDOTES RESPECTING THE BIBLE.

There are a few anecdotes relating to the publication of the first authorised translation of the Bible, which are well worth recording, as demonstrative of the temper in which our ancestors received the blessing, and the use they made of it. A command was issued that every church should be provided with one of these folio Bibles. It was done; but the anxiety of such of the people as could, to read the precious volume, and of such as could not, to handle and turn over the pages of that book, which they had been in the habit of regarding as a thing of mystery and prohibition, was so great, that it was found necessary to chain them for security to the desks. In a country church I have seen the very Bible, and the very chain, preserved as relics, which, three hundred years ago, attested the popular feeling on this subject. But so deeply rooted were the old prejudices of the governing authorities, that it was four years after the Bible was placed in the churches, before the king could be persuaded to revoke the decrees which forbade his subjects to have it in their private possession. At last they were *graciously permitted, by royal license*, to purchase Bibles for their own reading at home. Then it was that every body who could afford it, bought a copy of the Scriptures; such as could not buy the whole, purchased detached passages. A cart load of hay was known to be given for a few chapters of St. Paul's Epistles. And many there were, who, having learned to read in their old age, that they might have pleasure in poring over the written word, and reading with their own eyes the wonderful things of God, exclaimed with the prophet, "Thy words were found and I did eat them; and thy word was unto me, the joy and rejoicing of my heart." The crosses and public places, often presented the moving sight of men, women and children, crowding round a reader who was rehearsing the songs of Zion, and the prophecies of the seers of Israel, or the tender discourses of the Redeemer of mankind.

One poor man, named John Marbeck, was so desirous of making himself master of a Bible, that he determined to write one out, because he had not money enough to buy one; and when he had accomplished that laborious task, he set about the still more trying toil of making a concordance.

"They would hide the forbidden treasure under the floors of their houses," says Blunt in his admirable 'Sketch of the Reformation,' which every body should read, "and put their lives in peril rather than forego the book they desired; they would sit up all night, their doors being shut for fear of surprise, reading or hearing others read, the Bible; they would bury themselves in the woods, and there converse with it in solitude : they would tend their herds in the fields, and still steal an hour for drinking in the good tidings of great joy.

Such being the avidity with which the Scriptures were cherished, let the reader imagine the consternation which overwhelmed the pious of this country, when the capricious Henry reversed his former decrees in favour of biblical learning, and threatened his people with imprisonment, confiscation, and fine, if any below the privileged classes should presume to search the Scriptures. This terrible stretch of royal prerogative was confirmed by act of parliament in 1543 ;—and it seemed like a seal of human folly and infatuation, forced by a tyrant king, and a subservient senate, to refute future calumnies against Protestantism, and to be handed down to posterity, as proof that the reformation was carried on, not by the cold mechanism of state politics, but by the fervent zeal, and undaunted devotion of holy men, in spite of kings and parliaments. Our protestant forefathers would have been crushed, and their names and their labours clean forgotten, if the will of their temporal and spiritual rulers could have been accomplished. This proclamation of 1543 set forth that " No books were to be printed about religion without the king's consent ; none might read the Scripture in any open assembly, or expound it, but he who was licensed by the king or his ordinary. Every *nobleman* or *gentleman* might cause the bible to be read to him in or about his house. Every merchant, who was a housekeeper, might also read it, but no woman, nor artificers, apprentices, journeymen, serving-men under the degree of yeoman, and no husbandman, nor labourer, might read it."

Such were the struggles of Protestantism !— Nearly two hundred years after Wickliffe's translation first appeared, even after the authorised version was published and circulated, the king, who is falsely described by our opponents as the nursing-father of our faith, strove by every means with which absolute power invested him, to stifle the infant religion, which he is said to have engendered.

There is a curious document still in existence, which shows what was felt by the humble and lowly Christians of that day, who were thought too degraded in intellect to be permitted to read in the bible. It is in the form of a note, made by a shepherd, in the spare leaf of a book, which he bought after the passing of the act above referred to :—" At Oxford in the year 1546 brought down to Seynbury, by John Darley, price 14d. When I kept Mr. Letymer's, I bought this book, when the Testament was abrogated, that shepherds might not read it. I pray God amend that blindiness. Writ by Robert Williams, keeping sheep upon Seynbury Hill, 1546."— *Our Protestant Forefathers, by W. S. Gilly.*

From Murray's Encyclopedia of Geography.

KARNAC AND LUXOR—UPPER EGYPT.

" Above Kous, for some miles, is a sandy plain, after which the rocks approach close to the river. Beyond a projecting point, however, the view opens upon a scene to which the world presents nothing parallel ; an ex-

tensive plain covered throughout its whole extent with the most amazing ruins. This is Thebes ; the city of the hundred gates, that mighty capital, the foundation of which is unknown in history, and belongs only to the dim ages of traditionary poetry, whose report would have been denounced as fabulous, had not such mighty monuments proved that it fell short of the reality. This work of the first age of the world almost eclipses, as to grandeur, all that art and power have since produced. At first, the observer sees only a confusion of portals, obelisks, and columns, all of gigantic size, towering above the palm trees. Gradually he is able to distinguish, on the eastern, or Arabian side, the palaces of Karnac and Luxor ; on the western or Syrian side, Medineh, Ava, the Memnonium, and the tombs cut in the mountain behind.

Karnac surpasses in grandeur every other structure in Thebes and in the world. The French engineers on horseback were an hour and a half in performing its circuit, which they therefore conceive, cannot be less than three miles. On the northeast entrance the Egyptians appear to have lavished all their magnificence. The approach is by a long avenue of sphinxes, the largest of any known in Egypt, leading to a succession of portals with colossal statues in front. These structures are distinguished, not only by the grandeur of their dimensions, but by the variety of the materials. A calcareous stone, compact like marble, a variegated siliceous limestone, beautiful rose coloured and black marbles of Syrene have been severally used. " Most points of view present only the image of a general overthrow, rendering it difficult to distinguish Karnac as a series of regular edifices.—Across vast ruins appear only fragments of architecture, trunks of broken columns, mutilated colossal statues ; obelisks, some fallen, others majestically erect ; immense halls, whose roofs are supported by a forest of columns, portals and propylæa, surpassing in magnitude all similar structures. From the west, this chaos assumes an orderly appearance ; and the almost endless series of portals, gates, and halls appear ranged in regular succession, harmonising with each other. When the plan is thoroughly understood, its regularity appears wonderful, and the highest admiration is excited by the arrangement and symmetry of all the parts of this vast edifice.

Not only the general extent, but all the particular features, of this extraordinary structure are distinguished by a magnitude elsewhere unparalleled. There are two obelisks of 69, and one of 91 feet high; this, the loftiest of any in Egypt, is adorned with sculptures of perfect execution.—The principal hall is 318 feet long, and 159 broad, having the roof still supported by 134 columns.—These are about 70 feet high, and 11 feet in diameter, and a long avenue of others have all, except one, fallen down entire, and lie on the ground still ranged in their primitive order. All the sculptures are adorned with colours, which, though they ought, it should seem, to have most experienced the ravages of time, shine still with the brightest lustre. Of the largest sphinxes, fifty are still remaining, and there are traces which show that the whole avenue once contained 600.

The palace is entered with great difficulty, and its interior, being dark and filled with rubbish, presents few objects to attract the attention ; but on reaching the roof, the spectator enjoys a distinct and most magnificent view of the whole range of surrounding ruins. All who have visited this scene describe the impression made by it as almost superior to that caused by any other earthly sight. According to Denon, the whole French army, on arriving in sight, stood still, struck as it were with an electric shock. The scene, according to Jollois and Devilliers, appears to be rather the produce of an imagination surrounding itself with images of fantastic grandeur, than any thing belonging to real existence.

Belzoni, in particular, declares that the most sublime ideas which can be formed from the most magnificent specimens of our present architecture, would give a very inadequate picture of these ruins. It appeared to him that he was entering a city of departed giants. He seemed alone in the midst of all that was most sacred in the world. The forest of enormous columns, adorned all around with beautiful figures and various ornaments ; the high portals seen at a distance from the openings to this vast labyrinth of edifices ; the various groups of ruins in the other temples ; these, altogether, had such an effect upon his mind, as to separate him in imagination from the rest of mortals. For some time he seemed unconscious whether he was on terrestrial ground or some other planet.

If Karnac is unrivalled in the grandeur and extent of its remains, the temple of Luxor, as a single and beautiful object, seems superior to any thing else in Egypt. The view from the river is peculiarly beautiful, when, across the verdant islands with which it is studded, appears a white plain covered with palm trees, over which these colossal masses throw their shadows; while, behind, the Arabian mountain chain forms the boundary of the landscape. The approach is through the village of Luxor, whose crowded and miserable huts form a strange contrast with these monuments of ancient splendour. At length the portico appears, by the side of which are seen two of the most beautiful obelisks in the world, each rising to the height of eighty feet, yet composed of a single block of the finest granite from the quarries of Syrene. By what means such colossal masses were conveyed to so great a distance, and placed in their present position, surpasses the conception of modern art.

Behind them are two colossal statues, now studiously defaced and deep sunk in the sand, but which must have been forty feet high, and composed of a single block of the same granite.—The propylon is 200 feet in height, rising forty-seven feet above the present level of the soil ; the interior is equally grand. It presents to the view upwards of two hundred columns of different dimensions, many of them ten feet in diameter, and most in an entire state. But nothing is more remarkable in this edifice than the profusion of sculptures with which the obelisks, the walls, and all the apartments are covered. These, indeed, are favourite ornaments of all the Egyptian edifices, and remarkably frequent in the palace of Karnac ; but they occur here in unexampled profusion, and executed with as much care and delicacy as if they had been the work of the most skilful seal engraver. They appear to represent the history and triumphs of an ancient Egyptian sovereign, probably the founder of the edifice. One compartment, in particular, exhibits a great battle, in which the Egyptians, armed with bows and arrows, gain a complete victory over their Asiatic enemies, armed with the spear and the javelin.

The forms of pursuit and retreat, the attitudes of the victors, the wounded, and the dying, are so varied and striking, that Hamilton imagines it probable, this, and a similar representation at Karnac, may have furnished Homer with materials for many of the varied descriptions with which his narrative is filled. In another compartment, the conqueror is represented as seated on his throne, while the captive monarch is fastened to a car, and the chiefs are treated with all that studied and ruthless cruelty which the ancient laws of war were supposed to authorise.

A HEART-SICKENING PICTURE.

From a sermon preached in Hollis street church, Boston, on the 2d inst., by John Pierpont, and published in the last New World, we extract the following: It is part of the preacher's argument to prove against Great Britian and the United States, the awful charge that "these two nations—the freest nations of the world, and the most enlightened, if we may receive as true their opinions of themselves—live not as Christian nations, if their own boastings are to be trusted—are doing more, at this hour, by means of their wars for conquest, by their oppression of the conquered, and by their poisonous drugs—to desolate God's earth, to break down his kingdom upon the face of it, and to efface his image from the human soul, than is done by all other nations, Christian, Mahomedan and Pagan combined; and where, after all their boasting, these nations, between them, have invested one dollar in the means of Christian salvation, they have invested ten to corrupt and destroy their fellow men in body and in spirit, for time and for eternity!

"The sanguinary wars by which she (Great Britain,) has subjugated the hundred millions of India, and the stern despotism with which she rules and starves them, that her merchant prinçes may roll in splendour and lap themselves in voluptuousness, have a voice, which the whole thickness of the globe cannot keep out of our ears. 'A more beautiful country,' says a brother clergymen, recently of this city, 'than that from Cuddalore to Tanjore, (in Madras,) cannot possibly be imagined. The dense population and rich soil give their energies to each other, and produce a scene of surpassing loveliness. But the taxes and other causes keep down the labourers to a state below that of our southern slaves.' 'Turn your eyes backwards,' says a speaker of their own, no longer ago than last September, 'Turn your eyes backward upon the scenes of the past year. Go with me into the north-west provinces of the Bengal presidency, and I will show you the bleaching skeletons of five hundred thousand human beings who perished of hunger in the space of a few short months.

Yes—died of hunger in what has been justly called the granary of the world. The air, for miles, was poisoned with effluvia emitted from the putrefying bodies of the dead. The rivers were choked with corpses thrown into their channels. Mothers cast their little ones beneath the rolling waves because they would not see them draw their last grasp and feel them stiffen in their arms.' 'Jackals and vultures approached and fastened upon the bodies of men, women and children, before life was extinct. Madness, disease, despair stalked abroad, and no human power present to arrest their progress.'

And this occurred in British India, in the reign of Victoria the first. Nor was the event extraordinary or unforeseen. Far from it. Eighteen hundred thirty-five witnessed a famine in the northern provinces. Eighteen hundred thirty-three beheld one in the eastern. Eighteen hundred twenty-two saw one in the Deccan. They have continued to increase in frequency and extent, under our sway, for more than half a century. Under the administration of Lord Clive, a famine in the Bengal provinces swept off three millions! and, at that time, the British speculators in India had their granaries filled to repletion with corn. Horrid monopoly of the necessaries of life! Three millions died, while there was food enough, and to spare, locked up in the storehouses of the rich. To add to the horror with which we are now called upon to regard the last dreadful carnage, (that of the last year,) we are made acquainted, by the returns of the custom house, with the fact, that as much grain was exported from the lower parts of Bengal as would have fed the half million, who perished, for a whole year! Yet this awful oppression, and these desolating famines must go on, that England may extort her hundred millions of dollars every year from her hundred millions of Hindoos; and poppies must grow instead of wheat, that at her cannon's mouth she may force her opium upon the three hundred millions of the Chinese; while some one solitary Marshman, perhaps is translating the Bible of the Christians, to bring these countless millions to accept the religion of a nation that stands ready, at this moment, to destroy one half of them by war, that it may destroy the other half by poison !"

THE TEA PLANT IN BRAZIL.

The tea plant was imported from China into the Brazils about 20 years ago, and is cultivated very extensively in some parts, particularly near St. Paul, about 80 leagues from the capital. One proprietor alone possesses 60,000 feet of tea plants, some of which are six or eight years old. The tea is commonly gathered in October, November, December, January, and February; a good workman can collect 16 pounds a day. The leaf is afterwards dressed and dried. The youngest leaves form the "imperial tea," while the less tender constitute the "hyson," and other varieties. 1,500 feet of tea plants have recently been placed in the Jardin des Plantes, at Paris, and M. Guillemin, who imported them, is of opinion that certain parts of France, from their analogy to the Brazils

in climate and soil, are well fitted for the cultivation of the plant.

STATISTICS OF MORTALITY.
[From a late London paper.]

Dr. George Gregory gave a lecture, at the Royal Institution, on the statistics of mortality, which, from the manner of delivery, and the number of little facts brought together in illustration of the subject, showed with how much interest a man of talent, possessing a statistical mind, may invest that which might at first be supposed "dry," as the subject matter of a lecture. He commenced by remarking on the perfection of the present system of registration under the late act of parliament; next took a survey of London and the metropolitan districts, including the whole as "the metropolis," and remarking on the metropolitan character of the most distant suburbs of London, which he accounted for by the facility of intercommunication with all its parts: and thence proceeded with his observations on mortality and population—its increase, the number of births, the number of deaths, the increasing value of life under the improved condition of our city, and the different diseases affecting it, taking a glance, en passant, at the climacteric theory. It appears that the rate at which the metropolitan population increases is about eighteen per thousand annually, and that every year the metropolis increases to the extent of, or in other words, amalgamates into itself a population equal to that of the city of York. At the census of 1821 the population of London was, in round numbers, 1,328,000 ; in 1831, 1,500,000 ; and at the next census, which government are already making preparations for, it is expected to exceed 2,000,000. The proportion of births to deaths in the metropolitan districts is about 30 to 20.. The proportion between the deaths of the young, the adult, and the old, is pretty nearly the same, it seems, in all countries—namely, twice as many of old as adults, and six times as many children as of the old. The proportion of the sexes born, is 83 males to 79 females, or 21 males to 20 females. The excess of males disappears, however, in early age, so that, at the age of 15 the females preponderate. In the metropolis, the relative proportions are eight females to seven males. It was a question, under the present improved system, whether a single death escaped registration, and it was due to the British Association of Science to say that the plan was of their suggestion. This was not the case, however, with regard to births, as it was not compulsory on the part of the parent to initiate the registration, although it was compulsory to give information when called upon to do so. The value of human life (la vie probable et moyenne, as the French called it) had considerably increased; the number of deaths in 1740 was greater than it was now, a century afterwards, notwithstanding the enormous increase of the population. The number of deaths was equal to one every ten minutes throughout the 24 hours, so that if the great bell of St. Paul's tolled ten minutes for each person who died in the metropolis it would never cease tolling from the 1st of January to the 31st of December. The most healthy portions of the year, or the periods when the smallest number of deaths took place, were the summer and autumn; and the most unhealthy, or the periods during which the greatest number died, were the spring and winter. The last ten weeks had been the most healthy of the same period of the year known for many seasons past, and he had been informed by the surgeon of the metropolitan police, that he had never known the force to be in so healthy a state as they had been during the last ten weeks. With regard to the mortality among children, it appeared that half the number of males that are born die at the age of 7 years, and half the number of females at 13. In London, about half the number born die at the age of 21; and this showed an improvement of one third in the value of human life, when compared with that of the last century. The proportions of deaths between the young, the adult, and the old, are as, 40, 16, and 97 per thousand; of the 658 members of which the house of commons consisted, 13 might be expected to die annually! As the mortality in early life is much greater among boys than girls, the fact of there being a greater number of males born is doubtless intended as a compensating principle by the great Author of nature. In all healthy localities there is a less number of deaths in the warm than during the cold seasons; and in unhealthy localities, the reverse—a less number of deaths occurring in the cold than the warm seasons. In great cities like London, the mortality depended much on the nature of the locality; the healthiest parish was that in which they were at present assembled, namely St. George's Hanover-square. In this parish the number of deaths as compared with the number in Whitechapel was only 17 to 39. So that it would seem they had more than twice the chance of life here which the inhabitants of Whitechapel possessed. Mortality was always greater in cities than in rural districts. The proportion of deaths in London compared with the rural districts was 24 to 18, or 4 to 3. The two most unhealthy towns, or those in which there was the greatest mortality, compared with their population, were Manchester and Leeds.

The learned doctor concluded his lecture by some observations on the diseases most destructive of human life, and stated that it had been observed that whenever one disease was got rid of which proved fatal to large numbers, it was found that the numbers of those who died by other diseases always increased, so that it would seem by closing one avenue of disease, we merely opened the door to another. This fact had been particularly remarked in reference to the small-pox after the introduction of vaccination.

The hemp of Russia may be superseded, ere long, by the flax of New Zealand. It is believed that the labour of obtaining the latter in its coarse state, and the charges of importation, will be fully compensated by a price of 18l. per ton here; the expense of dressing will be about 12l. more; so that at about 30l. per ton, New Zealand flax, in a state to supersede Russian hemp, will be delivered in this country. The price of Russian hemp, in 1839, was 45l. per ton, it is now 36l., and 40l. may be deemed the average.

To dairy women.—To preven nauseous flavour which is too oft in cheeses, even when made o milk, and which, otherwise, w cious, salt the milk as soon as it the cows: I mean the evening's is kept in pans during the night, mixed with the new morning's quantity of salt to be used on th about a table spoonful to each ga and is generally sprinkled on t the pan, and the milk poured u and they soon become incorpo early salting has enabled many c whose cheese was before alway detestably rank, now to produce well-flavoured cheese, and on fa been pronounced totally unfit f system.

POTATO GLUE.

Take a pound of potatoes, pe boil them well, pound them w hot in three or four pounds of b then pass them through a hair wards add to them two pounds o very finely powdered, previously four pounds of water, and stir t gether. The result will be a spe or starch, capable of receiving colouring matter, even of powde brick, or lamp black, which may as an economical means of p posts, walls, pailings, and other i ing exposed to the action of the r

---

From the Chr

SPRING.

The sweet South wind, so
Sleeping in other climes, on sunny s
Or dallying gaily with the orange tr
   In the bright land of song.
Wakes unto us, and laughingly swe
Like a glad spirit of the sunlit sky.

The labourer at his toil
Feels on his cheek its dewy kiss, an
His open brow to catch its fragrant
   The aromatic spoil
Born from the blossoming gardens o
While its faint sweetness lingers ro

The bursting buds look up
To greet the sun-light, while it ling
On the warm hill side,—and the vio
   Opens its azure cup
Meekly, and countless wild-flowers
Their earliest incense on the gales o

The reptile, that hath lain
Torpid so long within his wintry to
Pierces the mould, ascending from i
   Up to the light again—
And the lithe snake crawls forth fro
To bask as erst upon the sunny hill

Continual songs arise
From Universal Nature—birds and
Mingle their voices, and the glad ea
   A second paradise !
Sunshine, and song, and fragrance—
Thrice blessed Spring !—thou beare

Nor unto Earth alone—
Thou hast a blessing for the human
Balm for its wounds and healing fo
   Telling of winter flown,
And bringing hope upon thy rainbo
Type of Eternal Life—thrice blesse

THE FRIEND.

A RELIGIOUS AND LITERARY JOURNAL.

VOL. XIII.   **SEVENTH DAY, FIFTH MONTH, 23, 1840.**   **NO. 34.**

EDITED BY ROBERT SMITH.

PUBLISHED WEEKLY.

Price two dollars per annum, payable in advance.

Subscriptions and Payments received by

GEORGE W. TAYLOR,

NO. 50, NORTH FOURTH STREET, UP STAIRS,

PHILADELPHIA.

SPEECH OF AMBROSE H. SEVIER,

OF ARKANSAS.

In U. S. Senate, March 17, 1840.—In Executive session, on the treaty with the New York Indians.

(Concluded from page 266.)

This letter of Mr. Crawford construes, and *properly construes,* the senate's resolution of the 11th June, 1838. Having submitted his letter to the secretary of war, containing his opinions, &c. the secretary advised upon the subject, and gave Mr. Crawford instructions for *future operations,* and these instructions Mr. Crawford embodied in his letter to Mr. Gillett, of the 30th of October, 1838, and which is as follows, viz :

"Sir: Your report and the treaty with the New York Indians, assented to as amended in the senate of the United States, have been submitted to the secretary of war. He is of opinion that the consent of a majority of *all* the Seneca chiefs must be obtained, but that, as you have heretofore met the requirement of the senate, by full explanations to them in council, you may proceed to the Seneca reservations, *and there obtain the assent of such Indians as have not heretofore given it.*

"You are accordingly authorised and requested, at your earliest convenience, to proceed to the Seneca reservation in New York, and to carry out the above views. Your service among the people qualifies you fully for the discharge of this duty, and gives assurance of its fair, honest, and capable performance.

"Very respectfully, your most obedient servant,
T. HARTLEY CRAWFORD.

"Hon. R. H. GILLETT, now at Washington."

Here we have, sir, what I consider a false step in this negotiation, which was not warranted by the resolution of the 11th of June, 1838, nor sanctioned by usage or sound policy, in making treaties with any nation or Indian tribe whatever. Here, sir, is the red book, which contains all of our Indian treaties from the earliest period to the present day, and I boldly challenge any senator to show me in it a single treaty ever made by us with an Indian tribe, which was not made with them in *council,* or else by delegates, duly authorised by the council to make such treaty. Sir, the McIntosh treaty, which was made at the Indian Spring, in Georgia, forms no exception to the principle I have here laid down. That treaty purported to have been made in *council,* and to have been assented to by a majority of the chiefs, and to have been agreeable to a majority of the Creeks. These important, and leading, and controlling facts, were *vouched for* and *asserted* by our commissioner, on that occasion, in his report. Relying upon the truth of that statement, the senate *ratified that treaty*—and what followed? McIntosh was murdered, and his followers were driven, for refuge and safety, out of the Creek nation into the white settlements. President Adams refused to carry that treaty into effect; and, at the following session of congress, laid the *facts* of that treaty before the senate—and what did the senate do with it? The senate investigated it, and finding it had been made by a *minority* of the chiefs, and by bribery and unfair means, the senate declared it *null and void ;* and yet, sir, with a knowledge of the proceedings of the senate upon that treaty, we find, by Mr. Crawford's instructions to Mr. Gillett, which I have just read, that our commissioner was authorised to proceed, for a third time, to the Seneca reservation, and there obtain "*the* assent of such Indians as had not heretofore given it."

This mode of hunting up Indians, and of getting their signatures, *out of council,* in the woods, or any where, wheresoever they may be found, seems not to have been very cordially approved of by General Dearborn; and upon ascertaining this fact, we find Mr. Crawford addressing another letter to Mr. Gillett, of the 19th of November, 1838, in which he says : "The instructions given you when here, it seems to me, *would justify your assembling of the Senecas,* should you deem it *necessary.* But to remove any doubt, I am directed by the secretary of war to say, *that if General Dearborn desires it,* you are authorised, *at your discretion,* to hold such council."

Here we find in a *matter of doubt* whether Mr. Gillett's instructions would authorise him to convene a council, and is stated that *he is not to convene the council,* unless General Dearborn *should desire it,* and not even then, unless *at his discretion.* And he never did convene the council, although it will be remembered that, on the 20th of October previous, the commissioners had not closed the council which he was then holding, but had publicly adjourned it to the 15th of November. This public pledge, which was *studiously violated,* seems to have given the parties concerned in it no sort of uneasiness, or to have needed any sort of apology. This violation of a public pledge by a duly authorised commissioner, is justified, though not avowed, on the ground, I suppose, that we are not bound, according to modern ethics, to keep faith with heretics or infidels ; and we are called upon as the high priests of the United States, on the alleged, but fallacious, pretext of *expediency,* to endorse this code of morality.

Mr. Gillett says, in his report upon this mission, that "*he visited such places on the reservations* as he was desired to by any of the chiefs. Eight of the signatures were received at *his room in Buffalo*—one at his former lodgings at Buffalo Creek, and one at the residence of the sub-agent." These ten, added to the thirty-one before received, makes forty-one altogether, which is a majority of one, and then he insists that the treaty had been assented to ; if not according to the resolution of the senate, it was assented to according to the instructions of the war department.

General Dearborn's report, in the main, varies but little from that of Mr. Gillett. He states, however, that he thought there ought to have been a council, but seems to have acquiesced in the other mode, as Mr. Gillett showed him the instructions he had received of Mr. Crawford of the 13th of October, by which he considered himself *prohibited from calling a council.* It is *denied* that Mr. Gillett said any thing to General Dearborn about his *subsequent instructions* of the 12th of November, 1838. As Mr. Gillett no doubt intended to avail himself of the *discretion these instructions* gave him, and finding the pliant New-Englander acquiescing in his views of expediency, he never did inform General Dearborn of those instructions. General Dearborn, in his letter to Governor Everett of the 19th January last, says, he *never saw or heard of the instructions of Mr. Crawford to Mr. Gillett of the 12th of November, 1838,* and yet the credulous general, after he had found out the existence of such *secret instructions,* some time after the negotiation was ended, and after the whole proceedings were published, seems to take no offence at the circumstance, but states that he believes (a belief, to say the least of it, which shows, on his part, a marvellous credulity) that not seeing those instructions was *undesigned* and *accidental.*

Mr. Crawford, in his letter to the secretary of war of the 15th of January, 1839, upon the subject of the last reports of Mr. Gillett and General Dearborn, says :

"That ten additional assents have been obtained, but that two of which are not manifested, by the *party appearing and signing in person.* The reasons given for their not appearing and signing, in person, the treaty as modified, are, that *one of them was absent,* and the other prevented from doing so by the acts of chiefs opposed to the treaty."

These are important details, and are not to be found in the printed report of Mr. Gillett, before whom these transactions occurred, and which probably accounts for the fact that several of the chiefs, whose signatures appear to the treaty, deny ever signing -or assenting to the treaty, or of *authorising any other person to do so for them.* I say important, because it will be observed that those two, signing by attorney, constitute what is claimed as a majority of the chiefs. Mr. Crawford concludes his letter by submitting the treaty, signed in the manner we have seen, by forty-one chiefs, for the consideration of the secretary of war.

The secretary of war reports upon this treaty to the president, of the 19th January, 1839, and recommends the president to submit it to the senate. Here let me remark, that the president is authorised by the terms of the resolution of the senate of the 11th of June, 1838, to promulge this treaty, without again consulting the senate about it, *whenever* he is satisfied that it has been assented to, according to the true meaning and intent of the resolution of the 11th of June, 1838. The president deemed it advisable, for reasons set forth in his message to the senate of the 21st January, 1839, not to promulge this treaty, but he submitted it again for our advice. By doing so, he has shown that our confidence has not been misplaced. He has shown, most abundantly, that though he appreciated the wishes and interests of New York and of Massachusetts, that he was, at the same time, not disposed to gratify even those two powerful states, at the expense and sacrifice of the just claims of even a small fragment of wretched and miserable Indians. He had the power to speak but a single word, and close up this controversy forever. But, sir, he wisely preferred adhering to the immutable and eternal principles of justice, to the pecuniary gains of Massachusetts or New York; he preferred preserving, with scrupulous fidelity, our national character, and honour and honesty, to the contemptible spoils and laurels which might be gathered in triumphing, by forced and unlawful means, over a handful of ignorant savages. Sir, he resisted importunities, and refused to promulge the treaty, and sent it back to the senate, to his impartial constitutional advisers, for their consideration. And how did the senate dispose of it? Let the report of the committee on Indian affairs of the last session, and of the resolution of the 2d of March last, founded upon that report, answer the question. What is the resolution of the 2d of March?

"*Resolved*, That whenever the president of the United States shall be satisfied that the assent of the Seneca tribe of Indians has been given to the *amended* treaty of June 11, 1838, with the New York Indians, according to the true intent and meaning of the resolution of the senate of the 11th June, 1838, the senate recommend that the president make proclamation of said treaty, and carry the same into effect."

Sir, we adopted that resolution for the purpose of giving the parties interested another opportunity, which they desired, to get the treaty assented to by the Senecas. This was done on the 2d of March, the day before we adjourned the last congress.

On the 7th of that month, four days after the adjournment, and before the treaty we had thus disposed of had left the secretary's office, so far as I know, but certainly before it had left the war department, we find Nath. T.

Strong, a Seneca chief, in a letter to the president, misrepresenting the views and proceedings of the senate upon that treaty, and urging him to ratify it. On the 9th of March, we find Mr. Allen, the agent of the land company, of whom I have before spoken, in his letter to the president, urging him to ratify the treaty, which the senate had refused to do, but seven days before. He furnishes the president the same list of chiefs we had had before us, which he contended was a majority of the Senecas.

On the 11th, we find Mr. Wilcox, another prominent individual throughout the whole of this long protracted negotiation, in his letter to the president, urging him to ratify the treaty, and endorsing the truth of Allen's statement relative to the number of chiefs.

On the 11th, we find Mr. Stryker, the subagent, in his letter to the president, furnishing a list of the chiefs, with the same view.

On the 4th of April, we have a letter to the president, from the Ogden land company, with the same view; and on the 6th of March, two days after we adjourned, we find that two of our brother senators, Messrs. Tallmadge and Norvell, furnished to this same Mr. Allen, for the purpose of showing (what they no doubt believed, and for which I attach no blame) that the requirements of the senate, by the resolution of the 11th of June, 1838, that the treaty should be assented to in open council, was dispensed with by the resolution of the 2d of March. I can only say that that was not my understanding of the resolution of the 2d of March. What is that resolution? The resolution of the 2d of March authorised the president to make proclamation of the Seneca treaty *whenever* he should be satisfied that the amended treaty had been assented to, *according to the true intent and meaning of the resolution of the 11th of June*, 1838. And how was that resolution of the 11th of June construed? Let the report of the committee on Indian affairs answer. And how was it construed by the *commissioner*, and by the war department, until it was found *expedient for them to give it a different construction?* Let the history of this negotiation, which the published documents fully furnish, answer the question. How was it construed by the president? Let his message of the 14th of January last answer the question.

Construing these resolutions as we did, the president refused to promulge the treaty, notwithstanding all the efforts made to induce him to do so. He despatched the secretary of war, last August, to Buffalo, for the purpose of submitting the amended treaty to the Senecas, containing the views of the senate, as re-affirmed by the resolution of the 2d March. He convened a council for this purpose, and what was the result? The secretary has given us nothing but the speeches of himself, of General Dearborn, of the agent, and of the Indian chiefs, for and against the treaty. But the president, in the message of the 14th of January last, transmitting this treaty again, and for the third time, to the senate, for *ratification*, has given us the result of the secretary's negotiation in *three italicised* lines, (multum in parvo,) which is, that "*no advance towards obtaining the assent of the Se-*

necas to the amended treaty, in council, was made, nor can a majority of them in council, be now obtained."

I have now, sir, endeavoured to give the senate a full and impartial, though I fear a tedious, history of what I consider the important points of this whole matter, from the beginning up to this day; and in doing so, I have based my statements upon the official published documents emanating from the public agents and officers of the government. I have not relied, because such testimony, however unjustly, in some instances, might be cavilled at, upon Indian statements and Indian affidavits. Nor have I relied, for any thing I have said, upon the written statements of the Quakers, who are viewed by some gentlemen as officious intruders and intermeddlers in this affair—not because I do not consider their statements as entitled to the fullest belief, but because I have not found such reliance necessary.

Now, sir, having wholly failed, after two years of expense and trouble, of trials and tribulations, backed by the potent influence of New York and Massachusetts, and of the *active members* of the land company and their *rewarded* chiefs, to obtain, in open council or otherwise, the voluntary assent of a majority of the Seneca chiefs to the very liberal treaty we are now considering—a treaty by which we agree to give to the Senecas, for their part of the Green Bay lands, their portion of the $400,000 in cash, and their portion of the 1,800,000 acres of land west of the state of Missouri—having failed in all this, what shall we do? Shall we throw our treaty in the fire, and *take by force* what we have been unable to accomplish by negotiation? It is a grave question for the senate to decide. If history is to be credited, it is not an unusual occurrence for the weak and helpless to be robbed and preyed upon by powerful civilised communities *professing* Christianity. Sir, when Cæsar demanded the public treasure of Rome, he scorned the production of any other warrant than his sword. And if we *really* want the lands of the Senecas for our masters—for this huge and overgrown land company—we have but to use a similar argument, and no doubt it will be attended with similar success. Sir, if we decide upon such a step, let us accomplish our purpose in the bold spirit of the valiant highwayman, and not by the trick and trap, the shuffling and legerdemain of a spurious treaty? If we have determined to give up our honesty, I hope we shall at least preserve our reputation for courage.

By a census of the Senecas, which has been furnished us, it appears that not only a majority of the chiefs, but also, about fourteen-fifteenths of the whole population, are against the treaty, and opposed to emigration. This proportion, we find existing now among them, after all the influences I have before alluded to have been brought to bear upon them for upwards of two years. And, sir, what has been, after endeavouring, in addition to all this, to *starve them into submission*, by withholding from them until late in the summer of 1838, their annuity of 1837. I will read to the senate, for their information, the letter of Mr. Harris of the 14th of March, 1838.

War Department.

Office of Indian Affairs, March 14, 1838.

"Sir:—In regard to the inquiries contained in the honourable Mr. Marvin's letter of the 2d instant, referred by you to this office for a report, I beg leave to observe, that it is known here that the Seneca annuity for 1837 has not been paid. Remittances *were made for the purpose in June last, but owing to various causes, among which were the absence of an exploring party to the West, the pendency of a negotiation with the New York Indians,* and the engagement of the disbursing agent in the suppression of the hostile movements on the Canada border, the payment has not been made. *The sub-agent, now here, informs me that it is not desirable it should be made until the return of the delegation now in this city.*

Very respectfully, your most obedient servant,
C. A. HARRIS, Commissioner.

Hon. J. R. POINSETT, Secretary of War.

Sir, the Indians now are, as they have been from the beginning, agitated, excited, and unhappy, about this treaty; and I now hope that, on this day, the Senate will quiet their agonizing apprehensions by finally disposing of it—by ratifying or rejecting it.

I had thought the treaty an advantageous one to the Indians. I think so still. But I am not disposed to force upon them a measure, though calculated, as I believe, to redound to their advantage, which they *literally abhor.* Whenever they may manifest a disposition to go westward, I, for one, will be willing to give them a home. But, in any future treaty we may have with them, should this one be rejected, I hope we shall have nothing to do with the Massachusetts land company. Let this company extinguish their right of occupancy themselves. And I here call upon those senators who are so opposed to monopolizing companies and corporations—so averse to paying state, or company, or corporation debts, with public money or public lands, for objects of state or company purposes *exclusively,* to stand by me on this trying occasion, and prevent such a conversion of the public treasure to such unworthy purposes—to local purposes in which we have not a shadow of interest.

We have had before us a great mass of testimony (*ex parte* always) upon both sides, criminating and recriminating each other. We have looked over it all; and we of the committee congratulate ourselves upon being able to make up our minds upon the merits of this treaty from the fulness of our official documents, without relying, in any great degree, upon this *ex parte* testimony.

I conclude, Mr. President, by expressing the hope that the senate will adopt the resolution reported by the committee on Indian affairs, which is a resolution to reject the treaty.

CENTRAL AMERICA.

The following extracts respecting an interesting portion of the American continent, rarely visited by travellers, and comparatively but little known, is from the "Narrative of a journey to Guatemala, in Central America," by G. W. Montgomery, who went there under a commission from the government of the United States, in the summer of 1838.

The territory called Central America extends from the eighth to the eighteenth degree of north latitude, and is bounded on the north by Mexico and the bay of Honduras; on the east by the Carribean sea and Veragua; and on the west and south by the Pacific ocean. It may be considered as a great isthmus, separating the Atlantic from the Pacific, and connecting the two grand divisions of Spanish America. This isthmus presents a coast-line of nearly a thousand miles on either side. Its breadth from sea to sea in no place exceeds four hundred miles, and at the narrowest point is scarcely one hundred.

The situation of this country is peculiarly favourable for commercial intercourse with every other part of the world. On the south-western side its shores are washed by the Pacific; and the whole of the northern border lies open to the Atlantic and the Gulf of Mexico. Both the Pacific and Atlantic coasts are indented with numerous bays and harbours, of which the principal is the bay of Honduras, in the latter sea, comprising the ports of Truxillo, Izabal, and Omoa, and communicating with the interior by means of a river which leads up to the lake called *Golfo dulce.* In the same bay is situated the port of St. Thomas, of which mention has also been made in another part of this narrative. On the Pacific shore is the bay of Conchagua, and the ports of la Union, Realejo, Sonsonate, and Istapa, of which the latter is the nearest to Guatemala, but is only a roadstead, and by no means safe, owing to the heavy swell constantly rolling in from the ocean.

The most considerable of the Central American islands are Bonaca and Ruatan, in the bay of Honduras; the archipelago of Chiriqui, in the Carribean sea; and the islands in the bay of Conchagua, in the south.

The principal rivers are the Usumasinta, which falls into the bay of Campeachy; the Polochie, which discharges itself into the Golfo dulce; the Balize, the Hondo, and the Motagua, also called the Gualan, which flow into the bay of Honduras; the Pasa, Lempa, and Esclavos, which contribute to the Pacific. These rivers are navigable for many miles into the interior. There are others of less note, which are not navigable. The country also abounds in warm and medicinal springs.

The lakes most deserving of notice are those called Golfo dulce, or Great Fresh Water Lake of Izabal, and Amatitan, which have been mentioned before, and especially the great lake of Nicaragua, which is connected with that of Leon.

The lake of Nicaragua is situated in the province of that name, at a distance of about a hundred miles from the Atlantic ocean, with which it communicates by the river St. Juan. This river is now considered the most advantageous and most practicable point for establishing a connection between the two oceans. It is believed to be navigable for vessels of three or four feet draft from its port to the lake; and for vessels of twice that depth, as far as the point where the falls commence, which are the great difficulty to be surmounted. The surface of the lake, according to the statement of a Spanish engineer who executed a survey in 1781, is forty-six feet above the level of the Pacific; its depth, about fifteen fathoms. The distance from that sea to the south-western extremity of the lake of Leon, which communicates, as before stated, with that of Nicaragua, is, by the report of the said engineer, fifteen geographical miles, and the intervening land is said to be sufficiently level to admit of the opening of a canal that should unite those lakes with the Pacific.

Should the grand work of uniting the waters of the two oceans be undertaken and accomplished, a revolution would be caused in the commercial world, attended with results in the highest degree beneficial to the inhabitants of both hemispheres. This part of the continent would become the great thoroughfare of nations; and Central America would at once rise to an importance, both commercial and political, which otherwise she never can attain.

Proposals for opening this communication were made by a company of English merchants in 1824. The following year similar proposals were made by some merchants of the United States. But in neither case does it appear that any specific attention was given to the subject by the government of the country. Subsequently, a proposition to the same effect was made by the Dutch, which was admitted, and the king of the Netherlands was to be stockholder to the amount of one half of the capital that might be invested. But, from whatever cause, this plan also fell through, and matters remain in the same state as before.

It seems singular that a subject so peculiarly interesting to the United States should not have attracted more attention in our country. The enterprise, however, could only be successfully undertaken under the auspices of the government, and with the sanction of congress. Were the subject properly recommended to the consideration of the national legislature, its importance could hardly fail of being perceived and duly appreciated; and the result, whatever it might be, could not but reflect credit on the administration. There is also reason to believe, that any steps that our diplomatic agent in Guatemala might be instructed to take towards a negotiation with the Central American government on this subject, would be met by that government with alacrity. There exists on the part of the people and authorities of that country a decided predilection for Americans, and for every thing that is American. They imitate the institutions, the laws, the policy of the United States, and look up to this country as their great political model. They at one time solicited to be admitted into the Union as a new state in our republic. While France and England are trying in vain to effect a treaty with their government, the United States have renewed, or are on the point of renewing, one that was concluded several years since. Thus every thing seems to favour and facilitate the recommplishment of an enterprise, which, besides enhancing in no slight degree the national glory of the United States, would be productive of the greatest commercial advantages to its citizens.

That some difficulties exist towards realizing this object, cannot be denied. One is the disturbed state of Central America at the present moment, and the civil commotions to which it is subject at all times. Another would be to obtain a grant of land on each side of the river St. Juan, with the sovereignty of the country ceded, without which a sufficient security would not be afforded to the persons and properties of our citizens who might establish themselves there.

But returning to the subject of this chapter: the face of the country is generally mountainous. It presents, as I have heretofore observed, a succession of sierras, or mountains, with intervening vallies, except in the neighbourhood of Guatemala, where the table-lands commence, which are vast undulating plains, spreading for many leagues around. All the physical and natural peculiarities of other countries are united in the formation of the general aspect of Central America: delightful vallies teeming with animal and vegetable life, extensive prairies clothed with verdure, gentle rivulets and foaming torrents, huge broken rocks, inaccessible mountains and fiery volcanoes, dense gloomy forests, grassy knolls, and shady groves. The same variety is remarkable in the climate, as will be shown anon, and in the vegetable productions of the country.

That elevated range forming the spine of the whole continent, styled in South America the Andes, and in the United States the Rocky Mountains, may be traced in its regular continuance through Central America, though at a less elevation, dividing this country into two grand sections ; the waters on the north of the ridge falling into the Atlantic, and on the south flowing into the Pacific.* This great range approaches to the Atlantic, and recedes from the Pacific, in Central America, in a greater degree than in any other part of the American continent, and is more abrupt in its slope towards the former ocean than towards the latter. It traverses the western part of the state of Guatemala, and constitutes that region called *los Altos*, or highlands, of Totonicapan and Quesaltenango. It is interrupted in its course by two transversal vallies, in one of which is situated the lake of Nicaragua ; in the other are the plains of Comayagua. Nearly the whole coast of the Pacific is bordered by an alluvial plain, varying in breadth ; and the line where this plain joins the base of the range, is crowned by a succession of volcanoes. Of these, the most remarkable are Amatitan, Isalco, Cosiguina, and another called the water volcano, from the circumstance of its emitting torrents of water instead of fire. The latter is said to be the loftiest of the volcanoes, its summit being 13,000 feet above the level of the sea. There are a vast number of others of less note. They are supposed to be the great causes of the earthquakes in Central America; yet the country in their vicinity is more thickly inhabited than elsewhere. Omotepeque is the only inhabited island in the lake of Nicaragua, and is at the same time the only one in the lake in which a volcano is found.

One of the great advantages of this country, is that of enjoying a climate peculiar to itself; a mild, temperate, and delicious climate, which has none of the varieties of the seasons; for although the tropical heats are experienced in

* A rivulet is pointed out in the vicinity of Guatemala that may be considered a curiosity. At a little distance from its source it branches off into two streams, one of which can be traced to the Atlantic; the other flows into the Pacific.

the low lands along the coast, in the rest of the country a perpetual spring prevails, and the earth is clothed with a rich and never-failing verdure. The cause of this temperature is the great elevation of this part of the American continent, which is some five thousand feet above the level of the sea, while the summits of some of the mountains rise to twelve or fourteen thousand feet above that level. In the interior, the variation of the thermometer of Fahrenheit is not more than 15° in the course of the year, the mercury seldom rising above 75° or falling below 60. The difference between the temperature of the coasts and that of the *altos*, or highlands, is much greater, and comprises, under the same degree of latitude, the extremes of heat and cold. The climate is also very healthy, except in the immediate vicinity of the coasts and on the banks of the great rivers, where fevers and other diseases are prevalent.

The seasons are divided into the dry and the rainy : the first, which is called summer, lasts from January to June, and the other, which is winter, comprises the remaining six months of the year. Nothing can be more regular than the commencement of the rains at the period presented by nature, and their cessation after they have lasted their appointed time. It is also a singular fact, that the rain scarcely ever falls in the morning, but almost always about two hours after the sun has passed the meridian. As the country is every where provided with numerous springs and rivers, the continuation of dry weather for nearly six months is not attended with any great inconvenience. In one respect it is highly advantageous, as it is not only favourable, but indispensable, to the production of cochineal, one of the great staple commodities of the country.

The soil in Central America is for the most part exceedingly fertile. In the plains, and especially in the vallies, it is a dark rich mould of alluvial formation, which might serve as manure for lands in other parts of the world, and is in some places six feet deep. The overflowings of some of the rivers and the numerous springs by which the country is watered, give to the land a green and fresh appearance, even in the dry season. To this fertility of soil, and to the graduation of temperature—the natural consequence of an advantageous scale of altitudes—may be attributed the variety and abundance of the vegetable productions of Central America, which embrace nearly all those of Europe and the West Indies, besides some that are peculiar to the country. Of these the most valuable are indigo, cochineal, tobacco, cocoa, mahogany, logwood, vanilla, cotton, and sassafras, which are the great staples of the country, and the chief articles of exportation. Indian corn, sugar, and coffee, are also produced in considerable quantity, and a variety of dye woods, as also gums, spices, and balsams, especially the balsam of Tolu, so much esteemed.

Of dye woods, the following, next to logwood, are the most valuable: the St. Juan and the Poro, which yield a beautiful yellow, and particularly the *Annona reticulata*, the peculiarity of which is that its wood, though perfectly white, changes colour on being cut or slit, and turns to a clear brilliant red, that is easily extracted, and is quite durable.

The gums most in esteem are copal, arabic, quitipi, guapinol, (an excellent perfume,) incense, chiracca, and the gum of the chesnut tree. An oily substance is also extracted from the fruit of this tree, from which candles are made, as fine as those of white wax, and burning with a clear, steady light, without giving out much carbon.

Besides the mahogany tree, there are others which are remarkable for their size and beauty, or for their peculiar fitness for cabinet work ; as cedars of gigantic dimensions, the *Ceyba*, or silk-cotton tree, the *Palma real*, or wild cabbage tree, the wild tamarind and the cocoanut tree. Also the lignumvitæ, the oak, the quachepelin, a very strong wood suitable for stakes to build on, as not rotting in the ground, the quiebrahacha, which is also remarkable for its durability and hardness, and the *comenegro*, or iron tree, so highly esteemed in the East Indies and in other countries.

Of the vegetables of this country, one of the most useful is a small species of bean, perfectly black, which is very extensively cultivated, and constitutes the chief nourishment of the working classes. Another is the plantain, which thrives well there, and is consumed in great quantities.

The fruits deserving any notice, are the chirimoya, a species of annona, which is very luscious and refreshing, the quanávana, another species of annona, the aguacate, or alligator pear, (*Persica gratissima*,) the corozo, which is a cocoa-nut in miniature, being not larger than a hen's egg, the pine-apple, the sapote, (*cucurbita citrullus*,) the caymito, commonly called in English the star apple, and the well known bannana. The fruits peculiar to higher latitudes are also produced there, but not in the same perfection.

The mineral productions of Central America are also deserving of consideration. The gold mines of Costarica, and the silver of Honduras, are rapidly increasing in their products. Those of Aguacate, in the former state, have produced great riches since their discovery. The extreme richness of this mine, and the circumstance of its being situated on the coast of the Carribean sea, were the cause of this part of the country being called *Costa rica*, or rich coast. There are other mines in the province of Comayagua, in New Segovia, in Nicaragua, and in the state of St. Salvador ; some of them so productive, that every one hundred pounds of ore extracted yield seventeen marks six ounces of silver, or nearly twelve per cent.* In other parts of the mountainous regions of Central America, there are strong indications of the existence of mines. The ore sometimes is found quite near the surface of the earth. A valuable piece of silver ore was shown me, while I was at Truxillo, by a man who said he had obtained it from the mountains in the neighbourhood of that place, just beneath the surface of the earth, and that by searching for ore in places that he was acquainted with, he could any day earn five ·or six dollars. It was by this kind of industry that he maintained himself.

* A mark of silver is eight ounces.

The seas of Central America abound in pearls and tortoise shell.

(To be continued.)

From the Boston Recorder.

POWER OF HABIT.

We find in all directions, examples of the power of reiterated effort to overcome great obstacles, and to render easy and pleasant what had been toilsome and irksome. And it is noticeable, lover as man is of variety, what an influence habit has upon his happiness. "The providence of God," says Bishop South, "has so ordered the course of things, that there is no action, the usefulness of which has made it a matter of duty, and of a profession, but a man may bear the continued pursuit of it without loathing or satiety. The same shop, and the same trade that employs a man in his youth, employs him also in his age. Every morning he rises fresh to his hammer and his anvil; custom has naturalised his labour to him; his shop is his element, and he cannot, with any enjoyment of himself, live out of it."

But this subject has a most deeply interesting relation to moral character. The repetition of moral acts tends as directly to strengthen the moral principles of the soul, as the wielding of the hammer to strengthen the arm that uses it. The difference between religious character in the maturity of Christian life, and in its earliest stage, is the result of reiterated acts and emotions of piety. Every act of self-denial, every repulse given to temptation, all the vigorous actings of faith—every instance of the gushing forth of fervent love for holy objects—all this has been fuel to the growing flame of piety. Every prison visited by Howard, and every scene of human misery that roused his heart, contributed to deepen the determination of his mind, and make its zeal more intense in his work of mercy. Each repetition of acts of holy benevolence, constitutes a step by which the mind ascends to a higher personal position than it had previously enjoyed. We cannot deny ourselves the privilege of quoting on this point from Dr. Chalmers, who in his recent and very valuable work on the Adaptation of External Nature to the Moral and Intellectual Constitution of Man, thus remarks: "And this law of habit, when enlisted on the side of righteousness, not only strengthens and makes sure our resistance to vice, but facilitates the most arduous performances of virtue. The man whose thoughts, with the purposes and doings to which they lead, are at the bidding of conscience, will, by frequent repetition, at length describe the same tract almost spontaneously —even as in physical education, things, laboriously learned at the first, come to be done at last without the feeling of an effort. And so, in moral education, every new achievement of principle smooths the way to future achievements of the same kind; and the precious fruits, or purchase of each moral victory, is to set us on higher and firmer vantage ground for the conquests of principle in all time coming. He who resolutely bids away the suggestions of avarice, when they come in contact with incumbent generosity; or the suggestions of

voluptuousness, when they come into conflict with the incumbent self-denial; or the suggestions of anger, when they come in conflict with the incumbent act of magnanimity and forbearance—will at length obtain, not a respite only, but a final deliverance from their intrusion. The oftener that conscience makes good the supremacy which she claims—the greater would be the work of violence and less the strength for its accomplishment, to cast her down from that station of practical guidance and command, which of right belongs to her. It is just because in virtue of the law of suggestion, those trains of thought and feeling which connect her first biddings with their final execution, are the less exposed at every new instance to be disturbed, and the more likely to be repeated over again, that every good principle is strengthened by its exercise, and every good affection is more strengthened by its indulgence than before. The acts of virtue ripen into habits; and the goodly and permanent result is the formation or establishment of a virtuous character."

These are noble thoughts, and eminently cheering too, to any humble soul that mourns over the power sin had acquired over him, and that is willing and ready for action, and persevering effort to rise above its power. One virtuous act—one resolute resistance of evil impulses—one bold rebuke of a pressing temptation, is one step towards recrossing the territory which the sinner had been traversing in its wanderings from God. The distance may be great which is to be retraced; opening his eyes on the immensity of the interval between himself and God, he may be tempted to despair; but let him not be overwhelmed. The power of habit may be successfully turned, through the grace of God, to the overthrow of sin, as it had been to increase its dominion. Reiteration of unholy acts had rendered it unholy. The reiteration of holy acts will restore the moral ruin to order and beauty again. He may have, indeed, gone so far that the declivity may be fearfully steep, and the difficulty of reascending very great. But he need not, with all his guilt and peril before him, despond. God's eye of kindness is on him that casts a look of sadness over the distance he has wandered from him. And for no act of mercy is he more ready than " to lift up the heads that hang down and to confirm the feeble knees."

Selected for the Episcopal Recorder.

Hints to Professors of Religion.

I cannot help feeling astonished that persons professing godliness, and really seeking salvation through the death and sufferings of a crucified Saviour, can enter into the pleasures and amusements of the world; and even go so far as to vindicate those very vanities, which, if they are sincere in their desire of serving God, and becoming *true* disciples of Christ, their own conscience must assuredly condemn. We may well inquire of such persons,—Is this honouring your Saviour in your lives and conversation? Are you prepared to receive the summons of your master while sitting in the theatre or at a card-table? Can you conscientiously say that your lamps would then be

trimmed and your lights burning? Conceive the transition (were it possible) of being removed from a card-assembly to that heavenly host who surround the throne of the Lamb, and triumph in that marvellous grace which has redeemed them from the power of sin, and made them more than conquerors through his redeeming mercy!

We may inquire again, have we any sanction in the conduct of the apostles, or those of their followers, for practices of this kind? Certainly not; their language continually was, "Abstain from all appearance of evil." "Come out from among them, and be ye separate, and touch not the unclean thing." "Friendship with the world is enmity with God." These, and many more equally striking passages in the pages of inspiration, might be quoted to prove the necessity of Christians being a peculiar people, if they intend to realise what they profess to be seeking. Moreover, can it be supposed that Christians, whose duty it is to reprove sin in others, will be able to perform that duty effectually, when they countenance amusements which are decidedly contrary to a life of holiness? Let them be assured their endeavours will neither have God's blessing nor the attention of those they endeavour to reform, but most justly will they draw down upon themselves this rebuke, "Physician, heal thyself."

But a still more painful view than this may be taken of the subject; the lamentable stumbling-blocks which are thus placed in the way of young inquirers. It is natural when we first set out on our way to Zion, to seek direction from those who have long before avowed themselves to be travelling thitherward. Alas, how great is our surprise, when we discover in those very individuals follies and inconsistencies for which we are now filled with shame and remorse! O, did they but know how increasingly difficult they render the road to young beginners by this conduct, we are inclined to think their walk and conversation would be widely different. Surely they are not aware how much doubt and unbelief they occasion, and how often they excite a suspicion whether there really is a necessity for walking in the narrow way to heaven.

But here we must stop, and take the word of *truth* for our guide. "Strait is the gate and narrow is the way which leadeth unto life, and few there be which find it. Because wide is the gate and broad is the road which leadeth to destruction, and many there be who go in thereat." This solemn consideration and express declaration of Christ himself, ought surely to convince every one of the positive necessity of separating from the world, and determining henceforward to know nothing save Christ Jesus and him crucified. Very many are the difficulties which must be encountered when first the decisive measures are taken; there are enemies within and without, but in the name and strength of Jesus we have nothing to fear. *Constant* and *fervent* prayer will assuredly be followed by success; and our severest trials will well be compensated by the glorious hope of a house not made with hands, eternal in the heavens. Prospects like these should animate every heart to press forwards for the prize of our high calling; to devote ourselves entirely to the service of our Lord and master; to walk as he walked, pure, undefiled, separate from sinners, looking daily for the mercy of God unto eternal life.

From the Irish Friend.
Interesting Testimony respecting William Brockway.

The following copy of a certificate of removal, was given, many years ago, by a friend of mine, who appeared to be aware of its authenticity; and, as I have no reason to doubt its genuineness, I forward it for insertion in the Irish Friend. Although an *uncanonical* document, it is a pleasing instance of individual integrity of conduct in the Friend, whose solitary situation, as to religious companionship, it describes; as well as an honourable testimony of the good-will and esteem which his neighbours bore towards him :—　　　J. P.

Islington, 1840.

Newport, (Isle of Wight,) Feb. 1, 1777.

Whereas, William Brockway, and his daughter, Ann Brockway, who resided in this town, and were of the people called Quakers, having lately removed from this place to Colchester, in the county of Essex, and there being now of that persuasion now residing in the island, to give testimony concerning their conduct and behaviour, the said Wm. Brockway has applied to us for that purpose, and we, being willing to comply with his request, having known him and his family for many years, do certify: That the said William Brockway and his family have always acted with credit and reputation amongst us,—their behaviour having been sober and just, and honest in their dealings with the inhabitants, and, therefore, universally respected. Previous to his leaving the island, he advertised his departure several times in the public papers, signifying, that all who had any demands upon him should bring in their accounts; which is an express proof of his integrity, and worthy imitation.

He ever maintained the principles of his society, in refusing the payment of tithes and church rates; for the first of which he suffered much in his property, permitting himself to be distrained upon, from the year 1737, to that of leaving the island, which was in the year 1776; and even when the constable offered to pay him the overplus of money arising from the distress, he constantly refused it. The churchwardens never made any distress for church rates, as far as we know or believe; although he was a renter in two parishes; they being satisfied that his refusal arose from principle.

He was an example to those in affluence, being charitable to the poor; and, by this means, he obtained their prayers and good wishes.

He came into the island in the year 1728, and was apprenticed to John Bevis, gardener and nurseryman—one of the same persuasion. In the year 1736 he was married, and set up his trade. He had nine children by his wife, five of whom died in their infancy; the other four, we hear, are at Colchester. His wife died in the year 1775: she was a sober, virtuous woman; a good example to her sex, and respected by all who knew her.

Signed by [sixty one persons : the first six names only are here given—viz.]

Francis Rogers, ⎫
Richard Drake, ⎬ Churchwardens of Newport;
Philip Ballard, ⎭
Francis Pike, Overseer of Newport;
R. Cowlam, ⎫ Having had the medical care
E. O. Cowlam, ⎬ of the family ever since 1738.

From the Irish Friend.
WAR.

[In the following communication, from an authentic source, we have a gratifying instance of the progress which our testimony against fighting is making among those of other societies—it should have the effect of stimulating Friends to increased faithfulness in the support not only of this, but of the various testimonies which they believe themselves called upon to bear.]

[To the Editor of the Irish Friend.]

Third month 19th, 1840.

Respected Friend,—It will probably afford you and your readers pleasure to learn, that the following resolution was passed at a missionary meeting, held in Huddersfield, in the Methodist New Connection Chapel, on the 17th of 3d month, 1840 :—

Resolved,—" That this meeting laments to learn, from the reports of the mission in Canada, that many of our best members have fallen in the field of battle, and that some congregations have been broken up by the ravages of war, and would recommend to all our Christian friends, in every land, to abstain from all carnal warfare, as a thing altogether at variance with the religion of Jesus Christ."

The resolution was passed with the greatest apparent unanimity, by a company of ten or eleven hundred of people. A similar resolution was cordially, and, to all appearance, unanimously passed, by a missionary meeting at Sheriff-Hill, Gateshead Circuit, Durham, a few months ago. The principles of peace are prevailing, and I hope they will continue to prevail, until wars shall cease unto the ends of the earth. I am yours, respectfully,

JOSEPH BARKER,
of Gateshead.

Extracts from an Address to the society of Friends. By Thomas Shillitoe.

Dear Friends :—In the first place, let me put you in mind of the nature and importance of that religious profession, we, as a society, are making among men; which I believe would be found to be above that of every other society of professing Christians—to wit, the absolute necessity of our living, acting, and moving in all our civil as well as religious engagements, under the influence and government of the Spirit of Christ Jesus our Lord and Lawgiver; that, "whether we eat or drink, or whatsoever we do, God the Father may in all things be glorified."

This, my friends, is the chief corner-stone of our building, our fundamental principle; therefore, let us consider how far the general tenour of our conduct corresponds therewith, how far we are each endeavouring earnestly to be found, in all things, conformable to the example and precepts of the great and holy pattern of all Christian perfection, of Him who has trod the path of temptation and trial before us, but who rejected every snare of the enemy. If this should not be the case with us, is there not a danger of our becoming to others, who, from our exalted profession, may be looking to us for example and encouragement in the way to the heavenly Canaan, like the evil spies unto the children of Israel formerly ; or that our examples may prove as lets and hindrances to such, instead of helps to press through difficulties and discouragements towards the mark for the prize—which is, " Ye shall be holy, for I, the Lord your God, am holy ;" " Be ye perfect, even as your Father which is in heaven is perfect ?"

Let us remember, however, we may be at peace with ourselves by thus professing; but not doing the very best in our power to attain this perfect stature of the Christian, we are but branding ourselves in the estimation of the more serious and thinking part of the community with the odious character of hypocrites; neither do I believe that we escape at all times the like censure from the more unthinking and irreligious part. And let us remember, that the sad effects of thus dissembling will not end here; for if this conduct be persisted in, we must expect to incur the woe pronounced by our blessed Lord. " Woe unto you, Scribes and Pharisees, hypocrites ; for ye shut up the kingdom of heaven against men; for ye neither go in yourselves, neither suffer ye them that are entering to go in." For if every one that nameth the name of Christ is to depart from iniquity, is it not obligatory on the part of such as make the high and holy profession we do, to endeavour to attain to such a state of purity of conduct and converse among men ?

I believe our first Friends were raised up as a people, to bear testimony to the sufficiency of that pure principle of light and life in all mankind, which would direct them in the way to the heavenly Canaan, and strengthen them to walk therein. They confirmed the truth of their testimony by the general tenour of their conduct, giving ample proof to bystanders, that, through submission to its holy appearance in their hearts, they were mercifully redeemed from the world and its spirit, not only from its pleasures, but also from its treasures, and were enabled to count all things appertaining to this life but as dross and as dung, so that they might win Christ. Hereby they became as an ensign to the nations, for the fame of them spread far and wide: they became instrumental in the Divine Hand to gather souls unto God, and had to proclaim the glad tidings of the church being added unto daily. But alas, my friends ! how is the gold become dim, and the most fine gold changed ! how is the love of God, and that humility and self-denial so manifest in them, now, by too many amongst us, turned into the love of other things, such as gold and silver, and a desire to make an appearance of greatness in the world.

Do not these things, my friends, loudly call upon us, as a religious body, making a high profession, to be willing, each one for himself, to enter timely into the closet of the heart, and seek for divine help to shut to the door thereof against carnal reasoning, great natural acquirements, and love of the world, which there is cause to fear have overpowered the better judgment of many among us. Hereby, as we become willing to stand open to divine conviction, we may be favoured each one to see in what manner, and how far, we may have contributed to this sorrowful declension, and timely amend our ways and our doings; seeing we are yet mercifully followed, both immediately by the Great Head of the church, and instrumentally, with line upon line, precept upon precept. O, how applicable to His dealings, as respects our society, is the language of the Most High, formerly uttered, "How shall I give thee up, Ephraim? how shall I deliver thee, Israel? how shall I make thee as Admah? how shall-I set thee as Zeboim? Mine heart is turned within me; my repentings are kindled together. I will not execute the fierceness of mine anger; I will not return to destroy Ephraim; for I am God and not man: the Holy One in the midst of thee: and I will not enter into the city." May we no longer be found walking unworthy of these his multiplied mercies, but be prevailed upon to return to the good old ways, that we also may be found in those paths of holiness of life and conversation, in which our forefathers walked, under sore travail of mind and great suffering of body, and waste of outward substance, through persecutions. Oh! let us no longer be found trampling, as it were, upon their testimony, by slighting the many great and precious privileges of this day of outward ease, we who are uninterruptedly eating the fruit of the vineyards and oliveyards we never planted, but which they were made instrumental to plant for us; thus making the way easy to us, as it now is, to assemble for the purpose of divine worship, for transacting society concerns, and for the support of our various religious testimonies.

How many among us are pursuing their worldly concerns, as if they counted gain godliness, and not, as must be the case with the true disciples and followers of Christ, godliness with contentment to be the greatest riches, proclaiming in the language of conduct, that all is fish that comes to their net, regarding neither quantity nor quality, so there be a prospect of a good profit attached to it. O, these professing worldlings, who say they are Jews and are not, but whose fruits testify they are of the synagogue of satan, I have been persuaded, have been the greatest enemies to the spreading of our religious principles and the enlargement of our borders; those who maintain an uniform, consistent warfare against the Babylonish garment, but with all their might grasp at the wedge of gold, and aim at making a splendid appearance in their way of living. I believe no character is more odious in the estimation of those termed libertines, than these, especially where it is known they are taking an active part in society concerns. For in neighbourhoods where meetings are held, it is pretty generally known by those out of

the society, who are what the world calls our pillars; though it cannot be doubted, that such must at times prove stumbling-blocks to honest inquirers after Zion, and be instrumental in turning the blind out of the right way of the Lord.

I believe I am safe in saying, I have not been wanting at times in endeavouring to cast a veil of charity over the conduct of some of my friends, who it is evident have in this way become satan's bond-slaves, and my heart is made sad on their account: I have an assurance, that whatsoever our temptations and besetments may be, if we are but in good earnest, willing to resist and overcome them, he that covets great trade, great riches, and to make a figure in the world, as well as he that takes strong drink, will experience a way, a sure and certain way, to be cast up in due time by the Lord, for his escape from this otherwise impassable gulf between him and an eternal resting-place with the righteous. For the self-same divine principle of light and life, which our worthy forefathers believed in, followed, and were actuated by, is still with us, as the cloud by day and the pillar of fire by night, is still experienced by those who wait for it, and found by such as submit to its government, which is an all-regulating principle, subduing every inordinate affection and disposition.

How remarkably was this manifest in the members of our society in the beginning; until the enemy was permitted to try us with the bait, which has not failed to take with some of all classes in society—riches and worldly prosperity. In proportion as the mind has been let out, and desires increased after these, it has become indifferent as to consequences; neither fearing the overcharge of quantity, nor properly regarding the quality of business. Happy had it been for many, had they willingly and timely yielded to those divine intimations; for I believe none ever turned aside from the path of safety totally ignorant thereof, but that in the beginning of their erring and straying, the witness for God followed them, and at times smote them: but if we disregard its invitations and secret monitions, it is then most just on the part of Almighty God, to leave us to the power and insinuations of satan; the god of this world, who rules in the hearts of the children of disobedience. But even while thus promoting the cause of the evil one, such may continue to make a fair show in the flesh, as to a profession of religion, and be very tenacious respecting some externals, as were the Pharisees—things comparable to the mint, the anise and cummin, and in which satan will not oppose them, so long as they rest therewith satisfied, and continue to rebel against the light, refusing to submit to the heart-cleansing operation of God's word and power, which only can effectually cleanse the inside of the cup and the platter.

(To be continued.)

Report of Tract Association of Friends, for 1839-40.

At the annual meeting of the Tract Association of Friends, held 4th month 21st, 1840, the report of the proceedings of the managers for

the past year was received and read; which is as follows:

To the Tract Association of Friends.

The managers report, that during the past year they have endeavoured to perform the duties assigned them by the Association.

At the time of our last report, there were 60,327 tracts on hand. We have printed 104,-721 during the year, and 132,636 have been taken from our depository in the same period, leaving in our possession at the close of the year, 32,412. Of the number furnished for distribution, which is much larger than in any previous year, our auxiliaries have taken 19,-965, and 39,986 have been purchased by the New England Tract Association of Friends. Of the balance, a few have been sold; the rest have been distributed by the managers and other members of the association, or have been furnished by them to individuals interested in disseminating sound views on moral and religious subjects. Committees of the board have during the past season furnished tracts on steamboats; the shipping in the port and canal boats; in railroad cars; to the inmates of the Moyamensing prison, the Eastern penitentiary and the Blockley almshouse. Our tracts have been distributed monthly by an individual, amongst the residents at the navy yard, to the seamen at their dwellings, or at their places of worship. They have also been furnished to the crews of United States vessels leaving this port. Through other persons they have been placed in the hands of the attenders at various First-day schools, some for white and some for coloured persons, in different sections of the city. Two of these schools were for the children of seafaring men, and were held in the Mariners' meeting-houses. In our general distribution through the city, some have been given to applicants at the soup-houses, others have been left at the dwellings of the poor.

Statistical table of distribution as far as ascertained.—200 have been distributed among our butchers; 72 among draymen and charcoal men; 7815 at First-day and other schools for white and coloured children; 3250 among the mariners and sailors at our navy yard, and on boa,d U. States vessels; 2079 on board steamboats and vessels in our port; 1250 among persons confined in the Eastern penitentiary and Moyamensing prison; 4968 for general distribution amongst our citizens; 1889 were placed on railroad cars or canal boats; 7475 have been given to merchants from the south and west; 2940 were furnished for the whale ships and steamboats in New England; 1512 have been forwarded for the use of the yearly meeting boarding school, and for general circulation, in N. Carolina; 1000 for Maine and New Hampshire; 1612 for New Jersey; 625 for New York; 167 for Maryland; 675 for Kentucky; 515 for Ohio; 150 for Georgia; 196 for Missouri; 175 for New Orleans; 1101 for Indiana and Iowa; 500 of Dymond on the right of Self Defence were furnished for circulation among the ministers belonging to the Methodist community.

Believing that the almanac heretofore prepared by us had been favourably received, and had been productive of benefit, we were induced to issue one for the present year, the whole edition of which, being 5000, was disposed of early in the season. We have made some progress in collecting matter for one for the year 1841, which will of course be placed in the hands, and subject to the judgments of our successors. Through the kindness of the publishers, 200 copies of a new edition of that excellent essay, "The Rise and Progress of the Religious Society of Friends," by Wm. Penn, have been given to us for distribution.

We have been obliged, during the past year, in consequence of the increased demand for our tracts, to call upon the friends of the association for an addition to our funds; and a number, in responding to this appeal, have consented permanently to increase their annual contributions. If this should be done by our members generally, it would enable us materially to extend the usefulness of the association.

Two auxiliaries have been recognized since our last report; one located at Spiceland, under the title of the "Youth's Tract Association of Spiceland ;" the other at Walnut Ridge, under the title of the "Youth's Tract Association of Walnut Ridge," both in the state of Indiana. It would be gratifying to receive more frequently than we have done of late, such evidences of an interest in the objects of this association ; and to have greater indications from those already formed, of their continued care in promoting the interesting work in which we are engaged. We have had to regret that from some of our auxiliaries we have had no demand for tracts for some time past.

But two new tracts have been added to our collection since our last report; one is entitled "The Origin and Objects of Civil Government," designed to show the views of Friends on this subject; the other, "Extracts from the Address of Thos. Shillitoe to the Society of Friends ;" both of them, we think, will be found well adapted for circulation at the present time.

We believe the publications of this association, in upholding the doctrines and testimonies of the religious society of Friends, do but advocate the cause of vital Christianity ; for this reason, we think that their distribution is calculated, with the divine blessing, to be productive of good ; especially now, when strenuous efforts are made to circulate, in very alluring garbs, reading matter of a highly pernicious and demoralising tendency. Impressed with these feelings, we are encouraged in reviewing the operations of the past year, by the wide and increased circulation which they have received ; and if they have a tendency to counteract the poisonous effects of immoral sentiments, or avert in any degree the desolating effects of libertine principles, we think there is ample inducement to continue their distribution.

Although we have frequently had reason to conclude that our tracts have been instrumental in enlightening and consoling the sincere seeker, and in awakening the indifferent to a consideration of heavenly things, yet it has not often been our privilege to have accurate information relative to the individual effects. We have, however, had our feelings recently much interested in the case of an aged mariner, to whom the perusal of some of our

tracts appears to have been peculiarly blessed. On one occasion, when under the reproving visitation of the holy spirit, he took the tract entitled "Thoughts on the Importance of Religion," and a copy of the Holy Scriptures with him into his chamber, intending to refer to every text he found in the publication. As he read and compared, the powerful influence of truth accompanied the exercise, and tendered his heart. Softened and subdued, he found the spring of supplication opened within him, through which he was enabled to ask for mercy and forgiveness in the name of Jesus. Submitting to the operation of that which thus visited him, he witnessed a blessed change, to which his conduct and conversation have in some degree borne testimony. Since the change in him, other members of the family have given evidence of the heart-cleansing operation of that power, which in his case had been so signally displayed. Instances such as this, while they are truly gratifying and encouraging, are calculated to raise feelings of thankfulness to Him who alone can bless our humble efforts to promote the cause of truth and righteousness.

Signed on behalf and by direction of the managers,

JOSEPH SCATTERGOOD, *Clerk.*

The following Friends were appointed to fill the respective offices of the association for the ensuing year.

Clerk.—John Carter.

Treasurer.—John G. Hoskins.

Managers.—Wm. Hodgson, Jr. ,Alfred Cope, George M. Haverstick, Wm. Henry Brown, Nathan Kite, John C. Allen, Wm. M. Collins, James Kite, Joseph Scattergood, Edward Ritchie, Josiah H. Newbold, Nathaniel H. Brown, Paul W. Newhall, Horatio C. Wood, Jonathan Evans.

Alfred Cope, Walnut street wharf, Philadelphia, is appointed Corresponding Clerk of the Board of Managers.

The Annual Meeting is held in the Arch street house, on third-day evening, during the week of the Yearly Meeting.

Hymn composed by Dr. Hawksworth, about a month before his death.

In sleep's serene oblivion laid,   •
   I safely pass'd the silent night,
At once I saw the breaking shade,   \
   And drink again the morning light.

New-born I bless the waking hour,
   Once more with awe rejoice to be ;
My conscious soul resumes her power
   And springs, my gracious God, to thee.

O guide me through the various maze,
   My doubtful feet are doomed to tread ;
And spread thy shield's protecting blaze,
   When dangers press around my head.

A' *deeper shade* will soon impend,
   A *deeper sleep* my eyes oppress :
Yet still thy strength shall me defend,
   Thy goodness still shall deign to bless.

That *deeper shade* shall fade away,
   That *deeper sleep* shall leave my eyes :
Thy light shall give eternal day,
   Thy love the rapture of the skies !

THE FRIEND.

FIFTH MONTH, 23, 1840.

With the present number is brought to a close the speech of Ambrose H. Sevier, in the United States senate, on the subject of the vexatious and complicated controversy between the pre-emption claimants, the United States, &c., on the one part, and the shamefully and cruelly imposed upon Seneca Indians on the other. We were induced to transfer the document to our pages at the suggestion of a much respected Friend, who has evinced a lively interest in the welfare of the aboriginal tribes, and during many years of his life devoted much of his valuable time in labours for their benefit, temporal and spiritual. The speech is a plain-dealing and able exposition of the case, unraveling, sometimes with sarcastic severity, but without exaggeration, the tangled web of a most vile scheme of intrigue and fraud, and all grasping avarice, perpetrated upon a helpless, unoffending, and unsuspecting people. It will be right to mention, for the information of those who may be ignorant of the fact, that these are the Indians who, for more than forty years, have been the continued objects of benevolent solicitude and care of our yearly meeting, accompanied with a large expenditure of funds, as also of time and labour, and whose beautiful, greatly improved, and comfortable settlements, with all their fond associations and predilections—homebred attachments, are now to be for ever abandoned, in exchange for a dreary, inhospitable wilderness, in a far distant and strange land.

The annual report, on another page, of the unpretending but truly useful institution, the Philadelphia Tract Association of Friends, we call attention to, as possessing matter of interest to many of our readers. The latest printed of the tracts in their catalogue, No. 64, consisting of extracts from an address by the late venerable Thomas Shillitoe, we have decided to place in our columns, in the belief, that the Christian admonition contained in it merited a wider circulation.

HAVERFORD SCHOOL ASSOCIATION.

A Special Meeting of Haverford School Association will be held in the Committee Room, Friends' Meeting House, on Arch street, on second day, the 1st of 6th month, at 4 o'clock, P. M.

CHARLES EVANS, *Secretary.*

HAVERFORD SCHOOL.

Letters and small packages for the students, may be left at the store of Kimber & Sharpless, No. 50 North Fourth street, Philadelphia, where the superintendent will send for them once a week—mostly on seventh day.

An experienced book-keeper and accountant being at present disengaged, is desirous of obtaining a situation, either in a merchant's counting house, or in a company's office, as book-keeper or secretary. Apply at the office of "The Friend."

THE FRIEND.

A RELIGIOUS AND LITERARY JOURNAL.

VOL. XIII.   SEVENTH DAY, FIFTH MONTH, 30, 1840.   NO. 35.

EDITED BY ROBERT SMITH.

PUBLISHED WEEKLY.

Price two dollars per annum, payable in advance.

Subscriptions and Payments received by

GEORGE W. TAYLOR,

NO. 50, NORTH FOURTH STREET, UP STAIRS,

PHILADELPHIA.

CENTRAL AMERICA.

(Continued from p. 209.)

In respect to the animals of the country, the most important are those which are not indigenous to the continent, but which have been introduced by the Spaniards, as cattle, horses, sheep, goats, and hogs. The horses are not of a very superior breed, but the mules are exceedingly hardy and useful. The woods and mountains contain some wild animals, but none very fierce or powerful. The most remarkable are tigers and wolves. The former are rather a species of leopard, and seldom attack a man, but live on game, and sometimes come into the villages and seize on the dogs and cattle. They are hunted for the sake of their skins, which are very beautiful. The zorillo is a small fox, which emits an effluvia so powerful and offensive, that it stupifies, and has been known to cause the death of a dog that had killed it. The same effluvia leaves a blue dye on every thing it comes in contact with. The tapir, commonly called the mountain cow, is the largest of the quadrupeds in a wild state, but in appearance is something between a hog and elephant. The zahino and the striped boar are also found in Central America, and a great variety of monkeys. Deer and wild hogs are common in the woods. Of the latter, there is a species with an excrescence on its back, from which a fetid matter is constantly exuding. This excrescence the natives call the navel, and say it must be immediately cut out on the animal being killed, as it contaminates the flesh. The otter and the manati are to be found in the rivers, which also abound with alligators. The latter are sometimes very large and dangerous.

Of snakes, lizards, and other reptiles, there is a great variety and abundance. The most dangerous are the rattlesnake, and another species called the Tamagazo; but particularly the latter, which is so venomous, that its bite occasions instant death. Happily, there exists an infallible antidote to the venom of these reptiles in a plant called *el Guaco*, the leaves or roots of which pounded and applied to the wound, or used internally by chewing them, and swallowing the juice, very rarely fail to effect a cure. This plant is also worn round the legs or ankles by persons in the woods, to prevent the bite of a snake. It is always to be found near places frequented by venomous animals. Its effect on them is believed to be narcotic and soothing—a sort of intoxication, which disarms them of their malignity. I was told by a merchant at Izabal, that having allowed the guaco to grow up in his garden, the place in a short time was infested by snakes; but that on rooting up the plant, and clearing his garden of it, these unwelcome visitors disappeared. The mica is another snake, the reputed peculiarity of which is, that it does not bite, but lashes with its tail, which it uses like a whip. The boa is also found in some parts of Central America. The armadillo and the iguana are common, and are said to be excellent eating. Scorpions and centipedes are also numerous, and the more troublesome, as they infest the dwellings of the inhabitants.

The birds of Central America are deservedly celebrated for their great variety, and the extraordinary beauty of their plumage. Among the most conspicuous, is the quesal, or trogon resplendens, which is to be found only in the wild and remote regions of Central America and the south of Mexico. Those frequenting the forests of Quesaltenango, from which they derive their name, are much the finest. The bird is of the shape and size of a pigeon. Its plumage is of a metallic golden green, except that of the wings, which is spotted with a brilliant red and black. The head is adorned with a soft silky crest of short barred feathers, of a beautiful green. But the distinguishing feature of this bird, and that which constitutes its peculiarity and beauty, is the plumage of its tail, which consists of three or four loose wavy feathers of a rich green, powdered with gold. These feathers are barred, and about three feet long. They used to be worn by the aborigines of America as ornaments for the head. In brilliancy of plumage, and in symmetry of form, this bird—even setting aside the grace and beauty of its pendent plumage—is unrivalled among the feathered tribe. When deprived of the ornament of its tail, the quesal seems sensible of the injury: it sickens and dies. Such is the importance it attaches to this part of its gorgeous dress, that the nest it makes is provided with two apertures, one for egress, the other for regress, in order to avoid the necessity of turning, by which the feathers of its tail might be broken or disordered. For the same reason it seldom makes a short or sudden turn. The Indians held it sacred, and used to say that the Creator, when he formed the world, assumed the form of a quesal.

The chorcha, a species of oreole, is remarkable for the curious construction of its nest, which is of the kind called pensile, from the circumstance of its being suspended in the air, by a mere thread, from the extremity of a lofty branch. In the construction of this nest, an architectural conception is displayed, the most ingenious, artificial, and complicate that it is possible to imagine. It is a bird of small size, and its plumage is black and yellow. It is to be found also in the United States; and as a very correct account of it is given in Wilson's Ornithology, any description of it here would be superfluous.

The sinsonte may be styled the American nightingale. It has also some affinities with the mocking-bird of the United States. From the peculiar softness and clearness of its note, it ranks the first among the singing birds of Central America. Parrots, perroquets, and mackaws, abound in the woods. The gay plumage of the latter, in its contrast with the deep green foliage of the trees, has a beautiful effect.

Besides these birds, there are numerous others equally remarkable, which it would be tedious to enumerate; for in no part of the world is the ornithological department more rich than in this country.

The population of Central America is estimated at one million nine hundred thousand souls, of all descriptions, besides the Mosquito Indians, who live in a state of independence. This population is divided into four grand castes, namely, Indians, whites, blacks, and ladinos—a mixture of the other three. The relative number of these classes is approximately as follows:

Indians,	. .	685,000,
Whites,	. .	475,000,
Ladinos,	. .	740,000,

Total, 1,900,000.

The number of blacks is too inconsiderable to be taken into account. It may also be remarked, that the ladinos of this country cannot be assimilated to the West Indian mulattoes, as their complexions are much fairer, and many are scarcely distinguishable from the whites.

The Indians of Central America, with the exception of one or two small tribes, are domesticated, and subject to the government of the country; many of them speak the Castilian, and are blended in their manners with the mass of the population. But, as I have heretofore had occasion to observe, they preserve in a great degree their aboriginal languages and customs. They even retain some vestiges of their ancient religious rites and superstitions, and it requires all the vigilance of the curates to prevent their falling back into idolatry. In Costarica there is a small tribe called the Valientes, who are allowed to retain their independence. They inhabit the woods and forests of that state, but are in constant intercourse with the rest of the population, and are peaceable and honest. The Mosquito Indians, before alluded to, are an ignorant indolent race, settled in the northern coast of Honduras, who in like manner disclaim the authority of the government, but are, in some sort, under the control of the English, to whom they are much attached.

The territory of Central America is capable of containing an infinitely greater population than that specified in the preceding statement. A large portion of it is unsettled, and in a state of nature. There are vast tracts in the interior, enjoying a fine climate and a fertile soil, where the most flattering prospects are held out to foreign emigrants, and where agricultural industry could not fail of reaping an ample compensation. Conscious of this, and of the advantages of recruiting its population from foreign countries, the government has adopted the policy of encouraging emigration. But the attempts made towards effecting this object have been hitherto unsuccessful, owing no doubt to the constantly disturbed state of the country and the insecurity of property.

[The author, sailing from New York, first arrives at Havana; from thence, after a stay of a few days, proceeds on his voyage and lands at Truxillo, a port of Central America, in the Bay of Honduras.]

The town stands close by the sea, at the foot of a lofty mountain crowned with trees, and clothed with a rich vegetation reaching to the very edge of the water. It is an isolated solitary place, of antiquated appearance, with few houses, and those in a ruinous condition.

During my stay in Truxillo I took a ramble in the woods, accompanied by the captain of the vessel. There is a brook in the neighbourhood of the town which pursues a winding course through the woods, and among the rocks, till it falls into the sea: we resolved to explore its banks as far as circumstances might permit. We sat out, accordingly, each of us armed with a stout stick, in the apprehension of encountering snakes. Indeed, so exaggerated were the accounts I had received of the number of these reptiles infesting the woods, that I had conceived it impossible to move a step without danger of being attacked by them.

As we proceeded on our excursion I was agreeably surprised by the beauty of the scenery. The size and loftiness of the trees, some of them in blossom, and the deep verdure of their foliage, surpassed anything I had ever seen of the kind. There was the tamarind tree, the wild lemon, loaded with fruit, and the sassafras. There, too, was the mahogany tree, which, like the sassafras, furnishes a staple commodity of the country; and a variety of other trees, with whose properties and names we were wholly unacquainted. There was a vast number of plants also, that seemed to me curious and well worth the attention of a botanist. Parrots, pelicans, and other birds of brilliant plumage, were flying all around us; there were singing birds among the trees; while, in the limpid waters of the brook, might be seen, now and then, the silvery sides of a fish glistening in the sun, as it darted across the stream. The leafy branches of the trees, overhanging the water from either bank, formed, in many places, a delightful shade. The brook sometimes rushed and foamed noisily among groups of rocks or through narrow passes; and at other times glided peacefully on, on an almost imperceptible current. At one place a little bay was formed, deep and cool, where the smooth and placid surface of the water, which was beautifully transparent, reflected, as in a mirror, the overhanging trees. It was impossible not to be affected by the solitude and beauty of the scene: the charm was felt and acknowledged by my companion as well as by myself. A pleasant breeze, blowing at the time, effectually prevented our being annoyed by mosquitoes; and, singular as it seemed to me, we met with no snake, nor any dangerous animal, in our path.

[Our traveller leaves Truxillo for Izabal, a port at the head of the Bay of Honduras, from whence to commence his overland journey to Guatemala, the place of his destination.]

It was late in the evening before our vessel gained the mouth of the Izabal. This river takes its rise in a great fresh-water lake called *Golfo dulce*, and pursues a meandering course for some fifty miles, before falling into the sea. At the head of that lake is situated the town of Izabal, the port of our destination. The entrance to this river is scarcely discernible, even in the day-time, to an unpractised eye, till within about a hundred yards of it, when an opening is perceived in the mountains like the opening of an immense cavern. The effect, as we approached it in the night, was still more striking; a starry sky affording just light enough to guide us on our path, but not sufficient to make objects distinctly visible. On entering the opening just mentioned, we seemed penetrating into the bowels of the earth. On each side of us towered the lofty and precipitous mountains that form the banks of the river; and immediately in front rose a completely our further progress. Towards this land, which appeared to recede as we advanced, the boat kept her way, steadily and at a good rate, for a full half hour, with her bows apparently not more than half a cable's length distant from it. There were moments when I trembled lest she should run against it, and be dashed to pieces. But this interposition of land was only an illusion, caused by the windings of the river, and heightened by the confused appearance of objects in the night.

About midnight the moon rose, and the effect of her pale silvery light on the trees and water was beautiful beyond description. I could now see objects more distinctly, and felt satisfied that if there is anything picturesque, beautiful, and sublime in nature, it must be the entrance to this river. The banks rise from a height of from two to three hundred feet, and are clothed with a rich and impenetrable foliage, the branches of the trees spreading several yards over the water. In some places this foliage suddenly disappears, and a vast naked rock, smooth and flat, and perfectly perpendicular, rises like a stupendous wall, at the foot of which the depth of water admits a vessel, brushing the very face of the precipice, without danger. Here and there may be seen a rill of water, as clear as crystal, coursing from top to bottom of this natural wall, or gushing out from a fissure in its side. At other places, a group of rocks assumes the appearance of an old castle or ruinous fortification. The stream varies in width from a hundred and fifty to three hundred feet, and is in many places thirty fathoms deep. It is dotted at intervals with little islands covered with reeds; and the sharp turnings it makes, give continual interest and variety to the scenery.

As we proceeded, the noise of the water thrown up by the paddles startled the tenants of this beautiful wilderness; and every now and then we heard a plunge, like that of an alligator, or an otter, seeking the deepest recesses of the river, or the scream of an aquatic bird flying across the stream: the only sounds that disturbed the silence of this solitary scene.

In the course of the night the boat stopped at a little fort called San Felipe, to take in fuel. During this detention I allowed myself a little rest, but was up again the next morning by daylight, when I found that the boat was not yet ready to start. The scene around, illuminated by the first rays of the sun, appeared to me even more striking and beautiful than when I had beheld it by moonlight. The lofty and umbrageous trees exhibited every variety of green, from the deepest tint to the lightest, and were alive with singing birds, while parrots and mackaws kept up a continued scream. Now and then a monkey would show himself, for an instant, swinging by his tail from a twig, or leaping from branch to branch. The little fort, with its ruinous battlements, could be seen partly reflected in the water, the surface of which was skimmed by the alcatrazes intent on their prey, and seemingly unconscious of our presence.

(To be continued.)

From the Advocate of Peace.

CHINA.

From Medhurst's recent and very valuable work on China, we condense a few items appropriate to our pages.

I. *Its Extent.*—China proper, consisting of eighteen fertile and extensive provinces, covers 1,298,000 square miles, or about 830,720,000 English acres, for the most part densely populated. This central territory is enlarged by the addition of Chinese Tartary, a vast but thinly peopled region; and the power and grandeur of China are augmented by her authority or influence over Thibet, Corea, and Loo-Choo, over Cochin-China, Camboja, Burmah and Siam; including within 35 degrees of latitude, and 70 of longitude, more than 3,000,000 square miles.

II. *Its Population.*—This has long been a subject of dispute among learned men; but recent inquiries and disclosures pretty fully confirm the highest estimates hitherto reported. Dr. Morrison investigated the point with great care, and gathered full and satisfactory information from official documents. China is furnished with the best means of an accurate census. "Every district has its appropriate officer; every street its constable; and every ten houses its tithing-man. Every family is required to have a board always hanging up in the house, and ready for the inspection of the authorized officers, on which the names of all persons, men, women and children in the house, are inscribed." From these boards, or from the reports of heads of families, an annual census is made for the purposes of internal policy ; and the results given in these " statistical accounts of the empire," so far from being exaggerated for the gratification of national vanity, are likely, for various reasons stated by Morrison and Medhurst, to fall below the actual number. We subjoin the following progressive view of the population from 1393 to 1812, the date of Morrison's inquiries :

In 1393,	. . . .	60,545,811
1662,	. . . .	21,068,600
1668,	. . . .	25,386,209
1710,	. . . .	23,312,200
1711,	. . . .	28,605,716
1753,	. . . .	102,328,258
1792,	. . . .	307,467,200
1812,	. . . .	361,221,909

The following are estimates of different writers at the periods designated :

In 1743, according to Amiot,	157,301,755
1792, " Grosier,	198,214,553
1790, " Morrison,	143,126,234
1792, " Staunton,	333,000,000

These estimates do not profess to be accurate ; but the former were copied from official returns of the population at the specified dates. Nor is it difficult to account for the alternate increase and decrease. From 1393 to 1662, they were reduced from 60,000,000 to 21,000,000, and continued very much the same for nearly a century, when they rose to more than 100,000,000. The first reduction was occasioned by the wars attending the Tartar conquest of China ; by large portions of the empire in the south and west not being completely subdued, so as to be reckoned as subjects ; and by the mode of raising the revenue in the form of a capitation tax, which led vast multitudes to evade the enrolment of themselves and their families. At length, however, the capitation tax was converted into a land tax, and the effect was soon visible in the results of the annual census. The comparatively rapid increase of the population from 1711 to 1753, and thence to 1792, was occasioned mainly by the almost uninterrupted peace of China ; and the diminished rate of increase from 1792 to 1812, was owing to emigration and to the use of opium.

Morrison and Medhurst both suppose China to contain not less than 361,000,000 inhabitants. Nor is this incredible. China proper alone embraces 830,720,000 English acres ; and this would give nearly 2½ acres for every inhabitant ; while an English physician has calculated that a single acre cultivated with potatoes, would subsist nearly 50 persons. Three hundred and sixty-one millions would be only 200 to every square mile ; and there are in Holland 210 to the square mile, in England 244, in Ireland 256, and in Belgium 333.

III. *Destructive influence of Opium on the population of China.*—From the close of the Tartar wars to the introduction of opium near the close of the eighteenth century, the population increased during long periods at the annual rate of about three per cent.; but mainly through the influence of this pernicious drug, the ratio of increase has been reduced to about one per cent.

"Those who have not seen the effects of opium-smoking in the eastern world, can hardly form any conception of its injurious results on the health, energies and lives of those who indulge in it. When the habit is once formed, it grows till it becomes inveterate. In proportion as the wretched victim comes under its power, so is his ability to resist temptation less strong ; and, debilitated in body as well as mind, he is unable to earn his usual pittance, and not unfrequently sinks under the cravings of an appetite which he is unable to gratify. Thus they may be seen hanging their heads by the doors of the opium-shops, which the hard-hearted keepers, having fleeced them of their all, will not permit them to enter ; and shut out from their own dwellings, either by angry relations or ruthless creditors, they die in the streets, unpitied and despised. In fact, every opium-smoker may calculate upon shortening his life ten years from the time when he commences the practice ; and, reckoning the shortened lives, the frequent diseases, and the actual starvation which are the result of this practice in China, we may venture to assert, that this pernicious drug annually destroys myriads of individuals."

Before 1796, opium, admitted on the payment of a duty, was imported to the extent of only a few hundred chests ; but, though since that time prohibited under heavy penalties, its importation has increased, especially within a few years, at the fearful rate of the following table.

Imported in	Chests	Valued at
1816,	3,210,	$3,657,000
1820,	4,770,	8,400,800
1825,	9,621,	7,608,205
1830,	18,760,	12,900,031
1832,	23,670,	15,338,160
1836,	27,111,	17,904,248
1837 in July	4,000,	
during the year	34,000,	about 23,000,000

IV. *Military establishment of China.*—The government of China includes under its cabinet of ministers six tribunals,—the tribunal of civil office, of revenue, of rites, of war, of punishments, and of public works. The tribunal of war superintends all the military affairs of the empire. The army, rated at 700,000, is a sort of militia, "being employed a part of the year in cultivating the ground, and contributing to their own support. These generally clothe and arm themselves according to their own fancy, and are distinguished by the character *robust* stitched on their jackets in front, and the word *brave* behind ! The regularly organised troops of the present dynasty are the Tartar legions, which amount to 80,000 effective men, arranged under eight banners, and always at the disposal of the government. These are so distributed throughout the empire as to keep four thousand times their own number in order,—80,000 × 4,000 = 320,000,000.

Chinese preparations for war compared with those of Christendom.—We have in former numbers given some estimate on this subject ; but though very low in contrast with those of Christian nations, we now ascertain them to have been much too high. It seems from Mr. Medhurst's account, that the regular army of China amounts merely to 80,000

men ; that all the other soldiers (700,000) resemble our militia more than they do the standing armies of Europe ; and that the entire military force of an empire containing a population of more than 361,000,000, is only 780,000.

Contrast this with the military establishments of Christendom. With a population of little more than 200,000,000, she maintains even in peace between three and four millions of soldiers ; an average of one soldier to about 70 inhabitants ; while China, if we reckon only her 80,000 Tartars, has barely one to 4,512, and, if we include her 700,000 militia, only one to 463 ; a proportion, according to the first estimate, of less than one to 600, and, according to the second, of little more than one to seven, in comparison with nations reputedly Christian. With less than fifteen millions of people, we ourselves have on our militia rolls probably 1,500,000, an average of one soldier to ten inhabitants, while China has at most only one to 463 !

Is it possible to conceive a fouler libel on Christianity, a keener satire on her professions of peace and good-will? Christendom, an immense range of barracks, a nursery of warriors, a vast slaughter-yard drenched age after age with Christian blood, shed by baptized hands ! Such a religion offer peace to China ! Could we make the Chinese credit such a promise, belied by the whole history of warring Christendom ? Yet the church, which has for centuries upheld this accursed system as an ordinance of God ! is said, even by some professed friends of peace, to have been in all ages essentially correct on this subject ! ! and the gospel, *as thus understood and practised*, is confidently expected to banish war from the face of the earth ! !

From the same.

HISTORY OF NANTUCKET.

An illustration of the efficacy of pacific principles.

Our secretary, who visited this interesting island last spring, was presented with a copy of its history, by Obed Macy, from which we might, would our limits allow, the slightest sketch, gather many facts to illustrate the safety and wisdom of a pacific policy.

The persecution of the Quakers led to the settlement of this island. Thomas Macy, having given shelter in his house to four Quakers for three quarters of an hour in a rain-storm, was compelled to seek among savages an asylum from the intolerance of our fore-fathers ; and, in the autumn of 1659, he took his family, in an open boat, around Cape Cod to Nantucket, of which the patent-right had already been purchased by ten men belonging to Salisbury. These purchasers soon after associated with themselves ten more, and subsequently extended the number to twenty-seven, by inviting seven mechanics to settle with them. This division of the island into twenty-seven shares, called *commonage*, continues to the present day, with a large number of subdivisions.

The whole history of Nantucket is curious and deeply interesting ; but we are concerned mainly with the progress of its pacific policy. This policy did not originate with the Quakers; for they had no meeting or society there till half a century after the settlement of the island, and they have always formed only a small minority. The great body of the people have never adopted the strict principles of peace; but influenced chiefly by their situation and employment, they have from the first entertained "a strong and almost universal opinion, that wars are wrong." They suffered intensely from our last and the revolutionary war; but their well-known aversion to war has proved a far better shield to them than fleets and fortifications could have been. Exposed on all sides, without the possibility of defence, without a single fort, arsenal, or military company, they have been left secure in their homes, and permitted to enjoy in war exemptions and privileges granted to no others. Nantucket, though utterly defenceless, was actually safer from plunder and conflagration "than fortified seaports, or even many inland towns."

Our militia system is entirely disregarded on this island. Nor is it found necessary for the enforcement of law, or any domestic or foreign purposes of government. The people, almost to a man, are opposed to its introduction; and no military organisation of any kind has ever been attempted with any success. Public opinion executes law; and their pacific character is a surer guarantee against foreign invasion than a rampart bristling with cannon all around the island. This is not mere theory, but the actual result of experiments tried there for nearly two hundred years.

From the same.

A PEACE SOCIETY IN THE FAR WEST.

The name of Dr. Nelson, the founder of the Mission Institute, in Quincy, Illinois, is familiar to all our readers; and we were happy to receive a few days ago, through our worthy friend and coadjutor, L. D. Dewey, of New York, a letter giving an account of a peace society organised in that seminary on the 10th of July, at the suggestion of Dr. Nelson. We copy the preamble and constitution sent by the secretary, William Fithian, who informs us, that "fifty persons had subscribed their names as members of the society."

PREAMBLE TO THE CONSTITUTION.

"Whereas the horrid custom of war has been prevalent among all nations, and even those called Christians have spent the greater part of their time, energies and revenues, in making havoc of the human family, and in contending with each other about matters that might be settled by arbitration; whereas the warrior, the destroyer of his race, has been crowned with glory for his deeds of blood, and extolled by the poet and the orator, while the peaceful benefactor of his race is forgotten; whereas war is chiefly set on foot by rulers who are liable to little personal suffering, while the mass of people pay their money, and spill their blood; and whereas, this war-spirit is universally prevalent, and because the church has neglected to testify against it; therefore, we unite and promise that we will endeavour to discourage the custom of war by all lawful means, and diffuse, as far as our influence

goes, a *spirit of peace;* that we will strive to quell wrathful passions in ourselves and others; that we will collect and diffuse information calculated to discourage war and promote universal peace; that we will have stated seasons of prayer for this object, and unite with others so far as we can, to promote the object, until ' peace on earth' shall be diffused every where."

THE FRIEND.

FIFTH MONTH, 30, 1840.

The present season has been peculiarly marked with atmospheric phenomena in various parts of the country—hurricanes, hail storms, inundations, &c. have been frequent. But a tornado, with which the city of Natchez was visited on the 7th of the present month, must have been awful to a degree seldom equalled in this country. About one o'clock on that day the attention of the citizens " was attracted by an unusual and continuous roaring of thunder to the southward, at which point hung masses of black clouds, some of them stationary, and others whirling along with under currents, but all driving a little east of north." The following is from the Natchez (Miss.) Free Trader, extra:—

The dinner bells in the large hotels had rung a little before two o'clock, and most of our citizens were sitting at their tables, when suddenly the atmosphere was darkened so as to require the lighting of candles, and in a few moments afterwards the rain was precipitated in tremendous cataracts rather than in drops. In another moment the tornado, in all its wrath, was upon us. The strongest buildings shook as if tossed with an earthquake; the air was black with whirling eddies of house walls, roofs, chimnies, huge timbers, torn from distant ruins, all shot through the air as if thrown from a mighty catapult. The atmosphere soon became lighter, and then such an awful scene of ruin as perhaps never before met the eye of man became manifest. The greater part of the ruin was effected in the short space of from three to five minutes, although the heavy sweeping tornado lasted nearly half an hour. For about five minutes it was more like the explosive force of gunpowder than any thing else it could have been compared to. Hundreds of rooms were burst open as sudden as if barrels of gunpowder had been ignited in each. As far as glasses or the naked eye can reach, the first traces of the tornado are to be seen from the Natchez bluff down the river about ten miles, bearing considerably west of south. Sweeping across the Natchez island it crossed the point below the plantation of David Barland, Esq. opposite the plantations of P. M. Lapice, Esq. in the parish of Concordia. It then struck the Natchez bluff about a mile and a half below the city, near the mansion called the "Briers," which it but slightly injured; but swept the mansion late of Charles B. Green, Esq. called the "Bellevue," and the ancient forest, in which it was embossed, into a mass of ruins. It then struck the city through its whole width of one mile, and included the entire

river and the village of Vidalia on the Louisiana shore—making the path of the tornado more than two miles in width. At the Natchez landing, on the river, the ruin of dwellings, stores, steamboats, flat boats, was almost entire from the Vidalia ferry to the Mississipi cotton press. A few torn fragments of dwellings still remain, but they can scarcely be called shelters.

In the upper city, or Natchez on the hill, scarcely a house escaped damage or utter ruin. The Presbyterian and Methodist churches have their towers thrown down, their roofs broken, and their walls shattered. The Episcopal church is much injured in its roof. Parker's great Southern Exchange is level with the dust. Great damage has been done to the City Hotel and the Mansion House, both being unroofed, and the upper stories broken up.

The destruction of property,—of houses, merchandize, &c., appears to have been immense, and yet more to be deplored; many human lives were lost. Our space will only admit of an additional short extract or two:—

The estimate of a little more than a million and a quarter of dollars for the damages done to the buildings merely, may be nearly correct for the compact part of the city; but to cover the loss of merchandise, provisions, goods of various kinds, and furniture destroyed, there should, in the opinion of some of the practical and clear minded men, be at least four millions more added—making the entire loss of property in the city of Natchez more than five millions of dollars. It is said there were 50 persons buried in one of the hotels. Seven were taken dead from the railroad depot, and seven dead and one injured from the hotel under the hill. Rumour says that, in all, 200 persons had been taken dead from the ruins. Of course, many not killed were more or less injured.

WESTTOWN SCHOOL.

The committee to superintend the boarding school at Westtown, will meet in Philadelphia on sixth day, the 12th of next month, at 3 o'clock, P. M.

The committee on instruction meet on the same day at 10 o'clock, A. M. And the visiting committee attend at the school on seventh day, the 6th of the month.

THOMAS KIMBER, *Clerk.*

Phila. 5th mo. 30th, 1840.

INSTITUTE FOR COLOURED YOUTH.

The managers are desirous of procuring a suitably qualified person (a member of the Society of Friends) to have the care of, and instruct a limited number of boys at the above institution.

Applications may be forwarded to either of the undernamed committee.

George Williams, 71 north Seventh street, Philip Garrett, Noble street, first door above Sixth, Blakey Sharpless, 50 north Fourth street, M. L. Dawson, corner of Tenth and Filbert streets. *Phila.* 5th mo. 30th, 1840.

HAVERFORD SCHOOL.

Letters and small packages for the students, may be left at the store of Kimber & Sharpless, No. 50 North Fourth street, Philadelphia, where the superintendent will send for them once a week—mostly on seventh day.

Extracts from an Address to the society of Friends. By Thomas Shillitoe.

(Concluded from p. 271.)

Those who covet an evil covetousness, must expect to possess leanness of soul; the sorrowful consequences of which will be unfruitfulness towards God, which, although it may appear to be very slow in its gradations, yet such may rest assured that it will take place, whatever they may have known aforetime of an enlargement of heart towards him and his cause. Some among us, not satisfied when a kind Providence has so favoured them, as that there has been an ample supply from their present business for basket and store, to satisfy their thirst of more, have infringed upon the rights and privileges of others, adding one fresh business to another. How does such a mode of procedure comport with a people professing, as we do, to be dead to the world, and alive unto him, whose apostle declared, "If any man love the world, the love of the Father is not in him?" From whence proceeds this conduct? Let the just witness tell us, my friends; and may it arouse us before it be too late! Let such no longer continue to say, "To-day or to morrow we will go into such a city, and continue there a year, and buy and sell, and get gain;" whereas they know not what shall be on the morrow: but let them be willing to yield to the restraining influence of God's word and power.

Consider from whence this determination proceeds, which many among us appear to have made; this willingness to sacrifice every thing that should be nearest and dearest to them, in order to add ten thousand to ten thousand, and twenty thousand to twenty thousand, and double and treble it again and again, if possible. Let those things speak for themselves: can they proceed from any other disposition than the love of the world? O, let such consider if the apostle's declaration be not true as to them, that the love of the Father is not in them. For many years I have esteemed it a reproach to such a society of professing Christians as we are, when any of our members have been summoned from works to rewards, and have left behind them such large sums of money of their own accumulation. O what a cloud has it brought over their very best actions, however conspicuous they may have stood in society! O the sorrowful feelings I have been dipped into at times on the account of such!—language fails me to set them forth. It is painful for me thus to expose myself on this sorrowful subject, for such I have often experienced it to be; but I believe that, if my feeble efforts be accepted as a peace-offering, that which appears to be the whole counsel must be imparted.

Some have replied, when remonstrated with on these subjects, that they are at a loss to define the word "enough;" but this difficulty, I am of the mind, rests with themselves: in the first place, through an unwillingness to have their wants circumscribed by that power which is from above; and in the next, for want of a sincere desire to have this word defined for them, by that wisdom which is as competent to direct in this as in any other important step of life. As it is a duty we owe to the body,

to make suitable provision for its comfort and convenience, especially for old age, that we may rather be helpful to others than require their help: so likewise to put our children in the way to get their living by moderate industry, and provide for such of them as may not be in a capacity to help themselves: when a kind Providence has entrusted to us so much as may answer these purposes, if after this there remains a disposition to accumulate, then I believe we are violating that command of the Divine Master, "Lay not up for yourselves treasures upon earth," and we are giving full proof where our hearts are: not that I apprehend it would be better for all such who have thus attained, to quit their trades and occupations; because some may be more in the way of their duty in continuing to pursue them honourably; when, besides introducing deserving persons as their successors, they may be the means of helping those who are not able to help themselves, with which description of persons the world abounds, such as the widows and the fatherless, and the infirm, who frequently are obliged to labour under extreme pain and suffering; but there must be no adding to the "enough," lest that enough which has been mercifully dispensed, be taken away again.

I am now under the necessity of claiming your attention, my dear sisters, in order that you may do your part in facilitating the escape of your husbands and parents from the troubled waters and sunk rocks of commercial difficulty, which the keen eye of human policy is so often unable to discover; for with you generally rests the management of household affairs: it is also principally for the supply of these that the labouring oar is kept tugging. You must be willing, mothers and children, to examine closely the mode and circumstances of your expenditure, with a mind made up to relieve, as far as in you lies, the head of the family, who may have both wind and tide to contend with. Search your houses, search your tables, search your garments; and where any expense can be spared without lessening your real comforts, seek for holy help to rid the vessel of it. I am well aware it will require holy help to take such steps; but this I am assured will not be wanting if sought after in a proper disposition of mind. And we shall find that those things which have been sacrificed, being calculated only to gratify the vain mind in ourselves and others, and pamper a depraved appetite, had not the effect of adding real comfort to our hearts. Regard not the world's dread laugh, but set your intimates and neighbours this salutary example; show them the way to live well at little expense; an example I believe we are called upon in a peculiar manner to be holding up.

And, Friends, you that are of ability of body, learn to wait more upon yourselves, and bring your children to do the like: I find I am never better waited on, than when I wait upon myself. Teach your children industry and a well-regulated economy; I fear there is too much need in the present day to press this wholesome practice; for next to a truly pious example, you cannot bestow upon your children a better portion. This appears to have been much the case with our first Friends;

and it had been better for many of our youth, had their parents trod more in the footsteps of these. Labour is a part of the penance enjoined by the fall. "By the sweat of thy brow shalt thou get thy bread." This sentence pronounced upon Adam descends to all his posterity. Suitable employment under the regulating influence of an all-wise Creator, is salutary both for mind and body, and qualifies us the better to feel for, and proportion labour, to those who may be placed under us. It may even prove a secondary means of keeping our nature under subjection, which we cannot be ignorant is corrupt, and requires much subduing; something to check its impetuosity, and bear rule in all our actions. There is yet another precious advantage results from bringing up children in habits of well-regulated industry and economy; little business will then be found sufficient to bring up a family reputably, when our wants are confined to real comforts and conveniences, which truth allows as far as ever our circumstances will warrant them.

When we are content to move in this humble sphere, we are prepared the better to meet such reverses as may come upon us. Let none among us say in his heart, I am out of the reach of reverses, because none are out of the reach of them; for however variously our outward substance may be secured, all sublunary things are unstable as the waters; and various as may be our resources, every supply may be cut off; the Philistines may be permitted to stop up all the wells which we have dug for ourselves and our children. The Most High may permit his little army to enter into our vineyards and oliveyards, and strip us of all, without power on our part to prevent the devastation; for when the palmerworm leaves, the canker-worm may eat; and what the canker-worm leaves, the caterpillar may so destroy, that not the least vestige of our once greenness and greatness may remain. This has been the case with many within my memory. The crafty have been so taken in their own craftiness, and the lofty so brought down from their seats, and the men of low degree exalted, that he who was the servant has become the master of his once master, and even his master's children have served his children. What has been may be again; for thus has the all-wise Disposer, to whom belong the cattle of a thousand hills and every visible thing, for nothing is mine or thine any longer than he sees meet we should possess it, evinced his sovereignty and power to humble his creature man; convincing him thus of the great uncertainty of all visible things. And may these turnings and overturnings which we hear of, and some more keenly feel the smart of, in commercial concerns and in families, prove the means of stimulating us to leave things that are behind, all of which are perishing, and press forward to those which are before, which are eternal.

I am afraid, my dear sisters, to close this subject without adding another hint, as essential to our being the better able to keep our family expenditure within its proper bounds; having myself experienced its salutary effects, when I had a numerous family around me. It is, to determine to purchase with ready money the various articles consumed for family use, and that we resolve to perform this, however mortifying it may prove, by depriving us of many things the natural disposition may crave in ourselves and children. I believe great advantage will be found to result from such a practice, both to parents and children, more particularly to such as at times feel themselves straitened, to carry on their business reputably. For when these difficulties are felt by an honest mind, it becomes obligatory on such, if they get through them, closely to inspect the manner of their expenditure, and this will afford an opportunity of timely checking any unnecessary expense that may have crept into the family. But when things for family consumption are mostly, if not all, had upon credit, this opens a wide door both for parents and children to greater indifference, both as respects expediency and cost, than truth at all justifies; and the children of such parents are in danger of being brought up ignorant of the real use or value of property. When numbering my blessings, I esteem this as not one of the least that my heavenly Father has bestowed upon me, that he kept me in a little way of business, and a care to keep my family expenses within proper bounds, and taught me the lesson of contentment with little things; because now I am advanced in life, I am satisfied I escaped manifold perplexities, which would have been at this time my attendants, had I sought after greater things as to this world. The purchasing goods for family consumption on credit, often proves a serious inconvenience to those on whom such are depending for their supplies, especially if they are not before-hand in the world; for it too frequently proves that such purchasers are not very ready to make payment in due time, and when this is the case, are they doing as they would be done by?

I want us more frequently to recur to that which we are making profession of, and as frequently compare our practice therewith, bringing all our deeds to that light, by which, in a future day, they will be judged; for I cannot refrain from expressing a jealousy, that too many amongst us are swerving into this dangerous track of the world. One of the diadems with which our first Friends were decked—one of the many jewels that shone in their character, and adorned their profession, was the care they manifested to have nothing but what they could well pay for; so that should reverses come, from the many perils they were in various ways liable to, none might be losers by them. This, in due time, with an uniform, consistent, upright conduct in other respects, procured for them that confidence in the minds of all ranks, and that respect which they so long maintained. I am not able to close this subject without entreating such, to whom these remarks may apply, not to set light by them. Look seriously at the subject, and make a stand, and hold up your testimony by example, against this baneful practice, for so I doubt not it has been to thousands, and the inlet to those embarrassments that have at last overtaken them. If we are willing to be found thus standing in our proper allotment, we may prove in a degree instrumental, in the divine hand, to check that torrent of evil, which so sorrowfully pervades

all classes: for the practice has overspread the nation of supporting an expensive manner of living upon credit, which, if not timely checked, there is reason to fear may contribute, amongst other evil practices, to work its ruin. We have stood high as a religious society in the esteem of others, for nearly a century and a half; in regard to honesty, integrity, and an exemplary conduct. Can we with truth say, we believe we have been rising higher in this respect, of later years? I fear this has not been the case; but that the many sorrowful failures, the multiplied instances of want of punctuality that have of late years occurred among us, with various departures in other respects from our well-known principles, have given a severe shock to that confidence in us, which once had place in the public mind.

The door has of late been set open much wider than was the experience of our first Friends, for the members of our society to associate with those of other religious professions, in the management of the various institutions for benevolent purposes that are on foot. Let us be careful that this does not lead us to assimilate ourselves to the world. The world hated our first Friends, because they maintained a faithful protest against its spirit, its maxims and manners; but in proportion as we put away from us the weapons of the Christian's warfare, and join in league with the world, a wider door of admittance into all companies and all societies will be opened to us. Thus we have, indeed, occasion to look well to our steppings and standing; remembering, that so far as we join ourselves to the world in any respect, we shall be condemned with the world. "If ye were of the world," said our blessed Lord to his immediate followers, "the world would love its own; but because ye are not of the world, but I have chosen you out of the world, therefore the world hateth you."

In order that we may not further forfeit the confidence of the public, but regain that which we may have lost, let me again repeat the caution, that by others' harms we may take warning; and by our future conduct give proof of our belief in this incontrovertible truth, that a man's life, or the true enjoyment of it, consisteth not in the abundance of the things which he possesseth. Let us learn that essential lesson of contentment with little things as to this world, remembering that he, whom we profess to take for our leader, declared respecting himself, although Lord of the whole world, "The foxes have holes, and the birds of the air have nests, but the son of man hath not where to lay his head," so void was he of any earthly inheritance. It was the exhortation of the prophet to Baruch, the son of Neriah, "Seekest thou great things for thyself? seek them not; for behold I will bring evil upon all flesh, saith the Lord; but thy life will I give unto thee for a prey, in all places whither thou goest." Whilst then we are engaged to circulate more generally, among mankind at large, publications explanatory of our religious principles, and religious tracts, may we give proof, in the first place, of their happy effects upon our minds; for example will do more than precept,—actions will speak louder than words; so shall we each one become a

preacher of righteousness, that cannot fail to reach to the pure witness in the minds of others.

Let us all retire to our tents; for, if I am not mistaken, such are the signs of the times, that they loudly call upon us so to do, and there closely to keep. The Lord is this tent, unto which the true Israel of God must flee to be safe; and as there is thus an abiding in him, who is the munition of rocks, should the potsherds of the earth begin to smite one against another, such will be preserved from smiting with them, in word or deed, and escape that danger which will more or less follow those who are found so meddling; and that perturbation of mind, that instability of confidence and want of support, under the various probations that may, in unerring wisdom, be permitted to overtake, which ever was and will be, the case of those who make flesh their arm.

And, Friends, let us not dare to meddle with political matters, but renewedly seek for holy help to starve that disposition so prevalent in us to be meddling therewith. Endeavour to keep that ear closed, which will be itching to hear the news of the day, and what is going forward in the political circles. I have found, that if we suffer our minds to be agitated with political matters, our dependence becomes diverted by little and little, from the true centre and place of safety, where perfect peace is experienced, though the world and all around us may speak trouble. Such as have this dependence will know it to be a truth fulfilled in their own individual experience, that "They that trust in the Lord shall be as Mount Zion, which cannot be removed; but abideth for ever;" and that, "as the mountains are round about Jerusalem, so the Lord is round about his people from henceforth even for ever."

I must now conclude, with expressing the earnest solicitude I feel, that we may each of us be found willing to unite with that all-sufficient help, which, I believe, yet waits our acceptance; and suffer it so to operate in and upon us, that we may become a people wholly separated in heart and mind, love and affection, from everything that has a tendency to dim our brightness, to prevent us from being as lights in the world; and be clothed with those beautiful garments, which so adorned our worthy ancestors—humility, self-denial, and an entire dedication of heart to the work and service of our God; a disposition truly characteristic of the disciples of him, who declared, "My kingdom is not of this world:" and thus may the enemy no longer be permitted to rob and spoil us, but the language go forth respecting us, "Happy art thou, O Israel, who is like unto thee, O people; saved by the Lord."

Thomas Shillitoe.

Hitchin, 1st of Eleventh month, 1820.

For "The Friend."

JOHN GRIFFITH.

The following account of John Griffith's first appearance in the ministry, and his remarks on that important service, are instructive, and appeared to me suitable for the columns of "The Friend." If those who apprehend themselves called to this solemn engagement were alike concerned to wait for the divine command to stand forth, and were alike careful to feel a qualification, renewed from season to season, there would be but few unsanctified offerings. The communications of such, although they might not be clothed in the "words which man's wisdom teacheth," would be attended with what is of far more consequence, "the power and demonstration of the spirit." The fact of one hundred appearances in the ministry within the compass of our yearly meeting in one year, ten of whom were in the particular meeting of Abington, is certainly interesting, and indicates a remarkable visitation to the church: the consideration of which ought to encourage us to faithfulness and strengthen us in the belief that, as we are concerned from day to day to wait upon the great Head of the church, he will in due season call and qualify "counsellors as at the first, and judges as at the beginning."

"About this time I had a distant view of being called into the work of the ministry; my mind being at times wonderfully overshadowed with the universal love of God in the glorious gospel of his Son, to mankind, to that degree that I thought I could, in the strength thereof, give up to spend and to be spent for the gathering of souls to him, the great Shepherd of Israel; and that I could lift up my voice like a trumpet, to awaken the inhabitants of the earth; but I found all this was only by way of preparation for this important work, and that I had not yet received a commission to engage therein. A fear was upon my mind, and care lest I should presume to enter upon this solemn undertaking without a right call; it appearing to me exceeding dangerous to speak in the name of the Lord without a clear evidence in the mind that he required it of me; which I then fully believed he would in his own time, which was to be waited for. From this time until I was really called into the work, I frequently had, but especially in religious meetings, openings of Scripture passages, with lively operations of the divine power in my mind; and sometimes with so much energy that I have been almost ready to offer what I had upon my mind to others. But as through an holy awe which dwelt upon my heart, I endeavoured to try my offerings in the unerring balance of the sanctuary, I found it was too light to be offered, and was thankful to the Lord for his merciful preservation, in that I had been enabled to avoid offering the sacrifice of fools. But when the time really came that it was divinely required of me, the evidence was so indisputably clear that there was not the least room to doubt, yet through fear and human frailty I put it off, and did not give way thereunto. But oh! how was I condemned in myself! The divine sweetness which had covered my mind in the meeting, was withdrawn, and I left in a very poor disconsolate state, wherein I was ready to beg forgiveness, and to covenant with the Lord, that if he would be pleased to favour me again in like manner, I would give up to his requirings. At the next first-day meeting, the heavenly power overshadowed me in a wonderful man-

ner, in which it was required of me to kneel down in supplication to the Lord in a few words: I gave way thereunto in the dread of his power with fear and trembling. After which, oh how my soul was filled with peace and joy in the Holy Ghost; I could then sing and make sweet melody in my heart to the Lord. As I remember I was 21 years of age the very day I first entered into this great and awful work of the ministry, which was the 21st of the fifth month, old style, 1734.

I have found my mind engaged to be somewhat particular concerning the manner of my entering into the work of the ministry to stand by way of caution and proper encouragement to others who may peruse the same, having, in the course of my observation, had cause to fear some have taken the work of preparation, as before hinted, for the thing itself, and so have proceeded very far to their own great wounding and the hurt of others in bringing forth untimely fruit, which is exceedingly dangerous and carefully to be avoided. Nothing is a sufficient guard to preserve therefrom but the single eye, through the divine blessing, awfully considering what a great thing it is for dust and ashes to speak as the apostle Peter directs, viz: "as every man hath received the gift, even so minister the same one to another, as good stewards of the manifold grace of God. If any man speak, let him speak as the oracles of God; if any man minister, let him do it as of the ability which God giveth." The author to the Hebrews saith, that "no man taketh this honour to himself but he that is called of God, as was Aaron." So that whatever some may pretend to and intrude themselves into, unless they are really called of God, they will have no share in that honour that cometh from God only.

The church of Christ hath not been without its trouble from false ministers, neither in the primitive times nor in ours. That excellent gospel liberty of all who feel themselves inspired thereunto, whether male or female, speaking or prophesying one by one, hath been, and still is, abused by false pretenders to divine inspiration: yet the liberty ought to be preserved inviolable, and other means found out to remedy this great inconveniency: which would not be difficult were the members in a general way spiritually minded, rightly savouring the things that be of God. Forward and unsanctified appearances by way of ministry would then be easily awed and suppressed so as not to disturb the peace of the church. The case has been otherwise, as I have observed in some places; but little minded if the words and doctrine were sound, and nothing to blame in the conversation. Here the main thing, which is the powerful demonstration of the holy spirit, is little regarded; and if a few are deeply pained at heart with such lifeless ministry, they find it exceeding difficult to lay hands thereon, for want of more strength; especially when they perceive what strength there is against them; for formal professors love to have it so rather than to sit in silence. And I have observed such pretenders all mouth or tongue, and no ears to receive instruction; fond of teaching others, but very unteachable themselves. I pray God to quicken his people, and raise the society into a more lively sense

of that blessed arm of power which gathered us to be a people; or I fear the great evil above hinted at will prove a very growing one: profession without possession being the proper element for such a ministry to grow and flourish in. I am not quite free to omit a remark on this head, as I am fully persuaded the living members of the church of Christ groan under a painful sense of this sorrowful token of a declined society. May the Lord of Sabbaoth hear their cries, and regard the anguish of their souls in secret, so as to work by his invisible power for his own name's sake, and their enlargement, by turning his hand again upon our Zion, to purge away her dross, and to take away her tin and reprobate silver, that her judges may be restored as at the first, and her counsellors as at the beginning; that many having their feet shod with the preparation of the gospel of peace, may yet appear beautiful upon the mountains: so be it, saith my soul.

I have given some hints how it was with me by way of preparative for the great and important work of the ministry, and the danger of my being misled; even at sometimes when I had right openings, and felt the sweet efficacious virtue of the love of God through Jesus Christ to mankind, which doubtless is the sensible experience and enjoyment at times of every faithful follower of Christ, who never was called to the work of the ministry. I was in those days apprehensive of some danger of being led out at that door; but I have since more fully and perfectly seen the danger of this and other by-paths, which would have led me to give that away to others, which I was to live upon myself; and out of the humble dependent state, in which only there is safety, to have a will and way of my own that I might be furnished and enriched with much treasure. But sincerity of heart, and my endeavours to preserve the single eye, through the watchful care of Divine Providence over me, brought the day of the Lord upon it all; so that I came clearly to see that away to others, which I was to live upon and experimentally to know my sufficiency was of God; that there must be a steady dependence on the Lord to be immediately fitted and supplied, every time I was to engage in this solemn service. I ardently desire, that all who have the least apprehension of being called into the work of the ministry may dwell in an holy dread of the divine presence, and know their own wills wholly subjected to the divine will, waiting for a distinct and clear certainty upon it at first, but also at all other times. And as self comes to be laid in the dust for ever, they will receive undeniable evidence in their own minds of the certainty of their mission; and they will not be without a testimony thereof from the witness of God in the consciences of mankind, amongst whom they are sent to minister. They will be a savour of life to the living in the truth, and of death to those who are in a state of death. Let it ever be remembered, that nothing of or belonging to man can possibly add any lustre or dignity to so divine a gift. Neither will the best and most curiously adapted words or doctrine, ever so truly and consistently delivered, be any more than as sounding brass or as a tinkling cymbal, without the power, light and demonstration of the spirit of Christ.

There is no occasion at all, for those who regard his power as the substance of their ministry, to be any wise solicitous about words; as the lowest and most simple are really beautiful when fitly spoken under. that holy influence.

Having thus entered upon the solemn and awful service of the ministry, I gave up for the most part, as. I found the requirings of truth through the divine power and efficacy thereof moving upon my heart and subjecting my will, to utter a few words in a broken manner, with fear and trembling; the Lord being exceeding merciful to me as a tender father, taking me by the hand, and making me willing by his mighty power, to be counted a fool for his sake and the gospel's.

The meeting I then belonged to was large, and a valuable weighty body of Friends therein; who, as far as I could observe by their carriage, did own and approve of my weak and low appearance in this service: yet they used Christian prudence not to lay hands suddenly, but gave me full opportunity to make proof of my ministry, and to feel my feet therein.

About this time a fine spring of ministry was opened within the compass of our yearly meeting; there having, by account, about one hundred opened their mouths in public testimony, in little more than a year; divers of whom became powerful, able ministers, and some of them withered away like unripe fruit. About ten appeared within that time in the particular meeting of Abington, to which I belonged.

As I was enabled to wait on my ministry, I experienced a considerable growth and enlargement; and in a faithful discharge of duty therein, great peace and heavenly consolation, like a pleasant refreshing stream, flowed into my soul. I also found that it was a means of engaging the minds of friends in a sweet and comfortable nearness of unity with me, which I had never before so largely and lovingly felt. Many young well minded people, and some others of little experience, seemed to admire my gift, and would sometimes speak highly of it, which they did not always forbear in my hearing. But oh how dangerous this is, if delighted in by ministers. It may be justly compared to poison, which will soon destroy the pure innocent life. My judgment was against it; yet I found something in me that seemed to have no aversion thereunto, but rather inclined to hearken to it, yet not with full approbation. The same thing in me would want to know what such and such, who were in most esteem for experience and wisdom, thought of me. I sometimes imagined such looked shy upon me, which would cast me down; all which, being from a root or fibre of self, I found was for judgment and must die upon the cross, before I was fit to be trusted with any great store of gospel treasure. I begun also to take rather too much delight myself in the gift; which, had not divine goodness in mercy by a deep and distressing baptism, kindly prevented, might have opened a door for spiritual pride (which is the worst of pride) to have entered in, to my ruin. I have reason to think, that solid friends, by observing my large growth in the top, with spreading branches, were in fear of my downfall in

case of a storm. However, in the midst of my high career, the Lord was pleased to take away from me for a time that which he had given me, viz: the gift of the ministry, and with it all sensible comforts of the spirit; so that I was, as I thought, in total darkness; even in the region and shadow of death. In this doleful state of mind I was grievously beset and tempted by the false prophet, the transformer, to keep up my credit in the ministry by continuing my public appearances. It might well be said of him that he would "cause fire to come down from heaven in the sight of men to deceive them;" for so I found it. It is hard to imagine how near a resemblance he could make, how exact an imitation he could form of the very thing itself, to the state of mind I was then in; even to that degree that I have at times been ready to say, "ah! I see and feel the fire of the Lord coming down to prepare the offering," and have been almost ready to give up thereunto, when a godly fear would seize my mind, and a desire yet to try it; by which means the strong delusion hath been discovered, and the false fire rejected. My soul hath been plunged into deeper anxiety, by this false heat, than I was in before. No tongue nor pen can set forth to the full the deep and almost constant anguish of my soul for about the space of four or five months; being as near as I can remember the time this sore affliction was upon me. It fared with me, in some degree, as it did with Job, respecting my friends; some conjecturing one thing, and some another thing, to be the cause of this fall, as it was apprehended; though through mercy they could not charge me with any evil as the cause thereof. The most probable reason to them of this alteration was, that I had been too much set up by others, and so had lost my gift; and this, I think, came nearest to the truth of the case. Yet it was not so lost, but that when my gracious helper saw my suffering was enough, he restored it again and appeared to my soul as a clear morning without clouds; everlasting praises to his holy name; my mind was deeply bowed in humble thankfulness under a sense of the great favour of being again counted worthy to be intrusted with so precious a gift; therefore I was careful to exercise the same in great fear and awfulness, and more in a cross to mine own will than before; as that which was but too likely to have decked itself therewith, was, for the present at least, in a good degree slain. I have very often in the course of my religious experience had cause to adore and admire divine wisdom, in his dealings with me for my preservation in the way of peace; being well assured that he will so work for mankind if they are sufficiently given up in heart and soul to him, that it will not be possible for them to miss of everlasting happiness; for none are able to pluck those out of his almighty hand who do not first incline to leave him.

In the splendid regions of the "far west," which lie between Missouri and the Rocky Mountains, there are living at this moment on the Prairies various tribes, who, if left to themselves, would continue for ages to live on the

buffalo which cover the plains. The skins of these animals, however, have become valuable to the whites, and, accordingly, this beautiful verdant country, and these brave and independent people have been invaded by white traders, who, by paying to them a pint of whiskey for each skin, (or "robe," as they are termed in America,) which sell at New York at ten or twelve dollars, induce them to slaughter these animals in immense numbers, leaving their flesh, the food of the Indian, to rot and putrefy on the ground. No admonition or caution can arrest for a moment the propelling power of whiskey; accordingly, in all directions these poor thoughtless beings are seen furiously riding under its influence in pursuit of their game, or, in other words, in the fatal exchange of food for poison. It has been very attentively calculated by the traders, who manage to collect per annum from 150,000 to 200,-000 buffalo skins, that at the rate at which these animals are now disposed of, in ten years they will all be killed off. Whenever that event happens, Mr. Catlin very justly prophesies that 250,000 Indians, now living in a plain of nearly three thousand miles in extent, must die of starvation and become a prey to the wolves, or that they must either attack the powerful neighbouring tribes of the Rocky Mountains, or in utter phrenzy of dispair rush upon the white population in the forlorn hope of dislodging it. In the two latter alternatives there exists no chance of success, and we have therefore the appalling reflection before us, that these 250,000 Indians must soon be added to the dismal list of those who have already withered and disappeared, leaving their country to bloom and flourish in the possession of the progeny of another world!—*Quart. Rev.*

MORNING.

BY WILLIAM H. BURLEIGH.

Up, sluggard, from thy pallet! Lo, the East
Heralds the coming of another day!
The burning sun advanceth in his might,
To fling his wealth of light upon the world;
And the gray mists that in the vale have slept
Through all the solemn night, are curling up,
Slowly and sullenly, as if to steal
The golden splendour from the fount of day,
And weave it in their undulating folds!
The conscious earth is blushing in the light,
As a coy maiden, when she meets the glance
Of an impassioned lover—and the streams,
Leaping and sparkling in the morning ray,
Send gaily forth their gurgling melody,
As if they knew another day was born.
The breezes, fragrance-laden, have awaked
From their brief slumber, and are flitting now,
On their light pinions over hill and plain,
Wooing the perfume from the opening flowers,
And dallying with the leaflets. Every tree
Is vocal with the melody of birds;
And the awakening herbage flings abroad
Its dewy incense on the odorous air,
As conscious that its Maker will accept
The grateful offering—and many a voice,
From vale and mountain and from shady grove,
Joins in the general anthem.

Experience teaches, it is true; but she never comes in time. Each event brings its lesson, and the lesson is remembered; but the same event never occurs again.—L. E. L.

THE FRIEND.

A RELIGIOUS AND LITERARY JOURNAL.

VOL. XIII.   SEVENTH DAY, SIXTH MONTH, 6, 1840.   **NO. 36.**

EDITED BY ROBERT SMITH.

PUBLISHED WEEKLY.

Price two dollars per annum, payable in advance.

Subscriptions and Payments received by

GEORGE W. TAYLOR,

NO. 50, NORTH FOURTH STREET, UP STAIRS,

PHILADELPHIA.

CENTRAL AMERICA.

(Concluded from page 274.)

[A few disconnected extracts will close our selections from the narrative. Just before our last extracts, occurs the following passage.]

I went on deck, and found that we had arrived in the bay of St. Thomas, and had anchored within a few yards of the shore. A finer or more interesting view than that which presented itself on this occasion, I have seldom seen. The bay of St. Thomas lay before me like an immense basin, exhibiting a smooth and glassy surface, and a clear, sandy bottom, illuminated by the rays of the sun, which was then just rising over the mountains, and pouring a flood of light over hill and valley. The shores of the bay, making a wide circular sweep, gave to a circumference of some twenty miles. The land—which was clothed with a luxuriant verdure—rose higher in proportion to its distance from the water, till it terminated in a range of towering mountains, forming a magnificent amphitheatre. There was depth of water there for the largest ship ever built, and room enough for the whole navy of Great Britain to ride at anchor.

This splendid bay is situated on the right of the embouchure of the river Izabal, and at the head of the great bay of Honduras. Being protected against the winds by the surrounding land, it affords a safe harbour; and from its situation on that part of the coast most favourable for communicating with the interior, and its numerous other advantages, seems destined by nature for a great commercial emporium. But, thus far, the place is almost a perfect solitude. There was not a single vessel in the harbour but our own, nor a house to be seen on shore, except two or three miserable huts. These huts were the commencement of a settlement projected by the government of Central America, but abandoned almost in the onset, from want either of means, or of energy, on the part of the government in promoting objects of public utility. An establishment there had also been contemplated by a company of English merchants, who made proposals to that effect, with an offer of opening a communication across the mountains to the nearest point of the road leading from Izabal to the capital. But the same fatality that attends all efforts at improvement in this country, rendered this plan abortive, and it was in like manner abandoned.

Our object in coming hither was to take in fuel. While this was doing, I landed with two or three of the passengers, and proceeded to the huts just mentioned. We found there only a white man and two negro women; the latter inhabiting one of the huts, and the former lodged in a sort of barn, open to the four winds, except at one extremity, which was boarded off, and served as a bed-chamber. The man was a sort of commandant in the place. He had erected a flag-staff close by his dwelling, and wore a cockade as an indication of his authority. He received from the government a salary of eight hundred dollars for remaining there, but was now, he said, pretty nearly tired of the solitude of the place and the insignificance of his office, and was about to resign. All his furniture consisted of a truckle-bed, a few stools for chairs, and a rude table of rough boards. There was a hammock suspended from the beams of the roof, a rusty fowling-piece, in one corner, and a fishing-net in another. He had some pigs and plenty of poultry, who had the range of the house, and seemed quite at home in it. He also had a kitchen garden, which I looked into and found well stocked with plantains, pumpkins, and other vegetables. In one of the largest huts, or rather in a large shed supported by upright shafts, there was a quantity of boards and shingles, which had been procured by the government and sent thither for the erection of houses. But there was now no probability that this lumber would be used for the purpose for which it was intended, or for any other, as it was in such a state of decay as to be almost useless. We remained in this Robinson Crusoe establishment only a short while, the mosquitoes becoming so troublesome, that we were glad to return to the vessel.

[A little further on is presented the following picture of simple and secluded life.]

During the detention incurred by the grounding of the boat, I made another visit on shore, as well from curiosity as for the sake of procuring vegetables and fruit. On an elevated spot near the mouth of the river, and in a romantic situation, there is a little village consisting of forty or fifty huts, shaded by cocoa-nut trees. Thither I proceeded with two of the passengers, and found the place inhabited entirely by negroes, of the class called, as I have elsewhere observed, *Caribes*. We entered one of the best-looking huts, which we were told was the dwelling of the *Alcalde*, or civil magistrate, and found there an old negro lying sick in a hammock. He seemed glad to see us, and addressed to us a few words in a language almost unintelligible, being a mixture of French, Spanish, and English; but we made out that he had been for some time suffering from an affection of the lungs, and would take it as a great favour if we would recommend something for his relief. It is proper to remark here, that the country-people in Central America look upon every foreigner as a doctor, and place implicit faith in his prescriptions. One of us *did* prescribe to him, but whether to a good or bad purpose, I cannot pretend to say. As I had no part in this, my conscience has never troubled me on the subject. The old man had a little image of *Nuestra Señora del Rosario* suspended from his neck. He was a great devotee of the virgin of this name, and counted largely upon her favour and protection. He also wore a little bag containing a relic of some saint, in which, too, he had great faith. The cabin he lived in—like all the others—was built of mud and cane reeds, and thatched with palm leaves, with only one door, and no windows. Though the largest in the village, it could not have exceeded fifteen feet square in extent. His furniture could not be more poor and homely; the only seat I was able to procure, being a barrel set on end. My companions accommodated themselves on an old chest. He insisted on our taking something to drink, and gave us some gin and water out of a calabash. He then, agreeably to our request, gave directions for the people to bring to him whatever fruit or vegetables they could spare; and in a short time, a much larger quantity than we wanted was supplied. This we procured for a mere trifle.

On our way back, we took a better view of the hamlet, and were pleased with its picturesque and primitive appearance. There was a fine spring of fresh water gushing out from the rocks in a shady place. The huts were scattered round without any order, each with one or two cocoa trees in front to protect it from the sun, and a patch of cultivated ground in the rear for raising vegetables. The inhabitants of either sex wore scarcely any clothing. We saw nobody at work, though it was not a holyday; yet they looked quite happy and free from care; and in this quiet and secluded state, apart from the rest of the world, they seemed to live forgetting and forgotten.

[The lake of Izabal is thus described:]

In the course of a walk in the afternoon, I took a passing view of the town; but seeing nothing in it to interest me, I turned my steps to the mountain that commands it, and ascended to a spot where the roots of an old tree afforded a pleasant resting-place. Here a fine view is obtained of the lake and of the surrounding country. Before me were scattered the thatched roofs of Izabal, and on each side, as far as the eye could reach, might be seen a series of mountains, towering over each other, and piled up like Pelion upon Ossa. How deeply I regretted not being an adept at drawing, to have made a sketch of the scene before me! Yet it was not without defects. No vessels were to be seen on the lake, with the solitary exception of the steamboat; no signs of cultivation, not a hamlet nor a house were visible on the land, save the little town beneath me.

When I considered the natural advantages of this country, I could not but lament that so little had been done by human industry to improve them. The idea, however, suggested itself, that some day this lake, now little better than a watery desert, might be traversed in every direction by steamboats and sailing vessels engaged in profitable trade; when the country around, instead of being encumbered with a wild and useless vegetation, might smile with fields of corn, and the neat cottage of the peasant, the thriving hamlet, and even the flourishing town, enliven the quietude of these solitary shores.

[Salvador is one of the places on the route to Guatemala, and is thus noticed:]

St. Salvador, which may be considered the second city of Central America, is the head of the state, or department, of that name, and contains a population of about fifteen thousand souls, including Indians and mulattoes. The other towns of any note in this state are St. Vincente, Santana, and Sonsonate. It is situated some fifty miles from the Pacific. Its trade and manufactures are very limited; the wealth of the place consisting chiefly in its agricultural productions. The city is laid out with considerable regularity; the streets crossing each other at right angles, except in the suburbs, where this plan has not been so strictly adhered to. In the centre of the city is the *plaza,* or market-place, three sides of which are lined with shops, with porticos before them, supported by a colonnade. On the other side is the church, a fine edifice, in a good style of architecture. There is also, on this side, a large house, where the members of the legislature assemble when congress is in session. The plaza just mentioned is crowded on market days with country-people, bringing the produce of their farms. All the fruits and vegetables of the tropics may then be seen exposed for sale on mats and *mantas* spread upon the ground. The variety of costumes and complexions, and the noise and bustle of the buyers and sellers, constitute a picturesque and animated scene. The primitive custom of trading by barter, I found, to my surprise, was still in existence there; Indian corn, or cocoa, being used in such cases as a substitute for a metallic currency.

[The following is from the succeeding chapter.]

Soon after leaving St. Salvador, we came to a wild tract of country, and travelled along a rough and rocky path, which, after a few miles, brought us to a deep ravine, called *el Barranco del Guaramal.* This ravine, formed by the waters descending from the neighbouring mountains, is overhung by rocks and bushes, and its banks, which rise to a height of thirty or forty feet, are covered with every variety of fern and moss, and with wild flowers and

weeds without number. There was, in particular, a species of bamboo, the branches of which fell in beautiful festoons on either side of us, or spreading from bank to bank, formed verdant arches over our heads that looked like the work of art. The bed of the ravine, in some places, consisted of loose stones, and, in others, of solid rock, and was the channel of a stream which, it being now the dry season, was not more than two feet deep in any part. The place was a fantastic assemblage of rocks, trees, and water, forming altogether the most wild and romantic scene I had yet beheld.

This ravine we were obliged to follow for the space of half a league, making its rough and watery bed our road for want of any other. At length we succeeded, by clambering up the banks, in gaining a smoother ground, and proceeded along a narrow path till we came to a dense forest. Here we had to unravel the mazes of a labyrinth of verdure for quite two hours, when we reached a plain, where we saw the village of Ateas.

Although it was early in the afternoon when we arrived, and the distance travelled had not been much, we had determined, in consideration of the fatigue our beasts had undergone from the nature of the roads, to proceed no further till the following day. At night I was provided with a good bed. The officer attending me wrapped himself up in the folds of his chamarra, and stretched his limbs on a mat under the piazza of the house.

Starting early the next morning, we proceeded along the plain of Ateas, till we came to another wood. Here my conductor directed the muleteers not to lag behind, examined his pistols, and asked me if mine were in proper order. He observed, at the same time, that this was a necessary precaution to prevent our being taken by surprise; for though he apprehended no danger from the insurgents in that quarter, there was a possibility of our falling in with deserters and fugitives from jail, who might be roaming about the country. He then placed himself at the head of our little party, and rode on in silence till we passed the wood.

As we proceeded on our way, a deep rumbling noise was heard, like distant thunder. It was occasioned by the eruptions of the volcano of Isalco, from which we were only a few miles distant. A little further on, having ascended an eminence, we came in full view of the volcano, and could see the smoke bursting in a thick column from the crater. The scoria and ashes emitted by the eruption fell in a shower round the mountain, and a stream of lava, though not then visible to the eye, could be traced by a line of smoke reaching from the crater to the base of the volcano. We approached within a mile of the base of this burning mountain, where the ground was covered with pumice stones and fragments of solid lava. It was a volcano of recent formation; its commencement dating not more than fifty years back. It broke out from the top of a hill of no great elevation; but the quantity of stones and lava emitted by it since its first eruption, have already formed a respectable mountain. The peculiarity of this volcano is, that the eruptions are almost continual; so that if not exhausted by constant performance, it

will becom[e]
able in the
eruptions,
emitted, th[e]
of the vill[a]
miles from
waste a larg[e]
ing a fertile
Passing
mentioned,
and can b[e]
houses, we
pretty Indi[a]
a grove of
were built
tered round
bitants, fro[m]
seemed to
when the c[o]

As we a[p]
a view of t[he]
for the first
tions of su[r]
pretend to
towards the
teen miles.
part of the
gazed upon
if its waters
those of ot[her]
two month[s]
ever, have [I]

It was e[a]
Sonsonate,
from an En[glish]
become acq[uainted]
ly received
merchants

This is t[he]
Salvador, n[ot]
is situated a
is the princi[pal]
Pacific, bei[ng]
from Panam[a]
mala. The
country, de
difficulty an[d]
ance over-la
shipped at t[he]
and circuito[us]
for the san
which are in
factures int[o]
of Central A[merica]

That ever
view of the
in the darkn[ess]
striking and
At intervals
issue from t[he]
dred feet, il
lurid light o
tions were
distant thun[der]
but though fi
for after bla[zing]
sided, when
down the r
fully throng
was one of
spectacles I

On the Habits and Instincts of Animals. By William Swainson, A. C. G., Fellow of the Royal Society, and of several Foreign Academies.

(Continued from p. 261.)

In *Birds*, we shall find the faculty of instinct exhibited in many curious, and several highly interesting, particulars; such as the construction of their habitations—the process of nidification — the methods of procuring food—and the migrations which so many undertake. Of their skill in forming their nests, the small birds of Southern Africa are striking examples, displaying, in many instances, the most surprising foresight in their formation. Some of the *Ploceanæ*, or weaving finches, suspend their nests to the branches of trees which overhang the water, shaping the fabric exactly like a chemist's retort, the aperture being placed at the bottom of the shank, which is eight or nine inches long; while others, it is said, fence their nests round with thorns. The *Icterinæ*, or hangnests of America, as their name implies, construct theirs on the same principle,—the fabric being composed of the stalks of the inward hair of a wiry sort of grass, the blades and stems of which they weave together, and hang to the extremities of lofty trees: in the forests of Brazil we have seen settlements thus formed of 200 or 300. The pensile warbler (*Sylvia pensilis*, Lin.) shows equal ingenuity: her nest is formed of dry blades of grass, the ribs of leaves, and very small roots, all twined together in the most skilful and artificial manner, formed into a compact ball, and carefully worked into binders, again suspended to a netting, which she has previously drawn from tree to tree,—so that this curiously constructed mansion rocks to and fro with the wind, secure from the assaults of her numerous enemies. The mode which these little artificers pursue, is not, however, always the same—but varies with that instinct which is observed so frequently to suit itself to new and peculiar circumstances: and thus, in our own island, although the nests of each particular species, when built in the open country, are always essentially on the same principle; yet, when found near towns or villages, where the same materials are not to be procured, their formation is adapted both to the situation in which they are placed, and to the substance of which they are constructed. The nest of the common wren (*Troglodytes Eurepæus*) illustrates the above fact: if built against a haystack, it will be uniformly made of hay; if attached to a tree covered with white lichen, it will chiefly be covered with the same substance; and so on, according to the place which it may chance to occupy. The obvious intention, however, in every instance, is to provide against discovery, by assimilating the exterior of the nest as near as possible to the object close to it.

In rearing their young, other instincts become developed. The ostrich will exemplify this second branch of our subject; and this unjustly slandered bird is now relieved from the odium which the ancients attached to her, since it is proved that she not only hatches her eggs, but that she reserves others, to provide the young with nourishment when they

first burst into life. In Senegal, where the heat is extreme, the ostrich, it is said, sits at night only, upon those which are to be rendered fertile; but at the Cape of Good Hope, where the sun has less power, the mother remains constant in her attentions to the eggs, both day and night. The instinct of this bird, in providing food for its young, appears to be without parallel, and is thus noticed by Le Vaillant:—"During this day's journey, I met with the nest of an ostrich, upon which the female was hatching: there were three eggs deposited on the bare ground, lying before her; and she was sitting upon nine others, the young of which were in so advanced a state as to be ready to burst the shell." The separation of the eggs in this manner—into two parcels—one parcel intended to supply the first food of the young which are hatched from the other—was considered incredible, when first announced as a fact by this well-known traveller; but subsequent observations have, in this instance, and in many others, only proved his veracity. The number of eggs which the ostrich usually sits upon is ten. But the Hottentots, who are very fond of them, upon discovering a nest, seize fitting opportunities to remove one or two at a time: this induces the bird to deposit more; and in this manner she has been known, like the domestic hen, to lay between forty and fifty in a season. The pelican is stated to preserve her eggs from injury, by hiding them in the water until the fancied danger is removed. The razorbill fixes hers on the smooth rock, with so exact a balance, that, if removed, and afterwards attempted to be replaced, it is difficult, if not impossible, to adjust it safe in the same position. Le Vaillant remarks, that the African *Ankinga*, or darter, which is a completely aquatic bird, nevertheless, builds its nest and rears its young on rocks and trees; yet the former is so constructed, that, at any moment of pressing danger, when the young are once able to swim, the mother can plunge them into the water beneath.

The expedients by which birds provide their food is often equally sagacious; none, however, show a more wonderful instinct in effecting this purpose, than those of the genus *Indicator*, or honey-guide. Dr. Sparman, the African traveller and naturalist, was the first who made the singular statement. He says, that, when this bird discovers a nest of honey, it flies eagerly to the first person it can find, and, by its chirping and fluttering, invites him to follow,—faithfully leading him to the spot, watching whilst he takes possession of the treasure, and patiently waiting for that portion which is always left by the African hunters as a reward to their feathered guide.

The address which the secretary eagle evinces in fighting with a serpent, has been thus described by an eye-witness:—"The battle was obstinate, and conducted with equal address on both sides. But the serpent,—feeling the inferiority of his strength,—in his attempt to flee and regain his hole, employed that cunning which is ascribed to him; while the bird, guessing his design, suddenly stopped him and cut off his retreat, by placing herself before him at a single leap. On whatever side the reptile endeavoured to make his

escape, his enemy was still found before him. Then, imitating at once bravery and cunning, he erected himself boldly to intimidate the bird, and, hissing dreadfully, displayed his menacing throat, inflamed eyes, and a head swelled with rage and venom. Sometimes this threatening appearance produced a momentary cessation of hostilities; but the bird soon returned to the charge, and, covering her body with one of her wings, as a buckler, struck her enemy with the horny protuberances upon the other, which, like little clubs, served the more effectually to knock him down as he raised himself to the blow: at last he staggered and fell; the conqueror then despatched him, and with one stroke of her bill laid open his skull."

The instinct of the nestling cuckoo is not more remarkable than that of the parent. The European species, as is well observed by White of Selborne, does not lay its eggs in other birds' nests indiscriminately, but, by a wonderful instinct, selects only those of soft-billed insectivorous birds,—such as the wagtails, hedge-sparrow, titlark, whitethroat, and redbreast,—to whom it can intrust the proper feeding of its progeny. The North American cuckoo, however, being of a different species, more frequently lay their eggs in the nests of the cowpen birds (*Molothrus pecoris*, Sw.), whose bills, from being larger and thicker than those of a sparrow, might lead to the belief that they feed their young upon the grain which the old birds are known to be fond of. It seems, however, that although this species, in their adult state, are granivorous, yet that they are also insectivorous, and feed their young with this latter aliment rather than with the former. Hence it is that the young cuckoo is still nourished with insects until it can fly, when it quits the nest and shifts for itself.

Quadrupeds claim our next attention. It is in this class, more than in any other, we find that kind of superior instinct which makes them not only the companion, but the friend, of man. The elephant, the horse, and more particularly the dog, afford familiar illustrations of that attachment towards mankind, implanted in their nature by Omnipotence, but withheld from all other animals. The skill and ingenuity of quadrupeds are, in many instances, very great, particularly in some of the smaller kinds. The jerboa, the beaver, and harvest mouse, are both architects and weavers; and the habitation of the latter ingenious little creature, according to White, is most artificially platted, being composed of the blades of wheat, perfectly round, and with the aperture closed in the nicest manner; the one he examined was " so compact and well fitted that it would roll across the table without being discomposed, though it contained eight little mice that were naked and blind."

The manner in which other quadrupeds preserve, and others obtain, their food, is indicative of this faculty. The fox, when possessed of a larger booty than it can at once consume, never allows itself to gratify its appetite, until it has secured the whole of its prize, by placing it in different holes, which it digs for the purpose, and which it endeavours to conceal by placing upon them a quantity of loose earth. Some of the *Glires*, or mice, provide a winter

Selected for "The Friend."

THE THREE SONS.

BY J. MOULTRIE.

I have a son, a little son, a boy just five years old,
With eyes of thoughtful earnestness, and mind of
gentle mould.
They tell me that unusual grace in all his ways appears,
That my child is grave and wise of heart beyond his
infant years.
I cannot say how this may be. I know his face is
fair,
And yet his chiefest comeliness is his sweet and serious air.
I know his heart is kind and fond, I know he loveth
me,
But loveth yet his mother more, with grateful fer-
vency.
But that which others must admire, is the thought
which fills his mind,
The food for grave inquiring speech he every where
doth find.
Strange questions doth he ask of me, when we to-
gether walk;
He scarcely thinks as children think, or talks as
children talk,
Nor cares he much for childish sports, dotes not on
bat or ball—
But looks on manhood's ways and works, and aptly
mimics all.
His little heart is busy still and oftentimes perplex'd,
With thoughts about this world of ours, and thoughts
about the next.
In childhood's gentle confidence he bends his knees to
pray,
And strange, and sweet, and solemn then, are the
words which he will say.
Oh should my lovely child be spared to manhood's
years like me,
A holier and a better man I trust that he will be ;
And when I look into his eyes, and stroke his thought-
ful brow,
I dare not think what I should feel were I to lose him
now.

I have a son, a second son, a simple child of three ;
I'll not declare how bright and fair his little features
be ;
How silver sweet those tones of his when he prattles
on my knee,
I do not think his light blue eye is like his brother's
keen,
Nor his brow so full of childish thought as his hath
ever been ;
But his little heart's a fountain pure of kind and ten-
der feeling,
And his every look a gleam of light, rich depths of
love revealing.
A play fellow is he to all, and yet with cheerful tone,
Will sing his little song of love, when left to sport
alone.
His presence is like sunshine sent to gladden home
and hearth,
To comfort us in all our grief, and sweeten all our
mirth.
Should he grow up to riper years, God grant his heart
may prove
As sweet a home for heavenly grace as now for
earthly love ;
And if beside his grave, the tears our aching eyes
must dim,

which he doth feel—
Are numbered with the secret things which
not reveal.
I know that we shall meet our babe, (his m
and I,)
Where God for aye shall wipe away all
every eye.
Whate'er befals his brethren twain, his bl
ver cease,
Their lot may here be grief and fear, but
tain peace.
It may be that the tempter's wiles their
bliss may sever,
But if our own poor faith fail not, he m
forever.
When we think of what our darling is, an
still must be—
When we muse on that world's perfect blis
world's misery ;—
When we groan beneath this load of sin, a
grief and pain,
Oh ! we'd rather lose our o'ber two, than
here again.

At the late General Conference of
thodist Episcopal Church, the commit
western book concern at Cincinnati
the value of the property there to be $
and the profit of the last four years
The committee of the book concern
York reported the value of that prop
$593,786.

Beware of satan and the flesh.

There is great beauty and deep ir
in the following lines ; taken from (
from Luther's Letters, translated for
Journal.

(To John Agricola of Eisleben.) I w
told a story about you, my dear Agr
one who persisted in repeating his affi
until I said that I would write to you,
out the truth.   It was a report that
beginning to contend for some new
namely, that faith can be without wor
said, moreover, that you were vain
propagating this opinion with much
rhetoric, and controversial use of Gre
Now as I have been taught by the sa
satan to be afraid even where there
danger, I write to you, not merely or
of my promise, but that I may seri
monish you to be on your guard agai
and the flesh.   For you know we a
sufficiently fortified against the wiles
unless we be perpetually guarded from
and also that there is much poison an
his snares, that a conflagration may co
a spark, or as Paul says, a little leave
eth the whole lump.   In so great
therefore, we must not, however sligh

THE ARAB RACE.

The New York Observer of the 30th ult. contains a condensed report of a speech delivered at a meeting of the American Board of Missions by Eli Smith, who, as a missionary, has for some time been a resident at Beyroot. From it we extract the following interesting account of the Arab race.

In selecting this people as the subject of the present address, I have given scope to my personal predilections. In my intercourse with nations I have observed that, like individuals, they are marked by distinctive peculiarities, well-defined and highly interesting. And as in the case of individuals, the heart will attach itself to one rather than another, so it is with nations; and among all the nations I have met with, the Arab race is my favourite. But here it is necessary to state distinctly who the Arabs are. The people who have exercised control for several centuries over the countries where the Mohammedan religion prevails, are usually called Turks. But the Turks do not belong to the Arab race, although it might be so inferred from the language of travellers. The Turks, properly so called, are a northern race; they came originally from northern Tartary, and the countries north and east of the Caspian sea. The Arabs, before the time of Mohammed, were confined to Arabia; there they had lived from the earliest times, contiguous to the other descendants of Abraham, and very frequent allusions are made to them in the Scriptures, particularly in the prophecies. Isaiah especially predicts the final ingathering of these sons of Ishmael in the following expressive strains: "The multitude of camels shall cover thee, the dromedaries of Midian and Ephah; all they from Sheba shall come; they shall bring gold and incense; and they shall show forth the praises of the Lord. All the flocks of Kedar shall be gathered together unto thee, the rams of Nebaioth shall minister unto thee; they shall come up with acceptance on mine altar, and I will glorify the house of my glory."

Sheba, Kedar, and Nebaioth are all countries of Arabia. I consider it a great privilege to be called to labour among a people who are named in the prophecies, and of whom it is expressly foretold that they shall one day submit to the sceptre of Christ.

When Mohammed arose, the enthusiasm and fanaticism of his religion kindled all their energies, and they poured forth as locusts upon all the surrounding countries, nor did they rest till they had overrun one half of the old world. On the east, they invaded and subdued Syria, Persia, Northern India, even to the Oxus, where their characteristics still remain. On the north, they rushed through Asia Minor, crossed the Dardanelles, and laid siege to Constantinople, which was then the capital of the Greek empire. In the west, they subdued Egypt and all Northern Africa to the straits of Gibraltar, crossed there, founded a kingdom in Spain, and planted their power even on the mountains of Switzerland and the frontiers of France. But the waves of this Saracen deluge receded, and now the Tigris is the eastern limit of the race. From the north they have passed back through Asia Minor, and a line

stretched from the northeast corner of the Mediterranean to the Tigris, bounds their wanderings in that direction. In Spain there is little left of them except a few traces of their language and a mixture of their blood. In Africa they still exist as a numerous and powerful people, and occupy all the north of it from the extreme east to the extreme west—a greater distance than from the Atlantic to the Pacific shores of our own continent. In Syria, though there is a mixture of races, there is but one language, and that the Arabic. Such is the extent and situation of the people among whom I sojourn, for whose welfare I labour, and for whom I plead.

But to be a little more particular as to their civil and political condition. The Arabs are divided into two grand classes—the *Hooderee*, or resident Arabs, and the *Bedawee*, (Bedouin) or wandering Arabs. The Bedawee is an inhabitant of the desert. He has flocks and herds, but he despises the cultivation of the soil. He is of the original Arab stock—a nomade, a wanderer. In the Bedawee you see the primitive characteristics of the Ishmaelitish race. As a class they are poor, indeed, but proud, constituting the *nobility* of the race, and boasting of a long line of noble ancestry, running farther back than any of the crowned heads of Europe. No potentate of any part of the world was ever more high-minded, or more careful to avoid intermarriage with a plebeian than the Bedawee Arab. They pride themselves in being as free as the wind in all their movements over the desert. They roam about like the shifting sands, scorning to submit to the government of the neighbouring nations. Small tribes or fragments of tribes may be an exception to this remark, but it holds good of the mass. You may see their black tents scattered here and there over the hills of Mount Lebanon, and tenanted by those who bear the name of some of the great tribes of the desert, from whom they have been separated by domestic feuds. But these broken hordes, though living thus, will not brook oppression. They detest the Turk and hate the Russian; and on the least attempt to curb them, they fly into the deserts, and luxuriate in poverty and freedom.

The other class are cultivators of the soil, and many of their original characteristics disappear. They are also more or less addicted to trade, and are more patient of subjection to other powers; as we find them tributary in Mesopotamia, Turkey, Syria, and Egypt. In the extreme west, as in Morocco, we find a native Arab kingdom, and in the southeast another in Muscat.

There are several characteristics of the Arab race of great interest and importance to the missionary. Is it of no consequence to the missionary whether the people among whom he labours are possessed of intelligence, and strong national character, or are sensual, sunk, degraded, and depraved? Nothing can be of more importance, inasmuch as we must depend mainly upon native agency to accomplish the great results we have in view. One trait in the Arab character of special interest is a nice sense of honour. Though there is good and bad among them, yet they all have a high sense of honourable obligations. It may not

lead to the positive practice of private virtue, yet it helps to prevent open vice or gross wrongs. This trait shows itself in their universal hospitality. This has come down to them from of old. In their lofty poetry, which will bear a comparison with that of any other people, they land and extol that Arab who consumes his substance to entertain strangers. Nor can they speak of one in higher terms than to say, "The fire never goes out on his kitchen hearth," but is always burning to cook for the stranger, his guest. Dismount from your horse in the desert and enter the Arab's tent, and he will entertain you as Abraham did of old, if not with the fatted calf, yet with the lamb or kid, with milk and butter. For to be economical on the score of food is, with the Arabs, the height of meanness. This makes the Arab generous, and thus a feeling of sacredness attaches to the character of *guest*. Some few are treacherous: but if you want to pass alone through the deserts of Arabia, you will be told there is no difficulty; "We will pass you over to a tribe that is friendly with us, and they will pass you on to one that is friendly with them, and so you will go safely through." When Prof. Robinson and myself were at Jerusalem, wishing to visit the region of the Dead Sea, which was infested by a band of Bedaweens regarded as robbers, we consulted a native friend, and the next day he brought us the captain of the band for our guide. We visited Bethlehem, slept where Jacob slept at Bethel, and returned in safety.

Again, as to the *vindictiveness* of the Bedaween, he is not natively blood-thirsty. But he is jealous of his rights, and it has been considered, from time immemorial, a sacred duty to avenge the blood of a relative. It is this feeling which gives them a decided character for independence—a trait possessed even by menial servants, who stand up and raise their voice in the presence of their masters, like the sons of republicans. This was shown when one of the Syrian bishops threatened to excommunicate those Arabs who came to hear us preach. The consequence was, that on the next Sabbath our chapel was fuller than ever.

That the Arab possesses great force of character no one can doubt who is acquainted with ancient history. But we see the same character developed now. We see it in the contrast between the Turks under the Sultan, and the Arabs under Mehemet Ali. See, too, how difficult it is for the French, with all their tactics, to subdue the brave Arab troops under Abd el Kader in the province of Algiers. Another proof of their independence and bravery was shown by the Druse Arabs. A small party had rebelled and fled to a volcanic region called Lija, or the *Asylum*, near which I have myself travelled. Here these Druses planted themselves, and 40,000 of the Pasha's troops could not dislodge them. A single Druse is said to have defended a defile against 500 men.

And then there is much to admire in the patience, perseverance and endurance of the Arab. The Bedawee considers it degrading to cultivate the soil. He would rather wander in the desert. And how does he live? I can scarcely tell. He lives upon the most meagre fare. He will start in the morning with a few pounds of meal, and a small quantity of water. If he finds no more when that is gone, he will endure hunger and thirst, and the severest privations, rather than complain. I once encountered a party who had been driven out of their territory, and were approaching Palestine in search of pasture for their flocks. So far as appeared, a few camels was all that furnished them food. I offered one of them a biscuit, and a cup of milk was returned; and they offered to exchange more. We gave them some barley which we had brought for our horses; and they ground it, husks and all, made it into a sort of dough on a sheep-skin, buried it in the ashes, and baked it. When they took it out, it was burned as black as a coal; yet they ate it with a good relish. Bread baked in this way, with camels' dung for fuel, is ordinary fare. Sanctify this trait in their character, what devoted missionaries, what sufferers for Christ's sake, what noble martyrs would they make!

The Arabs are, besides, a very talented race. Soon after the establishment of the Caliphate of Bagdad, almost all the learning and literature of the world was among the Arabs. I have examined some of their books of science, mathematics, &c. with intense interest. It is curious to see how they will start from the same point and arrive at the same results, by a process entirely different from ours. Algebra owes its origin to them; the very name is Arabic. In astronomy they are equally renowned; and by their observations have corrected the calculations made by the Greeks at Alexandria. The Arabic names of several of the stars and constellations now stand upon our celestial globes. In philosophy, though misled by a false religion, they have shown capacity of the brightest order. Their histories I regard as beautiful models. They are simple narratives of facts, much after the style of the Hebrew, dispensing with reflections and inferences, and leaving the naked incidents to make their due impression on your mind. But pass from history to poetry, and you look as from earth to heaven. It is perhaps the most beautiful in the world. It is the soul of sublimity, and for the boldness of its metaphors, the beauty of its rhythm, and the brilliancy of its language, it cannot well be surpassed. In literature, no nation, of equal age, can probably boast more books in the native tongue; and I found a learned German translating a Bibliotheca in nine large volumes, containing only the names or titles of native Arab books. As to language, we love our own, and think very highly of its richness, force, and finish. But with all its copious treasures and polished elegance, it must yield the palm to the Arabic. This is so nicely adjusted in all its parts, that it reminds you of the frame of a building, with every mortice fitted to every tenon, and ours compared with it is little better than a *patois*. It is, moreover, the language of the Turk, the Tartar, the Malay, and the East Indian.

Another trait in the Arab character is, that he is not disposed to infidelity. Just before going to Armenia, I found it stated in the publication of a Jesuit missionary that the Armenian is religiously inclined. I have since studied the Arab character with reference to

this point, and found it true also of them ; for while their neighbours the Greeks grow up and go over to infidelity, you will scarcely find any infidels among the Arabs. Indeed, you cannot insult an Arab more than by calling him an infidel. The religion of the Arab now is Mohammedan, and the impostor had the wisdom to adapt his religion to their character; but an acquaintance with them will show that the Bedaween knows hardly any thing of his religion. Few of them at the present day can read the Koran: and though it prescribes a penalty for those who do not say their prayers five times a day, scarcely one in a hundred knows enough to say his prayers. It is, however, a striking fact, that while all nominal Christians in the East have prayers in an unknown tongue, they have theirs in Arabic.

PHYSIOLOGICAL PHENOMENON.

The case of Thomas Bradley, of Deighton, still continues to attract much attention. We have received the following particulars from an individual who has been to the place and made inquiry into the circumstance, and also respecting the previous habits of the sleeper. Thomas Bradley is the son of John and Martha Bradley, of Deighton, near Huddersfield. He was born on the 4th of November, 1817, and was consequently 22 years of age last birth-day. He stood five feet ten inches high, weighed about eleven stone, and was particularly straight and well made. From his birth till he was fifteen years of age he was not subject to any serious disease, and none of the family were ever subject to fits. When in his sixteenth year he fell into a sleep which continued nine weeks. In the same year he again relapsed into a sleep which continued without intermission forty weeks. During this long period he was greatly emaciated, and a considerable length of time elapsed before he was able to stand alone; he, however, gradually recovered, regained his strength, and continued in good health up to the latter end of August of last year, when he became more than usually drowsy, with loss of appetite. On the 30th of that month, whilst at his tea in the afternoon, he again sunk into sleep, in which he has ever since remained, being a period of thirty-two weeks. His parents, acting under the instructions of the surgeons who have attended him, have been enabled to keep him in a better condition than on the previous occasion. His position in bed is altered three times a day, the linen is repeatedly changed, and nourishment regularly administered. The nourishment he receives consists chiefly of beef tea, given in minute portions, which, on reaching the top of the gullet, is swallowed down by a convulsive effort. By this means he receives sufficient sustenance for the state he is in.—*Bradford Observer.*

VACCINE ESTABLISHMENT.

Return to an address of the house of commons, dated March 10, 1840, for a copy of the last report from the National Vaccine Institution to her majesty's principal secretary of state for the home department.

To the Lord Marquis of Norma
secretary of state for the home

My lord,—The experience of
has confirmed our conviction of
of vaccination as the best securi
tion against smallpox, and has
moreover, proofs of the proprie
sent state of our knowledge, of p
cine matter, the produce of the
furnished by Dr. Jenner, which I
ed happily through successive g
subjects in the course of forty
and which forms the principal i
supply, to any which may hav
recently from the cow.

We admit that it is sometime
by our correspondents, that the
he had sent them has failed; but
has generally brought us intellig
material supplied from the very sa
succeeded elsewhere, and that i
efficacious in Somersetshire, whe
to be inefficient in Wiltshire. V
cluded, therefore, either that it ha
somehow in its transmission, or
ents submitted to it were not in c
to receive its influence, in cor
some eruptive disease having i
their constitution, or of some p
demic disorder having rendered i
ceptible of another and a new e
a time.

The number of patients dead
within the bills of mortality, if i
them, has been less this year th
since vaccination has been pract
are justified, by a careful retrosp
years, in stating that 4,000 lives, c
are saved every year within the c
hills only by vaccination having i
largely the practice of inoculatior
We have vaccinated at our se
13,144 persons, and have sent
charges of vaccine lymph since c
in parliament in 1839.

HENRY
President of the Royal College o
President of the b
ROBE
President of the Royal College
THO
Senior Censor of the Royal Col. c
CLEMENT HUE, M. D.
National Vaccine Establishment, .

"The influence of religion,"
"is not to be sought for in th
princes, in the debates or resolut
lar assemblies, in the conduct of
towards their subjects, or of sta
reigns towards one another; of
the heads of their armies, or c
triguing for power at home, (topic
almost occupy the attention and i
of history;) but must be perceivec
at all, in the silent course of priva
tic life. Religion operates most
whom history knows the least,
and mothers in their families, u
vants and maid-servants, upon
tradesman, the quiet villager, the
er at his loom, the husbandmar

Among such, its influence collectively may be of inestimable value, yet it effects, in the mean time, little upon those who figure upon the stage of the world. From the first general notification of Christianity to the present day, there have been in every age many millions, whose names were never heard of, made better by it, not only in their conduct, but in their disposition ; and happier, not so much in their external circumstances, as in that which is *inter præcordia*, in that which alone deserves the name of happiness, the tranquillity and consolation of their thoughts. It has been since its commencement, the author of virtue and happiness to millions and millions of the human race. Who is there that would not wish his son to be a Christian ?"

New British Niger Expedition.

Our readers will be pleased to learn that the British government have resolved to send out several iron steamers to the coast of Africa, to ascend the Niger, with the hope of making arrangements with the native chiefs for the suppression of the slave trade. The London Nautical Magazine for May, says :—

The principal object of the expedition is to put an end to the slave trade, by entering into treaties with the native chiefs, " w."'in whose dominions the internal slave trade is carried on, and the external trade supplied with its victims."

The expedition will embrace other important objects, though its leading feature will be an endeavour to suppress the inhuman traffic now carried on by those whose true interest it is to retain their subjects at home, and cultivate their native soil, so fruitful in natural productions, and so capable of being made the source of a legitimate and profitable commerce.

By proceeding up the Niger a large portion of the native chiefs engaged in the slave trade, may easily be communicated with ; and should the rapids or other obstructions about Boussa not be found impassable, a reasonable hope may be entertained of reaching the immediate vicinity of Timbuctoo, and navigating to Sansanding, from whence Park commenced his downward voyage, which terminated so fatally. —*New York Observer.*

Destruction of the Packet Ship Poland by Fire.

The packet ship Poland, Capt. Anthony, which left here May the 12th, for Havre, was fallen in with on the 18th, in lat. 41 12, lon. 56, by the ship Clifton, Capt. Ingersoll, which arrived here from Liverpool—the Poland being then on fire, which had made such progress that there was no hope of extinguishing it. There were on board of her 63 persons, viz : 24 cabin passengers, 11 steerage passengers, and the ship's company, comprising 28 persons, including the captain and mates ; all of whom were taken off by the Clifton, and have safely arrived in this city.

The Poland belonged to William Whitlock's line, and is insured, as is most of the cargo. Freight not insured. Most of the specie, we understand, is insured in France.

The fire was caused by lightning, which struck the ship on the 16th, in lat. 41 35, lon. 58 30, at 3 o'clock P. M., during a severe shower from the south west, and ran down the foremast into the lower hold, where it is supposed it set fire to the cotton which was stowed near the mast.

After an ineffectual attempt to get at the fire to extinguish it, the men being driven from their work by the smoke, the hatches were closed about 8 o'clock, and the boats were cleared and got out, and about 10 P. M. the females and children, with as many men as was thought proper, were put into the long boat, and moored astern, where they remained all that night, and the next day and night, until the morning, 18th—the ship being hove to, in order to be easy, and in hopes of being discovered by some passing vessel.

On that morning, the wind having very much increased, with a rising sea, and the fire not appearing to have increased much, the boats were hoisted in again, and sail made to the N. E. About one o'clock P. M. a sail was discovered and the ship was put before the wind to speak her. She proved to be the Clifton, as mentioned above. When the Poland was abandoned, the fire was very fast increasing, and the decks were growing hotter every minute. The passengers and crew saved but little except the clothes they had on, and a few light articles of small value.—*Journal of Commerce.*

EMIGRATION.

The tide of emigration from Great Britain flows both to the western and eastern worlds. There were lately in the London and St. Katharine docks no fewer than fourteen vessels bound for Sydney, and four for Hobart Town. The Cork Reporter says :—

" For the last eight or ten days our streets present great numbers of, generally, to all appearance, intelligent farmers and their families, on their way to the quays where the emigrant ships, advertised for the States and the Canadas, lie. A large portion of our countrymen and women, who are thus about to expatriate themselves from scenes of home, come from the western and northern districts of the country."

It is stated in other papers, that a party of 165 emigrants from Wurtemburg to the United States passed through Mayence, from Rotterdam, a few days since. They were led by their spiritual pastor, who, with a family of eleven children, was accompanying his flock to the new world. It is remarked, in Germany, that at no period has there been so much emigration to the United States as at the present moment ; entire caravans are constantly passing through the town of Mayence to reach Havre, overland, for the purpose of embarkation. The emigrants, many of whom are men of some property, generally average thirty years of age. On the 13th and 14th of March, as many as 600 took the direction above mentioned ; besides a vast number before and since, during the present winter, from various parts of Rhenish Prussia, and the small German States.

DISCOVERY IN TANNING.

A discovery has been made which seems likely to revolutionise the trade. By means of a tanning machine, or pair of horizontal rollers fixed over a tan-pit, between which is introduced a belt or band of hides attached by ligatures to each other, to the number of 50 to 100, and by which the rollers are constantly fed or supplied, the hides are lifted out of the pit on the side of the machine ; as they pass between the rollers, the exhausted ooze or tanning liquor is pressed out of them, and they are deposited in folds in the pit on the other side of the machine, where they absorb another supply of fresh ooze. The first hide having been inserted between the rollers, the others follow in succession, and upon arriving at the end of the band, the motion of the roller is reversed, to receive another squeeze. This alternating motion is constantly repeated, the pit being replenished from time to time with fresh solutions of tan, till the operation is completed. The effects produced by this simple plan, as we have satisfied ourselves by the inspection of documents from those who have been working on the patent method for many months, and from those who have purchased, manufactured, and worn the leather, are—1st. The shortening the time of tanning to one fourth of that generally required. 2d. The production of a considerable increase of weight. 3d. The leather tanned by this method resists water longer than that tanned by the old process. 4th. The new method is cheaper to work on than the old. 5th. That it is applicable to the existing tan-yards, at a comparatively trifling expense, with a capability of working in rounds or sories, and of expending tan and liquor. 6th. That it is available for all sorts of leather. —*English Paper.*

For "The Friend."

THE REMEDY.

BY THOMAS FOWELL BUXTON.

Some notices have at different times appeared in " The Friend" of a recent work by T. F. Buxton, portraying the present condition of the African slave trade. In it the author hinted at a remedy for this monstrous evil, which he did not then deem it expedient to make public. The reason, it seems, was, that a negotiation was at that time pending between the governments of Great Britain and Portugal, to which some of the views held out in the plan might have proved prejudicial. That objection having ceased, the "Remedy," as the publication is entitled, has come out, and, it is expected, will shortly be reprinted in this country.

The propositions therein developed are said to have received the sanction of the English government, which has already adopted the incipient measures for their execution.

According to a statement by R. R. Gurley, at a meeting of the " friends of African colonization and civilization," held last sixth day evening in New York, the outlines of this great scheme are these.

The main object to be sought in order to suppress the slave trade, is to elevate the mind, or, in other words, to civilize the character of the African people.

The instruments -to be employed in this work are the descendants of Africa—the coloured race.

The specific measures to be adopted for this end, are—

First. To impede and check by force the traffic in slaves.

Second. To establish and encourage legitimate commerce.

Third. To promote and teach agriculture.

Fourth. To impart moral and religious instruction.

To effect the first, the naval squadron of England is to be increased and concentrated on the coast, and treaties for the abolition of the slave trade to be formed with the tribes of the coast, the rivers and interior.

To effect the second, commanding positions must be obtained, factories established, and trading ships sent out.

For accomplishing the third, an agricultural company must be formed ; lands obtained for cultivation ; and the labourers guarded against the slave trade. These tracts should be selected with care in regard to soil, health and navigable rivers.

To accomplish the fourth, is the more especial object of the " African Civilization Society of England."

In co-operating in this grand design, the English government are to secure Fernando Po as a naval station, and there augment their naval force. To send three iron steam vessels (at an expense of more than $250,000) to explore the Niger—to negotiate treaties with the African chiefs—to secure the abandonment of the slave trade—make arrangements for legitimate commerce—obtain grants of land, &c.

The African Civilization Society is to aid in securing information and promoting education, the arts, and all other means of civilization, and especially to send out agents by the government expedition. The proposed agricultural company is to send out men qualified to develope all the resources of the soil. No monopoly—no slave trade—are to be fundamental principles in the whole scheme.

The author urges that Great Britain should, if requisite, couple an official pledge with her effort, that she will not claim for herself a single benefit which shall not be shared by every nation uniting with her in the extinction of the slave trade, and especially :—

First. That no exclusive privilege in favour of British subjects shall be allowed to exist.

Second. That no custom house shall ever be established at Fernando Po.

Third. That no distinction shall be made there, whether in peace or war, between her own subjects and those of any such foreign power, as to the rights they shall possess, or the terms on which they shall enjoy them. In short, that England purchase Fernando Po, and hold it for no other purpose than the benefit of Africa.

Such was the brief outline. Nothing higher, nobler, says the reporter, was ever proposed by a great Christian nation. England has already expended about $375,000, for the suppression of the slave trade, on a system proved to be ineffectual. But she is ready to expend more. Will not America share in the honours of an enterprise which is to raise millions from disgrace and chains, and secure in the commerce of those who engage in the work ample rewards for the treasures they expend ?

It was stated at the meeting, that the British abolitionists were encouraging some of the emancipated young men in the West India Islands, who are pious, to prepare to go to Africa in furtherance of the work.

THE FRIEND.

SIXTH MONTH, 6, 1840.

The Yearly Meeting of Friends for Virginia held the present year at Summerton in that state, convened at the regular time, second day the 18th ult. From information received, we are enabled to state, that this interesting though, compared with former days, much diminished company of Friends, were favoured through their several sittings, with renewed evidence, that the gracious Head of the church is yet mindful of them, they being enabled through the ability received, to transact the several concerns which came before them in love, harmony, and brotherly condescension. Located as they are in the midst of a slaveholding community, their trials and difficulties, arising from that circumstance, are many and their faithfulness in the support of our Christian testimony against slavery, and especially, in defending the claims of persons *illegally* detained in bondage, occupies a large portion of their time and attention. May they be encouraged in the path of duty, not doubting, that their firm, but discreet endeavours (for wisdom dwells with prudence) to plead the cause of the oppressed, will continue to give them place in the hearts of those in authority, while the light of their example will not be ineffectual on those around them.

We have been disappointed in the expectation that some one of our friends who were present would have furnished for insertion a notice of New York Yearly Meeting, which occurred last week. Perhaps the deficiency will be supplied in time for the next number.

The condensed view furnished by a correspondent, of T. Fowell Buxton's stupendous scheme for the extinction of the slave trade and slavery, and for meliorating the condition of the African tribes at home, will be gratifying to our readers. One feature in the plan, the increased naval equipment, it is true, is in conflict with the peaceable principle as professed by Friends ; but seeing it is to be a national or government concern, it is not to be expected, in the present state of the world, that such provision would be dispensed with, and the hope, perhaps, is not an unreasonable one, that the contemplated force is intended to intimidate by an overwhelming display of strength, and thus to prevent, rather than occasion, the effusion of blood.

THE FRIEND.

A RELIGIOUS AND LITERARY JOURNAL.

VOL. XIII.   SEVENTH DAY, SIXTH MONTH, 13, 1840.   **NO. 37.**

EDITED BY ROBERT SMITH.

PUBLISHED WEEKLY.

Price two dollars per annum, payable in advance.

Subscriptions and Payments received by

GEORGE W. TAYLOR,

NO. 50, NORTH FOURTH STREET, UP STAIRS,

PHILADELPHIA.

For "The Friend."

ASSAM TEA.

Abridged from Chambers' Edinburgh Journal.

The recent difficulties between the English and Chinese have turned the attention of the former to the possibility of procuring tea from a different source. A kindred plant, used in Paraguay, has been pointed out; and of this article accounts have been received from a great variety of travellers. A prospect of obtaining the ordinary tea from an Asiatic soil, near to, but independent of, China, has also arisen. In 1834, a committee was formed at Calcutta, for the purpose of promoting the culture of the tea-plant in British India; but it soon thereafter became known that the plant grew naturally in Assam; a large region 500 miles to the north of Calcutta, situated on the great Bramah-poota river, and, though not subject to the East India Company, yet under British influence. C. A. Bruce (who, it appears, made this discovery fourteen years ago) was immediately appointed by the committee to survey the district, and report on its capabilities of producing the plant, under culture. A report from Bruce has been received, from which it appears that the districts of Muttock and Singpho, to which his inquiries had as yet been confined, lie in the same latitude as the best tea-districts in China. The country, with respect to agriculture and social institutions, is in a very deplorable state; the people are of migratory habits, and dreadfully addicted to opium. It is amidst the wide-spread natural woods or jungles which cover a large portion of the country, and under favour of their shade, that the tea-plant is found growing, in tracts generally a few hundred yards in extent, with occasional trees, forming a sort of connection between one another. C. A. Bruce has now found a hundred and twenty such tracts.

He says, "in going over one of the hills behind Jaipore, about 300 feet high, I came upon a tea-tract, which must have been two or three miles in length—in fact I did not see the end of it; the trees were in some parts as thick as they could grow, and the tea seeds, fine and fresh, literally covered the ground; this was in the middle of November, and the trees had abundance of fruit and flower on them. One of the largest I found to be two cubits in circumference, and full forty cubits in height. At the foot of the hill I found another tract, and, had time permitted me to explore those parts, there is no doubt but I should have found many of the Naga hills covered with tea. I have since been informed of two more tracts near this. In going along the foot of the hills to the westward, I was informed that there was tea at Teweack, or near it; this information came too late, for I had passed it at a place called Chiridoo; here I found tea, and no doubt, if there had been time to examine, I should have found many more tracts. I crossed the Dacca river at the old fort of Ghergong, and walked towards the hills, and almost immediately came upon tea. The place is called Hauthoweak. Here I remained a couple of days going about the country, and came upon no fewer than thirteen tracts. A Dewahiah who assisted me to hunt them out, and who was well acquaintad with the leaf, as he had been in the habit of drinking tea during his residence with the Singphoes, informed me that he had seen a large tract of tea-plants on the Maga mountains, a day's journey west of Chiridoo. I have no reason to doubt the veracity of this man; he offered to point out the place to me, or any of my men if they would accompany him; but as the country belonged to Raja Poorunda Sing, I could not examine it. I feel convinced the whole of the country is full of tea.

Again, in going farther to the southwest, just before I came to Gabrew hill, I found the small hills adjoining it, to the eastward, covered with tea-plants. The flowers of the tea on these hills are of a pleasant delicate fragranee, unlike the smell of our other tea-plants; but the leaves and fruit appear the same. This would be a delightful place for the manufacture of tea, as the country is well populated, has abundance of grain, and labour is cheap. There is a small stream called Jhamgy river, at a distance of two hours walk; it is navigable, I am informed, at that period for small canoes, which would carry down the tea, and the place is only one and a half day's journey from Jorehaut, the capital of upper Assam. Southwest of Gabrew Purbut (about two days' journey) there is a village at the foot of the hill, inhabited by a race called Norahs; they are Shans, I believe, as they came from the eastward, where tea abounds. I had long conversations with them, and the oldest man of the village, who was also the head of it, informed me, that when his father was a young man, he had emigrated with many others, and settled at Tipum opposite Jaipore, on account of the constant disturbances at Munkum; that they brought the tea-plant with them, and planted it on the Tipum hill, where it exists to this day.

This was the only man I met with, in my jouneys about the country, who could give any account of the tea-plant, with the exception of an Abrum, who declared to me that it was Sooka, or the first Kacharry raja of Assam, who brought the tea-plant from Munkum; he said it was written in his Putty or history.

To the west of Gabrew, I did not find any tea; but to the westward of the Dhunseeree river I found a species, though not the same as that we use."

Bruce has also been engaged in experiments on the character of the tea produced in Assam.

Ninety chests of the article prepared by him and his assistants, were imported in London in 1838, and found, we are told, to be of good quality. In his report we find some notice of these operations:—

"Until lately, we had only two Chinese black-tea makers. These men have twelve native assistants; each Chinaman with six assistants, can only superintend one locality, and the tea-leaves from the various other tracts, widely separated, must be brought to these two places for manufacture. The leaves suffer when brought in large quantities from a distance, as they soon begin to ferment, and the labour of only preparing them so far as to prevent them from spoiling is excessive. The leaves last gathered are also much larger than they ought to be, for want of hands to collect them earlier. I mention this to show the inconvenience of having so few tea-makers.

The samples of black tea, made by the twelve assistants, having been approved of by the tea committee in Calcutta, it was my intention to have distributed the men among the different tracts; but the late disturbances on our frontier have prevented this arrangement, and I have been obliged to employ two men in Assam, two others having gone to Calcutta in charge of tea at the tract called Kahung, which is becoming a very extensive and important tea locality, so many others being near it. When we have a sufficient number of manufacturers, so that we can afford to have some at each tract or garden, as they have in China, then we hope to compete with that nation in cheapness of produce, nay, we might and ought to undersell them; for if each tract or garden had its own tea-maker and labourers, the collecting of the leaves would not perhaps occupy more than twelve days in each crop; after which the men might be discharged or profitably occupied on the grounds. It is true we have gained twelve black tea makers this year, in addition to the last; and twelve more native assistants have been appointed, who may be available next year to manufacture tea independently. We have also had an addition to our establishment of two Chinese green tea manufacturers, and twelve native assistants have been placed under them to learn; but

known, that the black and green tea are gathered from the same plant, and that the difference
is entirely owing to the different states of the
leaves, and modes of preparation. His account of the manufacture of green tea by his
Chinamen is extremely curious, but too long
to be here admitted. .

The demoralization produced by opium, and
a liking for independent labour which characterises the Assamese, throw difficulties in the
way of a large production of tea in Assam.
Bruce thinks it not impossible that the leaves
may be exported in a certain state, and subjected in England, by the cheap means of machinery, to those nice and tedious processes
which they have to undergo from manual
labour in China. "After a year's instruction
under Chinamen," says he, "it might be left
to the ingenuity of Englishmen to roll, sift and
clean the tea by machinery, and, in fact, reduce
the price of the green tea nearly one half, and
thus enable the poor to drink good unadultera-
ted green tea without the admixture of indigo
and sulphate of lime."

Five tea-tracts were under culture in Assam
in 1838, the produce of which amounted to
5274 lbs. Seven new tracts will be added in
1840, when it is thought the total produce
will be 11,160 pounds. These operations are
at the cost of the company ; but it is designed
ere long to throw the business open to private
speculation. Bruce enters into some calculations to show the probable profits of private
adventurers in this line. He takes ten tracts,
each 400 by 200 yards, and reckons the whole
expenses of cultivation the first year, at 16,-
501 rupees [$8,295], of which 4304 will not
need to be repeated the second year; and the
value of the produce he estimates at 35,554
rupees, thus giving a profit of upwards of cent
per cent.

Upon the whole, there seems little reason
to doubt that Assam is physically capable of
producing that important article, on which
forty to forty-five millions of dollars are annually spent in Great Britain.

To live like those that have their hope in
another life, implies that we keep under our
appetites, and do not let them loose into the
enjoyments of sense.—*Atterbury.*

various changes made as
employed therein, until we fir
blocks of wood, and tables of
place to the neat and conven
the present day. We shall spe
of authorship, and, giving an
of letters, show the manner
taries have obtained a recomp
bours both in ancient and mod
shall note the growth of a tas
the gathering of libraries, the
transcribers, the origin and
trade in books. Pursuing the
cal path thus laid out before u
ther deviate into disquisitions
language, nor enter into critici
ral literature. We shall baza
respecting the characters inscr
lars of Seth, nor the alphabet
the lost book of Enoch ; being
much instruction may be gath
vestigation of the records we h
most acute speculations upon
not. We shall pass by the es
poetry, and though we may giv
lingering glance, we shall not
an analysis of their waters, w
the deep pure gushing of the
or the shallower currents of Gr
so often turbid with earthy im

Did the plan of this lecture
treating of the literature of th
should call on you to listen
the dying patriarch Jacob, so
spirit of poetry, so grand with
of inspiration. I should invite
gate with me the writings of
his clearness and simplicity
his force and beauty as a poet,
vision as a prophet, his stern
giver, his meekness as a saint.
you to listen to the heavenwar
the royal psalmist of Israel,
with the poetic glory of Isai
you weep at the lamentation
mourn at the sorrowful note
trumpet of Joel, and trembl
stricken Habakkuk. In an e
of lectures on the history of li
drinking into the spirit of ancie
be as appropriate to the design
inciting to the intellect and

lived round stony heap or rudely reared pile, tribe after tribe of them have been swept from existence, and the records of their forefathers have none left to interpret them. Yet round these monuments there is a voice lingers which the conscience of the Anglo-Saxon usurpers of the soil may well startle to hear; —it is historic, for it speaks of the wrongs and outrages through which nations have perished; it is prophetic, for it tells of judgment to come on the head of the guilty oppressors.

In the same class of historical records we must place the belts of wampum, given by our Indians, in commemoration of speeches made, messages sent, presents delivered, or treaties adopted. These belts were carefully preserved, and the important particulars connected with them being often repeated, the whole tribe was made familiar with the facts, and each individual memory became a faithful historical record. Thus from year to year were events so accurately preserved, that it was no uncommon thing for their orators to repeat, at the time of after treaties, the agreements made, and the speeches delivered to their fathers, before those who now sat by their council fire had been ranked amongst men; and this, too, with admirable correctness and precision, as attested by printed copies, although the original witnesses, whose tongues had uttered the speeches, whose heads had planned, and whose hands had executed those agreements, had been joined to that quiet company from whom the living can gather no memorial.

From monuments which only appealed to the memory, and left the preservation of the whole train of incidents to its faithfulness—the next step towards the permanency of historical facts was in a rude imitation, either sculptural or pictorial, of the forms and figures connected therewith. This was an evident advance towards rendering knowledge fixed, inasmuch as the event was set forth to all beholders, and the names alone of the parties concerned intrusted to tradition. Rocks now, under the chisel, grew animate with representations of life, or bore witness to fields of battle and death in the figures traced on them by the painter.

The earliest of the Egyptian hieroglyphics are of the pictorial kind, which, delineating matters of fact, required little effort of the imagination to comprehend. Soon, however, figures became symbolical, and represented things which could not be made apparent by painting. The records formed at this period in the progress of literature, combine actual representation of events with symbolical additions readily understood by a poetic people. In the second class of the inscriptions by the Nile, the eye is found as a token of a superintending providence, a bird with extended wings an emblem of swiftness, and a scaling ladder a memorial of a siege.

A similar method of conveying information by records combining absolute representation with conventional symbols, appears to have been made use of by the aborigines of this country when the Spaniards first landed amongst them. The Mexicans, by a painting upon linen cloth, sent information to Montezuma that a band of white strangers had set foot

upon their shore. The natives of these more northern regions still employ this mode of conveying knowledge, and display no little ingenuity in representing continuity of action. When Henry Schoolcraft a few years since was on a journey of observation in the northwest part of the United States, his whole company, consisting principally of Indians, became so bewildered that they could not tell which way to direct their steps. The Indians, not knowing what might be the result, set themselves to prepare a historical record on a piece of birch bark, which, if found by any of their tribe, might give information concerning the expedition. They represented the military officer by drawing a man with a sword, a mineralogist by one with a hammer, and a lawyer by one with a book. Eight muskets signified so many soldiers; and three ascending columns of smoke betokened, that when they set up their tents for the night they made three encampments. Heckewelder thus speaks of the tribes he was familiar with: "On the bark of a tree, or on the side of a tree stripped of its bark, they can give every necessary information to those who come the same way. They will picture forth a war party—the number it consists of, the nations and tribes which compose it—which of them furnished the chief who led it, and in what direction they struck the enemy—the number of days they were going and returning, and the number of the enemy killed and taken. All this will be so clearly delineated, that at a single glance those who see it can understand." Amongst the multitude of illustrations which might be given, I shall bring forward but one more, which it seems to me might readily be comprehended by the most unpoetic and matter-of-fact intellect. A Shawanese and a white man both laid claim to right of ownership in a horse, which was in the Indian's possession. The white man was by no means disposed to be satisfied with his red brother's reasoning concerning their respective claims, until the latter, taking a coal from the hearth, drew on the door of the house two striking pictures, and asked him if he could read that Indian writing. The first picture represented the horse as being seized by the white man, whom the Indian, in the second, was delineated as scalping. These drawings seemed to come with the force of an irresistible argument, and the red man's title was no longer called in question.

When I had proceeded thus far in the preparation of this lecture, being led by the subject into the consideration of the language and literature of our aborigines, the peculiarity of their oratory forcibly arrested my attention. The idea suggested itself that this peculiarity was dependent upon the means they employed to make their knowledge visible. A volume of ancient Indian treaties furnished me with a great variety of speeches from some of their most accomplished orators. An investigation of these has confirmed the thought that led me to the search, for I found that every speech was but a symbolical painting, which the orator having formed in his own mind, describes to those around him. Does he dwell upon friendship between nations? he gives to the ear a description of that which his ready fingers could soon have represented to the eye—

an open pathway between two countries—a chain uniting the representatives of different tribes. Does he speak of a breach of that amity? he throws a tree over that pathway— he breaks or he rusts that chain. Does he tell of war? he scatters blood on that path, he takes the hatchet in his hand, he paints it in an enemy's head. Would he make peace? behold, he is rubbing that chain, he is sweeping the path, he is gathering the bloody leaves, bones, and hatchet, and burying them out of sight. A clear sky is with him also a token of peace, and clouds that overcast it are outrages or wars. Does he paint a river with a crimson current? then be sure many lives have been sacrificed; does the smoke curl from the calumet pipe? he remembers the quiet of peace, when the warrior could sit down and enjoy it. Would he tell of secrecy and stealth? he points to a man half concealed in the bushes; does he speak of being deceived? some one is closing his eyes, or is stopping his ears. Thus with him every speech is a picture, and such an one as every Indian could draw, or when drawn, comprehend.

When the written language was symbolical, we can have no difficulty in conceiving that figurative and poetic forms of speech should abound. Authors through such alone could render their works permanent, and readers were obliged to drink into their spirit that they might comprehend. In the introduction of the alphabetic characters which enabled a writer to leave nothing to the imagination of those for whom he wrote, the universal poetry of literature, of language, and of thought, gradually subsided.

On the Habits and Instincts of Animals. By William Swainson, A. C. G., Fellow of the Royal Society, and of several Foreign Academies.

(Continued from p. 284.)

The instinct of the black American bear, in procuring the acorns and chesnuts from the branches of particular trees, is worthy of attention. To procure these fruits in greater quantities, the animal ascends the tree; and as his weight will not allow of his going far from the trunk, he breaks the branch on which he has observed the most fruit, by grasping it in one of his fore paws. "I have seen some of these branches," observes Michaux, "of such a diameter that the animal must have possessed an extraordinary strength to break them so effectually as to fall upon the ground." Another singular and almost incredible instance of adapted means to an end is mentioned by Plutarch, who writes, "When I saw a dog in a ship—the sailors not being present—dropping small stones into the oil which was in a jar but partly full, I was astonished at his conceiving and understanding the overflow which takes place when heavy bodies sink in the lighter." The contrivance of the elephant to raise himself from the bottom of a pit is conducted on the same principle as that pursued by Plutarch's dog. When the natives have discovered his capture, he is retained in the pit until they judge he is sufficiently tractable to be conducted forth. Large bundles of jungle grass are then thrown to him; and he is thus gradually raised to the surface, or, at least, to such an elevation as will enable him to step out. The sagacity of elephants on such occasions, or when bogged in swamps, is truly admirable. The cylindrical form of an elephant's leg—which is nearly of equal thickness—causes the animal to sink very deep in heavy ground, especially in the muddy banks of small rivers. When thus situated, the animal will endeavour to lie on his side, so as to avoid sinking deeper; and, for this purpose, will avail himself of every means to obtain relief. The usual mode of extricating him is much the same as when pitted; that is, by supplying him liberally with straw, bought grass, &c.; these materials being thrown to the distressed animal, he forces them down with his trunk, till they are lodged under his fore feet in sufficient quantity to resist his pressure. Having thus formed a sufficient basis for exertion, the sagacious animal next proceeds to thrust other bundles under his belly, and as far back under his flanks as he can reach; when such a basis is formed, as may be, in his mind, proper to proceed upon, he throws his whole weight forward, and gets his hind feet gradually upon the straw, &c. Being once confirmed on a solid footing, he will next place the succeeding bundles before him, pressing them well with his trunk, so as to form a causeway by which to reach the firm ground. The instinct of the animal, and probably the experience of his past danger, actuates him not to bear any weight, definitely, until, by trial both with his trunk and the next foot that is to be planted, he has completely satisfied himself of the firmness of the ground he is to tread upon. Indeed, the caution with which this, and every part of his conduct on these occasions, is marked, evinces how forcibly nature has impressed him with a sense of his great weight. The anxiety of the animal, when bemired, forms a curious contrast with the pleasure he so strongly evinces on arriving at *terra firma.*

In their various modes of defence, or avoidance of their enemies, quadrupeds, like other classes of animals, frequently display wonderful instinct. The jerboa makes a burrow under ground, at the end of which a store of herbs is safely deposited. The cavern has but one entrance; but the wary inhabitant forms another, which reaches so nearly to the surface, that, in case of being taken by surprise, it can immediately burst through and escape. The chamois, and several other species of antelopes, ill-provided will defensive means, uniformly employ a sentinel, which, by a sharp hiss, advertises the herd of the approach of danger,—when all fly off with the greatest rapidity. The same habit is attributed to the wild horses of South America and Tartary. Several of the Brazilian monkeys have likewise a similar guard during the hours of repose; but whether Smellie is correct in stating that, if they find their sentry has neglected his duty, they fall on and tear him to pieces, we had no means of discovering. It is interesting to observe the manner in which instinct will sometimes overcome a difficulty which might even puzzle a reasonable creature. It has been stated, that if two mountain goats encounter each other upon a narrow ledge of rocks, where to pass or to turn is utterly impossible, one will imme-

diately lie down, while the other steps over his back. Nor is it less singular to remark the mode by which animals in similar situations communicate their wants and their distresses. An anecdote of this nature is told of a number of sheep who surrounded a cow, as if they wished to bespeak her favour for a poor gravid ewe, which was unable to recover herself from her miserable situation until the cow, advancing towards her, placed the tips of her horns beneath her side, and gave her a slight but dexterous toss, which instantly replaced the sufferer upon her feet. We must place this, however, among the questionable list of stories handed down of animal instinct.

But the most astonishing developement of instinct—at least among quadrupeds—will be found in the following account of the decoy elephants of India, the fidelity of which may be fully depended upon, as the facts are well known to almost every one who has resided any time in India:—" The females selected for this extraordinary undertaking are always those uniting the qualities of great docility and affection to their drivers, with a full grown stature; for, without this latter qualification, the animal cannot conceal her driver from the sight of the intended victim of her allurements, or, in the event of his being discovered, afford him protection. A particular time, however, is requisite for these operations; this is, during the rutting season, when the weaker males having been driven away from their former herds by those of greater strength and courage, are wandering about singly in the woods, uttering 'disconsolate trumpetings,' the cause of which is well known to the experienced hunter. These bachelor elephants are called *saums;* and, being considered very valuable, are especially selected for enticing. It is generally thought best to employ three females, called *koomkies,* in the capture of one *saun,* or wild male. Each of these is attended by a driver, or *mofrout,* who is provided with a black blanket, and a small quantity of strong rope: the former is used to cover the driver, who crouches in such a manner as not to be easily distinguished from the female he rides upon. She, also, aids in this deception; for, if the situation is favourable, both she and her driver furnish themselves with green boughs, which the former carries in her trunk, playing with it in such a manner as to favour the concealment of the latter. When the party thus approach the male, it is usual for the driver to dismount in some contiguous cover with their blankets and ropes, leading the females to the *saun,* towards which they proceed with the utmost caution. A most extraordinary scene then follows. The *koomkies* begin to caress their intended victim, as if with the utmost tenderness and affection. During this courtship, however, the females contrive to place themselves in such a manner as to favour the approach of their keepers, who, watching their opportunities, pass the repes with wonderful dexterity round the fore legs of the infatuated lover, who is thus speedily secured. When a large tree is at hand, the females artfully lead the male towards it, in the first instance; thus the approach of the keeper is not only greatly facilitated, but an opportunity is given of affixing to the hind legs of the *saun* a pair of

wooden clasps, armed inside with spikes; these are joined to a strong rope, which is passed round the tree, and made completely fast. During all this process, the conduct of the females is peculiarly artful. They not only exert themselves, with astonishing address, to divert the attention of their intended victim, and to cut off his view, downwards, by means of their trunks, but they even aid in effecting the ligatures therewith,—sometimes passing the rope, when the keepers might either be exposed to danger, or unable to reach it. It may be observed, that the spikes within the clasps, above mentioned, are so small, as only to inflict pain when the animal, finding himself captured, struggles violently to free himself from the shackles.

Notwithstanding all these precautions, however, it sometimes happens that the enamoured male in some way discovers the presence of the keeper, in which case not even the caresses of his agreeable companions can control his violence. This is a severe trial on the fortitude and fidelity of the females, who have been known to expose themselves to the *saun's* utmost fury, while attempting to aid the escape of their keepers. It all goes well, however, as soon as the *saun* is secured, the whole party commence a retreat; since nothing further is requisite, after these measures have been taken, than to leave the captured elephant to expend his strength in vain efforts to regain his liberty. Awakening, as it would seem, to a full sense of the deceit that has been practised upon him, his fury becomes ungovernable: he destroys whatever may be in his way; tears up the tufts of grass by the roots; rends from the tree such branches as he can reach; and, eventually, straining to throw down the tree itself by his weight, or to pull it up with his trunk. In short, his whole powers are in action on this occasion; and it is only on being completely overcome with fatigue, and nearly dead from thirst, that he subsides into a sort of tranquillity." We may pass over much that has been said on the preparatory measures adopted for reconciling the captive to his new situation, where he remains until he is sufficiently tamed to be led or driven to the premises occupied by the tame elephants. The same females and keepers who ensnared him are employed in this preliminary process. At first, he will only partake of water; but the impulse of nature soon operates,—and he is then induced to pick at tender branches of plantain trees, sugar canes, &c. Thus subdued, he is taken, under charge of other elephants,—generally superior to himself in strength and bulk,—to the dwelling he is in future to occupy. Sometimes, however, when he is on his way, or, perhaps, on his legs, being liberated, he will make a last and desperate effort to regain his liberty. When this happens, the conducting elephants, extending to the length of their tow ropes, urge forward as fast as may be practicable, while one or more sturdy males goad him behind with their tusks. This latter circumstance is not the least extraordinary part of the narrative; for animals to be driven into confinement by their own species is unexampled, we believe, except in the case of the elephant.

(To be continued.)

[From the Boston Courier.]

THE BURNING OF THE POLAND.

Boston, May 29, 1840.

As the loss of the unfortunate ship Poland excites considerable interest in this community, I take an early opportunity to give as complete a detail of the occurrences connected with it as my memory will allow. We sailed from New York, or rather we were taken in tow by the steamboat Wave, from pier No. 3, in the harbour, about 11 A. M., on the 11th instant, the wind being quite light, and were towed down to Sandy Hook, where the pilot and the steamboat left us.

Counting all hands, men, women and children, we had on board sixty three persons. We had good weather and favourable breezes, passing about twenty-five miles to the south of Nantucket Shoals, and going on prosperously and fast enough to satisfy those most impatient for a short passage, until the 16th. At 12 o'clock, noon, of that day, we were in latitude 41 35, and longitude 58 30, nearly one third of the passage, and with every hope of not being on board more than eighteen days.

At 2 P. M., or within a few minutes of that time, it began to rain, and so continued, in showers and squalls, until about three o'clock, when a severe shower commenced with large drops, like some of our summer showers after a hot and sultry day. As most of the male passengers were in the house on deck, looking out at the rain and sea, Captain Anthony standing at the door, a large ball of fire, apparently about twice the size of a man's hat, suddenly descended in a horizontal line from the clouds, which appeared to be meeting from two different points of the compass ahead of us, and struck the end of the foretopsail yard, on the left hand side; it descended the ties, or some chains, to the end of the foreyard, and ran on the yard to the cap of the foremast, where it exploded, with a report similar to that of a cannon, and giving the appearance of the explosion of a bomb, or similar, although on a much larger scale, to the explosions of some of the firework circles which we have had exhibited on the common on public galas, throwing out rays in every direction, like the rays of the sun. The whole was instantaneous, and was witnessed by two or three of us, it came and passed off in a flash, and was followed almost at the same instant by a peal of thunder, sharp and loud, but not long or rumbling. It was the only flash of lightning or peal of thunder that we saw or heard.

Almost immediately, Captain Anthony went forward with one or two of the passengers, being aware that we had been struck with lightning, to ascertain if the ship was damaged. It was ascertained that when the ball exploded, the electric fluid ran down the foremast to the lower deck, where the chain cable was stowed. We found that the fluid did run round the chain, but could not see where it escaped. On going into the forecastle, we discovered some signs of the lightning, and were led to suppose, on a very close examination, that after entering the steerage, it passed through into the forecastle out of the companion way. A piece of the *fid*, about eight inches long, and two or three thick, was knocked off the foretop, and two or three of the halyards were found to be

cut off, which the captain immediately set his men to repairing.

Although the cabin and steerage were filled with a sort of smoke, which had a sulphurous smell, no one really supposed the ship to be on fire, or that the appearances indicated any thing more than the gas usually following a stroke of lightning. Some alarm and anxiety was very naturally felt, particularly by the ladies, and those who were connected with them; but still, as there was no increase of smoke, and no appearance of fire, the crew went about their regular business, and at four o'clock dinner was served as usual, the cabin at that time being clear of every thing indicative of danger. Some of us could not eat—while there was uncertainty, we had no appetite, and the meal which had heretofore been one of pleasure, accompanied by the reciprocation of good feelings, and sallies of wit, passed off with dulness, and almost in silence. Captain Anthony looked in upon us as we sat at table, but he was too anxious to sit down, and did not cease in his endeavours to ascertain with certainty our position. The first mate and the steward opened the run and went into it, to ascertain if there was fire or smoke in that part of the ship, but came out without being satisfied either that there was or was not —the smell was the same as that we had at first, mostly of gas, like sulphur.

Our dinner was a short and silent one; and when we went on deck, the captain said that he had little doubt that the ship was on fire, and that we must endeavour to get at it. On a suggestion that we might be obliged to take to the boats, it was immediately remarked by one of our French passengers, and responded to by others, "Let us take care of the women and children first." I mention this as honourable to those who made it, and as showing that there was, even at that first moment of danger, a praiseworthy abandonment of self to the protection of others who are naturally more helpless. Not a moment was lost in clearing the main hatch, the captain himself leading the way, and commencing by throwing over the empty water casks and useless lumber which was stored round the long boat. The mate, with another gang of hands, was at the fore hatch, and, in a few minutes, all hands, including many of the cabin and steerage passengers, were at work hoisting out and throwing overboard flour and cotton.

The work of discharging the cargo between decks went on cheerfully, amid a severe rain, until about eight o'clock; the fire not appearing to increase, and at times appearing to be altogether extinguished, even if there had ever been any except in the imagination; but at that time, and when the forward lower hatch was reached, we were at once convinced of the awful fact, that the cotton in the lower hold was on fire. The hatch was immediately closed as tight as possible, the upper hatches were also closed and partially caulked, and preparations were made to get out the boats.

In answer to many inquiries why we had not in the mean time got our baggage on deck, I will remark, that until now there was a hope that we were still safe, or that, if there were fire on board, we should be able to get at and extinguish it. So great was our confidence,

that the children were undressed and put to bed for the night, not, however, without many anxious forebodings on the part of their parents. When the dreadful certainty was forced upon us, our first object was to get the women and children on deck, and in fact this was rendered the more necessary from the circumstance that the hatches being closed, the gas must escape somewhere, and it immediately got vent through the run and the steward's pantry, into the cabin, rendering it impossible for any one to remain below long at a time. Captain Anthony coolly, calmly, and quietly gave his orders, and they were obeyed in the same spirit by his men. He remarked, that it was useless to bring up any thing but such light articles as we could easiest find, as the boats would not be able to carry any baggage. One caught a carpet bag, and another a cloak; some opened their trunks and took out their money, leaving every thing else behind; and some caught blankets from the berths. The steward got up a barrel of bread, and others assisted him in putting whatever of eatables there was in his pantry into bags, &c. A barrel and two or three jugs of water were put into the long-boat, with such casts, cloaks, &c. as could be got at in a few minutes, and then she was launched overboard. The women and children were first handed over the side of the ship, and then the cabin passengers, all except three, a few of the steerage passengers, the second mate, and four sailors. The other boats were also got out, and two men placed in each. All this was done with order and regularity, without any pushing or crowding, and in tacit obedience to the captain's orders, in a very short time. It was ten o'clock before the long-boat was pushed off, and a line attached to her and the ship—having on board thirty-five persons. Nothing was said at the time about the other two boats, and those of us who remained on board the Poland were waiting for the first break of morning to learn the fate to which we were doomed—knowing that it would be madness to put more into the long-boat, and that not more than half of those of two. The ship, at the time we first supposed ourselves in danger, was put upon a southeasterly course, in the hope of falling in with or cutting off the ship we had passed in the morning, and signal lanterns were hoisted in the rigging, but when we commenced getting out the boats she was hove to, and she rode very easy all night, the sea not being very boisterous, and there being very little wind. It rained at intervals all night, and although it was daylight and clear about four o'clock in the morning, the time seemed very long. After the long-boat was hoisted out, an attempt was made to save some articles from the cabin, and the steward succeeded in saving the captain's watch and chronometer, and trunk, with a small box containing about three hundred dollars in specie, but the gas and the smoke soon obliged us to abandon all further attempts, and to close all the doors to the cabin and to the house over them.

We walked the deck all that night, and said but little. Captain Anthony was watchful, and going silently about in every part of the deck, stopping up a crack here and adjusting a rope there, or giving some order for the safety of those whom at that moment he must have felt were dependent almost entirely upon his discretion for their lives. Morning broke, and the sun rose, but no sail was in sight. There we lay on the broad ocean, a fine ship smoking at every crack, with three frail boats attached to her by a single rope, and no hope of rescue except through the goodness of the Almighty. Whatever may have been the religious feelings, or the want thereof, among those sixty-three persons so awfully situated, there was no cowardice exhibited, no sudden outbreak of prayer and repentance, no murmuring. But there did appear to be a confidence in the breast of every one that the God who had thus suddenly afflicted us, would not leave us to perish in that desert sea.

We remained in this state of suspense all day Sunday, making ourselves as comfortable as possible. Every crack where we could find the smoke coming out, was stuffed with cotton, or plastered over with pipe clay, of which the captain found a small lot on board attached to the gallery erected for the steerage passengers. The ice house on deck contained fresh meat, such as beef, chickens, ducks, &c., and the cooks were employed all day in cooking. We sent some warm coffee and fresh milk, with some boiled fowls, to our friends in the long-boat, and made every exertion to lighten their misfortunes. But still no ship came in sight, and evening at last found us in the same perilous situation that we were in the night before. During all this day the deck was quite warm, on the right hand side, forward of the main-mast, indicating, as we supposed, that the fire was under that part of the vessel; the thick glass dead lights, set into the deck, at intervals of about two feet, from stern to stem, were also quite hot. But towards night the deck and glasses began to cool off, and there was less smoke apparent; the forward hatches, too, were not quite so hot at night as they were in the morning, and we began to have more hope. We had got a man over the stern in the fore-noon, on a spar, to fasten down the shutters to the cabin windows and nail them down, but this did not prevent the smoke from coming through. The wooden shutters to the sky-lights on deck were put on to prevent the glass being broken by accident, and towards night we thought that the glass under those shutters had cooled off.

About ten o'clock on that night, most of the unfortunate people on board the ship sunk to sleep on the deck from mere exhaustion, leaving only three people awake to watch for help, or to warn us of what we most dreaded, a bursting out of the flames. No language can tell of the sufferings of that night, which was more dreadful than the last. We were like people confined on the top of a burning mine, with no power to escape—death almost certain to be our portion within a few short hours, and our minds tortured with suspense.

During the night, Captain Anthony laid down and caught a short sleep. The weather was tolerably fair, but silence reigned through-out, except so far as it was broken by the oc-casional rumbling and dashing of the sea. Just before two o'clock I laid down beside him to wait my fate, leaving only one man walking

the deck, and in doing so, I disturbed him. He waked, and turning over, he took my hand and remarked, "I feel that we shall be saved— I have had a pleasant dream." This circum-stance, slight as it was, had its effect, and did impart some consolation to both of us.

About this time the weather was changing, and the sea had risen, and the people in the long-boat became alarmed. Mr. Wainwright hailed the ship, to know if it would not be best to take the boat in. Captain Anthony answered that they had better wait patiently until daylight, and then walked forward to examine into the state of the ship. We now found that the fire had evidently increased, the deck and hatches were still quite warm, and the pitch was beginning to boil or melt in the seams between the planks. A short conference convinced us that but little time could elapse before the fire would burst through the deck, and then there would be no further hope. What we said and what we felt between that time and daylight, is not to be told here—it is sufficient that we thought we knew the worst; the two small boats could not hold more than fifteen persons, and there were nearly thirty on board the ship; under the best of circum-stances some of us must be lost; and it is needless to say, that Captain Anthony deter-mined that he should stick to his vessel and run the risk, rather than crowd the boats with too many people, or exclude any one else.

At daylight, Mr. Wainwright came on board in one of the small boats, and we explained our situation to him. There was but a chance for any of us. If he and his party remained in the boat, they *might* be saved, but if they were taken on board the ship, and the fire should break out, it would be then impossible to put the people into the boats again, and the launch them over the side, and death by fire or drowning would be the certain lot of all. The case was too strong, and the horrid con-viction was too apparent to be disputed, and as was his duty, he prepared to return to his family and meet his fate. It is not for me to say what were then our feelings. Three of us, in the fulness of our strength and the ripe-ness of years, were then parting, as we all supposed, for ever; and nearly every one else was asleep. Words were useless, and we could not utter what we wanted to express. We commended our families to each other, in case either should be saved; and with a silent shake of the hands he returned to the boat, to make such preparations as prudence suggested, to protect his almost helpless companions in case we should find it necessary to cut his boat adrift.

From this time the sea became more bois-terous, and at last, after some hours of anxious watching, we sent for Mr. Wainwright to come on board again, and he was told that there were fears that his boats would swamp. Captain Anthony was afraid to make sail on the ship, as the working of the masts might create a current of air below, which would either increase the fire, or operating upon the gas in the hold, blow off the hatches and thus seal our fate at once. After some considera-tion, it was concluded to run the risk and take in the boats, and put the ship before the wind, in the hope of falling in with some other ves-

sel, [...] no ti [...] tion. [...]

W [...] on b [...] wors [...] had t [...] our p [...] fema [...] a day [...] unabl [...] their [...] bodie [...] dashi [...] had b [...] whol [...] bust [...] out se [...] a firn [...] serve [...] weds [...] havin [...] ment [...] ready [...] boat [...] altoge [...] than [...] On [...] comfo [...] some [...] all fel [...] allevi [...] joined [...] was t [...] the no [...] vation [...] gitude [...] the se [...] bound [...] States [...] saved [...] were [...] ship v [...] part o [...] pitch, [...] out of [...] ed up [...] men [...] the te [...] water [...] Ab [...] vered [...] seen [...] disco [...] be de [...] almos [...] saw o [...] lewar [...] to be [...] Capt. [...] New [...] age p [...] Antho [...] in the [...] off, t [...] board [...] can." [...] Be [...] mann [...] mate [...] and t [...] ship v [...] high, our task a long and dangerous one; from three until nine o'clock the two boats were passing and repassing with people, and such articles as could be saved from the deck.

The gale was now blowing from the northwest, and both captains remarked that they did not recollect ever to have seen a worse sea for many years. We were all safely on board by nine o'clock, and Captain Ingersoll, not thinking it safe to risk his own ship any longer by laying to, in the vain hope of saving property, made sail on his ship, and we left the unfortunate Poland to burn up and sink, a fate which she undoubtedly met within two or three hours.

At the time the last boat's load left the Poland, the decks had become too hot to stand upon, and her sides were so warm, that as she rolled in the sea, the water would run off as from hot iron, and she would instantly become dry, and too hot to bear the hand upon. An effort was made to get out some articles from the house over the cabin stairs, but on opening the doors, the smoke, heat, and deleterious gas drove the people away instantly, and a second attempt proved alike fruitless. A like attempt near the main hatch met with the like success, and the ship was abandoned with tears and regret, for sailors imbibe an affection for the craft in which they have sailed, and they feel the loss more keenly than many people feel the loss of their friends and relatives.

On board the Clifton we met with a most cordial reception from Captain Ingersoll and his whole crew. We had been saved in life, but we had all lost our clothing, and the chests of the sailors and the trunks of their commander were freely opened, and their contents were as freely offered for our use. What inconveniences were suffered from the crowded state of the Clifton, and our own destitute condition, were of no moment. We were safe, and all things else were forgotten in a feeling of gratitude and thankfulness to Almighty God for saving us from the death we had so long seen almost certain to us.

There were many incidents connected with this eventful period, the recollection of which is interesting to those concerned, but I have already taken up more room than I at first intended. I cannot conclude, however, without remarking that to Captain Anthony belongs all the credit that belongs to any one for preserving us so long; the card published by the passengers under their signatures, awards him no more than justice, and might with equal justice have been made much stronger. He has acquired a hold upon our hearts that cannot be loosened but with life itself, and if ever man could retire with a confidence that he had done his duty faithfully in the hour of danger, unflinching at the last moment, that satisfactory consolation must be his.

As for the passengers and crew, they deserve all praise. It appears now almost impossible that so much could have been done, so much have been suffered, without confusion and without a murmur. From the first moment to the last, there was order and regularity observed, and each one appeared to strive to make the burthens of the others as easy to bear as possible; the calm confidence of our female companions, and their firm reliance

upon the goodness of the Power which was afflicting them, served in a great measure to encourage their friends in the hard task of sustaining them until assistance came to hand.

J. W. B.

The memorial of the Monthly Meeting of Friends, held in New York, concerning our beloved friend Sarah Waring.

The memory of those who have devoted themselves, their time and talents, to the service of the Militant church, cannot but be precions in its view:—and for the edification and encouragement of survivors;—and in the hope that a greater detachment from the things of time and sense, and an increased devotion to the cause of our Holy Redeemer may thereby be induced; it has ever been thought right that the distinctive traits in the characters of such, and the peaceful close of their earthly pilgrimage, should be placed upon record.

Sarah Waring, the subject of this memoir, was the daughter of Solomon and Lydia Underhill, of Cow Neck, now Manhasset, Queens County, New York:—from her childhood, she was religiously inclined, and, with added years, there was an increase of her love to God, and a desire to do his holy will.

She was married to our friend William Waring, of New York, in the year 1809, and, feeling her augmented responsibility, she was concerned to discharge with diligence the various duties of life—knowing that the work is to be done whilst it is yet day—and with the feeling which she manifested in the following expression: "how much is to be done and how little time to do it in!" she faithfully discharged the relative and social duties, and exercised the hospitality of primitive days—not for show—but for the refreshment of the weary traveller. She was diligent in visiting the sick, the destitute and the afflicted; and was especially careful to seek out, in their lowly situation, the dwellings of the stranger and of those who had but recently removed amongst us; to inquire into their circumstances, and sympathise with them in their trials; an incumbent Christian duty, the right performance of which, will often open the way for much usefulness, but which, it is apprehended, is too much neglected in populous cities.

She served, to the satisfaction of Friends, as clerk of several important meetings for discipline for a number of years, and was extensively useful in maintaining the order of the society: she long occupied, diligently and faithfully, the station of overseer, and, for some years, that of an elder in the church, and was strongly attached to its distinguishing testimonies.

She was sound in the faith of the gospel of our Holy Redeemer, which was manifested by her steady and firm adherence to it when many forsook it and fled; and she highly prized the written records of its truths, which was evinced by her diligent engagement in their perusal.

She was attacked with a pulmonary affection, under which she appeared declining in health, and went to the Island of St. Croix, in the West Indies, in the first month, 1839, where, in about a week after her arrival, she

had a hemorrhage of the lungs, during which, she was strikingly peaceful and quiet in her mind. After about four months' absence, she returned home in a state of increased bodily weakness. Her decline was very gradual, and she was long confined to her bed.

Possessing a mind of more than ordinary sensibility, she had been deeply affected under several afflictive dispensations of her life, and now, when her bodily frame was reduced to so great a degree of weakness, that life was long with difficulty sustained, she was, from the inexplicable connection between the mind and its material dwelling, again at times subjected to great depression.

In a state of great strippedness and a feeling of poverty and unworthiness, she earnestly desired to receive a peaceful assurance of her acceptance; and in seasons of comparative exemption from the sinking sensations peculiar to her disease, she was mercifully favoured with it: such, however, was her diffidence, and her low estimate of her attainments, that she spoke but little of these seasons of enjoyment, lest she should exhibit a greater degree of Christian advancement than she was willing to admit to be her experience; but in seasons of depression she was enabled to derive comfort from the unity and sympathy of the friends to whom she was attached in gospel love, and from the rich treasures which she continued to find in Holy Writ, many interesting passages of which recurred to her mind from time to time, and, by the divine blessing, were made the means of soothing and comforting her spirit: of the expression of her feelings and views, the following have been preserved:

The 27th of 6th month, 1839—she said that, at times, she felt the supporting arm, but, at others was weak and poor;—that, her peace was not from works of righteousness that she had done; and that she feared to apply to herself the favourable view of her state that her friends had presented to her; And, some days after, observed that, in a season of domestic affliction, and also whilst at St. Croix, she had been comforted by the application of the 20th Psalm to her condition.

Her spiritual state became increasingly comfortable, and, about the middle of the following month, she remarked that she felt a more full assurance of acceptance, which she had to witness for herself, not having dared to trust to the favourable views of her friends in relation to her state;—and observed that all her weakness and sufferings were not too much—and evinced a great interest in the prosperity of the cause of truth.

Towards the close of the same month, she expressed a hope that her patience would hold out—remarking that she felt an increasing quiet of mind, that she knew her nervous system was apt to be affected.

On the 15th of the 8th month, she remarked that she had not much aboundings to speak of, but that she was in peaceful quiet;—that, if her friends thought her state less than that, she was desirous of being told of it. A few days after, she said that, at times, she felt peaceful and quiet; at others, she remembered she had strayed through unwatchfulness; that she did not want to trouble her friends with her low feelings, for she knew she was excitable, and that she was constitutionally so.

About this period, in a time of great poverty of spirit, the assurance of divine acceptance was so far withheld from her that she was for a season unable to apply the promises to herself; but subsequently remarked to the young people around her "I do want you to know that the Lord is good"—again—"The Lord is my strength and my song, and he also is become my salvation."

The forepart of the 9th month was a time of much enjoyment—her mind being peaceful, and her countenance plainly indicating her feelings. She often recurred to a visit of a ministering friend, and said, "Oh, those sweet words!—in quietness and in confidence shall be thy strength, until thy change—which in the Lord's time will be a glorious change—shall come."

She could not at any time, without evident dissatisfaction, hear any allusion to the exemplary tenor of her past life, or to any good she had done; and about this time remarked, "Whatever judgment my friends may have formed, I am sensible I have been very deficient in humility."

On the morning of the 11th, continuing to be favoured to rely upon him who first loved her, she said she felt a peaceful calm pervading her mind, and a willingness to be released;—but, if it was the design of Divine Wisdom, she was willing to remain; it might be for the good of others.

She was not expected to survive the night of the 12th, and, on the afternoon of the following day, was much unsettled in mind: on the succeeding evening the excitement passed away and returned no more. She inquired if her pulse was not very low; and requested that her husband and sons should come into her room. She repeated several passages of Scripture, expressive of her feelings of quietness and thankfulness, and said her mind had been so affected by her poor body that she had become weak, very weak, that she had greatly desired she might not thereby injure any;—that the time of her departure was concealed from her, but that she felt there was much more cause for rejoicing than for mourning;—and continued through the night in a very peaceful frame of mind—frequently expressing her willingness and desire to depart, and was much engaged in thanksgiving for past mercies, and in prayer that He, whom she had endeavoured to serve, would be her staff and support in her passage through the valley of the shadow of death.

The night following she again asked the state of her pulse; and on being told it was, sometimes, scarcely perceptible, her countenance immediately brightened, and she said, "How grateful I ought to be to a merciful Providence,"—and shortly after, "Farewell! all my dear friends."

On the morning of the 15th of the 9th month, she requested to hear several passages of Scripture read;—one of which, from the triumphant song of Moses, was, "The horse and his rider hath he cast into the sea;" and the last, "I will give up to thee the sure mercies of David." In the afternoon she again made inquiry about the state of her pulse, say-

ing the best information in relation to it had been given her the night previous,—adding, "Why, why do you wish to detain me here? I desire to be patient, I strive to be patient and to say, 'Thy will and not mine be done.'" "The sufferings of this present time are not worthy to be compared with the glory that shall be revealed." Shortly after, she said, with much emphasis, "The Lord is good!— He is good!—He is very good!" And afterwards, "I am almost insensible to every thing around me—I am sinking away—I hope to be preserved from manifesting impatience."

In the evening she said she had no pain, and asked if it were not almost over. She spoke with her usual strength of voice until about fifteen minutes of her close, and was entirely conscious to the last.

A little before 9 o'clock, her purified spirit forsook its earthly tabernacle, in the 57th year of her age.

Signed by direction and on behalf of the meeting aforesaid,

WILLIAM BIRDSALL, *Clerk.*
ELIZABETH UNDERHILL, *Clerk.*

NATURE'S BEAUTIES.

I love, upon the foaming deep,
  Sweet breezes to inhale;
I love to have them gently beat
  Against the spreading sail!

I love upon the beach to roam,
  And listen to the surf;
I love to wander far from home,
  And lightly tread the turf!

I love to lay me on the grass,
  And gaze upon the sky;
I love to watch the clouds that pass
  O'er the expanse on high.

I love on Nature's charms to look,
  No mortal being near;
I love to sit me by a brook,
  Its rippling waters hear!

I love to tread the dreary waste,
  Of mountain's airy top;
I love the crystal water's taste,
  That from cool springs is got!

I love to hear the wild birds call,
  As through the air they soar;
I love to hear a waterfall,
  Or mountain torrent roar!

I love to wander by moonlight,
  In some sequestered spot;
I love to be, in silent night,
  Where other men are not!

I love to see the morning's sun
  Clearing the mist away;
I love, when he his course has run,
  To see him close the day!

I love ALL that in Nature's grand
  And beautiful to see;
From mountains wild to pasture land,
  All, all is joy to me!

                                    H. E. G.

Added by another hand.

But most of all they wake my love,
  That in their every feature,
They tell of Him enthroned above,
  The life of every creature.

There is no man but God hath put many things in his possession, to be used for the common good and interest.—*Calamy.*

THE FRIEND.

SIXTH MONTH, 13, 1840.

The Yearly Meeting of Friends held in New York, it appears, commenced on second day the 25th of last month, and continued by adjournments to the afternoon of sixth day, the 29th. In reference to the state of the society, as brought into view by the reading of the reports from subordinate meetings, religious concern was felt and expressed, inciting to increased faithfulness in the discharge of religious duties; especially in regard to the solemn and indispensable obligation of a diligent attendance at the appointed times of meetings for divine worship, as well on the first day of the week as on week days. The reports from the Quarterly Meetings on schools were fraught with interesting details, and a concern was felt on the subject in a good degree commensurate with its importance. Monthly Meetings were requested to make appointments yearly to co-operate with appointments by the Quarterly Meetings, for promoting the momentous object of a religiously guarded education for their children. The subject of slavery and the slave trade renewedly engaged attention, and the reading of the minutes of the Meeting for Sufferings furnished evidence that it had occupied the special consideration of that body, which resulted in the presentation to Congress of a memorial relating to the trade to Africa for slaves, and to the internal traffic in the persons of men. That meeting likewise presented a memorial to the legislature of the state, on behalf of the free people of colour, and the civil disabilities to which they are subjected. The concern relative to slavery was continued under the care of the Meeting for Sufferings, with authority to act in it on behalf of the society, as way shall open for it.

We have been induced to insert a more extended account of the burning of the Poland. It is abridged from a letter of J. W. Buckingham, of Boston, one of the passengers, and is a truly affecting statement, without the least appearance of exaggeration, of circumstances attendant on that most awful occurrence, which cannot but be deeply interesting to many of our readers who have not frequent access to the journals of the day.

Our readers will please correct a typographical error in our paper of last week. In line 44 of the poem "The Three Sons," for *senseless,* read *sinless.*

INSTITUTE FOR COLOURED YOUTH.

The managers are desirous of procuring a suitably qualified person (a member of the Society of Friends) to have the care of, and instruct a limited number of boys at the above institution.

Applications may be forwarded to either of the undernamed committee.

George Williams, 71 north Seventh street, Philip Garrett, Noble street, first door above Sixth, Blakey Sharpless, 50 north Fourth street, M. L. Dawson, corner of Tenth and Filbert streets.

Phila. 5th mo. 30th, 1840.

THE FRIEND.

, A RELIGIOUS AND LITERARY JOURNAL.

VOL. XIII.   **SEVENTH DAY, SIXTH MONTH, 20, 1840.**   **NO. 38.**

EDITED BY ROBERT SMITH.

PUBLISHED WEEKLY.

Price two dollars per annum, payable in advance.

Subscriptions and Payments received by

GEORGE W. TAYLOR,

NO. 50, NORTH FOURTH STREET, UP STAIRS,

PHILADELPHIA.

Communicated for " The Friend."

Two Lectures on the History of Literature, with a brief sketch of the various materials made use of for the preservation of Knowledge.

LECTURE FIRST.

(Continued from p. 291.)

The works of the earliest authors which have descended to us, are in a poetical form. From the symbolical character of the times, the poetry of imagery might be looked for, but is it not remarkable, that early literature should have trammelled itself with " an artificial division of sentences, and those minor elegancies of style which promote the harmony of rhythm." This form was, however, well adapted to facilitate the preservation of compositions, which could have no other repository than the memory of hearers. The difficulty of accurately retaining prose in remembrance may in part account for the fact, that poetical works alone survived to that period at which the invention of written characters furnished the means of recording them for posterity. Perhaps, however, it was those only who had a keen perception of the unwritten poetry of the universe, and who were sensitively alive to the harmony of measured sounds, who felt within them that stirring of intellect and feeling which led to composition. However this may be, " poetry," to use the words of a poet, " was the first fixed form of language, the earliest perpetuation of thought. It existed before prose in history, before music in melody, before painting in description, and before sculpture in imagery. Anterior to the discovery of letters, it was employed to communicate the lessons of wisdom, to celebrate the achievements of valour, and to promulgate the sanctions of law."

From figures symbolical of things, the next step was to such as were representative of sounds. What nation had an alphabet first in use amongst them cannot now be ascertained. The Greeks ascribe the invention to the Phenicians, but the weight of evidence seems greatly in favour of the Egyptians or Assyrians. Of this, at least, we are certain, that the most ancient alphabetic inscriptions to which we have access, and which date from a period of time anterior to the fabled invention of Cadmus, are found amongst the monuments of the Pharaohs, and on the bricks from the ruins of Babylon. The introduction and simplification of the alphabetic characters in any country, was probably the work of centuries, and due to the inventive genius of a nation rather than of an individual.

Champollion has traced a gradual change in the inscriptions of Egypt:—first, characters purely symbolical, passing into conventional, and thence into a series of signs having reference only to sound. At first, the figures made use of were the absolute representatives of visible objects, which, to increase the facility of composition, became, in time, reduced to a few marks, bearing little or no resemblance to their originals. Moses Stuart, in a note to Greppo's Essay on the hieroglyphic system, says, " one need only to read the interpretation of the names of the Hebrew alphabet successively, in order to believe that, originally, there was some analogy between the shape of the respective letters, and the objects by whose names they are called. For example, beginning with the alphabet, we proceed thus: ox, house, camel, hollow, hook, arrow, travelling-scrip, serpent, hand, hollow-hand, ox-goad, water, fish, prop, eye, mouth, screech-locust, ear, head, tooth, cross. These make out the whole original alphabet of the Hebrews; and no one can suppose that these names, rather than others, were given to the letters, except on account of some resemblance between them and the objects which bore these names."

Having thus briefly touched on the origin of letters, the next subject of inquiry will be the material on which they are most commonly inscribed. We find Job, who is supposed to have partaken of his cup of affliction and sorrow in the days of the patriarch Abraham, thus pouring out the anguish of his soul. " Oh that my words were now written ! oh that they were printed (or traced out) in a book ! that they were graven with an iron pen and lead in the rock for ever." At first the alphabetic characters were much confined to public monuments, and the letters were engraven upon stone and brick, or inscribed upon plates of metal or blocks of wood. The bark and the leaves of various kinds of trees soon came into use, and were employed to receive compositions whose durability was of less consequence to the public. Palm leaves in particular were at a very early period devoted to literature, and of these the first books appear to have been composed. These consisted of a number of leaves sufficient to contain an historical record or a poem, strung together on a cord. In conformity with the above quotation from Job, they engraved upon rocks with an iron chisel, and wrote upon wood, bark, and leaves, with a style or sharp-pointed instrument. The impression of the letters, thus traced out, were rendered more legible by being filled up with a composition of pounded charcoal and oil. We know nothing of the materials employed by the ancient Assyrians for their historical and literary records, except their tiles and bricks. Many of these, dug out of the ruins of Babylon, are in the British Museum. Egypt has preserved, in the sealed solitude of her pyramids, and in the dark recesses of her city of the dead, (Necropolis,) many testimonies to the state of the arts and sciences of the elder time.

The investigations of a Champollion and others, during the few last years, in lifting up the curtain from Egyptian history, have brought amusement for the curious, knowledge for the student, satisfaction for the Christian believer, and confusion to the infidel. When Volney, wandering amid the then voiceless hieroglyphics, declared that they needed but a Daniel to interpret them to prove that the evidences of the Christian religion had been weighed in the balance, and found wanting; when he presumed to say that the sacerdotal colleges of Egypt had been founded more than 13,000 years before the Christian era, he little thought that these monuments of antiquity would find a tongue to bear witness against the falsehoods of his pen. The ever varying spirit of infidelity urged a sneering Voltaire to declare that in the time of Moses no written character but the hieroglyphic was known, and that no mode of producing it but that of engraving on polished stone, brick, lead, or wood was practised. Having made this assertion, he proceeds—first, to deny the possibility of the Hebrews at that time writing at all, and then scoffingly enters into a calculation as to the amount of rock, metal, and wood which would be required for a hieroglyphic inscription sufficient to convey all the writings of Moses. He wist not of that discovery which, by throwing sunshine on the past history of Egypt, has dissolved the darkness which had proved to the imaginative infidel a refuge of lies. The tongue which now speaks from those records, confirms the truth of the sacred volume, both as to the history of kingdoms and the literature of ages. Those records which Volney fancied must go back through twice ten thousand years, are, in truth, in harmonious concord with the writings of Moses, and commence posterior to Noah. The assertion of Voltaire has an equally satisfactory answer, not only from ancient paintings, which represent scribes and clerks engaged in the very act of writing, but from rolls of papyrus, containing particular judicial acts of monarchs, written 200 years before the exode from Egypt. These rolls, of which multitudes have been taken from the place of the tombs to give knowledge and instruction to the living, have settled the very early use of papyrus as a writing material beyond a doubt. Thus we find placed in the hands of Moses, a light, convenient paper, of which a few pounds weight would contain all he wrote in the wilderness.

The writing papyrus (from which is derived our name, paper) is obtained from an aquatic plant growing in swamps by the Nile. It is found in this day in upper and lower Egypt, by the side of Jordan, in Sicily, and along the borders of some of the western rivers of Africa. A cloth which is prepared from it is made use of for sails, and sometimes for wearing apparel, and Bruce found it in Abyssinia employed as a lining for boats.

The stem of the plant is triangular, rising to the height of 12, 15, and it is said sometimes 20 feet, tapering gradually towards the extremity, which is surmounted by a flowing plume. The paper was prepared from the inner bark of the stem, by dividing it with a kind of needle into thin plates or pellicles, each of them as large as the plant would admit of. These plates, being trimmed and made smooth, a sufficient number to form a sheet of the requisite width, were laid side by side on a table, and then crossed by another layer at right angles to the first. The mass being then moistened with the waters of the Nile, was subjected to pressure, which caused the glutinous juices of the plant to exude, and to bind the whole firmly together. This paper, being first manufactured in Egypt, became in early time a very important article of its commerce. I have devoted some time to the description of it, for it was the principal material employed for books until long after the Christian era; and in the reign of Tiberius, a popular tumult arose in Italy in consequence of a scarcity of it.

Before treating of early literature, we shall briefly touch on the other writing substances employed in ancient time, and amongst literary and partially cultivated men in various ages. The skins of beasts rudely prepared, or more carefully dressed, have been amongst most nations in high repute for their durability, and of course the preservancy of the records committed to them. They were anciently written but on one side, and when a work exceeded that which a skin would contain, two or more were glued together so as to form an extended sheet. This, when not in use, was rolled upon a rod, after the manner of a modern map. The book was then called a volume, from being rolled. The form which originated the name has long been scarce in our oldest libraries; but the name itself had become of general signification, and is now synonymous with book. The title was written upon that part of the back of the skin which would be visible when the whole was rolled up. When Eumenes king of Pergamos, 170 years before the Christian era, was endeavouring to gather a library which should rival that established by the Ptolemies at Alexandria, the king of Egypt, to frustrate his intentions, prohibited the export of papyrus from the Nile. This it is said caused a more general use of skins at Pergamos, and led its scribes

to that preparation which has since been called parchment. It was in Pergamos, and about this period of time, that the square form was first adopted in books. This proved an economical arrangement, enabling the writers to make use of both sides of the sheet. The parchments were folded to the requisite size, and the book was no otherwise bound than by being stitched through the back.

A variety of other animal materials have also been pressed into the service of literature. Both Gibbon and Heeren tell us of a manuscript once in the library at Constantinople 120 feet in length, which was written on a membrane obtained from a serpent. Sea shells have given permanency to the thoughts of some, and the bones of animals, particularly the shoulder blade, to the wisdom of others. Both these materials were used by the philosopher Cleanthus, who was accustomed to write on them the lectures of his master Zeno. He flourished 260 years before the Christian era. Gibbon says, that much of the original copy of the Koran was on the shoulder blades of sheep. Perhaps the most beautiful animal production ever made use of was ivory, cut into very thin sheets. Some of the works most in esteem in eastern countries are still written on such. Linen cloth was employed in ancient, as it has been in modern time. It is however, not well adapted for the purpose, unless covered with a composition of wax or some other material which will give to it a smooth surface. Hesiod, 907 years B. C., wrote his compositions on leaden table. The laws of Solon were recorded on tables of wood, 596 B. C. The Romans, for the preservation of their treaties, caused them to be etched upon plates of brass. Even brass, however, did not always preserve the records committed to its trust, for we find it narrated in the Roman annals, that those plates which contained their laws of the twelve tables were struck by lightning and melted. Of the tables of wood, the ancients preferred those formed of cedar, not only because of their durability, but from the fragrance they continued to emit. It was a common saying of the Romans, respecting their favourite works, that they were worthy to be written on cedar; and the manuscripts which they most valued were anointed with an oil prepared from it.

Writing on rods or bars of wood is several times mentioned in the Scriptures. The ancient Britains made use of such, and their bars of wood being either square or triangular, when they wrote their poetic compositions upon them, the one received their four line stanzas, and the other, the triplets. A number of these bars being set in a frame, in which they could readily be turned according to the will of the reader, might contain a short narrative, a poem, or a sonnet. The Icelandic authors were accustomed to make a literary use of the smooth walls of their houses, and Olof, according to their Sagas, had a very large dwelling, not for the comfort and convenience of his family, but that he might have room wherein to deposit the fruit of his genius.

As the Romans, for their earliest productions, made great use of the inner bark of trees, the word "liber," inner bark, became their appellative for a book. The English

"book" is derived from the Saxon boc, beech tree, on the bark of which the prose and poetic legends of our fathers were written.

The books at Tanjore and other parts of India are written on palm leaves, and are strung together on cords after the ancient fashion. Most of the public libraries of Europe have copies of the Bible written on such, which are of comparatively recent execution. The Ceylonese still employ palm leaves, or the strips of those obtained from the talipot tree.

According to the substance to be written on was the instrument made use of by the ancient writers:—a chisel, a style, a pencil, or a reed. The reed, which may be considered to have been the pen of ancient times, was split and shaped to a point as those made now of quills.

The ink they employed was sometimes soot or ivory-black mixed with gum, and sometimes the coloured liquor obtained from the cuttle fish. A red ink they prepared from cinnabar. The liquor which is found in the cuttle fish, and which it makes use of in discolouring the waters to facilitate its escape from an enemy, is a very deep and enduring pigment. Some that Dr. Buckland obtained from fossil specimens of this tribe which had been buried, he supposes, several thousand years, had lost none of its characteristic colour. He submitted to a celebrated painter a portion on trial, who inquired where the colourman could be found who could furnish such excellent sepia.

We find Moses saying, "yet now if thou wilt forgive their sin, and if not, blot me, I pray thee, out of the book which thou hast written." This blotting out has been thought to have had reference to some of the vegetable inks employed in that time which might readily be washed from their leaves or bark. Others have imagined it to allude to writings made with a sharp style on tables covered with wax, which could be erased and renewed at pleasure. It was the practice of some of the Roman authors to compose at such a writing table, and not give any production a more enduring form until it had received a thorough revision, and endured the criticism of the author's literary friends.

(To be continued.)

For "The Friend."

HOW ROCKS ARE FORMED.

Some of the most curious philosophical experiments of the present age have consisted in imitations, on a small scale, of operations which nature carries on upon a very grand one. A popular view of some of these cannot fail to prove interesting.

Limestone is a rock found in great abundance throughout the crust of the earth. Marble, chalk, and calcareous spar, are modifications of it. Dr. Black ascertained that the process so familiar to us all, of burning limestone and thus making the quick-lime used in building and for agricultural purposes, is simply a discharging, from the original stone, of carbonic acid, which goes off in a gaseous form. Limestone he therefore made out to be the carbonate of lime. It was, some time after, propounded by Dr. Hutton, the geologist, that limestone, in its various modifications, had been formed under the influence of the heat which he assumed to exist in the interior of the earth, while a pressure of superincumbent materials prevented the carbonic acid from flying off. This was an ingenious idea, but deficient in positive proof. Sir James Hall, who was a supporter of Dr. Hutton's theory of the earth, subjected it to the test of experiment.

He commenced his experiments in 1798, at his country house of Dunglass, in Berwickshire. He took a common gun-barrel, and charging it with a quantity of chalk, or pulverized limestone, filled it up with brick-dust, and closed the muzzle by welding its lips together. He then introduced the breech into a furnace, heated to 25° of Wedgwood's pyrometer. Many barrels, thus treated, gave way; but, in others, at the conclusion of the experiment, the chalk was found *agglutinated into a stony mass*, which required the smart blow of a hammer to break it, and felt under the knife like common limestone. He afterwards changed the gun-barrels for porcelain vessels prepared on purpose, and used fusible metal for ramming, instead of brick-dust. He also took many ingenious methods for ascertaining how much carbonic acid made its escape during the operation. When an escape to the amount of twenty per cent. took place, the contents had no appearance of stony matter; but when it was about 3 or 4 per cent., the stony character was perfect. Ultimately, by allowing a little aqueous vapour to remain in the barrel, in order to counteract the expansion of the fusible metal, he succeeded in reducing the proportion of escaped gas to about one fourth per cent. The pounded chalk was then brought into the condition of saline marble, accompanied with crystallization and other marks of fusion. One specimen, formed from pounded spar, was so complete as to deceive one of Sir James' workmen, who remarked that, if the marble were a little whiter, the quarry from which it was taken would be very valuable. This particular specimen afterwards fell into dust, but many other pieces, the produce of the Dunglass laboratory, resisted the air and kept their polish for years; nor do we know that these are yet otherwise than in the condition of marble.

By calculations, which cannot well be explained here, Sir James concluded that a layer of the carbonate of lime, at the bottom of a sea 1700 feet deep, would, if a due degree of heat were applied, be formed into limestone; and into a complete marble, if the depth of the sea were 3000 feet; the pressure being in one case as 52, and in the other as 86, atmospheres.

Sir James spent seven years in his experiments, which were one hundred and fifty-six in number, and he showed in them a degree of patience, care, and philosophic ingenuity, which excited universal admiration when the result was published. He was considered as having proved—not exactly that our beds of limestone and marble were formed by heat under a pressure confining the carbonic acid—for nature might have other ways of bringing about the end, but that such at least was a mode in which the effects could be brought about. The probability that such were really

the circumstances under which the strata in question were formed, is so great, that practically, such is the doctrine as to their formation held by the philosophical world.

He afterwards made some interesting experiments relative to basaltic rocks; but, in these, as he was not the first inquirer, we pass them by in order to notice his investigations respecting the formation of sandstone. This rock is also a very abundant one throughout the crust of the earth, forming numerous beds, alternating with nearly all the other aqueous rocks. Its utility in building is well known. Sandstone is easily seen to be a composition of sand, for it may readily be reduced to that form; but the wonder is how sand has assumed so hard a consistence. He performed a series of experiments, which showed at least one way in which great layers of loose sand might be agglutinated at the bottoms of seas, so as to form rocky strata.

In the little valley of Aikengaw, at the eastern extremity of the Lammermuir hills, Scotland, he observed the gravel which occupies its bottom, agglutinated in several places into a mass of conglomerate, very solid in the centre, but becoming gradually looser on both sides, till it passed into the state of moveable gravel. He was soon satisfied, by applying chemical tests, that the agglutination was not produced, as in some cases, by calcareous matter. A few miles lower down the valley he found a crag of sandstone, which yields much to the action of the air, and in dry weather is covered with a white efflorescence, having exactly the taste of common salt. Combining the two facts, he inferred that sea salt might be the substance which, by serving as a cement, produced the consolidation, both of the sandstone rock and the conglomerate. He immediately resolved to follow out this idea by experiment, and, after many trials, succeeded in forming artificial sandstones of various qualities, some of which were firm enough to be dressed by the chisel, and some have resisted exposure to the elements for years.

In his first experiments, he put into a large crucible a quantity of dry salt and a quantity of loose sand; the whole being heated from below, the salt ascended in fumes through the sand, and converted it into a solid stone. The fumes seemed to act as a flux on the siliceous matter of the sand, and, in fact, to serve a purpose exactly analogous to what they do in glazing potters' ware.

Sir James' object, however, was to illustrate the Huttonian formation of rocks at the bottom of the sea; and he wished to show that the presence of a body of water above the sand, even at a moderate temperature, was not incompatible with the necessary degree of heat nor the success of the experiment. He filled an iron crucible, 18 inches high, to the brim, with sand and strong brine, the water rising three inches above the sand. An empty gun-barrel, closed at the lower end, was amidst the sand to within an inch of the bottom of the crucible, that by looking in at the upper and open end of the barrel, the temperature of the saline mass at different heights might be seen. The crucible was exposed to a strong heat, fresh brine being constantly added as it boiled

off; and it was distinctly seen by means of the gun-barrel, that while the sand at the bottom became red hot, the water at the top was merely in a state of moderate ebullition. After remaining in the fire for some hours, it was suffered to cool, and when examined, it was found that the sand at the bottom had concreted into a solid cake of most perfect sandstone, while the part above, which was still drenched with brine, remained permanently loose.

He used black-lead crucibles at first, but found that the action of the brine upon them impeded the success of the experiment. He found, also, that the process succeeded better with common sea water instead of brine, only it was necessary to continue the operation for three weeks, always maintaining the supply of water, till sufficient salt was accumulated. The substitution of a strong brine, containing one third of its weight of salt, merely shortened the process without altering the result. He observed too, that the longer the operation was continued, the more solid and durable was the sandstone produced; and hence, as nature has unlimited time for her processes, we see why her products should be so much more perfect than those of man.

Common sand was at first used by Sir James, but he afterwards found that pounded quartz or gravel could be solidified by the same method. For the sake of negative evidence, fresh water was tried, every other circumstance being the same; but there was not the slightest symptom of consolidation.

He now proceeded a step farther in his imitation of nature. Sandstones are often tinged or streaked with colours, and the colouring matter is generally metallic. A little oxide of iron (in powder) was therefore mixed with the salt, and this being put into a crucible with quartzose sand, it was found that the fumes of the salt bore up the metallic oxide along with them, and the cake of sandstone produced was curiously stained with iron.

Basalt has been the subject of similar experiment so early as 1804. The general character of this rock is well known. It is of igneous, or volcanic origin—generally of a blackish colour, and always very hard, being composed mainly of felspar and augite, with titaniferous iron, and, finally, is often of a columnar structure—that is, disposed in masses as of pillars closely joined together. The island of Staffa, one of the Hebrides, is a rock a mile and a half in circumference, consisting of three beds more or less horizontal, of which the central is formed of nearly upright columns of basalt, in which several caves have been worn by the waves. Another such specimen is found in the Giant's Causeway, on the northern coast of Ireland. "This," says Pictet, "is a sort of promontory or jettee, which slopes very gradually down to the sea, and terminates in a point, against which the waves dash with great violence. This jettee forms the left part of a semicircular bay, surrounded on all sides by a steep and lofty coast, which displays, in all its extent, the finest specimens of basaltic phenomena—nothing is to be seen, on every hand, but groups of columns in an upright position. The Giant's Causeway, properly so called, is one of these groups, but so much lower than the rest, that the tops of the pillars are seen [but] a little way above the level of the sea. The uniform appearance of the upper ends of these innumerable columns makes it seem, at a little distance, like a pavement of polygonal [many-cornered] stones. Upon a nearer approach they are found not to be altogether on the same level; and in walking along the causeway, one is obliged to step continually up and down. They are nearly all in perfect contact, without the interposition of other substance. The number of their corners is not uniform; there are some with eight, and some with four, but the most common form is six cornered." The columns are composed of blocks piled on each other, projecting on the upper, and hollow on the under surface, so as to fit accurately.

These objects are the wonder of their respective countries, yet the secret of their formation has at length yielded to persevering investigation. About 1804, Gregory Watt fused seven hundred weight of an amorphous or unshaped basalt, named Rowley Rag; the fire was maintained for six hours, and the mass was then suffered to cool very gradually, so that eight days elapsed before it was removed from the furnace. The experimenter found in it spheroids, or flattish globular masses, in some cases extending to a diameter of two inches. When two of these came in contact, they did not melt into each other; they kept distinct, but pressed against each other, and formed plane sides, just as soap bubbles may be observed to do when they press each other. When several spheroids met, they formed prisms, or acquired flat sides all round. Where the centres of a number of these spheroids were at equal distances from each other, it was calculated by Watt, that, in spreading out, and meeting each other, they must necessarily form six-sided figures. Where the centres were at unequal distances, it was not less clear that figures of other shapes must be formed. [The formation of the joints in the columns he did not succeed so well in elucidating. Latterly, that, too, has been accounted for, though by a process which cannot readily be explained without a diagram.] Thus, what was once thought one of the most mysterious of all nature's operations, was so far mimicked in a chemist's workshop, as to lead to a nearly certain knowledge of how the operation took place in nature's own greater laboratory. Staffa, the Giant's Causeway, and other well known basalts, must have once been fused masses, which assumed their columnar structure as a simple consequence of the manner in which they were cooled.

More recently, crystals like those found in rocks have been formed by Becquerell and Mitcherlich, European mineralogists, by means of electricity acting upon a solution containing the ingredients; and Crosse, of Somersetshire, has, by means of the same power, acting with small force, but during a considerable space of time, exactly simulated a process going on in the Quantock hills, where water, percolating through limestone, forms calcareous spar. The latter gentleman has also made crystals of silver, chalcedony, and quartz, out of various solutions.

Experiments like these are chiefly of value for the illustration they give to a very interesting and instructive truth which lies at the bottom of all philosophy, namely, the invariableness of the laws which govern the operations of nature, whether they act upon a large or small scale; they form the globe destined to sustain millions after millions of intelligent beings, and shape the dew-drop which sparkles on the hawthorn blossom, with equal accuracy, and in conformity to the same general principles; they form alike the stratum of rock which traverses an extensive country, and the handful of materials collected in the crucible of the philosopher; a small quantity of basalt, subjected to a common furnace, exemplifies those mighty workings which, countless ages ago, produced a Staffa and a Giant's Causeway.—*Abridged from Chambers' Edinburgh Journal.*

On the Habits and Instincts of Animals. By William Swainson, A. C. G., Fellow of the Royal Society, and of several Foreign Academies.

(Continued from p. 252.)

Out of the many other curious anecdotes which have been given of the sagacity of quadrupeds, we shall add one more, which, as recorded of an animal considered as proverbially stupid, is proportionably singular. An ass belonging to Captain Dundas, R. N. was shipped on board a frigate proceeding from Gibraltar to the island of Malta. The vessel struck on some sands off the Point de Gat, and the poor ass was thrown overboard, the sea at the time running so high that a boat which tried to reach the shore was lost. A few days after, however, this identical ass presented itself at the gates of Gibraltar, and hastened to the stable which it had formerly occupied. The fact was, that the poor animal had not only escaped safely from the waves, but actually travelled a distance of 200 miles through an intricate country, in a space of time which could not allow of his having even mistaken his road.

A most singular instance of the instinct of a cat for discovering its home is too remarkable to be omitted, particularly as it occurred under my own observation. This cat was an excellent mouser; and the house of a neighbouring friend being greatly infested with rats, it was agreed that the animal should take up its residence for a time in his house, that it might be cleared, in some degree, of these troublesome pests. Pussy, however, had then a kitten about two or three months old; and as we thought she was more likely to remain in her new habitation if she had her little one as a companion, both animals were sent; and, that the mother should not discover her way back, both were tied up in a sack, and in that state conveyed to our friend's house, a distance of near a mile and a half from Tittenhanger Green. The mother, finding herself with her kitten, and in a good hunting locality, made no effort to escape. To our utter astonishment, however, she made her appearance next morning, at the breakfast-room door, at her usual hour! She had come—no one knew how—over fields and through coppices, as it was conjectured, early in the morning, by a route she never could have traversed before, and without any other guide but instinct. Having partaken of her usual breakfast from the hands of her young mistress, she was seen no more that day; next morning, however, she was again at her post; and these daily journeys were continued for more than a week. On mentioning this to our friend, he stated that he always missed the cat at his breakfast hour; but that, soon after, she regularly returned to her kitten, which remained quietly in the house during the morning visits her mother paid to her real home. Our cat, like all good mousers, is such a thief, that, not wishing to kill it, we have frequently tied it in a sack and turned it loose a considerable distance from home; but, somehow or other, she invariably finds her way, "through brake and through briar," to Tittenhanger Green, where she now is.

The instincts of insects are so singular, and yet so various, that a volume might be filled with this subject alone. The grave beetles (*sylphidæ*) are so called from their habit of entering the bodies of small animals, in which they afterwards deposit their eggs. Astonishing, but well authenticated accounts have been given of the sagacious industry with which these little creatures accomplish labours, which must be to them enormous. Among other experiments, a glass cucurbit was half filled with earth, on which were placed four beetles and their young, and then, after being covered, it was lodged in the open ground: at the end of fifty days, the bodies of four frogs, three birds, two grasshoppers, one mole, the entrails of a fish, and part of the lungs of an ox, were buried by these indefatigable creatures.

We may here notice a most singular story of bees, related by Stedman. We should not have given it a place, but for the general accuracy of this traveller, and from the very pointed manner in which its veracity is vouched for. It will certainly amuse the reader, if it fails to convince him that bees know those who live about their nests. " On one occasion, I was visited at my hut by a neighbouring gentleman, whom I conducted up my ladder; but he had no sooner entered my aerial dwelling, than he leaped down from the top to the ground, roaring like a madman with agony and pain; after which he instantly plunged his head into the river. I soon discovered the cause of his distress to be an enormous nest of wild bees, or *wassee-wassee*, in the thatch, directly above my head, as I stood within my door; when I immediately took to my heels, as he had done, and ordered the slaves to demolish them without delay. A tar mop was now brought, and the devastation just going to commence, when an old negro stepped up, and offered to receive any punishment I should decree, if ever one of these bees should sting me in person. ' Massera,' said he, ' they would have stung you long ago had you been a stranger to them; but they being your tenants, and allowed to build upon your premises, they assuredly know both you and your's, and will never hurt either you or them.' I instantly assented to the proposition; and, tying the old black man to a tree, ordered my boy Quad to ascend the ladder quite naked; which he did, and was not stung. I then ventured to follow, and I declare, that even after shaking the nest, which made its inhabitants buzz about my ears, not a single bee attempted to sting me. I next released and rewarded him for the discovery. This swarm of bees I afterwards kept unhurt as my body-guard. They have made many overseers take a desperate leap for my amusement; as I generally sent them up my ladder upon some frivolous message, when I wished to punish them for injustice and cruelty to the negroes,—which was not seldom. The same negro assured me, that on his master's estate was an ancient tree, in which had been lodged, ever since he could remember, a society of birds, and another of bees, who lived in the greatest harmony together. But should any strange birds come to disturb or feed upon the bees, they were instantly repulsed by their feathered allies; and if strange bees dared to venture near the bird's nests, the native swarm attacked the invaders, and stung them to death. He added, that his master's family had so much respect for the above association, that the tree was considered as sacred.*

Memory, as well as instinct, appears to be given to animals, as necessary for their well being. An instance of the powers of memory evinced by an elephant is given by Williamson, as a fact, well known in Bengal at the time, and attested by the signatures of several gentlemen, who were eye-witnesses to the occurrence. An elephant, that had been some years domesticated, got loose during a stormy night, and rambled into his native jungles. About four years afterwards, when a large drove had been captured in the *Keddah*, the keeper of the lost one, along with others of the natives, had ascended the barricade of timber by which it was surrounded, to inspect the new guests; among them, he fancied he recognised his former charge; and, though ridiculed by his comrades, he called to the elephant in question by the name it had formerly borne. To the wonder of all present, the animal came towards him; the man, overjoyed at the event, got over the barrier, and, ordering the elephant to lie down to be mounted, he bestrode its neck as in former times, and exultingly led it forth, to the admiration and surprise of all present. Another instance of recollection in this quadruped must not be omitted here. An officer in the Indian army, who was quarter-master of a brigade, found it needful to put a heavier load than usual on a very large elephant, called the *paugul*, or fool; but he soon intimated that he was only disposed to take his usual load. The officer, seeing the animal repeatedly shake off the superabundant portion, lost his temper, and threw a tent-pin at the animal's head. Some days after, as the latter was going with others to water, he happened to pass the officer, whom he very deliberately lifted up into a large tamarind tree, leaving him to cling to the boughs, and to get down as well as he could. And this brings us to notice an instance of generosity manifested by this very individual,

* The best part of this pleasant and very pleasantly told story, in our estimation, is, the sagacity and truly philosophical cast of mind evinced by the old negro man, that would have done no discredit to many a modern *savan*, with the aid of all his vaunted book. knowledge.—*Ed.*

which, together with a small female, was subsequently under the command of Captain Williamson, and both animals were used to carry the tents of the party. "Unluckily," observes the captain, "after the first day's march, we found that the female was rather overladen, and began to gall, but we could not get the *paugul* to carry an ounce more than his first day's burden; the feet of the little female, however, becoming very sore, the animal relaxed from his obstinacy, and generously took as much of her burden as gave her relief during the rest of the journey.

(To be continued.)

For "The Friend."
A FATHER'S COUNSEL.

1. Be diligent in thy calling, and upright in all thy dealings.
2. Cultivate thy mind carefully, and it will afford thee a store of pleasing reflections.
3. Make choice of a course of virtue, and imitate a high pattern.
4. Do all the good in thy power, and let every action be useful.
5. Investigate affairs closely, and engage in them cautiously.
6. Lay all thy plans with prudence, and conduct them with economy.
7. When thou engagest, do it cheerfully, and when thou executest do it energetically.
8. In difficulties be patient, and by perseverance overcome them.
9. Arrange thy affairs systematically, and despatch them in order.
10. Have for every thing a time, and do every thing in time.
11. Select for every thing a place, and keep every thing in place.
12. What requires being often done, do well, and dexterity will be attained by habit.
13. Keep correct journals in business, and a record of all thy affairs.
14. Examine thy concerns carefully, and thy own character impartially.
15. Correct and reform what is wrong, and make amends for past injuries.
16. Complete all your engagements, and prepare for a state nearer perfection.

THE INFLUENCE OF EXAMPLE.
(A Fragment by Zeller.)

Young minds can at all times be acted upon without words,—simply by example. The further any person is from what he ought to be, the more does he experience this influence. The less his mind is developed, the more is he urged by a propensity to *imitate*, to direct and govern himself according to what he sees and hears in the society of other men, better, older, stronger, more skilful, and more experienced than himself. This is a truth that cannot be too often dwelt upon, especially in these days, when we attribute so many wonders to the power of words. Yes: example alone, a life of practice without display, exercises a most marked influence on the soul, the character, and the will; for the *conduct* of a man is the true expression of his being, and gives a tone to (or animates) every thing around him; consequently nothing can re-

main uninfluenced within the sphere of a living being. There emanates from the active noiseless life of a single individual, power which is to others, either " a savour of life unto life, or a savour of death unto death."

This explains to us why parents, simple, and without culture, especially mothers, who perhaps have never opened a book on education, and speak very little to their children, yet offer them every day the example of a lively affection, and a well employed though retired life, bestow an excellent education; while, on the other hand, we see the children of well instructed parents, frequently turn out ill, who have been acted upon by words alone, rather than by example, and who contemplate around them a class of beings who exercise no good moral influence. Alas! that all parents and instructors knew how much power there is in being virtuous, and how little in only *appearing* to be so!

It concerns all who are called to occupy themselves in education, to consider the holy lesson taught by a well beloved disciple of the Saviour, in these words: " Be thou an example of the believers, in word, in conversation, in charity, in spirit, in faith, in purity." 1 Tim. iv. 12. " In all things showing thyself a pattern of good works: in doctrine showing uncorruptness, gravity, sincerity, sound speech that cannot be contemned; that he that is of the contrary part may be ashamed, having no evil thing to say of you." Titus ii. 7, 8.

Here we address the following exhortations to all persons, parents, or tutors, who are charged with the task of education, beseeching them to give serious attention thereto.
1. Be what the children ought to be.
2. Do what they ought to do.
3. Avoid what they should avoid.
4. Aim always that not only in the presence of the children, but also in their absence, your conduct may serve them for an example.
5. Are any among them defective? *Examine what you are yourselves*, what you do, what you avoid,—in a word, your whole conduct.
6. Do you discover in yourselves defects, sins, wanderings? Begin by improving yourselves, and seek afterwards to improve your children.
7. Think well that those by whom you are surrounded, are often only the reflection of yourselves.
8. If you lead a life of penitence, and seek daily to have grace given you, it will be imparted to you, and through you to your children.
9. If you always seek Divine guidance, your children will more willingly be directed by you.
10. The more obedient you are to God, the more obedient will your children be to you; thus in his childhood the wise Solomon asked of the Lord " an obedient heart," in order to be able to govern his people.
11. As soon as the master becomes lukewarm in communion with God, that lukewarmness will extend itself among his pupils.
12. That which forms a wall of separation between God and yourselves, will be a source of evil to your children.
13. An example in which love does not

form a chief feature, is but as the light of the moon; it is cold and feeble.

14. An example animated by an ardent and sincere love, shines like the sun; it warms and invigorates.

ACCOUNT OF JONATHAN MAGEE.

[Translated from Tract No. 21, of the Children's Series of the Jaffna Tract Society.]

This youth was born of heathen parents in Connagam, a village in the parish of Oodooville. All his ancestors were of high caste and strong in the religion of Siva. When he was five years old he went to the village school and studied Tamul, and committed to memory some verses written against the Christian religion, and was forward in disputing with Christians. Being desirous of entering the seminary at Batticotta, he studied English, and was eventually received to the seminary. While there, his feelings against Christianity gradually changed, and he appeared to read the Bible with much interest, and to consider himself a great sinner. At this time he went home in vacation and spoke with his father and mother, and told them that the gods which this people worship, and the idols, are all without life and useless, and that trusting them is useless. His father and mother replied: "Son, is not the god whom our fathers worshipped the true God? Speak not thus profanely that the idol which our wise men and others from the commencement of the Siva religion, worshipped as God, is vain. If you speak thus, you will go to hell." In reply, he gave an account of the Christian religion, and said, that without faith in Jesus Christ, no one could go to heaven, and that disobedience to the commandments of God, and the worship of idols, and divine honours paid to many gods, are sin and lead to hell; but that speaking the truth could never lead to hell. In reply, they said, "While you are so young don't enter into so great subjects. Never speak lightly of any god." The boy replied, I am not afraid to leave off the worship of these gods and idols; but I fear because I have so long neglected to worship my Maker, and because I have walked contrary to his commandments so long. Therefore, I am resolved to go to Christ, to follow him, and to enter into his religion, that this sin may be taken away. His father was angry at this, and said, "You must not enter into the Christian religion now. If you do, all our relations will cast us off, the whole world will despise and ridicule us. See to it that you do not thus disgrace our family. Not only this, you are young, and there is no special haste to embrace the Christian religion. You may attend to that hereafter when you have studied and become learned, and have gotten a situation, and are respected." To this the boy made no answer, kept quiet, and went back to Batticotta. After a few days, he joined the church, and then wrote a note to his father telling him what he had done. The father read the note, and told it to no one but his wife. In the next vacation, the boy was afraid to go to his house for fear of his father and mother, and so went to a neighbouring schoolmaster's house, and made his case known to him. As the master understood the whole case, he accompanied the boy to his father's house. His father and mother were angry, and would not speak with their son. When his uncle and other relations understood the case, they were in a great rage, and came to beat him. The schoolmaster seeing this, snatched the stick from the uncle's hand, and broke it, and exhorted them to be quiet. They then refrained, and said, "Well, you may go and live with the missionaries, but never set foot again in this place, nor come into our presence." He bore all this with much patience, and returned to Batticotta. While there, he was constantly sorrowful, because some of the boys who studied in the same class with him were careless about their souls. He used daily to call some of them into a private room, exhort them, and pray with, and for them. He used to call them one by one and exhort them. When others talked with the boys, he also would tell his feelings, and speak of the importance of their also joining the Christian church. From the day he joined the church, till the time of his death, he was consistent in his conduct, very elevated in his piety, and in learning excelled. As he was thus distinguished in every thing, he was much beloved by all his class, and by his teachers, and by the missionaries. He fell sick on the 12th of November, 1836. His disease increased more and more until he died.

From the (Boston) Common School Journal.
Management of Disobedient Children.

The management of disobedient children is one of the most difficult of duties, whether in school or at home. In this branch of government, ignorance and bad temper run into mistakes, as certainly as water will run down hill. They cannot proceed rightly. It requires all possible prudence, calmness, consideration, judgment, wisely to govern a refractory child. It is a common saying, that anger should never be manifested towards the young or the insane. This, though true, is but a feeble expression of the truth. Feelings of wrath, madness, are as absurd and incongruous, in the management of a disobedient child, as they would be in a surgeon, when amputating a limb or couching an eye. Suppose we were to witness an operation upon the human eye, and the oculist, as he approached his work, should begin to redden in the face and tremble in the joints, to feel all the emotions and to put on the natural language of wrath; and should then spring upon his patient like a panther, and strike his knife into the eyeball at hazard;—should we call this *couching* or *gouging?* But are the moral sensibilities of a child less delicate in their texture than the corporeal senses? Does the body require a finer touch and a nicer skill than the soul? Is less knowledge and discretion necessary in him who seeks to influence the invisible and immortal spirit, than in him who operates in the visible and material frame? Is the husk more delicately wrought than the kernel? No; so much more exquisite as the painting is than the frame, or the jewel than the casket, so much more excellent is the soul than the body it inhabits; and he who does not approach in this faith, wants one of the essential prerequisites for acting upon it wisely. Firstly, then, let teachers discipline their own feelings to the work they have undertaken.

Teachers have their severest trials with disobedient children. To instruct the beautiful, the affectionate, the intelligent, the grateful, is unalloyed delight. But to take an awkward, gawky, unclean, ill-dressed, ill-mannered, ill-tempered child, and to work up an interest in it, to love it, to caress it, to perform a full measure of duty to it;—this draws upon all the resources of conscience, virtue and religion. Yet, in the eye of true benevolence, of Christian duty, this class of children presents the dearest of objects—the first to be attended to, the last to be forgotten.

The motive of duty also coincides with the motive of interest. If the teacher truly consults his own ease and comfort, he will treat the less amiable children in his school with great kindness and regard; because, by this course of conduct, he will save himself from a vast amount of labour and vexation in the end. When he knows that wounds actually exist, the true question of policy with him is, whether it is better, even for himself, to inflame and aggravate, or to soothe and heal them. At a common school convention in Hampden county, we heard Dr. Cooley relate an anecdote, strikingly illustrative of this principle. He said, that, not many years ago, a young man went into a district to keep school, and before he had been there a week, many persons came to see him, and kindly told him that there was one boy in the school whom it would be necessary to whip every day; leading him to infer that such was the custom of the school, and that the inference of injustice towards the boy would be drawn whenever he should escape, not when he should suffer. The teacher saw the affair in a different light. He treated the boy with signal kindness and attention. At first this novel course seemed to bewilder him. He could not divine its meaning. But, when the persevering kindness of the teacher begot a kindred sentiment of kindness in the pupil, his very nature seemed transformed. Old impulses died. A new creation of motives supplied their place. Never was there a more diligent, obedient, and successful pupil; and *now*, said the reverend gentleman, in concluding his narrative, that boy is the chief justice of a neighbouring state. The relator of this story, though he modestly kept back the fact, was himself the actor. If the Romans justly bestowed a civic crown upon a soldier who had saved the life of a fellow soldier in battle, what honours are too great for the teacher who has thus rescued a child from ruin?

One great error in the management of untoward children, consists in expecting too much from them at once, and immediately. Time is an important element in the process of weakening and subduing bad principles of action, as well as in the growing and strengthening of good ones. All actions proceed from some internal faculty or propensity; and it is not in accordance with the course of nature to expect that an overgrown and over-active propensity can be reduced to its natural size and vigour in a day. Whenever a child has yielded to an impulse to do wrong, but has been induced, by expostulation or discipline, to do right, the peculiar circumstances under which he was tempted to the wrong should be avoided, if possible, until the resolution to do right has had time to be confirmed; that is, those faculties or sentiments of his nature, from whose ascendency we hope improvement and reform, must have time to grow, and to become superior to their antagonists, if we expect they will prevail over them.

From the Farmers' Cabinet.

TARE.

In the "American Farmer" for the present week, there is honourable mention of the English tare, the most valuable crop that can be cultivated on a farm for summer soiling; but as it is evidently written by one who has not had the means of an intimate acquaintance with it, it is not wonderful that there are some inconsistencies in the account; the writer, however, deserves all praise for bringing it into notice, and it only remains to be put to the test of experience, when its superlative value for soiling all kinds of cattle will be made manifest.

The writer observes, "there is no hindrance in our climate to its cultivation," and yet he adds, "it is doubtful whether tares sown in the fall or autumn would survive our winters." He also says, "tares are of two kinds, winter and spring, but not distinguishable from the appearance of the seed." Now, every one acquainted with the subject knows, that there is a very marked difference in the appearance of the seed of the winter and summer tares, the first being round, small, and black; the latter much larger, flatter, and light coloured; and it is very generally believed, in the tare-cultivating districts, that the winter variety will not produce large crops if sown in the spring; nor will those of the summer variety, if sown in the autumn, even should they survive the winter; and I have been led to make the same remark.

Professor Low observes, very justly, "it is one of the most esteemed crops of England, when used as green forage; they are cut for this purpose after the pods are formed, but long before the seed is ripe;" but he is very wrong when he adds, "being in the class of crops not allowed to *mature their seeds*, they are not exhausting to the soil;" for it is well known that *all crops* begin to exhaust the soil when they begin to bloom, as the blossom is not furnished with any return sap-vessels: the custom of cutting as soon as they begin to blossom, however, obviates very much this objection. In the sheep-breeding countries, it is customary to feed off the tares by folding them with sheep by means of trundles, and if this is commenced early in the season, a second growth takes place, which gives an additional crop of great luxuriance. This is not, however, a mode of management to be recommended, for another important use of the tare culture is, to do away with the necessity of naked summer fallowing; and to this end they should be sown as early after harvest, on those lands designed for the wheat crop the next autumn, as possible: and if they are mown off and given to the cattle as soon as they are fully grown, and the land ploughed up as they are cleared, there will be sufficient time to give it a thorough cleaning before the time of wheat sowing, a preparation for that crop superior to almost every other, especially if the land has been manured for the tares, which it should always be, if possible, as it enables the crop to overcome the weeds, and to add exceedingly to the *size of the dunghill*; and it is remarked, that wheat after tares that have been manured for, is not liable to be affected by rust.

By the turnip and tare culture it is, that the system of naked fallowing is entirely done away in England. The turnips on light lands, the tares on heavy soils, each furnishing sufficient opportunity to clean the land thoroughly, before sowing barley after turnips, or wheat after tares. Arthur Young's observation, "that not a tenth of the stock could be maintained without them," is nothing but the truth; and it they will fatten horses, cattle, sheep, and hogs, without any other food, especially if they are allowed to perfect their seed—by which, however, is not meant to ripen it.

Tares produce more green food than the best meadows, and the land may be cleared of them in June, time enough for a crop of turnips, or even potatoes, or of being prepared for wheat. They will fatten all kinds of cattle, suit every soil and climate, and on good soils will produce twelve tons of green food per acre. Winter tares are sown from the middle of August, to the middle of October, two bushels or two bushels and a half per acre. Spring tares may be sown from March to midsummer.

They begin to blossom in May, when they should be mown and taken to the cattle in the stables until they pod, when the remainder should be made into hay; whilst making into hay, they require a good deal of sun; rain is very injurious. If all the farmer's stock is kept upon them while green, they are taken off the grass land, consequently, there will be more grass to make into hay; and they should be sufficiently plentiful to keep the cattle on them until after hay-making, when they might go into the mown meadows. Good land, well manured, will yield ten tons green per acre, which will make three tons of the best hay on the farm. If preserved for seed, they have been known to yield forty bushels per acre, and sell from one dollar to seven dollars per bushel, according to the seasons. They are of such infinite importance for summer soiling, that Mr. Davis, of Beddingham, England, says, he could not maintain one-tenth part of the stock he does without them. This plant maintains more stock at that season of the year than any other whatever. Upon one acre of tares he can maintain four horses, in much better condition than upon five acres of grass; upon eight acres he has kept twelve horses and five cows for three months—June, July, and August, and no other food given them. Cows give more butter while feeding on them than on any other food."

I have sown crops of tares in succession during the spring and summer; the last sowing, on the 21st day of June, proving a heavy and most valuable crop for soiling working horses on a railroad until the month of September—these were raised upon land which had been cleared of turnips in the spring and early summer, and which was sown upon the same by the 29th day of September.

JAMES BEYNON.

May 15, 1840.

From the same.

IRRIGATION.

Upon the borders of Sherwood Forest, (England,) are the water meadows of which he was speaking; a little river ran through the forest in this part, at the bottom of the valley, with sides moderately sloping, and of considerable extent, between the river at the bottom, and the common level of the surrounding country above. This little river, before reaching the place, ran through a small town, and gathered, doubtless, some refuse matter in its course. From this river the water was taken, at the upper end of the valley, conducted along the edge or bank, in a canal or carrier, and from thence, at proper times, it was suffered to flow out very gently, spreading over and irrigating the whole surface, trickling and shining when he saw it (November) amongst the light green of the new-springing grass, and collected below into another channel, from which it was again let out to flow, in like manner, over land lying still further down towards the bottom of the valley. Ten years ago, this land, for production, was worth little or nothing; he was told that some of it had been let for no more than twenty-five cents per acre: it has never been manured, and is yet now most extensively productive. It is not flooded; the water does not stand upon it, it merely flows gently over it, and is applied several times in a year to each part—in March, May, July, and October. In November, when he saw it, the farmers were taking off the third crop of hay cut this season, and that crop was certainly not less than two tons to the acre. This last crop is generally used as green food for cattle: when he spoke of tons, he meant tons of dried hay. After this crop was off, sheep were to be put upon it, to have lambs at Christmas, so as to come into market in March, when they command a high price: and upon taking off the sheep in March, the land would be watered, the process lasting from two to eight or ten days, according to circumstances, and repeated after taking off every successive crop. Now, although this water has, no doubt, considerable sediment in it, yet the general fact shows how important water is to the growth of plants, and how far, even, it may supply the place of other sources of sustenance.—*Webster's Speech.*

It is a fact, however, that the grasses growing on those watered meadows are quite of a different species from those indigenous to a dry sand upland soil; and this accounts for the numerous crops which they yield—the herbage is peculiarly coarse and long. Thousands of acres of the most productive water meadows, could be formed, comparatively at little expense, in many parts of our country.—*Ed.*

[From the Farmers' Cabinet.]
Slacking Lime and Churning Butter.

The reason of things should be found out.

All bodies, on changing from a *fluid* to a *solid* state, give out heat; and when *solid* bodies become *liquid*, heat is absorbed.

The heat which is given out during the slacking of lime, escapes from the water, in consequence of its changing from a liquid to a solid form, by its union with the lime. The same effect is produced in making butter; when the cream changes from a fluid to a solid, a considerable degree of heat is produced. Hence the importance of turning the churn slowly when the butter is about forming, so that the heated air which is expanded in the churn may gradually escape by the vent, (which should be kept open at this period of the operation,) and not operate to soften and injure the butter in very warm weather.

Some butter-makers put a portion of cold water in the churn when the butter is forming, in order to lower the temperature, and to contract the effect of the heat, set at liberty at this juncture; but experienced dairymen say, that water should *never* be brought into contact with butter, either in the churn, or during the process of working out the buttermilk. It destroys its fine flavour, and reduces its standard of perfection. The buttermilk should be *thoroughly extracted* by working, and absorbed by the application of a cloth in which a sponge is inclosed, and *no water* used in the process.　　　　　　　　　　O.

In the choice of water, always select that which is softest; for hard water, as it is called, is always rendered so by its impurities. Any substance will soften and cook sooner, and with less fuel, in soft water, than when hard water is used; and the essence will be more quickly and thoroughly extracted by the former, than by the latter, as is observed in making tea or coffee.

AGE OF SHEEP.

The age of a sheep may be known by examining the front teeth. They are eight in number, and appear during the first year, all of a small size. In the second year, the two middle ones fall out, and their place is supplied by two new teeth, which are easily distinguished by being of a larger size. In the third year, two other small teeth, one from each side, drop out, and are replaced by two large ones; so that there are now four large teeth in the middle, and two pointed ones on each side. In the fourth year, the large teeth are six in number, and only two small ones remain, one at each end of the range. In the fifth year the remaining small teeth are lost, and the whole front teeth are large. In the sixth year, the whole begin to be worn; and in the seventh, sometimes sooner, some fall out or are broken.—*Ib.*

Many who would startle at an oath, whose stomachs as well as conscience recoil at an obscenity, do yet slide glibly into a detraction. —*Government of the Tongue.*

For "The Friend."

THE EMIGRANT.

From eastern states where wealth and plenty reign,
And fickle fashion holds her gay domain,
When first we come to seek a dwelling here,
How comfortless our prospects oft appear!
The objects of delight no more we find,
But all our pleasant things seem left behind.
Yet let us not in sullen pride complain,
If well improved, this change may not be vain;
For solitude and hardships oft have brought
Far better lessons than in ease were taught;
The salutary lore which they impart
Strengthens the mind and purifies the heart,
And leads to nobler, more substantial joys,
Than e'er were found in grandeur, show and noise.
The still small voice brought to Elijah's ear,
In Jezreel's crowded walks he did not hear;
Nor, till on Horeb's solitary brow,
His future business did the prophet know.
Accustomed long to full and prosperous days,
Carmel's and flattered, bent in all our ways,
We oft regard these comforts as our due,
Nor honour Him from whom all blessings flow.
But then our long loved idols once removed,
With virtuous crosses and besetments proved,
Our helpless state we come to understand,
And own with rev'rence his almighty hand.
Thus Babel's king the God of Israel chose,
Till all the neighbouring lands were forced to yield;
On mighty kings his servile yoke was laid,
And e'en the beasts his bound'less power obey'd.
But grown too great and towering up to heaven,
He owns the God of heaven's eternal sway;
Who from the dust the meanest wretch can raise,
And all the proud is able to abase.
Augusta, Ohio.

THE FRIEND.

SIXTH MONTH, 20, 1840.

It has become our painful duty to notice an event deeply affecting many minds here and hereaway, as the announcement of it will be to very many in other parts, on both sides of the Atlantic. We allude to the death of our beloved and revered friend DANIEL WHEELER, which took place at the residence of John Clapp, in the city of New York, at about 12 o'clock on the night of sixth day, the 12th instant. It is known to most, perhaps all our readers, that this dear friend returned to his native land last autumn in consequence of the illness of two of his sons. One of these, Charles, who had been his faithful companion in the voyage to the South Sea islands, soon after the father's arrival in England, died. Some weeks subsequent to this affecting occurrence, Daniel again embarked in one of the Liverpool packets, and arrived at New York on the 28th of the 4th month last, in a state of great debility, having been ill during most of the voyage, so that it was with difficulty he was removed from the ship. The transition doubtless was grateful and relieving to him, from the privations incident to a sea voyage, to ample accommodations of the most comfortable kind, surrounded by an affection-

ate and sympathising family, tenderly solicitous to anticipate and supply all his wants, and having the further advantage of experienced and skilful medical advisers, indefatigable in their endeavours to do whatever was in their power for his relief. But the disorder proved to be too deep seated to be reached by medical art, and he ultimately sunk under it. The interment took place in the afternoon of second day, the 15th instant, after a solemn meeting held on the occasion in the Orchard street meeting-house. Thus far we deemed it right to state respecting the demise of this dedicated servant of Jesus Christ, hoping that some person having access to the requisite facts, will prepare for insertion a more extended notice.

It will be pertinent to remark in reference to the two lectures, of which a portion was given in the last, and a continuation is in the present number, that they were delivered in the course of last winter to a crowded and gratified audience, at Friends' Reading rooms, on Appletree alley; and that the lecturer has yielded to the solicitation of several that were present at the delivery, who believed that the insertion of them in this journal would be acceptable to many.

NOTE.—In the portion of the lecture published last week, there were several typographical errors. In the 6th line in the first column " our" should have been " one." In the 2d column, 22d line from the bottom, " perhaps" should be " heaps." In the same column, 11th line from the bottom, " wash" should be " waste."

HAVERFORD SCHOOL.

Letters and small packages for the students, may be left at the store of Kimber & Sharpless, No. 50 North Fourth street, Philadelphia, where the superintendent will send for them once a week—mostly on seventh day.

INSTITUTE FOR COLOURED YOUTH.

The managers are desirous of procuring a suitably qualified person (a member of the Society of Friends) to have the care of, and instruct a limited number of boys at the above institution.

Applications may be forwarded to either of the undernamed committee.

George Williams, 71 north Seventh street, Philip Garrett, Noble street, first door above Sixth, Blakey Sharpless, 50 north Fourth street, M. L. Dawson, corner of Tenth and Filbert streets.

Phila. 5th mo. 30th, 1840.

DEPARTED this life, second month 29th last, after a short illness, DEBORAH, wife of Bennet Smedley, a member of Goshen Monthly, and Willistown Particular Meeting, aged 41 years. In the decease of this our valued friend, we sensibly feel that we are bereaved of one who was peculiarly gifted for usefulness in the church; entering into feeling with exercised mind, and handing a word in season to those that were weary. She loved retirement, to seek for a renewal of spiritual strength, and esteemed it a privilege to be permitted to enjoy our silent meetings. Though at seasons tried with poverty of spirit, she was enabled to rely on the mercy of God, through Jesus Christ, her redeemer, and to feel that his grace was sufficient for her.

DIED, at her residence in Adams, Mass., on first day, the 7th inst., CHARLOTTE KELLEY, a maiden lady, aged 70 years. She was a worthy member of the Society of Friends. "Sweetly she sunk to sleep in Jesus' arms."—*Pittsfield Sun.*

THE FRIEND.

A RELIGIOUS AND LITERARY JOURNAL.

VOL. XLII.   SEVENTH DAY, SIXTH MONTH, 27, 1840.   NO. 39.

EDITED BY ROBERT SMITH.

PUBLISHED WEEKLY.

Price two dollars per annum, payable in advance.

Subscriptions and Payments received by

GEORGE W. TAYLOR,

NO. 50, NORTH FOURTH STREET, UP STAIRS,

PHILADELPHIA.

Communicated for "The Friend."

Two Lectures on the History of Literature, with a brief sketch of the various materials made use of for the preservation of Knowledge.

LECTURE FIRST.

(Concluded from page 295.)

Writers amongst the early Hebrews were probably but few. The Levites in the temple, the Scribes about the court, and those who presided in the schools of the prophets. The Levite received his support as a priest, the teacher had his emolument, the prophets their peace offerings and gifts, and the scribes of the king their rewards; but beyond these no recompense appears to have attended literary labour. Their compositions which have descended to us, are all connected with their history, or devoted to their religion.

That there was a high degree of civilization, and a very extensive acquaintance with many of the arts and sciences in Egypt as early as the time of Moses, the discoveries of Champollion have established beyond question. Almost all trace of their literature has, however, perished, as has that of the Chaldeans, Assyrians, and Phenicians.

Of Grecian writers, Homer and Hesiod appear to be the earliest of whose compositions any part has reached us. The period assigned by learned men as that wherein they flourished, was about 900 years before the Christian era. It would appear that the poets of that age obtained their subsistence by travelling through the land, and reciting their compositions at the assemblies of the citizens, the palaces of princes, and at public sacrifices and feasts. These wandering minstrels were not, however, considered by the Greeks as beggars, or as intruders upon hospitality. On the contrary, their company was solicited with eagerness, their poetry heard with rapture, and their wants ministered to with delight. Tracing the general stream of Grecian literature, we shall find her poets keeping a proud preeminence amongst her learned children even after her "wise men" and historians had entered the race for literary glory. As we draw near to the Christian era, we find that not only in Greece, but in Persia, in Pergamos,

and in Egypt, and probably at other of the eastern courts, the historian, the philosopher, and the poet received public patronage and honourable rewards. The poets and historians were considered as the arbiters of fame, the dispensers of ignominy, and the bestowers of glory. The philosophers, beside that they frequently received rewards as poets and historians, had generally their schools from which they derived a competent support.

The philosophy of the Greeks appears at first to have been contained in a few sententious maxims committed to memory, or of opinions received on the authority of tradition without investigation as to their origin or end. As their keen wit and inventive imagination came to be directed to its study, great changes were produced, and many sects and schools of philosophy arose. With many good principles and wise reflections, there was so much darkness and corruption in their various systems, that they have been severally classed as atheistical, vicious, hypocritical, covetous, impudent, fantastical, quarrelsome, and licentious.

A few remarks may now be hazarded respecting the tendency of the literature of the Hebrews compared with that of the Greeks. Much of the poetry of the Hebrews is prior in point of antiquity, and superior in sublimity to the most polished periods of the Grecian muse. Having its origin in religion, elevated by a sense of spiritual as well as intellectual inspiration, it bursts forth in animated and impassioned tones, and reaches an elevation of sentiment and diction to which the fervour of Grecian enthusiasm never attained. The first efforts of the muse were, no doubt, directed to the praise of Him, who, creating the world, made man a mind capable of appreciating it. Poetry, then, amongst the Hebrews, had its root in religion, and was watered by the dew of divine inspiration. If the heart of the poet Seer ascended to God with grateful ascriptions from that fountain of unerring truth, it returned laden with wisdom and knowledge for the rebuke of the sinner, the instruction of the ignorant, and the consolation of the mourners. The aim, the tendency of his writings, is to lead others to the source of true elevation of thought, and perfect purity of soul. For this purpose he points out the beauty of holiness, he dwells on the goodness of God, he seeks to stir up all the noblest emotions of nature, and to awaken a loathing of sin.

The poetry of the Greeks had its origin in the fountains of natural feeling, and depended upon the intellect and affections of men for its energy, its eloquence, and its power. These affections were corrupt, that intellect misguided, and poetry, under such influence, run riot in the licentiousness of fiction. Departing

from the inward word of truth, giving loose to a sensual imagination, they formed to themselves an artificial religion, and peopled heaven with a host of gods and goddesses impelled by as evil passions, and subject to as deep corruptions as could debase poor human nature. Divinities impure could not ask for immaculate worshippers; and the authors who hymned forth the praises of such gods, have given the fascinating graces of poesy to render the grossest abominations attractive. There flows not a streamlet from the crystal fountain of the Grecian Helicon in which is not mingled some portion of the waters of corruption. Through the whole range of Hebrew and Grecian literature, the same difference in the general tendency is apparent. The one calls for purity, meekness, and love, the other authorises anger, revenge, and many of the evil and impetuous passions. So loose were the Grecian ideas of virtue, that Pindar applies that epithet to those who succeeded at the Olympic games, or who bore off the prize in the chariot races. The effect of such writings must have been injurious to the national character, although, doubtless, in every individual bosom there was a purer spirit at work, which unfolded to their souls clearer perceptions of right, and higher principles of action, than could be gathered from the works of their poets, philosophers, and historians. Had the worshippers, at the marble altar of the unknown God, but listened to his oracle in the secret of their own souls, they might have left their beautiful models of literature alive with the original principles of correct morals, elevated philosophy, and religions truth.

At the public feasts in Greece, besides the contests in athletic exercises, musicians and poets contended, and philosophers, historians, and orators recited their own compositions. Herodotus made public his history at the Olympic games. Thus the Greek writers were accustomed to submit their works to the public, and to avail themselves of the critical judgment of others whilst they still lay open to revision. Others circulated their manuscripts amongst their literary friends, that they might point out defects, or suggest improvements in the margin. This trial before able critics and acute judges of style, no doubt diminished the quantity whilst it improved the quality of the literature of the country. The high price of papyrus and other writing materials, and the great labour of transcriptions, no doubt, had also a happy effect in checking the exuberance and preventing the circulation of the efforts of folly and dulness. But, alas, for the present day, we seem to have no guard against the overwhelming torrent of literature. On paper of little cost, compositions of less value are produced, and through the stupid columns of an illiterate periodical press, are furnished for the depraved appetite of an all-devouring public.

As a taste for literature spread, the schools of the philosophers increased, readers multiplied, and this stirred up a demand for books. The transcribers or copiers of manuscripts now became numerous. The multiplication of copies appears to have been attended with no reward or recompense to the author except fame. Libraries began to be formed under the patronage of the rich, a proof of an increasing literary taste which, at the same time, they served to stimulate. The first library is said to have been at Memphis; but no certain account concerning it is to be found. The first in Greece was collected at Athens, by Pisistratus, 527 years before the Christian era. When Xerxes desolated Attica, 480 B. C. he carried this collection with him across the Hellespont. Seleucus Nicater, king of Syria, an eminent encourager of letters, after 180 years, restored this library to Athens. At the same time he returned to Greece all the other monuments of art which had been taken away by Xerxes. For this the Athenians erected a statue to his memory at the portico of the academy. This library was taken and sent to Rome by Sylla, say 85 B. C. It was either restored again by Hadrian, or a new one was founded by him in its place. King Attalus, and his son Eumenes, about 200 years B. C. collected a large library at Pergamos. This library, containing from 2 to 300,000 volumes, was seized by Anthony and Cleopatra, and conveyed to Alexandria, to swell the royal library there. The Alexandrian library, commenced by Ptolemy Philadelphus, jointly with his father, Ptolemy Soter, B. C. 285, became probably the largest ever gathered before the invention of printing. It is said to have been begun at the suggestion of Demetrius Phalereus, an Athenian writer, who having found it necessary to flee from his country, had taken up his abode at Alexandria. Demetrius was appointed to superintend the collecting books, and was very industrious in gathering the literature of all nations—Jewish, Chaldee, Persian, Ethiopian, Greek, and Latin. Before the death of Ptolemy Philadelphus, the library contained more than 100,000 volumes. The successors of Philadelphus, being patrons of learning, devoted much attention to increasing this, until Ptolemy Physcon commenced a second in Alexandria. So eager was this king to urge on the growth of the new concern, that he seized on every manuscript which came into Egypt, and having had it carefully transcribed, he gave the copy to the owner, and kept the original for his own library. The first collection is said to have contained at one time 700,000 volumes. These volumes were, however, small, being many of them no more than a chapter of a history, or a book of a poem. When Julius Cæsar besieged Alexandria, the second library was accidentally burnt, and the old one appears to have been much lessened, if not totally dispersed. The 200,000 volumes from Pergamos, deposited by Anthony and Cleopatra, again revived the library, which continued to increase until Theophilus, Patriarch of Alexandria, in his zeal against heathenism, destroyed the temple of Serapis in which it was kept, A. D. 390. How many of

the volumes perished with the building we have no knowledge; some, it is said, were committed to the flames, and the rest dispersed. It appears, however, that the fragments were either gathered together, or a new library sprung into existence, which continued to flourish, as also did literature, in Alexandria until the capture of the city by the Arabs, under Omar. The books were then either burnt to heat the public baths, according to the generally received opinion of the literary world, or became so dispersed that the library ceased to exist. Connected with that established by Ptolemy Physcon, there had been a museum where learned men had been supported at the public expense. Within its bounds they had unbroken leisure, and every facility in the pursuit of knowledge. On the destruction of this library, the museum was attached to the elder one, and continued in literary health and vigour, until that also was destroyed. In the museum, the sciences of mathematics, astronomy, and geography had been successfully studied, and the works of Euclid, Appollonius, and Eratosthenes were composed under its fostering influence.

In Rome, libraries may date from that founded by Paulus Emilius, 167 B. C. Sylla brought a larger one from Athens, but neither were at all to be compared with that established by Lucullus, with the books he gathered in the Mithridatic war. Asinius Pollio gave one for the use of the public, as did Julius Cæsar, who placed his under the charge of the learned Varro. Augustus established two, one in the portico of Octavia, the other in the temple of Apollo.

My first lecture will close with the Christian era. At this time Hebrew literature was dormant. The poet-prophets had ceased from the fountains of Israel, and her noble strains of harmony and devotion were now scarcely known to her children in the language in which they were written. The Hebrew was no longer the spoken language of the shepherds and the vine-dressers on her mountains, the tillers of her vallies, or the merchants and artisans of her Roman governed cities. Her scribes, her lawyers, and her priests might be able to read the sacred records in its native tongue, but the Greek translation made at Alexandria under the auspices of Ptolemy Philadelphus was generally in use.

Greece had been plundered of her stores of learning and art, which, with many of her literary children, were now located at Rome. Grecian literature had been highly patronised at Pergamos, and was still at Alexandria, and in the capital of the world in a flourishing condition. At home and abroad it was vigorous, yet gave evident tokens of having passed its prime. Athens, however, bore 'a pre-eminent character for learning and refinement, and in her schools were educated many of the most illustrious citizens of Rome. These schools continued to flourish until suppressed in the sixth century by the emperor Justinian. At Rome, at the commencement of this era, literature was at its height, whether we consider the talent and vigour of her native writers, or the polish and learning of the foreign ones who found patronage within her. In India, at this period, the arts and sciences

were carried to considerable perfection, but of its literature we know little. It has been said that many of the fables which have come to us in a Greek dress, and are accredited to Esop, were of Hindoo origin.

Throughout the rest of the East, under the destructive influence of bloody and exterminating wars, darkness had gathered upon all the shrines of learning. The Chaldean written wisdom was no more, the light of Persian literature was extinguished, and the efforts of Armenian intellect were checked or destroyed by Parthian barbarism, or Roman devastations. By the gradual waste of time, where there was none to replace, through the more rapid destruction by fire sweeping away the only copies, the works of Chaldea and Persia have utterly perished, and Armenia has saved but one relic of her earlier writers.

The material of books at this time amongst the Greeks and Romans was very much confined to parchment and papyrus. Of the papyrus, a great variety was brought to Rome, of every different quality and appearance. The fairest and finest was called Augustus, after the emperor. Transcribers were now a very numerous class, and in the cities of Greece and at Alexandria they held an honourable rank in society, and were amply repaid for their labour. In Rome, however, those employed at this business were chiefly educated household slaves, who not only transcribed books, glued the copies into volumes, polished them with pumice stone, and took charge of their masters' libraries, but wrote their letters, read to them, and assisted them in their studies. The amount of books daily produced had very much increased, and they now became an article of merchandise, and the sale of them a distinct trade. Although many libraries had been destroyed, and many books once known had perished before the Christian era, yet at that time, in their public libraries, and in their private dwellings were hundreds of thousands of volumes, the result of active imagination, acute reasoning, and deep research, which have never come down to us.

Here, then, I close my first lecture, amid the light and glory of that literary sunset already passing away :—a sunset soon lost in evening shadows, which were to deepen and darken until the blackness of mental midnight enveloped the universe of mind.

On the Habits and Instincts of Animals. By William Swainson. A. C. G., Fellow of the Royal Society, and of several Foreign Academies.

(Continued from p. 301.)

Chapter III. treats of the passions of animals. We shall select a few passages.

Among reptiles, one species of the tortoise, the *Testudo caretta*, is exceedingly bold, and fierce, attacking its adversaries with its feet and strong jaws with the utmost vigour. The crocodile, though very voracious, does not appear to be an untameable animal,—instances having been quoted of its becoming tame, and in some degree gentle to its keeper. The male of the common Iguana is stated to exhibit a warm attachment towards the female, whom he will, though usually of a gentle disposition, defend with the most obstinate fury. The nimble and the green lizard of Carolina, we are told, "has every quality that can delight the eye, or interest the beholder in its favour," being at once beautiful, active, useful, patient, and industrious. Most of the venomous serpents, particularly the *cobra di capello*, or hooded snake, are extremely irritable and revengeful: but others, like the boa tribe, and most of the innoxious genera, are at once courageous and peaceable; powerful, indeed, when assailed, but never attacking except from necessity.

In birds the passions are much more acute and perceptible. It is when we enter the umbrageous woods, and look around amongst its feathered inhabitants, that sounds of joy, and indications of love open before us. A thousand varied notes, and some of the sweetest melody reach our ears; while all, from the soft cooing of the dove to the cackling of the common hen, express some latent feeling of tenderness or fear, hope or expectation. The turtle-dove woos his bride with his plaintive song, placing himself in the most winning attitude, and overwhelming her with caresses; while the little love-parrot sits beside his mate, and feeds her by disgorging into her bill. If one dies, the other is impressed with the deepest sorrow, and seldom survives its beloved partner. Many of the parrot family are well known to evince a strong and lasting affection towards each other. Bonnet mentions the mutual affection of a pair of those called love birds, who were confined in the same cage. At last, the female falling sick, her companion evinced the strongest marks of attachment; he carried all the food from the bottom of the cage and fed her on her perch: and when she expired, her unhappy mate went round and round her, in the greatest agitation, attempting to open her bill and give her nourishment. He then gradually languished, and survived her death only a few months.

It is in the parental character, however, that birds evince their strongest feelings. It is in this capacity that every nerve is exerted, every power employed, every sacrifice cheerfully made. Self seems no longer to be considered, danger no more dreaded; and death itself is braved, if it secure the safety of their young. The timid hen, casting away her fears, appears with a new spirit when surrounded by her youthful progeny; and she assumes an air of courage and defiance which evinces a determination to assault any enemy who may approach. The most feeble birds, at the season of incubation, assault the strong and fierce; the weakest will assail the most powerful. It is a well known fact, that a pair of ravens, which dwells in a cavity of the rock of Gibralter, would never suffer a vulture or eagle to approach the nest, but would drive them away with every appearance of fury. The missel thrush, during the breeding season, will fight even the magpie or jay. And the female titmouse will frequently allow herself to be made a prisoner rather than quit her nest; or if she herself escape, she will speedily return, menacing the invaders by hissing like a snake, and biting all who approach her: this we have ourselves experienced. The artifices employed by the partridge, the lapwing, the ring plo-

ver, the pewit, and numerous other land birds, to blind the vigilance and divert the attention of those who may come near their little ones, is equally curious. The partridges, both male and female, conduct their young out to feed, and carefully assist them in their search for food. But, if disturbed in the midst of this employment, the male, after first giving the alarm by uttering a peculiar cry of distress, throws himself directly in the way of danger, and endeavours, by feigning lameness or mability to fly, to distract the attention and mislead the efforts of the enemy,—thus giving his mate time to conduct her little brood to a place of security. "A partridge," says White, "came out of a ditch, and ran along, shivering with her wings, and crying out as if wounded, and unable to get from us. While the dam feigned this distress, a boy, who attended me, saw the brood, which was small, and unable to fly, run for shelter into an old fox's hole under the bank." The lapwing pushes forward to meet her foes, employing every art to allure them from the abode of her young: she rises from the ground with a loud screaming voice, as if just finished from hatching, though, probably, at the same time not within a hundred yards from the nest; she afterwards whines and screams round the invaders; and invariably becomes more clamorous as she retires further from the nest. The ring plover will flutter along the ground as if crippled; and if pursued, will hasten to a short distance, stretch out its feathers, and appear to "tumble heels over head," till it has enticed its enemy to a distance; while, on similar occasions, the pewit resorts to the same expedient of appearing wounded as soon as it perceives the approach of a stranger. Sheldrakes are equally ingenious: during the period of incubation, which lasts thirty days, the male keeps watch on some adjoining hillock, which he only leaves that he may satisfy the calls of hunger, or occupy the post of the female while she quits it for food. After the young are hatched, the parents lead, or sometimes carry them in their bill, towards the sea; and if interrupted in their progress, it is said they employ numberless arts to draw off the attention of the observer.

The eider duck, and some other birds, pluck the down off their own bodies to shelter and comfort their helpless young. Others will voluntarily undergo the pains of hunger for the same object; refusing to leave their nests until perfectly exhausted from want of sustenance; while some, again, are carefully provided with food by their mates,—most of whom, like the sheldrake, watch somewhere near, to ward off, or to give timely notice of the approach of danger, and to while away the time by his song. The blue-bellied parrakeet is an instance both of parental and connubial attachment. This bird, like the eider duck, lines its nest with the down stripped from its own breast; and La Vaillant informs us that it receives the most assiduous attentions from the male during the whole progress of nidification, —both afterwards uniting to display the same affection towards their young; these latter, for the first six months after they are hatched, are frequently seen seated by the side of their mother, while her faithful partner places himself

close by, and if unable to reach the little ones, he gives their food to her, and she distributes it to her progeny. Innumerable instances may be quoted of other birds which train their young in a manner equally indicative of parental love. Thus, some of the eagles take out their young before they are fully grown, on purpose to teach them the art necessary for securing their prey. The female lark conducts here to exercise their powers of flight, herself fluttering over their heads, directing their motions, and preserving them from danger. Even the butcher-bird, or common wood-chat shrike, continues her regard for her offspring even after they have obtained maturity; while the latter reward her care by assisting her in providing for the support of all. until the following spring. We may close these familiar instances of parental tenderness, exhibited more particularly by our native birds, with the following anecdote, recorded by White, of Shelborne:—"The common flycatcher (the *stoparola*, of Ray) builds every year in the vines that grow on the walls of my house. A pair of these little birds had, one year, inadvertently placed their nest on a naked bough, perhaps in a shady time, not being aware of the inconvenience that followed: but a hot sunny season coming on before the brood was half fledged, the reflection of the wall became insupportable, and must inevitably have destroyed the young, had not affection suggested an expedient, and prompted the parent birds to hover over the nest all the hotter hours, while with wings expanded, and mouths gaping for breath, they screened off the heat from their suffering offspring." The courage of the drongo shrikes, found in Africa, is not less striking than that of their natural allies or prototypes, the tyrant shrikes of America. "This bird," observes Dr. Burchell, "is remarkable for its boldness: whenever hawks or ravens approach its nest, it flies out upon them with incredible fury, and drives them away with a harsh, angry noise, attacking the obtruder on its dwelling in the rear, and pursuing him to a considerable distance. That a bird, not much larger than a swallow, should have courage to attack another so many times larger, and that, too, a hawk, is a singular fact, but not more extraordinary than the evident fear and precipitation with which its enemy hastens to get out of its reach."

Birds, however, like men, experience other besides the gentler passions. The fierceness of the rapacious order is well known; and the obstinacy with which combats are carried on, even by domestic fowls, is known to every one. But who would suppose that the smallest of all the feathered tribes—the humming birds—would exhibit the most violent, though, at the same time, ludicrous paroxysms of rage. Pennant, when speaking of the *trochilus colubris* of North America, observes, "The most violent passions sometimes agitate their little breasts: they often have dreadful contests, when numbers happen to dispute the same flower: they will tilt against each other with such fury, as if they meant to transfix their antagonists with their long bills." It may be truly said, that these little creatures are sadly prone to quarrel over their cups—not of wine, but of flowers. We have frequently seen

r or five engaged in a flying fight, when
outing the possession of a flowery tree in
forests of Brazil. At such times they fly
swiftly that the eye can scarcely follow
m. The violent quarrels of sparrows, par-
larly in the pairing season, is familiar to
it of our readers; but although desperate
the moment, they appear to be soon re-
ciled.

(To be continued.)

*suvius, Herculaneum and Pompeii, in
1839.*

Vhoever sojourns at Naples, were it only
a day, experiences the irresistible desire
going to see what is passing at the bottom
hat crater which perpetually smokes. It is
ecially towards evening, when the sun has
ppeared beneath the horizon, that the va-
rs of Vesuvius assume a denser tint, and
k its summit with a bouquet of brighter
iteness. At Resina you find horses, don-
s, and conductors, who convey travellers
f way up the mountain to the spot called
"Hermitage." This first ride is not an
nteresting one. Here nature is not yet
d. You pass through vineyards, planted in
es, which yield the celebrated *Lachryma
rista* wine, two sorts of which there are
ch inferior to their fame; then come some
neless trees, the foremost sentinels of vege-
on, which the next eruption will devour,
, lastly, you reach the "Hermitage," sur-
nded on all sides, save one, by the lava of
14, 1810, 1813, and 1822. Here you alight,
i enter a region of chaos. No more trees,
etation, birds, or insects are to be seen.
ery thing is dark, bristling with points, rent
deep and rugged fractures, covered with
ria, of a sulphurous smell, which tear your
; before they burn them. You are now at
foot of the cone; all that remains to be
e is to ascend vertically along the external
e of the volcano, halting on your way to
t a glance at a lateral plateau, called La
nma, which was no doubt, at one time, the
n focus of Vesuvius.

f your heart has not failed you along this
ler of dried lava, you will reach the top of
volcano in three quarters of an hour. Here
sight begins—a terrible, original, and un-
eeted one, notwithstanding all the descrip-
s given of it. Imagine a funnel five hun-
d *metres* deep, whose upper edges present
umerable crevices, whilst from the lower
t rise clouds of sulphurous vapour, which
ape by numberless apertures, bordered with
t of a lively orange colour. If you stop to
ire in the distance the city of Naples softly
ading round the gulf, and at your feet the
r-smoking crater, you feel the fire penetrat-
your boots, and the guide will urge you to
k, in order to avoid accidents. The ground,
n strongly struck, yields a certain metallic
ad, and as you go round the mountain you
t with gaping apertures, at the bottom of
ch burns a red and fattish flame. I have
iged into one of these pits a long chestnut-
stick, fresh cut, and covered with its still
st bark, and it has instantly caught fire. As
kneel before these infernal gates to ascer-

tain their depth, you distinctly perceive within hand-reach the flame bending upon itself,
dense, quiet, and almost limpid; it discharges
clouds of sulphuric acid gas, which excite
a cough, and soon compel the observer to
quit the spot. The ground, if such a name
can be given to the dangerous floor which
covers the orifice of the volcano, is strewed
with gray lava, ashes, melting sulphur, and
pyrite substances, whence escapes, at intervals, a white smoke, which affects your eyes
and lungs, and yet you cannot retire without
reluctance from that awful scene. One can
scarcely conceive how that crater, so narrow
in its lower part, has vomited heaps of lava
large enough to form a mountain four times as
bulky as the Vesuvius itself, without mentioning the ashes, small pebbles, and masses of
boiling water, which the wind has sometimes
carried to enormous distances.

Notwithstanding its fearful aspect, the Vesuvius may be easily approached even when its
irruptions take place. The lava itself, whose
progress is so formidable and inflexible, advances with extreme slowness. One has time
to avoid or fly before it. The slightest obstacle stops it; it turns round objects, burns them
if they be combustible, and envelopes and pe-
trifies them as it cools if they be not so. Thus
it is that the city of Herculaneum has been
sealed into a semi-metallic mass, and, as it
were, cast in the lava which now covers it.
Pompeia has disappeared under a discharge
from Vesuvius, under a shower of ashes and
little stones, which have gradually, though rapidly, covered it, just as certain Alpine villages
disappear beneath the snow in our severe winters. Such is the reason why so much money
has been expended in uncovering but a few
small parts of Herculaneum, namely, its theatre, which continues hid in utter darkness:
whilst a third part of Pompeia has been cleared, exhibits itself to the open sky, and renders
us contemporary with its inhabitants. Let us,
therefore, hasten down the Vesuvius and view
its ravages, which have been miraculously preserved for us in its whole splendour, a city of
thirty thousand souls buried for eighteen hundred years past.

Herculaneum and Pompeia seem both very
distant from the focus of Vesuvius. They are
now separated from it by inhabitants and cultivated spaces, which have been conquered
from the lava and recovered from the volcano.
The village of Portici is built *upon the roofs*
of the first of these two cities, which was pe-
trified on the day of its death, and into the
tomb of which one descends as into a mine,
by a sort of shaft, ending at the theatre where,
it is conjectured, the inhabitants were assembled when the eruption surprised them. It
was in 1689 that the ruins of the city made
their appearance for the first time in an excavation made at random, which was resumed in
1720, and finally organised in 1738 with admirable success. The discovery of the theatre
and of every thing else has taken place since
that period. The theatre is of Greek architecture, it is ornamented with a fine front, and
with marble columns standing on the stage
itself; the spectators occupied twenty-one rows
of steps, with a gallery above embellished with
bronze statues.

One
to the
actors
excite
and em
a forur
ples, w
and a g
prisone
of all t
blem oi
leave t
made E
tended
tivi, yc
lava, pi
um was
suvius.
The
at so gr
tions of
Hercul:
of Pom
ing inte
catacom
revive;
and ort
the cell
in more
found o
guests 1
where
which
cient bc
as ours
melts ir
by a sul
and wal
by Rom
there ar
the hor
sign ove
of these
ashes, 1
Every
affected.
epitaph
"*Servil
advance
of the
box cut
there ar
ways,
footway
wheel-r
Who
have bo
the doo
Here is
in phial
sams sti
Let u
baker's
suppose
tinguish
the oth
them,
wretche
the han
surprise
read th
carbonir
that cuj

olives, dried figs, lentils, and eatables of all descriptions. A saucepan has been carried to the Naples Museum, containing a piece of meat, as well preserved as by Apperi's process. What a number of meals Vesuvius interrupted on that woful day!

I nevertheless do not think that the Romans were great eaters. I have carefully explored a number of kitchens and dining rooms at Pompeia, and I have found, even in the richest houses, but very trifling cooking apparatus, and miniature table utensils. Their plates were real stone or marble, which could hold but one dish at a time. The guests lay down around as soldiers round their mess. What is admirable, delightful, charming, and overwhelming to us barbarians of the nineteenth century, is the exquisite pureness and delicacy of shape of all the utensils which served in Roman domestic life. One must see those candelabras, lamps, vases of all sizes, those charming little bronze calefactors (for every thing was of bronze,) those tripods, scales, beds, chairs, those graceful and so ingeniously wrought shields which fill up whole rooms at the Naples Museum. One must, above all, see the toilet arsenal of the Roman ladies, their combs, tooth-picks, curling irons, and the pots of vegetable or mineral rouge found in a boudoir. Thus the Roman ladies used rouge and deceived people, just as is practised now-a-days; they wore, like our ladies, those necklaces, rings, and ridiculous ear-rings which add nothing to beauty and diminish not ugliness. How times resemble one another, in spite of the space that separates them.

Above thirty streets of Pompeia are now restored to light; it is a third part of the town. The walls which formed its ancient inclosure have been recognised; a magnificent amphitheatre, a theatre, a forum, the temple of Isis, that of Venus, and a number of other buildings have been cleared. The secret stairs by which the priests of those times slily crept to prompt the oracles have been detected. On beholding so many monuments which display in so lively a manner the importance of public and the independence of private life among the Romans, it is impossible to resist a feeling of sadness and melancholy. Behold, along that fall of earth, the vestige of the breast of a woman who was buried alive and stiffened by death—behold the stones of that well, worn by the rubbing of the ropes—examine that guard-house, covered with caricatures of soldiers;—one might suppose that the Roman people still existed, and that we were but strangers in one of their towns. Who knows what future discoveries may be made in those august ruins! Murat employed upon them 2000 men every year. Only 60 men and 1000l. are now employed upon them. The excavations proceed, in consequence, with dismal slowness, however great may be the interest which his Sicilian majesty takes in their success. It is not to Rome—devastated and disfigured Rome—that one must go to study the Romans—it is to Pompeia. Pompeia, as regards antiquities, is worth all Italy together.

Origin of the Names of the several United States.

Maine was so called as early as 1623, from Maine, in France, of which Henrietta Maria, queen of England, was at that time proprietor.

New-Hampshire was the name given to the territory conveyed by the Plymouth Company to Capt. John Mason, by patent, Nov. 7, 1629, with reference to the patentee, who was governor of Portsmouth, in Hampshire, England.

Vermont was so called by the inhabitants in their declaration of independence, Jan. 16, 1777, from French *verd mont*, green mountain.

Massachussets was so called from Massachusetts Bay, and that from the Massachusetts tribe of Indians in the neighbourhood of Boston. The tribe is thought to have derived its name from the blue hills of Milton. "I had learned," says Roger Williams, "that the Massachusetts was so called from the Blue Hills."

Rhode Island was so called in 1644, in reference to the island of Rhodes, in the Mediterranean.

Connecticut was so called from the Indian name of its principal river. Connecticut is a Moheakaneew word, signifying *long river*.

New-York was so called in 1664, in reference to the Duke of York and Albany, to whom this territory was granted by the King of England.

New-Jersey was so called in 1664, from the island of Jersey, on the coast of France, the residence of the family of Sir George Carteret, to whom this territory was granted.

Pennsylvania was so called in 1681, after William Penn.

Delaware was so called in 1703, from the Delaware Bay, on which it lies, and which received its name from Lord de la War, who died in this bay.

Maryland was so called in honour of Henrietta Maria, queen of Charles I., in his patent to Lord Baltimore, June 30, 1632.

Virginia was so called in 1584, after Elizabeth, the virgin queen of England.

Carolina was so called by the French in 1564, in honour of King Charles IX. of France.

Georgia was so called in 1732, in honour of King George II.

Alabama was so called in 1817, from its principal river.

Mississippi was so called in 1800, from its western boundary. Mississippi is said to denote the *whole river*, i. e., the river formed by the union of many.

Louisiana was so called in honour of Louis XIV. of France.

Tennessee was so called in 1796, from its principal river. The word Ten-assee is said to signify a *curved spoon*.

Kentucky was so called in 1792, from its principal river.

Illinois was so called in 1809, from its principal river. The word is said to signify *the river of men*.

Indiana was so called in 1809, from the American Indians.

Ohio was so called in 1802, from its southern boundary.

Missouri was so called in 1821, from its principal river.

Michigan was so called in 1805, from the lake on its border.

Arkansas was so called in 1819, from its principal river.

Florida was so called by Juan Ponce de Leon in 1572. [Robertson says they called it Florida on account of its flowers.]

Columbia was so called in reference to Columbus.

Wisconsin was so called from its principal river.

Iowa was so called from its principal river.

Oregon was so called from its principal river.

LITTLE CHILDREN.
BY MARY HOWITT.

Sporting through the forest wide;
Playing by the water side;
Wandering o'er the heathed fells;
Down within the woodland dells;
All among the mountains wild;
Dwelleth many a little child!
In the baron's hall of pride;
By the poor man's dull fireside;
'Mid the mighty, 'mid the mean;
Little children may be seen!
Like the flowers that spring up fair,
Bright and countless every where!

In the fair isles of the main;
In the desert's lone domain;
In the savage mountain glen;
Among the tribes of swarthy men;
Wheresoe'er a foot hath gone;
Wheresoe'er the sun hath shone;
On a league of peopled ground;
Little children may be found!

Blessings on them! They, in me,
Move a kindly sympathy!
With their wishes, hopes, and fears;
With their laughter and their tears;
With their wonders so intense,
And their small experience!

Little children, not alone
On the wide earth are ye known;
'Mid its labours and its cares;
'Mid its sufferings and its snares.
Free from sorrow, free from strife,
In the world of love and life,
Where no sinful thing hath trod
In the presence of our God!
Spotless, blameless, glorified,
Little children, ye abide!

SINGULAR PATENT.

A patent of a somewhat singular description has lately been taken out; it is for an invention to supersede the ordinary wooden letters usually fixed upon the facia of shop windows. The new letters are made of porcelain, of every form and hue, and when fixed up, present a beautiful and attractive appearance. The facility of cleansing them is not the least of their qualifications; for with a sponge they are immediately brought to their pristine beauty and elegance. They will not exceed the old wooden letters in price, and they will last for ever; therefore, with beauty, economy, durability, and facility of cleansing to back them, it will be strange indeed if they do not succeed in charming the shopkeepers into their speedy adoption. Some of the patterns are positively quite elegant, particularly the golden ones, and, being glazed, present a dazzling and animated appearance. They are not quite ready for public use; but it is expected they will soon arrive from the manufactory in Staffordshire.—*Foreign Paper.*

The editor of the Friend is requested to republish the article on Charity, signed J. K. contained in the number dated 10th mo. 24, 1835. It was written at the time Elisha Bates was giving so much uneasiness to some Friends by his sentiments and the course he was pursuing; and when the charge of tale-bearing and detraction was pretty freely and openly advanced against those who were honest enough to express their uneasiness respecting him. Advantage sometimes arises from bringing into view the opinions which individuals have expressed when they thought it was proper to raise their voices against error, and when they rejected the charge of tale-bearing and detraction as utterly futile, as applied to those who spoke "against the principles and conduct of persons," "in order that the community, whether civil or religious, may be warned of the danger arising from their teaching, their influence or example."

For "The Friend."

CHARITY.

That charity which is the bond of perfectness, which neither thinketh nor maketh evil, and which, while it abhorreth whatever is wrong, cleaves to those things that are good, is essential to the preservation of every religious community. Between this heavenly affection, and that busy, tattling spirit, which is prying into the failings of others, and reporting them to the disadvantage of a brother or sister, there is as wide a separation as between light and darkness, Christ and Belial. The former is the accompaniment of the wisdom which cometh down from above, and is first pure, then peaceable, gentle, and easy to be entreated, full of mercy and of good fruits; while the latter is the product of the wisdom from beneath, which is declared to be earthly, sensual, devilish. The contrast is strong, yet not more so than the fruits of the two fully justify; for as one tends to strengthen the bonds of Christian union, to increase our love for the brethren, to cover those weaknesses to which our frail nature is incident, and teaches us to forgive as we hope to be forgiven: the other magnifies the failings of our friends, and creates many imaginary ones; makes us censorious and severe toward them, sows the seeds of disesteem and discord, and breaks the ties both of social and religious union. It was a deep conviction of the ruinous consequence resulting from this vice, which induced our early Friends so strongly to deprecate it, to caution their brethren against the first temptations to its commission, and endeavour to fortify their good resolutions by the strongest guards. The yearly meeting has again and again repeated those advices, and in order to incite to constant vigilance the query is required to be answered every three months, "Are tale-bearing and detraction discouraged?"

Perhaps there is no error to which we are more liable, through mere inadvertence, than detraction. Without any malevolent feeling or intention, we begin to converse, respecting acquaintances, perhaps advert to their conduct in some particular case, and almost without thought, pass an opinion respecting it; this leads to something further, and other disclosures are made to corroborate or justify the

opinion we have advanced. Th[...] given to conversation soon dege[...] scandal or tale-bearing, and a frier[...] in his reputation, or judged and [...] without the opportunity of being [...] defence. It would require a vol[...] scribe the various forms which thi[...] habit assumes in order to insinuat[...] its secret and plausible devices for [...] foundations of fellowship and un[...] stroying the character and influen[...] who are the unconscious and oft[...] victims of its machinations. How [...] conducive to the general good of [...] the increase of love and harmony, [...] therance of united and persevering [...] great cause of religion and virtue, [...] own purity and peace of mind wo[...] limit our conversation to things c[...] edify one another in love, to anim[...] courage in good works, and to str[...] faith in those precious doctrines [...] nies, which, from the concurrent [...] the Spirit of God and the Holy Sc[...] Society has been convinced are th[...] the gospel as it is in Jesus.

The remedy for this evil must [...] sought in the renovation of heart [...] the work of the Holy Spirit to ef[...] us. A patient endurance of its r[...] baptism will thoroughly change [...] character, new desires and affecti[...] induced, new dispositions and he[...] tives will actuate us, holier and hig[...] occupy our minds, and the whole r[...] a more exalted and dignified cha[...] grand distinguishing feature of wh[...] love to God, and love to the whol[...] mankind.

But in checking the evil under [...] there are many instrumental help[...] were disposed to listen to tale-b[...] detraction, few would be found ha[...] to persist in it. The relish with [...] listen, the readiness with which we [...] censure, and the pleasure we evin[...] ing something new, are the reward [...] bearer. If we withhold these, m[...] inducement for continuing the prac[...] taken away. Let us then watch [...] another in love; endeavour to disc[...] the practice by kind and tender a[...] and to direct conversation to useful [...] topics, and always avoid introd[...] friends or their characters as subjec[...] mon and familiar discourse.

I must not, however, conclude [...] without drawing a distinction wh[...] the support of truth against error [...] to make. It is not always detracti[...] bearing to speak against the prin[...] conduct of persons. There are cir[...] which demand an open and hones[...] of the course pursued by individu[...] principle and practice, in order tha[...] munity, whether civil or religion [...] warned of the danger arising from [...] ing, their influence, or example. [...] the improper conduct or the false p[...] others, where that concealment wc[...] them to pursue that conduct with [...] or to spread those principles more st[...] to the injury of others, would be to

tagion, is branded as a tale-bearer and calumniator.

Where a person publicly avows sentiments adverse to the faith of a religious body with which he is connected, and persists in that avowal, or where his practice contravenes the principles of that society, and his example, teaching, or influence, is likely to draw others after him, it becomes a duty to warn others against his conduct and principles.

The elders of Philadelphia did so in the case of Elias Hicks, and there are many who, to this day, will have cause to bless the Lord for it, as the means of preventing them from running into those soul-destroying errors, which were so plausibly presented to them. To charge this set of the elders, so salutary in its effects, to the account of detraction or breach of unity, would be indeed to put darkness for light, and evil for good. While, therefore, I would earnestly exhort against the sin of tale-bearing and detraction, it is important, in my view, that we should make right distinctions, and know what these words mean, lest we pervert them into an engine for throwing down the barriers necessary for the preservation of sound doctrine and Christian practice in the Society, proclaiming unbridled license for the promulgation of sentiments, however repugnant to our established principles, and leave every man to exercise all the influence he can acquire, in promoting among us whatever opinions he may choose to adopt.

J. K.

The following memorial, soliciting the interference of congress in suppressing the African slave trade, carried on under the American flag, and by citizens of the United States, was presented to the senate and house of representatives, directed to be printed, and, by the latter, referred to the committee on commerce.

Memorial of the Society of Friends in Pennsylvania, New Jersey, and Delaware, on the African slave trade. To the senate and house of representatives of the United States in congress assembled.

The memorial of the representatives of the religious Society of Friends, commonly called Quakers, in Pennsylvania, New Jersey, Delaware, &c.,

Respectfully represents:—That your memorialists are induced, by apprehension of religious duty, and regard for the present and future welfare of our common country, to solicit the attention of congress to an evil of great and appalling magnitude, in which we have reasons to believe that many of our citizens are deeply involved.

We are encouraged to hope that our application will be judged worthy of serious consideration, from the circumstance that the President of the United States, at the opening of the present session, called the attention of your body to the same subject: we allude to the African slave trade. We are fully aware that this traffic is prohibited by the laws of nearly all the governments in the civilized world, whose subjects or citizens have ever been engaged in its prosecution; and that the two most active and extensive maritime nations on

the globe have denounced it as piratical, and prescribed for those who may be found employed in it the awful punishment of death; yet the information which we have obtained from various sources of unquestionable authenticity, has led to the sorrowful conviction that this iniquitous commerce has, for several years past, been prosecuted to a greater extent, and in a manner more destructive to its victims, than it ever was before.

Under all the difficulties attendant upon this inquiry, and with ample allowance for all the questionable cases, an estimate, founded chiefly on official documents, leads to the conclusion that no fewer than one hundred and fifty thousand African slaves are annually landed on the coasts of Brazil, Cuba, and Porto Rico. A large number is known to be carried into Texas; and we have reason to apprehend that many are also introduced into the United States.

It is needless to expatiate upon the scenes of havoc and desolation from which this commerce is supplied; the sanguinary conflicts, the midnight conflagrations, and the toilsome march through inhospitable deserts, and under a burning sun, must be familiar to the mind of every person who is conversant with the history of the slave trade. From the concurrent testimony of numerous witnesses, we are warranted in the conclusion, that the number who perish by fatigue, famine, and the sword, considerably exceeds the number who reach the coast alive.

The diseases generated in the holds of the slave ships, while the traffic was tolerated, are well known to have given to the march of death more than ten times its usual speed.

But the circumstances under which it is now prosecuted have greatly increased the horrors and mortality of the middle passage. The ships engaged in it are constructed for rapid sailing; hence the space allotted to the slaves is more limited now than before the prohibitory laws were enacted. Other causes, sufficiently obvious, augment the suffering and mortality attendant upon the passage across the Atlantic. A comparison, founded upon a considerable collection of ascertained cases, appears to support the conclusion that rather more than one fourth of the number embarked on the African coast perish before they reach the place of their destination in the western world. Connecting this conclusion with the estimate already given of those who perish in procuring the slaves actually disembarked, we are brought to the dreadful conviction that the African continent is annually despoiled, by means of the slave trade, of from four to five hundred thousand of its inhabitants; or considerably upward of a thousand a day.

If we could believe that this desolating traffic was carried on exclusively by foreigners, it might still be worthy of consideration whether the influence of the United States with the other governments of the world ought not to be exerted toward arresting or mitigating so enormous an evil. But we have sorrowful evidence that a large part is prosecuted under the protection of the American flag, and that American citizens and American capital are deeply engaged in it. It is an undeniable fact, that numerous vessels are built in the

United States and sent to Cuba and ports in the Cape de Verd islands, where a sale, real or pretended, is effected to a foreigner, and a few foreigners are taken on board—the American officers still retaining their places. With this mixed crew the vessel proceeds, under the American flag, to the African coast. If visited by a British cruiser, the American character is assumed, as an efficient protection; but in case one of our national vessels falls in their way, the foreigners figure as the crew, and the Americans take the character of passengers. The flag of the United States, being found the most efficient protection, is generally displayed until the slaves are embarked, when it disappears, and that of Spain or Portugal usually takes its place. It is even said, that the American flag has been used to cover this nefarious traffic, in its preparatory stages, in cases where neither the vessel nor crew had any claim to the American character.

If the transfer to foreigners of ships built in the United States by American citizens, equipped and prepared in all respects for the African slave trade, should even be proved to be real *bona fide* sales, still such transactions must be considered as deeply participating in the criminality of that horrid traffic. Trading with known pirates, furnishing them with stores, or fitting out vessels for their purposes, has been regarded as a crime of equal atrocity with piracy itself.

We respectfully but earnestly solicit the serious attention of congress to this affecting subject, and desire that they will adopt such measures as to rescue the citizens of the United States from the infamy and guilt of participating in this foul opprobrium of the Christian name. The federal government has been highly applauded for its early and active exertions for the abolition of this traffic; and we ardently desire that those who are intrusted with the legislation of this great and growing republic may humbly seek and experience the wisdom which comes from above, to direct them in the adoption of proper measures; and that the powerful influence of the United States with other maritime nations of the world may be judiciously exerted for the final and total suppression of a traffic so revolting to humanity, and so totally irreconcilable with the character of a Christian community.

Signed by direction, on behalf of a meeting of the representatives aforesaid, held in Philadelphia the 17th of the 4th month, 1840.

WILLIAM EVANS, *Clerk.*

Magnanimity and Gratitude of a Lion.

Prince, a tame lion, on board his majesty's ship Ariadne, had a keeper to whom he was much attached; the keeper got drunk one day, and, as the captain never forgave the crime, the keeper was ordered to be flogged; the grating was rigged on the main deck, opposite Prince's den, a large barred up place, the pillars large and cased with iron. When the keeper began to strip, Prince rose gloomily from his couch; and got as near to his friend as possible; on beholding his bare back, he walked hastily round the den, and when he saw the boatswain inflict the first lash, his eyes sparkled with fire, and his sides resounded with the strong and quick beatings of his tail; at last when the blood began to flow from the unfortunate man's back, and the "clotted cats" jerked their gory knots close to the lion's den, his fury became tremendous, he roared with a voice of thunder, shook the strong bars of his prison, as if they had been osiers, and finding his efforts to break loose unavailing, he rolled and shrieked in a manner the most terrific that it is possible to conceive. The captain, fearing that he might break loose, ordered the marines to load and present at Prince; this threat redoubled his rage, and at last the captain desired the keeper to be cast off and go to his friend. It is impossible to describe the joy evinced by the lion; he licked with care the mangled and bleeding back of the cruelly treated seaman, caressed him with his paws, which he folded round the keeper as if to defy any one renewing a similar treatment, and it was only after several hours that Prince would allow the keeper to quit his protection and return among those who had so ill-used him.—*Foreign paper.*

The Falls of Riukan-Fos, Norway.

But hark! we are still far away from the falls, and yet their roar is already heard. We had been climbing without intermission for several miles, and there is another terrible hill before we dismount; at its foot several large and dangerous torrents are yet to be crossed. As we rise, houses, even at this remote and elevated point of the valley, are seen nestling among the copse, or completely overshadowed by some trees of nobler growth. The track rises higher and higher, so steeply that it seems impossible for our wearied horses to reach the top. At last the path seems to terminate—a huge precipice bars all advance. Leaving the horses in a deserted hut, we get round the interposing rock—climb on our hands and knees —turn a soft green point—and in another moment the fall bursts upon us in all its beauty and sublimity. Above the fall, the river is seen slanting through a naked ravine in a long inclined bed, where it flows smoothly and swiftly, without a pool to rest in, or a rock to break on, till in one moment, from clear and foamless water, it vanishes in white clouds of spray; with a single plunge it has fallen four hundred and fifty feet into a vast gulph scooped from the solid marble! So tremendous is the shock, that even at this distance the mountain trembles. From the immense height of the fall, the body of the water is lost sight of long before it reaches the bottom; instantly it recovers itself, however, and rises back to the very summit in light vapoury clouds, bounding and curling upwards, till the whole basin and the retreating hollows are full of wreaths upon wreaths of fantastic beauty. A matchless sight! The floating masses are ever varying their forms; now they are like the rich foliage of lofty trees waving in the summer gale, now like the gilded clouds at even. Their beauty is singularly heightened by the blackness of the surrounding rocks, and the deep green of the sward above. Lofty as the fall itself is, there are yet loftier mountains round it, whose imposing masses greatly increase the effect of the impressive scene. The sound of the cataract is at times louder than the loudest thunder, filling the air for miles with peals of terrible distinctness. On listening to it for a while, the head begins to turn. Altogether, the height—the mass of water— the ebon darkness of the surrounding rocks— the silence of the green spot we cling to in viewing it, backed by a huge triangle of swarthy basalt—the streaks of snow on the heights —the small hut creeping near the brink—the river rushing triumphantly out of the chaldron it has escaped from in despite of so fierce a trial—every adjunct required by taste unite to make this scene one of the most magnificent that nature presents.—*Bremner's Excursions in Norway.*

God sends the poor to *try* us; as well as he tries *them*, by being *such:* and he that refuses them a *little*, out of the great deal that God has given him, lays up poverty in store for his own posterity.—*Wm. Penn:*

Property of Numbers.—Joseph Hall, a teacher of mathematics, at Macclesfield, has discovered that the sum of the products contained in the 144 cells of the common multiplication table is 6084, a square number, the root of which is 78, and which root is equal to the sum of the numbers contained in the first column. If the table is extended to 20 times 20, or indeed to any given number of times, still the operation will exhibit a similar result, the sum contained in the first column squared, will be equal to the sum of all the products in the number of cells which the table may contain.—*Foreign Paper.*

The New Zealand Land Company in London has learned from its agent, that he has effected the purchase of the harbour of Port Nicholson, in Cook's Straits, with a territory of fifty miles long and thirty miles broad, including a million of acres. It is about thirty miles from Queen Charlotte's Sound, well wooded and full of foliage. The harbour is directly in the way from New Holland to England.

Mathew, the Catholic priest, administered the teetotal pledge in Nenagh, the most protestant district of Tipperary, one day last week, to 16,000 persons. The society now consists of 700,000 members. The number of grocers and spirit retailers in this city and liberties is reduced from 450 to 100. There are but three applications for spirit licenses in this city, to be made at quarter sessions, before the mayor, recorder, and magistrates, to-morrow.—*Limerick Chronicle.*

THE FRIEND.

SIXTH MONTH, 27, 1840.

With respect to the Yearly Meeting of Friends for New England, recently held, the information we have been enabled to obtain is very limited, and too indistinct to justify entering much into detail. It appears, however, that the select meeting of ministers and elders met on seventh day the 13th instant, at Newport, and that the Yearly Meeting convened at the same place, on second day following, continuing by adjournments until the morning of sixth day, the 19th instant. We learn generally, that, beside the regular course of proceedings relative to the state of the society as exhibited in the reports from subordinate meetings, several other subjects of interest were considered and acted upon; particularly in regard to the Indian tribes who have been compelled to abandon their ancient settlements, and to remove into a wilderness country beyond the Mississippi. The Newport Mercury of the 20th instant contains a short notice of the meeting, which concludes thus. "We learn that the deliberations were conducted with great harmony and unanimity, and the correct principles of the society duly maintained. The meeting closed with friendly and Christian feelings."

We commend to the attention of our readers the memorial, on another page, of the Society of Friends in Pennsylvania, New Jersey, &c. addressed, and recently presented to congress, on the African slave trade, carried on under *the American flag,* and by *citizens of the United States.* It is a document well becoming a body of Christian professors—dignified, energetic, yet respectful; and should be read and pondered by every man, woman and child among us, competent duly to appreciate the deep interest of the subject.

Correction.—In line 17 of The Emigrant, inserted last week, for the word *an* read *on.*

DIED, on the evening of the 22d instant, at her residence in this city, ELIZABETH ARCHER, aged 77 years, relict of the late Samuel Archer.

—— on the 24th instant, ELIZABETH KAIGHN, of this city, widow of John Kaighn, late of Kaighn's Point, Camden, New Jersey.

—— suddenly at Friends' Meeting House, in the northern district, Philadelphia, on the morning of the 23d instant, JOHN NORTH, aged about 55 years. Born in Ireland, this Friend had there seen the nature of the spirit of infidelity, which, many years ago, found a footing in that land, and when, in 1827, it showed itself within our borders, he was prepared to detect and testify against it. He was zealously concerned to support the testimonies of our society on their original foundation, and mourned over the innovations which the spirit of the world and the deceitfulness of riches produced amongst us. He had of latter times repeatedly informed his friends that he believed he should be suddenly taken from them; and with this belief impressed upon his mind, it is consolatory to think that he endeavoured to have his lamp trimmed and his light burning. Sometimes he expressed a few words in our meetings. On third day morning he rose in our meeting for worship, with the language, "Let no man take thy crown. The way to the kingdom is the same now that ever it was, a tribulated and narrow way—the way of the cross." He recited the reply of Peter to the query of our Lord, "Whom do ye say that I am," and concluded with these words: "'blessed and praised be the name of the Lord, who hath hid these things from the wise and prudent, and revealed them unto babes in Christ." Having solemnly pronounced these words, the latter sentences of which were uttered in a tremulous tone, he quietly took his seat; placed one hand to his cheek, to support his head in his usual contemplative position; then presently let both hands fall by his side, and his head inclined over towards the Friend on his right hand, as though he had fainted away. He was lifted up and carried out. The heart continued to act for a few minutes, but consciousness had ceased, and he gently passed away without a struggle.

THE FRIEND.

A RELIGIOUS AND LITERARY JOURNAL.

VOL. XIII.   SEVENTH DAY, SEVENTH MONTH, 4, 1840.   **NO. 42.**

EDITED BY ROBERT SMITH.

PUBLISHED WEEKLY.

Price two dollars per annum, payable in advance.

Subscriptions and Payments received by

GEORGE W. TAYLOR,

NO. 50, NORTH FOURTH STREET, UP STAIRS,

PHILADELPHIA.

Communicated for "The Friend."

Two Lectures on the History of Literature, with a brief sketch of the various materials made use of for the preservation of Knowledge.

LECTURE SECOND.

Our first lecture closed at a period when the haughty Roman scholar in his city-palace or his rural villa, surrounded by the living thoughts of poets, philosophers and historians, was fostering that luxurious refinement, which eventually destroyed the energy of mind through which alone true literary eminence can be supported. The Roman empire now had attained the zenith of its power. The Atlantic Ocean was its western boundary, the sandy deserts of Libya and Zahara were its southern limits and defence. The Armenian mountains, the bed of the Euphrates and unconquered Arabia marked out its eastern borders, whilst its northern line was yet shifting and changing as the Roman legions advanced into or retired from Gaul. Amid all this apparent strength and prosperity there was mingled much weakness—and the very root of desolation and degradation was there. The empire of Rome was an empire of slaves. The brilliant literature, the learned education, the freedom of thought and of action, were confined to the few. Ignorance, as dark as that which rested on the uncultivated Goth, was the portion of the multitude. Moral instruction was unknown, but new theatres and circuses for the amusement and corruption of the people, were every where erected. A want of the true principles of morals and philosophy had lately led the Roman to consider that military glory was the highest object which mankind could toil after—a lack equally lamentable now rendered them contented with the grossness of sensual delights, enjoyed in luxurious idleness.

The higher classes, with all their civilization and literature, were neither wise as philosophers, nor virtuous as moralists; and the great mass, despised and degraded, without education, or motives to improvement, were sunk in the grossest corruption. Christianity, although neither opposed to sound literature nor true philosophy—in its first introduction into the world was brought into collision with the principles of Gentile authors, and the wisdom of the Grecian and Roman schools. Its doctrines and its morals, pure and simple, were at variance with heathenism in theory, and sensuality in practice; there can be little wonder then that its followers gave no encouragement to the literature of the age. Some of the earliest followers of Jesus, under the pressure of a sense of duty became authors. Illiterate men took the pen, and prompted by the spirit of truth, they wrote what they had seen and heard, in simple, yet expressive language. In their writings, the words of their master, the sayings of the Blessed One are recorded, in which divine wisdom sheds its illuminating rays, in the doctrine delivered, and the morality enforced, whether by parable or by precept. . As the doctrines of Christianity became known, they were so in conformity with the living testimony of the light within, that the heathen felt their force. The grossness of their divinity became too glaring, and as the religion fell into disrepute, the literature which was so closely connected with it, sunk likewise. Heathenism continued for a time to furnish authors, who advocated the philosophy of the ancients—who sang of Jupiter, and the divinities of his court; but the light of genius was departing from the Roman world of letters; and the efforts of present intellect bore as little comparison to the past as the ashes upon the deserted shrines of her deities did to the ever fed fires which once kindled upon them. A few fast fleeting years, and the learning of Europe, the records of wisdom and science, were left to the fostering care of nominal Christians. These were too much engaged in defending their own principles, and in confuting heresies, in suffering for their religion or in contending about forms, to enter the literary arena, or to seek after polish and perfection in style. Although schools were established at various places in the empire, and supported at the public expense, in which lectures were delivered on philosophy, rhetoric, and law, yet real learning and correct taste every where declined. Luxury had rendered the mind as well as body effeminate, and vitiated the judgment in philosophy, in morality, in taste. In composition gaudy ornament took place of the true beauty of simplicity, affectation supplanted nature, and quibbles and sophistry took the gown of philosophy. It was now the autumn of time in the elder progression of science. On the fair tree of Roman literature the buds of its mental spring, had passed into the foliage of an intellectual summer, which now in its maturity was touched by decay, and although gorgeous and rich in appearance beyond even the glory of its earlier days, was ready to perish, like the beautiful frostbitten leaves of the trees of our forest, which now scatter at every blast.* The inroads of barbarians became frequent into Italy, and stores of ancient learning, classic beauty, and marble magnificence perished as they passed. Literary darkness increased; the sun of science had fairly set in western Europe when the seat of empire was removed to Byzantium; and the last rays of its reflected light departed when Rome was taken and sacked by the Goths. Over the muse sung, and art decorated land of Italy, over the civilized borders of Spain, over those German and Gaulish cities where schools of art, of law, and philosophy had flourished—a mingled flood of ignorance, barbarism and bloody superstition from the dark regions of the north spread its devastating waters. The learned men from all these places flocked to the ark at Constantinople, whilst the illiterate race who ruled the country as conquerors, drove the Latin language and literature from every western city in down-trodden Europe.

Greek literature had been applied to by some of the earlier Christians, for weapons with which to repel the adversaries of truth. There were those, however, who denied the propriety of the measure, and who contended that the advocates of a purer religion and a holier practice should draw none of their weapons from these armories of evil. In A. D. 398 the council at Carthage formally condemned the study of the heathen authors of Greece.

If we look to the far east, we shall find the Chinese, soon after the Christian era, in their cool and deliberate manner, cultivating literature and many of the sciences. The Chinese were good at invention but poor at improvement; they made many discoveries but generally failed to perfect them. In the 4th century the Arabians gave attention to poetry, and had annually a kind of literary fairs, which were held at Mecca and other of their cities. These were the scenes of poetical contests, and the poem to which the prize was awarded being written in letters of gold on a very fine cloth called Byssus, was hung up in the Kaaba or temple at Mecca. The Arabians at this time, although a poetic, were a very unlearned and uncivilized people. And thus they continued until after the time of Mohammed, who himself could not write.

This illiterate reformer arose, and overthrowing an ancient superstition, he established a new one. He pointed out to his followers the folly and absurdity of their old creeds, whilst he framed another for them, made large enough and easy enough to take in the joys of this world, and the hope of another. Reasoning against error, he strengthened argument

* Delivered in the eleventh month.

with eloquence, and enforced it and his new dogmas with the sword. Whilst he exhorted his followers to meditation, and bid them descend into their own bosoms, to the light of reason, he stirred them up with a zeal, which admitted not the coolness of reflection, and gave no quiet wherein the whispers of truth might be heard. In the same excitement in which they slaughtered their enemies and dreamed of the Houries, he set them to praying five times in the day. The Arabians embraced these doctrines, they meditated zealously upon them, prayed fervently in conformity therewith; considered opposition as an offence against God to be punished with death,—and heard not that voice whose whispers are peace, and whose word is of mercy and truth. They went forth to conquer, and literature, every where glimmering in the socket, expired as they passed. Scarcely, however, were they known as the destroyers of ancient dynasties, and the enemies of literature, before they established new kingdoms, and the sciences they had trampled on became the objects of their fostering care. With a zeal like that which drove them on to victory, they entered on the race for literary glory. The authors of Greece were soon translated into Arabic, were taken as the text books for schools, and received as supreme in their colleges. The Koran had given permanency to the language—and the invention of cotton paper amongst them, A. D. 708, had furnished an abundant material for the reception of their increasing literature. Under the patronage of the Abbasides at Bagdad the arts and sciences attained a high degree of perfection. Haroun Al Raschid invited the learned men from all countries to make that city their home, and paid them princely salaries. So eager were that race for literary distinction, that Al Mumum the successor of Haroun offered the Greek Emperor at Constantinople 10,000 pounds in gold, and perpetual peace, if he would send the philosopher Leo to instruct him. Al Mumum established excellent schools at Bagdad, Bassora, Bochara, and Cufa,—and large libraries at Alexandria, Bagdad, and Cairo. The Arabian conquerors sweeping through all the northern parts of Africa, had passed into Spain at the straits of Gibralter. A Mahommedan kingdom was established there, in which, under the fostering hand of the Ommiades, literature rivalled the brightness in which it appeared at Bagdad. In Spain there were 15 academies and 70 libraries, and at some of the schools, particularly that at Cordova, in the tenth century, many students from Christian countries sought instruction in mathematics, and a knowledge of medicine.

The learning and literature, however, of the Arabians, depended on the patronage of princes, and not on the taste of the people. It was an exotic, alike unnatural to the religion, and the habits of the nation. That patronage withdrawn, and with the speed of its ascent it regained its ancient level. When learning was reviving in Europe in the thirteenth century, it had already disappeared from the Arabic nations of Africa, and their Asiatic compeers. Adopting the words of Sismondi, we may in truth say, "The vast regions where Islamism rules or has ruled, are dead to all the sciences.

Those rich fields of Fez and Morocco, made illustrious through five centuries by so many academies, so many universities, so many libraries—are nothing more than deserts of burning sands where tyrants contend with tigers. All the laughing and fruitful fields of Mauritanea, where commerce, arts, and agriculture, were raised to the highest prosperity, are at present mere retreats for pirates." "Bagdad, formerly the seat of luxury, of power, of knowledge, is in ruins. The farfamed universities of Cufa and Bassora are closed forever. The immense literary wealth of the followers of Mohammed exists no more in any region where Arabians rule or Mussulmen govern. We are no longer to seek there for the fame of their great men or for their writings. Whatever has been preserved has been by the hands of their enemies; in the convents of monks, or the libraries of European princes. Yet these extensive countries have never been conquered—it is no stranger that has plundered them of their riches; that has annihilated their population—that has destroyed their laws, their manners, and their national spirit. The poison has sprung from themselves; it has arisen indigenously, and has destroyed every thing."

Persian literature partially revived and was encouraged by the Arabian monarchs, during the dominion of the Abbasides. It brightened during the tenth century, and lingered indeed until the close of the fourteenth, when the desolations of Timour the Tartar, came as a flood upon its expiring embers.

Amongst the rude inhabitants of the north of Europe, soon after the Christian era, we find that historical and descriptive poetry was cultivated and encouraged. The skalds or travelling minstrels of that day, were considered as companions for princes, and were liberally rewarded by them. There was little, however, in their poetry, to soften, to humanize the heart of the hearers, or to polish and elevate the taste. The glory, the slaughter of war, absurd mythological fables, all tending to foster ferocity, were enwreathed with the flowers of their literature, were the themes and the charm of their verse. Yet learning found some encouragement at the north, and in the Icelandic region of frost and fire, it was quickened into life, before it revived in the sunnier climes of the south.

Of all places once bright with knowledge, Constantinople was the only one in which, from the Christian era almost to the very period of the revival of literature, learning found a constant asylum, and the arts a home. But even there, though surrounded by libraries, though books were abundant, though close study was not wanting, the cause of knowledge was not onward. The memory was laden with information of the poetry, the philosophy, the history of the past, but the operation of original thought, the manifestation of unfettered genius, never kindled along the lines of their histories, to make room for which, the burning words of their forefathers had been erased from the parchment. Possessed of the intellectual wealth of past ages, they had not energy to turn it to account; acquainted with the philosophy of the ancients, they adopted its sophistry, whilst they fell far short of its

wisdom. With the volume of the sacred writings at hand, and ever contending on points of divinity, their morality stretched no further than heathenism, nor their religion than ceremonies. They had learning without thought, knowledge without invention, philosophy without wisdom, and religion without virtue. The following reflection which is found in the pages of Sismondi, and which is peculiarly adapted to the condition of things at that time in Constantinople, seems to me worthy of consideration in all ages. He says "It is not books that we want to preserve, it is the mind of man; not the receptacles of thought, but the faculty of thinking. Were it necessary to choose between the whole experience which has been acquired and collected from the beginning of time, the whole rich store of human wisdom, and the more unschooled activity of the human mind, the latter ought without hesitation to be preferred. This is the precious and living germ which we ought to watch over, to foster, to guard from every blight. This alone, if it remain uninjured, will repair all losses; while on the contrary, mere literary wealth will not preserve one faculty nor sustain one virtue."

Charlemagne of France and Germany, in the eighth century, and Alfred of England, in the ninth, encouraged literature in their respective dominions. Charlemagne could not write himself, yet he complains of the ignorance of his clergy, and Alfred declared, that from the Thames to the Humber there was not one priest who understood the service he recited. The literary taste which Charlemagne infused quickly subsided, and the coal which Alfred enkindled, though never totally extinguished, required the breath of centuries to fan it into vigour.

In the tenth century, the faint fires of learning were kept burning in the monasteries, and the literature of the people was confined to the love and war songs of the Troubadours. It was the age of chivalry and slavery. Of nobility without taste or learning, of a people without acknowledged rights. During this and two subsequent centuries, the sword was esteemed more than knowledge, and knightly honour than virtue or religion.

From the sixth to the fourteenth centuries the loss of classical manuscripts had been going forward with great rapidity. Time had decayed, and the fire had thinned them; but when the Saracens closed the manufactories of papyrus, in Egypt, they gave a new impetus to the work of destruction. In the quiet retreats of monastic seclusion, literary men found time to compose, and as new parchment and papyrus were scarce to be met with, the ancient manuscripts were erased to make room for the new. Thus the beautifully wrought heathenish divinity, where fact and fable were told in that style of classic elegance which admitted no impurity but that of morals, gave place very frequently to as absurd tales clothed in barbarous language by some dreaming monk, which though nominally Christian, was only better than its predecessor in that its dulness consigned it to oblivion.

(To be continued.)

On the Habits and Instincts of Animals. By William Swainson. A. C. G., Fellow of the Royal Society, and of several Foreign Academies.

(Continued from p. 308.)

HYBERNATION, TORPIDITY, AND MIGRATION OF ANIMALS.

The changeful breezes of spring have passed, and the glowing warmth of summer's sun gladdens and revives all nature. Every thing looks bright and joyous; and the animal, as well as the vegetable world, appears endued with fresh life, and strength, and vigour. The note of love, and the voice of happiness resound through the woods and meadows, united in one sweet and general chorus; while, to the pious heart, this universal concert seems, in the accents of harmony, to speak the praises of that great and gracious Being whose creative hand first formed, and still sustains the wondrous whole. But the bloom of spring passes away; winter, with its stern and chilling aspect, closes the annual circle of time. What, then, becomes of that variety of animals, many of whose delicate forms are incapable of sustaining the rigour of this inhospitable season? Are they left, unprotected, to meet their destiny, or struggle with their fate? No : the same wise and merciful God, who first called them into life, now directs them by unerring instinct, in what manner to prepare for the storm and the tempest. And, perhaps, in no part of the wise economy of nature is the Almighty agency more clearly apparent, than in these several preparations for a period which none of them could foresee, and the approaches of which many of them had never before experienced.

Animals avoid extreme cold in three different ways,—by hybernation, by torpor, and by migration. We shall now take a rapid view of the animal circle, and slightly touch upon such as afford us examples of these instincts. The first two will be treated of conjointly ; the migration of animals, separately.

Of the manner in which such zoophytes and animalculæ as survive the year, pass the winter months, in cold latitudes, we know very little. The greater part of those which are not formed to survive the year, naturally perish, having reached their destined age ; but such as are of longer life, and are endowed with locomotion, in all probability retire to the deep recesses of the ocean, or, at least, beyond the influence of atmospheric air ; while, according to Ellis, they are generally found to be contracted or torpid during this period. With regard to the molusca, or shell fish, our information is equally defective. From the number of empty shells frequently seen on the margins of our fresh water ponds, it seems probable that several of our native fluviatile univalves perish in autumn, while the rest retire to the deepest crevices. Most of the land shells close the opening to their habitations, at the beginning of winter, with a thick white coon, or false operculum, by which it is securely sheltered; they also seek a further protection in the hollows of banks and trees. The garden slug generally forms for itself a winter retreat beneath the earth, close to the roots of plants.

Reptiles are particularly subject to the law of torpidity. The Greek tortoise (Testudo Græca), and probably others of the same group, burrows a hole in the ground, into which it retires for several months. White, of Shelborne, who attentively observed the manners and habits of one of these animals, states, that it regularly took up its subterranean station in November, and did not reappear until the following-April. Having occasion to carry it from the residence of the lady to whom it belonged, to his own home in Hampshire, it was dug up in March, 1780, and conveyed in a chaise to the place of its destination. An eighty miles journey had so far recovered it from its torpor, that it walked about for a short time on being turned into the garden; but towards evening, the weather being cold, it again insinuated itself into the earth, and remained in concealment for a month. The green lizard of Carolina hastens, on the approach of winter, into the hollows or crevices of decayed trees ; and the chamelion retires into the holes of rocks, or some other equally safe retreat, where it is supposed to become torpid. Similar retreats, we suspect, are chosen by the numerous lizards of the south of Europe, more especially as they are always more numerous near stone walls and rocks, in the spring, than in any other localities. Serpents, inhabiting cold and temperate climates, become torpid during the winter. They are said principally to retire under ground, from whence they emerge upon the return of warm weather. We are told, by an American writer, that, on a fine spring day, numbers of rattlesnakes may be seen creeping out, in an apparently languid state, and assembling together, for the object of basking in the rays of the sun.

Passing over the class of birds, in which no well-authenticated instance of hybernation or torpidity is known, it may be observed, that quadrupeds have three different modes of guarding against winter, viz., migrating, burrowing, or becoming torpid. Few species, comparatively, are migratory animals ; for their locomotive powers being much more confined than those of birds, it would be impossible for them to pass over such enormous distances as would produce a change of climate.

The Alpine hare and the field mouse are interesting examples among the instances of burrowing quadrupeds ; and the sagacious care with which these animals provide for their winter support is truly admirable. The most remarkable of the torpid quadrupeds are the bears of North America, who are well known to form caves, in which they fall into a state of complete or partial somnolency. Bats, in the same manner, retire into caverns, hollow trees, or old buildings, in vast numbers, where they pass the winter in a state of torpidity. The loir, or fat dormouse, however, is a more interesting example : it rolls itself into a ball, and in that state, as it has been said, may be tossed about without its being awakened to consciousness—nothing appearing to effect its resuscitation but long exposure to heat.

The jumping mouse of Canada, according to a communication made by General Davies, makes a very curious and artificial preparation for the cold season, a specimen of which was discovered in a gentleman's garden, about two miles from Quebec, in the latter end of May, 1787. "It was," we are told, "inclosed in a ball of clay, about the size of a cricket-ball, nearly an inch in thickness, perfectly smooth within, and about twenty inches under ground. The man," it is added, " who first discovered it, not knowing what it was, struck the ball with his spade, by which means it was broken to pieces, or the ball would also have been presented to me." The mus cricetus, or hamster, however, above all other quadrupeds, appears to fall into the most complete torpidity,—every animal function being so completely deadened, that it is said the creature may be cut open without exhibiting any signs of sensibility : the heart, however, may be observed to contract and dilate alternately, but with a motion so slow, that the pulsations do not exceed fourteen or fifteen in the space of a minute. The strongest stimulants are of no avail ; and the electric shock may be passed through the animal without exciting any appearance of irritability.

Amphibious animals of cold and temperate climates generally pass the winter, like the tortoises, beneath the surface, in a state of torpidity. Frogs and toads both burrow into the earth at this season. Hearne, the traveller, when in Arctic America, met with frogs in such a completely frozen state, that, although their legs were broken, the injury did not appear to cause the slightest sensation to the animal. He, however, adds, that, by wrapping them up in skins, and exposing them to a slow fire, they have been restored to activity.

The generality of insects, during winter, pass into a state of temporary torpor. "The sites chosen for their hybernacula," as Kirby and Spencer well observe, " are very various ; some merely insinuate themselves under a very large stone ; others prefer a collection of dead leaves, or the moss on the sheltered side of an old wall or bank ; others seek a retreat in the moss itself, or bury themselves deep in the rotten trunk ; while numbers penetrate into the earth to the depth of several inches. Those insects which bear considerable cold without injury, are less careful about their winter retreats ; while the more tender species either enter the earth beyond the reach of frost, or prepare for themselves artificial cavities in various substances, such as moss and rotten wood, which conduct heat with difficulty, and defend them from an injuriously low temperature." The same authors also state, that the first cold weather which occurs after insects have entered their winter quarters, produces precisely the same effect upon them as upon many species of the larger animals. " At first, a partial benumbment takes place ; but the insect, if touched, is still capable of moving its organs. But, as the cold increases, all the animal functions cease ; the insect breathes no longer, and has no need of a supply of air ; its nutritive secretions cease, and no more food is required ; the muscles lose their irritability, and it has all the external symptoms of death. In this state it continues during the existence of great cold ; but the degree of its torpidity varies with the temperature of the atmosphere. The recurrence of a mild day, such as we sometimes have in winter, infuses a partial animation into the stiffened animal; if disturbed, its limbs and antennæ resume their power of extension; and even the faculty of spurting out their defensive fluid is reacquired by many beetles. But, however mild the atmosphere in winter, the great bulk of hybernating insects, as if conscious of the deceptive nature of their pleasurable feelings, and that no food could then be procured, never quit their quarters, but quietly wait for a renewal of their insensibility by a fresh accession of cold."

(To be continued.)

JANE STUART.

OF WISBEACH, IN CAMBRIDGESHIRE.

[TO THE EDITOR OF THE IRISH FRIEND.]

A * * *, 4th month 10th, 1840.

Respected Friend,—A friend of mine, travelling some time since in Cambridgeshire, found a curious and interesting entry in the Friends' Register of Burials at Wisbeach, respecting Jane Steward, or, rather, Stuart, of that place. The following, including the erasure, is an exact copy of the Register :—

J. S. } "Jane Stuart departed this Life on 12th
of 7th mo., on first day, about one o'clock, } 1742
ye. 14th, aged 88.   King
Supposed to be descended from James 2nd she lived in a cellar in the old Market Wisbech—the house has been rebuilt by Cha. Freeman—

Respecting this extraordinary individual, the following notices appeared, thirty years ago, in the 28th and 29th vols. of the "Monthly Magazine, or British Register:" at that time one of the most influential periodicals of the day :—

From the Monthly Mag., 30th mo. 1st, 1809.

"*Extracts from the Portfolio of a Man of Letters.*

"A natural daughter of King James 2nd, was convicted of *Friends'* principles, and imprisoned for the same with Thomas Ellwood, &c. Upon her being engaged to a young man for marriage, and the day fixed, as they were on the road the coach overturned, and her intended husband was killed, and his brother broke his leg. She stayed in London, and nursed the young man till he recovered; when, assuming some habit of disguise, she travelled on foot to the Isle of Ely, and, inquiring at some *Friend's* house for employment, the master asked her 'What she could do?' She answered, 'she was willing to put her hand to any thing.' He then said, 'canst thou reap?' She replied, 'she could hardly tell; but, if he pleased, she would try.' So he sent her into the field; and, before evening, she discovered herself to be so great a proficient at reaping as to be called 'Queen of the Reapers.' She constantly attended the adjacent meeting; and, observing a rock hard by, she either put up with a natural cave in the rock, or had a cell made therein, where she lived, quite recluse, spinning for her employment. She told Sarah Taylor, that she 'enjoyed such contentment and peace, that she would not leave her cell and spinning-wheel to be Queen of England.' She had been at most of the European courts, particularly at the Hanoverian and Prussian; and the Pre-

tender being her supposed brother, she once travelled, by chaise, into Scotland to see him."

From the Mo. Mag., 2d mo. 1st, 1810.

"*To the Editor of the Monthly Magazine.*

"Sir,—Jane Stuart, the extraordinary character, of whom some account is given in the Monthly Magazine, for October last, supposed to be a natural daughter of King James 2nd, after renouncing the world, and splendour of courts, resided at Wisbech, in Cambridgeshire. It is to be regretted that few memorials remain of her; but two ancient and respectable inhabitants, now deceased, have related to the writer of this the following incidents :—

"When she first came, she sought employment by standing (as is usual with labourers, at this day, who want work) on or near the foot of the bridge, where, in hay-time and harvest, the farmers resort every morning to hire. She selected for her abode a cellar, in a part of the town called the Old Market, where she spun worsted ; to dispose of which, she regularly had a stall on the market-day. Being once thus employed, she recognised, by the arms and livery, a coach and attendants, going to the principal inn, (the ' Rose and Crown,') near to which her stall stood; upon which, she immediately packed up her worsted, retired to her cell, and carefully concealed herself. The owner, who was said to be the Duke of Argyle, endeavoured to find her; but without effect. The house, under which she lived, has been since rebuilt; and part of it is now occupied by the Lady Mary Knollis, aunt to the present Earl of Banbury. She constantly attended, when in health, the meeting of the Society of Friends, in Wisbech ; was humble and exemplary in her conduct; well esteemed by her neighbours—invariably avoided all conversation relative to her family connections ; and, when in the freedom of intercourse, any expression inadvertently escaped, leading to an inquiry, she stopped short, seemed to regret having disclosed so much, and silenced further research. She read the New Testament in Greek ; but even this circumstance was discovered accidentally, by an unexpected call ;—was fond of birds, which were frequently allowed to leave their cages, and fly about in her apartment. When near eighty, she had a new set of teeth. She died (according to the Friends' Register) the 12th of 7th mo., 1742, aged 88, and was buried in the society's grave-yard, at Wisbech ; where, out of respect to her memory, box has been planted round her grave, with her initials, age, and date, which still remain to mark the spot of her interment.

"Yours, &c., A."

I may add to these extracts, that the box-planting on the grave is yet preserved ; and is trimmed short, so as still to exhibit the initials, &c., arranged as under :—

J. S.,

aged 88,

1742.

Selected for " The Friend."

TO THE NORTH STAR.

Beautiful star !
The brightest jewel on night's ebon brow,
For ages thou hast gazed as thou art gazing now,
  On this world's feverish jar.

Far in the northern pole
Thy clear and steady flame burns without end :
While other planets on their journeys tend,
  For ever doomed to roll.

But thou, O beacon bright in heaven's blue sea !
Dost never from thy moorings break away ;
But hangest out thy constant flame for aye,
  That shipwrecked men may look to thee.

The mariner, when his bark
Is driven across the ocean, bleak and drear,
And cheerlessly the breeze screams in his ear,
  And midnight shrouds his billowy track,

Casts o'er the waste his straining eye,
And through the driving tempest looks to thee ;
From the torn deck, and from the boiling sea,
  He turns for guidance from the sky.

The moon shines when the eve grows dim ;
She fills her golden horns with light, and then
Fadeth away and is obscured again
  Through all her curved rim.

But thou dost never pale thy flame.
But steadily, throughout the lapse of time,
Dost keep unmoved thy lonely throne sublime,
  —For ever still the same !

The planets in their orbits disappear,
The twinkling stars haste on their cloudy path,
The round red sun an endless journey hath,
  But thou art fastened in thy sphere.

Then art a beauteous type, bright star !
Of that pure star, religion ! on whose ray
The Christian looks for guidance on his way,
  When human passions wage their war.

Upon the troublous seas of life,
When tumults stir the bosoms of mankind,
Then to religion's steady light, his mind
  Turns for a refuge from their strife.

WESTERN AFRICA.

In the Missionary Herald for June, 1840, is a general letter from the missionaries, at Cape Palmas, Dec. 6th, 1839, from which we make the following extracts:

"We would remark here, as it is the subject of frequent inquiry with our correspondents, that we do not think the capacities of African children for learning is any way inferior to that of children in our own country. And it may be safely affirmed, that they pursue their studies with more eagerness, and in some instances with more success, than any children we have known. To adduce a solitary proof of this assertion, it may be stated that we have boys of not more than ten years of age, who write without any assistance, sensible and connected compositions upon such subjects as the early history of England, origin of the English language, etc." The same letter states, " in this vicinity they have not bought slaves for many years past, but it has been a favourite resort for the purchase of rice for the slave factories ; and the article which the purchasers have usually given in exchange for rice, has been rum, the influence of which upon a community like this needs not to be told."—*Anti-Slavery Reporter.*

PRINTED BY ADAM WALDIE,
Carpenter Street, below Seventh, Philadelphia.

For "The Friend."

EARLY FRIENDS IN NEW ENGLAND.

It would be interesting could one have the opportunity of rummaging among the old records of our eastern brethren for the notices, doubtless therein to be found, of the persecutions endured by some of the early Friends who felt themselves constrained to preach the truth in those regions in primitive times. Much curious matter might be anticipated; some, it may be, which we had rather not " dig out of the dust of antiquity,"—for there may have been weak ones upon the skirts of our flock, who, not having perfectly triumphed over the infirmities of the flesh, shrunk at the prospect of suffering for the testimony.;—though, on the other hand, knowing how the arm of the Lord was with many of his faithful servants, whose memorial is among us, we might reasonably expect to find—should those records at all approach the truth—some noble, and perhaps forgotten examples of that Christian firmness and valour, so wonderfully tempered with meekness and resignation, which has always distinguished the true soldier of the cross.

That such records, yet unpublished to the world, do exist, would seem to be a fact, from a little volume which issued no great while ago from the Boston press, containing some particulars relative to sufferers for the name and testimony of Jesus, in that town; which, from the standing of the author, Abel Cushing, formerly senator from Norfolk, Mass. it is not to be supposed are imaginary, though evidently somewhat coloured, either by the recorder, or by Cushing himself.

The author, we must remember, however, is a politician, a profession, at this day, whatever it may once have been, not much afflicted with those troublesome scruples which sometimes beset the honest historian, and impel to many a tedious and toilsome chase after the exact truth: he is therefore to be read with caution. He had an object in writing his little book; he says, and perhaps he thinks, it was the edification of his republican brethren; for strange fancies seize upon knowing men sometimes. And truly his fellow republicans might find, would they read aright, instruction therein, though not in way and manner designed. He appears to be what is called a leveller—an enemy to many of the established modes of mutual co-operation—the determined foe of corporations, and especially of banks—and to entertain a thoroughly democratic horror of all attempts by the state to take care of the religious interests of its citizens, except in so far as to prevent their meddling with one another on that account. Whether he would confess to such a portrait is doubtful, probably not; such, nevertheless, is the semblance of himself shadowed forth in the "Historical letters on the first charter of Massachusetts government." He would establish a parallel between the religious persecutors of old, and those whom he holds to be the financial persecutors of this generation—between the old Puritans and the modern bankers! He tells how the former erred in hanging Quakers and drowning witches, and would have his reader aroused to, what he possibly may himself believe to be the fact, that the latter are imbued with a sufficient share of the very same malignant spirit, and may, if not tightly reined, likewise plunge into some horrible excess! However, any notice of these whims and alarms has nothing to do with my object, except to give the reader of what follows a clue to some of his expressions and turns of thought.

The book is divided into twenty-five chapters or "letters," six of which are chiefly devoted to a narration of the persecutions inflicted upon Friends. Some of the particulars given are not contained in any other work that I have seen, and probably they will be new to the generality of readers. I purpose transcribing below the greater part of them, not binding myself, however, always to adhere to the language of the original. The first four letters treat of the banishment of Roger Williams, and the Hutchinsonian heresy, the fifth was intended for a sketch of the rise of Quakerism, and takes some notice of Mary Fisher. What follows is from

LETTER VI.

There can be no doubt but the early Quakers were conscientious missionaries. Perhaps none in any age or country were ever more sincere. And what a modicum of true Christianity, or humanity even, would have taught those to whom they came, to bear with them. It is easy to discern what kind of influences ruled here, under free forms of government, when the advent to these shores of six female and two men Quakers should have caused a law in substance thus:—

That any citizen causing a Quaker to come into the country, should, on conviction, pay a penalty of one hundred pounds; and for entertaining a Quaker, knowing him to be such, was finable at the rate of forty shillings an hour. For the first offence of Quakerism, by citizen or stranger,—if a man, he should have one ear cut off; and for the second offence, the other ear; if a woman, first to be whipped, and put into the house of correction, and for the second offence to lose one of her ears, and for the third offence, by man or woman, to have his or her tongue bored through with a hot iron.

The first application of this law was to two English women, Sarah Gibbons and Dorothy Waugh. These coming to Boston ventured to address the people on lecture-day after the regular services were over, and they were taken up, thrust into the house of correction and whipped.

Not long after, a woman named Gardner, coming to Weymouth with her infant child, was proved to be a Quakeress. She was carried to Boston and whipped, as also a young damsel; her companion, with a three-corded knotted whip, and after the punishment she kneeled down and prayed to the Lord to forgive her persecutors.

The two next were William Brend and William Leddra. These being taken up at Salem for being Quakers wrongfully in the jurisdiction, they were carried to Boston, and put into the house of correction and ordered to work. This they refused; for which they were whipped twenty blows each with a three-corded whip, and then commanded to depart from the charter limits. But the marshal's fees were demanded of them. They declined paying the cost of their own punishment, and were still detained to work it out. The next morning William Brend still refusing to work, the jailer in a rage seized a tarred rope, and beat him therewith until the prisoner fainted. Upon this a report went abroad that the man was killed in prison; and a tumult among the people was feared; whereupon, Endicot, the governor, and the magistrates posted notices on the church doors and other public places, that Brend had revived, and was well, but that the jailer should be punished for his cruelty.

But J. Norton, a preacher, a mortal enemy to Quakers, and a great instrument of the laws against them, declared publicly that the stripes were good enough for men who had, come here to beat their gospel ordinances black and blue.

John Copeland and Christopher Holder came over about the time of Mary Fisher; and two years after, they were arrested at Dedham, carried to Boston, and imprisoned with one named Rouse. At the next court of assistants they were brought in for trial, Endicot presiding, who said, " since you three, in contempt of the magistrates and ministers, have come here to seduce the people, whether you lose your ears or your lives, your blood will be on yourselves."

To this the Quakers boldly answered, that the Lord God had sent them here.

Nay, said the governor, but under pretence of peace you have come to poison the people. How do you prove the Lord hath sent you?

You scourge and persecute us, was the reply; and Christ told his disciples they should suffer such things for his name's sake.

Then, said Major Denison, one of the assistants, every malefactor who is whipped, suffers for Christ's sake.

But do ye not know, said Rouse, that if we were malefactors, God's judgments would be far heavier upon us than your punishments?

John Copeland, John Rouse, again. said the major, you are yet a youth, and I hear are well born and bred, your father being a king's officer at Barbadoes, and a gentleman: what heavier judgment of God do you look for, (unless it be a halter,) than to be driven from home, and to run about here with a set of vagabonds and deceivers?

I was not driven from my father's house, said Rouse, but at the command of the Lord I left it, and when he shall clear me of this land I will gladly return home again.

But why do we parley, said Endicot. You see these Quakers have no commission but the spirit within them, and that's the devil;—secretary, read the law to the prisoners: and when this was done, one of them said, we have seen many of your laws having much scripture reference in their margin, but what scripture have you for cutting off ears?

What scripture is there for hanging people, said Endicot?

Perhaps, said Denison, they would like to be crucified; there's scripture enough for that.

After consultation, Endicot called the prisoners by name, and said, the sentence of the court is, that each of you have his right ear cut off by the hangman.

Here the Quakers earnestly protested against the proceeding. They declared that they were Englishmen, and not subject to the colonial laws; they were subject only to English laws and the English court. But Endicot called out; no appeal to England; we shall allow of no appeal to England.

The marshal then took them to the apartment where execution was to be done, and when he had let in the hangman and one or two others, he locked the door, and read the order of the court.

Again these three protested against the illegality and injustice of the procedure; and Holder further said that such an execution should not be done in private: but they told him it was to prevent their appealing to the people. There is no doubt that Norton, Endicot, and their associates, feared a public execution of this character.

The executioner then took Holder by the head, and as he brushed away the hair to come at the ear, the marshal turned away in manifest disgust and sorrow; but Rouse said, thou must turn again and see the execution, for such is the order. True, true indeed, said he, I was to *see* it done, we must look on; and he saw the blood follow the hangman's knife most profusely, as he threw the ear on the floor.

Thus these three unresisting Quakers suffered this ignominious mutilation with patience, and even without a sigh.

When it was over, they declared, that the ignorant they forgave. For those who had done this thing maliciously, every drop of their blood would sit heavy on their souls at the great day of accounts.

After this they were ordered out of the jurisdiction.

CONVERSION OF AN INFIDEL.

From the Irish Friend.

About the year 1799 I became acquainted with a native of Ireland, who, in his early youth, went to Germany, where he was educated at one of the colleges, and was brought up in the Roman Catholic persuasion, the inconsistency of which, he told me, he very early saw. The bigotry, superstition, and wickedness of the priests was such as to give him a disgust to religion—believing, he said, that the foundation of it was dissimulation and priestcraft. When he left the university, he was introduced to the emperor, Joseph the Second, to whom he was one of the lords of the belchamber, and he soon became an officer of rank in the German army. The emperor made him a count, in addition to his hereditary titles of marquis and viscount, and a grandee of the first order in Spain. He was related to some of the first nobility in England and Ireland. At the commencement of our acquaintance, he expressed a wish to know something of the principles of Friends; and, having read Barclay's Apology, in returning it to me, he told me it was the best written book on divinity he had ever seen; and, if it were possible to act according to the sentiments contained in it, no man could act wrong; but he added, "I have something to say to you in private, and which I hardly dare say to any other man. Unfortunately for me, I do not believe in any system of religion—I do not believe in the existence of a God. You may be sure it is a subject that has given me a great deal of thought; and, when I came into this Protestant country, I had hoped I should have discovered the essence of truth, and that the Protestant clergy would have given the lie to the impressions I had imbibed, from my early prejudices, on account of the dissolute and abandoned lives of the Romish clergy; but, alas! I see that there is the same system of deception carried on in England as in Germany. The clergy have only one thing in view, and that is the accumulation of wealth, and where it can be done, to endeavour after splendour and aggrandizement. As to their flocks, 'tis a matter of no consequence whether they are ignorant or wise. It appears no part of their study to aim at their religious improvement, so that I find myself just where I was. I observe that all mankind are alike—they pretend to religion, they talk of it, and there they leave it. As a confirmation of what I say, I beg inform you, that, on my first coming into these parts, I paid a visit to my relations in Ireland, who showed great hospitality and kindness to me, and, as is usual in that country, there were large convivial parties, where neither the manners nor the conversation would bear much reflection, even in an infidel, (as I suppose I should be called.) It happened that the conversation one evening took a religious turn, in the course of which I inadvertently leaned towards scepticism *at least*; on which one of the company hastily said—'Surely, sir, you do not doubt the existence of a Supreme Being?' to which I replied—'What are your sentiments on that subject?' Why, sir, my sentiments are these: I look upon the Almighty as of infinite purity; as the object of both love and fear—and that I am in his immediate presence—it is through him I live and move and have my being—I consider that I am amenable to him for every action of my life—that if I do evil voluntarily, I run the risk of his eternal displeasure, and wretchedness will be my portion, but if I act according to his will, I shall be eternally happy.' 'Is this, sir, really and truly your belief?' 'Yes, sir, it undoubtedly is, and is also the belief of every well-regulated Christian.' 'Then, sir, how comes it to pass that your actions correspond so little with your professions? Is it possible that such a hearsay evidence as this would convince me, were I an atheist, of the truth of God's existence? Has any part of your conduct, since we have been so often together, manifested either *love, fear,* or *reverence,* for this object of your pretended regard? I wish not to give you offence; but see whether there be any thing like consistency in your declarations and the conduct I fear you are habitually in the practice of.' My friend seemed confused and thoughtful, and I immediately turned the discourse to another subject." I was much struck with so much of this conversation, and was considerably more so when he told me in confidence that he had left Germany on account of his objection to serve any longer in the army—that the thoughts of taking away the life of a fellow-man had become distressing and perplexing to him, so much so, that he could, in no way, be accessory to the death of a fellow-creature. He added, that since he had been in England, a relation of his, the Marquis of B——, had kindly offered to raise a regiment of horse in Ireland, and to get him the command, which he politely refused on the above ground; which was the occasion of the marquis's displeasure, and the loss of his friendship. I felt much interested about this person, and carefully concealed from every one what his sentiments were. I apprehended, when there appeared such great sincerity, the Almighty would, in his own time, reveal himself to him. He seemed much gratified in attending our religious meetings, and I had many times seen him much affected, and in tears in them. He used frequently, in a modest way, to argue the point of his disbelief with me; but never, I believe, as to himself to much purpose. I lent him several books, in which the existence of God was treated on, but all seemed unavailing. He had made notes on a Bible I had lent him almost through the whole book, in opposition to its precepts and doctrines.—Towards the close of the period of his infidelity he requested I would lend him Newton's Principia, which I refused, on the ground that he had wandered so much in the dark by seeking for that without, which was only to be found within, that I advised him to keep his mind still and quiet; adding, that I believed the Almighty would one day make himself known to him, but he must not be surprised if he should do it in such a way, as to all outward appearance would, in his view, be contemptible.

A few weeks after this, two female friends, A—— C——, and D—— M——, having a concern to visit the families and friends who attended Westminster Meeting; as he had now been a pretty constant attender, his name was set down with two others, and I requested the Friends to let me sit with them. Very soon after we sat down, Divine goodness was pleased to overshadow this little assembly, I mean in the silent part of it. The poor object of this little narrative in a few minutes burst into tears, and continued in this humble state for near twenty minutes, before a word was spoken. When one of the females, unlettered and unlearned as to human attainments, but who waited for Christ to be her instructor, in a few words expressed herself to this effect: that she had felt an extraordinary solemnity on our first sitting down, so much so, that she feared to speak, though she feared to keep silence, more especially, as the subject which had come before her was of a truly awful nature. "Surely," she added, "there is no person present who has any doubts respecting the existence of a supreme being; if there is, I would have such to look into their own hearts, and observe the operation of something they cannot but feel, more especially when they have committed an evil action—how does it torment the poor mind, and render it for a time in continued uneasiness; on the other hand, when they have acted well, avoid the temptation to evil, what a sweet glow of approbation has covered the mind! From whence proceeds this uneasiness or this approbation? It must proceed from something,—

man could not communicate these sensations to himself! Be assured they come from God —nay, it is God himself who thus speaks in the inmost of the heart." The Friend said but little more, but to the person to whom it was addressed, it was a volume—it was as though the windows of heaven were opened. To myself it was an opportunity never to be forgotten. About two days from the above period, my Friend called on me in the evening, and requested to have some conversation with me, which I readily agreed to: he, without much preface, told me that he knew not how he could be sufficiently grateful to me, for the patience I had endured with him, and for the kind concern I had manifested for his welfare; but added, " I believe it will give you inconceivable pleasure to be informed that I have not a doubt remaining. I am abundantly thankful to that Almighty Being, who, in mercy, has made himself known to this poor benighted heart of mine in some degree, through the instrumentality of that dear woman, though I may acknowledge to you, that, before a word was spoken, the business was completed. I had taken great pains, as you know, to invalidate the Scripture testimonies, but, at that solemn and heavenly opportunity, all the arguments I had made use of for this purpose, reverted back, and I became confounded and ashamed. I felt, as it were, all at once the certain evidence of a merciful and kind God, which so overcame me, that I could only show my love and gratitude by my tears, so that for a while, I appeared as in heaven; that is, in a situation of mind far beyond what any earthly object could bestow. The dear woman was doubtless sensible of my situation, and confirmed to me the evidence I felt in my own soul. I this evening thought, that though I had been thus favoured, it would be difficult to point out the divinity of Christ, a thing which I then conceived as altogether absurd; but on coming up your steps, and waiting to speak to you, the whole mystery was unfolded; and I now have no doubts on this subject." He also entered on the subject of the creation of man, and other religious subjects, in a way that astonished me. His very nature seemed altered, and his countenance seemed changed, as from the haughtiness of a man possessing outward rank in society, he now became mild and passive, like a little child, joined to the disposition of a lamb. He lamented, several months after, his being obliged to return to Germany; previous to which he requested some of Friends' writings, acknowledging that he felt more satisfaction in reading them than any other; and he attended Friends' meetings, till he left England.

From the Irish Friend.

REFUGE FOR THE HOUSELESS POOR.

Islington, 4th Mo. 1st, 1840.

Respected Friend—A few weeks ago, I went, in company with a friend, after our evening meeting on a first day, to view that remarkable and philanthropic establishment, " The Refuge for the Houseless Poor"—situate in an obscure yard near Whitecross street in the city. Having felt a singular, but melancholy satisfaction in the scene which presented itself, I am induced to lay the account of our visit before thy readers, many of whom, more particularly those in the country, may not have heard of the existence of such a receptacle of human destitution; and, it is more than probable, they may not have at all conceived the necessity of providing such an establishment. But, when we bring into view, the well known fact, that, in this great Metropolis, there are thousands of our fellow beings who have no place of their own wherein to rest their weary limbs at night, and are driven for shelter to the cellars and other abodes of misery in which they are provided with a lodging, such as it is, on prepayment of 4d. per night; and that frequently in the winter season, whilst out of work, even this poor accommodation is beyond their means to purchase; then the great importance of providing a temporary shelter for the " houseless poor" becomes self-evident to every reflecting mind. For want of such a protection in the night, many have perished in the inclement seasons of the year, in the markets of the city, under sheds, and other exposed places—not having elsewhere to lay down their heads.

The spacious building, to which I have alluded, consists of three large floors, above the ground, and appears to have been built as chambers for wool, or such like merchandise, which have since been roughly, but conveniently, adapted to the several purposes to which they are now appropriated. On entering the outer doors, from the street, there is a small office, at the bar of which every fresh applicant presents himself, and gives his name, his age, and his parish, or the town from which he comes. Here he tells his tale of woe, and the causes which have led to his present destitution ; (and the same routine is observed in the case of the females;) all these particulars are carefully noted by the proper officer, in a large book kept for the purpose; and it is easy to imagine, that this singular volume portrays an epitome of human wretchedness, not often put upon record. After the poor man has passed his examination, he is shown to a large trough of water, where he undergoes a tolerably good purification of his person: when he is examined by the surgeon, who reporting him free of infectious disorders, he is directed to his place amongst his new companions. In this way, hundreds of poor objects, of both sexes, during the winter months, are received every night, and dismissed in the morning; many, like Noah's dove, not finding any rest for their weary limbs, return again and again; whilst others, happily procuring better quarters, are seen no more: the absentees, however, are generally outnumbered by the newcomers, particularly if the weather prove inclement, and work, out of doors, at a stand. This asylum is open to all ; it needs no certificate of character, letter of recommendation, or humble petition, to gain admittance within these hospitable walls; neither native or alien, age or sex, black or white, saint or sinner, is excluded : all may come who will, and be received freely. Here the puling infant, in its poor mother's arms, and all the intermediate gradations of age, to the hoary-headed man or woman of threescore years and ten, can lay them down, and, *for a while*, forget their sorrows. One only exception to this noble rule is made—an instance of which occurred whilst we were there :—A middle aged man, in great apparent destitution, applied for admission for the night; but, on being examined by the surgeon, he was reported to have a cutaneous disease, of an infectious character; and, from this cause, was necessarily denied admittance. He was, however, dismissed with expressions of kindness from the manager on duty ; a ration of bread was given him, and a shilling ; with directions where he might apply in the morning for medical assistance.

As I before observed, the building is large, and consists of three lofty airy rooms, one on each floor above the ground floor. The lowest is appropriated to the men's sleeping room, and the upper floor to that for the women and little children ; the middle floor is used as a chapel on First days, where, when we arrived, the company (about 300) were assembled. (The numbers vary every night more or less, and have sometimes even exceeded 600 men, women, and children.) They were then at their worship, and chanting songs of praise to the great Creator, to " Him from whom all blessings flow ;" in which they were joined by several gentlemen present, who appear to devote much of their time to these poor outcasts. The religious service is conducted by one of the royal chaplains ; and it very frequently happens, that he does duty in the morning before the Queen and her household in the Chapel Royal, and in the evening, he repeats the same service to this interesting congregation of some of her meanest and poorest subjects. After the service was ended, the women and children proceeded, one by one, up stairs, to their own sleeping apartment, accompanied by their respective matrons ; each of the women, as they passed a person who was stationed with a large basket, received a ration of the best white bread —(about half a pound ;) and, if the woman had a child under her care, she received a double allowance. When the females were all withdrawn, the men advanced singly, in the same orderly manner, and they received a like portion of bread, with which they *descended* into *their* dormitory ; and we understood, that the same allowance is dispensed to them all, when they are dismissed in the morning; accompanied with a kind welcome to return again, at night, if they cannot provide for themselves better. The men's apartment, which we inspected, (and that for the females, is similar,) is partitioned off into single berths, on the spacious floor, by means of boards, ten inches wide, placed edgeways, forming compartments about seven feet by two ; each man has one of these divisions to himself, which is plentifully supplied with clean dry straw, upon which he lies down with his clothes on.

The width of the floor admits of two of these berths across the room, the men lying feet to feet with their heads towards the opposite walls ; but part of the floor, which is wider, we observed had more than two divisions across, and the boys slept upon a small floor by themselves, elevated above the other. There is a large powerful stove with iron flues, that affords an agreeable warmth, in the cold winter nights, throughout the apartment, which is also cheerfully lighted with several gas lamps.

After the men had retired, we went into their apartment, and the scene was both novel and affecting to behold; all the men (in number about 150) had lain down, each in his comfortable berth, or was reclining thereon, eating his dry bread, apparently with the savoury relish of a good appetite. Little or no conversation was going forward in the room, but every one seemed intent upon his own immediate comfort. About nine o'clock, not a whisper is heard, and very soon afterwards all are buried in a short, but sweet oblivion to all their woes. Besides the matrons, who superintend the women's apartment, there are officers in the house, on duty all night, whose business it is to prevent any disorderly conduct which might arise; to look after the fires and lamps, and answer the bell at the gate, should any midnight wanderer seek the friendly roof, which is not unfrequently the case; and such are sure not to seek in vain. Besides those of the poor, who inherit penury from their forefathers, we sometimes meet in this humble asylum with minds of higher grade; even men of good education, and some classical scholars have been known to be brought so low and reduced, as to become candidates for a night's lodging and a meal of dry bread, at this refuge for the forlorn and friendless. Those who feel an interest in the study of the countenance, as showing a reflex of the human mind, may here contemplate a series of living portraits, not often found grouped together in the same family. But the Christian philanthropist will take a still higher estimate of this interesting company of human beings, as having each a soul to be saved or to be lost, and will breathe a sigh that all might come to the knowledge of the Saviour who died that they might live to Him whilst here on earth, and with Him hereafter in heaven for ever.

J. P.

N. B.—"The refuge for the houseless poor" has been established many years, although not opened every winter, when the weather happens to be very mild. It is liberally supported by ample contribution. In aid of its objects a messenger from court was lately sent down to inquire if any assistance to the funds was needed, and the answer returned was, that they were quite sufficient.

INDUSTRY OF MASSACHUSETTS.

From an official report made to the legislature, it appears that the product of the great branches of *manufacturing* industry in Massachusetts, during the year ending in April, 1837, was $91,700,000; of which sum the three principal items were, cotton fabrics, $17,409,000; woollen fabrics, $10,399,000; and fisheries, $7,592,000. If to the products of manufacturing industry be added the earnings of *navigation* and *agriculture*, it is estimated that the whole annual product of the industry of Massachusetts exceeds $100,000,-000; which, divided by 700,000, the population of the state, gives $140 as the average value of the annual labour of each man, woman, and child, in the community. The whole value of the industry of the cotton-growing country of the southern states, with a popula-

tion of 2,500,000, is not equal to $100,000,-000; and. the annual value of the labour of each man, woman, and child in the slaveholding states is estimated at only $40.—*N. Y. Obs.*

A Liverpool paper states that 4800 people departed from Drogheda alone, via Liverpool, for America, during the six weeks preceding the 16th May, and that they took with them, on an average, twenty pounds each, or not less than 100,000*l.* in specie.—*Late paper.*

THE FRIEND.

SEVENTH MONTH, 4, 1840.

The following, extracted from one of our exchange papers, relative to the proceedings of the United States Senate on the subject of the slave trade, will be interesting to our readers. What influence the memorial of Friends on the subject, inserted last week, had in the case, does not appear.

IN SENATE.—THE SLAVE TRADE.

Wednesday, June 17.—The bill to aid in putting an end to this diabolical and inhuman traffic in human blood and misery, so far as the flag of this country is concerned, was taken up, at the earnest solicitation of Mr. Davis, who explained the object of the bill, by showing that American vessels were built for this purpose and sold to Spanish and Portuguese merchants, the transfer not being made until the vessel reached the coast of Africa, and the vessel being, in the mean time, protected by her flag—that after the transfer was made, the slaves were put on board, and the vessel depended on her *heels* for the safety of the return voyage. The object of the bill before them was to prevent the flag from being used for any such purpose.

Mr. Calhoun thought the measure would rather be embarrassing than lead to any good practical results. He was inclined to think the bill had grown out of the interference of another power, which was setting itself up as a general arbiter to regulate the internal concerns of other nations. He had understood that, while all this show of feeling was kept up, on the part of England, about suppressing this trade, the very manacles used to fetter those unhappy beings were manufactured, by thousands, at Birmingham. Had England taken any steps to put an end to that? For his part, he never could think of the interference of that power in the case of the Amistad with any degree of patience, and he thought it was time for this country to look to herself and assert her own dignity.

Mr. Davis replied that the bill was offered rather to carry out the policy of our own country than that of Great Britain. He could say that Great Britain had vindicated herself—he admitted that manacles had been manufactured there, but, then, there was a law on the statute book which authorized their seizure wherever found, but the law was evaded by the slavers taking out bolt iron and manufacturing them on the voyage.

Mr. Grundy condemned the interference of the British government in the case of the Amistad as highly improper.

Mr. King was sorry to say that there had been a correspondence with the British government, and it was there among the voluminous documents furnished to the committee. The British government had pressed upon them the right of search, but had been promptly told that no such claim would be tolerated. Mr. King avowed himself favourably disposed towards the bill—he regarded the measure as necessary to prevent the prostitution of the flag.

Mr. Webster made some remarks in support of the bill, contending that every possible step should be taken to prevent the glorious flag of the country from being prostituted for the aggrandizement of Spanish and Portuguese adventurers.

The bill was ordered to be engrossed, without division.

From the American and Foreign Anti-Slavery Reporter we copy the annexed paragraph, as an additional evidence that conscience is at work among the slave-holders.

EMANCIPATION OF 163 SLAVES.

Munroe Edwards, Esq., of Iberville Parish, Louisiana, (about 88 miles above New Orleans, on the Mississippi,) has taken 163 slaves to Cincinnati, Ohio, and there given them all full deeds of emancipation. He then distributed the whole proceeds of the last two years' crop of his plantation (upwards of $20,000) among them! He could have sold these men, women, and children for upwards of a hundred thousand dollars, but nobly preferred giving them their liberty. These joyful emancipated persons have gone, some to Kentucky, some to Illinois, some into the interior of Ohio, and some have returned to Louisiana among their relations. We have a full account of the particulars of this most interesting occurrence, but have nó space at present to enlarge. Laus Deo !

From the same.

NEW YORK LEGISLATURE.

Two important laws were enacted at the late session, in compliance with the petitions of abolitionists, highly beneficial to people of colour. The first secures the right of trial by jury to persons claimed as slaves, and the other protects the free citizens from being kidnapped or reduced to slavery. The governor is authorised to employ an agent, at the expense of the state, to effect the restoration of any free citizen of this state who may be kidnapped or held in slavery in any of the states or territories of the United States. These acts, so honourable to the legislature of New York, make the "servile" bill of Ohio appear still more infamous by contrast.

From the number of the "Irish Friend" for 5th mo. 1st last, we have transferred to our pages several articles possessing interest. That headed "Conversion of an Infidel" is without reference to authority, but carries internal evidence of its truth. By request of the editor of The Irish Friend, we insert the subjoined note.

To Subscribers.—Those who are in arrear with their subscriptions will please to bear in mind, that the terms are—"payable in advance."

AGENT APPOINTED.

Thomas Newby, P. M., Newby's Bridge, Perquimans county, N. C.

A meeting of "The Philadelphia Association of Friends for the Instruction of Poor Children," will be held at half past 8 o'clock, on second day evening, the 6th inst., at the usual place.

JOSEPH KITE, *Clerk.*

MARRIED at Friends' meeting house, Adrian, Michigan, on fifth day, the 21st of fifth mo. 1840, BENJAMIN G. WALKER, of Adrian, to MARY ANN, daughter of Abraham West, of the same place.

THE FRIEND.

A RELIGIOUS AND LITERARY JOURNAL.

VOL. XIII. SEVENTH DAY, SEVENTH MONTH, 11, 1840. **NO. 41.**

EDITED BY ROBERT SMITH.

PUBLISHED WEEKLY.

Price two dollars per annum, payable in advance.

Subscriptions and Payments received by

GEORGE W. TAYLOR,

NO. 50, NORTH FOURTH STREET, UP STAIRS;

PHILADELPHIA.

On the Habits and Instincts of Animals. By William Swainson. A. C. G., Fellow of the Royal Society, and of several Foreign Academies.

(Concluded from p. 316.)

HYBERNATION, TORPIDITY, AND MIGRATION OF ANIMALS.

Insects, whether in the egg or pupa state, are, by the efforts of instinct, placed in such situations as will best secure them from the effects of cold. Thus, the majority of grasshoppers, as well as several other insects, insinuate their eggs deep into the earth, where they will be out of the reach of frost; while the female of *Bombyx Neustria* covers hers with an unusually strong and hard shell, and gums them in bracelets round the twigs of hawthorn, &c., firmly securing them to the bark with a very adhesive gum: thus they are protected from the blasts and storms of winter, and, being impenetrable to rain, they remain uninjured. Those insects which continue, during winter, in the pupa state, are often protected by cocoons of silk and other materials; but such as are more hardy, as the pupa of the common cabbage butterflies, receive no injury from being naked, although they are usually suspended in some such sheltered situation as the corners of palings, the south side of walls, &c. Those, on the other hand, which hybernate in the larva state, either conceal themselves in some hole or cavity, or, if aquatic, bore into the sand or mud round the pools which they inhabit. It is a most extraordinary but well-attested fact, however, that some species of larva become so entirely frozen, as to appear literal masses of ice, which will yet afterwards revive. In proof of this, Lister asserts that he has found caterpillars that have actually chinked like stones when dropped into a glass, but which have -yet recovered to life and vigour. It is unfortunate that he has not left us a sufficient clue to discover the particular species in question.

The hybernation of insects, as it has been justly observed, cannot be ascribed altogether to the effect of cold, since it is proved that the period of their seclusion is not regulated by the state of the atmosphere. Insects are uni-

formly found to retire at a certain period, without any reference to these variations of the climate which would otherwise cause corresponding variations in their disappearance. To what, then, is to be attributed this apparently wise forethought with which animals prepare for a season, the rigours of which they are neither formed to endure, nor have had any experience of? Most assuredly, to that same instinct which accounts for so much in their habits and economy, otherwise inexplicable to us. It is clearly impossible that this apparent forethought can be any thing else but inbred instinct, of which they knew neither the cause nor the effect, because they have had no experience to guide them, or to show them the necessity of the preparations they thus make. Reflection and forethought cannot be employed upon things or events which are totally unknown; neither can it be put down to the force of example and imitation—as may be urged in the case of swallows, or other animals, which migrate or perform certain acts in society. Nearly all insects select their winter quarters singly; and this, not until they are compelled by cold, as Kirby and Spence justly observe, but at certain periods, uninfluenced, as far as we know, by any change of the atmosphere. The hybernation of insects, in short, is one of the best proofs that animals do not enjoy reason, and of the real difference between that faculty and instinct, that can possibly be adduced.

The migration of animals, and the sociability with which it is generally accompanied, is one of the most interesting subjects in the economy of nature. It might, indeed, have been treated of, under the following chapter, as a modification of the imperfect societies of the animal world; but, being more intimately connected with hybernation, we introduce it in this place. These unions, independent of other and more paramount causes, would seem to be produced by a love of sociability, or by some feeling corresponding to that propensity of timid people congregating at the time of any common danger or hazardous enterprise. It does not appear, however, that, upon these occasions, the stronger assist the weaker, or the courageous protect the pusillanimous,—at least this mutual support is not put forth when man is the aggressor; and we, consequently, have few or no opportunities of judging in respect of their conduct when attacked by other foes. But be this as it may, the associations in question are of a very different character from those last mentioned. They are essentially peaceful, and carry the mind back to those primitive ages of the world, when the patriarchs of families, accompanied by their descendants, journeyed to fresh fields and more fruitful valleys, as those spots successively became inadequate for the entire and increased community. They

seem to congregate, not for the mere gratification of a sensual appetite, but to live together for a season in peace and harmony; journeying and feeding together, and generally moving under the direction of sagacious leaders. We have numerous and familiar instances of such associations, both among vertebrated and the annulose animals, for in both classes is the instinct of migration, in certain families, strongly implanted. Looking to quadrupeds, we find those of the Old) changing their quarters, according as the seasons bring to perfection different species of fruit upon which they feed; when these become exhausted, they bend their course to other localities, in joyous and agile troops, the females carrying their young; and thus, leaping from bough to bough, they travel a long chain of forests, many leagues in extent, until they reach the next fruitful district, which is, in turn, abandoned for others more distant. We shall not here speculate upon the causes of migrations generally, since these simultaneous movements appear to originate from various motives, but of which a necessary supply of food seems to be the chief: our present purpose is to show its effects.

As united migration implies a great development of the social principle, we find it most remarkable among quadrupeds in the class of *Ungulata*, comprising the ruminants, and all those tribes whose docility towards man is most conspicuous. A few instances may be briefly noticed. The Saiga antelopes (*Antelope Colus*, H. Smith) are sociable and migratory, especially in the autumn, when they assemble, sometimes to the number of ten thousand, in a herd, and traverse towards more southerly deserts, returning in the spring in smaller troops. They are unwilling to reside far from water; are seldom seen single; and the herd, when in a state of repose, always keep a few stationed to look out. But perhaps the most striking instance of this instinct is afforded by the springer antelope, or springbock of the Cape colonies. This species resides on the plains of Southern Africa, to an unknown distance in the interior, in flocks, assembling in vast herds, and migrating from north to south, and back, with the monsoons. These migrations, which are said to take place in their most numerous form only at the intervals of several years, appear to come from the northeast, and in masses of many thousands, devouring, like locusts, every green herb. The foremost of these vast flocks are fat, and the rear exceedingly lean, while the direction continues one way; but with the change of the monsoon, when they return towards the north, the rear become the leaders, fattening in their turn, and leaving the others to pick up a scanty subsistence. Burchell, speaking of the same species, observes, that it is one of the most numerous in Africa, sometimes being seen in flocks of two thousand. The most animated account, is that of Le Vaillant, which we shall give in his own words. " Being informed that the herd was approaching, I immediately set out with Haripa, my attendant, who posted me in a defile of the plain, through which the antelopes must necessarily pass. We had not long remained in this position, when we saw rising from the sides of the hills clouds of dust, which seemed every moment to extend themselves and become larger. He then desired me to lie down upon my belly, with my face towards the ground; and in this posture, which appeared to me very little proper for hunting, I waited the event in silence. The antelopes advanced full speed, and did not fail to direct their course towards us, as he had foreseen. As the situation we had taken did not permit them to see us, they were not startled, but proceeded forward without altering their direction. When about two thousand of them, however, had passed us, he rose up, began to discharge his arrows, and desired me to fire at the same time. I was fully sensible that, when the herd was once put in motion, the antelopes in the rear would follow the rest; and that during the impression of their fear, which made them fly and press forward in crowds towards us, they would not be able to perceive us. I saw, also, that the savages, by despatching them silently with their arrows, ran no risk of scaring them; but I was apprehensive that, if I fired my gun, the explosion would spread terror among them, and that they would then return the way they came. My apprehensions, however, though founded in reason, were not verified. I fired repeatedly in all directions, but the column continued to advance as before, and fear produced on them no other effect than that of making them move on faster. I frequently poured the contents of my gun into the middle of this confused multitude, and each of my balls often brought down several of them at a time. Had I wished, I might easily, in this manner, have procured a hundred; and I only ceased firing, merely because such a quantity of game would have been of no use to me. Every time I discharged my piece at these antelopes, all their rumps immediately, and at the same moment, became white; and those thousands of red backs flying before me formed, as it were, one sheet of snow—which seemed displayed only to disappear again in an instant." It is difficult, as our author well observes, to account for "the prodigious multiplication of these antelopes in a country so infested with carnivorous animals as the whole of Southern Africa. I had," he says, "in other places met a few of their numerous flocks; but when I beheld this, I often wondered how so many thousands of animals, which, by their number, must have dried up the streams and consumed the pasturage of a whole district, could live in a place so barren and destitute of water. But though antelopes, as well as goats, have not the same need of drink as other animals, they doubtless inhabit more fertile cantons,—and there were such in the neighbourhood. In short, to give my readers an idea how numerous this herd was, I shall only say that, notwithstanding the rapidity of its course, it employed three whole hours in passing the spot where I was stationed."

The antelopes and ruminating quadrupeds of America appear also to assemble in very large numbers, at particular seasons. Dr. Richardson remarks, of the *Caribou* or Barren Ground reindeer, "that it travels in herds, varying in number from eight or ten to two or three hundred." And Captain Lyon adds, that they regularly visit the polar regions at the latter end of May or the early part of June, and remain until late in September. The woodland reindeer (*Rangifer sylvestris*, Sw.) cross the Nelson and Severn rivers, in immense herds, in the month of May, pass the summer on the marshy shores of James's Bay, and return to the northward in September. These instances, taken almost at random from among the true ruminants, sufficiently establish the frequency, in this order of quadrupeds; of regular migration.

Communicated for "The Friend."

Two Lectures on the History of Literature, with a brief sketch of the various materials made use of for the preservation of Knowledge.

LECTURE SECOND.

(Continued from page 314.)

In the 15th century Greek literature was no more, for Constantinople had fallen;—Roman lively in tradition ;—Arabian was now a relic of the past. Yet mind was awakening in every country in Europe. Native intellect began to display itself, and native literature to grow. The invention, or rather the introduction into Europe of the manufacture of cotton and linen paper, as it tended to the multiplication of books, greatly facilitated the new progress of mind.

In China, even before the Christian era, paper had been prepared from a variety of materials. As, perhaps, the very same mode of manufacture is still preserved amongst that stationary people, we shall briefly allude to their modern preparations. The bamboo, of which many of the houses they live in are constructed, as well as the light neat furniture which fills them ;—which furnishes fences for their gardens, poles for their palanquins, and floors and supporters for their bridges ;—which supplies them with boxes and cases to hold ; with their baskets to carry; with life boats to save them in shipwreck ; with greens for their tables ; with the masts and sails for their vessels ; with the conduits for their water courses, and with pipes for tobacco smoke ; with canes for support, and rods for correction, adds yet this item to the list of its uses,—it furnishes abundance of paper.

The green bamboo is cut into short pieces, which having been first softened by exposure to water, is submitted to the action of lime. After this it is boiled, and then being beaten with heavy hammers, is reduced to a soft pulp, is prepared for the moulds. The wheat, after having been dried, is dipped into a solution of alum, which hardens and prepares it to bear ink. From the bark of one of the varieties of that tree, the name of which has not been un-

frequently on some of our tongues of late, (I mean the morus,) they also manufacture paper. It has been generally believed that fine paper can be obtained from silk, and that the Chinese made an early use of it for that purpose. I believe there is no other foundation for this latter opinion than this ; the Chinese did, in early time, write upon woven silk. If good paper can be made from it at all, it must be by some different process from that employed in the manufacture of that from linen and cotton. The officers of the Bank of the United States, a few years since, had an experiment made, on a pretty extensive scale, in the neighbourhood of this city, as to the practicability of making their bank note paper of silk. In vain was it submitted to the long continued action of the grinders, it absolutely refused to be reduced to that pulpy consistence suited to the formation of *good* paper.

In the province of Kiangnan, the Chinese collect the skins of the silk worm,—and from them they prepare paper. The most sanguine believer in the silk culture will hardly think us ready for a manufactory of this sort, even if the worms who die in feeding be added to the skins of those who have lived out their days. The Japanese also make use of one of the morus tribe, from which they prepare paper ; this they sometimes make so thick and strong that it is used for mats and for wearing apparel. Perhaps I had better stop and describe the mode of its manufacture, as it may suggest a *speculative* application of its many-leaved cousin, should the public ever grow tardy in buying them. The young shoots are boiled, and the bark scraped off. This bark is then put in clear ley, and again boiled. It is then carefully washed, well beaten, and mixed with a glutinous extract obtained from rice and the root of the plant oreni. This prepares it for the mould. A very similar mode is adopted in India in preparing paper from the bark of the set-burooa or paper shrub. The pulp produced from this is said to resemble in colour milk and water.

Rice paper is cut out of the stem of an herbaceous plant called shola by the Bengalese. The stem is entirely composed to the very centre, of a fine white cellular tissue, marked by two or three delicate concentric circles. In order, therefore, to procure a sheet of this substance, it is necessary to cut it in a circular manner, unrolling it, as it were, like a scroll. The rice paper plant grows abundantly in the marshy plains of Bengal, and in the neighbourhood of the lakes in almost every province in India. The plant is perennial, and the stem seldom exceeds two and a half inches in diameter. The natives form artificial flowers from this paper, and various fancy ornaments. The straw of the rice plant, and even the thistle, furnishes the eastern Asiatic nations with material for paper.

In A. D. 704 the Arabians at Bucharest invented a mode of manufacturing paper from raw cotton. The cotton was first subjected to partial fermentation, by being wet and left in heaps. This rendered the mass tender, which was then beaten to pulp, macerated in water, and formed into sheets on moulds. When the Arabians introduced the manufacture of paper into Spain, they substituted water power for manual labour in reducing cotton to pulp. It appears from specimens of paper manufactured in that country in the 12th century, that they had begun to make use of linen and cotton rags. About the commencement of the 14th century, paper composed entirely of linen was in use in Germany, as various records, still preserved of that period, show. Until after the middle of the last century, the old system of half rotting the rags, previously to the grinding, was continued. It was then found that they could be reduced to a homogeneous pulp by a suitable mill, without that weakening of the fibre which necessarily resulted from the partial decomposition. Paper has been moulded by hand until within a few years,—but a variety of machines are now employed to effect this purpose. A full description of paper, and improvements in paper mills, would of itself furnish matter enough for an evening lecture.

Oat straw and various of the grasses of our country have been tried with success in the preparation of paper. In France they are making it from shavings of green wood. A tracing paper of repute in Germany is formed from poplar. In Ireland a very excellent pressboard is obtained from the peat or turf. Paper has been formed of asbestos. The inventor was desirous of obtaining a substance which might endure the action of fire. He succeeded in this, but found, that although the paper remained unharmed by the heat, the printing that had been upon it was entirely obliterated. The English and French manufacture the best paper, as the Germans and Italians do the cheapest.

The rags produced in our country are not nearly sufficient to supply the quantity of paper demanded by its multiplying presses. The rag merchants of Germany, Holland, and Italy, are put in requisition, and even Turkey contributes to our stores. A modern writer says, " the material of which the sheet of paper I now have in my hand is formed, existed perhaps a few months ago in the shape of a tattered frock, whose shreds, exposed for years to the sun and wind, covered the sturdy shepherd watching his sheep on the plains of Hungary ; or it might have been part of the coarse blue shirt of the Italian sailor on board some little trading vessel of the Mediterranean, or it might have pertained to the once tidy Camicio of the neat straw plaiter of Tuscany, who on the eve of some festival, when her head was intent upon gay things, condemned the garment to the rag merchant of Leghorn. It may have constituted the coarse covering of the flock bed of the farmer of Saxony, or looked bright in the damask tablecloth of the burgher of Hamburg."

The Chinese, as is well known, were possessed of the art of printing from carved blocks of wood, long before it was practised in Europe. A similar mode of printing was either invented in, or introduced into, Europe early in the 15th century. Representations of scenes from scripture history, or from the lives of their saints, with a text (or two annexed), were rudely carved on wood. From these impressions were printed, and being bound as books, they became very popular, and supplied an inducement to children to acquire the know-

ledge of letters. In this manner a selection from scripture history was printed as " the Bible for the poor." This was soon followed by other similar books. It appears that John Guttenburg was the first man who seized upon the idea, that those scripture texts and saintly legends might be composed of separate letters, capable of re-arrangement after one impression had been taken off. By this thought he had secured the principle upon which the art of printing depended. Its progress soon led him from one line to many, from a page to a book. As early as 1436, being then at Strasburg, he was engaged in making experiments upon engraved blocks. In 1442 he had invented movable types, which were cut by hand. Having spent much of his estate in his various efforts to bring his art to perfection, he returned to his native city, Mentz, where, in 1449, he connected himself in business with a rich citizen, John Fust, or Faustus. The art of cutting types out of wood, lead, and tin, which substances he severally employed, was very expensive. Peter Schoeffer, first servant, then son-in-law and partner to John Faust, an ingenious mechanic, discovered the art of casting types. An early writer says, " Peter Schoeffer, of Gernheim, perceiving his master Faust's design, and being himself ardently desirous of improving the art, found out, by the good providence of God, the method of cutting the characters in a matrix, that the letters might be singly cast instead of being cut. He privately cut matrixes for the whole alphabet, and when he showed his master the letters cast in these, Faust was so pleased with the contrivance, that he promised Peter to give him his only daughter, Christiana, in marriage, —a promise which he soon after performed." The first edition of the Bible, now called Guttenberg's Latin Bible, was finished in 1455. Faustus and Schoeffer, who separated in 1456 from Guttenberg, printed both a Latin and German Bible. When these were offered for sale, the monks, who had hitherto made large sums by copying them, became alarmed at the wonderful increase of the number of copies. As the art was yet concealed, they ascribed it to the father of evil, and Faustus was more than once in danger from their interested zeal. In 1462, the Archbishop Adolphus having taken and sacked Mentz, the servants who had been employed in its printing offices were scattered abroad, and carried the knowledge of the business with them. Printing was speedily commenced in various places in Italy, as well as in Germany and Holland. Roman characters were first employed at Rome in 1467, the Gothic having been used by the printers at Mentz. Aldus Manutine introduced the 'Italic' at his office in Venice in 1490 ; it is said to have been a fac-simile of the writing of the poet Petrarch.

Caxton, the first English printer, who flourished from 1471 to 1491, was encouraged by presents from the nobility, as well as by the sale of his books. He says, in the preface to a work of his called " The Legends of the Saints," that he was desired to translate and print it by William, Earl of Arundel, who " promised to take a reasonable quantity of them, and sent me a worshipful gentleman, promising that my said lord should, during my

life, give and grant to me a yearly fee,—that is to say, a buck in summer and a doe in winter." He was better off than some of his brethren; for we find Sweynham and Pannartz, printers at Rome, presenting a petition to the pope in 1471, wherein, after stating that they had printed 12,475 volumes, they continue thus: "A prodigious heap, and intolerable to us, your highness's printers, by reason of those unsold. We are no longer able to bear the great expense of housekeeping, for want of buyers ; of which there cannot be a more flagrant proof, than that our house, though otherwise spacious enough, is full of quire books, but void of every necessary of life."

As readers multiplied, the demand for books did also. To meet the wants of an increasing literary public, enlarged editions were printed, which, of course diminishing the cost and price, again extended the sale.

The ink used by the ancients in their writings was generally some vegetable carbonaceous matter as lamp-black, diffused in some liquid gum. The Chinese and other oriental nations use such yet. The India ink is ivory lamp-black combined with a very transparent glue. Our common writing ink is composed of gall-nuts, sulphate of iron, gum Arabic, and water. Printers' ink is composed of lampblack and nut, flaxseed, or linseed oil. The colouring matter in these inks is easily destroyed by almost any of the acids. I have observed, by a communication presented last summer by John Redman Coxe, of this city, to the Linnean Society of Great Britain, that he has obtained an inky fluid from a species of fungi or agarici, of a very indestructible nature, resisting acids and even chlorine gas. The doctor is disposed-to believe that the deposit left by the liquor when dried, mixed with oil, will form a fine composition for copperplate printing, and, diluted with water, a free writing ink ; neither of which can be erased, he says, without destroying the paper it has been printed or written on.

We may now return to the history of the progress of the human mind. War and conquest in the Roman empire had given place to ease and luxury, at the time that literature was at its perfection. Ease and· luxury weakened the mind, and cut the sinews of its· energies. A flood of barbarism swallowed up the literature of Italy ; then war and ignorance prevailed, to which, with the poetry of the troubadours, chivalry was added. A sense of individual rights was quickened in the people, and corporations were formed to protect them. The works of the ancients began again to be studied, not as treasures of wisdom to be wondered at and commented on, but as models for the moderns to endeavour to equal. It is natural for man to pursue with energy that path in which there is something to attain. The very love of gain which stimulated the study of alchemy, in its powerful effects on the human mind, spurred it on in the career of observation, which furnished new data for science. The press gave the discoveries of one to the many, not to be received as truths without investigation, but for them to test, if possible overthrow, and, if not, extend. It is the belief that our fathers have attained to the perfection of poetry, and that nothing can be in true taste which is not in conformity with their writings, which has crippled original thought, and made the compositions of the nineteenth century so correct and so commonplace: and it is in the physical sciences, the persuasion that the brightest attainments are but the forerunners of greater, that is urging on the human mind in the race of progressive improvement.

On the revival of letters in Europe, Italy started first in the race for literary distinction. Printing presses were established in every Italian state. Poets and historians, universities and literary institutions, flourished under the patronage of the polished and profligate Leo Tenth. Literature had been closely connected with licentiousness in ancient writers, and the poets of Italy took them for their patterns.

Indeed, the first authors throughout all re-animating Europe adapted their writings to the state of morals which the era of darkness had produced. Compositions, which then found patronage and applause, which were read in the presence of princes without offence, which were written for the amusement of the fair occupants of thrones, are rebuked by the purer spirit of this age, and driven from the family circle.

The reformation of Luther touching on religion, of all subjects that which most interests the mind of man, stirred up all Europe to reflection. The desire after knowledge generally prevailed; students grew numerous, eager to grapple with the doctrines of others, and prepared to defend their own.

As books increased, it was soon apparent that literature was to be an engine of evil as well as of good. Some writings tended to vitiate taste, others were opposed to the prevalent doctrine of the day, and many corrupted the morals. It is probable that taste and morals might have suffered without the arm of the law interfering for their succour, but that which touched the craft by which they obtained their bread brought the whole power of the priesthood into action. Books that contained passages which offended them were driven from the book-stores, were burnt by the hangmen, and the public forbidden either to purchase or read them. This censorship of the press was established in every country in Europe, and indexes were drawn out and printed containing a list of prohibited books. It was soon found, however, that this did not stop the sale. Regular inquisitors of the press were therefore called into requisition, without whose sanction no volume was to be printed. Ignorant men, devoid of sound judgment and correct taste, were often employed to examine writings which they were not competent to comprehend, much less to correct. These frequently struck out passages necessary to the complete connection of the whole, and introduced others contradictory to the general scope of the author. Sometimes a book which had been published was condemned by the censors of one city and approved by those of another. It is said that these literary inquisitors at Paris had a manuscript forty years before them, ere they came to a decision respecting it. Printers, however, at different places, continued secretly to publish works not licensed, and the public bought them. The eager desire which the world had of reading whatever was prohibited, was so

well known, that the publisher of Erasmus's Colloquies, not finding the sale rapid enough, actually intrigued to get it publicly condemned. He succeeded, and in consequence had such an increase in the demand for them, that he parted with twenty-four thousand copies—a sale unprecedented in that day.

Tonstall, bishop of London, in the time of Henry VIII. to display his zeal for the church of Rome, purchased all the unsold edition of Tindal's translation of the New Testament, and had them publicly burnt in Cheapside. This act excited no little indignation among the citizens of London, and so inflamed their desire to read, that on the appearance of a second edition, it sold with great rapidity. Unable to understand from whom the Tindalites could have received the support and encouragement which enabled them to enter the London market with a new edition, the lord chancellor of England sent for one of the principal amongst them to a private examination. The chancellor told him, that if he would only reveal who it was that supported and encouraged them, he should not be made to suffer. This he readily answered, by assuring the judge that the greatest encouragement they had ever received, was from the bishop of London, who, by purchasing the half of one edition, had enabled them to publish a second.

During the variable state of things in England in the time of Henry VIII. books on all sides in religion were at different times publicly burnt. During the time of Edward VI. they were confined to the writings of Catholics, whilst those of Protestants fed the flames in the days of Mary. The fuel supplied by Elizabeth was principally political, and her Stuart successors kept it burning with libels. Elizabeth, in her royal zeal against the authors of works that displeased her, had one hanged, and caused another, with his publisher, each to lose their right hands. A third was saved by a pleasant turn of Francis Bacon. When the fair fury demanded of him whether the author was not guilty of treason, he replied : " Not of treason, madam, but of robbery, if you please; for he has taken all that is worth noticing from Tacitus and Sallust." When the celebrated English writer, Camden, in the time of James 1st, undertook to publish his annals of the reign of Elizabeth, part was condemned by the censors. As soon as the mutilated work was published, Camden sent one, with a copy of the part that had been stricken out, to his friend, De Thou, the French historian, who immediately published the work entire in Paris.

Milton, whose Paradise Lost narrowly escaped suppression, indignantly expresses his opinion,—that after an author had summoned up all his reason and deliberation, had meditated and consulted, to be obliged to bring the efforts of his midnight watchings to the hasty view of an unleasured licenser, perhaps his younger in years, and far his inferior in judgment, cannot but be a dishonour and degradation to the author, to the book, to the privilege and dignity of learning.

The licensers of England lost their office at the time of the revolution, and freedom of the press was established in 1694. The minister from Copenhagen, not exactly understand-

ing the security of English subjects and the freedom of their press, told William III. that if a Danish subject had taken as much liberty in his writings with the king of England as Lord Molesworth had with the king of Denmark, he would have been executed therefor. The English king coolly replied, that he durst not serve subjects so: " But," said he, " if you please I will tell Lord Molesworth what you say, and he shall put it into the next edition of his book."

Literature had continued to flourish in all countries in Europe, except in Italy, Spain, and Portugal. In the classic clime of Italy mind had started first in the race for improvement, but, clogged by an inquisitorial priesthood, burdened by a licentious community, it struggled for more than a century, and then sunk back again to imbecility and ignorance.

(To be continued.)

"MANY LITTLES MAKE A MICKLE."

"The capital invested in poultry and rabbits in Great Britain is estimated at £10,000,000 sterling." "When we look," says McQueen, "at the immense number of eggs brought from Ireland, (50 tons of eggs, and 10 tons of live and dead poultry have been shipped from Dublin in one day,) and 66,000,000 eggs imported from France for London alone; and this immense number a trifle certainly to what are produced in this country, we shall cease to wonder at the large capital here stated to be invested in poultry of all kinds. The quantity of eggs imported into Liverpool from Ireland in 1832, was 4097 crates, value £81,940 sterling ; which, at 6d. per dozen, gives 3,277,600 dozens, and the number, 39,331,200. In 1832 the import had increased to 7,851 crates, or upwards of 70,000,000. The number imported into Glasgow from Ireland in 1835, by the custom-house entries, was 19,321 crates, which, at nine eggs to a pound, gives the number, 17,459,568.

The production and consumption of poultry, game, &c. in Great Britain and Ireland, may be judged of by the consumption of Paris, in 1822, of the following articles and animals, according to Count Chaleon:— 931,000 pigeons, 1,289,000 chickens, 549,000 turkeys, 328,000 geese, 131,000 partridges, 177,000 rabbits, 174,000 ducks."

This shows the magnitude of an interest which is deemed by most farmers of too trifling consideration to be worth making any calculation about.

It is, without doubt, a proportionately great interest in this country, yet who, in this respect, deems it worth attending to ?—New England Farmer.

War.—"Seven years' fighting," says Jeremy Bentham, " sets a whole kingdom back in learning and virtue to which they were creeping, it may be a whole age."

A writer in the Journal of Commerce states that in fourteen states of the Union, there are 12,897,638 sheep, yielding nearly 42,000,000 pounds of wool, valued in 1826, from an average of ten years, at $21,168,000. In the whole state of New York there were 4,299,879.

For "The Friend."

EARLY FRIENDS IN NEW ENGLAND.

(Continued from p. 318.)

LETTER VII.

For the honour of our countrymen let us not believe that the law of death against Quakers was easily obtained. The people needed preparation. The pulpit was the press of that age, and the church power controlled it, as does the money power in these times. An intelligent witness of their movements declared, that "he who could not whip and persecute those who differed from the rulers in matters of religion, could not sit on the bench, or sustain any office in the commonwealth." How much the people's common sense of justice was perverted by the ruling power, we can learn from the fact, that the judges who condemned to stripes, imprisonment, and death, were elected by the people.

John Norton and the other leading ministers of the colony first petitioned the general court for a law to banish Quakers on pain of death.

In the aristocratic branch, or court of assistants, there was no difficulty. They passed the law to punish by death even without a jury, and at county courts where three magistrates only sat. But the popular branch—the deputies—were of different minds. These were then twenty-five in number. A portion of them refused to sanction a law so contrary to common justice and their charter, and by which a majority of three might hang at pleasure. Yet it passed 13 to 12, the speaker of the house of deputies voting against it.

The minority, thus strong, resolved to enter their dissent upon the record; this the ruling power feared, and contrived to insert the clause, "to be tried by a special jury," to make it popular. Yet were the dissenting deputies much distressed by the measure, and particularly one Worzel, who was sick and absent, and who wept for grief when he learned the result, saying, he would rather have crept on his hands and knees to court, than such a law should have passed.

This act is a legislative curiosity; about as much so as the charter of the first bank under our present constitution, and some later charters. It begins with the preamble, "that whereas, no one hath a right to lord it over men's consciences," &c.: and under this specious declaration of equal rights, stands as great an outrage of all rights of person and property, as the records of despotism can produce; and the administration of it was as cruel as its provisions were derogatory to just and democratic legislation.

This contemptuous enactment greatly excited the Quakers; and within one year two of them sealed their testimony against it with their blood.

Marmaduke Stephenson was in youth an humble ploughman in old Yorkshire, in England; and whilst, on a certain time in 1655, he walked after his plough, the power of the living God, as he declared after his condemnation, so filled him as did ravish his heart; and the word came to his conscience, saying, I have ordained thee a prophet unto the nations.

At the appointed time Barbadoes was set before him as the place to which he must go; and without delay he made ready to depart; and bade farewell to his kind wife and four tender children for the last time, for the Lord had said he would take care of them; and he took passage for the designated island. Here, whilst at his master's work, he heard of the Massachusetts law to put his brethren to death, and his heart burned within him; and finding a vessel bound to Rhode Island, he went thither. And here, whilst he visited the seed which the Lord had blessed, the word came to him a second time, to go to Boston with his brother, William Robinson, who had come there as a merchant, from London, and to do business.

But scarcely were the two arrived in Boston, when they were seized and imprisoned; as also one Nicholas Davis, who had the temerity to come from the Plymouth patent into the charter limits. Mary Dyer, also, who came from Rhode Island to see and encourage these prisoners, was herself imprisoned with them.

At the next court of assistants these four were sentenced to banishment on pain of death; and two days only allowed them to free the jurisdiction from their hated presence. Mary Dyer and Davis returned home; but the other two, being bound in spirit to remain, went down to Salem to build up their friends in the faith.

But their movements were narrowly watched, and they were soon brought back to Boston, and cast into prison; and in less than a month Mary Dyer returning, was cast into prison also. And thus the charter government had in their custody three persons whose lives, by the Quaker law, were forfeited; and all sober and moderate men regarded the event with intense anxiety.

It was on the 20th of October, 1659, that they were brought before the court of magistrates to receive their sentence. Governor Endicot then presiding, first ordered the officer to pluck off their hats; (these Quaker hats seemed as disagreeable to the charter authorities as their tenets;) he then said, as no punishments hitherto could keep the Quakers away, and although the court did not desire the death of any, yet they must now give ear and hearken to their sentence. Here Robinson desired to read divers reasons, which he had prepared, why he had not left the jurisdiction,—but his request was refused.

The paper was published after his execution, and was in substance,—that, being in Rhode Island, the Lord commanded him to go to Boston and testify against the rulers there, and to offer his life for the truth. He did not hesitate to obey as a child, believing it became him thus to show his obedience to the Lord; and that at the time of his banishment on pain of death, he was still under God's command.

The sentence pronounced on him was this: "William Robinson, you shall be led back to the place from whence you came, and from thence to the place of execution, and to be hanged on the gallows until you are dead"—and he was taken away.

The governor then said,—"Marmaduke Stephenson, you are at liberty to speak." But he, seeing how Robinson had been treated, was silent: but, after sentence, he thus addressed the court:—"Give ear, all ye that are guilty, for the same day that ye put the servants of the Lord to death, your visitation will come, and you will be accursed forever. If you put us to death our blood will be upon your own heads. Take warning, then, in love I exhort you, before it is too late, that so the curse may be removed, for the Lord hath spoken it, and will perform his word upon you."

Mary Dyer next received sentence, to which she only responded, the will of the Lord be done; she seemed even joyous, and said to the marshal, as he offered to take her away, that he might let her alone, as she would go back to prison without him. I believe you, Mrs. Dyer, said he, but I must obey my orders.

Seven days after, these three were led out to execution. A multitude attended, anxious to learn the end; still doubtful whether their free charter rulers would proceed to blood. But when they saw a strong body of horse-guards moving in front, and two hundred foot soldiers in the rear of the prisoners, with drums near them, to drown their voices if necessary, many became sad.

Mary Dyer, it is true, could not denounce the woes of guiltiness upon her destroyers in bold and solemn strains, like her companions, yet in this death scene she manifested the superiority of her sex in patient suffering. She was now turned of sixty, a widow, and a mother of pious sons and daughters, settled in Rhode Island; and to her companions she appeared as a mother, holding each by the hand as she walked to the gallows between them, and strengthening them by her example and her words. She said, "that now was her greatest hour of joy; that tongue could not describe the sweet influences and refreshings of the spirit of the Lord which she then felt;" indeed an eye-witness said that her deportment confounded her enemies and astonished the beholders, and all were constrained to confess that hers was the faith of martyrs.

When they came to the foot of the gallows ladder, they took an affectionate leave of each other, and Stephenson prayed to God to regard his wife and little ones beyond the ocean.

Robinson's turn came first, and as he went up the ladder, he said, "this is the day of your visitation; the Lord has arisen in his mighty power to be avenged on all his adversaries. I suffer not as an evil doer, but for Christ. I charge you all that you mind the light of Christ which is in you, of which I have testified, and for which I offer my blood." But Robinson's earnestness and strength seemed to irritate preacher Wilson, who stood by and said, "hold your tongue, man, you will die with a lie in your mouth." As the rope was placed about his neck, and he saw that they would have his blood, he said, "now are ye made manifest," and was swung off.

Stephenson was also swung off, earnestly protesting that he suffered for no crime, but for conscience sake, and his last words were, "this day shall we be at rest in the Lord." These executions were on lecture day, that great day of council during the first charter.

When Mary Dyer saw both her companions hang dead before her, she also went freely up the ladder. There they put the halter about her neck, secured her clothes, and covered her face with a handkerchief, which Wilson lent the hangman; and as she was about to swing off, a voice came as from the crowd crying, "stop, stop, a reprieve, a reprieve, the woman is reprieved;" and it was so; her life was saved at this time by the intercession of her son; which plainly shows that Endicot and his councillors had power over the lives of their fellow citizens.

In the mean time Mary Dyer's purpose was not shaken. She seemed to hesitate, and with the rope yet about her neck, she declared that she was willing to suffer like her brethren there before her, unless they would repeal their wicked law. But as the people began to cry, "take her away," she was conveyed back to prison; from whence she wrote to the court, the next day, that she did not wish to receive her life from those, who with wicked hands had shed the blood of her friends. "I choose to die rather than to live as from you, as guilty of their innocent blood!" were her own words. But, notwithstanding this, they saw fit to send her home, at their own charge, hoping to see her face no more.

But they had to deal with one of the most remarkable of recorded martyrs, for in the following spring she returned, and appearing openly, they were constrained to notice her. And when she was brought before the court, Endicot said, are you the Mary Dyer sentenced here the last court? And she said, yea, I am; and when he told her that to-morrow at 9 o'clock she must go to the gallows, she replied, "thou saidst this before. I came here before to warn you to repeal your wicked law. I am upon the same work now." "Take her away, take her away," said the governor. On the following day she was led out to execution, guarded by horsemen and soldiers as at the former time. When she was put upon the ladder, and prepared for execution, it was intimated to her that if she would recant she might save her life. "Nay," said she, "I cannot, for in obedience to the will of the Lord God I came, and in his will I abide faithful to the death." "What," said they, "will you be guilty of your own blood?" "Nay," she replied, "I come to keep you from blood guiltiness—repeal your unrighteous law against the servants of the Lord." They asked her if she would have the prayers of the elders. She said, "I know never an elder here." "Will you have any of the people pray for you?" "I desire the prayers of all God's people;" and being now ready to depart, she signified the same to the executioner, and he swung her off, and she died without a struggle. "She hangs like a flag to warn all Quakers," said a church partizan.

(To be continued.)

LETTER FROM THE FAR WEST.

Asa Turner, Jr., of Denmark, Lee Co., Iowa Territory, writes to James G. Birney, Esq., under date of April 22d, that an anti-slavery society has been formed at that place, and also at Salem, Henry Co. I. T. He says "Our little church and society are almost to a man on the right side of this great question. As to the territory generally there is but little light, and less action on the subject. We need some judicious and efficient men to lay before

the people the nature of this abomination of abominations. The inhabitants of Salem are mostly Quakers, and many of them take a deep interest in the subject of slavery. Last summer two slaves passed through Salem, and were soon overtaken by their pretended masters. As they returned with the fugitives, some inquired by what authority they were carrying away these men captives, and called upon them to show their authority. The justice was sent for, and the trial was about to commence, but the black boys chose to take leg bail. So the poor mensealers had to return without their prey. A few weeks after the slaves discovered themselves to their new 'Friends,' who undertook to help them on their way to the land of liberty. Two hundred dollars were offered for the apprehension of the fugitives. Three Quakers sat out with the two runaways in a covered wagon. Four men, armed, way-laid them, and demanded the slaves on pain of death. No resistance was made, and the poor men were taken to Missouri, and one of them was immediately sold to go down the river. For this act the perpetrators received $200. Three or four are professors of religion, and two of them officers in the Methodist church! The Quakers were apprehended and tried under the black law of the territory, and fined $500. The laws of the territory are much the same as in Ohio and Illinois—making it the duty of the county commissioners to apprehend and sell every black man who has no free papers,—and imposing a fine of $500 on any one who shall aid one of these outcasts in obtaining the birthright given by heaven."

A. Turner communicates the following heartrending fact. "A black man in Missouri married a free woman, who now lives at Quincy, Ill. His master told him, if he would pay him $1200 he should have his liberty. Being a good blacksmith he went to work, and in three years paid the amount, but last fall he came over to see his wife, rejoicing to think he was soon to breathe with her the air of liberty. He returned to Missouri for his free papers. His master was offered $1800 for him, which he accepted, and in a day or two, instead of returning to his wife, he was on his way in chains to New Orleans!"—*Anti-Slavery Reporter.*

From the Franklin Farmer.

On the Cultivation of Fruit Trees.

Description of a method of cultivating peach trees, with a view to prevent their premature decay; confirmed by the experience of forty-five years, in Delaware state, and the western parts of Pennsylvania. By Thomas Coulter, Esq. of Bedford county, Pennsylvania.

The death of young peach trees is principally owing to planting and pruning *the same stock*, which occasions it to be open and tender, with a rough bark, in consequence of which insects lodge and breed in it, and birds search after them, whereby wounds are made, and the gum exudes, and in a few years the tree is useless. To prevent this, transplant your trees as young as possible, if in the kernel it will be no check of growth. Plant them sixteen feet apart. Plough and harrow between them, for two years, without regard to wounding them, but avoid tearing them up by the

roots. In the month of March or April, in the third year after transplanting, cut them all off by the ground, plough and harrow among them as before, but with great care, to avoid wounding or tearing them. Suffer all the sprouts or scions to grow, even if they should amount to half a dozen or more, they become bearing trees almost instantaneously, on account of the strength of the root. Allow no animals but hogs to enter your orchard, for fear of their wounding the shoots, as a substance drains away through the least wound, which is essential to the health of the tree, and the good quality of the fruit.

If the old stalk is cut away the third year after transplanting, no more shoots will come to maturity than the old stump can support and nourish, the remainder will die before they bear fruit, and may be cut away, taking care not to wound any other stalk. The sprouts when loaded with fruit will bend, and rest on the ground in every direction for many years, all of them being rooted as if they had been planted, their stock remaining tough, and their bark smooth, for twenty years and upwards. If any of the sprouts from the old stump should happen to split off and die, cut them away, they will be supplied from the ground by others, so that you may have trees from the same for 100 years, as I believe. I have now trees from one to thirty-six years old, all from the same stump. Young trees formed in this manner will bear fruit the second year; but this fruit will not ripen so early as the fruit on the older trees from the same stump. Three years after the trees are cut off, the shoots will be sufficiently large and bushy to shade the ground so as to prevent the growth of grass, that might injure the trees; therefore ploughing will be useless, and may be injurious by wounding them. It is also unnecessary to manure peach trees, the fruit of manured trees is always smaller and inferior to that of trees which are not manured. By manuring you make the peach tree larger, and apparently more flourishing, but its fruit will be of a bad kind, looking as green as the leaves, even when ripe, and later than that of trees which have not been manured. Peach trees never require a rich soil; the poorer the soil the better the fruit; a middling soil produces the most bountiful crop. The highest ground is the best for peach trees, and the north side of the hills the most desirable, as it retards vegetation, and prevents the destructive effects of late frosts, which occur in the month of April, in Pennsylvania. Convinced by long experience of the truth of these observations, the author wishes they may be published for public benefit, and has been informed, that Col. Luther Martin and another gentleman in the lower part of Maryland, have adopted a similar plan with great advantage.

EDUCATION IN MASSACHUSETTS.

The number of public schools in Massachusetts in 1837 was 2,918, and the number of academies and private schools, 854; total, 3,772, or, one school, on an average, for 186 souls.

The number of scholars that attended the public schools, in winter, in 1837, was 141,837, and the number of scholars in the private schools was 27,266; total, 169,103. At the same time the whole number of children in the state between 4 and 16 years of age was only 177,053.

The number of students from Massachusetts in the New England and New York colleges at one time has been, for several years past, nearly *one thousand*, or about one student for every 700 inhabitants.

The money raised by *direct tax* for the support of public schools in Massachusetts, in 1837, was $465,228, and the amount raised *voluntarily* to prolong the continuance of these schools was $48,301. At the same time, the amount paid for tuition in the private schools was $228,026. If to these items be added the amount paid for tuition in the colleges, the whole sum paid for education by the people of this state, will be found to be nearly a million dollars annually ! There is probably no district of equal population on the globe in which the inhabitants are more numerously and thoroughly educated. The people are opposed to the formation of a large fund for the support of their schools, but prefer the system of direct tax, and there is no tax which is any where more promptly levied or more cheerfully paid.—*N. Y. Obs.*

HORRORS OF THE SLAVE TRADE.

When will the horrors of this traffic be fully disclosed! When will the wrath of heaven cease to slumber, or the energies of earth be roused to put an end to it forever. The Cape of Good Hope shipping list, received by the last arrival, contains the following dreadful account of the suffocation of *six hundred* human beings, fastened in the hold of a slave ship, that they might be kept quiet during a gale !

"The last accounts from the Mozambique state that two slavers, one a ship, and the other a brig, were wrecked in Mozambique harbour during a hurricane from the south-east, but the crews of both, and 200 slaves on board the brig, were saved. The ship had arrived the preceding day, and had not taken in any slaves. It was reported of the brig, which was commanded by a Spaniard, that she originally had on board nine hundred slaves, but during a hurricane (in the prosecution of her voyage) the hatches were battened down, and on opening them after the hurricane had subsided, it was discovered that 300 of the slaves had died from suffocation and want of food. The gale re-commenced, the hatches were battened down a second time, the consequence of which was an additional 300 slaves perished from the same causes, and 100 of the remaining 300 slaves died on the passage to Mozambique harbour, whither she repaired for the purpose of getting a farther supply."—*Ib.*

DISGRACEFUL LAW.

The law for the expulsion and exclusion of all free persons of colour from Texas, makes it the duty of sheriffs and constables to arrest all such persons coming into the republic, after giving them ten days notice, and take them before a judge, who shall exact from them a bond, in the penalty of $1,000, conditioned for removal out of the republic. The third pre-

scribes that, if unable to give bond, the coloured person shall be sold at public auction, to be a slave for one year. The fourth provides that the coloured person may give the required bond at any time within the year; but if he does not, at the end of the year, he shall again be placed in the custody of the sheriff. By the fifth section it is provided that at the end of the year he shall be sold for life. The eighth section allows two years for coloured persons to leave the republic. All found after that time to be sold. The ninth section forbids masters of vessels, &c. to bring free coloured persons within the limits of the republic under penalty of not less than $1,000, nor more than $10,000—with the exception of cooks and other hands employed on board vessels.—*Ib.*

The world represents a rare and sumptuous palace; mankind the great family in it: and God, the mighty lord and master of it.

We are all sensible what a stately seat it is : the heavens adorned with so many luminaries, and the earth with groves, plains, valleys, hills, fountains, ponds, lakes, and rivers ; and variety of fruits and creatures for food, pleasure and profit. In short, how noble a house he keeps, and the plenty, and variety, and excellency of his table ; his orders, seasons, and suitableness of every time and thing. But we must be as sensible, or at least ought to be ; what careless and idle servants we are, and how short and disproportionable our behaviour is to his bounty and goodness : how long he bears, how often he reprieves and forgives us : who, notwithstanding our breach of promises and repeated neglects, has not yet been provoked to break up house, and send us to shift for ourselves. Should not this great goodness raise a due sense in us of our undutifulness, and a resolution to alter our course, and mend our manners, that we may be for the future more worthy communicants at our master's good and great table. Especially since it is not more certain that we deserve his displeasure, than that we shall feel it, if we continue to be unprofitable servants.

But though God has replenished this world with abundance of good things for man's life and comfort, yet they are all but imperfect goods. He only is the perfect good to whom they point. But, alas ! man cannot see him *for* them ;—though they should always see him *in* them.—*Penn's Reflections and Maxims.*

THE HOOF OF OPPRESSION.
"A man's a man for a' that."—*Burns.*

The other day an officer of the American and Foreign Anti-Slavery Society received a note from a gentleman, formerly a member of congress from a slave state, and now a resident of the vicinity of the city of New York, introducing a tall and fine looking black man, a native of the same state, who wished to beg a sufficient sum to purchase his oldest son, now in slavery. The note states, "for a long term of honest industry and praiseworthy service, mostly in command of a trading vessel, an act of manumission was passed, at the instance of his late master, in his favour. He has paid by his earnings to his late master, and the owners of his children, $2100, and he has six of his children with him, in New York. There being

another, the oldest, a boy about 16 years of age, living in servitude with J. B. J. Esq. Mr. J. is willing to part with him on reasonable terms, and David is desirous of raising a sum to purchase his freedom. You could not bestow a favour on a more worthy object, as I have lived many years a neighbour to David, and know him to be an uncommonly smart, active, and very honest fellow, &c."

David had a certificate, almost worn out, signed by no less than eight individuals and firms of the highest respectability in the place of his late residence, addressed to six firms in this city, as follows—"The undersigned, citizens of the Borough of ——— do hereby certify, that we have long been acquainted with the bearer of this, D. B., of colour, (black, about 50 years of age, over six feet high, and respectable in his manner and appearance,) who is about to remove with his family to a free state—most likely to New York. D. B. has always sustained a good character for industry, honesty, and integrity ; and we take pleasure in recommending him to the favourable notice of all good persons in whatever city, neighbourhood or state he may locate. Witness our hands, &c."

In conversation with D. B. he said, "I am a member of the church. My former master used to send me to Philadelphia and New York in command of a vessel, with cargoes of wheat and flaxseed, for many years. I could not read nor write, and therefore a man was sent with me to keep the accounts, but the business was left to my judgment ! When my master died, 12 years ago—I was sold, and my old mistress bid me off. I gave my young master $825 for my freedom ; I also earned $1300 and paid for my wife and four children ; and was eleven years paying it. Two children were born free. I now want my oldest boy, and then we shall all be together."

Does any one say this is a solitary case ? We say in reply, we have heard of many similar instances, and doubtless there are thousands. Is it answered, slavery is more tolerable than we had thought, if slaves have such advantages, and fare so well. What ! is it an advantage for such men to be deprived of the privilege of learning to read and write ? 'Is it faring well to be robbed of one's wages for half a century ? Is it good treatment to require of such a man as David, who had served his master so ably, so honestly, and for such a length of time, to pay $2125 for his own freedom, and that of his wife and his four children ? Is it good treatment and faring well for the old man to be obliged to go about begging for money in a free state to redeem his oldest boy from slavery ? And to be cast upon the world, in his old age, after toiling day and night for so many years to enrich another ! If slavery had done no more evil than to trample upon a hundred or two such men as David, for 50 long years, it should arouse the manhood of every citizen of this country to put down a system of such complicated villany, as John Wesley was wont to call it, wherever the people of the United States have the constitutional right ; and to cry shame on those who, in this age, continue to sustain by example or argument, such a detestable "institution."—*Anti-Slavery Rep.*

PREACHING OF FLOWERS.

FROM AN OLD ENGLISH POET;

Your voiceless lips, O flowers, are living preachers,
Each cup a pulpit,—every leaf a book,
Supplying to my fancy numerous teachers,
From loneliest nook.

'Neath cloistered boughs each floral bell that swingeth,
And tolls its perfume on the passing air,
Makes Sabbath in the fields, and ever ringeth
A call to prayer;

Not to the domes where crumbling arch and column
Attest the feebleness of mortal hand,
But to that fane most catholic and solemn
Which God hath planned ;

To that cathedral, boundless as our wonder,
Whose quenchless lamps the sun and moon supply,
Its choir, the winds and waves,—its organ, thunder,
Its dome the sky.

There, amid solitude and shade, I wander
Through the green isles, and stretched upon the sod,
Awed by the silence, reverently ponder
The Ways of God.

ANTHONY BENEZET.

(From Thorp's Letters.)

Manchester, 12 mo. 25, 1804.

My dear Friend :—I will relate to thee, at this time, a short anecdote which I had from James Thornton, one of the first of the first rank who have visited us from that quarter of the world. He said, when Anthony Benezet was in his last illness, and very near his death, he went to see him. Anthony had been long distinguished as a lover and benefactor of mankind; but when James came into the room, he said he never had been more deeply impressed with a sense of spiritual poverty than he was at that time; and as he sat under these feelings, a view opened, how little all the merits of good works can avail, or be relied on, at such a time, or any thing short of our holy Redeemer. He took leave of him under these impressions, and the good man died, I think, very soon after, and James attended his burial; but, he said, when he entered into the house, it felt to him as if it were divinely perfumed—something so like the opening of heaven, and a sense of the Divine presence, as he had at no other time experienced. What a striking conformity between the death of this good man and that of his blessed Master! I thought this little story deserved to be remembered.

With the salutation of love, in which I wish us both a continual increase, I am thy affectionate friend,

JOHN THORP.

The following pleasing anecdote, illustrative of the strong attachment of the Ass for his master, is related by Bingley:

An old man, who some years ago sold vegetables in London, used in his employment an ass to convey his baskets from door to door. Frequently he gave the poor industrious creature a handful of hay, or some pieces of bread, or greens, by way of refreshment and reward. The old man had no need of any goad for the animal, and seldom indeed had he to lift up his hand to drive it on. This kind treatment was one day remarked to him, and he was asked whether his beast was apt to be stubborn. "Ah, master, (he replied,) it is of no use to

be cruel; and as for stubbornness, I cannot complain, for he is ready to do any thing, or go any where. I bred him myself. He is sometimes skittish and playful, and once ran away from me. You will hardly believe it, but there were more than fifty people after him, attempting in vain to stop him; yet he turned back of himself, and never stopped till he ran his head kindly into my bosom."

Effects of the Natchez Tornado.

Dr. Tooley has published, in the Natchez papers, some striking facts observed during the dreadful storm in that city. The external rarefaction of the atmosphere was so great and rapid, that several houses exploded from the pressure of the air within. The leaves and buds of plants were seared, many of them having their vitality destroyed, and the growth of others so much suspended, that they did not revive for eight or ten days after. The latter effects are accounted for by the great influence exerted on the absorption of plants from the sudden rarefaction of the air. They are peculiar to tornadoes, but are seldom observed to produce so marked an effect as is above stated.—*New York Obs.*

THE FRIEND.

SEVENTH MONTH, 11, 1840.

We continue to receive unequivocal testimony to the successful working of the free labour system in the British West India colonies. Statements of a different character occasionally appear, but these, in most instances, proceed from persons under selfish or pro-slavery influences, and form, at most, but exceptions to the general prosperity. The British and Foreign Anti-Slavery Reporter, published in England under the sanction of the British and Foreign Anti-Slavery society, is regularly forwarded to this office. The number for 5th mo. 6th and 20th are now before us. Of their various and interesting contents, our limits, at present, will admit only of one short article. As the opinion of a chief justice, by the nature of his office, accustomed to the sifting and balancing of disputed questions, it is reasonable to suppose it to be the result of cool reflection and deliberate investigation.

St. Lucia.—The late chief justice of this island, to the assessors of the royal court, affords the following satisfactory extract:—'I now proceed to direct your attention to the more immediate object of our meeting in this hall, viz. the state of the calendar ; and here, again, there is fresh subject of congratulation for us all. Attribute the great diminution of crime (particularly of the more heinous offences) to what you may, the fact is indisputable, that there has been a great diminution of crime amongst the people. The wayward and savage passions, the rude revenge, which manifest themselves amongst the lower classes of society in every community, have displayed themselves here much less frequently than heretofore. Since the apprenticeship ceased, we have had (with one single and sad

exception) neither the atrocities nor the wild vengeance of former times to repress and deplore. All the jealousy of mastership, on the one side; all the impatience of restraint and turbulence which mastership, as it existed, gave birth to on the other,—have passed away, nor, most fortunately in this island, left a trace of bad feeling or exasperation behind: all the dissensions and evil passions of a former state of things having been lost in the gratitude and fruition of the present.

"It would not be fitting from this place to discuss the general question of the negro character, his capacity or his abilities, but certainly a more contented, peaceful, and well-disposed race than the population of this island can no where be met with. That they are not *all* industrious, that they have not *all* found out their own true and best interests, that they have not *all* yet learned that the chief charm of existence in every rank of life is to be found in well apportioned, and active, and useful exertion of body and mind,—or that the destiny of man on this earth is, to gain 'his bread by the sweat of his brow,' may be fairly laid more to their misfortune than their fault—to the former system of slavery and its consequences—to the want of proper and patient instruction, and oftentimes to the want of proper management on the part of those whom Providence has placed in a higher grade of society. And if labour has in some instances been directed into other hands, or, from circumstances, into other channels than formerly, there cannot be a doubt but that the *number* of labourers now at work on your rich and beautiful valleys, and the amount of labour performed by them in the aggregate, is not less than during any period of the apprenticeship, or proportionally of former times. Give, then, your peasantry the same encouragement and opportunities, and, the same training which others have had in more favoured islands, and you will not find them either falter or fail, and under a bountiful Providence you may speedily enjoy a prosperity which you have not yet known."

FRIENDS' ASYLUM.

Committee on Admissions.—John G. Hoskins, No. 60 Franklin street, and No. 50 North Fourth street, up stairs ; E. B. Garrigues, No. 185 North Seventh street, and No. 41 Market street, up stairs ; Isaac Collins, No. 129 Filbert street, and No. 50 Commerce street; Edward Yarnall, southwest corner of Twelfth and George streets, and No. 39 Market street ; Samuel Bettle, jr., No. 73 North Tenth street, and 26 South Front street.

Visiting Managers for the Month.—Joseph R. Jenks, No. 5 Vine street; John G. Hoskins ; William Jones, No. 326 Arch street.

Superintendents.—John C. and Lætitia Redmond.

Attending Physician.—Dr. Charles Evans, No. 201 Arch street.

Resident Physician.—Dr. Pliny Earle.

DIED, 7th mo. 2d. 1840, REBECCA B. PEIRCE, daughter of Caleb Peirce, of this city, aged thirty-one years.
—— In this city on the 4th inst. WILLIAM NEEDLES, late of Talbot county, Maryland, in the 79th year of his age.

THE FRIEND.

A RELIGIOUS AND LITERARY JOURNAL.

VOL. XIII.   **SEVENTH DAY, SEVENTH MONTH, 18, 1840.**   **NO. 42.**

EDITED BY ROBERT SMITH.

PUBLISHED WEEKLY.

Price two dollars per annum, payable in advance.

Subscriptions and Payments received by

GEORGE W. TAYLOR,

NO. 50, NORTH FOURTH STREET, UP STAIRS,

PHILADELPHIA.

Communicated for "The Friend."

Two Lectures on the History of Literature, with a brief sketch of the various materials made use of for the preservation of Knowledge.

LECTURE SECOND.

(Concluded from page 334.)

We have already shown, that at Rome the sale of books had become a regular business before the Christian era. The trade continued until literature was banished by northern invasions. Constantinople was perhaps the only place from the 6th to the 11th or 12th centuries where collections of books were offered for sale. Throughout western Europe, during that period, the monasteries were the sole manufactories of books. Of these at times a Bible, a missal, a homily, a saintly legend, might be purchased by the rich. These books were transcribed on parchment, and were bound with thick lids of wood covered with leather, and studded with brass headed nails. Such volumes were seldom sold to any but the clergy. "Laymen," said one of the old bishops of Durham, "to whom it matters not whether they look at a book turned wrong side upwards, or spread before them in its natural order, are altogether unworthy of any communion with books." Bartholin expressed his great admiration for books in words,—which show the lamentable darkness of his own mind, who could think that the Almighty Creator, upholder, and preserver of learned and unlearned, civilized and uncivilized man, speaks only to him through the medium of books ; he says, "without them, God is silent, justice dormant, physic at a stand, philosophy lame, letters dumb, and all things involved in Cimmerian darkness."

I have selected the following incidents, setting forth the scarcity of books, and the value attached to them. In the 9th century the abbot of Ferrieres sent to borrow Cicero on Oratory, and Quintillian's Institutes of Pope Benedict III. stating that there was no perfect copy of either in France. The Countess of Anjou purchased the homilies of Harmon, bishop of Halberstadt, and paid for the work 200 sheep, 5 quarters of wheat, and the same amount of rye and millet. In 1299 the bishop of Winchester,

in borrowing a Bible with marginal notes from the cathedral convent of St. Swithens, gave a bond drawn up with great solemnity of expression for the return of it. This Bible had been presented to the convent, and a daily mass was said for the soul of the donor,—it being considered by the monks that such a gift merited eternal salvation. The prior and his brethren at the convent of Rochester, threatened to pronounce the irrevocable sentence of damnation on any person who should steal their Latin translation of Aristotle's poetics, or even obliterate the title. Even so late as the 15th century, when Louis XI. of France borrowed a volume written by Rhoses, the Arabian physician, he deposited, by way of pledge, a considerable quantity of plate ; besides which, he was obliged to find a nobleman to join with him as surety in a deed, binding himself under a great penalty to restore it.

Such was the value attached to books in this time of priestly prerogatives and popular ignorance ; a value affixed to them rather as saintly relics for ignorance to wonder at and worship, than as fountains of knowledge, and storehouses of thought for furnishing the intellect, or strengthening and refreshing the mind. Learning was deemed by many as a sanctified garment, appropriate to the church, and which none but its members might wear. But with the first efforts of awaking thought, laymen became students. The learning, the literature, the freedom of thought which had characterised the past, the illiterate ignorance, the mental inertness and slavery of the present, engaged their attention ; and whilst mind indignantly broke the bonds which enthralled it, the lore of the ancients was released from the cobwebs of libraries.

Cotton paper furnished the monk in his cloister, and the scholar in his study, with an abundant material for the multiplication of books. The increase of these gave employment for booksellers, whose literary storehouses accumulated throughout the cities of Europe. Learning had, however, been so long exclusively an ecclesiastical attribute, that the vendors of books were placed under their government, to be controlled by their caprice, and limited by their ignorance, superstition, or prejudice. At Paris, from the 13th to the close of the 15th centuries, booksellers were appointed by its priest-governed university,—and it was illegal for any one to vend a book valued at more than 10 sons, without its permission and sanction. The individual thus chosen was considered a part of the academical body; as such, he was bound by its laws, he partook of the rights, and enjoyed the immunities of its members. But he dared not refuse to loan books to any of them, under a read or to copy ; he had to give security for his good behaviour, and was deprived, at the

pleasure of the university, of his trade and privileges. The price of each book was settled by the heads of the university, who took care of *themselves*, as well as the interests of learning, by reducing the gain on those which were sold to their members to less than a two per cent. profit. But vain were the trammels which licensers, priests, and universities imposed upon literature ; it lived, and it flourished. The invention of printing facilitated its nourishment. The reformation came, and in the zeal it enkindled, the productions of mind started up with a vigorous luxuriance, like the growth of young leaves, the expansion of blossoms, the extension of shoots in the sunniest seasons of spring. With their release from the spiritual dominion of Rome, Germany and Holland had obtained intellectual liberty, and established for themselves the freedom of the press. From their printing offices—those distributing fountains of literature, the free thought, the noble sentiment, the religious truth, were in various languages profusely scattered to all European countries. England might restrain, France might control, Spain might bind, and Italy might fetter, but the productions of the authors of each found a way to posterity through the freedom of Holland, or the presses of Saxony.

At the present time the book trade and printing is comparatively unshackled in most places in Europe. Spain and Portugal are yet, however, under bondage as deep as ever ; and every manuscript endures the scrutiny, and receives the sanction of several tribunals of censorial criticism before it can reach the eyes of the public.

Books are sold at very low prices in Germany, and the book trade is there systematized as it is in no other country. Leipzig is considered as the grand literary emporium ; and in it all the principal publishers, from the Vistula to the Rhine, and from the Danube to the Baltic, have their accredited agents. These receive the volumes as they are issued from every press, and from these they are distributed to every book mart in Germany. A yearly fair for the sale of books was established in Leipzig soon after the invention of printing. In 1667 it was attended by 19 booksellers from other places. A catalogue of the books offered for sale is printed every year, which contains a list of all books published since the last fair. This furnishes a curious statistical detail of literary labour in Germany. In 1816 more than 3000 new works came from the press;. In 1828 more than 5600, and in 1838 the number exceeded 6000. At this fair, booksellers from all parts of Germany, Sweden, Denmark, the Russian Baltic provinces, the Netherlands, and some from England and France, to the number of more than 300, annually meet. Perhaps there is no one town in the world which has so great a proportion of its inhabitants connected with literature as Leipzig. There are more than 100 resident booksellers, and the capital employed in printing is several millions of dollars. It has 32 printing offices, one of which employs 40 ordinary presses, and 3 driven by steam. Forty millions of sheets are annually printed there, and the average weight of the books which are brought to it every year for sale, is 3,360,000 pounds, or 1500 tons. I can find time but for a few remarks respecting the book trade of the present day. Throughout Europe and America it is fast growing into two branches, the one embracing those who publish, the other those who retail. Periodic public sales of books in quantities to the trade are held in many places. In America, at Boston and Baltimore, there is one held yearly; at New York and Philadelphia, two. At the sales at Philadelphia, the average amount received for books sold is about $80,000.

When we consider the immense multiplication of books from the many thousand presses in America, and the ten thousand presses of Europe; the idea of keeping up an intimate acquaintance with modern literature appears to be absurd. A knowledge of the names of books, and the subjects they treat on, which has been called the erudition of title pages, may soon be sufficient to occupy a lifetime. A writer in the Edinburgh Review in 1816, calculates that up to that period, there had been printed in Europe since the time of Faust and his servant 3,641,960 different works. Leibnitz, in mock consternation at the increase of books, declares that cities would soon not be sufficient to contain the libraries. D'Israeli, however, comforts himself with the recollection of the patriotic labours of the grocers and trunkmakers, those alchemists of literature, who annihilate gross bodies without injuring the finer spirits.

Since the springing up of literature in Europe, authors, by profession, have suffered perhaps more than those of earlier ages. It is true, that writers whose works are popular, —the demand of the public outrunning the rapidity with which they are produced, sometimes receive immense profits, and gather together estates. Yet, as a body, the literary labourers have little present pecuniary recompense, and small chance for future fame. Those who, by their situation in life, are raised above want, who care not for an increase of fortune, who write for their own satisfaction, may distribute their volumes amongst literary friends, and take their applauses for fame. But in the great literary cities of Europe, there are thousands of men who, with indefatigable industry, good talents, and not unfrequently much erudition, toil day after day, night after night, in the drudgery of composition, the illy paid recompense of which just keeps them on the brink of starvation, until death releases from earthly troubles, or a premature old age consigns them to the long dreaded poor-house. Many whose works have been popular, who have received considerable sums from their sale, with a prodigality too often attendant on professional authorship, have squandered it away, and perished in poverty, wretchedness, and want. Tom Nash, a popular professional

author, in the reign of Queen Elizabeth, thus describes his own condition. "Sat up late, and rose early, contended with cold, and conversed with scarcitie;" "all my labours turn to losse. I was dispised and neglected, my pains not regarded, or slightly rewarded, and I mysself in prime of my best wit, laid open to povertie." "How many base men that wanted the parts I had, enjoyed content at will, and had wealth at command. I called to mind a cobler that was worth 500 pounds; a hostler that had built a goodly inn ; a carman in a leather pilche that had whipt a 1000 pounds out of his horses tail. And have I more than these, thought I to myself ; am I better born ? am I better brought up ? yea, and better favoured, and yet am I a beggar!"

The great-antiquarian, Stow, who spent his estate in investigating the ancient monuments of Great Britain, applied for, and obtained, in his 80th year, letters patent from King James 1st, to take up alms as a beggar. I cannot take time to speak of the sufferings of a Goldsmith, who, by profuse prodigality, was kept always in poverty; nor of a suicidal Chatterton, whose history shows the depth of degradation to which a fine mind may be brought, when destitute of virtue, and void of religion, it is caught in the storms of adversity. I must hasten to a close. Those who would know the difficulties which young men of talents may have to contend with, who, through literature seek after fortune and fame, I would recommend to read the private journal of the late George Crabb during the first three months of his residence in London. He sought patron after patron without success, and when rejected did not sit down in despair. Booksellers and noblemen were appealed to in vain. But in the midst of discouraging incidents, with the most unfailing good humour, he points out the daily reduction of cash, the sale of his books, the pawning of his watch, and the thinning of his wardrobe. The very perfection of the serio-coimico is to be found in his lamentations over an unfortunate rent in his last coat.

Our literary men in America become politicians, and get offices whereby they live, or they edit newspapers, or they flourish in the "cotton line," or they are clerks in banks, and devote no more time to the desk of the author, than they can spare without detriment to the pocket. One might suppose the poems of Halleck and Bryant were popular enough, and returned them profit enough, to entice (even in this bank note world) the one more frequently from his cotton bags, and the other from his editorial chair into the bowers of the muses. But perhaps 'tis a matter of calculation;—one knows the profit of his business, the other the salary of his party. Let but another Caracalla arise, and offer a piece of gold for every verse, and straightway the gliding of goose quills and the scratching of steel pens would be visible from the line of New Brunswick to the borders of Texas. What a forsaking there would be of cotton bags and banks, of parties and politics, whilst the whole race would be foremost in the art of turning rhymes into guineas. The love of money is in truth the characteristic of our country ; and this may (perhaps) save us from being afflict-

ed with a very large number of nearly starved authors. I had intended to have devoted some time in particularising the sums of money received by some of the fashionable authors of the present day, but I am warned to be brief. A Milton, in the 17th century could obtain but £5 for a Paradise Lost ; a Moore, in the 19th, receives £3,000 for a Lalla Rookh, and a Scott the same for a Rokeby. Our Cooper and Irving have probably each received more than $50,000 for their writings.

The fashions in literature I must pass by with as brief a notice. At different periods particular forms of books have been generally adopted,—and there has been the reign of folios, quartos, octavos, or twelves. We can all remember when the public taste run upon miniatures, and nothing was relished but in homoopathic doses. Fashion has also some influence in the naming of books. If "Every man his own lawyer," is published, there instantly follows, "Every man his own physician," "Every man his own surgeon," "Every man his own gardner," and "Every man his own cattle doctor." If a "Child's book" is invented, straightway comes a "Boy's book," just preceeding a "Girl's book,"—and a "Young man's" and "Young ladies'" book succeed. The "Father's" and "Mother's" book" soon engage our attention, and then the "Family book" completes out the circle. Then comes the "Child's own book," which brings out the whole coterie of relatives with their own books also.

The task I assigned to myself has been accomplished. I have in some manner explained the means adopted, and the materials employed in different ages to render knowledge permanent, and have also endeavoured to give a brief sketch of the history of literature. Many of the facts which we have heard, have no doubt been deposited in the storehouse of memory ; but what knowledge have we gained which may beneficially influence our mental, our moral, or our religious opinions ? If we have seen, through the discoveries of industrious investigations and scientific search, the assertions of a Volney proved as false as they were presumptuously positive,—if we have seen the sneering arguments of Voltaire proved lighter than vanity, and robbed of every semblance of verity, shall we not feel a firmer conviction than ever, that the labours of learning, the testimony of literature, yea, even the inquiries of infidels, do all eventually tend to confirm the language of scripture and the truths of our holy religion. If we have felt the superiority of sacred to profane literature, in eloquence, in purity, in wisdom, and in power, shall we not seek to participate in the waters of that fountain from which the Hebrew writers drew all their inspiration. If we have observed in the heathen poets the evils resulting from the unsanctified intellect, and corrupt imagination of man building up for himself a religion, shall we not learn, in the concerns of the immortal soul, to beware of ourselves, to trust not to reason, to lean not on others, but to seek for the witness of truth, which directs from all error, presumption, and sin.

The dangerous effect of a depraved literature upon the morals and judgment of nations has claimed our attention, and may well stir up the inquiry in each of us, how far in our reading, we are quaffing at the modern waters of literary corruption. Are we poisoning our own minds, and is the influence of our example encouraging others to a course of reading calculated to give a dangerous latitude to their imaginations, to impair the purity of their morals, or to destroy their confidence in religion.

We have seen that whilst the human mind was in onward progress, access to libraries excited the intellect, and urged on the literature of nations ;—but when the active zeal for advancement and perfection had ceased in an age, collections of books became but as dead monuments of the past, awaking no sensation in the living : and we have been convinced, that it was better for nations or individuals to feel within them a spirit that would inquire, investigate, and reason, than without this to be possessed of the records of all human knowledge, the pages of all earthly wisdom, and the volumes of all scientific truth.

From the incidents of the past, this conviction has perhaps been forced upon us all, that, though wars may give matter for history, may furnish out themes for the poet, yet the influence they exercise is always opposed to the permanent prosperity of learning and literature. We have seen the monuments of mind perishing from the path of the conqueror,—we have seen science wither in the cities of the conquered. A continued course of victory, giving birth to luxury and pride, which have tended to foster a taste repugnant to true learning, and an imbecility of mind unfriendly to attainments in knowledge.

If we look at the snail-like pace which learning has traveled in China, its retrograde motion among the Hindoos, its sudden extinction in every kingdom of the Arabians, its failure in Goth-trampled Europe, its second declension in priest-ridden Italy,—we shall be led to conclude, that established errors in doctrine, general corruption in morals, and national servitude to arbitrary rule, give no promise of permanence to literature, of increase to knowledge, or advancement to science. On the contrary, we may remember that in Europe on the re-awakening of the human mind, it exercised the liberty of thought,—it quickened to a perception of social, political, and religious rights, and then, and not till then, nations really started on the race of mental, of moral, and religious improvement.

We may sum up the whole of these observations in a few words. Undoubted facts in science, certain discoveries in philosophy, true histories of the past, will always be found in accordance with the revelations of Him who is truth :—and that nothing that is corrupt in morals, erroneous in religion, or false in philosophy, will permanently improve the intellect, or add to the happiness of man.

To conclude—there is not a subject which can furnish a theme for a lecture from which we may not draw some proof of the superintending goodness, creative wisdom, or retributive justice of God. We may read this in the records of literature, it speaks from the pages of history. Go ask our anatomist as he lectures, appeal to our physiologist if it is not true, that a hand of unbounded power, controlled by consummate wisdom, has built up the framework of human existence,—has fitted it "bone to his bone," prepared every part for its functions, and clothed the whole fabric with beauty. All life, through its various unfoldings, speaks the praise of *that* mercy, tells the tale of *that* might, which controls e'en the dust of unorganized matter, which wheels the whole systems of worlds, and yet has prepared for each atom in nature the laws which must govern and guide it. Our chemist can show us,—for his daily employments compel him to trace the manifold powers of the simplest material around him. Adaptations, preparing for action, are so plain, attractions drawing, and affinities binding for beneficent ends, are so striking, that he fain must acknowledge the goodness of him whose wisdom has planned, and whose power has implanted the laws that control them. The voice, then, of history, the learning of ages, the unfoldings of science, break forth in harmonious concord with the language of nature, as "day unto day uttereth speech, and as night unto night showeth knowledge" of unfathomable wisdom, unutterable goodness, and inimitable power.

A DANGEROUS ADVENTURE.

[We extract the following account of a hazardous adventure from "Julius Rodman's Journal of the first passage ever achieved across the Rocky Mountains," published in Burton's Magazine.—*Bost. W. Mag.*]

During our sojourn here, an incident of note occurred. The banks of the Missouri in this neighbourhood are precipitous, and formed of a peculiar blue clay, which becomes excessively slippery after rain. The cliffs, from the bed of the stream back to the distance of a hundred yards or thereabouts, form a succession of steep terraces of this clay, intersected in numerous directions by deep and narrow ravines, so sharply worn by the action of water at some remote period of time as to have the appearance of artificial channels. John Greely, the prophet, the interpreter Jules, and myself started out after breakfast one morning, to ascend to the topmost terrace on the south shore, for the purpose of looking around us ; in short, to see what could be seen. With great labour, and by using scrupulous caution, we succeeded in reaching the level grounds at the summit opposite our encampment.

Upon reaching these level grounds we all sat down to rest, and had scarcely done so, when we were alarmed by a loud growl immediately in our rear, proceeding from the thick underwood. We started to our feet at once in great terror, for we had left our rifles at the island, that we might be unincumbered in the scramble up the cliffs, and the only arms we had were pistols and knives. We had scarcely time to say a word to each other before two enormous brown bears (the first we had yet encountered during the voyage) came rushing at us open-mouthed from a clump of rose-bushes. These animals are much dreaded by the Indians, and with reason, for they are indeed formidable creatures, possessing prodigious strength, with untameable ferocity, and the most wonderful tenacity of life. There is scarcely any way of killing them by a bullet, unless the shot be through the brains, and these are defended by two large muscles covering the side of the forehead, as well as by a projection of a thick frontal bone. They have been known to live for days with half a dozen balls through the lungs, and even with very severe injuries in the heart. So far we had never met with a brown bear, although often with its tracks in the mud or sand, and these we had seen nearly a foot in length, exclusive of the claws, and full eight inches in width.

What to do was now the question. To stand and fight with such weapons as we possessed was madness ; and it was folly to think of escape by flight in the direction of the prairie ; for not only were the bears running towards us from that quarter, but, at a short distance back from the cliffs, the underwood of briar bushes, dwarf, willow, etc. was so thick that we could not have made our way through it at all, and if we kept our course along the river between the underwood and the top of the cliff, the animals would catch us in an instant ; for, as the ground was boggy, we could make no progress upon it. while the large flat foot of the bear would enable him to travel with ease. It seemed as if these reflections (which it takes some time to embody in words) flashed all of them through the minds of all of us in an instant—for every man sprang at once to the cliffs without sufficiently thinking of the hazard that lay there.

The first descent was some thirty or forty feet, and not very precipitous: the clay here also partook in a slight degree of the loam of the upper soil; so that we scrambled down with no great difficulty, to the first terrace, the bears plunging after us with headlong fury. Arrived here, we had not a moment for hesitation.— There was nothing left for us now but to encounter the enraged beasts upon the narrow platform where we stood, or to go over the second precipice. This was nearly perpendicular, sixty or seventy feet deep, and composed entirely of the blue clay which was now saturated with late rains, and as slippery as glass itself. The Canadian, frightened out of his senses, leaped to the edge at once, slid with the greatest velocity down the cliff, and was hurled over the third descent by the impetus of his courser. We then lost sight of him, and of course supposed him killed ; for we could have no doubt that this terrific slide would be continued from precipice to precipice, until it terminated with a plunge over the last into the river—a fall of more than a hundred and fifty feet.

Had Jules not gone in this way, it is more than probable that we all should have decided, in our extremity, upon attempting the descent ; but his fate caused us to waver, and in the meantime the monsters were upon us. This was the first time, in all my life, I had ever been brought to close quarters with an animal of any strength or ferocity, and I have to no scruple to acknowledge that my nerves were completely unstrung. For some moments I felt as if about to swoon, but a loud scream from Greely, who had been seized by the foremost bear, had the effect of arousing me to exertion, and when once fairly aroused, I experienced a kind of wild and savage pleasure from the conflict.

One of the beasts, upon reaching the narrow

'edge where we stood, had made an immediate rush at Greely, and had borne him to the earth, where he stood over him, holding him with his huge teeth lodged in the breast of his overcoat—which, by the greatest good fortune, he had worn, the wind being chilly. The other, rolling rather than scrambling down the cliff, was under so much headway when he reached our station, that he could not stop himself until the one half of his body hung over the precipice ; he staggered in a sidelong manner, and his right legs went over while he held on in an awkward way with his two left. While thus situated, he seized Wormley by the heel with his mouth, and for an instant I feared the worst; for in his efforts to free himself from the grasp, the terrified struggler aided the bear to regain his footing. While I stood helpless as above described, through terror, and watching the event without ability to render the slightest aid, the shoe and moccasin of W. were torn off in the grasp of the animal, who now tumbled headlong down to the next terrace, but stopped himself, by means of his huge claws, from sliding farther. It was now that Greely screamed for aid, and the prophet and myself rushed to his assistance. We both fired our pistols at the bear's head ; and my ball, I am sure, must have gone through some portion of his skull, for I held the weapon close to his ear. He seemed more angry, however, than hurt; the only good effect of the discharge was in quitting hold of Greely, who had sustained no injury, and making at us. We had nothing but our knives to depend upon, and even the refuge of the terrace below was cut off from us by the presence of another bear there. We had our backs to the cliff, and were preparing for a deadly contest, not dreaming of help from Greely, (whom we supposed mortally injured,) when we heard a shot, and the huge beast fell at our feet, just when we felt his hot and horrible fetid breath in our faces. Our deliverer, who had fought many a bear in his lifetime, had put his pistol deliberately to the eye of the monster, and the contents had entered the brain.

Looking now downwards, we discovered the fallen bruin, making ineffectual efforts to scramble up to us ; the soft clay yielded to his claws, and he fell repeatedly and heavily. We tried him with several shots, but did no harm, and resolved to leave him where he was for the crows. I do not see how he could ever have made his escape from the spot. We crawled along the ledge, on which we stood, for nearly half a mile, before we found a practicable path to the prairie above us, and did not get to camp until late in the night. Jules was there all alive, but cruelly bruised—so much so, indeed, that he had been unable to give any intelligible account of his accident or of our whereabouts. He had lodged in one of the ravines upon the third terrace, and made his way down its bed to the river shore.

From the Journal of the American silk Society.
THE GRAPE VINE.

There are few things that afford more pleasure for the expense of time and trouble than a good and well-managed grape vine. From considerable observation the editor of this journal was led to conclude, that a very erro-neous practice was generally pursued in relation to grape vines ; and three years ago determined to try an experiment. The error in practice alluded to is this : the vine is permitted to grow to the full extent of its ability, and thus every season a large portion of wood has to be cut off and thrown away. It occurred to the writer that this waste of the power of the plant might and ought to be prevented. Accordingly, in the spring of 1837, he obtained an Isabella vine, one year old, from the layer, having a very good root, and planted it in an ordinary soil, of rather a sandy quality, putting a wheel-barrow load of wood-yard ma-nure and old lime mortar about the root. As soon as it began to grow he rubbed off all the buds but one, and trained that perpendicularly, rubbing off during the season all side shoots ; and when it had reached to the top of a second story balcony, nipped the end off, thus stopping its further growth. In the spring of 1838, he rubbed off every bud but two at the top of the vine, and trained these two along the front of the balcony, having stretched a large wire along the posts for their support. He rubbed off every side bud during the season, as at first. Both shoots made about thirty-five feet of growth this season. In the spring of 1839 every joint on the horizontal shoots was permitted to send forth its buds, and to grow un-molested, till the branches had fairly set fruit, generally until they were about 18 inches long. Then the end of each branch was nipped off, and its further growth prevented. The perpendicular stem was carefully prevented from sending out buds. The whole plant was carefully watched that no more buds might be permitted to grow—each one being rubbed off as soon as it appeared. Thus, from about the middle of June, the vine was not permitted to form any new wood. During the season the grapes grew uncommonly well, and every one ripened in good season, and was very fine, as was proved by the numerous company at the Horticultural Society exhibition, who unanimously pronounced them the finest grapes there. The produce of this vine was *three hundred and fifteen bunches*, all very large, and the berries of uncommon size. The society awarded to them its first premium for native grapes. Almost every body, however, doubted whether the plant had not been injured by this excessive bearing of fruit; and many old gardeners considered that it would be killed by it. The writer never doubted on this score. He had only compelled the plant to *make fruit*, instead of wood to be cut off and thrown away, and has no doubt that if he had been able to get the season before a greater length of wood for fruit branches, the plant would have supported a much larger quantity of fruit. On trimming the vine preparatory to its bearing in 1840, there was very little wood to be cut off. Only two buds were left on each branch of last year's growth, and these are now growing and showing fruit buds very finely. The vine is not dead, nor does it appear to have been injured in the least by last year's hard work. So far, the experiment is beautifully successful, and we now feel authorized to recommend this plan to all who love fine fruit. It must be borne in mind that the experiment was made with the Isabella grape ;

we of course cannot say any thing about its applicability to other kinds from *experience ;* but the same reasoning applies with equal force to all kinds. If the powers of a plant can be turned from the formation of wood to that of making fruit, as we have proved it can in the case of the Isabella grape, we do not see any reason why the experiment may not be successful with all kinds of grapes and fruit. One thing we do know, that a plant that hears fruit does not grow as much as one that does not; and we are hence authorized to infer, that the power of the plant may be directed at pleasure, either to the growth of fruit or wood —that by suppressing the one, you may in-crease the other, to a very great extent. The vine above described has attracted the attention of numerous persons, and many have determined to follow the example. It may be observed that this vine occupies no room at all in the garden. It grows close in the corner of the house, a single stem ascending fourteen feet to the balcony, when it starts off horizontally, as above described, along the balcony. Thus every house in any city that has a yard at all, so that the vine may be set in the earth, may have just such a supply of delicious grapes as the writer of this had last fall.

G. B. S.

In the Annual Monitor for 1840, published at York, England, is the following striking account of resignation under affliction of long duration.

DIED, the 12th of 10th mo. 1838, HANNAH MYERS, of Leeds, aged about 82 years.

We believe it may be truly said of the ex-perience of this dear friend, that " godliness with contentment is great gain ;" for through her long protracted life it is not known, by her nearest connections, that a murmur ever esca-ped her lips, no repining at her lot, but a con-stant, cheerful acquiescence in the divine will. Her allotment was a truly secluded one ; hav-ing, through bodily infirmity, been confined to her house nearly 70 years ; not being able to walk, nor move herself from one place to an-other for that period. The uniform serenity of her mind was very instructive to those about her; and many can bear witness, that their faith has often been strengthened by see-ing the power of religion so strongly exem-plified, in supporting her mind under the nu-merous privations of society, to which she was necessarily subject.

The humbling view she took of her reli-gious attainments was an evidence of true dis-cipleship ; and she often remarked that she had been an unprofitable servant, and had nothing on which she could rely, no work of her own; but only on the merits of God, in Christ Jesus, our Lord.

THE BURNING OF A COAL MINE.

Letters and papers from the department of the Allier, bring accounts of a remarkable con-flagration, which broke out in the coal mines of Commentry, and had been burning for a week, with daily increasing fury. It appears that this fire, which, for the last four-and-twenty years, has been silently smouldering in the bowels of the earth—revealing its existence by perpetual smoke, and occasional outbreaks of flame, which, however, had always been confined within the limits abandoned to its dominion—had, at length, made its way through some breach into one of the vast galleries of these extensive workings ; and there, meeting with the air current so long denied it, had spread through all the subterranean chambers and passages with a rapidity before which resistance became utterly powerless ; showing itself at every crevice and outlet of the vast labyrinth, and flinging its points and columns of fire far up into the air, through all the shafts that led into the wide field of the rich deposit. Luckily the solemnities of the day [being the first day of the week] had emptied the workings of their human tenants, for no mortal aid could have availed them against the suddenness with which the fiery flood swept over all things. The authorities of the district were early on the spot, but have hitherto been little more than idle and awe-struck spectators. Neither Vesuvius, nor any other eruption, say the accounts, can give a notion of the dreadful and sublime scene. " If," says one writer, " it were possible to forget that the flames have been for three whole days devouring the immense wealth, and that by this conflagration three ·hundred fathers of families will be thrown out of employment, there would be room for no other sentiment than that of admiration at the magnificent spectacle. Imagine a deep ravine nearly circular, in the form of a reversed cone, with its edges, however, hourly enlarging. Through fourteen large openings, issuing at about twenty feet above the ground of this ravine, and giving access to the innumerable galleries of the mines below, as many torrents of flame are poured forth with frightful violence from the caldrons within—flames of a thousand hues rushing forth like fiery whirlwinds—dividing, and crossing, and mingling, and rising, and falling, and rising again. At times, a hollow cracking sound echoes through the abyss ; this is some huge block of coal detaching itself from the roof or sides of one of the galleries, and falling into the blazing gulf. Then rises up a thick column of black dust ; till it reaches the openings of the galleries, two gaping mouths shoot into the air their dazzling columns of fire. Suddenly one of these ceases. It seems for a moment as if checked in its wrath. Then comes a long and startling groan from the entrails of the earth : and forth again rushes the flame, blood red, roaring and terrible, threatening in its fury to lift up the burning mountain altogether, and bury the spectators beneath its dreadful ruins. Again, look around you ; it is midnight, and two thousand faces are there, some grouped on the opposite crest of the ravine, some sheltered in the cavities of the rocks. Yet no sound meets the ear save that of the roaring flames." The latest accounts state that the rafters of the galleries had all fallen, and the founts of flame nearly ceased to play. The whole had become one burning gulf. The loss is said to be incalculable; millions of hectolitres of coal had been consumed. The engineers were preparing to turn a stream, which flows at a league's distance, and direct it upon the burning mountain. Workmen were employed night and day in

this operation, by which it was hoped to lay the mines under water.—*French paper.*

COLOURED PEOPLE IN LONDON.

John T. Norton, an American, writes from London to the Hartford (Ct.) Courier as follows :

" There are not many coloured people in England, but I see one or more every day. And where do you think I see them ? The first I saw was a mulatto woman walking arm in arm with a gentleman in Hyde Park. The next was an African man entirely at home in an omnibus filled with white gentlemen and ladies. The next was an elegantly dressed and beautiful young lady, sitting by the side of a black lady, on terms of perfect equality, in one ·of the most splendid coaches in Hyde Park, with liveried servants. Yesterday, whilst riding in an omnibus in Regent street, a coloured young woman beckoned to the driver, and he stopped and opened the door at once. She did not get in, as she found it was not going where she wished to go.

" This afternoon I attended the church in Blackfriars, formerly Rowland Hill's. The largest and most respectable and solemn audience was present that I ever witnessed—the sexton told me 4,000. On looking round, I saw a head and face that marked the purest African descent. Was he perched up in a corner ? No : he was in a pew near the middle of the church. On my walk home, I saw a black man with an elegantly dressed white lady leaning on his arm, and immediately following them, a white and black gentleman arm in arm. I followed them a little, and soon, on coming to another street, the lady shook hands with the two black gentlemen, (for they had every appearance of such,) and they both put their arms into the white gentleman's, and walked on. What I noticed more particularly in all these cases was, that not the least attention was attracted. I could not perceive that any individual besides myself, knew that there was any difference in the colours.

" My paper is full, and I am

" Yours truly,

" JOHN T. NORTON."

From the New York Observer

TREATMENT OF THE SICK.

The first care of friends for friends, when they are brought down by disease or casualty, is, to relieve them from pain and restore them to health. . To this end, physicians are called in, and various remedies are administered. It is agreed on all hands, too, that good nursing is as important as good medical advice. In some cases it is much more so. Many a patient, under the most skilful practice, has been carried off for want of proper attention to diet, and to the prescriptions of the doctor. In the crisis of a disease, especially, every thing often depends upon following his directions *implicitly*. A dosing nurse, who has an ear for every new remedy that happens to be recommended by the neighbours, is unsafe. Wait till the physician comes ; ask his advice, and if he approves of it, try it. Otherwise, beware how you experiment upon the life of a fellow being.

Though many suffer for want of proper attention, even *good* nursing may be carried too far. There is such a thing as over-doing, as well as not doing enough. Some persons are so extremely anxious when friends are sick, that they must all the while be doing something. They are sure that if a little medicine does some good, a great deal would do much more. And that if taking it once in four or six hours abates the disease, taking it twice as often would conquer it twice as soon ; so they kill the patient with kindness. He went down, they say, in spite of all they could do ; whereas, had they done but half as much, he might have been saved.

And here, let me say, that the sick are sometimes exceedingly injured by calling in too many watchers. I am aware that, in acute disease, it may be necessary to have some one by the bed-side continually ; and in extreme cases, more than one watcher may be wanted. The members of the family, perhaps, are quite worn out with anxiety and toil. In such cases they ought to send out for help ; and it would argue any thing but kindness and fellow-feeling to refuse. But is not this often done when the sick man would be far better off with the little attention which some one in the house might give him, without much interruption of sleep ; and are not two persons frequently called in when one would do better? What the sick want, in the night time, is *rest*. Nothing is more important than to get every thing still at an early hour ; but how can this be done if one or two persons are up in the room all night, however careful they may be in all their movements? Some families, in which members are afflicted with lingering diseases, will go through a whole winter without sending for a single watcher, while others, under precisely similar circumstances, will wear out a whole neighbourhood. Where a sick person needs only that kind of attention, two or three times in a night, which a father, mother, brother or sister can render by sleeping in the room, why should friends be taxed to come in and sit up all night, however cheerfully they may offer to do so ? It is hardly necessary to add, that in cases of great mental excitement, it is commonly very injurious to bring in strangers as watchers. It adds fuel to the fire, and sometimes, I have no doubt, hastens diseases to fatal issues. . It is not very uncommon for the sick, when the brain is bewildered, to imagine that they are threatened with some personal violence ; and, where this happens, the sight of strange faces is almost sure to create alarm, as if their greatest fears were about to be realised.

May I add, that the custom which extensively prevails of calling in to see the sick is very injurious? There is a preposterous, not to say cruel, curiosity in regard to this, which ought to be discouraged, and even frowned upon, if it cannot be otherwise restrained. The neighbours want just to step into the sick room and see how the patient *looks*; but what possible good can it do? And who that is writhing with pain, or reduced to extreme debility, wants to be made a gazing-stock to any body? If you can do any thing for your sick neighbour as a nurse or a watcher, very well. Offer your services, and render them most cheerfully where they are needed ; but otherwise, it is a kindness to keep away. I think I have known many sick persons very much injured by this sort of neighbourly kindness. By crowding around the door and the bed, they have excluded and consumed the oxygen, which was more essential to the sick man than all his medicines.

There is apt to be a strong desire, too, when a patient begins to recover, to visit him in a friendly way, before he is able to bear the fatigue and excitement. Physicians will tell you, I believe, that there are more relapses from this cause than almost any other. "The patient is worse—he had too much company yesterday." How often have I heard this remark from the lips of doctors and experienced nurses. Many, I have no doubt, are confined to their rooms weeks or months longer than necessary, by being visited too early and too frequently, from the best motives in the world. There are other and better ways of showing our sympathy and our friendship, till the sick have gained sufficient strength to see us.

I only add once more, that it is a great calamity for a sick man himself to be a dabbler in physic. This is sometimes the case. The patient has his theory about various classes of diseases. He has studied the symptoms, and thinks that some other remedies than those which his physician prescribes would do better. Now it is notoriously unsafe, where a disease is violent or in any way critical, for the most skilful practitioner to rely upon his own prescriptions—how much more for a person who has a mere casual smattering in domestic pharmacy. And yet individuals of this class not unfrequently give their medical attendants a vast deal of trouble. They are so much wiser than the greatest masters of the healing art, that it is difficult to bring them under any regular course of treatment. They *feel* so and so; and say what you will, they are persuaded that such and such medicines would help them. Under these morbid impressions, patients even of strong minds will sometimes take the matter into their own hands, and venture upon the most dangerous experiments.

An acquaintance of mine, a very respectable clergyman, had been confined with a slow fever for a number of weeks, and under the mild, but I have no doubt judicious, treatment of his family physician, was beginning to recover. All the symptoms were favourable. But the good man was impatient. He wanted to be in his pulpit and his parish;' and he was fully convinced that he needed more active medicines. The physician tried every way to beat him off from the notion, but in vain. He was confident, he said, that his stomach and bowels were in a particular state which he described, and that he should never be well till they were thoroughly cleansed. Accordingly, finding that the doctor could not be induced to yield to his wishes, he, in an evil hour, prepared a heavy portion of drastic physic for himself. He took it, and the next day he was a corpse. H.

ANTARCTIC CONTINENT.

Latest from the Exploring Expedition—Highly Important Discovery.—Capt. Wilkes, in the Vincennes, has ascertained, beyond all question, the existence of a great Antarctic Continent, and has actually skirted along its coast throughout more than 56 degrees of longitude. The particulars of this important discovery, so far as they are known to us, are contained in the following extract from a Sidney (New South Wales) paper of March 12th, for which we are indebted to a commercial house, who received it from their Sidney correspondent. The same paper also contains (from the Hobart Town Courier) information of the same continent having been seen, *on the same day*, though in a different longitude, by the French exploring expedition; but the latter was unable to approach the coast save at a single point, and does not appear to have seen even more than a few miles of it, whereas the American expedition saw and examined it, as before stated, for a distance of more than 54 degrees of longitude. Probably the same continent was seen some years ago by Captain Fanning, (see Fanning's Voyages, p. 447.) We subjoin the two extracts above referred to.—*Jour. of Commerce.*

[From the Sidney Herald, March 12th.]

Discovery of the Antarctic Continent.—Amongst the arrivals to be found in our shipping list of this day, is that of the United States ship Vincennes, under the command of Charles Wilkes, Esq. The Vincennes has been absent from this port almost eighty days, most of which time has been spent in southern exploration; and we are happy to have it in our power to announce, on the highest authority, that the researches of the exploring squadron after a southern continent have been completely successful. The land was first seen on the morning of the 19th of January, in latitude 66 deg. 20 min. south, longitude 154 deg. 18 min. east.

The Peacock, (which ship arrived in our harbour on the 22d ultimo, much disabled from her contact with the ice,) we learn, obtained soundings in a high southern latitude, and established beyond doubt the existence of land in that direction. But the Vincennes, more fortunate in escaping injury, completed the discovery, and run down the coast from 154 deg. 18 min. to 97 deg. 45 min. east longitude, about seventeen hundred miles, within a short distance of the land, often so near as to get soundings with a few fathoms of line, during which time she was constantly surrounded by ice islands and bergs, and experiencing many heavy gales of wind, exposing her constantly to shipwreck. We also understand that she has brought several specimens of rock and earth procured from the land, some of them weighing upwards of one hundred pounds.

It is questionable whether the discovery can be of any essential service to commerce, but it cannot be otherwise than gratifying to Captain Wilkes, and the officers engaged with him in this most interesting expedition, to have brought it to a successful termination the high trust committed to them by their country; and it is hoped that so noble a commencement in the cause of science and discovery will induce the government of the United States to follow up, by other expeditions, that which is now on the point of termination.

[From the Hobart Town Courier.]

We have to acknowledge the receipt of a French letter, containing a succinct account of the expedition of the two French corvettes, the *Astrolabe* and *Zelee*, under the command of Commodore D'Urville, which, from its length, and the late hour at which it reached our office, we are unable to give in type this week. Our readers will be pleased to learn that the exertions of the French commodore have been crowned with success. On the evening of the 19th January, in latitude 66 deg. S. and about 130 deg. east longitude, land was descried; and on the 21st the corvettes approached to within five or six miles, and two boats' crews put off to collect specimens of rock from a point which was clear of ice. The land is described as stretching from the south to the W. S. W. as far as the eye could discern. Commodore D'Urville was desirous of continuing his discoveries, but was stopped on the 23rd by a bank of ice stretching out from the land directly north to an immense distance, and was consequently compelled to alter his course. The following day the vessels encountered a most furious gale of wind, during which the *Zelee* very narrowly escaped being wrecked. Further progress was prevented by (*la banquise*,) which hindered any further progress towards the south. Although not much will have been gained by this enterprise in point of utility, it will add greatly to our geographical and scientific knowledge. It does not appear that any living beings or animal exist in these cold and dreary regions; not even a seal was seen, nor any very useful kind of whale. Captain Dumont D'Urville has, by this discovery, earned an additional title to the honours of his country, distinguished as his name has already been in scientific navigation. (The *Astrolabe* and *Zelee* had arrived at Hobart Town.)

Postscript.—Since putting the above in type, we have been favoured with the annexed letter from an officer of the Vincennes, which, with some variations from the newspaper account, contains many additional particulars.

U. S. SHIP VINCENNES, }
Sidney Harbour, March 12th, 1840. }

We arrived here yesterday from our southern cruise, upon the success of which we all have reason to congratulate ourselves. We have discovered land within the Antarctic, and cruised along the edge of the barrier ice (seeing the land frequently) upwards of seventy degrees of longitude. All are convinced there is an extensive continent there: whether it will be of any benefit to mankind, or not, time alone can show.

For my part, no inducement could be held out that would make me volunteer to return there, unless one of the other vessels should have been unfortunate enough to be wrecked. We were unfortunate in not being able to land, take possession, and plant the stripes and stars. When the weather permitted us to do so, no boat *could* land—the land being very high, covered with snow, and sloping gradually to the water, where it was terminated by ice, descending one hundred or two hundred feet perpendicularly.

The weather was, part of the time, good, and part blowing from fresh to heavy gales, with thick snow storms, making the navigation extremely hazardous, on account of the icebergs by which we were generally surrounded.

I have at times counted one hundred large ones from the deck, without the aid of a glass, taking no notice of the small ones.

We found the Peacock here repairing, almost a perfect wreck, having had her stern frame lifted, and all the *timbers* broken above the main deck, as far forward as the gangway, rudder knocked off, forefoot carried away, and planking knocked up to within an inch and a half of her wood-ends. How she arrived here, it seems impossible to conceive. I did not suppose a vessel in her condition could hold together long enough to do so: she was caught in the ice, and jammed by the closing of the passage after she went in. I hope that the brig and schooner have escaped, and that we shall find them at New Zealand.

By the arrival to-day from Hobart Town, (Van Diemen's land,) we learn that the French expedition is there, and that they discovered land the same day we did, in 66 S. and 130 east. It is no doubt a continuation of what we saw, and will render the honour of being first disputed for some time. I do not think they can boast much, as they were satisfied with a single sight, owing to the Zelee's being near lost. *We* have coasted the new continent thirteen hundred miles.

For "The Friend."

EARLY FRIENDS IN NEW ENGLAND.
(Continued from p. 326.)

LETTER VIII.

William Leddra was the fourth Quaker hung for his religion in Boston. He also was a missionary to Massachusetts, to warn the people of their errors, and he was a very talented and popular teacher. But during his three years' residence among them, our first charter rulers ceased not to ply him with hot persecution; ofttimes they imprisoned, ofttimes they scourged him, and during the whole winter preceding his execution they kept him in irons like a burglar or a robber; yet, as himself declares, "he never turned his cheek from the smiter, nor his feet from following the flock; and the whip on his back, and all his imprisonments, and banishments on pain of death; and even loud threatenings of a halter, did no more move him than if they had bound a spider's web upon his finger." When brought before his persecutors, who were also his judges and his judges' counsellors, he demanded to know his crime.

"You stand with your hat on," said they; "you say thee and thou, and are a Quaker; and you, moreover, have declared those Quakers, whom we have executed, to be innocent."

"What," said Leddra, "will you hang a man for speaking good English, and defending the servants of the Lord?" "A man," said Dennison, "may speak treason in good English."

"Will you go to England, and trouble us no more?" said Bradstreet. "I have no business there," said Leddra. "Then you shall go that way," said this merciful judge, pointing towards the gallows.

"I understand you," said Leddra; "I am to die for breathing the air of your jurisdiction; but mark me, I am an Englishman and your fellow-subject, and I appeal to the laws of my own nation and country, and if by them I am criminal, I am ready to suffer." "Appeal to England, three thousand miles off!" said Dennison with a sneer; "and what will you gain by that? Send over your complaint; the next year parliament will send over here to know what's the matter, and the third year the government of England will be changed. Be better advised—renounce your errors, and save your life."

"What," said Leddra with indignation, "and join such murderers as you!—then let every one who meets me point and say, lo! this is the man who has forsaken the God of his salvation." As he said this, Wenlock Christison, who was also sentenced to banishment on pain of death, walked into court and stood by the prisoner. For a moment the judges were silent, and seemed confounded at this voluntary offer of human life, and which they now began to dread the necessity of taking.

Here's another Quaker, said one.

Bring him forward, Mr. Marshal, said Secretary Rawson: Yea, said Wenlock. Were you Christison? Yea, said Wenlock. Then what doest thou here? said governor Endicot fiercely. I came here, said Wenlock, with a loud voice, to warn you to shed no more innocent blood, and to see my friend; for the blood you have already shed now cries to the Lord God for vengeance. Take him away, jailor, said Endicot, and as they seized him he desired to remain with his friend William, whom he boldly affirmed they were about to murder.

But the faith and courage of Leddra, and fidelity of Christison—virtues which savages even reverence, were powerless upon the charter assistants and their advisers. So full of "holy" zeal were they, and so blind to mere "carnal" virtue, though of the highest order; and without delay they passed sentence of death upon the prisoner; and on the 14th of March, 1661, it being lecture day, and after "divine service," he was led out to be hung, and to preserve the public peace, and to keep off the mob, and to maintain the supremacy of the first charter law, Endicot himself, with a strong military guard, conducted the victim from prison to the gallows.

When he arrived at the foot of the ladder, he saw Edward Wharton in earnest expostulation with the multitude against the execution and the injustice of the rulers, and he said, "friend Wharton, remember that all who would be Christ's disciples must take up the cross;" and to the people he said, "for the testimony of Jesus, and for testifying against deceivers, I am brought here to suffer." This Wharton was a Salem man, and under banishment on pain of death. As the martyr went up the ladder, one in the crowd regarded him with peculiar interest: Leddra called to him also and said, "friend, know that this day I am willing to offer up my life as a witness of Jesus." Upon this the man became greatly agitated, and begged that he might speak. "Gentlemen," said he, "I am a stranger to you and your country, and yet a friend to both; for Jesus' sake, for the Lord's sake, I pray you not to take away that man's life, but remember Gamaliel's counsel to the Jews. I am a seaman, and lately arrived from England, and when I heard this man was to die for his religion, I went to see him in prison; and me thought the Lord did mightily appear in his words. I then sought out one of the magistrates who condemned him, and asked what was his crime. He is a rogue, said he, a very rogue, and has also abused magistracy. But I said, what has that to do with the question? Why do you kill the man? what is your rule, your law, your authority? But he did not answer. Gentlemen, you have no rule, no warrant from the word of God, no precedent from England, nor have you authority from the king, whose name you presume to use, to hang that man.

"But they tell me he may go away if he will. Is it so? Then let him go—let me have him; I command a stout ship, and will gladly take him away from your country. William Leddra come down, come down from that cursed tree; they say you may go away if you will; come down to me, William, and I will take care of you."

Here a murmur of applause ran through the crowd, but to quiet them, Allen, minister of Boston, who, probably, on that day had preached, called out to the people, that such willingness to die in the criminal, should not move them; for the apostle had said, "that some should be given up to strong delusions, and even dare to die for them."

And the captain of the guard said to the stranger, "sir, what have you to do in the matter? William cannot go away, *you* may go away, and if you take my advice, you will do so quick'ly." "I shall go away," said the seaman, "for of all sights, to my eyes this is the most cruel."

Orders were given to make haste, and the ladder was turned to throw him off; Leddra had only time to say, "Lord Jesus receive my spirit," and these were his last words.

And when he was dead, and about to be cut down, Wharton, whose own life was then forfeit, and at the mercy of the charter rulers, with other friends, stood under; and as the body fell, they caught it in their arms: and after he was stripped by the hangman, they laid him in his grave.

Is the production of the beet root sugar profitable without a protecting duty? The most important fact we have met with lately, bearing upon this question, is that the business is extending from France, into Germany, Prussia, Austria, and Russia.

An important improvement has been recently introduced into the manufacture of beet sugar in France, which consists in refining the sugar at the time of making it, by one continuous operation, without taking it from the mould until it is converted into the most beautiful lump. Such importance is attached to this discovery, that it has obtained the prize of 20,000 francs.—*Late paper.*

LONDON POLICE.

From the private letter of an American in London.

One of the most striking and admirable institutions of the city is its police. This is the result of Sir Robert Peel's labour and skill. In the space of every half square, or from twenty to fifty rods, you see a man, idling about, as if he had just come to London. He has a narrow leather strap buckled upon his wrist, and a strip of silver edging upon his collar, with one or two letters and figures worked into the cloth of the collar. He has also a peculiar hat on, which looks like oil cloth highly varnished, with the body covered with crape, and the top exposed to the weather. He has no arms or other weapons, and if it rains you see him with a cape over his shoulders like our firemen. Once in a while he stops and looks up and down, or if there is any collection or confusion of any kind, he slowly walks up to the scene of it. If there is a collection of coaches at a stage-house or mail-office, one of these men is always looking on. If there is a public meeting of any kind, one of these men is in the street, two or three in the entry, one or two at the inside door, and half a dozen in the crowd or near the platform. In markets, on the wharves, at the steamboat landings, near the bridges,—in fact, wherever you go you meet these stragglers. They walk very lazily ; you seldom see two of them together, and you never see them with any body unless as a protector. These are policemen. They are the men to ask the way to any given place, the name or design of any building,—in short, any thing that the citizen or stranger needs to inquire about. They are perfectly civil, and seem to seize every opportunity to be useful. There are two commissioners of police, and the force is divided into seventeen departments, marked with initials and numbers. Each division has one superintendent, four inspectors, sixteen serjeants, and one hundred and forty-four constables—making a force of two thousand eight hundred. Each of these policemen receives nineteen shillings, or nearly five dollars a week, and his clothes, and coals for one fire—perhaps one dollar per day. I have seen no man drunk, and but one case of a squabble in the street, and that was in the suburbs. The principal business of the lord mayor appears to be, to do the honours of the city on public occasions. I have seen him preside at two public meetings—one, of the Society for the propagation of the Gospel in foreign parts, and the other a public meeting to petition parliament respecting the condition of the colony at New Zealand. He has the title of Right Honourable, from being a member of the privy council *ex officio*. The office is held for a term of years, and the next oldest in commission of the two sheriffs of London succeeds. The office is said to be worth six thousand pounds per annum. He wears a broad gold chain on the neck, a profusion of rings on his hands, and a gold snuff-box. His robe is a light blue, edged with fur, and hanging quite to the ground. Wherever he goes the coast is clear, and all respect is paid.—*S. S. Journal.*

Agriculture feeds us to a great extent ; it clothes us, and without it we *could* not have manufactures, and *re should* not have commerce ; these all stand together, but they stand together like pillars—the largest in the centre—and that largest is AGRICULTURE.—*Webster.* ·

For "The Friend."
To the Memory of Daniel Wheeler.

Seal not the sympathetic fount, whose inmost depths are stirred,
Whose crystal waters overflow at each remembered word,
Which, from those lips now closed in death, like dews refreshing fell,
The gospel's joyful tidings in distant lands to tell.
Check not the fount of sympathy, but bid its waters flow,
To mingle with the daughter's tears, the sons' o'er-whelming woe—
To swell the tide which overleaps the broad Atlantic's wave,
Or gushes where Pacific's tides the distant islands lave,
Since both on Honolulu's shore and Russia's snowy steep,
The Christian and the heathen world bow down the head to weep. .
As when, with overwhelming force, the fierce tornado's wrath
Uproots the venerable trees along its forest path,
We scarcely give a passing thought, or heed the ruin made,
Though many a tall, time-honoured tree prone to the earth is laid.
But, when some isolated oak, of high majestic form,
Which yielded shade in summer's heat, and shelter from the storm,
Beneath whose shadow sire and son successively have strayed,
And many a generation has wandered to its shade,
To some insidious disease becomes a gradual prey,
Till root and branch are withered quite by slow, yet sure decay,
We gaze upon its vacant place in loneliness of soul,
And mourn its loss in after years, as on their course they roll.
So, when a Christian patriarch falls, the vacancy how drear,
To those who loved his counsels high, his kindred ex-ample here.
One who unmoved amid life's storms and tempests seemed to stand,
Like to some stately beacon rock, upon a sea-bent strand.
What high companionship was his, as oft alone he stood
Upon the Freeling's narrow deck, above the briny flood,
When of his numerous earthly friends but one beloved was near,
With converse sweet each heavy hour and moment lone to cheer;
Since faith was there with angel light, a radiance bright and warm,
And resignation placed her bow upon the darkest storm.
Then wherefore mourn, since, as we trust, thy pure and ransomed soul,
Borne upward to the mercy seat, has reached its final goal,
" Where faith is lost in certain sight, where partings never come,
And prayer is changed to endless praise in the Redeemer's home."
ADA.

THE FRIEND.

SEVENTH MONTH, 18, 1840.

·Once more it seems needful to offer a few words on the subject of obituary notices, though, perhaps, but a repetition of what has been remarked more than once heretofore. Brevity ; in our estimation, is the point chiefly to be aimed at in these mementos, and eulogy, or delineation of character, if indulged in at all, should be with the strictest regard to condensation. If the partialities and affectionate

THE FRIEND.

A RELIGIOUS AND LITERARY JOURNAL.

VOL. XIII.　　　　SEVENTH DAY, SEVENTH MONTH, 25, 1840.　　　　NO. 43.

EDITED BY ROBERT SMITH.

PUBLISHED WEEKLY.

Price two dollars per annum, payable in advance.

Subscriptions and Payments received by

GEORGE W. TAYLOR,

NO. 50, NORTH FOURTH STREET, UP STAIRS,

PHILADELPHIA.

Notes of an Excursion to the Susquehanna at Wilkesbarre.

From the North American.

An esteemed friend, and an accurate observer of men and things, who has recently made a tour to Wilkesbarre by the Philadelphia and Reading and Tamaqua railroads, and the Lehigh canal and railroad, has afforded us an opportunity of making some extracts from notes taken by him during his excursion.

At Mauch Chunk there are three schutes for the delivery of coal into boats. From one of these they now deliver daily rising 600 tons, and they can, when necessary, deliver 1,000 tons each per day. The loaded car in descending, draws an empty one up an inclined plane 750 feet, overcoming in this distance 212 vertical feet. An iron band is used in place of rope, on one of the Room Run planes. Three men attend at the head of the schute now in use, and can let down and discharge one car per minute.

Though business is dull generally, there seems to be a good deal doing here. Little can be accomplished any where without labour. He who does not work must pay others for working;—this puts the rich and the poor more on a level than some may suppose. Here this principle is completely exemplified.

It is thought that the Lehigh company's coal lands could yield a million of tons annually, for more than a century,—and why not for many centuries? These lands extend to within a few rods of the Little Schuylkill lands, near Tamaqua. They are in one direction about fourteen miles long, and amount to about 15,000 acres in this place; on the Lehigh, elsewhere, the company has about 7,000 more, part worth but little, and some very valuable for water power, sites for villages, &c. The Nesquehoning, a powerful stream, passes some miles through the Mauch Chunk tract; it has 240 feet descent, every twenty of which will afford a mill seat. Iron ore is also found in several places on these lands. Killed two rattlesnakes in our rambles to-day.

Departed in a canal boat for White's Haven, distant twenty-five miles. This canal is formed by a succession of pools. These pools approach so near together as to form the semblance of a large placid navigable river, interrupted by dams and locks, and occasionally by a short canal. The water in the pools is of an average depth of twenty feet. High mountains line the shores on both sides, some of them said to be from 1,000 to 1,200 feet elevation. Very few spots fit for habitations are visible. It is interesting to see the splendid dams and locks so completely subduing a bold torrent, and contrasting so strikingly with the savage wildness of the scene. These locks and dams surpass any thing of the kind in this country, and perhaps in any other part of the world. Until Josiah White taught otherwise, a lock of six feet was deemed the only safe lift; seven and eight feet were thought rather hazardous;—here we have them twenty, twenty-five, and even thirty feet, with cascades from the dams proportionally grand—in the spray of which, when the sun shines, dances continually the inimitable rainbow. There are twenty-nine locks, and twenty dams between Mauch Chunk and White's Haven. The locks are one hundred feet long and twenty wide, and pass two boats at a time, side by side. 205,000 cubic yards of solid masonry were used in their construction between these points, and more substantial structures I have not seen. From the foundation to the coping of the thirty feet lock, the distance is forty-five feet. This lock was filled, and a boat passed in six minutes, and the water discharged in less than two minutes. Josiah White says that if the work was to be constructed again, he would have but three locks and three pools between these points.

Landed at Lowrytown, 15 miles above Mauch Chunk, and ate a well prepared dinner in a log house. Here a small stream discharges into the Lehigh. The Buck Mountain company's coal mines are five miles distant, and a railroad is now constructing to them, which is nearly completed. They have also a landing here, with a handsome basin, but the valley is narrow, and the hills on each side are very steep. The pool at Lowrytown is thirty feet deep. Near lock No. 28, the rocks along the shore look like masonry, and are said to present the same appearance to the bottom of the pool, forty feet below the water level. At Taylor's Retreat, two saw mills are constructing, calculated to cut annually three millions of feet of boards. The Lehigh company own the land, and the owners of the mills are to pay $3 per inch on two hundred inches of water, or $600 annually, on a lease for twenty years. The head of water is twenty feet. On reaching White Haven, ten miles from Lowrytown, we had an opportunity of viewing the Lehigh company's property. They possess good water power, and there are several saw mills, &c. in operation. During the day we met a number of boats descending, laden with lumber, each carrying from 35 to 45,000 feet. This will soon become a considerable trade, and will prove a source of no small revenue to the Lehigh company. Boats can go hence to market at all periods of the year, unless prevented by ice, and will thus have an advantage over boats and rafts that descend by freshets only, and which often arrive at a glutted market—as at Port Deposit. There is an immense body of white pine timber in this vicinity, the only market for which must be down the Lehigh. It is said that no less than five million thousand feet of lumber will find its only market by this route, exclusive of that which may arrive from the river Susquehanna, which it is believed will be considerable, as being the nearest and safest course to Philadelphia and New York.

From White's Haven our company proceeded on horseback on the line of the railroad to Wilkesbarre. The tracks on this road are constructed of solid masonry, extending about two feet under ground, the coping being heavy, flat hard stones, laid even with the surface. The cost is not more than to have formed it of rubble stone, the materials being at hand to make a solid wall, and it is less liable to settle. On the two lines of this masonry, timber is placed crosswise for sleepers, and on these rest the rails, which are called the T rail, weighing about fifty pounds the running yard. It is a most substantial structure. The tunnel, three fourths of a mile long, is not yet commenced. On our way we examined the wheels preparing for the inclined planes, of which there are three, to overcome a descent of 1000 feet. Two wheels for each plane are thirty feet in diameter, over which iron bands are made to pass in place of ropes, as used at the inclined plane on the Columbia railroad. The value of the iron band for security and durability, is no longer a problem, it having been in use for more than one year at Mauch Chunk. It is the offspring of Josiah White's ingenuity. Should it by possibility give way, he has provided for the safety of the passing car, which will, in that event, descend by an easy and slow motion to the level. The band is subjected to a proof of three or four times greater strain than will at any time be applied to it when in operation. The railroad is twenty miles long, fifteen of which are nearly completed, the rails being already laid nearly the whole of this distance.

From Chambers' Edinburgh Journal.

ASCENT OF THE PIC DU MIDI.

[The following letter is the composition of an English gentleman residing at Bagueres de Bigorre, in the South of France. The adventure which it describes took place last July.]

* * It has occurred to me that you might wish to hear of my adventurous journey to the Pic du Midi, one of the highest mountains of the Pyrenean range. The party consisted of the Countess of C——, the Count de V——, and myself. We left Bagneres at eight o'clock in the evening, and reached the village of Grippe at eleven. The windows of the small inn command an interesting view of the valley of the Adour, and the mountains overhanging it, and which we had made a previous excursion to visit. At midnight we mounted our horses to commence the ascent of the celebrated Pic du Midi, which is between eleven and twelve thousand feet above the level of the sea. There was not a cloud in the heavens, and the stars shone so brilliantly in this pure atmosphere, that we had sufficient light to guide us over the narrow and precipitous path, though not more than to enable us to distinguish the outlines of the mountains which surrounded us. I am not sure, however, if this uncertain light, aided by the dashing of the three cataracts, did not rather enhance the effect of the scene, by leaving so much to the imagination. The waterfalls are formed by the river Adour, which rises in the Pic du Midi, and after passing through Bagueres, Jarbes, and Pau, empties itself into the sea at Bayonne. The sound of these immense masses of water was very imposing in the stillness of the night. After a rapid ascent of an hour, we reached a small plain, on which were scattered a few miserable shepherds' huts, which they dignify by the name of the village of Tremesaigne. On leaving this we entered upon a gorge, through which the ascent was so steep, and the path so rugged, that we were compelled to dismount, and scramble up as well as we could; and this was difficult enough, as the mountains on each side cast their shadows over the path, and prevented our seeing where we were about to place our feet—water, rolling stones, and boggy ground, alternately receiving them. This difficulty surmounted, we again took to the saddle, and in half an hour reached another plain, on which there was one solitary hut. This place rejoices in the name of Areze, so called from a giant said once to have inhabited these regions. The sound of our horses' feet attracted the attention of the shepherds' dogs, who, fourteen in number, saluted us with their deep-toned mouths, which, with the noise of the cascades falling in every direction, and the hollow-sounding bells round the neck of the cattle, disturbed the silence of the night, and broke in upon the solitude of the place in an impressive manner. These dogs, the faithful guardians of their masters and their masters' property, are of immense size, and perfectly white; the manner in which they extract the sheep from the snow is quite marvellous. The barking of the dogs soon brought out one of the shepherds, who, knowing our errand, presented us with poles with iron points, so indispensable upon these expeditions as to merit the name of a *third leg*. Having taken the bridles off of our horses, and turned them loose on the plain, we collected our forces, which consisted of two guides and Madame de C—— and servant, and set forth at two o'clock in the morning on our hazardous ascent. Our reasons for setting out in the middle of the night were, to avoid the heat of the day, and to see the sun rise. This, however, we soon found impossible, as Madame de C—— was obliged to stop every two or three minutes, in consequence of the steepness of the path. Seeing that our great object was likely to be defeated by the slowness of her progress, she begged us to leave her with the guides, and to go forward. I was most unwilling in the first place to leave her, and also I did not relish the idea of going without a guide. My companion, however, laughed at the idea of danger, and the guides said we could not miss the way; and so on we went. The young are apt to think the old fools, whilst the old *know* the young to be so. Accordingly, we had not proceeded very far before we had to choose between two paths, one along the glaciers, which we had now fairly reached, and the other between two mountains, which had evidently been torn asunder by some sudden effort of nature. The intermediate space was this dubious way, so precipitous, and difficult to ascend, that I was relieved when our guides answered our call from beneath, by saying " All right," though the alternative was a glacier. The light of the stars now yielded to that of the moon, which, though shorn of its fair proportions, rose majestically above the tops of the hills we had left. Its light was most acceptable. No sooner had we surmounted the difficulty of this glacier, (and how small and insignificant does it now appear when compared with those we afterwards encountered,) than a choice of roads was again offered us, and our voices could now no longer reach the guides.

We differed about these roads. I was for continuing along the glacier; my friend, with the activity of the chamois which inhabit these mountains, was disposed to climb the ravine. His reasons appeared good, and we chose the latter, which proved wrong, though the mistake did not involve us in any natural difficulty beyond unnecessary additional fatigue. We now reached a plain of three or four hundred yards square, and found the level ground a great relief to those muscles which had been kept so long on the stretch by the rapidity of the ascent. This plain was covered with snow, whereon we saw the recent foot-marks of a bear. It was here where Plantade perished, surrounded by his philosophical instruments, with which he had been making observations. At half past three we began to perceive the approach of day. The effect of the gradual increase of light was interesting; the lofty summits of the mountains first receiving its influence, threw the valleys into still deeper shade. On this plain I perceived blocks of granite and gneiss: whence they came I cannot tell, as the mountain, as far as I could judge, is entirely composed of schiste. Their angles were rounded by attrition, so that the adjoining mountains, which, from their pointed summits, seemed granitic, may have once owned them. The side of the glacier being laid bare, proved to me the immense depth of the snow over which we had been walking; it was at least thirty feet in thickness! We now began to look with anxiety for the lake Ouchet, which is only two thousand five hundred feet below the Pic. In a few minutes we perceived it, entirely frozen over, though the snow upon it was partially melted. The basin in which it is situated is circular, its circumference about a quarter of a mile, and it has all the appearance of the crater of an extinct volcano. From hence, the mountain rises so abruptly that our hearts almost failed us, and we now felt the difficulty of our position, and the folly we had committed in undertaking such an ascent without a guide. We were now nine thousand feet above the level of the sea, and the keen air began to penetrate through our thin clothes; but you know well the exhilarating effects of mountain air, particularly at high elevations. We now commenced the ascent of the cone, and though we saw the summit illuminated by the rays of the sun, we were sorely embarrassed to know which direction to take. We first attempted to ascend in a straight line, to the top, but were soon obliged to abandon this for a zig-zag. An opening in the valley gave us a view of the sun, which shed its purple light over the whole range of the mountains; we saluted it with all the enthusiasm of its ancient adorers. Nothing, in fact, could exceed the grandeur and sublimity of the scene. After gazing for a few minutes upon this glorious sight, we resumed our dangerous journey over the glaciers, between which and the lake there was not a projecting rock, nor an obstacle in the way of the unfortunate man who should make a false step, so difficult to avoid on the frozen snow. Now, indeed, we felt the danger of our situation, when to retreat were as dangerous as to advance; in short, the very act of turning round might have proved fatal. My head began to fail me, and I no longer dared to look down to the lake beneath; it was not, however, till afterwards, that I was aware of the full extent of our danger. We had, unfortunately, no crampons, or spiked shoes; and as we traversed the side of the glaciers inclined like the roof of a house, we had to make a hole in the snow with our sticks before we could advance. Luckily, this side of the mountain being exposed to the south, there were considerable intervals from which the snow had disappeared; here the danger was less, but still so great, that at every step, after seeing where to put my foot, I closed my eyes and laid hold of the rocks, for the precipice of a thousand feet was too appalling for an unaccustomed eye to look upon without emotion. My companion was considerably above me on the face of the hill, and, ignorant or regardless of danger, was singing with all the gaiety of a French heart, when his attention was attracted by a voice (and no one who has not heard it, can tell how striking is the sound of the human voice in such solitudes): the voice was that of a guide who had nearly gained the summit, warning M. de V—— of his danger, and telling him to pass below the guide. He prudently listened to the voice of experience, and joining me, we passed the last of the glaciers in safety. We had now a most painful, though not dangerous ascent to gain the summit. The path lay over a bed of schiste, which, being reduced to small fragments by the operation of those causes always in activity at such a height, gave way so under our feet, as to double the fatigue, and to render the ascent as tedious as it is over the cinders of Vesuvius.

My chamois-footed companion was up before me, and had taken my Mackintosh, of which I had now great need; for although in the most profuse perspiration, the piercing wind of these elevated regions appeared to go through me. I seemed as if I could now lay hold of the Pic itself; but how fallacious are distances in this rare atmosphere! I soon, however, touched the goal I had so long in sight. It was now five o'clock. I will not add to this already too long letter by giving a description of the view from the Pic du Midi: suffice it to say, that the whole chain of the Pyrenees, from east to west, was visible under the most favourable circumstances; the course of the Garonne as far as Toulouse, and the Adour as far as the sea. Such scenes fill the mind with a thousand agitating and overwhelming feelings: the omnipotence of the hand that formed, and the insignificance of the creature that contemplated, these magnificent works of the creation, were painfully brought to the mind. Placing our backs against a rock to shelter us from the wind, and with the sun full upon us, we gazed for nearly an hour upon all the wonders by which we were surrounded.

An incident happened, which proved the courage and insensibility to danger of these intrepid mountaineers. M. de V—— let fall his drinking cup, which rolled down the glacier out of sight, and as we thought into some unfathomable abyss. The guide, however, starting up, said he would soon fetch it. We did all we could to dissuade him, by pointing out the great risk, and the utter insignificance of the thing lost; but he hesitated not a moment, and was soon suspended from the rocks on the side of the glacier. I closed my eyes, not daring to look upon what I deemed inevitable destruction. He disappeared; was absent about five minutes, during which we imagined all sorts of horrors, but at length returned with the cup in his hand. Whilst seated on the summit, four vultures came close to us, continuing to fly for a while over our heads, increasing the circle at each revolution, and ascending still higher, till they were apparently the size of swallows. M. de V—— discharged a pocket-pistol for the sake of the echo, but it was but faintly answered, and that at an interval of several seconds, probably by some higher Pic. We now thought of returning, but a ceremony, deemed indispensable upon such occasions, was first to be performed, namely, that of engraving our names upon the rock. We found a considerable variety of flowers on the very top, and the blue iris amongst the number. The summit is entirely composed of talcose schiste, and bears evident marks of having been struck by lightning. Having inscribed our names, (as monuments of our folly perhaps,) we began to descend, preceded by the guide, who reached the bottom of the schistous path before described almost at a bound. We descended with more measured steps, but faster than was agreeable. Each person detaching fragments of rock, which, collecting others in their course, and acquiring fresh impetus as they descended, produced a singular effect, and as they tumbled into the ravine, sounded like distant thunder. We now reached the first glacier, where an accident happened to one of the party, which must have proved

fatal but for the intrepidity and presence of mind of the guide, who had first descended to the foot of the glacier. I went down next, and by forcing my heels into the snow, arrived safely, though I had acquired such an impetus, that had not the guide arrested my progress, I never could have stopped myself. Next came one of the strangers, who, contrary to the advice of the guide, seated himself on the snow, and in this manner began to slide down the smooth surface of the glacier. He had not, however, proceeded far, before he had acquired such a velocity that he became terrified; his head took the place of his heels, and he came towards us with an appalling rapidity, uttering the most piercing cries of "I am lost!" "I am lost!" Nothing can ever efface from my remembrance this awful sight. At this moment, between him and the lake, two thousand feet below, there was nothing but fragments of rocks to arrest his progress. The guide, with a promptitude and courage beyond all praise, ran from the spot where he was standing, to place himself between a fellow creature and inevitable death, and this at the imminent peril of his own life; for the impetus the man had gained in falling through a space of three or four hundred yards, was likely enough to hurry them into the abyss beneath. Regardless, however, of himself, he rushed to the spot, placed his staff firmly in the ground, held it with his left hand, and was prepared to receive the terrified man with the right. Fortunately for both, at the bottom of the glacier there was a large stone, which broke the fall against the guide, though it covered the poor fellow with wounds and blood. For a second I thought the guide had lost his balance; it was one of the most painful moments I ever remember to have passed. The poor man bled from several parts of his body; his hands were cut, his nose and eyes dreadfully swelled, but fortunately no bone was broken, and he was enabled to continue his descent. This event impressed us all with the greatest alarm, particularly M. de V—— and myself, as this was the very glacier we had crossed in our way up. The guide was in a state of great agitation, and his trembling hand as he took hold of my arm by no means gave firmness to my feet. However, we reached the lake once more. To our great surprise we found Madame de C——; but great, indeed, was our astonishment on hearing that she had gained another of the summits of the mountain. The keenness of the air, however, caused her to spit blood. After taking a hasty view of the scene, she descended to a more genial atmosphere.

After sitting some time contemplating this dreary scene, and listening to the personal adventures of the guides, in whom the *sacrarandi* had not suffered by their libations of brandy, we thought it time to continue our descent. One of the guides mentioned a singular position in which he was once placed on the summit of the mountain, with a bright sun over head, and a storm of thunder and lightning raging below. The guide imagined himself at once transformed into a Jupiter, and the Pic du Midi into an Olympus. The effect must, however, have been singular. We here saw a chamois, which had much the appearance of a roe-buck. Nothing material occurred in our

descent, excepting my falling on a glacier, and going from the top to the bottom with such a velocity that I lost my breath; I, however, preserved my presence of mind so far as to guide myself with my hands, and to keep my feet foremost. The only damage done was to my nails, which were broken by my rapid motion over the snow. We reached the peasant's hut at nine, the ascent and descent having each occupied three hours. Madame de C——, whose courage I never saw equalled in any woman, was a good deal exhausted after a walk on glaciers of seven hours. We left the kind-hearted shepherds, thirty of whom inhabit the same small hut, and, mounting our horses, reached Grippe at half past eleven, and Bagneres at one, under the most scorching sun possible.

MISCELLANY.

[From late Foreign Journals received at this office.—*N. Gaz.*]

The Pulse.—At a late meeting of the Royal Academy of Sciences and Belles Lettres in Brussels, M. Rameaux laid before the academy the results of his inquiries as to the mean number of pulsations in man. These, it is said, establish so positive a relation between the number of pulsations and the stature of the individual, that, by using the tables of growth which M. Quetelet has given in the Physique Sociale, for the two sexes, the corresponding number of pulsations for each age may be deduced; and the numbers so calculated agree in the most satisfactory manner with the numbers obtained by observation.

THE ALCHEMIST.

Alchemy has been defined by Harris to be "An art without art, the beginning of which is falsehood, the middle labour, and the end poverty." It has also been esteemed as a kind of "visionary chemistry," and the ages that produced those men known by the name of alchemists, have been always considered as having contributed little or nothing to the advancement of that noble science, chemistry, which is now pursued with such eagerness and success.

However absurd and preposterous the pursuits of alchemy were, however visionary the hypotheses that were started, yet the ardour with which they were followed, the amazing number of experiments that were made, and the prodigious care that was taken to observe their results, could not fail to contribute much to the discovery of many facts and combinations to which chemistry, even at this day, is highly indebted, and thus the activity of error was favourable, eventually, to the cause of truth.

The alchemists of former times, mostly men of profound learning and great abilities, led away from the investigation of the truth by the dazzling prospects that appeared likely to arise, from the discovery of the philosopher's stone, that *ignis fatuus* of the philosophers, discovered many useful combinations, as the metallic salts, and other substances, which have been so successfully applied in medicine. To them we are indebted for the discovery of sulphuric, nitric, and muriatic acids, to them also we are indebted for the discovery of phosphorus, which was first found to exist as a simple substance, by Brandt, at Hamburg, in 1777, while searching for some substance capable of acting upon the baser metals to convert them into *gold* or *silver*. To Roger Bacon, a monk of the Franciscan order, the world owes the discovery of *gunpowder*.

Though many alchemists descended to the vale of humble experience, the world, unable to receive and appreciate the intelligence they were able to communicate, raised its voice against them, and while their talents and progress in the science raised the admiration of the more intelligent, they failed not to excite the envy of the illiterate, who, regardless of the value of their discoveries, and of the benefits that were likely to arise from them, failed not to impress the world with the belief that they had dealings with the devil—and, accordingly, under the excuse that they practised the *black art*, we read that some of them were imprisoned. Genius, thus cramped, could not exert its full strength, and, doubtless, had it not met with such obstacles, the world would have witnessed many more wonderful discoveries. But it is not to be wondered at, that, in a barbarous age, one who was skilled in any deep science should be accused of *magic*.

What has been said of Roger Bacon individually, can be applied to the whole flock of alchemists. "Tradition framed their characters on the vulgar notions entertained in their days of the results of experimental science, and the learned alchemists searching for the *philosopher's stone* in their laboratories, aided only by infernal spirits, were substituted for the real inquirers into the phenomena of nature."

Not only do we owe to them the discovery of many useful combinations, but to those inventive geniuses we are indebted also for the formation of much useful apparatus, and "not only were they expert in their formation, but sometimes happy in their application." That some of the lower order of alchemists devoted their whole lives to endeavour to discover the *philosopher's stone*, or the universal remedy, or other things equally absurd, is not to be denied, but with those of a higher order the case was far different—"they often indulged in the insane caprices of the mere searchers for the *philosopher's stone*, but their madness had a method in it, and their wanderings were not without a plan."

Sulphur Mines of Naples: or the Solfatara.

Near Puzzoli, in Italy, is that great and famous mine of sulphur, called Solfatara.

It consists of an oval plain, about two hundred yards in diameter, surrounded by steep rocks on all sides, which are perpetually decomposing and falling down in ruins. The plain is elevated about two hundred and fifty yards above the level of the sea, and is regarded as the crater of an ancient volcano. The plain is sensibly hotter than the atmosphere in the warmest days of summer, and burns the feet through the shoes. From the cavities in this part, vapours exhale, which are nothing else than sulphur subliming through the crevices. The sulphur adheres to the sides of the rock, where it forms enormous masses;

which sometimes fall down by their own weight. In calm weather the vapours rise twenty-five or thirty feet from the earth.

In the middle of the plain there is a kind of basin, three feet lower than the rest of the surface, which sounds hollow when any person walks over it, as if there were a great cavern beneath. Further on is a small lake, called Agano. Beyond this lake are the excavations from whence the earth is dug which furnishes the sulphur; it is light and tender.—The workmen always dig into the plain for the earth, and neglect the sulphur, which is formed on the surface in considerable quantities, and of a bright yellow colour. They say the latter has lost its nature, and does not make sulphur of so good a quality as that which is procured from the soft stone under the surface.

Solfatara was styled by the ancients, the "Court of Vulcan," to the south of the city of Naples. The Solfatara has not emitted flames within the memory of man, so that it is a kind of half extinct volcano; but wet weather increases the quantity of its smoke. Its form is circular, with vines and fruit trees on the outer declivity. Tiles placed over vent holes, and serving as retorts, collect the condensed sulphur. Pure virgin sulphur is formed in all the hot crevices of the inside and outside of the cone of the Solfatara.

Ever since the days of Pliny the Solfatara has supplied a considerable part of the sulphur of commerce in Europe. According to M. Brieslak, the sulphur is formed by the decomposition of sulphuretted hydrogen gas, which is plentifully disengaged in this place.

In token of the great value of these mines, it need only be stated, that the amount of the *pot de vin* alleged to have been received by his Neapolitan majesty from the sulphur company, was no less than 1,000,000 ducats, or about 175,000*l.*

Steam Boilers.

Steam Boilers.—A gold medal was recently decreed to the elder M. Chaussenot by the Society for the Encouragement of National Industry, for an apparatus to render the explosion of steam boilers impossible. His invention is said to be perfect, both as regards its improvements on the safety-valve, and an ingenious contrivance to give due notice of danger to the crew: while in the event of all the warnings of his machinery failing, or being disregarded, the steam flows back upon the furnace, and instantly extinguishes the fire.

Discovery of Ancient Royal Treasure.

A few days since a large collection of valuable Anglo Saxon coins, and other relics of olden times, were discovered close to the river Ribble, at Cuerdalehall, near this town. It appears that a number of workmen were employed in repairing the embankments of the Ribble, (which had become partially undermined by the action of the water,) in order to prevent the encroachments of the river, when they were suddenly surprised and overjoyed at the discovery of the buried treasure. It was contained in a leaden chest, which, however, had become so decayed and corroded, that it broke asunder in the attempt to extricate it from its hiding place, and the inclosed valua-

bles of course rolled out before the astonished gaze of the "bankers."—There are, we understand, about 10,000 coins, and the average weight is about twenty grains each, which are principally of the reigns of Etheldred, Alfred, and Edward the elder, besides which there are ingots of silver, bracelets, bridle bits, some ring-money, &c. &c.

The money, we are informed, weighs about 290 ounces, and the other articles, about 756 ounces, in all, 986 ounces of silver. The probable time of the deposits of this valuable treasure was, as nearly as can be estimated, about 1000 years ago. The prevailing opinion, from the extent of the property, and other circumstances, is, that it was the royal treasure. Some odd pieces of the booty have found their way into the hands of a few individuals, and are, of course, highly valued. Indeed, the numismatic collectors and connoisseurs are quite in a *furor* about the matter, and the spot where the treasure was found, has, since the discovery, been more zealously scratched than any dunghill in the best populated poultry-yard. The appropriation and ownership of the property will, we apprehend, become a question between the crown and Mr. Assheton, but, in all probability, the claim of the latter will not be interfered with. The circumstance has created a lively sensation in this neighbourhood.—*Preston (Eng.) Chronicle.*

On the Influence of Women.

On the Influence of Women.—There is nothing, indeed, by which I have through life more profited than by the just observations, the good opinion, and the sincere and gentle encouragement of amiable and sensible women.—*Memoirs of Sir S. Romilly.*

Sulphuric Acid.—60,000 tons are manufactured annually, in England alone.

Method of Restoring Life to the Apparently Drowned.

Method of Restoring Life to the Apparently Drowned—Recommended by the "Royal Humane Society of England," instituted in the year 1774. Avoid all rough usage. Do not hold up the body by the feet, nor roll it on casks or barrels, or rub it with salt or spirits, or apply tobacco. Lose *not a moment* in carrying the body to the nearest house, with the head and shoulders raised. Place it in a warm room if the weather is cold. Preserve silence, and positively admit *no more* than *three* intelligent persons. Let the body be instantly stripped, dried, and wrapped in *hot blankets,* which are to be frequently renewed. Keep the mouth, nostrils and throat free and clean. Apply warm substances to the back, spine, pit of the stomach, arm-pits and soles of the feet. Rub the body with heated flannel, or cotton, or warm hands. Attempt to restore breathing by *gently* blowing with a bellows, into one nostril, closing the mouth and the other nostril. Press down the breast *carefully,* with *both* hands, and then let it rise again, and thus imitate natural breathing. Keep up the application of heat—continue the rubbing—*increase it when life appears, and then give a tea-spoonful* of warm water, or *very weak* brandy and water, or wine and water. *Persevere for six hours.* Send quickly for medical assistance.

For "The Friend."

EARLY FRIENDS IN NEW ENGLAND.

(Continued from p. 325.)

LETTER IX.

The "March term" of the court of assistants for 1661 closed with the execution of William Leddra, and that, too, under circumstances the most gloomy and terrible.

The government in their apology to the king, had professed only to stand at the entrance, and to have offered "the point" to intruders in self-defence; those, therefore, who rushed upon it, they said, were suicides, whose absence only they desired.

Four we have seen had already rushed upon that point and perished; and five others were ready, walking openly to and fro within the charter limits, after sentence of banishment on pain of death, and some of these last were freemen of the colony. And now whose turn next? was the general and anxious inquiry. If the Quakers would so freely offer themselves for sacrifice, would the ministering priests and magistrates at all shrink from the slaughter, acting as the agents, and in the name of the people of the people's government, and making the whole community responsible for their doings—and to the world the popular government of Massachusetts seemed engaged in the work of popular persecution, and well might it excite the wonder of that age. But when the Massachusetts Quakers seemed without defence before their enemies, save in the common sympathy which their sufferings might excite, and acting on the fears of the charter authorities, help came suddenly from another quarter.

The news of Leddra's death, with the danger of others, reached England, and the brethren there, in their alarm, applied to the king for protection, and the result was most happy. Charles the 2d was not fond of our first charter ancestors. They held their patent of self-government by the gift of his father, yet they belonged to that school of politics and religion which cut off his head; and they favoured Cromwell, and cherished the regicides who fled to America. All this the English Quakers well knew, and they put into the monarch's hands George Bishop's book on the cruelties to their sect here. It was in the 13th year of his reign, and when he read the famed sarcasm of Assistant Denison on the stability of his throne, to those Quakers who claimed an English trial, " that this year they apply to England, the next, parliament will send over to inquire, and the third year the government of England will be changed."— Charles noted the passage, and calling to the lords and dignitaries about him, read it aloud, saying, " Lo ! these are my loving subjects of New England, they seem already to see with delight my throne shaken, as my father's, but I'll stop their career." Whilst in this turn of mind, Edward Burroughs, a distinguished Quaker, obtained an audience, and thus addressed him. " O king, there is a vein of innocent blood opened in thy dominions, which, if not stopped, will overflow the whole realm." " But I will stop that vein," he replied, and he directed that a mandamus should be made out, of which the following is the substance :—it

was directed to John Endicot, and all other governors of New England, and to the ministers and officers of all plantations there.

Charles R.—Trusty and well beloved, we greet you well. Having been informed that several of our subjects, among you, called Quakers, have been, and are imprisoned by you, whereof some have been executed, and others in danger to undergo the like, we do hereby require that if there be any of those people among you, called Quakers, now condemned to suffer death or other corporeal punishment, or that are imprisoned and obnoxious to the like condemnation, you are to forbear, and proceed no further therein, but forthwith to send said persons (whether condemned or imprisoned) over into this our kingdom of England, together with the respective crimes or offences laid to their charge, to the end that they may be dealt with agreeable to our laws and their own demerits; and for so doing, this shall be your sufficient warrant and discharge.

Given at our court at Whitehall, the 9th day of Sept. 1661.
By his majesty's command.
WILLIAM MORRIS.

Strange mandate, indeed, from a despotic throne, and to a self-governing community! What tyranny is worse than that of a special interest in power, operating through free forms, be it of wealth, of the church, or combinations of monopolists?

It now remained to pass the royal mandamus over to the colony, and for this purpose it pleased the king to grant his deputation to Samuel Shattuck, a Quaker of Boston, and then in London under banishment from his native land on pain of death; and as the business required haste, a ship was chartered, Ralph Goldsmith, another Quaker, master, for three hundred pounds, to sail in ten days, goods or no goods.

In June, 1661, Wenlock Christison was brought before the court of assistants; there, both Endicot and Bellingham told him that unless he would renounce his Quakerism, he should surely die. " Nay," said he firmly, "do not deceive yourselves, I shall not change my religion, or seek to save my life; you can take it when you will." But, to the surprise of all, instead of proceeding to trial, he was ordered back to prison.

The court went into consultation how they should dispose of him. But they were divided, and for two weeks sat in debate, during which time it was said the sun shone not in the firmament, as if in sadness at the guilty work. A sure token of the feelings of the people, who are prone, on like occasions, to look through nature up to nature's God.

At last intolerant pride prevailed, and Christison was put on trial, and the jury soon returned a verdict of guilty; and when asked what he had to say why sentence of death should not be passed on him, he said he had done nothing worthy of death. " But," said they, " you come among us in rebellion, which is like the sin of witchcraft, and should be punished." " By what law do you put me to death ?" asked Christison.

Endicot. We have a law which condemns you to death.

C. Who empowered you to make that law ?

E. We have a patent, and are the patentees; judge if we may not make laws.

C. But can you make laws repugnant to those of England ?

E. Surely not.

C. Then in your laws against the Quakers you have gone beyond your bounds, and have forfeited your charter. Tell me, are you the king's subjects ? yea or nay.

" What good will an answer do you?" said Secretary Rawson. " To know," said Christison, " if you will own your late petition to the king, wherein you desire to kneel among his most loyal subjects."

" We are among his most loyal subjects," said Endicot. " So am I," said Christison, " and, for aught I know, as good as yourselves, if not better; for did the king but know your hearts as God knows them, he would soon see their rottenness towards himself; but, as we are equally subject to the same king and laws, what have you to do with my life here, upon a law of your own making, and not approved by our king or nation ? I never yet heard of English law to hang Quakers."

" But there is to hang Jesuits, though," said Endicot.

" But you presume to hang me as a Quaker, and not as a Jesuit, therefore, I appeal to the laws of my own nation."

" We have you in our power," said a surly assistant, " and shall dispose of you whether you will or no."

" Guilty or not guilty ?" said the secretary.

" I deny all guilt."

" But the law condemns thee," said Endicot.

" And the Lord doth justify me," said Wenlock. " Who art thou that condemnest?"

The vote for sentence of death was then put, but there was a division among the assistants; a number would not vote to sentence the prisoner. Endicot seeing this, became angry, and declared that he could find it in his heart to go home.

" Far better for thee to be at home than here," said Wenlock, " for thou art about a bloody work."

Even the second vote was confused and uncertain, which so incensed the governor, that he stood up and said, " I thank God I am not afraid to give judgment;" and he then pronounced sentence of death; to which Christison replied, " the will of the Lord be done."

But to the court he said, " Note my words, if you have power to take my life, being as I am in your hands, yet this will be your last; you shall never more have power to take Quakers' lives from them. Do not think to weary the living God by slaying his servants. For the last man you have put to death, here are five come in his room; if you kill me, God will send others of his servants in my room, that you may have torment upon torment,— which is your portion; there is no peace for the wicked, saith my God."

Upon this scene comment is unnecessary. Wenlock was sent back to prison, and in five days after, the marshal and constable came with others for his liberation, with twenty-seven more of his suffering companions, who had long pined in a dungeon in Boston, for their testimony to what they believed the truth.

What means this? said Wenlock, when

such, persecution itself would require courage; though usually its office is most cowardly.

And even now the prison doors were thrown open in the spirit of malignity. For, of the twenty-seven to be liberated, they took Peter Pierson and Judith Brown, stripped them both to the middle, man and woman, fastened them to a cart's tail, side by side, and whipped them through the town of Boston, twenty stripes each, the cart driving slowly that the lash might be laid on deliberately. The peculiar offence of Peter and Judith was refusing to plead to the charges brought against them in court, and remaining dumb before their persecutors.

(To be continued.)

From the Alexandria Gazette.

A GLANCE AT THE MORMONS.

TO THE EDITOR.

Since the Mormons were expelled from the state of Missouri, they have purchased the town of Commerce, a situation of surpassing beauty, at the head of the lower rapids, on the Illinois shore of the Mississippi river. The name of the place they have recently changed to Nauvoo, the Hebrew term for fair or beautiful. Around this place, as their centre, they are daily gathering from almost every quarter; and several hundred new houses, erected within the last few months, attest to the passing traveller the energy, industry, and self-denial with which the community is imbued. They have also obtained possession of extensive lands on the opposite side of the river, in that charming portion of Iowa Territory, known as the "Half Breed Reservation;" and there, upon the rolling and fertile prairies, they are rapidly selecting their homes, and opening their farms. As the traveller now passes through those natural parks and fields of flowers, which the hand of the Creator planted there, he beholds their cabins, dotted down in most enchanting perspective, either on the borders of the timber, or beside the springs and streams of living water, which are interspersed on every hand.

Nor are they unmindful of their interests abroad, while they are thus accomplishing so much at home. No sect, with equal means, has probably ever suffered and achieved more in so short a space of time. Their elders have not only been commissioned and sent forth to every part of our own country, but they have left their families and friends behind them, and gone to Europe, and even to the Holy Land, to reveal the wonders of the " new and everlasting covenant," and to preach " the dispensation of the fulness of times."

a winning asylum for all the disaf satisfied of other persuasions, ɑ much that is congenial to almost of erratic or radical religious ch ɑn illustration of this, it is state number of their own journal, cal and Seasons," that, on a single England, one of their elders late among others, no less than thirtec of one denomination of Christians.

The name of *Mormon* they di affirm that it was given to them b mies. They call themselves " *Th Jesus Christ of Latter Day S* number among their chief ecclesiɑ taries, a prophet, patriarch, and a priests, bishops and elders. The stood to disavow the truth and vali churches, and to believe that their siastical constitution entitles them the full enjoyment of all the gifts ɑ of the church in ancient times. that all who are baptised by immen proper authority, are legally entitle mission of their sins, and the gift Ghost. Among other religious exe meet together to testify, to prophec with tongues, to interpret, and to visions and revelations, and in shc cise all the gifts of God, as set in o the ancient churches. They belie restoration of Israel to Palestine; t of Jerusalem; and the second adv Messiah, are near at hand; and tl calamities which have recently bef of the cities of our land, are set ɑ their records as prophetic signs of coming of the Son of Man in the heaven to open the millennial era.

As to the "Book of Mormon," place implicit confidence in its trut ny that it is a *new* Bible, to exclu but a historical and religious record ancient times, by a branch of the h rael that peopled America, from wh dians are descended. The metalli which these records were engraved they were at length discovered and by Joseph Smith, Jr. and found, ɑ corroborate and confirm the truth oi but also to open the events of an rica, as far back at least as the flo believe that this book pours the ligl day upon the history of a nati mounds, and cities, and fortificatiou pose, in grand but melancholy ruin bosom of the western prairies; an son that it is not more generally the same that operated to prevent

few inquiries relative to some of his peculiar tenets, I observed that it was commonly reported of him that he believed in the personal reign of the Messiah upon earth, during the millennial era.

I believe in no such thing, was his reply. —At the opening of that period, I believe that Christ will descend; but will immediately return again to heaven. Some of our elders, he continued, before I have found time to instruct them better, have unadvisedly propagated some such opinions; but I tell my people it is absurd to suppose that Christ "*will jump out of the frying-pan into the fire.*" He is in a good place now, and it is not to be supposed that he will exchange it for a worse one.

Not a little shocked at the emblem employed by the prophet, we descended from his chambers, and the conversation turned upon his recent visit to Washington, and his interview with the President of the United States. He gave us distinctly to understand that his political views had undergone an entire change; and his description of the reception given him at the executive mansion was any thing but flattering to the distinguished individual who presides over its hospitalities.

You hold in your hands, I observed, a large amount of political power, and your society must exert a tremendous influence, for weal or woe, in the coming elections.

Yes, said he, I know it; and our influence, as far as it goes, we intend to use. There are probably not far short of an hundred thousand souls in our society, and the votes to which we are entitled throughout the union must doubtless be extensively lost to Van Buren.

Not being myself disposed in any way to intermeddle in party politics, I made no definite reply; but, immediately taking leave, we returned to Montrose, abundantly satisfied that the society over which he presides has assumed a moral and political importance which is but very imperfectly understood. Associated on the religious principle, under a prophet and leader whose mysterious and awful claims to divine inspiration make his voice to believers like the voice of God; trained to sacrifice their individuality; to utter one cry; to think and act in crowds; with minds that seem to have been struck from the sphere of reason on one subject, and left to wander, like lost stars, amid the dark mazes and winding ways of religious error, these remarkable sectaries must necessarily hold in their hands a fearful balance of political power. In the midst of contending parties, a single hand might turn their influences, with tremendous effect, to whichever side presented the most potent attractions; and should they ever become disposed to exert their influence for evil, which may heaven prevent, they would surround our institutions with an element of danger, more to be dreaded than an armed and hundred-eyed police.

SINGULAR INDIAN CUSTOM.

A custom prevalent, and almost universal, amongst these Indians, is that of flattening or mashing in the whole front of the skull, from the superciliary ridge to the crown. The appearance produced by this unnatural operation is almost hideous, and one would suppose that

the intellect is materially injured by it. This, however, does not appear to be the case, as I have never seen, with a single exception, (the Kayouse,) a race of people who appeared more shrewd and intelligent. I had a conversation on this subject, a few days since, with a chief who speaks the English language. He said, that he had exerted himself to abolish the practice in his own tribe; but, although his people would listen patiently to his talk on most subjects, their ears were firmly closed when this was mentioned: "They would leave the council fire one by one, until none but a few squaws and children were left to drink in the word_s of the chief." It is even considered among them a degradation to possess a round head; and one whose *caput* has happened to be neglected in his infancy, can never become even a subordinate chief in his tribe, and is treated with indifference and disdain, as one who is unworthy a place amongst them. The flattening of the head is practised by at least ten or twelve distinct tribes of the lower country, the Kliikatats, Kalapooyahs, and Multnomahs of the Wallammet, and its vicinity; the Chinooks, Klatsaps, Klatsonis, Kowalitsks, Kailammets, Killemooks, and Chekalis of the lower Columbia and its tributaries, and probably by others, both north and south. The tribe called Flatheads, or Salish, who reside near the sources of the Oregon, have long since abolished this custom. The mode by which the flattening is effected, varies considerably with the different tribes. The Wallammet Indians place the infant, soon after its birth, upon a board, to the edges of which are attached little loops of hempen cord, or leather; and other similar cords are passed across and back in a zigzag manner through these loops, enclosing the child, and binding it firmly down. To the upper edge of this board, in which is a depression to receive the back part of the head, another smaller one is attached by hinges of leather, and made to lie obliquely on the forehead, the force of the pressure being regulated by several strings attached to its edge, which are passed through holes in the board upon which the infant is lying, and secured there. The mode of the Chinooks, and others near the sea, differs widely from that of the upper Indians, and appears somewhat less barbarous and cruel. A sort of cradle is formed by excavating a pine log to the depth of eight or ten inches. The child is placed on it, on a bed of little grass mats, and bound down in the manner above described. A little boss of tightly plaited and woven grass is then applied to the forehead, and secured by a cord to the loops at the side. The infant is thus suffered to remain from four to eight months, or until the sutures of the skull have in some measure united, and the bone become solid and firm.— It is seldom or never taken from the cradle, except in case of severe illness, until the flattening process is completed. I saw, to-day, a young child from whose head the board had just been removed. It was, without exception, the most frightful and disgusting looking object I had ever beheld. The whole front of the head was completely flattened, and the mass of brain being forced back, caused an enormous projection above. The poor little creature's eyes protruded to the distance of half

an inch, and looked inflamed and discoloured, as did all the surrounding parts. Although I felt a kind of chill creep over me from the contemplation of such dire deformity, yet there was something so stark-staring and absolutely queer in the physiognomy that I could not repress a smile; and when the mother amused the little object, and made it laugh, it looked so irresistibly, so terribly ludicrous, that I and those who were with me burst into a simultaneous roar, which frightened it and made it cry: in which predicament it looked much less horrible than before.—*Townsend's Sporting Excursions in the Rocky Mountains.*

FINGAL'S CAVE IN STAFFA.

We advanced along a sort of giant's causeway, the pavement of which was the heads of basaltic columns, all fitting together in the most beautiful symmetry, and, turning round the precipice to our right hand, found ourselves at the entrance of the great cave. The sea was too stormy to allow us to enter it, as is often done in boats, we had, therefore, to clamber along one of its sides, where a row of columns is broken off at some distance above the waves, and presents an accessible, but certainly very formidable causeway, by which you may reach the far end. I do not believe that any stranger, if he were there alone, would dare to pass along that irregular and slippery causeway, and penetrate to the obscure end of the cave; but numbers animate one another to do any thing. We clambered along this causeway or corridor, now ascending and now descending, as the broken columns required, and soon stood—upwards of seventy of us—ranged along its side from one end to the other. Let it be remembered that this splendid sea cave is forty-two feet wide at the entrance; sixty-six feet high from the water; and runs into the rock two hundred and twenty-seven feet. Let it be imagined that, at eight or ten feet below us it was laved with the sea, which came rushing and foaming along it, and dashing up against the solid rock at its termination; while the light thrown from the flickering billows quivered in its arched roof above us, and the whole place was filled with the solemn sound of the ocean; and if any one can imagine to himself any situation more sublime, I should like to know what that is. The roof is composed of the lower ends of basaltic columns, which have yet been so cut away by nature as to give it the aspect of the roof of some gigantic cathedral aisle. Lichens of gold and crimson have gilded and coloured it in the richest manner. It was difficult to forget, as we stood there, that, if any one slipped, he would disappear for ever, for the billows in their ebb would sweep him out to the open sea, as it were, in a moment. Yet the excitement of the whole group was too evident to rest with any seriousness on such a thought. Some one suddenly fired a gun in the place, and the concussion and reverberated thunders were astounding. When the first effect was gone off, one general peal of laughter rang through the cave, and then nearly the whole company began to sing, "the sea! the sea!" The captain found it a difficult matter to get his company out of this strange chantry—where they, and the

winds and waves seemed all going mad together—to embark them again for Iona.—
William Howitt.

THE MESSENGER.

ON THE DEATHS OF J. N., E. K., R. B. P., M. W. B. AND W. N.

Death's wing, raven-coloured, sweeps over our land,
  Yet we mark not his course when we feel not his
      power;
He silently strikes with his mist-covered hand,
  And the slain is forgotten ere passes the hour!
We deem him but one of the crowd we pass through;
With our friends and our kindred death's nothing to do!

Why should we be thoughtful?—no cause of alarm
  Has enter'd our dwelling to break our repose;
We live to our liking; we dream not of harm;
  From our goblet of pleasure no bitter stream flows;
Yet we start—as did he who beheld on the wall
The hand writing of old—when we see a friend fall.

How often, when death is abroad in his power,
  When onta-gion goes forth on the wings of the wind,
When pestilence has a full chart to devour,
  And terror is with their dread presence combin'd,
Does it seem as though mercy has shielded our friends,
While no message to part to our kindred descends.

Again—when all palmy and fresh is the air,
  And health smiles upon us with promise of life,
Do the shafts of the spoiler, unwilling to spare,
  Fall thick in our circle with ravages rife:—
One after another our friends are laid low,
As in rapid succession comes blow upon blow.

      *   *   *   *

One came to the altar and offered his gift;
  Where the people were gathered his turtle doves lay;
When beyond mortal ken came the messenger swift,
  And offering and offerer were taken away!
The incense remained as a cloud round the mount,
But the soul that presented had gone to account.

A mother, by children most dearly belov'd,
  Who travail'd for Israel and mourned for her woe,
Ere the sun through another set circle had mov'd,
  To the house for all living was cited to go;
Friends and kindred lamented—the church mourn'd
    her loss,—
The pathway she trod led her steps to the cross!

Scarce a week sped space in the journey of time,
  Ere one who in patience had long borne her load,
Though youthful in years, yet attain'd to her prime,
  Pass'd from trouble and earth to the joy of her God;
With calmness surrender'd her life—and her woes
Forever were gone as her spirit arose.

Ere the earth pressed her coffin there came a new call,
  To a young wife and another, the joy of her home;
A kinsman's sweet infant she cloth'd in its pall,
     the summons "the bridegroom
    has come."
And the dear little infant for whom she had striven,
Press'd onward to bliss, her forerunner to heaven!

Within the same hour that this lov'd mother's head
  Was laid in the earth, as all living must lay,
A humble old Christian sought his " narrow bed"
  Beside her;—and joyfully wing'd the same way.
Yea;—we may believe *all* the spoiler hath slain,
In this little circle, are risen again !
                      J.

MADNESS AND MONARCHY.

It is a singular fact, that there are now confined in the public and private establishments
for the treatment of insanity in London and
the neighbourhood, no less than sixty men and
women who consider themselves the legitimate, but unacknowledged sovereigns of the
country!—One female patient insists upon asserting that she is the real Victoria, and that
she was confined in a madhouse, in order
to prevent her from ascending the throne of
her forefathers. This patient most pertinaciously affirms, that she was sent to the asylum by Lord Melbourne, in order to make way
for a lady with whom he was in love, and who
now occupies the throne. It is amusing to
witness the pomposity with which this poor
mad creature struts about the ward, exclaiming, "Fall back, clear the way for your illustrious Queen Victoria."—*Physic and Physicians.*

Moderation is the silken string running
through the pearl chain of all virtues.—*Bishop
Hall.*

THE FRIEND.

SEVENTH MONTH, 25, 1840.

In addition to the statement already given
of the late New England Yearly Meeting, the
following items have since been furnished by
an unknown hand.

"A peculiar solemnity seemed at several
times to be spread over many minds, from the
painfully affecting intelligence of the demise of
our beloved friend Daniel Wheeler—who had
mingled with us when last assembled in this
capacity, much to our edification and comfort.
"Appended to our epistle to the Yearly
Meeting of London, was a brief testimonial in
relation to the services of this dear departed
friend, and expressing our sense of the loss
that his bereaved family and the church have
sustained in his removal from works to rewards."

"At this time acceptable epistles were received from each of the Yearly Meetings in
Great Britain and on this continent, which ar-
ticulations of gospel fellowship tended renewedly to assure us that it is good for us, as it is
our duty as brethren of the same "household
of faith," to maintain a lively interest in each
others' welfare. During the several sittings
of the meeting, much valuable counsel was imparted by concerned friends in attendance, and
especially during the consideration of the state
of society as introduced by the answers to the
queries."

"The Report of the Boarding School Committee was read, and printed copies directed
to be furnished to the subordinate meetings.
From this it appears, that the number of
scholars for the past year exceeds that of the
year previous, and that the number for the
last term is larger than for several preceding
terms; and encouragement was extended to
friends to avail themselves of the opportunities
afforded by this institution for the education of
their children. Although no written ' returns'
on the subject were called for the present year,
it is believed that the interesting cause of education is by no means disregarded among us.
"The committee having a care of the Pe-
nobscot Indians, submitted a favourable report
in relation to that tribe; and information having been received that the Passamaquoddies in
the same state are desirous of having Friends'
care extended to them, the committee were desired to inquire into their condition, and report
to a future meeting.
"The state of the tribes west of the Mississippi, also claimed the sympathy of the
meeting, and a committee was continued to

make farther inquiries into their situation,
either through an agent specially commissioned, or otherwise, as may be deemed expedient."

There must be but few of our readers that
have not heard something of the famous " Joe
Smith"—of his ridiculous pretension to the
discovery of the " Book of Mormion," engraved on metallic plates, after concealment
for centuries in the earth, and, of the still
stranger circumstance, that the stupid imposition should have gained numerous proselytes.
We transfer from the National Gazette an article on the subject, which will be read with
interest. The editor of that paper accompanies the insertion with the following pertinent
remarks:—
Upon our outside page is a very interesting
account of the Mormons, given by a correspondent of the Alexandria Gazette. Any
fears of the continued increase or influence of
these infatuated people we think ill-founded.
Christianity has at all times had silly sects
upon its skirts, which soon quit their hold if
unnoticed. Johannah Southcote had quite as
formidable a train at one time as Joe Smith
now has. Many men and women, grave in
years of experience, were happy in the blessed
assurance that she was destined to give birth
to a Messiah. The whole sect has dissolved,
and no vestige of the congregation remains.
So, too, Mathias the Prophet had cajoled many
respectable persons, and was in a fair way of
establishing wider faith in his mission, when
his villany, paramount to his cunning, brought
him into a court of justice and dissolved his
scheme of deception. It is melancholy to
know that well-meaning and even well-informed people can become the dupes of South-
cotes, Mathiases and Joe Smiths; but the evil
can hardly fail to work its own cure. Had the
latter been let alone when he commenced his
game of imposture, it would have fallen long
ago by its own weight. But opposition and
injury clothed him with the attributes of a
martyr, and hence his greater success. There
is now but one mode to circumscribe the
growth of the Mormons—to let them alone.

Butler's Character of a Translator.—A
translator dyes an author, like an old stuff,
into a new colour, but can never give it the
lustre of the first tincture: as silks that are
twice dyed lose their glosses, and never receive a fair colour.

A stated meeting of the Female Branch of
the Auxiliary Bible Association of Friends, in
Philadelphia Quarterly Meeting, will be held
on the 30th instant, at 4 o'clock P. M. in
Friends' Reading Room, Appletree alley.
  7th mo. 25th.

Departed this life 1st of 4th mo. last, after a lingering indisposition, REBECCA C. wife of Nathaniel Gilles-
pie, a member of Sadsbury Monthly and Lampeter
Particular Meeting, in her 43d year.

     PRINTED BY ADAM WALDIE,
  Carpenter Street, below Seventh, Philadelphia.

THE FRIEND.

A RELIGIOUS AND LITERARY JOURNAL.

VOL. XIII.   SEVENTH DAY, EIGHTH MONTH, 1, 1840.   NO. 44.

EDITED BY ROBERT SMITH.

PUBLISHED WEEKLY.

Price two dollars per annum, payable in advance.

Subscriptions and Payments received by

GEORGE W. TAYLOR,

NO. 50, NORTH FOURTH STREET, UP STAIRS,

PHILADELPHIA.

From the North American.

Notes of an Excursion to the Susquehanna at Wilkesbarre.

(Concluded from p. 337.)

At Wilkesbarre we visited the coal mines of the Baltimore coal company in the vicinity. The openings are numerous, running into each other; the vein appears to be about twenty-five feet thick. The miners pointed out one stratum low in the vein, which they called the Blacksmith, being about twelve inches thick, and more friable than the rest of this stratum: they allege it is universally found in this vein fifty miles in extent. The company are mining at the rate of 100 tons daily, and sell it delivered on the river shore, or at the basin, at $1.50 per ton. People here are much in favour of the railroad to the Lehigh, and say that not only from the town, but from up the river, a large trade will pass on it to Philadelphia; as being their shortest and best route. This view seemed confirmed by an intelligent gentleman from Towanda, who expressed his opinion that an active business will be carried on from his district along this line in lumber, agricultural produce, and bituminous coal. A body of the latter has recently been discovered between Wilkesbarre and Towanda, about 40 miles above the former place. He also estimates very profitable results from the completion of the railroad, and is sanguine that when the North Branch canal shall be connected with the New York improvements by means of the Chemung canal, a considerable trade will be derived to the road and Lehigh navigation, from the state of New York.

Our return was by the Pine Forest. In the outskirts of Wilkesbarre we were shown the land purchased by the Lehigh company for a basin, depot, &c. when required. Here they are making bricks, which cost by contract $5 per thousand, into which coal dust is mixed. These bricks are quickly burned, are very hard, rough, and strong. This process of making bricks is said to save expense—ten cords of wood answer in place of forty cords required by the usual method. Stopped half way at the Boiling Spring—it bubbles up no doubt through veins of sandstone, bringing with it minute grains of sand. It bubbles constantly, and makes a pretty appearance. The water is fine. We partook of refreshments at the house of the engineer, a rough, uncultivated spot on the mountain, 1600 feet above the level of Philadelphia. Every thing was neat within, and the viands well prepared and excellent. Notwithstanding the experience of our guides, we lost our way in the woods, and for a considerable time scrambled over pathless wilds at the hazard of our limbs, if not of our lives; our horses blundering over rocks, entangled roots, and quagmires, brambles, &c.; fallen trees intercepting our passage, and often from their great size compelling us to retrace our steps to get round them. At length we discovered a blind path, which eventually conducted us out of this wilderness into a pine forest of very large trees, destined at no distant day to be felled by the unsparing axe, and to be applied to the use of man. These must necessarily find a market down the Lehigh, near to which we had approached. We were now at Pine Forest, and speedily commenced our downward voyage in a boat built of inch boards, in the scow form, having a steering paddle at the bow, one at the stern, and another for a rudder. This boat had three attendants, one of whom had steady employment in bailing out with a tin bucket the water which rushed in through the seams. From Pine Forest to White Haven, a distance of two and a half miles, the river descends seventy-five feet. Many ripples, rapids, and rocks lie in the river, to steer through which requires skill and experience. The forward steersman receiving his instructions from the helmsman, not indeed in seamen's phrase, but by calling out "to the right," "to the left"—and where a sailor would sing out "steady," our steersman called out "whoop." No matter, the men understood each other, and conducted us safely along, being ourselves not a little satisfied with the novelty of all we witnessed. Before the Lehigh company improved this navigation, no rafts could descend this stream.

We saw some rafts, but more boats loaded with lumber going down to-day. The company receives one dollar per 1000 feet tollage on all lumber. These improvements have converted a rapid rocky dangerous stream, by means of successive pools, into a placid, deep, and broad river.

Spent the night at White Haven. On repassing the thirty foot lock, I found that the water, being 67,500 cubic feet, was discharged in less than two minutes. It passes out of the sides instead of the tail of the lock, and has the additional advantage of not agitating the water in the canal below, frequently very inconvenient on an approaching boat. The company have been, it would seem, singularly fortunate in having honest, intelligent, and well-trained men in their employment; they have been generally brought up and educated by the board, and appear attached to the service. It is particularly gratifying to be enabled to say, that we have not heard an oath, seen a drunkard, or witnessed any indecencies among the workmen or boatmen, since we have been on the Lehigh and mixed with the labourers employed on the works. All appear civil, busy and contented. Observing with how much ease a woman and her little daughter managed the several movements of the gates at the locks, I asked their weight, and was answered, that the gate to which I pointed weighed 45 tons. Notwithstanding the gloom that hangs over business in general throughout the country, there is here the appearance of considerable activity; boats full and empty are constantly passing, and the Beaver Meadow railroad has its share. Two trains of cars, consisting of near thirty each, pass down and return daily; they carry from two and a half to two and three quarters tons each car, and make a considerable show. This company expect to bring down 30,000 tons of coal this season, and other companies in this vicinity about 70,000 tons, in addition to that brought from the Lehigh company's mines.

The construction of the dams on the Lehigh is such as to render it very improbable that they should be injured by freshets; the greater the weight of water on the dam, the greater is the resistance to the flood; and so deep and calm is the water in the pools, that the ice, instead of breaking up and descending in masses, melts gradually without injury to any thing. Moreover, whenever it is desirable, large bodies of water can be discharged through the sluices formed in the dams.

The Lehigh is a powerful stream; the water in the upper section looks as black as ink, owing, doubtless, in part to colouring matter from the roots of hemlock, and in part to the dark shade of the high mountains that bound the shores.

About four miles above Allentown, the Crane company for smelting iron with anthracite coal have their foundry. We stopped to examine the works. These works will soon be in operation.* They have a very substantial appearance, and no doubt will answer the purpose designed. The bellows, of which there are two, are of heavy iron, and circular, five feet in diameter, and six feet stroke, piston rod 4½ inches in diameter. The water is taken from the Lehigh canal by a sloping cut and returned into it immediately. Water wheel 25 feet broad and 12 feet diameter. Heated air is used, and they can give from 600° to 1000° Fahrenheit. We lodged at Bethlehem last night, and in our rambles visit-

* This furnace is now turning out about three tons of pig metal daily.—Eds. N. A.

ed their graveyard. Here rest the remains of Wm. Jones, at one time secretary of the U. S. navy, and then president of the Bank of the United States. He died here in 1831, a few days after I saw him last. . His grave is furnished with the same simple prostrate marble slab that distinguishes the other abodes of the dead in this ground, with the like simple inscription, recording only the birth and death of the deceased. Here also lies the body of my old friend John Heckewelder, and some others of the brethren formerly well known to me. The bodies of the male tenants of this resting place of the dead, are divided from those of the sisterhood by a path which runs through the centre of the yard dividing it into two equal parts; on the sisters' side they pointed out to me the spot where is deposited the body of a young lady from the West Indies, who had been placed at school in this town by her father, a West India planter. She it seems had African blood in her veins, but was so nearly white as to render the sable hue perceptible by close examination only; it was, however, at length detected by the other girls and made known to her. She was herself, until then, unconscious of the circumstance, and wrote to her parent for information. His answer confirmed the fact, to her great mortification and surprise. She henceforth became melancholy, pined away, and soon descended to the grave; and thus a blooming and interesting girl fell an early victim to prejudice and her own embittered feelings.

From the New York Observer.

WYOMING VALLEY.

Wilkesbarre, Pa. July 6, 1840.

This valley lies along the Susquehanna, and is, in fact, one with the Lackawana valley lying on the Lackawana river. Its direction is north-east and south-west, having Carbondale on the north-eastern extremity, and Nescopeck creek on its south-western. Its length is about fifty miles, and its greatest breadth eight. On either side are continuous ranges of mountains from 800 to 1500 feet in height. Through the western range, about the centre of the valley and near the mouth of the Lackawans, at a place called Camel's Ridge, the Susquehanna breaks, forming a romantic glen. In the centre of this valley lies Wilkesbarre, a borough of 3000 inhabitants, and seat of justice for Luzerne county. On the opposite bank of the Susquehanna lies Kingston, a flourishing village and township of farmers. North are New Troy, Pittston, Exeter, and Providence; and south, Plymouth, Hanover and Newport. On the mountain east of Wilkesbarre, at a point called Prospect Rock, the eye commands a view of nearly the whole of this valley. That part which is under distinct vision, from Camel's Ridge on the north-east to Nanticoke Falls on the south-west, is exquisitely beautiful. The extensive flats of the Susquehanna are all under cultivation, and at this season covered with the richest crops, of which by far the most extensive is wheat. The eye of the greediest husbandman must water, when he looks at this ample field bearing its rich burden. Here Virgil might find an abundant theme for Geor-

gies and Bucolics; here Cowper might expatiate on the beauties of the country, and here Campbell might write a far more touching "Gertrude" than his unaided imagination produced at the distance of three thousand miles from the scene itself. From this point you look right down upon the spot which marks the most dreadful massacre recorded in the history of the revolution. It is situated in the village of New Troy. On this spot the inhabitants of the valley are erecting a monument to commemorate the tragedy. The material is a hard, compact, dark-coloured sandstone, very much resembling granite. Its form is square; first, a triple base two feet six inches high, of which the lowest is twenty-eight feet broad; next, a pedestal, a cube of twenty feet, bearing on three sides inscriptions, and having on the fourth a portal; and lastly, the frustrum of a pyramid, its base thirteen feet, its summit four feet in breadth, and its height forty feet; making a total height of sixty-two and a half feet. Beneath are deposited the remains of those slain at the massacre. It is affecting to stand here and contemplate the events commemorated; the contending bands—one peaceful, defending all which to them was sacred; the other savage and mercenary, the instruments of oppression; the contest—the ranks of those who had right on their side broken, routed, tomahawked, scalped; the consternation, flight and murder of defenceless women and children; dwellings burning; rich harvests, just ready for the sickle, destroyed. Yet such is the price at which kings purchase glory.
* * * * Perhaps the most interesting topic in relation to this valley is the anthracite. The whole valley, according to the dimensions given above, rests on coal, affording to the geologist a very interesting field of observation and speculation. The country is transition, and has evidently been under the action of fire, which has rent, and heaved, and bent the strata in all directions. In some places there is one bed of coal, in others several beds lying one above another, with alternate strata of sandstone, slate, conglomorate, &c. The following are the strata at one place where they have driven a tunnel to strike the lowest bed of coal and at the lowest point of the bed, for here the strata describe the arc of a large circle. First, and lowest, red slate; 2d, conglomorate, 125 feet thick; 3d, sandstone, 30 feet; 4th, coal, 22 feet, with very thin layers of slate at intervals; 5th, sandstone, 30 feet; 6th, diluvion, 10 to 20 feet; 7th, coal, 10 feet; 8th, sandstone, 25 feet; 9th, coal; 10th, sandstone, 30 feet; 11th, small top vein of coal. On one side of this basin, where the coal appears on the surface, or in miners' language, *crops out*, the dip is four degrees, and on the other ten. Generally slate lies next above and next below the coal, and this is filled with vegetable impressions. These are so perfect in their lineaments that the vegetable must have been enclosed in full vigor, and they are so carefully deposited, that not a leaf is folded or disturbed. Many of them resemble ferns and flags with which we are familiar, and many of them are gigantic and *outre*, such as find no place in the classes of Linnæus, and evidently date back to periods of a former world. Their number and qauntity too, are amazing. Every lamina you

raise discloses one or more, and their presence is almost as constant as the coal. Where this immense wilderness of plants came from, and how they were so orderly disposed in this their vast cemetery, are questions difficult to be answered. Nor do they throw any light on the origin and formation of the coal itself; for in the coal no trace of a plant is found. Some have tried to account for the existence of the coal by supposing it to be the product of vast forests carbonized. But where could the forests grow that, in the condensed state of the anthracite, would produce such quantities? In this single coal field there are nearly two hundred miles; the field next south-east, the Lehigh region, is much more extensive; and the next, the Schuylkill region, not much less. To what depth the coal extends is not yet determined, but the superficial extent with its known depth is sufficient to refute the idea of such an origin. As yet its origin is a stumbling block to geologists.

The process of mining is effected more easily here than in other anthracite regions. Often, the *croppings out* are so favourable as to require no tunnel, and the excavation of coal is begun in open daylight. In other cases a horizontal tunnel is driven for a short distance to strike the vein, and then the excavations are made laterally. A railway is then laid, and the tunnel serves both to remove the coal and to drain off the water. I have noticed but one perpendicular shaft, and here the rubbish, and the water, and the coal must all be raised by the main strength of steam. The places of favourable excavation, however, are becoming scarce, and perpendicular shafts will become common. The time is not distant when there will be a large subterranean population here, and the valley a great colliery.

The importance of this valley in a commercial view is daily magnifying. Hitherto it has been cut off from market by want of communication; but since the princely improvements of the state of Pennsylvania have approached a completion, an outlet is afforded for the products of Wyoming. This season, for the first time, the Susquehanna canal has been opened to the tide waters of the Chesapeake, connecting the valley with Baltimore. Before, indeed, it was connected with Philadelphia by the canals from Harrisburg and the Columbia railroad; but this did not avail for the coal business, on account of the competition with the coal mines of the Lehigh and the Schuylkill. The Susquehanna is now hastening to its completion to the New York state line. There it will connect with the various canals and rail and water courses of New York, laying open the whole interior of that state as a market for the coal of this valley. Indeed, it will have a monopoly of that market. Another market has just presented itself in the iron regions of Danville, fifty miles below this. Recently very extensive beds of excellent iron ore have been discovered and opened at Danville, Bloomsburg and Catawissa, and furnaces erected. But it was not till a few weeks since that the experiment of smelting iron with anthracite succeeded. It has now succeeded most satisfactorily. Both pigs and bar iron of prime quality are now produced from anthracite; and it is estimated that next season ninety thousand tons of anthracite will be needed at Danville alone for the furnaces. A railroad is just now completed from Wilkesbarre to Whitehaven on the Lehigh, whence there is canal navigation to the Delaware, and so on to Philadelphia, and also to New York by the Morris canal. On this railroad it is intended to take boats with their loads from the Susquehanna canal, and transport them to Whitehaven, a distance of seventeen miles, and set them down on the Lehigh canal.

With such communication with markets south, east and north,—with such treasures of coal, iron and agricultural produce, it is obvious that this valley is destined to become a very busy place and an important part of this commonwealth, not to say of the nation. * * * * On the east of this place, some ten miles, is a dismal forest and swamp, in which, at the massacre, great numbers of aged men, women, and children perished in their flight, from starvation and fatigue, and the tomahawk. From this, the place has received the appropriate appellation, " Shades of Death." I was forcibly reminded of these things on the recent fourth of July, when 700 children, of the Sabbath schools of this borough and vicinity, marched in procession, with displayed banners, from the church to a retired grove, and listened to the story how " God brought your fathers here and preserved them, through dangers great and fearful, till they subdued the wilderness and drove out the wild beasts and the savage foe, and made this place the pleasant land and delightful home it now is."   J. R.

MANAGEMENT OF THE INSANE.

In Dr. Woodward's report relating to the State Lunatic Asylum, occurs the following interesting passage:—

Of the *one thousand and thirty-four* patients who have been in the hospital since it was first occupied, there have not been *twenty* who have not taken their food at the table with others more or less of the time ; of these *twenty*, more than three-fourths were so ill and feeble when they arrived at the hospital as to be unable to do so, and died without amendment in a few days. While this sheet is being written, we have not a solitary individual who has not for a very considerable time taken food with others, with knives and forks. No injury has ever been done by allowing patients all the means of comfortably taking their meals.

The difference between eating food in solitude from a tin or wooden dish with the fingers or a spoon, and going to a neatly furnished table, and taking meals from crockery with a knife and fork, is the difference between a savage and a civilized man, of a brute and a human being.

No one thing contributes more to awaken self-respect and restrain the furiously insane, than this indulgence at table, and the confidence which he feels is placed in him by those who have him in keeping. The same is true in respect to dress and the treatment he receives from those whom he looks upon as superiors and whom he feels bound to obey. If he is neatly and comfortably clad, like those whom he meets, he feels that he is as good as

others, respects himself as they appear to respect him, and is careful to do nothing by which he shall " lose caste." If his garments are tattered or dirty, he will tear them off or soil them more ; if neat and tidy, he will preserve them with care, and even feel proud of them.

Within a few days, a patient was brought to the hospital who had been confined *three* years in a cage ; he had not used knife or fork to take his meals during this period, and had not felt the influence of a fire for two winters. The gentleman who brought him to our care manifested praiseworthy benevolence in his efforts to ameliorate his condition, and get him into more comfortable winter quarters, and hoped that in a few months we should be able to improve his state, and that he would observe the decencies of life and take his food in a proper manner ; while he remained conversing respecting him, the patient below was quietly seated at the table taking his supper with knife and fork in his hand ! On the second Sabbath from his admission, he attended chapel quietly, and gave it as his unqualified opinion that he was " *well off.*"

Another man came into the hospital quite recently, furious as a wild beast, noisy, violent and outrageous ; he was placed in a solitary room with wristbands upon his arms to save his clothes and keep them on. For many days in succession he tore his clothes and stripped himself constantly. A few days ago, I found him in a state of perfect nudity. I proposed to him to be dressed and go into the gallery ; he promised that he would be quiet and tear no more clothing ; upon his pledge he went in—he has been quiet, has kept his clothes upon him, takes his food at the table with others, and is quite civil, in a state of entire *contrast* to what he had been before.

If, in our daily intercourse with the insane, we should treat them as inferiors, or pass them by without notice or attention, refuse to hear them, and evince towards them a feeling of superiority, we should find them in a constant state of irritation and excitement. If we treat them kindly and politely, inquire after their welfare, and hear patiently their story, we awaken in them a spirit of mildness and affection, we can control them without severity, and gain their confidence and esteem.

If there is any secret in the management of the insane, it is this ; respect them, and they will respect themselves ; treat them as reasonable beings, and they will take every possible pains to show you that they are such ; give them your confidence, and they will rightly appreciate it, and rarely abuse it.

From the Newport Mercury.

ANTIQUITIES OF AMERICA.

We learn from the New York Daily Express, that Stephens, United States Charge d'Affairs to Guatemala, and Catherwood, of the Panorama, have met with the most encouraging success almost at the outset of their researches for antiquities in Central America. At Quirigua they made the following discoveries :—

" One statue 10 feet high, lying upon the ground. One ditto, 10½ feet high, lying

upon the ground, face looking towards the heavens. One ditto 26 feet high, inclining similar to the steeple or tower at Pisa. A monument 23 feet high perpendicular, in the form of an obelisk, full of hieroglyphics, with a human statue cut upon its top, and has some figures in its hands. Another statue 6 feet high, representing a woman. One other statue 19 feet high, representing on the other a man, in good preservation. Another, the head of a giant, 6 feet in diameter. Two altars, most elegantly sculptured. One obelisk, 12 feet in height. Four other monuments in distinct places, one of which is of a circular form, and upon a small eminence formed of stones, apparently brought from the river. In the centre between these four human monuments, there is a huge round stone, which is wholly covered with hieroglyphics and inscriptions ; beneath the stone are two human heads, covered nearly with vegetation, upon which the stone rests.

" The above monuments are found about 3000 feet from the river Montagua. The time of Messrs. Catherwood and Stephens being short, they were unable to make more discoveries in that place; but they are satisfied that these monuments, &c. can be removed and taken to the United States of America, which is their intention ; while those of Palenque are so far in the interior, it would be impossible to remove them. We also learn that the human figures, and the ornaments which appear about them, are all similar to those of Palenque. In fact, this we consider only as a prelude to what we shall expect from these distinguished, persevering and scientific travellers. We learn these gentlemen will continue their journey, and after their visit to Palenque, will proceed to Mexico."

The New York Star, (edited by Noah, a Hebrew,) offers the following comments upon the above facts :—

" The people of this country must be prepared for extraordinary developements in researches throughout Central America, Peru, and Mexico. We must as a nation relinquish our unbelieving propensities, our uniform practice of doubting every thing which we cannot exactly comprehend, and believing all things to be a hoax or a humbug excepting men or a silver dollar, and prepare ourselves by a proper study and discipline of mind to know and to believe that this new world, so called—the discovery of a few centuries—was settled by the descendants of Peleg, and that the statues above described, together with the altars and obelisks, the temples at Palenque, the hieroglyphics, the aqueducts, viaducts, and military highways, are from the same people who built Tyre, Babylon, the Tower, the Pyramids, and Carthage —the Phœnicians ! who, driven down the Mediterranean by Joshua, after they had circumnavigated Africa, visited Britain and the Western Islands, found themselves, nearly 4000 years ago, in the Gulf of Mexico, and there made their settlement—spread over the peninsula to the Pacific Ocean and to Cape Horn. Let our people be prepared for something yet more startling—the downfall of the powerful people who built these cities. Let them be prepared to believe that 1500 years after the Phœnicians had settled in America, the nine and a half tribes of Israel, after the capture of

Samaria, took their departure for 'an unknown country,' and after taking in train the Tartars and Chinese disposed to follow, crossed at Behring's Straits, and passed down on the Pacific side until they reached the Isthmus of Darien, and there they came suddenly upon the Canaanites and destroyed them a second time, and in the new world, and with them destroyed their temples and their pagan altars, as they were ordered to do by the Almighty wherever they found them. Let our people know that the red men spread over this continent are the descendants of what was called the lost tribes, who bear, at this day, the proofs in their religion, language, and ceremonies, of their early origin."

Peaches.—A correspondent of the Journal of Commerce, speaking of peach trees, and their liability to be destroyed by " hard winters," states that Judge Judson, of the U. S. District Court of Connecticut, who resides at Canterbury, caught the idea that it might be the too early springs which created the difficulty. He, therefore, in January, after the ground had become thoroughly frozen, covered the roots a foot deep with hay or straw, which had the effect to keep the frost in the ground, and so prevent the sap from starting until the spring was fairly opened. He succeeded completely ; for the last spring the trees all around, and of his neighbours in the adjoining yard, were all destroyed, but his were fresh and blooming. The fact seems to be, that not the cold weather, but warm weather does the mischief. The trees are killed by the frost after the sap starts.

The National Intelligencer contains a notice of Kercheval's History of the Valley of Virginia, and speaking of the Ice Mountain in Hampshire county, in that state, it says :—
" The Table Ice Mountain, Kercheval thinks ' the most extraordinary and wonderful work of creation, and deserves the highest rank in the history of the natural curiosities of our country.' ' It is washed on one side by the Capon, and its west side for about a mile, is covered with loose stones of various sizes, and of diamond shape. It is from six to seven hundred feet in height, and on the western side for about one hundred yards, and ascending some thirty feet, when the loose stones are removed, the most perfect, pure and crystal looking ice *at all seasons of the year*, is to be found in blocks of from one or two pounds to fifteen or twenty pounds weight.' "

In the extremity of pain the Christian feels there is no consolation but in humble acquiescence in the Divine will. It may be that he can pray but little, but that little will be fervent. He can articulate, perhaps, not at all, but his prayer is addressed to one who sees the heart ; who can interpret its language ; who requires not words, but affections. We have a striking instance of an answer to silent prayer in the case of Moses. In a situation of extreme distress, when he had not uttered a word, the Lord said unto him, I have heard thy crying.

Communicated for " The Friend."

TO THE MEMORY OF DANIEL WHEELER.

Oh, dearly loved,
And worthy of our love ! No more
Thy aged form shall rise before
  The hushed and waiting worshipper,
In meek obedience, utterance giving
To words of truth, so fresh and living
That ever to the inward sense,
They bore unquestioned evidence
Of an anointed messenger !—
Or, bowing down thy silver hair,
In reverent awfulness of prayer,
  The world—its time and sense shut out,
The brightness of Faith's holy trance
Gathered upon thy countenance,
As if each lingering cloud of doubt—
The cold dark shadows floating here
In Time's unluminous atmosphere
  Were parted by an angel's hand,
And through them on thy spiritual eye
Shone down the blessedness on high—
  The glory of the better land.

We mourn for thee :
Yet, full of hope and strong in faith
That, through the ministry of death,
From weary works our blessed Lord
Hath called thee to the rich reward,
Of those who in His holy name
Have borne the cross—despised the shame,
  And counted not their own lives dear ;
Knowing no other will than His—
Nor hope but of His love—nor fear
Save of their own unworthiness—
'No shelter save beneath the wing
  Of Ancient Goodness,—and no life
  Save in their death to outward strife
The burial of their human will—
In meek submission draining still
Each bitter and afflicting cup
Vouchsafed to them, while filling up
The remnant of His suffering.

The oak is fallen !
While, meet for no good work, the vine
May still its worthless branches twine.
Who knoweth not that with thee fell
A great man in our Israel ?
Fallen, while thy loins were girded still,
  Thy feet with Zion's dews still wet,
  And, in thy hand retaining yet
The Pilgrim's staff and scallop-shell.
Unharmed and safe, where, wild and free,
  Across the Neva's cold morass
The breezes from the Frozen Sea
  With winter's arrowy keenness pass,
Or, where the unwarming tropic gale
Howled through thy Freeling's tattered sail ;
Or, where the noon-hour's fervent heat
Against Tahiti's mountains beat ;—
The same mysterious Hand which gave
Deliverance upon land and wave—
Tempered for thee the storms which blew
  Ladoga's frozen surface o'er,
And blessed for thee the baleful dew
  Of evening upon Eimeo's shore,
Beneath this genial heaven of ours,
Midst our soft gales and opening flowers,
Hath given thee a grave !

His will be done !
Who seeth not as man—whose way
Is not as ours : and oh, for thee,
Nor anxious doubt, nor dark dismay
Disquieted by closing day,
But evermore thy soul could say
  " My Father careth still for me !"
Called from thy childhood's home—from her
  The last bud on thy household tree,
The last dear one to minister
  In duty and in love to thee,—
  From all that Nature holdeth dear,
Weary with years and worn with pain
To seek our distant shores again :
Bound in the spirit, yet unknowing
  The things that should befall thee here,

Whether of labour or of death,
In child-like trust serenely going
  To that last trial of thy faith !

Oh ! far away
Where never shines our Northern star
  On that dark waste which Balboa saw
From Darien's mountains stretching far,
So strange, Heaven-broad and lone, that there
With forehead to its damp winds bare,
  He bent his mailed knee in awe ;—
In many an isle whose coral feet
The surges of that ocean beat,
In thy palm-shadows Oahu,
Amidst Owhyee's hills of blue,
  And taro groves of Tooboonai,
Are gentle hearts which soon shall be
Sad as our own at thought of thee—
  Worn sowers of Truth's holy seed,
Whose souls, in weariness and need,
Were strengthened and refreshed by thine,
  For blessed by the Master's hand
To them and theirs, thy tender care,
Thy ministry and fervent prayer—
Grateful as Eshcol's clustered vine,
  To Israel in their weary land !

And they who drew
By thousands round thee in the hour
Of prayerful seeking, hushed and deep,
That He, who bade His islands keep
  Silence before Him, might renew
Their strength with His slumbering power,
Will they forget the pilgrim old—
  The gray haired voyager on the wave—
Who in their solemn gatherings told
Of Him who came to seek and save
The wanderers from His Father's fold ?
They too may weep that thou art gone ;
  That ne'er more thy faithful lip
Shall soothe the weak—the erring warn
Of those who first, rejoicing, heard
Through thee, the Gospel's glorious word—
  Seals of thy true apostleship !
Yet, if the brightest diadem,
  Whose rays of living lustre burn
Around the ransomed ones in bliss,
Be evermore reserved for them,
Who here, through toil and trial, turn
Many to righteousness,—
May they not think of thee as wearing
That star-like crown of light, and bearing
Amidst heaven's bright and blissful band
The fadeless palm-branch in thy hand ;
And jotting with a seraph's tongue
In that new song the elders sung,
In offering to its blessed Giver
Thanksgiving, praise and love, forever.

Farewell !—
And though the ways of Zion mourn
  When her strong ones are called away
Who like thyself have calmly borne
  The heat and burden of the day ;
Yet He who slumbereth not nor sleepeth,
His ancient watch about us keepeth,
Still, sent from His preparing hand
New witnesses for Truth shall stand—
New instruments to sound abroad
The Gospel of our risen Lord,
To gather to the fold once more
  The desolate and gone astray—
  The scattered of a cloudy day,
And Zion's broken walls restore ;
And, through the travail and the toil
Of true obedience, minister
Beauty for ashes, and the oil
  Of joy for mourning unto her !
So shall her holy bounds increase
With gates of praise, and courts of peace ;
So shall the Vine which martyr tears
And blood sustained in other years
  With fresher life be clothed upon
And to the world in beauty glow,
As the rose plant of Jericho,
  And glorious as Lebanon !

                           J. G. W.

For "The Friend."

EARLY FRIENDS IN NEW ENGLAND.

(Continued from p. 342.)

LETTER X.

Ralph Goldsmith's ship arrived in Boston harbour near the close of 1661, and on the first day of the week. On board was Samuel Shattuck, the banished Quaker, but now the king's deputy, and having charge of the royal mandamus to the colonial officers and ministers. And, to preserve the secrecy of the mission, no intercourse was allowed by the captain between the ship's company and the town's people on the day of their arrival. Early on the following morning Ralph and Shattuck repaired to John Endicot's house, and on knocking at the door, a man came from his excellency to know their business. They bid him say to his master that they had a message from King Charles of England to the governor, which they could communicate in person only.

On being introduced, Endicot's countenance changed when his eye fell upon Shattuck; he knew that Quaker, for he had pronounced his sentence of banishment, and he ordered his hat to be taken off. But when he read the deputation and the mandamus, his countenance changed again, and the parties seemed suddenly to have shifted positions, for they gave Shattuck his hat, and Endicot took off his own, in respect to the vice-royal deputy.

Endicot then left the two and sought out Bellingham for consultation; and they soon returned an answer that they would obey the king's commands. Goldsmith and Shattuck then returned to the ship and delivered their letters from England; and all the company, which was supposed to consist of Quakers, went on shore, and with their friends in town returned thanks to God for their great deliverance.

At this time the assistants were in session; the subject was brought before them, and in a short time there was a general jail delivery of the Quakers then imprisoned in Boston.

The king's mandate produced a great sensation in the colony. They knew that Charles was jealous of their loyalty, and would lend a willing ear to the numerous complaints now gathering against them. They therefore appointed two agents to London—Norton, preacher at the first "church" in Boston, and Bradstreet, the distinguished persecuting assistant. These were to learn the king's suspicions against them, and to represent the people here as his most faithful subjects. The supposed dangers of the mission may be learned from the fact, that the agents took surety of the government to make good all damage by detention of their persons in England. They sailed in the second month of 1662.

At Whitehall it was said that their reception was most flattering; but to the English Quakers they were objects of great interest; and in London many of these, with George Fox, gathered round them, to learn what part they sustained in the cruelties to the Friends in America. Norton, it was said, denied any participation in those cruelties, but Bradstreet confessed his acts and defended them. And when Fox, the father of the sect, asked him by what law they put his friends to death, he replied, by the English law against Jesuits. But, said Fox, did you believe those you hung were Jesuits or Jesuitically affected? and Bradstreet was constrained to say no. Then, said Fox, you murdered them! The charge of murder in London was unpleasant to the charter ruler, and he exclaimed, What, have you come here to entrap and catch us? Thou hast caught thyself, replied the Quaker; and upon thine own admission may be brought to answer here in England for the lives of those men, and we are daily advised to bring thee to answer, by the most loyal of the king's servants, but we shall leave thee with the Lord.

This was a most startling intimation. The idea of a trial for murder, in England, was a vision of terror to the charter agents; who saw at once, in the actual state of the public mind, a strong token of the most fatal result. In their present position the subject assumed a new and frightful aspect; alone and friendless in a distant land, they could now appreciate the feelings of those Quakers they had slain in Massachusetts.

Upon Norton's more susceptible mind the impression was never effaced, for from the time of their return, which was quite hasty after this, all accounts agree that he pined, and not long after died in melancholy mood.

From the reception of the king's mandamus the charter powers ceased capital persecutions for religion; but, as if loth to take their hands off the Quakers, they for a long season, and almost to the end of the charter, continued to whip, fine, and imprison them almost without measure. By a law as late as 1677, the year after Philip's war, they renewed the slumbering fires of persecution, because, as they alleged, God's judgments were upon them, in that calamity, for their toleration of Quakers. In these persecutions more than three hundred citizens of the republic suffered in their persons and estates; and many were ruined by heavy fines, whippings, and imprisonments, and in discouragement left the country. So numerous were the law-made offences against the church power, a man could hardly speak or move without hazard. To go to a Quaker meeting was penal, to stay at home was penal, and Quakers could not be made to attend the regular charter worship in company with their persecutors; hence prosecutions and punishment were of almost daily occurrence. Those who had property would rather see it wasted than submit, and when they had none, they were doomed to hard labour, and in one case two were ordered to be sold out of the country as slaves to pay their fines, for not attending the regular public worship.

Lawrence Southic, and Cassandra his wife, whom God had blessed with two dutiful children, a son and a daughter. They once had property of lands and cattle, but by long and continued prosecutions, and the law against their sect, and by banishment, they were now very poor. Their children refused to attend the established worship. Upon this they were taken before a magistrate and fined, and having no property were ordered to work; this they also refused, and the public treasury was like to lose its dues, and thus the case was carried before the general court, which, to raise money, gave the following order.

"Whereas, Daniel Southic and Provided Southic, son and daughter of Lawrence Southic, have been fined by the courts of Salem and Ipswich, pretending to have no estate, and refusing to work; the court, upon perusal of a law which was made on account of debts, in answer to what should be done, for the satisfaction of the fines, resolves, that the treasurers of the several counties are and shall be fully impowered to *sell* said persons to any of the English nation at Virginia or Barbadoes, to answer for said fines.

"EDWARD RAWSON, Sec."

Under this order one of the treasurers actually undertook to send Southic's children to a slave market at Barbadoes. But to the lasting honour of the profession, no shipmaster could be found to take them; and one especially, affirmed that, should he be tempted to engage in so foul a business, he would never trust himself at sea again in the best ship that ever swam, and he bade the wicked treasurer go home and repent.

How soft a word is religious intolerance for such an act of charter despotism as this!

There was a law in those days, also, by which Quakers might be whipped as vagabonds from town to town through the charter limits, and the several constables, as they passed them on from hand to hand, whipped them southerly into the wilderness between Dedham and Rhode Island.

On a certain time three young and delicate Quakeresses went down to Dover, then the most northerly town in Massachusetts, and where there were many Quakers. Here their movements and exhortations became offensive to Richard Waldron, one of the charter magistrates, and the following order, issued by him, will serve as a sample of many others, and of itself conveys more knowledge of the temper of the times than any description.

"To the constables of Dover, Hampton, Salisbury, Newbury, Rowley, Ipswich, Wenham, Lynn, Boston, Roxbury, and Dedham, and until these vagabond Quakers are carried out of this jurisdiction.

You and every of you are required, in the king's name, to take these vagabond Quakers, Anne Colman, Mary Tompkins, and Olive Ambrose, and make them fast to the cart's tail, and driving the cart through your several towns, to whip them upon their naked backs, not exceeding ten stripes a piece in each town, and so to convey them from constable to constable, till they are out of this jurisdiction, as you will answer it at your peril; and this shall be your warrant.

Per me, RICHARD WALDRON."

In Dover, on a cold winter's day, Waldron saw the execution of his own order. The young women were stripped to the waist before him, tied to a cart's tail and whipped, and when some present ventured to condemn his cruelty, he put two of them in the stocks. From Dover they were passed on to Hampton, and there whipped; and thence to Salisbury, At Salisbury, Walter Barefoot through compassion persuaded the constable to give him the warrant to take the prisoners to Newbury;

but having obtained it, he set the females at liberty, and thus, no doubt, saved their lives. For, by the order, they could be whipped through eleven towns, ten stripes in each, and over a distance of eighty miles!

This cruelty soon built up a Quaker society in Dover, which long outlived the charter despotism; and this is the Waldron who was tomahawked in his own bedchamber by the Indians for his cruelty and treachery to them, they not being of Quaker forbearance.

LETTER XI.

Although I do not propose to detail further the Quaker persecutions, yet it is not for lack of matter. The collection of fines in those days for mere law-made offences, was a lucrative business. The constables and marshals levied upon the cattle, wearing apparel, the farming and household utensils of the people, by appraisement. So numerous were these appraisements, that as they now stand recorded, a correct estimate may be formed of the gold and silver value of all the necessaries of life under the first charter. Cotemporary writers affirm that more than forty thousand pounds were thus levied for the use of the government and the ministry; an immense sum, when we consider the poverty of the country, and the fact that seventy-five pounds would then buy as much as one hundred now. It brought down a wide spread ruin, although many fattened upon the spoils of their fellow citizens. The rights of property were violated by that government which was designed to protect it. It might be lost without sloth or improvidence, or won without industry or virtue. But the most deplorable wrong was the corruption of the public mind. It was the pollution of the fountains of justice: and to sustain those persecuting measures, required the excitement of the worst of passions among the people.

In 1665 Governor John Endicot died. He was older than the charter, being one of those to whom it was originally granted. He was nominated as a first assistant, in 1629, by the king, and came over soon after. The close of his life and administration was marked by the prosecution of five anabaptists. They were degraded and deprived of the power to vote as freemen, and when they would not cease the exercise of their religion, they were first imprisoned, and then banished.

But the king never forgot or forgave the necessity of his mandamus. In the execution of Englishmen, not for any crime known to British law, that jealous monarch saw the assumption of sovereignty in his own dominions and by his own subjects. In his letter to the colony in 1662, he commanded that only wisdom, virtue, and integrity should entitle to office, and that all freeholders of competent estates, not vicious, though of different religious persuasions, should be allowed to vote. In lieu of obedience, they sent the king a load of mats for his royal navy, with a most loyal letter. From this period we date the decline of the charter. And it was so that this British king, tyrannical and intolerant at home, seemed here the advocate of all good freedom, and the great refuge of all the oppressed. Yet it was not till 1683 that he dispatched the quo warranto against the charter; and then it was with

a promise, that if the colony would submit, he would regulate the government merely, and not destroy it.

Upon this the assistants, as was quaintly said, "showed more of the willow than the oak," and they passed a resolve "that they would not contend in law with his majesty, but would humbly lay themselves at his *royal feet* in submission to his pleasure." Another spirit this, from that which animated Mary Dyer, the defenceless woman, whom they slew in the days of their power.

"The wicked flee when no man pursueth: but the righteous are bold as a lion:"—"the Lord upholdeth the righteous."

PRAYER.

Henry Scougal, in his treatise entitled, "The Life of God in the Soul of Man," after reference to the promise of the Holy Spirit, thus proceeds: "In prayer, we make the nearest approaches to God, and lie open to the influences of heaven; then it is, that the Sun of Righteousness doth visit us with his directest rays, and dissipateth our darkness, and imprinteth his image on our souls." "As there is one sort of prayer, wherein we make use of the voice, and another wherein, though we utter no sound, yet we conceive the expressions and form of words, as it were in our minds; so there is a third and more sublime kind of prayer, wherein the soul takes a higher flight, and having collected all its forces by long and serious meditation, it darteth itself, if I may so speak, towards God in sighs and groans, and thoughts too big for expression. As when affections, appearing in all his works of wonder, it addresseth itself unto him in the profoundest adoration of his majesty and glory:—or when, after sad reflections on its vileness and miscarriages, it prostrates itself before him with the greatest confusion and sorrow, not daring to lift up its eyes, or utter one word in his presence—or when, having well considered the beauty of holiness, and the unspeakable felicity of those that are truly good, it panteth after God, and sendeth up such vigorous and ardent desires, as no words can sufficiently express; continuing these acts as long as it finds itself upheld by the force and impulse of the previous meditation."

"This mental prayer is, of all other, the most effectual to purify the soul, and dispose it to a holy and religious temper, and may be termed the great secret of devotion, and one of the most powerful instruments of the divine life; and it may be, that the apostle hath a peculiar respect to it, when he saith, 'the Spirit helpeth our infirmities, and maketh intercession for us with groanings which cannot be uttered,' or, as the original may bear, that cannot be worded."

ON WATERSPOUTS.

Extracted from Reid's work on the Law of Storms.

Of the different atmospheric phenomena, none is more curious than the waterspouts. That they cause small whirlwinds there seems no reason to doubt.

That which renders the waterspout so remarkable is the circumstance of a double cone being formed when the phenomenon is complete, one cone pointing downwards from a cloud, whilst another points upwards from the sea. The thin semi-transparent columns which stalk, as it were, on the surface of the ocean in calm weather, though no cloud is to be seen above them, as well as the small agitated circles, which are only seen by their marking the smooth surface of the sea in their gyrations, may probably have the same origin as the waterspout. One of these circles, which appeared too insignificant to do harm, after performing many gyrations near a ship commanded by Captain Marquis, on the coast of Malabar, suddenly approached her, as she lay becalmed, with her sails loose, and passing across her bows, carried off her flying jib and jib-boom into the air, higher than the mast-head. I have myself witnessed these semi-transparent columns, within the tropics, without being able to decide which way they turned round; and the spiral form in which they are said to revolve may be the reason: for it is very difficult to pronounce which way a screw revolves when turning rapidly. The figure being double, and the cones pointing in opposite directions, it should be observed whether the cloud above the spout also revolves, and if the gyrations of the upper portion of the phenomenon be in the same or in the contrary direction to those at the surface of the sea.

Notwithstanding diligent inquiry of a great many persons who witnessed waterspouts at sea, I have only been able to obtain one account in which the gyrations of the wind are satisfactorily explained; and in this instance it proved to be on the surface of the sea, turning in the contrary direction to the apparent law in great storms, in south latitude. The instance alluded to is the waterspout described by Capt. Beechey, in the published account of his voyage in the Pacific, when he commanded the Blossom. That account says,—

"While we were off Clermont Tonnerre, we had a narrow escape from a waterspout of more than ordinary size. It approached us amidst heavy rain, thunder, and lightning, and was not seen until it was very near to the ship. As soon as we were within its influence, a gust of wind obliged us to take in every sail, and the topsails, which could not be furled in time, were in danger of splitting. The wind blew with great violence, momentarily changing its direction, as if it were sweeping round in short spirals; the rain, which fell in torrents, was also precipitated in curves, with short intervals of cessation. Amidst this thick shower, the waterspout was discovered, extending in a tapering form, from a dense stratum of cloud to within thirty feet of the water, where it was hid by the foam of the sea, being whirled upwards by a tremendous gyration. It changed its direction after it was first seen, and threatened to pass over the ship: but being diverted from its course by a heavy gust of wind, it gradually receded. On the dispersion of this magnificent phenomenon, we observed the column to diminish gradually, and at length to retire to the cloud from whence it had descended, in an undulating form.

"Various causes have been assigned for

these formations, which appear to be intimately connected with electricity. On the present occasion a ball of fire was observed to be precipitated into the sea, and one of the boats, which was away from the ship, was so surrounded by lightning, that Lieut. Belcher thought advisable to get rid of the anchor by hanging it some fathoms under water, and to cover the seamen's muskets. From the accounts of this officer and Mr. Smyth, who were at a distance from the ship, the column of the waterspout first descended in a spiral form, until it met the ascending column a short distance from the sea; a second and a third were afterwards formed, which subsequently united into one large column, and this again separated into three small spirals, and then dispersed. It is not impossible that the highly rarefied air, confined by the woods encircling the Lagoon Islands, may contribute to the formation of these phenomena.

"Neither the barometer nor sympiesometer were sensibly affected by this partial disturbance of the atmosphere; but the temperature underwent a change of eight degrees, falling from 82° to 71°: at midnight it rose to 78°. On the day succeeding this occurrence, several waterspouts were seen at a distance, the weather being squally and gloomy."

Clermont Tonnerre is in south latitude, and is one of the group of islands called "Dangerous Archipelago," about lat. 19° S. long. 137° W.

Having applied to Captain Beechey in the hope that he might be able to explain in which way the gyrations of wind which accompanied this waterspout revolved, I received from him the following explanation:

"The gyrations were in a direction *contrary* to that of the hands of a watch; if it had been otherwise the ship would have changed her tack, whereas she only broke off. She was on the starboard tack, and the waterspout came upon the weather beam, and passed under the stern. At first the ship broke round off seven or eight points, and afterwards kept coming up and breaking off, as the gusts of wind varied their direction, but the wind continued on the starboard side the whole time, and the ship did not alter her position more than a quarter of the circle. It was quite clear, from the peculiar manner in which the rain (if such large drops can be so designated) fell, that we were within the vortex of the spout, and that the gusts which laid the vessel on her side were part of the phenomenon, and consequently that the gyration must have been as I have stated. I have observed many waterspouts between the tropics, but, with the exception of that off Clermont Tonnerre, never noticed the direction in which they turned, and regret that the subject was never before mentioned to me, as I have had many opportunities of determining the fact.

"As it appears to me that any observations upon this extraordinary phenomenon will be interesting, I extract from my journal a few lines, which I wrote when I last crossed the equator:—

"'The day had been very sultry, and in the afternoon a long arch of heavy cumuli and nimbi rose slowly above the southern horizon: while watching its movement, a waterspout began to form at a spot on the under side of the arch, that was darker than the rest of the line. A thin cone first appeared, which gradually became elongated, and was shortly joined with several others, which went on increasing in length and bulk, until the columns had reached about half down to the horizon. They here united and formed one immense dark-coloured tube. The sea beneath had been hitherto undisturbed; but when the columns united, it became perceptibly agitated, and almost immediately became whirled in the air with a rapid gyration, and formed a vast basin, from the centre of which the gradually-lengthening column seemed to drink fresh supplies of water. The column had extended about two thirds of the way towards the sea, and nearly connected itself with the basin, when a heavy shower of rain fell from the right of the arch, a short distance from the spout, and shortly after another fell from the opposite side. This discharge appeared to have an effect upon the waterspout, which now began to retire. The sea,' on the contrary, was perceptibly more agitated, and for several minutes the basin continued to increase in size, although the column was considerably diminished. In a few minutes more the column had entirely disappeared; the sea, however, still continued agitated, and did not subside for three minutes after all disturbing causes from above had vanished.

"'This phenomenon was unaccompanied by thunder or lightning, although the showers of rain which fell so suddenly seemed to be occasioned by some such disturbance.'"

The circular motion imparted to the water of the sea during waterspouts, is probably not confined merely to the surface, for the ocean, to an unknown depth, may partake of the impulse.

In 1815, the Orontes frigate, commanded by Captain Cochrane, was in company with the Newcastle, the flag-ship of the late Admiral Sir Pulteney Malcolm. The ships were near the equator, between Teneriffe and St. Helena, when two large waterspouts were observed a-head of the Orontes, one on each bow, about a mile and a half distant, whilst the Newcastle was nearly the same distance on the larboard beam.

It was perfectly calm at the time; yet the Orontes was observed to be going a-head of the admiral; and it was proved by throwing paper into the sea, that the vessel was making no way through the water. The officers were of opinion that the Orontes was carried forward by a partial current which did not affect the Newcastle, and the circumstance was mentioned to the admiral by Captain Cochrane, on their arrival at St. Helena, as a curious coincidence, viz. the Orontes being carried forward, whilst the waterspouts were a-head of her.

The moving pillars of sand described by Bruce as having been seen in Nubia, though the account may be familiar to many, is here reprinted, because these moving pillars probably originated from the same cause, whatever that may be.

"On the 14th of November, at seven in the morning, we left Assa Nagga, our course being due north; at one o'clock we alighted among acacia trees at Waadi el Halboub, having gone twenty-one miles. We were here at once surprised and terrified, by truly one of the most magnificent sights in the world. In that vast expanse of desert from west to northwest of us, we saw a large number of pillars of sand at different distances, at times moving with great celerity, at others stalking on with a majestic slowness; at intervals we thought they were coming in a very few minutes to overwhelm us; and small quantities of sand did actually more than once reach us. Again they would retreat, so as to be almost out of sight, their tops reaching to the very clouds. Then the tops often separated from the bodies; and these once disjoined, dispersed in the air, and did not appear more. Sometimes they were broken near the middle, as if struck with a large cannon shot. About noon they began to advance with considerable swiftness upon us, the wind being very strong at north. Eleven of them ranged alongside of us, about the distance of three miles. The greatest diameter of the largest appeared to me at that distance as if it would measure ten feet. They retired from us with a wind at southeast, leaving an impression upon my mind to which I can give no name, though surely one ingredient in it was fear, and a considerable deal of wonder and astonishment. It was in vain to think of flying; the swiftest horse, or fastest sailing ship, would have been of no use to have carried us out of the danger.

"15th Nov.—At 7 A. M. we left Waadi Dimokea. The same appearance of moving pillars of sand presented themselves to us this day, in form and disposition like those we had seen at Waadi el Halboub, only they seemed to be more in number and less in size."

THE TORNADO AT NATCHEZ.

We have just conversed with an observant and scientific citizen of Natchez, who was an eye-witness of the late desolating tempest, and he has communicated to us some particulars which go towards explaining the rationale of tornadoes. This gentleman lives in a house built after the Spanish model, and which is more substantial than the great majority of houses in Natchez. Its chimneys were blown down and its windows driven out, and one of its wings, built more recently, and not so securely as the rest of the edifice, was prostrated. The main body of the building was uninjured, and the family escaped.

The gentleman's gardener had just left his own house, close by, and its windows and doors were by accident left open; it received no injury. The gardener of a friend, living in his immediate neighbourhood, hastened to his house when he saw the storm approaching, and succeeded in closing his doors and windows, which he had scarcely done when the house fell and crushed him under the ruins. Dr. Tooley, the neighbour of our informant, a man of science, with a just conception of the action of the tempest, threw open all the windows and doors of his house, not already open when the storm commenced, and, although the structure of it was frail, it sustained no injury: not even a pane of glass was broken. It was saved by the free outlet given to the air in the rooms seeking to restore the balance in the atmosphere.

Houses, that were made as air-tight as the closing of doors and windows could render them, were in the condition of the sealed bottle under the exhausted receiver of an air-pump: the pent-up air of which shivers it into a thousand fragments. The destruction of houses was entirely owing to the sudden expansion of the air within, said to have been equal to the explosive force of gunpowder. They were exploded—the roofs shot up into the air, and the bricks in the walls were projected with violence in all directions around. In many cases the upper rooms, or garrets, which were most confined, alone exploded, the other apartments escaping in consequence of the exit afforded to the air by doors and windows. Our informant represents it as having been the work of an instant. The wind did not seem to blow harder than it [does in storms of ordinary severity.] It appeared that the common air was suddenly and strangely rarefied—as if its pressure had been at once annihilated—and, in this state, the atmosphere confined in houses rushing out into the void, threw down every wall not of remarkable strength, or having large outlets by which it might escape. He walked forth a moment after his own house felt the concussion, and beheld on all sides houses prostrate, and his neighbours crawling forth from under their ruins. He confirms the statement already given, that a marvellously small number of persons perished, considering how many houses full of inhabitants were demolished in a single moment of time.

Those persons who heard the lectures of Dr. Espy, on his late visit to our city, will be struck with the confirmation which the tornado of Natchez gives to his theory of storms. As he maintained was the fact in all such tempests, the buildings in that ill-fated city were thrown down by an explosion—the instantaneous expansion of the air within the houses. And the practical lesson to be drawn from the whole is, that the windows of our dwellings should be raised and the doors thrown open during a tornado, to allow free egress to the air, in case of the sudden rarefaction of the atmosphere without.—*Louisville Journal.*

It is a fact well known in the history of knowledge, that men, gifted with singular intelligence, have broached the grossest errors, and even sought to undermine the grand truths on which human virtue, dignity and hope depend. And on the other hand, there are instances of men of naturally moderate powers of mind, who by a disinterested love of truth and their fellow-creatures, have gradually risen to no small force and enlargement of thought. Some of the most useful teachers of mankind have owed their power of enlightening others, not so much to any natural superiority, as to the simplicity, impartiality and disinterestedness of their minds, to their readiness to live and die for the truth. Thought expands as by a natural elasticity, when the pressure of selfishness is removed. Moral and religious principles fertilize the intellect. Duty faithfully performed, opens the mind to truth, both being of one family, alike immutable, universal and everlasting.

The Yearly meeting of Friends in London gave, in their Epistle of 1826, the following truly excellent advice to its members—advice as applicable now as then, and to others, as well as those within the pale of the Society of Friends. "We would tenderly invite those who may have acquired a competency of outward substance, to watch the proper period at which they may withdraw from the cares of business, and when disengaged from the regular concerns of trade, to beware how they employ their property in investments which may involve them anew in care and anxiety. We affectionately desire that neither these nor any other cares may disqualify them from acting the part of faithful stewards in the employment of their time, their talents, and their substance, or from being concerned above all things, through watchfulness unto prayer, to have their lamps trimmed, and oil in their vessels; that when the solemn close of life shall come, they may, through redeeming love and mercy, be prepared to enter into the joy of their Lord."

Faithfulness to God.—The man who would be faithful to his God, would rather be rebuked by the wise and religious, than applauded by the foolish and profane.

Perhaps nothing would tend so efficaciously to diminish the general evils of insolvency as a sound state of public opinion respecting the obligation to pay our debts. The insolvent who, with the means of paying, retains the money in his own pocket, is, and he should be regarded as being a dishonest man. If public opinion held such conduct to be of the same character as theft, probably a more powerful motive to avoid insolvency would be established than any which now exists.

THE FRIEND.

EIGHTH MONTH, 1, 1840.

Within a few days past, we have received more than one intimation, from respectable sources, that we have been guilty of an indiscretion by inserting, the week before last, the article headed "Coloured People in London." In answer we may say, that it was copied from one of our exchange papers, with no other view than as showing the kind of feeling with which coloured people were regarded there; and, being unaccompanied by note or comment, it was only by a strained inference that we could be supposed to hold it up as an example for imitation among ourselves. We should be very sorry to be so understood. We are not, nor ever have been connected with the anti-slavery societies, and although among those associated with them are many estimable individuals, and not a few of them in the list of our particular friends, yet we have uniformly believed, that one of the greatest mistakes committed by the anti-slavery people, is the mixing up with the abolition question, the warfare against what they are pleased to call

prejudices in regard to the coloured race. The great object, it is our settled judgment, should be the extirpation of slavery, by striking at the root; leaving those minor appendages to time, and the gradual but certain effects of advancing light and knowledge. In short, it continues to be, as it has been, our desire to act in consistency with the temper and principles of Old School Abolitionists—such as influenced the James Pembertons, the Warner Mifflins, the Benjamin Rushes of former days,—or, which is still more in accordance with our convictions, we desire to regulate our movements in relation to this subject, so that they may continually harmonize with the principles and mode of action "professed and practised by the Society of Friends—that is safe and proper." In the mean time, we wish our friends to bear in mind, than an editor has a difficult and often a perplexed path to tread—that with the best intentions he is liable to err, either on the right hand, or on the left, and therefore has a reasonable claim to kindness on the part of those who judge.

It has been mentioned to us, that we omitted to note, according to our general practice in similar cases, the return of our Friend Jacob Green to his home in Ireland. The omission was altogether unintentional, and it may be satisfactory to distant subscribers, even yet to state, that he embarked in the steamship British Queen (directly after attending New York Yearly Meeting) on or about the 1st of the 6th month last. We have now to add, that our Friend Joseph John Gurney embarked at New York, on seventh day the 25th ultimo, in the packet ship Roscius for Liverpool.

MORAL ALMANAC.

We have on our table the Moral Almanac for the year 1841, published by the Tract Association of Friends, and to be had at their depository No. 50, North Fourth street. It bears a neat, and we think improved appearance, and with the tables and calculations essential to an almanac, contains besides equivalent to about twenty-three pages of judiciously selected moral and religious reading matter, of itself worth at least three times the selling price. The demand last year, it appears, considerably exceeded the number printed; consequently many who neglected to apply early were disappointed. This we are desired to mention for the benefit of those who wish a supply, lest by neglecting to call seasonably, a like disappointment ensue.

The lines inserted to-day to the memory of D. Wheeler, were kindly furnished us by a friend of the gifted author. Their beauty and appropriateness, we think, will not be questioned.

Died, at his residence in Wilmington, Delaware, on the 19th ult. WILLIAM WETHERELL, in the 72d year of his age.

PRINTED BY ADAM WALDIE,
Carpenter Street, below Seventh, Philadelphia.

THE FRIEND.

A RELIGIOUS AND LITERARY JOURNAL.

VOL. XIII.   SEVENTH DAY, EIGHTH MONTH, 8 1840.   **NO. 45.**

EDITED BY ROBERT SMITH.

PUBLISHED WEEKLY.

Price two dollars per annum, payable in advance.

Subscriptions and Payments received by

GEORGE W. TAYLOR,

NO. 50, NORTH FOURTH STREET, UP STAIRS,

PHILADELPHIA.

For " The Friend."

THE REMEDY FOR THE SLAVE TRADE.

I have been much interested in looking over Buxton's remedy. The scheme is a magnificent and noble one indeed, and an honour to the great nation which has undertaken to carry it out. If successful, it will shed incalculably more glory upon her than all the conquests ever won by her or any nation, however brilliant in the estimation of men who are more disposed to glorify their oppressors than their benefactors; and if unsuccessful, even defeat in such a cause will be no small praise. We have read of many nations brought to degradation and destruction by more powerful neighbours, but the pleasing example has not yet found a page in history, of the most powerful nation of the earth attempting, under the influence of Christian philanthropy, to raise a people who have been trodden down as near to the level of the brute as, perhaps, it is possible for the cruelty of man to sink his fellow. A project so novel and so vast, seems, at first, more like the dream of some benevolent visionary, than the deliberate determination of cool-headed, calculating men.

Let those who think so examine the foundation upon which its author stands, and if they are not quite convinced that his feet are on a rock, they will in candour acknowledge that he has foothold on what wears the appearance at least of solid substance. In his book, he gives in the first place a summary of the present legitimate commerce of Africa, and contrasts it with her capabilities as they are represented by numerous travellers of high standing. He shows the prodigious cost of the brutal traffic in the bodies of men, and compares the paltry profit gained in this way with that which would result from the labour of those whom she banishes from her teeming soil, if properly applied to the cultivation of it. He holds up the temptation of a lucrative trade, waiting for the merchants of all nations who will co-operate in this great scheme, and illustrates both by theory and fact the practicability of inducing the indolent, marauding African to quit the slaughter and sale of his fellows for the peaceable and harmless pursuit of regular and lawful trade combined with agriculture.

Religion, acting upon the susceptible mind of the negro, is the chief corner stone of Buxton's expectations. His system rests upon religious instruction in the first place, to be immediately followed by the arts and sciences, and above all, the commerce of civilized life. Religion is to give the impulse which is to rescue Africa from her miserable thraldom.

The chief obstacle to affording her people religious instruction heretofore has been the destructiveness of her climate to the constitution of the white man; but the emancipation of the West India negroes seems likely to be the means of setting numbers of pious individuals at liberty for this work, who, moved with compassion for the deplorable condition of the land of their fathers, are willing and already are freely offering themselves for the service.

Buxton says: My first object is to show that Africa possesses within herself the means of obtaining by fair trade, a greater quantity of our goods than she now receives from the slave trade; and secondly, to point out how this truth may be made plain to the African nations. I have further to prove, that Great Britain, and other countries have an interest in the question only inferior to that of Africa, and that if we cannot be persuaded to suppress the slave trade for the fear of God, or in pity to man, it ought to be done for the lucre of gain. The present condition of Africa in relation to commerce is deplorable. Even the feathers received at Liverpool from Ireland reach an amount exceeding all the productions of central Africa; the eggs from France and Ireland exceed one half of it; while the value of pigs from Ireland into the port of Liverpool is three times as great as the whole trade of Great Britain in the productions of the soil of central Africa. The whole amount of goods exported direct from Great Britain to all Africa is considerably within one million sterling.

The imports, though they have increased since the year 1820, are still extremely limited; and it is observable that they scarcely embrace any articles produced from the cultivation of the soil. Their estimated value, in 1834, was about two and a quarter millions of dollars (exclusive of gold dust, about one and one third millions); they consisted chiefly of palm oil, teak timber, gums, ivory, beeswax, &c. all extremely valuable, and in great demand, but obtained at comparatively little labour and cost.

After quoting a number of writers on the capabilities of Africa and the feasibleness of his scheme, he remarks : There is no species of argument which carries with it a greater force of conviction to my mind, than the concurrence of a variety of persons, who, being competent to judge, and having opportunities of

forming a sound judgment, examine a given object with very different purposes, from very different points of view, yet arrive, without concert, or previous communication, at the same conclusion. In the case before us we collect the unpublished dispatches, letters, and journals of the several governors of Sierra Leone, Fernando Po, the Gambia, and the Gold Coast. These documents were written at different times, with no view to publication, and there was no connection between the officers who wrote them. Differing on many points, they harmonize exactly on those which affect my case. Each speaks of the exuberant fertility of the soil; each laments the desolation which, in spite of nature prevails ; and each looks to the cultivation of those fertile lands, and to the growth of legitimate commerce, as the remedy to the distractions of Africa, and the horrors of the slave trade. For example. it appears that General Turner at Sierra Leone, and Colonel Nicolls of Fernando Po, had in view much such a plan as I have suggested, when they spoke in their dispatches of putting an end to the slave trade in two or three years. This unconscious union between themselves is not all. The views of these gentlemen correspond with those which I find in the private journals of the missionaries, who have gathered their experience, and formed their opinion, while labouring among the native tribes of the Gambia. That which is the opinion of these soldiers and of these teachers of religion turns out to be the opinion of the most distinguished travellers and of intelligent traders. Captain Becroft, who traded on the western coast, and Captain Raymond, who did the same on the eastern, tell me—that trade, springing from the cultivation of the soil, will, and that nothing else will, abolish the slave trade.

Buxton quotes a number of authorities to show how readily the natives of Africa may be induced to devote themselves to agriculture and trade. The testimony of a gentleman named Ferguson, who has resided seventeen years at Sierra Leone, and for the last eight years has been at the head of the medical department there, is interesting and important. He says: " Keeping steadily in sight your principle of substituting a harmless and profitable trade for one that is illegal and worse than profitless, I am also desirous of directing your attention to what has been going on during the last year or two in the Rio Nunez. This river, though now little spoken of, was in former years notorious for slave trading.

" At Kaikandy, the chief trading place, situated about 100 miles from the sea, and in the country of the Landemas, numerous factories, occupied by French and English traders, are established ; to which Foulahs, Seracoolies, Bambarras, and people of other nations, resort in great numbers. I spent some time there in February last, and was assured by the merchants that the Foulahs were gradually weaning themselves from the slave trade, and that they had of late years brought down a much larger quantity of native produce than formerly.

"About three years ago, some of the Foulah traders who resort to Kaikandy, brought down small parcels of coffee, and offered them for sale. The coffee was so eagerly purchased by the European merchants, that the Foulahs immediately turned their attention to the further supply of it. It appears that there are vast forests of indigenous coffee in the Foulah country, and of much finer quality than that of the West Indies or South America. The Foulahs evince great satisfaction in the possession of such an unexpected source of wealth, and the quantity supplied has of course greatly increased.

"They are an intelligent people, and are very anxious to extend their commercial dealings with the British. They seem to have already perceived that it is more profitable for them to preserve the element of labour in their own country, than to deprive themselves of its assistance by selling each other to strangers ; so that it may be said, without a metaphor, that in every hundred weight of coffee which they collect and take to Kaikandy, at least one human being is preserved from slavery."

The Gambia was formerly a great mart for slaves. The population along its banks are now eager for lawful commerce, in which alone they are now engaged. The trade is extended about 400 miles up the river ; a new and lucrative branch has also been lately opened there in gum ; and the only exception to the cheerful picture occurs in the French establishment at Albreda, where still some slaves are said to be harboured. This great change is ascribed to two causes ; first, to the vicinity of the British colony, and its command over the river ; and, secondly, to the existence of a good market for the produce of the soil. Now that the natives can find a ready market for the produce of their lands, the cultivation of the soil increases every year ; and the aborigines have been heard to say, that they now wish they had their slaves back again, because they could get more by their labours in husbandry than they did by selling them to Europeans.

We know that a slave fetches, in interior Africa, about 3l. ; in Brazil, at least 70l. ; Africa, then, has this advantage over America, that it can be cultivated at one-twentieth of the expense. The soil being equal, a labourer in Africa will raise as much produce as the same labourer transported to America, but at less expense ; for you can hire ten labourers in the former at the price that one costs in the latter. Hence I infer, that the labour and produce of Africa, if fairly called forth, would rival the labour employed, and the produce raised in America, throughout the markets of the civilized world.

For "The Friend."

FACTS IN THE NATURAL HISTORY OF REPTILES.

In vol. 39, No. 1, of "The American Journal of Science and Arts," is an article compiled from the Proceedings of the Boston Society of Natural History, which contains several curious facts. Under date of February 19, 1840, it is stated that "Dr. Storer presented the following report on Bell's British Reptiles," some extracts from which may be interesting for the readers of the Friend.

From an examination of the splendid "monograph of the Testudinata" of our author, we had a right to expect a rich treat from the pages before us ; nor have we been disappointed. The " History of the British Reptiles" is written by a *true naturalist*, by one whose every page is stamped with accuracy and truth, who never finds it necessary to exaggerate in order to interest, but who seems to feel his responsibility in the statements he makes, and that his reputation is associated with the subjects he is endeavouring to elucidate.

The descriptions of each of the sixteen species which constitute the Reptilia of Great Britain, are all clear and interesting—such descriptions as satisfy the naturalist. I will glance at some of the species. Singular as it may appear, but *one of the Colubridæ* is found in Great Britain—the natrix torquata, common snake ; which we are here told, " inhabits most of the countries of Europe, from Scotland and the corresponding latitude of the continent, to Italy and Sicily." The following curious anecdote is related of the manner in which they manage their prey and each other :—

"On placing a frog in a large box in which were several snakes, one of the latter instantly seized it by one of the hinder legs, and immediately afterwards another of the snakes took forcible possession of the fore leg of the opposite side. Each continued its inroads upon the poor frog's limbs and body, until at length the upper jaws of the two snakes met, and one of them in the course of its progress, slightly bit the jaw of the other; this was retaliated, though evidently without any hostile feeling ; but after one or two such accidents, the most powerful of the snakes commenced shaking the other, which still had hold of the frog, with great violence, from side to side against the sides of the box. After a few moments' rest, the other returned the attack, and at length, the one which had last seized the frog, having a less firm hold, was shaken off, and the victor swallowed the prey in quiet. No sooner was this curious contest over, than I put another frog into the box, which was at once seized and swallowed by the unsuccessful combatant." Our author, immediately after relating this anecdote, observes : " The frog is generally alive, not only during the process of deglutition, but even after it has passed into the stomach. I once saw a very small one which had been swallowed by a large snake in my possession, leap again out of the mouth of the latter, which happened to gape, as they frequently do immediately after taking food. And on another occasion, I heard a frog distinctly utter its peculiar cry several minutes after it had been swallowed by the snake." This reminds us of the anecdote related by Harlan,[*] who, speaking of the tenacity of life exhibited

[*] Descriptions of several species of Batracian Reptiles, &c. by Richard Harlan of Philadelphia.

by the *Rana clamata*, observes : " A dog of Mr. Bartram's having accidentally swallowed one of these animals, it was observed to struggle and cry piteously for at least *half an hour*, to the great diversion of the spectators, and no small confusion of the dog, who was at a loss to comprehend this species of intestinal eloquence." Like many of our snakes, the *torquata* may be easily tamed. Our author remarks : " I had one many years since, which knew me from all other persons ; and when let out of his box, would immediately come to me, and crawl under the sleeve of my coat, where he was fond of lying perfectly still, and enjoying the warmth. He was accustomed to come to my hand for a draught of milk every morning at breakfast, which he always did of his own accord ; but he would fly from strangers, and hiss if they meddled with him."

The history of the *Rana temporaria*, common frog, is very interesting ; the changes which take place in its developement from the *ovum* to the perfect animal, are pointed out with a clearness which shows how well they are understood by the describer. In a pleasing anecdote, our author proves its capability of being tamed ; he states that his friend, Dr. William Roots, of Kingston, informed him, " that he was in possession for several years, of a frog in a perfect state of domestication. It appears that the lower offices of his house were, what is commonly called under ground, on the banks of the Thames. That this little reptile accidentally appeared to his servants, occasionally issuing from a hole in the skirting of the kitchen, and that during the first year of his sojourn, he constantly withdrew upon their approach ; but from their showing him kindness, and offering him such food as they thought he could partake of, he gradually acquired habits of familiarity and friendship ; and during the following three years, he regularly came out every day, and particularly at the hour of meal time, and partook of the food which the servants gave him. But one of the most remarkable features in his artificial state of existence, was his strong partiality for warmth, as during the winter seasons, he regularly (and contrary to the cold-blooded tendency of his nature) came out of his hole in the evening, and directly made for the hearth in front of a good kitchen fire, where he would continue to bask and enjoy himself until the family retired to rest. " There happened to be at the same time a favourite old domestic cat, and a sort of intimacy or attachment existed between these two incongruous inmates ; the frog frequently nestling under the warm fur of the cat, whilst the cat appeared extremely jealous of interrupting the comforts and convenience of the frog. This curious scene was often witnessed by many besides the family."

The manner in which the *Bufo vulgaris*, common toad, sheds its cuticle, is described very instructively :—

" Having often found, among several toads which I was then keeping for the purpose of observing their habits, some of brighter colours than usual, and with the surface moist and very smooth, I had supposed that this appearance might have depended upon the state of the animal's health, or the influence of some peculiarity in one or the other of its functions ;

on watching carefully, however, I one day observed a large one, the skin of which was particularly dry and dull in its colours, with a bright streak down the medial line of the back; and on examining further, I discovered a corresponding line along the belly. This proved to arise from an entire slit in the old cuticle, which exposed to view the new and brighter skin underneath. Finding, therefore, what was about to happen, I watched the whole detail of this curious process. I soon observed that the two halves of the skin, thus completely divided, continued to recede further and further from the centre, and became folded and rugose; and after a short space, by means of the continued twitching of the animal's body, it was brought down in folds on the sides. The hinder leg, first on one side and then on the other, was brought forward under the arm, which was pressed down upon it, and on the hinder limb being withdrawn, its cuticle was left inverted under the arms, and that of the anterior extremity was now loosened, and at length drawn off by the assistance of the mouth. The whole cuticle was thus detached, and was now pushed by the two hands into the month in a little ball, and swallowed at a single gulp."

For "The Friend."

JAMAICA FREEDOM.

We often hear of the bad working of emancipation in Jamaica. As many of the readers of "The Friend" may be at a loss to know *why* it works badly, the following extract from the "British and Foreign Anti-Slavery Reporter," is offered for their information.—Read and see.   E. N. R.

JAMAICA.

Our attention has been called to a pamphlet entitled, "Conciliation, a Letter addressed to the Planters of Jamaica,"—an extract or two from which we give in our present number. We shall have occasion to recur to it. After a few words on the duty of *every* one of the queen's subjects, to abstain from all contravention of the law bestowing absolute freedom at once on those in bonds, J. J. Gurney proceeds:—

"Now, the very essence of slavery is compulsory labour. I apprehend that I can make no mistake in asserting, that all attempts to *compel* labour, be they weak or be they stringent, be they temperate or be they violent, are opposed to the true meaning and purpose of the act of emancipation, and to the principles of justice as they bear on the circumstances of the case.

"One of the methods which has been resorted to in this island, for compelling work, is the mixture of the question of tenure with that of labour; and I am confident that a little calm reflection will serve to convince any man that such a mixture is not only at variance with the commonplace rules of political economy, but also with the rule of right. It is a system which classes under slavery, and is in its nature opposed to that law of liberty, in which, I trust, we all now rejoice.

"Allow me to explain myself. A planter

of Jamaica, at the close of the apprenticeship—the date of full freedom by law—finds himself in possession of a number of cottages and provision grounds, occupied by certain freemen, who, I suppose, in such a case, might be regarded as tenants at will. Allowing some short interval for the almost inevitable temporary unsettlement, it must soon become evident that *something* is due to the planter, in return for such tenancy. Now, what is that something, according to the universal principles which regulate the relations of landlord and tenant? Certainly not labour—much less a personal restriction to work on a particular spot—but a fair rent—such a rent as represents the true money value of the property tenanted. This is the only *quid pro quo*, as I conceive, which justice can demand on the occasion.

"To require of the tenant the regular payment of such a rent, and *legally to eject*, in case of the non-payment of it, are neither of them proceedings to which any reasonable objection can be urged. But to require not merely that the tenant should pay rent, but that he should work on a certain estate, at a certain rate of wages, and for a certain number of days in the week, and to eject him if these latter provisions are not complied with—appears to me unjust in principle—a recurrence, as far as it goes, to the old system of slavery. *It is the compelling of labour by a penal infliction.*

"I presume that ejectments from tenements on the grounds now mentioned, cannot be legal; and it appears that the object has, in many cases, been effected by manual force. Cocoa nut and bread-fruit trees have been felled—cottages have been unroofed, and sometimes demolished—pigs have been shot—provision grounds have been destroyed—the pleasant fruits of God's earth uprooted by the rude hand of violence, or trodden under foot of oxen. I conceive that *such acts of spoliation are, in point of fact, nothing more or less than substitutes for the cart-whip*. Notorious as the facts are to which I have now alluded, I mention them, because necessary to be mentioned, and with no other than Christian feelings towards those who have perpetrated them."

J. J. Gurney supposes, what we wish were true, that the planters dislike this mode of compelling labour quite as much as he does. We fear that many of the highest and proudest of them are guilty of these deeds of wrong.

He proceeds:—

"Another method of compelling labour has been the arbitrary increase of rents, with distraint, imprisonment, and ejectment in the train, in case of their not being paid. A labourer on a certain estate is under an agreement with its manager, to pay two shillings sterling per week as rent for his house and ground. Some cause of dispute and dissatisfaction arises with regard to his labour, and the rent is immediately raised, by way of penal exaction, to twice, thrice, or four times the amount; or, *strange to say*, it is demanded for his wife, and each of his children respectively, as well as for himself. He of course is unable to pay it. Complaint is made against him by the overseer to some of the magistrates in the neighbourhood; the debt is adjudicated to be a valid one; his goods are distrained; and if

there be a deficiency in the amount thus levied to pay the debt and the fees, he is imprisoned for ten days. But this is not all; after he has been discharged, the remainder of the debt still hangs over his head, and whenever his petty articles of comfort and convenience again accumulate, he may be exposed to another distraint. In case of his removing any of his goods to avoid the effect of this second seizure, he is liable as a fraudulent debtor to imprisonment, at the discretion of the magistrate, for any term not exceeding three months; and any members of his family who assist him in so doing, may be subjected to the same punishment. Now all this is monstrous. It is a screw of prodigious power, of which the obvious application is to *compel labour*, or in other words, *to reduce freemen, a second time, to slavery*."

THE ATMOSPHERE OF CITIES.

In an annual report by a register-general of births, deaths, marriages, &c. which we find in a late English print, there is an appendix, embracing statements of the comparative mortality of great towns and rural districts. The person who prepared the calculations, consulted on one side, returns from thirty-two metropolitan cities, and twenty-four of the largest towns in England, such as Birmingham, Manchester, Liverpool, &c., and on the other hand possessed himself of statistics from the counties of Cornwall, Devon, and others, containing an equal amount of population. In six months the deaths from twelve principal causes of disease, were as arranged in the following table:—

	In London and 24 other towns, containing a population of 3,653,000.	In rural districts, containing a population of 3,500,000.
Epidemic, endemic and contagious diseases,	12,766	6,015
Sporadic diseases,	25,398	14,230
Of uncertain seat,	4,396	3,730
Age,	2,924	3,102
Violent deaths,	1,370	929
Not specified,	1,104	1,657
Total,	47,953	29,693

This comparison, he thinks, establishes completely the fact of the increased mortality in crowded communities, and the immense influence of the state of the atmosphere in augmenting disease. The classes of disease upon which the difference between the mortality of town and country districts chiefly hinges, are precisely those in which the air is most influential.—*Eve. Post.*

From Chambers' Edinburgh Journal.

ANIMAL COTTON.

In an age when fine loaves of bread are manufactured from sawdust, and superior wine from rhubarb and turnips, it is surprising that but little advantage has been taken of the natural production of an insect, very common and much dreaded in the West Indies, the Capada worm or insect fly-carrier. It is a deadly enemy to the indigo and capada plantations, sometimes destroying whole fields in a night: a circumstance which gave rise to a saying once current in the western hemisphere, that the planters of indigo go to bed rich, and rise in the morning beggars. Attention has been turned more to the most efficient methods of destroying the animal, than to turning it to some useful purpose. Yet this might easily be done, for in a certain state it produces a substance which appears to be equal, if not superior, to the finest silk or cotton. It is of the most dazzling whiteness and the greatest purity, answering the purposes of lint in the hospitals of the negroes, when silk and vegetable cotton serve only to inflame wounds by the asperities of their filaments. We abridge an account of it from Burt's "Observations on the Curiosities of Nature," a very bad title for an ingenious book.

The capada worm, or insect fly-carrier, is produced, like the silk-worm, from the eggs which its mother scatters every where, after she has undergone her metamorphosis into a white butterfly. It begins to live at the end of July, and at its birth is arrayed in a robe of the most brilliant and variegated colours. When on the point of undergoing its metamorphosis in August, it throws off this superb livery, and puts on another of an admirable sea-green hue. This fundamental colour reflects all its various shades, according to the different undulations of the animal, and the different accidents of light; but this new decoration announces the approach of a period when it is doomed to undergo great tortures. It is immediately assailed by a swarm of ichneumon flies, one of which inserts itself into each of the pores of its body, not an opening being left unoccupied. All its struggles to get free of its tormentors are in vain. These flies, which are so small that they can only be studied by the microscope, drive their stings into the skin of their victim, over the whole extent of its back and sides. Afterwards, and all at the same moment, they slip their eggs into the bottom of the wounds which they have inflicted. No sooner is the operation performed, than the ichneumon flies disappear, and the patient remains for an hour in a drowsy and even motionless state, out of which it awakens to feed with its former voracity. It then appears much larger, and its size increases every day. Its green colour assumes a deeper hue, and the tints produced by the reflection of the light are more strongly marked. About a fortnight after the worm has been encumbered with this factitious pregnancy, the prospect of a numerous progeny begins to be apparent. By the aid of a microscope the eggs may be seen hatching in the body of the animal; and as they are all produced at the same instant, a single glance reveals the capada worm covered with a living robe of ichneumon flies. They issue from every pore, all the body being covered with them, only the top of the head appearing bare. Its colour then changes to dirty white, and the little worms assume a black appearance to the eye, although their true colour is a deep brown. This operation lasts about an hour, and it is followed by another, which is not much more protracted, but still more singular.

Immediately that the ichneumon worms are hatched, without quitting the spot where they separate themselves from the eggs, they yield a liquid gum, which becomes solid on exposure to the air. At the same time, and by a simultaneous motion, they elevate themselves on their lower extremities, shake their heads and one half of their bodies, and swing themselves in every direction. And now they commence a very curious operation. Each of these animalcules works himself a small and almost imperceptible cocoon in the shape of an egg, in which he wraps himself up. The formation of these cocoons occupies only about two hours, and myriads of them being crowded close together, form a white robe, with which the capada worm appears elegantly and comfortably clothed; but while they are thus busily arraying him in his new attire, he remains apparently unconscious of their assiduities—he is then in a state of insect paralysis. As soon as this covering has been completed, and the little artists who wove it have retired to their cells, the worm endeavours to rid himself of his officious guests, and of the robe which contains them, but he does not succeed in the attempt without the greatest efforts. At length he contrives to get rid of the encumbrance, but instead of his former fat and shining appearance, he presents all the decrepitude of extreme old age. He is flaccid and dull; his skin is wrinkled and dirty; and, in short, symptoms of approaching dissolution begin to show themselves. He still makes a desperate attempt to gnaw a few leaves, but he no longer devours them with that voracity which indicates a vigorous constitution. Shortly afterwards he passes into the state of a chrysalis, and in giving life to thousands of eggs, he relinquishes his own. The cotton produced in this remarkable manner may be used without any preparatory process, as soon as the flies have quitted the cocoons, which is generally eight or ten days after their seclusion. Indeed, there is no need for the precautions which the silk-worm requires, the robe which covers the fly-carrier being worked every where so perfectly well, and in such abundance, that in less than two hours the quantity of one hundred pints has been collected. This highly interesting animal certainly deserves some attention, for we are not aware that any has been given to it, except in so far as its destruction was concerned. We know not that experiments have been made to weave this silky substance into a wearable tissue, but if the description which we have given above be correct, (and there is no reason to doubt but it is,) there seems no obstacle to its being used for this purpose.

We may here notice a singular fact, established by Dr. Mitchell of New York, that vegetable fungi grow on the bodies of living insects. He states that these vegetable productions are not peculiar to one insect, but are to be found on the bodies of the wasp, sphynx, and others; that the bodies of insects nourish more than one species of vegetable fungi; that some of these parasitical plants begin their works of annoyance, like the larvæ of the ichneumon, in the body of the living insect, and continue it till the animal is killed by its destructive operations; that these mixed associations of vegetable with animal life are not prone to rapid putrefaction, but remain long enough to be collected by naturalists, and become the objects of scientific investigation. Dr. Mitchell seems to be of opinion that vegetable fungi, in attaching to the insect class of animals, perform an important purpose in the economy of nature, by preventing the inordinate increase of such animals.

From the Boston Courier.

The following lines were written on the occasion of an accidental meeting, a few evenings since, of all the surviving members of a family, the father and mother of which (one eighty-two, the other eighty years old) have lived in the same house *fifty-three* years.

THE FAMILY MEETING.

We are all here!
    Father, Mother,
        Sister, Brother,
All who hold each other dear,
Each chair is filled, we're all AT HOME,
To-night let no cold stranger come;
We hnot often thus around
Our old familiar hearth we're found,
Bless then the meeting and the spot,
For once be every care forgot;
Let gentle peace assert her power,
And kind affection rule the hour,
        We're all—all here.

We're not all here!
Some are away—the dead ones dear,
Who thronged with us this ancient hearth,
And gave the hour to guileless mirth.
Death, with a stern, relentless hand,
Looked in and thinned our little band,
Some like a night flash passed away,
And some sank, lingering, day by day;
The quiet graveyard—some lie there,
And cruel Ocean has his share—
        We're not all here!

We ARE all here!
Even they—the dead—though dead, so dear.
Fond memory, to her duty true,
Brings back their faded forms to view
How life-like through the mist of years,
Each well-remembered face appears;
We see them as in times long past;
From each to each kind looks are cast;
We hear their words, their smiles behold,
They're round us as they were of old—
        We ARE all here.

We are all here!
    Father, Mother,
        Sister, Brother,
You that I love with love so dear—
This may not long of us be said,
Soon must we join the gathered dead,
And by the hearth we now sit round,
Some other circle will be found.
O then that wisdom may we know,
That yields a life of peace below,
So in the world to follow this,
May each repeat, in words of bliss,
        We're all—all here.

Interesting Literary Discovery.—The indefatigable oriental scholar, Professor Lee, has brought to light, in a Syriac translation, one of the lost works of the celebrated Eusebius, author of the Church History.

Widows—No city in the world contains so many widows as Paris. There are 53,625 in the city, and 64,082 in the department.—*British Journal.*

DIED, in Baltimore on the 1st inst, ELIZABETH, wife of Dr. William W. Handy, after a protracted illness, in the 50th year of her age. To her surviving friends, it may be a consolation to know that she made a peaceful close, being fully resigned to the Divine will, and in hope of a happy eternity through the merits of her Saviour.

THE FRIEND.

357

MEMORIALS.

Memorials received through the kind attention of a friend, respecting John Barclay, Hannah Fisher, and John Dymond, are handed to the editor of "The Friend" for insertion.

Nearly all the Yearly Meetings in the society, have adopted the plan of printing such of these documents as are deemed suitable for publication, early after they have passed the inspection and approbation of the meetings whose province it is to prepare them for that purpose. A few years since, the Yearly Meeting of Philadelphia authorised its meeting for sufferings to print the unpublished memorials whenever it might be judged expedient. There are several concerning Friends who were highly valued in their lives, which remain locked up from public view, and which would be very acceptable to the younger part of the society. Would not a benefit arise from giving them the opportunity of contemplating these bright examples, who, through obedience to the grace and power of the Lord Jesus, were made lights in the world, and proved by their practice the excellency of that heartfelt religion which subdues sin, purifies the soul, and gives a solid ground for the hope of everlasting salvation?

A testimony from Gracechurch Street Monthly Meeting, concerning John Barclay, *who died on the 11th of 5th month, 1838, and his remains were interred at Winchmore Hill, on the 18th of the same.*

Blessed are the pure in heart, for they shall see God.—Matt. v. 8.

This, our dear friend, was the son of Robert and Ann Barclay, was born at Clapham, in Surrey, in the year 1797. His parents were members of our religious society. His mother died whilst he was very young. From his own memorandums we find that he was early visited with the convictions of divine grace; but becoming exposed to the influence of bad example at a public school, the sinful propensities of the natural mind were strengthened; yet the strivings of the Holy Spirit were graciously continued, and he was often brought into deep humiliation and sorrow on account of his transgressions; and his tears of repentance and his prayers for preservation were poured forth in secret places. In reference to the state of his mind at this time, he says, "As the evil tree cannot but bring forth evil fruit as long as it is suffered to live and thrive in the heart; so this being the case with me, the fruits did show themselves abundantly indeed. Oh! that all who have been injured by my evil example could be shown a fiftieth part of the remorse and repentance, sorrow and trouble, which has been, through unutterable mercy, experienced by me." He was made willing to abide under the judgments of the Lord, and was favoured to know that these chastisements from his Heavenly Father's hand were administered in love; in a sense of which his heart was often made to overflow with thankfulness, and he was brought into a state of submission to the Lord's will, and humble dedication to his requirings. Alluding, some years afterwards, to the circumstances of this eventful period of his life, he writes thus: "This

I may say and leave upon record, that though many almost indescribable temptations and presentations of evil had been permitted to come about me, sometimes like a mighty flood, so that in hours of extreme weakness I have been many and many a time ready to give up the 'fight of faith;' yet to this day the Lord, strong and mighty, has been pleased in his abundant compassion, to encamp around me, and to give me songs of deliverance, songs of triumph and of praise. In his name will I set up my banner, who is a Rock of defence, and sure Refuge to my poor weary soul. Oh! young man or young woman, to whom this may come,—my friend, my brother, my sister, who art seeking the better country, and Him who is the Way and the Guide; oh! though thou art weary and heavy laden, take courage; there is a staff, a stay, and strength and succour with him and in him who hath gone before, and who leadeth on his little ones gently and sweetly, as they are able to follow. Take this as the counsel of one who writes from a sure and living experience, and who hath indubitably known his name (which is above every name) to be a strong tower indeed. He will be with *his* even to the end of the world."

His mind for several years after his father's decease, was brought under much concern on the subject of business; and he felt it to be his duty to give up an offer which was considered to be very advantageous. In a retrospective view of this step, he says, in a letter, "I know not that I have taken any measure, that now in seasons of calmness seems to afford the like peace to me." Alluding to this again, he adds, "The ground upon which I think it best for me to be not much engrossed with the things of this life is, that having experienced no small share of the forbearance and mercy of the Lord, having been delivered from the pit of destruction, having sincere, hearty, and very fervent desires for my own preservation and salvation, as well as for that of my poor fellow creatures every where, I have inclined towards the belief, that the Lord will make use of me, if I am faithful to his requirings, in the way, time, and for the purposes which he sees best; under this impression it is, and not to encourage or give way to an apathy, or want of energy or exertion, that I believe it right for me to sit loose to this world and the anxieties thereof, lest I should be incapacitated for performing that service, which may be shown to be my duty. I believe it safest for me, if in any business, it should be one of moderate profit, and not involving much attention."

He believed himself required to observe much simplicity and economy in providing the needful accommodations of life; and in reference to this subject he says, "I am clearly of the belief, that it is my duty to live in such a humble, plain, homely, simple manner, as that neither in the furniture, food, or clothing used, any misapplication of the gifts of Divine Providence be admitted or encouraged."

About this time, which was in the twenty-second year of his age, he writes thus: "O the love that the Lord hath shed abroad in my heart!—O the divine joy, the unspeakable peace, the blessed presence of the Most High, how it seems to flow through me, making up

for all trial, and tears of disquietude and distress!—O may this feeble testimony speak out his adorable mercy, when this poor frail flesh shall be laid low in the dust; may it induce others to fear Him that made the heavens and the earth, and to trust in Him for ever! Praises to the Lamb that liveth, yet was slain. —Amen."

Early in the year 1820, he believed it right for him to remove from the family circle, and to reside for a time at Poole in Dorsetshire, and about the end of the same year he was married to Georgiana Hill. Their union was short, for in less than three years his dear companion was taken from him by death, at Marazion, in Cornwall, whither they had removed for the benefit of her health.

His mind had for several years been impressed with an apprehension that he should be called to the work of the ministry; and in the prospect of it he was preserved in a waiting dependent state; and fervent was his concern to be entirely given up to serve the Lord in the way of his holy requirings. At the interment of his beloved wife, in the 6th month, 1823, he was engaged in vocal supplication; and in the autumn of that year he spoke as a minister. In allusion to this solemn and important work, after describing the fear and caution with which he had entered upon it, he says, "The weight and sweetness that dwelt on my mind after this surrender, cannot be set forth. O how it rested on my spirit all the day in an unutterable manner! and yet such freedom of spirit, so that nothing seemed a trial, or that to which I was unequal. I shall not easily forget how comfortable and at ease in my mind I felt. O! it was a heavenly feeling, and nothing short of Him that is in heaven could give it."

He was acknowledged as a minister by his Friends in Cornwall in 1825, and in the following year was married to Mary Moates, and removed to Alton. After a residence of three years at that place, he settled at Croydon, and in 1835 he removed to Stoke Newington, within the compass of this Monthly Meeting, where he resided during the remainder of his life. In the course of the before-mentioned period, he paid several religious visits, with the unity of his friends, and in one of these journeys he travelled into Scotland as far as Aberdeen.

He had been from his youth of a tender constitution, and for the last few years of his life he had suffered much from a disease in the knee, which rendered walking or other active exertion difficult to him. He was, however, very exemplary in his efforts to attend our religious meetings, in which the exercise of his dedicated spirit was strengthening to many. His engagements in the line of ministry amongst us were not frequent; but he was at times led to address his friends in a weighty and feeling manner, endeavouring to turn their attention from a dependence on man, and from all that is superficial in religion, to a single reliance on the great Head of the Church, "The minister of the sanctuary and of the true tabernacle, which the Lord pitched, and not man." Our dear Friend was remarkable for integrity and uprightness of heart; and in the private walks of life his conduct was strikingly circumspect, and his conversation, whilst innocently cheerful, was instructive, being seasoned with grace.

Notwithstanding he was, in the ordering of unerring wisdom, much confined at home from bodily infirmity, yet his concern for the prosperity of our society remained unabated, and his mind was actively employed in endeavouring to promote the spiritual welfare of its members. With this object, his time was much occupied in editing a series of publications, selected from the writings of our honoured predecessors in religious profession.

In the 11th month of 1836, he paid an acceptable visit, in the love of the Gospel, to the families of Friends at Brighton; and in the 11th month 1837, he felt attracted by the same precious influence, to a similar engagement in his own particular meeting of Stoke Newington. After going through nearly half the families, wherein his service was much to the comfort of his friends, finding his constitution increasingly feebled, he returned to the Monthly Meeting its minute granted him for that purpose, accompanying it with a letter, replete with the expression of religious concern, from which the following is extracted : " On proceeding in the weighty engagement before me, I may acknowledge that although no wonderful outpouring of Divine Power was my portion, I was mercifully favoured, during the few days that I entered upon the work, with such a sense that the Lord preserveth the simple and the upright, that it was my meat and drink to be thus among my friends ; hard things were made very easy, and bitter things full of sweetness ; a gently flowing stream of heavenly goodness being extended in every hour of need, though in a way humiliating to the creature, and so as nothing of the flesh could glory."

His health continuing to decline, he went to Brighton; but there his indisposition increased, and on the 8th of the 5th month, he was, by medical advice, removed to Turfbridge Wells ; after which he survived but a few days. On the evening of the 9th, when about to retire to rest, on rising from his chair, and leaning on the couch and on the arm of his beloved wife, he supplicated thus ; " Oh, gracious Father ! if it please thee, spare us to each other a little longer, and make us more entirely devoted to thee and thy precious cause of Truth in the earth : nevertheless not our will, O Lord ! but thine be done." On the next day, which was the one immediately preceding his decease, he uttered many weighty expressions, amongst which were the following : " The Truth shall prevail. Truth shall reign over all.—None that trust in the Lord shall be confounded, but they shall be as Mount Zion, which cannot be moved.—You all know my desire to be preserved near unto the Lord.—I only want to be strengthened and upheld by the Lord; to be found in him ; this is the way of peace.—I trust we shall be strengthened and animated to go through our day's work ; then we shall find mercy at the hands of the Lord.—Let us look to the Lord for strength, at all times, and under all circumstances." ·

In the latter part of this day his voice, though feeble, appeared to be making a constant melody ; during which those around him distinguished the words, " O Lord—dear Lord

—come.—I bless the Lord.—I am the Lord's—for ever.—Cleave to Him—O—cleave to Him—love Him with all your heart." The name of Jesus was often to be heard, and the word Hallelujah was frequently repeated.

About four o'clock in the afternoon of the 11th of 5th month, 1838, he peacefully passed away, aged forty-one years, a minister about fifteen years ; and is, we reverently trust, united to the redeemed before the throne, who sing the new song, " Worthy is the Lamb that was slain, to receive power, and wisdom, and riches, and strength, and honour, and glory, and blessing."

Given forth by our Monthly Meeting, held at White Hart Court, the 10th of 10th month, 1838, and signed by—

[*Here follow the signatures of men and women Friends.*]

Read and approved in our Quarterly Meeting for London and Middlesex, held in London this 25th day of the 12th month, 1838, and in and on behalf thereof signed by

           GEORGE STACEY, *Clerk.*

Signed in and on behalf of the Women's Quarterly meeting, by

           MARY FORSTER, *Clerk.*

(Remainder next week.)

For "The Friend."

FIRST DAY MEDITATIONS.

The declaration of our Holy Redeemer, " By this shall all men know that ye are my disciples, if ye have love one to another," would seem to have more meaning than is usually attributed to it by those who profess to be his followers and disciples, and as it points out such a distinguishing feature, ought to claim from us more attention, and to awaken the inquiry whether we are participators in it ? In order to be seen of *all* men, there must be some obvious fruits of its inward operations which would prove to the world at large, that we are really the disciples of Christ. As we cannot question the truth of the declaration, let us in a glance at the multitude of those who profess his name, see whether it is in reality the badge of Christianity as it now exists in the world. A moment's reflection will convince us, that among the nations of Christendom there subsists little of that fraternal regard which leads to seek one another's welfare as their own, but that pretexts are sought and found for the most sanguinary conflicts. To turn to individual nations, to communities, to neighborhoods, and even to associations professedly religious, do we find among them those marks which make it evident that their members are truly followers of the Lord Jesus ? It will not be difficult to answer this question by a simple reference to what lies within reach of our own observation, for selfishness is too obviously the predominating feeling.

The love which subsists among the followers of Christ, and which is designed to be perpetually their distinguishing mark, must arise from their being actuated by a common principle, by something universal in its nature, and operating in the minds of all. We cannot imagine a uniformity of feeling and action as arising from diverse and contrary desires and inclinations, from various motives and various interests. This characteristic must therefore

arise from the prevalence in the minds of believers, of that which makes them " of one heart and one soul." We must be sensible as a religious community, that there is a shortness among ourselves, notwithstanding our high profession, in this essential qualification of Christian discipleship ; and it behooves us to inquire wherein lies the cause of this lamentable deficiency ;—lamentable because the light which might, through the prevailing of the Spirit of Christ in our hearts, shine with lustre in the eyes of the people, is dimmed for want of faithfulness in following him.

The apostle John declares, " If we love one another, God dwelleth in us, and his love is perfected in us." How many there are who can *say* they *love* their fellow professors, and yet on a close examination would hardly venture to determine that " God dwelt in them, and that the love of God was perfected in them." This love then, or charity, which is declared of in the New Testament, must be something else than that ordinary feeling of good will which subsists between individuals who have no occasion to be dissatisfied with each other ; but would wish to promote one another's temporal comfort, and which would even bear with some inconveniences for the sake of accommodating their neighbours : different even, it must be, from that ordinary friendship which subsists among the members of any religious body, seeing that many such there are, who are deficient in some of the prominent traits of being ingrafted into the true vine.

What then is it? is the solemn inquiry which should present itself to all of our minds. What is this blessed and heavenly fellowship which is to mark us as the disciples of the crucified Redeemer ? What is it that is to unite us as individuals to those whose fellowship is with the Father and with the Son?

" *Herein is love,* not that we loved God, but that he loved us and sent his Son to be the propitiation for our sins." The beginnings of love are in the Divine fountain, which flowing forth towards us poor lost and undone creatures, brought the Son of God into the world a propitiation for our sins, that he might reconcile us to God, and not only reconcile us, but redeem us from the wayward course of our own lusts and unsanctified propensities. In order to bring about this change in us, our Saviour more than once declares that we must *lose our lives*; a most emphatic expression, and conveying in a very cogent manner the mode of his operation in the soul of man to effect that new creation unto righteousness, which must be experienced if we become prepared to join the general assembly and church of the first born who are written in heaven. This process is also expressed by the apostle as " putting off the *old man* with his deeds," and the change wrought, as " putting on the *new man* which is renewed in knowledge after the image of him that created him." Various other similitudes are used to designate that entire change which takes place in the true believer and disciple of Christ, which change is essential in order to a participation in the benefits of his coming, and without which we are but nominal professors of his adorable name. As then this work is not wrought of, or by ourselves, but is expressly declared to be *his* work from the beginning to the end, it must be perfected by the operation of his own Holy Spirit, and free from the contrivance of the creaturely will. The sensible direction of Christ in his children and people, is aptly compared to the connection of the head with the natural body, in which are concentrated those organs of sense which are essential to its welfare, and from whence are supposed to flow tô the extremities the incentives to action. Thus are the followers of Christ compared to a body, of which he is the head, and as close as is the connection between the head of the natural body and its members, so is that of Christ with his church, all the members being actuated by one will, and that "the good and acceptable, and *perfect* will of God."

This may serve to illustrate that perfect concordancy among the true members of his body which our Lord designed to indicate, when he set forth love as the badge of discipleship, inasmuch as the possibility of dissension among the members of his mystical body, the church, is as unlikely as any difference among the members of the natural body. This love then, also includes *unity*, oneness, for the apostle expressly declares "there is no schism in the body of Christ," and thus points out that perfect condition in which they are harmoniously united in him.

How then is it, that among us as a religious body, there is so little of this *true* fellowship, this blessed evidence of Christian discipleship, this influence which would unite us together as the heart of one man, make us strong in the Lord and in the power of his might for the overturning of evil, and advancing his glorious cause in the earth? Is it not because many have failed in a willingness to endure that first requisition of *losing their lives*, of becoming dead with Christ by baptism, of submitting to that stroke which would destroy the old man with his deeds, with his unsanctified will, his unsanctified knowledge even of divine things, and are unwilling to receive as little children the ingrafted word which is able to save the soul? Till we know more of this, we shall always be a divided people, a halting people, and shall fail in coming up to that condition which was pointed out as characteristic of the Zion of the Holy One of Israel, "An eternal excellency, a joy of many generations."

M. D.

Communicated.

FRIENDS' SELECT SCHOOLS.

The school for boys will open in the schoolhouse on Orange street, on 2d day the 31st of the 8th month, under the superintendence of the principal, Samuel Alsop, assisted in the elementary department by William Ivins. The classical school is taught by Joseph Thomas.

The course of study embraces all the usual branches of a solid and practical education, and the school is believed to offer advantages which are surpassed by few or none.

The new building on Cherry street above Eighth, designed for the accommodation of this school, is now in the course of erection,

and is expected to be ready for occupancy in a few months. As the accommodations and advantages which this will give for a better classification and arrangement of the pupils, will render some changes in the organization of the school expedient, it is thought unnecessary to publish a synopsis of the course of studies until those changes are completed.

Parents wishing to enter their children will do well to attend to it early, so that the pupils may commence their studies at the opening of the session, this being found to be of great advantage to them.

Application to be made to Samuel Alsop at the school on Orange street below Eighth, or at his residence, No. 200 Noble street above Fifth.

The girls' select school for the education of the children of Friends, is held in a commodious building erected for the purpose, in James street, near the corner of Sixth and Market streets.

The year is divided into two terms of twenty-three weeks each: the first commencing the last second day in the Eighth month: the second at the close of the first term, and ending at the beginning of the summer vacation, which continues six weeks.

The price of tuition per term for those in the sewing department, is $8: those in the first class, $18, and for those in the other classes, $11. Stationary, 50 cents; and the usual charge for fuel.

No pupils will be admitted for less than one term; and it is particularly requested that they enter the school at the commencement of the term. No deduction from the price will be made for those who enter after that period.

The school convenes as follows: From the 15th of the Third month to the 1st of the Fifth month, and from the 1st of the Ninth month to the 15th of the Tenth month, at half past eight: from the 1st of the Fifth to the 1st of the Ninth month, at eight o'clock in the morning; and during the remainder of the year at 9 o'clock. The afternoon session commences throughout the year at half past two o'clock.

The design of the monthly meetings in the establishment of the select schools, is not merely to give to our youth the advantages of a solid and useful literary education, but also to guard them from the corrupting influence of improper company and example; to imbue their minds with correct principles, and to train them to love and observe our Christian doctrines and testimonies.

Sensible of the responsibility which rests upon them, and desirous of promoting the real welfare of the pupils, as well as the support of those testimonies, the committee earnestly solicit the cordial co-operation of parents and guardians in supporting the following rules, and in giving the children an education both at home and at school, consistent with our religious profession, since without this co-operation, the labours of the committee and teachers will be, in a great degree, frustrated.

Plainness of dress and language being important branches of our testimonies, it is particularly requested that parents may not send their children to school in apparel which is not consistent with simplicity.

RULES.

The plain Scripture language of Thou and

Thee to a single person, shall be exclusively used.

The pupils will be required to dress in plain apparel, consistently with our well-known testimony in this respect; all superfluous trimmings such as lace, or ribbons merely for ornament, being prohibited.

All the scholars will be required to attend meetings for Divine worship with their teachers in the middle of the week.

Punctual attendance at the stated hour for opening the school is required; and for every absence or detention from school, each girl is to bring a note, signed by the parent or guardian, stating the fact.

It is requested that none of the pupils without permission from the teacher, should come to school more than 15 minutes before the time, and that they leave the premises as soon as they are dismissed.

No books not used in school, nor newspapers, shall be introduced.

STUDIES.

Sewing Department and Fourth Class.

Spelling,—Primary Dictionary and Progressive Spelling book. Defining,—Book of Commerce. Geography,—Parley's, Mitchell's, and Geographical Exercises. Philosophy,—Swift's, 1st and 2d Part. Arithmetic, —Pike's. Religious Instruction,—Scripture Lessons and Catechism.

Second Division of Third Class.

Spelling,—Progressive Spelling book. Geography,— Mitchell's. Arithmetic,— Pike's. Grammar,—Comly's. Book of Commerce. Galladuet's Natural Theology. Religious Instruction,—Scriptural Questions and Conversations for Youth.

First Division of Third Class.

Spelling. Geography. Grammar. Religious Instruction. Arithmetic,—Pike's and Lewis's. Philosophy,—Comstock's. History, —Worcester's Elements. Botany,—Lincoln's.

Second Class.

Spelling. Geography. Grammar. History. Botany. Philosophy. Arithmetic,—Lewis's and Emerson's. Chemistry,—Comstock's. Religious Instruction,—Scriptural Questions and Bevan's View.

Second Division of First Class.

Spelling. Grammar. Botany. Arithmetic. Chemistry. Religious Instruction. Geography,—Goodrich's. Astronomy,—Guy's. Natural History,—Smellie's. Geometry,—Legendre. Algebra.—Colburn's.

First Division of First Class.

Spelling. Botany. Arithmetic. Geometry. Geography. Religious Instruction. Algebra,— Colburn's and Lewis's. Rhetoric,—Mill's Blair. Mental Philosophy,—Abbott's Abercrombie. Paley's Natural Theology.

Senior Class.

Spelling. Botany. History. Algebra. Geometry, &c. Roget's Animal and Vegetable Physiology. Religious Instruction.

Reading, Writing and Composition attended to by all the classes.

Latin and French taught at an additional charge.

Persons wishing to enter children in this school, may apply at the school-house on James street, or to Hannah Allen at her residence, in Pine near Sixth street.

INFANT SCHOOL.

The School Association of Women Friends, having for several years observed the great decrease in the number of scholars in the Infant School during the warm weather, and believing it would conduce to its benefit, on consideration of the subject, have concluded to divide the school year into two terms. The first, to commence the last Second-day in the Eighth month, and continue to the last day of the First month. The second, to commence, with the first of the Second month, and continue to the end of the Sixth month, when a vacation of two months will take place.

The price of tuition per term is eight dollars.

Reading books, cards, and slates are provided by the Association, for the use of which a small charge is made of twenty-five cents per term. Children will be furnished with other books at the usual store prices.

Fuel charged as customary,—one dollar.

Punctual attendance at the stated hour of opening the school is requested.

The scholars are required to dress simply; and parents are particularly requested to aid the Association in this important testimony of our religious society, endeavouring to avoid the changing fashions of the world. Ribbons, trimmings, and buttons, merely added for ornament, will come under this restriction, and the boys are prohibited from wearing caps.

The design of the Association in the establishment of this Seminary, was, that the children of our society, while they were receiving their early school instruction, might at the same time have a guarded, religious care extended over them, and an endeavour maintained to train them in the love and observance of our Christian doctrines and testimonies.

Philadelphia, 7th month, 1840.

THE FRIEND.

EIGHTH MONTH, 8, 1840.

The "Irish Friend," of 6th mo. 1st, contains some account of the late yearly meeting in London, from which we extract the following :—

"The yearly meeting in London concluded, we understand, on sixth day evening, the 29th ult.—there was about as large an attendance as in past years—nearly 40 Friends were present from Ireland. Epistles were received from Ireland and all the American yearly meetings, except Virginia. Epistles in reply to all the before mentioned meetings, Virginia included, were issued, and also a general epistle to the American yearly meetings, on the subject of slavery; encouraging Friends to a faithful discharge of their duty in this respect. A document was also issued on the spirituality of the gospel dispensation, as held by Friends, testifying against the continuance of all types and shadows in the Christian church—against

tithes and other ecclesiastical demands for the support of the ministry, &c.

"Several very instructive testimonies of deceased Friends in the ministry were presented to the meeting, viz. Wm. Rickman, of Rochester, John Wigham, Aberdeen, Sarah Jago, Plymouth, Mary Hagger, Ashford, Francis Dixon, Gainsboro', Elizabeth Janson, York, and Elizabeth Hoyland, Northampton; some of these will be printed. The yearly meeting was also deeply impressed with the suffering condition of the Aborigines in the several parts of the globe; much sympathy and feeling for them was expressed, and a desire that none under our name who emigrate to British colonies, might, in any degree, compromise the golden rule of a Christian's conduct towards them, in doing unto others as they would wish others should do to them. A considerable degree of feeling was manifested on account of the warlike preparations which have lately been made in several of the ports and arsenals of the country. It is to be lamented that the awful prospect of war with a heathen nation has become so popular, and that many pious and influential persons of other communities are found to defend it, as being, in their estimation, permitted, if not ordered, by Divine Providence to open the hitherto closed kingdom of China to the reception of the gospel.— Strange! that reflecting minds can ever believe that the wrath of man will be able to work the righteousness of God: and still as strange, that they can be brought to hope or desire that the gospel of Jesus Christ may be, or can be, brought home to the minds of unbelievers by the sword; or that, through the slaughter of thousands of our fellow mortals, the kingdom of the Prince of Peace is to be established !!"

To the foregoing is appended as follows :— "A school to combine manual labour with instruction is about to be established in Oxfordshire for the children of poor Friends, and those whose parents may have had a claim upon our society. This plan of education appears to have answered well at Brookfield in this country, and also at Penketh in Lancashire. A subscription in aid of the object was entered into at the yearly meeting."

FRIENDS' ASYLUM.

Committee on Admissions.—John G. Hoskins, No. 60 Franklin street, and No. 50 North Fourth street, up stairs; E. B. Garrigues, No. 185 North Seventh street, and No. 41 Market street, up stairs; Isaac Collins, No. 129 Filbert street, and No. 50 Commerce street; Edward Yarnall, southwest corner of Twelfth and George streets, and No. 39 Market street; Samuel Bettle, jr., No. 73 North Tenth street, and 26 South Front street.

Visiting Managers for the Month.—William Jones, No. 326 Arch street; Thomas P. Cope, No. 277 Spruce street; John Farnum, No. 116 Arch street.

Superintendents.—John C. and Lætitia Redmond.

Attending Physician.—Dr. Charles Evans, No. 201 Arch street.

Resident Physician.—Dr. Pliny Earle.

DIED, in Lynn, Mass. on the 21st of 6th month, of pulmonary consumption, MARIA MOTT NEWHALL, daughter of Estes and Miriam Newhall, in the 20th year of her age.

In the early part of her illness, after becoming aware of the improbability of her recovery, it was her lot to pass through deep baptisms, and severe conflicts, during which she was given to see the exceeding sinfulness of sin; and although she was possessed by nature of an affectionate disposition, and had been careful in the fulfilment of her moral, social, and relative duties, yet she was now brought to acknowledge that she had not yielded sufficiently to the pointings of truth in her own mind; that, without true repentance and the washing of regeneration, she had no ground to hope for Divine acceptance; and that if she was ever saved, it must be by the one great offering.

As her disease progressed, she became increasingly interested for the promotion of the principles of our society, and maintenance of its testimonies; and on hearing an article read, which had appeared in print, calling in question the propriety of continuing to support our testimony with respect to plainness of dress, she remarked—"We cannot serve God and mammon —Oh, it is reasoning—they may reason the truth all away." And at another time after a season of meditation, she said—"Those who prophesy the downfall of our society will find they are mistaken—the principles are immutable, and there will continue to be supporters."

The light and trifling manner in which some were in the practice of speaking upon serious things, particularly the ministry, and of repeating passages of the Holy Scriptures in an irreverent manner, was cause of much concern with her; the tendency thereof she considered, was to undermine all that was good, and to be in the way of hearing such things, she believed had a deleterious effect upon the mind.

A deep sense of gratitude and love to her Heavenly Father pervaded her mind, for the mercies and favours bestowed upon her; and although from the nature of her disease, she passed through much bodily suffering, yet patience and humble resignation appeared to be the clothing of her spirit. She was frequently heard to say, "How much I have to be thankful for"—"How many blessings?" And one evening she was led to exclaim, "Bless the Lord, oh my soul, and forget not all his benefits !"

In conversing with some of her particular acquaintance, she frequently adverted to the Divinity of our Saviour, saying—"There is no other name under Heaven, whereby we can be saved but that of Jesus— he that denieth the Son denieth the Father also. We are commanded to worship and adore him, and how can we except we believe?"

Shortly before her death she informed her friends, she had been aware for several days, that her final change was very near, and that she was ready and willing to go. Thus she continued calm and tranquil, with a bright and cheerful countenance, and apparently free from suffering, until like one in a peaceful slumber she quietly departed; and we doubt not has joined that happy number, whose robes have been washed in the blood of the Lamb.

——, at Indian Springs, Ann Arundel county, Maryland, on the 4th of 4th month last, ELIZABETH HOPKINS. This valuable friend was one of the small number of that neighbourhood, who, about the period of the separation in Baltimore Yearly Meeting, maintained their allegiance to the ancient doctrines of our religious society. She was an humble Christian, characterised by the possession of that " meek and quiet spirit which is in the sight of God of great price."

——, in this city, on the 20th ult. in the 23d year of his age, HENRY HILL COLLINS, son of Isaac Collins. The deceased was in the full bloom of vigorous health, when his career, so full of hope, was suddenly arrested by a severe disease, which terminated his life after a few days illness. He had active habits, manly principles, amiable dispositions, and warm affections; and it is a consolation to his friends, to believe that his mind had been gradually preparing for the awful change; that the latter months of his life were marked by increased seriousness and self-examination, and that he was mercifully favoured before his departure to trust and to rejoice in his Redeemer.

THE FRIEND.

A RELIGIOUS AND LITERARY JOURNAL.

VOL. XIII. SEVENTH DAY, EIGHTH MONTH, 15, 1840. NO. 46.

EDITED BY ROBERT SMITH.

PUBLISHED WEEKLY.

Price two dollars per annum, payable in advance.

Subscriptions and Payments received by

GEORGE W. TAYLOR,

NO. 50, NORTH FOURTH STREET, UP STAIRS,

PHILADELPHIA.

For "The Friend."

THE REMEDY FOR THE SLAVE TRADE.

(Continued from p. 354.)

To any one familiar with the earlier period of the slave trade controversy, it will not be necessary to say, that the Gold Coast was perpetually referred to as the district which furnished by far the greater part of the slaves taken to the British colonies. We not only established forts there for the express purpose of encouraging that trade, but there seems to have been no difficulty in obtaining from parliament munificent grants for their maintenance —£30,000 was the annual sum thus applied. "These establishments," says the governor of the colony, "constituted the great emporium whence the British West India colonies were supplied with slaves. Such being the ease, and considering also the vast number of slaves which were annually exported in order to meet the demands of so extensive a market, we are fully warranted in affirming, that in no part of Africa was the slave trade more firmly rooted, or more systematically carried on, than in these settlements."

What is now termed legitimate commerce, was, previously to the passing of the abolition act, but little thought of, or only attended to so far as it was auxiliary to the grand object—the acquisition of slaves. "Daily accustomed to witness scenes of the most cold-blooded cruelty, the inhabitants became utterly callous to human suffering: each petty chieftain oppressed and plundered his weaker neighbours, to be in his turn plundered and oppressed by one stronger and more powerful than himself. In no portion of Africa, in short, was the demoralising, the brutalising influence of the slave trade more fearfully displayed, than in those extensive tracts of country which now form, or are adjoining to, our settlements on the Gold Coast."

But, happily, this state of things no longer exists. Within a few short years, so complete a revolution has been effected, that, in the expressive words of Governor McLean, " From Apollonia to Accra, not a single slave has been exported since the year 1830."

It becomes, then, highly interesting to ascertain how the slave trade has been eradicated from a portion of Africa, comprehending a space which Governor McLean rates at 4000 square miles inland, and a line of coast 180 miles in extent, where it had been planted, protected, fostered, and munificently encouraged for centuries.

This great object has not been accomplished by our naval squadrons. Her majesty's cruisers have certainly been in the habit of visiting the settlement, but only for the purpose of procuring supplies, and of affording, if called upon, aid to the local authorities. No cruiser (says the governor) has ever, at least for many years, been stationed off the Gold Coast for the purpose of intercepting slaves.

This revolution has been effected by the very agency which I desire to see tried on other parts of the coast, and on a greater scale, by the establishment of a station, which, while it multiplies the difficulties and dangers of the slave trader, will afford protection to the native in the cultivation of the soil, by giving security to the trader, and opening a market for the sale of the productions he rears. Crops have been grown, and articles produced, and labour bestowed, because he who sowed knew that he should reap, and he who laboured was no longer exposed to the probability of seeing his acquisitions rifled, and himself hunted after, by the marauders whom his prosperity had attracted.

It is not to be denied that there were great difficulties in the outset. The trade in man has its attractions—it combines the hazard of the chase, with the name and profits of merchandize. It affords a field for the exercise of skill—for the display of courage—for the employment of stratagem—for the gratification of revenge. It calls forth all those martial passions in which savages, and others than savages, conceive that all glory resides. To some, no doubt, it yielded wealth: a successful sally—a fortunate adventure—a sudden and daring surprise—rendered a profit larger than a month's labour would produce. It was, moreover, the inveterate custom of the country. The inhabitants knew the art of kidnapping, and knew no other art: there seemed to them no other way by which they could obtain those supplies of foreign manufacture and produce, which long habit had rendered necessaries of life.

These difficulties stood in the way of the effectual abolition of the slave trade: they were only to be overcome by proving to the natives experimentally that it was their interest to suppress it; in other words, that they would gain by the sale of their productions a larger amount of those foreign luxuries which they craved, than by the sale of man. It was therefore necessary to create some other species of traffic, whereby the native could procure his wonted supplies. This end could not have been effected without the aid of resident merchants and a local government: the one to afford a perpetual and ready supply of the articles which the African needed, and to urge him to provide the goods which would be taken in exchange; the other, to protect legitimate commerce, and to redress, and, if needful, to punish the exportation of slaves.

The experiment has been successful. The difficulties and perils which, after the abolition law, attached to the slave trade, called into existence various articles of commerce previously unknown. The soil, which formerly did not yield sufficient for the sustenance of the inhabitants, now exports a very large amount of corn to Madeira; and the natives, as we are expressly told by the governor, are better supplied with European and other merchandise than formerly, when it was the chief mart for slaves.

It does not diminish my satisfaction to know that this result was brought about by slow degrees. For many years after the slave trade was abolished by law, the conflict between lawful and unlawful trade continued. It was not likely that the natives would be weaned in a moment from the customs of their forefathers, or by any thing short of a succession of experiments. But innocent commerce has at length fairly won the victory, and the last case of slave trading occurred in 1830. Buxton gives some description of it because it proves the check already given to the trade, and because it incidentally shows in an official form, the customary horrors of the traffic, which, as far as the Gold Coast extends, we have been so happy as to repress.

In the month of January, a Spanish slaver appeared off Apollonia, (an ally merely of the British,) and asserted that he had liberty to trade from the English. The king sent messengers to Cape Coast Castle to ascertain the fact, which not being confirmed, he refused either to sell a slave or to restore the Spaniard's cargo, which, meantime, he had got possession of. But the Spanish captain contrived to entrap several of the king's family, and intimated that he would carry them off if the slaves were not forthcoming. "Whereupon the king mustering his more immediate attendants and adherents, sallied out into the town, in the night time, and seizing all without distinction whom he could find, sent them, to the number of 360, on board in irons, at daybreak, receiving in return the persons detained as hostages. " Here were 360 free people, living in their own houses, in perfect peace and apparent security, seized, without the shadow of pretext, by a rapacious and remorseless tyrant, whom they had been taught to look up to as their father and protector. One of them, a mulatto girl, about 16 or 17 years of age, was afterwards redeemed, and she described the consternation and horror of the poor people when they found themselves ironed in the slaver's hold."

In a letter which I received from Governor McLean, dated 29th September, 1838, he again adverts to the formerly disordered state of the colony, which he thus contrasts with its present condition :—" In 1830 all communication with Ashantee, and through it with the interior, had been entirely stopped for ten years previously ; and the only trade done was for what gold and ivory could be procured in the districts adjoining the coast. The whole country was one scene of oppression, cruelty and disorder ; so much so, that a trader dared not go twenty miles into the ' bush.'

"At present our communication with the interior is as free and safe as between England and Scotland ; single messengers can, and do travel from one end of the country to the other with perfect safety ; and no man can oppress another with impunity." Such is the important change which a local government, with but limited resources at its command, has been enabled to effect throughout this extensive territory, in the short period of eight years, and principally by means of a strict and impartial administration of justice.

The trade of the Gold Coast already repays more than twenty-fold the sum granted by parliament for the support of the local establishment. Its exports to Great Britain amount to $900,000 per annum, forming one fifth of the whole commerce of Africa ; although the country is by no means so fertile as many other parts of that continent, and has not the advantage of navigable rivers.

We do not give Africans the credit due to them for mechanical ingenuity. Clarkson in 1818 exhibited to the Emperor Alexander articles made by them, in leather, in iron, in gold, in cotton cloth, mats, &c. The emperor, surprised, inquired if he was to understand that these were made by Africans in their own country, that is, in their own villages ; or after they had arrived where they had the opportunity of seeing European manufactures. Clarkson says, " I replied, that such articles might be found in every African village, both on the coast and in the interior ; and that they were samples of their own ingenuity, without any connection with Europeans. ' Then,' said the emperor, ' you have given me a new idea of the state of these poor people. I was not aware that they were so far advanced in society. The works you have shown me are not the works of brutes, but of men endued with rational and intellectual powers, and capable of being brought to as high a degree of proficiency as other men. Africa ought to be allowed to have a fair chance of raising her character in the scale of the civilised world.' "

Buxton has collected much interesting testimony to their aptness for manufactures, agriculture, and navigation ; in the latter department the Kroomen have already earned among sailors a high reputation for good seamanship. They are an intrepid, generous race, who neither sell nor allow themselves to be made slaves.

(To be continued.)

History of the Lehigh Coal and Navigation Company.

In the year 1793 a company was formed under the title of the " Lehigh Coal Mine Company," who purchased from Jacob Weiss the tract of land on which the large opening at Summit Hill is made, and afterwards " took up," under warrants from the commonwealth, about ten thousand acres of land, embracing about five sixths of the coal lands now owned by the Lehigh Coal and Navigation Company. The Coal Mine Company proceeded to open the mines, and made an appropriation of ten pounds ($26.67) to construct a road from the mines to the landings, (nine miles ! !) After many fruitless attempts to get coal to market over this nominal road, and by the Lehigh river, which, in seasons of low water, in its unimproved state, defied the floating of a canoe over its rocky bed, and after calling for contributions of money from the stockholders until calling was useless, the Lehigh Coal Mine Company became tired of the experiment, and suffered their property to lie idle for some years.

In the mean time they endeavoured to get the navigation of the Lehigh improved, and several laws were passed by the commonwealth without effecting this object.

To encourage and bring into notice the use of their coal, the company, in December, 1807, gave a lease upon one of the coal veins to Rowland and Butland for twenty-one years, with the privilege of digging iron ore and coal, gratis, for the manufacture of iron. This business was abandoned, together with the lease, as, from some cause, they did not succeed in their work.

In December, 1813, the company made a lease for ten years of their lands, to Miner, Cist and Robinson, with the right of cutting lumber on the lands, for building boats; the whole consideration for this lease was to be the annual introduction into market of ten thousand bushels of coal, for the benefit of the lessees. Five ark loads of coal were despatched by these gentlemen from the landing at Mauch Chunk, two of which reached Philadelphia, the others having been wrecked in their passage. Four dollars per ton were paid to a contractor for the hauling of this coal from the mines to the landing over the road above referred to, and the contractor lost money. The principal part of the coal which arrived at Philadelphia was purchased at twenty-one dollars per ton, by White and Hazard, who were then manufacturing wire at the Falls of Schuylkill. But even this price did not remunerate the owners for their losses and expenses in getting the coal to market, and they were consequently compelled to abandon the prosecution of the business, and, of course, did not comply with the terms of the lease.

In December, 1817, Josiah White and Erskine Hazard, being desirous of supplying their works with anthracite coal, and finding they could not obtain it as cheaply from the Schuylkill region as they were led to believe it could be procured from the Lehigh, determined that Josiah White should visit the Lehigh mines and river, and obtain the necessary information on the subject. In this visit he

was joined by George F. A. Hauto. Upon their return, and making a favourable report, it was ascertained that the lease on the mining property was forfeited by non user, and that the law, the last of six which had been passed for the improvement of the navigation of the river, had just expired by its own limitation. Under these circumstances the Lehigh Coal Mine Company became completely dispirited, and executed a lease to White, Hauto and Hazard, for twenty years, of their whole property, on the conditions that, after a given time for preparation, they should deliver for their own benefit at least forty thousand bushels of coal annually in Philadelphia and the districts, and should pay, upon demand, one ear of corn as an annual rent for the property.

Having obtained the lease, these gentlemen applied to the legislature for an act to authorise them to improve the navigation of the Lehigh, stating in their petition their object of getting coal to market, and that they had a plan for the cheap improvement of river navigation, which they hoped would serve as a model for the improvement of many other streams in the state. Their project was considered chimerical, the improvement of the Lehigh particularly being deemed impracticable, from the failure of the various companies who had undertaken it under previous laws, one of which had the privilege of raising money by lottery. The act of 20th of March, 1818, however, gave these gentlemen the opportunity of " ruining themselves," as many members of the legislature predicted would be the result of their undertaking. The various powers applied for, and which were granted in the act, embraced the whole scope of tried and untried methods of effecting the object of getting " a navigation downward once in three days for boats loaded with one hundred barrels, or ten tons," with the reservation on the part of the legislature of the right to compel the adoption of a complete slack-water navigation from Easton to Stoddartsville, should they not deem the mode of navigation adopted by the undertakers sufficient for the wants of the country.

White and Hazard, having levelled the river from Stoddartsville to Easton, in the month of April, 1818, with instruments borrowed of the Delaware and Schuylkill Canal Company, (the only instruments at that time to be met with in Philadelphia,) and having also taken the levels from the river to the coal mines, to ascertain that a road could be constructed altogether on a descending grade from the coal to the navigation, and having ascertained from the concurrent testimony of persons residing in the neighbourhood, that the water in the river never fell, in the driest seasons, below a certain mark in a rock at the Lausanne Landing, were satisfied that there would always be a sufficiency of water in the river to give the depth and width of water required by the law, if the water were confined by wing dams and channel walls in its passage over the " riffles" from pool to pool. This plan was therefore decided upon for the improvement of the navigation, as well as the use of flat-bottomed boats, to be constructed for each voyage from the timber lands which were purchased for this purpose on the upper section of the Lehigh.

It may not be uninteresting to state the situation of the country along the Lehigh, as they found it at this period. From Stoddartsville to Lausanne, a distance of thirty-five miles, there was no sign of a human habitation; every thing was in the state of nature. The ice had not yet left the shores of the river, which runs for almost the whole of this distance in a deep ravine between hills from four hundred to one thousand feet high, and so abrupt that but few places occur where a man on horseback can ascend them. The adjacent country, though in many parts well covered with timber, had only a nominal value, as all hope of getting it to market was extinguished by the repeated failures of all attempts to improve the navigation, which was now considered impossible. The fall in this part of the river was ascertained to be, from Stoddartsville to Mauch Chunk, nine hundred and ten feet; or, on the average, about twenty-five feet to the mile. Above the gap in the Blue Mountain there were but thirteen houses, including the towns of Lausanne and Lehighton, within sight from the river. Below the gap the country was improved. Rafts were sent, during freshets, from Lausanne downward, but no raft had ever come from above that point. From Mauch Chunk to Easton the fall was three hundred and sixty-four feet, making the whole fall from Stoddartsville to Easton twelve hundred and seventy-four feet.

The great first and second anthracite coal regions were then entirely unknown as such. Coal had been found on the summit hill, where the great opening of the Lehigh Company now is, and also at the Beaver Meadows. But there was then no knowledge that there were, in each location, continuous strata of coal, for many miles in extent, in each direction from these two points. Indeed the old Coal Mine Company for some years offered a bonus of two hundred dollars to any one who should discover coal on their lands, nearer to the Lehigh than the summit mines, but without its being claimed. The use of the coal from these locations was confined to the forge fires of the neighbouring blacksmiths and the bar room stoves of the taverns along the road. Wood was almost the only fuel used in Philadelphia; and that and bituminous coal supplied the fireplaces of New York and eastern cities. The only canal in Pennsylvania, at that time in navigable order, was one of about two miles in length, at York Haven, on the Susquehanna, and one made by Josiah White, at the Falls of Schuylkill, with two locks, and a canal three or four hundred yards long.

It was under these circumstances that the legislature of 1818 granted the privileges of the "Act to improve the navigation of the river Lehigh" to Josiah White, George F. A. Hauto, and Erskine Hazard, which are now considered of such immense magnitude that they ought never to have been granted, and that those gentlemen were at that time pointed at as extremely visionary, and even crazy, for accepting them.

Having obtained the law, the lease on the coal mines, and the necessary information, respecting them, and decided upon the plan of making the improvements, the next step of the pioneers was to raise the necessary capital for carrying on the work. Preliminary to this,

they published, in pamphlet form, a description of the property, and the privileges annexed to it, and proposed to create a company to improve the navigation and work the coal mines.

The stock of this company was subscribed for on the condition that a committee should proceed to the Lehigh, and satisfy themselves that the actual state of affairs corresponded with the representation of them. The committee consisted of two of our most respectable citizens, both men of much mechanical experience and ingenuity. They repaired to Mauch Chunk, visited the coal mines, and then built a batteau at Lausanne, in which they descended the Lehigh and made their observations. They both came to the conclusion, and so reported, that the improvement of the navigation was perfectly practicable, and that it would not exceed the cost of fifty thousand dollars, as estimated, but that the making of a good road to the mines was utterly impossible. "for," added one of them, "to give you an idea of the country over which the road is to pass, I need only tell you that I considered it quite an easement when the wheel of my carriage struck a stump instead of a stone!!" This report of course voided the subscription to the joint stock.

It very soon appeared that there was great diversity of opinion relative to the value of the two objects. Some were willing to join in the improvement of the navigation, but had no faith in the value of the coal, or that a market could ever be found for it among a population accustomed wholly to the use of wood. On the other hand, some were of the opinion that the navigation would never pay the interest of its cost, while the coal business would prove profitable. This gave rise to the separation of the two interests; and proposals were issued for raising a capital of fifty thousand dollars, on the terms that those who furnished the money should have all the profits accruing from the navigation up to twenty-five per cent., all profits beyond that to go to White, Hauto and Hazard, who also retained the exclusive management of the concern. The amount was subscribed, and the company formed under the title of the "Lehigh Navigation Company" on the 10th of August, 1818. The work was immediately commenced, the managers taking up their quarters in a boat upon the Lehigh, which moved downwards as the work of constructing the wing-dams progressed. The hands employed had similar accommodations.

On the 21st of October of the same year "The Lehigh Coal Company" was formed, for the purpose of making a road from the river to the mines, and of bringing coal to market by the new navigation. The capital subscribed to this company was fifty-five thousand dollars, and was taken on the same plan as that of the Navigation Company; but the managers were to be entitled to all the profits above twenty per cent., they conveying the lease of the coal mine company's land, and also several other tracts of land which they had purchased, to trustees for the benefit of the association. The road which now, for seven miles, constitutes the grading of the rail road to the summit mines was laid out in the fall of 1818, and finished in 1819. This is believed to have been the first road ever laid out by an instru-

ment, on the principle of dividing the whole descent into the whole distance, as regularly as the ground would admit of, and to have no undulation. It was intended for a rail road, as soon as the business would warrant the expense of placing rails upon it. A pair of horses would bring down from four to six tons upon it in two wagons.

(To be continued.)

THE LUMINOUS SEA.

Extracted from an article in the Nautical Magazine.

Curiosity has not been oftener excited by the phenomena of nature, nor with more pleasing sensations, to those who have witnessed its full effects, than by the luminous appearance of the sea. In the tropical regions where nature spreads her richest treasures, this phenomenon is seen in its greatest splendour, and the mariner, with no great stretch of the imagination, has often fancied himself in a sea of liquid fire. On the coast of Mexico, in the Pacific Ocean, during the calm of night, when stars only are visible above, the sea has assumed this appearance to such a degree that a ship actually seems floating in a bed of sparks of living fire, and as she rises with the swell, or dashes it from her, by any sudden effect of a wave, it curls from her side as a sheet of fire throwing a broad glare of light. This appearance, so gratifying to the eye, is sufficient to fill the mind of the beholder with wonder and astonishment, and the cause of it is naturally his first question. That it proceeds from animalcule is generally known, but their nature and the circumstances under which the light is emitted is with many persons still a matter of speculation.

On the passage from Madeira to Rio Janeiro, the sea was observed by Sir Joseph Banks to be unusually luminous, flashing in many parts like lightning. He directed some of the water to be hauled up, in which he discovered two kinds of animals that occasioned the phenomenon; the one a crustaceous insect which he called the cancer fulgens, the other a larger species of medusa, to which he gave the name of pellucens.

The cancer fulgens bears some resemblance to the common shrimp; it is, however, considerably less, the legs are furnished with numerous seta. The light of this animal, which is very brilliant, appears to issue from every part of its body.

The medusa pellucens measures about six inches across the crown or umbella; this part is marked by a number of opaque lines, that pass off from the centre to the circumference. The edge of the umbella is divided into lobules which succeed each other, one large and two small ones, alternately. From within the margin of the umbella, there are suspended a number of long cord-shaped tentacula. The central part of the animal is opaque, and furnished with four thick irregularly shaped processes, which hang down in the midst of the tentacula.

This zoophyte is the most splendid of the luminous inhabitants of the ocean. The flashes of light emitted during its contractions are so vivid as to affect the sight of the spectator. In the notes communicated to Sir Joseph Banks by Capt. Horsburg he remarks, that the luminous state of the sea between the tropics is generally accompanied with the appearance of a great number of marine animals of various kinds upon the surface of the water; to many of which, however, he does not attribute the property of shining. At other times when the water which gave out light was examined, it appeared to contain only small particles of a dusky straw colour, which dissolved with the slightest touch of the finger. He likewise observes that in Bombay, during the hot weather of May and June, he has frequently seen the edges of the sea illuminated by minute sparkling points.

At sunrise, on April 12th, 1798, in the Arabian sea, he perceived several luminous spots in the water, which, conceiving to be animals, he went in a boat and caught one. It proved to be an insect somewhat resembling in appearance the woodlouse, and was about one third of an inch in length. When viewed with a microscope it seemed to be formed by sections of a thin crustaceous substance. During the time that any fluid remained in the animal, it shone brilliantly like the firefly.

In the month of June of the same year, he picked up another luminous insect on a sandy beach, which was also covered with a thin shell, but it was of a different shape and a larger size than the animal taken in the Arabian sea,

Comparing the above description with an elegant pen and ink drawing which was made by Captain Horsburgh, and accompanied his paper, I have no doubt that both these insects were monoculi; the first evidently belongs to the genus *limulus* of Muller; I shall therefore beg leave to distinguish it by the name of *limulus nocticulus*.

My pursuits and the state of my health having frequently led me to the coast, I have had many opportunities of making observations upon the animals which illuminate our own seas. Of these I have discovered three species, one of which is a *beroe* not hitherto described by authors; another agrees so nearly with the *medusa hemispherica*, that I conceive it to be the same, or at least a variety of that species; the third is a minute species of medusa, which I believe to be the luminous animal, so frequently seen by navigators, although it has never been distinctly examined or described.

I first met with these animals in the month of October, 1804, at Herne Bay, a small watering place on the northern coast of Kent. Having observed the sea to be extremely luminous for several nights, I had a considerable quantity of the water taken up. When perfectly at rest no light was emitted, but on the slightest agitation of the vessel in which the water was contained, a brilliant scintillation was perceived, particularly towards the surface; and when the vessel was suddenly struck, a flash of light issued from the top of the water in consequence of so many points shining at the same moment. When any of these sparkling points were removed from the water, they no longer yielded any light. They were so transparent that in the air they appeared like globules of water. They were more minute than the head of the smallest pin. On the slightest touch they broke and vanished from the sight. Having strained a quantity of the

luminous water, a great number of these transparent corpuscles were obtained upon the cloth, and the water which had been strained did not afterwards exhibit the least light. I then put some sea water that had been rendered particularly clear by repeated filtration into a large glass, and having floated in it a fine cloth, on which I had previously collected a number of luminous points, several of them were liberated, and became distinctly visible, in their natural element, by placing the glass before a piece of dark coloured paper. They were observed to have a tendency to come to the surface of the water, and after the glass was set by some time, they were found congregated together, and when thus collected in a body, they had a dusky straw colour; although, individually, they were so transparent as to be perfectly invisible, except under particular circumstances. Their substance was, indeed, so extremely tender and delicate, that they did not become opaque in distilled vinegar or alcohol until immersed in these liquors for a considerable time.

On examining these minute globules with the microscope, I found that they were not quite perfect spheres, but had an irregular depression on one side, which was formed of an opaque substance, that projected a little way inwards, producing such an appearance as would arise from tying the neck of a round bag and turning it into the body.

The motions of these creatures in the water were slow and graceful, and not accompanied by any visible contractions of their bodies. After death they always subsided to the bottom of the vessel.

From the sparkling light afforded by this species, I shall distinguish it by the name of *medusa scintillans.*

The night following that on which I discovered the preceding animal, I caught the two other luminous species. One of these I shall call the *beroe fulgens.*

This most elegant creature is of a colour changing between purple, violet and pale blue; the body is truncated before, and pointed behind; but the form is difficult to assign, as it is varied by partial contractions at the animal's pleasure. I have represented the two extremes of form that I have seen this creature assume; the first is somewhat that of a cucumber, which, as being the one it takes when at rest, should perhaps be considered as its proper shape; the other resembles a pear, and is the figure it has in its most contracted state. The body is hollow, or forms internally an infundibular cavity, which has a wide opening before and appears also to have a small aperture posteriorly. The posterior and two thirds of the body are ornamented with eight longitudinal ciliated ribs, the processes of which are kept in such a rapid rotatory motion, while the animal is swimming, that they appear like the continual passage of a fluid along the ribs. The ciliated ribs have been described by Professor Mitchell as arteries in a luminous beroe, which I suspect was no other than the species I am now giving an account of.

When the beroe fulgens swam gently near the surface of the water, its whole body became occasionally illuminated in a slight degree. During its contractions, a stronger light

issued from the ribs, and when a sudden shock was communicated to the water, in which several of these animals were placed, a vivid flash was thrown out. If the body was broken, the fragments continued luminous for some seconds, and being rubbed on the hand, left a light like that of phosphorus. This, however, as well as every other mode of emitting light, ceased after the death of the animal.

The hemispherical species that I discovered, had a very faint purple colour. The largest that I found measured about three quarters of an inch in diameter. The margin of the umbella was undivided, and surrounded internally by a row of pale brown spots and numerous small twisted tentacula: four opaque lines crossed, in an arched manner, from the circumference towards the centre of the animal: an opaque, irregular shaped process hung down from the middle of the umbella; when this part was examined with a lens of high power, I discovered that it was enclosed in a sheath in which it moved; and that the extremity of the process was divided into four tentaculas, covered with little cusps or suckers like those on the tentacula of the cuttle fish.

This species of medusa bears a striking resemblance to the figures of the medusa hemispheris published by Gronovious and Muller.

In this species the central spot and the part round the margin are commonly seen to shine on lifting the animal out of the water into the air, presenting the appearance of an illuminated wheel, and when it is exposed to the usual percussion of the water, the transparent parts of its body are alone luminous.

In the month of September, 1805, I again visited Herne Bay, and frequently had opportunities of witnessing the luminous appearance of the sea. I caught many of the hemispherical and minute species of medusa, but not one of the beroe fulgens. I observed that these luminous animals always retreated from the surface of the water as soon as the moon rose. I found, also, that exposure to the day light took away their property of shining, which was viewed by placing them for some time in a dark situation.

In that season I had two opportunities of seeing an extended illumination of the sea produced by the above animals. The first night I saw, this singular phenomenon, was extremely dark; many of the medusa scintillans and medusa hemispherica had been observed at low water, but on the return of the tide they had suddenly disappeared. On looking towards the sea, I was astonished to perceive a flash of light of about six yards broad, extend from the shore for apparently the distance of a mile and a half along the surface of the water. The second time that I saw this sort of light proceed from the sea, it did not take the same form, but was diffused over the surface of the waves next the shore, and was so strong, that I could for the moment distinctly see my servant, who stood at a little distance from me; he also perceived it, and called out to me at the same instant. On both these occasions the flash was visible for four or five seconds, and although I watched for a considerable time, I did not see it repeated.

(Remainder next week.)

MEMORIALS.

(Concluded from p. 356.)

A Testimony of Frenchay Monthly Meeting, respecting HANNAH FISHER, *deceased 27th 2d month,* 1830.

Our late dear and valued Friend, Hannah Fisher, of Hillside, near Bristol, widow of the late George Fisher, of Bristol, and daughter of William and Hannah Jepson, of Lancaster, died on the 20th day of the 6th month, 1838, whilst on a visit to her son-in-law at Harrow, in the seventy-third year of her age, and was interred in Friends' burial ground at Winchmore Hill, on the 27th of the same. She had been an acknowledged minister in our society about twenty-two years, and a member of this meeting nearly fourteen years.

Although the attack which proved fatal was sudden, it appears not to have been unexpected, as she had previously sustained a very similar, but slighter seizure, on recovering from which she remarked to some of her family, that it was a gentle warning. In conversation on the subject of death, she frequently remarked of how little importance it appeared to *her* in what way it came, so that a preparation for it had been realized. That this had long been her own favoured experience, many very interesting and valuable private memoranda indicate, at the same time clearly recording a humbling sense of her own unworthiness, and of her whole reliance upon the mercy of God in Christ Jesus. In writing to a friend respecting the bereavements which some others had then recently sustained, she says, " I think if we viewed death as Christians should do, we should consider it a gate opened to set the captive free, and as a passage to *life,* and *liberty,* and *joy.*"

Her communications as a minister were neither frequent nor in many words, yet they were acceptable and instructive, and evidenced a mind deeply exercised for the spiritual advancement of those around her. It was the lot of this valued friend, after the decease of her husband, to experience great and varied trials, through all of which her character, as a sincerely humble and practical disciple of our Lord and Saviour, was instructively shown. Her whole deportment was dignified, securing respect from all, and the love of those who knew her. She possessed a remarkably clear and sound judgment, which was acceptably exercised in the disciplinary proceedings of our society, as well as in the concerns of private life.

Under a sense of the loss we have sustained by her removal, and in the hope that it may stimulate others to follow her, as we believe she was concerned to follow Christ, we think it right to record this brief tribute of our esteem and love.

Signed in Frenchay Monthly Meeting, held at Frenchay the 27th of the 2d month, 1839.

[*Here follow the signatures of men and women Friends.*]

Read and approved in the Quarterly Meeting of Gloucester and Wilts, held at Melksham the 26th of 3d mo. 1839, and signed in and on its behalf by

JOHN FOWLER, } Clerks.
REBECCA FOWLER, }

A Testimony from the Monthly Meeting for the East Division of Devonshire, on behalf of JOHN DYMOND, *deceased.*

Our late valued friend, John Dymond, was born in the 9th month, 1761. He died on the 31st of the 5th mo., and was buried at Exeter on the 6th of 6th mo., 1838, a minister about forty years.

He was the eldest son of George and Ann Dymond, of Exeter, both honourable elders of that meeting, from whom he received a guarded and religious education. Their pious efforts being accompanied by fervent aspirations to the Father of mercies for his blessing, and enforced by their own exemplary conduct, were a means of producing a permanently beneficial influence on his character.

He was preserved from uniting in most of the follies incident to youth ; and exhibited a steady and consistent example to the younger members of the family. Early desires were raised in his heart, to endeavour unreservedly to follow his heavenly guide ; and as he ripened in age, we believe he was increasingly favoured to feel the precious visitations of redeeming love. He was thus gradually prepared for further discoveries of the divine will concerning him ; and he came forth in the important work of the ministry about the thirty-sixth year of his age. His early communications were expressed in few words, in great humility, and under deep exercise of mind. His gift becoming gradually enlarged, and being attended by the baptizing power of the holy spirit, he became an instrument of strength and edification to those of his own quarterly meeting, beyond the compass of which his labours for many years seldom extended. At subsequent periods of his life, with the full unity of his friends, he visited the meetings of Friends in London and Middlesex, Yorkshire, and many other of the English counties ; also in Scotland and Ireland. In the course of these weighty services, he was frequently engaged in visiting families ; also in appointing meetings for those of other religious societies ; and there is reason to believe that his labours were very acceptable, and have left a sweet and lasting impression on the minds of many.

Our dear friend was zealous in promoting the abolition of the slave trade and slavery ; objects, which for a long series of years, obtained his earnest and persevering attention.

Highly appreciating the value of the Holy Scriptures, and being himself a diligent reader of them, he. rejoiced in the establishment of the Bible Society, and became, in the place of his residence, one of its earliest, and continued, to a very late period of his life, one of its most efficient supporters. He also actively co-operated with his fellow citizens in various measures of public utility, and objects of benevolence : and in these pursuits he evinced a soundness of judgment, and an integrity of purpose, which secured to him their confidence and attachment.

In the year 1828, three of his children, who had arrived at mature age, and who were a comfort and stay to him in his declining years, were removed by death within the short space of two months. Deeply afflictive was this bereavement, yet he was enabled to bow in Christian submission to the will of his

Heavenly Father, exemplifying in a remarkable manner the truth of that declaration of the prophet, " Thou wilt keep him in perfect peace whose mind is stayed on thee, because he trusteth in thee."

His ministry was sound, weighty, and instructive. He was concerned to preach " Christ crucified," as the great propitiatory offering made " once for all," as well as to inculcate attention to the immediate teachings of the Holy Spirit, and unreserved submission to the divine will manifested in the soul. He mourned the late divisions within the borders of our society ; but he had faith to believe, to adopt his own words when writing to a friend, that "the foundation upon which our early worthies built, will stand the test of the most rigid examination, and still be held dear by many." And again, at a subsequent date, "The longer I live, the more firmly is the conviction fixed upon my mind, that if ever our society fills that station in the Christian church, which I believe our Heavenly Father calls us to, we must walk by the same rule, and mind the same thing, which our early friends were led into. It was, I believe, in their assemblies (often) when no words were spoken, that they were brought to a deep sense of the need in which they stood, of redeeming love and power, and that they were instructed in things pertaining to life and salvation."

During an illness of many months, he was preserved in much patience and cheerfulness. On the 24th of 4th mo. he remarked to his daughter-in-law, " I have been for some weeks in a precarious situation. I have not been able to feel anxious about it ; I hope it is not apathy, but it seems as if I could not be uneasy." She remarked that she believed there was no *cause* for uneasiness, and that all was ordered in best wisdom. He rejoined, " I trust so. I have often thought of what a friend in the ministry said to me not long since, ' *Thy sacrifices have been accepted,*' and oh ! *it deeply humbled me.* They have been little and imperfect ; yet this I trust I can say, I have endeavoured to be faithful." After a pause, " My day's work *is done,* but I have nothing to trust to but the mercy and goodness of the Almighty. I may not be able to express much more, yet may say that I have a quiet hope."

As our dear friend's bodily strength declined, and the last solemn event drew near, it was evident to those about him, that under an humble hope in divine acceptance, " His heart was fixed, trusting in God." Thus he departed in peace, and his memory is precious.

While we mourn the loss which ourselves and the church have sustained, we are consoled by the belief, that through the mercy of God in Christ Jesus, he has exchanged this probationary state for one of unsullied and endless joy ; and that his purified spirit is united to the just of all generations.

Signed in the Monthly Meeting aforesaid, held at Exeter, the 5th of 12th mo. 1838, by

[*Here follow the signatures of men and women Friends.*]

Read and approved in the Quarterly Meeting for Devonshire, held at Plymouth the 26th of 12th month, 1838, and signed by direction and on behalf of the meeting, by

JOHN DYMOND, *Clerk.*

Signed in and on behalf of the Women's Quarterly Meeting for Devonshire, by

SARAH JOHN DYMOND.

From the Irish Friend of 6th month 1st.

Reasons why Christian Women should exercise the Gifts of the Holy Spirit, particularly in reference to the Ministry of the Gospel. W. EADE, Lindfield, 1839.

This little tract, although published anonymously, is understood to have been revised by "The Morning Meeting," in London, and may therefore, be said to express the sentiments of the society, on the subject of women's preaching. It may be safely handed, as information, to those of other societies; many of whom, it is apprehended, are unacquainted with our reasons for adopting views so contrary to the practice of almost all other denominations of the Christian church.

We are informed, that a large edition of this little work has been translated into French, for distribution on the continent, by our Friends, who have lately been travelling on religious service there. It may readily be imagined, that great ignorance, upon this subject, prevails, in those places where people, in general, give themselves but little trouble to inquire whether these things are so; having been educated in the belief, that such matters belong not to themselves, but to the priest.

The author of the work under notice, has treated the subject of it in a clear and forcible style of reasoning, which every *really* unprejudiced mind must allow, has truth, equity, and Scripture to support it. The arguments in defence of the ministry of women are fairly drawn from holy writ, and are supported by reason, and by analogy, as well as by the evidence of learned and pious individuals, not of the Society of Friends. A stronger proof than those, we have in the abundant evidence amongst us, of the baptising influence of the Holy Spirit being wrought upon the heart, through the instrumentality of women's preaching,—even to the converting the soul to God. The author, very properly, sets out with observing, that the ministry of the gospel, as a characteristic privilege of the Christian dispensation, has been restricted, either by ecclesiastical domination, or by the prejudices and preconceived opinions of many who profess the name of Christ.

The writer then proceeds to notice that memorable day, when the company of disciples, consisting, as there is good reason to conclude, of both men and women, "were ALL with one accord in one place, and were ALL filled with the Holy Ghost, and began to speak with other tongues as the Spirit gave them utterance." "This is that," said Peter, "which was spoken by the prophet Joel. And it shall come to pass in the last days, saith God, I will pour out my spirit upon all flesh, and your sons and your daughters shall prophesy, and your young men shall see visions, and your old men shall dream dreams, and on my servants and on my hand-maidens I will pour out of my spirit, and they shall prophesy." This outpouring of the spirit, this gift of prophecy, our author truly asserts, was as unequivocally declared to be bestowed upon the

daughters and on the *handmaidens*, as on the *sons* and the *servants.* That women *did* continue to exercise this gift of prophecy, is sufficiently manifest by the Apostle Paul referring to certain women by name, in his epistle to the Romans, who were his fellow-workers in the gospel; and, in his epistle to the Philippians, be speaks of those *women* who laboured with him in the gospel, and as being amongst his fellow-labourers. In addressing the Corinthian church, the same apostle gives some particular directions, how both men and, *women* should behave themselves when engaged, in the holy assemblies, in the exercise of the gift of prophecy, or of prayer. As the apostle thus decidedly recognises the public praying and prophesying of females—giving injunctions concerning their dress and deportment, when so employed—it is self-evident, that some *women,* as well as men, laboured in the ministry of the word. In the 21st chapter of Acts, there is mention made of Philip, the evangelist, who had four daughters which did prophesy. The Apostle Paul, himself, defines the term here used prophesying, in the way and manner which we now call preaching:— "He that prophesieth," saith he, "speaketh unto men to edification, to exhortation, and comfort." And, thus, Adam Clarke, in accordance with the views of John Locke, says, that, "prophecy, in the New Testament, often means the gift of exhorting, preaching, or expounding the Scriptures." From these observations, and much more which might be adduced in proof that, "male and female are all one in Christ," we are brought to the conviction, that the same apostle, whom we have before quoted, when he forbade women to speak in the church, did not apply the restriction to the exercise of any spiritual gift, but solely with a view to correct certain abuses which had rendered their assemblies for worship at Corinth, both unprofitable and disorderly. Ecclesiastical writers concur in asserting, that it was lawful and customary for any man in the Jewish synagogue, who had a mind so to do, to ask of his teacher, explanation of any thing which he had heard only; this privilege was not permitted to the women—they were to ask their questions at home. This custom of asking questions in the synagogue—Benson and others inform us—was transferred to the Christian church, with the approbation of the apostle, who, however, restricted these interrogatories to the men. In the Corinthian church this practice had been introduced, which the apostle forbade to the women, referring them, for answers to their questions (probably, very unsuitable ones) to their husbands at home. Grotius, on this passage, remarks, that "the apostle suffers not the women to perform such an office—[teaching]— that is to say, unless they have the prophetical impulse." "Prophecy," adds he, in another place, "is beyond the reach of positive law." Adam Clarke, on this text, fully admits, that the apostle's prohibition to women speaking in public, "by no means intimated, that, when a woman received any particular influence from God, to enable her to teach, she was not to obey it; on the contrary," adds he, "she was to obey that influence; and the apostle lays down directions for regulating her

personal appearance when thus engaged." It is well known, that the late John Wesley approved of women's preaching: for, said he, "God owns them in the conversion of sinners; and who am I, that I should withstand God!"

"In tracing the history of the Christian church," the author of the tract under notice very justly and forcibly remarks, "we may observe, how very soon was the brightness of the gospel day eclipsed by the power of the 'man of sin.' Then, no longer was the choice and the qualifications of the ministers referred to Him who is ordained to be the only 'Head over all things to the church;' but, men, swayed by temporal interests, appointed to this sacred office, such as were the fit instruments for promoting or securing the wealth and the power of worldly princes. And, although the Christian church has, to a considerable extent, emerged from the darkness of the apostacy, yet she has, perhaps, been, in no respect, more slow to avail herself of the blessings and privileges of this glorious gospel day, than in allowing the free and unrestricted exercise of the ministry." "Put me, I pray thee, into one of the priest's offices, that I may eat a piece of bread," is, too generally, the prevailing language of the Christian ministry. Divinity is taught as a science, and preaching as an art, in the colleges and schools of Christendom; and, acquirements thus obtained for money, are too often made objects of pecuniary calculation. "The enticing words of man's wisdom" are suited to those "who have itching ears;" and thus, whilst the people will have it so, the buyers and sellers continue in the temple. But those who are taught in the school of Christ, and are commissioned, by him, to preach his gospel, and are content to labour on his own terms—"Freely ye have received, freely give." "How many (says our author) have yet to learn, that, in Christ Jesus, there is neither male nor female; that, as God is a Spirit, so his communications, through whatever medium conveyed, are directed to the *souls* of his rational creatures; that no external circumstances necessarily influence these communications; that, to suppose they do so, is to estimate the dispensation of the gospel as far below that of the law. Can we believe, that the Holy Spirit is *now* more limited in its manifestations, and in its requirements, than when, by its inspiration, Miriam prophesied and sang the praises of Jehovah?—when Deborah, under the palm trees of Mount Ephraim, prophesied, and judged Israel by the law, and the Spirit of the living God?—and, when Huldah the wife of Shallum, together with cotemporary prophets, declared the judgments of the Most High, as impending over a rebellious and gainsaying people? And, when the Sun of Righteousness was about to rise upon a benighted world, how remarkably were women employed to announce his coming and advent! when Elizabeth and Mary were filled with the Holy Ghost, and when Anna, the prophetess, spoke of the infant Messiah to all those that looked for redemption in Israel! His coming was effectually declared to the inhabitants of Samaria, through the instrumentality of a woman; and it was to women that the joyful tidings were communicated, by the two men in shining garments: 'He is not here, but is risen.' It was *they* (the women) who were commanded to 'go quickly,' and tell his sorrowing disciples of his resurrection. It was a woman that received that most sacred commission—'Go to my brethren, and say unto them, I ascend unto my Father, and your Father, and to my God, and your God.'" In conclusion, our author very forcibly remarks—"So effectually have the glad tidings of salvation been declared by females, that many have been, through their instrumentality, converted from the error of their ways, and brought from darkness to light: many hungry and thirsty souls have been refreshed and strengthened; and many living members of the Church edified together. And, though this preaching may not be 'with excellency of speech or of wisdom,'—but 'in weakness and fear, and in much trembling,'— yet many can feelingly testify, from heartfelt experience, that it has often been exercised 'in the demonstration of the Spirit, and of power.' Did professing Christians, with a more lively faith, appreciate their high privilege, as offered through this most blessed gift —were they seeking to obey its teachings— and to live under its sanctifying power—and, with a true hunger and thirst after righteousness, thankfully accepting every medium, through which the great Shepherd and Bishop of souls condescends to feed, and to instruct his people—there would be no disposition to dispute the authority of the instrument through which he may, in his infinite compassion, extend to sinners the invitations of his grace, and cause the glad tidings of his gospel to be proclaimed."

From the same.

PUNISHMENT OF DEATH.

A circumstance worthy of note occurred a few years since to a Friend residing in the neighbourhood of ——, in Essex, which furnishes a lively proof of the energy of the principle of Christian love, in producing conviction in the mind of an obdurate offender, and of drawing forth a confession of guilt and penitence which all the terrors of revenging law failed to effect. The anecdote is ascertained to be literally true. J—— ——, was one evening returning home rather late, it being nearly dark, when he was met by two men, whom he suspected were soldiers. They spoke to each other in a low voice as he passed, when he was almost immediately knocked down, and robbed of a considerable sum of money and his watch. Being severely hurt, it was with considerable difficulty that he reached his own dwelling, not far distant, and was there confined under surgical care about two months. During this time, no information could be obtained which might lead to a discovery of the perpetrators of the deed, but some time after, he understood that a robbery had been committed in the neighbourhood, and that two soldiers had been taken up, one of whom was tried, convicted, and condemned to death for the crime, and then lay in —— jail, waiting his execution. Being now sufficiently recovered from the injuries he had sustained, he determined, if practicable, to obtain an interview with the unhappy man, judging it at least possible that he might know and be prevailed upon to reveal something relating to his own circumstance. Accordingly, accompanied by a Friend, he applied to the keeper of the jail for admission to him. The request was, with reluctance, acceded to, on account of the dark state of mind which the person had all along evinced, and the determination which, from the first, he had shown, not to be prevailed upon to make the least disclosure. J——, persevering, however, in his endeavours to see him, the criminal was at length brought up into the master's room, and urged to acknowledge if he knew any thing which related to the robbery committed upon him. He sullenly and obstinately rejected every inquiry, and although the jailer also expostulated with him, "how much better it might be, if he knew any thing to tell the gentlemen, seeing it could not make him own case worse, which was now awfully decided;" yet he persisted in avowing his entire ignorance of the matter. When all endeavours thus proving fruitless, he was about to be returned to his cell, J—— ——'s mind became affected with tender compassion towards the man, and stepping up to him as he was in the act of withdrawing, he affectionately grasped his hand, and said—"If *thou* art the man who robbed me, I freely forgive thee, and I hope the *Almighty* will!" on which, with great emotion, he immediately exclaimed—"*I am the man.*" Truth and conviction forced their way into his mind —trembling and amazed, and with tears, he voluntarily made full confession, and mentioned particularly how the stolen property had been in different ways disposed of, by which a part of it was, in consequence, recovered. Not so the man. Desirable as it was, under circumstances of contrition and confession, that he might have been privileged with time and opportunity to prove the sincerity of his repentance by an amended life, it is affecting to consider that the sanguinary edicts of his country forbad it, and the unsparing rigour of a human law conferred no mercy on *one* whom the Divine Judge, in *his* mercy, appears to have visited.
W.

From the same.

A Biographical Notice of the late JOHN PICKERING.

Extracted from Lettsom's Memoirs of Dr. Fothergill.

The late Major John Pickering, of Tortola, was, in early life, brought up to a mechanical employment, but, by strength of genius and dint of self-exertion, he acquired a competent share of learning and an extensive acquaintance with mathematics; by industry he became possessed of a large tract of uncultivated land, and by perseverance he covered it with canes and cotton, and he gradually rose to be one of the wealthiest planters in the West Indies. He was, about his fortieth year, made governor of the island of Tortola, and had the rank of major in the insular militia. At length he publicly professed the religious principles of the Quakers, and relinquished all his civil and military honours and employments. He afterwards rarely attended the courts of judicature, unless he thought some poor person, some orphan or widow, was oppressed by some more powerful neighbour, when he voluntarily attended, and publicly pleaded the cause of the weak, if he deemed them oppressed; and his justice and weight were such as generally preponderated. I frequently accompanied him to his plantations, through which, as he passed, his numerous negroes saluted him in a loud chorus or song, which they continued as long as he remained in sight. I was also a melancholy witness of their attachment to him after his death. He expired suddenly, and when few of his friends were near him. I remember I had hold of his hand when this fatal period arrived; but he had scarcely expired his last breath before it was known to his slaves, and instantly about five hundred of them surrounded his house and insisted upon seeing their master. With this they commenced a dismal and mournful yell, which was communicated from one plantation to another, till the whole island was in agitation, and crowds of negroes were accumulating around us. Distressed as I was with the loss of my relative and friend, I could not be insensible to the danger of a general insurrection; or if they entered the house, which was constructed of wood, and mounted into his chamber, there was danger of its falling by their weight, and crushing us all in its ruins. In this dilemma I had resolution enough to secure the doors, and thereby prevent sudden intrusion. After these precautions, I addressed them through a window, assuring them, that, if they would enter the house in companies of twelve (only) at a time, they should all be admitted to see their deceased master, and that the same lenient treatment they had experienced from him should he still continued; to this they assented, and in a few hours quiet was restored: but it affected me to see with what silent, sullen, fixed melancholy, they departed from the remains of this venerable man. He died in 1768, aged about 60. Dr. Lettsom himself became possessed of a large property in slaves in Tortola, bequeathed to him by John Pickering or some other relative. On this circumstance he subjoins the following reasoning and conclusion. "The repeated proofs of fidelity and love which I received from my own people, gave me, at length, so settled a confidence in their integrity, that, without the least apprehension of danger, I have frequently found, that I had left not only my liberty but my life entirely at their disposal. The beneficence of the powerful, and the gratitude of the dependent, form an union of interests that never fails to heighten mutual regard; my own happiness became at length so closely connected with the happiness of my negroes, that I could no longer withhold from them the natural privilege of freedom which Heaven had conferred upon me; I therefore delivered them from bondage, and thus restored them to the character of beings, into whom the Author of Nature and Giver of all good has breathed the breath of life."

From the same.

It may not be generally known that George Pilkington, accompanied by his wife, sailed some months ago for the Brazils, where he appears, by the latest accounts, to be engaged in promoting that cause to which he has been for some years so zealously devoted. The only information which we possess relative to his proceedings, is comprised in the following extract from the *"Jornal Do Commercio"* published at Rio de Janeiro, and dated 2d month, 27th last :—.

"George Pilkington, late captain of the corps of royal engineers, who, under a conviction of duty, has during the last six years, traveled on his own responsibility, and without being the missionary or agent of any religions sect, society or political party, through the British empire, and addressed large assemblies in upwards of 500 of its cities and towns, on the unchristian principle of every description of war, affectionately invites those who feel an interest in the gospel of the Prince of Peace, to attend a lecture on the subject, at the grand saloon, Pharoux Hotel, on the evening of the 27th inst., at a quarter before seven o'clock precisely.

From the same.

PROVIDENTIAL DELIVERANCE.

The late J. A———, of Leeds, when in the meridian of life, was traveling in Scotland. In descending a hill, at the foot of which a river meandered, he found himself forcibly struck with the scenery ; not only on account of its beauty, but because he was certain he had seen it before. As he had never previously been even on the borders of Scotland, he could not account for this strange though clear remembrance of the country around him, but after a few minutes, he recollected a dream he had some time before :—

He thought he was descending the same hill, in order to cross the river by a ferry at the foot of it ; and that a little ragged boy opened him a gate, and held his horse while he got into the boat, and then followed him with it—that when they had reached the middle of the river the boat sunk, and all were drowned. As this was passing in his mind, the same little ragged boy opened a gate for him. At first, he endeavoured to discard all apprehension from his dream, as unworthy a man of sense and education : he was a man of liberal and unprejudiced mind, and earlier in life, had been accused of free-thinking ; how then would it be compatible with his former principles, to surrender himself the child of a romantic imagination—to an idle dream ? As these reflections crossed his mind, he determined to go on ; but he found the impulse too strong to be resisted ; and to avoid the ferry, he resolved to pursue his way by the nearest bridge, about twenty miles off. From that moment he thought no more of his dream, till some weeks after, as he was returning from his journey; he stopped at an inn, on the opposite side of the same ferry to dine. The landlady observed him with a melancholy earnestness which distressed him. "Are you not, sir," she said, with great emotion, "the gentleman who, a few weeks ago, refused to cross the ferry, and went round by Stirling bridge instead?" "Yes," he answered, "I am; why do you ask?" "Then, sir, you may thank God for it; for either by the boat's being too much laden, or from some unknown cause, it sank in

the middle of the river, and every one, among whom was my son, perished." Let those who affect philosophical incredulity, disprove this if they can, to be the interposition of Providence in favour of a man so estimable and so necessary to his family! Let them prove it if they can, to be the effect of blind chance or of a distempered imagination! Those to whom he was dear, bowed with humility and admiration to inscrutible wisdom, who, in so extraordinary a manner, had preserved to them a life so precious. The ways of the Most High are, indeed, past finding out.

A remarkable instance of the strength of maternal affection is related in a French paper. The inhabitants of an inn at Roulers, in Belgium, were surprised in their beds by the house being on fire, and were obliged to make their escape in their night clothes. The young mother of two children, in the terror of the moment, came away with only one of them, an infant at her breast, but the panic almost instantly subsided, and, recollecting the other was left behind, she laid her infant on the ground, and rushed into the flames to save the other, or rather to perish herself, as every one present felt confident would be her fate. Her courage and affection, however, were rewarded ; for in a few minutes she returned with a child in her arms, though her own face was scorched, her hair singed, and her scanty covering in flames. She had scarcely got clear of the house, when the whole building fell—a burning mass of ruins!

American Mechanics.—The mechanics in this country are fast equalling, if they do not surpass, those of Europe. A self-taught artist (by name Holcomb) in a small town in Massachusetts, has constructed some of the most perfeet telescopes ever made. One in the possession of an academy at Albany, is said to be unrivaled for its beauty and accuracy. He is now constructing one for the Girard College in Philadelphia, which will surpass in size, if not in exquisite power of observation, the celebrated telescope of Herschell. We saw in the upper part of this city the other day, a beautiful astronomical apparatus designed for Williams' College, inimitably finished, and embodying more various uses than any other apparatus ever constructed. It was made by a modest and worthy brass-founder of the name of Phelps.—*Troy Mail.*

THE FRIEND.

EIGHTH MONTH, 15, 1840.

The magnitude and importance of the anthracite coal-fields of Pennsylvania—the immense influence which they already have, and are destined to have upon the prosperity of the state, and even of the United States, renders the subject one of deep interest to the community at large. We therefore have thought proper to transfer to our pages a considerable part of a pamphlet recently put forth, entitled, "A History of the Lehigh Coal and Navigation Company, published by order of the Board of Managers." The history of this company is

in fact essentially the history of the introduction into use amongst us of anthracite coal, and our readers will be well repaid in tracing, by means of this narrative, its progress, from small beginnings, through all the various discouragements and impediments, to its present triumphant and magnificent developement.

FARMERS' CABINET.

We copy from the number for the present month the following spirited notice, from the pen of the able editor of the Farmers' Cabinet; and we sincerely wish for this useful periodical a degree of success commensurate with the talent and zeal with which it is conducted.

NOTICE TO SUBSCRIBERS.

The 5th volume of the Cabinet commences with the present number. We rejoice in the avenues which are opening around us for the cultivation of agricultural knowledge; and the hope of assisting others in their pleasing task, and fulfilling our own engagements with credit to ourselves and usefulness to our subscribers, adds not a little to the present reward of our labours.

We sincerely thank our contributing friends for their unremitted favours, and beg to apprise them, that the time is coming when those who have done most will have *most to do*, for agricultural science is rising in all her majesty, throughout all lands; the sword is beaten into the ploughshare and the spear into the pruninghook, and millions are enabled to sit under their own vine and under their own fig-trees, none *wishing* to make them afraid. And it never can be, that America will content herself to sit and receive as a boon instructions, either in this or any other department of science, without feeling a proud desire to add her share to the general fund. But if "of those to whom much is given, much will be required," she has indeed a debt upon her hands! Let her, therefore, bestir herself, and show that she *feels* the world is "traveling west."

Nothing facilitates so much the diffusion of agricultural knowledge as the circulation of periodical works on that subject; it is a mistake to suppose or to expect that such publications ought to contain nothing but what has been tried and found correct, and deserving of general adoption into practice,—it is merely a means of communication between man and man, and the detail of failure in an experiment might be made equally interesting and profitable, even to him who has been "exercised thereby," as might the most perfect instance of success; by comparing notes, we shall find which way the current lies, and then we shall steer forward in unison to the haven of success. One thing is certain—agriculture will no longer be a subject upon which persons will be able to sleep comfortably—it is the scientific manager only who will henceforth be able to live on his labours, or what is called—make both ends meet.

DIED, of a short and severe illness, at the residence of his mother, Poplar Ridge, Fayette county, Indiana, on the 4th of 7th month, 1840, ISRAEL WRIGHT, son of the late Joel Wright, in the nineteenth year of his age. His loss will be severely felt, not only by those constituting the domestic circle to which he immediately belonged, but likewise by numerous relatives and friends.

THE FRIEND.

A RELIGIOUS AND LITERARY JOURNAL.

VOL. XIII.   SEVENTH DAY, EIGHTH MONTH, 22, 1840.   NO. 47.

EDITED BY ROBERT SMITH.

PUBLISHED WEEKLY.

Price two dollars per annum, payable in advance.

Subscriptions and Payments received by

GEORGE W. TAYLOR,

NO. 50, NORTH FOURTH STREET, UP STAIRS,

PHILADELPHIA.

For " The Friend."

THE REMEDY FOR THE SLAVE TRADE.

(Continued from p. 362.)

The venerable Thomas Clarkson strongly commends the plan proposed by Buxton. He says: " As far as our knowledge of Africa and African manners, customs, and dispositions goes, a better plan could not be devised—no other plan, in short, could answer. Had this plan been followed from the first, it would have done wonders for Africa by this time, and it would do much for us now: in two years from the trial of it, it would become doubtful whether it was worth while to carry on the slave trade; and in five years I have no doubt that it would be generally, though, perhaps, not totally, abandoned. Depend upon it there is no way of civilising and Christianising Africa, which all good men must look to, but this."

Among the practical evidence in favour of his proposition, he makes mention of the happy effect of an attempt made a number of years ago by some Friends, on a small scale, but of a somewhat similar character. " The experiment failed, or it seemed to fail, owing to the death of the agent whom they had sent; but it was with no small pleasure that I found, in the papers of the brother of a deceased governor of the colony at St. Mary's, this evidence that their labours were not entirely lost. After stating that they had established a school and farm on a point of land forming Cape St. Mary's, ' as eligible a spot for such an undertaking as could be found in the country,' he goes on to say, ' the natives of the neighbourhood must have observed, with some degree of attention, the mode adopted by these settlers in their agricultural pursuits. Indeed, it must be inferred that many of them assisted on the works of the farm, as at this date (viz. 14 years after) they conduct matters in a more neat and satisfactory manner than is to be observed in other parts of the country. Their grounds are well cleaned and enclosed; vegetation, of one kind or other, appears to be kept up during the year; the quality of their articles is superior to their neighbours; and altogether there is a superiority among these people, a neatness about their persons and villages that pleases the eye, particularly as these things do not ex-

ist in other parts of the country. The old chief of the district loses no opportunity of making the most particular inquiries after his friends, the Quakers, and of expressing his regret that such good people should not have remained amongst them, as their kindness will ever live in the memory of the inhabitants. The chief and his son are worthy, good folks, and much attached to the English. The seeds which W. Allen and other gentlemen have sent to the Gambia, have been of infinite service in improving the quality of the cotton and rice.' "

I hardly know any thing more encouraging than the facts which have thus unexpectedly come to light. Here an effort has been made exactly in conformity with the views which I am endeavouring to urge, but it was soon abandoned; yet the effect of that imperfect experiment is still visible in the improvement of the face of the country, and in the manifest distinction between that district which had been thus befriended, and the desolate regions which surround it.

The fact, too, that these simple people retain a lively and grateful recollection of their benefactors, and cease not to pant for their return, proves that in the minds of the people, as well as in the quality of the soil, there are materials on which we may work. When so much was effected by a slight effort, what may we not expect to be accomplished, when the same merciful measures shall be adopted permanently, and upon a large scale?

Commerce will follow agriculture. I do not, however, anticipate that this commerce will, in the first instance, be large. Africa is only capable of producing: as yet, she does not produce. When it is found that there is security for person and property, and that products of industry find a ready market, and command a supply of European articles which the natives covet, an impulse will, no doubt, be given to internal cultivation. But it is greatly to be desired, that this impulse should be as strong, and operate as speedily as possible. What we want is, to supplant the slave trade by another trade, which shall be more lucrative. We cannot expect that savage nations will be greatly influenced by the promise of prospective advantage. The rise of the legitimate trade ought, if we are to carry the good will of the natives along with us, to follow as close as possible upon the downfall of the trade in man: there ought to be an immediate substitute for the gains which are to cease. In short, the natives must be assisted, and by every method in our power, put in the way of producing those things which will bear a value in the market of the world. It is impossible that we can be in error in assuming that Africa, under cultivation, will make more

from her exports than she now receives from the sale of her population.

There is no danger that the experiment will fail, if time enough is allowed for the full development of its results: but there is very considerable risk that the experiment, while advancing to maturity, will fail, from the impatience of a barbarous people, who are not in the habit of contemplating distant results, and who, finding themselves stripped of one species of customary trade, have not as yet been remunerated by the acquisition of a better source of revenue. For this reason, I suggest that we should, for a time, subsidise the chiefs of Africa, whose assistance we require; and, for the same reason I propose that we should give all natural, and even some artificial stimulants to agricultural industry.

If at the moment when the African population find themselves in unaccustomed security, and feel, for the first time, a certainty of reaping what they sow; when they see their rivers, which have hitherto been worse than useless to the bulk of the people [having been but the highway of armed banditti]—transformed into the cheapest, the safest, and the most convenient channel of intercourse between themselves and the civilised world, and discover this to be the choicest blessing which nature has bestowed upon them; if at the moment when a market is brought to their doors, and foreign merchants are at hand, ready to exchange for their productions the alluring articles of European manufacture, of which, sparingly as they have hitherto tasted, they know the rare beauty and surpassing usefulness,—if at this moment, when so many specific and powerful motives invite them to the diligent cultivation of their soil, they are visited by a band of agricultural instructors, who offer at once to put them in possession of that skill in husbandry which the rest of the world has acquired, and they are enabled to till their ground in security, and find opened to them a conveyance for its productions, and a market for their sale; and if simultaneously with these advantages we furnish that practical knowledge, and those mechanical contrivances which the experience of ages, and ingenuity of successive generations have by slow degrees disclosed to ourselves—I cannot doubt that those combined benefits and discoveries will furnish an immediate, as well as an ample compensation for the loss of that wicked traffic, which, if it has afforded profit to the few, has exposed the great mass of the inhabitants to unutterable wretchedness.

No more daring attempt was ever made to form a settlement in Africa than that undertaken by Captain Beaver, near the close of the last century. His object was to establish a colony on the island of Bulama. In negotiating for the purchase of territory, the natives wondered that he and his company would not buy slaves; and, by steadiness on this point, they got the character of being the first white men the natives had heard of " who could not do bad."

The two first who came to Captain Beaver were full of suspicion, and soon departed. He did not even ask them to remain, but paid them off, and dismissed them with presents. He never after wanted labourers: in one year he employed nearly 200 of them. The Africans of these parts, says he, always go armed, and never voluntarily place themselves in the power of even a friendly tribe. " They came to me unarmed," says Captain Beaver, " and remained for weeks and months at a time on the island, without the least suspicion of my ever intending them evil." The captain believes that by fair dealing, and by the wealth which is to be raised from the soil of Africa, the slave trade is to be overthrown. " If," says he, " we could substitute another commerce, and at the same time that other be more certain and more abundant, the great object in trading in slaves will be done away. This may be done by the produce of the earth." " And, as far as my little knowledge of the Africans will enable me to judge, I have no doubt of their readily cultivating the earth for hire, whenever Europeans will take the trouble so to employ them. I never saw men work harder, more willingly or regularly, generally speaking, than those free natives whom I employed in the island of Bulama. What induced them to do so? Their desire of European commodities in my possession, of which they knew that they would have the value of one bar at the end of a week, or four at the end of a month."

Captain Beaver's opinions are considered peculiarly important by Buxton, because published before the controversy as to free and slave labour had arisen, and because that gentleman took nothing upon the authority of others, but formed his opinions from his own personal experience in Africa.

(To be continued.)

History of the Lehigh Coal and Navigation Company.

(Continued from page 363.)

Every thing was thus making satisfactory advances toward the accomplishment of the object, when, late in the season of 1818, the water in the river fell, by an unparalleled drought, as was believed, fully twelve inches below the mark which has been mentioned as shown by the inhabitants to be the lowest point to which the river ever sunk. Here was a difficulty totally unanticipated, and one which required a very essential alteration in the plan. Nature did not furnish enough water, by the regular flow of the river, to keep the channels at the proper depth, owing to the very great fall in the river, and the consequent rapidity of its motion. It became necessary to accumulate water *by artificial means*, and let it off at stated periods, and let the boats pass down with the long wave, thus formed, which filled up the channels.

This was effected by constructing dams in the neighbourhood of Mauch Chunk, in which were placed sluice-gates of a peculiar construc-

tion, *invented for the purpose* by Josiah White, (one of the managers,) by means of which the water could be retained in the pool above, until required for use. When the dam became full, and the water had run over it long enough for the river below the dam to acquire the depth of the ordinary flow of the river, the sluice-gates were let down, and the boats, which were lying in the pools above, passed down with the artificial flood. About twelve of these dams and sluices were made in 1819, and with what work had been done in making wing-dams, absorbed the capital of the company (which, on the first plan of improvement, would have been adequate,) before the whole of the dams were completely protected from ice freshets. They were, however, so far completed, as to prove, in the fall of that year, that they were capable of producing the required depth of water from Mauch Chunk to Easton. In the spring of 1820 the ice severely injured several of the unprotected dams, and carried away some of the sluice-gates. This situation of things, of course, gave rise to many difficulties. It was necessary that more money should be raised, or the work must be abandoned. A difficulty also arose among the managers themselves, which resulted in White and Hazard making an arrangement with Hauto for his interest in the concern, on the 7th of March, 1820. On the 21st of April following, the *Lehigh Coal Company and the Lehigh Navigation Company agreed to amalgamate their interests, and to unite themselves into one company, under the title of the " Lehigh Navigation and Coal Company,"* provided the additional sum of twenty thousand dollars was subscribed to the stock by a given date. Of this sum nearly three-fifths were subscribed by White and Hazard. With this aid the navigation was repaired, and *three hundred and sixty-five tons of coal sent to Philadelphia, as the first fruits of the concern!* This quantity of coal completely stocked the market, and was with difficulty disposed of in the year 1820. It will be recollected that no anthracite coal came to market from any other source than the Lehigh before the year 1825, as a regular business.

The money capital of the concern was soon found to require an increase. The work was done, with the exception of one place at the " slates," where the channel and wing walls were made over the smooth surface of slate ledges, which projected alternately from one side of the river nearly to the other, and rose to within four inches of the surface of the water for a considerable distance along the river. From the nature of the ground, it was impossible to make the wing walls remain tight enough to keep the water at the required height, and it was evident that a dam must be resorted to, to bury the slates permanently to a sufficient depth below the surface. This, it was estimated, could not be erected at a less cost than twenty thousand dollars. To raise this sum, in the circumstances of the company, was a difficult task. The small quantity of coal which had been brought down having so completely filled the market, and the inexperience in the use of that species of fuel having excited so many prejudices against it, that many of the stockholders doubted

whether it would be possible to introduce the coal into general use, even if the navigation were made perfect. While this difficulty was in the process of arrangement, the work was kept alive by the advances of one of the managers. At length, on the 1st of May, 1821, a new arrangement of the whole concern took place, by which all the interests became more closely amalgamated. The title of the company was changed to " *The Lehigh Coal and Navigation Company.*" It was agreed that the capital stock should be increased by new subscriptions, and that in consideration thereof, and of certain shares of the stock to be given to them, J. White and E. Hazard would release to the company all their reserved exclusive rights and privileges, and residuary profits, and convey to trustees, for the use of the company, all their right to the water power of the river Lehigh, and come in as simple stockholders; the company, at the same time, assuming the settlement of Hauto's claim upon White and Hazard. It was, however, agreed that the subscribers to the new stock should have the benefit of all the profits up to three per cent. semi-annually; then the original stockholders became entitled to the profits until they derived semi-annual dividends of three per cent.; and, finally, any excess of profit beyond these was to go to the stock allotted to J. White and E. Hazard, until the profit in any six months should be sufficient to produce a three per cent. dividend on all the stock. From that time all discrimination in the stock was to cease, and all the owners to come in for an equal share of the profits in the proportion of shares of stock held by them.

The business of the company was to be carried on by five managers, two of whom were to reside at Mauch Chunk, under the title of acting managers, and superintend the navigation and coal department, while the others took care of the finances.

After this agreement was made, a number of the stockholders and their friends visited the works and property of the company, and although they expressed themselves measurably disappointed in the appearance of things, yet the doubt of the possibility of getting a market for the coal, induced a timidity in subscribing to fifty thousand dollars of new stock, which was only overcome by J. White and E. Hazard transferring, as a bonus to those who would subscribe, an amount of the stock held by them equal to twenty per cent. on the amount of the new subscription. In this way the whole fifty thousand dollars was subscribed. The dam and lock at the slates were erected, and one thousand and seventy-three tons of coal were sent to Philadelphia in 1821.

The unincorporated situation of the company, now that its operations were becoming more extensive, caused uneasiness among the stockholders with regard to their personal liabilities, and necessarily operated as a check to the prosperous extension of the business. In addition to which, the whole property and interests of the concern were virtually mortgaged to the holders of the fifty thousand dollars of new stock, which would render any extension of the capital excessively difficult. To remedy these difficulties, application was made to the legislature, who, on the 13th of February,

1822, granted the act of incorporation under which the company are now operating. In this year the capital stock of the company was increased by new subscriptions amounting to $83,950, and two thousand two hundred and forty tons of coal were sent to market.

The boats used on this descending navigation consisted of square boxes, or arks, from sixteen to eighteen feet wide, and twenty to twenty-five feet long. At first, two of these were joined together by hinges, to allow them to bend up and down in passing the dams and sluices, and as the men became accustomed to the work, and the channels were straightened and improved as experience dictated, the number of sections in each boat was increased, till at last their whole length reached one hundred and eighty feet. They were steered with long oars, like a raft. Machinery was devised for jointing and putting together the planks of which these boats were made, and the hands became so expert that five men would put one of the sections together and launch it in forty-five minutes. Boats of this description were used on the Lehigh till the end of the year 1831, when the Delaware division of the Pennsylvania Canal was partially finished. In the last year forty thousand nine hundred and sixty-six tons were sent down, which required so many boats to be built, that, if they had all been joined in one length, they would have extended more than thirteen miles. These boats made but one trip, and were then broken up in the city, and the planks sold for lumber, the spikes, hinges, and other iron work, being returned to Mauch Chunk by land, a distance of eighty miles. The hands employed in running these boats walked back for two or three years, when rough wagons were placed upon the road by some of the tavern-keepers, to carry them at reduced fares.

During the low water upon the Delaware it was found necessary to improve several of the channels of that river, and in this way about five thousand dollars were expended by the Lehigh Company, under the authority of the commissioners appointed by the state for the improvement of the Delaware channels, whose funds were exhausted.

The descending navigation by artificial freshets on the Lehigh is the first on record which was used as a permanent thing; though it is stated that in the expedition in 1779, under General Sullivan, General James Clinton successfully made use of the expedient to extricate his division of the army from some difficulty on the east branch of the Susquehanna, by erecting a temporary dam across the outlet of Otsego lake, which accumulated water enough to float them, when let off, and carry them down the river.

The descending navigation of the Lehigh was inspected, and the governor's license to take toll upon it obtained on the 17th of January, 1823, it having been in use for two years previous to the inspection. No toll was charged upon it till 1827.

The great consumption of lumber for the boats very soon made it evident that the coal business could not be carried on, even on a small scale, without a communication by water with the pine forests, about sixteen miles above Mauch Chunk, on the upper section of

the Lehigh. To obtain this was very difficult. The river, in that distance, had a fall of about three hundred feet, over a very rough, rocky bed, with shores so forbidding that in only two places above Lausanne had horses been got down to the river. To improve the navigation it became necessary to commence operations at the upper end, and to cart all the tools and provisions by a circuitous and rough road through the wilderness, and then to build a boat for each load to be sent down to the place where the hands were at work by the channels which they had previously prepared. Before these channels were effected, an attempt was made to send down planks, singly, from the pine swamp, but they became bruised and broken by the rocks before they reached Mauch Chunk. Single saw-logs were then tried, and men sent down to clear them from the rocks as they became fast. But it frequently happened that, when they got near Mauch Chunk, a sudden rise of the water would sweep them off, and they were lost. These difficulties were overcome by the completion of these channels in 1823, which gave rise to an increase of the capital stock, at the same time, of ninety-six thousand and fifty dollars, making the whole amount subscribed five hundred thousand dollars. In this year, also, five thousand eight hundred and twenty-three tons of coal were sent to market, of which about one thousand tons remained unsold in the following spring, there being still a great prejudice against the domestic use of coal. This prejudice was, however, on the wane, and very soon after this time became nearly extinct.

In 1825, the demand for coal increased so much that twenty-eight thousand three hundred and ninety-three tons were sent down the Lehigh, and the coal trade on the Schuylkill now commenced by their sending down by that navigation seven thousand one hundred and forty-three tons.

(To be continued.)

THE LUMINOUS SEA.

Extracted from an article in the Nautical Magazine.
(Concluded from p. 304.)

A diffused luminous appearance of the sea, in some respects different from what I have seen, has been described by several navigators.

Godehen de Riville saw the sea assume the appearance of a plain of snow on the coast of Malabar.*

Captain Horsburgh, in the notes he gave to Sir Joseph Banks, says: There is a peculiar phenomenon sometimes seen within a few degrees distance of the coast of Malabar, during the rainy monsoon, which he had an opportunity of observing.

At midnight the weather was cloudy, and the sea was particularly dark, when suddenly it changed to a white flaming colour all around: this bore no resemblance to the sparkling or glowing appearance he had observed on other occasions in seas near the equator, but was a regular white colour, like milk, and did not continue more than ten minutes. A similar phenomenon, he says, is frequently seen in the Banda sea, and is very alarming to those

* Mem Etrang. de l'Acad. des 8c. Tom. 3.

who have never perceived or heard of such an appearance before.

This singular phenomenon appears to be explained by some observations communicated to me, by Langstaff, a surveyor in the city, who formerly made several voyages.

In going from New Holland to China, about half an hour after sunset, every person on board was astonished by a milky appearance of the sea : the ship seemed to be surrounded by ice covered with snow ; some of the company supposed they were in soundings, and that coral bottom gave this curious reflection, but on sounding with 70 fathoms of line no bottom was met with. A bucket of water being hauled up, Langstaff examined it in the dark, and discovered a great number of globular bodies linked together, each about the size of a pin's head.

The chains thus formed did not exceed three inches in length, and emitted a pale phosphoric light. By introducing his hand into the water, Langstaff raised upon it several chains of the luminous globules, which were separated by opening the fingers, but readily reunited on being brought again into contact, like globules of quicksilver, (the globules were so transparent that they could not be perceived when the hand was taken into the light.) This extraordinary appearance of the sea was visible for two nights. As soon as the moon exerted her influence, the sea changed to its natural dark colour, and exhibited distinct glittering points as at other times. The phenomenon, he says, had never been witnessed before by any of the company on board, although some of the crew had been two or three times round the globe.

I consider this account very interesting and important, as it proves that the diffused light of the sea is produced by an assemblage of minute medusæ on the surface of the water.

In June, 1806, I found the sea at Margate more richly stored with minute medusæ than I have ever seen it. A bucket of the water being set by for some time, the animals sought the surface, and kept up a continual sparkling, which must have been occasioned by the motions of individuals as the water was perfectly at rest. A small quantity of the luminous water was first put into a glass jar, and on standing for some time, the medusæ collected at the top of the jar, and formed a gelatinous mass, one inch and a half thick, and of a reddish or mud colour, leaving the water underneath perfectly clear.

In order to ascertain if these animals would materially alter their size, or assume the figure of any other known species of medusæ, I kept them alive for 25 days, by carefully changing the water in which they were placed ; during which time, although they appeared as vigorous as when first taken, their form was not in the slightest degree altered, and their size but little increased. By this experiment I was confirmed in my opinion of their being a distinct species, as the young actiniæ and medusæ exhibit the form of the parent in a much shorter period than the above.

In September 1806, I took at Sandgate a number of the beræ fulgens, but no other species : they were of various dimensions, from the full size down to that of the medusa

scintillans on different parts of the coast of Sussex, also at Tenby, and at Milford Haven. I have likewise seen this species in the bogs of Dublin and Carlingford in Ireland.

In the month of April, last year, I caught a number of the *beröe fulgens* in the sea at Hastings; they were of various sizes, from about the half of an inch in length, to the bulk of the head of a large pin. I found many of them adhering together in the sea; some of the larger sort were covered with small ones, which fell off when the animals were handled, and by a person unaccustomed to observe these creatures, would have been taken for a phosphoric substance. On putting a number of them into a glass, containing clear sea water, they still showed a disposition to congregate upon the surface: I observed that when they adhered together, they showed no contractile motion in any part of their body, which explains the cause of the pale or white colour of the diffused light of the ocean. The flashes of light which I saw come from the sea at Herne bay, were probably produced by a sudden and general effort of the medusæ to separate from each other, and descend in the water.

The *medusa scintillans* almost constantly exists in the different branches of Milford Haven that are called pills. I have sometimes found these animals collected in such vast numbers in those situations, that they bore a considerable proportion to the volume of the water in which they were contained: thus, from a gallon of sea water in a luminous state, I have strained above a pint of these medusæ—I have found the sea, under such circumstances, to yield me more support in swimming, and the water to taste more disagreeably than usual—probably the difference of density, that has been remarked at different times in the water of the sea, may be referred to this cause.

All my own observations lead me to conclude that the *medusa scintillans*, is the most frequent source of the light of the sea around this country, and by comparing the accounts of others with each other, and with what I have myself seen, I am persuaded that it is so likewise in other parts of the world. Many observers appear to have mistaken this species for the *nereis noctiluca*, which was very natural, as they were prepossessed with the idea of the frequent existence of the one, and had no knowledge of the other. Some navigators have actually described this species of medusa without being aware of its nature. Bajon during his voyage from France to Cayenne, collected many luminous points in the sea, which he says, when examined by a lens, were found to be minute spheres; they disappeared in the air. Doctor le Roy, in sailing from Naples to France, observed the sparkling of the sea, which is usually produced by the medusa scintillans. By filtering the water, he separated the luminous particles from it, which he preserved in spirits of wine: they were, he says, like the head of a pin, and did not at all resemble the *nereis noctiluca* described by Vianelli; their colour approached a yellow brown, and their substance was extremely tender and fragile. Notwithstanding this striking resemblance to the medusæ scintillans, Le Roy,

in consequence of a preconceived theory, did not suppose what he saw were animals, but particles of an oily or bituminous nature.

The minute globules seen by Langstaff in the Indian Ocean, were, I think, in all probability, the scintillating species of medusæ, and on my showing him some of these animals I have preserved in spirits, he entertained the same opinion.

Professor Mitchell of New York, found the luminous appearance on the coast of America to be occasioned by minute animals, that from his description, plainly belonged to this species of medusa, notwithstanding which he supposed them to be a number of the nereis noctiluca.

The luminous animalcule, discovered by Forster off the Cape of Good Hope, in his voyage round the world, bears so strong a resemblance to the medusa scintillans that I am much disposed to believe them the same. He describes his animalcule as being a little gelatinous globule, less than the head of a pin; transparent, but a little brownish in its colour, and of so soft a texture, that it was destroyed by the slightest touch. On being highly magnified, he perceived on one side a depression, in which there was a tube that passed into the body, and communicated with four or five intestinal sacs.

Many writers have ascribed the light of the sea to other causes than luminous animals. Martin supposed it to be occasioned by putrefaction: Silberschlag believed it to be phosphoric: Professor J. Mayer conjectured that the surface of the sea imbibed light, which it afterwards discharged. Bajon and Gentil thought the light of the sea was electric, because it was excited by friction. Forster conceived that it was sometimes electric, sometimes caused from putrefaction, and at others by the presence of living animals. Fougeroux de Bondaroy believed that it came sometimes from electric fires, but more frequently from the putrefaction of marine animals and plants. But these authors have left their speculations unsupported by either arguments or experiments, and they are inconsistent with all ascertained facts upon this subject.

I shall terminate this paper by an enumeration of the several conclusions, that are the result of the observations I have been able to make upon the phenomena of animal light.

The property of emitting light is confined to animals of the simplest organization, but in general, exists only at certain periods, and in particular states of the animal's body. The power of showing light resides in a peculiar substance or fluid, which is sometimes situated in a particular organ, and at others diffused throughout the animal's body. The light is differently regulated, when the luminous matter exists in the living body, and when it is abstracted from it. In the first case, it is intermitting, or alternated with periods of darkness; is commonly produced or increased by a muscular effort, and is sometimes absolutely dependent upon the will of the animal. In the second case the luminous appearance is usually permanent until it becomes extinct, after which it may be restored by friction, concussion, and the application of warmth, which

last cause operates on the luminous matter (while in the living body) only indirectly by exciting the animal. The luminous matter in all situations, so far from possessing phosphoric properties, is incombustible, and loses the quality of emitting light, by being dried or much heated. The exhibition of light, however long it may be continued, causes no diminution of the bulk of the luminous matter. It does not require the presence of pure air, and is not extinguished by other gases.

The luminous appearance of living animals is not exhausted by long continuance, or frequent repetitions, nor accumulated by exposure to natural light; it is therefore not dependent upon any foreign source, but inheres as a property in a peculiarly organized animal substance or fluid, and is regulated by the same laws which govern all the other functions of living beings.

The light of the sea is always produced by living animals, and most frequently by the presence of the medusa scintillans. When great numbers of this species approach the surface, they sometimes coalesce together, and cause that snowy or milky appearance of the sea, which is so alarming to navigators. These animals, when congregated on the surface of the water, can produce a flash of light, somewhat like an electric corruscation. When the luminous medusæ are very numerous, as frequently happens in confined bays, they form a considerable portion of the mass of the sea, at which times they render the water heavier, and more nauseous to the taste; it is therefore advisable to always strain sea water before it is drunk.

From the Philadelphia Courier.

HARVEST.

Husbandman, lift up thine eyes and see
How the Lord of the harvest is blessing thee !
He causes the sun on thy fields to glow ;
He speaks the word, and the waters flow ;
The evil and good his bounties share,
The just and unjust are still his care ;
The grass at his bidding grows up around,
And herbs for the service of man abound ;
The cattle are his on a thousand hills,
They quench their thirst at crystal rills
Which spring up for them at the sound of his voice,
And the forests, and mountains, and valleys rejoice !
Husbandman, bow thy heart and knee,
For the Lord of the harvest calls to thee—
He calls to thee from the waving plain,
From the ripening corn, and the standing grain ;
He speaks to thee in the rolling thunder—
In each passing breeze—then listen and wonder :
" Hearken, O man, unto thee I call,
I am thy Maker, the God of all !"
Man, who goes forth in the morning to toil,
Who reaps the fruits of the teeming soil,
As evening advances thy labours close,
And wearied thou seekest the sweets of repose ;
O man, ere in slumber thy pillow is pressed,
Think of the God who has given thee rest !
Thine heart in grateful penitence raise,
O breathe unto him an hymn of praise ;
And the Lord of the harvest, who cares for thee,
Thy Father, thy Friend, and Redeemer will be !

Of all parts of wisdom, the practice is the best. Socrates was esteemed the wisest man of his time, because he turned his acquired knowledge into morality, and aimed at goodness more than greatness.

The Military Profession, unlawful for a Christian.

The following extracts from Letters on the Unlawfulness of the Military Profession for a Christian, are taken from the "Memoir of Gordon Hall, A. M., one of the first Missionaries of the American Board of Commissioners for Foreign Missions, at Bombay, by Horatio Bardwell." Glasgow, 1834.

"It will be perceived by the following extracts, as well as by a preceding letter,* that G. Hall was an advocate for the doctrine of peace. He uniformly and zealously opposed the principle of war in every shape, and on every occasion. He was not altogether unsuccessful in his efforts to lead others to adopt the same sentiment. It is known that two young English officers in the India service, with whom G. Hall was conversant, were brought into the same sentiments, chiefly through his instrumentality. It is believed both of these young gentlemen consider G. Hall as instrumental in their conversion to God, as well as of abandoning the principle of war.

"The following letters were written by G. Hall, to one of these young men."

"*Bombay, Aug.* 25, 1813.

"My dear Friend,—Yours of the 23d came to hand last evening. I rejoice that the Lord has not forsaken you, that he does not leave you to sin, without being sensible of it, that he is teaching you the depravity of your heart, the vanity of this world, the necessity of Christ, and the duty of taking up the cross and following him. How great is that grace, which inclined your heart to think of the Saviour!

"When we think of the treachery of our hearts, where should we find any hope, had not God said, I will not forsake my people! In our hearts all is discouragement—in Christ, all is encouragement. Without Christ, we can do nothing—through Christ strengthening us, we can do all things.

"You desire me to be very explicit on 'the matter of war, and respecting its being justifiable or not.' You cannot mean that I should enter into a full discussion of the whole subject; it would require a volume. I perfectly agree with you in viewing the three cases of war which you have mentioned, as entirely contrary to the gospel. If these three are the only cases in which you are liable to be called to fight, and if you deem it contrary to fight in either of these cases, then your way is clear. You must leave the army, or do violence to your conscience.

"As to war and violence, in every shape, I am as confident that it is utterly contrary to the spirit of the gospel, as I am that theft or any other immorality is so. You cannot expect me to collect and arrange the arguments against it. Just look at this command, 'Put ye on the Lord Jesus.' Assume his character —be holy and harmless as he was—be meek, lowly, gentle, and inoffensive as he was. Love your enemies. pray for them, and do them good, as he did. Peter, in his zeal to defend his master (and what cause could be more justifiable?) cut off an ear of one of the mob. But Peter was reproved for drawing the

_____
* See last paragraph.

sword, and Christ wrought a miracle to heal his enemy. And when he was seized by his enemies, he was led like a lamb to the slaughter, he opened not his mouth. Such is the character we are to put on, and never, for a moment, to put off. Now, can the man who thus puts on Christ, thus abides in Christ, thus conforms to Christ, can he draw his sword and take the life of his fellow man, and hurry him to the bar of God?

"'Whatever ye would that men should do to you, do ye the same to them.'—Now is it possible for a man to commit any kind of violence, without breaking this command?

"We are commanded to *pray* for *all* men, and to pray without ceasing.—Who can reconcile this with the business of *killing* them?

"It is our duty to pray that *wars* may cease. But how would such a prayer sound on the lips of a man girded with the *sword?*—Let your heart be open to conviction—keep the Saviour before your eye, and you cannot remain in doubt on this subject."

"*Bombay, Sept.* 1813.

"Dear friend,—You say that your sins and your Saviour are constantly before your eyes. I rejoice at this. May it never be otherwise. David, that eminent servant of God, said, 'My sin is ever before me,' and again, 'I set the Lord always before me.' These were doubtless two important means, which he employed, in his becoming a man after God's own heart.

"You do well in making every step a subject of prayer. Could I say any thing to impress this duty still more deeply upon your mind, I should deem myself inexcusable in not doing it. Your trying circumstances do, in a very special manner, call you to prayerfulness.

"Concerning your resignation, I think you have taken a right course. It is unquestionably correct to reduce your inquiry to the single point,—' Is the profession of arms right, on *Bible* proof, or is it wrong?' If wrong, if sinful, it must be abandoned, come what may, —nothing is so daring and presumptuous as living in known sin. But, my friend, *feel* the importance of being taught by the *Holy Spirit.* If you see your duty, you will not pursue it, unless moved forward by the grace of God. If you begin the pursuit, you will finish it only through Christ strengthening you.

"The question before you is, whether you shall abandon what the world calls honourable, lucrative, and wise; and, in the place of it, take what the same world esteems folly, ignominy, and poverty. In this, you will find the world, satan, and all the wickedness of your own heart combined to oppose you. They will not mind defeats—if they do not succeed in one attack, they will plot another. In the great work of salvation, it is satan's policy, first, to hold the sinner in perfect stupidity; if he fails in this, he will endeavour to induce him to put it off for the present; if he does not succeed here, he will attempt to substitute error for truth. These are his devices, not only in the article of personal salvation, but in every step of Christian duty. May you be enabled to take refuge in Christ, who has overcome principalities and powers, and can

easily give you the victory over all these mighty foes."

"*Bombay, Sept.* 27, 1813.

"My dear friend,—Your's of the 18th came to hand on the 21st. We unitedly blessed God for his mercy to you. Neither we nor you can ever ascribe to him one thousandth part of that praise, which is his due; but let us do all we can, and pray for strength to do more. If God has truly enlightened your mind by a knowledge of his truth, and enabled you, in any measure, to do his will, how great the mercy! Such knowledge does not spring from any acuteness of mental discernment; for the natural man understandeth not the things of the Spirit, nor can he know them, because they are *spiritually* discerned. —You say, you are ignorant—and well may you say this. The Christian is a perpetual student; he has many things to study and to learn, before he can fully know what the Lord would have him do. So far as you have obtained a knowledge of God's will, you cannot hold it fast, unless you are strengthened by divine grace; much less can you, without the same grace, derive peace and comfort from that knowledge. While you fear that you are leaning to your own understanding, see well to it, that you do not fear still more to submit yourself to be taught of God—to sit at the feet of Jesus, with an entire willingness to hear and obey every direction he may give.

"You seem decided on the subject of war. I think all your subsequent reflections, if devout, will only confirm your decisions, and render you more thankful for that spiritual light and grace, which enabled you to make them. You request me ' to search, if there are any scriptural proofs in favour of war:' I could as soon look for proof that men may lie one to another, as that they may slaughter one another. The last passages on which my mind received satisfaction were Rom. xiii. 1—8; 1 Cor. vii. 20, 21. The objection arising from the first of these, you have answered, incontrovertibly; the second no more proves that the soldier must abide in his calling, than it does that the highwayman must abide in his.

"You say you cannot remain in the army, with a clear conscience, and shall therefore resign your commission,—but by retaining it and going to England on a furlough and then resigning, the passage will cost you only 1500 rupees, whereas if you resign *here* your passage will cost 4000. If your profession in the army is incompatible with your duty as a Christian, it can be no less sinful for you to continue in that profession for a *moment,* either on board ship or in England, than here; and to do it, for the sake of saving money to benefit your aged parents, or for any other purpose, would be 'doing evil, that good may come.'

"In the present stage of the business, I advise you to bring distinctly before your mind this solemn inquiry,—by what course of life you can do *most* for the glory of God, and retain a *conscience* void of offence."

"The following and last letter to this young officer, contains a discussion of a principle of very general application, and on which multitudes are deceived to their own ruin and the great injury of community; it therefore deserves the particular consideration of the reader."

" *Bombay, Oct. 5, 1813.*

" My dear sir,—The questions you propose are important, and not without difficulties. I consider myself as fearfully responsible to God for every word I write to you. I need much time to meditate upon and examine the subject. But as you desire me to write immediately, and as I shall only have time to receive another letter from you, before my expected departure, I send you such thoughts as occur to my mind without much meditation.

" Your first inquiry is this,—' Can I relinquish the present means of subsistence, which God has given me, till I have some reasonable hope of gaining my bread?'—You admit that your profession is a sinful one, which you cannot conscientiously follow. But, dear sir, will you charge God with putting you into this sinful profession, or providing such unholy means for your subsistence? Ought you not rather to consider, that in the pride, vanity, and thoughtlessness of your heart, *you put yourself* into this situation, contrary to his will, as made known to you in his word? And that God might justly call you to want and disgrace for it? Again, if your profession is a sinful one, is it better to run the risk of continuing a while in a course of sin, than to run the risk of wanting bread?

" You say, ' till I have some *reasonable* hope of gaining my bread ;' I would have you examine Pss. xxxiv. 9, 10, and lxxxiv. 11 ; Matt. vi. 25—34, and Mark x. 28—31. Now, do not the numerous promises of this kind, which God has made to his children, amount to so much as ' a *reasonable* hope of gaining your bread ?' Do not the terms of this inquiry look something like this ? If I could but *see* that my bread would be sure, then I would *trust* in God for it, and do what he commands; but till I have this ' reasonable hope,' I must take care of *myself.*—My dear sir, we are to walk by *faith,* and not by sight.

" You argue from the command, ' Abstain from all *appearance* of evil,' as though giving up a reasonable hope of gaining your bread had the ' appearance' of evil. But has it not something more than the ' appearance of evil' —is it not evil *itself*—to remain in an evil employment, though you might in your heart intend to make a pious use of the avails of that employment?

" But, after all, if the course you contemplate should bring you to hunger and even to death, would that be any argument against it? What has the faith of those of whom the world was not worthy, brought them to? (See Heb. xi. 36—39.) Can you suffer more than they did? and does their suffering prove that they chose a *wrong* course?

" Your next inquiry is, ' What shall you do for your dear parents in this trying situation?' This is a tender point. I shall only observe at present, that if your profession is a sinful one, *they* sinned in putting their son into it, and God might justly make them suffer for it. Certainly neither they nor any other persons have a right, for a moment, to bind you to that situation, which you cannot occupy,

without violating the precepts and will of your Saviour, nor can any consideration justify you in sustaining a profession, which you *know* to be disallowed by Christ."

The following extract is from the letter alluded to in the first paragraph.

" As to war, you may mark me for a thorough Quaker. I believe it is utterly opposed to the spirit of the gospel, for man, in any case, to draw his sword and stab his brother, —' bone of his bone, and flesh of his flesh.' I wish every body would read Barclay, Clarkson, and Dodge, on this subject. Though they have not advanced the whole weight of argument that might be presented, yet I think enough to convince every pious mind. How long did many good men advocate the slave trade,—but now what a phenomenon to such a man ! So it will soon be with war."

Extracts on the subjects of Slavery, from the journal and writings of John Woolman, of Mount Holly, New Jersey, a minister of the Society of Friends, who died at York, England, A. D. 1772.

1753.—A person at some distance lying sick, his brother came to me to write his will. I knew he had slaves, and asking his brother, was told he intended to leave them as slaves to his children. As writing is a profitable employ, and as offending sober people was disagreeable to my inclination, I was strained in my mind; but as I looked to the Lord, he inclined my heart to his testimony: and I told the man, that I believed the practice of continuing slavery to this people was not right; and had a scruple in my mind against doing writings of that kind :—that though many in our society kept them as slaves, still I was not easy to be concerned in it; and desired to be excused from going to write the will. I spake to him in the fear of the Lord, and he made no reply to what I said, but went away; he also had some concerns in the practice, and I thought he was displeased with me. In this case I had a fresh confirmation, that acting contrary to present outward interest, from a motive of divine love, and in regard to truth and righteousness, and thereby incurring the resentments of people, opens the way to a treasure better than silver, and to a friendship exceeding the friendship of man.

A neighbour receiving a bad bruise in his body, sent for me to bleed him ; which being done, he desired me to write his will; and amongst other things, he told me, to which of his children he gave his young negro. I considered the pain and distress he was in, and knew not how it would end; so I wrote his will, save only that part concerning his slave, and carrying it to his bedside, read it to him; and then told him, in a friendly way, that I could not write any instruments by which my fellow creatures were made slaves, without bringing trouble on my own mind. I let him know that I charged nothing for what I had done, and desired to be excused from doing the other part, in the way he proposed. We then had a serious conference on the subject; at length he agreeing to set her free, I finished his will.

Being on a religious visit in the southern provinces, he thus writes :

Soon after I entered this province, a deep and painful exercise came upon me, which I often had some feeling of, since my mind was drawn towards these parts.

As the people lived much on the labour of slaves, many of whom are used hardly, my concern was, that I might attend with singleness of heart, to the voice of the true Shepherd, and be so supported as to remain unmoved at the faces of men.

As it is common for Friends, on such a visit, to have entertainment free of cost, a difficulty arose in my mind, with respect to saving my money, by kindness received, which to me appeared to be the gain of oppression. Receiving a gift, considered as a gift, brings the receiver under obligations to the benefactor, and has a natural tendency to draw the obliged into a party with the giver. To prevent difficulties of this kind, and to preserve the minds of judges from any bias, was that Divine prohibition; " Thou shalt not receive any gift: for a gift blindeth the wise, and perverteth the words of the righteous."

Being helped to sink down into resignation, I felt a deliverance from that tempest in which I had been sorely exercised, and in calmness of mind, went forward, trusting that the Lord Jesus Christ, as I faithfully attended to him, would be a counsellor to me in all difficulties ; and that by his strength I should be enabled even to leave money with the members of society, where I had entertainment, when I found, that emitting it would obstruct that work to which I believed he had called me. And as I copy this after my return, I may here add, that oftentimes I did so, under a sense of duty. The way in which I did it was this: when I expected soon to leave a Friend's house where I had entertainment, if I believed that I should not keep clear from the gain of oppression, without leaving money, I spoke to one of the heads of the family privately, and desired them to accept those pieces of silver, and give them to such of their negroes as would make the best use of them ; at other times, I gave them to the negroes myself, as the way looked clearest to me. Offering them to some who appeared to be wealthy people, was a trial both to me and them ; but the fear of the Lord so covered me at times, that my way was made easier than I expected ; and few, if any, manifested any resentment at the offer, and most of them, after some talk, accepted them.

On the way, happening in company with a colonel of the militia, who appeared to be a thoughtful man, I took occasion to remark on the difference, in general, between a people used to labour moderately for their living, training up their children in frugality and business, and those who live on the labour of slaves ; the former in my view, being the most happy life : with which he concurred, and mentioned the trouble arising from the untoward, slothful disposition of the negroes ; adding that one of our labourers would do as much in a day, as two of their slaves. I replied that free men, whose minds were properly on their business, found a satisfaction in improving, cultivating, and providing for their families ; but negroes labouring to support others, who claim them as their property, and expecting nothing but slavery during life, had not the like inducement to be industrious.

After some further conversation, I said, that men having power, too often misapplied it; that though we made slaves of the negroes, and the Turks made slaves of the Christians, I, however, believed that liberty was the right of all men equally; which he did not deny, but said, the lives of the negroes were so wretched in their own country, that many of them lived better here than there. I only said, there is great odds in regard to us, on what principle we act; and so the conversation on that subject ended. And I may here add, that another person, sometime afterward, mentioned the wretchedness of the negroes, occasioned by their intestine wars, as an argument in favour of our fetching them away for slaves; to which I then replied, if compassion on the Africans, in regard to their domestic troubles, were the real motives of our purchasing them, that spirit of tenderness being attended to, would incite us to use them kindly; that as strangers brought out of affliction, their lives might be happy among us; and as they are human creatures, whose souls are as precious as ours, and who may receive the same help and comfort from the Holy Scriptures as we do, we could not omit suitable endeavours to instruct them therein; but while we manifest, by our conduct, that our views in purchasing them, are to advance ourselves; and while our buying captives taken in war, animates those parties to push on that war, and increase desolation among them: to say they lived unhappy in Africa, is far from being an argument in our favour. And I further said, the present circumstances of these provinces, to me appear difficult; that the slaves look like a burdensome stone, to such who burden themselves with them; and that if the white people retain a resolution to prefer their outward prospects of gain, to all other considerations, and do not act conscientiously towards them, as fellow creatures, I believe that burden will grow heavier and heavier, till times change in a way disagreeable to us: at which the person appeared very serious, and owned, that in considering their condition, and the manner of their treatment in these provinces, he had sometimes thought it might be just in the Almighty so to order it.

The sense I had of the state of the churches, brought a weight of distress upon me. The gold appeared to me to be dim, and the fine gold changed; and though this is the case too generally, yet the sense of it, in these parts, hath, in a particular manner, borne heavy upon me. It appeared to me, that through the prevailing spirit of this world, the minds of many were brought to an inward desolation; and instead of the spirit of meekness, gentleness, and heavenly wisdom, which are the necessary companions of the true sheep of Christ, a spirit of fierceness, and the love of dominion, too generally prevailed. From small beginnings in errors, great buildings, by degrees, are raised, and from one age to another, are more and more strengthened by the general concurrence of the people: and as men obtain reputation by their profession of the truth, their virtues

are mentioned as arguments in favour of general error; and those of less note, to justify themselves, say, such and such good men did the like. By what other steps could the people of Judah arise to that height in wickedness, as to give just ground to the prophet Isaiah, to declare, in the name of the Lord, that "*none* calleth for justice, nor *any* pleadeth for truth." Is. lix. 4. Or for the Almighty to call upon the great city of Jerusalem, just before the Babylonish captivity, "If ye can find a man, if there be any who executeth judgment, that seeketh the truth, and I will pardon it." Jer. v. 1. The prospect of a road lying open to the same degeneracy, in some parts of this newly settled land of America, in respect to our conduct towards the negroes, hath deeply bowed my mind in this journey; and though, briefly to relate how these people are treated, is no agreeable work, yet after often reading over the notes I made as I travelled, I find my mind engaged to preserve them. Many of the white people in those provinces, take little or no care of negro marriages; and when negroes marry, after their own way, some take so little account of those marriages, that with views of outward interest, they often part men from their wives, by selling them far asunder. * * * Many, whose labour is heavy, are followed, at their business in the field, by a man with a whip, hired for that purpose, and have in common little else allowed, but one peck of Indian corn, and some salt for one week, with a few potatoes; the potatoes they commonly raise by their labour on the first day of the week.

The correction ensuing on their disobedience to overseers, or slothfulness in business, is often very severe, and sometimes desperate.

Men and women have many times scarce clothes enough to cover them, and boys and girls, ten and twelve years old, are often without clothing amongst their master's children.

A few use some endeavours to instruct those they have in reading; but in common, this is not only neglected, but disapproved. These are the people, by whose labour the other inhabitants are in a great measure supported, and many of them, in the luxuries of life; these are the people, who have made no agreement to serve us, and who have not forfeited their liberty that we know of; these are the souls for whom Christ died: and for our conduct towards them, we must answer before Him, who is no respecter of persons.

They who know the only true God, and Jesus Christ, whom He hath sent, and are thus acquainted with the merciful, benevolent, gospel spirit, will therein perceive that the indignation of God is kindled against oppression and cruelty; and in beholding the great distress of so numerous a people, will find cause for mourning.

To rational creatures bondage is uneasy, and frequently occasions sourness and discontent in them: which affects the family, and those who claim the mastery over them: and thus people and their children are many times encompassed with vexations, which arise from their applying to wrong methods to get a living.

Treasures though small, obtained on a true principle of virtue, are sweet in the possession; and while we walk in the light of the

Lord, there is true comfort and satisfaction. Here neither the murmurs of an oppressed people, nor throbbing uneasy conscience, nor anxious thoughts about the event of things, hinder the enjoyment of it.

A Friend of some note in Virginia, who hath slaves, told me, that, being far from home on a lonesome journey, he had many serious thoughts about them; and that his mind was so impressed therewith, that he believed he saw a time coming, when Divine Providence would alter the circumstance of these people, respecting their condition as slaves.

He thus speaks of attending the Yearly Meeting, of which he was a member, held in Philadelphia, 1759:

In this Yearly Meeting, * * * the case of slave keeping lay heavy upon me. * * * When this case was opened, several faithful Friends spake weightily thereto, with which I was comforted; and feeling a concern to cast in my mite, I said in substance, as follows : " In the difficulties attending us in this life, nothing is more precious than the mind of truth, inwardly manifested; and it is my earnest desire, that in this weighty matter, we may be so truly humbled, as to be favoured with a clear understanding of the mind of truth, and follow it; this would be of more advantage to the society, than any medium not in the clearness of Divine wisdom. The case is difficult to some who have them; but if such set aside all self-interest, and come to be weaned from the desire of getting estates, or even from holding them together, where truth requires the contrary, I believe way will open that they will know how to steer through those difficulties."

Many Friends appeared to be deeply bowed under the weight of the work, and manifested much firmness in their love to the cause of truth, and universal righteousness on the earth: and, though none did openly justify the practice of slave-keeping in general, yet some appeared concerned, lest the meeting should go into such measures, as might give uneasiness to many brethren ; alleging, that if Friends patiently continued under the exercise, the Lord, in time to come, might open a way for the deliverance of these people. I, finding an engagement to speak, said, " My mind is often led to consider the purity of the Divine Being, and the justice of his judgments; and herein my soul is covered with awfulness. Many slaves on this continent are oppressed, and their cries have reached the ears of the Most High. Such are the purity and certainty of his judgments that he cannot be partial in our favour. In infinite love and goodness, he hath opened our understandings from one time to another, concerning our duty towards this people; and it is not a time for delay. Should we now be sensible of what he requires of us, and through a respect to the private interest of some persons, or through a regard to some friendships, which do not stand on an immutable foundation, neglect to do our duty in firmness and constancy, still waiting for some extraordinary means to bring about their deliverance; it may be by terrible things in righteousness, God may answer us in this matter."

(To be continued.)

[From the Farmers' Cabinet.]
FRUIT TREES.

The following extracts from a foreign work will show the young people of our country how they keep up a succession of fruit trees in Germany, and perhaps it may stimulate some of them to imitate so laudable an example.

"In the duchy of Gotha, in Germany, there are many villages which obtain a rent of many hundred dollars a year for their fruit trees, which are planted on the road-side, and on the commons. Every *new-married couple* is bound to plant two young fruit trees. The rent arising from the trees thus planted is applied to the uses of the parish or town.

In order to preserve the plantations from injury or depredation, the inhabitants of the parish are all made answerable; each of whom is thus on the watch over the other; and if any one is caught in the act of committing any injury, all the damage done in the same year, the authors of which cannot be discovered, is attributed to him, and he is compelled to atone for it, according to its extent, either by fine or corporal punishment."

"A gentleman at Colchester, England, makes it a rule, whenever he builds a cottage, to plant a vine against its walls, and two or three apple and pear trees near to it, or in the garden, and thus he confers a greater benefit on his tenant, by giving him an innocent source of gratification to his children, and an excitement to a little extra industry on his own part, than if he had let him a comfortless, mean-looking hovel, at half the rent."

A few ornamental trees and shrubs, disposed with good taste about a farm-house, add much to the beauty and pleasantness of the scene; and they never fail to make a favourable impression, on the mind of a visitor, of the character of the inmates of the mansion. A season should never be suffered to pass by without some addition being made, by the young people, to the ornaments of the yard, garden, or lane leading to the house. Some families have displayed their industry, taste, and good judgment, in this respect, so conspicuously as to command the admiration of their neighbourhood, and to excite the curiosity of travellers to inquire "who lives there?" Z.

Green vegetable matter for manure.—The value of green vegetables, when put under the soil and submitted to the process of decomposition, does not appear to be fully appreciated by the farmer. The more rapid the growth of a plant, the more efficacious is it in restoring exhausted soils, a result, perhaps depending on the fact, that such plants derive a large portion of their support from the atmosphere, and of course return to the earth more than they take from it. Buckwheat and clover are striking instances of this power in green crops to fertilize soils, and both have been extensively used for this purpose. Green manuring has been more used for grain crops than for roots, but the following experiment made by Professor Parks, in 1839, will show that the good effects are not less conspicuous on roots than on grain.

"I had a trench opened of sufficient length to receive six sets of potatoes, under three of which I placed green cabbage leaves, while the other three had nothing but the soil. When the crop was dug up, the plants over the cabbage leaves yielded about double the produce of the other."—*Cultivator.*

THOUGHTS FOR PARENTS.

Here we address the following exhortations to all persons, parents or tutors, who are charged with the task of education, beseeching them to give serious attention thereto.
1. Be what the children ought to be.
2. Do what the children ought to do.
3. Avoid what they should avoid.
4. Aim always, that not only in the presence of the children, but also in their absence, your conduct may serve them for an example.
5. Are any among them defective? *Examine what you are yourself*, what you avoid—in a word, your whole conduct.
6. Do you discover in yourself defects, sins, wanderings? Begin by improving yourself, and seeking afterwards to improve your children.
7. Think well that those by whom you are surrounded, are often only the reflection of yourself.
8. If you lead a life of penitence, and seek daily to have grace given you, it will be imparted to you, and through you to your children.
9. If you always seek Divine guidance, your children will more willingly be directed by you.
10. The more obedient you are to God, the more obedient will your children be to you; thus in his childhood the wise Solomon asked of the Lord "an obedient heart," in order to be able to govern his people.
11. As soon as the master becomes lukewarm in communion with God, that lukewarmness will extend itself among his pupils.
12. That which forms a wall of separation between God and yourself, will be a source of evil to your children.
13. An example in which love does not form a chief feature, is but as the light of the moon; it is cold and feeble.
14. An example animated by an ardent and sincere love, shines like the sun; it warms and invigorates.—*London S. S. Mag.*

THE FRIEND.

EIGHTH MONTH, 22, 1840.

Among other proofs of the kindness of friends in England received by the recent arrivals, is a little tract, "The Military Profession Unlawful for a Christian,"—the perusal of which has afforded us peculiar satisfaction; and believing that its more extensive circulation will be useful, we have placed it entire on our pages of to-day. To the meek and the simple—the truly humble seeker, most of the leading truths of the gospel may respectively be couched in a single proposition and very brief commentary; they become obscure only through the sophistications of carnal reasoning. Take for example the following from the tract

"Just look at this command, 'Put ye on the Lord Jesus.' Assume his character—be holy and harmless as he was—be meek, lowly, gentle, and inoffensive as he was. Love your enemies, pray for them, and do them good, as he did."

We would suggest to the Tract Association of Friends in this city, the propriety of adding this to their list of truly valuable publications.

The extracts on the subject of slavery, from the journal and writings of John Woolman, are part of a tract published for an association of individual members of the Society of Friends, in the city of New York, and were forwarded with a view to insertion in "The Friend," by an esteemed individual of that city. We agree with her that a recurrence to the manner of proceeding of that bright example of what a Christian should be, in the prosecution of a cause which he had so much at heart, may be of use in the present day.

Agent Appointed.—Garret Pim, East Rochester, Columbiana county, Ohio.

MARRIED, on the 4th of sixth month last, at Friends' Meeting, Weston, Marion county, Ohio, GRIFFITH LEVERING, of West Nottingham, Cecil county, Maryland, to ESTHER L. BENEDICT, of the former place.

——, at Friends' Meeting, Blue River, Indiana, on the 9th of seventh month, 1840, MATTHEW TRUBLOOD, son of William Trublood, to MARTHA, daughter of William Draper.

DIED, 8th month seventh, JOHN HUMPHREYS, of this city, aged 49 years. He was religiously concerned to maintain the principles of our society, and was of exemplary deportment. He endured a painful illness with much patience and resignation, and towards the close of his life, the language of thanksgiving and praise to his Heavenly Father was heard to flow from his lips. His friends have the consoling assurance that his end was peace.

——, at Jamestown, Island of Canonicut, on the 11th instant, JOSEPH GREENE, in the 81st year of his age; an exemplary and useful member, and for many years an overseer of Rhode Island Monthly Meeting. His parents were valuable members of our religious society, and careful to instruct him in the principles and testimonies which distinguish us as a people. As he advanced in years, he gave ample evidence that the principles in which he was educated had become those of conviction and judgment. Living on an island, rendered communication with the main land and with Rhode Island difficult as he advanced in years; and the infirmities of old age increasing, he did not get much abroad; but continued until the last autumn diligent in the attendance of the meeting at Canonicut—always walking; and a part of the road being occasionally covered with the tide, he was sometimes even in winter under the necessity to wade through it barefoot. Possessing a strong and discriminating mind, and being deeply interested in the welfare of society, and concerned for the prosperity of truth, he attentively watched the introduction and spread of unsound principles in some of the neighbouring Yearly Meetings by E. H. and his followers; maintaining his testimony to the close of his life against all innovation in doctrine, and every departure from the faith once delivered to the saints, however specious the garb under which such a disposition might appear. His bodily sufferings were great during his last illness; but the language of the Psalmist seems to represent both the state of his mind and the feelings of those who were with him at the close: "Mark the perfect man, and behold the upright, for the end of that man is peace."

——, on the 1st day of the eighth month, 1840, at his residence near Canton, Indiana, after a short illness, CHARLES POOL, a member of Blue River Monthly Meeting, in the 33d year of his age.

THE FRIEND.

A RELIGIOUS AND LITERARY JOURNAL.

VOL. XIII.   SEVENTH DAY, EIGHTH MONTH, 29, 1840.   NO. 48.

EDITED BY ROBERT SMITH.

PUBLISHED WEEKLY.

Price two dollars per annum, payable in advance.

Subscriptions and Payments received by

GEORGE W. TAYLOR,

NO. 50, NORTH FOURTH STREET, UP STAIRS,

PHILADELPHIA.

For "The Friend."

THE REMEDY FOR THE SLAVE TRADE.

(Continued from p. 370.)

The natural productions and commercial resources of Africa are inexhaustible; from experienced merchants and travellers into the interior, we gather that nature has scattered her bounties with the most lavish hand; and that what is required to make them available to the noblest purposes, is a legitimate commerce sustained by the government, and directed by honourable men.

Besides the wild beasts whose skins are valuable, immense herds of cattle, incalculable in number, range its plains; and excellent beef may be obtained at some of our settlements, at from 2d. to 3d. per pound. Sheep and goats are numerous; pigs can be had in any numbers; poultry literally swarms, and fish of all kinds visit the waters in immense schools.

The mineral kingdom has not yet been explored, but enough is already known to show that the precious metals abound, particularly gold. Iron is found in Western Africa. The ore from Sierra Leone is peculiarly rich, yielding 75 per cent. according to M'Cormack; that from Upper Senegal was found to be good. It is also found near Timbuctoo; and wrought by the Arabs. The mountains of Congo are said to be almost all ferruginous. Copper is so abundant in Mayomba, that they gather from the surface of the ground enough for their purposes. Sal ammoniac is found plentifully in Dagwumba, and is sold cheap in the Ashantee market; nitre, emery, and trona, are found on the border of the desert.

But Buxton regards the productions of the vegetable kingdom as of infinitely more value. He looks to the forests, and the plains, and the vallies, and the rich alluvial deltas, which it would take centuries to exhaust of their fertility and products. Fifty miles from Sierra Leone is the delta of the Seeong Boom, Kitiam and Gallinas rivers, containing from 1000 to 1500 square miles of the richest alluvial soil, capable of growing all tropical produce.

From Cape St. Paul to Cameroons, and from thence to Cape Lopez, extends the richest country that imagination can conceive. Within this space from forty to fifty rivers enter the ocean, forming vast flats, to the extent of 180,000 square miles! With a few inconsiderable exceptions, the whole coast of Western Africa, accessible to trading vessels, presents immense tracts of land of the most fertile character. But it is not to the coast alone that the merchant may look for the results of his enterprise. The interior is represented as equally fertile, and its productions would probably embrace all the marketable commodities of both Indies.

Mahogany, teak, ebony, lignum vitæ, rosewood, and many other beautiful and hardgrained trees, as yet unnamed by Europeans, grow most abundantly in the woods—with great quantities of ship-timber of the choicest kinds. Dye-woods of great variety abound, and the most precious gums. Nuts, some of which are scarcely known to us yet, are beginning already to form an important article of trade. There are the palm-nut, the shea-nut, highly valuable for their oil, the cola-nut, the ground-nut, the castor-nut, the nitta-nut, and the cocoa-nut. All the tropical fruits, and many of the grains of the temperate zones thrive luxuriantly. Of drugs, there are aloes and cassia, senna, frankincense, cardamums, and grains of paradise, or Malagetta pepper. A beautiful cordage is made from the fibres of the aloe, by Mr. Pavy of Paris, who also manufactures glossy stuffs from those of the palm and banana trees. Hemp grows wild on the Gambia, and the same may be said of tobacco. Indigo grows so freely, that, in some places, it is difficult to eradicate it. "Immense quantities" of it spring up in the streets of Freetown. It is known to grow wild as far inland as the Tchad, and gives a beautiful dye to the native cloths. Sugar canes grow spontaneously in several parts of Africa, and when cultivated become very large.

But before all these cotton should claim our attention; because it requires little capital, yields a steady return, is in vast demand in Europe, and grows naturally in the soil of Africa. The vast tropical districts along the southern side of the Great Desert, the fine plains, and gently rising country from the northern bank of the Rio de Formosa, and from the Niger to the base of the Kong mountains, are adapted to the culture of the finest cotton. This portion of Africa alone, so rich in soil, so easy of access, offers an independent and abundant supply of it.

But it may be said, centuries must elapse before the land can be made to yield any quantity of that article. An anecdote, however, which I heard stated to the Marquis of Normanby, by a gentleman whose mercantile knowledge would not be disputed by any one, may serve to forbid despair. He stated that the person who first imported from America a bale of cotton into this country was still alive, and that the custom-house officer at Liverpool (the port of importation) refused to admit it a American, because no cotton could be grown there; yet that country which could grow no cotton, now, besides supplying her own demand, and that of all other countries, sends annually to Great Britain a quantity valued at about £15,000,000 sterling.

I propose then that an effort shall be made to cultivate districts of Africa; we should touch at a few prominent points,—at each of these a mart should be established, and something might be done towards the education of the children of those who entered our service.

Great, no doubt, are the difficulties; yet, such are the discoveries of the last ten years, that we may now lay aside the impression of an impenetrable continent, and of interminable wastes of sand, which have accompanied us from our childhood. We now know that a mighty river which discharges itself into the Bight of Benin, by upwards of twenty mouths, is navigable, with little interruption, from thence nearly to its source, a distance of more than 2600 miles. We also learn from the travellers who have navigated the Niger, that there are many tributary streams, some of which, especially the Tschadda, or Shaderbah, are equally navigable, and afford every facility for intercourse with the numerous nations and tribes who inhabit the countries in their vicinity.

Here then is one of the most magnificent rivers in the world, introducing us into the heart of Africa: at a central point it opens a way by its eastern branch, to the kingdoms of Bornou, Kanem and Begharmi; by its western, to Timbuctoo,—each bringing us into communication with multitudes of tribes, and unfolding to us the productions of a most extensive and fertile territory.

The problem is, how shall that stream be closed to the passage of slaves to the coast; while it is at the same time opened as a secure and accessible highway for legitimate commerce. The solution seems almost self-evident: we must obtain the positions which command the Niger; and, without doubt, the most important of these is Fernando Po. It is situated about twenty miles from the main land, in the Bight of Biafra, and commands the mouths of those great streams, about forty in number, which penetrate so deeply into central Africa, along the coast from the Rio Volta to the Gaboon. It is exceedingly fertile, yet healthy. Its length is twenty-four miles, breadth sixteen, and extreme height above the sea 10,000 feet.

Laird thus describes its aspect: "The splendid scenery that distinguishes this beautiful island, is well known from former descriptions, and to persons coming from the low marshy shore of the main land has indescribable charms.

"The view from the galleries of the government-house, on a clear moonlight night, I never saw equalled, nor can I conceive it surpassed. To the north east, the lofty peak of the Camaroons throws its shadow half way across the narrow strait that separates the island from the main land; while the numerous little promontories and beautiful coves that grace the shores of Goderich bay, throw light and shadow so exquisitely upon the water, that one almost can imagine it a fairy land. On the west, the spectator looks down almost perpendicularly on the vessels in the Clarence Cove, which is a natural basin surrounded by cliffs of the most romantic shape, and a group of little islands, which nature seems to have thrown in to give a finish to the scene.

"Looking inland, towards the island, the peak is seen, covered with wood to the summit, with its sides furrowed with deep ravines, and here and there a patch of cleared land, showing like a white spot in the moonlight."

We are also informed that from the elevation of 3500 feet above the sea, there is always found the climate of an European summer.

The shores are bold, and, with hardly an exception, free from those swamps, which, on the coasts of the main land, generate the fatal malaria so destructive to Europeans. The island, moreover, is free from hurricanes, and there are several bays of convenient access, and good anchorage. Commodore Bullen says, scarcely a vessel could leave the Bonny, Calabars, Bimbia and Camaroons rivers, without being observed time enough to notify any vessel in Maidstone bay to intercept her. "You have not," said a gentleman who had resided there nine years, "an island, either in North or South Atlantic, equal to Fernando Po for shipping: a vessel may anchor there all the year round in perfect safety." Laird says, "My proposal is, to make the government's head-quarters at Fernando Po, which is the key to central Africa. It is also the only place upon that whole coast, on which hospitals, &c. could be erected above the reach of fever, where invalids might recruit in a pure and bracing atmosphere."

Fernando Po, therefore, possesses in a remarkable manner the advantages of which we stand in need [whether the object be to capture the slave-trader, or to encourage legitimate commerce]. I confess I look forward to the day when Africa shall unfold her hidden treasures to the world; and as a primary means of enabling her to do so, this island is of incalculable value. And, whereas, we now consign the negroes captured from slavers, in vast numbers, to the destruction, consequent on a long voyage to Sierra Leone, they could be landed here within a few hours or days; and if located here, would afford material for a normal school, for the introduction of agriculture, civilization, and Christianity into the interior of Africa.

(To be continued.)

NATCHEZ TORNADO.

We derive the following from the Medical Examiner, a respectable journal, published in this city, in which it is quoted as having originally appeared in the Western Journal of Medicine and Surgery. Besides reciting a number of circumstances not included in the previous notices which we have given of this memorable event, it discusses the subject in a more regular and philosophical way, and in a manner, we think, calculated to interest the readers of "The Friend."

—

We have seen several short notices of this desolating tempest by gentlemen of Natchez, from which we propose embodying some of the more remarkable facts. According to Dr. Tooley, whose account is the fullest that we have read, the morning of the fatal 7th of May was densely overcast, and very warm, with a brisk south wind which increased about noon, veering to the east. The southwestern sky at mid-day assumed a darker and more tempestuous aspect, the gloom and turbulence increasing every moment; and by forty-five minutes after twelve the storm began to be distinctly heard, the wind blowing a gale from the northeast. The roar of the tempest, which grew louder and more terrific as it advanced rapidly upon the city, was attended with incessant flashes of forked lightning. At 1.45, Dr. Tooley describes the storm-cloud as assuming "an almost pitchy darkness, curling, rushing, roaring above, below, a lurid yellow, dashing upward, and rapidly approaching, striking the Mississippi some six or seven miles below the city, spreading desolation upon each side, the western side being the centre of the annulus. At this time a blackness of darkness overspread the heavens; and when the annulus approached the city, the wind suddenly veered to the S. E. S, attended with such crashing thunder as shook the solid earth. At 2.10 the tornado burst upon the city, dashing diagonally through it, attended with such murky darkness, roaring and crashing, that the citizens saw not, heard not, knew not the wide wasting destruction around them." The rush of the tornado over the city occupied a space of time not exceeding five minutes, and the destructive blast not more than a few seconds. At this moment the barometer fell, according to one writer, to nearly 29.

The disastrous effects of the storm are too well known to the readers of the Journal to require a lengthened description. "Natchez under the Hill," with the exception of one or two houses, was razed to the ground, and nearly every private dwelling and public edifice in the city sustained more or less injury. Hundreds of houses were unroofed, or had their gable ends or windows blown out; of three steamboats at the wharf, two were sunk, and the third, which was freighted with lead, had its upper works blown away to the water's edge; not less than sixty flat boats parted their cables, and were swamped; and three hundred human beings, it is computed, perished on the land and in the river during the few moments in which the tempest was passing. Few such storms are recorded in the history of the United States; but as hurricanes of destructive violence occur almost every year in some part of the country, it becomes a matter of somewhat more than curious interest to ascertain the laws by which they are governed, and the mode in which they exert their tremendous force. We were informed by Dr. Cartwright, that Dr. Tooley preserved his house from all injury, even the breaking of a pane of glass, by adopting the measures which his theory of storms suggested. That theory was the explosive one—that, where houses are demolished by a tornado, it is in consequence of the sudden expansion of the air within, caused by the instantaneous rarefaction of the external atmosphere. Dr. Tooley observed, that as the storm approached, the mercury in his barometer sunk rapidly; and he prepared for the expansion of the air in his house by raising all the windows, and throwing open the doors. His house was not so well built to resist a storm as many of those in his neighbourhood which were prostrated, or sustained more or less damage, and its escape can only be accounted for by the fact, that he provided for the exit of the air which, confined, must have blown out the windows, as happened in many instances, if it had not blown down the house. A wing of Dr. Cartwright's house was blown down, but the main body of it, which was of a very substantial structure, escaped with the loss of its chimneys, and the bursting out of the windows.

What is the rationale of tornadoes? Is the force exerted owing to the gyratory motion of the atmosphere, or to a sudden rarefaction in some portion of it, causing a corresponding expansion of those portions immediately under it or around it? In many storms there can be no doubt, that the gyrations of the atmosphere do the mischief, as where forest trees are seen twisted off. In other cases the violent sweep of the atmosphere bears down all before it. But in Natchez the wind is said not to have been more violent than the persons who were present had often seen it when no extensive mischief was done; and this tornado, from a multitude of facts collected, seems to have been of the class in which the ruin results from explosions. The following may be cited from a great number:

1. The gardener of Dr. Cartwright had just quit his employ, and in leaving his house neglected to close the doors and windows. It escaped without injury. The gardener of a friend, living in his immediate neighbourhood, hastened when he saw the storm approaching, and succeeded in closing his doors and windows, which he had scarcely done when the house fell upon him and killed him.

2. The garret of a brick house, mentioned in the account of Dr. Tooley, being closely shut up, both ends were burst outward, and with such explosive force, that some of the bricks of the windward end were thrown upon a terrace nearly on a level with it, to a distance of not less than twenty feet, in the face of the wind.

3. A brick house on the north side of Main street had its leeward gable end blown out, the windward end remaining uninjured.

4. The windward gable end of a large house adjoining the Commercial bank, bursted outward in the face of the storm, the leeward end escaping without injury.

5. The gable ends of a large three-story brick house on Franklin street were thrown

out with great violence, in opposite directions, and one, of course, against the wind.

6. The leeward ends of two brick stores were thrown outward with violence, while the windward ends escaped. The same happened to the leeward side of a large brick house close by.

7. In the neighbourhood of the last mentioned, another brick house had the windward gable end thrown outward.

8. The desks in the Agricultural bank, which were locked by the president as the storm commenced, were found open shortly after, with their locks bursted. In another instance, the drawer of a bureau was thrown quite out, while the bureau itself was found in its previous position.

9. The leeward walls of two front rooms of the Tremont House were thrown outward with great force, without injuring or disturbing the furniture within.

10. The gable ends of a large brick store on Main and Pearl streets were blown out; the roof of the fire-proof brick office of the Probate court exploded to windward; and in a house on State street a large trap-door in the roof was bursted open, giving an outlet to the air, and saving the roof.

Hundreds of such facts, it is said by persons who have surveyed the ruins, might be adduced, showing, that where sufficient openings were not afforded to the expanding air, the roof, windows, or some other part of the house gave way, and most generally to the leeward. A writer in one of the Natchez papers pledges himself to point out to the incredulous, in a walk through the city, *five hundred explosions* —instances in which the violence done can only be explained by the outward action of the atmosphere.

We have a parallel case in the *break-bottle* experiment with the air-pump, in which a thin square bottle, hermetically sealed, is shivered into a thousand fragments, under the exhausted receiver, by the expansion of the confined air. The pressure of the atmosphere over the city was suddenly diminished nearly one thirtieth, as was shown by the fall of the barometer, and rooms containing four thousand cubic feet of air, were thus subjected, it has been estimated, to a pressure from within of eighty-six tons more than from without. The consequence was, that the windows were blown out when the walls were strong, and the equilibrium was thus restored; and in garrets, where the air was more confined, trap-doors were blown open, or gable ends thrown out with immense force. In some cases roofs were heaved up and removed, and often, as has been shown, walls were shot out in the face of the wind. The pressure of the atmosphere over the city being thus diminished nearly one thirtieth. Garrets being closer were oftener exploded than other apartments which were relieved by windows and doors; and for the same reason brick houses sustained more damage than those composed of wood. And, finally, in the "explosive" theory we have an explanation of the well-authenticated fact, that where doors and windows were unclosed, leeward and windward, houses, as was strikingly the case with Dr. Tooley's, escaped all injury. Whatever, therefore, may be the *modus operandi* of hurricanes generally, the conclusion seems irresistible, that in the tornado at Natchez the

demolition of buildings was occasioned by the rarefaction of the outer atmosphere, and a corresponding expansion of the air within, equalling the explosive force of gunpowder. Still, there are phenomena connected with the storm for which nothing but the supposition of " a mighty rushing wind" will account; and such a wind, in fact, is inseparable from the rarefied state of the air which led to the explosions. Into the air which thus presented a comparative vacuum, the surrounding atmosphere must have rushed with great violence; and it was this wind that uprooted forest trees, raised the immense waves in the Mississippi, and forced the boats from their moorings.

The quantity of rain which fell during the passage of the tornado, according to Dr. Tooley, was only 83-100ths of an inch, but holding in suspension mud and particles of leaves and other vegetable matter in such quantities as not only to darken the air, but leave a thick coating upon whatever it came in contact with.

Dr. Tooley closes his account of the tornado with a description of some curious effects produced by it upon the leaves and buds of plants: they were in a manner *seared* by it. Those which were not killed outright were crisped, and their growth suspended for ten or more days. Some very thriving grape cuttings in the garden of Dr. T. were killed, and the old vines were also stunted and injured. An arbour vitæ in his yard seemed blighted and dying; the leaves of the succulent morus multicaulis appeared for some days as if an eastern sirocco had passed over them ; and fruit trees, grass, and weeds, assumed the same appearance.

History of the Lehigh Coal and Navigation Company.

(Continued from page 371.)

It became evident that the business on the Lehigh could not be extended as fast as the demand for coal increased, while it was necessary to build a new boat for each load of coal; besides, the forests were now beginning to feel the waste of timber, (more than four hundred acres a year being cut off,) and showed plainly enough that they would soon disappear, in consequence of the increased demand upon them ; while, at the same time, the Schuylkill coal region had an uninterrupted slackwater navigation, which would accommodate boats in their passage up as well as down, and, of course, admitted any extension of the coal trade that might be deemed advisable. It should also be mentioned that almost the whole of the shares of the stock of the old " Coal Mine Company" had been purchased, so that the mines had become nearly the sole property of the Lehigh Coal and Navigation Company. These shares represented fiftieth parts of the whole property, and the purchase of them commenced at one hundred and fifty dollars per share ; the last was purchased for two thousand dollars, after the slackwater navigation had been made. Under all these circumstances, it was concluded that the time had arrived for changing the navigation of the Lehigh into a slackwater navigation. The acting managers, who resided at Mauch Chunk,

formed a plan for a steamboat navigation, with locks one hundred and thirty feet long, and thirty feet wide, which would accommodate a steamboat carrying one hundred and fifty tons of coal. These locks were of a peculiar construction, adapted to river navigation. The gates operated upon the same principle with the sluice-gates in the dams for making artificial freshets, and were raised or let down by the application or removal of a hydrostatic pressure below them. The first mile below Mauch Chunk was arranged for this kind of navigation. The locks proved to be perfectly effective, and could be filled or emptied, notwithstanding their magnitude, in three minutes, or about half the time of the ordinary lock. Application was then made to the legislature for an act for the improvement of the river Delaware upon this plan, but the commonwealth decided upon the construction of a canal along that river, provided the estimate of the expense of its construction should not exceed a limited amount per mile. This, of course, put an end to all thought of continuing the steamboat plan upon the Lehigh. Had this plan been adopted, there can be no doubt the transportation of coal upon it could have been effected *at an expense not exceeding four mills per ton per mile*, and the same steamboat could proceed (when the Delaware and Raritan canal was done) to New York, Albany, Providence, &c. &c. without transhipment.

The large quantity of coal which had been brought to market and sold in the previous year produced a profit which brought the semi-annual dividend fully up to three per cent. on the 1st of January, 1826, and placed all the stock of the company upon an equality from that time forward. In the previous years the dividend account stood as follows : January 1, 1822, the first dividend made, was confined to the preferred subscribers, who then received three per cent. on their subscription of fifty thousand dollars, and from that time larly afterward. July, 1822, gave the original subscribers one per cent., and from that time they regularly received three per cent., except in July, 1824, when the dividend to them was omitted. On the stock allotted to J. White and E. Hazard, a dividend of one per cent. was made, January, 1824, and of two and a half per cent. January, 1825. These were the only dividends in which they participated, previous to the one which equalized the stock.

In 1826, there were thirty-one thousand two hundred and eighty tons of coal sent down the Lehigh. The business was now becoming so large that it was difficult to keep the turnpike to the mines in good working order, without coating it with stone, and it was determined that the best economy would be to convert it into a railroad. The only railroad then in the United States was the Quincy railroad, about three miles in length, made in the fall of 1826. There had previously been a short wooden railroad, not plated with iron, at Leiper's stone-quarry, of about three quarters of a mile in length, but this was worn out, and not in use. The railroad from Mauch Chunk to the summit mines was commenced in January, and completely in operation in May, 1827. It is nine miles in length, and has a descent all the way from the summit mines to the river. The road is continued beyond the summit about three fourths of a mile, and descends into the mines west of the summit about sixty feet. With this exception, the whole transportation of the coal upon it is done by gravity, the empty wagons being returned to the mines by mules, which *ride down* with the coal. This, also, was an arrangement made at the suggestion of Josiah White, entirely novel in its character; and enabled the mules to make two and a half trips to the summit and back, thus travelling about forty miles each day. Numerous branch railroads are now constructed into the different parts of the mines.

In February, 1827, the balance of the stock, amounting to five hundred thousand dollars, was subscribed for; and, it having been decided that the Delaware division of the Pennsylvania canal would be made, it was determined to go on with a canal and slack-water navigation upon the Lehigh, from Mauch Chunk to Easton. Canvass White, whose character as a canal engineer stood as high as any in the country, was invited to take charge of the work. He recommended a canal to be constructed of the then ordinary size, to accommodate boats of twenty-five tons. But the acting managers argued that the same hands could manage a much larger boat, and the only additional expense for a boat of one hundred, to one hundred and fifty tons would be for a larger boat, and for an additional horse or two to tow it. The whole lading being coal, which could always be furnished in any quantity, there need be no detention for a cargo for the larger boat, and the expense per ton would be very much lessened. It was at last concluded that the engineer should make two estimates, the one for the canal to be forty feet wide, and the other for a canal of sixty feet wide, each with corresponding locks. The difference in the estimates for the two canals in that location was so small (about $30,000) that the largest size was unanimously adopted. The wisdom of this decision has been most clearly demonstrated, and other canal companies in the United States have since followed the example. The dimensions of the navigation were fixed at *sixty feet wide on the surface, and five feet deep; and the locks one hundred feet long, and twenty-two feet wide, adapted to boats of one hundred and twenty tons.* The work was at once laid out and let to contractors, who commenced their operations about midsummer.

The canal commissioners met soon after at Bristol, for the purpose of deciding upon letting the Delaware division of the Pennsylvania canal. They were applied to, to construct it so as to correspond with the work going on upon the Lehigh; it was, however, insisted that the experience of Europe had proved that a twenty-five ton boat was the size most cheaply managed; and that even upon the New York canal, which would admit of boats of forty tons, it rarely happened that the packets carried more than twenty-five tons. The commissioners at length concluded to make the locks of *half* the width, and of the same length as those on the Lehigh, so that two of the Delaware boats could pass at once through the

Lehigh locks, and thus save half the time in lockage. Had not the "experience of Europe" thus thwarted a noble work, sloops and schooners would, at this day, have taken in their cargoes at White Haven, *seventy-one miles up the Lehigh*, and have delivered them, without transhipment, at any of our Atlantic ports. The canal commissioners of the present day have already officially expressed to the legislature their anticipations that it will soon be necessary to enlarge the whole of the Delaware division, to enable it to pass the immense trade that will undoubtedly be poured into it from the Lehigh.

This enlargement of the Delaware canal must unquestionably take place soon, or the enlargement of the Morris canal, by our spirited neighbours of New York, will take off a very large proportion of its trade. The enlargement of twenty-six miles of the Delaware canal, and of thirteen of its locks below Easton, with an outlet to the river Delaware at Black's Eddy, opposite the feeder of the Delaware and Raritan canal, would *yet* admit sea vessels to load or discharge at White Haven. The Delaware division is now only calculated to pass boats of sixty tons through the locks.

As so large a portion of the Delaware division was made by embankments along the river, the probability is, that the full-sized canal would not have cost more than the one now constructed, and the transportation upon it would not have cost so much by one fourth. The Lehigh slackwater navigation, from Mauch Chunk to Easton, was opened for use at the close of June, 1829, while the Delaware division was not regularly navigable until nearly three years afterwards, although it was commenced but about four months after the Lehigh. The contractors upon the Delaware division were suffered to use improper materials, and when finished by them the canal would not hold water. It was, at length, left to the care of Josiah White to make it a good and permanently useful navigation.

The want of the Delaware division, after the Lehigh was completed, caused the failure of eight dividends to the Lehigh company, as they were obliged to continue the use of the temporary boats, which were very expensively moved on the Lehigh navigation, but were the only kind that could be used upon the channels of the Delaware river, which were still necessarily used to get to market. This not only prevented the increase of the company's coal business on the Lehigh, but also turned the attention of persons desirous of entering into the coal business to the Schuylkill coal region, which caused Pottsville to spring up with great rapidity, and furnish numerous dealers to spread the Schuylkill coal through the market, while the company was the only dealer in Lehigh coal. In this manner the Schuylkill coal trade got in advance of that of the Lehigh.

The capital of the company being limited, by the act of incorporation, to one million of dollars, which amount had been expended in the operations of the company prior to the completion of the slackwater navigation, it became necessary, in 1828, to consider the means to raise the necessary funds to carry on the

work. By this time a total change had taken place in the views of the community respecting the undertaking of the Lehigh company. The improvement of the Lehigh had been demonstrated to be perfectly practicable, and the extensive coal field owned by them was no longer considered to be of problematical value. The legislature of 1818 was *now* censured for having granted such valuable privileges, and all the "craziness" of the original enterprise was lost sight of. Hence applications to the legislature for a change in their charter were thwarted by the influence of adverse interests. With such opposition, it was in vain to apply to the legislature for an increase of capital, as it was evident that such a change could not be effected without a sacrifice of some of the valuable privileges secured by the charter of the company. Resort was therefore necessarily had to loans, to enable the company to complete the work required of them by law, and these were readily procured, in consequence of the good faith always evinced in the business of the company, and their evidently prosperous circumstances. The first loan was taken in 1828.

The claim upon the company arising from their assumption of the agreement of J. White and E. Hazard with G. F. A. Hauto for the purchase of his interest, before mentioned, was finally settled in 1830, by the purchase by the company of the remaining shares of the stock into which Hauto had converted his claim.

Upon the completion of the Delaware division of the Pennsylvania canal, the operations of the coal business were very much simplified by the change from temporary to permanent boats, and the consequent discharge of the host of hands required in chopping, hauling, sawing, rafting, piling, and otherwise preparing the large amount of lumber necessary for building, on the average of some years, of eleven to thirteen miles in length of boats, sixteen to eighteen feet wide. In 1831 the company constructed a railroad, about five miles long, from the landing to the mines which had been opened along Room Run, which, like the one from the summit mines, operates by gravity, but has a more gradual descent toward the river.

(To be continued.)

A medal of honour has been given by the French government to a young female, named Louise Roulland—who, at the age of 17, entered herself on board the fishing sloop Bon Pere, of Ligny, and has since been sharing in all the duties of the crew—for having saved, on different occasions, four persons from drowning, in the most courageous way. Another female, named Justin, has received the medal for having, with her brother, who has also had the medal, gone in a small boat through a heavy sea, to the relief of a vessel which was being wrecked, at a league from the shore, on the coast of Brittany, and saved three men and a woman who were on board. Another female, named Gernot, at Dinan, has had the medal for saving a child in the river Rance, although she could not swim, being the mother of four children herself, could hardly have expected to risk her life for a child not her own.—*Late pap.*

Extracts on the subject of Slavery, from the journal and writings of John Woolman, of Mount Holly. New Jersey, a minister of the Society of Friends, who died at York, England, A. D. 1772.

(Concluded from p. 373.)

As persons setting negroes free in our province, are bound by law to maintain them, in case they have need of relief; some who scrupled keeping slaves for term of life, in the time of my youth, were wont to detain their young negroes in their service till thirty years of age, without wages, on that account. With this custom I so far agreed, that I, being joined to another friend, in executing the will of a deceased friend, once sold a negro lad till he might attain the age of thirty years, and applied the money to the use of the estate.

With abasement of heart, I may now say, that sometimes, as I have sat in a meeting, with my heart exercised towards that awful Being, who respecteth not persons or colours, and have looked upon this lad, I have felt that all was not clear in my mind respecting him; and as I have attended to this exercise, and fervently sought the Lord, it hath appeared to me, that I should make some restitution, but in what way I saw not till lately; when being under some concern, that I may be resigned to go on a visit to parts of the West Indies; and under close engagement of spirit, seeking to the Lord for counsel herein: that of my joining in the sale aforesaid, came heavily upon me; and my mind for a time was covered with darkness and sorrow; and under this sore affliction, my heart was softened to receive instruction. Here I first saw, that as I had been one of the two executors, who had sold this lad nine years longer than is common for our own children to serve, so I should now offer a part of my subsistence, to redeem the last half of that nine years; but as the time was not yet come, I executed a bond, binding me and my executors, to pay to the man he was sold to, what to candid men might appear equitable, for the last four and a half years of his time, in case the said youth should be living, and in a condition likely to provide comfortably for himself.

[Being under great exercise of mind, respecting his prospect of duty to visit the West Indies; and also doubting the propriety of taking passage in a vessel, engaged in the West India trade, on account of the "oppression the slaves lie under, who raise the West India produce," he wrote the following. which he showed to the owners of a vessel engaged in this trade, and to sail about that time.]

" To trade freely with oppressors, and without labouring to dissuade from such unkind treatment, and seek for gain by such traffic, tends, I believe, to make them more easy respecting their conduct, than they would be, if the cause of universal righteousness was humbly and firmly attended to, by those in general with whom they have commerce; and that complaint of the Lord, by his prophet, ' They have strengthened the hands of the wicked,' hath very often revived in my mind; and I may here add some circumstances, preceding any prospect of a visit there. The case of David hath often been before me of

late years: he longed for some water in a well, beyond an army of Philistines, at war with Israel; and some of his men, to please him, ventured their lives in passing through this army, and brought that water. It doth not appear that the Israelites were then scarce of water, but rather, that David gave way to delicacy of taste; but having thought on the danger these men were exposed to, he considered this water as their blood, and his heart smote him that he could not drink it, but poured it out to the Lord. And the oppression of the slaves, which I have seen in several journies southward, on this continent, and the report of their treatment in the West Indies, hath deeply affected me; and a care to live in the spirit of peace, and minister just cause of offence to none of my fellow creatures, hath, from time to time, livingly revived on my mind. And under this exercise, I, for some years past, have declined to gratify my palate with those sugars."

"I do not censure my brethren in these things; but believe the Father of mercies, to whom all mankind by creation, are equally related, hath heard the groans of this oppressed people; and is preparing some to have a tender feeling of their condition: and the trading in, or frequent use of, any produce known to be raised by the labours of those, who are under such lamentable oppression, hath appeared to be a subject, which may yet more require the serious consideration of the humble followers of Christ, the Prince of peace."

"After long and mournful exercise, I am now free to mention how things have opened in my mind, with desires that if it may please the Lord, further to open his will to any of his children in this matter, they may faithfully follow him in such further manifestation."

Being visited with a fit of illness, and brought very low, he dictated to a Friend, as follows:

1 mo. 4, 1770. " I have seen in the light of the Lord, that the day is approaching, when the man that is the most wise in human policy, shall be the greatest fool ; and the arm that is mighty to support injustice, shall be broken to pieces: the enemies of righteousness shall make a terrible rattle, and shall mightily torment one another; for He that is omnipotent is rising up to judgment, and will plead the cause of the oppressed."

Extracts from a pamphlet written by J. Woolman, entitled Some Considerations on the Keeping of Negroes. Recommended to the professors of Christianity of every denomination.

" He, who, of old, heard the groans of the children of Israel, under the hard taskmasters in Egypt, I trust, hath looked down from his holy habitation, on the miseries of these deeply oppressed people. Many lives have been shortened through extreme oppression, while they laboured to support luxury and worldly greatness; and though many people in outward prosperity, may think little of these things, yet the gracious Creator hath regard to the cries of the innocent, however unnoticed by men.

The Lord, in the richness of his goodness, is leading some into the feeling of the condi-

tion of this people, who cannot rest without labouring as their advocates ; of which, in some measure, I have had experience, for in the movings of his love in my heart, these poor sufferers have been brought near to me. The unoffending aged and infirm, made to labour too hard, kept on a diet less comfortable than their weak state required, and exposed to great difficulties under hard-hearted men,—to whose sufferings I have often been a witness ;—and under the heart-melting power of Divine love, their misery hath felt to me like the misery of my parents. With the condition of the youth, my mind has often been affected, as with the afflictions of my children ; and in a feeling of the misery of these people, and of that great offence, which is ministered to them, my tears have been often poured out before the Lord.

If we bring this matter home, and, as Job proposed to his friends, ' Put our souls in their souls' stead ;' Job xvi. 4, if we consider ourselves and our children, as exposed to the hardships which these people lie under, in supporting an imaginary greatness ; did we, in such case, behold an increase of luxury and superfluity amongst our oppressors, and therewith felt an increase of the weight of our burdens, and expected our posterity to groan under oppression after us ;—under all this misery, had we none to plead our cause, nor any hope of relief from man, how would our cries ascend to the God of the spirits of all flesh, who judgeth the world in righteousness, and in his own time is a refuge for the oppressed !

If they, who thus afflicted us, continued to lay claim to religion, and were assisted in their business by others, esteemed pious people, who, through a friendship with them, strengthened their hands in tyranny ;—in such a state, when we were hunger-bitten, and could not have sufficient nourishment, but saw them, pleasing their taste with things fetched from far:—when we were wearied with labour, denied the liberty to rest, and saw them spending their time at ease ; when garments, answerable to our necessities, were denied us, while we saw them clothed in that which was costly and delicate :—under such affliction, how would these painful feelings rise up as witnesses against their pretended devotion ! And if the name of their religion was mentioned in our hearing, how would it sound in our ears, like a word which signified self-exaltation and hardness of heart !

If these negroes had come here as merchants, and with their ivory and gold dust, in order to trade with us, and some powerful person had taken their effects to himself, and then put them to hard labour, and ever after considered them as slaves, the action would be looked upon as unrighteous. * * * * * * In the present case, relating to home-born negroes, if we have any claim to them as slaves, that claim is grounded on their being the children or offspring of slaves, who, in general, were made such, through means as unrighteous, and attended with more terrible circumstances, than the case last supposed ; so that when we trace our claim to the bottom, these home-born negroes, having paid for their education, and given reasonable security to

ned them, in case of their be-
able, we have no more equitable
service, than we should if they
dren of honest merchants, who
uinea in an English vessel to

If we claim any right to them
en of slaves, we build on the
d by them, who made slaves of
s; so that of necessity we must
he trade, or relinquish our right
ng the children of slaves.
command of the Lord, through
i shalt not suffer sin upon thy
shalt, in any wise, rebuke thy
halt not suffer sin upon him.'

d it seem right to honest men, to
re by these people more than by
' * * —These have made no
ve; been no more expensive in
n others, and many of them ap-
to make a right use of freedom
ple; which way then can an
ithhold from them that liberty,
free gift of the Most High to his
res? The upright in heart can-
he wicked in their wickedness;
nant to the life they live, to hold
age unjustly gained.
d by many, that the means used
n, are unrighteous, and that buy-
en brought here, is wrong; yet
a free is attended with some diffi-
) not comply with it; but seem
opinion, that to give them food
and keep them servants, without
ges, is the best way to manage
y know of. While present out-
is the chief object of our atten-
ll feel many objections in our
t renouncing our claim to them,
en of slaves; for being prepos-
rrong opinions, prevents our see-
arly, which to indifferent persons
i seen.
iusly consider, that liberty is the
ient men; that the Mighty God
or the oppressed; that in reality
ted to them; that they being set
i liable to the penalties of our
likely to have punishment for
is other people: this may answer
tions: and to retain them in per-
de, without just cause for it, will
ts, in the event, more grievous
hem free would do, when a real
and equity was the motive to it.
re our fellow-creatures, and their
ition requires our serious consid-
) know not the time when those
ich mountains are weighed, may
Parent of mankind is gracious;
ver his smallest creatures; and a
men escape not his notice: and
r of them are trodden down, and
: he remembers them: He seeth
m, and looketh upon the spread-
ng exaltation of the oppressor.
channels of power, humbles the
r people, and gives deliverance to
d, at such periods as are consis-
infinite justice and goodness."

For "The Friend."

FIRST DAY MEDITATIONS.

Admonished by the duties of this day of reflection, when, in some degree, those who are
not altogether indifferent to those things that
" are not seen," look a little into their condition as responsible beings, it may be well for
some of us who are sincere in our desires after
good, and may, in a course of religious duties,
seem to be seeking it in good earnest, to inquire, how far we are pursuing that path
which is pointed out in holy writ for the attainment of salvation, and to know, if possible, whether we are indeed in the right track
or not.

It is plain, that as we have but once to
make our journey, and no opportunity in a
future condition to correct our errors, or ability
to call back again the day that is past, it is of
the highest consequence that every step we
take should be based in certainty, and that
above all, the course of life, religious profession, or religious duties which we are counting
upon to secure us an inheritance in the regions
of light, should be such as to leave no doubt of
ultimate attainment in this solemn undertaking.
Can it be possible that our Creator has endued
us with faculties for the pursuit of bodily comfort in this life, a capacity to pursue certain
means to certain ends in things pertaining to
our present existence, and left us to grope in
darkness, or even the least uncertainty with
respect to that unchanging condition to which
we are all hastening with steady and rapid
footsteps?

The reflections which arise from this view
of our condition ought to affect us deeply, and
inasmuch as it is not possible that our beneficent Creator should have left us thus, ought
we not to be engaged, if we are making any
profession of attending to it, to know our
hearts established, by faith in Him, upon a
sure foundation, not to be removed by human
reasonings, or the doubts and fears and questions which may arise from the unstable and
uncertain devices of men? This ground of
certainty then, as the subject is one out of the
reach of our outward senses, and beyond the
comprehension of our natural understanding as
men, must arise from some assurance other
than that derived from any conclusions we may
draw by comparing one thing with another, or
as regards our *individual* condition by drawing inferences from the character of our Creator as a merciful, condescending, and long
suffering being.

If we have any confidence in the declarations of the Holy Scriptures, we must believe
that in our natural condition, as the offspring
of Adam, we are in a state of alienation from
God; that our thoughts, pursuits and desires,
are contrary to him, and that " in us, that is,
in our flesh (or carnal nature) dwelleth no good
thing." This is sufficient of itself to affect us
deeply, and if we were sufficiently humbled
under it, would lead us to entertain very different views of ourselves from what too many
of us who make a high profession of religion
often take. Our utter depravity, the death and
incapacity for good in which we all are by nature, is a subject to which we are little prone
to turn our attention, and the pride of our

hearts would rather l
we can do something
prostrate before him
that he would take t
immediate protection
would be pleased to
and afterward receive
the difficulty which
to encounter arises fr
take this view of then
may seem at times to
before the Most Hig
abandonment of self,
to see ourselves as no
which are essential
upon the Lord alone.

All who profess to
ment in religious ex
who have made none
testimony of Scriptur
ourselves, to take of
natural and undone
help. There are ma
serve to illustrate thi
one is, that parable o
out to hire labourers i
is set forth the call wl
made by the heavenly
pleases himself, goes
are standing idle an
they had no occasio
shown where he stant
He must come to the
his company; he do
ding. As then, he t
knocks, so, as he ha
design in it, he afford
a capacity to yield to
his reproofs, to cease
cions will, and as w
thus afforded, he cat
a change; the grour
mission to the heaven
the seed of the king
resisted, grows up ar
rooting out of the olt
tablishes itself as th
tions.

Now, as his first
his own free grace, ar
for him in our unrege
us nothing, so, after
measure subjected t
that we should wait f
ence, to qualify us f
what may be suited
wants. Having, ho
raised in us, there is
renewed soul after t
this, in its essential c
are times, when, und
want of help, we are
to God for a special
sons in which we m
groans and vocal int
prayer, and as we d

mission to the operations of divine grace, we shall not fail in knowing something of praying without ceasing, which, as it consists in an inward sense of the divine presence, and a longing for him, must introduce us to an acquaintance with the God of our lives. We shall perceive by the victory he gives over our souls' enemies, that he is a God hearing and answering prayer, and this victory will be of so obvious and undoubted a character, that we shall be enabled to adopt the language of the Apostle, " There is therefore now no condemnation to them which are in Christ Jesus, who walk not after the flesh, but after the spirit; for the law of the spirit of life in Christ Jesus hath made me free from the law of sin and death." His Spirit will, indeed, " bear witness with our spirits, that we are the children of God." Here is no uncertainty or doubt—here is no guessing or drawing conclusions from the declarations of others, but the sure and clear evidence of his Spirit with our spirits, that we are his children, " heirs of God, and joint heirs with Christ."

From the Irish Friend.

FELICIA HEMENS.

It will doubtless be interesting to many of the readers of the IRISH FRIEND, to peruse some account of the last days of this gifted female, who died the 16th of 5th month, 1836. Within the previous three months, having been for some time at Archbishop Whateley's, it became necessary to take her back to Dublin, that she might be nearer to her physicians. She had now nearly lost the use of her limbs, and was rapidly declining ; but her trust being in her Redeemer, she was kept in perfect peace and serenity, and submission to her own state, and the kindest consideration for others shed their sweet influence over her. She very frequently spoke of the unutterable comfort she derived from dwelling in the contemplation of the atonement, declaring, that this alone, was her rod and her staff, now all earthly prospects were failing. " At times (remarks her sister) her spirit would appear to be half etherealized, her mind would seem to be fraught with deep, and holy, and incommunicable thoughts ; and she would entreat to be left perfectly alone, in *stillness and darkness*, to commune with her own heart, and reflect on the mercies of her Saviour. Her affections, warm, and eager, and sensitive, as they had been, were subdued into the same holy calm ; and meetings and partings which, in other days, would have thrilled her with joy, or wrung her heart with grief, were now sustained with the sweet, yet solemn composure of one whose hopes have ' surely there been fixed'—where meetings are for ever, and partings are unknown. After the exhausting vicissitudes of days, when it seemed that the night of death was indeed at hand —of nights, when it was thought that she never could see the light of morning—wonderful was the clearness and brightness of the never-dying. principle amidst the decay of its earthly companion." It further appears, by the sister's statement, that, on the 26th of the 4th month, being the first day of the week, " she dictated to her brother ' The Sabbath Sonnet;' the last strain of the ' sweet singer,'

whose harp was henceforth to be hung upon the green willows :—

How many blessed groups, this hour are bending,
Through England's primrose meadow-path, their way
Toward spire and tower, 'midst shadowy elms ascending,
Whence the sweet chimes proclaim the hallowed day.
The halls, from old heroic ages, grey,
Pour their fair children forth ; and hamlets low,
With whose thick orchard bloom the soft winds play,
Send out their inmates in a happy flow,
Like a freed vernal stream. I may not tread
With them, those pathways,—to the feverish bed
Of sickness bound : yet, O my God, I bless
Thy mercy, who, with Sabbath peace, hath filled
My chastened heart, and all its throbbings still'd,
To one deep calm of lowliest thankfulness.

To this quotation, her sister beautifully and pathetically adds—

" Little now remains for the biographer, but—

A soft and miserere chant,
For a soul about to go."

After this last effort, the shadows of death began to close in apace: the wing once so buoyant and fearless, was now meekly folded, and the weary wounded bird longed only for rest. When all was fast drawing to a close, she said to those who attended her dying bed, and were waiting to witness her last breath, that she had made her peace with God, and that she felt all at peace within.

Islington. J. P.

The Folly of trying to please Every Body.

As some pretend to care for none, there are those who, on the other hand, try to please all, by becoming—not in its best sense—"all things to all men." Some do it from selfish designs altogether ; and others from a too yielding temper. These last cannot bear in any case, to be opposed or to oppose : and so readily fall in with the sentiments and views of their present company, and side with every man they meet. Often this pliability of mind or temper is owing to a sort of amiable weakness, but it is destructive of all respectability of character.

I know not how to illustrate this point better than by the following story, which as to substance and pith, may be regarded as undoubtedly true.

Some very long time since, M. M——, of Massachusetts (then a British colony,) being at Boston, bought him a wig there, and returning home, wore it at church the next Sabbath. As a wig of such a size and shape was quite a novelty in that obscure place, it gave offence to almost the whole congregation, who, both male and female, repaired the next day to their minister's house, and stated their complaint, the burden of which was, that the wig was one of the Boston *notions*, and had the look of fashion and pride. The good-natured minister thereupon brought it forth, and bade them fashion it to their own liking. This task they set about in good earnest, and with the help of scissors, cropped off lock after lock, till at last they all declared themselves satisfied,—save one—who alleged, that wearing any wig at all was, in his opinion, a breach of the commandment, which saith, " Thou shalt not make

unto thee any graven image, or any likeness of any thing that is in heaven above, or that is in the earth beneath." This last objector M—— silenced by convincing him that the wig, in the condition it then was, did not resemble any thing either above or below.

Even so fares it with the characters that make it their aim to please every body. Slashed on this side and on that, and twisted into every shape and out of all shape, they finally come to the condition of his reverence's wig.—*Late paper.*

The following from the Phœnix (Edinburgh) newspaper, gives a striking view of the mutations which have occurred within the eventful period it embraces, although the catalogue of remarkable incidents might have been greatly extended.

THE PROPHET OF 1770.

Let us suppose ourselves carried back seventy years in the stream of time, and to live again, the youthful subject of the young King George III. Let us likewise imagine that in those days the divine spirit of prophecy had come upon us, unveiling to our sight the events of the future. In seven years from this time the British empire shall be rent in twain (American war in 1776.) In fifteen years men shall rise from the earth and fly through the air (invention of balloons 1785.) In twenty years the French monarchy, the oldest that ever was, and now so flourishing, shall come to an end. A virtuous prince, (Louis XVI. 1793,) not yet king, shall in twenty-three years lay down his life on the scaffold: his wife and sister shall share the same fate. In those same days news shall travel with the speed of the wind, and what was done at mid-day shall be known at the farthest bounds of the kingdom ere the setting of the sun, (the telegraph, 1794.) In twenty-six years a conqueror shall arise, (Bonaparte,) who shall water his horses in the Nile, the Jordan, the Tagus, and the Borythenes. This conqueror shall restore the chair of St. Peter, and throw down what he had restored (dethronement of Pius VII.) Finally, he whom the world could not contain shall die a captive on a rocky island, (St. Helena,) neither in Europe, Asia, Africa, nor America : but in the midst of the vast ocean: a few feet of earth his empire, a willow his monument. In those days metals shall be found which float on the water and burn under it, (sodium and potassium discovered by Sir Humphrey Davy.) Ships shall stem the stormiest ocean without sails or oars, (steamships.) Carriages shall run without horses, with the speed of the wind, (locomotive engines.) (The ordinary speed of the wind is 35 miles an hour ; that of the engines on the Great Western railway is 39.) Men shall be conveyed from India to the mighty Babylon in a month ; from America in ten days ; from one end of England to the other in eight hours. Bridges shall hang by a chain over the sea, while roads shall be made under it, (the Menai bridge and the Thames tunnel.) The very beasts in those days shall have laws to protect them. Those days shall be days of great light. Men shall plough without horses, (steam plough ;) they shall spin without hands, (power-loom ;) they shall calculate by wheels, (Babbage's machine ;) the sun shall engrave for them, (the Daguerrotype ;) they shall write with the lightning, (electric telegraph.) One machine shall print in an hour many thousand books, each of which shall take a man many days to read; a man may buy a book for a penny; for a penny he may send it to the ends of the empire. They shall read the rocks instead of a book, (geology,) and decipher the history of beings which lived and died ere man existed. In the heavens new stars shall be discovered; some, sisters of the earth; some, brothers of the sun, (the planets, five in number, discovered since the American war; and the double stars by Sir William Herschel ;) and of all the colours of the rainbow. In those days, likewise, they shall read the pyramids, (Young's and Champollion's discoveries.) They shall find out the mouth of the Niger and the magnetic pole; the way to every thing shall have been discovered but the way to be happy.

FILIAL DUTY.

"Grieve not thy Father, as long as he liveth."

Thy Father! Why with locks of snow
Are thus his sacred temples clad?
Why droops he o'er his staff so low
With trembling limbs and vision sad?
Care hath his brow with wrinkles scarr'd.
His clustering ringlets shred away,
And time with tyrant sceptre marr'd
The glory of his manhood's sway.

How oft that palsied hand hath led.
Thine infant footsteps weak with fear,
How gently bow'd that reverend head
Thy childhood's broken tale to hear;
And when those wayward feet have stray'd
'Mid youthful follies rashly free,
Those lips invoked at midnight shade
The pardon of thy God for thee.

If from his speech should dotage flow,
Or eye, or ear, be dull and dead,
Then to his second childhood show
The love that smooth'd thy cradle bed.
Grieve not thy sire! for if his love
Unblest, or unrequited be,
He whom thou call'st thy sire above,
Will bend a judge's frown on thee.

L. D. S.

The Great West.—It is computed that the "Valley of the Mississippi," including under this name the whole region whose waters flow into the ocean through that mighty river, contains 1,300,000 square miles, and its soil is remarkably luxuriant and fertile. Its natural facilities for internal communication are probably unsurpassed in the world. The steamboat which starts from the head waters of the Alleghany, may land its passengers at the distance of five thousand miles, at the sources of the Missouri, and this without approaching within a thousand miles of the ocean, into which the waters of the Mississippi are discharged!

At the close of the American revolution, there were no inhabitants in this vast region, except the aborigines, and a few hunters and trappers. The whole country was a wilderness—a stranger to civilized life. In 1830, its population was 3,700,000, and it now probably numbers hard upon 5,000,000 souls. If this vast extent of country should become as thickly settled as Massachusetts, it would contain 67,000,000. If it should be as populous as England and Wales, it would number 17 000,000, and if as populous as Holland, 2 000,000—and the soil is so rich, and the country produces in such abundance every thing which contributes to the comforts of life, that it is impossible to predict the limits of its population.—Bost. Jour.

The Tomato.—Now is the time for gathering this healthy and most desirable vegetable which is cooked in various ways according to the peculiar taste of people. As a salad it is good—as an omelet, with butter, eggs, and crumbs of bread, capital—it is good stuffed and baked—good stewed down close with a piece of beef and Lima beans—in short, what position is it not good? Recently tomato has been successfully used in medical cases. It is good for a cough—soothing to the lungs. Use it freely in the hot months to check the accumulation of bile. If you wish to pack them away in bags for winter; gather them when ripe and scald them to get the skin off—then boil them with a little sugar and salt but no water—spread them in thin cakes in the sun, and when dry pack them away in a dry room.—N. Y. Star.

THE FRIEND.

EIGHTH MONTH, 29, 1840.

It will probably be expected by many of our readers that we give some account of the meeting of the British and Foreign Anti-Slavery Convention. It assembled, it appears, at Freemason's Hall, in the city of London, on the 12th of 6th month last. The venerable philanthropist Thomas Clarkson was chosen president. The Anti-Slavery Reporter of 6th month 1st, says,—"The list [of delegates] exhibits the names of nearly five hundred constituent members, and comprehends not only men of various climes and colours—for men as black as ebony, and men once slaves, are there—but men of the highest distinction in various countries for virtue, talent, and philanthropy." The same paper of 7th month 1 supplies us with the following summary statement:

"At the period of our last issue we announced that the anti-slavery convention was sitting; we have now to announce that its session has closed. From day to day—the Sabbath alone excepted—its deliberations were continued, until late in the evening of Tuesday the 22d ultimo. Ten complete days were thus spent in its business, and certainly they were spent in a most business-like manner. The attendance of delegates and the interest the proceedings were sustained to the last. it was felt difficult in anticipation to understand what the convention might find to do, was not long before all such difficulties vanished away. Foreign delegates have expressed noble and uncompromising sentiments, reports of which will be of incalculable influence in the countries from whence they came —of which the speeches of the American delegates present an eminent example. Treasur

THE FRIEND.

A RELIGIOUS AND LITERARY JOURNAL.

VOL. XIII.   SEVENTH DAY, NINTH MONTH, 5, 1840.   NO. 49.

EDITED BY ROBERT SMITH.

PUBLISHED WEEKLY.

Price two dollars per annum, payable in advance.

Subscriptions and Payments received by

GEORGE W. TAYLOR,

NO. 50, NORTH FOURTH STREET, UP STAIRS,

PHILADELPHIA.

For " The Friend."

THE REMEDY FOR THE SLAVE TRADE.
(Continued from p. 378.)

Next in importance to Fernando Po, is a settlement at the confluence of the Niger and the Tschadda. It can hardly be doubted, I think, even by those who are most sceptical with regard to predictions of future commercial greatness, that this position will, hereafter, become the great internal citadel of Africa, and emporium of her commerce. It commands the Niger, with all its tributary streams in the interior, while Fernando Po exercises the same control over its numerous mouths. With these two positions, and with our steamers plying between them, it is not too much to say, that this great river would be safe from the ravages of the pirate and the man-hunter, and would be open to the capital and enterprise of the legitimate merchant. I must here avail myself of a passage from a work published nearly twenty years ago, (M'Queen's View of Northern Central Africa.)

" The extent of country and population, whose improvements, labours and wants, would be dependent upon, and stimulated to exertions by a settlement on the Niger, is prodigious, and altogether unequalled. The extent comprehends a country of nearly 40° of longitude from west to east, and through the greater part of this extent, of 20° of latitude from north to south, a space almost equal to Europe. Where the confluence of Tschadda with the Niger takes place, is the spot to erect the capital of our great African establishments. A city built there, under the protecting wings of Great Britain, would ere long become the capital of Africa. Fifty millions of people, yea, even a greater number would be dependent on it. * * * * *

" The rivers are the roads in the torrid zone. Nature seems to have intended these as the great help in introducing agriculture and commerce. Wherever the continents are most extensive, there we find the most magnificent rivers flowing through them, opening a communication from side to side. What is still more remarkable, and becomes of great utility, is, that these mighty currents flow against the prevailing winds, thus rendering the navigation easy, which would otherwise be extremely tedious and difficult. The prevailing trade-winds blow right up their streams. This is the case with the Niger, and in a more particular manner during the time it is in flood. For ten months in the year, but more particularly from May till November, the prevailing wind in the Bights of Benin and Biafra is from south-west, thus blowing right up all the outlets of the Niger. In the Congo, Tuckey found the breeze generally blowing up the stream. It is needless to point out, at length, the advantages which may be derived from this wise regulation in the natural world."

I have dwelt thus much on the Niger and the settlements connected with it, because it clearly holds the foremost place among the great inlets to Africa; but the number and situation of many other navigable rivers on the western coast of Africa have been much remarked by those who have visited them, as affording the noblest means for extending the commerce of this country to the millions who dwell on their banks, or occupy the cities and towns in the interior. Along the coast, commencing at the southern point of the Bight of Biafra, and embracing the coast of Calabar, the Slave Coast, the Gold Coast, the Ivory Coast, the Grain Coast, the Pepper Coast, the coast of Sierra Leone, and thence northwards to the Senegal, there cannot be less than ninety or one hundred rivers, many of them navigable, and two of them rivalling in their volume of water and extent the splendid rivers of North America. It is reported that a French steam vessel plies more than 700 miles up the Senegal, and that the Faleme, which flows into it eight leagues below Galam, is navigable in the rainy season for vessels of sixty tons burden. The Faleme runs through the golden land of Bambouk, where the French traders obtain considerable quantities of the precious metal. The Gambia is a noble river. It is about eleven miles wide at its mouth, and about four opposite Bathurst. How far it extends into the interior is unknown; it is said, however, that it has been ascended for some hundred miles. It is also asserted, that from the upper part of this river the Senegal can be reached in three, and the Niger in four days.

In addition to the mighty rivers above referred to, it has been ascertained, that from Rio Lagos to the river Elrei, no fewer than twenty streams enter the ocean, several of surprising magnitude, and navigable for ships, (M'Queen,) and that all the streams which fall into the sea from Rio Formosa to Old Calabar inclusive, are connected together by intermediate streams, at no great distance from the sea.

I entirely disclaim any disposition to erect a new empire in Africa. Remembering what has been disclosed of the affliction of that quarter of the globe, and of the horrors and abominations which every spot exhibits, and every hour produces, it would be the extreme of selfish cruelty to let a question so momentous be decided with an eye to our own petty interests; but there is another view of the case,—it would also be the most extreme folly to allow ourselves to swerve one iota from a right decision, by any such indirect and short-sighted considerations.

What is the value to Great Britain of the sovereignty of a few hundred square miles in Benin or Eboe, as compared with that of bringing forward into the market of the world millions of customers, who may be taught to grow the raw material which we require, and who require the manufactured commodities which we produce?

It appears to me, however, that the danger of our indulging any thirst for dominion is rather plausible than real. In the first place, the climate forbids the employment of European armies, if armies indeed formed any part of my plan, which they do not. I look forward to the employment, almost exclusively, of the African race. A few Europeans may be required in some leading departments; the great body of our agents must have African blood in their veins, and of course to the entire exclusion of our troops.

I have satisfaction in finding that from among the liberated Africans in our West Indian colonies, we are likely to be furnished with a number of persons, in whom are united the desirable qualifications of fitness for the climate, and willingness to enter upon the work.

An important feature of the present time is this, that the exertions of the missionaries in the West Indies are beginning to tell on their converts in the missionary spirit which they have imparted. There is a feeling in the hearts of our emancipated negroes towards the land of their origin, which seems to have arisen spontaneously.

Buxton, hoping for the existence of such a feeling, had written on the subject a circular to the missionaries, but before answers could be returned, he received a letter on behalf of one of their congregations in Jamaica as follows :

" We beg to press upon your attention a subject of vast importance, and shall feel thankful if, at the very earliest opportunity, you will bring it before the committee ;" * * * " and without delay, adopt measures to realise the desires of many thousands of their fellow-Christians in this island. The subject is, a mission to the interior of Western Africa ; the land from which the beloved people of our charge, or their forefathers, were stolen, and which is at present without the light of the gospel, and suffering under accumulated wrongs. We, their ministers, feel on the subject an intense interest, while in *their* hearts the strongest emotions are excited for the perishing land of their fathers."

A highly respectable gentleman, more than four months after the date of this, wrote to him from Kingston, Jamaica, on the same subject:

"It is very remarkable, he says, that before being acquainted with the movements in England, *we* had been acting in some measure practically on your principle. Three or four months ago a large meeting, consisting of betwixt 2000 and 3000 persons, was held in this city, for the purpose of considering the best means of Christianizing Africa, by such Christian agency as we could collect in this island. I was president of that meeting, and on my return home, what was my surprise to find upon my table Mr. Trew's circular, inquiring to what extent a Christian commercial agency for operations in Africa could be procured here! * * * I think you may rely on securing from the West Indies an agency of negro and coloured persons, efficient for establishments either civil or commercial, as might be thought advisable. * * * *

"One poor African, named James Keats, left this country a few months ago, really on a pilgrimage to his native land, that he might carry the gospel there. We are anxious to hear of him. He had reached Sierra Leone, and had, I believe, embarked for the Congo river, which he intends to ascend."

The Church Missionary Society have a normal school for the education of teachers at Sierra Leone; by the last statement it appears that sixteen are now in the course of education, under the effective instruction of G. A. Kissling, who speaks favourably of his scholars. By a summary, issued May, 1839, it appears that there are 5098, of all ages, under the care of this society; and the report of this year states, "with thankfulness to Almighty God, the steady progress of this first established of the society's missions."

The Wesleyans are likewise engaged on the African coast in the preparatory steps for this great work, and feel much encouraged with the result of their efforts thus far.

Buxton remarks: The elevation of the native mind is the truest, the cheapest, and the shortest road to the downfall of the slave-trade, and of those frightful superstitions which it has tended to preserve.

In what way then can this advance of mind be most effectually and speedily attained? I answer in the words of Burke, when speaking on a kindred subject: "I confess I trust more, according to the sound principles of those who have at any time ameliorated the state of mankind, to the effect and influence of religion, than to all the rest of the regulations put together."

(To be continued.)

GROTTO OF ADELSBERG.

The following graphical account of a remarkable natural curiosity is extracted from one of a series of letters published in the Episcopal Recorder of this city.

Adelsberg, (Illyria,) June 15, 1840.

I have just returned from a visit to one of the most celebrated grottos on this continent,

and am now seated to give you some account of this most interesting illustration of the beauties of the works of God. The grotto is within fifteen minutes walk of this village, after which it is called. The village is on the great road from Trieste through Gratz to Vienna, between thirty and forty miles from the first named place, and as it fell in our way from our landing place on the Adriatic to the Austrian capital, we thought it worth while to stop a few hours to see it. For a long time, the threshold of the great cave was known to all who lived in the neighbourhood, but it was not till about twenty years ago that the vast chambers beyond that, making the finest grotto in Europe, were discovered. In 1819, some peasant, while working in the part of the cave then known, accidentally broke through a screen of stalactite, which had till then been supposed to be the end of the cavern. A series of subterranean chambers was there opened, displaying a variety of grand and beautiful formations, and running on to the distance of perhaps a mile and a half or two miles, making in all a vast temple of nature to which the previously known portion of the cave was but the vestibule. The country around is picturesque, hills and mountains giving it variety. The entrance to the grotto is in the side of a rocky mountain, bearing on its summit the ruins of an old castle. The small river Poik, after winding through the lowland at the west, suddenly sinks in the porous limestone, and is afterwards heard in the cave murmuring in the darkness, and seeking its way into the heart of the mountain where it is lost for ten or twelve hours, after which it re-appears on the opposite side of the Uns. The mouth of the cave is closed by an iron gate locked, which is opened for all visiters who pay the prescribed sum for the guides and lights. In somewhat more than 160 yards from the door is an immense chamber, called the Dome, 300 feet long and 100 feet high, which was the furthest part known till the discovery of 1819. Beyond that is a deep descent by steps, well made for the purpose, to the bed of the Poik in its subterranean passage, over which a wooden bridge has been thrown, and then there is a corresponding ascent to the level of the cave, and there begins the magnificence of this nocturnal temple. Stalactites in every form of fancy and beauty adorn the great chambers. Some of these are delicate in colour and shape, like the finest and richest tracery of a Gothic building of marble or alabaster; some stand like the light shafts of Ionic columns, and some in the full size of a pillar that supports some grand cathedral tower. The formations have such fanciful shapes that the guides have given them names from the objects which they are supposed to resemble. One is the prison, a chamber up on one side separated from the main passage by a stalactite screen made in the form of massive bars, behind which a lad went with a dim light and thrust his hands out and held his hat like some prisoner seen through a grated door asking charity of the passenger. Again high up among cloud-shaped formations, the lad lighted up by a distant lamp an aperture, which, seen from a proper position, was the moon. Then came the butcher's stall, hung round with meat, several large sides of pork,

which certainly was represented in a most striking manner, being pointed out by the guide. In a large chamber in this region of the cave, there is an annual assembling of the peasantry for an entertainment. On one side of this chamber, high up, is a natural orchestra of beautiful stalagmite, and here the musicians are placed on the day of the merry-making. The great cavern is illuminated, while the strains of a strong band and the dancing and mirth of the peasantry from all the surrounding country break the midnight quiet, which, through all the rest of the year, reigns in the inner chambers of the mountain.

In another place the guides show the pulpit on which a lad mounts to illustrate the propriety of the name. Again, there is the waterfall, a beautiful representation of water frozen in the act of falling over a series of rocks. Then we are shown in several places the cauliflower, a pile of pure stalactite formed into the image of that plant, and of a size that would suffice for a host. In one place, two hearts are formed of the crystallized stone, and in another is a set of church bells, the pendant crystals of different sizes resounding with different notes when struck, so as to give various changes. The lad who was charged with the performance, satisfied us fully of the power of these bells of the great subterranean cathedral. In one place was the representation of a skull or death's head, and in another a fanciful figure standing upright in the midst of the cave, like a carved head, into the mouth of which the guide put his pipe, and called it the "guardian of the grotto." In one place was the garden, a large space overgrown with stalagmites beautifully set, and of various forms and sizes, so as to look in the twilight produced by the lamps, like a great shrubbery. The most beautiful, perhaps, of all the specimens we saw, is called the curtain, which it perfectly resembles. It is transparent, and hangs in graceful folds from the arch, one side being drawn up as if by a cord. At the farther end of the grotto stands a figure of white stalactite, looking like a draped statue, and called by the guides the pope, and certainly when seen from a distance it is an excellent picture of statues of him which we have seen in Italy. Some of the stalactites were as white as pure alabaster, and many of the thinner ones transparent. Two hours were spent in traversing the grotto, and the interest continues to the last. Two days would be required to explore it satisfactorily.

In a pond of pure water in the cave is kept a specimen of a remarkable animal called *proteus anguinus,* which is found in a subterranean lake a few miles from Adelsberg in the *Magdalenen grotto.* One has been transferred to the cave I have just been describing as a specimen. It is eight or ten inches long, and shaped partly like a fish, and partly like a lizard. Its colour is that of the flesh of an infant, its tail is that of an eel, it has four legs like those of a lizard, and there is a red crest about the throat, supposed to be the lungs. It is said to have no sight, for it lives in subterranean water in perpetual night, and it suffers when exposed to the day. In one other place, within forty miles of this, (at Sittich,) it is said to be found, rarely, however, and, (as has been said,) in Sicily also, but it is not known to exist elsewhere in Europe.

From the New York Observer.

They hated me without a cause.—To hate, in scripture phrase, is frequently, to love less. To hate an object is to love it less than another. Thus, Jacob have I loved; Esau have I hated; i. e. I have loved Esau less than Jacob. If any man come to me, and hate not his father, and mother, and wife, and children, and brethren, and sisters, yea, and his own life also, he cannot be my disciple; i. e. except he love these less than me, and let every worldly object have but a subordinate place in his affections, he cannot be my disciple. Every man, therefore, who does not love Jesus Christ supremely; who does not give him the first and chief place in his affections; who does not by his conduct show that every other object has but a subordinate place; may truly and emphatically be said to hate the Saviour of sinners!

We see then why a change of heart is necessary. The heart is the seat of hatred to Christ. Hatred dwells in the heart. The only true reason why men have ever hated, and will ever hate the Saviour, is because of the depravity of their hearts. Other reasons may be named, but they are only occasions of stirring up the enmity which reigns within. The hatred is all there, and the occasion need only be furnished for it to burst forth, and crucify the Son of God afresh, or persecute his followers unto death! Can man, with such a heart, enter heaven? Can he enjoy God any where? Ye must be born again!

Then we see, too, the necessity of the Holy Ghost, to renew and sanctify the heart, and shed abroad within us a Saviour's love. The heart is full of hatred. As the Jews were the more opposed to Christ the stronger his claims, and the clearer the evidence in support of them, even so it is now. The clearer the truth is presented, the more convincingly duty is urged; the more strongly obligation is pressed, the more the carnal heart rebels, and the more bitter is its opposition to the truth, and the more decided the manifestations of its hatred to Jesus Christ. Now how is the heart to be subdued? The power of the Holy Ghost must effect it. W. J. M.

History of the Lehigh Coal and Navigation Company.

(Concluded from p. 380.)

As the time at which the original act granted to White, Hauto and Hazard required the navigation to be completed to Stoddartsville was now approaching, and the attention of the public was awakened to the second, or Beaver Meadow coal region, it became necessary to look to the commencement of that part of the company's work. It was evident that the descending navigation by artificial freshets would not be satisfactory to the legislature, who had reserved the right of compelling the construction of a complete slackwater navigation. The extraordinary fall in the upper section of the Lehigh rendered its improvement by locks of the ordinary lift impracticable, as the locks

would have been so close together, and would have caused so much detention in their use, as to render the navigation too expensive to be available to the public. The plan of high lifts was proposed by the managers as one that would overcome this difficulty, and in 1835, Edwin A. Douglas, Esq. was appointed as engineer to carry it into execution. The work, as high as the mouth of the Quakake, was put under contract in June, 1835, and from thence to White Haven in October of the same year. The descending navigation above Wright's creek was also put under contract in the same year.

On the 13th of March, 1837, the legislature passed an act authorizing the Lehigh Coal and Navigation Company to construct a railroad to connect the North Branch division of the Pennsylvania canal with the slackwater navigation of the Lehigh, and increasing their capital stock to one million six hundred thousand dollars; at the same time *repealing* so much of the former act as required or provided for the completion of a *slackwater* navigation between Wright's creek (near White Haven) and Stoddartsville. This act was accepted by the stockholders of the company on the 10th of May, 1837.

The whole work of the navigation required by the acts of the legislature was completed, and the governor's commission given to the inspectors to examine the last of it, on the 19th of March, 1838. The following is the report of the commissioners to the governor, showing their opinion of the work:—

To the Governor of the Commonwealth of Pennsylvania.

The commissioners appointed in the commission whereof a copy is hereunto appended, report, that in pursuance of their appointment they met at Mauch Chunk, and from thence proceeded, on the 11th of June, inst., on board of a canal boat, up the navigation to the mouth of Quakake creek, passing through lock No. 12, the point at which they closed their inspection in October last; commencing their present examination at this point, situated in the upper or second grand section of the Lehigh improvements, from thence passing along the navigation upwards, to lock No. 29, at White Haven, a distance of sixteen miles and $1\frac{18}{100}$ths; one mile and $\frac{76}{100}$ths thereof being canal, and the remaining fourteen miles and $1\frac{8}{100}$ths slackwater navigation. On their way they carefully viewed and inspected the improvements in said section, consisting of sixteen stone locks and thirteen dams, all of which being constructed in the most substantial manner, and of the best materials (the dams of timber and stone,) and perfected in a complete and workmanlike manner, and the whole of the improvements throughout being found in good and navigable order, and the tow-paths along the slackwater navigation all lined with stones. The dimensions of the largest of the locks (No. 27, called "Pennsylvania lock") being as follows: twenty-seven feet thickness of solid wall at the bottom, and ten feet on the top; thirty feet lift, three feet working guard, chamber of twenty feet in width, and one hundred feet in length, eighty-six feet clear of the swing of the gates, and containing nine thou-

sand nine hundred and seventy-two cubic yards of masonry, and two hundred and forty-two thousand four hundred and nineteen feet, board measure, of timber work; and the largest of the dams being of the height of fifty-eight feet, and of the width of one hundred and ninety feet at the combing. For a particular description of the remaining locks and dams the commissioners refer to the table hereunto appended. On the said section there will yet be erected a bridge across the river, the solid stone abutments of which are completed, and the superstructure, of one span of one hundred and ten feet, is now under contract, to be finished by the 1st day of September next: in the mean time, the navigation will be kept in complete operation by means of a rope ferry, established at this point. The amount total, of lockage, in the sixteen miles before described, is three hundred and sixty-eight feet.

It will be seen by the report made on the 27th of October last, by the undersigned, that about eighteen miles of the second grand section or division of the river Lehigh were then in hand, but not yet finished. The commission, under which the undersigned now act, authorizes and enjoins upon them to examine and report upon that section, and which has been done by them in the manner herein set forth. In addition to the particulars therein contained, they must state, that they found the river unusually full of water, which had risen so high as to float, from the pool at White Haven, nearly all the logs that had been accumulating for a length of time, and formed a very large mass of heavy timber, from one to three feet diameter, which they found lodged upon the dams, or lying on the face, or at the foot of them, the whole distance from White Haven to Mauch Chunk, thus testing the strength of the dams and locks by the united pressure of the water and the timber. In no instance have the noble works been injured, except the angle of one of the abutments, which was a little fractured by the fall of a large tree against it, in passing the dam. The undersigned are assured by Mr. Douglas, the able engineer, that a trifling expense will replace the broken stones, and give additional strength to the abutment.

The company having now fully complied with the law, and in a manner honourable to themselves, and, (as Pennsylvanians, the undersigned say, with pride,) most honourable to the state, we deem them entitled to a license for charging and collecting the legal toll.

In ascending this division of the Lehigh, the commissioners passed through a succession of the largest, best constructed, and most easily managed locks within their knowledge, and of such magnitude as greatly to exceed every public work of the kind in the United States. They were filled with admiration and delight as they examined these stupendous works, erected on that river, which, three years ago, was wild, shallow, and useless, and has now been converted into a calm and beautiful stream, suited for all purposes of navigation, either for trade or pleasure, and will, as it is hoped and contemplated, be, at no distant day, navigated by sea vessels, so constructed as to load at White Haven, and discharge at the ports along the Atlantic shore; to these may be added packets for passengers, which, by their size and comforts, will convey to the centre of this district of country, visiters and travellers to whom it has hitherto been both closed and unknown.

The undersigned would farther state, that on the 10th of June inst. a boat laden with forty tons of merchandise was carried through the Lehigh improvements, or navigation, from Mauch Chunk to White Haven, in fourteen hours, drawn by one set of two horses—and that the locks on the whole of said navigation are of a capacity to pass boats of from one hundred and twenty to one hundred and fifty tons burden.

Witness the hands and seals of the commissioners, at Mauch Chunk, this 12th day of June, in the year of our Lord 1838.

SAMUEL BRECK, [L. S.]
N. BEACH, [L. S.]
OWEN RICE, [L. S.]

Northampton county, to wit :

On the 12th day of June, A. D. 1838, before me, the subscriber, one of the justices of the peace in and for said county, personally appeared the within named Samuel Breck, Nathan Beach, and Owen Rice, who, on their solemn oaths and affirmations, duly administered according to law, severally declared and said, that the facts set forth in the foregoing report are just and true, to the best of their knowledge and belief.

In testimony whereof, I have hereunto set my hand and seal, at Mauch Chunk, the day and year aforesaid.

J. S. WALLACE, J. P. [L. S.]

PENNSYLVANIA, ss.

In the name and by the authority of the Commonwealth of Pennsylvania.

SEAL OF THE STATE OF PENNSYLVANIA.

JOSEPH RITNER, *Governor of the said Commonwealth.*

To all to whom these presents shall come, sends greeting :

Whereas, pursuant to the eleventh and fifteenth sections of an act of the general assembly, entitled, "An act to improve the navigation of the river Lehigh," passed the 20th day of March, 1818, commissioners were appointed by me, on the 19th day of March, 1838, to view and examine the remaining portion of the navigation of the river Lehigh, from lock No. 12 to lock No. 29, at White Haven, a distance of sixteen miles and $\frac{7}{10}$ths : one mile and $\frac{29}{100}$ths thereof being canal, and the remaining fourteen miles and $\frac{7}{10}$ths slackwater navigation ; upon the notification for making the same, that the said remaining portion of the navigation of the river Lehigh was made and perfected agreeably to certain acts of assembly, referred to in the first section of an act passed the 13th day of March, 1837, entitled, " An act authorising the construction of a railroad to connect the North Branch division of the Pennsylvania canal, at or within the borough of Wilkesbarre, with the slackwater navigation of the river Lehigh," which authorise the making of the same—And whereas, the said commissioners, Samuel Breck, Nathan Beach, and Owen Rice, Esquires, have reported to me in writing, under their respective hands and seals, and under their oaths and affirmations, that they have viewed and examined the said remaining portion of the navigation of the river Lehigh, specified in their report, and that it is made and perfected in a complete and workmanlike manner, agreeably to the true intent and meaning of the acts of assembly on the subject : Now know ye, that I, the said Joseph Ritner, governor of the said commonwealth, do hereby permit, license and suffer the said president, managers and company to fix and appoint so many places on the said remaining portion of the navigation of the river Lehigh, so made and perfected as aforesaid, as will be necessary and sufficient to collect the tolls and duties granted by law to the said company, from all persons having charge of all boats, arks, vessels, crafts and rafts passing up and down the same.

Given under my hand, and the great seal of the state, at Harrisburg, this 19th day of June, A. D. 1838, and of the commonwealth the sixty-second.

By the Governor.
J. WALLACE, *Deputy Secretary.*

We have here the official evidence of the whole work of the navigation, required by the legislature, being completed, and in a manner highly satisfactory to the authorities. In its execution no money has been expended in ornament, nor withheld where it was deemed necessary for permanence and security.

The following tables show the detail of the whole.

[These tables and other matter, of much value to those more immediately concerned, we pass over, and close our extracts with the concluding paragraph of this interesting history.]

A history of the Lehigh Coal and Navigation Company, from its earliest infancy, has thus been furnished. Its growth has been seen till it has nearly reached manhood. Examine its present position. See its immense property in coal and other lands ; its navigation and railroads penetrating the vast regions of timber, and coal, and iron, ore, and limestone, with abundant power for manufacturing them ; and at the same time connecting the two best Atlantic markets, by the shortest, cheapest, and most southern route, with a boundless country intersected by upwards of seventeen hundred miles of canals, and several times that amount of lake and river navigation, teeming with all the products of agriculture, and requiring all the manufactures of our own and of foreign countries in return,—and then decide if there can be a doubt of such an institution proving prosperous, affording perfect security for the regular repayment of all the loan-holders, and amply reimbursing the stockholders for their investments.

FOWLER SPARE THAT BIRD!

I know of few things more calculated to disturb the equanimity of mind, and ruffle the feelings of a humane man, one who lives among animals and birds, and feels as if they were all personal friends, than to see a shock-headed, straddling thing calling itself a man, with rusty musket or rifle creeping about our highways, woodlands or orchards, and popping away at the harmless little creatures, that give to the landscape half its charms, and to the eye and ear half their pleasures. I know these men cannot look upon birds as I do, or they would not have to be guilty of homicide to know what the feelings of a murderer are when they wantonly destroy these creatures of the air. I plead for the beautiful songters, that greet the morn with a hymn, flutter over and through our meadows and orchards, and exhibit an instinctive happiness, that might reconcile even a misanthropist to life and its cares. I never heard the blue-bird without a feeling of gladness, that "the winter is over and gone, and the time of the singing of birds is come ;" and this feeling is increased as day after day the robin, the sparrow, yellow-bird, bobalink, brown thrush, oriole and wren successively arrive, and enliven the woods and fields with their presence and fill the air with their music. And what is the crime charged upon these beautiful birds, that they are doomed to death by every boy or man, who is disposed to show his prowess in shedding their blood ? Why they eat our cherries, or perhaps occasionally peck our trees or our sweet apples. This charge is true ; but only a very small part is guilty, if guilt there is about it: and must all the acknowledged harmless species suffer for the act of one or two ? Yet these are sought after and destroyed with as much avidity and hot-haste, as the most predatory ones. The urchin or the ragamuffin raises his weapon, and the half-warbled song remains unfinished for ever.

I have admitted the charge, but if true in its fullest extent, would it justify extermination ? Is there no good deed performed—no services rendered to the gardener or the agriculturalist ? I think there are many, and that the good they do, overbalances many fold, as a strict matter of profit or loss, the trifling injuries they produce. I saw this morning in my garden, a robin hopping along on the ground, I saw it seize a black grub or cut worm, and in a few moments another. Those two worms among my melons or cucumbers, would have done me more injury than a dozen robins in my cherry trees, and yet these two formed but a small part of the worms of various kinds this single bird would devour in a day. Before you destroy a bird on your premises or permit any one else to do it, be certain that you are not about to destroy one of your most faithful friends. Think of the pleasure and instruction they afford ; arise on one of our beautiful mornings before the sun, and hear from copse and orchard, and lawn and grove the thousand voices of joy and melody that are rising and mingling, and if you have a single feeling that belonged to man in paradise, it will not be necessary to repeat to you, *Fowler spare that bird!*—A FRIEND TO MEN AND BIRDS.—*Exchange paper.*

The blessing of the Lord shall slip, from thee, without doing thee any good, if thou hast not ceased from doing evil.—*Taylor.*

Epistle from the Representatives of Indiana Yearly Meeting.

Having carefully watched with a hope of seeing the following epistle in the columns of " The Friend," and being from time to time disappointed, I thought it best to forward a copy, hoping it will meet the approbation of the editor, being unwilling that the readers of that interesting Journal should miss the privilege of perusing it, in particular, as rumours have been industriously circulated that Friends of Indiana Yearly Meeting are joining anti-slavery societies.   A SUBSCRIBER.

Gilead, Marion co., Ohio, 8th mo. 15th, 1840.

To the Quarterly, Monthly, and Preparative Meetings of Indiana Yearly Meeting, and to Friends individually.

Dear Friends—The attention of this meeting has been arrested by the commotions and excitements which at present agitate the public mind in this country on the subject of slavery ; and during the consideration thereof, an earnest desire has prevailed, that Friends may so demean themselves in their intercourse with the public on this great question, as still faithfully to maintain the testimony of our religious society against slavery, and be preserved in that, calmness and Christian firmness which accords with our religious profession, and will show forth our good example to the world. In the progress of the light of truth, many advocates for the cause of the oppressed and degraded African have been raised up in our land ; and many benevolent associations have been formed, with a view, as appears by the articles of their organization, to promote the abolition of slavery on peaceable principles.

We rejoice that others are coming up to the work in which our society has been long engaged ; and most earnestly hope that the light of truth and righteousness may continue to spread until it pervades our whole country, from one end of the land to the other.

But the sphere in which our society has thought it right to labour, appears to be different from that of most other associations. We profess to occupy religious ground, and to wait for divine ability to labour as the followers of Christ in the spirit of his gospel, hoping for the eradication of all evil things by its holy influence and universal prevalence in the hearts of men ; hence our labours should all be in accordance with our peaceable principles and peculiarities ; instigated by considerations of religious duty, no political considerations or party strifes should be suffered to draw us off from our own ground, for whenever we leave that, we are subject to act very inconsiderately.

We have many other testimonies to bear besides that against slavery, and we affectionately exhort our members to keep this in mind in all their intercourse with others for the promotion of schemes of benevolence. Among these, our testimony against war, whether offensive or defensive, stands conspicuous. In the peculiarities of our religious worship also, and of our profession in regard to plainness in dress and address, we are still called upon to distinguish ourselves, not only from the world, but from most other professors of the religion of Jesus. From the danger of compromising our principles in several of these testimonies, in cases that may occur during excitements and political commotions, we feel ourselves called upon to renew and impress the advice heretofore issued to our members by our yearly meeting, to abstain from connecting themselves with the abolition and colonization societies.

We wish to say nothing to discourage any Christian effort in the cause of freedom by the first of these ; nor to call in question the benevolent motives which influence many who are engaged in the last. Our desires and prayers are, that the Lord, in his mercy, may overrule the whole for good : and we would have none to think, that because the light of the gospel in its advances has made many coadjutors in the cause of justice and of mercy, that we are now to indulge in apathy, or lukewarmness, or relax our labours in all suitable openings for the benefit of the coloured race.

The foregoing epistle was produced to this meeting by a committee appointed for the purpose, and being read, and deliberately considered, was united with, and approved, and directed to the serious attention of all our members.

Extracted from the minutes of the Meeting for Sufferings of Indiana Yearly Meeting, held at White Water, 6th mo. 4th, 1840.

THOMAS EVANS, *Clerk.*

FIRST DAY MEDITATIONS.

The subject of prayer, adverted to in a former paper, is one much misunderstood by many who make a profession of religion, and great mistakes are thus made in our approaches to Him who seeth not as man seeth. As it is the means of communion of the soul of man with its Maker, and when rightly understood and practised, at once the highest privilege and most exalted enjoyment allotted us in this state of existence, we ought not to fail in its right exercise, but seek to know how, and what, and when to pray. The observations of Scripture upon this necessary duty are very striking, and may afford to the rightly exercised mind much encouragement to apply to our beneficent caretaker for daily supplies, and to strengthen our faith in the unfailing fountain of all good. It is well said by the apostle, that " We know not what to pray for as we ought." The reflections that arise from this declaration, should make us very humble ; that in our natural condition we do not even know what we need, that we are blind and insensible, and until we receive light from heaven, incapable of seeing the state we are in. No conjectures formed from the declarations of Scripture as to our being reprobate, lost and sinful creatures, are sufficient to enable us to ask aright ; there must be light upon our own individual state, upon our special need ; there must be a little of that influence extended to us, which is compared to a fire or a hammer, to a knocking at the door of our hearts, arousing us from the sleep of death in which we all are, until we hear the voice of the Son of God. When our souls are thus aroused, and a sense given us of our abject, destitute, and wretched condition, that we have been living in opposition to the divine will—seeking our own gratification, indulging in carnal, sensual thoughts, and pursuing the things of this present unstable world, instead of living in conformity to the will of our Creator, we are brought very low, and in our earnestness we cry out, " What shall I do to be saved !" This is the first breathing and cry of the converted soul ; it is the first evidence of conversion, and the answer now is the same the apostle gave the jailer, " Believe on the Lord Jesus Christ, and thou shalt be saved and thy house."

Well, in order to believe rightly, we must have some direct and sensible apprehension of what is to be believed in. We cannot suppose that the apostle meant that there should be a bare acknowledgment that the man Christ Jesus, who was crucified and slain by the Jews, was a divine person, and that what he had done in Jerusalem and Judea, was very beneficial to the salvation of souls ; this the awakened jailer could assent to from the testimony of competent witnesses, from the examination of the prophecies respecting him, and from seeing the miracles which he performed. What then was that belief in him which he declared was sufficient to save his soul ? Was it not an inward sense and conviction, that that which had thus caused him to come trembling to his prisoners, was the power and spirit of that same Lord Jesus Christ, whom the apostles preached, and for whose sake they were then suffering imprisonment and stripes ? It was his mighty power that shook the foundations of the prison, and reached the heart of this jailor in a manner which made him sensible that he was a lost and undone creature, unless some way of escape was afforded him. *Faith* then was the first step which this poor man was to take towards salvation, faith in the Lord Jesus Christ, not only as respected the forgiveness of his past transgressions, by virtue of the one offering on the cross, but faith in his inward power and presence, which had thus aroused him from the sleep of indifference and death, and prompted the solemn inquiry which should be in every soul, " What shall I do to be saved ?" As this inquiry is raised in any, and that which thus awakens, is taken heed to and believed in, it has power in it to save the soul, and the answer of the apostle, " Believe in the Lord Jesus Christ and thou shalt be saved," will be found sufficient for every poor sinner that may be thus driven to seek him. " In him are hid all the treasures of wisdom and knowledge ;" he is all powerful to help those that trust in him, and the exercise of true faith in him comprises perfect confidence in his all-sufficient attributes.

Faith then is the one essential requisite which prepares the soul to apply, availingly, to the fountain of all excellency for help, and the promises to those who thus apply, are most ample and encouraging in their character. Our Saviour expressly declares, that " *Whatsoever* we ask in his name we *shall* receive ;" and the apostle John says, " If we ask any thing according to his will, he heareth us." Why then should so many of the professors of the Christian name be all their life-time praying with many words, and taking the name of the Redeemer into their mouths, and yet oftentimes sit down in the sorrowful conclusion, that their prayers have not availed them? That they are still the servants of sin, and that sin still *reigns* in their mortal body, so that they seem compelled as it were to fulfil the lusts thereof? Is it not because they "ask amiss?" For the Lord's promises are, "Yea and amen, forever;" there is no qualification in the solemn assurance, that whatsoever we ask we *shall* receive. As therefore prayer is as it were the vehicle through which we receive all that is availing to our spiritual life and health, and that by which we are enabled to hold communion with our Maker, how important that we entertain correct views of it, and rightly enter upon its performance.

We have seen that the first qualification for its exercise is faith, not a bare assent to truths declared to us outwardly, but an inward, living, apprehending faith, whereby we have entire confidence, that what we ask we shall receive. This being in our hearts, or as the apostle expresses it, Christ dwelling in our hearts by faith, we have a sense administered, in his light, of our respective wants, of our inward deficiency; the soul thus taught secretly seeks the supply, and as it is not the divine will that we should remain in a state of sinfulness and backsliding all our lives, so, as he thus awakens us to a feeling of our weakness, our short coming, our emptiness, he administers, as we ask for it, strength, restoration and fulness. Our prayers must, however, be *according to the divine will*, or it will avail us nothing to pray. He must be moving in our hearts, instructing us what we should pray for as we ought, and until he thus makes us sensible, truly sensible, our prayers will not be made according to his will.

In the true prayer of the soul, words are not essential; indeed the *frame of mind*, which at all times longs and pants after God, is much the most likely praying to reach effectually the divine ear. He who knows our innmost thoughts, by whom the very hairs of our head are all numbered, needs only to see the bent and desire of our souls, to know their uprightness to him, and our prayers for his help;—this, indeed, after all, is the very essence and substance of prayer,—without which, the very best words are nothing, and which being lived in, and dwelt under, words are not needed; "He knoweth what we have need of before we ask him." This, however, is not to prevent individuals, at some times, in their private devotions, making use of words, if so called upon; neither, of course, does it apply to the exercise of an assembly of worshippers, to whom words are needful to convey from one to another the sense of a united engagement.

The use of words in prayer, the presenting of our bodies before him, and speaking in his holy presence, is surely the most awful position in which, as mortals, we can venture to place ourselves; and to mock God by the expression of unfelt and unbidden words, is that which, in religious exercises, must be the most unacceptable in the divine sight. To know then the nature of true prayer, to be in the daily exercise of it, in a word to know what it is to pray without ceasing, is the highest at-

tainment of the Christian life, a state in which the soul may be said to follow hard after God, to desire him more than hid treasures, and to glory only in knowing a thorough submission and conformity to his blessed and holy will.

From the Irish Friend.

THE DIVINE POWER DISPLAYED.

At a time when immediate revelation is called in question, and those who most assuredly, yet reverendly, believe therein, are considered little better than enthusiasts by many of the wise of this world; it may not be unprofitable to relate a remarkable instance which occurred within our borders, not in the earliest times of our society, but at a later period; and there are now living those who have had the opportunity of hearing it confirmed by such as were conversant with the circumstances, and eye and ear witnesses thereunto.   E. H.

In the particular meeting of Woodbridge, in Suffolk, it was, about a century back, the custom with a number of men Friends to meet together alternately at each other's houses on one evening in the week: it was, at the commencement, little more than a social meeting, but after a time it assumed a somewhat different character, it was found to intrude on family convenience, and to prevent this, it was concluded to meet at the meeting-house, in the room appropriated to the holding of the women Friends' meeting for discipline. After a time, Friends were almost imperceptibly drawn into retirement, and a regular evening weekly meeting was established for men Friends—one of these Friends (well known and highly appreciated by the individual making this statement) was in the station of elder, and was held by his friends generally as an elder worthy of double honour; his faithful and exemplary conduct truly adorning the station he filled in the society, although never raised above the station of a servant, and which place he filled in the family of Jonathan Peckover, who also was highly esteemed as an elder in the church.

This servant and worthy elder, whose name was Robert Artis, has repeatedly named to the individual furnishing this account, that his sister, Sarah Artis, had long felt that it was a sacrifice required of her to propose being admitted to sit one evening with the men Friends, but standing in awe of her brother's master, it became a great trial to propose it. Ultimately it was effected by her brother, at her request, submitting her concern to his master; whereupon the way was made for her admission to meet with the Friends assembled at their next meeting, when she presented herself. Although she had never previously appeared as a minister, a testimony was then and there given her to bear; but feeling great reluctance to speak the word of the Lord, and endeavouring to excuse herself, whilst sitting with her hands clasped together, in deep conflict of spirit, and almost indescribable agony of mind, it was awfully impressed upon her mind, that if she refused to be faithful at that time, a fearful effect of the divine displeasure awaited her. She at length yielded, and a wonderful and solemnizing influence on those assembled, attended her communication, and

left no doubt upon their minds of its being a divine requiring. So far as can now be recollected, her opening was the quotation of the 7, 8, 9, and 10 verses of the 24th psalm, "Lift up your heads," &c. What further was expressed is not remembered. At the next meeting for worship her mouth was again opened, to declare of the deep things of God; likewise, at several succeeding meetings, until about *the day month* of the time above related, which, being the monthly meeting, she believed it required of her to lay a concern before her friends to pay a religious visit to the meetings of Norfolk and Lincolnshire. Such was the power attending her offerings in the ministry, and such the evidence in the minds of her friends of the rectitude of the concern, that she was at *that time* acknowledged as a minister in unity, and furnished with the needful document to proceed on her journey. She accordingly left Woodbridge, and without much, if any stopping at any intervening place, (though she passed through several where meetings were held,) went direct to Wells, on the sea coast of Norfolk, where resided that eminent servant and minister of the Lord, Edmund Peckover, brother to the before-mentioned Jonathan Peckover; in this meeting she was commissioned to address an individual, who, she said, had, for many years past, been required to pay a religious visit to a foreign land, but who had been unfaithful to the requiring, and that she had to declare, that unless he now gave up to what he knew was required of him, that the time was at hand when his gift in the ministry would be taken from him, urging him to faithfulness ere it was too late, attended with much encouragement if dedication and obedience should ensue, &c. At the following monthly meeting, Edmund Peckover, in great brokenness of spirit, laid before his friends a concern to visit America, acknowledging that, for *twenty years* past, he had been unfaithful, in not giving up thereto. This meeting is described by Joseph Oxley, in his journal, in the following words:—"About this time, my dear uncle, Edmund Peckover, laid before our monthly meeting a concern which had been on his mind for a *great many years*, to pay a religious visit to the churches in America; and requested our approbation and certificate. It was a singularly moving time; and almost the whole meeting was broken into tears; so deeply exercised was all within him for the cause of righteousness, and for the prosperity of our Zion. He spoke with divine power and authority; and the Lord's love and gracious regard was largely manifested to us that day." J. Oxley also adds the following interesting account of his leaving his home:—"All things being in readiness, we, divers of us, went with him as far as Swaffham, (12 miles,) at which place it was agreed, that Joseph Ransom and I should continue with him up to London; for which purpose we returned back, after we had rode a few miles, to get some few necessaries for our own journey, and returned to our company as expeditiously as we well could. We found they had dined at Swaffham, and gone from thence. Still moving forward, we saw them at some distance, going but a foot's pace, and in much stillness. The nearer we approached, the more awful and solemn they appeared. When we got up to them, we found they were all retired into silence, and our spirits were also gathered and united with theirs in the holy solemnity. In this manner we continued some time, and then my dear uncle made a full stop, and so did all the rest, and alighted from our horses. My uncle being filled with the power and love of God, kneeled down on the wide heath, and supplicated the Almighty with that fervency of spirit, and we were all so affected, and reached by the power of truth, which was over all, as was to our inexpressible joy, consolation, and comfort. This was a renewed confirmation and opportunity to my dear uncle and us, of his concern being grounded upon a right bottom. I never, at any time, felt and enjoyed any thing to the like degree as this: it was to us, at that time, even as if the very heavens were opened; the fragrancy thereof remains sweet in my remembrance to this day. In this heavenly pause we saluted one another, whilst tears plentifully trickled down our cheeks: we knew not how to part, and yet, it must be; thus, in much brokenness and contrition of soul and spirit, we took an affectionate leave one of another; but, indeed, we were so overcome, as was almost past ¹utterance. After some little time more, we mounted our horses, and turned our backs one upon another; but the heavenly virtue still remained with us. When at some distance, my dear uncle turned about to take another look of his relations and friends; and they, also, in like manner, shaking their heads, and waving their hands, with hearts full up to the brim, bidding farewell: and, even whilst he sorrowed, he rejoiced; so we passed on our journey, filled with divine love."—*J. Oxley's Journal, page 226.*

A testimony from Woodbridge Monthly Meeting, concerning our deceased friend Sarah Artis.

She was born at Woodbridge, aforesaid, in the county of Suffolk, in the 9th mo., 1714, of religious parents, who were both taken away whilst she was young.

She early discovered a sincere desire after the saving knowledge of the truth; and became, not only a hearer of the word, but a diligent observer of the same, in which she grew, and took deep root, downwards. She was much afflicted, and preserved humble in spirit, that her heart became like the good ground in which the seed of life broke through plentifully to the refreshing many hearts. She was often concerned to visit particulars, more especially of the younger sort, and was made instrumental to the opening of their present states; and to administer the wine and the oil, as the occasion required; and, as she was much given up to do her master's work, she profited greatly therein.

She came forth in a public ministry, in the 26th year of her age; in which she was, at times, gifted with a *discerning spirit*, that it might be truly said of her, she was one of the wise-hearted women in our Israel, in whom the spirit of wisdom and understanding dwell.

She was clear in her delivery—sound in judgment—easy in expression—tinctured with gospel savour—which has often, like the stone

out of the sling of David, smote the enemy in the forehead! She was careful to be in the practice of what she preached to others, that her life might truly be said to be a pattern thereof. She travelled in the work of the ministry three times into the north of England, and several times into the west; and twice visited Ireland. Her service, in the intervals of her longer journies, was much in visiting the neighbouring counties. The time of her illness was pretty long and heavy, being afflicted with a cancer in her mouth, which much affected her speech, so as that she could not utter words, but with great difficulty. She continued languishing several months, and was earnest in spirit, that she might be preserved in the patience, to an entire resignation to the Lord's will, whether to live or die. She expressed great satisfaction in that she had been faithful in the discharge of her duty; and, near her latter end, had great desire of being dissolved, in full assurance of entering into that rest which is prepared for them that die in the Lord.

She departed this life about the 44th year of her age: a minister eighteen years; and was buried in Friends' burying-ground, at Woodbridge, the 19th of 4th mo., 1758.

Robert Artis, the brother of Sarah Artis, who is mentioned in the foregoing account, also related to the writer of this the following anecdote regarding himself:—When young in years he was prone to violent passion, and once when following the plough on a hot summer day, the horses were rendered very troublesome from the bite of flies, and his choler rising he was unmerciful to the poor animals, for which he felt such close conviction, that after a time he stopped his horses, and kneeled down to supplicate for forgiveness, and strength to abstain for the future, from such offence in the sight of his Almighty Father; it proved such a time of humiliation and deep religious feeling, as induced his continued desire, to be for ever after preserved in the fear of the Lord, and he told the writer of this he was never after tried alike with passion; indeed, during the several years the writer was personally acquainted with him, he possessed a large share of meekness, gentleness, and humility, and these Christian graces were eminently conspicuous in his character.

When far advanced in life, he was robbed, by a neighbour breaking into his cottage when he was attending an evening meeting on a first day, of fifty guineas, part of his savings; and when condoling with him on his loss, he expressed great disinclination to take any step to punish the offender, and concluded with this observation to the writer of this memorandum —"Let it go, it has cost me many a sweat of the brow;" and he passively and patiently yielded to the loss, although it was one third of all he possessed, and objected to the amount being restored to him by his friends.

Robert Artis had three sisters, all of whom he outlived, and all his relations; stating before his decease, he was not aware that he had any one relation left, even the most distant. He lived more than half a century as a servant in the family of Jonathan Peckover, but not of the same generation; he was a pleasing and

very instructive companion; his company was quite a treat to children, from the pleasing and instructive anecdotes he related to them. The writer of this helped to bear his remains to the grave, from the love he bore to him.

HAPPY CONFIDENCE IN GOD.

Some Hottentots accompanying Dr. Phillip, in what they deemed a dangerous journey, in South Africa, one was seized the first night he joined them with inflammation of the lungs. Dr. P. says, " My Hottentot driver could bleed and always carried a lancet with him. We made a bed for our suffering companion under a bush, and the night being serene, and the moon at the full, shining on his countenance, we had a good opportunity of observing so much of the expression of his mind as could be seen in his face. During the whole time of the operation, and while his countenance exhibited every mark of internal joy, he continued discoursing in the most rational and elevated strain of piety. 'What mercy,' said he, ' that I have not now a Saviour to seek! How awful must my state have been, had I deferred making religion my concern till now! I know in whom I have believed, and he is able to keep that which I have committed into his hands till that day.'

" When we had bound up his arm, he turned his head to me, and with a smile upon his countenance, remarked, ' you are on the king's business, and it requires haste. You must not wait for me. Leave me here under this bush; my heavenly Father, who careth for the young ravens, will take care of me!' (They of course would not leave him.)

" I never knew a more amiable and excellent man—he still lives a most exemplary and truly Christian life."

Reader, is this God your God? How many, like this suffering Christian, had to declare, that unless they had sought God in health, they never could have sought him, and must have died in sorrow and despair! If God is your God, rejoice in such a portion: but if you have neglected him hitherto, O seek the Lord while he may be found !

THE BISHOP OF ALST AND HIS FRIENDS.

A person who had practised many austerities without finding any comfort or change of heart, was once complaining to the bishop of Alst of his state. "Alas!" said he, " self-will and self-righteousness follow me every where. Only tell me when you think I shall learn to leave self. Will it be by study, or prayer, or good works?" " I think," replied the bishop, " that the place where you lose self, will be that where you find your Saviour."

A person, once pleading with the same bishop for going into worldly society, said, " You know, believers are called to be the salt of the earth." " Yes," said the bishop, " but if the salt be cast into the ocean, from whence it was first drawn, it will melt away, and vanish entirely."

At another time, a person was excusing himself for not attending public worship, by observing, that the manner and appearance of the minister were disagreeable to him. " Let us," said the bishop, " look more at our Saviour, and less at the instruments. Elijah was as well fed when the bread from heaven was brought by a raven, as Ishmael, when the spring of water was pointed out by an angel. Whether, then, we are fed immediately from God, as the Israelites with manna, in the wilderness, or by the glorious means of those who may seem to us as angels, or by the base means of those who seem to us contemptible, let us be content and thankful if they are but appointed by God, and if it be the bread and water of life which they bring."

Selected for "The Friend."

THE POOR MAN'S DEATH-BED.

Tread softly—bow the head—
Is reverend silence bow !
No passive bell doth toll,
Yet an immortal soul
Is passing now.

Stranger ! how great soe'er,
With lowly reverence bow !
There's one in that poor shed,
One by that wretched bed,
Greater than thou.

Beneath that pauper's roof,
Lo ! Death doth trust his state
Enter—no crowds attend ;
Enter—no guards defend
This palace-gate.

That pavement, damp and cold,
No whispering courtiers tread ;
One silent woman stands,
Clasping with pale thin hands,
A dying head.

No busy murmurs sound ;
An infant wail alone—
A sob suppressed—again
That short, deep gasp—and then
The parting groan.

O change, oh, wondrous change !
Burst are the prison bars !
This moment there so low
In mortal pangs—and now
Beyond the stars !

O change ! stupendous change !
There lies the senseless clod ;
The soul from bondage breaks,
The new immortal wakes—
Wakes with his God.

Lunatics and Idiots in New Jersey.—In the spring of last year, a committee of five was appointed to ascertain the number and condition of the lunatics and idiots in the state of New Jersey. This committee have made their report, from which we learn that the whole number of lunatics in the state, so far as they have been able to ascertain them, is 338 ; the number of idiots is 358. The commissioners are of opinion, however, that there are many cases of insanity in the state which have not come to their knowledge. The report strongly recommends the erection of a state asylum or hospital, as the best and most effectual means for the relief of the unfortunate subjects of the inquiry of the committee.—*N. York Com. Ad.*

A curious circumstance has lately occurred to an elderly woman, of the name of Sweatman, now living in Southampton, aged 92, who, after having lost every tooth in her head, has, within the last few weeks, cut a tooth, and there is every probability of her soon cutting another.

THE FRIEND.

NINTH MONTH, 5, 1840.

The National Gazette of 31st ult. devotes nearly a column and a half of editorial matter under the head of " Emancipation of Free Coloured People," for the purpose of holding up to the view of that class of our population inducements for removal and settlement in Jamaica. It appears from the article, that the legislature there " by an act passed in April last, organised a plan and appropriated means to encourage emigration of free coloured persons to that island." Not entering, at present, upon the question of emigration, we merely quote so much as will suffice to indicate the character of the act :—

" It is enacted that the governor shall appoint agents and sub-agents, and a commissioner to proceed to the United States, whose duty it shall be to publish the proposition of the government, avoiding all misrepresentation, and explaining the real advantages which the emigrant may derive by accepting it. The agents are required to examine the vessels carrying out colonists, before they leave our ports, to ascertain that they are properly constructed for the comfort and health of the passengers, and fully provisioned for the voyage ; and the masters of vessels who may fail in any requisition specified in the act, are made subject to certain penalties. On arriving at the island, the emigrants will be received by agents there, and directed in the choice of their pursuits, &c. They are expressly exempted from militia duty.

" All the expenses of the passage, the agents' salaries and fees, and the support of emigrants for a limited period after their arrival, are paid for by the government, except in certain cases fully explained, in which a moiety of the passage money is subsequently refunded.

" For all these purposes, the legislature appropriates fifty thousand pounds sterling a year, from the 11th of April last, until the 31st of December, 1843, making a total sum of nearly *one million of dollars.* This liberal provision exhibits the interest and determination of the government in the project."

NOTICE TO SUBSCRIBERS.

If those subscribers who are in arrears for " The Friend," would avail themselves of the kindness of post-masters, by asking them to forward to us what is due, *under their frank,* which they are permitted by law to do, it would be very acceptable. Very few, if any, post-masters would object to doing it, if the statement of name, amount enclosed, and necessary direction were handed him on a sheet of paper with the money to be sent ; leaving the letter of course for his signature.

HAVERFORD SCHOOL.

The Semi-Annual Examination will commence on fifth day the 10th inst. and close on third day the 15th inst. Parents and others interested in the school are respectfully invited to attend.

9th month 3d, 1840.

DILLWYN'S REFLECTIONS.

Occasional Reflections, by George Dillwyn, a valuable collection of religious and moral sentiments, well adapted for schools and private reading, and may be recommended as a convenient text book for editors of periodicals, from the great number of small paragraphs and detached sentences, suitable for filling up.— For sale at the office of " The Friend."— Prices 25 and 31 cents.

Haddonfield Boarding School for Girls,

Under the care of Amy Eastlack and sister, is again re-opened, and ready for the reception of pupils ; and those who wish to place their children in this institution this fall or winter, are requested to forward their names early. Terms are thirty dollars per quarter, of twelve weeks, payable in advance. Application may be made at the school, or to

WILLIAM EVANS, No. 184 south Front st.
THOMAS KITE, No. 132 north Fifth street.
HENRY WARRINGTON, Westfield, N. Jersey.
JOSEPH B. COOPER, Newton, New Jersey.
8th mo. 25th, 1840.

FRIENDS' ASYLUM.

Committee on Admissions.—John G. Hoskins, No. 60 Franklin street, and No. 50 North Fourth street, up stairs ; E. B. Garrigues, No. 185 North Seventh street, and No. 41 Market street, up stairs ; Isaac Collins, No. 129 Filbert street, and No. 50 Commerce street ; Edward Yarnall, southwest corner of Twelfth and George streets, and No. 39 Market street ; Samuel Bettle, jr., No. 73 North Tenth street, and 26 South Front street.

Visiting Managers for the Month.—Thomas P. Cope, No. 277 Spruce street ; John Farnum, No. 116 Arch street ; Isaac Collins.

Superintendents.—John C. and Lætitia Redmond.

Attending Physician.—Dr. Charles Evans, No. 201 Arch street.

Resident Physician.—Dr. Pliny Earle.

DIED, at the residence of her father, Christopher Marshall, on the Ridge road, on the 21st year of her age, PRISE MARSHALL, junr, in the 21st year of her age.

——, suddenly, on the evening of the 21st ultimo, at the residence of Joseph Lownes, Springfield, Delaware county, Pennsylvania, SARAH EDWARDS, of Philadelphia, widow of the late Griffith Edwards, in the 63d year of her age. She left home in usual health on the 14th ult. on a visit to her friends, and on the evening that her family were joyfully expecting her return, she was suddenly removed, we believe, to a better inheritance. Although this afflicting dispensation was thus unexpected to her friends, they are consoled by the belief, that she was found watching when the Lord came. She had frequently expressed to one of her children, that " She believed her dissolution would be sudden ;" and about three weeks previous to her decease, said, " I should not be surprised, if I were to be taken without being able to speak one word," adding, " I am deeply solicitous that my lamp may be trimmed and burning—that I may have oil in my vessel when the bridegroom shall come."

——, on the 16th of 7th month, of a lingering sickness of two months, JOSHUA JOHNSON, of Orange county, N. C., a member of Cane Creek Monthly Meeting. Being fully sensible of his approaching dissolution, he was favoured to become, not only reconciled, but anxious to depart and be at rest. He exhorted his family to love every body, and try to live nearer the Redeemer.

THE FRIEND.

A RELIGIOUS AND LITERARY JOURNAL.

VOL. XIII.   **SEVENTH DAY, NINTH MONTH, 12, 1840.**   **NO. 50.**

EDITED BY ROBERT SMITH.

PUBLISHED WEEKLY.

Price two dollars per annum, payable in advance.

Subscriptions and Payments received by

GEORGE W. TAYLOR,

NO. 50, NORTH FOURTH STREET, UP STAIRS,

PHILADELPHIA.

For "The Friend."

THE REMEDY FOR THE SLAVE TRADE.
(Continued from p. 396.)

One important feature of Buxton's plan remains to be described. He feels that nothing could be more unfortunate or discreditable, than that Great Britain should give any colour to the suspicion of mercenary motives. It should then be made manifest to the world by some signal act, that the moving spring is humanity; that if England makes settlements on the African coast, it is only for the more effectual attainment of her great object; and that she is not allured by the hopes either of gain or conquest, or by the advantages, national or individual, political or commercial, which may, and he doubts not, will follow the undertaking. Such a demonstration would be given, if, with the declaration, that it is resolved to abolish the slave trade, and that in this cause we are ready, if requisite, to exert all our powers, Great Britain should couple an official pledge that she will not claim for herself a single benefit, which shall not be shared by every nation uniting with her in the extinction of the slave trade; and especially,

First,—That no exclusive privilege in favour of British subjects shall ever be allowed to exist.

Secondly,—That no *custom-house* shall ever be established at Fernando Po.

Thirdly,—That no distinction shall be made there, *whether in peace or in war*, between our own subjects and those of any such foreign power, as to the rights they shall possess, or the terms on which they shall enjoy them. In short, that we purchase Fernando Po, and will hold it for no other purpose than the benefit of Africa. I am well aware that these may seem startling propositions. I am, however, supported in them by high authorities; the suggestion as to the custom-house was made to me by Mr. Porter of the board of trade; and that respecting neutrality in peace or in war, originated with the learned judge of the British vice-admiralty courts. Supported by his authority, I may venture to say, that, though a novel, it would be a noble characteristic of our colony. As it is intended for different ends, so it would be ruled by different principles, from any colony which has ever been undertaken: it would have the distinction of being the neutral ground of the world, elevated above the mutual injuries of war; where, for the prosecution of a good and vast object, the subjects and fleets of all nations may meet in amity, and where there shall reign a perpetual truce.

Let us look to the tendency of the proposition, that no custom-house shall be established at Fernando Po, or at the post to be formed at the junction of the Niger and the Tschadda: we might then hope that the history of these stations would be a counterpart to that of Singapore, which is described as having been, in 1819, "an insignificant fishing-village, and a haunt of pirates," but now stands as an eloquent eulogy on the views of its founder, Sir Stamford Raffles, proving what may be effected, and in how short a time, for our own profit, and for the improvement of the uncivilized world, "by the union of native industry and British enterprise," when uncurbed by restrictions on trade.

How far the English government have entered into the plans thus developed, we may form some judgment from a letter addressed by Lord John Russell, a distinguished member of the British ministry, and "secretary for the colonies," to the lords commissioners of the queen's treasury, which was laid on the table of the house of commons, the 8th of the second month of this year.

He first refers to the dishonour inflicted on the government by the continued existence of the slave trade, and enters into some statement of the extent to which it is prosecuted at this day—notwithstanding the costly efforts which have for many years been so ineffectually made for its suppression, and finally, comes to the conclusion, that "to repress the foreign slave trade by a marine guard would scarcely be possible, if the whole British navy could be employed for that purpose;" and he proceeds to state, that "Her majesty's confidential advisers are therefore compelled to admit the conviction, that it is indispensable to enter upon some new preventive system, calculated to arrest the foreign slave trade in its source, by counteracting the principles upon which it is now sustained. Although it may be impossible to check the cupidity of those who purchase slaves for exportation from Africa, it may yet be possible to force on those, by whom they are sold, the persuasion that they are engaged in a traffic, opposed to their own interests when correctly understood.

"With this view it is proposed to establish new commercial relations with those African chiefs or powers within whose dominions the internal slave trade of Africa is carried on, and the external slave trade supplied with its victims. To this end the queen has directed her ministers to negociate conventions or agreements with those chiefs and powers, the basis of which conventions would be; first, the abandonment and absolute prohibition of the slave trade; and, secondly, the admission for consumption in this country on favourable terms, of goods the produce or manufacture of the territories subject to them. Of those chiefs, the most considerable rule over the countries adjacent to the Niger and its great tributary streams. It is therefore proposed to despatch an expedition which would ascend that river in steamboats, as far as the points at which it receives the confluence of some of the principal rivers falling into it from the eastward. At these, or at any other stations which may be found more favourable for the promotion of a legitimate commerce, it is proposed to establish British factories, in the hope that the natives may be taught that there are methods of employing the population more profitable to those to whom they are subject, than that of converting them into slaves, and selling them for exportation to the slave traders.

"In this communication, it would be out of place, and indeed impracticable, to enter upon a full detail of the plan itself, or of the ulterior measures to which it may lead, or of the reasons which induce her majesty's government to believe, that it may eventually lead to the substitution of an innocent and profitable commerce, for that traffic by which the continent of Africa has so long been desolated. For my immediate purpose, it will be sufficient to say, that having maturely weighed these questions, and with a full perception of the difficulties which may attend this undertaking, the ministers of the crown are yet convinced that it affords the best, if not the only prospect of accomplishing the object so earnestly desired by the queen, by her parliament, and her people.

"Having instituted a careful inquiry as to the best and most economical method of conducting the proposed expedition, I find from the enclosed communication from the lords commissioners of the admiralty, that it will be necessary to build three iron steam vessels for this service, and that the first cost of those vessels, including provisions and stores for six months, will amount to £35,000, (about $175,000). It further appears, that the annual charge of paying and victualling the officers and men will be £10,546 (say $53,000). The salaries of the conductors of the expedition, and of their chaplain and surgeon, will probably amount to £4,000. In addition to this expenditure, presents must be purchased for the chiefs, and tents and mathematical instruments, with some other articles of a similar kind, will be indispensable for the use of the persons who are to be engaged in this service, when at a distance from their vessels. I have some time since given directions for the completion of this additional estimate, but with those directions 'it has not hitherto been found practicable to comply. The charge for this branch of the proposed service will not be very considerable.

"I have to convey to your lordship my recommendation that in the estimate to be laid before the house of commons for the services of 1840, the sums may be included which are necessary to provide for the expenses of the proposed expedition to the Niger, on the scale already mentioned, under the several heads of expenditure." I have, &c.
(Signed) J. RUSSELL.

I have quoted this letter so much at length, because it is official evidence of the manner in which the British queen and her government view this important subject, and that their co-operation therein is not designed to be in word only, but in deed and in truth. That the Omnipotent Ruler of the universe, may, if consistent with his inscrutable will, bless their efforts, and ultimately crown them with success, must be the sincere desire of all true friends of wretched Africa the world over.

For "The Friend."

ALPINE EXCURSION.

Early on a fine morning, in the latter end of the ninth month, 1839, we left Geneva upon an excursion to the valley of Chamony, at the foot of Mont Blanc, of whose towering height we had a distinct, although distant view from the town. Having obtained the requisite permission from the consul of the king of Sardinia, which was readily granted, upon paying the usual fee, we passed the frontiers of Savoy with but little delay and inconvenience from the usual examination, and reached Bonnville, five leagues from Geneva, after a ride of four hours to breakfast. Upon one side of the town flows the river Arve, which is passed by a good stone bridge, and near it is a column not long since erected in honour of Carlo Felice, in gratitude for his having added to the security of the town, by the formation of strong embankments, to restrain the fury of the river during freshets. After passing Cluses, three leagues beyond Bonnville, the road is carried through defiles on the borders of the Arve, and beneath precipices which mark the first grand entrance into the Alpine region, the banks of which are well wooded, and the scenery wild and beautiful. We arrived at Sellenches,* situated at the entrance of the valley of Chamony, about an hour before sunset; and the Postillions discouraging us from going further that evening, on account of the danger of being benighted among the mountain passes, we rested for the night at the Hotel Bellevue, from which we had a fine prospect of Mont Blanc, distant more than twelve miles in a direct line, but to an eye unaccustomed to such bold mountain scenery, does not appear one third that distance. We had no cause to regret the delay, as the interest of the scene was much increased by the parting rays of a fine autumnal sunset upon its snow-capped top, blending

* I have been informed, since our return, by a friend, whose brother resides in Geneva, this romantic little village, containing fifteen hundred inhabitants, has been almost destroyed by fire.

with the white, the most delicate tints of purple, and so variegated as to give to it the appearance of a rich icing, long after the light had ceased to be reflected in the valley below. About midnight, the moon over the whole " her silver mantle threw," adding an air of solemnity to this truly sublime and beautiful scene. The next morning we proceeded in a char à banc, a kind of sofa placed on four wheels, drawn by two horses, and capable of carrying three persons. Upon one of the horses rode the postillion, a very important personage in this valley, dressed in a military livery. After a romantic ride of five hours along a narrow road, in many places so much washed by the Arve and other mountain streams, as to be almost impassable, we arrived at the village of Chamony. It is situated in the deepest and most retired part of the valley, which is here but from one half to three quarters of a mile in width, twenty-five hundred feet above the sea—mountains rising upon three sides, from seven to thirteen thousand feet, their tops covered with perpetual snow, and the glaciers extending down the ravines, like immense slides into the valley. From under the largest, called the Glacier du Bois, the terminus or outlet of the Mer de Glace, (sea of ice,) issues the Arve, making its appearance in the valley from under an arch way, or cavern of solid ice, from fifty to sixty feet in height, and rushing out amidst masses of rock and blocks of ice which have rolled down the glacier, or fallen from the arch above. Every spot that admitted of cultivation was improved, and their mountain houses, which are only used in the summer while making cheese, were perched so high that they appeared quite inaccessible ; but the inhabitants looked sickly,—every one in six were afflicted with the goitre, a disease incident to these deep valleys, which gave them a forbidding appearance,—although considered here, as we were told, a mark of beauty.

After having taken some refreshment, and procured guides and mules, we ascended the Montanverte, which rises thirty-five hundred feet above the valley, to have a view of the Mer de Glace. The ascent was difficult and dangerous. Our path was sometimes a mere shelf in the rock, just wide enough for a mule to walk, where one misstep of those sure-footed creatures would have proved fatal both to itself and rider. This path lay across the track of a recent avalanche, that had swept away the trees which hid the frightful depth below, presenting an appalling scene of desolation. Upon reaching the top, the air, which below and ascending was warm and sultry, suddenly changed, the wind blowing from the Mer de Glace and fields of snow as piercing and cold as winter. Before descending upon the Mer de Glace, which lay about fifty feet below us, we wrapped ourselves in our cloaks, which the guides had advised us to bring along. We were unable to proceed but a few hundred yards, on account of the great fissures or crevices, from five to six feet wide, of various lengths, and extending down the whole thickness of the ice, a depth of three hundred feet, through which we could distinctly hear the river running below. The top is covered with stones and dirt, which are ejected to its surface, and thrown over its edges, called the moraine

of the glacier, forming a strik[...] its beauty and purity in the [...] of which were partly buried [...] of rock, having been thus [...] downward progress. From [...] a view of the Mer de Glace [...] the ravine or valley, and op[...] of those pinnacled mountai[...] striking a feature in the Cl[...] The loftiest part of this s[...] called the Aquilleverte, rises n[...] thousand feet perpendicular [...] tanverte. The whole scene is [...] ginable, and defies the feebl[...] to do it justice in the descri[...] its character. Long before [...] to leave a scene so interesting [...] mated it was time to return, if [...] to spend the night upon the m[...] danger of being benighted wa[...] risked ; so we were compell[...] yield. In descending, we fe[...] boys who were calling togethe[...] afforded us company the rem[...] tance down, and we reached [...] an absence of between nine [...] de Londres, a very neat and [...]

The next morning we ascen[...] on the opposite side of the [...] ride of two hours we reached tl[...] the same height as the Montan[...] directly opposite across the va[...] left the mules, it becoming to[...] to proceed further. Taking [...] our party and myself ascende[...] two thousand feet higher. Th[...] season favouring us, we were [...] the snow, by climbing over w[...] debree, formed by the washin, [...] and stones, and from which th[...] appeared ; until we had gaine[...] twelve to thirteen hundred feet [...] compelled to wade through it, [...] ascent so fatiguing, that it wa[...] ficulty my companion, with th[...] guide, was able to reach a deb[...] us a timely resting place. Be[...] chain of Savoy Alps, invol[...] perpetual snow, stretching as [...] could reach, a distance betwee[...] miles—the monarch (Mont I[...] above all the rest, "on a thron[...] a diadem of snow ;" but for [...] not in " a robe of clouds," an[...] glaciers winding down the mo[...] valley beneath, which seemed [...] mere pass running between. [...] was magnificent and sublime [...] degree, and the stillness profo[...] sive, occasionally broken by tl[...] sound produced by the sliding [...] posito, which greatly increa[...] Our voices were so clear and [...] startled us, and each word [...] responded by an echo from a [...] towards Mont Blanc. We we[...] of the chamois, but not one of [...] timid creatures would show its [...] approached under the directio[...] (who was a hunter,) with the [...] the edges of the precipices do[...]

are found. But we could form a very correct idea of the danger of hunting them, it being necessary to descend into ravines that made us shudder to look into. The only living animal we saw was a marmot, endeavouring to hide himself among the rocks. After remaining as long as our guide thought prudent, we descended to the cottage and joined our party, who anxiously waited our arrival. Before we reached the valley, his majesty began to be invested in his robes, whose ample folds showing indications of reaching to us—we consequently hastened our return. The clouds moved gradually over the valley, encircling one mountain, and then another, until they spread themselves like a canopy over the whole—the mountains rising like walls, on all sides, far above the opening by which we entered, being hid by the winding of the valley, seemed to make our loneliness and seclusion from the rest of the world the more complete. The next morning the scene was changed, the clouds having disappeared, and the sun again shining brightly upon the mountain tops. We made an excursion on our return to the Glacier des Pyramids, upon the side of Mont Blanc, up which we ascended twelve to thirteen hundred feet. The ice, in melting, assumed the form of pinnacles of various heights, from thirty to fifty feet; their pellucid masses glistening in the sun, had a novel and pleasing effect. After crossing over this great body of ice, we descended upon the other side to our charā bane, and proceeded to the baths of St. Gervais, which lay a little out of our route, but so pleasant a deviation all travellers should go or return by them. The site is a little fairy spot with excellent accommodations, hot mineral baths, &c. At the back of the house, a short distance up the glen, which seems to end here, is a fine cataract—one of the pleasures of this place is its unbroken solitude. After stopping at several water-falls that abound among the Alps, reached the Hotel Bellevue by dusk. The next day we returned to Geneva, visiting, while our horses rested, the Grotto de Balme, a league from Cluses, within the Alpine defile, the entrance to which is eight hundred feet above the road, the access to it by a mule path made with considerable labour and expense. We penetrated into it between seven and eight hundred feet; from its regularity, it has the appearance of an artificial tunnel. The roof or ceiling is circular, from fifteen to twenty feet high, all of solid rock. From. an enclosure at the mouth, we had a charming prospect of the picturesque valley beneath.   M.

From the Sunday School Journal.

NEW ZEALAND.

We have seldom found so much information in the same space, as in the following passages from an article published, some months since, in a foreign review, (the Monthly Chronicle.) It relates to a very interesting section of the globe, about which little has been known until lately, and that little was known very imperfectly. The facilities of intercourse between distant regions are becoming so multiplied, that ignorance of their position, and their peculiarities of climate, soil, population and productions, will be impatiently borne. We shall probably follow up this sketch of the history and present condition of New Zealand, with some more particular account of its religious customs and prospects.

Lying in the southern pacific, between the thirty-fourth and forty-eighth parallels of S. latitude, and 166th and 180th degrees of E. longitude, there is an island, or, more correctly, there are two islands, separated by a strait four or five leagues broad, upon which nature has bestowed a delicious climate, a fertile soil, and such bounteous resources of the earth and waters, as indicate almost inexhaustible means of prosperity and happiness. This island, or double island, was discovered in 1642, by a Dutchman, Captain Abel Janeen Tasman, who was appointed to the command of an expedition for determining the extent of the continent then called Terra Australis, supposed by some people to stretch to the pole. Tasman had not been many days upon his course, after leaving the Mauritius, when he discovered a great quantity of duckweed floating on the sea, which raised his expectations of short-ly making land; and, in order to encourage the zeal of his crew, he declared that whoever should first descry a ridge of land, or even a break of shoals, should receive as a reward, three reals and a pot of arrack. A month elapsed, however, before the reward was earned, the weeds still fast accumulating upon the path of the ships. At last high mountains were seen; and as the adventurers approached, they discerned a variety of trees scattered over the surface, but planted so thinly as to offer no obstruction to a view of the country. Some of Tasman's followers went ashore, but were disappointed to find no inhabitants in this strange region, although there were evident traces of human beings in some ingenious steps cut in the trees, to assist the ascent of people in search of birds' nests. They had no sooner returned to the boat, however, than they saw the clear outlines of living men moving rapidly between the trees, and the smoke of watch-fires, or encampments, wreathing up from the distant woods. The curiosity of Tasman was strongly excited by these circumstances, and he prosecuted his voyage until he cleared the southernmost point of the land, setting at rest the tradition that it extended to the pole. Soon afterwards he steered to the east, and lost sight of this newly-discovered but unexplored land, which, in honour of the governor-general who had prepared the expedition, he called Van Dieman's Land—the name by which it continues to be known.

Nine -days afterwards—on the 14th of December, 1642—land was again discerned in the direction of the east. The clouds hung so low as to bury the heads of the mountains, which were invisible to the navigators when they had even arrived so close that they could distinctly hear the breaking of the waves against the shore. Towards evening, they came to anchor in a tranquil sheltered bay. Throughout the day they could not discover any movement of life on the land, which appeared to be barren and uninhabited; but as the sun had no sooner set, than a display of lights, hurrying to and fro, inspired the whole scene

with sudden animation; and four vessels, crowded with islanders, blowing an instrument that resembled a Moorish trumpet, and calling to the strangers in coarse, vigorous tones, put out to the ships. The Dutch returned the salutation of trumpets, but could not comprehend the language of the natives, which was wholly unlike any vocabulary with which they had been previously acquainted. That night no further approaches towards a friendly intercourse were established, the natives returning to the shore when it became dark; but the next morning they re-appeared in greater numbers: seven canoes hovered near the ships; and, observing a boat full of Dutch sailors in constant employment, conveying orders from one to another, the canoes surrounded it, nearly upset it with their beaks, and assailed the crews so ferociously with clubs and paddles, that they killed three of them, and mortally wounded one, escaping back to land with one of the dead bodies. This incident, discovering too plainly the savage character of the islanders, determined Tasman to stand out to sea; but his vessels were scarcely under weigh, when twenty-two canoes rapidly followed, and persisted in keeping close in their wake, until the Dutch, opening a brisk cannonade, compelled them to make a precipitate retreat. In commemoration of this inhospitable reception, Tasman named the bay *Moordenaere's*, or Murderer's Bay, and, in honour of the States General, called the country Staten Land.

From that period until 1770, when Captain Cook sailed through the groups of the Pacific, nothing further was ascertained concerning Staten Land, and the general impression was, that it formed part of a great undefined southern continent. Captain Cook, however, circumnavigated it, and found it to consist of two large islands, divided by a strait, to which he gave his own name, changing the name of the islands from Staten Land to that by which they have ever since been known in Europe—New Zealand.

The extent of country embraced by these islands—which, although distinctly separated by the waters of the strait, are yet in such close proximity to each other, as to form of necessity one common nation—considerably exceeds the entire surface of Great Britain and Ireland. The accounts of the actual length and average breadth of New Zealand, vary in a very remarkable degree in different publications, especially in those which affect to favour the public with clear summaries of popular miscellaneous information, crowding an inconvenient diversity of topics into a surprisingly narrow compass—a class of books which, of all cheap ducts of knowledge going, are the last to be relied upon for correctness in the most accessible matters of fact. Indeed, so profound is the ignorance which prevails concerning New Zealand, that in many of our school geographies its name is altogether omitted, except in the dwarf map of the world which sometimes accompanies such books, and where the curious explorer may perchance detect it occupying an obscure place south wards in the Pacific. This desideratum will no doubt be speedily supplied by the results of the inquiries which recent circumstances have

on the islands, and which
1 to a complete survey of
mean time, it is of the ut-
iat all the information that
pon, in reference to their
s, natural resources, and
be fully, honestly, and
ie English public.

1g difference between the
ern islands of New Zea-
is agreeably diversified by
chly clothed with foliage,
merous navigable rivers:
nous and barren in the in-
able of being brought into
1,) but luxuriantly wooded
most to the water's edge.
this material difference in
cultural characteristics of
hern portion has naturally
share of attention; and it
ie rush of settlers, mission-
s hitherto been almost ex-
A chain of mountains runs
rough both islands. The
in abundance nearly in all
in the north; pines of five
cluding the Koudi pine,
1 timber of the Baltic, and
npetent judges to be supe-
ard kinds of wood adapted
1 of almost every descrip-
are found in great luxuri-
of vast extent. In 1773,
the experiment of planting
1nd with European garden
he returned to the island
ds, he found, in many of
e had deposited the seed,
onions, radishes, leeks,
and fine potatoes, nearly
1ut considerably improved
1ange of soil. The coun-
aneously wild celery and
1g out of the fissures of the
found in every cave; yams
plentifully grown; and the
1ealand are, perhaps, the

1tions of New Zealand are
With these alone a large
mmerce might be secured;
f grain, roots, and fruits,
1o, olives, potatoes, some of
1ducts of the east, and the
1dom of Europe, might be
in the rich alluvial tracts
the banks of the rivers.
resident, introduced the
success. The climate of
1urable to almost every
t luxury. It does not for-
1at class of exquisite cli-
found only in paradise or
e equable than the climate
in the winter, and not so
. All travellers agree in
remarkably fine and ge-
y or the south of France,
1eezes from the sea; yet,
1 combination of advan-
is said to furnish no quad-
1ats, and no game of any

kind. Captain Cook, perceiving this want,
introduced some European poultry into the
islands, and, on a subsequent visit, was gratified by finding that they had increased, both in
their wild and domestic states, with unparalleled rapidity, and to an extent that rendered
their extinction extremely unlikely.

The bays and roadsteads abound with a variety of excellent fish. The shell-fish is
described to be of a superior quality, better
flavoured, and more delicate than any found in
Europe. The whale fishery on the coast is
also so prolific, as to point out New Zealand
as the most desirable point for establishing the
head-quarters of a whale fishery for the whole
of the southern Pacific.*

The aborigines of New Zealand are amongst
the most interesting of the primitive races that
have escaped the desolating progress of the
white man. In stature they resemble the inhabitants of the Three Kings' Island, as
described by Tasman, who tells us that they
are very tall, and in walking take great strides.
The New Zealanders are generally between
six and seven feet in height, sometimes more,
and rarely less, of great strength and activity,
muscular and large, but unlike the people of
Otaheite or the Society islands, having no tendency to obesity. One traveller observes, that
if they were properly fed, he has no doubt
they would be the largest and best made men
in the world. The women are finely formed,
and graceful in their persons, and both sexes
mark their bodies with black stains, called
amoco, which is similar to the process of tat-
tooing. This fashion is general, but by no
means arbitrary in its regulations, as every
person tattoos himself agreeably to his taste,
sometimes commemorating particular events
by particular dots or incisions; until at length
each individual may be identified by his own
special marks. The costume of the sexes
does not present any very prominent points of
difference. It consists chiefly of the skins of
dogs, cut lengthwise in divers colours, attached
to a strong matting called pui, and tied over
the shoulders from two corners, and then girded loosely with matting round the waist. In
addition to these articles, the New Zealanders
exceed all other nations in the display of
trinkets, shells, feathers, &c.; and they carry
this love of finery to such a height, that their
canoes are held to be the most picturesque vessels of any savage tribe afloat. The Roman
Catholic missionaries appear to be quite aware
of this frailty of the natives, and turn it zealously to account for the benefit of their objects,
by loading them with presents of pretty little
brass crucifixes, and images of the Virgin Mary, which the New Zealanders exhibit to the
best advantage, suspended from their ears, or
glittering round their necks, amongst sharks'
teeth, birds' wings, bits of coloured glass,
bright stones, tin-foil, and buckles. Sometimes

* Dr. Lang mentions an important fact, illustrative
of the productiveness of the whale fishery on the New
Zealand coast, namely, that during 1838, a single mercantile house in Sydney imported from New Zealand
no less than seventy-one tons of whalebone, which usually sells for 145 pounds per ton in London. As each
whale yields about 500 pounds weight of bone, there
must consequently have been not fewer than 284
whales killed to produce this quantity.

they decorate the collar
these emblems of redem]

A race with such a h
lishments may be expe
touch of poetry in their
especially as nature has
them the pleasures of tl
meaner enjoyments of b
ingly we find them in
usages which are not c
selves, but which are 1
provoke European curio
the most singular of the
eating each other upon
and of even getting up br
in the scramble to kill a
beings for their festiva
modes of cooking are
which generally satisfy
they are certainly not e
rieties of food to which
not numerous. We do
they use vegetables with
temporary meat, but the 1
of fish is undoubtedly kn
are eaters of fish as well
birds and dogs for domest
instead of bread, they eat
fern, which they scorch c
beat with a stick until tl
It is usual with them t
over some neighbouring
quet; and on these occas
generally open with a
spirited movement in wh
ing as high into the air a
is followed by a sham fi
sit down to eat the bodie
enemies. In the winter
of the most distinguished
chiefs, gave a feast of th
consisted of one hundred
cumoras, and greens,
weight of whale oil, som
and several baskets of hu
pearance and character
ceived as a fair exemplar
"Echo's personal appear
knew these people well,
ing: he is tall and well
carriage; has the finest fa
and his hair, which curl
shoulders, is ornamented
which proclaims his ran
ever, is of another comple
ning, cruelty, and treache
characteristics. He visits
that arrives, for the purp
ever he can lay his hand
he is so ably assisted, that
been an hour at anchor b
of almost every moveabl
guage of the eyes is, w
made an auxiliary in thei
ings."*

It is worthy of remark
of the New Zealanders in
catalogue of crimes as to 1
pose, at first sight, that

* Communicated to Lieut
mander of a vessel trading
Zealand. See Holman's Voyag

most fastidiously moral people on the face of the earth. But the severity of the laws, which visit with death a variety of minor offences that are elsewhere punished by fine, imprisonment, or expatriation, is susceptible of this solution—that the New Zealanders eat the criminals they execute.

The houses of the islanders are irregular and poorly provided. Mats and baskets are the principal pieces of furniture, and in the formation of these articles, the natives exhibit as much skill as in their cannibal legislation. Their settlements are scattered villages, containing from 200 to 1000 persons each, recognising, but hardly governed by, the authority of a chief. The constant employment of these numerous parties is that of making war upon each other. Any one who has examined a drop of water through a powerful microscope, and watched the perpetual activity with which the work of destruction proceeds amongst its myriad inhabitants, has seen a fac-simile of the state of society in New Zealand. The natives carry on the same sort of warfare, and for exactly the same purpose,—they fight for their dinners, and dine upon the dead bodies.

For "The Friend."

FIRST DAY MEDITATIONS.

It is a most happy and blessed circumstance that there have been preserved from one time to another, ever since the foundation of the world, and the creation of man, abundant testimonies to the goodness and mercy of our Creator; and evidence is thus afforded that he is mindful of us, and regards us with tender and compassionate solicitude. Much of what is recorded on this subject is contained in the Holy Scriptures, and, consequently, they have a value, far above that of any other book in the world, and have doubtless been providentially cared for in the many mutations which have occurred during the periods of which they speak, and since they were written. Highly should we esteem these testimonies, confirming as they do those offers and evidences of divine mercy which are daily before our eyes, or inwardly conveyed to us through the medium of the Holy Spirit. The diligent perusal of these holy records is calculated to stimulate us to an examination, as to how far our lives correspond with the lives of such as have received evidence of divine approbation, and may confirm and explain, and enlarge our hearts to understand more fully, the dispensations of divine goodness to ourselves.

In order, however, rightly to understand them, and participate in the feelings of those who wrote them, we must be walking in the same paths—we must be influenced by the same motives, and something of the same zeal must animate us which operated in them to promote the glory of their Creator. If our minds are bent upon the world, and worldly things; if the wealth, the honours, or the pleasures of this present time have the predominating place in us; if we love our own ease, our own gratification, our own selfish desires, more than the will and glory of our Creator, we are not very likely to be benefited by perusing those accounts of his doings among the children of men, which indicate his abhor-

rence of such a course of life. If we read at all in such a state of mind, it must be with listless indifference, or with such thoughts as these :—these are good things,—very desirable to practice and pursue, but they are too hard for me, I cannot do such and such things; it may even be said, I am not called to do thus and so, they are too great attainments for me, I must be content with a lower state; if I can maintain a good character among my neighbours, and deal honestly with them, so as to avoid reproach, this is all that seems required of me. Let some of us who sit down to-day, perhaps for the only time in the week when we take our bibles, ask ourselves whether these are not the thoughts that too much occupy our minds when we look over the pages of the sacred volume, and take notice of the holy lives, the righteous conversation, the undaunted zeal of those who served the Lord in their day, and have fallen asleep in Him. Well, let us consider in what respect we differ from them. We may not, it is true, be called upon to perform as public a part as some of them, or to endure outward suffering or persecution, but are we not called upon to lead holy and blameless lives, to honour our Creator in all our ways, and instead of living to ourselves to become conformed to his holy and blessed will ? This cannot be considered beside our proper business ;—it presents itself to us in almost every page of the bible as our important and necessary duty, and if we read the scriptures from time to time, without knowing something of the purifying virtue of which they speak, we are in danger of mocking God by a pretence of devotion, without having a spark of the living substance in us.

Let us then, when we take up our bibles to-day, ponder in our hearts, what good the reading of them has done us heretofore, what have we gained in a spiritual sense ; is there in us an evident increase of divine life and favour, and do we feel more and more united from one time to another, with " the spirits of just men made perfect ?" Or do we, on the other hand, find ourselves in the same situation as in years past, our minds much intent upon the things of this life, and no evident advancement in the spiritual journey heavenwards ? It will do none of us any harm to dwell seriously on these reflections, and if, haply, we find that there is in us no clear evidence of Christian advancement, no substantial ground of Christian hope, no longing to be made perfect in holiness, we may very reasonably conclude, that our reading hitherto has been to but little profit.

In order to read the scriptures availingly, we must read them humbly, we must read them with a reverent eye to him that gave them forth, and we must, above all, have a little of the' same faith which those had who wrote them. Our humility, too, must be of the right kind, not " voluntary humility;" that which is put on for the occasion, and dropped with each returning gust of temptation, but that inward abiding sense of our own unworthiness and incapacity for good, which qualifies the soul to rise in living aspirations to the source of all wisdom and power. As we thus read, with our eye fixed in steady attention upon the one interpreter, we shall be enabled

to perceive the excellencies with which the sacred volume abounds ; we shall experience living fellowship with the righteous of past generations, and shall know the truth of the apostolic declaration, " Whatsoever things were written aforetime were written for our learning, that we, through patience and comfort of the scriptures, might have hope."

SOCIALISM* SILENCED; OR, THE LOGIC OF THE LIFE.

A true story—by Hugh Stowell, M. A., of England.

It makes one sad to find how widely the canker of socialism has spread amongst some classes of our working men. In some large manufacturing towns, there are few factories or workshops into which it has not crept, and it does most mischief where there is most ignorance. Sometimes one pert, prating, forward fellow will dupe and mislead a whole set of men because he talks boldly, uses big words, and seems to be very knowing and deep. What a pity that our plain men are not more of them able to handle the evidence of Christianity, and to beat such pretenders with their own weapons. There is, however, one way, and that, after all, the best way, in which the simplest and least learned believer may meet and put down the subtlest infidel—a way in which he may face the scorner as David the uncircumcised Philistine, with nothing save a sling and a stone, yet in " the name of the Lord of hosts," be " bold as a lion." The way I mean is, to contend, not so much by words as by deeds ; not so much by the logic of the'lip, as by the logic of the life.

I shall best make my meaning plain by a simple account, which, I can promise you, shall be quite true, because it will be about what lately happened in my own parish, and partly under my own eye. John ——— is a dyer, who lives in a corner of my district. Some years ago, he was as bad a character as you can well conceive ; a drunkard, a blasphemer, a cruel husband, a noted boxer, a practical infidel. As is usual in such cases, his 'house was the home of wretchedness, unfurnished and deserted ; his wife was in rags, his cupboard empty, and debt and shame were his constant companions. About three years ago, however, he came under the notice of an assistant of mine. His wife was induced to open her house for a cottage lecture, and the husband, after a time, began to steal into the back part of the dwelling during the little services, and to lend a half-unwilling ear to what was going on. It pleased Him, " who leads the blind by a way that they know not," to reach his conscience in this manner. He became very uneasy, and in spite of his mean clothes, began to attend the place of public worship. For a time his anguish of mind was greater than can be told. But at last that Saviour who came " to bind up the broken-hearted," and who died on the cross to save sinners, manifested

* A scheme of infidelity in England, of which the notorious Robert Owen, we believe, is the founder. It is proper to mention, that we have made some small changes in the phraseology of this interesting and instructive article, the better to adapt it to our pages.— Ed. of " The Friend."

himself to him as he doth not to the world, giving him " beauty for ashes, the oil of joy for mourning, the garment of praise for the spirit of heaviness." Isa. lxi. 1—3.

The calm morning after a stormy night is not a greater change than that which followed in the life and lot of happy John. All things became new. He set himself at once to wipe away the heavy scores which stood against him at the tavern and the shop, till at last he owed no man any thing but love. His house was made clean and tidy, and one piece of furniture after another was purchased, till the whole face of his cottage was changed. On the first day of the week, his wife and himself, decently dressed, were regularly in their places at the time appointed for worship.

A light thus put on a candlestick could not be hid. So striking a change in one who had been so notorious called forth much notice. He became a wonder unto many. Some admired; others mocked, and many persecuted him. His former infidel companions were more especially mad against him. They jeered him, reproached him, enticed him, and did all in their power to draw or to drive him from his Saviour. But, deeply sensible of his own utter helplessness, he clung to the strength of God, and thus, out of weakness being made strong, his enemies only served to prove his faith, exercise his patience, and increase his watchfulness. The blast of temptation, which lays in the dust the plant which our heavenly Father hath not planted, only roots the deeper every " tree of righteousness" which he has planted in the garden of his grace.

John had most to bear at his daily labour in the dye-house. It was his hard lot to work amongst a band of " Socialists," and they had it nearly all their own way. For a time, indeed, two men, members of a religious body, timidly took the Christian's part; but after a while, even those, worn out by annoyance, and ashamed of the cross, deserted both him and their profession of religion, becoming apostates, the vilest of the vile. The humble confessor was thus left alone, like a sheep in the midst of wolves; but he was not alone, "for the Lord stood by him." He was enabled to walk blamelessly and unrebukeably before them. Sometimes he reasoned with them, at other times he entreated them, but most commonly he did as his Master had done when beset by his accusers, " he answered not a word." His meekness was the more lovely, because he had been aforetime a terror to his companions, nor was there one of them who would have dared to provoke him. But now the gentleness of the lamb restrained the strength of the lion.

The quiet influence of John's consistent walk could not fail to be felt. His life was harder to answer than his tongue. A beautiful proof of this occurred one day, and shall form the point of my little narrative. His fellow-workmen had been nearly an hour decrying Christianity as the source of all crime and wretchedness, whilst they boasted what their system would do if fairly tried—what peace, and purity would reign in their " New Moral World." John held his peace for a long time, till at last " the fire kindled," and lifting up his voice, he turned upon them and said feelingly,

but firmly, " Well, I am a plain-dealing m〈a〉 and I like to judge of the tree by the fru which it bears. Come then let us look at w〈〉 your principles do. I suppose they will do a little way what they would do in a gre Now there," said he, pointing at the two ap〈〉 tates, " there are Tom and Jem, on whom y have tried your system. What, then; has done for them? When they professed to Christians, they were civil, sober, good-te pered; kind husbands and fond fathers. Th were cheerful, hard-working, and ready oblige. What are they now? What have y made them? Look at them. How chang they are! But not for the better. They se〈〉 down-cast and surly; they cannot give on〈〉 civil word; their mouths are full of curs〈〉 and filthiness; they are drunk every wee. their children are nearly naked; their wi〈〉 broken-hearted, and their houses desola There is what your principles have don This is the ' New Moral World' they ha made.

" Now I have tried Christianity, and wh has it done for me.? I need not tell you wh I was before; you all too well know. The was not one of you that could drink so deepl or swear so desperately, or fight so fiercely was always out of humour, discontented, a unhappy. My wife was starved and ill-use〈〉 I had no money nor could I get anything up〈〉 trust; I was hateful and hating. What am now? What has religion made me? Tha〈〉 God, I am not afraid to put it to you. has helped me to walk carefully amongst yo Am I not a happier man than I was? C you deny that I am a better servant to my ma ter, and a kinder companion to you? Wou I once have put up with what I daily bear fro you? I could beat any one of you as easily ever: why don't I do it? Do you ever he a foul word come out of my mouth? Do y ever catch me in a public-house? Is there a one that has got a score against me? Go a ask my neighbours if I am not altered for th better. Go and ask my wife: she can tell yo Go and see my house, let that bear witnes God be praised for it: here is what Christiani has done for me; there is what Socialism h done for Tom and Jem."

He stopped. The appeal was not to 〈〉 withstood. For that time, at least, the scoffe had not a word to answer. They were ove powered by the eloquence of example.

My brethren of the working class, follow th beautiful pattern—" With well-doing put silence the ignorance of foolish men." " I not afraid of their terror," 1 Pet. ii. 15; iii. 1 " Witness a good confession," 1 Tim. vi. 1 Stand fast like Daniel before the den of lion or Shadrach, Meshach and Abednego, befo the burning fiery furnace. If you cannot arg you can act. If you cannot reason down yo can live down the artful infidel. There is logic of which, through grace, you may masters; a logic so simple that a child c understand it, so conclusive that a philosoph cannot disprove it; it is the logic John ma use of—it is the logic of the life.

━━━

Effects of Camphor on Vegetables.—T stimulant effects of camphor upon the hum

BEET SUGAR.

We see it stated that the sugar imported into Great Britain last year, compared with the average import of the years from 1830 to 1839 has fallen off to the extent of 40,000 tons; and as compared with the ten years preceding, from 1820 to 1829, 50,000 tons; in consequence of which the wholesale and retail grocers, confectioners, &c., have got up a petition to parliament, praying for the admission of foreign sugars for home consumption at a fair reduction of duty.

England will have to commence the cultivation of the beet root. The quantity of sugar manufactured from this root on the continent of Europe, where it was first introduced by Napoleon, is astonishing, and is constantly increasing. In France, the quantity of beet sugar manufactured from 800 manufactories, is about 60,000 tons. According to accounts in the Dutch papers lately, the manufacture of sugar from beet root is extending there rapidly, and one establishment is cited at Vosterbick, in Gulderland, which alone consumes in the process from 4,000,000 to 5,000,000 lbs. weight of beet root per annum. In Prussia and Central Germany, the same efforts are making to extend the cultivation, the average yearly production from 1836 to 1838, for which alone the returns are given in the papers, being estimated at about 11,000,000 lbs. weight of sugar. But it is calculated that the quantity now made is very considerably more. Austria is not behind in the same branch of industry and cultivation. At the close of 1838, the quantity of sugar produced from the beet root exceeded 9,000,000 lbs. weight, or from 12 to 13 per cent. of the whole annual consumption, calculated at about 115,000,000 lbs. In Bohemia alone, the number of beet root sugar establishments is stated for October, 1838, in the Commerce, French paper, at 87. In Russia, the cultivation and manufacture of the beet root sugar is equally on the increase, and is pushed with great activity, and in numerous instances the culture of hemp has been abandoned for that of beet root sugar, to which the peasantry are encouraged by premiums from the land proprietors. In Moscow and the neighbouring governments, the beet root establishments are said to have increased in number since 1832, at the average of 40 per annum.

The amount of sugar manufactured in Louisiana is about 70,000,000 of pounds, or 35,000 tons annually, a very small part of our consumption. Sugar plantations have lately been established in the Sandwich islands.

An attempt is now making to introduce the culture of the beet root into the United States. According to the statement of Mr. Fleichman, an acre of good cultivated land, will produce on an average twenty tons of the beet root; one ton of which yields, when treated after the new method, 180 pounds of refined sugar. The cost of manufacturing a ton of beets into sugar, is estimated at six dollars at the highest; and 180 pounds of refined beet sugar would sell for $11, or 6 1-10 cents per pound. —*Boston Evening Journal.*

The Industry of Massachusetts.—According to an official report made to the legislature, it appears that the product of the great branches of *manufacturing* industry in Massachusetts, during the year ending in April, 1837, was 91,700,000 dollars, of which sum the three principal items were, cotton fabrics, 17,409,000 dollars, woollen fabrics, 10,399,000 dollars, and fisheries, 7,592,000 dollars. If to the products of manufacturing industry be added the earnings of navigation and agriculture, it is estimated that the whole annual product of the industry of Massachusetts exceeds 100,000,000 dollars; which divided by 700,000, the population of the state, gives 140 dollars, as the average value of the annual labour of each man, woman, and child in the community.

For "The Friend."

BREAD AND WINE.

Another great objection they had was, that the Quakers denied the sacrament, as they called it, of bread and wine, which they said, they were to take and do in remembrance of Christ, to the end of the world. A great deal of work we had with the priests and professors about this, and the several modes of receiving it in Chistendom so called; some take it kneeling, some sitting, but none take it, that I could find, as the disciples did. As to the matter, Christ said, " Do this in remembrance of me;" he did not tell them how often they should do it, or how long; neither did he enjoin them to do it always as long as they lived, or that all believers should do it to the end of the world. The apostle Paul, who was not converted until after Christ's death, tells the Corinthians that he had received of the Lord, that which he delivered unto them concerning this matter, and relates Christ's words respecting the cup thus: " This do ye, as oft as ye drink it, in remembrance of me;" and the apostle adds, " For *as often as* ye do eat this bread, and drink this cup, ye do show forth the Lord's death till he come." According to what the apostle here delivers, neither Christ nor he enjoined people to do this always, but leaves them to their liberty, " *as oft as ye drink it.*"

The Jews used to take a cup, and to break bread and divide it among them in their feasts, as may be seen in the Jewish antiquities; thus the breaking of bread and drinking wine were Jewish rites which were not to last always. After the disciples had taken the bread and wine, some of them questioned whether Jesus was the Christ; they said, " We trusted that it had been he which should have redeemed Israel." Although the Corinthians had the bread and wine, and were baptized in water, the apostle told them they were reprobates, if Christ was not in them, and bid them examine themselves. Christ said that he was the bread of life that came down from heaven, and that he would come and *dwell in them*, which the apostles did witness fulfilled, and exhorted others to seek that which comes down from above; but the outward bread and wine, and water, are not from above, but below.

Now ye that eat and drink this outward bread and wine in remembrance of Christ's death, will ye come no nearer to Christ's death than to take bread and wine in remembrance of it? After ye have eaten in remembrance of his death, ye must come into his death, and die with him, as the apostles did, if ye will live with him. This is a further advanced state, to be with him in the fellowship of his death, than only to take bread and wine in remembrance of it. You must have fellowship with Christ in his sufferings; if ye will reign with him, ye must suffer with him; if ye will live with him, ye must die with him; and if ye die with him, ye must be buried with him, and being buried with him in the true baptism, ye also rise with him. Then having suffered and died with him, and been buried with him, if ye are risen with Christ, " seek those things which are above, where Christ sitteth on the right hand of God." Eat the bread which comes down from above, which is not outward bread, and drink the cup of salvation which he gives in his kingdom, which is not outward wine. Then there will not be a looking at the things that are seen, as outward bread and wine, and water are; for, as says the apostle, " the things that are seen are temporal, but the things that are not seen are eternal."

The fellowship that stands in the use of bread, wine, and water, things that are seen, will have an end; but the fellowship which stands in the gospel, the power of God, which brings life and immortality to light, by which people may see over the devil that has darkened them, this fellowship is eternal and will stand. All that are in it seek that which is heavenly and eternal, which comes down from above, and are settled in the eternal mystery of the fellowship of the gospel, which is hid from all eyes that look only at visible things. The apostle told the Corinthians, who were in disorder about water, bread and wine, that he " desired to know nothing amongst them, but Jesus Christ and him crucified."   Fox.

Bees.—In Livonia the inhabitants make hollow places in the trees of the forest to receive and cultivate bees. Some of them had hundreds, and even thousands of these beehives. Butner, a Livonian clergyman, says the air, at some distance from the ground, is better for the bees than that of the bee-houses which receive the exhalations of the earth. Where forests are not conveniently situated, he says it is advantageous to place the hives upon trees standing alone, at 12 or 15 feet above the ground.

Progress in China.—Sclawuskowski, a Polish noble, who was banished to Siberia, but afterwards received permission to visit China, has established a school of the French and Polish languages at Maimotsky, for the last two years, and has now between four and five hundred scholars, among whom are many of the sons of Mandarins and Tartar nobles. Maimotsky is the frontier town between which and Kiahkta, the Russian and Chinese trade is carried on.

Mammoth bones.—The mammoth bones may not inaptly be called the peculiar produce of Siberia and the Northern Islands. The further the traveller proceeds to the north, the smaller in size, but the more abundant in quantity become these relics of a former world. In e Lœchŏw islands it is a rare circumstance to scover a mammoth's tusk weighing more an 78 lbs., whereas, in the interior of Sibe-, it is not an uncommon thing to meet with e of four times that weight. On the other nd, the immense quantity of these bones and in the Siberian islands, forms one of the st remarkable phenomena connected with se singular remains. The first of the Lœ-ow islands is little more than one mass of ammoth's bones—and though for upwards of hty years the Siberian traders have been inging over annually large cargoes of them, ere appears as yet to be no sensible diminu-n in the apparently inexhaustible store. The th found in these islands, are also much iter and fresher than those of the continent. e most valuable were met with on a low nd bank of the western coast; and there, en after a long prevalence of easterly winds, sea recedes, a fresh supply of mammoth nes is always found.

IE DYING BELIEVER TO HIS SOUL.

Deathless principle, arise :
Soar, thou native of the skies ;
Pearl of price, by Jesus bought,
To his glorious likeness wrought,
Go, to shine before his throne ;
Deck his mediatorial crown :
Go, his triumphs to adorn ;
Made for God, to God return.

Lo, He beckons from on high !
Fearless to his presence fly :
Thine the merit of his blood ;
Thine the righteousness of God.

Angels, joyful to attend,
Hov'ring round thy pillow bend ;
Wait to catch the signal giv'n,
And escort thee quick to heav'n.

Is thy earthly house distrest ?
Willing to retain her guest ?
'Tis not thou, but she, must die :
Fly, celestial tenant, fly,
Burst thy shackles, drop thy clay,
Sweetly breathe thyself away:
Singing, to thy crown remove ;
Swift of wing, and fir'd with love.

Shudder not to pass the stream :
Venture all thy care on Him ;
Him, whose dying love and pow'r
Still'd its tossing, hush'd its roar.
Safe is the expanded wave ;
Gentle, as a summer's eve :
Not one object of his care
Ever suffer'd shipwreck there.
See the haven, full in view !
Love divine shall bear thee through.
Trust to that propitious gale:
Weigh thy anchor, spread thy sail.

'Saints, in glory perfect made,
Wait thy passage through the shade:
Ardent for thy coming o'er,
See, they throng the blissful shore.
Mount, their transports to improve:
Join the longing choir above:
Swiftly to their wish be giv'n :
Kindle higher joy in heav'n.
—— Such the prospects that arise,
To the dying Christian's eyes!
Such the glorious vista, faith
Opens through the shades of death!
                                    Toplady.

Something New.—Among the candidates ered yesterday for admission to the freshman ss at Cambridge, was a pupil of the Perkins stitution for the Blind—a youth of sixteen, ind from his birth. He passed a perfectly tisfactory examination in all the branches,

and was duly admitted. He has been a pupil of the institution over six years, and has ac-quired, besides an acquaintance with the branches requisite for admission to college, a knowledge of the French language and of the science of music.

We were anxious to know how this youth who has entered college was to progress in his studies, as all the books are not printed in raised letters, and we learned that he is as-sisted by a lad with a pair of eyes, who reads his lesson, looks out words in the dictionary, consults the grammarian, &c. His lesson once committed, he goes to his tutor, who reads passages to him, for instance in Greek ; these he will translate and parse with ease, and such is the increase of the power of memory by this practice, that it goes far to counterbalance the loss of sight.—Boston Journal.

THE FRIEND.

NINTH MONTH, 12, 1840.

An article in the American and Foreign Anti-Slavery Reporter for the present month, after some introductory remarks, proceeds as fol-lows :—

" We have made these remarks preliminary to a proposal we are about to make, to aboli-tionists and all other friends of the people of colour. Let a fund be raised, and entrusted to a board of wise and philanthropic men, for the benefit of coloured youth. Let this board seek out those who are endowed with superior talents, who possess high moral worth, who are skilful, industrious, enterprising—and af-ford them the necessary aid to acquire me-chanical trades, and a good education. What an incalculable blessing such an organization might be to the subjects of it, to the coloured people in general, to society at large, to the cause of emancipation !—There are those who would gladly contribute to such a fund, and we doubt not an efficient committee might be se-lected to appropriate the funds wisely and ad-vantageously.

" Since the above was penned, the executive committee of the American and Foreign Anti-Slavery Society have passed the following resolutions :

" Resolved, that this committee recommend the formation of a Board of Relief, for the pur-pose of securing funds from benevolent indi-viduals, to be loaned or expended for the bene-fit of meritorious persons of colour, especially young men of uncommon abilities and moral worth, with a view to aiding them in acquiring a knowledge of mechanical arts, and in obtain-ing a good education.

" Resolved, that the following gentlemen be requested to act as such committee, to supply vacancies, and add to their numbers: William Jay, S. S. Jocelyn, Lewis Tappan, S. E. Cornish, S. E. Morse, and Christopher Rush."

We like the spirit of these resolutions. They indicate a mode of benevolent action for the benefit of the coloured people which we have long considered of primary importance, and equally so, whether we look to their colo-nization in Africa or in Canada, to their emi-gration to the British West India colonies—or

to their remaining among us as a component part of the body politic ; and we would fondly cherish the hope, that the scheme of raising funds for this object will be liberally sustained. With regard to the members of our own reli-gions society, at least within the compass of this Yearly Meeting, we have within our borders an institution originating in principles of kindred character, which will, or ought to, monopolise the whole of their liberality in this way for some time to come. We allude to the Institute for Coloured Youth. This inter-esting establishment, favourably situated some six or eight miles from the city, is about com-mencing its operations upon a limited scale ; but though patronised by and under the con-trol of some of our most enterprising and gene-rous minds, must, without additional aid, of necessity be cramped, if it does not languish, through inadequacy of pecuniary means. This ought not, and we trust will not be permitted to be long the case, among a people so emi-nently blessed " in basket and in store" as we have been and remain to be.

A young woman, a member of the Society of Friends, wants a situation as teacher in a Friend's school. She is well qualified to teach the usual branches of an English education, and would have no objection to going to the country. A note addressed to B. D. and left at the office of " The Friend," will meet with immediate attention.

WEST TOWN BOARDING SCHOOL.
An adjourned meeting of the Committee on Instruction will be held on 6th day, the 18th instant, in the Committee room, on Mulberry street, at 3 o'clock in the afternoon.
                    THOMAS KITE, Clerk.

Haddonfield Boarding School for Girls,
Under the care of Amy Eastlack and sister, is again re-opened, and ready for the reception of pupils; and those who wish to place their children in this institution this fall or winter, are requested to forward their names early. Terms are thirty dollars per quarter, of twelve weeks, payable in advance. Application may be made at the school, or to
WILLIAM EVANS, No. 134 south Front st.
THOMAS KITE, No. 132 north Fifth street.
HENRY WARRINGTON, Westfield, N. Jersey.
JOSEPH B. COOPER, Newton, New Jersey.
8th mo. 25th, 1840.

HAVERFORD SCHOOL.
The Semi-Annual Examination will com-mence on fifth day the 10th inst. and close on third day the 15th inst. Parents and others interested in the school are respectfully invited to attend.
9th month 3d, 1840.

DIED.—At his residence in Delaware county, Penn-sylvania, on seventh day, the 29th of 8th month, in the 84th year of his age, MOSES PALMER, a valuable mem-ber of Concord Monthly Meeting, in the station of an elder.

—— , in Baltimore, on the 18th of 8th month last, SARAH WEBSTER, in the 70th year of her age. Through-out a long protracted illness she evinced the patience of a Christian, and has left on the minds of her friends a consoling belief, that through the merits of a cruci-fied Saviour, her reward is with the spirits of the just in the kingdom of Heaven.

THE FRIEND.

A RELIGIOUS AND LITERARY JOURNAL.

VOL. XIII.   SEVENTH DAY, NINTH MONTH, 19, 1840.   NO. 51.

EDITED BY ROBERT SMITH.

PUBLISHED WEEKLY.

Price two dollars per annum, payable in advance.

Subscriptions and Payments received by

GEORGE W. TAYLOR,

NO. 50, NORTH FOURTH STREET, UP STAIRS,

PHILADELPHIA.

LIFE IN SIBERIA.

A late number of the Foreign Quarterly Review has an article, the subject of which is the narrative of an expedition by order of the Russian government, under direction of Lieutenant, now Admiral, Von Wrangel; undertaken for the purpose of completing the survey of the north-eastern coast of Siberia, and to determine, if possible, the long pending enigma, of the existence of a large polar continent. The reviewers pronounce the work one of the most attractive of the kind that has for some years passed through their hands. The publication, say they, has been unaccountably delayed for more than ten years, and appears at length in the form of a translation; while the original Russian manuscript is still allowed idly to repose in the archives of the admiralty at St. Petersburg.

We propose transferring to our pages a considerable part of the article. On the 23d of the 3d month, 1820, the author left St. Petersburg, and on the 2d of the 11th month arrived at Nishney Kolymsk; which for three years was destined to form the centre of his operations.

The cold became more severe as our author advanced further towards the north, and before reaching Sredne-Kolymsk, though yet in the middle of October, the thermometer had already marked 29° below zero. He thought it high time, therefore, to make his winter toilette, the particulars of which may be interesting to those of our readers who are desirous of studying foreign fashions.

"Over my customary travelling uniform I had first to pull a *camisole* with sleeves and breast-piece, both lined with the fur of the silver fox. Over my feet I drew double socks of soft young reindeer skin; and, over these, high boots or *torbassy* of similar material. When riding, I put on, in addition, my *nakolenniki* or knee-pieces. Lastly came the *Kukhlanka*, or over-all, a sort of wide sack, with sleeves, made of double reindeer skin, with fur inside and out, and a hood of fur hanging down the back. There were also a number of small pieces to protect the face; the *nanosnik* for the nose, the *naborodnik* for the chin, the *naushniki* for the ears, the *na-*

lobnik for the forehead, &c.: and to complete my costume came an immense fox-skin cap with long ears. I was so embarrassed by this cumbersome, and to me unaccustomed dress, that it was only with the assistance of my attendant I was able to mount my horse. Fortunately, the skin of the reindeer is exceedingly light, considering its warmth and closeness; otherwise it would be impossible to bear the weight of so many pieces of fur."

Nishney-Kolymsk is a wretched fishing village, consisting of a church and forty-two houses or huts, into which the inmates creep for shelter during their nine months' winter, but which are left to take care of themselves during what are called the summer months, when the whole population wander away to catch fish and reindeer, of which the meat when frozen is laid by as a stock for the winter. Completely exposed to the piercing winds that come sweeping from the north pole, the climate of the place is even more severe than its latitude would imply. On the 2d of November, when M. von Wrangel arrived, the thermometer stood at 32° (36° below zero of Fahrenheit); and though in summer the temperature sometimes rises to 18° (70° of Fahrenreit) yet the average for the year is not above 8° below the freezing point of Réaumur. During the first week in September the Kolyma is usually frozen over, and in January the cold reaches 43° (50° below Fahrenheit's zero), when the very act of breathing becomes painful, and the snow itself throws off a vapour! The intense cold is usually accompanied by a thick mist, a clear day being of rare occurrence during the whole winter. For eight-and-thirty days the sun never rises, and for fifty-two it never sets. The summer itself brings little enjoyment with it, for in the early part of July the gnats or mosquitoes appear in such countless swarms, that they fairly darken the atmosphere, when large fires are lighted of dried moss or leaves, under the smoke of which not only the inhabitants but even the cattle seek shelter from the persecutions of their diminutive tormentors. These insects, however, perform one most important office for the good people of Nishney-Kolymsk, by driving the wild reindeer from the forest to the open heath or *tundra.* The herds wander by thousands during the gnat season towards the sea-coast, when, more particularly while crossing the rivers, large numbers of them are easily killed by the hunters.

Vegetation is almost extinct in this northern region. A few berries are in favourable seasons collected by the women; but with this exception no plant grows that can be used for food. The soil never thaws; and of the few stunted trees that still linger about the Lower Kolyma, the roots seldom strike into the ground, but lie for the most part stretched

along the surface, as though they shrunk from the thick strata of ice below. A few wild flowers adorn the heaths in summer; the rose and the forget-me-not then invite the sentimental lover to expatiate on their beauty, if love and sentiment can indeed exist where all nature is covered with an almost perpetual shroud,—a north wind, even in summer, scarcely ever failing to bring with it a snow-storm.

The district of Kolymsk is calculated to contain 2498 male inhabitants, including 325 Russians and Cossacks. Of this population, 2173 are subjected to the *yassak* or direct tax, which produces 803 fox-skins, 98 sables, and 10,847 rubles in money. The Russians are mostly the descendants of real or supposed criminals; the Cossacks claim the original conquerors of Siberia as their ancestors, form a distinct corporation, and are exempt from the *yassak.* Our author speaks much of the social virtues of these simple-minded denizens of the north, who, during their long and dreary winter, find means to relieve the tedium and monotony of their existence by song, dance, and various other unpretending in-door amusements.

The dwellings of the Russians along the Lower Kolyma vary but little from those of the Yakoots and other Siberian aborigines. The trees in this part of the country being too stunted to afford any materials for building, the inhabitants depend for their supply of timber wholly upon the drift wood brought down the river by the annual inundations which seldom fail to accompany the breaking up of the ice. As soon as a sufficient number of trees has been collected, a kind of log hut is constructed, the interstices of which are filled up with moss and clay, and for the sake of warmth, a mound of earth is raised all round to a level with the window. These huts measure usually from two to three fathoms square, and one and a half fathom in height. In one corner stands the *tshuval*, or fire-hearth, the smoke of which escapes by a small hole in the roof; but, in a few houses, luxury has extended already to the adoption of regular Russian stoves with chimneys. Low and incomplete partitions divide the sleeping places of the several members of the family, and the rest of the dwelling is made to serve all the multifarious offices of kitchen, workshop, sitting and reception room, broad benches being placed around, on which reindeer skins are spread as a ready couch for an occasional guest. Such a hut is usually provided with two small windows of ten or twelve inches square, through which, if glazed, a scanty light would find its way, but as a substitute for glass fish-bladders are used in summer, and in winter plates of ice, seldom less than six inches in thickness, through which only a very feeble portion of daylight is able to pierce. A small store-house usually stands by the side of the dwelling, and the roofs of both are fitted up with a scaffolding for the drying of fish.

Little value appears to be set on cleanliness of any kind. Public baths are maintained by the order of government, though rarely visited by the inhabitants. Linen or calico is worn only by the more wealthy, and among them the use of it is mostly confined to the women. A shirt of soft reindeer skin with the fur inside, is generally worn next the skin. The outer side of this garment is. dyed with a red colour obtained from a decoction of alder bark, and round the edges and the sleeves it is ornamented with narrow stripes of beaver and other skin, which are obtained at high prices from the Tshuktshi. The trousers, likewise of reindeer skin, descend half way down the leg, and over the whole comes the *kamleya* of thick tanned reindeer skin, without the fur. The *kamleya* soon receives a dark yellow tint, from the smoky atmosphere by which the wearer is almost always surrounded. The above constitutes the home costume; but when the Kolymskite dandy ventures abroad he takes care to array himself in various other descriptions of fur, of which some conception may be formed from the account given a few pages back, of M. von Wrangel's travelling accoutrements.

Except on state occasions, the dress of the women differs but little from that of the men, unless in the arrangement of the head gear.

"To form a just conception of life on the banks of the Kolyma," says M. von Wrangel, "one must have spent some time with the inhabitants. One must have seen them in their winter dwellings and in their summer *balagans* ; one must have shot down their rapid streams in the light canoe, must have climbed mountains and rocks with them, or dashed in their light dog-drawn sledges through the most piercing cold over the boundless tundra ; one must in short have become one of themselves. Such was our life during the three years we spent here. We lived with them, dressed like them, fed on their dried fish, and shared with them the hardships and privations inseparable from the climate, and the frequent want even of food which it brings along with it.

"Let us begin with the spring. The fishery forms their most important pursuit; indeed the very existence of the whole population depends upon it. The locality of Nishney-Kolymsk, however, is unfavourable, and the inhabitants are obliged to migrate at this season to more suitable parts of the river. As soon as the winter ceases, they accordingly abandon their dwellings in search of some convenient spot, where they forthwith construct a *balagan*, or light summer hut, and immediately commence their hostilities upon the piscatory tribe. Most of the Nishney-Kolymskites have regular country-houses of this description at the mouths of the several creeks and rivulets, which they begin to visit in April, in order to prepare for the campaign. In the middle of May, when the merchants arrive from the fair of Ostrovnoye, on their return to Yakoutsk, the whole population abandons the little place, leaving the whole town to the guardianship of one Cossack sentinel, and perhaps one or two old

women, whom age prevents from joining in the general pursuit.

"Spring is the most trying season of the whole year. The store collected during the summer and autumn has usually been consumed for some time; the fish do not always make their appearance immediately, and the dogs, exhausted by their winter work, and yet more by the severe fast to which they have for some time been subjected, are too feeble to allow their masters to avail themselves of the *nast*,* to catch a few elks and wild reindeer. Famine then appears in its most horrible form. Crowds of Tungusians and Yukaheers come flocking into the Russian villages in search of some subsistence. Pale and ghost-like, they stagger about, and greedily devour every species of garbage that falls in their way. Bones, skins, thongs of leather, every thing in short that the stomach will receive, is eagerly converted into food. But small is the relief they find ; for the unthrifty townspeople are by this time almost as ill off themselves, and living upon the scanty remnant of fodder stored up for the use of the dogs, so that many of these faithful and valuable animals perish nearly every year of hunger. There is a store-house established by the government, where rye flour is sold to every comer ; but the expense of conveying it from so enormous a distance enhances the price to such a degree that few are able to avail themselves of the facility thus afforded them. Although the additional accommodation is granted them of not paying before autumn, still there are not many who can afford to give twenty rubles for a pood of flour, which moreover has often been damaged during the protracted journey it has had to perform. Three of these periods of horror did I witness, during three succeeding springs, and even now I shudder when I reflect on the scenes of suffering which I beheld, and of which it would be utterly impossible for me to attempt a description.

It is just when famine is at its worst that relief arrives. Suddenly countless swarms of birds make their appearance. Swans, geese, ducks, and several descriptions of snipes. These are the first heralds of spring, and at their coming hunger and want are at an end. Old and young, men and women, all that can walk or run, now rush out with guns, bows, and sticks, to kill as many as they may. In June the ice breaks up, a profusion of fish comes crowding into the river, and all hands are in movement to avail themselves of the short season of grace to provide a store for the coming year. But here a new misfortune often assails them. The stream is not strong enough to float away with sufficient rapidity the mighty masses of ice. These accumulate in the narrows and shoals, and the water, arrested in its course, quickly overflows the whole of the low country, and, if the inhabitants are not

* When the warmth of the spring's sun thaws the surface of the snow, it freezes again during the night, whereby a thin crust of ice is formed, strong enough to bear a sledge with its team of dogs. In this condition the snow is called *nast*, over which the elks and the reindeer are pursued during the night, and, as owing to their greater weight, they are constantly breaking through the ice, they are caught by the hunters with little trouble.

quick enough in driving their hor[ses] hills, the poor animals are infallibly [lost]; the summer of 1822 we had such [condi]tion at Nishney-Kolymsk, which c[ould] us so suddenly that we had only j[ust] take refuge with a few of our most i[mporta]ble articles upon the flat roofs of [the huts] where we were forced to remain fo[r] of a week. The water rushed w[ith] rapidity between the houses, and [the] place looked like a little archipelago [of] tops, among which the inhabitants [mer]rily rowing about in their canoes, p[aying] another friendly visits and catching f[ish].

" More or less these inundations o[ccur every] year, and when the waters subside [the] fishery with nets begins. Fish form[s the] food of man and dog, and for the y[early] sumption of the hundred families tha[t form] the little community of Nishney-Ko[lymsk at] least three millions of herrings are [caught]. Many other kinds of fish are caug[ht at this] time, among which is the *Nelma*, a [de]scription of salmon trout ; but the fi[sh are] generally thin, and are mostly conve[rted into] *yukhala* for the dogs ; that is to say, [fish] cleaned, and dried in the air. Fro[m the] trails an abundance of train oil is [obtained] which is used for food as well as for f[uel]. *yukola* is distinguished from the [one] merely by the selection of a better ki[nd of fish] and by greater care in the preparatio[n.]

" The proper season for bird h[unting is] when the animals are moulting, whe[n they] lost their feathers they are unabl[e to fly.] Large detachments are then sent of[f to the] fishing stations, and numbers of s[wans,] geese are killed with guns, bows, a[nd sticks.] The produce of this chase is said to [have dim]inished greatly of late years. Fo[rmerly it] was no unusual thing for the hunters [to bring] home several thousands of geese in [a day,] whereas now they are content if they [bring] as many during the whole season.

" While the men are fishing and [shooting] the women make the best use of th[e days] of fine weather, to collect the scant [produce] which the vegetable kingdom yields [in] the shape of a few berries and aroma[tic herbs.] The gathering in of the berries is a [season of] gaiety, like the vintage in souther[n countri]ties, spending the nights in the ope[n air] amusing themselves with song and d[ance, and] other innocent diversions. The ber[ries them]selves are preserved by pouring o[ver them] over them, and freezing them, in w[hich con]dition they form one of the favourite [foods] during the winter. Besides the ber[ries they] collect at this time the *makarsha*, [a] root found in large quantities in the [subter]nean storehouses of the field-mice. T[he] girls have a peculiar tact in discov[ering the] magazines of these little notable [animals,] whom, without the least remorse, the[y plunder] of the fruits of their provident indust[ry.]

For " The Friend."

SLAVERY IN INDIA.

It is a matter of interest to those conscientiously scrupulous of partak[ing in] products of slave labour, to know wh[ether] articles of East India origin, which many such persons have been in the habit of using, on the supposition that they were the result of free labour, actually are so or not. The negative has often been asserted and denied. The slavery acknowledged to exist in India, has been described as an institution growing out of the religion of the country, and the system of " caste,"—and as differing so essentially from what we understand by slavery, as no more to deserve the name than do those political institutions of many other countries, which degrade certain classes of men, and debar them from the enjoyment of privileges destined by the creator for the common benefit.

There has been a great want of accurate information on this subject, in this country especially—a want which will in a good degree be supplied, I hope, by the circulation of the little book, the title of which stands at the head of this article. It is the work of William Adam, a native of England, and formerly in the service of the East India company, from both of which, circumstances have separated him : he is now a resident of Cambridge, Massachusetts, and holds a professorship in the college there. He addresses himself in the form of letters to T. Fowell Buxton.

His chief object is to draw the attention of the British people to the great extent of slavery in India, and to the prevalence of those abuses necessarily connected with the system ; of which neither they, nor the world, seem to have been sufficiently sensible. He appears from his residence there, and the nature of his pursuits, to have had favourable opportunities of collecting facts, though the difficulties of doing so are such that on some points he is not able to be very precise. This is especially the ease in regard to the number of slaves in India ; no general census having yet been taken, nor any other official return of population in such form as to distinguish the bond and free. He relies, therefore, mainly, upon the estimates of the most intelligent writers upon the subject, and arrives at the conclusion, that there cannot be less than 500,000 slaves in that country, and that in all probability the actual number reaches a full million.

The condition of these slaves is various, and to understand this clearly, it is necessary to explain the origin of the system. When India was entered by the British, it was under the dominion of the Mahommedans, who had brought the Hindus into subjection by force of arms. The Hindus themselves were also conquerors of a race who had preceded them, and who are reputed to be the aborigines of the land. Many of these were reduced to slavery by the Hindus, and their descendants still remain in bondage under the Hindu law ; for their Mahommedan masters allowed them, with certain reservations, the enjoyment of their own customs and laws, and even permitted them to hold in bondage thousands who were not taken captive in war, notwithstanding the law of Mahommed expressly forbad the followers of the prophet themselves from enslaving any but prisoners of war and their descendants. Under the latter law, many of the Hindus became slaves, and still continue so ; for the English, practising the same policy, allowed both them and their Hindu predecessors to retain those

usages which were not deemed inconsistent with the commercial and political aggrandisement of the East India company.

As before stated, besides these victims of war, there are great numbers held in bondage, by the Hindus, under the sanction, one may say, of the company, though, as it is alleged, in many instances, contrary to their laws. Adam tells us, that a prolific source of slavery in India, is the sale of free children by their parents. The existence of this practice is so notorious that it seems scarcely necessary to support the statement by any authority. He however does quote several creditable writers in proof of the assertion. Colebrooke, he says, represents that during a famine or a dearth, parents have been known to sell their children for prices so very inconsiderable, and so little more than nominal, that they may in frequent instances have credit for a better motive than that of momentarily relieving their own necessities, namely, the saving of their childrens' lives. by interesting in their preservation persons able to provide nourishment for them. He is however mistaken, says Adam, when he goes on to state that there is no reason to believe that they are ever sold from mere avarice and want of natural affection in the parent.

There is perhaps no country in the world that has been subjected in modern times to so many and heart-rending famines as British India, and we may hence infer how considerable the number of those who by means of slavery have been preserved from starvation, and in times of famine have been consigned to slavery. This, at least in Bengal, in Colebrooke's opinion, is the chief source of domestic slavery.

The next is kidnapping, an evil the extent of which cannot be fully known ; it appears to be practised at the present day, under the very eye of government, and in the very heart of Calcutta.

Chaplin's official report shows that, in the Mahratta country, subject to the Bombay presidency, the practice of kidnapping has arisen out of the sale of children by their parents in times of famine. " A great number," says he, " have within these few years been imported into the Dekhan. Under these circumstances, and this mode of disposing of a famishing offspring, it seems beyond all doubt to have been the means of alleviating scarcity. One great evil has however resulted, that of kidnapping children for the purpose of selling them in distant countries as slaves. This is a common practice amongst the Lumans and Brinjarees ; but it may be prevented by forbidding the sale of all children, of whom a satisfactory account of the manner of procuring them is not given."

In the Madras territories also, kidnapping exists to a great extent. Baber states, that while he was in India, the duties led to constant official intercourse, upon a variety of subjects, with the political residents at the courts of the neighbouring states of Mysore, Coorg, Cochin, and Travancore, some of which related " to slaves who had been kidnapped in Travancore," a native state, " and sold to British subjects ; and even to free-born children of various castes of Hindus, subjects of the Cochin or Travancore Rajas, reduced to slavery in the honourable company's dominions, who

had been procured by the most fraudulent and violent means, and deprived of their caste by cutting off the lock of hair (the distinguishing mark of their caste), by making them eat prohibited food, and otherwise disguising and polluting them." He further states, that one of the varieties and sources of domestic slavery in the western provinces south of the Kistna to Cape Comorin, is " kidnapped persons brought by Bingurries and other travelling merchants from distant inland states, and sold into slavery." In 1787, when Fra Paulino wrote his account of Travancore, " several thousands of persons were being sold annually like cattle, and sent out of the country ;" and in 1811, Baber relates that he discovered and suppressed a traffic consisting in the kidnapping of slaves and free-born children from the Cochin and Travancore states, and importing them into Malabar, and this traffic he states had been carried on for a period of twelve years by the overseer of the company's plantation in Malabar, and under authority alleged to have been granted by the Bombay government. He thinks, with truth, that he could point out hundreds of these slaves in every town in Malabar, there being few Mahommedan and Christian houses in which there were not some of them.

A. D. Campbell also states, that " there can be no doubt that children are sometimes kidnapped and sold as slaves without the knowledge of their parents, among the lowest and poorest of the Hindus ; and their anxiety to recover infants whom they in all probability found it very difficult to support, would have done honour to the highest classes of European society."

Adam refers to an instance of this nefarious traffic in Madras, brought to light no longer ago than the eleventh month of last year. The case is related by the superintendent of marine police at that place. He detected a party smuggling off eight young children to a native brig. This led to a search, and resulted in the discovery and rescue of twenty-eight children, two of them girls, and all between the ages of three and ten years. " It appears," says the superintendent, " by all the evidence adduced, that these poor children have been stolen, decoyed, and purchased ; two from Bimlipatam, twenty-six from Caliogapatam ; and I have no doubt, if the case is properly handled in the supreme court, that the nacoda, or master of the vessel, his owner, and his passengers, all Musalmans, will be convicted as slave dealers, and the brig—the Magdien—will be confiscated. The children have deposed that they were brought away by the above parties ; some of them say they were stolen, some that they were decoyed away, and a few that their parents sold them ; they have given their former names, and their present names as fixed by their masters ; they are all Gentoos ; they have been converted, or rather, forcibly changed, by their masters from that caste to Musalmans."

On this, Adam justly remarks, that while slavery continues, kidnapping must be expected. Kidnapping is one of the sources of slavery, and increases the number of slaves ; but it is also one of the fruits of slavery, for it exists only in slave-holding countries. There can be no effectual suppression of kidnapping,

much we may profess to abhor it, cherish or even only tolerate its cause titution of slavery.

ext source of slavery in India is the on of slaves either by land or sea. s been greatly diminished by legal on the part of the company ; but, good grounds to suspect, not wholly od : indeed Chaplin distinctly asserts, n to that extensive district of country e Dekhan, or Deccan, that although rt of slaves from foreign states now ohibited by the orders of the supreme nt, "this has increased the price, utting a stop to the traffic."

ekhan is a large part of all India, em- he whole country south of the Ner- which river, judging from a map be- rises about 500 miles west of Calcutta, harges into the gulf of Cambia, at -west angle of the peninsula of Hin-

understands the traffic mentioned by o be overland, but he adduces the tes- f a number of individuals, and relates cumstances himself, to prove that the on by sea has not ceased. He men- instance, that during part of the time as resident in Calcutta, he was tenant e belonging to an Armenian landlord, occupied by an Armenian family, and n Amratola street, in which, and in ourhood, there are several Armenian one of the appurtenances of the house olam-khana, or slave-keep, a roomy uncomfortable apartment, but with ars and a padlock on the door like of wild beasts. He has also been hat African slaves not uncommon medan families, and he found a con- of this statement in the fact that by a ich he made of the population of the oorshedabad, in 1836, under the au- government, it was shown that there to the household of the Nuwab of labad, sixty-three eunuchs, stated by ers of the Nuwab's family, to be of n birth.

rd helpeth Man and Beast.—During . to conquer the world, Alexander the an, came to a people in Africa, who remote and secluded corner in peace- nd knew neither war nor conqueror. him to the hut of their chief, who re- m hospitably, and placed before him ates, golden figs and bread of gold. at gold in this country ? said Alexan- ke it for granted, (replied the chief) wert able to find eatable food in thou try. For what reason then art thou ng us ? Your gold has not tempted t, said Alexander, but I would wil- ome acquainted with your manners ms. So be it, rejoined the other, so- ng us as long as it pleaseth thee. At of this conversation, two citizens en- ato their court of justice. The plain- I bought of this man a piece of land, vas making a deep drain through it, I easure. This is not mine, for I only for the land, and not for any treasure

that might be concealed beneath it ; and yet the former owner of the land will not receive it. The defendant answered : I hope I have a conscience as well as my fellow citizen. I sold him the land with all its contingent, as well as existing advantages, and consequently the treasure inclusively.

The chief, who was at the same time their supreme judge, recapitulated their words, in order that the parties might see whether or no he understood them aright. Then after some reflection said : Thou hast a son, friend, I be- lieve ? Yes ! And thou (addressing the other) a daughter ? Yes !—Well then, let thy son marry *thy* daughter, and bestow the treasure on the young couple for their marriage portion. Alexander seemed surprised and perplexed. Think you my sentence unjust? the chief asked him. Oh, no, replied Alexander, but it astonishes me. And how, then, rejoined the chief, would the case have been decided in your country ?—To confess the truth, said Alexander, we should have taken both parties into custody, and have seized the treasure for the king's use. For the king's use ! exclaimed the chief, now in his turn astonished. Does the sun shine on that country !—O yes ! Does it rain there ?—Assuredly. Wonderful ! but are there tame animals in the country that live on the grass and green herbs ? Very many, and of many kinds. Aye, that must be the cause, said the chief ; for the sake of those in- nocent animals the All-gracious Being continues to let the sun shine and the rain drop down on your country.—*Coleridge.*

Effects of the temperance reformation in Ireland.—It has been asserted by temperance men, as a strong argument in favour of abolish- ing the traffic in intoxicating drinks, that in- temperance was, directly or indirectly, the cause of a large portion of the crimes which were committed in civilized society. The late accounts from Ireland show a wonderful dimi- nution in crime, as appears by the criminal courts in that country. The judges in their charges, in almost every case, congratulating the juries on the meagre aspect of the criminal docket, presented a marked contrast to similar addresses at the assizes in England. At Lim- erick assizes, Mr. Justice Ball, in his charge to the grand jury, bore the following testimony to the temperance reformation and its effects : " I am happy to find," said he, " on referring to the Crown book, that there are only three cases for trial, and but one prisoner in the city jail, a circumstance which is probably with- out parallel. I learn from the inspector of the prison, that his experience leads him to at- tribute it in one degree to the vastly improved moral habits of the people, from sobriety. The vice of drunkenness has become so rare, that it is now looked on as a most improper thing. I hope the operation of this improved moral habit will increase, so that the judges who fol- low me will also have to congratulate you on the same subject, and it reflects high credit on the local authorities, that the exertions they have made to suppress intoxication, and reform the habits of the people, have had a salutary influence. This happy state of things affords a model to every other city in Ireland, and I

hope the good example w lowed."

A good conscience, i health is to the body. It ease and serenity within countervail all the calamit can befal us. I know n generous mind to get ove proach, and nothing palli than our consciousness th them. If any one speaks tetus, consider whether i side, and if so, reform thy may not affect thee. Wh told, that the very boys la —aye, says he—then I m ter. Plato, being told th mies who spoke ill of hi said he, I will live so th them. Hearing at anoth mate friend of his had sj him—I am sure he would he had not some reason surest, as well as the nobl the sting out of a reproach of preparing a man for thi lief against the pains of cal *science.*

[From the Farmer

CONDUCTIN

Among conductors of t metallic substances are, pre-eminence ; iron, altho it answers the purpose p score of economy, has b use of conducting-rods. dence of its entire efficie stance can be cited, of a bt sixty feet in extent from th arranged conducting-rod e electricity.

Conductors should be rods, half an inch in diam a point of platinum, or o these metals are preferred remaining unchanged by mosphere, and bright surfa the electric fluid with th putting up conductors, it should extend six or most elevated part of the is attached, and coming d to be connected with a ba more square, and eight or is to be buried in the ear extending at an angle of 4 building. Preparatory to sufficient excavation shoul of three or four bushels of c around its lower terminati wet with water before repl is a very important part c the charcoal being indestr exceedingly retentive of w conductor, it serves to diff to the general mass of r descends the conducting-ro

For "The Friend."

The collector of the following fragments has for many years been in the practice, when he met in his reading with any fact which could illustrate the rise of our society in America, of noting it down, and the authority upon which it rested. Being desirous of placing the information thus obtained in a form accessible to others, he planned a series of biographical sketches, of which those concerning George Rofe and Robert Barrow, which have already appeared in "The Friend," were part. He now proposes, with the permission of the editor, to commence the publication of these notices in chronological order, in connection with facts and documents necessary to enable the reader to gather a general outline of the first spreading of our religious principles on the western continent, and its adjacent islands. In the first attempt at obtaining a satisfactory feeling of certainty, in respect to the order of events, many difficulties occurred. The small amount of information furnished by Sewell was derived from George Bishop, whose object in his "New England Judged" was not to settle the times, but to prove that the rulers of all the patents, except those of Providence and Rhode Island, were guilty of persecution. For this purpose he gathered together a mass of conclusive facts, to which dates are but seldom attached. Some of the errors into which Sewell and others have been led by this want of chronological arrangement, I have been enabled to rectify by reference to the publications of John Rouse, Christopher Holder, John Copeland, and Humphrey Norton, from whom Bishop principally derived the facts which he has narrated.

—

Historical fragments, illustrating the early religious labours of Friends in America, with biographical sketches of the first ministers who visited it.

"In 1655 many went beyond seas, where truth also sprang up."	*George Fox's Epistles.*

The first ministers of the gospel in the Society of Friends who visited America were Anne Austin and Mary Fisher. Anne Austin appears to have been a resident of London; she was, at the time of her leaving England on this religious visit, a wife, and the mother of five children. Mary Fisher, who was one of the earliest labourers in the work of the ministry in England, appears from the number of imprisonments she endured within its borders, to have been an inhabitant of Yorkshire. She was, when she joined Anne Austin, a maiden of about thirty years of age. Towards the close of the year 1655, they were together at Barbadoes, but whether they left England as companions, or became banded together in the fellowship of the gospel after reaching that island, we have now no means of ascertaining. Of the amount of their ministerial labour there, we are ignorant; but from the after visits of Friends, it is evident that the seed which they were commissioned to sow, found entrance in the hearts of some. Several members of the family of Thomas Rouse, a lieutenant-colonel in the army, then a resident of the island, appear to have been convinced at this time.

In the spring of 1656 they sailed for Boston in the ship Swallow, of which Simon Kempthorn, of Charlestown, was master. Before we proceed to narrate the particulars of the reception they met with, it may be proper to describe the feeling of the public mind at that time in New England on the subject of religious liberty. The first settlers were men firmly persuaded of the truth of the puritanical doctrines of their fathers, and who deemed the toleration of any other opinions little less than a direct alliance with the devil, and connivance at his work. They individually saw the propriety of being themselves allowed the liberty of judging, and bore their testimony against prelacy, and whatever else they deemed to be error; but freedom of thought, which did not coincide with their views, they held to be licentiousness, and all dissent from their doctrine, "damnable heresy." With such sentiments, operating in men of stern and unbending characters, whose religion lay much in the intellect, and whose hearts had been but little softened by the operation of that word which alone can bring into the meekness and gentleness of Christ, we need not wonder if persecution for differences in doctrines should speedily arise. We shall not go into an account of the dissensions which sprang out of these attempts to enforce conformity; it will be sufficient to say, that whilst all religious freedom was banished or suppressed, the minds of many of the inhabitants became secretly dissatisfied with the arbitrary proceedings of the magistrates and priests.

Of those persecuted for their sentiments, Roger Williams was one, and on being banished in 1636, he, with some of his followers, founded the settlement at Providence, on land freely given him by the Indians. In 1637, William Coddington, John Clarke, William Hutchinson, John Coggshall, William Aspinwall, Thomas Savage, William Dyer, (the husband of Mary,) William Freeborne, Philip Shearman, John Walker, Richard Carder, William Baulstone, Edward Hutchinson, Edward Hutchinson, jr., Samuel Wilbore, John Samford, John Porter, and Henry Bull, disgusted with the intolerant spirit displayed in the Boston Patent, determined to seek an asylum for themselves, and for religious liberty in the wilderness. William Coddington had been a magistrate from the time of his first arrival in the country in 1630, and was one of the principal merchants in Boston.

He describes the rise of the spirit of persecution in Massachusetts in the following, which is an extract from a letter he wrote in 1679, to the governor of that colony.

"Friend, there was a time, about seven years from our first coming, which was to Salem, June the 12th, 1630, we brought over the Massachusetts patent, myself being chosen in England an assistant to the governor; and for that seven years a magistrate and treasurer; which was the best time that ever the Massachusetts saw—God exercising us with sickness and wants. But after seven years, the New England ministers, so called, being out of persecution, began to persecute about the testimony of the spirit, the light within. "Now was the time the magistrates were priest-ridden, and now others and myself did draw up our remonstrance as members of the court against persecution for succeeding times. Now it was that the priests would have accommodations of lands, with the best houses built for them, and they hired for their preaching, some at £100 per year, some more, some less. Now they were grown warm in their accommodations, so that John Cotton preached against them, as having lost their garment which they should not have been found without, which they kept in the blustering times of the bishops in England, but now the warm sunshine of their great accommodations and revenues had got their cloak from them. Now they were like them that having suffered in the times of Queen Mary, in Queen Elizabeth's days, became bishops; and some of them, *said he*, had lost the inward consolation of the spirit, and that they never saw good days after. Now was the iron bed, like that of the tyrant, made use of, that cut all according to it shorter or longer. Now was contention about the grace of God within us, and without us." "The priests began to usher in persecution in the Massachusetts. They attributed all to man. Cæsar might take God's share, and his own too, against the scriptures—Luke xx. 21, 25. For if men in reference to soul and body, things appertaining both to this and the other world, shall be subject to their fellow-creatures; what follows, but that Cæsar (however he has got it) has all God's share and his own too, and being lord of both, both are Cæsar's, and nothing God's. Now it was that that royal law began to be neglected, 'Whatsoever ye would that men should do unto you, do ye even so to them.' John Cotton did teach you how to distinguish between the scriptures and the spirit, and that the one was a dark lantern without the other, and that the things of God should not be given to Cæsar, and yet Cæsar should have his own."

So much at present for William Coddington's letter. John Clarke, who had made the original proposition that they should seek a refuge in the wilderness, was now chosen, with a few others, to select a suitable place. The previous summer (1637) had been unusually warm, and this led them to direct their steps to the north. Within the limits of what is now New Hampshire they first sought a situation, but the winter coming on, the keen blasts of the north warned them to seek a more southerly clime. The exploring expedition accordingly sailed south. They now thought of Long Island and of Delaware Bay; but whilst their vessel was coasting round to Narraganset, some of them passed over by land to Providence, and making their intentions known to Roger Williams, he recommended them to settle on Aquetneck, now Rhode Island. Finding, by application to the inhabitants of Plymouth, that the island was not considered within their limits, the adventurers returned to Boston. Here, on the 7th of the 1st month, (March,) 1638, they incorporated themselves into a body politic, and chose William Coddington their judge, or chief magistrate. The sachems of the Narraganset tribe of Indians sold them Aquetneck, and several smaller islands in the bay, for fifty fathoms of white beads.

The Indians resident upon it were induced to remove before winter, in consideration of a present of ten coats and twenty hoes. Having thus obtained peaceable possession, they settled upon Aquetneck, and gave to it the name of the Isle of Rhodes. At this settlement, and at that of Roger Williams, religious liberty and all freedom, consistent with the good of society, were tolerated. I have been thus particular in the description of the settlement of Rhode Island, because many of the original inhabitants became Friends, and because it proved a quiet resting place for the poor persecuted members of our society when whipped out of the adjoining patents.

At the town of Sandwich, although within the limits of Plymouth, a number of those who were dissatisfied with religious bigotry and political intolerance, had found shelter—some of them had already seen into the unlawfulness of war, and many were apparently waiting, scarcely attached to any sect, for the annunciation of a society of purer principles, and a more spiritual worship than those by whom they were surrounded. Indeed, a few of this description were found in every patent.

We may now return to Anne Austin and Mary Fisher. Early in the 5th month, 1656, the Swallow anchored in the port of Boston. Intelligence of the arrival of two Quakers was quickly communicated to Richard Bellingham, the deputy governor, who, in the absence of Governor Endicott, bestirred himself with notable diligence to prevent the threatened inroad of heretics among them. There was then no law against Quakers, for none had as yet set foot in the colony. In 1646 they had enacted a law against heresy and error, which decreed to banishment the opposers of the baptism of infants, and the deniers of the lawfulness of war, and this it was thought might be enforced against Anne and Mary. To prevent any person from being instructed in their principles, or convinced by their ministry, Bellingham commanded that the women should be closely confined on board the ship, and that their books should be taken from them and burnt. Of these they had with them about one hundred. Humphrey Norton having described the seizure of the books, says, " which being done, as thou mayest understand by their order, the common executioner was appointed to destroy them, (O, learned and malicious cruelty,) as if another man had not been sufficient to have burnt a few harmless books, who, like their masters, can neither fight, strike, nor quarrel."

The council being called together, the following order was issued:

"At a council held at Boston the 11th of July, 1656. Whereas, there are several laws long since made and published in this jurisdiction, bearing testimony against *hereticks* and *erroneous persons*, yet, notwithstanding *Simon Kempthorn, of Charlestown*, master of the ship *Swallow, of Boston*, hath brought into this jurisdiction, from the island of *Barbadoes*, two women, who name themselves *Anne*, the wife of one *Austin*, and *Mary Fisher*, being of that sort of people commonly known by the name of *Quakers*, who, upon examination, are found not only to be transgressors of the former laws, but do hold very dangerous *heretical* and blasphemous opinions, and they do also acknowledge, that they came here purposely

to propagate their said errors and *heresies*, bringing with them, and spreading here sundry books, wherein are contained most corrupt *heretical* and blasphemous doctrines, contrary to the truth of the gospel here professed among us.

The council therefore tendering the preservation of the peace and truth enjoyed and professed among the churches of Christ in this country, do hereby order:

First—that all such corrupt books, as shall be found upon search, to be brought in and spread by the aforesaid persons, be forthwith burned and destroyed by the common executioner.

Secondly—that the said *Anne* and *Mary* be kept in close prison, and none admitted communication with them without leave from the governor, deputy-governor, or two magistrates, to prevent the spreading of their corrupt opinions, until such time as they be delivered aboard of some vessel to be transported out of the country.

Thirdly—the said *Simon Kempthorn* is hereby enjoined, speedily and directly to transport, or cause to be transported, the said persons from hence to *Barbadoes*, from whence they came, he defraying all the charge of their imprisonment, and for the effectual performance hereof, he is to give security in a bond of one hundred pounds sterling, and on his refusal to give such security, he is to be committed to prison till he do it."

After this the two females were brought on shore, and, as one of them in speaking to the deputy used the word "thee," he said, he needed no more to prove them Quakers, and on this evidence committed them to prison. They were now closely confined, and a fine of five pounds was threatened against any who should speak to them even through the window of the prison. It is probable that the women found themselves constrained to publish the glad tidings of the gospel to the people, who, by curiosity or compassion, were led to look in upon them. The window was therefore boarded up. Their pens, ink and paper were now taken from them, lest, through the instrumentality of these, some communication should take place with the citizens. The rulers seem to have designed the death of these two innocent women, but they did not dare so far to offer violence to the feelings of the community, as to proceed to that extremity against those who had violated no law. But the inhabitants of New England were superstitious in no ordinary degree, and the belief in witchcraft which was every where prevalent, seemed to offer an opportunity to get rid of them without awaking the compassion of the multitude. Throughout the various patents, a number of females had already been put to death on that charge. Those executed at Boston were Margaret Jones in 1648, and Ann Hibbins, Bellingham's sister-in-law, but a few months before the arrival of Anne Austin and Mary Fisher. The cry of witchcraft was now raised against the prisoners, and their persecutors were eager in looking out for evidence to substantiate it. They could find no overt act, for the community had not yet learned that facility in manufacturing evidence on this subject, which, in after years, so completely destroyed the harmony of society, broke up

the peace of families ber of innocent ind death. In want of were stript, and t cruel and indecent were no mark of w popular superstition unusual sign was se who had thus sold t would have gone ha any singular mark, parent. But nothin found, and now the furnish them with p zens of Boston to su their extremity, Nic habitant of the city, ing him five shilling of furnishing them Kempthorn, we are arbitrary requisition probably paid for the try.

After remaining weeks, Anne and M a vessel bound to l liam Chichester was was bound, under a them to that island, to land in New E any of its inhabitant bible were detained They were sent fro 6th month.

(To be

(To be

A MINISTRY OF

In the course of came to Swarthmor Fell, in the year 165 tended his ministry markable degree in great change among garet Fox, speaking Swarthmore, my dw brought the blessed gospel, which I and parts have cause to t then husband, 'Thom of the assize, was go our house being a ministers and religio Fox's friends broug staid that night. N fast day, he went to but came not in until I and my children ha and when they had upon a seat, and des liberty to speak, and said he might. His not a Jew that is that circumcision whi Jew that is one inwa sion which is of the l said, that Christ was and lighteth every m world, and that by gathered to God. I wondered at his doctr such before.

"He went on and opened the scriptures, and said ' they were the prophets', Christ's, and the apostles' words, and what as they spoke, they enjoyed and possessed, and had it from the Lord.' He then said, ' What have any to do with the scriptures, but as they come to the spirit that gave them forth ? You will say Christ saith this, and the apostles say this ; but what canst thou say ? Art thou a child of light, and hast walked in the light, and what thou speakest, is it inwardly from God ?' This opened me so that it cut me to the heart, and I saw clearly we were all wrong. I sat down in my pew and cried bitterly ; and I cried in my spirit to the Lord, ' We are all thieves, we are all thieves ; we have taken the scriptures in words, and known nothing of them in ourselves.' So that served me, that I cannot tell what he said afterwards ; but he went on declaring against the false prophets, priests, and deceivers of the people. He came to our house again that night, and spoke in the family among the servants, and they were generally convinced. I was struck into such sadness, I knew not what to do ; I saw it was the truth, and could not deny it, and I received it in the love of it. I desired the Lord that I might be kept in it, and then I wanted no greater portion.

"In about three weeks my husband returned home ; many were in a rage, and captains and great ones went to meet my husband as he was coming, and informed him that a great disaster was befallen his family ; that they (George Fox, J. Naylor, and R. Farnsworth) were witches, and had taken us out of our religion, and that he must send them away, or all the country would be undone. He returned greatly offended, and what a condition was I likely to be in, either displease my husband or offend God. James Naylor and R. Farnsworth were there, and I desired them to speak to him, which they did very moderately and wisely ; but he was at first displeased with them, until they told him they came in love and good will to his house. He became pretty moderate, and his dinner being ready he went to it, and I went in and sat down by him. While I was sitting, the Power of the Lord seized upon me, and he was struck with amazement, and knew not what to think, but was quiet and still. The children were all quiet, and grown sober, and could not play on their music, which they were learning ; and all these things made him quiet and still.

"At night George Fox came, and after supper I asked my husband if he might come in. He said, yes. So George came in without any compliment, and began to speak very excellently, as ever I heard him ; that if all England had been there, I thought they could not have denied the truth of what he said, and my husband came to see it clearly. Several Friends being at our house, and speaking of the number who were convinced in that place, and their difficulty in getting accommodations to hold a meeting, my husband overheard them, and of his own accord said, ' You may meet here if you will.' Notice was given, and there was a large meeting on first day. My husband went that day to the steeple house, and none with him but his clerk and groom ; the priest and people were all troubled ; but praised be the Lord, they never got their wills upon us to this day."

Referring to the rise of Friends, George Fox gives a summary account, as " the appearance of the Lord's everlasting truth breaking forth, wherein the Lord's mighty power and word of life hath been richly and freely preached to the gathering of many into reconciliation with God by it, to the exaltation and glory of God, through the bringing forth of the heavenly and spiritual fruits from such as have been gathered by his eternal light, power and spirit unto himself. By sowing to the spirit in the hearts of people, life eternal has been reaped ; the flocks have been gathered, which have the milk of the word *plenteously;* the riches of the word have flourished and mightily abounded, and God's heavenly plough with his spiritual men have gone on cheerfully, to the turning over the fallow ground of the hearts that had not borne heavenly fruit to God. God's heavenly threshers, with his heavenly flail have with joy and delight threshed out the *chaff* and the *corruptions* that have been atop of God's seed, and wheat in man and woman, and thus have they threshed in hope, and are made partakers of their hope ; through which God's seed is come into his garner." "O, the inexpressible excellency of the everlasting glorious truth, gospel, and word of life, that the infinite, invisible, and wise God, who is over all, hath revealed and manifested ! How have the professors, priests, and powers risen up in opposition against his children, that are born of the immortal seed by the word of God ! How great have been the persecutions and reproaches, and spoiling of goods that have been executed upon them ! But they who are as dear to God as the apple of his eye, how hath the Lord manifested himself to stand by them, in overthrowing powers, priests, and states ! What changes have there been since 1644, 1650, and 1652 ! How have the jails been filled in this nation with the heirs of life, God's chosen ones, who had *no helper in the earth* but the Lord and *his Christ ?* So that truth's *faithful witnesses* were scarcely to be found *but in jails* and in *prisons,* where the righteous were numbered among the transgressors ; who had neither *staff* nor bag *from man,* but the staff, the bread of life, and the bag that holds the treasure that waxes not old. But the Lord Jesus Christ, *that sent them forth,* was their exceeding great *supporter* and *upholder* by his eternal power and spirit, both then and now." G. F.

Although many, like Demas, have forsaken the truth and loved this present world, its changeable friendships and religions, there are many who hold fast their integrity, and prefer Jerusalem as their chief joy. Their confidence is in the same Lord Jesus Christ, and it is their delight to feel his eternal power and spirit supporting them in all conflicts, and giving them the victory over their soul's enemies. They travail for the welfare of Zion, and the extension of her borders, and from time to time experience their faith renewed, that the blessed truth which visited their forefathers in a night of great darkness and apostacy, will yet visit and break forth in thousands, raising them up to testify the same blessed gospel of salvation, through the spiritual appearance of the Lord Jesus in the heart, who loved us, and died for us, and rose again for our justification.

STARTING IN LIFE.

It is of great importance that persons, in early life, should prepare themselves for the part they are to act in society. There is a strong desire in both sexes to rise to respectability ; and this is highly commendable ; but many persons err in their attempts to gain their object.

A principal cause of the failure of young people to reach the object of their desire, is, the attempt to *get rich without labour.* In this way, they often aim at an object without the means to accomplish it.

Young friends, learn wisdom. It is not the order of Providence that mankind should have blessing and prosperity without labour. It is best for mankind that this should be the order of things ; good moral habits are formed by industry ; sudden acquisitions of property tend to prevent the formation of such habits ; they are often ruinous to morals. Moderate acquisitions of property generate good habits—the habits of prudence, of foresight, and correct calculation of what is practicable.

The desire of reaching a respectable standing in life, has led many to renounce labour for books, with the expectation that they can live by learning. But the number of persons who can gain subsistence by learning, is comparatively small. By far the greatest part of mankind are destined to labour, without which society cannot be supported.

In forming a plan of business for life, therefore, the first requisite is to determine the course to be pursued, the occupation which is to be followed, and then to devote all possible attention to gain the qualifications essential to success in *that occupation.* In this preliminary to success, persons very often make great mistakes.

If a young man is to be a farmer, he must begin when a boy, and continue in that business. He must gain knowledge by experience, and muscular strength by labour. Books and learning will never make farmers.

If a young man is to be a mechanic, he must begin his art when young, and persevere in it, and be thoroughly master of every part of his business. Books and learning cannot supply the want of labour and experience. Farmers and artisans cannot be made in the school-house or college. Most of the studies cultivated in our seminaries of learning, however useful to professional men, are not applicable at all to the common occupations of life.

Most of the people of this country possess small estates, which, when divided, will not support their children. Hence it often happens that children, whom the father can support in a genteel style, fail, at his death, of the means of subsistence. Hence probably no country presents so many instances of young persons of both sexes, *educated above their condition,* as the United States. Many persons and families, within the knowledge of the writer, have been ruined, or doomed to struggle with adversity all their lives, from this mistake. They begin wrong ; they expect to be gentlemen and ladies, without the means of supporting themselves in such style.

Equally mistaken are many of the daughters of poor families. Some of them enter manufactories, where they get good wages, and dress in rich attire; neglecting to gain a thorough knowledge of housekeeping, the very knowledge they most want to insure them a good settlement.

In no particular, is the folly of females more remarkable than in their estimate of labour. They seem to think it disgracing to labour in the family as domestics, when they will labour in manufactories without objection. They do not consider that the proper sphere of females is in the family, and that they cannot fill that sphere without serving an *apprenticeship*, and they should no more disdain it, than young men should disdain to be apprentices to mechanics. The young of both sexes must be subordinate to those who are older, for it is from the experience and knowledge of older persons that they are to qualify themselves to be respectable masters and mistresses themselves. Girls who have no property should seek to be domestics for two or three years, in respectable, well-ordered families; for it is in these they are to learn, not only to do all kinds of work, but to improve their minds and their manners. It is the best, if not the only chance which many of them can have, thus to improve, and become respectable mistresses of families.—*S. S. Journal*.

* "*Troubled about many things.*"—What an exact description of the heart of every man who has not found "peace in believing." A heart that is set upon many things, must of necessity be troubled. It is tossed about from one side to the other, as the little bark upon the angry waters, or like the chaff driven by the wind. It flies to one after the other of the many things between which its affections are divided, seeking rest and finding none.

Yet strange as it may seem, the rest which many objects cannot bestow it may find in one. Its faculties, its capacities, its desires all point one way. In a multiplicity of objects then, it cannot find its chief good. Weariness, vexation and disappointment will be the result of the trial. How true and how striking then, the words of Christ, one thing is needful! And how wise the petition of David, "there be many that say, who will show us any good: Lord, lift up the light of thy countenance upon us!"

Stucco Wash.—Six quarts of clean lime, slaked in boiling water, two quarts of salt, five gallons of water—boil and skim, then add one pound of copperas, and three quarters of a pound pot or pearlash, gradually, and four quarts sifted wood-ashes—colour to taste or fancy: applied while hot.

2. Clean, fresh-burnt lime, same as above, quarter of a pound burnt alum, powdered, one pound sugar, three pints rice flour, made into a jelly, one pound clean glue, first dissolved —five gallons water: will retain its brilliancy for a century.—*Farmers' Cabinet*.

Selected for "The Friend."
LOST TIME.

The arrow parting from the bow—
   Though drawn with mighty strain,
May still be traced in rapid flight,
   And be replaced again.

But who in all the lapse of years,
   Since time began his race,
Has e'er regained a moment lost,
   Or filled his vacant place?

The bird when from its cage escaped,
   By soothing voice and word,
May still, perchance, again be caught,
   And to its perch restored.

But for the moments misemployed,
   In folly or in crime;
No voice nor word has e'er prevailed
   To stay the hand of time!

THE FRIEND.

NINTH MONTH, 19, 1840.

Having a strong predilection for the country and for country life—for whatever pertains to rural concerns and scenery, we accepted an invitation, nothing loath, a few days since to visit Haddington nursery, Samuel Rhoads, jr. proprietor, situated a short distance beyond the pleasant little village of the same name, west of the Schuylkill. The ride of about four and a half miles, can be varied at pleasure by the choice of several roads, diverging but little from the direct route, and through a pleasantly diversified and highly cultivated country. The object that first attracted attention on our arrival, was the neatness of the dwelling house, in which, without needless expense, architectural effect was tastefully combined with convenience in the arrangement of the apartments, in a way that might, with advantage, be imitated in other cases. The nursery grounds are in front of the house, on a slope displaying to the south-east, and though but moderate in extent, are well stocked with a carefully selected assortment of trees and shrubbery, a large proportion of which are of a size suitable for transplanting. Of apples, there are upwards of fifty varieties; of pears about eighty, a choice collection, many of them imported from Europe; to which may be added, plums, cherries, peaches of the most approved sorts. Also, apricots, quinces, English walnuts, upwards of thirty kinds of English gooseberries, currants, raspberries and grapes. The department of flowering shrubbery is rich, including fifty varieties of roses. Among the ornamental or shade trees, we may note as specially worthy of attention the English sycamore, the English ash, the weeping ash, (a tree of very singular character,) and the genuine sugar-maple, the latter to be recommended not only for its intrinsic beauty, but as remarkably free from insect depredations. But though last in this enumeration, yet not least as objects to be admired, are the evergreens, and pre-eminently among these, we refer to the balm of gilead or black spruce, and the Norway spruce. Of these beautiful species there is a finer display, both in number and perfection of form, than we remember to have before seen, and at prices comparatively low. In fine, whoever wishes

THE FRIEND.

A RELIGIOUS AND LITERARY JOURNAL.

VOL. XIII.　　　　　SEVENTH DAY, NINTH MONTH, 26, 1840.　　　　　NO. 52.

EDITED BY ROBERT SMITH.

PUBLISHED WEEKLY.

Price two dollars per annum, payable in advance.

Subscriptions and Payments received by

GEORGE W. TAYLOR,

NO. 50, NORTH FOURTH STREET, UP STAIRS,

PHILADELPHIA.

LIFE IN SIBERIA.

(Continued from page 402.)

Such is life on the Kolyma during the short summer, a season of activity for all, for in addition to the chief occupations of which we have just laid a brief epitome before our readers, there are many other, though less momentous, calls upon the industry of the inhabitants. Their huts perhaps want repairing, their boats have to be mended, and in the forests the traps must be looked after. The Russians at Nishney-Kolymsk are supposed to set about 7500 traps in the neighbouring country, which are visited about eight or ten times during the winter, and at each time they expect to find something in every tenth trap. The animals mostly caught are sables and foxes. The elks, the wild reindeer, and the wild sheep, also offer an attraction for the adventurous hunter, while others more ambitious wander forth in search of the mightier bear. The bear-hunters are the heroes of the Kolyma, and tales of their marvellous achievements form the standing topic during the long winter evenings, when old and young crowd about the warm *tshwal*, to while away their idle hours by the songs and traditions of their Russian ancestors as well as of their adopted land.

The best friend of man in almost every clime is the dog, but in northern Siberia existence would scarcely be possible without the aid of this invaluable animal. All along the Arctic ocean the dog is almost the only beast of burden. He is harnessed to the light sledge, or *narte*, which will carry no inconsiderable load, and in which, during winter, the natives perform journies of incredible length. The Siberian dog bears a strong resemblance to the wolf. He has a long pointed snout, sharp upright ears, and a long bushy tail. Some of them have short hair, others a tolerably thick fur, and they are met with of all imaginable colours. Their size also differs very much, but a dog is not thought fit for the sledge if less than one arshin and two wershok high, and one arshin and five wershok long.* Their barking resembles the howling of a wolf. They always remain in the open air. In summer they dig holes in the frozen earth to cool

* Three Russian arshins make seven English feet, and each arshin is divided into sixteen wershok.

themselves, and sometimes they will spend the whole day in the water to escape from the persecution of the gnats. Against the intense cold of winter they seek shelter by burying themselves under the snow, where they lie rolled up with the snout covered by the bushy tail. Of the cubs, the males only are usually kept, the females are mostly drowned, only one or two being entertained by each father of a family to preserve the breed. The rearing of these dogs forms an important occupation, and requires no little skill and judgment. A dog may be put to the sledge when a year old, but cannot be subjected to hard work before his third winter. The team of a sledge seldom consists of less than twelve of these dogs, of whom one is used as leader, upon whose breeding and docility the safety of the whole party depends. No dog must be used as a leader unless he be perfectly obedient to the voice of his master, nor unless the latter be certain that the animal will not be diverted one moment from his course by the scent of any kind of game. This last point is one of the highest importance, and if the dog has not been well broken in, but turns to the right or left, the rest of the dogs will immediately join in the pursuit, when the sledge is of course overturned, and the whole pack continue the chase until some natural obstacle intervene to arrest their course. A well-taught leader, on the other hand, not only will not allow himself to be seduced from his duty, but will often display the most astonishing tact in preventing the rest of the team from yielding to their natural instinct. On the boundless tundra, during a dark night, while the surrounding atmosphere is obscured by the falling snow, it is to the intelligence of his leading dog that the traveller is constantly indebted for his preservation. If the animal has once been the same road before, he never fails to discover the customary halting-place, though the hut may have been completely buried under the drifting snow. Suddenly the dog will remain motionless upon the trackless and unbroken surface, and by the friendly wagging of his tail, announce to his master, that he need only fall to work with his snow-shovel to find the door of the hut that offers him a warm lodging for the night. The snow-shovel, on these winter excursions, appears to be an appendage without which no traveller ventures upon a journey.

In summer the dog is no less serviceable than in winter. As in the one season he is yoked to the sledge, so in the other he is employed to draw the canoe up against the stream, and here they display their sagacity in an equally surprising manner. At a word, they halt, or where an opposing rock bars their progress on the one side, they will plunge into the water, swim across the river, and resume their course along the opposite bank. In short,

the dog is as indispensable to the Siberian settler, as the tame reindeer to the Laplander. The mutual attachment between the Siberian and his dog is in proportion to their mutual dependence on each other. M. Von Wrangel relates remarkable instances of the extent to which he has seen some of the people carry their fondness for their dogs. In 1821 an epidemic disease broke out among the dogs in Siberia, and carried off many thousands of them.

"A Yukaheer family had lost the whole of the twenty dogs of which they had recently been possessed, and two newly-born cubs were all that remained. As these animals were still blind, and without a mother's care, it scarcely appeared possible to preserve them. The Yukaheer's wife, to save the last remnant of the wealth of her house, resolved that the two dogs should share the milk of her breast with her own child. She was rewarded. The two adopted sucklings throve wonderfully, and became the ancestors of a new and vigorous race of dogs."

The sufferings of the poor inhabitants, in consequence of the loss of the dogs, through the epidemic malady that raged in 1821 and 1822, were dreadful in the extreme. Yet will it be believed, that an order was once actually issued by the government at St. Petersburg, to destroy all the dogs throughout the north of Siberia, "on account of their consuming such quantities of provisions, and thereby occasioning such frequent famines." The order was not executed, because it would have required the whole Russian army to enforce the command, and after a while means were found to enlighten the rulers upon the absurd tyranny of their proposed "reform." We see thus that England is not the only country where a colonial minister will at times indulge in the most extravagant vagaries.

Let us now accompany the Siberian into the interior of his hut, to which he returns as soon as the frost has put a stop to his fishing and hunting. The walls are carefully caulked with clay and moss; a fresh mound of earth is collected outside; the *tshwal* is repaired, and fresh ice-panes fastened into the windows. All this is seldom finished before the beginning of December. Then the several members of the family begin to creep more and more closely around their warm hearth, where a crackling fire yields the native of the arctic zone his only substitute for the absent sun. The flame of the *tshwal*, and of one or more lamps is then seen glimmering through the ice-panes, while from the low chimney arises a glowing column of smoke, carrying up with it, every now and then, a complete shower of sparks. The dogs crouch about the house, and three or four times a day, at tolerably regular intervals, more frequently perhaps when the moon shines, they raise a most tremendous howling, which is audible to a great distance over the plain. A low door, lined with the skin of a reindeer, or, if possible, with that of a white bear, admits the stranger into the interior of this dwelling. There the father and his sons are seen mending their nets, or making bows, arrows, and hunting-spears. The women are seen sorting and dressing the furs which the men have perhaps brought home from their last visit to the traps, or they may be engaged in the feminine task of repairing their own or their husbands' garments, on which occasions the sinews of the reindeer are made to supply the place of thread.

The dainties prepared by the culinary skill of the Kolymska matrons are not exactly calculated to excite the appetite of a Parisian gourmand. Fish and reindeer flesh form the invariable *pieces de resistance*, and train oil is the constantly recurring sauce. Yet, even with these scanty materials to go to work upon, female ingenuity is seldom at a loss to vary the bill of fare. An accomplished French cook will boast of his ability to dress eggs in three hundred and sixty-five different ways, and the housewife on the banks of the Kolyma shows herself almost equally inventive. Thus we have cakes made of the roe of the fish, or of the dry fish flour pounded in a mortar. Then the belly of the fish is chopped small, and, with the addition of a little reindeer flesh and makarsha root, thickened with train oil, the delicate compound appears before us in the shape of a savoury forced ball. Smoked reindeer tongues are seldom produced, unless in honour of a guest, and small slices of frozen fish eaten raw are esteemed in these distant regions as highly as the *glace a la vanille* at the Café de Paris. Salt never enters their food, but is always produced if a stranger partakes their meal. Tea and sugar are seen only at the tables of the wealthy, on which occasions the *yukola* or dried fish supplies the place of toast or biscuit, bread being a delicacy which few can afford to indulge in. Flour, always an expensive article, is seldom seen except in the aristocracy of the place, and is generally used for the composition of a beverage called *saturan*. This is prepared by roasting the flour in a pan, and stirring it into a paste, with a little melted butter or fish oil. Upon this is poured boiling water, and the infusion is drank warm out of cups. Our author assures us the beverage is both nutritive and agreeable; but he had gone through a three years' seasoning, and custom may go far to reconcile the palate even to the *bonne bouche* of a Siberian *cuisine*.

Flirtation, courtship, love, and jealousy, still maintain their empire over the youthful heart, even in the remote north. It is the daily office of the young ladies of Kolymsk to fetch water from the river, where a well is cut in the ice. Here the love-sick youth never fails to watch for the arrival of his mistress, and manifests his attachment by filling her pails, and perchance even carrying them home for her. Such an act of gallantry is looked on as a formal declaration of love, and always excites the envy and *medisance* of less favoured rivals. The hole in the ice is the daily gossiping place for the young of both sexes, and we can easily believe what we are told, that the fair damsels are exceedingly careful that the water pails shall be freshly filled every day.

Shortly after M. Von Wrangel's arrival at Nishney-Kolymsk, the little place was put quite into commotion by the arrival of Captain Cochrane, whose delightful account of his *pedestrian* excursions through these regions are already well known to the British public. Our countryman remained some time there, and manifested a wish to accompany the expedition over the ice of the Arctic ocean, for which the Russian seaman was preparing; "but such an increase to our party," says our author, "on a journey where every additional pound weight of luggage had to be seriously considered, would have occasioned so many difficulties with respect to sledges, provisions, and the like, that I deemed it expedient not to avail myself of his offer." Disappointed in his wish to join the main expedition, Captain Cochrane contented himself with accompanying a small party to the fair of Ostrownoye, whither Von Wrangel despatched one of his officers to cultivate the good graces of the Tsheskoes, whose country he was about to visit. Previously to the departure of the Englishman, however, our author determined to astonish the good people of the town by a splendid entertainment in honour of the stranger.

"It was on twelfth night that I invited all the élite of the place to a *wetsherinka* or ball. I chose one of the largest houses for the occasion. It belonged to a Cossack, who happened to be something of a violin player. The ball-room, about eighteen feet square, was sumptuously illuminated by several lamps of train oil. The walls and benches having been subjected to a washing (an operation which it would be impossible to say when they had last undergone) were ornamented with some attempt at drapery, and on the floor some yellow sand was scattered. By way of refreshments for the ladies, I had procured tea and lump sugar, together with a few plates of cedar-nuts. The supper consisted of some fish-cakes, yukala, and frozen reindeer marrow. At five o'clock our guests appeared, in their best furs, and their gaudiest holiday attire. After the first few exclamations of wonder and admiration at the luxury and splendour of the entertainment, the ladies took their seats on the benches along the wall, and commenced singing some of our national melodies. The younger part of the company amused themselves with a variety of *jeux innocens*, and danced slowly and heavily, as though it had been a task, to the unaccountable tones which the not very pliant fingers of our musical host, an old reindeer hunter, contrived to draw from his cracked fiddle, two of the strings of which were of reindeer sinews, the other two of twisted silk. The men were grouped around the *tshuval*, and seemed exceedingly to enjoy the little addition of brandy which I offered them as a qualification to their tea. At ten o'clock the party broke up, and my guests departed with endless assurances of gratitude for the costly manner in which I had entertained them. Nor were these mere set speeches; on the contrary, they were honestly meant, for even in the subsequent years of our stay, the magnificent and delightful *Prasdnik* was often referred to, as a bright point in the gloomy uniformity of their customary manner of living."

M. Von Wrangel found on his arrival at Nishney-Kolymsk, that the necessary preparations for his expedition had been neglected, and all his endeavours to collect the requisite number of sledges, and the requisite quantity of food for the dogs having failed, he was obliged, for that year, to renounce his journey to the north over the icy surface of the Arctic ocean. Not, however, wholly to lose his time, he determined to attempt a month's excursion along the coast, of which only a very small portion was at that time known. The inhabitants had long stood greatly in awe of the Tshuktshi or Tsheskoes, and had therefore seldom ventured farther than the Baranow Rocks, which were deemed the frontier mark of the Russian territory. It was known, however, that the Tsheskoes themselves were little in the habit of venturing so far towards the Russian line, the coast from the Baranow Rocks to Cape Shelagskoi being generally left unoccupied by both parties, as a sort of neutral ground. Our author resolved accordingly to devote the time that remained to him to a survey of the coast as far as the above cape.

The place of rendezvous was Sukharnoye at the mouth of the Kolyma, a "town" consisting of two uninhabited houses, to which a few families are in the habit of repairing during the fishing season.

"Fifty versts before reaching Sukharnoye we lost sight of the stunted shrubs, and found ourselves on one unbounded plain of snow, unbroken, unless here and there by an occasional fox-trap. A man accustoms himself, no doubt, to every thing in time, but the first impression produced by this gigantic shroud admits of no comparison with any other object in nature, and night, by obscuring the spectacle, comes as a positive relief."

(To be continued.)

For "The Friend."

THE THEORY OF STORMS.

The facilities afforded by the peculiar position and geographical features of North America, for extensive simultaneous observations on the phenomena of the great northeast storms of our latitude, very early drew the attention of the intelligent men. Dr. Franklin first recorded the main fact respecting them—namely, that they begin at the southwest, and travel against the wind. But little further progress, in our knowledge, was made for a long period. The investigations and theories of our countrymen, Espy and Redfield, and of Col. Reid, the present governor of Bermuda, respecting the phenomena of storms, have latterly excited much curiosity and discussion.

The attention of the writer has been recalled to the subject, by the publication in the recent number of the Transactions of the American Philosophical Society, of a paper "on the storm which was experienced throughout the United States, about the 20th of December, 1836, by Elias Loomis, professor of mathematics and natural philosophy in Western Reserve College." As this paper is the most elaborate and extended investigation of the kind that has yet been made, it is likely to give us clear views, and to substitute facts upon many points that were before conjectural, and it therefore deserves to be widely circulated. It is only by extensive simultaneous observation that any very accurate data can be obtained. The storm in question fell within the period at which hourly observations on all the phenomena of the weather are made in various places for thirty-seven successive hours. The idea of making these observations is due to the younger Herschel, who proposed that on the days of the equinoxes and the solstices, and on the following day, an hourly register should be kept by meteorologists throughout the world. This proposal has been acted on in this country, at Baltimore, New York, Albany, Flushing, New Haven, Gardiner, Me., Montreal and Quebec. The regents of the university in New York require registers to be kept at all the academies under their care; and from this source Professor Loomis obtained observations at 42 points in that state. By a regulation of the war department, registers are kept and regular returns made of the weather at all the military stations, which furnished our author with data from 28 posts, most of them in the far west, and extending from the southern part of the peninsula of Florida to Wisconsin and the upper Missouri. He also obtained more than thirty private records from various parts of the United States, and from many stations in Europe, and procured access to the log books of several vessels at sea. He has made the most of these ample materials, and the memoir which he has prepared from them, will serve as a model for similar investigations.

The principal facts established by our author are, 1st, that a great atmospheric wave, as shown by the depression of the barometer in its trough, passed over the continent from west to east, the progress of which he traces over a space of 20° of latitude and 36° of longitude, from Fort Jessup, lat. 31° 35′, long. 93° 42′; Fort Leavenworth, lat. 39° 28′, long. 95° 14′; and Fort Snelling, lat. 44° 53′, long. 93° 12′, to Bermuda lat. 32° 44′, long. 63° 28′, and St. Johns, in Newfoundland, lat. 47° 34′, long. 52° 38′. 2d. That this depression of the barometer was followed by its rise, and that at the same time the thermometer suddenly fell many degrees.

3d. That when the barometer had attained its greatest depression, the wind which had previously blown from the southeast, suddenly shifted to the northwest, and blew violently from that quarter.

1st. *The movement of the barometer.* The reader who will trace the following named places on the map, will see that the progress of the wave was nearly uniform. At Natchez, the barometric minimum was at 10 A. M.; on the 20th at Pensacola, 6 P. M.; at Lexington, Ky., and Springfield, Ohio, 7 P. M.; at Marietta and Twinsburg, Ohio, 11 P. M.; at Savannah, Geo., and Rochester, N. Y., it occurred at 5 A. M.; on the 21st, at Syracuse, N. Y., Sunbury, Pa., and Washington City, at 7 A. M.; at Baltimore, at 7½h.; Montreal, 9h.; Philadelphia, 10h.; Albany, 11h.; New York, 11½h.; at Flushing, L. I., and Quebec, at noon; at Hanover, N. H., and New Haven,

at 1h. P. M.; in Boston and New Bedford, at 4h.; at Gardiner, Me., 5h.; at Halifax, at 8 A. M.; in Bermuda, at midnight of the 22d; and in St. Johns, at 9 A. M. of the 23d. The curves of depression, as projected by our author, show so close a resemblance to each other as to leave no doubt of their being the effect of the same wave. The line of simultaneous depression was decidedly convex in front; and when first observed to the west of the Mississippi, was nearly north and south, but the northern end travelled faster than the southern, so that it gradually bent to the northeast. Its velocity, in the southern border of the U. States, was from 17 to 29 statute miles per hour, and on the northern border from 17 to 37 miles per hour, so that it was not uniform. The depression of the barometer increased with the latitude. At Indian Key it was 26 hundredths of an inch, at Pensacola .46, at Savannah .65, at Philadelphia .97, at Flushing 1.042, at Albany 1.173, at Montreal 1.266, and at Quebec, the most northern station heard from, 1.57. As Quebec could not have been to the north of the point of greatest depression of the barometer, the probability is that the storm when raging most violently there, extended as far to the north as it did to the south. That point of greatest depression appears to be the commencement of the clearing up of the storm, for it is accompanied by the change of wind which is the prelude of a change of weather. We find upon examining the chart annexed to the memoir, that the line of the barometric minimum at midnight of the 20th, passed through Tallahassee, in Florida, near Milledgeville, in Georgia, the junction of the three states of Virginia, Tennessee and North Carolina, Wheeling, Va., and Thunder Bay, in Lake Huron. At the same time the rain extended from the west of this line and nearly parallel with it, to a considerable distance out to sea on the east. The western limits of the rain at midnight of the 20th, were Saganaw Bay in Lake Huron, a few miles east of Springfield, Ohio, Lexington and Brainard, Tenn. Passing in a curve to the east of Pensacola, its boundary may be traced through East Florida to the south of St. Augustine, where it takes a N. E. course, following the direction of the coast at a distance of 100 to 200 miles, till it passes between Martha's Vineyard and Nantucket, through Cape Ann, and in a N. N. W. direction to Montreal. The space inclosed by these boundary lines probably represents the actual figure of the storm as it then raged, being an oval space not less than 1200 miles in length, by nearly 700 at its greatest breadth. Yet in a line passing through Philadelphia, and Twinsburg in Ohio, the eastern limit of the rain was considerably more than 500 miles to the east of the line of greatest depression, while the western limit was not more than 140 miles to the west of that line. By the time the centre of the storm reached Quebec its circumference must have greatly enlarged, so that it seems probable it extended 800 or 900 miles to the north of that place.

2d. *The movement of the thermometer.* While the barometer was falling under the influence of the storm, the thermometer was every where rising, and as the barometer rose the thermometer fell with extraordinary rapidi-

ty. As most of the ... tions were only taken ... cannot therefore asce ... which the fall begat ... where hourly records ... with the minimum o ... may therefore be ass ... But at Fort Leavenw ... Fort Snelling, it was ... 19th and morning of t ... Augusta, Ill., St. Lou ... morning and noon of ... Lexington, Springfie ... tween evening of the ... 21st; at Savannah, Su ... Philadelphia, Albany, ... between morning and ... New Bedford, Boston ... noon and evening. ... greater at the north a ... south and the east; ... the northwestern stat ... fell 50° in 24 hours ... at Augusta, Ill., fou ... for the daily variatio ... an almost unexample ... tions to the northwes ... Detroit and St. Lou ... below zero.

3d. *The amount o* ... throws into a tabula ... he received of the fa ... marked, that no pa ... register is so little to ... gauge; for no accura ... to overcome the unce ... the unequal action of ... alike and near each o ... in the elevation of t ... the conical funnel, in ... to the nearest house ... affect the quantity ... same storm, and w ... raging, no unexcepti ... find accordingly th ... stated to have fallen ... each other, varies ... keepsie for instance ... Point, 46 hundredth ... burg, 8 miles north ... the latter place 3.40 ... allowance however ... and for errors in co ... the most remarkable ... the extreme inequal ... over the vast space ... also in the duratio ... many of the report ... it rained and then ... St. Louis, about 1 ... snowed and hailed ... ter 3 tenths of an ... hours, the rain begin ... between 10 and 11 ... Batavia, about 30 ... south of west, it be ... the 20th, turned to ... 5 P. M. on the 21 ... enowed or rained a ... of the 21st at Onc ... At New York it ra ... P. M. on the 20th to

Flushing, Jamaica, and Flat Bush, it did not begin to rain till 4 A. M. of the 21st, and ceased at the same time as in New York; yet it began to rain at New Bedford, Boston, and Gardiner, on the evening or night of the 20th. Upon a careful comparison of all the returns, our author is of the opinion that the average depth of the rain throughout the United States was seven eighths of an inch. On the northern limits of the storm, only snow fell—at the southern stations only rain; while at the intermediate points, the rain changed into snow.

(To be continued.)

TEMPERANCE IN IRELAND.

The following is the copy of a letter, says the Philadelphia North American, addressed by a lady who has been for many years at the head of the female writers of Great Britain, to a Philadelphian in London, on the subject of the Irish temperance reform and Father Mathew, which has been kindly furnished us :—

"The accounts you see in newspapers, of Father Mathew and his temperance medals, and his influence over the Catholics, in Ireland, in making them take and keep the pledge, or vow, against drinking all fermented liquors, are true, and so far as I can learn, not exaggerated. I saw a gentleman, who witnessed the wondrous sight of the sober procession of tens of thousands in Dublin, (on St. Patrick's day,) who marched through the streets with temperance badges and ensigns, and "walked sober off at last" in the evening, or at night, to their town or country abodes.

In the counties of Cork and Kilkenny, from whence we have accounts from long resident friends, we hear of tens of thousands who voluntarily flock to take the pledge, many of them reeling drunk immediately before they take it, as a last farewell to whiskey and spirits! A fact most extraordinary, but certain! The wonder seems to me as great, that these people, so fond of drinking, and so habituated to it, should, of their own accord, go to vow against it, and when sober, keep religiously afterwards the vow they made when drunk. Yet so it is. The voluntary taking the pledge shows beyond all doubt that there is a real and strong desire in even the slaves to intemperance, to free themselves from the vice; and also it proves the power of the Catholic faith. There are but few instances, hitherto, of any having forfeited their pledge.

There can, I think, be no doubt that this preservative against intemperance, whether superstitious or not, religious, moral, or political, is, has been, and will be, of the greatest advantage to Ireland, and to the lower orders, and all orders of the Irish.

Merely in an economic point of view, it saves the sums squandered in whiskey, and in whiskey shops. The whiskey shops are shut up in many towns, and the calculations prove that the amount saved in Ireland is equal to the expense of the new poor laws!! Marriages probably premature—improvident marriages—at all events, marriages have decreased one third in many districts. Then in point of health the change for the better is incalculable among these temperance tribes—the bettering of the diet, as well as the habits of the people, wonderful! In the county of Kilkenny (to speak of which I know from the best authority,) there is bread now sold instead of whiskey, in all the villages and little towns, in every house where only whiskey formerly was sold.

I should think that the influence of Father Mathew and his medals, would last so long as it shall not be publicly proved that any or many have broken their pledge with impunity.

Though we cannot pronounce what length of time the teetotallists will be able to hold out before the pledge be broken or convicted of being broken, yet it is even now apparent that Father Mathew foresees the danger of their breaking their pledges, and has begun to provide against it thus : by permitting some who feel they cannot keep their vow, to give up the medal pledge. This I am assured has been done in some instances, but only in few hitherto. I have no doubt that Father Mathew has provided this allowance to give up the pledge, under all these circumstances, to prevent the greater danger, and scandal and obstruction to his whole power, of the vow being broken.

Long may it be before his power over the Irish may fail, and soon may it be converted into power over themselves! and permanent power of self-control !

So far as it has gone, I think this medal charm has done more in Ireland, numbers and space, and inveterate bad subjects considered, than was ever accomplished in any other country.

I have heard circumstances which give me a high opinion of Mathew's integrity, truth, and simplicity of character."

From the Farmers' Cabinet.

BOILED FOOD FOR POULTRY.

It is customary for some poultry-men to cook the different grains which they use for fattening poultry, and this they do by boiling, continuing the process until the mass swells, and becomes so soft as to break the envelope by which each grain is surrounded, conceiving that such food is better for the purpose, and the use of it far more economical than the dry grain. Now, whether this idea is or is not correct, still it is of importance to know the difference of expense between the two, and interesting to ascertain whether more or less of it is eaten than of that which has not been submitted to the culinary process. To discover this, I find that Reaumur caused four pints of each of the six grains following to be boiled until they were well bursted, and he found that the increase of bulk of each sort was as follows :

4 pints of oats, after boiling, filled 7 pints.
4 do.   barley,   do.   do. 10 do.
4 do.   buckwheat, do.   do. 14 do.
4 do.   Indian corn, do.   do. 15 do.
4 do.   wheat,   do.   do. 10 do.
4 do.   rye,   do.   do. 15 do.

Rice was not tested, but swells much more than either of the above: it is seldom, however, used for the above purpose.

On experiment, it was found that poultry were not uniformly partial to boiled grain, although occasionally a preference was shown for it; nor did it appear that they entertain a decided partiality for one species over that of every other; wheat, however, being sometimes preferred and rye disapproved of; it therefore follows, that we might make choice of that grain which happens to be most plentiful or cheapest, always excepting rye, which must not be used unless other sorts cannot be had.

Other experiments were made, to ascertain whether there be any economy in feeding with boiled grain, and this was done by knowing, first, how much dry grain sufficed for one or more fowls, and then boiling the same quantity, and trying how much in that state would suffice for a meal; the result was as follows. Rye, although so very considerably increased by boiling, instead of being more satisfying, becomes less so, more of it being consumed when boiled than when dry. Oats, although increased by boiling nearly one half, are not, on this account, more satisfying for poultry, which, if in two days they will consume four pints of dry oats, will, in the same period, eat seven pints when boiled ; so there is no economy in the additional trouble. Mowbray is of the opinion that oats scour, although they are supposed to promote laying, and are in many places used for fattening. Buckwheat swells still more than oats by boiling, but poultry will consume fourteen pints boiled, in the same space of time that four would be sufficient, and it is thought to be an unsubstantial food. But Indian corn is more profitable when boiled than raw, the saving being one third, or near it; while the fowls which ate two pints of barley in its dry state, consumed but three pints of the boiled grain ; therefore, as ten pints of boiled barley are produced from four pints of dry grain, the experience in dry barley is to that of boiled, as ten fifths to six fifths, or as ten to six, or five to three ; amounting to a saving of two fifths by giving boiled instead of dry barley ; thus it is far more profitable and effective when boiled than raw, and, if fed to the poultry while warm, it will hasten materially the period of laying, promoting in a high degree the health and thrift of all kinds of poultry. Wheat, as shown in the above table, increases in bulk on boiling, nearly the same as barley ; and these experiments go to show that the use of boiled wheat, barley and Indian corn is a matter of economy, while on the contrary, in the boiling of oats, rye, and buckwheat, you have the loss of fuel, time, and trouble, out of pocket.

These things are worth remembering, especially at the present time, when the fattening of poultry is carried to so great a length, our steam-boats and rail-ways requiring such quantities to feed their passengers, poultry being, in so many ways, the standing dish of their public tables. For the keeping of poultry before fattening, no food is at all to be compared to boiled potatoes, mixed with a small portion of boiled barley, the process of which is very much expedited, if the grain is broken in the mill before cooking; but in that state it will require stirring while boiling, to prevent it from burning.

It is found, by actual experience, that there is no saving in the substitution of bran for grain ; some persons take the trouble to boil this, but it does not even increase its bulk, and not at all its quality. Two measures of dry bran, after boiling, will not go so far as one measure of boiled barley, thus showing a striking difference in favour of barley, even in point of economy.   S.

For "The Friend."

Historical fragments, illustrating the early religious labours of Friends in America, with biographical sketches of the first ministers who visited it.

(Continued from p. 405.)

The vessel which bore Anne Austin and Mary Fisher back to Barbadoes had scarcely spread her white sails o'er the bosom of the Atlantic, when a ship from London, of which Robert Lock was the commander, came to anchor in Boston bay. For the two Quaker ministers sent away in the one vessel, there were eight brought in by the other. These last were Christopher Holder, Thomas Thurston, William Brend, John Copeland, Mary Prince, Sarah Gibbons, Mary Weatherhead, and Dorothy Waugh; four men and four women. According to their own testimony, they had "been brought here in the will of God, having been made sensible of the cries and groans of his seed, which was crying unto him for help and deliverance from under cruel bondage." When the commander of the ship went on shore, which was the 6th of the 7th mo. 1656, he took with him a list of his passengers, and on furnishing it to the governor, he was no doubt questioned; whether there were any Quakers among them. On being informed that there were, the marshal and a constable were immediately sent on board the vessel with a warrant, commanding them "to search the boxes, chests and trunks of the Quakers for erroneous books and hellish pamphlets." They were also directed to bring the bodies of the eight Quakers, and that of Richard Smith, an inhabitant of Long Island, who came with them from London, and was termed their proselyte, before the court then sitting at Boston. Here they were subjected to a long and frivolous examination, the greatest part of which was concerning their belief in the Trinity. The account the prisoners have left, says: "Unto which we answered according to the scriptures, that the Father, Son and Spirit we own, but a Trinity the scripture speaks not of: and so the Father, who then was with us, preserved us by his power as in the hollow of his hand, so that they could not touch us." John Norton, the priest, in endeavouring to prove the scriptures to be the rule and guide of life, brought forward these verses from the 10th chapter of Romans: "But the righteousness which is of faith speaketh on this wise, Say not in thine heart, who shall ascend into heaven? (that is to bring Christ down from above:) or, who shall descend into the deep? (that is to bring up Christ again from the dead). But what saith it? The word is nigh thee, even in thy mouth, and in thy heart; that is the word of faith which we preach." This quotation seemed full as much against the proposition he wished to establish as for it, so he instantly turned to the 2d Epistle of Peter, 1st chapter and 19th verse, and read, "We have a more sure word of prophecy; whereunto ye do well that ye take heed, as unto a light that shineth in a dark place, until the day dawn, and the day-star arise in your hearts." Here he was interrupted by one of the prisoners, who asked him, What is the light there spoken of which shineth in a dark place?

J. Norton. It is the eternal Word.

William Brend, who had his hand on his own breast, then asked, What is the dark place?

J. Norton. I think it is under your hand.

Brend. Then thou meanest the heart?

J. Norton. Yea.

One of the prisoners then said, Is not the eternal Word a sufficient guide?

J. Norton. Yea.

Prisoner. Is it thy rule and guide?

J. Norton. Yea, when I am guided aright.

Upon this, some of the magistrates demanded of John Norton, What difference there was between his doctrine and the doctrine of the Quakers. The governor declared that he could not say as Norton had said. Upon this, the priest became alarmed, and would have denied that he had expressed himself as they represented; but the magistrates were positive, and much dissension arose among them. They then committed Friends to prison, postponing their examination until the following day. When they were again called before the court, they found that the examination was to be public, the first having been in private. The same questions were put to them which they had already answered. These the prisoners declined replying to, except by referring the court to what they had previously said, and which had been all written down. They then demanded what law it was for the violation of which they had been imprisoned. Endicott did not answer the question, but said, "Take heed how ye break our ecclesiastical laws, for then ye are sure to stretch by a halter." Upon their asking for a copy of these, he told them they should not have one. This reply displeased some of the townsmen present, and one of them spoke out in the hearing of the court, "How shall they know then when they transgress?" At the close of the examination, the court passed sentence of banishment upon the eight Friends, ordering that they should be sent to the prison again, and there be kept without bail or mainprize, until such time as they shall be sent away in the ship that brought them, to the place from whence they came. Richard Smith was also committed to prison, there to remain until they had an opportunity of sending him round by water to Long Island, they being afraid to trust him to go to his family through their patent.

The court then sent for Robert Lock, the captain of the ship in which the Quakers came, and required him to give bond to carry them back at his own charge, and to land them no where but in England. Deeming this a violation of his rights as a free-born Englishman, who had infringed no law of his country in carrying her citizens to any part of her dominions, he refused to submit. Irritated by the man's independence, they committed him to prison, to lay there until he should be obedient to their will. After remaining in confinement four days, his determination to support his rights was overbalanced by his fears of pecuniary losses which must result from his being unable to attend to the procuring a cargo, and re-loading his ship. He accordingly submitted to the yoke, entered into the bonds required, and was thereupon set at liberty.

About ten days after the Friends were com-

mitted to prison, the following order was issued to the keeper:

"You are by virtue hereof, to keep the Quakers formerly committed to your custody as dangerous persons, industrious to improve all their abilities to seduce the people of this jurisdiction, both by words and letters, to the abominable tenets of the Quakers, and to keep them close prisoners, not suffering them to speak or confer with any person, nor permitting them to have paper or ink.

EDWARD RAWSON, *Secretary.*
August the 18th, 1656."

During the examination of Richard Smith, Governor Endicott told him that he was deluded, and that he ought to have a discourse with three or four of their godly ministers, who might convince him of his error. On considering the subject, Richard felt willing to have a conference, and on a first day of the week, asked the jailer's permission to attend at the public place of worship. Here, when the usual service of the day was over, he arose, and briefly reciting the governor's language, added, "If there are any such as are godly here who can convict me of any error I hold, I am ready to hear."

Governor E. I intended the conference should be in private.

R. Smith. It is my desire that it may be in public.

On this he was immediately hurried back to prison, without any attempt to show forth his errors, or convince him of them. After three weeks confinement, which must have kept him until about the first of the seventh month, he was released, an opportunity presenting of sending him round by water to his own residence. Of this individual I find very little authentic information. Bishop says, *some* of those taken from Lock's ship had municipal rights in Boston; of these, John Copeland was one, for he says, "I was called out from amongst them, and sent unto them." Richard Smith was probably another. There had been a merchant in Boston of that name, who, in 1641, "purchased of the sachems a tract of land in the Narraganset country, remote from the English settlements, where he erected a house of trade, and gave free entertainment to all travellers." His land was among the thickest of the Indians, and his house was erected on "the great road of the country."* This was in what is now Warwick, Rhode Island; and as that district was the scene of the war between the New England colonies and the Narragansets in 1654, he was doubtless obliged to leave it, and seek a shelter elsewhere.

On the seventh of the seventh month another order was received by the jailer, directing him to search as often as he saw meet, the boxes, chests and things of the Quakers, formerly committed to his custody, for pen, ink and paper, papers and books, and take them away. This order was signed by the governor and deputy.

At a meeting of the governor and magistrates of Massachusetts, held at Boston the second of the seventh month, 1656, a letter was pre-

* Holmes' Annals and Mass. Hist. Society's Transactions, vol. v.

pared and addressed to "The Commissioners of the United Provinces," who were about to sit at New Plymouth. In this they recommend, "That some generall rules may bee alsoe comended to each Generall Court to prevent the coming in amongst us from forraigne places such notorious heretiques as Quakers, Ranters, &c." This letter was read at the meeting of the commissioners, who accordingly determined on the fourth of September, to " Propose to the several Generall Courts, that all Quakers, Ranters, and other notorious heretiques bee prohibited coming into the United Colonies, and if any shall heerafter come or arise amongst us, that they bee forthwith cecured or removed out of all the jurisdictions." *Hazard's State Papers, vol.* 2, *p.* 347–349.

All that had as yet been done to the Quakers had been without even the shadow of law, for in neither case had they allowed them the opportunity of violating those issued against the anabaptists by disseminating their opinions. The knowledge of this had urged the rulers of Boston to lay the case before the commissioners as before recited; and now, having the sanction of that body, a law was soon prepared to cover former misdoings, and to legalise future tyranny.

" At a general court held at Boston the 14th of October, 1656.

Whereas, there is a cursed sect of *heretics* lately risen up in the world, which are commonly called *Quakers,* who take upon them to be immediately sent of God, and infallibly assisted by the spirit, to speak and write *blasphemous opinions,* despising government, and the order of God in the church and commonwealth, speaking evil of dignities, reproaching and reviling magistrates and ministers, seeking to turn the people from the faith, and gain proselytes to their pernicious ways. This court taking into consideration the premises, and to prevent the like mischief, as by their means is wrought in our land, doth hereby order, and by authority of this court, be it ordered and enacted, that what master, or commander of any ship, bark, pink, or catch, shall henceforth bring into any harbour, creek or cove, within this jurisdiction, any *Quaker* or *Quakers,* or other *blasphemous hereticks,* shall pay, or cause to be paid, the fine of one hundred pounds to the treasurer of the country, except it appear he want true knowledge or information of their being such, and in that case he hath liberty to clear himself by his oath, when sufficient proof to the contrary is wanting : and for default of good payment, or good security for it, shall be cast into prison, and there to continue till the said sum be satisfied to the treasurer as aforesaid. And the commander of any catch, ship or vessel, being legally convicted, shall give in sufficient security to the governor, or any one or more of the magistrates, who have power to determine the same, to carry them back to the place whence he brought them, and on his refusal so to do, the governor, or one or more of the magistrates, are hereby empowered to issue out his or their warrants, to commit such master or commander to prison, there to continue till he give in sufficient security to the content of the governor, or any of the magis-

trates aforesaid. And it is hereby farther ordered and enacted, That what *Quaker* soever shall arrive in this country from foreign parts, or shall come into this jurisdiction from any parts adjacent, shall be forthwith committed to the house of correction, and, at their entrance, to be severely whipt, and by the master thereof to be kept constantly to work, and none suffered to converse or speak with them during the time of their imprisonment, which shall be no longer than necessity requires. And it is ordered, If any person shall knowingly import into any harbour of this jurisdiction any *Quaker* books, or writings concerning their devilish opinions, shall pay for such book or writing, being legally proved against him or them, the sum of five pounds ; and whosoever shall disperse or conceal any such book, or writing, and it be found with him or her, or in his or her house, and shall not immediately deliver the same to the next magistrate, shall forfeit or pay five pounds for the dispersing or concealing of every such book or writing. And it is hereby further enacted, That if any person within this colony shall take upon them to defend the *heretical* opinions of the *Quakers,* or any of their books or papers as aforesaid, if legally proved, shall be fined for the first time forty shillings ; if they shall persist in the same, and shall again defend it the second time, four pounds ; if notwithstanding they shall again defend and maintain the said *Quakers'* heretical opinions, they shall be committed to the house of correction till there be convenient passage to send them out of the land, being sentenced by the court of assistants to banishment. Lastly, it is hereby ordered, That what person or persons soever shall revile the persons of magistrates or ministers, as is usual with the *Quakers,* such person or persons shall be severely whipt, or pay the sum of five pounds.

This is a true copy of the court's order, as attests

EDWARD RAWSON, *Secretary.*"

Humphrey Norton, who addressed an answer to this law to the rulers of Boston, shows them that in it they "blaspheme God, belie his people, transgress his laws, and limit his spirit." He reminds them that they were either banished men themselves or such as fled for conscience sake, and that although He who provides for all that love him, had provided the land for them, they were now striving to limit his spirit which was seeking to gather his scattered seed to himself. He tells them that their persecuting law is "contrary to God, Christ and the scriptures," and particularises fifteen untruths contained therein. He then desires them to examine into the ground from which it originated, "seeing the devil only is the author of all unrighteousness, malice and lies." N. E.

For "The Friend."

CHRISTIAN GRAVITY.

Men differ naturally in their temperaments and dispositions, and education and society have also an influence in making up the variety. When divine grace is permitted to take the government of the mind, it curbs and regu-

lates the natural vivacity, and often gives a degree of cheerfulness to the dull and phlegmatic. Persons habitually taciturn are sometimes considered wise and discreet, and because they have few ideas to communicate, or want energy to utter them, they may be overtaken with a disposition to censure as volatile others who give a proper license to their cheerfulness. We may err in judgment in pronouncing the silent and reserved man to be a solid Christian, as well as in deciding that another is light and unguarded, because he is more free in imparting his thoughts and feelings. In the great variety of mental constitution, it is doubtless the design of the Creator that we should exert a beneficial influence on each other, and in the order and harmony which grace produces, show forth the wisdom and goodness and glory of Him who made us.

But whatever men may be by nature, or however a sprightly temperament may render them agreeable companions to the volatile and the gay, when they take the character of religious persons, a sober, circumspect deportment best becomes their profession, and will not only contribute to their own preservation, but promote a religious life in others. In the first effectual visitations of the grace of Christ upon the young and active, the discoveries of divine light are often clear and very impressive. The heart not having become hardened, when the spiritual senses are awakened to the excellency of the truth as it is then opened, there is a lively apprehension of its purity, and of the importance of its requisitions ; and very tender scruples are not unfrequently felt by the newly convinced soul. How important that the actions and sentiments of older Christians should comport with the fruits of the same Holy Spirit, and enforce its convictions in the hearts of such who are as babes in Christ. But if unhappily they should indulge in unbecoming volatility, or should speak slightingly of the scruples of sincere exemplary persons, or of the instances of divine guidance in smaller matters which eminent servants of the Lord have recorded in their lives; how are they likely to stumble the inexperienced, and perhaps lay waste the work of truth in their hearts. What distress and conflict have these sometimes brought upon serious young persons ! Between the convictions of divine grace, and the example and sentiments of older professors, they have been greatly puzzled ; the insinuations of the subtle serpent, that they need not be so scrupulous, that there is not so much in their apprehensions of duty as they imagine, have received force from such examples. Should they have no experienced friend to counsel and strengthen them, to keep to the impressions of duty which their Saviour has made on their minds, they may be grievously misled and entangled, unless he, who is a father to the fatherless, rebukes Satan, and arms them with double courage to take the yoke of Christ upon them and follow Him, notwithstanding the obstacles they meet in the way.

Could we scan the secret history of those who have turned against the principles which they once advocated, we should probably find that many of them had never fully yielded to the baptism of the Holy Spirit, so as to have the chaff consumed with unquenchable fire. Much of this light nature has been permitted to remain. Though they have felt the operation of the flaming sword, the wound has been healed, and they have come to rest satisfied with the early administrations of condemnation, and with the sacrifices which they then made. Unwilling to go again and again into the refining furnace, the unsanctified nature has revived, and the enemy has succeeded in persuading them that it is not necessary they should be as particular in some things, and as self-denying as they were once convinced was their indispensable duty. Getting off the watch and losing ground themselves, they have then begun to find fault with those who were keeping their habitations in the truth, as being very strict; then they have thought them very narrow minded, and then very uncharitable, because they firmly maintained their testimony, which the Lord required of them, against all undue liberties, and all performances which were without life and power, and which they, abiding in the light, saw, were not free from the first and fallen nature. Some of this class have become enemies to the cross of Christ. They have thrown off the yoke, and have secretly and openly ridiculed the straitness of the watchful circumspect follower of Christ, despised doctrines and principles for which men and women, better than themselves, have suffered persecution even unto death, and have finally left the society.

Of the sad consequences of throwing the yoke off the neck, and leading the children into a broader way where they may take greater liberties, we have had lamentable proofs. The restraints of religion are irksome to the unsubdued mind. A religion without the cross, without mortification, that can participate in the fashions, and language, and friendships of a vain world, is very congenial to the carnal mind. But such is not the religion of Jesus Christ. The New Testament gives us no evidence that he entered into any alliance with the spirit or the friendships of the world—it gives no trait of levity or humour in all his actions or discourses. He declared, that "Every idle word that men shall speak, they shall give account thereof in the day of judgment." And yet our Lord did not inculcate a sanctimonious exterior as constituting the substance of religion. "Moreover, when ye fast, be not as the hypocrites, of a sad countenance; for they disfigure their faces, that they may appear unto men to fast." He was opposed to all deceit and hypocrisy, in appearing to be what we are not, for the purpose of making a false impression. The gravity which his religion induces proceeds from a watchful reverent state of mind, and the cheerfulness, from a peaceful and grateful consciousness of divine approbation.

Our Saviour commanded his disciples to watch and pray, lest they entered into temptation, for the spirit may be ready, but the flesh is weak. The apostles exhorted the believers to gravity. "Let your speech be always with grace seasoned with salt, that ye may know how ye ought to answer every man." "A bishop must be blameless, vigilant, sober, of good behaviour—one that ru-

leth well his own house, having his children in subjection with all gravity. Likewise must the deacons be grave, not double-tongued—holding the mystery of the faith in a pure conscience. Even so must their wives be grave, not slanderers. These things I write unto thee, that thou mayest know how thou oughtest to behave thyself in the house of God, which is the church of the living God, the pillar and ground of the truth." "Speak thou the things that become sound doctrine, that the aged men be sober, grave—that the aged women, likewise, be in behaviour as becometh holiness—that they may teach the young women to be sober—young men, likewise, exhort to be sober-minded—in all things showing thyself a pattern of good works—in doctrine, showing uncorruptness, gravity, sincerity." "Wherefore gird up the loins of your mind, be sober, and hope to the end for the grace that is to be brought unto you at the revelation of Jesus Christ."

William Penn says, respecting himself and his fellow members, "We held the truth in the spirit of it, and not in our own spirits. They were bound and brought into subjection. Our liberty stood in the liberty of the spirit of truth, and no pleasure, no profit, no fear, no favour, could draw us from this retired, strict and watchful frame. Our words were few and savoury, our looks composed and weighty, and our whole deportment very observable. True it is, that this retired and strict sort of life, from the liberty of the conversation of the world, exposed us to the censures of many as humourists, conceited self-righteous persons; *but it was our preservation from many snares to which others were continually exposed.*"

George Fox gives this counsel—"Live in the pure life of God, and in the fear of the Lord; so will you be kept in the life, in the solid and seasoned spirit, and preach as well in life as in words. None must be light or wild. For the seed of God is weighty; brings to be solid, and leads into the wisdom of God."

For "The Friend."

THE FARMERS' CABINET.

Although I am no farmer, I take the Cabinet, and call myself one of its regular readers. There is something in the business-like air of this spirited agricultural paper that is very captivating. Every well conducted farm is in fact a laboratory and work shop, in which experiments on some of the most curious and interesting phenomena in nature are continually going on. And when the farmers of a well cultivated, prosperous district, can be induced frequently to correspond with the agricultural paper of their neighbourhood, we are sure of a rich treat. As there is no attempt on their parts at fine writing, they escape most of the faults of newspaper writers, and tell their plain story in short and few words, that is to say, in the very best style. It is like smelling the fresh ploughed earth, to sit down and listen to these details about sugar beets, and Indian corn, and turnips, and these sharp satires upon city speculators. The very homeliness of the subjects that are treated of recommends them

to our notice, for they discuss that do not find their way into books. The Farmers' Cabinet, plain and homely wisdom, suit and well adapted to reconcil means and moderate expectatio

The numerous papers of this in the United States, speak we ligence and activity of the farmi although each paper must be particularly for the benefit of i yet, even the farmers of the —of that of the Merrimack, o find profit and interest, in les men of Chester and Delaware gomery and Philadelphia are price of these papers is so lo out time so lightly to read thei refrain from commending the net to the notice of the distan Friend, and advising our sub ahead of us in agriculture, for ing what is doing abroad.

DELAW.

Tiger Catching.—Tigers by the natives in India, by s set in a stretched bow, with a t the path. Another way is by in a strong bamboo lattice ca goat inside with him to give when the tiger comes, the ma spears, or poisoned arrows, th stices of the wicker work. Bu annoys the tiger most, is lue and is done by covering the l lime, and strewing them thic If by chance the animal shou of these smeared leaves, his fa dered as decided. He comme his paw, with a view to reme incumbrance, but finding no expedient, he rubs the nuis jaw, with the same intention, his eyes, ears, &c. become occasion such uneasiness as c perhaps among many more leaves, till at length he become veloped, and is deprived of s situation, may be compared to been tarred and feathered. T duced by this strange and no soon discovers itself in dreadfu serves to call the watchful peas state find no difficulty in shoot their detestation.—*Late paper*

The Shetland Pony.—Th diminutive breed, varying fro half to nine and a half hands in in Shetland, and all the islan and west of Scotland; they ar formed, and possess prodigio their size: one of these, nine only, carried a man of twelve forty miles in a day! the man knees parallel with the pony prevent his feet from touching dering it a question which pitied, the horse or his rider

nall and of remarkable features of charac-
rith a very large and flowing mane, and
xtending to the ground. Their backs are
, their quarters finely expanded and pow-
their legs flat and fine, their pasterns
, and feet most exquisitely moulded and
)g, black as ebony and impenetrable as
they are seldom shod in their native
nds, and are sure-footed to a proverb :
are extremely high-spirited and courage-
)ut tractable in their nature. They are
caught in their native pastures, by being
n into a bog ! or are hunted up precipices,
, the nearest pursuer catches the animal
e leg, and it not unfrequently happens
)oth man and horse come tumbling down
)er ! In winter, and the early part of
g, these animals have a very ragged ap-
nce, with their coats long and thick, and
manes and tails matted together, but still
iful to look upon.
gentleman was presented with one of these
iful animals, docile as elegant, and mea-
g only seven hands (28 inches) in height,
)cing desirous of conveying his present
as early as possible, yet at a loss to do
)nveniently, his friend said, " can't you
him in your chaise !" He made the extent, and the Sheltie was lifted into the
m of the gig and covered with the apron,
bits of bread being given him from time
ie to keep him quiet : he lay quite peacea-
ntil the gentleman reached his destination,
exhibiting the novel spectacle of a horse
 t in a gig !
L. Meason, Esq., of Lindertis Kinic-
, Forfuirshire, has a remarkably fine breed
se exquisite little ponies, which he keeps
e highest state of grooming ; they are,
fore, quite pictures in miniature of the
an courser ; and these he crosses with the
Arabian steed, their progeny being re-
able for fine symmetrical proportions, with
speed and grand action.—*Farmers' Cabi-*

RESIGNATION.

BY SUSAN WILSON.

sider the work of God : for who can make that
it, which he hath made crooked ?—*Eccl.* 7, 13.

Though thy path-way be uneven,
  Do not murmur or repine,
But to the will of Heaven,
  In submission humble thine ;
Did we find no cross or trial
  With our hopes and joys allied,
No cause for self-denial,—
  How would our faith be tried ?

Oh ! let us strive, when bending
  Beneath a load of care,
To turn to Him who's lending
  An ear to humble prayer ;
And pray—not that no longer
  Sorrow or care we find,—
But that our faith grow stronger,
  Our spirits more resign'd.

Led by our wishes blindly,
  How should we go astray,
If crosses were not kindly
  Placed sometimes in our way :
Then—though " crooked" or uneven
  Our path-way,—may we still
In submission bow to Heaven
  Our wayward, selfish will.

HOME IN THE SKIES.

From a series of hymns which have recently appeared in Blackwood's Magazine, purporting to be the
productions of a Hermit.

When up to nightly skies we gaze,
Where stars pursue their endless ways,
We think we see from earth's low clod,
The wide and shining home of God.

But could we rise to moon or sun,
Or path where planets duly run,
Still heaven would spread above us far,
And earth remote would seem a star.

'Tis vain to dream those tracts of space,
With all their worlds approach his face :
One glory fills each wheeling ball—
One love has shaped and moved them all.

This earth, with all its dust and tears,
Is his no less than yonder spheres ;
And rain-drops weak, and grains of sand,
Are stamped by his immediate hand.

The rock, the wave, the little flower,
All fed by streams of living power
That spring from one Almighty will,
Whate'er his thoughts conceived, fulfil.

And is this all that man can claim ?
Is this our longing's final aim ?
To be like all things round—no more
Than pebbles cast on Time's gray shore ?

Can man, no more than beast, aspire
To know his being's awful sire ?
And, born and lost on nature's breast,
No blessing seek but there to rest ?

Not this our doom, thou God benign !
Whose rays on us unclouded shine :
Thy breath sustains yon fiery dome,
But man is most thy favoured home.

We view those halls of painted air,
And own thy presence makes them fair ;
But dearer still to Thee, O Lord !
Is he whose thoughts to thine accord.

The Business of Tanning is carried on
more extensively, in the region of the Cats-
kill Mountains, than in the same limits in any
other portion of the country. In 1820 only
three tanneries of any size could be found in
that region, turning out annually about 40,000
sides of leather. Now there are more than
fifty-six tanneries of magnitude in that region
which annually manufacture 650,000 sides of
sole leather, valued at nearly $2,000,000 ! The
leather business, which includes the manufacture of boots and shoes, if the statistics could
be obtained, would be found to equal if not exceed almost any other branch of business in
the state of New York.

Hen's Eggs.—A writer in the Farmers'
Cabinet, corroborates a fact, mentioned by a
writer more than two thousand years ago, viz :
that hen's eggs which are nearly *round*, invariably produce female chickens, and those
which are *long* or pointed, produce males.

THE FRIEND.

NINTH MONTH, 26, 1840.

With the present number is brought to a
termination another volume of " The Friend."
We have in a state of forwardness an index of
the contents, which will immediately be put to
press, and sent to subscribers as soon as practicable.

From our exchange papers we have pe[
ceived, for some time past, symptoms of i[
creasing dissension in several of the religiou
denominations, growing out of the slaver
question. We copy the following from on
of those papers.

Zion's Watchman contains a call to the min
isters and members of the Methodist Protestan
church, " to meet in convention, in the city o
New York, on the 3d day of November next
for the purpose of adopting such measures a
will, forever, exclude the principle, practice
and influence of slavery from the church. I[
making this call," they say, " we are actuate[
by no other motive than that of love to th[
church to which we belong, and for whose in
terests we have, heretofore, and are still, will
ing to suffer much and longer ; but believin[
as we do, that it is morally wrong to identif[
ourselves longer with a church that is unwillin[
to express itself fully upon a point of so muc[
magnitude, we are impelled to this course as [
matter of DUTY, and stand upon the elevate[
ground marked out by the elementary principles of our constitution."

Agent appointed.—Isaiah Pope, Windham[
Maine, instead of Wm. Cobb, resigned.

WEST TOWN SCHOOL.

The Committee to superintend the Boarding
School at West-town, will meet there, on Fifth
day the 8th of next month, at 3 o'clock, P. M.
The Committee on Instruction will meet at
the School on the same day, at 1 o'clock, P. M ;
The winter Committee on the preceding
Seventh day, the 3d of the month.
          THOMAS KIMBER, Clerk.
Phila. 9th mo. 26th, 1840.

The winter term of Franklin Park Boarding
School will commence on Second day the 5th
of the 10th month, next.
          M. M'VAUGH,
          WM. DENNIS,
          B. H. DEACON.
9th mo. 26th, 1840.

HAVERFORD SCHOOL.

The winter term of this institution will commence on fourth day, the 14th of tenth month
next. The charge for board and tuition is $200
per annum. Applications for admission will
be received by Charles Yarnall, secretary of
the board of managers, No. 39 Market street.

Philadelphia, 9th month, 1840.

DIED, at Moreland, Montgomery county, Pa., on
the 26th ult., HANNAH, daughter of Charles Spencer, in
the 23d year of her age.

——, recently, at the residence of her brother, John
Tudor, of Hampden, in Adams county, Pa., DEBORAH
T. TUDOR, daughter of John and Phebe Tudor, in the
24th year of her age. She was a member of Deer
Creek Monthly Meeting, in the vicinity of which she
had passed much of her time for the last few years.

PRINTED BY ADAM WALDIE,
Carpenter Street, below Seventh, Philadelphia.